1993

Merchants and Revolution

MERCHANTS

AND

REVOLUTION

Commercial Change,
Political Conflict, and
London's Overseas
Traders,
1550–1653

ROBERT BRENNER

PRINCETON UNIVERSITY PRESS

Library of Congress Cataloging-in-Publication Data

Brenner, Robert, 1943–
Merchants and revolution : commercial change, political conflict, and London's
overseas traders, 1550–1653 / Robert Brenner.
p.   cm.
Includes index.
ISBN 0-691-05594-7 (acid-free paper)
1. Merchants—England—London—History. 2. London (Eng.)—Commerce—
History. 3. Political leadership—England—London—History.
4. Social structure—England—London—History.
5. London (Eng.)—Politics and government. I. Title.
HF3520.L65B74   1991
382'.09421—dc20   90-26252

This book has been composed in Linotron Caslon and Caslon Open

Princeton University Press books are printed on acid-free paper,
and meet the guidelines for permanence and durability of
the Committee on Production Guidelines for Book Longevity
of the Council on Library Resources

Printed in the United States of America

10   9   8   7   6   5   4   3   2   1

DESIGNED BY LAURY A. EGAN

FOR LAWRENCE STONE

Contents

Tables

Map

Preface

THIS WORK seeks to lay bare the relationship between the evolution of English commerce in the century after 1550 and the political activities and alignments of London's overseas traders in the conflicts of the first half of the seventeenth century. I begin with an account of the transformation of English trade and the associated transformation of London's merchant community during the late Tudor and early Stuart period. I describe the economic opportunities and difficulties that confronted English traders in this epoch; show how London's merchants organized themselves politically, as well as commercially, to respond to these economic opportunities and difficulties; and explain the sociopolitical effects of commercial development—the social groups to which it gave rise and their changing economic fortunes and evolving relationships with the centers of political power. On the basis of this sociopolitical account of commercial change, I go on to offer what might be termed a socioeconomic interpretation of London merchant politics during the early Stuart period. I explain the affiliations, initiatives, and alliances of the several sociocommercial groups that constituted the overseas trading community in each successive phase of the developing conflicts from the early 1620s to the early 1650s, and I discuss the implications of those activities and alignments for the development of City and national politics.

Part One describes and interprets the transformation of English commerce during the period 1550–1650. This process of growth and change encompassed three distinct and relatively discontinuous (if chronologically overlapping) stages: (1) an enormous quantitative expansion of the traditional broadcloth export trade with northern Europe between 1480 and 1550, which gave rise to a long period of stagnation and disruptions between 1550 and 1614, and ultimately issued in a definitive crisis and decline from 1614 to 1640; (2) the creation and long-term expansion of long-distance, primarily import and re-export, trades with the Near and Far East—with Russia, the Levant, and the East Indies—over the century from 1550 to 1650; and (3) the rise, from the early part of the seventeenth century, of the Virginian and West Indian plantation trades, based originally on tobacco, but, from 1640 onward in the West Indies, centered on sugar and slaves. Each of these stages laid the basis, to a limited extent, for its successor. But each ultimately gave rise to and was controlled by a separate social group of merchants, had its own distinct modes of organization and operation, and experienced its own, quite autonomous, evolution. Chapter I uncovers the underlying dynamics of commercial change over the whole of the Tudor—Stuart period. Chapter II describes the emergence and rise to prominence of those merchants who exploited the growing opportunities for long distance trade in imports with the Near and Far East, in relation to the economic and political experience of the hitherto hegemonic Merchant Adventurers, whose fortunes were tied to the oscillations of the short-route export trade in cloth to northern Europe. Chapter III explains the very lukewarm response of the great company merchants of London, now prominently including Levant—East India Company traders as well as Merchant Adventurers, to the new possibilities offered by the emerging trades with the Americas. Chapter IV charts the meteoric rise of an entirely new group of traders, originating almost totally outside the company merchant community, which assumed the task of developing American plantation production and commerce from about 1618 through the 1640s.

Part Two describes and interprets the complex evolution of merchant political activity and alliances from the 1620s to the outbreak of the Civil War. Chapter V exposes the company merchants' close alliance with the Crown and alienation from the House of Commons during the first two decades of the seventeenth century and, in that context, analyzes what new factors lay behind the sudden rise, from 1625 or 1626, of a new and powerful movement of company merchants that was staunchly allied to the parliamentary opposition in its struggles against the Crown during the later 1620s. Chapter VI describes the critical processes of alignment and realignment among the Crown, leading aristocratic oppositionists, and key sectors of the merchant community during the "reign of Buckingham" and the years of the Personal Rule that helped shape the character of political conflict from 1640. These processes encompassed, most crucially, the alienation of critical sections of the parliamentary aristocratic opposition leadership from the City merchant elite; the alliance of that same aristocratic opposition leadership with the emerging group of non-company traders, the new merchant leadership, behind colonial commercial and plantation development; and, correlatively, the Crown's wooing of the majority of the top company merchant leaders. Chapter VII offers a perspective on the outbreak of political conflict between November 1640 and the summer of 1642 by describing the activities and alignments, both nationally and within the municipal context, of the leading sociocommercial groupings within the London merchant community. To this end, it traces the developing interconnections between parliamentary reform and City revolution, on the one hand, and the rise of royalism and the growth of reaction in the City on the other. It does so by charting the emerging alliances between the parliamentary chieftans, the new-merchant leadership of the colonial-interloping trades, and a radical mass movement of London citizens, at one pole, and between the Crown, the merchant elite, and, ultimately, the overwhelming majority of the company merchants, at the other pole.

Part Three follows the activities and alignments of the different sections of the merchant community from 1642 to 1653. Chapter VIII charts the spectacular, though temporary, rise to influence, both nationally and within London during the years 1642–1643, of a dynamic City radical movement, composed largely of nonmerchant citizens, in which the new-merchant leaders of the colonial trades and their allies among the Independent ministers played a central leadership role carrying a London parliamentary war-party alliance to the peak of its power. Chapter IX describes the consolidation in power in London, during the middle 1640s, of what can be seen as a moderate proparliamentary party. This new ruling group—which included a relatively small, but significant, group of company merchants who had stood largely aloof from the City revolution of 1641–1642 but ultimately sided with Parliament—sought to achieve a settlement nationally and within the City that would ensure its own position and restore social order largely through the imposition of a strict Presbyterian national settlement. Chapters X through XIII show how the triumph of the political independents, imposed on London by Cromwell's victorious army, carried the new-merchant leadership of the colonial trades to positions of unprecedented influence. These chapters explain, first, how the colonial-interloping traders achieved power, both nationally and in London, within a much broader alliance, whose London component was almost entirely devoid of company merchants and heavily dominated by nonmerchant political independents who first learned to work together in the City radical movement of 1640–1643; and, second, how they used their new preeminence to bring about radical programmatic departures over a wide range of fields—in politics, religion, and the law, but above all in commercial and colonial policy and in foreign policy more generally during the Commonwealth.

The postscript seeks to determine the implications of this work for the broader interpretation of political conflict in Stuart England.

Acknowledgments

THE PROCESS by which this book was created was long and tortuous: it could not have reached completion without a great deal of help from a great many people. It is especially gratifying to be able finally to thank at least some of them.

Like many other Americans who go to London to begin their research with only the most superficial understanding of the manuscript sources, I was touched by the extraordinary generosity of so many British scholars. They were willing not only to spend their time directing me in the archives and discussing the tidbits I had found, but also to share with me substantial blocks of material that they had gleaned through long and painful labor. In this regard, I owe a special debt to the late Prof. F. J. Fisher, who offered me invaluable advice for initiating my study of Tudor–Stuart commerce, and handed over to me large-scale lists of merchants compiled from the London port books that were critical in getting my research started. I wish to express my gratitude also to Prof. Barry Supple and to Mr. Harlan Taylor for similarly allowing me to make use of port book materials they had compiled. Discussions with Mr. Taylor about long-term developments in Stuart commerce and his articles on the Spanish trade were crucial to the evolution of my own views on the subject. Analogous discussions with Dr. David Fischer, who generously allowed me access to his important dissertation on the origins of the Levant trade, were similarly indispensable.

It is unfortunately impossible to thank most of the hundreds of scholars whose studies provide the foundation of this work, except through recognition in the footnotes. However, I want to express my appreciation explicitly to two authors who have offered me valuable help and counsel and whose works on London have provided the indispensable groundwork for my own research. The first is Dr. Valerie Pearl, whose *London and the Outbreak of the Puritan Revolution* (Oxford, 1961) remains the standard in the field and provides the point of departure for my own study of the merchant community; the second is Prof. Robert Ashton, whose *City and the Court, 1603–1643* (Cambridge, 1979) allowed me to extend the scope of my study of merchant politics back into the early seventeenth century in a way that would otherwise have been impossible.

I want also to thank a number of people who read the manuscript at various stages. Prof. Conrad Russell gave me invaluable encouragement at a pivotal juncture, while making several important criticisms and bringing to my attention a number of factual errors; his suggestion that

the manuscript be reworked to take into account certain recent developments in the historiography of the field was on target and helped determine
the final form of the book. Perry Anderson, with his customary generosity, read at least two drafts of the manuscript cover to cover and offered
many powerful criticisms and pregnant suggestions: because of his in-
sights, the book has been much improved, and would undoubtedly have
been substantially better had I been able to take all of them into account.
I am deeply grateful to him. Prof. Jacob Price of the University of Mich-
igan read and very helpfully commented on several drafts of the manuscript; his long-term support for the project has been a major source of
encouragement to me. Professor Paul Seaver of Stanford University has
offered support for this project over many years, in many different forms,
I want to express my gratitude to him. Sharon Lloyd went systematically
through most of the manuscript, attempting, against the odds, to improve
its style, and also offered several important criticisms of substance. I want
to thank Christopher Thompson, who read parts of the manuscript at an
early stage, and who over many years has helped me in myriad ways,
calling my attention to important manuscript documents and new work in
the field and pursuing with me an ongoing discussion about how to understand the political history of the Stuart period. Johanna Brenner made a
truly fundamental contribution to the project as a whole, helping me in
myriad ways with its conceptualization and arguments, with its organization and style, and with its research. I am profoundly grateful to her.

A number of people read sections or chapters of the book at various
stages, and provided indispensable comments and criticisms, substantive
and stylistic. In this regard, I wish to thank Julia Adams, Richard
Ashcraft, Lutz Berkner, John Brewer, Temma Kaplan, the late Franklin
Mendels, Sherry Ortner, Ted Rabb, Eleanor Searle, Joe Slavin, and Scott
Waugh. I also wish to express my deep appreciation to Jack Felman for
subjecting himself to endless hours of invaluable discussion of this work
in progress and for offering his ideas, his unstinting support, and his
friendship.

I am very grateful to the following institutions for fellowship, or other
material, support in the research and writing of this work: The American
Council of Learned Societies; The Center for European Studies, Harvard
University; The Guggenheim Foundation; The Institute for Advanced
Study, Princeton; The National Endowment for the Humanities; Princeton University; The University of California at Los Angeles. I wish to
express my gratitude to the Yale Parliamentary Diaries Project, especially
to Maija Jansson, for allowing me to consult the typescript of the Parliamentary diaries of 1626 in advance of publication, and more generally for
helping me to make use of the parliamentary diary materials held by the
Project.

I wish to express my gratitude to Mrs. Damaris Inie for permission to reproduce the portrait of Sir Thomas Andrews on the jacket.

I want to express my profound appreciation to Princeton University Press for seeing me through the extended, and (for the Press) unquestionably maddening, process of turning this work from a manuscript into a book. In this regard, I owe a really enormous debt to Joanna Hitchcock, who has overseen the project from the very beginning and offered me nothing but the warmest encouragement, most massive assistance, and unstinting toleration—confronted by my inveterate inability to leave well enough alone. I really cannot thank her enough.

It was the intellectual excitement of studying with Professor Richard Jones at Reed College that initially induced me to take an interest in early modern English History. I cannot thank him adequately for the inspiration and encouragement—as well as the model of scholar-critic—that he so generously offered me at Reed and over the years.

My greatest debt—an incalculable one—is to Lawrence Stone, who oversaw this work from beginning to end, systematically read and criticized every draft, and, most important, offered the warmest friendship and unflaggingly good-humored encouragement in the face of the most persistent procrastination and frustratingly self-defeating behavior on my part. But for Lawrence, this book would never have been completed. I dedicate it to him, as a very small token of my gratitude.

Abbreviations

Add. MSS   Additional Manuscripts
A.H.R.   American Historical Review
A.O.   Acts and Ordinances of the Interregnum, 1642–1660, ed. C. H. Firth and R. S. Rait, 3 vols. (London, 1911)
A.P.C.   Acts of the Privy Council
A.P.C. Col. 1613–1680   Acts of the Privy Council, Colonial Series, 1613–1680, ed. W. L. Grant and J. Monro (London, 1908)
B.I.H.R.   Bulletin of the Institute of Historical Research
BL   British Library
C.C.M.E.I.C.   Calendar of the Court Minutes of the East India Company, ed. E. B. Sainsbury, 11 vols. (Oxford, 1907–1938)
C.J.   Journals of the House of Commons
CLRO   Corporation of London Record Office
C.P.R.   Calendar of the Patent Rolls
C.S.P. Col. 1574–1660   Calendar of State Papers, Colonial Series, America and the West Indies, 1574–1660, ed. W. N. Sainsbury (London, 1860)
C.S.P. Col. E.I.   Calendar of State Papers, East Indies, China, and Japan, ed. W. N. Sainsbury, 6 vols. (London, 1862–1884)
C.S.P.D.   Calendar of State Papers, Domestic
C.S.P. Ven.   Calendar of State Papers, Venetian
Dictionary of Seventeenth-Century Radicals   Biographical Dictionary of British Radicals in the Seventeenth Century, ed. R. L. Greaves and R. Zaller, 3 vols. (Brighton, 1982–1984)
D.N.B.   Dictionary of National Biography
Ec.H.R.   Economic History Review
E.F.I.   The English Factories in India, 1618–1660, ed. W. Foster, 13 vols. (Oxford, 1906–1927)
E.H.R.   English Historical Review
H.J.   Historical Journal
H.M.C.   Historical Manuscripts Commission
J.B.S.   Journal of British Studies
J.Co.Co.   Journals of the Common Council
J.Ec.H.   Journal of Economic History
KCA   Kent County Archives
L.J.   Journals of the House of Lords
Mass. Hist. Soc. Coll.   Massachusetts Historical Society Collections
Md. Hist. Mag.   Maryland Historical Society Magazine

New Eng. Hist. Gen. Reg. *New England Historical and Genealogical Register*

PRO   Public Record Office

T.R.H.S. *Transactions of the Royal Historical Society*

Va. Co. Recs. *Records of the Virginia Company of London*, ed. S. M. Kingsbury, 4 vols. (Washington, D.C., 1906–1935)

V.M.H.B. *Virginia Magazine of History and Biography*

Note: All dates are Old Style, except that the beginning of the new year is taken to be 1 January. Spelling and capitalization have been modernized except in the case of titles.

[PART ONE]

The Transformation of English Commerce and of the London Merchant Community, 1550–1650

The Dynamics of Commercial Development,

1550–1640: A Reinterpretation

A T THE TURN of the seventeenth century, the Company of Merchant Adventurers, "the most famous company of merchants in Christendom," held unquestioned leadership in London's merchant community. Its predominance was of long standing, and reflected the perpetuation of a traditional commercial pattern. As it had for a century, semifinished woolen cloth remained England's chief overseas commodity, and the Merchant Adventurers monopolized its major export markets by virtue of their royal charter. During the first decade of the seventeenth century, cloth composed by value three-quarters of London's exports, and three-quarters of all cloth exports were sent to Germany and the Low Countries, the privileged trading area of the Merchant Adventurers. The Merchant Adventurers thus controlled about one-half of London's total export trade. It is understandable that this company of merchants constituted England's outstanding commercial group by any test of wealth or power, and that its leading members enjoyed a disproportionate share of London's highest political positions.[1]

By the eve of the Civil War, however, the locus of commercial and political power in the London merchant community had shifted. The Merchant Adventurers had lost their overwhelming dominance. A different group of merchants, who based themselves in the newly emerging commerce of the Elizabethan expansion, especially the closely linked trades with the Levant and the East Indies, had joined and, to an important extent, replaced the Merchant Adventurers at the top of London's mercantile society. In the space of several crisis-filled decades, the Merchant Adventurers saw their traditional north European cloth export markets cut in half.[2] Meanwhile, the newer trades with southern Europe, the

---

[1] A. Friis, *Alderman Cockayne's Project and the Cloth Trade* (London, 1927), p. 70, and in general, ch. 2. See also R. G. Lang, "The Greater Merchants of London, 1600–1625" (Oxford University, Ph.D. diss., 1963), pp. 149–50; P. Ramsey, *Tudor Economic Problems* (London, 1963), pp. 63–65.

[2] B. E. Supple, *Commercial Crisis and Change in England, 1600–1642* (Cambridge, 1959), pp. 258–59.

Mediterranean, and the Near and Far East experienced an extended period of remarkable growth and prosperity. In 1638, Lewes Roberts, a contemporary authority on commercial matters, could reasonably contend that the Levant Company "for its height and eminency is now second to none other of this land."[3] Its membership, according to another contemporary witness, was "composed of the wealthiest and ablest merchants in the City."[4] The Merchant Adventurers remained a very important group of merchants, but accelerating processes of commercial crisis and transformation had deprived them of the best trading opportunities, and they were obliged to relinquish their position at the summit of London's mercantile hierarchy. By 1640, representatives of the Levant–East India combine had become preponderant within what might loosely be termed the City *merchant establishment*, which consisted of the top socioeconomic layers among London's privileged company merchants, and had come to constitute the core of a recomposed City *merchant political elite*, which exercised its authority through the aldermanic court, the East India Company board of directors, and the customs farming syndicates. To begin to see how this came about, one must reexamine the shifting sources of commercial development over the Tudor–Stuart period.

Commercial Crisis and the Interpretation of Commercial Change

According to what has become the traditional interpretation of Tudor–Stuart commercial change, the transformation of English commerce in the late sixteenth and early seventeenth centuries was primarily an adaptation to the short-term crises and the secular decline of the traditional export trade in broadcloths with northern Europe. In this view, the dynamic expansion of the cloth export trade during the early Tudor period came to a cataclysmic conclusion with the crisis of 1551–1552; stagnation and a series of deep depressions during the reign of Elizabeth followed; and, ultimately, a disastrous long-term drop-off of the trade under the early Stuarts brought irreversible decline. English merchants were thus driven to develop the new trades with southern Europe and the Near and Far East in this era in order to provide new markets for cloth, both broadcloths and "new draperies," so as to compensate for the fall in the north

---

[3] L. Roberts, *Merchants Mappe of Commerce* (London, 1638), ch. 273, p. 259. According to Roberts, the company had "grown to that height that (without comparison) it is the most flourishing and beneficial company to the commonwealth of any in England" (pp. 79–80).

[4] H. G. Tibbutt, ed., *The Tower of London Letter Book of Sir Lewis Dyve, 1646–1647*, Publications of the Bedfordshire Record Society 37 (Bedford, 1958), p. 54.

European commerce.[5] Although containing important elements of truth, this interpretation is seriously misleading. It misstates the depth, timing, and remediability at different junctures of the problems of the traditional trade. It fails to take fully into account all of the merchants' options in responding to these problems. And it overestimates the capacity of the new trades to resolve these problems. As a result, the traditional interpretation fails to grasp the fundamental forces behind the new trades—the motivation for their initiation, the conditions that made possible their consolidation, and the foundations for their long-term success.

The rise of the new trades of the Elizabethan era, extending from Morocco, Russia, Persia, and Guinea to Turkey, Venice, and the East Indies, was based, from the start, on imports. Merchants were thus moved to found these new trades far less by chronic economic crisis in the cloth export commerce than by the periodic physical disruptions of their traditional trade routes—especially those to the Antwerp and Iberian entrepôts. These disruptions compelled certain merchants interested in imports to seek better access to the ultimate sources of supply. English merchants found it feasible to establish the new trades in large part because of the weakening hold of Portugal and Spain over their commercial empires, as well as certain other favorable political shifts in the new areas of commercial penetration. Even so, they could successfully capitalize on the openings presented to them only because of the growing political, as well as economic, strength of English commerce and shipping in this period. Finally, what made possible the new trades' extraordinary long-term growth and continuing high profits over more than a century was the remarkable secular rise of domestic demand for imports in England, as well as the growth of the reexport trades with Europe.[6]

[5] For this cloth export-centered approach, see F. J. Fisher, "Commercial Trends and Policy in Sixteenth Century England," *Ec.H.R.* 10 (1940): 105–7. In Fisher's words, "the more important results of the depression have to be sought elsewhere. An obvious measure was to seek new markets for English cloth . . . and those markets were, of necessity, sought further afield. The immediate result of the slump induced by the over-production of the forties and the revaluation of 1551 was, in fact, to launch England on the quest for Eastern and African trade. . . . The later depressions served only to intensify the movement." See also F. J. Fisher, "London's Export Trade in the Seventeenth Century," *Ec.H.R.*, 2d ser. 3 (1950): 157–59 and Supple, *Commercial Crisis*, ch. 7; G. D. Ramsay, *English Overseas Trade during the Centuries of Emergence* (London, 1957), pp. 20–30; Ramsey, *Tudor Economic Problems*, pp. 68ff.; R. Davis, "England and the Mediterranean, 1570–1670," in *Essays in the Social and Economic History of Tudor and Stuart England*, ed. F. J. Fisher (Cambridge, 1961); G. D. Ramsay, *The City of London in International Politics at the Accession of Elizabeth Tudor* (Manchester, 1975), p. 62.

[6] The view that imports, as well as reexports, powered commercial expansion in this era was initially presented in my doctoral dissertation, "Commercial Change and Political Conflict: The Merchant Community in Civil War London" (Princeton University, 1970), pp. 1–52, as well as in my articles "The Social Basis of Economic Development," *J.Ec.H.* 32 (1972): 361–69, and "The Civil War Politics of London's Merchant Community," *Past & Present*, no. 58 (1973): 56–60. The works

The Elizabethan Expansion: Causes and Character

The crisis of the 1550s did mark the end of a long period of growth of the English cloth trade with northern Europe. But to assess properly the traditional claim that a search for new cloth markets to compensate for cloth trade depression was what lay behind the geographic expansion of commerce in the subsequent era, we must specify the longer-term trends in the cloth export commerce, both before and after the mid-century dislocations.

Cloth exports from England enjoyed a powerful rise in the early Tudor period, increasing some two and a half times during the years from the late 1480s to the mid–sixteenth century. Cloth exports from London grew even faster, and during this period London's share in the national cloth export totals expanded at the expense of the outports, as English trade focused increasingly on the London-Antwerp route and English cloths came to be shipped almost exclusively to Antwerp, and from there to their ultimate destinations in various parts of Europe. The long-term expansion of the cloth trade took place almost entirely in two relatively short bursts. Almost half the increase came during the reign of Henry VII, that is, from the late 1480s to the early 1510s. From that point, national cloth exports more or less stagnated for close to a quarter of a century, although London's cloth trade continued to grow in this period, while the outports' cloth trade declined. Finally, from the middle 1530s to midcentury, there was a new and rapid rise in national cloth exports, perhaps fueled in its final stages by government coin debasements.[7]

During the early 1550s, both national and London cloth exports dropped off drastically. Moreover, at no time during the subsequent half century did these totals regain the heights they had attained at the zenith

---

of K. R. Andrews and Harland Taylor on the Spanish trade and of David Fischer on the Levant trade also point in this direction, and were very helpful to me. See especially Andrews's *Elizabethan Privateering* (Cambridge, 1964) and Taylor's "Price Revolution or Price Revision: The English and Spanish Trade after 1604," *Renaissance and Modern Studies* 12 (1968) and "Trade, Neutrality, and the 'English Road,' 1630–1648," *Ec.H.R.*, 2d ser., 25 (1972), as well as Fischer's "Development and Organization of English Trade to Asia, 1553–1605" (University of London, Ph.D. diss., 1970). I wish to express my thanks to Dr. Fischer for allowing me to refer to his dissertation. I also benefited greatly from discussions with Mr. Taylor on this subject. I want also to express my appreciation of Andrews's very important work *Trade, Plunder, and Settlement* (Cambridge, 1984). Andrews's interpretations in this work converge at many points with my own, and I have incorporated specific results of his at various points in the text. F. J. Fisher, revising somewhat his earlier emphasis on cloth exports, put forward positions similar to those adopted here in "London as an Engine of Economic Growth," in *Britain and the Netherlands*, ed. J. Bromley and E. Kossman, vol. 4 (The Hague, 1971).

[7] J. D. Gould, *The Great Debasement* (Oxford, 1970), pp. 118–26, esp. table 12, p. 120.

of the final boom from 1548 to 1550.[8] Nevertheless, it is doubtful whether either the short-term crises or the long-term relative stagnation of cloth exports of the second half of the sixteenth century impelled a search for new cloth markets or the opening of the new trades, as alleged by the traditional interpretation.

First, if one separates the London cloth export figures into totals for denizen (English) merchants and totals for alien merchants, the crisis of the early 1550s is seen to be much less severe and more short-lived for English cloth exporters than it has sometimes appeared.[9] In the aggregate, the decline of London cloth exports was indeed quite dramatic, with totals falling from the record highs of 125,298 and 132,660 cloths in 1549 and 1550 to 112,710 in 1551 and 84,968 in 1552. But most of this decrease was accounted for by the sharp decline in the Hanse merchants' export totals from 43,584 and 44,302 in 1549 and 1550, to 39,854 and a remarkable 13,829 in 1551 and 1552, the greater part of which resulted directly from the government's canceling of the Hanse merchants' trading privileges in early 1552. London denizens' exports declined only from 80,353 and 87,181 in 1549 and 1550, to 69,859 and 65,690 in 1551 and 1552. Unfortunately, figures do not survive for 1553, 1555, and 1556, so it is impossible to evaluate properly the significance of the record-high figures for 1554, both for London cloth exports (135,559) and London denizen cloth exports (96,993). However, by the years 1557, 1559, and 1560 (figures for 1558 are not available), London denizen exports had climbed to an average of 85,433, a figure that was higher than for any previous, recorded three-year period during the sixteenth century.[10]

Second, although total London export figures stayed below their mid-century record highs during the remainder of the sixteenth century, they held at roughly the levels they had reached in the early 1540s. Between 1538 and 1544, London cloth exports averaged 96,114 cloths a year. Between 1559 and 1600, they averaged 93,275 a year (98,017 if we exclude two three-year periods when trade was disrupted as a result of political dislocations on the Continent).[11]

Third, the so-called depressions of the late sixteenth century simply did not pose fundamental problems for the cloth export trade, as is often im-

---

[8] Compare table 12 in Gould, *Great Debasement*, p. 120, with the table in Fisher, "Commercial Trends and Policy," p. 96.

[9] This point is made in Fischer, "English Trade to Asia," pp. 27–32.

[10] For these results, see ibid., pp. 23, 27–30. See also G. D. Ramsay, "The Cloth Trade at London in Mid-Sixteenth Century: The Merchant Adventurers and Their Rivals," in *Produzione, commercio e consumo dei Panni di Lana (nei secoli XII–XVIII)*, ed. M. Spallanzani (Florence, 1976), pp. 380–81ff. For this and the following three paragraphs see tables 1.1 and 1.2.

[11] Fisher, "Commercial Trends and Policy," p. 96; Gould, *Great Debasement*, p. 120.

plied. These crises were, in every case, of relatively short duration and attributable to politically induced disruptions of the English merchants' marts in Europe, of which the most severe came between 1561 and 1563 and between 1571 and 1573, when Spain issued prohibitions on English imports into the Spanish Netherlands. In themselves, these dislocations signaled no problem with the market, that is, with the demand for English cloths, but merely a difficulty in accessing outlets. In order to transcend the problem, therefore, English merchants did not find it necessary to discover new customers but only to secure suitable places at which to sell. Their existing customers could then renew their purchases. This is what happened in each case, as either more peaceful political conditions allowed the English merchants to resume trading at their old mart(s), or the English merchants simply relocated their mart(s). There was, as a result, no extended drop-off of trade.[12] On the contrary, over the whole Elizabethan period, cloth exports are notable for their constancy. Between 1559 and 1600, the three-year averages of London cloth exports compiled by F. J. Fisher do not fall below 93,681 or rise above 103,132 (except, again, for the two brief periods when trade was disrupted). These levels were sustained, or exceeded, until after 1614.[13]

Finally, it needs to be emphasized that the London cloth export merchants had ways to respond to stagnation in demand for their goods other than by seeking to discover new markets. In particular, they could, and did, more effectively exploit the existing market. During the 1550s and the 1560s, the Company of Merchant Adventurers, which controlled the cloth export trade with northern Europe, achieved a remarkable strengthening of its privileges. Above all, foreign competitors, who had controlled a major part of the cloth export commerce, were deprived of their privileges and ultimately largely excluded from the trade. At the same time, entering the trade was made much more difficult for domestic merchants. As a consequence, those English merchants of London who remained in possession of the north European cloth trade were able actually to increase their trade, to regulate it much more tightly, and to profit more from its operation.[14] The result was that although total London cloth exports stagnated over the half century after 1550 at approximately the level they had reached by the early 1540s, London exports by English merchants actually increased significantly during that period. Most of the

---

[12] Fisher, "Commercial Trends and Policy," p. 96; Friis, *Alderman Cockayne's Project*, pp. 51–54; Ramsay, *City of London*, pp. 251ff.

[13] Fisher, "Commercial Trends and Policy," p. 96; Fisher, "London's Export Trade," p. 4; Friis, *Alderman Cockayne's Project*, pp. 78, 93.

[14] For tighter regulation of the cloth trade as a response to the cloth crisis, see Fisher, "Commercial Trends and Policy," pp. 109–12ff.; Ramsay, *City of London*, pp. 45–48, 60; Ramsay, "Cloth Trade at London," pp. 379–83.

TABLE 1.1

London Cloth Exports: Denizens, 1488–1614

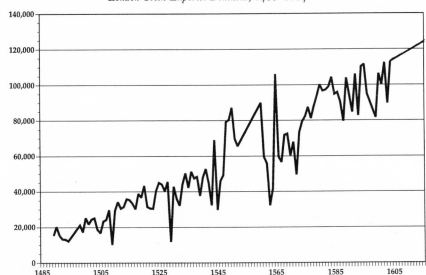

SOURCES: Compiled from E. M. Carus-Wilson and O. Coleman, *England's Export Trade, 1275–1547* (Oxford, 1963), tables; Gould, *Great Debasement*, app. C; Fischer, "English Trade to Asia," pp. 23–25; Fisher, "Commercial Trends and Policy," p. 96; Supple, *Commercial Crisis*, tables 1–3; PRO, Enrolled Customs Accounts 28, 29 (1559–1581, 1582–1593, 1598–1603); PRO, Customs Accounts 213/19, 90/45, 213/19 (1594, 1595, 1596).

growth came at the start of the period, with denizen cloth exports increasing from an average of 57,100 cloths a year between 1541 and 1550, to around 75,000 a year by the 1560s. It is doubtful if London denizens' exports to the Adventurers' marts expanded much further over the remainder of the period before 1600. The fact remains that London denizens' exports to the Adventurers' markets over the whole of the Elizabethan period were, on average, at least 30 percent higher than they had been during the export boom of the decade before 1550,[15] a time in which the London cloth export trade as a whole reached what had been, up to that point, record highs.

[15] Fischer, "English Trade to Asia," p. 23; Fisher, "Commercial Trends and Policy," p. 96; Fisher, "London's Export Trade," p. 153. Total London cloth exports by denizens were averaging perhaps 97,000 cloths a year in the decade 1591–1600, assuming alien merchants were, at this point, exporting no more than 5 percent of the total. But by this time London denizens' cloth exports to markets in the Levant, the Baltic, and elsewhere constituted 20 to 25 percent of that total. Thus, cloth exports to the Adventurers' markets were probably no greater than at the start of Elizabeth's reign. Cf. H. Zins, *England and the Baltic* (Manchester, 1972), p. 185.

[9]

TABLE 1.2

London Cloth Exports: Total, Denizens, and Aliens, 1488–1614

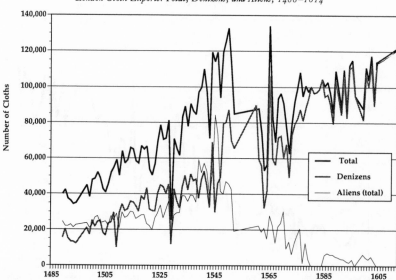

SOURCES: Compiled from Carus-Wilson and Coleman, *England's Export Trade*, tables; Gould, *Great Debasement*, app. C; Fischer, "English Trade to Asia," pp. 23–25; Fisher, "Commercial Trends and Policy," p. 96; Supple, *Commercial Crisis*, tables 1–3; PRO, Enrolled Customs Accounts 28, 29 (1559–1581, 1582–1593, 1598–1603); PRO, Customs Accounts 213/19, 90/45, 213/19 (1594, 1595, 1596).

The stasis of the London export trade during the half century or so after 1560 was thus certainly in some contrast to its dynamism during the period before 1550. But in view of the relatively limited extent and brief duration of the crisis of the 1550s (at least for the English merchants of London), the short-term and remediable character of the commercial disruptions of the reign of Elizabeth, the trade's relative stability between 1559 and 1600, and, above all, the significant increase in cloth exports enjoyed by English merchants of London trading with northern Europe in the half century after 1550, there is strong reason to question the thesis that depressed and crisis-prone cloth markets compelled the merchants to search for new markets in which to sell their cloth—and that it was this search that led to the Elizabethan commercial expansion. That thesis appears all the more questionable when one takes into account the ever more tightly controlled conditions under which the cloth export commerce was pursued—and, specifically, the Merchant Adventurers' success, precisely from the 1550s and 1560s, in getting the government to increase their privileges considerably. Indeed, in view of the relatively favorable conditions that actually prevailed for London denizen merchants in the traditional cloth trade with northern Europe from the late 1550s to the early 1600s, it is not easy to see why they would have felt the need to seek alternatives farther afield.

Whatever may have been the merchants' fears for their traditional trade or hopes for new cloth markets farther away, none of the new trading areas that the English developed after 1550 could even begin to provide significant new demand for English cloth, and it is hard to see how such a result could have been expected. During the sixteenth century, cloth exports to Morocco never exceeded 3,000 cloths a year; those to Russia never surpassed 2,500 annually.[16] The Levant Company was exporting no more than 6,000 cloths each year by 1600 (and the figure did not rise appreciably before 1630).[17] The East India Company did not even attempt cloth exports.[18] A simple comparison of these numbers with the average of perhaps 70,000 to 80,000 cloths annually exported by the Merchant Adventurers in this period[19] reveals the essential irrelevance of the new areas as cloth markets, let alone as markets that could counteract any serious decline in the traditional cloth markets or even distract the Adventurers from their established trade. Cloth problems alone could hardly have motivated the Elizabethan expansion, nor could the cloth export markets provided by the new trades have sustained it.

The fact is that every one of the new trades with southern and eastern areas founded in the half century or so after 1550 *concentrated from the very start on imports.* They represented successive and interconnected phases in a cumulative process of commercial innovation. They were developed by a unified group of merchants who had the common goal of tapping the lucrative markets for silks, spices, and other products of the Mediterranean and the Near and Far East. In this drive for imports, the decline of the Antwerp entrepôt very likely marked a turning point, for it encouraged English merchants to go themselves directly to the sources of supply.[20] But well before Antwerp's demise, English merchants had set the expansionary process firmly in motion.

---

[16] T. S. Willan, *Studies in Elizabethan Foreign Trade* (Manchester, 1959), pp. 275–76; T. S. Willan, *The Early History of the Russia Company, 1553–1603* (Manchester, 1956), p. 252; Supple, *Commercial Crisis,* p. 258. The Guinea trade was for gold, as well as other imports, and does not seem to have at all involved significant cloth exports (Andrews, *Trade, Plunder, and Settlement,* pp. 103–6).

[17] Davis, "England and the Mediterranean," p. 120; Supple, *Commercial Crisis,* p. 258; Friis, *Alderman Cockayne's Project,* pp. 70–71 n. 2. The Russia Company's Persian voyages, which preceded the founding of the Turkey Company, involved only very small cloth export totals, on the order of seven hundred cloths a year (Fischer, "English Trade to Asia," pp. 86–92).

[18] K. N. Chaudhuri, *The English East India Company* (London, 1965), pp. 10–13.

[19] Fisher, "Commercial Trends and Policy," p. 96. See also above, note 15.

[20] Chaudhuri, *East India Company,* pp. 6–7.

The voyages to Morocco in 1551 and the Chancellor-Willoughby expedition seeking a northeast passage in 1553 were the first major steps in the expansionary thrust. These ventures were initiated at about the time of the most intense dislocations in the cloth export trade of the sixteenth century, but neither of them responded in any direct way to the problems with cloth export markets. Even those contemporary commentators, such as Clement Adams and Thomas Edge, who connected the new adventures to the difficulties in the cloth trade did not argue that the new areas were sought as export markets for English cloths. In their view, the crisis provided the stimulus or the occasion for generalized commercial experimentation—above all, the attempt to imitate and compete with the Portuguese and Spanish in the discovery and exploitation of new and lucrative import markets. As Edge remarked, "The trade of this kingdom waxing cold and in decay . . . the merchants [were] incited with the fame of the great masses of riches brought home from both the Indies."[21] Moreover, at about this same time, political changes and disruptions in Spain, North Africa, the Mediterranean, and beyond were presenting English merchants with both new problems in, and new possibilities for, carrying on their established import trades. These dislocations, and the opportunities they created, were probably as crucial in providing the short-term motivation for the new ventures of the 1550s as was the sanction of cloth crisis.

The founding of the English trade with Morocco was conditioned by the destruction of the long-standing Portuguese hegemony over that region. During the 1540s, Muley Muhammed, the founder of the Saadian dynasty, had succeeded in expelling the Portuguese from their strongholds at Safi and Agadir, thereby making it impossible for them to continue controlling the trade with Morocco and so opening the way for the English. What induced English traders to start direct commerce with Morocco at this point was, very likely, the disintegration of the English import trade from Spain during the 1540s, which resulted from intensifying Anglo-Spanish political conflict. English merchants seem to have been obliged to open up the Moroccan trade in order to obtain commodities they formerly had gotten from middlemen in the Iberian peninsula. Leading traders with Spain played a central role in the founding of the Moroccan trade, and they likely viewed it as a natural extension of their

[21] S. Purchas, *Hakluytus Posthumus*, 20 vols. (Glasgow, 1906), 13: 5. Adams writes in a similar vein: "Our merchants perceived the commodities and wares of England to be in small request with the countries and people about us . . . and the price thereof abated . . . and all foreign merchandises in great account and their prices wonderfully raised. [C]ertain grave citizens of London . . . seeing that the wealth of the Spaniards and Portugals, by the discovery and search of new trades and countries was marvelously increased, supposing the same to be a course and mean for them also . . . thereupon resolved upon a new and strange navigation" (R. Hakluyt, *The Principal Navigations, Voyages, Traffiques, and Discoveries of the English Nation*, 12 vols. [Glasgow, 1903], 2: 239–40).

established commerce. The close connection between the Spanish and Moroccan trades would last out the century. In any case, the Moroccan trade was initiated much more to tap sources of sugar and gold than to open up a very limited cloth market. It was no coincidence that an important group among the pioneers of the trade had been associated with sugar importing and with sugar refining in England. Moreover, the series of voyages that founded the Moroccan trade began in 1551 before the cloth crisis had become obvious.[22]

The company for the discovery of a northeast passage of 1553, which evolved into the Muscovy Company of 1555 and detonated the whole eastward expansionary movement, had as its explicit purpose the opening of a route to the spices and gold of the Far East that would be free from Portuguese interference. A new direct trade with Russia—which included some cloth exports, but which was centered on the import of naval supplies and furs—grew up as a by-product.[23] Although there is no direct evidence, the immediate impulse for this new thrust eastward may very well have come, in part, from the disruption of the sea trade with the Levant that took place at this time, apparently due to the depredations of the Barbary corsairs and the rise of Turkish maritime power in the Mediterranean. The journey of the *Bark Aucher* in 1551–1552 is reported by Richard Hakluyt as the last successful English voyage to the Levant via the Mediterranean for some twenty years, and among its seamen was Richard Chancellor who, as it happens, became one of the two central figures who led the northeast passage venture of 1553.

In any case, the English merchants' inability to acquire eastern imports via the Mediterranean and the Levant must have further encouraged them to seek new routes to the East. In 1557 the Muscovy Company, after having failed to develop a northeast passage, founded a direct overland trade with Persia via Russia by which it could obtain at least some of the desired silks and spices. It may, moreover, be some indication of the connection between the decay of the Levantine trade and the rise of the Muscovy Company's Persian commerce that William Jenkinson, who initiated the overland trade with Persia for the Muscovy Company, had, in 1553, succeeded in procuring a privilege to trade throughout the Ottoman Empire from Sultan Suleiman in Aleppo, but apparently had been frustrated in his attempt to make use of it by the disruption of trade routes through the Mediterranean. The Muscovy Company continued the trade with Persia—sending out six voyages between 1557 and 1579—until the Turks cut off the route from Russia to Persia in 1580. And over this same pe-

---

[22] Willan, *Studies*, pp. 92–96, 220.

[23] Willan, *Russia Company*, pp. 1–3, 57–61, 90–91, 145–55; T. S. Willan, "Trade between England and Russia in the Second Half of the Sixteenth Century," *E.H.R.* 63 (1948): 308–9.

riod, the company launched a series of voyages to India itself, which traveled overland through Persia and by other routes, with the aim of establishing a direct trade.[24]

Meanwhile, beginning in 1553, a series of merchant syndicates sought to found a direct trade with Guinea, and it is not surprising that the originators of this commerce included many of the same merchants trading with Spain who were already developing the Moroccan trade. It is, indeed, testimony to the emerging unity of the whole commercial movement to the south and east for imports that of the thirty-four merchants interested in the Guinea voyage of 1558, twenty-two also had been named in the Muscovy Company charter of 1555.[25]

The character of merchant participation in the new southern and eastern trades thus increasingly reflected the distinctive commercial forces that set these trades in motion. It is true that significant numbers of Merchant Adventurer cloth traders were leaders in the Muscovy, Moroccan, and Guinean ventures of the 1550s.[26] But this, in itself, was of little economic or social significance. In view of the overwhelmingly dominant position of the Adventurers and their trade in London's commerce at this time, some Adventurers were bound to have been prominent in almost any sizable overseas venture. The point is that those Adventurers who continued to play a role in the new trades almost certainly did so for their import potential.[27] In consequence, from very early on a pattern of commercial specialization began to emerge that became ever more accentuated as the century progressed. The Merchant Adventurers tended, increasingly, to concentrate on their own traditional markets almost to the exclusion of all others. Meanwhile, those who were developing the new import trades to the south and east tended, increasingly, to constitute a unified group and to treat each new venture in the expansionary process as part of a single project.

The growing gap that had opened up between those merchants who were developing the new trades and the traditional Merchant Adventurer

[24] T. S. Willan, "Some Aspects of English Trade with the Levant in the Sixteenth Century," *E.H.R.* 70 (1955): 399–400; Fischer, "English Trade to Asia," pp. 73–107; S. A. Skilliter, *William Harborne and the Trade with Turkey, 1578–1582* (Oxford, 1977), pp. 6–11; Andrews, *Trade, Plunder, and Settlement*, p. 67.

[25] Willan, *Studies*, pp. 100–101; T. S. Willan, *The Muscovy Merchants of 1555* (Manchester, 1953), p. 27; Andrews, *Trade, Plunder, and Settlement*, pp. 103–4.

[26] For the traders with Russia, see Willan, *Muscovy Merchants*, pp. 22–25. For the trade with Morocco, compare Willan, *Studies*, p. 94, with, for example, the Merchant Adventurers' charter of 1564 in *C.P.R. 1563–1566*, pp. 178–79, or the list of 1559 cloth exporters in PRO, S.P.12/6/112–14.

[27] Examples of such leading traders who were very active in both the Merchant Adventurers' trade and the new commerce with the south and east in its early stages are Edward Jackman, Francis Bowyer, William Allen, and William Garrard.

cloth export specialists manifested itself during the 1570s in the conflicts surrounding the organization of the Spanish Company. The English trade with Spain focused heavily on imports; its profits were derived, to a large extent, from products from the Portuguese and Spanish empires, particularly sugar and spices, but also wines, fruits, raw wool, and iron produced in Spain itself.[28] For this reason, the Spanish trade seems to have served as the prototype and springboard for the developing trades with Africa, the Mediterranean, and the East, as well as a sort of dividing line—and point of friction—between these emerging trades and the north European commerce of the Merchant Adventurers.

Anglo-Spanish political conflict between 1569 and 1573 temporarily disrupted the commerce with Spain. But after Spain lifted its embargo, the trade started, once again, to experience substantial growth. And beginning in 1573, steps were taken to establish a corporate organization for it.[29] Nevertheless, from the time that plans were first set in motion for a charter for the Spanish trade, the traders with Spain seeking corporate privileges *and* the Company of Merchant Adventurers tried to prevent Merchant Adventurers from entering the new company. As originally framed in 1573–1574, the Spanish Company charter declared ineligible for membership any merchant already belonging to another merchant company, and this meant the Merchant Adventurers above all. The intent of this proviso was perfectly explicit. The merchants who traded with Spain wished to prevent Merchant Adventurers from using their superior access to Dutch finished woolens and other Dutch products highly valued in Spain to undersell them and thus to gain an advantageous position in the lucrative Iberian import markets.[30] Analogously, the Merchant Adventurers as a company feared that those of their members who traded with Spain would sell their cloth in Europe at cut rates or pay more for European products for reexport to Spain. In either case, the Adventurers who traded with Spain would outcompete their cloth export specialist colleagues in the Adventurers' markets, because (in the words of the company) "their gain lieth in the foreign commodities"—that is, in the trade in Dutch goods for imports from Spain.[31]

These events suggest that the personnel of the Merchant Adventurers Company were already largely separate from those in the Spanish trade. Equally important, they indicate that those Merchant Adventurers who did trade with Spain composed a distinct group within the Adventurers'

[28] Andrews, *Elizabethan Privateering*, pp. 13–14.

[29] P. Croft, *The Spanish Company*, London Record Society Publications 9 (London, 1973), pp. ix–xii.

[30] PRO, S.P. 12/99/8, 9; *A.P.C. 1575–1577*, pp. 330–31; Croft, *Spanish Company*, pp. xii–xv.

[31] R. H. Tawney and E. Power, eds., *Tudor Economic Documents*, 3 vols. (London, 1924), 2: 54; Andrews, *Elizabethan Privateering*, p. 14; Croft, *Spanish Company*, pp. xv–xvii.

company—a group with interests different from and in conflict with those of the typical Adventurers. These traders with Spain, who ran big, diversified operations,[32] sought to make the Adventurers' traditional bilateral commerce with northern Europe serve their broader, multilateral trade, which was designed especially to exploit the market in Spanish imports.[33] Almost all of that very small number of Merchant Adventurers who continued to play a part in the expansionary process to the south and east came from this group.

While the Merchant Adventurers' trade was thus an increasingly unitary one, and separated from the others, the southern and eastern trades experienced an increasingly intertwined growth, motivated by the same interlocking groups of merchants with common commercial goals. During the 1550s and 1560s, Muscovy Company merchants and traders with Spain were responsible, as noted, for opening up the overland route to Persia and for establishing direct trades with Morocco and Guinea. It was the efforts of Muscovy Company and Spanish Company merchants that gave rise, in turn, to the founding of the Turkey Company, the decisive step in the Elizabethan expansion. English trade with Turkey by way of the Mediterranean began to revive from the early and middle 1570s. From this time onward the Antwerp entrepôt was totally disrupted, and it became necessary to seek new ways to obtain the eastern products formerly available there. The commercial life of the Low Countries as a whole was also disturbed in this period as the result of the Dutch war for independence, and, at roughly the same time, Venetian maritime commerce with northern Europe was disrupted by Venice's war with Turkey (1570–1573). As a result of this collapse of their entrepôt and these temporary preoccupations of their competitors, English merchants were presented with both the motivation and the opportunity to penetrate the Mediterra-

[32] The leading Merchant Adventurers who were also major traders with Spain included some of London's most prominent citizens—men such as aldermen Thomas Starkey and Anthony Gammage, as well as Richard Saltonstall, Francis Bowyer, William Masham, and others. They were, in fact, powerful enough to force their way into the Spanish Company of 1577 over all protests. They can be identified especially from a list in *A.P.C. 1575–1577*, pp. 330–31, but also from the list of the original Spanish Company assistants in V. M. Shillington and A. B. Chapman, *The Commercial Relations between England and Portugal* (London, n.d.), pp. 316–17, and the roll of charter members in PRO, C.66/1158/1–6, which can be compared with lists of Merchant Adventurers compiled from the London Port Books for Cloth Exports, Easter–Michelmas 1565 and Easter–Michelmas 1571, PRO, E.190/2/1 and PRO, E.190/5/1, as well as the names on the Adventurers' charter of 1564 in *C.P.R. 1563–1566*, pp. 178–79, and the list of cloth exporters in 1559 in PRO, S.P.12/6/112–14.

[33] See, for example, the trade of the great Merchant Adventurer and trader with Spain Thomas Middleton, who carried on a complex multilateral operation among Spain, England, and various north European ports in a wide range of commodities, with a number of leading merchants as partners (A. H. Dodd, "Mr. Myddleton, Merchant of Tower Street," in *Elizabethan Government and Society*, ed. S. T. Bindoff et al. [London, 1961]).

nean.[34] The actual founding of the Turkey Company in 1580–1581 represented, in part, an attempt by Muscovy Company merchants to achieve the goals of their company's voyages to Persia by using the cheaper and safer Mediterranean route, after the Turks had disrupted the overland commerce to Persia by way of Russia. It represented, also, the increased determination of merchants trading with Spain and Portugal, after Portugal had been annexed in 1580 by a Spain hostile to England, to go behind their Iberian middlemen and enter directly the import markets of the Near and Far East formally under Portuguese jurisdiction. In fact, most of the Turkey Company founders turn out to be both Muscovy Company members and leading Spanish traders.

The original Turkey Company joint stock had twelve investors: nine of these were Muscovy Company investors; ten were Spanish Company members; and eight were both Muscovy Company investors and Spanish Company members (one was in neither company). In addition, the Muscovy Company, as a corporation, made a major direct investment in the Turkey Company. The involvement of most of the Turkey Company merchants in the Russian and Spanish trades had been substantial and of long duration.[35] Three were at one time or another governors of the Muscovy Company,[36] among them George Barne, who was Muscovy Company governor at the time he became a Turkey Company founder. Barne, in fact, represented a second generation of top leadership in the Elizabethan expansion. His father, who had also been a trader with Spain, was a chief promoter of the original northeast passage voyage of 1553 and a charter consul of the Muscovy Company in 1555, as well as a leading promoter of the voyages to Guinea in 1553–1554. Barne himself had married the daughter of Sir William Garrard, one of a family of merchants who led in the early development of the Moroccan trade. He was deeply involved in the Spanish trade from the 1560s on, and he was a founding director (or assistant) of the Spanish Company when it was chartered in 1577.[37] Indeed, the Turkey Company patentees held a remarkably dominant position in the Spanish trade at this point. Six of the twelve had been among

[34] Davis, "England and the Mediterranean," p. 117; R. Davis, "Influences de l'Angleterre sur le déclin de Venise au XVIIème siècle," in *Aspetti e cause della decadenza economica Veneziana nel secolo XVII* (Venice, 1961), pp. 186, 196–97, 230–31. Willan, *Russia Company*, pp. 153–54; Fischer, "English Trade to Asia," pp. 115–24, 161–62; Fisher, "Commercial Trends and Policy," pp. 106–7.

[35] Fischer, "English Trade to Asia," pp. 121, 169, and app. For a list of the original Turkey merchants, see BL, Cotton MSS, Nero B.8, fol. 53.

[36] George Barne, John Harte, Richard Martin. See Willan, *Russia Company*, pp. 285–88.

[37] Willan, *Muscovy Merchants*, p. 78. London Port Book for Imports, 1567–1568, PRO, E.190/4/2.

the thirty founding directors of the Spanish Company.[38] In 1584, the ten traders with Spain who were Turkey Company patentees included no fewer than five of the top ten importers from Spain that year, and among them they controlled more than 25 percent of that year's total Spanish import trade.[39] There were four Merchant Adventurers among the Turkey Company founders, but, as might have been expected, three of these were also prominent in the Spanish trade.[40] It was typical of the whole commercial thrust to the south and east that Richard Staper and Edward Osborne, the two main entrepreneurs behind the Turkey Company, were leading figures in the Spanish trade, but were *not* Merchant Adventurers.[41]

The chartering of the Venice Company in 1583 was part and parcel of the same movement into the Mediterranean and the Near East that had resulted in the Turkey Company charter. The handful of merchants who dominated the Venice trade from the start—including Thomas Cordell, Edward Holmden, William Garway, and Paul and Andrew Bayning—had all been active in the Spanish commerce. Both Holmden and Cordell, who started the Venice Company, also had been very active in the Moroccan commerce. In fact, it appears that Cordell had pioneered the reopening of the Turkish trade in 1575, actually preceding those who ultimately secured the Turkey Company patent.[42] In 1592, the Venice Company merchants joined the Turkey Company merchants to form the Levant Company, marking the firm establishment of English commerce in the eastern Mediterranean and the Near East.

During the 1580s and the 1590s, the same group of Spanish-Muscovy-Turkey-Venice Company merchants accelerated their efforts to open direct commercial access to the Spanish and Portuguese empires. In much the

[38] Edward Osborne, George Barne, John Spencer, Richard Saltonstall, William Marsham, and Richard Staper.

[39] BL, Lansdowne MSS 41 provides a full listing, apparently extracted from the port books, of the import traders with Spain of 1584 and the value of their trades. The Turkey Company patentees included George Barne (£1,797), William Marsham (£3,105, including £612 in partnership), Richard May (£1,377), Richard Saltonstall (£2,956, including £2,276 "and Co."), John Spencer (£1,345), and Richard Staper (£182).

[40] Martin Calthorpe, William Masham, Richard Saltonstall, and Henry Hewitt, the last three of whom were important in the Spanish trade.

[41] Osborne and Staper, as well as another leading Turkey Company patentee, John Spencer, are found on a list of merchants described as "not free of the Merchant Adventurers" who shipped kerseys out of London in 1577–1578. BL Harleian MSS 167, fols. 75ff, 91ff.

[42] For the Venice Company patentees, see PRO, S.P. 12/160/10. For the leading role of the above-mentioned traders, see Willan, "English Trade with the Levant," pp. 405ff., and Lang, "Greater Merchants of London," pp. 201–6. For the activity of these men in the trades with Spain and Morocco, see BL, Lansdowne MSS 41; Andrews, *Elizabethan Privateering*, pp. 109–11; PRO, E.122/196/1 (Barbary traders, 1567–1568); Willan, *Studies*, pp. 131, 161, 193–94. For Cordell's early activity in the trade with Turkey, see Skilliter, *William Harborne*, pp. 11–13.

same way as the Turkey and Venice companies had assumed the objectives of the eastward-looking commerce of the Muscovy Company and Iberian merchants by exploiting the sea route through the Mediterranean, the East India Company established itself to take over the commerce of the Levant Company merchants in Far Eastern commodities by developing the direct trade with India and the East Indies via the sea route around the Cape of Good Hope.[43] Meanwhile, the same groups of merchants took comparable steps to pry open the valuable import markets of the Portuguese empire in South America.

In 1578, at the same time that Richard Staper, with Edward Osborne, was moving to get behind Iberian middlemen to establish a permanent trade with the eastern Mediterranean, he was also in touch with one John Whithall about the possibility of going behind the Portuguese to trade directly with Brazil for sugar.[44] This same Whithall was also in contact with the Spanish-trade merchants John Bird and Robert Walkden. By 1580, Bird, along with Christopher Hoddesdon, Anthony Garrard, Thomas Bramley, and William Elkin, had sent the *Minion* on a trading voyage to Brazil. All of these men were already active in the Spanish trade and/or leaders in the Moroccan trade. In 1583, Thomas Cordell and William Garway followed up the effort of Bird and company by sending their ship *Merchant Royal* to Brazil with a cargo of victuals to relieve a famine. Cordell and Garway were in that very year establishing the Venice Company. Over the next several years, the same merchants attempted to carry forward the commerce with Brazil, but their efforts were cut short by the outbreak of hostilities between England and Spain in 1587–1588.

As it turned out, war proved to be a blessing to these men. Through the late 1580s and 1590s, leading traders with the Mediterranean and the Near and Far East secured enormous quantities of sugar without having to pay for it, by means of a series of highly successful privateering ventures against Portuguese ships returning from Brazil. A limited number of merchants were thus able to amass great fortunes through simultaneously exploiting opportunities for privateering in the Atlantic and for peaceful trade with the eastern Mediterranean and areas farther east. Prominent among them were the great Levant Company merchants–cum–Atlantic privateers Thomas Cordell, Paul Bayning, and William Garway. These men and others like them applied their earnings, in turn, to opening up the direct sea trade with the East Indies.

London merchants had been seeking to establish a direct trade with the Far East at least from the time of the Chancellor-Willoughby voyage of

---

[43] Chaudhuri, *East India Company*, pp. 10–14.

[44] The following two paragraphs are derived from Andrews, *Elizabethan Privateering*, esp. ch. 10. As I hope will be obvious, my debt throughout this section to Professor Andrews's important book is very great.

1553. The Muscovy Company claimed by its charter of 1555 the right to control all voyages of discovery to the east by way of the northeast or the northwest, and in 1556 and 1557 it sent out first Stephen Borough, then Anthony Jenkinson, to test a variety of possible passages via the northeast. During the 1560s, the Muscovy Company merchants remained deeply concerned with opening up trade with the Far East, but as a company, they sent out no new voyages until 1580; by that time, they had been joined in the effort by the other overlapping groups of southward- and eastward-trading merchants.[45]

Between 1576 and 1578, the veteran sea captain Martin Frobisher led three ventures to establish a trade route to the Indies by way of the northwest under a license from the Muscovy Company. Frobisher was the nephew of John Yorke, a leader in the Muscovy Company and an originator of the Guinean trade, and had himself participated in the pioneering voyages to Guinea in the 1550s. In addition to substantial court backing, Frobisher's voyages attracted significant support in the City, drawn for the most part from merchants already active in the Spanish, Moroccan, and Russian trades.[46] Next, in 1580, the Muscovy Company, under the leadership of Sir George Barne and Rowland Heywood, tried on its own to gain a northeast passage, sending out a voyage under the leadership of Arthur Pet and Charles Jackman.[47]

The Turkey Company merchants, meanwhile, concentrated at first on developing the land route to the Far East. By 1580, Richard Staper and Edward Osborne had already sent out John Newbury via Aleppo to survey the commercial possibilities in Persia and beyond. In 1582, the Turkey Company followed up this effort by dispatching Newbury, along with Ralph Fitch, to India itself. It was apparently Fitch's report, on his return, that led the Levant Company merchants to seek the inclusion of the overland route to the East in their renewed monopoly charter of 1592.[48]

Finally, in 1583, still another route was tried, in a voyage partly of plunder, partly of discovery, to the Molucca Islands by way of South America. Edmund Fenton took charge of this venture, which received the strong backing of the earl of Leicester and Lord Burghley. The Muscovy Company, as a body, played a central role in Fenton's voyage, making a

[45] See the preface by W. N. Sainsbury to *C.S.P. Col. E.I. 1513–1616*; also Fischer, "English Trade to Asia," pp. 74–81.

[46] For backers of Frobisher's voyages, see *C.S.P. Col. E.I. 1513–1616*, pp. 11, 17, 18, 29. Note especially alderman William Bond, Lionel Duckett, Matthew Field, Thomas Marshe, and Oliver Burr, all significant in the trades with Spain and/or Morocco. See also Andrews, *Trade, Plunder, and Settlement*, pp. 168–69ff.

[47] Willan, *Russia Company*, p. 133.

[48] W. Foster, *England's Quest of Eastern Trade* (London, 1933), pp. 79–109; Fischer, "English Trade to Asia," pp. 178–83.

large direct investment, just as it had in the original Turkey Company joint stock. The individual merchants who supported the venture once again came almost exclusively from among those groups of leading traders behind the Spanish, Turkey, and Venice companies. They included Thomas Pullyson, William Towerson, Thomas Aldersey, and Thomas Starkey (all Spanish Company directors); Sir George Barne (Spanish Company director and Turkey Company founder); Martin Calthorpe, "Customer" Thomas Smythe, and Sir Richard Martin (Turkey Company founders); and Thomas Cordell and Robert Sadler (Venice Company founders).[49]

In the long run, of course, the Dutch exposed the growing weakness of the Portuguese in the Indian Ocean and showed that the voyage around the Cape of Good Hope was the cheapest and safest route to the Far East. The Levant Company merchants ultimately had no choice but to follow the Dutch example if they wished to continue to compete in the East Indian commodities that they previously had obtained, at greater cost, from middlemen in the Near East. We do not know all of the persons who were behind the first English initiatives to develop this route (which actually preceded the Dutch breakthrough). But that close-knit group of Venice Company merchants with widespread operations who were at this very time helping to organize the new, consolidated Levant Company of 1592 provided a critical part of the leadership. The handful of merchants who, in 1589, first proposed a voyage of trade to the Far East by way of the Cape intended to employ the ships *Susan*, *Merchant Royal*, and *Edward Bonaventure* to carry out their purpose. These ships belonged to Paul Bayning and Thomas Cordell, the Venice Company merchants who were also active in the Spanish trade and leading privateers. Bayning and Cordell's ships, along with one other, were the vessels ultimately used in the pathbreaking voyage of James Lancaster to the Indian Ocean in 1591–1592.[50]

The East India Company was founded in 1599, and was dominated by the Levant Company merchants, who saw the project as essential to maintaining an important segment of their old trade. The East India Company initially met at the Levant Company's offices. Levant Company merchants composed more than one-third of those present at the first meeting of the new company in September 1599, and seven of the original fifteen directors elected at that meeting were Levant Company merchants. The first governor of the East India Company was the Levant Company governor Sir Thomas Smythe, and seven of the twenty-four directors (known as "committees") chosen under the original charter of 31 December 1600

[49] Andrews, *Elizabethan Privateering*, pp. 203–6; *C.S.P. Col. E.I. 1513–1616*, pp. 73–74.
[50] Chaudhuri, *East India Company*, p. 12; Andrews, *Elizabethan Privateering*, pp. 213–18.

were also Levant Company directors.[51] In addition, Levant Company members provided between one-fourth and one-third of the total fund invested in the first, third, and fourth joint stocks.[52]

As a joint-stock organization, the East India company was easily entered through investing, with no need for active involvement. But, symptomatically, members of the Company of Merchant Adventurers, which still included by far the greatest number of the City's wealthiest merchants, provided relatively little investment support.[53] The Adventurers seem, in fact, to have become even more obsessively focused on their short-route cloth trade with northern Europe—and even less connected to the new southern and eastern trades—as time went on. During the first quarter of the seventeenth century, approximately 35 men who made their fortunes primarily in the Merchant Adventurers' trade were wealthy and prestigious enough to assume the position of alderman of London. Of these, no fewer than 25 traded with the Adventurers' privileged marts to the complete exclusion of all other overseas commercial involvements.[54] Out of some 150 Merchant Adventurers actively trading in 1606, only 11 were among the 118 Levant Company charter merchants of 1605, and just a few of these could be said to be important traders with the Levant.[55] The

[51] A. C. Wood, *A History of the Levant Company* (London, 1935, repr. 1964), p. 31; Foster, *England's Quest*, pp. 144–53. Compare lists of original East India Company directors in *C.S.P. Col. E.I. 1513–1616*, pp. 101 (Sept. 1599) and 117 (Dec. 1600), with lists of Levant Company members and officers, which may be constituted on the basis of the lists of charter members of 1592, 1601, and 1605 printed in Hakluyt, *Principal Navigations* 5: 75–76 (1592), C. T. Carr, ed., *Select Charters of the Trading Companies, 1530–1707* (London, 1913), p. 32 (1601), and M. Epstein, *The Early History of the Levant Company* (London, n.d.), pp. 158–60 (1605).

[52] These results were obtained by comparing lists of Levant Company members derived from lists cited above in note 51 with lists of early East India Company investors and the amounts of their investments, which survive for the first, third, and fourth joint stocks. These East India investor lists have been printed in G. Birdwood, ed., *The Register of Letters, Etc., of the Governor and Company of the Merchants of London Trading into the East Indies, 1600–1619* (repr. London, 1965), pp. 275–81, 294–95, and *The Dawn of the British Trade to the East Indies*, printed by Henry Stevens (London, 1886), pp. 1–5.

[53] Merchant Adventurers contributed perhaps 15 percent of the total investment fund raised for the East India Company's first, third, and fourth joint stocks. This is necessarily a rough figure, derived by comparing a list of Merchant Adventurers, compiled from the London Port Book for Cloth Exports, 1606, PRO, E. 190/13/5, with the East India Company investor lists referred to above in note 52. These Merchant Adventurers of 1606 actually contributed about 11 percent of the total invested in the first, third, and fourth joint stocks. But this figure is likely somewhat low, since the list of Merchant Adventurers, here comprising traders active in a single year, is undoubtedly incomplete.

[54] Lang, "Greater Merchants of London," pp. 149–50.

[55] This result was obtained by comparing lists of traders of one hundred or more cloths with the Merchant Adventurers' privileged areas in 1606, compiled from the London Port Book for Cloth Exports, 1606, PRO, E.190/13/5, with Levant Company 1605 charter members in Epstein, *Levant Company*, pp. 158–60.

separation between the commerce with the Mediterranean and the Near and Far East and the cloth export trade to northern Europe, already evident at the beginning of the Elizabethan expansion, thus became ever more pronounced, powerful testimony to the divergent forces that drove each of these trades forward.

Commercial Crisis and Change in the Early Stuart Period

By the early seventeenth century, the commercial conquests of the Elizabethan period—above all the lucrative trade with the Levant—were already having a discernible effect on individual merchant fortunes in London. However, the new trades still remained dwarfed, in terms of value, by the overwhelming size of the Merchant Adventurers' cloth export commerce. The Adventurers' north European cloth markets were not expanding, and were plagued by certain chronic difficulties. But for a significant period there was stabilization and even a new burst of export growth and prosperity. In fact, during the first decade of the reign of James I, cloth exports by the Merchant Adventurers appear to have reached an all-time high, attaining levels perhaps 20 percent or more above the average for the reign of Elizabeth. As late as 1614, when the Jacobean cloth export boom was still near its peak, England's overseas commerce might have appeared, on the surface at least, to be dominated by woolen exports, much as it had been a century before.[56]

By 1640, however, there was no longer even the appearance of continuity. Long-term processes making for the transformation of English trade, at work since the middle of the sixteenth century, were accelerated rather suddenly. A substantially new commercial pattern took shape within the space of a few decades. It did not await, as historians have often contended,[57] the post-Restoration period, although it was of course confirmed and accentuated in that era.

Thus, while the Merchant Adventurers' export markets had been somewhat precarious over a long period, the actual fall, when it came, did not occur gradually. As late as 1606, 219 merchants shipped more than 101,000 cloths to the Merchant Adventurers' north European cloth markets; in 1614, the corresponding figures were still 182 active merchants

---

[56] Supple, *Commercial Crisis*, ch. 1 and p. 259 (table 3); Fisher, "London's Export Trade," p. 153; Friis, *Alderman Cockayne's Project*, pp. 78, 93. See above, pp. 8–9.

[57] See, for example, R. Davis, *A Commercial Revolution*, Historical Association Pamphlet no. 64 (London, 1967), pp. 8–9; Supple, *Commercial Crisis*, pp. 161–62.

shipping 99,000 cloths.[58] Then the bottom dropped out. In 1620, there were only 117 active merchants, and they shipped only about 59,000 cloths to the Adventurers' marts;[59] in 1632, the figures were 373 active merchants and 59,000 cloths.[60] By 1640, there were just 103 merchants active, exporting about 45,000 cloths to Hamburg and the Netherlands.[61]

The crisis of the Merchant Adventurers' trade was far from affecting all branches of overseas commerce. In fact, by 1640, it was "a general opinion that the trade of England was never greater,"[62] and the merchants trading with Spain, and in particular with the Near and Far East, were its primary beneficiaries. The growth of (often dyed) broadcloth exports, largely to the Levant, combined with the impressive rise of the lighter new-drapery (worsted and "mixed" woolen and worsted cloth) exports to southern Europe, roughly made up for the decline of cloth exports to northern Europe. It is thus possible that, by 1640, the value of English woolen exports was, in the aggregate, nearly as great as it had been in 1600. This fact has led historians to treat commercial change in the early Stuart period, as they have that of the Elizabethan era, as if it were powered primarily by crisis and decline in the traditional cloth export trade, which led to the rise of compensative new cloth markets and new cloth products.[63]

The fact is that the substantial growth of trade with southern and eastern regions during the first half of the seventeenth century was not motivated by the profits to be made from cloth exports, and it cannot properly be interpreted as an adaptation by English commerce and manufacturing to the disastrous decline of the old cloth trade. The problems and possibilities of the cloth export trade were no more central to the Stuart commercial expansion than they had been to the Elizabethan commercial expansion.

[58] Friis, *Alderman Cockayne's Project*, pp. 78, 93 for figures for 1606 and 1614, as amended in Supple, *Commercial Crisis*, pp. 258–59 (see esp. p. 258 n. 2).

[59] The figures for 1620 were compiled from the London Port Book for Cloth Exports, PRO, E.190/23/3. I am very grateful to Professor B. E. Supple for his kindness in putting this material at my disposal.

[60] Compiled from the London Port Book for Cloth Exports, 1632, PRO, E.190/36/5. The large increase in the numbers of traders in this year is accounted for by the suspension of the Merchant Adventurers' privileges between 1624 and 1634. See below, ch. 2, pp. 59–61.

[61] The figures for 1640 were compiled from complete notes on the London Port Book for Cloth Exports, 1640, PRO, E.190/43/4, made by Professor F. J. Fisher. I am very grateful to the late Professor Fisher for his kindness in making these notes available to me.

[62] "Sir Thomas Roe's Speech in Parliament" (1641), *Harleian Miscellany*, 12 vols. (London, 1809), 4: 456.

[63] Fisher, "London's Export Trade," pp. 153–59; D. C. Coleman, *The Economy of England, 1450–1750* (Oxford, 1977), pp. 64–65; Supple, *Commercial Crisis*, ch. 7. "It has already been made abundantly clear that [the] development of the new draperies, and the opening of the southern markets which it involved, was largely a response to the stagnation of the old draperies and to economic conditions in the early seventeenth century" (Supple, p. 153).

Imports and reexports continued to provide the real dynamic, and for this reason the commercial growth of the early Stuart period must be understood as an extension of the Elizabethan expansionary thrust. By the time of the Stuarts, however, it was no longer a question merely of *qualitative* shifts—of the establishment of new trading routes and the growing independence of English merchants from their former European suppliers of imports. From the late sixteenth century, growing English (and European) demand provided the foundation for an impressive overall *quantitative* increase in total imports (and reexports) from the newly developing commercial areas.[64]

First, raw-silk imports, which had totaled perhaps 12,000 pounds around 1560, grew to about 120,000 pounds by 1621, although a significant part of this total was still being brought in from the Near East by way of northern Europe.[65] By the late 1620s, some 90 percent of all raw silk was being imported directly from its source by Levant–East India Company merchants, and the totals reached about 172,000 pounds in 1630, 200,000 pounds in 1634, and 220,000 pounds in 1640 (see table 1.3).[66] Second, currants from the Greek islands, which were consumed throughout much of the population, were also providing a dramatically increased source of income for the Levant–East India Company merchants. Monopolized by the Levant Company, currants imports more than quadrupled between 1600 and 1640, rising from perhaps 12,000 or 14,000 hundredweight a year to about 50,000 hundredweight annually (see table 1.4).[67] East Indian spices, especially pepper, provided a third major source of profits from imports for this group of traders. In this case, a significant part of their income came from reexports, often to the Mediterranean, carried by Levant Company merchants.[68] Finally, with the disruption of the land route to Italy after 1621, many of the same group of merchants used the sea route to enter the Italian market to profit

[64] For the qualitative, as opposed to the quantitative, character of the Elizabethan expansion, see L. Stone, "Elizabethan Overseas Trade," *Ec.H.R.*, 2d ser., 2 (1949): 54–55. The rise of reexports is a major theme in Fisher, "London's Export Trade," pp. 160–61.

[65] A. M. Millard, "The Import Trade of London, 1600–1640" (University of London, Ph.D. diss., 1956), app. 2.

[66] These figures are based, in the first instance, on Millard, "Import Trade of London," app. 2. See, however, table 1.3 with explanation.

[67] London Port Books for Imports, 1630, 1634, 1636, 1638, and 1640; PRO, S.P.12/272/127; and PRO, S.P.14/10A/26. Professor Davis has stated that currants prices fell drastically over this period ("England and the Mediterranean," p. 136). However, available price data (and contemporary comment) seem to indicate that currants prices in fact held up fairly well over the period. See, for example, Henry Robinson's contention in 1641 that England paid out about £75,000 a year for currants imports (which averaged around 50,000 hundredweight) or about 30s. a hundredweight (in the islands). Compare this figure with indications on currants prices in 1627, given below.

[68] Chaudhuri, *East India Company*, ch. 7.

146767

[25]

TABLE 1.3
Raw-Silk Imports (in lbs.)

	Totals	Levantine	East Indian	Dutch	German	French
1560	12,000					
1621	125,000	40,000	5,000	41,000	5,700	5,000
1628–1629	142,000	80,000	58,000	4,000(?)		
1630	180,000	150,000	12,000	2,000	3,500	9,800
1634	191,000	136,000	33,000	18,000	1,750	2,400
1640	213,000					
1663	302,600	278,000	1,293			
1669	265,000	249,502	248			

SOURCES

1. All figures 1560–1640, except 1628–1629, are calculated from Millard, "Import Trade of London," app. 2. Figures are given approximately, since they had to be transformed from the value totals presented by Millard using port book valuations. Raw-silk imports for 1634, designated by Millard as from Leghorn, have been included with Levantine raw-silk imports because they were, according to the London Port Book for Imports for that year, brought in by Levant Company merchants who had almost certainly brought them from the Near East (their ship stopping at Leghorn).

2. Figures from 1628–1629, from PRO, E. 122/230/4, a list of importers of raw silk for those years, with amounts brought in, were apparently abstracted from the London Port Books. Totals are given as the annual average of two years.

3. Figures for 1663 and 1669 are from BL, Add. MSS 36785 (the totals for these years include 23,506 lbs. and 14,563 lbs., respectively, brought in from Italy, the only significant source outside the Levant for this commodity in these years).

TABLE 1.4
Levant Currants Imports

Year	Amount	Source
1591–1592	9,480	PRO, S.P. 12/272/127
1592–1593	8,710	PRO, S.P. 12/272/127
1593–1594	6,990	PRO, S.P. 12/272/127
1594–1595	10,120	PRO, S.P. 12/272/127
1595–1596	6,240	PRO, S.P. 12/272/127
1596–1597	869	PRO, S.P. 12/272/127
1597–1598	10,080	PRO, S.P. 12/272/127
1598–1599	10,180	PRO, S.P. 12/272/127
1601	14,000	PRO, S.P. 14/10A/26
1602	16,000	PRO, S.P. 14/10A/26
1603	20,000	PRO, S.P. 14/10A/26
1610	48,990	PRO, E. 122/91/6
1621	30,818	PRO, E. 190/24/4, or Millard, "Import Trade of London," app. 2.
1630	37,109	PRO, E. 190/34/2
1634	51,220	PRO, E. 190/38/5
1636	46,196	PRO, E. 190/37/13
1638	62,512	PRO, E. 190/42/1
1640	48,743	PRO, E. 190/43/5
1663	31,469	BL, Add. MSS 36785
1669	39,983	BL, Add. MSS 36785

from several different, growing lines of commerce. Of these, the most lucrative was the trade in Italian luxury silk fabrics. In 1621, some £62,000 worth of luxury silk fabrics had been imported into England from Italy, almost all by way of the land routes through Germany and the Netherlands. By 1634, the figure for this product had risen above £90,000, and much of it was being brought via the sea route by merchants who were members of the Levant Company. By the end of the pre–Civil War period, Italy was providing, in addition, several new sorts of import products, including olive oil and grogram yarn.[69]

Overall, by the 1630, imports by traders with Italy, by Levant Company merchants, and by the East India Company, taken together, composed perhaps 40–50 percent of England's total imports, excluding

[69] Millard, "Import Trade of London," app. 2; Davis, "England and the Mediterranean," pp. 133–37.

wines. In absolute terms, the combined value of their imports may have approached, or even possibly surpassed, that of the Merchant Adventurers' exports. In 1632, the Merchant Adventurers exported broadcloths that were worth about £480,000 (60,000 cloths), and they sent out, in addition, nonbroadcloth goods of uncertain value, largely new draperies. In 1640, the Merchant Adventurers' broadcloth exports were worth about £400,000 (50,000 cloths), with their exports of other sorts valued at about £94,000.[70] Meanwhile, the total combined value of Italian, Levantine, and East Indian imports in 1630 was £527,000 (£350,000 from the Levant alone); in 1634, it was £689,000 (£305,000 from the Levant alone).[71] But the change may, by this time, have been even greater than these figures indicate. Imports, particularly silks, were notoriously undervalued in the book of rates. In addition, the Merchant Adventurers' profit rates were probably lower than those of the merchants trading with Italy, the Levant, and the East Indies, because the Adventurers were experiencing a very difficult period of intensified international competition and falling prices.[72] In any case, by the time of the Restoration, these long-term trends had become even more pronounced, and the new pattern was fully established. In 1663, combined Italian, Levantine, and East Indian imports were valued at £1,031,000 (£373,000 from the Levant alone), whereas exports to the Adventurers' marts in Germany and the Low Countries totaled a mere £406,000. For 1669, combined imports from Italy, the Levant, and the East Indies totaled £1,208,000 (£467,000 from the Levant alone), while exports to the Low Countries and Germany reached only £601,000.[73]

In the foregoing context, the much-heralded rise of both broadcloth and new-drapery exports to Southern Europe and the Mediterranean in the early part of the seventeeth century must be understood largely as the re-

[70] London Port Books for Cloth Exports, 1632 and 1640, PRO, E.190/36/5 and PRO, E.190/43/4. Cloths here have been valued at £8 each. London Port Book for Exports (nonbroadcloths), 1640, PRO, E.190/43/1.

[71] See table 1.5. By 1663 the value of Levant–East India imports alone exceeded that of combined English exports to the Low Countries and Germany—by £768,000 compared with £406,000; the corresponding figures in 1669 were £903,000 compared with £601,000 (BL, Add. MSS 36785).

[72] Cranfield Papers, KCA, U.269/M.121–22, 632–42, provide data on the relationship between official customs rates and actual prices, although this is for the time around 1615. Cranfield estimated that imports, on average, were undervalued in the book of rates by about one-third. He claimed, in particular, that the real worth of raw silks was 50 percent more than the rated value; that all groceries (for example, spices, currants) except mace and nutmeg were undervalued; and that cloths were substantially overvalued, that is, by about one-sixth (although he noted that to get the true worth of cloth, it was necessary to add 20 percent to the value in the book of rates as normal profit to the exporter). See KCA, U.269/M.121, 637, 641. For the intensifying competition to which the Merchant Adventurers were being subjected in their north European markets, especially in the 1620s and the 1630s, see Supple, *Commercial Crisis*, pp. 138–49.

[73] BL, Add. MSS 36785.

TABLE 1.5

Levant and East India Imports

Official Values and Proportion of Total Imports, Excluding Wines and Trade with the Americas

	1621	1630	1634	1640	1663	1669
Levant	181,997	352,263	305,483	—	373,595	466,703
	18%	34%	25%		13%	16%
East Indies	87,070	164,206	205,734	—	384,671	438,869
	9%	16%	17%		14%	15%
(Germany and Low Countries)	(353,247)	(205,970)	(221,861)	—	(1,024,052)	(940,456)
	(34%)	(21%)	(18%)		(37%)	(32%)
Total Imports	1,028,857	987,522	1,216,497	1,222,099	2,770,489	2,944,175

NOTE

These figures must be taken as rough approximations, especially because official valuations are not always reliable or consistent. They do indicate very roughly the absolute growth trends in the several areas. They should be somewhat more accurate for relative trade distribution among areas within a given year.

SOURCES

1. Figures for 1621 and 1630 are calculated from Millard, "Import Trade of London," app. 2.

2. Figures for the Levantine trade for 1634 are derived directly from the London Port Book for Imports for that year. Included in this total are some £77,000 in goods, mostly raw silks, which were recorded as arriving from Leghorn but which were brought in by Levant Company merchants and which almost certainly had been brought by them from the Near East (their ship stopping at Leghorn).

3. Figures for German and Low Countries imports and also the total for 1634, as well as the 1640 total, are calculated from Millard, "Import Trade of London," app. 2.

4. Figures for 1663 and 1669 are calculated from BL, Add. MSS 36785.

sult of the fundamental expansion of the import trades. No doubt the ability of English manufacturers to produce new sorts of cloths at roughly competitive prices helped English merchants penetrate certain new markets. But, in almost every case, merchant importers increased their cloth exports in order to pay for increased imports, and they generally fell far behind.

Spain was possibly the leading market outside northern Europe for English cloths. Broadcloth exports to the Iberian peninsula seem to have been substantial as late as the 1580s. But during the first part of the seventeenth century they dwindled into insignificance. There was undoubtedly an important rise in the export of new draperies to Spain during the early Stuart period. But even here the point of saturation seems to have been reached relatively quickly. The growth in new-drapery exports to Spain appears to have ceased after 1620, at a time when imports from that area continued to grow. Moreover, throughout the period, English merchants commonly had to sell their cloths in Spain at below cost. They were apparently willing to do this in order to obtain lucrative imports, especially from the Americas.[74] At the same time, it is no doubt because the export of cloths to Spain was such a marginal business that we find only a tiny handful of cloth-specialist Merchant Adventurers entering the Spanish trade, despite its easy access, even when their own commerce entered deep crisis.[75]

The Italian commerce offers perhaps the best case for viewing the rise of the new southern and eastern trades, as the traditional interpretation would have it, as an adjustment by English industry and commerce to the north European cloth trade crisis. Certainly, the lighter new draperies did find a significant market in Italy, which seems to have absorbed increasing quantities throughout the period at the expense of Italian domestic production. Yet, even here, there is reason to suspect that the boom in new-drapery exports to Italy in the 1620s was a function of the marked rise of

[74] In Taylor's words: "It was imports rather than exports which counted for most in the calculations of merchants. New drapery exports to Spain were frequently subsidized by sales at or below cost price in order to command imports on which profits depended" ("Trade, Neutrality, and the 'English Road,' " pp. 237–38). See also Taylor, "Price Revolution or Price Revision?" pp. 11–15, 18–19, 29. Taylor contends that the Spanish market for English cloths, including new draperies, had reached its limit around 1620, ceasing to grow after that point. For the growth of imports from Spain in the 1630s, see Millard, "Import Trade of London," app. 2.

[75] For example, among 440 merchants exporting to Spain in 1640 (all products, including new draperies, besides traditional broadcloths), there appear to have been no more than a handful of Merchant Adventurers; in fact, I have been able to identify only three, who among them exported a minuscule part of the total sent to Spain that year. These figures are the result of comparing the list of exporters to Spain of 1640, compiled from the London Port Book for Exports (nonbroadcloths), 1640, PRO, E.190/43/1, with reasonably full lists of Merchant Adventurers, compiled from the London Port Books for Cloth Exports for 1620, 1622, 1628, 1632, and 1640. For the traders with Spain at this time, see below, ch. 2, pp. 85–87.

Italian imports at this time. Precise figures on new-drapery exports are unavailable to confirm or deny this hypothesis.[76]

Finally, the Levant was at no time in the early Stuart period a significant market for what are properly called new draperies (that is, worsteds such as says or mixed woolens and worsteds such as bays and serges), and only a minor one for broadcloths. In the early seventeenth century, English merchants did send to the Levant increasing quantities of dyed broadcloths. This product had only recently begun to be made in England, and does represent an adaptation of English industry to the difficulty of exporting its traditional product to its traditional market. Nevertheless, the growth of dyed-broadcloth exports to the Levant did no more than compensate for a corresponding decline of kersey broadcloth exports in the same period. Kerseys, initially, had been the Levantine-trade merchants' main export, but essentially disappeared from their shipments in the early seventeenth century. Overall, cloth exports to the Levant grew very little, if at all, before 1630, stagnating at a level of perhaps 6,000 to 8,000 cloths a year. This sort of market can in no way account for the intense, and increasing, activity of English merchants in this area in this period.[77] From 1630, cloth exports to the Levant began to rise somewhat, but they clearly did so as a faint and lagging response to the dramatically increased imports of these years (see table 1.6).[78]

During the first half of the seventeenth century, the value of exports to the Levant appears to have continued to constitute less than half the value of Levantine imports—as it had in the later sixteenth century.[79] In 1621, Lionel Cranfield singled out the Levantine commerce as particularly to blame for the nation's balance-of-trade problems, claiming that "upon the customs books we shall see that the Turkey Company hurts [the balance of trade] more than the East India Company. They now give two parts in

---

[76] Davis, "England and the Mediterranean," pp. 133–37.

[77] Ibid., pp. 118–20; Supple, *Commercial Crisis*, p. 258.

[78] Cloth exports to the Levant totaled 13,682 cloths in 1632 and 15,223 in 1640. These figures were compiled from the London Port Books for Cloth Exports for these years, PRO, E.190/36/5 and PRO, E.190/43/4. In 1638, Lewes Roberts claimed that, on average, cloth exports to the Levant totaled 14,000–16,000 cloths a year. (*Merchants Mappe*, pp. 139, 193).

[79] Davis concluded that the English enjoyed a favorable or at least an equal balance of trade with the Levant in the first half of the seventeenth century ("England and the Mediterranean," pp. 124–25). But it is almost certain that this is incorrect. This notion is controverted by (1) the conclusions of Willan and Fischer that the Levant trade was seriously unbalanced in the late sixteenth century; (2) the admitted stagnation of cloth exports to the Levant in the period 1600–1630 in the face of a very substantial rise in imports from the Levant; (3) the fact that the value of Levant exports even in the 1630s could not have been above £120,000 a year (15,000 cloths exported), while Levant imports in the 1630s were commonly above £250,000 annually; (4) official government figures that show Levant imports outdistancing exports by £373,595 to £167,661 in 1663 and by £466,703 to £191,458 in 1669 (Willan, "English Trade with the Levant," p. 410; Fischer, "English Trade to Asia," pp. 346–62; Millard, "Import Trade of London," app. 2; BL, Add. MSS 36785).

TABLE 1.6
Cloth Exports to the Levant

I. *Individual Years (based on London Port Books)*								
1598	1606	1620	1622	1628	1632	1640	1663	1669
8,883	8,291	9,501	8,036	2,034	13,682	15,223	12,460	14,349

II. *Averages (based on Levant Company Ledger Books)*			
1621–1626	1629–1635	1644–1650	1652–1656
6000	6,500	6,500	6,000
(+1000 kerseys)			

SOURCES

1. Figures for the individual years 1598–1628 from Supple, *Commercial Crisis*, p. 258. These figures include exports to Italy, which apparently averaged between 1,000 and 2,000 a year. The source for these figures is the London Port Books for Cloth Exports, except for 1598, for which the source is PRO, S.P.Dom.Eliz.I 268/101.

2. Figures for the individual years 1632 and 1640 from the London Port Books for Cloth Exports for those years, PRO, E.190/36/5 and E.190/43/4.

3. Figures for the individual years 1663 and 1669 are from Davis, "Influences de l'Angleterre," p. 205. The source for these figures is BL, Add. MSS, 36785.

4. Average figures for 1621–1626, etc., from Davis, "Influences de l'Angleterre." The source is the Levant Company Ledger Books, PRO, S.P.105/157–58.

money and the third in commodities."[80] Moreover, it has been demonstrated that English merchants trading with the Levant, like their counterparts trading with Spain, were obliged to sell their cloths at or below cost in order to secure their profitable imports. The price of cloth in Istanbul was practically the same as in London, clear evidence that English exporters were, in effect, dumping their cloths in the Levantine market.[81] Of course, the East Indies could not absorb cloth exports on any terms, and trade with the Far East had to be supported through the carrying of gold and by other means. In view of the import-centered character of the new trades and their limited capacity to absorb English exports, it is no wonder that contemporaries were deeply concerned with the balance of trade.

The early decades of the seventeenth century, and especially the years

[80] *Commons Debates, 1621*, ed. W. Notestein, F. H. Relf, and H. Simpson, 7 vols. (New Haven, 1935), 6: 300. William Towerson, deputy of the Merchant Adventurers Company, made the same point at the same meeting of Parliament, asserting that Levantine silks, currants, and indigo were being exchanged by the Levant Company merchants for English money (Friis, *Alderman Cockayne's Project*, p. 399). Similarly, the final report of the government's commission on trade of 1622 singled out the trade with Turkey in reference to its recommendation that increased care should be taken that fewer foreign commodities be bought with English money (ibid., p. 422).

[81] B. Braude, "International Competition and Domestic Cloth in the Ottoman Empire, 1500–1650: A Study in Undevelopment," *Review* 2 (Winter 1979): 442–46.

after 1620, have been aptly characterized as a "time of transition." The traditional cloth trade with northern Europe was in profound decline, and the new commerce with southern and eastern regions was on the ascent. But to interpret the latter in terms of the former, as is routinely done, is to miss the mark.[82] The commercial expansion to the Mediterranean, the Near East, and the Far East, dating from the latter part of the sixteenth century, must be understood as part of that long-term reorientation of English commerce that has come to be called the "commercial revolution." The growth of the Levantine–East Indian trade in this period, based as it was on the *import* of raw silks, of currants, and of spices—for domestic manufacturing, for broad home consumption, and for reexport to Europe—may be said to constitute the first phase in that reorientation. By 1640, this phase was already well advanced. In fact, at that point, the impact of a new, second stage—the rise of commerce with the Americas, also based on imports, in tobacco and sugar produced on farms and plantations—was already being strongly felt.

The Roots of Commercial Transformation: English Economic Growth versus European Economic Crisis in the Seventeenth Century

The sharply contrasting trends that marked English commerce in the first half of the seventeenth century must be interpreted in terms of the divergent evolutions of the English and the Continental economies in this period. English cloth exports diminished as they came up against declining European markets for cloths, the result of the secular crisis of production, above all in agriculture, that gripped seventeenth-century Europe. In contrast, English imports rose, partly in connection with the growing reexport commerce, but especially because of a growing domestic market, conditioned by the breakthrough in England in this period to ongoing economic development, rooted ultimately in the sociotechnical transformation of agriculture.[83]

THE CLOTH EXPORT CRISIS

According to the standard account, English cloth exports experienced stagnation and decline in the first half of the seventeenth century as a result

---

[82] The phrase and the associated interpretation are from Supple, *Commercial Crisis*, p. 135.

[83] For the general analysis of European economic development in the later medieval and early modern period on which this interpretation is based, see "The Agrarian Roots of European Capitalism," in *The Brenner Debate: Agrarian Class Structure and Economic Development in Pre-Industrial Europe*, ed. T. H. Aston and C.H.E. Philpin (Cambridge, 1985).

of intensified foreign competition. A good deal of contemporary commentary can be marshaled in support of this argument, and it is no doubt correct, up to a point.[84] But intensified competition itself needs to be explained. The English merchants' Dutch, Venetian, and Flemish rivals were also complaining about increased international competition in this period, and seem to have been badly hurt by it. There is, indeed, good reason to believe that not just the English, but the entire European, cloth export industry was in trouble. If English cloth exports were in decline, it was not because the cloth exports of England's competitors were on the rise.

The fact is that none of the European national cloth export industries gained ground in this period, and most lost substantially. The Flemish cloth export industry, which had reconstituted itself by specializing in only the highest-quality products, enjoyed a period of real growth during the sixteenth century. But during the seventeenth century, the Flemish cloth industry was unable to maintain its position, and its exports fell by half during the hundred years after 1600.[85] In a parallel manner, the much more significant Italian cloth industry, also heavily based on high-quality products for export, grew very substantially during the latter part of the sixteenth century. But after the turn of the century, it, too, suffered catastrophic decline, and in the cloth industries of Venice, Florence, Milan, and Como, output fell by more than half before 1650.[86]

Nor were the losses experienced by the Flemish and Italian industries offset by dramatic gains for the rising industrial powers of England and the United Provinces. The highly advanced Dutch industry had gone forward during the late sixteenth century on the basis of its superiority in producing new draperies (bays, says, fustians). But this branch of Dutch industry fell off precipitously after 1620, losing two-thirds of its output by 1700. Because it maintained the greatest concentration of skill and technique in Europe, the Dutch cloth industry was able partially to make up for the losses sustained in new-drapery production by increasing its output of traditional broadcloths during the same period. Even so, the overall picture was one of decline.[87] Finally, as noted, the once-overpowering English broadcloth industry saw its exports to northern Europe cut

[84] See Supple, *Commercial Crisis*, pp. 137–41.

[85] J. Craeybeckx, "Les industries d'exportation dans les villes flamandes du xvııe siècle, particulièrement à Gand et à Bruges," *Studi in onore di A. Fanfani* 4 (1962): 412–68; P. Deyon, "La concurrence internationale des manufactures lainières au xvıe et xvıie siècles," *Annales E.S.C.* 27 (Jan.–Feb. 1972): 27–28.

[86] D. Sella, "The Rise and Fall of the Venetian Wool Industry," and C. M. Cipolla, "The Economic Decline of Italy," in *Crisis and Change in the Venetian Economy*, ed. B. Pullan (New York, 1968).

[87] C. Wilson, "Cloth Production and International Competition in the Seventeenth Century," *Ec.H.R.*, 2d ser., 13 (1960).

in half in the short period between 1614 and 1640. Part of the loss was made up by the rapid growth of new-drapery exports, especially to southern Europe. But the balance sheet as a whole registered stasis at best.

The fact that the European cloth export trade as a whole stagnated and declined during the first half of the seventeenth century leads inexorably to the conclusion that merchants faced at this time a general problem in the market, not merely more formidable international competitors. After about 1600, there were many losers, but no real gainers; there was, at best, a *redistribution* of a flat or even shrinking export total.[88] It follows that a ceiling had been reached. The pattern is reminiscent of that previously experienced by the medieval European cloth industry in the early fourteenth century. Indeed, the long-term trends of growth and decline of the international cloth trade during the medieval and early modern era appear to have been closely bound up with those grand cycles of economic and demographic development and crisis that marked the European economy at least through 1700.

Massive industries producing cloth for export had arisen in Flanders in the eleventh and twelfth centuries, and in Brabant and Italy somewhat later, on the basis of their ability to capture significant portions of the Continent's luxury and semiluxury markets.[89] All these industries grew during the great period of economic expansion of the later twelfth and thirteenth centuries, as rising population and output provided the basis for rising upper- and middle-class incomes and, in turn, rising consumption. But the growth of upper- and middle-class consumption of manufactured goods was restricted in the last analysis by the sociotechnical limitations of medieval agriculture. In view of the long-term tendency of agricultural productivity to stagnate or decline, upper- and middle-class incomes and thus consumption were constrained by the restricted ability of the population to grow in the face of the finite supply of available land and by the ultimately limited possibilities for transferring income away from the peasant producers. A general crisis of productivity, population, and income was experienced almost everywhere in Europe at various points in the fourteenth century. Upper- and middle-class purchasing power was undermined, and the inevitable result was a structural crisis in the European cloth export industries. The sharp intensification of international competition between cloth-producing centers was the signal that markets had been saturated and that generalized growth was no longer possible.

In a similar manner, the European cloth export industries of the early

[88] Cf. Coleman, *Economy of England*, p. 132.

[89] See E. M. Carus-Wilson, "The Woolen Industry," in *The Cambridge Economic History of Europe*, ed. M. M. Postan and E. E. Rich (Cambridge, 1952), 2: 301ff.

modern period experienced a rapid rise on the basis of the broad-based upturn of the European economy that began in the second half of the fifteenth century. All across Europe, the peasant population and agricultural output grew rapidly and so, in turn, did upper- and middle-class incomes and demand. England's cloth industry was able to benefit disproportionately by capturing a major share of the expanding market. In fact, English cloth exports tripled in the period from about 1460 to 1550.[90] Even so, all of the leading national cloth export industries of Europe did well during much of the sixteenth century.

During the late sixteenth and early seventeenth centuries, however, almost everywhere in Europe, agricultural output and, in turn, population, sooner or later ceased to grow—a development that reflected, as in the fourteenth century, the continuing sociotechnical limitations of agricultural production. The fact that output had reached its limit was manifested, again as in the fourteenth century, by the great struggles of the epoch to redistribute income in the face of static or declining total production, leading to the growth of absolutist taxation (in France and West Germany) and the further intensification of serfdom (in eastern Europe), as well as to large-scale, often highly destructive, warfare, both internal and among nations. It was expressed also in the stagnation or decline of upper- and middle-class purchasing power, and ultimately in the profound crisis in the markets for cloth all across the continent. This decay of demand for cloth manifested itself in the decline of almost every national industry producing primarily for local consumption—the French, the Spanish, and those of eastern Europe[91]—as well as in the profound dislocation of the great European cloth centers producing for an international market— the Flemish, the Italian, the English, and the Dutch.

During the crisis in the international cloth trade of the later medieval period, the saturation of markets and the resulting intensification of competition had naturally put a premium on cheaper forms of production. Consumers at every income level demanded fewer goods and less expensive ones. In consequence, in all the great cloth-producing centers there was a drive to lower the cost of production. This found expression, first of all, in the rise of poorly made goods, based on cheap labor and a lower quality of workmanship—at the expense of well-produced goods made by careful, well-trained, and more expensive labor. It was reflected as well in

---

[90] Coleman, *Economy of England*, pp. 48–55, 61–65.

[91] For the difficulties in the various local industries, see, for instance, M. Malowist, "Poland, Russia, and Western Trade in the Fifteenth and Sixteenth Centuries," *Past & Present*, no. 13 (1958); M. Malowist, "L'évolution industrielle en Pologne du XIVe au XVIIe siècles," *Studi in onore di A. Sapori* I (1957): 574–603; P. Deyon, *Amiens, capitale provinciale* (Paris, 1967), pp. 167–72, 205–16; P. Goubert, *Beauvais et les Beauvaisis de 1600 à 1730* (Paris, 1960), pp. 585–94; J. H. Elliott, "The Decline of Spain," in *Crisis in Europe, 1560–1660*, ed. T. Aston (London, 1965); J. De Vries, *The Economy of Europe in an Age of Crisis, 1600–1750* (Cambridge, 1976), p. 103.

the dramatic growth of lower-wage production in smaller towns and the countryside where labor was plentiful and living costs were relatively low—at the expense of production in the urban centers where labor was costly, especially because living costs were high and production was sometimes under guild control. Finally, there was the appearance of new types of products (the new draperies), which were less costly in terms of skill, raw materials, and technology—at the expense of the traditional, high-quality products.[92]

The heightened international competition of the early seventeenth century led to essentially the same trends in the centers of cloth production for the international market as had that of the late Middle Ages. Thus, the changes in the cloth trade that took place in this period were not, for the most part, in response to changes in taste and fashion, as is sometimes alleged; the different sorts of cloth that appeared were, by and large, simply less expensive subsitutes for and copies of existing varieties. The generalized crisis of purchasing power and the declining demand for cloth at all levels of society led to a systematic deterioration of the cloth market and, in response, a systematic downgrading of the cloth product from the top to the bottom of the line. This process made for the substitution of cheaper, if often less well made, goods for more expensive ones; the appearance of lower-quality, but often quite attractive, imitations; and, finally, the rise of entirely new products using cheaper materials and less-skilled labor, which took the place of the older, finer ones in the shopping baskets of financially strapped consumers.

In the first place, then, all of the great cloth-exporting centers were hurt by competition from newly emergent local industries, usually based in the countryside and making cheap, poorly produced goods for local consumption. Declining incomes, resulting from agricultural depression, forced many consumers to turn to the lowest-cost items; meanwhile, the growth of population and the concentration of landholding created a mass of wretched, semiproletarianized peasant producers who required manufacturing employment to supplement their meager incomes from agriculture in order to make ends meet. Because the local industries relied on peasant producers, they generally could put out only the lowest-quality, worst-made goods. Nevertheless, they succeeded in drastically undermining the markets for the bottom-of-the-line cloth products that previously had been supplied to these regions by the great international manufacturers. In particular, at the turn of the seventeenth century, newly emergent local cloth industries in eastern and central Europe, in Spain, and in the Levant be-

[92] H. Van Der Wee, "Structural Change and Specialization in the Industry of the Southern Netherlands, 1100–1600," Ec.H.R., 2d ser., 28 (1975): 203–21; D. Nicholas, "Economic Reorientation and Social Change in Fourteenth-Century Flanders," Past & Present, no. 70 (1976): 3–29; M. M. Postan, "The Trade of Medieval Europe: The North," in Postan and Rich, Cambridge Economic History of Europe 2: 191–256.

gan to take over local markets that English merchants had captured during the sixteenth century (and before) on the basis of the export of cheaply made kerseys. Kerseys originally had been developed in the English countryside, and their sale on the international market represented, in Coleman's words, "the commercialization of a peasant technique, once supplying merely local or subsistence needs." It is not really surprising therefore that English producers of kerseys were unable to compete with the nascent, local, peasant-based industries of Europe and the Near East and that English kerseys were ultimately eliminated from the local markets for low-quality products.[93]

At the same time, almost all of the great exporting centers were adversely affected by a contracting demand for the very best types of cloth. Particularly hard hit in this respect were the English in their north and central European markets, the Venetians in their Levantine market and in Italy itself, and the Flemish everywhere. Only the Dutch seem to have had the skilled labor and technology (and the access to higher-quality Spanish wool) required to hold their own.[94]

Finally, as the obverse side of the foregoing process, there was a growing demand for new sorts of cloths—inevitably of lower quality—that could serve as less expensive, but more or less close substitutes for the traditional, high-quality products. Those manufacturers who could command relatively skilled, but nonetheless flexible and relatively cheap, labor were in the best position to meet this demand. For this reason, the English cloth industry, which could make use of a pool of experienced but unregulated and low-cost producers in the countryside—and which had unequaled access to unlimited supplies of the appropriate sort of homegrown wool—appears to have been able to prevail over all of its urban-based and sometimes guild-regulated competitors in the manufacture of the so-called new draperies. Although this did not happen overnight, the English exporters of new draperies appear ultimately to have beaten out their Dutch competition in both northern and southern Europe.[95] Similarly, the English new draperies sharply cut into the sales of

[93] Supple, *Commercial Crisis*, pp. 137–40; Taylor, "Price Revolution or Price Revision?" p. 15; Fischer, "English Trade to Asia," pp. 348–49; Davis, "England and the Mediterranean," p. 120; W. G. Endrei, "English Kerseys in Eastern Europe, with Special Reference to Hungary," *Textile History* 5 (Oct. 1974): 96–97. The quotation is from D. C. Coleman, "An Innovation and Its Diffusion: The 'New Draperies,' " *Ec.H.R.*, 2d ser., 22 (1969): 421–22.

[94] Wilson, "Cloth Production and International Competition," pp. 216–20; Supple, *Commercial Crisis*, pp.136–37; Sella, "Venetian Wool Industry," pp. 117–21; Deyon, "La concurrence internationale," pp. 27–28; Van Der Wee, "Structural Change and Specialization," pp. 216–18; Craeybeckx, "Les industries d'exportation," p. 422.

[95] Wilson, "Cloth Production and International Competition," pp. 213–15. For English difficulties with Dutch competition in the first part of the seventeenth century, see Taylor, "Trade, Neutrality, and the 'English Road,' " p. 238, and De Vries, *Economy of Europe*, pp. 101, 103.

the Italian producers in their own home market. Meanwhile, the English industry's newly developed line of dyed broadcloths was able to replace the Italians' better-quality, but more expensive, broadcloths in the Levant. It was indeed the invasion of new sorts of English cloth—both new draperies in Italy itself and newfangled broadcloths in the Levant—that appears to have been the immediate cause of the decline of the great Venetian cloth industry during the first several decades of the seventeenth century. Hampered both by high wages and by guild regulations that imposed the traditional quality and stylistic standards on local production, the Italian industry was unable to make the necessary adjustments to stand up to its more flexible rivals from the north.[96]

It should thus be clear why the intensification of competition in the international cloth market can provide only a superficial explanation for the secular crisis of the English cloth trade during the first half of the seventeenth century. In relative terms, the English and Dutch industries emerged the winners in the fierce war for markets of this period. Each came to dominate the international cloth market in which it enjoyed competitive advantages. Speaking very roughly: the English ultimately won out in the market for new draperies, ousting the Dutch from their formerly hegemonic position in this line; the Dutch prevailed, in the end, in the market for the traditional high-quality product, taking over the leading position formerly enjoyed by the English; and the Dutch and the English divided the market in the newer, less-than-highest-quality dyed broadcloths, which, in terms of quality and price, fell between the new and old draperies.[97] Meanwhile, the great Italian export industry collapsed, as did the less-significant Flemish industry. But because intensified international competition was itself a manifestation of an underlying problem of demand—the saturation of markets—the English victory in relative terms, like that of the Dutch, represented a decline in absolute terms. No national cloth export industry could gain in the face of the general crisis of the European economy.

THE RISE OF IMPORTS

Of course, the new English import trades were able to prosper at the very time that the traditional cloth export trades were languishing. And the divergent fates of these trades must be linked, in the last analysis, to the

[96] Davis, "England and the Mediterranean," pp. 121–24; Sella, "Venetian Wool Industry," pp. 119–23. See also R. T. Rapp, "The Unmaking of the Mediterranean Trade Hegemony: International Trade Rivalry and the Commercial Revolution," *J.Ec.H.* 35 (1975).

[97] The new English "Spanish" cloths, produced in the West Country, challenged comparable Dutch products in northern Europe and appear to have done especially well in the Levant (Supple, *Commercial Crisis*, p. 150). See also above, note 96.

different markets they served. This was the period in which the English economy was, for the first time, beginning to distinguish itself from those of its Continental neighbors. While general crisis gripped a European economy still structured by precapitalist agrarian forms, the English economy was able to sustain ongoing development on the basis, above all, of the transformation of its agrarian social and property structure in a capitalist direction.

The rise of capitalist property relations on the land had a dual significance: on the one hand, it meant the breakup of those decentralized or centralized systems of extraeconomic coercion by which a lordly class had exacted levies from the direct producers and thereby maintained itself (seigneurial dues or salaries from offices based on taxation); on the other hand, it meant the separation from possession of the land of the direct producers (peasants), who formerly had direct nonmarket access to (possession of) their full means of subsistence. The production structure that arose, therefore, was distinguished by the emergence of a new class of tenant farmers (of varying wealth): these producers were free from the older lordly controls, but, deprived of their direct possession of the soil and thus their direct access to their means of subsistence, they were rendered dependent on the market for their livelihood and subject to competitive rents, which provided the means of support for the dominant class of landlords. Having thus lost their shield from competition, the tenants had no choice, if they wished to hold onto their farms, but to produce competitively for exchange and thus to seek to cut costs: in consequence, in order to survive, they were obliged to specialize, accumulate their surpluses, and innovate.

Over time, the results for the economy as a whole of this subjection of the direct producers to the economic imperatives that derived from the emerging capitalist social and property structure—above all, competition in production—were epoch making. First, systemwide attempts to cut costs led to the improvement of agricultural production—specialization in crops by type of soil and regional ecology, innovations in technique, and, in the end, the dramatic growth of agricultural productivity. Second, processes of social differentiation arising from unequal success in responding to the market, as well as from the rapid growth of population, resulted, over time, in the accumulation of land and the means of production in the hands of a dynamic class of capitalist tenant farmers. The opposite side of the same coin was the appearance of a growing class of semilanded and propertyless people, who needed to take up employment to make ends meet and who provided a labor force for nascent industry. Third, the direct producers' increasing dependence on the market, not only for the means of production but also for the means of subsistence, and the resulting processes of specialization, brought about the decline of home production of necessities and the initial rise of a domestic market. Finally, the effect of intensifying competition on all producers, especially those who lacked the resources to produce at the requisite level of efficiency, was the inexorable intensification of labor, both industrial and agricultural, by both owner-operators and wage laborers. The long-term economic implications of all these processes can be deduced: the cheapening of goods, resulting from increases in productivity, especially in agriculture, and from the intensification of labor, especially in industry, had the indirect effect of increasing purchasing power; meanwhile, the growing market dependence even of agriculturists (who previously had produced for subsistence) and the relatively poor had the direct effect of increasing demand. The result was a continuing growth in the home market, which not only spurred economic development but ultimately helped to found the long-term rise of imports.[98]

The initial acceleration of English manufacture for home consumption did not, it is true, depend on rising demand. Occurring in the middle years of the sixteenth century, it took the form of the rise of import-substitution industries in products used in the manufacture of cloths—in particular, woad, madder, alum, and copperas. Nevertheless, in the latter part of the sixteenth century, there was the initial development of so-called consumer industries, most notably stocking knitting, ribbon making, and linen, thread, and lace production. Their emergence is a telltale sign not only of a vital middle-class market, but also of not insignificant lower-class demand. It is symptomatic of the trend that as early as 1578, in as remote a spot as Kirkby Lonsdale, a small market town in Lancashire, retail shops could stock a wide variety of both native and imported goods. The first several decades of the seventeenth century saw a continuation of the same development, highlighted now by the emergence of dynamic industries in pin making, starch making, and vinegar making. Indeed, examinations of inventories over the whole century between 1550 and 1650 reveal increasing numbers of poor people, including laborers, in a position to acquire larger quantities of domestic wares.[99]

In the foregoing context, the import boom of the second quarter of the seventeenth century is particularly revealing, precisely because it came at the time of the greatest crisis in the cloth export trade. Imports could grow at this juncture, even in the face of the economic dislocation caused by the

---

[98] For the foregoing analysis, see Brenner, "Agrarian Roots," and references there cited. For a very similar interpretation, see J. Thirsk, *Economic Policy and Projects: The Development of a Consumer Society in Early Modern England* (Oxford, 1978). I have relied a good deal on Dr. Thirsk's book in this section. For a different view of the period, see R. B. Outhwaite, "Progress and Backwardness in English Agriculture, 1500–1650," *Ec.H.R.*, 2d Ser., 39 (1986).

[99] Thirsk, *Economic Policy and Projects*, pp. 24–94; D. M. Palliser, "Tawney's Century: Brave New World or Malthusian Trap?" *Ec.H.R.*, 2d ser., 35 (1982): 350ff.

decay of cloth manufacture, only because the foundations of the English economy were already shifting. The cloth export crisis hit extremely hard, but its effects were apparently geographically limited to the cloth-manufacturing areas of East Anglia and the West Country.[100] Meanwhile, a growing English home market was absorbing record imports of commodities of all types.

According to Millard's figures, the value of total imports grew significantly over the whole period from 1600 to 1640, increasing from about £1,000,000 (including wines) in 1600 to about £3,000,000 (including wines) in 1640. But the really dramatic rise of imports came after 1615 as the traditional cloth export trade was turning down: the value of imports (including wines) averaged £1,240,000 over the period from 1603 to 1615; by 1630–1640, their value was averaging £3,000,000 a year.[101]

Given the skyrocketing rents of the first four decades of the seventeenth century, it is hardly surprising that this period was marked by a significant increase in luxury imports, in particular of fine manufactured silks from Italy. What was more expressive, however, of the new economic pattern was the dramatic rise of raw-silk imports to feed a newly developing English silk industry, which produced mostly low-quality items for middle- and even lower-class consumption. Between 1621 and 1640 raw-silk imports nearly doubled, increasing from 125,000 pounds to 213,000 pounds. As one contemporary remarked in 1617, "There is such a madness to be clothed in silk that we cannot endure our home made cloth." By the 1660s, raw-silk imports had increased to about 283,000 pounds annually. So widespread had the consumption of silks become by this time that the author of *Brittania Languens* was prompted to remark in 1680 that "silk is now grown nigh as common as wool," and "ordinary people, especially the female, will be in silk, more or less, if they can."[102]

Equally indicative of the growing purchasing power of middle- and lower-class English people in the early Stuart period was the rapid increase of all sorts of food imports. As already noted, currants imports rose enormously in this period. They leaped from about 31,000 hundredweight in 1621 to about 62,000 hundredweight in 1638 and about 49,000 hundredweight in 1640.[103] Currants were consumed very widely throughout the population. As the Venetian ambassador remarked in 1628, "A

[100] Supple, *Commercial Crisis*, esp. pp. 5ff., 52–54, 100–104, 111–12, and 123–25.

[101] A. M. Millard, "The Imports of London, 1600–1640," with attached "Analyses of Port Books . . . 1558–1640 . . . compiled by A. M. Millard, 1950–1959" (bound TS, BL Reading Room, n.d.), p. 50 and table 1.

[102] Table 1.3. The figure for the 1660s is an average of the figures for 1663 and 1669. Quotations are from D. Sella, "Industrial Production in Seventeenth-Century Italy," *Explorations in Economic History* 6 (1969): 246.

[103] Table 1.4.

general prohibition of currants cannot be made without exciting universal discontent. This people consume a greater amount of currants than all the rest of the world, and are so accustomed to this luxury and so fond of it, that men have been said to hang themselves because they have not enough money to buy them on certain popular festivals."[104] The consumption of various other imported edibles by the middle and even the lower class also increased significantly at this time, and the growing demand for raisins, tobacco, and sugar in this period was mainly responsible for the dramatic rise, after about 1620, in imports from Spain, which largely consisted of these products.[105]

Finally, the real takeoff in the import of commodities from the East Indies began in the 1620s. Here, however, it is not clear to what extent rising consumption was accounted for by increased demand consequent on increased purchasing power, and to what extent by declining prices resulting from the increased availability of East Indian commodities, due to the firm establishment of the East India Company and its trade. The skyrocketing consumption of tobacco during the 1620s and 1630s was certainly made possible by the collapse in its price.[106] In any case, there can be no doubt that the rise of English imports was conditioned not only by the rise of English purchasing power, but also by the growth of English commercial and colonial power, which brought much lower prices for some products. Indeed, as I shall have occasion to emphasize in a moment, the two went hand in hand.

It may well be that a fortuitous run of good grain harvests in the 1620s, which brought about unexpectedly low food prices, helped to mitigate the worst effects of the cloth crisis, and to keep imports buoyant. But it seems reasonable to argue that what was ultimately taking place was no mere short-run development but a secular transformation. Between 1500 and 1700 the English population increased about two and a half fold. An increase of nearly the same dimensions between 1150 and 1300 to approximately the same absolute level as in 1700 had brought about the demographic crisis of the fourteenth century. A similar doubling of population on the Continent, starting from record-low levels in the period from the late fifteenth Century to the late sixteenth century, had also led to demo-

---

[104] *C.S.P. Ven. 1628–1629*, p. 553. See also Salisbury's reference in 1608 to currants (along with sugar and tobacco) as products "of necessary important use to the poor." J. Spedding, ed., *Lord Bacon's Works*, 16 vols. [London, 1861–1872], 11: 58, quoted in Friis, *Alderman Cockayne's Project*, p. 198).

[105] Millard, "Analyses of Port Books," tables 30, 31, 33, 34, and 35. The very impressive increase in the import of the relatively cheap Spanish wines in these years is further indication of the same trend. Annual Spanish wine imports more than doubled between the 1600s and the later 1630s (Millard, table 27).

[106] See Chaudhuri, *East India Company*, pp. 140–72; R. R. Menard, "A Note on Chesapeake Tobacco Prices, 1618–1660," *V.M.H.B.* 84 (1976): 401–10.

graphic and agrarian catastrophe. By the early seventeenth century in England, however, subsistence crises were a thing of the past (and had not been severe by European standards even during the second half of the sixteenth century). Moreover, after falling steadily and sharply from the late fifteenth century, real wages bottomed out about 1600–1610 and from then on at least maintained their level, in the face of continuing population growth until 1650 or so, rising during the rest of the seventeenth century. Meanwhile, throughout the whole period of demographic growth, the English economy was able to sustain a steady movement of the population out of agriculture into various nonagricultural pursuits. Whereas in 1520 about 76 percent of the population was involved in agriculture, by 1700 only about 55 percent was so occupied. This change occurred, apparently, with relatively little strain, for by the latter part of the seventeenth century, English grain exports had grown to such a level as to drive east European competitors essentially out of the market.[107]

It was thus the continuing growth of agricultural productivity, coupled with increasing rural specialization, that made possible ongoing economic development and underpinned a rising home market in England straight through the seventeenth century, when general economic crisis was gripping virtually the entire Continent. Declining agricultural costs allowed for relatively low food prices and thus for more people off the land and in industry, as well as for rising discretionary incomes for both the middle and the lower class. The second half of the seventeenth century brought the further growth of the whole range of consumer industries that had had their beginnings in the late Tudor–early Stuart period, as well as the rise of a host of new industries making consumer products, such as knives, edge tools, and hats. In addition, not only London, but also Liverpool, Manchester, and Birmingham experienced dynamic growth. In the post-Restoration period there was a continuation of the boom in the import (as well as the reexport) trades with southern Europe and the Near and Far

[107] Thirsk, *Economic Policy and Projects*, p. 162; Coleman, *Economy of England*, p. 12; E. Le Roy Ladurie, "Les masses profondes: La paysannerie," in *Histoire economique et sociale de la France*, ed. F. Braudel and R. Labrousse, 3 vols. (Paris, 1970–1977), vol. 1, pt. 2, pp. 555–85; A. Appleby, "Grain Prices and Subsistence Crises in England and France, 1590–1740," *J.Ec.H.* 39 (1979); R. Schofield, "The Impact of Scarcity and Plenty on Population Change in England, 1541–1871," *Journal of Interdisciplinary History* 14 (Autumn 1983): 276 (on real wages); E. L. Jones, "Editor's Introduction," in *Agriculture and Economic Growth in England, 1650–1815* (London, 1970), p. 2; E. A. Wrigley, "Urban Growth and Agricultural Change: England and the Continent in the Early Modern Period," *Journal of Interdisciplinary History* 15 (Spring 1985): 700 (ratio of agricultural to nonagricultural population); J. A. Faber, "The Decline of the Baltic Trade in the Second Half of the Seventeenth Century," *Acta Historiae Neerlandica* 1 (1966): 125–26; A. H. John, "English Agricultural Improvement and Grain Imports, 1660–1765," in *Trade, Government, and the Economy in Pre-Industrial England*, ed. D. C. Coleman and A. H. John (London, 1976), pp. 46–68; Palliser, "Tawney's Century."

East, as well as in those with the Americas, which had begun under Elizabeth and prospered under James I and Charles I. Agricultural revolution thus continued to help pave the way not only for ongoing industrial growth, but for continuing commercial revolution.[108]

The Power of English Commerce

Finally, it needs to be emphasized that the growth of English imports would have been far more problematic for the English economy had it not been directed by English merchants. What made import-driven commercial expansion so beneficial was its control by English traders and English shippers. English merchants, as noted, were motivated to expand English commercial horizons by the desire to emulate and, ultimately, to displace the Spanish and the Portuguese in their trades for gold, spices, and other commodities. What actually drove them to initiate the new trades were the serious disruptions of their Iberian and Antwerp entrepôts and the consequent need to acquire on their own the goods that they had formerly obtained from middlemen. In order to accomplish this, they were compelled to invade and attack the privileged commercial strongholds of the Portuguese, Spanish, and Venetian empires. They were encouraged to persevere in their efforts by the perceptibly declining power of their competitors, especially the Venetians in the Mediterranean, the Portuguese in the Indian Ocean, and, at last, the Spanish in the Atlantic and the Caribbean. They found the new trades profitable over a very long period to a large extent because of the long-term growth of English home demand. Nevertheless, while all of the foregoing helps explain why English merchants embarked on and persisted in their expansionary drive southward and eastward, it does not fully explain why English merchants actually succeeded in their endeavors—in particular, why they were able to capture what were, in most cases, relatively long-established trades from those who previously had controlled them.

It would, of course, be wrong to deny entirely that the impressive, and unquestionably increasing, flexibility and strength of English textile manufacturing, dating from the late sixteenth century, facilitated English commercial expansion. The new products of English cloth manufacturers did, as noted, allow English merchants to make sales in certain critical (if limited) new markets. This was true, in particular, with respect to the

[108] Thirsk, *Economic Policy and Projects*, ch. 5 and Conclusion; Coleman, *Economy of England*, chs. 6, 7, 9, 11; A. H. John, "Agricultural Productivity and Economic Growth in England, 1700–1760," *J.Ec.H.* 25 (1965); D.E.C. Eversley, "The Home Market and Economic Growth in England, 1750–1780," in *Land, Labour, and Population in the Industrial Revolution*, ed. E. L. Jones and G. E. Mingay (London, 1967).

new draperies in Italy and the newly developed "Spanish" dyed broad-cloths in the Levant. The ability to market these new cloth products no doubt helped provide an advantage to English merchants at a time when European traders of all countries were chronically short of specie. Nevertheless, as I have tried to argue, outside northern Europe, English merchants were commonly compelled to sell their cloths at below the cost of production, and, in any case, they could not, in the really crucial markets, even begin to cover the cost of their imports with their exports. Even in the Levantine trade, exports paid for less than half of imports, and in the East Indies, of course, sales of English-made goods were minimal. The question, therefore, remains: What accounts for the strength of English commerce in the new areas of trade?

English merchants trading with southern and eastern areas were, it seems, able to prevail in these regions because, to put it crudely, they had the power to do so. They appear to have derived their power in this period largely from the growing effectiveness of English shipping in the Mediterranean and the Indian Ocean and from the increasing strength of English commercial organization, notably the Levant Company and its off-shoot, the East India Company. Their power was also much enhanced by the support of an English monarchy that had been historically—and now was increasingly—concerned with promoting commerce. Highly restricted, in comparison to a number of their Continental counterparts, in their capacity to tax the land, English monarchs were more and more dependent on returns from customs and, for this reason among others, had to facilitate, to the extent that they were able, the expansion of overseas trade. The specific processes by which English merchants achieved a preeminent position in the Mediterranean and a very powerful one in the Indian Ocean can be clarified when their commercial experiences in these areas are seen in light of their much less successful commercial experiences in the waters and ports of western Europe.

The initial focal point of the English expansionary thrust was the Iberian peninsula: it was here, to an important degree, that English merchants initially sought those highly valued products of the Far East and the Americas. Nevertheless, the inability of English commerce to stand up to that of the Dutch in this key arena exposed its weaknesses, at least in relative terms. During most of the first half of the seventeenth century, English new draperies could not really compete with Dutch-made products in Iberia. English merchants trading with Spain were thus commonly obliged to travel to the Continent to procure goods that could be sold in the Spanish market. Nor could English shipping compete with the more efficient Dutch flyboats on the routes to Spain. For these reasons, the achievement of peace between Spain and the United Provinces—as in the periods between 1609 and 1618 and after 1648—generally spelled disaster for English trade with Iberia, for it meant the return of Dutch competition, and, very quickly, of Dutch predominance.[109]

In sharp contrast, as Ralph Davis has made clear, English commerce exerted a growing hegemony in the Mediterranean starting in the late sixteenth century precisely because, in this region, mere industrial strength and shipping efficiency were insufficient to ensure commercial domination. For a very long period after English commerce began to penetrate the Mediterranean, those who wished to trade successfully in the region could do so only to the degree that they could command the naval power to ward off the attacks of successive generations of predators, from the Turks and Barbary pirates in the middle of the sixteenth century, to the Spanish in the latter part of the sixteenth century, to the North Africa-based multinational pirate communities in the first half of the seventeenth century. When English merchants first sought to exploit the opening provided by the temporary disarray of their Italian and Dutch opponents during the 1570s to reenter the Mediterranean, they had no choice but to devise the means to defend themselves. In the end, they did so by developing a new type of armed vessel that was actually more efficient in carrying out the combined operations of shipping and warfare required by Mediterranean conditions than were the ships of any of their competitors.[110]

It is thus no accident that the very same merchants who first developed the Turkish and Venetian trades under charters from Elizabeth turned out to be among the leading shipowners of the period: proprietors of a growing fleet of great armed vessels, their boats could hold their own against all comers, and do so more cheaply than could the vessels of their chief competitors, the Venetians and the Dutch (who could not make use of their highly efficient but militarily insufficient flyboats in this region). Not only

[109] Taylor, "Trade, Neutrality, and the 'English Road,' " pp. 237–39; Taylor, "Price Revolution or Price Revision?" pp. 15–17; H. Taylor, "English Merchants and Spanish Prices about 1600," in *Kölner Kolloquien zur Internationalen Sozial- und Wirtschaftsgeschichte* 1 (Cologne, 1970): 253–55; De Vries, *Economy of Europe*, p. 101; V. Barbour, "Dutch and English Merchant Shipping in the Seventeenth Century," *Ec.H.R.* 2 (1929–1930). The pattern was, in fact, roughly the same throughout most of Europe, notably in the Baltic. There, as in Spain, Dutch exporters of cloth took advantage of the period of peace after 1609 to erode and ultimately to destroy the position of English cloth traders. The English had achieved a temporary monopoly in the Baltic following the disruption of Dutch commerce after the revolt of the Netherlands and the collapse of the Antwerp market. In the Baltic as in Spain, the English proved unable to match either cheap Dutch manufacturers or cheap Dutch shipping (J. K. Federowicz, "Anglo-Polish Commercial Relations in the First Half of the Seventeenth Century," *Journal of European Economic History* 5 [1976]: 363–69; see also J. K. Federowicz, *England's Baltic Trade in the Early Seventeenth Century* [Cambridge, 1980], pp. 158–73, 185–87).

[110] Davis, "England and the Mediterranean," pp. 126–32; R. Davis, *The Rise of the English Shipping Industry in the Seventeenth and Eighteenth Centuries* (London, 1962), pp. 5–8; Davis, "Influences de l'Angleterre," pp. 212–20.

could the English Levantine-trade merchants directly manage their own private coercive force; they could command, as well, the state's support for their commercial initiatives. Elizabeth's government, as well as those of the early Stuarts, not only granted them monopoly charters for their trades and eventually a navigation policy, but also offered a significant level of direct diplomatic and political backing to their expansionary efforts (partly because the companies would, in return, perform diplomatic and political functions for the government). It appears to have been the combination of (armed) shipping superiority, company organization, and government backing that made for English commercial supremacy in the Mediterranean. In turn, English strength in the Mediterranean appears to have provided much of the foundation for the rise of English commercial power throughout the world during the following century.[111]

The same traders with Turkey and Venice who first developed the armed fleets that penetrated the Mediterranean were among the leaders of the privateering war against Spain during the 1580s and 1590s. This conflict brought enormous gains to English privateers, and so provided them with the means and the incentive to invest their profits in building still more large, armed ships. Levant Company merchants, as we know, provided most of the financing and entrepreneurship for launching the English trade with the East Indies. Equally important, it was the ships of great privateering Levantine-trade merchants, almost exclusively, that carried out the first East India Company voyages.[112]

During the first two decades of the seventeenth century, first the Anglo-Spanish peace of 1604 and then the Dutch-Spanish peace of 1609 put English merchants in serious difficulty through much of the commercial world. The huge field of Atlantic privateering was now closed to them. Equally significant, they suddenly faced withering Dutch competition through most of Europe proper: from the North Sea to the Iberian peninsula, the combination of cheap Dutch manufactures with cheap Dutch shipping seemed to constitute an insuperable barrier to successful English commerce.[113]

In sharp contrast, during these same decades the power of English commerce grew not only in the Mediterranean, but in the Far East. In the Mediterranean, where the Barbary corsairs received vast accretions of strength in the period after the Anglo-Spanish peace from unemployed English seamen who brought with them their advanced maritime techniques, English commerce reigned supreme. On the basis of both their superior shipping and their new lines of broadcloths, the Levant Com-

---

[111] Davis, "England and the Mediterranean," pp. 126–32; Davis, "Influences de l'Angleterre," pp. 212–20.

[112] Andrews, *Elizabethan Privateering*, pp. 104–12, 214–20.

[113] See above, note 109.

pany traders secured the strongest position in the trades with Turkey and the eastern Mediterranean, especially at the expense of the Venetians. At the same time, benefiting from their tight company organization, these same traders largely expelled the Venetians from the Greek islands of Zante and Cephalonia and established a commercial monopoly in the lucrative currants trade. As a by-product of these commercial developments, English shipping assumed a major place in the carrying trade within the Mediterranean, manifested in the dramatic rise of the Leghorn entrepôt in the years before 1640. Finally, to help protect the traders with the Levant from the competition of merchants using the overland routes through Italy and Germany, the English government, starting in 1615, began to implement an increasingly severe navigation policy, which eventually provided that all Levantine imports had to be shipped to England directly from their source and carried in English vessels.[114]

Meanwhile, the East India Company was also prospering, by employing a combination of private maritime power, commercial organization, and government support quite similar to that which the Levantine-trade merchants had used to such good effect. Having relied initially on ships built by Levant Company traders who were also privateers, the East India Company soon took over the task of constructing its own fleet, creating the dockyards at Deptford and Blackwall to do so. During the first forty years of the seventeenth century, it built some seventy-six ships, especially prepared for military-commercial combat, to ready itself to challenge the Portuguese at the heart of their empire in the Indian Ocean. After having established a foothold at Surat in 1608, the company required about a decade of direct military confrontations to construct the local alliances and maritime strength needed to dislodge the Portuguese and establish a firm commercial base in the Gujarat region of western India. Shortly thereafter the company was able to prevail over the opposition of the merchant communities of the area to establish a trading base at the Red Sea port of Mokha, where it was possible, through the trade of English commodities, to procure products that could then be exchanged at Surat (where English merchants previously had had to rely on the exchange of silver sent from England). Finally, between 1614 and 1622, the East India Company was able to exploit its own naval strength, as well as Portuguese conflicts with the Shah of Persia, to establish a very lucrative trade with Persia by way

---

[114] Davis, "England and the Mediterranean," pp. 126–32, 136. Note Davis's comment that "the Mediterranean was the first, and for a long time the only, region where English ships took a large part in the carrying trade between foreign countries. This situation was created by the special dangers of Mediterranean navigation; its basis was strengthened by the growth in the volume of English cargoes going to and coming from the Mediterranean, by the creation of an English commercial base at Leghorn" (p. 132). See also Millard, "Imports of London," pp. 126–28; Friis, *Alderman Cockayne's Project*, pp. 179–84. See also below, ch. 2, p. 66.

of the Gulf. An English commercial base in this region was ultimately secured through a series of direct battles in which the company's powerful fleets of East Indiamen were able to prevail over Portuguese squadrons and also to help the Shah's armies capture the Portuguese strongholds on Kishm Island and, ultimately, Hormuz.[115]

During the first forty years of the seventeenth century, then, English commerce consolidated its hegemony in the Mediterranean and established a powerful commercial base in the Indian Ocean. In so doing, it went a long way toward definitively destroying the power of the Venetians and the Portuguese commercial strength in their traditional commercial bastions. All this only further increased the commercial strength of those interconnected groups of merchants that had, from the start, developed the newly emerging southern and eastern trades. Meanwhile, taking advantage of Spain's declining strength in the Western Hemisphere, English commerce had begun to make serious inroads in North America and the Caribbean. In fact, by 1640, the English merchants' very triumphs in the expansionary process had brought them face-to-face with a new competitor. Up to this point, the continuing dynamism of the English international commercial expansion had depended on the ability of English merchants to wield sufficient commercial power to prevail over the declining mercantile nations of Italy and Iberia. But from this time onward, further commercial growth would be predicated on their capacity to stand up to the rising power of the Dutch. If English commercial expansion was initially driven forward by the crises of the entrepôts and the envy of old empires, and was sustained over time by the unquenchable demand for imports from an impressively expanding home market, it was, in the end, only made possible at all by the close and successful integration of commercial enterprise and the direct application of power.

[115] Foster, *England's Quest*, pp. 185–88, 234–43, 281–82, 288–313; Chaudhuri, *East India Company*, pp. 89–96ff.; Davis, "Influences de l'Angleterre," pp. 190–96; Andrews, *Trade, Plunder, and Settlement*, pp. 270–77.

Government Privileges, the Formation of

Merchant Groups, and the Redistribution

of Wealth and Power, 1550–1640

THE TRANSFORMATION of English trade dating from the latter part of the sixteenth century—highlighted by the rise of new import-centered trades with the Mediterranean and the Near and Far East and the decline of the traditional cloth export commerce with northern Europe—had far-reaching sociopolitical consequences for the London merchant community. First, it gave rise to a powerful new group of traders, quite separate from the long-dominant Merchant Adventurers, a fact that requires further explanation. Second, precisely because an essentially new and distinct group came to control the new trades, while the Merchant Adventurers remained basically locked into their traditional commerce, the contrasting commercial trends of the period had the effect of redistributing wealth and power away from the Merchant Adventurers, who were badly hurt by the decline of their north European markets, and toward the Levant–East India Company traders, who profited from the continuing growth and prosperity of the commerce with the Mediterranean and the Near and Far East. Finally, although the newly emergent Levant–East India combine took over a preeminent position within what I have termed the company merchant establishment, and largely displaced the Merchant Adventurers within what I have called the City merchant political elite, the rise of this group implied no serious discontinuity and no schism within the London merchant community. On the contrary, the Levant–East India Company traders, rich and well connected from the start, succeeded in maintaining and reinforcing the cohesiveness of the City merchant community, not only by means of their own extraordinary internal solidarity, but also by virtue of their capacity to forge ties with merchants outside their special commercial sphere and, in that way, to integrate top City merchants who were *not* Levant–East India Company traders within a reconstituted City political elite. Indeed, by 1640, the Levant–East India combine formed the core of a cohesive merchant leadership, closely identified with London's sociopolitical order and prepared to play a vanguard role in its defense. The aim of this chapter is to explicate the foregoing consequences of the commercial transformations of the late Elizabethan−early Stuart age.

Corporate Organization and Commercial Groups

The first half of the sixteenth century brought the increasing concentration of English trade on the Antwerp cloth market and the increasing concentration of the cloth trade in the hands of Londoners; the consequence was the increasing domination of English commerce by the Merchant Adventurers, who were foremost in the cloth trade from London to Antwerp. By 1550, on the eve of the first major commercial initiatives to the south and east, the Adventurers held unchallenged commercial supremacy and, had they sought to do so, could unquestionably have taken control of the expansionary process, at least at the start. That the Adventurers largely failed to lead the expansionary movement and were unable, over the long run, to reap the fruits from the very lucrative trades that subsequently developed thus requires explanation. That the emergent group of merchants trading with southern Europe and the Near and Far East not only seized control of the most profitable new trades, but succeeded, over time, in consolidating their stranglehold on this commerce must also be explained. It will then be possible to understand how the growth and decline of markets interacted with merchant political and organizational initiatives to determine the contrasting fortunes of the Merchant Adventurers and the Levant−East India combine over the period.

THE MERCHANT ADVENTURERS:
TEMPORARY CONSOLIDATION AND LONG-TERM COLLAPSE

That the Merchant Adventurers failed to take the initiative in originating the new southern and eastern trades during the second half of the sixteenth century is not really surprising. Throughout this era, the Adventurers simply had better opportunities for profit in their own trade than were available to them in the new lines of commerce.

The Adventurers were probably most tempted to experiment during the commercial dislocations of the early 1550s. But at this point the new trades were just getting off the ground and had relatively little to offer. The Chancellor-Willoughby voyage to find a northeast passage in 1553, which set off the expansionary process, was the largest voyage of discovery ever undertaken up to that point, yet it attracted a mere £6,000 to its joint stock. This figure needs only to be compared with the £500,000 or so in goods annually exported by the Merchant Adventurers in these years to give an idea of the minimal alternative the new trades could offer at this time.

By the end of the 1550s, the Adventurers' cloth export trade had stabilized. But the new trades still showed relatively little potential for providing new sources of profit in general or demand for cloth in particular. The Levantine trade was the most promising of the new cloth export markets, but it never absorbed more than six thousand cloths annually before 1600; in fact, it is doubtful if all of the new markets combined ever absorbed more than ten thousand cloths in any year during the sixteenth century. In comparison, during most years of the second half of the sixteenth century, each of some twenty to twenty-five Adventurers sent out one thousand to two thousand cloths on his own, while another fifty or so sent out between five hundred and one thousand cloths each.[1]

With the founding of the Turkey and Venice companies in the early 1580s, the eastern commerce did begin to yield quite sizable profits but these were overwhelmingly derived from imports. And, as will become evident, a relative handful of merchants quickly succeeded in monopolizing them. Nevertheless, it is doubtful if many of the Adventurers would have been interested in entering the new commerce, even at that point, had they had the chance. For during the 1550s and 1560s, they had taken a series of initiatives that would ensure, and indeed enhance, the value of their own commerce for at least another half century.

There can be no doubt that the relative stagnation of the traditional north European cloth markets beginning in the 1550s posed problems for the Adventurers. Between 1500 and 1550, the Adventurers had been accustomed to seeing London cloth exports rise at an annual rate of 2.7 percent. But beginning in the 1550s, London cloth exports to the Adventurers' traditional markets stagnated at levels substantially below those reached during the boom period of the 1540s and early 1550s.[2] The Adventurers did not, however, have to accept passively the limitation on their profits that might have been entailed by the end of the growth of their

---

[1] For the previous two paragraphs, T. S. Willan, *The Muscovy Merchants of 1555* (Manchester, 1953), p. 6; A. Friis, *Alderman Cockayne's Project and the Cloth Trade* (London, 1927), pp. 78, 93. The figures for individual shippers come from the early seventeenth century, but in view of the rough constancy of the trade over the period 1560–1614, there is little reason to think the figures were radically different in earlier years. For cloth exports in trade with the Levant before 1600, see R. Davis, "England and the Mediterranean, 1570–1670," in *Essays in the Social and Economic History of Tudor and Stuart England*, ed. F. J. Fisher (Cambridge, 1961), p. 120; B. E. Supple, *Commercial Crisis and Change in England, 1600–1642* (Cambridge, 1959), p. 258. See also above, ch. 1, p. 11.

[2] F. J. Fisher, "Commercial Trends and Policy in Sixteenth-Century England," *Ec.H.R.* 10 (1940): 96; J. D. Gould, *The Great Debasement* (Oxford, 1970), p. 125. This figure for the rate of growth is a simple average, not compounded. The calculation is based on a total growth of the London cloth export trade of 135 percent over the period 1500–1551.

market. They had the option of attempting to exploit that market more intensively by imposing a policy of increased restriction and regulation.

The point is that, throughout the sixteenth and early seventeenth centuries, the merchants of London secured their profits as much through collective political initiative and organization as through individual economic enterprise. In almost every case, they founded their trades on government privileges that provided the basis for monopoly companies and the close regulation of commerce. Trade by a government-chartered, regulated company was the long-established norm in England. And it had a good and sufficient rationale in the complementary needs of the larger overseas merchants and the monarchy.

The merchants' business involved the relatively simple process of carrying goods between export and import customers. Making profits depended on their being able to buy cheap and sell dear. But this was no simple matter. All else being equal, there was always an immanent tendency toward overtrading. If too many merchants entered the trade or if those merchants already active shipped too many goods, the supply of the goods they sold might outrun existing demand, leading to intensified competition, falling prices, and declining or disappearing profit margins. Analogously, if they did not control the demand for the goods they purchased abroad, they might so drive up prices as to be unable to sell the goods at a profit on the domestic market. These dangers could be particularly acute when purely economic barriers to entry, such as capital or skill requirements, were low or markets were stagnant. They could also be especially serious when domestic traders, retailers, artisans, or ship captains could enter the field and, by directly trading with the ultimate sellers or buyers, undercut the merchants' middleman profit. The merchants thus sought government-backed monopolies in order to restrict trade to members of their companies and to bar those who were not exclusively overseas traders. On this basis, they sought to regulate the shipments of the company traders, with the goal of manipulating markets for purchases as well as for sales.

The monarchical government had every reason to look favorably on the merchants' requests for company privileges. This was especially so, given its historic difficulty in taxing the land—a difficulty that only became greater during the Tudor–Stuart period—as well as its secularly increasing expenses. A prosperous merchant community could offer an unrivaled source of financial support. Merchants could grant loans to the monarchy and pay taxes on trade. They would, presumably, be more able and willing to do so to the extent that the monarchy granted commercial privileges that secured and enhanced their profits. Historically, the Crown had granted the Staplers Company monopoly trading rights in wool, which was England's main export commodity in the late medieval period. In turn, the Staplers paid the custom and the subsidy, the proto-typical tax on English trade, and performed a variety of important financial services for the Crown. This sort of quid pro quo came to typify arrangements between the monarchy and the greater City merchants, and as a rule they enjoyed the most intimate and symbiotic relationship.[3]

During the late Middle Ages, the Merchant Adventurers had followed in the Staplers' footsteps, securing royally sanctioned privileges to export cloth and, in return, paying the custom. In the last analysis, trade restrictions were especially significant for the Merchant Adventurers, because small investors with little capital or experience could easily enter the short-route London-Antwerp cloth commerce. Nevertheless, before the 1550s, the Adventurers appear to have exerted only limited controls over the trade. A government act of 1497 allowed English traders entry into the company's privileges for the minimal fee of ten marks (£6 13s 4d.).[4] Moreover, foreign merchants, especially those of the German Hanse, held a significant share of the cloth export trade. Still, with exports expanding very rapidly, it seemed that the Adventurers could survive the economic competition without much difficulty.

From the middle of the sixteenth century, however, pressures on both the monarchy and the Merchant Adventurers to strengthen their relationship drastically increased. The Crown, in the wake of the unprecedentedly burdensome wars of Henry VIII, found itself in deep financial trouble, faced with massive debts compounded by monetary disruption. The Merchant Adventurers were suffering from the short-term export crisis, and, as it turned out, the onset of a long period of stagnation of trade. In the course of the 1550s and 1560s, the Adventurers won a qualitative increase in royal protection of their trade. They procured much-enhanced privileges that allowed them to strengthen their internal organization decisively, as well as to control shipments and prices. In turn, the Crown gained greater, and far more systematic, access to the resources of the merchant community than ever before.

In fact, during the 1550s there was a small revolution in royal finances. First, beginning in 1551, Thomas Gresham's famous plan for restoring royal financial and monetary stability was implemented. Acting as the Crown's financial agent, Gresham required the Merchant Adventurers to hand over to him in Antwerp a large part of the proceeds in foreign cur-

---

[3] See G. Unwin, "The Merchant Adventurers Company in the Reign of Elizabeth," in *Studies in Economic History: The Collected Papers of George Unwin* (London, 1927); E. Power, *The Wool Trade in English Medieval History* (Oxford, 1941).

[4] G. D. Ramsay, *The City of London in International Politics at the Accession of Elizabeth Tudor* (Manchester, 1975), pp. 46–47; G. D. Ramsay, "The Cloth Trade at London in Mid-Sixteenth Century: The Merchant Adventurers and Their Rivals," in *Produzione, commercio e consumo dei Panni di Lana (nei secoli XII–XVIII)*, ed. M. Spallanzani (Florence, 1976), pp. 379–80.

rency from the sale of their cloths. This would be repaid in sterling in London at a fixed rate of exchange, with Gresham making sure to value the pound at appreciably more than it was quoted in Antwerp. This mechanism allowed the Crown to assure itself, on a continuing basis, of a massive source of short-term loans. It also allowed Gresham, acting for the Crown, to control the supply of sterling at Antwerp and, in this way, to force up the price of English currency on the international market. This system remained in effect for some two decades.[5]

Second, in 1558 the Crown radically revised the customs rates, so as to increase dramatically its returns from taxes on trade. It issued a new book of rates that effectively raised the duty on all included items by about 75 percent. The special duties on imported wine and on exported beer and cloths were also sharply raised. The cloth increase was especially large, with the duty on each undyed cloth exported raised from 14*d.* to 6*s.* 8*d.* for Englishmen and from 2*s.* 6*d.* to 14*s.* 6d. for (non-Hanse) alien merchants. The significance of this alteration for both the Merchant Adventurers and royal finances can be roughly calculated. In a normal year, given 95,000 to 100,000 cloths exported, the customs of London on cloth alone would now yield £30,000 or more. This figure should be compared with the parliamentary subsidy for all England, which yielded around £110,000 in 1559.[6]

Finally, all through this period, the Crown maintained its established practice of obtaining loans from the City government, which was at this time overwhelmingly dominated by the Merchant Adventurers. Queen Mary borrowed £10,000 within a few weeks of her accession. Her demands reached a high point in March 1558, when she made a request for 100,000 marks (£66,666), which had to be scaled down drastically. Queen Elizabeth borrowed £10,000 from the City in 1562 for her military expedition to Normandy and approximately £17,000 from leading City merchants in 1569.[7]

The reciprocal of the Crown's sharply increased financial demands on the merchant community during the 1550s and 1560s was a vast enlargement of the merchants' privileges. Stepped-up royal protection of trade was designed to compensate the merchants for their financial contributions, thereby encouraging their willingness, and increasing their ability, to pay.

First, the Crown helped the leading Merchant Adventurers defeat their opponents outside the company. Perhaps most important in this respect,

---

[5] Ramsay, *City of London*, pp. 51–53, 62; Ramsay, "Cloth Trade at London," p. 381; Unwin, "Merchant Adventurers Company," pp. 152ff.

[6] Ramsay, *City of London*, p. 50; Friis, *Alderman Cockayne's Project*, pp. 48–50.

[7] Ramsay, *City of London*, pp. 50–51; Ramsay, "Cloth Trade at London," p. 379; Unwin, "Merchant Adventurers Company," pp. 165–67.

foreign merchants, who hitherto had controlled a significant proportion of London's cloth exports, saw their effectiveness as competitors in the cloth trade sharply reduced. The powerful Hanse of German merchants was deprived of its trading privileges, while the Italian and Flemish merchants were essentially confined to their import operations. Meanwhile, the Crown quashed a series of attempts by the London cloth dyers to limit the Merchant Adventurers' shipments of undyed cloths abroad.[8]

Second, the Crown created the conditions that made it possible to regulate competition within the company itself. In the mid-1550s, the Adventurers received permission to raise the company entry fee from the nominal sum of 10 marks to the hefty fee of 100 marks (£66), and later to £200. The result was to reduce significantly the number of active traders. To the same end, the Adventurers effectively restricted entry into their privileges to "mere merchants," that is, specialists in overseas trade, specifically excluding artisans and retailers. The latter were especially dangerous, since they could render superfluous the Adventurers' middleman's function and undersell them in their export and import markets. The company consolidated these gains in 1564 with the issue of a royal charter.[9]

By means of their tightened control over the cloth export commerce, the Adventurers were able to regulate their trade more closely. The Crown further assisted in this respect by crushing a bid by the merchants who had entered the company by paying a fee (known as fining or by redemption) to gain a status equal to that of those admitted by apprenticeship (the so-called Old Hanse) and a greater role in directing company affairs. During the subsequent period the Adventurers began to restrict the export of cloth by members to times and ships designated by the company. In addition, the company introduced the "stint" system, by which each member was allowed to export only a certain maximum number of cloths each year. These rules were aimed at controlling the supply of cloths and thereby their price. In 1564, the Crown granted the company the right to station observers at the customs office, allowing the Adventurers to enforce their regulations better and to make sure that interlopers were barred from the trade.[10]

The Merchant Adventurers' strengthening of their extra-economic con-

---

[8] Ramsay, *City of London*, pp. 44–46, 51, 60–70; Ramsay, "Cloth Trade at London," pp. 379–83; G. D. Ramsay, "The Undoing of the Italian Mercantile Colony in Sixteenth–Century London," in *Textile History and Economic History*, ed. N. B. Harte and K. G. Ponting (London, 1973), pp. 27–32; Fisher, "Commercial Trends and Policy," pp. 107–9.

[9] Ramsay, *City of London*, p. 49; Friis, *Alderman Cockayne's Project*, p. 102; Ramsay, "Cloth Trade at London," pp. 379–80; Fisher, "Commercial Trends and Policy," pp. 109–14.

[10] Ramsay, *City of London*, pp. 48, 268–69; Ramsay, "Cloth Trade at London," p. 380; Friis, *Alderman Cockayne's Project*, pp. 89–93, 103–14.

trols over the cloth trade yielded remarkable results. First, the Adventurers significantly increased their share of the trade. During 1539–1546, when the non-Hanse alien merchants temporarily achieved equality with the English merchants with respect the the payment of customs, well over 60 percent of London cloth exports fell into the hands of foreign merchants (Hanse and non-Hanse combined). By the 1560s that figure had been reduced to 25 percent or less, and by 1600, to less than 5 percent.[11] This meant, as noted earlier, that even while *total* London exports essentially stagnated between the late 1550s and the turn of the century—averaging approximately 105,000 cloths a year in 1557, 1559, and 1560, and around 103,000 in 1598, 1599, and 1600—London *denizen* cloth exports grew noticeably over that period, averaging around 57,000 annually for the years 1541–1550, about 85,000 a year for 1557, 1559, and 1560, and about 98,000 a year for 1598, 1599, and 1600.[12] Since the Merchant Adventurers controlled virtually all of the London denizen cloth exports in the 1550s, but perhaps only 80 percent of that trade by 1600, it may be concluded that the Adventurers had achieved most of their increase in shipments of this period by the early part of Elizabeth's reign.

Second, through their system of regulation, the Adventurers succeeded in controlling the number of cloths shipped. Between 1560 and 1600, triennial averages did not rise more than 6 percent above or fall more than 6 percent below the yearly average of 98,017 for the entire period (except in two brief periods when the mart was disrupted).[13] Such consistency is inexplicable apart from reference to the Adventurers' tight regulation of the trade.

Finally, through company restrictions the number of active merchants was kept relatively low so that the trade was concentrated in the hands of a few. In 1606, 219 merchants shipped cloth to the Adventurers' privileged areas, dividing among themselves a trade of some 101,000 cloths worth close to £800,000. In 1614, 182 merchants shipped cloths to the Adventurers' privileged areas, sharing a trade of some 99,000 cloths also worth close to £800,000. In comparison, in 1609, for example, no fewer

[11] Another way of putting it is that aliens' cloth exports dropped from about 61,000 a year in the mid-1540s to about 5,000 annually in 1600 (Ramsay, "Cloth Trade at London," p. 383; Friis, *Alderman Cockayne's Project*, p. 62).

[12] Figures in the text were derived from D. Fischer, "The Development and Organization of English Trade to Asia, 1553–1605" (University of London, Ph.D. diss., 1970), p. 23, and Fisher, "Commercial Trends and Policy," p. 96. The number used for London total cloth exports in 1559 is an approximation, based on figures for denizens and non-Hanse aliens; a figure for Hanse cloth exports in 1559 was not available.

[13] Compiled from Fisher, "Commercial Trends and Policy," p. 96. The highest triennial average in this period was 103,032, and the lowest, 93,681. The average does not include the two three-year periods when the trade was severely disrupted.

than 176 traders active in the unregulated trade with Spain were compelled to divide an export trade worth a mere £31,744 (official value).[14]

The Merchant Adventurers thus maintained their prosperity in the face of the relative sluggishness of their trade essentially by developing a much more intimate relationship with the Crown. The informal system by which the Adventurers made a significantly deeper financial and political commitment to the Crown, receiving in exchange powerful protection of their trade, succeeded admirably from the viewpoint of both parties, at least for a time. It served as the model both for Crown-merchant relations and for the operation of overseas commerce by privileged companies throughout the pre–Civil War period.

Of course, the regulation of trade could achieve just so much. No amount of state protection could offset the disastrous effects of the deep depression of the north European cloth trade during the middle decades of the seventeenth century. Although cloth exports actually grew during the first decade of the reign of James I, after 1614, as noted, the Adventurers' cloth exports fell by some 50 percent, relative to the average for the previous half century. To make matters worse, the European wars of this period seriously disrupted the Adventurers' import markets. As a result of the breakdown of the overland routes from Italy to northern Europe, products from the Mediterranean and farther east began to be imported by sea directly into England, rather than by land via the Adventurers' marts in the Netherlands and Germany. In 1621, the value of English imports from Germany and the Low Countries totaled approximately £354,000. But the corresponding figures for 1630 and 1634 dropped to roughly £206,000 and £222,000, respectively.[15]

Most shocking of all to the Adventurers, in an era of intensified competition and chronic depression, when a protected trade was more important than ever to the Adventurers' commercial success, they were unable to count on their privileged position. The Crown suspended the Adventurers' charter between 1614 and 1617 in favor of the rival Cockayne Company. Then, in 1624, the House of Commons' alliance of growers, clothiers, and outport interests, which had fought the Adventurers for

[14] Friis, *Alderman Cockayne's Project*, pp. 78, 93; Supple, *Commercial Crisis*, pp. 258–59; London Port Book for Exports (nonbroadcloths), 1609, PRO, E.190/14/7. The figures for the trade with Spain may be somewhat misleading, since it is possible that these Spanish-trade merchants were exploiting an import trade significantly more lucrative than was the export trade. Figures for Spanish imports for this period are unfortunately unavailable.

[15] A. M. Millard, "The Import Trade of London, 1600–1640" (University of London, Ph.D. diss., 1956), app. 2; Davis, "England and the Mediterranean," p. 135. The Adventurers' import trade was, in this period, also hard hit by government policies, as the series of navigation acts promulgated by the Crown beginning in 1615 compelled merchants to bring in Levantine and Eastland goods directly from their source, thus eliminating the Adventurers' middleman role as reexporters of these goods from their north European marts to England. See below, p. 66.

decades, succeeded in getting the Adventurers' chartered privileges significantly weakened; they were not to be fully restored until 1634.[16] The company's loss of privileges drastically lessened its control over the trade, and this was reflected in a massive influx of new traders. In 1622, under the Adventurers' monopoly, 113 traders sent a total of approximately 50,000 cloths to the company's north European outlets. But by 1632, with the company's monopoly now sharply reduced, the number of active traders had tripled, with no fewer than 300 traders exporting a total of approximately 59,000 cloths to these ports. Then, in 1640, with the monopoly once again restored, the number of merchants sending out cloths was reduced by two-thirds, with 103 traders exporting a total of 45,000 cloths to the Adventurers' marts.[17] These figures testify to the effectiveness of the company's chartered monopoly in controlling competition in the cloth trade. They indicate, moreover, why the insecurity of the Adventurers' privileges in this era of contracting markets was so very disastrous for them.

As a result of the double blow of collapsing markets and the loss of privileges, relatively few Merchant Adventurers could, after around 1620, any longer secure from the trade the great accumulations of wealth that their predecessors had amassed. Moreover, the exclusive focus of most of the Adventurers on their own markets, as well as their traditional tendency to depend on the state's protection, left them largely unprepared to diversify as their trade suddenly and rapidly contracted. Diversification was, in any case, made especially difficult because of the powerful grip the Levant–East India merchants had come to exert over their own trades. Indeed, only the wealthiest and best-connected Adventurers were able to enter the extraordinarily lucrative commerce with the Near and Far East. Among 150 or so merchants who imported one hundred or more hundredweight of currants from the Levant in 1630, 1634, 1636, 1638, or 1640, no more than a handful had been or currently were Merchant Adventurers. Similarly, in 1640, out of 103 merchants who exported cloths to the Adventurers' marts, no more than 5 or 6 were also Levant–East India Company merchants.[18] Long before this time, the merchants trading with the southern and eastern areas had used their relationship with

[16] Friis, *Alderman Cockayne's Project*; Supple, *Commercial Crisis*, pp. 64–72. See also below, ch. 5, pp. 212–15.

[17] London Port Books for Cloth Exports, 1622, 1632, and 1640, PRO, E.190/26/2, PRO, E.190/36/5, and PRO, E.190/43/4.

[18] These results were derived from comparing full lists of Levant Company members, composed from the company's Court Minute Books, and of currants importers, derived from the London Port Books for Imports, 1630, 1634, 1636, 1638, and 1640, PRO, E.190/34/2, PRO, E.190/38/5, PRO, E.190/37/13, PRO, E.190/42/1, and PRO, E.190/43/5, with lists of Merchant Adventurers, derived from the London Port Books for Cloth Exports given above in note 17, as well as, for 1628, PRO, E.190/32/3.

the government, their company organization, and their business and family connections to establish a position of preeminence comparable to that formerly enjoyed by the Adventurers.

THE RISE OF THE LEVANT—EAST INDIA COMBINE

The leading merchants behind the Elizabethan expansion to the south and east were not, by and large, Merchant Adventurers, but they were in no way new men. On the contrary, many of them stood from the outset right beside the top Merchant Adventurers within the highest circles of London's economic and political mercantile leadership. There was no difference between the members of the two groups in terms either of wealth or of social status. The merchants trading southward and eastward were thus distinguished from the Adventurers only by the distinctive requirements for carrying out their new commercial tasks. Unlike the Merchant Adventurers, the traders with the Mediterranean and the East did have to innovate. But what made their field so inordinately attractive was their ability to reduce the need for risk taking even while they created novel commercial operations. Already ranked among the City's richest and most influential businessmen, they were able to make use of their close ties with the government to obtain, essentially from the start, powerful state backing for their voyages of exploration, as well as their corporate organizations. Like the Adventurers, they used their political connections to win exclusive company control over their valuable new trades; but, in contrast with the Adventurers of the early seventeenth century, they enjoyed their vast privileges during a period in which their commerce grew continuously. The result was the rise of a new commercial combine, whose wealth, power, and cohesiveness were to increase right up to the Civil War.

In 1575, Edward Osborne and Richard Staper, the merchants behind the revived trade with Turkey, sent Joseph Clements and John Wight to Constantinople to secure a safe conduct for travel there for their factor William Harborne. Clements and Wight appear to have obtained from the sultan not only a safe conduct but permission to trade, and in 1578 William Harborne returned to Constantinople to establish the basis for ongoing commerce. Interestingly enough, at just about the time Harborne was embarking, the queen's secretary Sir Francis Walsingham seems to have composed "A Consideration of the Trade into Turkey," in which he spelled out the advantages of a regular trade with Turkey both for English commerce and for English shipping, and recommended a voyage to establish the trade very much like that which Harborne actually undertook. This may very well indicate that Osborne and Staper and the English government closely collaborated in planning Harborne's mission. In any

case, as S. A. Skilliter has shown, the English government unquestionably
gave its unofficial backing to Harborne's voyage, both because of the potential gains for commerce and shipping mentioned by Walsingham and
because of the political and diplomatic advantages that might be secured
from the Ottomans in the conflict with Spain. Consequent on Harborne's
voyage, the sultan confirmed broad privileges of trade with Turkey for
the English merchants and shortly thereafter the queen issued the Turkey
Company charter. About the same time, English merchants began selling
tin, lead, and other military supplies to Turkey.[19]

By the Turkey Company patent of 1581, the Crown granted the whole
of the lucrative Middle Eastern market to a single joint-stock company of
just twelve merchants, and, almost immediately, this restricted body of
merchants was able to establish the trade on an extremely profitable basis.
The Turkey Company claimed to have made no fewer than twenty-seven
voyages to the Levant between September 1582 and September 1587. It
paid some £11,359 in customs on the cargoes of these voyages, so that the
rated value of the shipments was around £228,000. It has been calculated,
however, that the *actual* value of the Turkey Company's goods at this time
was some two to three times their rated value.[20] At a conservative estimate,
therefore, the twelve men who controlled the Levant commerce in these
five years drove a trade worth more than £500,000, or £100,000 a year.
One opponent of the company no doubt exaggerated when he stated, "It is
well known that the parts of Italy and Turkey will bear a greater trade
than all parts of Christendom in amity with her majesty."[21] Still, the burden of his remark was undeniable: the Levantine commerce would have
supported with profit many more than the handful of merchants who controlled it, were it not for the Turkey Company's government-protected
monopoly.

Such favorable conditions for trade could not have been procured by
just any merchants. The original Turkey Company patentees were a special group indeed.[22] These men were, as noted, already commercial leaders in the Spanish and Russia companies; we should not be surprised,
therefore, that they were wealthy and that a good number of them were
among the City's chief magistrates. Of the twelve patentees of 1581, no
fewer than eight were London aldermen, or became aldermen at some

---

[19] For the foregoing paragraph, see S. A. Skilliter, *William Harborne and the Trade with Turkey,
1578–1582* (Oxford, 1977), pp. 23–75ff. Skilliter advances strong evidence for dating Walsingham's memo at 1578, instead of 1580 as previously thought (pp. 27–32).

[20] M. Epstein, *The Early History of the Levant Company* (London, n.d.), p. 19; T. S. Willan,
"Some Aspects of English Trade with the Levant in the Sixteenth Century," E.H.R. 70 (1955):
408–9.

[21] Quoted in Epstein, *Levant Company*, p. 33 n. 14.

[22] See Fischer, "English Trade to Asia," pp. 166–69.

point during the 1580s. Three were sometime MPs.[23] Their average subsidy payment was £217 in 1582; in that year no more than sixty-five citizens in the whole of London made subsidy payments of £200 or more.[24] Finally, the Turkey patentees included three of the most important mediators between the Crown and the City merchant community of the Elizabethan period. Sir George Barne was the brother-in-law of Walsingham and, as governor of the Russia Company, worked closely with such leading court figures as Leicester and Burghley in organizing a number of the period's major voyages of discovery. "Customer" Thomas Smythe was either a collector or a farmer of the London customs during much of the later sixteenth century. Richard Martin was the son-in-law of Sir Julius Caesar as well as the master of the mint.[25] Walsingham was a key supporter of the Turkey Company's request for privileges. It was probably Martin's intervention that ensured that the patentees' £5,000 loan to the queen (later made a gift) was confirmed and that the charter was issued.[26] At the same time, the government appears to have made the new company a series of substantial loans of silver to facilitate its commerce with Turkey. Such exchanges of royal backing for financial support, and such instances of outright Crown support of merchant commercial initiatives, facilitated by close court-merchant connections, were the norm in this period, and they powerfully influenced the entire development of the Levant–East India trade.

At the expiration of their patent in 1588, the Turkey Company merchants tried to gain even broader privileges. They sought, in particular, to appropriate the lucrative currants trade with the Greek islands of Zante and Cephalonia that had been granted to the Venice Company merchants in 1583.[27] At the time they received their charter, the Venice Company merchants had not been of quite the same top caliber as the Turkey Company traders. Nevertheless, they were already well established as leaders in the Spanish and Moroccan trades. Even in 1582, the subsidy valuations for Thomas Cordell, Paul Bayning, Edward Holmden, and William

[23] Edward Osborne (1573), George Barne (1574), Richard Martin (1578), Martin Calthorpe (1579), John Harte (1580), William Marsham (1582), John Spencer (1583), and Richard Saltonstall (1588) were the aldermen among the patentees. For the City's aldermen and information about their officeholding, see A. B. Beaven, *The Aldermen of the City of London*, 2 vols. (London, 1908). George Barne, Edward Osborne, and Richard Saltonstall were the MPs.

[24] PRO, E.179/251/16; Fischer, "English Trade to Asia," p. 386. Edward Osborne (£250), George Barne (£240), Richard Martin (£260), Martin Calthorpe (£300), John Harte (£260), William Masham (£200), John Spencer (£300), Thomas Smythe (£150), Richard May (£180), Richard Saltonstall (£200), Richard Staper (£90), and Henry Hewitt (£170).

[25] Willan, *Muscovy Merchants*, p. 78; Fischer, "English Trade to Asia," pp. 401, 407.

[26] A. C. Wood, *A History of the Levant Company* (London, 1935, repr. 1964), p. 10; Fischer, "English Trade to Asia," pp. 152, 195–200.

[27] Epstein, *Levant Company*, ch. 4.

Garway, the four chief Venice Company merchants, had averaged a quite respectable £100; and they had enjoyed considerable commercial success since then, not only in trade, but also in privateering and shipping.[28] Such merchants as these could not simply be brushed aside, and the Turkey Company merchants were obliged to carry out a merger with them.

In 1589 and 1590, the merchants of the Turkey and Venice companies together petitioned the Crown for a new, expanded Levant patent, listing first thirty, then forty, merchants to whom they desired the trade to be restricted by charter. The men they named were almost all either Turkey Company or Venice Company members or close connections of theirs, servants or apprentices. Not surprisingly, therefore, their proposals provoked substantial protests from merchant outsiders anxious to get in on a valuable trade.[29] In response, nineteen of the most prominent Turkey and Venice company merchants haughtily laid down the conditions under which they would find it worthwhile to continue their trade:

> Assuredly no better success is to be expected in this trade if more should be admitted, for in very truth, the one half of us already traders are too many and in number sufficient to maintain that trade . . . most humbly beseeching your honour (the premises considered) to be a means that we may have use of that trade without receiving in of any . . . otherwise it will not only discourage us and others in like respect hereafter to attempt to go on with like charges and discoveries, but be utterly discouraged to enter into any new charge . . . and so rather to withdraw ourselves, giving over the trade.[30]

Although the merchants' scarcely veiled threat to leave the trade was hardly credible, it was certainly true that a free and open trade posed real dangers for them. This fact was brought home with force to traders for currants with the Greek islands in the years between 1589 and 1592, after the Turkey and Venice company charters had lapsed and before the Levant Company charter was issued. In these three years, there was no way to prevent anyone from entering the trade or to limit the amount shipped, and an average of 18,000 hundredweight of currants was imported each year. But with the issue of the Levant Company charter in

---

[28] PRO, E.179/251/16; Fischer, "English Trade to Asia," p. 386; R. G. Lang, "The Greater Merchants of London, 1600–1625" (Oxford University, Ph.D. diss., 1963), pp. 206–9; K. R. Andrews, *Elizabethan Privateering* (Cambridge, 1964), ch. 10.

[29] Epstein, *Levant Company*, pp. 27–31 and app. Fischer, "English Trade to Asia," pp. 276–91, presents a very full analysis of the negotiations and personnel involved at each stage in the process by which the Levant Company of 1592 was established.

[30] PRO, S.P.12/239/44. Edward Osborne, George Barne, John Harte, William Masham, John Spencer, Richard Martin, William Garway, Edward Holmden, Henry Hewitt, Roger Clarke, Paul Bayning, Andrew Bayning, Thomas Cordell, Henry Anderson, Henry Farrington, Richard Staper, Robert Sadler, and Leonard Poore were the petitioners.

1592, the situation was rectified. Between 1592 and 1599, an average of only 8,800 hundredweight of currants a year were brought into England.[31] This represented a decrease of more than 50 percent, clear evidence of the effectiveness of company controls in limiting supply.

By the charter of 1592, the Levant Company was restricted to fifty-three persons (twenty-one more than the Turkey and Venice company merchants had nominated), while twenty others were given the option to join within two months, if they would pay the not insubstantial admission fee of £130. The company was thenceforth to control entry to the trade on whatever terms it thought fit. This slight opening of the trade could not seriously diminish the value of a twelve-year monopoly of the Levantine commerce, which now included not only the Venetian currants trade, but exclusive rights to the overland route to the Indies.[32] Of course, this overland route was never established. Instead, the leading Levantine-trade merchants extended their trade to the Far East by developing the sea route, and they secured a royal charter for the East India Company in 1599.

During the early decades of the seventeenth century, the Levant Company merchants further tightened their grip on the trade with the Near East, although they were forced in the process to renegotiate their arrangement with the Crown. As before, the Crown expected a financial quid pro quo for privileges granted. Despite the inevitable frictions, the result was a further consolidation of the Crown-company partnership.

As it turned out, the Levant Company patent of 1592 did not last beyond the turn of the century.[33] From the 1580s, the company had arrogated to itself the right to collect an imposition of 5s. 6d. a hundredweight on currants imported by those who were not members of the company, whether Englishmen or aliens. When this levy was brought to the attention of Queen Elizabeth, she swiftly sought to usurp it for the benefit of the royal treasury. The resulting negotiations led to a settlement by which the Crown agreed in 1601 to renew the company's charter in exchange for an annual payment of £4,000, the estimated annual return to the company from the imposition.

By 1603, the Levant Company merchants appear to have come to the conclusion that they could gain a more advantageous arrangement. They renounced their patent, alleging that they could not pay the £4,000 each year. This was only a bargaining gesture, however. In 1605, they reaccepted the charter and agreed to a royal levy of 5s. 6d. a hundredweight

---

[31] Fischer, "English Trade to Asia," pp. 360–62; PRO, S.P. 12/272/12. See also table 1.4.

[32] Epstein, *Levant Company*, pp. 36–39.

[33] See Epstein, *Levant Company*, ch. 5. It is uncertain precisely when the Levant Company became a regulated company, but Fischer presents a strong case that it ceased to be organized on joint-stock lines right from the charter of 1592 (Fischer, "English Trade to Asia," pp. 307–12). See also Willan, "English Trade with the Levant," pp. 406–7, for the same conclusion.

on all currants brought into the realm, including those brought in by Levant Company members.[34]

In 1615, the Crown closed the last loophole in the Levant Company's commercial monopoly when it proclaimed that all goods imported from the Levant had to be brought to England directly from the Levant, and in English ships. This important ruling not only effectively cut off Levantine imports by foreign merchants; it also wiped out the Merchant Adventurers' import trade in Levantine commodities that had been carried by foreign merchants to the Adventurers' north European entrepôts.[35] Over time, this navigation act seems to have eliminated the indirect trade for currants, galls, cotton, and, finally, raw silks, and to have reserved these imports solely for the Levant Company.[36] As the counterpart of this gift, the Crown increased the imposition on currants by 2s. 2d. a hundredweight, restoring the levy to 5s. 6d. (it had been reduced to 3s. 4d. in 1608).[37] Even so, the government made this increase less painful for the company by decreeing that "no goods [from the Levant] shall be entered in the customs house without the [Levant Company's] husband's hand."[38] This ruling allowed the company itself to enforce the navigation act, as well as to directly enforce the company monopoly against interlopers.

The Levant Company's privileges were indispensable for its elaborate system of trade regulation and, in turn, for the reservation of the profits of the trade to a restricted circle of merchants. As members of a regulated company, the individual Levant Company merchants traded for themselves with their own capital, but were required to adhere to rules and policies set by the corporation's general court. These regulations were aimed at the control of company markets and the maintenance of favorable prices for company products. The Merchant Adventurers allowed their members to trade only at a designated mart town, during limited time periods, using ships especially chartered by the company. The Levant Company's regulations, as they took shape during the early seventeenth century, proved, if anything, to be even more highly restrictive. Their effectiveness was greatly enhanced, moreover, by formal and informal practices of recruitment to the trade that substantially limited the number

[34] Epstein, *Levant Company*, pp. 40–51; Wood, *Levant Company*, pp. 31–35; Friis, *Alderman Cockayne's Project*, pp. 158–60, 184–85, 193–95, 201–5; R. Ashton, *The City and the Court, 1603–1643* (Cambridge, 1979), pp. 90–92.

[35] Friis, *Alderman Cockayne's Project*, pp. 180–83, 189.

[36] For the intense enforcement of this regulation (which was greatly aided by the fact that leading merchants trading with the Levant held the customs farms for much of the period), see PRO, S.P.105/147/57v, 86, 92v, 97v; PRO, S.P.105/148/5ff., 44v, 69v, 92, 95, 102, 119, 124, 184. See also table 1.3.

[37] Friis, *Alderman Cockayne's Project*, p. 198.

[38] PRO, S.P.105/147/82v (18 Nov. 1616).

of effective participants, while giving significant control to the company's leading members over just who was to be admitted.

At the point at which the company's surviving court minutes begin, in September 1611, we find the company limiting all trade with the Levant proper, that is, Turkey (specifically Constantinople and Smyrna) and Aleppo, to two ships, while forbidding further commerce there until the following July at the earliest.[39] This policy of "joint" or "general" shipping was maintained in the trade with Turkey and Aleppo throughout the following two decades, with only a few lapses of short duration.[40] Apparently, limiting in this way the quantities that could be shipped by company members was normally sufficient to turn the prices of company products in the members' favor. However, on those occasions when prices were threatened, the company did not hesitate to take more direct action to repair the markets.[41]

Tighter controls were generally required to limit the import of currants from the Greek islands of Zante and Cephalonia, which constituted the other main branch of the company's trade. This was because the cheapness of currants tended to induce overtrading, whereas this problem seems to have arisen only occasionally in the commerce in raw silks, which was the mainstay of the Levantine trade proper. As already noted, the reestablished company succeeded in reducing currants imports during the 1590s by some 50 percent over the previous period of uncontrolled trade. By 1610, however, the amount of currants imported into England had ballooned to 49,000 hundredweight a year, as compared with around 11,000 hundredweight yearly at the start of the decade.[42] There are no figures for the following few years, but by 1616, for the explicit purpose of bringing down the price for currants in the Greek islands, the company had decided to carry on its currants trade by means of separate limited-period joint stocks in which company members held shares. These joint stocks were managed on an annual basis by small committees of leading Levant Company merchants, who were given responsibility for allocating shares to the company members, for determining the amount of commodities to be brought in, and for setting their prices, marketing them (sometimes by reexport to the Continent), and distributing the profits. This method seems to have achieved the desired results. By 1621, the number

[39] PRO, S.P. 105/147/3–7.

[40] The company's application of this policy over the period 1611–1631 may be followed in detail in the company's Court Minute Books, PRO, S.P. 105/147, 148.

[41] See, for example, the entry of 2 Aug. 1623: "Mr. Governor moved . . . that whereas silk had greatly fallen in price here . . . for that this kingdom was already overlaid with that commodity . . . [it] would afford a better price at Marseilles . . . which notion was well liked of" (PRO, S.P. 105/148/97).

[42] PRO, S.P. 14/10A/26, and PRO, E. 122/191/6. See also table 1.4.

of currants imported annually had been cut to around 31,000 hundred-weight, a reduction of close to 40 percent from 1610. After this point, the joint-stock method was allowed to lapse. But from July 1628, the company began to substitute a policy of setting a maximum price for the purchase of currants in the Venetian empire.[43]

Between 1631 and 1633, the body of Levant Company adventurers in their general court succeeded in perfecting their system of controls, promulgating a policy that remained substantially unchanged through the end of the decade. In its fully articulated form, this called for single annual shipments in company vessels to Constantinople and Smyrna (in the spring) and to Aleppo (in the summer), as well as the setting of a maximum price of 22 Venetian dollars (£5 10s.) for each ton of currants, which were to be bought only at certain periods of the year. In 1639–1640, a final twist was added when the company approved a policy of stinting on currants, limiting each member's maximum purchase. The Levant Company members monopolized valuable markets. Like all of the great London merchants in this period, they wished to leave as little as possible to chance in exploiting them.[44]

The company's actual success in controlling its markets is evidenced not only in the aforementioned data on the limiting of currants imports, but in certain bits of evidence on prices and costs in the currants trade—"the main trade of this Society," as reported in the company's minutes of 1619. In 1617, according to Lord Treasurer Sir Lionel Cranfield, currants sold in London for about 50s. a hundredweight (wholesale), although they could go as high as 70s. a hundredweight in holiday seasons. Cranfield's figure is roughly corroborated by the company court minutes, which quote a figure of 43s. 4d. a hundredweight as the price of currants to be sold to the City's grocers by the company's joint stock in early 1618.[45] Some ten years later, in 1629, according to the Venetian ambassador, "although currants have been increasing in price for some years owing to bad crops, the [Levant] Company, having a considerable capital, buy up beforehand the produce of the poorest of the inhabitants of these islands, much to its advantage, accommodating them with money or anything else in advance, so that for them the prices are almost always the same."[46] The ambassador

---

[43] For the currants joint stocks, from their original proposal to their dissolution, see PRO, S.P.105/147/70, 73, 75, 77, 80v, 82, 84, 85, 85v, and PRO, S.P.105/148/10, 13v, 14, 21v, 24, 37, 43v, 47, 47v, 61, 71, 72v, 73, 83. For the maximum, see PRO, S.P.105/148/186, 237. For the size of the currants trade, see PRO, E.190/24/4 and table 1.4.

[44] PRO, S.P.105/148/231, 232, 237, 249, 250v, and PRO, S.P.105/149/81–85. For the continuance of these policies, see PRO, S.P.105/149/104, 106, 148, 200, 209, 258, 293, 296, 298, 348, 366. For the currants stint, see PRO, S.P.105/149/303, 305, 327, 360, 387, 388.

[45] Epstein, *Levant Company*, p. 109 n. 1; Cranfield Papers, KCA, U.269/M.692 and KCA, U.269/O.N.6348; PRO, S.P.105/148/10 (7 Feb. 1618).

[46] *C.S.P. Ven. 1628–1629*, pp. 553–54.

went on to state that in England currants continued to sell "very well without further risk . . . they cost 13 Venetian soldi the pound." If the ambassador was right about these figures, then currants prices, while remaining the same in the islands, had increased somewhat in London. Thus, the Levant Company merchants were now selling currants for around 54s. a hundredweight (13 soldi a pound), as compared with 43s. 4d.–50s. a hundredweight in 1617–1618. The striking point is that beginning in December 1628, the company had begun to enforce a maximum purchase price for its members of 2 to 1.6 Venetian dollars a hundredweight for currants in the islands, that is, between 10s. and 8s. According to the company's representative in the islands, without such direct controls prices might go as high as 20s. a hundredweight, and they had in fact reached this figure at times in recent years. If this new 10s.–8s. maximum was even moderately well enforced, it must have ensured the company's membership a significant saving and further enhanced what was apparently an already substantial rate of profit.[47]

Finally, to ensure the effectiveness of its system of market controls, the Levant Company undoubtedly had to place some limits on the size of its active membership. Without a comparatively small active membership, the company would have found it difficult to implement regulations and to contain intracompany competition. The company's charter allowed three different routes of admission—by patrimony, by apprenticeship, or by paying a fee (fining, or by redemption). All sons of members were eligible for admission free of charge. Any apprentice to a company member who served for seven years, four of them within the company's privileged area in the Levant, was also allowed to enter without paying a fee to the company. Finally, admission was open to any merchant who paid a fee of £25 if he was under age twenty-seven, £50 if he was older. These provisions might appear somewhat lenient; in practice, they sharply limited the size and social composition of the active company membership.

Apprenticeship was by far the most common method of entry. Even sons of members were sometimes apprenticed before joining the company, and this was quite understandable. To carry on the trade, special skills were needed, and these could best be acquired under the wing of a merchant already engaged in the trade. Apprenticeship, moreover, was perhaps the best way to establish and consolidate those family and commercial connections on which fortunes in commerce so often depended. For an apprentice to become his master's partner and/or marry his daughter was a common occurrence. Finally, service in the Levant brought commissions and, during the last years of one's apprenticeship, the right to carry on a private trade; from these sources it was sometimes possible to accu-

---

[47] PRO, S.P. 105/148/186 (ruling made 11 July 1628), and PRO, S.P. 105/148/237.

mulate the initial capital necessary to launch one's own career upon admission to the company.[48] For these reasons, and because the Levantine trade could be so lucrative, the price of an apprenticeship to a Levant Company merchant was normally quite substantial. In the years around 1670, the minimum fee appears to have been about £300, and it was apparently quite common in this era to pay £500 to £1,000.[49] Before 1640, the cost may have been somewhat lower—perhaps £200 to £300 on average— but it was still certainly beyond the means of all but a very restricted layer of the population.[50] The complaint leveled at the Merchant Adventurers that company merchants took as apprentices "such only whose friends give great sums of money with them and are provided of great stocks" could have been made with equal justice against the Levant Company.[51] It was only natural that the Levant Company merchants should select their apprentices from families in high economic strata. Only substantial citizens or well-off gentry could afford the high fees; only their children would be appropriate partners or perhaps future sons-in-law.

The Levantine trade could be entered much more cheaply by paying the entry fee than by apprenticeship; but, of some 350 or more new members admitted to the Levant Company in the period 1611–1640, only 98 entered by the former route.[52] It is clear why this was so: merchants who

---

[48] For a very good discussion of apprenticeship and the reasons for its crucial importance to the prospective Levant Company merchant, see R. Davis, *Aleppo and Devonshire Square: English Traders in the Levant in the Eighteenth Century* (London, 1967), pp. 64–68.

[49] In his will, the Levant Company merchant Robert Abdy left instructions that any of his sons who wished to become apprenticed to a merchant should be given the sum of "£300 at the least if to a Turkey merchant, but if to any other merchant or tradesman . . . not exceeding £300" (PRO, will of Robert Abdy, 1670 PCC Penn 146). See also Wood, *Levant Company*, p. 215.

[50] The evidence on the cost of apprenticeship in the early seventeenth century is scarce. I have come across only three examples for the period before 1650. In the mid-1630s Quarles Brown was apprenticed to Lewes Roberts for £300 (PRO, will of Lewes Roberts, 1641 PCC Evelyn 48). Sometime in the 1640s, Christopher Oxinden was apprenticed to John Gayre for £200 (PRO, will of John Gayre, 1649 PCC Fairfax 133). In 1633, Thomas Smith, the son of Humphrey Smith, was apprenticed to Edward Abbot for £500 (Society of Genealogists, Boyd's Index of London Citizens: 1991).

[51] *The Golden Fleece Defended; or Reasons against the Company of Merchant Adventurers* (London, 1646), pp. 1–2.

[52] All entries into the Levant Company are recorded in the company's Court Minute Books. The figures on Levant Company admissions for the period 1611–1640 are as follows:

	1611–1620	1621–1630	1631–1640	Total
Apprenticeship	82	51	96	229
Patrimony	13	14	18	45
Redemption	9	34	55	98
	104	99	169	372

Each company member was allowed once in every seven years to admit a person of his choice free of charge. That person was not obliged to serve a seven-year apprenticeship, but since he was, in fact, usually a servant (apprentice) of the sponsor, I have counted such admissions with those by apprenticeship.

entered by paying a fee—that is, without the advantages of an apprenticeship—normally found it difficult to achieve much commercial success. During the 1630s, when the prosperity of the Levantine trade was responsible for attracting unprecedented numbers of new members, no fewer than 55 merchants, substantially more than the combined total of the previous two decades (1611–1630), entered the company by fining. However, of these men, only 23 appear among the currants importers of 1634, 1636, 1638, and 1640, and they controlled only a tiny portion of the total brought in during these years.[53] On the other hand, of the 31 merchants who each imported 1,000 hundredweight or more of currants a year in either 1634, 1636, 1638, or 1640, only 4 had entered the company by paying a fee.[54]

A merchant who had done well in other trades before joining the company by fining might make a go of it in the Levantine trade,[55] but to do so, he needed a large working capital, especially to support factors in the Levant and to withstand the relatively long turnover period when his money was tied up in commodities. He also had to find some way to gain knowledge of the trade, as well as the needed commercial connections, which were generally acquired by means of apprenticeship and difficult to come by without it. For most traders, admission by fining was not a paying proposition. For this reason, the Levant Company put up no real resistance when the Royal Commission on Trade proposed in 1623 to lower the company fee for admission from £50 to £20 or even to £10.[56] In contrast, because the economic and technical requirements for active participation in the north European cloth trade were so minimal—apparently little more than a bit of cloth to sell and the price of its transport—the Merchant Adventurers felt it necessary to charge the astronomical fee of £200 for admission to the company.[57]

Recruitment to the Levantine trade thus tended to require *both* wealth

---

[53] These results were arrived at by comparing the lists of those who entered the company by redemption with lists of active currants traders compiled from the London Port Books for Imports for the years noted: PRO, E.190/38/5 (1634), PRO, E.190/37/13 (1636), PRO, E.190/41/5 (1638), and PRO, E.190/43/5 (1640).

[54] Henry Andrews, Richard Beresford, Thomas Bowyer, Caleb Cockcroft, John Cordell, Matthew Craddock, Thomas Davies, William Ferrar, Francis Flyer, Thomas Freeman, Henry Garway, William Garway, John Gayre, Richard Hall, Hugh Hamersley, Henry Hunt, Abraham Jennings, John Langham, Huet Leate, Richard Mantell, Samuel Mico, Richard Middleton, John Munn, Thomas Mustard, Hugh Norris, Lewes Roberts, John Smith, Thomas Soames, William Vincent, Roger Vivian, and John Wilde—among whom only Craddock, Ferrar, Mantell, and Mico entered by paying a fee.

[55] This was apparently the case with Matthew Craddock, who was a successful Eastland merchant for many years before joining the Levant Company by paying a fee in 1627 (PRO, S.P.105/148/169; Friis, *Alderman Cockayne's Project*, p. 283). For Craddock's career, see below, ch. 4.

[56] PRO, S.P.105/148/86v, 89, 89v.

[57] Friis, *Alderman Cockayne's Project*, p. 102.

and family connections: sons of members could of course come in by patrimony, but they were often apprenticed to other company merchants and
many times ended up marrying their daughters; children of nonmembers
required an initial fortune (and, most probably, social connections) in order to secure an apprenticeship, and many of them also ended up as sons-
in-law of company merchants. In this light, it is hardly surprising that
between 40 and 50 percent of all active Levant Company traders had fa-
thers, fathers-in-law, or brothers already in the company when they
joined. What is truly impressive is the degree to which the leading merchants who originally established the trade in the later sixteenth century
were able to make their influence felt through their descendants. Even in
the 1630s, a dominant core of the company's membership could trace family connections back to the founders of the Levantine trade in the last
quarter of the sixteenth century, if not to the pioneers of the eastward
expansion of the previous generation. Thirty Levant Company merchants
who traded in currants in the 1630s can be linked, by their own direct
membership in the company, or by birth or marriage (often as a third
generation), to the generation of merchants who entered the Levantine
trade between the time of the Turkey Company charter of 1581 and the
Levant Company charter of 1605.[58] These men probably controlled half

[58] *Huet Leate, Richard Leate,* and *Nicholas Leate,* all sons of Nicholas Leate who was a charter
member of the Levant Company in 1592 and who had married Jane, the daughter of the Turkey
Company (1581) founder Richard Staper; *John Wilde,* who married Mary, daughter of Nicholas
Leate and Jane Staper; *Henry Hunt,* who married Mabel, daughter of Nicholas Leate and Jane Staper
(Society of Genealogists Boyd's Index: 1650; PRO, S.P. 105/147/34 and PRO, S.P. 105/148/121,
139; *Visitation of London, 1633–1635,* Harleian Society Publications 15 and 17 [London, 1880–
1883], 1: 403; 2: 376). *John Offley,* the son of Robert Offley, a charter member of the Levant
Company in 1592 who married Ann, daughter of the Turkey Company (1581) founder Edward
Osborne (Society of Genealogists, Boyd's Index: 22523; PRO, S.P. 105/148/26). *Job Harby,* who
married Elizabeth, daughter of Richard Wyche, a Levant Company charter member of 1605, who
had married Elizabeth, daughter of the Turkey Company (1581) founder Richard Saltonstall (*Visitation of London, 1633–1635* 1: 346; Lang, "Greater Merchants of London," p. 380). *John Munn,*
son of John Munn, Levant Company charter member of 1600 who was the stepson of Thomas Cordell
(and brother of Thomas Munn, one of the great Levant Company merchants of the early seventeenth
century); *Thomas Bowyer,* son of Margaret Cordell Bowyer, daughter of Thomas Cordell, and of
Robert Bowyer, a Levant Company charter member of 1600 who was the son of Francis Bowyer, one
of the leaders of the first generation of those involved in commercial expansion to Morocco, Russia,
and Spain in the 1550s and 1560s (*Visitation of London, 1633–1635* 1: 94, 189; *D.N.B.* 1183–86
[due to uncertainties in the Munn genealogy, the relationships here attributed to the "John Munn"
who traded in the Levant in the 1630s must remain in doubt]; T. S. Willan, *Studies in Elizabethan
Foreign Trade* [Manchester, 1959], p. 218). *Henry Garway* and *William Garway II,* both sons of the
Turkey Company (1583) founder William Garway; *William Garway III,* son of William Garway II;
Robert Sainthill, who married Elizabeth, daughter of William Garway II (*Visitation of London, 1633–
1635* 1: 304; PRO, S.P. 105/149/182; Society of Genealogists, Boyd's Index: 10131). *Henry Andrews,* who married Elizabeth, daughter of William Bond, Levant Company charter member in 1600
and 1605, who was the son of William Bond, one of the founders of the trade with Russia in the years

of the Levantine trade in the 1630s. They brought in 109,425 hundred-weight of the total of 231,106 hundredweight of currants imported by Levant Company merchants in the five years 1630, 1634, 1636, 1638, and 1640.[59]

By 1640, significant numbers of the Levant Company's richest and most active traders were thus joined in a highly ramified network of inter-locking family relationships, the members of which controlled a major share of the trade. This web of connections helps to explain why the Levant Company merchants were so successful in exploiting the valuable privileges they derived from their close ties with the government, in restricting effective membership in the company, and in closely regulating the trade. At the same time, the formidable barriers to successful partici-pation in the Levantine commerce go far to explain why so few Merchant Adventurers entered the Levantine trade, even from the 1620s when their own trade entered into crisis. It is no accident that of the handful of Ad-venturers who did trade with the Levant during the first part of the sev-enteenth century, a disproportionate number were recruited from among the Adventurers' leading representatives. Only the wealthier and better-connected among them seem to have succeeded in profiting from eastern trade. "Born rich and adding wealth to wealth by trading in a beaten road to wealth"—thus a seventeenth-century critic described the career pattern

---

after the middle of the sixteenth century; *Daniel Andrews*, son of Henry Andrews; *Samuel Mico*, who married Elizabeth, daughter of Henry Andrews (*Visitation of London, 1633–1635* 1: 86; 2: 99; Willan, *Muscovy Merchants*, p. 81; Society of Genealogists, Boyd's Index: 1265–66; PRO, S.P. 105/149/379; PRO, will of Henry Andrews, 1638 PCC Lee 127). *Thomas Salter*, son of George Salter, a charter member of the Levant Company in 1592, 1600, and 1605; *Nicholas Herrick*, who married Susan, the daughter of the Levant merchant William Salter, a son of George Salter (PRO, S.P. 105/147/75; *Visitation of London, 1633–1635* 1: 377; H.M.C., *Salisbury* 10: 215). *Caldwell Farrington*, son of Thomas Farrington who was trading with the Levant before 1600 (PRO, S.P. 105/148/118). *Simond Edmonds*, who married Mary, daughter of Thomas Boothby, a Levant Company charter member in 1605; *Francis Flyer*, who married Martha, another daughter of Thomas Boothby (*Visitation of London, 1633–1635*, 1: 246, 281). *John Smith*, son of Humphrey Smith, a Levant Company charter member of 1605 (PRO, S.P. 105/149/389). *Thomas Soames*, son of Stephen Soames, Levant Company charter member of 1605 (PRO, S.P. 105/147/5). *Thomas Hamersley*, the son of Hugh Hamersley, a charter member of the Levant Company in 1600 and 1605 (PRO, S.P. 105/147/75). *Edward Abbot*, son of Morris Abbot, a Levant Company charter member in 1600 and 1605 (Society of Genealogists, Boyd's Index: 1502). Finally, *Hugh Hamersley, Morris Abbot, Stephen Soames*, and *Ralph Freeman*, all of whom began to be active in trade with the Levant around 1600, if not before (*H.M.C., Salisbury* 9: 103; 10: 215; Lang, "Greater Merchants of London," pp. 194–96, 217–19, 222–23. It should be noted that the first seventeen traders mentioned above were all descended from either the leading Turkey Company (1581) founders Richard Staper, Edward Osborne, and Richard Saltonstall, the major Venice Company initiators Thomas Cordell and William Garway, or the great Russia Company and Morocco Company pioneers William Bond and Francis Bowyer, who were most active in the period before the advent of trade with the Levant.

[59] Compiled from London Port Books for Imports for these years. See also table 1.4.

of the typical Levant Company merchant.[60] On the available evidence, there is little reason to dispute his characterization, and it helps in understanding the meteoric rise to dominance of this extraordinarily successful commercial group.

The Redistribution of Commercial Opportunities and the Recomposition of the City Merchant Establishment

The ability not only to control access to expanding markets and to regulate the trade closely but, beyond that, to concentrate the commerce in relatively few hands within their company, allowed the leading Levant Company merchants to accumulate fabulous fortunes. Such great wealth routinely provided them with the opportunity for magistracy. This had been true for the Merchant Adventurers during the long period of their commercial hegemony; it was no less the case for the traders with the Mediterranean and the Near and Far East.

THE DISTRIBUTION OF THE TRADE

The differences among the Levant Company members with respect to the number and quality of their commercial connections and the amount of commercial capital they initially commanded yielded a radically skewed distribution of trade within the company. Here, once again, the Levant Company's experience was analogous to that of the Merchant Adventurers. Only a small proportion of the Merchant Adventurers' members were active at any given moment, and, among these, a far smaller number were dominant. For example, in 1606, a year in which 219 merchants shipped cloth to the Adventurers' markets, 26 merchants (21 percent), trading over 1,000 cloths each, exported 43 percent of the total. In 1614, the corresponding figures were 182 shippers, with 23 (16 percent) exporting 1,000 cloths or more and controlling 49 percent of the market.[61] The Levant Company's trade distribution was even more unequal.

During the first forty years of the seventeenth century, more than 500 merchants were admitted to the Levant Company, but there was always a substantial disparity between those eligible to trade and those who actually did so, as well as a great unevenness in the quantities traded by those who

---

[60] The relative handful of Adventurers who entered the Levant Company included such great traders as Richard Saltonstall, the Middletons, the Batemans, the Freemans, the Ferrars, and Henry Andrews. The quotation is from "Mr. Walwyn's conception, for a free trade," PRO, S.P.105/144/172.

[61] Friis, *Alderman Cockayne's Project*, pp. 78, 93.

were active.[62] From the very founding of the trade, the Levantine commerce was concentrated in relatively few hands. During the Turkey Company's first decade, when the trade was often worth £100,000 a year or more, the entire commerce was monopolized by a joint stock company consisting of between 10 and 20 members. In the same period, the Venetian trade, worth perhaps £30,000 to £50,000 annually, was run by a half dozen merchants.[63] The bits of evidence available indicate that little changed under the Levant Company of 1592. For the one voyage for which there is a full record of imports, that of the *Royal Exchange* in 1596, we find 2 among the 20 shippers controlling 51 percent of the total of £13,125 in rated value, or perhaps £30,000 in actual value.[64]

Nor did the charters of 1601 and 1605, despite the eased admission requirements, cause a break in the pattern. In 1610, some 250 traders (many of them non–Levant Company members bringing in trivial amounts) imported 48,990 hundredweight of currants. Thirteen merchants, each of whom brought in 1,000 hundredweight of currants or more, imported 56 percent of this total.[65] This pattern of trade distribution remained substantially unaltered in the 1620s and 1630s, as can be seen from analyses of the currants trade and the silk trade, as well as of the Levant Company's impositions (see table 2.1). The imposition was a comparatively light duty (1–2 percent of rated value) that was placed on all the members' imports and exports, and therefore provides probably the best evidence of the distribution of trade. During the period 1627–1635, when the value of the Levantine trade may have approached £200,000 to £300,000 a year, the impositions paid show that 24 merchants, or the top 12 percent, controlled 54 percent of the trade.[66]

THE LEVANT–EAST INDIA COMBINE

The Levant Company merchants' commercial base was not confined to the Levantine trade. During the 1630s, few of the Levant Company mer-

[62] One hundred eighteen were admitted as charter members in 1605. Some 370 or so were admitted between 1611 and 1640. An unspecified additional number were admitted between 1605 and 1611 (no court books survive for this period). See above, note 52.

[63] This estimate for the Venetian trade is very rough. It is based on the rated value of Venetian imports between 1 July and 20 September 1589 at about £15,000 (see Willan, "English Trade with the Levant," pp. 405ff.).

[64] Fischer, "English Trade to Asia," pp. 346, 421–22; BL, Lansdown MSS 81, fol. 125. Apparently less reliable data on three other voyages of this decade yield similar results (see PRO, S.P. Foreign, Levant, 109, fol. 116; PRO, E.122/218/16).

[65] PRO, E.122/191/16.

[66] The currants-import figures are based on the London Port Books for Imports for the stated years. The silk-import figures are from PRO, E.122/230/4. The impositions figures were compiled from the Levant Company Ledger Books, PRO, S.P.105/157–58.

TABLE 2.1
Levant Company Trade Distribution

IA. IMPOSITIONS PAYMENTS, 1621–1627

% Distribution (members)		Number of Members		% Total Distribution of Trade	
top	12 } 35		23 } 67		54 } 88
next	23		44		34
next	65		123		12
	100		190		100

IB. IMPOSITIONS PAYMENTS, 1627–1635

% Distribution (members)		Number of Members		% Total Distribution of Trade	
top	12 } 25		24 } 51		54 } 73
next	13		27		19
next	75		153		27
	100		204		100

II. RAW-SILK IMPORTS, 1628 AND 1629: TWO-YEAR TOTALS

Total Number Silk Importers	Total Silk Imported	Importers of 5000 + lbs.			Importers of 1000–4999 lbs.		
		No.	Total Amount Traded	% Total Silk Imported	No.	Total Amount Traded	% Total Silk Imported
93	168,657	10	80,657	48	32	68,419	40

III. CURRANTS TRADE, 1630–1640

Year	Number of Levant Co. Currants Traders	Total Levant Co. Currants Imports	Merchants Trading 1000 hundred weight or more		
			Number	Total Amounts Currants Traded	% Total Currants Imports
1630	46	35,623	14	23,988	67
1634	61	48,795	17	31,302	73
1636	38	45,072	11	37,917	84
1638	44	62,249	14	51,468	83
1640	61	44,367	10	22,808	51

NOTE

These totals are for Levant Company members. Total Levant currants imports differ slightly from these figures each year due to amounts brought in by nonmembers.

SOURCES

IA. H. Taylor, "Price Revolution or Price Revision? The English and Spanish Trade after 1604," *Renaissance and Modern Studies* 12 (1968): 13.

IB. Levant Company Ledger Books, PRO, S.P. 105/157–58.

II. PRO, E. 122/230/4.

III. London Port Books for Imports.

chants were interested in the City's established company trades with northern and western Europe. In 1640, for example, there were only six Levant Company members among the 74 active Merchant Adventurers (that
is, exporters of a hundred cloths or more to the Adventurers' markets).[67]
Similarly, only four Levant Company traders were among the 34 Eastland traders of London listed by Hinton.[68] Finally, only five Levant Company members were among the more than 175 traders in French wine
active in the year 1637.[69] On the other hand, the Levant Company merchants' influence in the newer and related trades with Russia and especially
with the East Indies was substantial, and of great significance to the overall
structure and character of London's merchant establishment.

The trade with the East Indies had, of course, developed as a direct
extension of the Levantine commerce, and it remained the special project
of the Levant Company traders. Part of the reason for this was purely
commercial: the East India Company remained heavily focused on the
spice import trade for which the Levant Company merchants had originally developed it. Moreover, as the trade expanded, goods imported
from the East Indies found ready reexport markets not only in Europe,
but also in the Levant, and were usually carried there by men who belonged to both companies.[70]

But there is also a more general explanation for the continuing preeminence of Levant Company merchants in the East India Company. With
a working capital of unprecedented magnitude at its disposal, the East
India Company was the largest joint-stock commercial venture of the period—and for much of the time, quite a profitable one.[71] As cause and
consequence of this fact, London's greatest merchants were naturally attracted to its board of directors, which very soon became the most important mercantile governing body in London. Unlike the Levant Company's
board of directors, which functioned merely as an executive committee for
the general court that actually governed the trade, the East India Company's twenty-four directors, or committees, substantially controlled the
East India business. The company's charter empowered the whole body of

---

[67] This result was derived from comparing full lists of Levant Company members, compiled from
the company's Court Minute Books, with the names of Merchant Adventurers active in 1640, compiled from the London Port Book for Cloth Exports, 1640, PRO, E.190/43/4. The Levant Company Merchant Adventurers included Anthony Bateman, Richard Bateman, William Bateman, Nicholas Bowater, Caleb Cockcroft, and William Williams.

[68] Christopher Clitherow, Matthew Craddock, Nicholas Leate, and Richard Mantell (R.W.K.
Hinton, *The Eastland Trade and the Commonweal* [Cambridge, 1959], pp. 219–20).

[69] Robert Charlton, James Traves, Sir Job Harby, Marmaduke Rawden, and Richard Beresford,
(London Port Book for Wine Imports, 1637, PRO, E.190/35/7).

[70] K. N. Chaudhuri, *The English East India Company* (London, 1965), pp. 12–13; L. Roberts,
Merchants Mappe of Commerce (London, 1638), p. 193.

[71] Chaudhuri, *East India Company*, pp. 209ff.

the company's membership assembled in its general court to make company policy. However, since the general court met only four times a year, it was unable in practice to control the directors, especially since the charter did not specifically limit the authority of the directors. Indeed, at several points during the early 1630s, when it was being challenged by the membership, the company's directorate seriously considered the total abolition of the general court.[72] Because of their elite social position, as well as their enormous investments in the company, the board members could get away with this sort of highhandedness. A minimum investment in the company of £2,000 was required for eligibility to the directorate. And at one point the twenty-four directors claimed that they held more stock than four hundred of the generality.[73]

During the 1630s, Levant Company merchants overwhelmingly dominated the East India Company's directorate. Of the forty-seven different directors chosen for the company court during that decade (1630–1639), no fewer than twenty-eight were Levant Company members.[74] The five men—Morris Abbot, Christopher Clitherow, Robert Bateman, Henry Garway, and William Cockayne—who among them controlled the positions of governor, deputy governor, and treasurer of the East India Company throughout the 1630s were all leading Levant Company merchants.[75] Not surprisingly, many of the East India Company directors played a leading role in the Levantine trade. In 1634, for example, among the East India Company's twenty-seven main officers (governor, deputy governor, treasurer, and directors) there were twenty Levant Company traders. Ten of these were active in that year in the Levantine currants trade, and they controlled about 20 percent of the total imported.[76]

To complete this picture, it need only be added that the Russia Com-

[72] India Office Library, Court Minutes of the East India Company 13: 110, 126; *C.C.M.E.I.C. 1635–1639*, p. vii. Note, in addition, the directors' decision to conceal the company accounts from the generality, 24 December 1634 (ibid., p. ix).

[73] *C.C.M.E.I.C. 1635–1639*, p. vii.

[74] The court minutes for the period July 1637–July 1639 have not survived, so the following list of Levant Company members who were East India Company directors is not perfectly complete: Hugh Hamersley, Henry Garway, Anthony Abdy, Jeffrey Kirby, William Spurstowe, Thomas Mustard, Job Harby, John Cordell, John Williams, John Gayre, William Cockayne, Giles Martin, John Langham, Richard Davis, Thomas Bownest, Abraham Reynardson, Thomas Munn, Humphrey Browne, Henry Andrews, William Garway, Robert Cambell, Richard Venn, Matthew Craddock, Daniel Harvey, Edward Abbot, Richard Bateman, Morris Abbot, William Ashwell, Lewes Roberts.

[75] Compiled from the calendars of the East India Company Court Minutes.

[76] The East India officers of 1634 active in the currants trade in that year included William Garway (598 hundredweight), Matthew Craddock (1,029 hundredweight), Henry Garway (3,206 hundredweight), Henry Andrews (1,875 hundredweight), John Langham (1,648 hundredweight), Thomas Mustard (640 hundredweight), John Gayre (1,701 hundredweight), William Cockayne (551 hundredweight), John Williams (660 hundredweight), and Job Harby (513 hundredweight).

pany and trade, at the core of the expansionary thrust eastward during the second half of the sixteenth century, remained throughout the early Stuart period firmly in the hands of Levant–East India merchants. Between 1601 and 1612 the East India Company and the Russia Company together organized and financed voyages for the discovery of a northwest passage. Shortly thereafter, the Russia Company went into deep financial crisis and the East India Company temporarily took it over.[77] In 1620, the great Levant–East India magnate Ralph Freeman purchased the entire Russia Company trade from the East India Company for £12,000. But shortly thereafter a new, regulated company was formed under the governorship of alderman Hugh Hamersley, who was then also governor of the Levant Company and an East India Company director.[78] In the later 1620s and 1630s, a handful of Levant–East India leaders, including Hamersley, Job Harby, William Bladwell, and Henry Garway, dominated the Russian trade.[79] Henry Garway's accession around 1640 to the governorships of the Levant, East India, and Russia companies was a true reflection of these trades' overlapping and interlocked development and directorates.[80]

THE REDISTRIBUTION OF WEALTH AND OFFICES

By 1640 the eastward-trading combine formed the heart of London's commercial establishment and provided the greatest source of merchant recruits for the City's highest social and political positions. The shift in the locus of wealth during previous seventy-five years or so can be seen, in gross terms, by comparing the relative socioeconomic position of the memberships of the various merchant groups at the beginning of the period with that at the end. In 1559, no fewer than sixteen of London's twenty-two wealthiest citizens were Merchant Adventurers, according to the subsidy of that year.[81] In 1576, on a list apparently drawn up by the government of "the names of sundry of the wisest and best merchants in London to deal with the weightiest causes of the City as occasion is of-

---

[77] *C.S.P. Col. E.I. 1513–1616*, pp. xxvii–xxxii; Lang, "Greater Merchants of London," pp. 242–45; W. R. Scott, *The Constitution and Finance of English, Scottish, and Irish Joint-Stock Companies to 1720*, 3 vols. (Cambridge, 1910–1912), 2: 54–55.

[78] Friis, *Alderman Cockayne's Project*, pp. 56–57 n. 5.

[79] By 1632, eight of twenty-six merchants who sent cloth to Russia were leading Levant Company traders, and these traders controlled some 60 percent of the total cloth exports—2,383 of a total of 3,910 cloths exported (London Port Book for Cloth Exports, 1632, PRO, E.190/36/5). In 1634, the Levant–East India director Job Harby controlled almost half the total imported from Russia (and the Levant Company trader William Bladwell brought in most of the rest) (London Port Book for Imports, 1634, PRO, E.190/38/5).

[80] V. Pearl, *London and the Outbreak of the Puritan Revolution: City Government and National Politics, 1625–1643* (Oxford, 1961), p. 299.

[81] Ramsay, *City of London*, p. 40.

fered," there were about twenty-six Merchant Adventurers, eleven traders with Spain and/or Morocco (who were not also Merchant Adventurers), and four Eastland merchants (who were not also Merchant Adventurers).[82]

By the 1630s, however, the rise of the eastward trading merchants had brought a major change. Several crude but revealing indicators of socioeconomic position can give a very general idea of the place of the once overwhelmingly dominant Merchant Adventurers in relation to the newly emergent Levant Company traders. Although none of the results of these tests, in isolation, can be regarded as entirely conclusive, they all point in roughly the same direction and provide evidence of a pattern.

In the first place, among the select group of citizens assessed at £100 or more in the parliamentary assessment lists of 1642–1643, there were twenty-one Merchant Adventurers and forty-one Levant Company traders.[83] There are, however, difficulties connected with the use of these assessments. First, there is no way of determining the degree to which political factors influenced them, in particular whether the parliamentarians who did the assessing charged their opponents more than they did their friends. Second, the assessment ordinance was directed especially at those who had not previously contributed to the parliamentary cause or who had not contributed in proportion to their estates.[84] Since there is no way to tell who had previously contributed, or to what extent, there is no way to determine to what extent this factor affected the figures.

The London Visitation, which can be taken as a general gauge of high socioeconomic position, seems to confirm the impression of the relative place of the Merchant Adventurers vis-à-vis the Levant Company traders conveyed by the assessments. Of seventy-four Merchant Adventurers active in 1640, twenty-nine (39 percent) were included in the London Visitation of 1633–1635.[85] In comparison, of the sixty-one Levant Company currants traders active in 1640, thirty-six (59 percent) were so included.

In the autumn of 1640, the Crown raised £50,000 from some 140 leading London citizens.[86] Although this was technically termed a loan, it seems that London's wealthiest citizens were more or less obliged to lend in proportion to their estates. The Crown had used this method for its loan of 1617,[87] and it appears that the loan of 1640 fits the same pattern (as

---

[82] BL, Lansdowne MSS 683. The numbers here must be taken as rough approximations, due to the incompleteness of the merchant lists on which they are based.

[83] PRO, S.P. 19/A.49. Only those merchants listed in the port books as trading one hundred cloths or more a year at the Merchant Adventurers' marts are counted as Merchant Adventurers.

[84] A.O. 1: 38–41.

[85] *Visitation of London, 1633–1635.*

[86] PRO, S.P. 28/162.

[87] R. Ashton, *The Crown and the Money Market, 1603–1640* (Oxford, 1960), pp. 123–24. The

does the comparable citizens' loan of £100,000 to the king in the spring of 1641). Among these wealthy contributors there were twenty-one Merchant Adventurers, whose average payment was £155, in comparison with thirty-one Levant Company traders, whose average payment was £275.[88]

But no doubt the most spectacular evidence of the decisive change that had taken place can be found in the representation of the different sections of the merchant community on the court of aldermen of the City of London. Election to this body was not merely an entrée to the most important municipal decision-making body; it was also a sign of elite socioeconomic position. A fortune of £10,000 was a minimum requirement for eligibility, and every alderman was expected to have the financial resources to cope with the heavy responsibilities for entertainment and hospitality associated with the office of lord mayor. In the period 1555–1570, 38 aldermen were chosen; some 25, perhaps a few more, were overseas traders. No fewer than 17 of these were Merchant Adventurers.[89] This overwhelming dominance was maintained into the first quarter of the seven-

---

City loan to the Crown in 1625 was made, apparently, in a similar fashion (Ashton, pp. 128–29). That the November–December 1640 "loan" was actually an assessment on the City's wealthiest citizens is further evidenced by the fact that, in a number of cases, individuals made separate payments on more than one date, apparently installments on a preset sum owed by each.

[88] These results were derived from comparing relatively extensive lists of Merchant Adventurers and Levant Company merchants, compiled primarily from the surviving port books and the Levant Company Ledger Books, but also other miscellaneous records, with the list of those who were assessed in November–December 1640 ("lenders"), as given in PRO, S.P.28/162. The Merchant Adventurers included George Clark (Clarke) (£300), Lawrence Halstead (£500), Matthew Craddock (£500), Isaac Jones (£400), William Essington (£200), George Franklin (£200), Edward Williams (£200), William Williams (£100), Richard Bateman (£100), Humphrey Berrington (£100), Samuel Avery (£100), Robert Lowther (£900), Robert Fenn (£200), Caleb Cockcroft (£100), Barney Reymes (£100), Andrew Kendrick (£100), Thomas Northey (£200), William Christmas (£100), James Fenn (£200), Christopher Packe (£100), and Richard Clutterbuck (£50). The Levant Company merchants included John Gayre (£500), John Ofield (£100), Francis Flyer (£200), Thomas Soames (£500), Robert Bateman (£500), William Cockayne (£300), Isaac Pennington (£800), John Cordell (£500), Matthew Craddock (£500), Morris Abbot (£400), Simon Edwards (£200), William Ashwell (£200), Samuel Vassall (£500), Thomas Hodges (£200), James Mann (£100), William Williams (£100), Thomas Freeman (£100), Christopher Clitherow (£500), William Langhorne (£100), Nathan Wright (£100), Henry Austin (£50), John Langham (£500), Caleb Cockcroft (£100), Joseph Brand (£100), Richard Bateman (£200), Robert Gayre (£100), Abraham Reynardson (£500), Robert Sainthill (£100), Hamon Gibbon (£100), Michael Gatward (£100), and Daniel Harvey (£300). One should note in passing the predominance of these two groups of merchants on this list of wealthy Londoners. Together, they constituted more than one-third of those assessed.

[89] This result was derived from comparing relatively extensive lists of Merchant Adventurers for this period, obtained from all of the surviving London Port Books for Cloth Exports, as well as the Adventurers' charter, with full lists of aldermen in the period 1555–1570. The Merchant Adventurers included Richard Malorye, Richard Champyon, Roger Martyn, Richard Foulkes, Thomas Rowe, William Allen, Humphrey Baskerfeld, Richard Chamberlyn, Rowland Heyward, Edward Jackman, Richard Lambert, William Beswick, Lionel Duckett, John Ryvers, Henry Beecher, William Bond, Richard Pype, and Alexander Avedon (?).

teenth century. Of the 140 aldermen elected in the period 1600–1625, about half, around 70, were overseas traders. Of these overseas trader aldermen, approximately three-quarters, or around 50, traded at one time or another with the Merchant Adventurers' privileged markets in Germany and the Low Countries, while one-third to one-half, that is, about 30, were mainly or exclusively occupied there.[90] This powerful representation of Merchant Adventurers far outweighed that of any other group. Only 8 aldermen were recruited from among the merchants trading with the Levant in this period.[91] By 1640, in contrast, almost half of the 26 aldermanic offices were in the hands of Levant Company traders and/or East India Company directors. In the period 1626–1640, 16 Levant Company traders, but only 9 Merchant Adventurers, were elected. Between 1631 and 1640, only 2 Merchant Adventurers were chosen aldermen, as against 8 Levant Company merchants.[92]

Insofar as overseas merchants were brought into important positions within the national government in the pre–Civil War period, they seem to have been chosen almost exclusively from among the Levant–East India combine. No large structure of offices was created in England in this period such as existed in France and other Continental countries. Moreover, insofar as offices were available, merchants rarely received them. The important exception to this rule was in state finance, and here the Levant–East India traders were overwhelmingly dominant. As Robert Ashton has shown, the farmers of the customs came to play an increasingly crucial role in providing credit for a crisis-ridden government in the 1620s and 1630s. Between 1620 and 1640, some twenty-eight different men headed syndicates in control of the farm of the great customs and of the lesser customs farms for currants, wines, and sweet wines. Of these, ten were East India Company directors, and eleven were leading Levant Company merchants (seven were both). At least eight of the others were not merchants at all, but were, rather, financiers and financial administrators. Among all these customs farmers, there were only two Merchant Adventurers.[93]

---

[90] Lang, "Greater Merchants of London," pp. 149–50, and Abstract. See p. 150 n. 1 for names.

[91] Lang, "Greater Merchants of London," p. 200.

[92] The Levant Company merchant aldermen included Christopher Clitherow (1626), Sir Stephen Soames (1626), Sir Morris Abbot (1626), Henry Garway (1627), Rowland Backhouse (1627), Humphrey Smith (1629), Jeffrey Kirby (1629), Robert Bateman (1629), Anthony Abdy (1631), Robert Cambell (1631), Henry Andrews (1634), John Cordell (1635), Thomas Soames (1635), John Gayre (1636), Isaac Pennington (1639), and Abraham Reynardson (1640). The Merchant Adventurer aldermen included Richard Venn (Fenn) (1626), Thomas Morley (1627), Sir Henry Rowe (1627), Rowland Backhouse (1627), Humphrey Smith (1627), Robert Jeffreys (1629), Robert Bateman (1629), Hugh Perry (1632), and Henry Andrews (1634).

[93] R. Ashton, "Government Borrowing under the First Two Stuarts, 1603–1642" (University of London, Ph.D. diss., 1953), pp. 264–66. See also Ashton, *Crown and Money Market; C.S.P.D.*

A Unified Merchant Community,
an Integrated Merchant Political Elite

The significance of the commercial transformations of the early Stuart period was not confined merely to their effect in elevating or depressing the economic and political fortunes of individual merchants in varyingly successful commercial lines. As emphasized, commercial change during the pre–Civil War period conditioned not only the rise of impressive numbers of eastward traders to positions of prominence, but also their emergence as a cohesive and dominant sociopolitical group. One should not, however, conclude that the Levant–East India merchants sought to oppose themselves to the other overseas company merchants in either social or political terms, or that a serious social or political gulf had grown up between them and the rest of the community of company merchants. On the contrary, the Levant–East India merchants remained at all points closely bound to the rest of the community of company merchants, both by critical common interests and by ties of family and business; they could therefore play an important role in providing leadership for the community as a whole.

MERE MERCHANTS VERSUS
THE CITY'S DOMESTIC TRADESMEN

Above all, the Levant–East India merchants shared with all of the other company merchants of London a profound dependence on the Crown-sanctioned commercial corporations that provided the foundation for their protected trades. This dependence united the generality of company merchants in defense of privilege and, all else being equal, in support of the royal government, which was of course the guarantor of their protected status. But it brought them together as well in sharp opposition to those various nonmerchant elements in the City that, by virtue of their own economic roles, appeared to threaten the merchants' trade and that were therefore largely excluded from overseas commerce. The aim of the chartered companies was not merely to keep out poorer, badly connected traders so as to restrict the numbers participating in the trade; it was, especially, to prevent entry into overseas commerce by the City's shopkeepers, small producers, and ship captains, whatever their wealth. These people were well positioned to undersell the "mere merchants" (overseas trading wholesalers), for they could dispense with the middleman's profit required

---

1627–1628, pp. 421, 423; Bodleian Library, Bankes MSS (catalogue), 38/28, 50/8. These figures must be rough approximations, since the records on which the identification of customs farm "leaders" is based appear to be somewhat arbitrary, in terms of the names listed as associated with each farm (and those left out).

by the mere merchants by going directly to the final consumer, either with English exports or foreign imports. Moreover, many of them were by no means poor, and an important minority succeeded in accumulating substantial fortunes and undoubtedly possessed sufficient wealth to pursue overseas trade, had they been allowed to do so. For the mere merchants to have permitted shopkeepers, small producers, or ship captains to enter their companies might therefore have proved disastrous. The Merchant Adventurers seem to have been the first to adopt the proviso confining membership in their corporation to mere merchants, and they did so explicitly in order to prevent retailers, artisans, and ship captains from "taking the living from their brethren." In turn, during the latter part of the sixteenth century, almost every group of merchants seeking government protection for its commerce made the confinement of its trade to mere merchants a central demand, and a clause to that effect became a standard provision of every company charter.[94]

The mere merchants, on the one hand, and the shopkeepers and artisans, on the other, had always had a direct and serious conflict of interest over the price of the goods they sold to one another. Indeed, struggle between the two groups had been a characteristic feature of the urban political economy since the later Middle Ages. The mere merchants' widespread adoption of the proviso excluding retailers and artisans from their companies had the effect, therefore, of deepening, extending, and making more explicit the already existing basis for conflict. In the first place, the mere-merchant proviso obviously obliged most of those shopkeepers and artisans who would otherwise have entered overseas commerce to confine themselves to their established line of work, for the price of entry was nothing less than the relinquishing of their established domestic business. Those retailers and direct producers who would have had the best chance of success as merchants were naturally those whose business had been most successful; so it was they who stood to lose most by the restriction of trade to mere merchants. Equally important, by keeping shopkeepers and artisans out of their companies, the overseas merchants very much strengthened their position over and against them as monopolists and monopsonists. They thereby improved their capacity to exploit shopkeepers and artisans in day-to-day exchanges. The result was naturally a significant hardening of the lines that already divided the company merchants from the rest of the City's business community, and an increase in the potential for open hostilities between the two.

The Merchant Adventurers appear to have devised the mere-merchant proviso especially to exclude from their overseas marts the City's artisan cloth producers. The ease with which these cloth producers could enter the Adventurers' trade in the absence of company restrictions was made

[94] R. H. Tawney and E. Power, eds., *Tudor Economic Documents*, 3 vols. (London, 1924), 2: 53.

amply clear in the years 1624–1634 when the Adventurers' privileges were suspended. In this period independent producers flooded into the trade, resulting in a threefold increase in the total number of traders.[95] What the Adventurers wished to prevent was exemplified in the rags-to-riches story of one William Kiffin, who started out as a poor runaway apprentice to a cloth worker. Kiffin founded a meteoric career as an overseas merchant by illegally carrying small parcels of cloth to the Adventurers' privileged markets during the 1640s, when there was a weakened enforcement of the company's monopoly.[96] It was, indeed, men of Kiffin's sort who eventually led the broad-ranging attack on the Adventurers' privileges during the later 1640s.

The merchants in the new southern and eastern trades of the Elizabethan period regarded the government-chartered monopoly corporation as essential, mainly because the City's grocers and retailers were in a particularly strong position to undersell them in their favored import commodities. Nevertheless, these merchants did not always get the protection they wanted, even in such long-cherished commercial fields as the trade with Spain. In those cases where they failed to receive the expected protection, many of them simply refused to go on with the trade. Their withdrawal, however, was fraught with danger, for it opened the way to socioeconomic advancement for traders from a social layer very different from and generally lower than theirs, with interests in conflict with their own.

When, in the early 1570s, the traders with Spain sought government privileges for the trade, they made the exclusion of the City's grocers, retailers, artisans, and mariners from the Spanish commerce a central demand. London's tradesmen were finding the Spanish market increasingly attractive because of the wide variety of consumer commodities—including tobacco, sugar, fruits, and cheap wines—that they could obtain there for sale in their shops. By the Spanish Company charter of 1577, all but mere merchants were barred from trading with Spain. But with the outbreak of war in 1585, the charter lapsed.[97]

At the restoration of peace in 1604, the government renewed the Spanish Company's privileges, which were immediately challenged by a group of retailers, shopkeepers, and others who had been excluded from the trade. Despite this outcry, by 1605 the government had drawn up and approved a new charter, which again barred "retailers, artificers, common mariners, and handicraftsmen."[98]

[95] See above, p. 60. See also *A Discourse Consisting of Motives for the Enlargement and Freedom of Trade* (London, 1645), p. 26.

[96] *Life of Mr. William Kiffin*, ed. J. Ivimey (London, 1883), pp. 28–30.

[97] PRO, S.P.12/99/8, 9; P. Croft, *The Spanish Company*, London Record Society Publications 9 (London, 1973), pp. ix–xii, xxxv; Friis, *Alderman Cockayne's Project*, p. 169.

[98] Croft, *Spanish Company*, pp. xxix–xxxix; Friis, *Alderman Cockayne's Project*, pp. 156–58.

But the Spanish Company did not long retain its privileges. In 1606, Parliament disallowed its charter, with dramatic effects on the trade. Many of the great City merchants behind the Elizabethan expansion southward and eastward clearly had hoped to retain their long-standing preeminence in the commerce with Spain. Of the thirty directors named in the new Spanish Company charter of 1605, nine were Levant Company merchants, and four of these were Levant Company charter officers in 1601 and/or 1605.[99] However, few of the greater merchants were willing to go on trading with Spain once government protection had been lifted. In 1609, among 176 active traders who sent out a total of £31,744 worth of goods (nonbroadcloths) to Spain, there were only 11 Levant Company merchants who exported a total of £3,682 worth of goods.[100] By 1615, among 49 traders with Spain who brought in 100 or more butts of wine (their total being 14,177 butts), there were only 4 Levant Company members (whose imports totaled 1,589 butts).[101]

Meanwhile, businessmen from the layer of domestic traders normally excluded from overseas trade had seized their chance. Literally hundreds of noncompany, nonmerchant traders invaded the Spanish commerce. Many of these had small operations, but they could still pose a serious threat to the mere merchants by virtue of their ability (as retailers) to operate on a relatively thin margin. No doubt even more discouraging was the entry of a significant group of really substantial domestic traders. For example, among the top 12 percent of exporters to Spain in 1609, around one-third came from outside the ranks of the mere-merchant overseas traders. These men were responsible for about 30 percent of the total exported by this top group.[102]

When the Dutch made peace with Spain in 1609, the problems of English merchants trading with Spain were further intensified. Given their access to cheap, Dutch-made cloths and to inexpensive Dutch shipping, Dutch merchants generally could undersell their English competitors in the Spanish market. Fortunately for the English, Spanish-Dutch hostili-

---

[99] Andrew Bayning, John Bate, Thomas Cordell, and Richard Staper were the Levant Company officers; the other members were Arthur Jackson, Sir Robert Lee, Robert Bowyer, Richard Wyche, and Lawrence Greene. See the Spanish Company charter of 1605, printed in Croft, *Spanish Company*, pp. 101–2, in comparison with the Levant Company charters of 1601 and 1605.

[100] London Port Book for Exports, 1609, PRO, E.190/14/7. Robert Bowyer (£84), Thomas Boothby (£280), John Dike (£527), John Eldred (£275), William Kellett (£499), Nicholas Leate (£40), William Masham (£283), Robert Middleton (£812), Sir Stephen Soames (£33), Richard Wyche (£209), William Woader (£155).

[101] London Port Book for Wines, 1615, PRO, E.190/18/2. Richard Wyche (176), Lawrence Greene (321), Robert Middleton (556), Humphrey Slaney (836). I went to thank Mr. Harland Taylor for generously allowing me to consult his lists and compilations from this port book. These results are based on his lists and figures.

[102] Taylor, "Price Revolution or Price Revision?," pp. 10–18.

ties were renewed after 1618, and the English trade with Spain enjoyed a new and extended period of growth and prosperity. Even so, the established merchants of the eastward trading group continued, for the most part, to abstain from the Spanish trade. Between 1605 and 1640, these important merchants made a series of attempts to organize a new Spanish Company, but none of these was successful.[103] As a result, the trade continued to be dominated, in the words of one commentator, by "divers who entitle themselves merchants trading for Spain, albeit most of them are no merchants at all, but mariners and ordinary retailers."[104]

The Levant traders found the mere–merchant provision to be indispensable, especially with respect to their commerce in currants imported from the Greek islands of Zante and Cephalonia in the Venetian empire. As noted, the trade in currants required neither the expertise nor the capital needed to participate in the trade in silks with Turkey and Syria. It was therefore especially attractive to the City's shopkeepers, who hoped to bypass their Levant Company middlemen. In the early seventeenth century, numbers of these retailers sought to circumvent the mere-merchant provision either by gaining admittance to the company while covertly retaining their domestic business, or by interloping illegally within the company's privileged areas. However, the Levant Company assiduously enforced its monopoly: it carefully scrutinized all prospective entrants, weeding out those who had no firm proof that they had given up their old business; and it strictly maintained the provisions against interloping.[105]

The mere-merchant provision thus remained a substantial brake on social mobility into the London merchant community, a powerful instrument of exploitation by the overseas company traders of the City's domes-

---

[103] Ibid., pp. 15–16, 30–31; H. Taylor, "Trade, Neutrality, and the 'English Road,' 1630–1648," *Ec.H.R.*, 2d ser., 25 (1972): 238–39. For the various attempts by the Spanish-trade merchants to secure a charter, see Friis, *Alderman Cockayne's Project*, pp. 156–58, 161–62, 169–71; PRO, P.C.2/41/130, 163, 182, 195–96, 308; PRO, P.C.2/42/571; Roberts, *Merchants Mappe*, ch. 270, p. 236.

[104] PRO, C.O.1/3/39. Note especially the merchants' continuing complaints that the retailers would sell their exports at below cost in order to get hold of prized import commodities. As the great company merchant Sir Thomas Middleton stated in the 1614 Parliament, "Shopkeepers of London send over all kinds of commodities and sell better cheap than he bought, and return it in tobacco" (*C.J.* 1: 469). Joseph Brand, Samuel Mico, Edward Abbot, Sir Henry Garway, Richard Middleton, Samuel Vassall, James Mann, Robert Oxwicke, James Traves, and Marmaduke Rawden are the Levant Company merchants I have been able to discover who were significant traders with Spain during the 1630s.

[105] For cases in which the Levant Company took action to be sure that a prospective member had relinquished his former trade and become a mere merchant, see PRO, S.P.105/148/138v, 140v, PRO, S.P.105/149/250, 253, PRO, S.P.105/150/265, and PRO, S.P.105/151/121. The trades proscribed in these cases were "mariner," "seaman," "shopkeeper," "cloth drawer," "warehouse helper," and "factor." See PRO, S.P.105/148/194 and PRO, S.P.105/149/185, 253 for examples of company action against shopkeepers interloping within their privileges.

tic tradesmen, and a continuing source of tension between them. During the early 1620s, more or less open hostilities broke out between the Levant Company and the City's grocers. In the summer of 1620, the grocers organized a sort of debt strike against the company, refusing to honor the obligations they had incurred upon their purchase of currants from the company's joint stock. On 18 October 1620, Morris Abbot, one of the directors in charge of the currants joint stock, reported to the general court: "The bad payment made . . . by the grocers in general for currants bought of the 2nd joint stock, diverse monies being yet unpaid that were due in July, June, and some in May, whereby it is conceived that they have combined themselves together to make the company bad payment."[106]

Clearly, the Venetian ambassador knew what he was about when, in early 1621, he sought to enlist the City's retailers as allies in his struggle to break the Levant Company's monopoly grip on the currants trade. "I have," he stated, "encouraged the grocers of the City, who sell raisins and muscatels, to present a petition [to Parliament], as they have since done against the tyrannical proceedings of the Levant Company." The Levant Company had to form a committee to represent its position before Parliament. Yet, as the Venetian ambassador sadly admitted, the chances of the grocers' success were slight, for the Levant Company had "a most remarkable influence over the lords of the council, some of whom have brothers and relations in the companies, some of whom being brought presents, and some having their own assignments upon the [currants] monopoly."[107]

Certainly, the Levant Company's membership seems hardly to have worried when, in 1626, the grocers again tried to launch an attack against them in Parliament, this time accusing them of engrossing, or monopolizing, the trade in galls imported from the Near East. The company's governor, Hamersley, warned his membership to "take care lest any complaint of that nature should be justly brought against any of the company"; but "divers then present" merely shrugged this off, saying that "they would maintain it in Parliament or any other place and make it appear that the fault lies not in the merchants, but in the grocers."[108]

While the Levant Company merchants did not feel seriously endangered by the grocers, they were in no doubt that their interests were fundamentally in conflict with the grocers', and that it was necessary to press for every advantage against them. In April 1642, when the Levant Company agreed to give its support to a proposal for establishing a new national court especially for commercial cases, it did so only with the express

---

[106] PRO, S.P. 105/148/46. See also PRO, S.P. 105/148/52, 53v–54, 66v, 70, 70v, 72v.

[107] C.S.P. Ven. 1621–1623, pp. 22–23; PRO, S.P. 105/148/52.

[108] PRO, S.P. 105/148/139v.

proviso that "this society conceived it inconvenient that others than mere merchants should be admitted as judges in the court."[109] The preceding years obviously had done nothing to ease the embittered relations between shopkeepers and company merchants.

Until 1625, the trade with Spain was the only really dynamic sector of overseas commerce that was open to the City's domestic tradesmen and ship captains. From that time onward, though, the rapidly expanding trades with Virginia and the West Indies in tobacco and sugar were also freed from company control. Not surprisingly, both of these areas became breeding grounds for increasingly powerful sociocommercial groups outside, and at odds with, the City merchant establishment. Indeed, the conflict between company merchants and the City's domestic tradesmen, above all those shopkeeper and mariner elements that had gravitated toward overseas commerce, either legally in the open areas of Spain and the Americas or illegally via interloping, was to constitute an important underlying basis for the political and ideological struggles in London during the Civil War.

THE LEVANT–EAST INDIA COMBINE
AND THE MERCHANT POLITICAL ELITE

In defense of their privileged position, the Levant–East India traders, and the City's merchants more generally, naturally turned first to their companies and to the royal government that sanctioned them. But they looked for leadership as well from London's aldermanic court, the oligarchic body that essentially governed the City. They could normally have confidence in this body to look after their interests, since to a large extent it was composed of top company traders, and it maintained the most intimate relationship with the Crown. During the decades preceding the Civil War, the Levant–East India merchants, who were at this time increasingly dominating the aldermanic board, appear to have contributed significantly to the capacity of the City's magistracy to represent London's merchant establishment by virtue of their ability to forge powerful direct ties, both familial and commercial, with great company merchants from corporations outside their own immediate sphere.

In this regard, the ability of the East India Company to attract leading representatives of London's other major overseas companies to its board of directors was particularly significant. For this body was able to function not merely as a commercial committee, but also as an integrating mechanism through which London's mercantile leaders could meet and construct business, family, and political connections. The case of the important City merchant Sir James Cambell was typical. Cambell, at one time or another

[109] PRO, S.P. 105/150/46.

the governor of both the French Company and the Company of Merchants of the Staple, as well as an alderman of London, was never an active Levant Company trader. Nevertheless, Cambell established a close relationship with the Levantine-trade merchants through long service beside them on the East India Company board of directors, a connection that was solidified by the marriages of two of his sisters to two of the greatest Levant–East India magnates of the period, Sir Anthony Abdy and Sir Christopher Clitherow. Abdy and Clitherow were themselves brothers-in-law (by Abdy's marriage to Clitherow's sister Abigail). Clitherow, one of the few Eastland merchants of the period who rose to the highest elite circles, was, moreover, the brother-in-law of Sir Henry Garway, the governor by 1640 of the Levant, East India, and Muscovy companies.[110] In analogous ways, through the pre–Civil War period, a striking number of the greatest non-Levant merchants were thus brought within a cohesive merchant elite given its dominant character by the traders with the East.

Characteristic of the merchant political elite that had emerged in the immediate pre–Civil War decades was the degree to which the still relatively large number of Merchant Adventurers who remained leading figures had become closely associated with the Levant–East India combine. Among the nine Merchant Adventurers who became aldermen in the years 1625–1640, seven previously had been connected commercially with the Levant–East India group: four were deeply involved in the Levantine trade, and six had been East India Company directors.[111] Only three citizens identifiable as merchants but commercially active outside the Merchant Adventurers or Levant Company trade seem to have become aldermen in the period 1626–1640, and one of these had become an East India Company director well before taking office.[112]

The Levant–East India combine thus succeeded to an important extent in bringing the leading traders from the other commercial areas, in particular the Merchant Adventurers, within their orbit. The unity of this mer-

---

[110] PRO, will of Sir James Cambell, 1642 PCC Cambell 1; PRO, will of Christopher Clitherow, 1641 PCC Evelyn 140; Pearl, *London*, pp. 288–89, 294–97, 299ff. Sir James Cambell's brother Robert was also a member of the Levant Company, as well as an East India Company director and an alderman (PRO, S.P. 105/147/18; Beaven, *Aldermen* 2: 62).

[111] Rowland Backhouse, Humphrey Smith, Robert Bateman, and Henry Andrews were the Adventurers active in the Levantine trade. Richard Venn, Humphrey Smith, Robert Jeffreys, Robert Bateman, Hugh Perry, and Henry Andrews were the East India Company directors.

[112] John Highlord, an Eastland merchant, Thomas Atkins, a Spanish-trade merchant, and John Warner, a trader with the Americas. Highlord was an important East India Company director. It is possible that there were still other overseas traders who were neither Levant Company merchants nor Merchant Adventurers who became aldermen in this period, 1626–1640, but my lists of traders in other commercial lines for the earliest part of the seventeenth century may not be full enough to allow me to identify them.

chant political elite from all the trades—centered in the court of aldermen, the customs farms, and the East India directorate, and dominated
by the Levant Company merchants—was to have critical consequences
for the political evolution of the entire merchant community from the end
of the 1630s. By offering a coherent leadership in control of the key directing institutions of London, these top traders were able to play a major
role in mobilizing the company merchants behind their common interests
in the maintenance of the established order—the traditional City constitution and their corporate privileges—against a threatened revolution.

The Company Merchants and
American Colonial Development

URING the first quarter of the seventeenth century, English
traders, for the first time, sought systematically to establish commerce with the Americas. Important City merchants had opened
up the new trades with Russia, Turkey, Venice, the Levant, and the East
Indies that highlighted the Elizabethan expansion, and, in each case, had
had recourse to their favorite commercial instrument, the Crown-char-
tered monopoly company. Not unexpectedly, some of London's greatest
merchants also took charge of the original colonial ventures of the Jacobean era and, in so doing, again made use of privileged companies.[1] But
the entrepreneurs behind the American colonial companies of this period
achieved neither organizational stability nor financial success. By the end
of the 1620s, all of the main companies had collapsed, and the great City
merchants had entirely forsaken the American trades.[2] The great spurt of
colonial economic development that occurred over the following decades
took place on a noncorporate basis, and was carried out by a new group of
traders from outside the circle of the City's overseas company merchants.

The Crown's dissolution of the Virginia Company in 1624 and the
granting of the West Indies to the earl of Carlisle under a proprietary
patent in 1627 effectively ended company control throughout most of
British America. Both of these events need to be understood, to a certain
extent, as the result of short-term political occurrences largely external to
the colonizing process.[3] The fact remains that the survival of the colonial

---

[1] The trade with Morocco, also established in this period, is something of an exception. See T. S.
Willan, "English Trade with Morocco," *Studies in Elizabethan Foreign Trade* (Manchester, 1959),
pp. 92–312.

[2] The only exception is the Somers Island (or Bermuda) Company, which formally lasted until
1684. However, this company had no de facto trading privileges because the tobacco trades with
Virginia and the West Indies were open. The Providence Island Company, begun in 1629–1630,
was the only major chartered company in the Americas founded after 1625. The Massachusetts Bay
Company charter served almost entirely as an instrument of government and had little commercial
significance. For the colonizing companies of the early seventeenth century, see T. K. Rabb, *Enterprise and Empire* (Cambridge, Mass., 1967).

[3] For some of the politics surrounding the Carlisle patent, see J. A. Williamson, *The Caribbee*

companies was, in any case, a doubtful proposition, since any attempt by the City's company merchants to adapt traditional commercial forms to the colonizing process faced insuperable obstacles. The Virginia Company, by far the greatest of the colonial commercial operations of the period, was initiated under relatively auspicious conditions. Yet from the start this venture had to confront fundamental problems that it could never overcome. By following the Virginia Company's rise and fall, one can see why the old forms were inappropriate to this new field, and discern the reasons why the great company merchants who dominated most of England's overseas commerce were ultimately obliged to withdraw from the colonial trades.

The Virginia Company

The Virginia Company was set up according to traditional joint-stock principles. By the charters of 1609 and 1612, the company received a monopoly of the trade with that portion of the American mainland located between 34 degrees and 40 degrees north latitude, and control of land allocation and utilization. All economic decision making was to be a company prerogative.[4] There was, in fact, little in its formal organization to differentiate the Virginia Company from the East India Company, chartered nine years earlier, or any of the other joint-stock commercial companies. Nevertheless, the growth of English commerce with Virginia presupposed the creation of a permanent, export-producing colony. The fact that productive plantations were a prerequisite for commerce crucially distinguished the project of the Virginia Company from those of the purely trading ventures of this era, and largely accounts for its deviant line of development.

The chartering of the Virginia Company in 1609 was accompanied by a full reassessment of the colony's potential. The stockholders relinquished earlier hopes of quick windfalls through the discovery of precious metals or trade with the Indians. Facing the hard reality that nothing substantial could be gained without the production of staple crops, they initiated a full-scale effort at colonization. The company took complete charge of production, which was carried out on company land by indentured ser-

---

Islands under the Proprietary Patents (Oxford, 1926), pp. 38–64. On the breakup of the Virginia Company, see W. F. Craven, The Dissolution of the Virginia Company (New York, 1932), ch. 10. See also below, ch. 5, pp. 215–17.

4 The Virginia Company charters of 1609 and 1612 are printed in A. Brown, The Genesis of the United States, 2 vols. (Boston, 1890), 1: 208–38, 540–53. For discussions of the significance of these charters, see C. M. Andrews, The Colonial Period of American History, 4 vols. (New Haven, 1934–1938), 1: 103–7; Craven, Dissolution, pp. 29–32.

vants sent and supplied at the company's expense. The company's chosen agents, a governor and council residing in Virginia, implemented decisions on planting, distribution, and trade, as well as government, in the colony. As sole proprietor, the company collected what was produced; as monopoly merchant, it carried out all colonial marketing functions.[5]

The fact remains that the Virginia Company's plantations required a good deal of time to reach a level of development sufficient to produce the staple exports required to yield profits. As a result, almost from the start, the company faced a crisis of investment. As early as 1610, the company had trouble covering the expenses of a projected major voyage, as many investors defaulted on the second and third payments on their stocks.[6] By 1612, it had to resort to lotteries to retain solvency.[7] Without fresh investment, the company found itself paralyzed, but it never came close to solving this problem. The consequence of the Virginia Company's failure to finance itself was a fundamental change in the nature of colonial enterprise under the company's auspices, and eventually the company's dissolution altogether.

Between 1612 and 1619, the Virginia Company saw its control over colonial development steadily eroded. Lacking the investment funds to carry out extensive activities of its own, the company was obliged to rely on individuals or groups acting independently within its nominal proprietary sphere. In 1614, the first indentured servants to complete their seven-year contracts gained their freedom, and those who chose to remain in the colony received from the company plots of their own to cultivate as they saw fit.[8] These plots constituted the first productive area within the colony that the company allowed to fall outside its own direct control. The ground for a second, more significant, noncompany sector was created when it became apparent in 1616 that the company could pay no cash dividends on the original investments in its joint stock. Instead, the company gave its stockholders grants of Virginia land at the rate of a hundred acres a share to develop as they wished.[9] The company opened the way for further individualistic colonizing efforts in 1616, when, to encourage prospective colonists, it found itself obliged to adopt the "headright" system, under which it gave land to whoever would finance his own or another's passage to Virginia, at the rate of fifty acres for each person transported.[10]

[5] Craven, *Dissolution*, pp. 32–33. For a discussion of this form of colonial organization, in which the whole of the colony's economy was under direct company control, see L. D. Scisco, "Plantation Type of Colony," *A.H.R.* 8 (1903): 260–70.

[6] Andrews, *Colonial Period* 1: 106–7.

[7] R. C. Johnson, "The Lotteries of the Virginia Company," *V.M. H.B.* 74 (1966): 259ff.

[8] Craven, *Dissolution*, p. 35.

[9] Ibid., p. 56; Andrews, *Colonial Period* 1: 124.

[10] Andrews, *Colonial Period* 1: 125.

The emergence of these opportunities for the acquisition of private holdings paved the way for the transformation of the process of economic development in Virginia. Especially after 1616, the corporation's activity radically contracted. Individual entrepreneurs, operating through a variety of partnership forms, now took over responsibility for colonial growth, and they devoted themselves with increasing intensity to one all-engrossing task: the production of tobacco for export to England. Sir Edwin Sandys summed up the dominant trend in 1619 when he observed that "as the private plantation began thus to increase, so contrariwise the estate of the publique [the company-operated sector] . . . grew into utter consumption." The consequence, in Sandys' view, was that the colony became so obsessively devoted to tobacco planting that the colonists soon "reduced themselves into an extremity of being ready to starve unless the Magazine [the subcompany that brought them their provisions and marketed their goods] . . . had supplied them with corn and cattle from hence."[11]

Beginning in 1619, the Virginia Company did make a desperate, last-ditch effort to reverse these trends toward individualistic and single-crop production. It suddenly sought to revive production on the company's own lands (the "estate of the publique") and sent over large groups of colonists to provide the labor force for this purpose. It tried, at the same time, to break the tobacco monoculture and to diversify the colony's economy. To that end it sought to compel the colonists to produce certain amounts of food and commercial crops besides tobacco, while itself taking charge of a series of ambitious projects—specifically, the construction of a colonial iron industry, the development of silk production, and the introduction of wine making. The company could sustain these efforts, however, for only a few years and, in the end, could make little impact on the overall direction of colonial development. The result of this brief period of intense company activity was actually to consolidate already existing trends.[12]

Virginia's development accelerated in the period between 1619 and 1623. W. R. Scott, following contemporary estimates, has found the total expenditure on the Virginian economy in these years to have been £80,000 to £90,000. But of this sum, the company laid out only about £10,000, while private entrepreneurs supplied the remainder.[13] At first, independent subcompanies, which were set up under patents issued by the company, may have played a leading role in the colony. A number of stockholders would combine their company shares, receive as dividends substantial grants of land (called "hundreds" or "plantations"), over

---

[11] The quotations of Sandys are from Craven, *Dissolution*, pp. 38, 40.

[12] Craven, *Dissolution*, pp. 81–104, 176ff.

[13] W. R. Scott, *The Constitution and Finance of English, Scottish, and Irish Joint-Stock Companies to 1720*, 3 vols. (Cambridge, 1910–1912), 2: 286.

which they were given limited governmental powers, and attempt to develop them from England at their own expense as small, private colonies.[14] But, at least from the time of the great Indian massacre of 1622, and probably before, organizations of this type fell into decay.[15] Individual migrating colonists who managed their own plantations and did their own shipping, or who worked in collaboration with merchant suppliers and marketers, now took over the primary entrepreneurial tasks. By the time of the company's fall in 1624, the basic pattern of Virginia's future development had thus been established. The dissolution of the company was a political act that destroyed, once and for all, every aspect of corporate control over the Virginian economy. But its economic effect was only to ratify an already existing situation.

The decline of the Virginia Company was the result of the overwhelming failure of its joint stock to attract investment funds. At least potentially, the London merchant community was by far the best source of capital for investment in commerce in general and colonization in particular. The City's great company merchants controlled the East India Company and were primarily responsible for the unprecedented financial support that company attracted. A group of elite City merchants around the great Levant—East India magnate Sir Thomas Smythe (who held the key position of company treasurer) also effectively led the Virginia Company during its early years and provided the major part of that company's meager funds.[16] However, when it very soon became clear that the Virginia Company would yield profits only in the long run, its merchant investors entirely lost interest. Even the East India Company had found it difficult to establish itself on a permanent basis before it had amply demonstrated its profit-making capacity to the City's cautious merchant investors. During the first six years of the East India Company's existence, its merchant backers commonly refused to venture capital in new company undertakings before they had received their returns from the previous effort. Only after the East India Company had been in existence for thirteen years, during which time nine out of ten of its voyages had shown a profit, did its merchant backers cease to resort to "terminable" joint stocks and establish a permanent joint stock.[17]

[14] W. F. Craven, *The Southern Colonies in the Seventeenth Century, 1607–1689* (Baton Rouge, 1949), pp. 120–22.

[15] On the failure of most of the great patents, see Andrews, *Colonial Period* 1: 131 and n. 4, 132; Craven, *Southern Colonies*, pp. 161–62; Craven, *Dissolution*, p. 174; C. Dowdey, *The Great Plantation: A Profile of Berkeley Hundred and Plantation, Virginia, from Jamestown to Appomattox* (New York, 1957), p. 49.

[16] Craven, *Dissolution*, pp. 25–26; Rabb, *Enterprise and Empire*, pp. 56–57. Rabb estimates that 55 to 60 percent of the money raised by the Virginia Company was contributed by merchants. For a complete list of the Levant Company merchants and East India Company directors in the Virginia Company, see Rabb., app.

[17] K. N. Chaudhuri, *The English East India Company* (London, 1965), p. 40. The first permanent

In contrast, the early activities of the Virginia Company never showed a profit. Thus, even at the start, between 1609 and 1613, the Virginia Company could elicit only a meager £30,000 through direct investment by its stockholders.[18] It raised only about £6,000 more from joint-stock investment in the years up to 1619,[19] and just about nothing after that.[20] In approximately the same period, 1609–1621, the East India Company raised over £2,000,000 for its joint stock,[21] while London commerce, by and large, experienced substantial growth and prosperity.[22] Clearly, there was no general shortage of investment funds in London, only a widespread reluctance on the part of the City's merchants to put money into the Virginia Company. As one writer put the problem at about the time of the Virginia Company's dissolution, "A great store of treasure and wealth must be spent and many years overpassed" before profits could be expected from colonial plantations. As was obvious to contemporaries, the great merchants of London were prepared neither to take the risk nor to wait.[23]

In consequence of this reluctance to invest in plantations, the great merchants who ran the Virginia Company in the period up to 1618–1619 appear to have been quite pleased to allow control of colonial production to fall into private, noncompany hands[24] and to concentrate instead on the purely commercial tasks of provisioning Virginia and marketing its to-

---

joint stock was organized in 1613. Up to that time, separate financial arrangements were made for each voyage.

[18] Scott, *Joint-Stock Companies* 2: 251, 254.

[19] Ibid., p. 258.

[20] Ibid., p. 288. In his *Enterprise and Empire*, Professor Rabb seems to confuse the total amount expended on the Virginia Colony before 1624 by both the company and private entrepreneurs with the total amount raised by the company on investment in shares in its joint stock. Rabb, quoting Scott, gives £200,000 as the amount invested in the Virginia Company's joint stock (*Enterprise and Empire*, pp. 58–59 n. 69, 66), but Scott clearly intends this figure to refer to "the whole cost of the plantation up to 1624" (*Joint-Stock Companies* 2: 286–87 n. 1). The total invested in the company's joint stock was, according to Scott, only about £37,000. The company was able to expend a total of approximately £76,500 on the colony, because it was able to raise about £39,500 over and above its joint-stock fund by means of lotteries (£29,000), loans (£5,000), and miscellaneous receipts (£5,500) (ibid., pp. 258, 286–87). Thus, in the period before 1624, the company contributed probably less than half of the total of £200,000 spent on the colony, private entrepreneurs contributing more than £100,000. Moreover, the direct investment in the colony by private entrepreneurs was probably three times as great as the expenditure there by way of investment in the company's joint stock (£100,000 plus, as compared with approximately £37,000).

[21] Chaudhuri, *East India Company*, p. 209.

[22] On the commercial prosperity of the early years of the seventeenth century, see B. E. Supple, *Commercial Crisis and Change in England, 1600–1642* (Cambridge, 1959), pp. 23–32; R. H. Tawney, *Business and Politics under James I* (Cambridge, 1958), pp. 14–18.

[23] R. Elburne, *A Plaine Pathway to Plantations* (London, 1624), p. 37, quoted in Rabb, *Enterprise and Empire*, p. 39 n. 27.

[24] It is true that starting in 1617, Sir Thomas Smythe did undertake to develop a private plantation in Virginia. But Smythe's efforts were unsuccessful. His plantation was never made to yield substantial profits, and its failure must have helped to dampen what little enthusiasm remained for plantation investment in the merchant elite (Craven, *Southern Colonies*, pp. 122, 161–62).

bacco. In 1616, when the growth of tobacco planting in Virginia offered, for the first time, the possibility of profitable colonial exports, sections of the company's merchant leadership formed a semiautonomous subsidiary company, secured full monopoly import and export privileges, and took control of carrying out the tasks of supplying the colony and bringing in its tobacco.[25]

This "Magazine," as it was called, was entirely dominated by representatives of the Virginia Company's merchant leadership. Its directorship included[26] Sir Thomas Smythe, who was at one time or another governor of the East India, Muscovy, French, and Somers Island companies, as well as a lord mayor of London;[27] Robert Johnson, Smythe's son-in-law and a director in both the Levant and East India companies, as well as a London alderman;[28] Sir John Wolstenholme, one of London's leading financiers, a customs farmer and later an East India Company director;[29] William Essington, a leading Merchant Adventurer who was the son-in-law of the Merchant Adventurer Sir Thomas Hayes, a lord mayor of London;[30] and William Canning, another important Merchant Adventurer, as well as deputy governor of the Bermuda Company and several times master of the Ironmongers.[31] At a time when the Virginia Company's general joint stock had reached its lowest ebb, with its treasury nearly £8,000 in the red and unable to finance company activities of any type, this small group of merchants was able, by itself, to raise £7,000 for its own private syndicate and to extract a substantial rate of profit from the colonists.[32] As an admittedly hostile contemporary described the period of merchant rule within the company,

> Those few that followed the business . . . were (by the governors here, for their own particular ends as is conceived, for, to their own private benefit it was only suitable) directed to bestow their monies in adventuring by way of Magazine, upon two commodities only, tobacco and sassafras, matters of present profit, but no ways founda-

[25] On the Magazine, see Andrews, *Colonial Period* 1: 126–27; Craven, *Dissolution*, pp. 33–34; Scott, *Joint-Stock Companies* 1: 256–57.

[26] *Va. Co. Recs.* 3: 598.

[27] G. E. Cockayne, *Some Account of the Lord Mayors and Sheriffs of the City of London . . . 1601–1625* (London, 1897), pp. 4–5.

[28] Cockayne, *Lord Mayors*, p. 80; A. B. Beaven, *The Aldermen of the City of London*, 2 vols. (London, 1908), 2: 54.

[29] Tawney, *Business and Politics*, p. 87 and index.

[30] London Port Book for Cloth Exports, 1640, PRO, E. 190/43/4; Society of Genealogists, Boyd's Index of London Citizens: 9377–78; A. Friis, *Alderman Cockayne's Project and the Cloth Trade* (London, 1927), p. 96.

[31] London Port Book for Cloth Exports, 1614, PRO, E. 190/18/4; Brown, *Genesis* 2: 842.

[32] Craven, *Dissolution*, p. 35; Scott, *Joint-Stock Companies* 2: 256. In an agreement of 1618 with the company, the Magazine's rate of profit was limited to 25 percent (Craven, *Dissolution*, p. 51).

tions of a future state. So that of a *merchant-like* trade there was some probability at least for a while; but of a *plantation* there was none at all (emphasis added).[33]

The contrast between the merchants' refusal to support the colony through the general joint stock and their willingness to exploit it through their commercial monopoly was a central theme in the successful movement against the merchant directorship that resulted in the company reforms of 1618 and the takeover of the company by Sir Edwin Sandys' "gentry party" from Sir Thomas Smythe's "merchant party" in 1619. As Lord Robert Rich observed of the period before 1619, "The merchants who then swayed the courts affected nothing but their immediate gain, though with the poor planters' extreme oppression as appeared by their Magazine."[34]

Sandys' gentry party was largely responsible not only for the ouster of Smythe's merchant party from the Virginia Company's leadership, but also for the attempt beginning in 1619 to revive the company's role in production in the colony (and to reverse the merchants' implicit strategy of allowing control of production to fall into private, noncompany hands and concentrating on the purely commercial tasks of provisioning and marketing tobacco). But Sandys and his friends failed miserably, and the reason is not far to seek: their noble and gentry supporters proved no more willing to provide the investment funds necessary to underwrite production in the colony than the City merchants had been. During their tenure in office from 1619 to 1623, Sandys and his supporters could attract so few new investments in the Virginia Company's joint stock that they did not even bother to list this source of funds as a category of (potential) income in their company accounts. Even worse, they were unable to induce those who already had subscribed to the joint stock to pay in their funds. By 1620, a total of £16,000 in uncollected subscriptions stood on the company's books. Sandys and his friends were thus compelled to rely almost entirely on lotteries and could therefore raise very little money for their ambitious projects—perhaps £10,000 out of a total of around £90,000 to £100,000 spent on the colony during the period of their control. Ironically, by the end of their tenure in office, Sandys and his collaborators were having to rely on a contract for the monopoly of the tobacco trade to keep the Virginia Company going, and were seeking to reward themselves for their efforts on the company's behalf by providing themselves unusually high salaries for managing this contract.[35]

With the accession to power of Sandys' party in 1619, the great London

---

[33] "Discourse of the Old Company" (1625), in *V.M.H.B.* 1 (1894): 158–59.

[34] The quotation is from Craven, *Dissolution*, p. 41.

[35] Ibid., pp. 33, 147–50.

merchants temporarily withdrew from Virginia Company affairs. They did not, however, relinquish their hope of regaining control. When Sandys' controversial tobacco contract proposal of 1622–1623 offered an opening, the merchants did everything in their power to overthrow the Sandys regime. Apparently, these great traders still hoped to monopolize the Virginian tobacco trade, and in 1623 they mobilized a new combination of forces to repossess the company. This alliance brought together two of the three warring factions that had vied for power throughout the Virginia Company's history. On the one hand, there was the "merchant party" led by the great City magnates Sir Thomas Smythe, alderman Robert Johnson, and Sir John Wolstenholme. On the other, there was the great aristocratic colonizing connection centered on Robert Rich, second earl of Warwick, and his kinsman Sir Nathaniel Rich.[36]

The Riches occupied a unique position in the colonizing movement. Unlike most of the landed-class investors, they played an active role—indeed a leadership role—in almost every colonial venture of the early Stuart period including the Virginia Company. In addition, the head of the Rich connection, Lord Robert Rich (who became in 1619 the second earl of Warwick) following in the footsteps of his father, a great Elizabethan privateer, maintained a large privateering fleet. Beginning in 1616, the privateering activities of Rich and his circle had led them into sharp conflict with Sir Thomas Smythe and the great City merchants who at that time led not only the Virginia Company, but also the East India Company and the other great City overseas trading corporations. In that year, Rich had sent out to the Red Sea two vessels, operating under a commission for privateering granted by the duke of Savoy, which attempted to plunder an enormously valuable ship belonging to no less a personage than the queen mother of the Great Moghul. As the East India Company had just secured a privilege for trade in the region from the Great Moghul and naturally wished to remain on good terms with him, several of its ships (which happened to be in the region) intercepted Rich's vessels, thereby frustrating Rich's mission, keeping him from a small fortune, and earning his enmity. Shortly thereafter, bad feeling between the Rich faction and Smythe's party was intensified when Smythe and his friends opposed Warwick's attempt to have his protégé Nathaniel Butler appointed governor of Bermuda. Tensions were no doubt further heightened when Smythe's son married Warwick's sister, a union of which Smythe did not approve. For these reasons, and also because they disapproved of the merchants' policies for the Virginia Company, Warwick and his circle initially backed the Sandys faction and made possible its accession to power in 1619.[37]

[36] On the tobacco contract and its upshot, see ibid., pp. 221–91ff.; Andrews, *Colonial Period* 1: 150–77.

[37] Craven, *Dissolution*, pp. 83–86ff.

Meanwhile, the temporary alienation of James I from the Spanish in 1618 provided a brief opening for Warwick to initiate a series of anti-Spanish colonizing and privateering ventures in the Americas. In 1619–1620, the Riches were among the main instigators of a new effort at colonization in Guiana within the Spanish empire in the Americas. In 1618, Warwick had sent his ship *Treasurer* on a voyage of plunder into the Spanish West Indies, after which he sought to use Virginia as a base for further privateering forays. But in the early part of 1620, Sandys and his friends, newly ascendant in the Virginia Company, intervened. They brought Warwick's anti-Spanish activities not only before the privy council but also to the attention of Gondomar, the Spanish ambassador. Since James I, shortly before this time, had revived once again the Spanish match, Sandys' actions not only resulted in the termination of Warwick's American ventures, but put his person in jeopardy.[38] The ultimate result was to push the Rich faction back into alliance with Smythe's merchants against the Sandys leadership.

Smythe's "merchant party" represented, in fact, the very cream of the City merchant community, the merchant elite mobilized to recover the same sort of hegemony inside the Virginia Company that they were accustomed to enjoying in all of the other great City overseas trading corporations. The composition of Smythe's faction can be adduced from a list that its members drew up in April or May 1623, in the heat of their battle to replace the Sandys faction in the company's leadership, of "Persons fit to be Governor and Deputy Governor of Virginia and Somers Islands Companies." The twenty-one men the merchant party nominated at this time included Sir John Wolstenholme and Sir William Russell, both of whom were leading Crown financiers, as well as major London merchants; Hugh Hamersley, Robert Johnson, Nicholas Leate, Anthony Abdy, John Dyke, Humphrey Slaney, Robert Bateman, Thomas Styles, and Richard Edwards, who were all important Levant Company traders and (with the exception of Edwards, Styles, and Slaney) at one time or another Levant Company officers; William Canning and Edward Bennett, who were consequential Merchant Adventurers; and Humphrey Handford, a top merchant in the French trade and an importer of European wares. Six of these men would, at one time or another, serve as aldermen of London, and eleven were sometime East India Company directors. Smythe's merchant party was certainly aptly named.[39]

---

[38] Ibid., pp. 125–40ff.

[39] *Va. Co. Recs.* 4: 90–91. For additional merchant-party opponents of Sandys, see "Names of Adventurers Who Dislike the Present Proceedings of Business in the Virginia and Somers Island Companies," *Va. Co. Recs.* 4: 80–81. Additional company merchant opposers listed there include the major Levant Company trader, East India Company officer, and sometime alderman Morris Abbot, the Levant Company officer Christopher Barron, and the top Merchant Adventurers William Essington, William Palmer, and Edward Palmer. Identification of merchants is based on London Port

Ultimately, the anti-Sandys alliance, composed of the Smythe and Rich factions, could regain power in the Virginia Company only by first destroying it. With the help of James I and his lord treasurer, Sir Lionel Cranfield, they were able to bring about the Virginia Company's demise in May 1624. But they did not intend that this state of affairs should be permanent. They hoped through dissolution simply to break the power of their opponents within the company, and then to reconstitute it with themselves in control. The merchants and their allies seemed close to success when, on 15 July 1624, only a few months after the old company's destruction, the king appointed a new commission for Virginia. This move seemed to clearly signal the government's intention to restore the anti-Sandys forces to power. The commission was totally packed with merchant-party stalwarts and adherents of the Rich faction. It had forty-one members, not including the ten commissioners who were leading officers in James's government. Among these forty-one, there were no fewer than fifteen of the twenty-one persons listed by the merchants the previous year as "fit to be officers" of the company. Moreover, twenty-six of the commission's forty-one (nongovernment) members were either among those nominated to be officers by the merchants or on another list of opposers of the Sandys leadership, "Names of Adventurers that Dislike the present Proceedings of Business in the Virginia and Somers Islands Companies," drawn up by Sir Nathaniel Rich in April 1623, or both. The commission also included an additional handful of great merchant magnates who were included on neither of these lists, but were unquestionably associated with Smythe's merchant party. James I explicitly charged the commission with reestablishing a corporate organization for Virginia with the same privileges that the old company had. The monopoly of Virginia's trade that the merchants so desired seemed on the verge of realization.[40] But with the death of James I, the Virginia commission was abrogated and never reestablished under Charles I.

City Merchants, the Landed Class, and Colonial Development

Understandably, the rise of new forms of colonial enterprise, in the wake of the decline and dissolution of the Virginia Company, had a powerful impact on the personnel of the American trades. Once it had become clear,

---

Books for Cloth Exports, Levant Company Court Minute Books, and East India Company Court Minute Books (calendars).

[40] *C.S.P. Col. 1574–1660*, p. 63; *A.P.C. Col. 1613–1680*, p. 78; *Va. Co. Recs.* 4: 490–91, 80–81. The additional merchant-party magnates who were on neither of the aforementioned lists of opponents included Sir Baptist Hicks, Sir James Cambell, and Sir Ralph Freeman.

following the establishment of direct royal administration in Virginia and of the Carlisle proprietorship in the West Indies, that company control would not be reinstituted in the Americas, the City's company merchants withdrew from colonial activity. A comparison of complete listings of London aldermen, Levant Company merchants, and East India Company directors, as well as reasonably full listings of Merchant Adventurers, French Company merchants, and Eastland Company merchants, with reasonably full listings of the hundreds of active traders with Virginia and the West Indies[41] shows hardly any overlap between the company merchants and the colonial merchants during the pre–Civil War period. There were, of course, some exceptions. Two of the most important were Samuel Vassall and Matthew Craddock. Another was Humphrey Slaney, who traded in partnership with his son-in-law, William Cloberry. The others who have been identified were Edward Bennett, Nathan Wright, Benjamin Whetcomb, Anthony Pennyston, and Richard Chambers (all Levant Company) and William Tristram (Merchant Adventurer).[42] It is impossible, however, to dispute the general verdict that the company merchants of London ceased to participate in American colonization after 1625 and that this task fell to an entirely new group.

The company merchants' withdrawal from colonial commerce after 1625 is not really surprising. Following the dissolution of the Virginia Company, the growth of Virginia commerce still presupposed plantation development, and it seems to have remained difficult to participate significantly in the former without investing in the latter. But this was something the City's company merchants still refused to do. The nascent plantation economy, unable as yet to expand by itself, needed constant injections of outside capital and manpower to keep it going. As a result, especially in the colony's formative years, those interested in marketing large amounts of tobacco could not easily obtain it without taking part in the production process. The more substantial Virginian planters appear to have controlled a significant portion of the early trade in tobacco. These men brought their capital with them and performed their own marketing with the help of colonial ship captains.[43] Then, too, some of the leading

[41] My lists of traders with the Americas depend, in the first place, on the London Port Books for Imports, from which the names of colonial tobacco merchants can be extracted. These are available for the years 1621, 1626, 1627–1628, 1630, 1633, 1634, 1638, and 1640. They have been substantially supplemented by a wide variety of government documents, petitions, judicial records, and the like.

[42] Toward the end of the 1630s, the overlap between the company merchants and traders with the Americas increases somewhat, but this is a result of American-trade merchants—including Richard Cranley, William Pennoyer, and Gregory Clement—moving into the Levantine trade, rather than vice versa. Samuel Moyer was another merchant apparently active in both spheres of commerce, but it is uncertain which he entered first.

[43] For example, Richard Stephens, the Virginia councilor, imported into England 27,000 pounds

tobacco merchants seem to have bought plantations of their own, thereby bringing all aspects of colonial development under their direct control. Perhaps the most common arrangement was for the merchant to enter into business in partnership with a local planter, advancing him the necessary capital in exchange for part of the product. As Richard Pares has written,

> The merchant and the pioneer were associated from the first in some kind of partnership. The merchant was able thus to place his surplus capital, and to receive his return in the form of colonial produce which he could sell; in addition, he was partly protected against the unfaithfulness of his agents—the chief risk in all colonial enter-prise—by the partnership which gave the planter an honest interest in the prosperity of his business. The planter, for his part, obtained perhaps the price of his transport, perhaps his outfit of tools and pro-visions for the first year; above all, the merchant would have re-cruited servants for the plantation and paid their passages across the sea, thus giving the planter a start in life which he could only have obtained for himself by several years' hard work.[44]

In addition to the reciprocal benefits to be derived from merchant-planter partnerships, the maintenance of the headright system of land grants in Virginia following the dissolution of the company further strengthened the tendency to interconnect trade and plantation. Under this system, those who transported colonists were awarded land at the rate of fifty acres per person transported. The effect was naturally to concentrate land in the hands of merchants (who were of course responsible for transporting large numbers of colonists) and thus to encourage merchant participation in plantations.

There were many possible variations on the basic merchant-planter combination, and all kinds of contractual arrangements were evolved to fit the requirements of the participants.[45] But even when there was no formal agreement, the same fundamental relationship appears to have been realized in practice as a result of an unavoidable interdependence. The financial requirements of subsistence and production before the har-vest commonly made it necessary for the planter to seek loans from the merchant. The merchant was therefore obliged to provide advances to finance production, if he hoped to have a crop to market. The debtor-

---

of tobacco in 1627–1628, by far the largest single shipment in that year (N. J. Williams, "England's Tobacco Trade in the Reign of Charles I," *V.M.H.B.* 65 [1957]: 421–49 [this is a printed, abstracted version of a surviving London Port Book for Tobacco Imports into England for 1627–1628]). For further details see below, ch. 4.

[44] R. Pares, "Merchants and Planters," *Ec.H.R.*, supp. 4 (1960): 5.

[45] Pares prints a number of these agreements in an appendix to "Merchants and Planters," pp. 52ff.

creditor relationship thus established often assumed a long-term character, involving the merchant more or less permanently in the planter's business. As the Virginia Assembly petitioned in 1632: "We the poor planters of this colony have a long time groaned under the cruel dealings of unconscionable merchants who have by needless and unprofitable commodities always pre-engaged the inhabitants in debts of tobacco to the value almost of their ensuing crops."[46]

The need to invest in plantations was not, however, the only aspect of colonial commerce that discouraged the participation of the major City merchants. Even had this impediment been removed, it is unlikely that their enthusiasm for the commerce with the Americas would have been much increased. The City merchants were accustomed to trade under the protection of monopoly privileges. Under the Virginia Company, they had established their Magazine for just this purpose and they had fought to have the Virginia Company reestablished to the same end. But after 1625, free trade became the rule in American commerce, and the expanding trades in tobacco and provisioning were opened up to anyone who could find the capital. By 1634, there were 175 men operating in the Virginian tobacco trade, and in 1640, there were 330. These figures should be compared with the total of 61 active Levant Company currants traders in each of these two years.[47] Fiercely competitive conditions therefore prevailed in a period of rising production. As a result, there was a rapid fall and general instability of commodity prices.[48] Whereas some of London's greatest merchants had been anxious to trade tobacco under the highly controlled monopoly conditions of the Virginia Company's Magazine, they were repelled by the anarchy of the new, free American commerce.

The failure of the great London merchants to participate in colonial trade is thus explained by those crucial characteristics that distinguished it

---

[46] *V.M.H.B.* 65 (1957): 468. Examples of planter debt to merchants can be found in *County Records of Accomack-Northampton, Virginia, 1632–1640*, ed. S. M. Ames, American Legal Records, vol. 7 (Washington, 1954). See p. 105 n. 23 for an instance in which a debt was ultimately settled through the transfer of a plot of land to the merchant creditors. A similar situation apparently prevailed in the Caribbee Isles. "The more wealthy of the early settlers, with money to charter their own shipping, were able to combine planting and trading, and so to gain a predominance over the small planters. The conditions of the time, as we have seen, favoured the merchants, who in a few years became the virtual if not the nominal owners of most of the land. The small men had not the resources to tide them over an unlucky season, and were obliged to mortgage their holdings to those who could give them credit" (Williamson, *Caribbee Islands*, p. 67).

[47] These figures were compiled from the London Port Books for Imports for 1634, PRO, E.190/38/5, and 1640, PRO, E.190/43/5.

[48] G. L. Beer, *The Origins of the British Colonial System, 1578–1660* (New York, 1908), pp. 817–95; R. R. Menard, "A Note on Chesapeake Tobacco Prices, 1618–1660," *V.M.H.B.* 84 (1976): 401–10.

from their regular corporate commerce. The regulated trades, typified by the Levant Company commerce and the Merchant Adventurers' trade, simply involved the carrying of commodities. They were operated under restricted, corporately controlled conditions designed to regulate competition, to minimize risk, and to ensure profits. Symptomatically, the great City merchants behind the East India Company consistently refused to allow it to involve itself in colonizing or plantation ventures of any kind, even though their recalcitrance in this respect made them vulnerable to effective attacks on their privileges. Correlatively, when the East India Company's monopoly was weakened during the 1630s and 1640s, many important merchants simply withdrew their support and the company came near to total collapse.[49] The contrast between the company merchants' regular operations and those of the colonial entrepreneurs who succeeded them in the Americas could not have been more stark. Given the high profitability and relatively controlled conditions of the great company trades, the conservatism of the establishment merchants was reasonable, their avoidance of the new trades predictable.

Paradoxically, then, the collapse of company organization for the Americas, and the consequent withdrawal from the trade of London's leading overseas traders, may actually have facilitated the colonizing process. Under the Virginia Company, the City's overseas traders had proven their unwillingness to invest in plantations, and the company's inability to develop Virginia can, in large part, be attributed to just that factor. On the other hand, it is doubtful if the new groups of small planters and traders who took over plantation development as the company declined would have been willing to invest in plantations had they been excluded from the profits of trade, or compelled to operate under the domination of a monopoly company. The reestablishment of a privileged corporation for the trade with the Americas might well have meant a continuation of that stagnation of plantation investment and that bleeding dry of the colonists by means of monopoly commerce that marked the merchants' rule under the company.

Aware of the City merchants' disdain for plantations and their aversion to high-risk, fixed-capital investments, contemporary backers of the colonization movement often looked to the landed classes to take up the slack. Sir Francis Bacon echoed a widespread opinion when he recommended that the leaders of the colonial plantations "be rather noblemen and gentlemen than merchants; for they [the merchants] look ever to their present gain."[50] Influenced by such contemporary statements and mesmerized by the sheer numbers of gentry stockholders in the colonizing companies,

---

[49] For details, see below, ch. 4, pp. 170–81.

[50] Quoted in Rabb, *Enterprise and Empire*, p. 39 n. 27.

some historians have been led to overestimate the landed-class contribution to the colonizing movement and, in the process, to misapprehend its nature. In fact, the nobles and gentry of England had neither the inclination nor the wherewithal to ensure the continuity of the colonizing movement. With some notable exceptions, their long-term effect—despite their momentary flutters of intense activity—was slight.

This point is nowhere better illustrated than in the case of the Virginia Company itself, where the participation of a great mass of gentry investors, as well as a famous group of aristocratic leaders, has tended to convey a false impression of the landed-class role in the colonizing movement. It is true, of course, that for a relatively short period Sir Edwin Sandys and his gentry and noble supporters did run the company and make serious efforts to support the plantations. Yet, as has been seen, colonial development during their tenure in office took place not because of them, but rather in spite of them. Above all, they totally failed to raise money for the Virginia Company's joint stock from among themselves and their landed-class friends. By 1622, they were hoping to use a tobacco contract to loot the project, having given up hope of profiting through the joint-stock operation itself.[51] By the time they were ultimately forced to cede control, the colony had been decimated by sickness and Indian massacre, and was having to start again almost from scratch.

The fact that there were no fewer than 560 gentry stockholders behind the Virginia Company tends, paradoxically, to point up the superficiality, rather than the depth, of the landed-class contribution. The amount raised by the joint stock in the entire course of the Virginia Company's existence was a mere £37,000; if the gentry contributed 50 percent of this amount (they composed around 45 percent of the stockholders and probably contributed less than that proportion), it would mean an average investment of less than £35 from each gentry investor. This was, of course, a trivial sum for commercial ventures in this period and more in the nature of a formal or token contribution than an expression of real financial interest. The fact that MPs, who were of course most subject to pressure from the court and to the pull of patriotic enterprise, comprised a disproportionate number of the investors only adds to the impression that the gentry invested more out of duty than in the hope of meaningful profit.[52]

Those nobles and gentry who backed the "hundreds" (or private plantations), which were financed and operated outside company control and often on a fairly large scale, could have contributed significantly to colonial development. Included among the supporters of these ventures were

[51] Craven, *Dissolution*, pp. 221–50.

[52] Rabb, *Enterprise and Empire*, pp. 92–96. Thus, my conclusion from T. K. Rabb's tabulations on colonial investment by members of the gentry and by MPs is that they show the insignificance of their contribution rather than point up its importance, as he contends.

such landed-class leaders as the earl of Southampton and Sir Richard Berkeley. But these ventures were short-lived and ultimately came to very little in terms of Virginia's longer-term evolution. Most of them had failed even before the company's demise. Certainly, without the injection of masses of new capital, which emanated from neither the gentry nor the City company merchants, the colonizing process in Virginia would have come to a halt following the Virginia Company's collapse.

Merchant and landed class investors behaved pretty much as did their counterparts in the Virginia Company in almost all of the ventures of the first phase of the colonization movement, extending from the late Elizabethan period through the reign of James I. It is true that, in a number of instances, nobles and gentry did take important steps to initiate colonizing projects. But only rarely did they carry through on their original commitments. Nor did the company merchants at any point take up the slack. The result was a dismal record of failure for almost all the formally patented colonizing companies.

Sir Humphrey Gilbert's attempt to plant a colony north of Florida between 1578 and 1583 and Sir Walter Ralegh's follow-up project for Roanoke from 1584 may perhaps be said to have initiated the English movement toward colonization in the Americas, and both these projects were led and financed largely by landed-class elements. Gilbert's venture sought to mobilize younger sons of the gentry and landed-class Catholics to establish estates in the new world, and a handful of courtiers and nobles, notably the queen's secretary Sir Francis Walsingham and the earl of Sussex, along with a number of landed-class stockholders and the gentry who actually went to settle, provided most of the financial support for it. Ralegh's somewhat more substantial project also attracted Walsingham's patronage, as well as the financial backing of a number of influential members of the landed class, such as Lord Charles Howard and Sir Richard Grenville. Nevertheless, for what would become all too familiar reasons, neither Gilbert's nor Ralegh's venture could sustain itself very much beyond its founding voyage. As it turned out, these projects, like their successors in the Americas, were unable to provide the quick returns for which their backers had hoped, because they yielded neither precious metals, nor already existing staples, nor an easy route to the East Indies. On the contrary, the fledgling settlements required a good deal of investment just to keep them going, and could be expected to yield no profits for a long time. Few investors had the wherewithal or the desire to take the risk and wait.[53]

[53] For the foregoing on Gilbert's and Ralegh's projects, see *The Voyages and Colonising Enterprises of Sir Humphrey Gilbert*, ed. D. B. Quinn, Hakluyt Society Publications, 2d ser., nos. 83 and 84, 2 vols. (London, 1940), 1: 31–100; *The Roanoake Voyages, 1584–1590*, ed. D. B. Quinn, Hakluyt Society Publications, 2d ser., no. 104, 2 vols. (London, 1955), 1: 17–34, 60–71, 75–76; K. R. Andrews, *Trade, Plunder, and Settlement* (Cambridge, 1984), pp. 186–97, 199–222.

In both Gilbert's and Ralegh's ventures, the backers appear to have made serious efforts to mobilize merchant support. In each case, a group of merchants did agree to participate, but each made it clear that it was primarily interested in the trading side of the venture, demanding commercial monopolies as the price of the involvement of its syndicate. In the end, for various reasons, neither of these merchant syndicates actually took part in the Gilbert or Ralegh ventures.[54]

In general the great City merchants had much better places to put their money than in colonizing projects, and, at the time of the Gilbert and Ralegh projects, in the latter part of Elizabeth's reign, they were especially distracted by the extraordinary opportunities for profit in the privateering war against Spain, not to mention the development of the Levant commerce and, ultimately, the East Indian trade. It is of course true that a handful of merchants did seek to make significant contributions to the American colonization movement even in this period, notably Sir Thomas Smythe and Sir William Sanderson, both leaders of the commercial expansion eastward. But these men were exceptional, and they appear to have participated less with the expectation of profits than out of a patriotic concern for colonial development.[55]

When peace with Spain came in 1604, there was a new burst of colonizing activity. Beginning in 1609, a series of noble and gentry syndicates sent out a succession of voyages for exploration and colonization in Guiana. Nevertheless, none of these companies for Guiana succeeded in securing long-term backing for the projects they initiated. Roger North, supported by the great colonizing connection around the earl of Warwick, did raise the significant sum of £60,000 for the Guiana venture of 1619, but the massive follow-up funds required were never forthcoming and the project was, in any case, cut short by the revival of negotiations for the Spanish match. The subscription to the Guiana Company of 1628 amounted to only £2,400 and, according to Pares, was a "mere china egg brought forth to make the London business class lay." But "the merchants for the most part stood aside," and after 1631 English activities in Guiana came to an end.[56] Over approximately the same period during which the Guiana experiments were taking place, the Virginia Company

[54] Quinn, *Sir Humphrey Gilbert* 1: 56, 60–62, 2: 313–35; Quinn, *Roanoake Voyages* 2: 569–76; Andrews, *Trade, Plunder, and Settlement*, pp. 193, 207, 219, 222ff.

[55] R. McIntyre, "William Sanderson, Elizabethan Financier of Discovery," *William and Mary Quarterly* 13 (1956): 184–201.

[56] On the Guiana ventures, see Rabb, *Enterprise and Empire*, pp. 65, 66, 104; J. A. Williamson, *English Colonies in Guiana and on the Amazon, 1604–1668* (Oxford, 1923), pp. 50–51. The quotations are from Pares, "Merchants and Planters," p. 12 n. 60, and A. P. Newton, "The Great Emigration," in *Cambridge History of the British Empire* (Cambridge, 1929), 1: 143. For an almost identical comment with regard to Harcourt's Guiana Company of 1609, emphasizing the deflection of the greater merchants' funds into other commercial projects, see Williamson, *Guiana*, pp. 50–51.

was of course seeking to develop settlements and trade in the Chesapeake region. But, as noted, neither landed-class leaders nor company merchants could offer sustained support for this venture, and the tasks of continuing colonization in and of developing commerce with Virginia were left to others.

Although facing very different conditions and problems and conducted on a smaller scale, the Newfoundland Company, established in 1610, went through an experience similar to that of the Virginia Company. Initially, great company merchants—such as Ralph and William Freeman, who were among the few City merchants to trade on a large scale in both the Merchant Adventurers' and the Levant Company trades, and John and Humphrey Slaney, whose commercial involvements were as wide-ranging as those of any other merchants of the day—provided much of the Newfoundland Company's leadership and financial backing. These men aimed to use the colony to gain better access to the great fishery off the coast of Newfoundland and in this way to achieve a competitive advantage in the rapidly developing triangular trade whereby fish from Newfoundland were exchanged in Spain for valuable imports, especially from the Spanish empire. Nevertheless, the costs of settlement and of developing plantations quickly offset any potential savings with respect to the fishing trade. The merchants therefore withdrew their support for the Newfoundland Company's joint stock and left the corporation to flounder. Under gentry leadership the Newfoundland Company could not raise sufficient funds to continue, and, like the Virginia Company, was obliged to cede control over the colony to groups of independent subcompanies.[57]

Finally, the English settlement of the West Indies, begun in 1625–1626, was dominated, almost from the outset, by the earls of Carlisle, who held the proprietorship of the Caribbee Isles. The Carlisles failed entirely to invest in production and simply milked the colony by way of taxes and impositions. As in Virginia, an entirely new group, which came from neither the ranks of the company merchants nor the landed classes, assumed the task of plantation and commercial development in the West Indies.[58]

Only the Providence Island Company and the Bermuda Company were able to function effectively on the basis of gentry leadership and finance, but here there were exceptional factors at work. During the 1630s Providence Island and Bermuda became outposts of Puritanism, at once ports of exile and staging posts for revolt. The parliamentary gentry who sup-

[57] For the progress and failure of the colony, see G. T. Cell, "The English in Newfoundland, 1577–1660" (Liverpool University, Ph.D. diss., 1964), pp. 125–28, 134, 135–37, 167, and esp. 182. For the merchant subscribers, see G. T. Cell, "The Newfoundland Company: A Study of Subscribers to a Colonizing Venture," *William and Mary Quarterly*, 3d ser, 22 (1965): 614–16.

[58] Williamson, *Caribee Islands*, pp. 83–89, 135–49.

ported them probably did so at least as much for their political and religious purposes as for their economic possibilities. At the same time, the Providence Island and Bermuda projects were backed by the extraordinary mercantile connection around Robert Rich, second earl of Warwick. The Riches were among the greatest colonial entrepreneurs of the day and were willing to combine trade, plantation development, and privateering in order to make a profit. They made no bones about their long-term economic interest in the colonies, and they expended large sums of money, as well as a good deal of energy, in order to supervise directly a wide range of overseas commitments.[59] But there were few like them among the English nobles and gentry.

The fact is that not many among the landed classes had the Riches' wealth; among those who did, hardly any were willing to spend the time and energy required to watch over vast overseas holdings effectively. This failure to invest in colonial enterprise does not, however, imply that the English landed classes of this era were either poor or possessed of a backward mentality—any more than the similar refusal of the established City merchants implies these characteristics. Neither company merchants nor landed gentry were attracted to colonial investments because they had such promising alternatives immediately open to them. The gentry naturally turned to the management of their estates, as this was a period in which rents were rising rapidly;[60] the merchants continued to focus on developing the very profitable southern and eastern trades. Both therefore left the Americas open to an entirely new group of traders from social strata much lower than their own.

As will be seen, the men who developed the American colonial commerce were from unimpressive, often obscure socioeconomic backgrounds. They lacked access to the great City merchants' monopoly trading companies and the security of broad landed estates. They were, in fact, probably led to enter the colonial field in large part because their economic options, compared with those of the company merchants, were so sharply

[59] For these ventures, see below, ch. 4. For the Riches, see A. P. Newton, *The Colonising Activities of the English Puritans* (New Haven, 1914), and W. F. Craven, "The Earl of Warwick, Speculator in Privateering," *Hispanic-American Review* 10 (1930): 457–79. The Calverts' colony in Maryland is also a notable exception, but here again, extraeconomic, particularly religious, factors enter the picture, especially the desire for a haven for harried Catholics.

[60] For the rising rents and great profit opportunities offered by moderately careful estate management in the period 1600–1640, see E. Kerridge, "The Movement of Rent," *Ec.H.R.*, 2d ser., 6 (1953); L. Stone, "Estate Management," in *The Crisis of the Aristocracy, 1558–1641* (Oxford, 1965); P. J. Bowden, "Agricultural Prices, Farm Profits, and Rents," in *The Agrarian History of England and Wales*, vol. 4, *1500–1640*, ed. J. Thirsk (Cambridge, 1967), pp. 694–95. These works have exploded the myth that landlords could not successfully adapt to the economic trends of the period. Especially by the early seventeenth century, landlords were doing extremely well, profiting from the rapidly rising rents of that era.

restricted. Indeed, the new men of the colonial trades succeeded in developing colonial plantations and commerce where the company merchants and the landed classes had failed largely because they were willing to accept profit margins, take risks, and adopt methods of operation that neither the merchants nor the gentry would seriously consider. In particular, these men were ready to invest in plantation production and to carry out the regular travel to, and sometimes settlement in, the colonies that overseeing plantation investment required. They were willing to do these things, moreover, without the benefit of monopoly trading privileges. Paradoxically, therefore, they were, from the start, far better fitted than were either the company merchants or the gentry to exploit colonial opportunities and to profit from them. The unexpected consequence was that, in the process of carrying out the arduous task of founding the colonial economies, these new men ended up preparing themselves far better than any other traders to grasp the truly spectacular economic oportunities the colonial field ultimately offered. From obscure and unimpressive beginnings, they altered their own economic activities and condition, while they worked a fundamental transformation of the English commercial world.

The New-Merchant Leadership

of the Colonial Trades

THE YEARS between the downfall of the Virginia Company and the outbreak of the Civil War mark the crucial period for the American colonizing movement. Only then were colonies permanently established, and only from that time did colonization and colonial production come to be carried on in a sustained and accelerating manner. Just one thousand people remained in Virginia at the Virginia Company's dissolution in 1624. But by 1640, eight thousand colonists were residing there. Over roughly the same period, the first permanent settlements in the West Indies were established, and the British population of these islands grew to about twenty-five thousand.[1] These two areas— Virginia (including Maryland) and the Caribbean Islands (including Bermuda)—became the chief productive centers in British America. Before 1640, settlers concentrated almost exclusively on producing tobacco to be shipped to England, and from there to the rest of Europe and the Near East. In the years between 1622 and 1638, tobacco imports from the American colonies to England leaped from about sixty-one thousand pounds to two million pounds a year, providing the basis for a new and increasingly important line of mercantile activity.[2] Meanwhile, New England was the scene of a series of dynamic colonizing efforts. By 1640, the most populous of its colonies, Massachusetts Bay, had attracted some twenty thousand people; it constituted, moreover, one leading pole of attraction in a transatlantic Puritan network of religio–political opposition to the Crown that included not only its offshoots, Connecticut and Rhode Island, but also the offshore colonies, Bermuda and Providence Island.

The rise of American colonial commerce was only made possible by the construction from scratch of an entirely new system of production. This

---

[1] W. F. Craven, *The Southern Colonies in the Seventeenth Century, 1607–1689* (Baton Rouge, 1949), pp. 147, 183.

[2] G. L. Beer, *The Origins of the British Colonial System, 1578–1660* (New York, 1908), p. 110 n. 3; BL, Add. MSS 35865, fol. 248, summarized by J. A. Williamson, *The Caribbee Islands under the Proprietary Patents* (Oxford, 1926), pp. 137–39; R. R. Menard, "The Tobacco Industry in the Chesapeake Colonies, 1617–1730: An Interpretation," *Research in Economic History* 5 (1980).

was a project radically different from any previously undertaken by English merchants. The unique nature of the enterprise can be brought out by characterizing the new groups behind it and the innovative methods they adopted.

The traders who were responsible for the crucial inputs of capital and entrepreneurship for colonial development were "new men" in several senses. Few of them had been members of the great London trading companies, or overseas merchants of any kind. Nor did they come from the upper ranks of either London or county society. Originally men of the "middling sort," they were mostly born outside London and were, in many cases, the younger sons of minor gentry or prosperous yeomen. A few came from borough commercial families.

From their provincial homes, many of these men directly entered into colonial entrepreneurship by emigrating to the colonies and starting up plantations, a path nearly universally eschewed by the City's company merchants. In this case, they often used their plantation profits to return to London and set themselves up as full-fledged overseas merchants. Even then, they tended to remain intimately involved with all aspects of the colonial economy, including plantations and politics as well as trade. Indeed, the tight connections retained by the leading colonial traders with the ruling Virginia Council and the West Indies proprietorship provided one important key to their dramatic success.

Those colonial traders who did not begin their careers by emigrating to America often started out as domestic traders, sea captains, or shopkeepers in London, and got involved in colonial trade as an extension of their domestic operations. By entering directly into colonial trade, City retailers could save themselves the substantial middleman's cost on tobacco. At the same time, they could gain access to a new and lucrative market for provisions. Men such as these, it will be remembered, lacked this option in all of those overseas trades that were regulated by companies; for the mere-merchant provision of the company charters barred shopkeepers, ship captains, and artisans from becoming company members so long as they retained their domestic businesses. Many of the new colonial merchants—including some of the most important among them—remained fully active in their old City businesses even as they immersed themselves in American commerce. Their enduring connection with the City's domestic trading community would powerfully influence not only their commercial careers but their political and religious formation as well.

By the end of the pre–Civil War period, colonial commerce had matured and was attracting scores of new traders every year. Nevertheless, a critical feature of the overall evolution was the emergence from the mass of small traders of what might best be termed a colonial entrepreneurial leadership. This collection of top colonial traders formed a coherent social group, which provided the most important source of motivation, capital, and organization for the whole colonization movement. Linked to one another by a multiplicity of partnership and family ties, these men overcame unimpressive initial economic endowments by getting in on the ground floor, by taking the initiative in high-risk ventures, and by exploiting their ties with the colonial political authorities. They were behind almost every important colonial adventure of the period and controlled a disproportionate share of the trade. They exploited the fur and provisioning commerce, which, in the initial phase of colonial development, offered the greatest opportunities for windfall profits. They dominated the rapidly developing tobacco trades with Virginia and the West Indies, which formed the heart of the new American commercial economy. They were responsible, moreover, for most of the larger speculative ventures of the period—including the autonomous colonial trading center on Kent Island in the Chesapeake Bay, an interloping syndicate in the Canadian fur trade, and Caribbean privateering. Finally, these traders were the major London backers of the Puritan colonies in New England, Bermuda, and Providence Island, and through their participation in these ventures they established critical ties with groups of Puritan aristocrats and gentry that would have great political as well as economic significance. To understand the early evolution of the colonial economy is, in large part, to follow the evolution of this group.

The complex of commercial and family connections that formed the skeletal structure of the colonial merchant leadership can be displayed through lists of business partnerships and family connections.[3] The common background of these men, which helped bring them together in the first place, can be demonstrated through statistical profiles of their social origins.[4] Nevertheless, to fully understand this group requires an examination of the process of its formation, as well as of the life experiences and modes of operation of its individual members. One especially convenient way to accomplish this is to follow the career of the colonial merchant who was at once the group's archetypical figure and its leading member. Maurice Thomson was certainly the greatest colonial merchant of his day. He was involved in almost every major colonial undertaking of the period, and he worked, directly or indirectly, with almost all of the other leading colonial entrepreneurs. The unusual success and the spectacular range of Thomson's enterprises hardly make him the average representative of the group. But the very breadth and depth of his involvements over the entire period make his career the ideal point of departure for describing the colonizing movement, introducing almost all of its other

[3] See tables 4.2 and 4.3, pp. 184–93 and 194–95.
[4] See table 4.1, p. 83.

leading figures, and tracing its path of development. Using Thomson's career to provide a thread of continuity, it becomes possible to follow step by step the maturation of the new-merchant leadership while tracing the major phases of colonial economic evolution over the pre–Civil War period.

Early North American Development: Furs, Provisions, and Politics

THE MERCHANT–COUNCILOR INTEREST

The decay of the Virginia Company and the subsequent weakness of royal control from England engendered a chaotic pattern of social, political, and economic development in the Virginia Colony. The 1620s and 1630s witnessed a struggle for spoils in which the leading members of the colonial government were the main participants. Almost all of these officials came to Virginia from undistinguished social backgrounds in order to enrich themselves through trade and plantations. They appear to have regarded the Virginia Council, through which they governed the colony, primarily as a means for the aggrandizement of their own clique. Throughout the period councilors joined with one another and with various friends in a series of business and political partnerships to milk the resources of the colony. As Bernard Bailyn has pointed out, most of the major political events for thirty years after the company's dissolution—including the overthrow of Governor Harvey—were incidents in the pursuit of their private goals.[5]

As noted, in plantation development in early Virginia, the distinction between merchant and planter tended to be blurred: merchants took up plantations, planters became merchants, and all sorts of merchant-planter partnerships were formed. This was especially true at the top level of the society, for in order to market large amounts of tobacco, it was generally necessary to combine plantation ownership with trade. As a result, the Virginia councilor elite, naturally including many of the leading planters, became closely connected with the greatest merchants in the field. Most of the councilors had partners among the merchants, and some councilors were themselves leading overseas traders.

The natural commercial bond between councilors and merchants was, moreover, strengthened as a result of their complementary resources. The planter-councilor, by virtue of his political position, had privileged access to the colony's most desirable economic opportunities; the merchant could

---

[5] For the foregoing paragraph, see B. Bailyn, "Politics and Social Structure in Virginia," in *Seventeenth Century America*, ed. J. M. Smith (Chapel Hill, N.C., 1959), pp. 90–98.

supply the capital and entrepreneurship needed to exploit these successfully. In consequence, from very early on, the leading merchants and chief councilors—quite often the same people—were brought together in a nearly irresistible bloc, which constituted the most powerful force in Virginia's early development.

It was largely through constructing alliances with members of Virginia's councilor clique that the new-merchant leadership was first able to establish itself. Working together, councilors and merchants penetrated all aspects of the Virginia economy. The specific trajectory of Viriginia's early economic evolution is, indeed, incomprehensible without reference to the emergence of a special *merchant-councilor interest* distinct from, and in important ways directly opposed to, the interest of the generality of planters. During the pre–Civil War era, the merchant-councilor combine engaged in a wholesale shareout of the colony's major resources—furs, lands, and commercial monopolies. At the same time, its members pursued pro-merchant commercial policies that were directly harmful to, and opposed by, most of the colony's planters—above all, the establishment of a new Virginia Company and the abolition of free trade with Virginia.

During the earliest years of North American development, the trade in furs, on the one hand, and in provisions, on the other, carried special importance, although for different reasons. From the time when the search for precious metals was given up to the point when the plantations became reliable producers of a staple crop, furs were the colonies' most valuable and dependable exports. Unlike other colonial products, furs required no heavy capital outlay or long-term investment. All that was usually necessary was access to Indian trappers. But because the supply of furs was so limited, yet at the same time so valuable, it is perhaps not surprising that the colonial authorities attempted to appropriate this lucrative business for themselves—in particular by restricting trade with the Indians to those to whom they granted licenses. This was the pattern not only in Virginia, but in New England as well.

The colonial magistrates were preoccupied with the provisioning trade not only because of its potential profitability but also because the very existence of the colony depended on supplying the planters. Control over the provisioning trade, insofar as it could be exercised by the colonial authorities, was thus a critical political issue and could become a source of severe conflict. In Virginia, controversy arose in part over the regulation of the price of supplies brought in from England, and in part over how to develop alternative sources of supply in the colony itself (through trade with the Indians and/or through the enforced cultivation of food crops). On these questions, the colony's councilors occupied an ambivalent position. They were under heavy pressure from the planters to prevent the commercial interests from exploiting the colony. At the same time, considering their capital and their mercantile connections, the councilors and their merchant friends were very well placed to take charge of provisioning themselves. As it turned out, the colony's councilors could not resist taking advantage of their position. They appointed themselves to carry out many of the early missions of trade for provisions with the Indians, while prohibiting other colonists from doing so. Meanwhile, they and that group of minor traders who got in early on the commerce with the colony (often as colonists themselves, sometimes as London-based sea captains, and usually as friends with one or another of the colonial councilors) made a killing in the provisioning trade from London. They exacted monopoly profits by exploiting colonists who had become dependent on suppliers from England as a result of their total concentration on tobacco planting and the still irregular nature of the trade with London.[6]

The core members of what was to emerge as the colonial entrepreneurial leadership made their initial colonial profits from the provisioning and fur trades. Maurice Thomson makes his first appearance in the commerce with Virginia among that relatively small group of merchants already active in these trades under the rule of the Virginia Company. Born around 1600, Thomson was the eldest of five sons of an armigerous Hertfordshire family.[7] He could hardly have expected much of an inheritance from his father, Robert, for by 1617 he had settled in Virginia.[8] Shortly thereafter he appears as a transatlantic ship captain, master of "a good ship burden 320 tons." Over the next several years, Thomson performed a number of passenger transportation and provisioning services for the Virginia Company and the Virginia Colony.[9] In the meantime, he accumulated a Virginia estate of 150 acres. In 1623 three of Thomson's younger brothers, George, William, and Paul, joined him in Virginia, transported there by their brother-in-law Capt. William Tucker, who apparently covered the

[6] On the pressures that emerged inside the colony as a result of the single-minded emphasis on tobacco growing and of the problems in acquiring provisions, as well as the potential for profit that arose in consequence, see E. S. Morgan, "The First American Boom: Virginia, 1618 to 1630," *William and Mary Quarterly*, 3d. ser, 28 (1971), as well as E. S. Morgan, *American Slavery, American Freedom*, (New York, 1975), pp. 92–130. See also Bailyn, "Politics and Social Structure," pp. 95–97. For the councilors and the early fur trade, see N. C. Hale, *Virginia Venturer* (Richmond, Va., 1951), pp. 115–22ff. See also *Va. Co. Recs.* 4: 6–8; H. R. McIlwaine, ed., *Minutes of Council and General Court of Colonial Virginia, 1622–1632, 1670–1676* (Richmond, Va., 1924), pp. 136, 193, 479.

[7] For Thomson's date of birth, see "Cloberry Transcripts," pp. 189, 217 (see below, note 22). *Visitation of London, 1633–1635*, Harleian Society Publications 15 and 17 (London, 1880–1883), 2: 282; *Visitation of Hertfordshire*, Harleian Society Publications 22 (London, 1886), pp. 97–98.

[8] According to Thomson's testimony in 1623, he had by then already been in Virginia for six years (*Va. Co. Recs.* 2: 386). This is verified in N. Nugent, ed., *Cavaliers and Pioneers: Abstracts of Virginia Land Patents* (repr. Baltimore, 1963), p. 4.

[9] *Va. Co. Recs.* 1: 277, 4: 245, 257.

expenses.[10] It was undoubtedly Thomson's business connection with William Tucker, facilitated by Tucker's marriage to a sister of Thomson's, that paved the way for Thomson's meteoric ascent as a colonial merchant.

Also originally a sea captain, William Tucker was one of the Virginia Colony's earliest settlers and among the first of its special breed of great merchant-planter-councilors. He arrived in Virginia in 1610 at the age of twenty-one.[11] In 1616 he was active with several London citizens in the foundation of a plantation in Virginia, and among his partners in this venture there were two in particular who were to play significant roles in his developing career.[12] One was Elias Roberts, a London trader whose son Elias would also enter the colonial field and marry in 1630 Dinah Thomson, another sister of Maurice Thomson's (and of Tucker's wife).[13] The other was Ralph Hamor, who, like Tucker, soon emerged in Virginia as a magistrate and an important political figure.[14] By 1619, William Tucker was one of the leading Englishmen in the colony, and was elected a representative to the first meeting of the Virginia House of Burgesses. Two years later, Tucker and Ralph Hamor were chosen to present the Virginia Colony's case in Parliament against the proposed tobacco contract of Sir Thomas Roe and others. In the following years, Tucker led numerous expeditions of trade with, and war against, the Indians under the auspices of the colonial government, no doubt further enriching himself in the process. He also served in a variety of local governmental and administrative positions in his home section of Kecoughtan (Elizabeth City).[15] In 1625 Tucker was among only fifteen men in the entire colony who had ten or more servants. The others in this category, among them his old partner, Ralph Hamor, were almost all members of that merchant-councilor clique that dominated the colony. By 1626, if not before, Tucker had been appointed to the Virginia Council, and according to George Sandys, the colony's treasurer, was one of the few councilors of that era sufficiently wealthy, honest, and industrious to carry out the responsibilities this office entailed.[16] It was natural that, as his relative, political connection, and business partner, Tucker should play a formative role in Maurice Thomson's career.

[10] Nugent, *Cavaliers and Pioneers*, p. 4; *Va. Co. Recs.* 4: 557; "Abstracts of Virginia Land Patents," *V.M.H.B.* 1 (1894): 190, 192–93.

[11] "Abstracts of Virginia Land Patents," *V.M.H.B.* 1 (1894): 190, 192–93.

[12] *Va. Co. Recs.* 3: 58; A. Brown, *The Genesis of the United States*, 2 vols. (Boston, 1890), 2: 1034.

[13] Society of Genealogists, Boyd's Index of London Citizens: 35124, 39168.

[14] For Hamor, see, for example, L. F. Stock, ed., *Proceedings and Debates of the British Parliaments Respecting North America*, 5 vols. (Washington, 1924), 1: 34; Morgan, "First American Boom," pp. 191, 193.

[15] *Va. Co. Recs.* 3: 154, 535–36, 623, 4: 6–8, 251, 284, 446; Stock, *Proceedings and Debates* 1: 34.

[16] *Va. Co. Recs.* 4: 111; Morgan, "First American Boom," pp. 188, 190.

By the time, then, of the dissolution of the Virginia Company in 1624, Maurice Thomson and William Tucker were partners and had established themselves among that group of small entrepreneurs that had taken over from the company the leading role in Virginia's economic development. Like others among them, such as William Felgate, who was another of Tucker's brothers-in-law, they had lived in the colony for a number of years while carrying out a variety of small-scale operations, often in provisioning.[17] During the period of the Virginia Company's rule they had acquired the requisite experience, capital, and connections to set themselves up as colonial merchants in the full sense. By 1626 Maurice Thomson had returned to London to extend their business interests throughout the breadth of the Atlantic economy. Tucker's powerful political base in Virginia, particularly his seat on the Virginia Council, appears to have encouraged him to remain a resident of the colony, although he often traveled to London for reasons of business, and he ultimately resettled there.

Over the next fifteen years, Thomson and Tucker remained partners and leaders in developing all aspects of the Virginian economy. This continued to require not merely plantation development and trade, but the deepening of political connections and the acquisition of privilege. For Thomson and Tucker, probably the critical moment was their entry into partnership with the great magistrate of Virginia, William Claiborne. The sealing of this alliance opened the way to an extended period of overpowering ascendancy within the colony for the emerging new-merchant entrepreneurial leadership.

THE KENT ISLAND PROJECT

William Claiborne may have been the most consistently influential politician in Virginia throughout the whole of the pre-Restoration period. Even so, in background, career, and economic objectives, he was not very different from William Tucker or such other leading Virginia councilors as Samuel Matthews, George Menefie, Thomas Stegg, and John Utie. All rose from "middling sorts" of backgrounds (or lower) to high positions in Virginia as merchant-planter-councilors; all were distinguished by their ability to combine planting with mercantile activity on a rather large scale;

---

[17] See, for example, Thomson's involvement in selling fish in Virginia in February 1626 ("Minutes of the Council and General Court, 1622–1629," *V.M.H.B.* 25 [1918]:126). For Felgate's activities, see, for example, *Va. Co. Recs.* 4: 245, 257. For Felgate's relationship with Tucker, see PRO, will of William Tucker, proved 17 Feb. 1644. Felgate was active in the trade with the Americas from the time of the Virginia Company (*Va. Co. Recs.* 2: 17, 25, 75, 90, 154). He was the son of a Suffolk yeoman (Skinners Company, London, Apprentices and Freeman Book, 1496–1602, fols. 418, 466, 489).

and all forged connections with the leading London colonial merchants.[18]
William Claiborne was a younger son of a King's Lynn, Norfolk, family. His father and grandfather engaged in a variety of shipping and small industrial enterprises—the manufacture of salt and Icelandic fishing, among others—and both held the office of alderman and lord mayor of King's Lynn during the last quarter of the sixteenth century. In 1598, Claiborne's father, Thomas, married the daughter of a London brewer and moved to a country house in Crayford, Kent, where both of his sons were born. Despite his civic prominence and social situation, Thomas Claiborne does not appear to have been a very wealthy man. His eldest son, Thomas, was apprenticed in London and eventually set himself up in the hosiery business, later becoming involved in the tobacco trade, perhaps in collaboration with his brother William. William Claiborne emigrated to Virginia in 1621, when he was offered the potentially lucrative position of Virginia surveyor.[19]

As an official in the government of Virginia, William Claiborne was from the start presented with valuable opportunities. Along with his office, worth £30 a year in addition to fees, he received a grant of 200 acres of land immediately upon his arrival. In the next several years he was able to secure from the colony's council additional land grants of 150, 250, and 500 acres. In the meantime, he succeeded in having his surveyor's salary doubled on a retroactive basis. By 1624, he had become a councilor of Virginia, and in 1626 he was appointed the colony's secretary of state.[20]

From this influential position, Claiborne was able to launch a major mercantile career. Under the protection of grants and monopoly commissions secured from the Virginia Council, he organized between 1627 and 1629 a series of increasingly ambitious fur-trading ventures with the Susquehannock Indians.[21] His goal was to develop a vast fur-trading and colonial provisioning network up and down the Atlantic coast and to center its operation on an island that he had discovered in the upper Chesapeake Bay. To this island, which he later named Kent, would come furs from the Virginia back country and as far away as Canada for shipment to England. At this place, the food and clothing needed in the fledgling colonies of New England and Nova Scotia, but also in Virginia itself, would be produced and distributed. So grandiose a project required a good deal more capital than Claiborne had, and would certainly necessitate outside

---

[18] For Menefie, see, for example, R. L. Morton, *Colonial Virginia*, 2 vols. (Chapel Hill, N.C., 1960), 1: 138, 142, 144, 145; see also below, pp. 135–36. For Matthews, see Hale, *Virginia Venturer*, index. For Utie and Stegg, see Bailyn, "Politics and Social Structure," pp. 94–95, 99, and see also below, pp. 139–40, 143, 147.

[19] For this biographical information on Claiborne, see Hale, *Virginia Venturer*, ch. 1.

[20] Ibid., pp. 55, 87–88, 101, 103–4, 108.

[21] Ibid., pp. 115, 122–28.

help. At the same time, as Claiborne realized from the start, the creation of a large-scale provisioning center in the Virginia Colony that was under the control of a private merchant syndicate would inevitably arouse hostility. Claiborne certainly expected opposition from the governor, and perhaps also from the assembly. He therefore found it advisable to secure the help of London merchants who had not only the requisite capital but also the connections in England needed to obtain a monopoly patent to secure the enterprise.[22]

Whether Claiborne first approached, or was approached by, the City merchant William Cloberry concerning the fur-trading and provisioning project on Kent Island is uncertain,[23] but the basis for their mutual interest in collaboration is not in doubt. Cloberry was the third son of an armigerous Devonshire family who had secured his future by becoming first apprenticed to, then business partner of, Humphrey Slaney, one of the most adventurous London merchants of his day, and by marrying Slaney's daughter.[24] Slaney, who participated in the Merchant Adventurers', Levant, Spanish, and Barbary trades, had been one of the few important company merchants to involve himself actively in the Americas. He was a founder of the Newfoundland Company, and after this venture fell apart he remained a leader in the Newfoundland fish trade, as well as in the developing commerce with Guinea.[25] William Cloberry was Humphrey Slaney's partner in the Newfoundland and Guinea trades, as well as in the American tobacco commerce.[26] Above all, by the time he met William Claiborne, Cloberry had become an important collaborator of Sir William Alexander, the English secretary of state for Scotland, in Alexander's latest attempt, begun in 1628, to settle the Nova Scotia proprietorship he had been awarded in 1622. Cloberry was also working with Alexander in developing the Canadian fur trade.[27] Cloberry could thus offer William

---

[22] The history of the Kent Island project from its inception can be reconstructed in detail as a result of the survival of extensive papers from the High Court of Admiralty on the case "Claiborne vs. Cloberry," which began in 1639. These papers have been transcribed by R. G. Marsden and are on deposit at the Maryland Historical Society as "The Cloberry Transcripts." A good part of these transcripts has been printed in *Md. Hist. Mag.* 26 (1931) and 27 (1932).

[23] Claiborne and Cloberry each accused the other of initiating contact. Compare PRO, H.C.A.24/98/278 (Cloberry's libel) with PRO, H.C.A.24/98/318 (Claiborne's libel); "Cloberry Transcripts," *Md. Hist. Mag.* 26 (1931): 385–87, 27 (1932): 19–20.

[24] *Visitation of London, 1633–1635* 1: 173; *Visitation of Devon, 1622*, Harleian Society Publications 6 (London, 1872), p. 60; Haberdashers Company, London, Apprenticeship Bindings, 1602–1611, 7 December 1610.

[25] G. T. Cell, "The Newfoundland Company: A Study of Subscribers to a Colonizing Venture," *William and Mary Quarterly*, 3d ser., 22 (1965): 615.

[26] J. W. Blake, "The Farm of the Guinea Trade in 1631," in *Essays in British and Irish History*, ed. H. A. Cronne, T. W. Moody, and D. B. Quinn (London, 1949), pp. 87ff.; G. T. Cell, *English Enterprise in Newfoundland, 1577–1660* (Toronto, 1969), p. 77 n. 106.

[27] C. Rogers, ed., *The Earl of Stirling's Register of Royal Letters Relating to the Affairs of Scotland*

Claiborne ample capital and broad experience; most important, through Sir William Alexander, he had the powerful connection at the English court needed to gain privileged status for trade throughout the American continent.[28] In addition, Claiborne and Cloberry had a common interest in developing Kent Island as a source of provisions for the colony in Nova Scotia then being developed by Sir William Alexander with Cloberry's help.

It is indicative of the eminence already achieved by the Maurice Thomson–William Tucker partnership that Claiborne and Cloberry asked Thomson to join them in the Kent Island project. From the mid-1620s Thomson had immersed himself in opening up the West Indian tobacco trade. Only very recently, moreover, he had launched a fur-trading venture in Canada, and this may have been an important reason why Claiborne and Cloberry sought his collaboration.[29] Since Cloberry and Sir William Alexander were themselves also already active in the Canadian fur trade, it is probable that some sort of eventual linkup was envisioned between the colony at Kent Island and that trade as well.[30] In any case,

---

and Nova Scotia from 1516 to 1635 (Edinburgh, 1885), p. 265; C. M. Andrews, The Colonial Period of American History, 4 vols. (New Haven, 1934–1938), 1: 314–15, 328, 329. See also below, note 30.

[28] Cloberry's claim to have this connection was, according to Claiborne, the major factor that induced him to enter the partnership (Md. Hist. Mag. 27, [1932]: 20; PRO, H.C.A.24/98/318).

[29] For Thomson's trade with the Caribbean, see below, pp. 125ff. For his fur trade with Canada, see below, note 30.

[30] As it was Thomson's project lasted only a short time, since it owed its existence to a set of diplomatic and legal circumstances that turned out to be only temporary. Thus, during England's war with France in the late 1620s, a group of English merchants trading with France, led by Gervase Kirk, William Barkeley, and Robert Charlton, seized the opportunity provided by the Anglo-French hostilities to carry out a series of successful voyages of conquest in French Canada under royal commission. By July 1629, after linking up with Sir William Alexander and his Scottish Company for Canada, these men, organized as the Canada Company, had captured all of French Canada and were preparing to exploit it under a royal monopoly patent. At this point, however, peace was made with France, and by the Treaty of Susa Charles I agreed to give back to France most of the area in Canada that had just been captured. This peace settlement naturally undermined the legal strength of the Canada Company's patent, and Maurice Thomson and his partners took advantage of this opening to launch an interloping project in the fur trade. The territory was not actually returned to the French for several years, and during this period, Thomson and Co. traded illegally but apparently quite profitably in the Canada Company's patented area. Nevertheless, the Canada Company pursued a case against Thomson, and it won a judgment of four hundred marks against him in 1632. Thomson refused to pay, and was temporarily thrown in prison with one of his captains. But by this time both the interlopers and the Canada Company were being forced to wind up their operations as a result of the French reoccupation. These events can be followed in A.P.C. Col. 1613–1680, pp. 134, 169–85; C.S.P. Col. 1574–1660, pp. 103, 106–7, 114, 119, 120, 128, 139, 143, 145, 151; and PRO, H.C.A.24/88/248, 320, 330. For further detail, see H. E. Ware, "An Incident in Winthrop's Voyage to New England," Massachusetts Historical Society Transactions 12 (1908–1909): 105–7. The relevant secondary works are H. Kirke, First English Conquest of Canada, 2d ed. (London, 1908), and H. P. Biggar, The Early Trading Companies of New France (Toronto, 1901). It should be noted

Claiborne, Cloberry, and Thomson constituted the nucleus that actually ran the Kent Island project. The partners obtained additional financial backing from John de la Barre, a leading City trader with France and Spain, who was at this time Thomson's collaborator in the Canadian fur trade, and also from Simon Turgis, a merchant and planter in Virginia.[31]

Plans for the operation were completed early in 1631. The partners made arrangements with the colony at Massachusetts Bay, as well as that in Nova Scotia, for provisioning from Kent Island. Most important, through Cloberry's friend Sir William Alexander they obtained a trading commission under His Majesty's signet for Scotland. This document, which fell short of a royal charter, authorized the partners to trade "for corn, furs, or any other commodities in all parts of New England and Nova Scotia where there is not already a patent."[32]

Claiborne took full command of the venture, and he sailed from England on 28 May 1631 with twenty servants and £319 worth of supplies aboard the ship *Africa*, hired for £700 from Thomson's partner and brother-in-law, William Tucker.[33] Tucker was at this time a colleague of Claiborne's on the Virginia Council. Not unexpectedly, the council gave the project its blessing. Claiborne arrived at Kent Island several months later, and over the next several years succeeded in constructing an active and highly productive plantation colony, while carrying on a substantial trade in furs.[34]

Nevertheless, it was not long before the Kent Island project ran into difficulties that threatened its very existence. The Virginia planters naturally resented the giveaway in England of valuable colonial trading rights to a partnership of merchant outsiders, and they organized in their assembly against it. Before considering the conflict that ensued,[35] however, it is necessary to sketch its broader context—the tumultuously expanding Atlantic tobacco economy.

in passing that William Barkeley, who at this time was a member of the Canada Company, was later to extend his colonial activities into New England, Bermuda, and the West Indies, especially in partnership with Maurice Thomson's brother-in-law Elias Roberts. See below, p. 189.

[31] For Turgis's trade, see, for example, PRO, P.C.2/44/63. Turgis was a younger son of a Petworth, Sussex, family, his father having served as lord mayor of Chichester (*Visitation of London, 1633–1635* 2: 300). For de la Barre's partnership with Thomson in the Canadian fur trade, see references in note 30. De la Barre's extensive European trade can be followed in the London port books for the period. De la Barre's father seems to have been a Huguenot immigrant from Flanders and some sort of London merchant (*Visitation of London, 1633–1635* 1: 224).

[32] *Mass. Hist. Soc. Coll.*, 5th ser., 8 (1882): 31; Hale, *Virginia Venturer*, p. 144; Rogers, *Earl of Stirling's Register*, pp. 265, 527–28.

[33] *Md. Hist. Mag.* 26 (1931): 389.

[34] Hale, *Virginia Venturer*, pp 156–58; J. H. Latané, *Early Relations between Maryland and Virginia*, Johns Hopkins University Studies in Historical and Political Science, 13th ser., nos. 3, 4 (Baltimore, 1895), pp. 12–14; *C.S.P. Col. 1574–1660*, p. 176.

[35] See below, pp. 130, 141–44.

The Atlantic Tobacco Economy:
The West Indies and Virginia

TRADE

By the 1620s Englishmen had begun to make their first serious inroads in the Caribbean. Although the whole area was legally a Spanish domain, and recognized as such at the peace with Spain in 1604, the decay of Spanish authority had enabled both English and Dutch merchants to continue their clandestine operations there. No permanent colonies were established, but the English government itself sanctioned a series of ventures to Guiana between 1609 and 1631. The Amazon Company of 1619, organized by the earl of Warwick and Capt. Roger North, actually planted a number of men at the head of the Amazon delta. However, the negotiations for a Spanish match obliged the Crown to terminate this venture, thereby setting in motion a chain of events that led to the first permanent English settlements in the West Indies.[36]

Among the colonists left to fend for themselves after the dissolution of the Amazon Company was one Thomas Warner, the son of an old but not very wealthy East Anglian landed family. In 1622, Warner found his way home by way of the Caribbee Isles and became interested in the possibility of founding a colony in the area. In England, he secured some capital from Ralph Merrifield, a London merchant previously interested in the undercover West Indian trade, and returned with a small party of settlers to St. Kitts, where he began planting tobacco in 1624. After the breaking off of the Spanish match, Warner again returned to England and, with Merrifield, obtained from the Crown in 1625 a royal commission for colonization and trade in Barbados, St. Kitts, Nevis, and Montserrat, as well as an appointment as governor and royal lieutenant of the Leeward Islands. In the same year the great Anglo-Dutch merchant Sir William Courteen organized the first English settlement on Barbados.[37]

At the time, then, of Maurice Thomson's original entry into commerce with the Caribbean in 1626, the English had just two fledgling colonial operations in the entire area. Thomson got in on the ground floor: in cooperation with partners and relatives he became involved, directly or indirectly, with the initial establishment of trading ventures on almost every island. Combining the requisite skill and daring with the right political connections, he built a veritable commercial empire in the Caribbean in the space of two decades. Thomson's own story of his introduction to

[36] A. P. Newton, *The Colonising Activities of the English Puritans* (New Haven, 1914), pp. 25–27. For the Guiana Voyages, see J. A. Williamson, *English Colonies in Guiana and on the Amazon, 1604–1668* (Oxford, 1923).

[37] Williamson, *Caribbee Islands*, pp. 21–22, 27–29. For the subsequent dislodgment of Courteen by the earl of Carlisle, see ibid., ch. 3.

business in the Caribbean provides a classic account of the relationships between commerce and plantation and between capital and privilege that characterized West Indian development, indeed all American development, in its earliest period.

> About . . . April 1626 . . . upon sundry . . . affairs [I] came into the town of Southampton and stayed there about six days . . . during which time one Thomas Combes of Southampton . . . pretending he had sustained some loss by furnishing a ship called the St. Christopher and sending her forth with men and provisions and victuals for the island of St. Christopher . . . intending to have planted tobacco there . . . by reason whereof the said Combes being loath to go on . . . and yet not willing to leave the same because then he must have undergone much more loss, to help himself therein he subtly and cunningly insinuated himself into [my] company falsely telling [me] that he had adventured to the said island and he had a very hopeful and profitable plantation there which should give a great quantity of tobacco and other profits there yearly and further affirmed that he had 8000 wt. of very good tobacco there at the time which he had appointed to be sent out into England . . . in the next ship that came there which tobacco had been worth £3000 and upwards at the time and used many other insinuating speeches whenever he could get any opportunity to speak unto [me], thinking thereby to have procured [me] to have been partner with him but failing thereof the said Combes further told [me] that the governor of the island Captain Warner was Combes's special and intimate friend and that the said captain had vowed he would serve seven years in the said island but he would make the said Combes a great gainer if he would adventure thither . . . Combes offered [me], if [I] would allow him but half the charges he had been already at for the said plantation and for getting the said 8000 lbs. of tobacco, that then [I] should be partner with him, but finding [me] yet to stand off, he at last urgently moved that [I] be partner with him in the said plantation and adventure promising faithfully that if [I] would allow the said Combes but one-quarter part of his . . . former charges [I] should be equal partner therein . . . whereupon [I] did accept the said offer.[38]

Although in his reply to the foregoing account Thomson's partner Thomas Combes claimed that it was Thomson who had taken the initiative, done all the "insinuating," and proposed the partnership, the basis for their

---

[38] From Thomson's bill of complaint in Chancery Court against his partner Thomas Combes, 12 June 1634 (PRO, C.2/Ch.I/T.24/64). Combes's reply is attached to the same document.

collaboration is clear. Combes had a plantation in St. Kitts that had so far been unsuccessful but that had great promise, especially because of Combes's close connection with Capt. Thomas Warner, the original settler and governor of the island. Thomson, as both men mention, had experience "as a planter in some other parts" and the cash on hand that Combes lacked. There was ample basis for a bargain. Thomson agreed to cover a good part of Combes's previous expenses and thereby became a full partner in the operation, putting up £4,000 of initial capital. This is some indication both of the impressive scale of this venture and of the success already achieved by Thomson and his partner William Tucker in Virginia.[39]

In April–May 1626, Thomson and Combes sent three ships carrying sixty slaves to their thousand-acre plantation on St. Kitts.[40] Governor Warner also traveled with this expedition and appears to have worked closely with Thomson and Combes in both provisioning and tobacco trading in the early days of the colony.[41] Within a year, a major new recruit joined the syndicate. Thomas Stone, fourth son of a Carhouse, Lancaster, family, had been apprenticed in London to the Haberdashers Company.[42] Like many others among the new colonial merchants, Stone was active in retail trade; he operated a shop in Cateaton Street, London, and appears to have entered the tobacco and colonial provisioning trade as an extension of his domestic business activity. It was probably because he wished to continue his shopkeeping business that he did not join the Merchant Adventurers Company (which would of course admit only "mere merchants") but instead illegally interloped within their privileged area for many years, exporting cloth and importing a variety of goods from several Low Country ports.[43] Stone may have been particularly attractive to Thomson and his friends because of his trading connections in Holland. In any case, by 1627 Thomson and Stone are found as partners, reexporting tobacco to Middleburgh, Flushing, and Amsterdam. Like Maurice Thomson, Stone became simultaneously active in commerce and production in both Virginia and the West Indies, and, also like Thomson, he

[39] PRO, C.2/Ch.I/T.24/64.

[40] Bodleian Library, Rawlinson MSS C.94, fols. 8–9; Williamson, *Caribbee Islands*, p. 31.

[41] In July 1627, for example, Thomson and Combes's ship *The Plough*, "by advice from . . . Captain Warner did supply [St. Kitts]," and returned to England with 10,500 pounds of the governor's tobacco as well as 5,500 pounds belonging to Thomson and Combes (*A.P.C. Col. 1613–1680*, p. 122; Bodleian Library, Rawlinson MSS C.94, fol. 9).

[42] Bodleian Library, Rawlinson MSS C.94, fols. 8–9; *Visitation of London, 1633–1635* 2: 266; E. Stone, "The Ancestry of William Stone, Governor of Maryland," *New Eng. Hist. Gen. Reg.* 49 (1895): 314–16.

[43] PRO, E.122/218/25 (list of tobacco retailers-licensees); A. Friis, *Alderman Cockayne's Project and the Cloth Trade* (London, 1927), pp. 110, 110 n. 3, 367, 369.

worked in close cooperation with a relative on the spot, in this case his nephew William Stone. William Stone operated the Stones' plantation in Accomac, Virginia, and became a leading official in the county and eventually the colony.[44]

In 1627, Thomson, Stone, and Combes sent Robert Wilding, an apprentice of Stone's in the Haberdashers Company, to St. Kitts to help oversee their plantation there and to manage the business.[45] In that year, however, the earl of Carlisle received the proprietorship of all the Caribbean Isles, and he compelled the partners to repurchase from him the patents for their land in St. Kitts and to pay for the right to export tobacco customs-free for the next ten years. When, in the following year, a new, redrawn grant was issued to the earl, these patents were again called in; but though the partners lost their customs privileges, they retained their plantation and continued their trade.[46]

Meanwhile, close kinsmen of Maurice Thomson helped launch very similar pioneering operations in the other Leeward Islands, probably under some arrangement with Maurice. A syndicate led by Anthony Hilton, who had received license from the earl of Carlisle, began the first colony on the island of Nevis in 1628, and among the leaders of the original settlement was Edward Thomson. Edward Thomson's precise family relationship with Maurice is unclear. But, like Hilton, he had been one of the earliest settlers on St. Kitts (in association with the Thomson-Stone-Combes group?), and over the next two decades he was a constant partner of Maurice's in commercial activities throughout the world.[47]

Similarly, Maurice's brother George Thomson helped found the first colony on Montserrat in the mid-1630s. William Tucker had brought George Thomson to Virginia in 1623 along with his two younger brothers, Paul and William. George established a plantation and, by the later 1620s, had become a member of the Virginia Assembly.[48] From there, like his older brother Maurice, he expanded his activities into the Caribbean. In 1635, George Thomson became a leading backer of Montserrat's

[44] J. R. Pagan, "Growth of the Tobacco Trade between London and Virginia, 1614–1640," *Guildhall Studies in London History* 3 (1979): 261 n. 89; S. M. Ames, ed., *County Records of Accomack-Northampton, Virginia, 1632–1640,* American Legal Records, vol. 7 (Washington, 1954), pp. xxx, 162–63; see also the index.

[45] Bodleian Library, Rawlinson MSS C.94, fol. 9; Haberdashers Company, London, Freemen Book (chronological), 1638.

[46] Bodleian Library, Rawlinson, MSS C.94, fol. 9; PRO, C.2/Ch.I/T.24/64; Williamson, *Caribbee Islands,* p. 65.

[47] Williamson, *Caribbee Islands,* pp. 66–68. It is likely, but not certain, that Edward Thomson was part of Hilton's founding syndicate, which included, most prominently, Thomas Littleton, a connection of the earl of Carlisle. In 1629, or shortly thereafter, Littleton assigned goods to Edward Thomson on Nevis (PRO, H.C.A.24/90/101).

[48] "Abstracts of Virginia Land Patents," *V.M.H.B.* 1 (1894): 190.

pioneer settler and first governor, Capt. Anthony Briskett, advancing Briskett supplies in exchange for the right to market his tobacco.[49]

Maurice, Edward, and George Thomson, as well as Thomas Stone, remained very active in the West Indies throughout the pre–Civil War period. Some indication of the scale of their business was given by Thomas Combes when he asserted that by 1634, the Thomson-Combes-Stone partnership had already returned £40,000.[50] At about the same time, Edward Thomson is found bringing in some 20,000 pounds of St. Kitts tobacco in a single shipment.[51] Nor does the influence of these men in the Caribbean seem to have declined as the years went on. In 1638, for example, Maurice Thomson brought in 38,000 pounds of St. Kitts tobacco (and an additional 25,000 pounds from Barbados); in 1640, Thomas Stone brought in 32,000 pounds of St. Kitts tobacco. Both these amounts were the largest imported from St. Kitts by any merchant in the respective years.[52] In the meantime, these men were continuing to operate, often together, on a large scale on the North American continent, expanding the size and scope of their businesses with the rapid development of the Virginian tobacco economy.

Tobacco production in Virginia, as in the West Indies, grew by leaps and bounds during the 1620s and 1630s, creating a huge potential for profit, but also very serious problems for the colonists.[53] From early on, the bulk of the planters faced two interrelated problems: on the one hand, plummeting tobacco prices, resulting from what seemed to be an infinitely elastic supply; on the other hand, the relatively high cost of provisions, reflecting the restricted amounts brought in by the merchants who controlled the trade. The result was widespread planter debt. Despite their recognition as a body of the need for economic diversification, the planters as individuals generally tried to overcome their financial difficulties simply by increasing their tobacco output. This naturally led to crises of overproduction, further falls in prices, and ever-deepening debt. It was the special ability of the new-merchant leadership and their friends on the Virginia Council to take advantage of the intensifying pressures within the Virginian tobacco economy that largely accounts for their extraordinary success in this field during the pre–Civil War period.

The planters sought to counter the merchants and break out of their

[49] PRO, H.C.A.24/92/26; PRO, H.C.A.13/53/21–22, 263–64; Williamson, *Caribbee Islands*, p. 94.

[50] PRO, C.2/Ch.I/T.24/64.

[51] PRO, H.C.A.24/89/96.

[52] London Port Books for Imports, 1638 and 1640, PRO, E.190/41/5 and PRO, E.190/43/5.

[53] On tobacco production in this period, and especially on crises of overproduction, see Menard, "Tobacco Industry," pp. 109–16, 128–35. See also R. R. Menard, "A Note on Chesapeake Tobacco Prices, 1618–1660," *V.M.H.B.* 84 (1976).

cycle of overproduction and rising debt by politically regulating the economy. Their program was straightforward: to use the Virginia Assembly to put limits on tobacco production and to keep up tobacco prices; so far as possible, to compel planters to produce their own supplies, especially food, within the colony; and to overcome their dependence on the merchants by destroying privileged trading syndicates and especially by opening up the colony to free trade, in particular with the Dutch. In attempting to implement these measures the planters had no doubt that their main obstacle was that small group of merchant-planter-councilors that in these years was attempting to secure a stranglehold on the tobacco economy as a whole.

The planters set out their full program in their petition of 6 March 1632 to the Dorset Commission on Virginia affairs, recently appointed by the Crown in England.[54] The planters explained to the commissioners that to pay off their debts, they had been "necessarily tied to the planting of that bad commodity from which otherwise [they] had willingly declined." The assembly members vowed that they "had rather want, than labor as slave to other men's purse, among whom we have good cause to complain of Capt. William Tucker who has far exceeded all other merchants in the prices of their goods."

The planters introduced their alternative program with a scarcely veiled assault on the Claiborne-Cloberry-Thomson syndicate, which was at that moment developing the provisioning center on Kent Island in Chesapeake Bay: "We are resolved to plant store of corn, where we desire that none that are not resident here may receive commission to trade in our Bay, whereby the benefits that might accrue to the planter will be frustrated by those that bear no public charge." But the planters did not confine themselves merely to complaints over particular cases of favoritism. The Virginia Assembly recently had passed legislation setting a minimum price on tobacco at $6d.$, and they asked the Dorset Commission to approve it. This would enable the planters to pay their "engagements and so set free [their] hands for other works of better consequences" (that is, diversification), or at least allow them to afford to pay for provisions. At the same time, to counter the merchants' monopolistic practices, they called for opening up the trade. "In particular, we recommend unto your honours' considerations that we may have all free trade to those parts and markets where such commodities by our industry shall raise." This simple program of the setting of tobacco prices, leading (it was hoped) to economic diversification, and free trade in the Virginian import and export com-

[54] "The Assembly in Virginia to the Commissioners for the Affairs of Virginia, 6 March 1632" (from Sackville MSS), *V.M.H.B.* 65 (1957): 461–63. See this document for material and quotations in this and following paragraph.

merce remained for many years the basis of the Virginian planters' struggle against their economic dependence on the merchants.

To head off the planters and to consolidate their hegemony, the leading
Virginian merchants were also obliged to use political means. They relied
mainly on the Virginia Council, although, when necessary, they also
sought backing for their policies from the government in England. Despite the aforementioned express opposition of the planters in their assembly to trading licenses for merchants, the Virginia Council had supported
the Kent Island project of Claiborne, Cloberry, and Thomson from its
inception in 1631. Moreover, just a few months following the assembly's
March 1632 petition to the Dorset Commission in favor of free trade with
Virginia, the council went so far as to grant the sole right to market the
entire Virginian tobacco crop for the following three years to a syndicate
consisting of William Tucker, Maurice Thomson, and their merchant-
planter partner Thomas Stone. Tucker was, of course, the very merchant
the assembly had just singled out for his monopolistic practices. But in
light of the fact that Tucker was at this time a Virginia councilor and,
along with Maurice Thomson, a partner of the colony's secretary of state
William Claiborne in the Kent Island project, the council's action in approving the monopoly grant to these merchants is not difficult to understand. Gov. William Harvey seems to have agreed to this contract only as
a last resort, perhaps under duress. In the very letter in which he grudg-
ingly sanctioned the tobacco contract for the syndicate, he was led to ask
the privy council in England "to take into your grave consideration why
Mr. [Thomas] Stone, Maurice Thomson, and Capt. [William] Tucker
cannot afford to allow a penny per pound for tobacco when our intruding
neighbors the Dutch do allow us eighteen pence per pound in the same
commodity." Harvey lamely justified approving the contract by saying it
was better to give these men who already had "the greatest trade of all
others in that commodity" an official monopoly at a negotiated price than
to allow them to continue to use their powerful market position to extract
exorbitant profits from the planters.[55]

The councilors' support for the merchants was not confined to the granting of privileges to a favored few among themselves and their friends.
They consistently pursued a broader strategy designed to assure the merchants' control over trade. This policy had two interrelated aspects: (1) the
establishment of a monopoly company in London for trade with Virginia,
and (2) the exclusion of all foreign, especially Dutch, merchants from the
Virginian trade. This program was, of course, precisely the opposite of
that advocated by the planters in their assembly.

The story of the attempt to form a new Virginia Company during the

[55] PRO, C.O.1/6/54; *C.S.P. Col. 1574–1660*, p. 151.

1630s remains to be fully unraveled. Still, it is evident that by the time of the establishment of the Dorset Commission in 1631, something like a three-cornered alliance had emerged in support of such a company, and that leading members of the Virginia Council formed a key element within this alliance. The pro-company agitation had its center in a hazy grouping in London referred to as the "Virginia Company." This was led by the customs farmer Sir John Wolstenholme and apparently included a number of other men who had been prominent in the old Virginia Company. The Dorset Commission seems to have been packed with "Virginia Company" members, including, apparently, George Sandys, Sir John Danvers, Sir Robert Killegrew, Sir Thomas Roe, Sir Robert Heath, Sir John Zouch, Nicholas Ferrar, John Ferrar, Heneage Finch, Gabriel Barber, and Sir Dudley Digges, as well as Wolstenholme. All of these men had been associated with the old Virginia Company and appear to have retained an interest in Virginian affairs. It was likely Wolstenholme's influence that was most responsible for getting the Dorset Commission to recommend to the Crown the reestablishment of a Virginia Company in late 1631, but it is doubtful if he faced much opposition.[56]

The second main group pushing for a reestablished Virginia Company was composed of the leading London merchants trading with Virginia. In general, the new-merchant leadership obviously had much to gain from a revived corporation to control the Virginia trade, but during the period in which the Dorset Commission was considering reconstituting the old company, Maurice Thomson, William Tucker, Thomas Stone, and their friends were seeking to secure their own private monopoly of the tobacco commerce, and so had little reason to come out publicly on the issue. However, the moment they lost this very special privilege, they did not hesitate to make their opinion known.[57]

Finally, the Virginia Council itself desired a revived company. This is understandable in view of the fact that many of the councilors were closely identified with the great merchant-planters, while a number of them maintained intimate connections with members of the "Virginia Company" in London. When the Dorset Commission recommended that a new company be established, the Virginia Council immediately gave its support. Moreover, on 6 March 1632, the council took the additional step of making it clear to the Dorset Commission that it supported restricting the trade in Virginian tobacco to the English market. Not accidentally, this was the very moment that the Virginia Assembly was petitioning for free trade.[58]

[56] *C.S.P. Col. 1574–1660*, pp. 130, 136. For the "Virginia Company" grouping in England, see also J. M. Thornton, "The Thrusting Out of Governor Harvey," *V.M.H.B.* 76 (1968): 13–16.
[57] See below, p. 133 and fn. 59.
[58] "Virginia in 1631," *V.M.H.B.* 8 (1901): 36–40 and esp. 44–45; "The Governor and Council

The question of the regulation of the trade with Virginia was not immediately decided, but clearly it was too important an issue for the merchant-planter-councilor clique to leave unresolved. In August 1633, William Tucker wrote to the privy council in England asking that the Virginia Company be resurrected and demanding that the government take action to exclude the Dutch from Virginia's commerce. Tucker argued that the superior competitiveness of the Dutch would soon drive the English merchants from the trade and thus leave the planters even worse off than they already were—a theme that was to be echoed by the merchants throughout a whole epoch, to the planters' extreme exasperation. Tucker's request was referred to the customs farmers Sir John Wolstenholme and Abraham Dawes, who naturally shared his interest in confining the trade to England and who previously had worked in support of a revived company. After "meeting with divers of the chief planters of Virginia," these men recommended both the exclusion of the Dutch from the Virginian trade and the reestablishment of the Virginia Company. Their report was cosigned by the "chief planters" whom they seem to have consulted—none other than the new-merchant leaders William Tucker, Thomas Stone, and Tucker's brother-in-law William Felgate (as well as one Thomas Collins who has not been identified).[59]

In mid-1633, following a strong plea from ten Virginia planters, including several members of the assembly, the privy council in England agreed to revoke the Thomson-Stone-Tucker monopoly contract. This action obviously induced William Tucker and his friends to make their plea for reviving the Virginia Company, but a new corporation for the Virginia trade was never established. On the other hand, the privy council *did* order the Dutch excluded from the tobacco trade from that time on.[60]

---

in Virginia to the Lords Commissioners, 6 March 1632" (from Sackville MSS), *V.M.H.B.* 65 (1957): 465, 461–63. The connections of the Virginia councilors with members of the "Virginia Company" in London can be seen in many ways. William Claiborne and Samuel Matthews, perhaps the two most powerful men on the Virginia Council at this time, maintained a close working relationship with Sir John Wolstenholme, probably the leader of the "Virginia Company" and, of course, a strong backer of a revived company; "Abstracts of Virginia Land Patents," (*V.M.H.B.* 1 [1894]: 428–29; *C.S.P. Col. 1574–1660*, p. 172; PRO, C.O.1/6/87; "The Aspinwall Papers," *Mass. Hist. Soc. Coll.*, 4th ser., 9 [1871]: 131–53). Other Virginia councilors, including William Ferrar and John West, had powerful ties with members of the Dorset Commission. Perhaps the most telling evidence of the intimate relationship maintained by the Virginia Council and the "Virginia Company" is the close collaboration between them during the Virginia councilors' conflict with Governor Harvey. At the time of Harvey's expulsion in the later 1630s, the Virginia Council and the "Virginia Company" presented identical programs for Virginia's economic and political development in opposition to Harvey's plans (see Bodleian Library, Bankes MSS [catalogue] 8/2 and 8/3; PRO C.O.1/6/58. Cf. Thornton, "Thrusting Out of Governor Harvey").

[59] PRO, C.O.1/6/80, 81, 82; *C.S.P. Col. 1574–1660*, p. 171; *A.P.C. Col. 1613–1680*, p. 190.
[60] PRO, P.C.2/44/63; *A.P.C. Col. 1613–1680*, pp. 187–88; PRO, C.O.1/6/81; Beer, *British Colonial System*, pp. 233–34.

The leading Virginian merchants made the most of their opportunities, both temporary and permanent, to consolidate their position in the trade. Quite possibly the influx of large numbers of traders served to make relatively weaker the viselike grip of Maurice Thomson and his immediate partners on the Virginian trade during the remainder of the 1630s. But during this period, Thomson and his friends were nonetheless able to strengthen their group substantially by building business and family ties with most of the leading merchants who had more recently entered the field. Even as they saw their hold on the trade decline in relative terms, they succeeded in increasing their power both by greatly increasing their trade in absolute terms and vastly expanding their circle of connections.

In 1633, the Thomson-Stone-Tucker syndicate brought in 256,700 pounds of tobacco out of the total of 405,000 pounds imported from Virginia into England in that year.[61] In 1634, Thomas Stone imported about 46,000 pounds of tobacco, about 10 percent of the entire volume imported. In the same year, Maurice Thomson's youngest brother William entered the tobacco trade (perhaps in partnership with Maurice). Although this was apparently his first such venture, he also brought in about 46,000 pounds of tobacco.[62]

Shortly thereafter, William Thomson married the daughter of the Virginian merchant Samuel Warner [63] and thereby significantly strengthened the Thomson connection by bringing it into alliance with one of the leading new families of the colonial trades. Samuel Warner had gotten in trouble in the late 1620s for breaking illegally into the East India Company's privileged trade. Samuel and his brother John Warner together ran a druggist business in London, and it is very likely that they entered the American tobacco commerce as an outgrowth of their domestic shopkeeping. By the early 1640s, the Warners and the Thomson group were operating together in a wide range of activities in the Americas and beyond.[64]

Also in 1634, Maurice Thomson himself sent out 155,000 pounds of tobacco from Virginia. This was by far the largest amount shipped in that year, amounting to some 25 percent of the total, and to make the shipment Thomson sought the help of Robert South, William Willoughby, and Gregory Clement. South's career is obscure. Both Clement, who had gotten in trouble in the late 1620s for trading illegally as a factor in the East

---

[61] Totals compiled from the London Port Book for Imports, 1633, PRO, E.190/38/1.

[62] Totals compiled from the London Port Book for Imports, 1634, PRO, E.190/38/5.

[63] J. R. Woodhead, *The Rulers of London, 1660–1689* (London, 1965), p. 161.

[64] V. Pearl, *London and the Outbreak of the Puritan Revolution: City Government and National Politics, 1625–1643* (Oxford, 1961), pp. 325–27. For the Warners' colonial trade, see London Port Books for Imports for the years 1627–1640; PRO, H.C.A.24/92/37; PRO, H.C.A.24/93/97; and PRO, E.122/196/24. The Warners were sons of a Bucknell, Oxfordshire family (*Visitation of London, 1633–1635* 2: 325).

Indies, and Willoughby, a ship captain with strong ties to New England, were to become two of Thomson's more important collaborators, and key figures in the colonial trades in their own right.[65]

The voyage of Thomson, Clement, Willoughby, and South never reached its destination; Dunkirk privateers took their ship. By 1637, however, Thomson and Clement had won from the Crown the right to seek reprisal, and in that year, they sent out the first of a long series of privateering voyages that would extend well into the 1640s. In their initial privateering effort, Thomson and Clement took as partners Richard Bateson, William Pennoyer, and Edward Wood. These three merchants would continue to work with Thomson and his friends and bring them into contact with a significant number of new and important collaborators.[66]

Bateson was from an obscure Wiltshire family. But by 1640, he had established himself among the significant traders with America, importing in that year 15,000 pounds of Virginian tobacco. Well before then, Bateson had helped his career by establishing a partnership with Samuel Vassall, one of the greatest figures in the colonial trades during the pre–Civil War period.[67]

Samuel Vassall was the son of a Huguenot emigrant sea captain and merchant. He appears to have secured his future by marrying the daughter of Abraham Cartright, a wealthy London merchant. Like his father-in-law, Vassall entered the Levant Company and carried on an active trade with the Mediterranean through the 1620s. Vassall's original contact with the colonies may have come as a result of his Puritan convictions: he was a founder of the Massachusetts Bay Company. In any case, by 1628, Vassall had begun the series of ventures to Virginia and the West Indies that were to occupy him over the following two decades. Vassall put his brother-in-law, the sea captain Peter Andrews, directly in charge of most of these voyages, and the two of them worked closely with the Virginian merchant-planter George Menefie, who was the third member of their partnership.[68] Menefie, like such other great Virginian merchants as Maurice Thomson, William Tucker, and William Claiborne, had begun

---

[65] *C.S.P.D. 1636–1637*, pp. 350, 554; PRO, C.2/Ch.I/C.59/29; *C.S.P. Col. E.I. 1625–1629*, p. 488; *C.S.P. Col. E.I. 1630–1634*, pp. 148, 164–65. For Clement's career as a colonial merchant, see PRO, C.24/733/51. For Willoughby, see "The Willoughby Family of New England," *New Eng. Hist. Gen. Reg.*, 30 (1876): 69–70.

[66] *C.S.P.D. 1636–1637*, pp. 350, 554; PRO, C.2/Ch.I/C.59/29; PRO, H.C.A.24/108/62–65, 116. The third partner, Edward Wood, who worked with Bateson on other projects, is unfortunately unidentifiable.

[67] PRO, C.2/Ch.I/C.90/28, PRO, will of Richard Bateson, 1667 PCC Carr 79. See London Port Book for Imports, 1640, PRO, E.190/43/5, for Bateson's tobacco trade.

[68] Pearl, *London*, pp. 189–90; PRO, will of Peter Andrews, 1650 PCC Pembroke 152; *C.S.P. Col. 1574–1660*, p. 190 and index.

his career by emigrating to Virginia and setting himself up as a small merchant in the colony. His rise to prominence was likely the result of his attachment to Vassall and Andrews, with whom he became associated in 1628. By the mid-1630s, Menefie had done well enough to gain appointment to the Virginia Council where he took his place among the core members of the colony's merchant-planter-councilor clique. Nevertheless, before settling permanently in Virginia around 1640, Menefie, like others among the merchant-councilor group, moved back and forth between London and Virginia, serving as on-the-spot representative for Vassall's firm in Virginia and coordinating the planatation side of the operation.[69]

The most spectacular of Samuel Vassall's projects was his unsuccessful attempt in 1630 to plant a colony in what is now South Carolina. This venture was probably connected with the religio-political upheavals of the period. It was initiated by a group of Huguenot refugees who hoped to find a new home within a territory to the south of Virginia granted by the Crown in 1629 to Sir Robert Heath. The project's leaders commissioned Vassall and Andrews to transport passengers and supply the colony in its early stages. But the operation miscarried when the prospective colonists were mistakenly landed in Virginia. As a result, Vassall ended up paying £600 in damages to his contractors after a long suit.[70]

In his more prosaic trading ventures with Virginia and the West Indies, Vassall often worked in partnership with a number of leading colonial traders who were also working with the Thomson connection. Two of these, Richard Bateson and Edward Wood, were, as noted, Thomson's privateering partners.[71] A third, Richard Cranley, originally a Levant Company trader, was a prominent American sea captain who worked, during the early 1630s, in Virginia and the Caribbean in collaboration with Edward Thomson, the founder of the Nevis Colony,[72] and also with Nathan Wright, a Levant Company merchant who traded with New England and interloped in both the Greenland and Newfoundland trades be-

[69] For Menefie's low-status origins and subsequent success in Virginia, see Bailyn, "Politics and Social Structure," pp. 94–97. For Menefie's career, especially his long assQciation with Samuel Vassall and Vassall's brother-in-law Peter Andrews, see PRO, H.C.A.24/92/299 and PRO, C.2/Ch.I/C.90/28, and PRO, will of George Menefie, 1647 PCC Fines 31, in which Andrews is mentioned as a friend and overseer.

[70] For this venture, see "Virginia Gleanings in England," *V.M.H.B.* 15 (1908): 297–98; *C.S.P. Col. 1574–1660*, pp. 112, 113, 115, 120, 190, 194, 197–99, 207. Also, see PRO, will of Edward Kingswell, 1639 PCC Pile 34.

[71] PRO, C.2/Ch.1/C.90/28. For Bateson and Wood, see above, notes 66 and 67.

[72] PRO, S.P.105/149/255; PRO, H.C.A.24/91/22–23. For Edward Thomson, see above, pp. 128–29. By 1642, Cranley was working with still another outstanding new-merchant leader, Richard Hill, this time in the Newfoundland fish trade. BL, Add. MSS 5489, fols. 49ff. For Hill, who was to play a leading role in the sugar and slave trades that developed during the 1640s, see below, p. 165 and n. 178.

fore involving himself in Virginia during the later 1630s.[73] By 1640, Vassall was collaborating with Maurice Thomson himself in a voyage to Virginia and the West Indies. The third partner in this latter venture was William Felgate, the leading American merchant who was the brother-in-law of Thomson's brother-in-law and trading partner, William Tucker.[74]

William Pennoyer, the fifth and final partner of Thomson, Clement, Wood, and Bateson in their privateering voyage of 1637, would emerge in the subsequent period as perhaps Maurice Thomson's most important commercial collaborator. Pennoyer was the son of a Bristol glover and began his career as a shopkeeper in London. Disallowed because of his profession from trading legally with the Near East by the mere-merchant provision of the Levant Company charter, Pennoyer became "a great interloper" in the Levant trade. During the later 1630s, he pioneered the import and reexport of Virginian tobacco to the Levant, and found it convenient to enter the Levant Company in 1637, probably so that he could expand his activities in this line. In the Virginia-England-Levant tobacco reexport commerce, Pennoyer worked with his brother Samuel who served as factor and junior partner in the Levant and, above all, with Matthew Craddock, one of the greatest traders with the Americas of the period.[75]

Matthew Craddock's career was similar to that of Samuel Vassall, and different from those of the great majority of colonial merchants in several respects. Craddock was the son of a cleric of Hasguard, Pembroke. His grandfather had been a Merchant Adventurer and Stapler of Stafford and his cousin (his father's brother's son) was a leading citizen and sometime lord mayor of that borough. Another relative, William Craddock, was the Hamburg factor of Sir William Cockayne, one of London's greatest merchant princes, and it was probably through this connection that Matthew was apprenticed to Cockayne in 1616. Craddock appears to have begun his commercial career in the Eastland trade, and, by the later 1620s, like Vassall, he was a major figure in the Mediterranean trade as well. Also like Vassall, Craddock seems initially to have become involved in the Americas as a result of his Puritan proclivities. He was the first governor of the Massachusetts Bay Company, and during the later 1620s established a plantation on the Mystic River in Massachusetts. By the later 1630s, he was among the leading figures in the Virginian and West Indian

[73] For Wright, see Pearl, *London*, p. 331; PRO, P.C.2/41/101-2, *C.S.P. Col. 1574-1660*, pp. 120, 307. Wright imported, for example, some 11,300 pounds of Virginian tobacco in 1638 (London Port Book for Imports, 1638, PRO, E.190/41/5).

[74] *C.S.P. Col. 1574-1660*, p. 305; "Virginia Gleanings in England," *V.M.H.B.* 32 (1914): 267-68; PRO, will of William Tucker, proved 17 Feb. 1644. For Felgate, see above, p. 120 and note 17.

[75] Clothworkers Company, London, Apprentice Register, 1606-1641, 16 March 1621; PRO, S.P.105/149/253; PRO, C.2/Ch.I/A.13/69; PRO, H.C.A.24/95/203; PRO, H.C.A.24/101/246.

tobacco and provisioning trades and stood at the center of a vast complex of family and business connections that encompassed some of the key merchants in the colonial field.[76]

Matthew Craddock's aunt, Jane (his father's sister), had married Edward Mainwaring of another Staffordshire armigerous family; their son Randall Mainwaring was therefore Matthew Craddock's cousin. Like Matthew Craddock, Randall Mainwaring was a younger son who had moved to London. There his marriage to Elizabeth Hawes connected him with still another of the important merchant families in the new American trades.[77] From the mid-1630s, Mainwaring traded with the Americas in partnership with his brothers-in-law, Joseph and Nathaniel Hawes, and their brother-in-law, the sea captain George Payne. In 1640, Joseph Hawes imported into London more tobacco from Barbados than did any other merchant.[78] One of Joseph Hawes's apprentices, George Snelling, traded with the Americas in partnership with Maurice Thomson around 1640.[79] Randall Mainwaring's son-in-law and apprentice John Brett had become, by the 1640s, a leading trader with the West Indies and was also involved in New England.[80] Mainwaring's nephew (his sister Elizabeth's son), John Jolliffe, who was to become a high-ranking London merchant in the 1650s and 1660s, began his career in the 1630s as one of Matthew Craddock's factors in the American trades.[81] Mainwaring's niece (Jolliffe's sister Anne) seems to have married Joseph Parker, another active tobacco importer in the pre–Civil War years.[82] Upon Parker's death, Anne married John Dethick, who may have been involved commercially

---

[76] Pearl, *London*, pp. 185–87; Skinners Company, London, Apprentices and Freeman Book, 1601–1694, fol. 8v; *Visitation of Staffordshire, 1614*, William Salt Archaeological Society, Collections for a History of Staffordshire, pt. 2 (Stafford, 1884), 5: 100. See also the valuable biographical folder on Matthew Craddock at Skinners Hall, London.

[77] *Visitation of Staffordshire, 1614*, pp. 100, 207–8; *Visitation of London, 1633–1635* 1: 366, 2: 79.

[78] PRO,H.C.A.24/92/33; D. O. Shilton and R. Halworthy, eds., *High Court of Admiralty Examinations, 1637–1638* (London, 1932), p. xxviii and index; Stock, *Proceedings and Debates* 1: 181, 197–200, and index (under Joseph Hawes); PRO, S.P.16/49/66. Out of the 64,000 pounds of tobacco imported form Barbados in 1640, 60,000 pounds came in under the name of Joseph Hawes (London Port Book for Imports, 1640, PRO, E.190/43/5).

[79] *C.S.P. Col. 1574–1660*, p. 195; *A.P.C. Col. 1613–1680*, p. 305; Society of Genealogists, Boyd's Index: 39750; Drapers Company, London, Apprentice Register, 1626–1650, alphabetical index.

[80] *Visitation of London, 1633–1635* 2: 79; Grocers Company, London, Index of Freemen, 1345–1645. Brett, like Mainwaring, was a London grocer. Like Mainwaring and Craddock he was from a Staffordshire family. For Brett's trade in the 1640s, apparently an extension of his City shopkeeping business, see below, p. 165 and n. 181.

[81] Woodhead, *Rulers*, p. 99; *Mass. Hist. Soc. Coll.*, 4th ser., 6 (1863): 127.

[82] Woodhead, *Rulers*, p. 99; Society of Genealogists, Boyd's Index: 14841. Parker, for example, seems to have imported 8,500 pounds of Virginia tobacco in 1640 (London Port Book for Imports, 1640, PRO, E.190/43/5).

in the Americas before 1640, who later joined Maurice Thomson in East Indian interloping, and who became a partner of John Jolliffe in the Spanish trade.[83] Finally, through the marriage of Matthew Craddock's daughter Damaris to Thomas, the son of Thomas Andrews, the Craddock family became associated with still another new-merchant family that was active in the colonial trades and also very prominent in Puritan causes throughout the period. The father, Thomas Andrews, often in partnership with his sons Thomas, Nathaniel, and Jonathan, promoted the Plymouth Colony in the 1620s, backed the Massachusetts Bay Colony in the 1630s, and participated in West Indian trade and East Indian interloping in the 1640s.[84]

By the later 1630s, Matthew Craddock seems to have been working directly with Maurice Thomson in the colonial trades, although this is not certain. In 1637–1638 they appear to have jointly operated the ship *Rebecca* in the tobacco and provisioning trades, and to have worked together in collaboration with their common Virginian factor Thomas Stegg.[85] Stegg had emerged by this time as a leading merchant-planter-councilor in his own right, and in 1640 he was one of the first to supply the West Indies with horses from Virginia[86] in partnership with still another lead-

[83] Dethick appears to have been involved in Caribbean privateering under the auspices of the Providence Island Company, but this is not entirely clear (*Admiralty Examinations, 1637–1638*, pp. 287–88; PRO, H.C.A.13/54/24v–25). For Dethick's partnership with Jolliffe, see PRO,H.C.A.24/111/197. Dethick was from a minor armigerous family of Norfolk (*Visitation of London, 1633–1635* 1: 227; D. C. Coleman, *Sir John Banks* [Oxford, 1963], pp. 16–19). For Dethick's later career, see below, p. 175 and n. 221.

[84] The marriage took place in 1642. Thomas Andrews, Sr., was from Feltham, Middlesex. His marriage to a yeoman's daughter with a dowry of £60 is an indication of his original social status. From the 1630s, in cooperation with his son John (Jonathan), he ran a wholesale linen drapery in Fish Street Hill, London. See J. C. Whitebrook, "Sir Thomas Andrews, Lord Mayor and Regicide, and His Relatives," *Congregational Historical Society Transactions*, 2d ser. (1938–1939), 13: 151–53; Pearl, *London*, pp. 311–13; W. J. Harvey, ed., *List of the Principal Inhabitants of the City of London, 1640. From Returns Made by the Aldermen of the Several Wards* (London, 1886), p. 4. For Andrews's activities in New England, the West Indies, and East Indian interloping, see W. Bradford, *A History of Plymouth Plantation, 1620–1647*, ed. W. C. Ford, 2 vols. (Boston, 1912), 2: 6; F. R. Rose-Troup, *The Massachusetts Bay Company and Its Predecessors* (New York, 1930), app.; *New Eng. Hist. Gen. Reg.* 39 (1885): 179, 181; Barbados Record Office, Deeds (recopied) 2/658,3/922. (This reference was transcribed for me at the Barbados Record Office.) See also below, pp. 162, 175, 178, 179, 182.

[85] In February 1637, Craddock ordered his agent, John Jolliffe, to be certain to send the ship *Rebecca*, victualed for three months, to Thomas Stegg, Craddock's factor in Virginia (*Mass. Hist. Soc. Coll.*, 4th ser., 6 [1863]: 127). In the following February (1638), there is a reference to a debt of 25,000 pounds of tobacco due "Maurice Thomson and Thomas Deacon and the rest of the Company of merchants belonging to the good ship the *Rebecca*." The additional fact that Thomas Stegg was Thomson's Virginia factor, as well as Craddock's, throughout the late 1630s adds to the presumption that they were sometime partners (PRO,H.C.A.24/97/5).

[86] For Stegg's partnership with Jeremy Blackman in shipping horses from Virginia, see *C.S.P. Col. 1574–1660*, p. 308. In 1639, Stegg received a 1,000-acre land grant (Nugent, *Cavaliers and Pioneers*, p. 118). For Stegg as a Virginia councilor, see *C.S.P. Col. 1574–1660*, p.292.

ing partner of Thomson's, Jeremy Blackman.[87] In any case, Thomson and Craddock were certainly closely linked through their common partner William Pennoyer, who was a major collaborator of both.

In both 1638 and 1642, Maurice Thomson was listed as by far the leading importer of tobacco into London, an indication of his own continuing preeminence and that of his immediate circle.[88] But much more important is the fact that by this time there had emerged a significantly broader colonial merchant leadership than the one that had originally come together during the 1620s around Thomson and his friends. By virtue of the mass of overlapping family and business connections just described (and others that will be specified shortly), this group developed an impressive degree of coherence, which gave it the power to take ever more ambitious initiatives across the whole colonial economy, and beyond. Its strength within the Virginian economy was increasingly expressed not only in its dominance of the tobacco and provisioning trades, but in the capacity of some of its leading representatives to establish themselves as great Virginian landholders.

LAND AND PLANTATIONS

The rapid growth of tobacco production put a high premium on land. The planters cultivated tobacco on a purely extensive basis: they simply used up the land and moved on to a new area. As a result, they were obliged, more or less continually, to demand that the size of the colony be increased, and to seek special land grants from those in or near government. Naturally enough, the merchant-councilor clique was especially active on this score, pushing for a more rapid extension of the colony's borders and a more liberal policy on land grants. Here, however, by the mid-1630s, they had run up against the implacable opposition of Gov. William Harvey, who was pursuing a land policy diametrically opposed to their own.

Governor Harvey had, from the outset, adopted a conservative approach to the question of land grants and the expansion of the colony, most likely because he wanted to avoid costly military mobilizations and to minimize what could be catastrophic military conflicts. Harvey had thus sought, above all, to maintain peace with the Indians. But unless the Indians were destroyed, the planters could not expand the colony at the desired pace. Harvey also had been stingy about granting land to the plant-

[87] For Blackman, see below, pp. 146–47 and n. 106, as well as pp. 162, 165, 175.

[88] For 1638, see London Port Book for Imports, 1638, PRO, E.190/41/5. Thomson's tobacco imports from Virginia in this year totaled 50,000 pounds (in addition to some 63,000 pounds from St. Kitts and Barbados). For 1642, see PRO, E.122/230/9. This document lists the amounts of customs paid by all importers of tobacco in the last six months of 1642. I owe this reference to the kindness of Dr. A. M. Millard.

ers, probably because a liberal land-grant policy would have led inexorably to the need to extend the colony's borders. Finally, as the king's servant, Harvey had fully backed Charles I's grant of a mass of territory to the north of Virginia to Cecilius Calvert, second Lord Baltimore, a direct affront to the Virginian planters' expansionist ambitions.[89]

Harvey had also confronted the merchant-planter-councilors on the question of the colony's commercial policy. He had opposed resurrecting the Virginia Company; he had supported free trade; and he had backed the assembly's program of controlling tobacco production and diversifying. Indeed, for thus standing up for the generality of the planters and against the colony's special merchant interest, Harvey had won the planters' gratitude and their full backing.[90] The fact remains that Harvey's land policies went directly against the desires of all layers among the colonists, high and low, merchant-councilor and mere planter alike. His attempt to implement these policies therefore had the paradoxical effect of forcing into alliance the hitherto bitterly opposed merchant-planter and planter groups. Indeed, Harvey's land policies allowed the merchant-planter-councilor clique to mobilize the generality of the planters behind their struggle against the governor. This eventuated in Harvey's overthrow in 1635 and in the untrammeled authority of the merchant-planter-councilor group within the colony.

It was the Crown's grant of the Maryland Colony to Lord Baltimore on 20 June 1632 that set off the chain of events that issued in the councilors' climactic showdown with Governor Harvey. This grant not only aroused the combined opposition of merchant-councilors and mere planters over the general question of the colony's expansion; it also provoked a confrontation with that small but strategic group of merchant-councilor leaders which was committed to defending the Claiborne-Cloberry-Thomson provisioning and fur-trading settlement on Kent Island in the Chesapeake Bay.[91] Apparently fearing the worst and hoping to head off the expected patent, the Virginia Assembly had included in its petition to the Dorset Commission of 6 March 1632 a request that "the limits of our plantation both to the northward and to the southward may be preserved against all intrenching undertakers." Then, immediately upon hearing of the grant of the Maryland patent, the council remonstrated that the land given to Baltimore rightfully belonged to the Virginia Colony because it had been included in the original Virginia Company patent. But the Virginians

[89] For Harvey's attitude on these questions, see Bailyn, "Politics and Social Structure," pp. 96–97, and Thornton, "Thrusting Out of Governor Harvey," pp. 20–26.

[90] PRO, C.O. 1/6/54; Thornton, "Thrusting Out of Governor Harvey," p. 20; Bailyn, "Politics and Social Structure," p. 96.

[91] Andrews, *Colonial Period* 2: 278–82. See also Latané, *Maryland and Virginia*, pp. 8–10.

were unable to change the king's mind, and as a result, the scene of battle shifted across the Altantic.[92]

Baltimore's particular program of colonial development for Maryland only exacerbated the conflict with the Virginian leadership. The other major proprietary regime in the Americas, the Carlisle patent in the West Indies, provoked resistance in this period because the proprietor exacted arbitrary payments while taking no direct interest in the islands' development. In contrast, the Calverts incited opposition in Maryland for attempting to establish a too-powerful grip on the whole colonizing process. The Calverts' original settlement of the Maryland Colony was a full-scale attempt to re-create a semifeudal sociopolitical structure in the American wilderness. This experiment was doomed to failure. Nevertheless, during the early years of the colony's existence, the Calverts did succeed in establishing a set of governing institutions through which they were able to exert a substantial influence over Maryland's economy, as well as its social and political life.[93] This tightly controlled archaic system, which was clearly intended for the proprietors' particular profit, disregarded the concerns of the planters and thus made any accommodation with Virginia that much more difficult. In addition, the Maryland Colony challenged the very existence of the Kent Island project, which lay formally within the Baltimore patent and was immediately claimed in its entirety by the Calvert proprietors.

The Virginia Council gave its wholehearted backing to the Kent Island organizers, for the councilors had a strong interest not only in supporting Claiborne and his friends but also in eliminating the Maryland Colony. Indeed, the Calverts' claim to Kent Island had the effect of making Kent Island an issue of political principle for the Virginians. The settlement was, from the start, incorporated within the Virginia Colony, and it sent representatives to the Virginia House of Burgesses beginning in 1632. Nevertheless, Calvert refused to recognize Kent Island's separation from his own grant, insisted on his right to license and control all of Maryland commerce including that of the Kent Island organizers, and launched an all-out campaign to annex the island.[94]

The struggle to defend Kent Island and to oppose the Calvert patent set off the decisive battles between the Virginia Council and Governor Harvey. Harvey, as the king's agent, accepted from the first the king's grant to Lord Baltimore and pursued a conciliatory policy toward the Maryland settlers. When he finally refused to defend Kent Island, he pushed the

---

[92] Latané, *Maryland and Virginia*, p. 13; Andrews, *Colonial Period* 2: 279; "Governor and Council in Virginia to the Lords Commissioners," pp. 461–65.

[93] Andrews, *Colonial Period* 2: 281–85, 293–99.

[94] Hale, *Virginia Venturer*, pp. 156–59; Andrews, *Colonial Period* 2: 305ff.; Latané, *Maryland and Virginia*, pp. 8–31.

councilors over the brink. In the spring of 1635, they succeeded in expelling Harvey from the colony after a series of brief and semiviolent encounters.[95]

The roots of this conflict are thus perfectly clear. Governor Harvey's failure to back William Claiborne merely hardened the resolve of councilors already opposed to him because of both his commercial and his land policies. Yet two aspects need to be stressed because they have been generally overlooked: first, the strongly mercantile stamp given the anti-Harvey revolt by its merchant-planter-councilor leaders and, in particular, the big gains for the merchant interest that were the immediate outcome of the revolt; second, the alliance against Harvey of the usually mutually hostile merchant-planter and mere-planter interests around the central issue of land and the colony's expansion.[96]

The handful of councilors who were the chief architects of the revolt—including William Claiborne, William Tucker, George Menefie, John Utie, and Samuel Matthews—were not only merchants in their own right but aligned with powerful London interests. William Claiborne and William Tucker and their extensive mercantile involvements and commercial connections have already been discussed at some length. George Menefie has also been previously introduced as a Virginian merchant, planter, and councilor whose successful career may be attributed in large part to his partnership over two decades in the London-based firm of the great colonial merchant Samuel Vassall. Similarly, the councilor John Utie was closely associated with the London-Virginia merchant-planter Richard Bennett. Bennett was a nephew, partner, and representative in Virginia of Edward Bennett, a leading City merchant who founded the big, Puritan-led Isle of Wight Colony in 1622 and traded with Virginia throughout the period in collaboration with Richard and other relatives. Finally the councilor Samuel Matthews had followed a career that closely paralleled that of William Claiborne and William Tucker. Beginning as a small trader in Virginia, Matthews had become a councilor by 1624 and was in 1625 one of only five men in the entire colony who had twenty or more servants. Throughout the 1620s, Matthews, like Claiborne, was a leading developer of the Chesapeake fur and provisioning trades under the auspices of the council. By the end of the 1630s, he would associate himself with Claiborne, Maurice Thomson, and a number of other Londoners in

[95] Morton, *Colonial Virginia* 1: 135–43; Latané, *Maryland and Virginia*, pp. 19–20; T. J. Wertenbaker, *Virginia under the Stuarts* (Princeton, 1914), ch. 3.

[96] In 1638, George Donne, a Virginia ally of Harvey, accounted for the revolt against the governor, at least in part, in terms of the plantation's "wholly depending on the wills and counsels of men of trade." T. H. Breen, "George Donne's 'Virginia Reviewed': A 1638 Plan to Reform Colonial Society," *William and Mary Quarterly* 30 (1973): 460.

a large-scale, though ultimately abortive, land and trading project to the north of Virginia.[97]

These merchant-councilors had sought, as emphasized, to have the Dutch excluded from the Virginian trade and also had worked for the incorporation of a new overseas trading company for Virginia. Moreover, almost all of them had maintained close ties throughout the 1630s with that ill-defined group in London that persisted in calling itself the "Virginia Company" and that continued to demand the reestablishment of a London corporation for the Virginian trade. The "Virginia Company" had backed the council against the Calverts from the very start, and its most influential member, Sir John Wolstenholme, actually had joined William Claiborne in 1633 in a petition to confirm the Kent Island Company's privileges. When the councilors' conflict with Harvey was brought to the attention of the royal government in England in 1635, the "Virginia Company" not only petitioned the privy council on their behalf, but did so on the basis of precisely the same set of grievances and demands as the councilors had presented. Governor Harvey, for his part, had no doubt that the London "Virginia Company," and in particular Sir John Wolstenholme, had opposed him all along, and he explicitly attributed the councilors' revolt, at least in part, to the continuing drive for a reestablished company for the Virginian trade by the council and the "Company."[98]

Despite the mercantile character of the council leadership of the revolt—and the fact that it had major commercial aims—there can be little doubt that the revolt was fundamentally about land questions. Immediately following the initial confrontation with Harvey that began the revolt, the councilors made a broad appeal to the planters, who seem to have responded with illegal assemblies and mass petitions against the governor. What won the councilors the support of the generality of the planters was the prominent place the councilors gave to grievances against Governor Harvey's land policies: Harvey's support of the Maryland Colony; Harvey's peaceful policy toward the Indians, which seemed to compromise Virginia's potential for growth; and Harvey's unwillingness to grant the planters new lands or legal security for those they already held.

The expulsion of Harvey brought the councilors to unopposed power

<hr />

[97] On Utie, see Morton, *Colonial Virginia* 1: 144; D. R. Ross, "The Bennett Family in the Early Seventeenth Century" (unpublished manuscript), pp. 3, 4, 12, 18. I wish to thank Mr. Ross for allowing me to consult his manuscript in advance of publication. On Matthews, see *Va. Co. Recs.* 3: 535–36, 4: 6–8; McIlwaine, *Minutes of Council and General Court of Colonial Virginia*, pp. 136, 198, 479; Hale, *Virginia Venturer*, p. 236; "Notes and Queries," *V.M.H.B.* 33 (1926): 310–11; Morgan, "First American Boom," pp. 188–89. See also below, pp. 157–58.

[98] PRO, C.O. 1/6/87; Bodleian Library, Bankes MSS (catalogue) 8/3, 19, and 13/27; Thornton, "Thrusting Out of Governor Harvey," pp. 15, 22.

within the colony, and they immediately began to implement their program. In the years leading up to his ouster, perhaps on the advice of the Crown, Harvey had largely suspended the established policy of granting land in exchange for the transportation of persons to the colony. This headright policy had originated under the old Virginia Company, but continued in effect when Virginia became a royal colony. It offered the merchants in particular an easy entrée into the colony's plantation economy and naturally proved extremely favorable to the economic interests of the leading stratum of merchant-planters. Nevertheless, even after the headright policy had been explicitly confirmed from London by the Laud Commission for Virginia in July 1634, Harvey had limited himself to granting just nine patents in the period up to his departure the following May.[99]

With Harvey's departure, the council drastically reversed this policy. During the brief period of Gov. John West's interim rule, while Harvey was in England, it issued 377 headright patents alone, in addition to numerous patents of other types.[100] The councilors themselves, involved as they were in overseas business, were among the chief beneficiaries of this policy, as were some of the biggest merchants. Several of the largest headright grants of the period went to councilors John Utie (1,250 acres), George Menefie (1,200 acres), Capt. Francis Eppes (1,700 acres), and William Pierce (2,000 acres) on the basis of their transporting numerous servants and other persons to Virginia. Others went to Thomas Stone's nephews and planter-partners, William and Andrew Stone (1,800 acres), and the major tobacco merchants John Sadler and Richard Quiney (1,250 acres), Richard Bennett (2,350 acres), and Cornelius Lloyd (850 acres).[101]

Similarly, as early as 1632 the councilors had complained to the Crown of the great waste of land resources resulting from the fact that the "general great hundreds lie unplanted and unsupplied," and asked for permission to regrant them to others in the colony.[102] These "hundreds" were the huge tracts of land that the old Virginia Company had granted to various individuals and syndicates as an incentive to large-scale investment and development. The plantations on these tracts were never very successful and most of them had, to all intents and purposes, collapsed in the period leading up to the company's dissolution. But the land remained legally in the hands of the original patentees. Clearly, the hundreds were great plums, and in early 1637 the council members saw to it that they were finally placed in the hands of their leading merchant friends. On 9 Feb-

[99] Thornton, "Thrusting Out of Governor Harvey," pp. 24–25.
[100] Ibid.
[101] Nugent, *Cavaliers and Pioneers*, pp. 211ff.
[102] "Governor and Council in Virginia to the Lords Commissioners," p. 465.

ruary 1637, the council granted the famous "Berkeley Hundred" to a syndicate consisting of nine London colonial merchants: Maurice Thomson, William Tucker, George Thomson, James Stone, Jeremy Blackman, William Harris, Thomas Deacon, Cornelius Lloyd, and James Dobson. This eight-thousand–acre tract was the largest patent granted in the entire pre-Restoration period. One month later, on 16 March 1637, the "Martin's Brandon" hundred went to a similar syndicate consisting of three leading London merchants, Richard Quiney, John Sadler, and Simon Turgis.[103]

Berkeley Hundred had been the scene of one of the more ambitious private plantation experiments carried out under the Virginia Company.[104] It owners, led by John Smyth of Nibley and including Sir William Throckmorton, Richard Berkeley, and George Thorpe, had spent around £2,000 on voyages of settlement and supply between 1619 and 1621. But just at the point when their little colony was beginning to establish itself, the Indian massacre of 1622 almost completely wiped it out. In the ensuing years, Smyth, now on his own, made several attempts to revive the plantation, and as late as 1632 he sent one Thomas Combes[105] to investigate the possibility of starting anew. Combes actually recommended that Smyth continue the enterprise under new leadership, but by this time any major economic undertaking in Virginia required the blessing of the colony's official elite. Smyth could no longer command the influence he had once wielded in Virginian governing circles and, as a result, "he could not even hold onto his cattle against the council's friends." In this case, apparently, the council's friends were none other than William Tucker, Maurice Thomson, and their associates, who bought out Smyth's rights—just how is uncertain.

The nine-man syndicate that took over the Berkeley Hundred was composed entirely of merchants who were already involved in Virginian trade and plantations. William Tucker, Maurice Thomson, and Maurice's brother George Thomson are familiar enough. James Stone has not been identified, but was very probably a relative of their partner Thomas Stone. Jeremy Blackman was a leading colonial sea captain, active in the passenger transportation business, as well as in a wide variety of commercial ventures. He was a substantial trader in Virginian tobacco, importing, for example, some twelve thousand pounds in 1634. Blackman had become connected with Maurice and George Thomson at least as early as the Kent

[103] Nugent, *Cavaliers and Pioneers*, pp. 53, 55.

[104] This paragraph is based primarily on C. Dowdey, *The Great Plantation: A Profile of Berkeley Hundred and Plantations, Virginia, from Jamestown to Appomattox* (New York, 1957), pp. 1–50. See also Craven, *Southern Colonies*, pp. 161–62.

[105] The "Thomas Combes" who was Maurice Thomson's West Indies partner in this period? See above, pp. 126–28.

Island project, for which he carried out certain shipping services, and he was to remain one of their most important partners for the rest of his life. By the end of the 1630s Blackman was among the first to begin transporting horses from the colony to the West Indies; here he worked with the Virginian merchant-planter-councilor Thomas Stegg, who happened also at this point to be Maurice Thomson's Virginian factor.[106]

William Harris and Thomas Deacon, two others in the syndicate that purchased Berkeley Hundred, were partners in a London cheesemongering business, and it seems to have been the potential profits from colonial provisioning that first attracted them to the Virginian tobacco trade, in which they were active starting in 1631 at the latest.[107] Their deepening involvement in plantations per se seems to have led them to take up temporary residence in the colony.[108] But during the later 1630s they were members of several, perhaps connected, London-based Virginian trading operations—in 1637 and 1638 with Maurice Thomson and William Tucker[109] and in 1639 with William and Thomas Allen, two other leading tobacco merchants of the pre–Civil War era.[110] The Allens were a father-son partnership and seem to have traded from time to time in association with still another important Virginian trading-planting combine, the brothers-in-law Richard Quiney and John Sadler.[111] Quiney and Sadler were members of the Grocers Company and partners in a grocers business;[112] as no evidence of their participation in other branches of overseas trade has been found, it is reasonable to suppose that their entry into the American commerce was an outgrowth of their previous domestic trading interests. It was Quiney and Sadler, along with their partner Simon Tur-

[106] *New Eng. Hist. Gen. Reg.* 4 (1850): 261, 27 (1873): 194; *C.S.P. Col. 1574–1660,* pp. 176, 308; *A.P.C. Col. 1613–1680,* p. 277; "Cloberry Transcripts," *Md. Hist. Mag.* 27 (1932): 17. For Blackman's 1634 tobacco trade, see London Port Book for Imports, PRO, E. 190/38/5. For Stegg as Thomson's Virginia factor and for other aspects of his career, see above notes, 85 and 86.

[107] *C.S.P.D. 1639–1640,* p. 563; New York Public Library, Smyth of Nibley Papers, no. 40; Harvey, *List of Principal Inhabitants of London, 1640,* p. 2. Deacon was the son of a Kelston, Somerset, yeoman family (*Visitation of London, 1633–1635* 1: 222; Clothworkers Company, London, Apprentice Register, 1606–1641, 19 July 1609).

[108] "Abstracts of Virginia Land Patents," *V.M.H.B.* 6 (1899): 91. See also land grants to a "William Harris, planter," in Nugent, *Cavaliers and Pioneers,* p. 12.

[109] Ames, *Records of Accomack,* p. 105; PRO, H.C.A.24/94/155.

[110] *A.P.C. Col. 1613–1680,* p. 259. In 1640, for example, 16,500 pounds of tobacco were imported under William Allen's name (London Port Book for Imports, 1640, PRO, E.190/43/5). William Allen was a younger son of an armigerous Essex family (*Visitation of London, 1633–1635* 1: 10; *Visitation of Essex, 1612,* Harleian Society Publications 13 [London, 1878], pp. 133–34).

[111] *C.S.P. Col. 1574–1660,* p. 321. In 1640, for example, 23,000 pounds of Virginian tobacco were brought in under Quiney's name (London Port Book for Imports, 1640, PRO, E.190/43/5). Quiney was the younger son of a Stratford-upon-Avon family (*Visitation of London, 1633–1635* 2: 184; PRO, will of Richard Quiney, 1656/7 PCC Ruthen 6).

[112] Grocers Company, London, Index of Freemen, 1345–1645 (alphabetical).

gis, who received the 4,500-acre Martin's Brandon grant from the Virginia Council. Turgis, it will be recalled, was one of the organizers of the Kent Island project.

It is unclear whether these specific groups of Londoners made these great acquisitions of land at this particular time in order to involve themselves more deeply in plantation production, or merely for speculative purposes. What is certain is that land was an excellent investment, and that the position of these merchants so near to the sources of political power left them particularly well placed to profit. The Virginia Council remained throughout this period committed to expanding the colony and continued to harbor a deep antagonism to the Baltimore Colony. Despite the privy council's confirmation of Calvert's patent in April 1638,[113] the potential for conflict remained only just below the surface.[114]

The Puritan Connection

The new merchants' deepening involvement in all aspects of the Atlantic tobacco economy led them to harden the ties that bound them to one another. The emergence of a veritable maze of interlocking business and family connections among the leading colonial traders is, as emphasized, one of the salient features of pre–Civil War colonial development. In part, of course, the merchants' growing solidarity emerged naturally. Common economic interests in similar projects often led directly to further collaboration. Business ties, once established, were reinforced through marital alliances, just as family ties often served as the original basis for business partnerships. However, at least from the later 1620s, there was an additional, extra-commercial factor at work behind the creation of family and business alliances among the new-merchant leaders. This was the growing involvement of many of the leading tobacco and provisioning merchants in the Puritan colonizing projects.

As is well known, the establishment of colonies in Massachusetts Bay and Providence Island, as well as the transformation of the already existing settlement in Bermuda, were closely linked to the parliamentary crisis of the late 1620s. It was the climactic parliamentary confrontations with the Crown in 1628–1629 over the issues of unparliamentary taxation, forced loans, arbitrary imprisonment, and, above all, Arminianism and the persecution of Puritans that induced the group of leading parliamentary oppositionists around the earl of Warwick, Lord Saye and Sele, and Sir Nathaniel Rich to evolve their colonizing schemes. In 1628, the earl

---

[113] *C.S.P. Col. 1574–1660*, pp. 267–68.
[114] See below, pp. 167–68.

of Warwick took over the governorship of the Bermuda Company with the purpose of transforming it into a Puritan project, and other leading parliamentary oppositionists soon entered this corporation to support him. In 1629, many of the same people formed the Providence Island Company as their own exclusive colonizing venture. Meanwhile in 1629–1630, the earl of Warwick, Sir Nathaniel Rich, and Lord Saye and Sele, as well as other Puritan magnates like the earl of Lincoln, played a critical role in patronizing the nascent Massachusetts Bay Company. They made sure that the government approved its charter, and they protected the company's transfer to Massachusetts. From the time of the dissolution of Parliament in 1629, these three colonies formed a crucial element within an ongoing Puritan opposition network, serving as ports of exile and organizing centers for continuing opposition.[115]

It was both as centers of colonial commercial development and as outposts of religio-political resistance that the Puritan colonies came to attract some of the most important of the new merchants and merchants-to-be. In a few cases, leading new merchants entered the field of colonial commercial enterprise through their support of the Puritan colonizing efforts. On the other hand, some of the best-established traders with the Americas became increasingly committed to Puritan religio-political activities through their commercial activities in the Puritan colonies. Either way, the effect tended to be the same. The linkup between the colonial merchants' commercial enterprises and the Puritan undertakings led to the creation and reinforcement of critical interconnections among the new men. Perhaps most important, it also brought growing ties between the American merchant leadership and the great Puritan aristocrats who ran the Bermuda and Providence Island companies, as well as the lesser gentry who governed the New England colonies. It will become necessary to consider, in some detail, the political and religious implications of these relationships in order to understand the ideological formation of the new-merchant leadership and its subsequent political activities.[116] But the section that follows will confine itself to the structure of connections and economic interests that emerged by way of the new merchants' involvement in Puritan colonial efforts.

THE MASSACHUSETTS BAY COMPANY

The Massachusetts Bay Company was founded in 1627 by a coalition of former participants in the Dorchester Company, several members of the East Anglian Puritan gentry, and London citizens with serious commer-

---

[115] For the preceding progression see Newton, *Colonising Activities*.

[116] See below, ch. 6, pp. 275–81.

cial as well as religious intentions. However, the political crisis of the later 1620s and the sudden determination of large numbers of Puritans to leave England forced the company to concentrate almost totally on the foundation of a haven for victims of religio-political persecution. In late 1629, the gentry-led group of emigrants under the guidance of such men as John Winthrop, Isaac Johnson, and Thomas Dudley was allowed to take over the government of the company and to move with the charter to Massachusetts the following spring. As a result of the transfer, opportunities for participation by London merchants in any aspect of Massachusetts economic development were kept to a minimum, and relatively few London merchants were active. Still, among those who do appear prominently, there were some central figures in the new-merchant leadership.[117]

A contingent of London citizens dominated the Massachusetts Bay Company at its inception, but they progressively lost ground as the emigrating gentry took over. These Londoners came almost entirely from outside the ranks of the overseas company merchants.[118] Few were overseas traders of any kind, and most were domestic traders of various sorts, especially London retailers. Among the Massachusetts Bay Company's total membership of around one hundred, there were just four who were either Levant Company members or East India Company officers—Francis Flyer, Matthew Craddock, Samuel Vassall, and Nathan Wright. And the whole approach to commerce of at least the latter three of these four radically distinguished them from the typical members of the company merchant establishment. I have already discussed the careers of Vassall and Craddock, and introduced Wright as well. In the later 1620s, Vassall was starting a long career in trading and planting in Virginia and the West Indies in partnership with his brother-in-law Peter Andrews, the ship captain, and the Virginian merchant-planter-councilor George Menefie. In 1630, perhaps in connection with the other Puritan colonizing ventures, Vassall took charge of an abortive attempt by a group of Huguenot families to start a colony in the region to the south of Virginia. Craddock, who was the first governor of the Massachusetts Bay Company and founder of a large-scale plantation on the Mystic River, was also, in the later 1620s, in the process of becoming a great tobacco and provisions trader with the Americas. By the end of the 1630s, Craddock stood at the center of one of the most powerful family-business networks in the American trades. Wright was a Levant Company merchant who would be jailed for interloping in the Greenland Company's privileges and who would get in

---

[117] See Andrews, *Colonial Period*, vol. 1, chs. 17 and 18; B. Bailyn, *The New England Merchants in the Seventeenth Century* (Cambridge, Mass., 1955), pp. 17–20.

[118] The following analysis is based on the biographical accounts of the Massachusetts Bay Company adventurers given in Rose-Troup, *Massachusetts Bay Company*, ch. 16, in relation to lists and accounts of various sections of the London merchant community previously presented in this work.

trouble with the Newfoundland Company for his activities in partnership with the American merchant Richard Cranley (who was also a partner of Samuel Vassall's). By the later 1630s, Wright had emerged as an active tobacco trader, and he later became involved in a variety of ventures with Maurice Thomson.[119]

The new-merchant leaders Craddock, Vassall, and Wright not only played important roles in establishing the Massachusetts Bay Company, but also were among the handful of London merchants who remained actively involved with the company after it moved to the colony. Craddock, Vassall, and Wright were among the original associates named in the charter; Vassall and Wright served on the eighteen-man board of directors; Craddock was the company's first governor and its chief leader until the decision to move to America.[120]

When the company was transferred to Massachusetts most of the investors who remained in London were simply squeezed out of the operation. The company placed practically the whole of the colony's trade in the hands of an independent subcompany of undertakers, composed of six merchants (including the treasurer) who were to remain in London and five emigrating colonists. The undertakers took over all the assets and debts of the company, agreed to bear all future commercial charges, and promised to pay back the company's investors their principal within seven years. In exchange, they received the sole right to transport goods and emigrants, the privilege of establishing a magazine for provisioning the settlers at fixed prices, the monopoly of the salt manufacture of the colony, and 50 percent of the beaver trade. Craddock and Wright were among the five undertakers who remained in London. Their subcompany seems to have played a significant part in the colony's trade throughout the 1630s, although the precise scope of its business is unclear.[121]

Since New England never did develop the kind of staple commodity that supported the southern and West Indian colonies, its commercial potential during the 1630s was never very large even for those men who had access to its trade. Furs were its only really important export and, for a while at least, a London-based subpartnership led by the new governor's son John Winthrop, Jr., the London lawyer Emanuel Downing, and the City merchant Francis Kirby carried out a series of fur-trading expeditions under the auspices of the company of undertakers.[122] By and large, however, London merchants were excluded from the fur trade, which

[119] For Craddock, Vassall, and Wright, see above.

[120] N. B. Shurtleff, ed., *Records of the Governor and Company of the Massachusetts Bay in New England*, 5 vols. (New York, 1853), 1: 4, 6, 11.

[121] Bailyn, *New England Merchants*, pp. 19, 26 n. 35; Andrews, *Colonial Period* 1: 398; Rose-Troup, *Massachusetts Bay Company*, chs. 10 and 11.

[122] Bailyn, *New England Merchants*, pp. 26–27, esp. 27 nn. 38–39.

soon fell almost entirely into the hands of politically well-placed merchants residing in the colony, just as it had in Virginia. Like most of the traders with Virginia and the West Indies, these men had only rarely begun their careers as overseas merchants. Almost always originating outside the City, they often entered the fur business on the basis of capital acquired through the sale of property in England and especially by virtue of their close connections with the new colonial government.[123]

On the other hand, London-based traders did largely retain control of the passenger transportation and provisioning trades for New England.[124] In these lines of commerce, the company of undertakers played an important role at the start, but during the later 1630s a significant number of other London traders also entered this business. Needless to say, there is no evidence that merchants belonging to the London chartered trading companies participated in this line.[125] Small London tradesmen who extended into the transatlantic field essentially the same line of business they were pursuing in London dominated this commerce as they did the other American trades. In so doing, they often worked in partnership with relatives who had emigrated to New England and set up shop there.

A small but significant nucleus of new colonial leaders took advantage of the opportunities in New England provisioning and passenger transportation. These naturally included most of that handful of new men who originally invested in the company, as well as Maurice Thomson and several of his other trading partners. Matthew Craddock was not only active in the fur trade, but operated a trading and shipbuilding business in Massachusetts on the Mystic River.[126] Samuel Vassall maintained a trading partnership with his brother William, who was a resident merchant and sometime magistrate of the Massachusetts Bay Colony during the 1630s and 1640s.[127] Thomson was apparently in touch with the aforementioned Winthrop-Downing-Kirby fur-trading syndicate, and Kirby refers to him as "cousin."[128] Thomson also worked in this period in association with a number of England's leading exporters to Massachusetts (for example, Joshua Foote, a London ironmonger), as well as with prominent New England businessmen (like Nicholas Trerice, a Massachusetts sea cap-

[123] Ibid., pp. 30–32.

[124] For this paragraph, see Ibid., pp. 34–39.

[125] This statement is based on the extensive, if incomplete, listings of traders with New England in *Notebook Kept by Thomas Lechford, Esq., Lawyer in Boston, Massachusetts Bay, from June 27, 1638, to July 29, 1641*, American Antiquarian Society Transactions and Collections 7 (Worcester, Mass., 1885); *Aspinwall Notarial Records, 1644–1651*, Boston Record Commissioners Report 32 (Boston, 1903).

[126] Bailyn, *New England Merchants*, p. 285; Andrews, *Colonial Period* 1: 363–69.

[127] Pearl, *London*, pp. 190, 191 n. 128; Bailyn, *New England Merchants*, pp. 36, 38, 88, 107.

[128] *The Winthrop Papers, 1498–1649*, 5 vols. (Boston, 1929–1947), 3: 55–56.

tain).[129] In this latter trade, Thomson may have collaborated with his brother Robert Thomson, who emigrated to Boston in the early 1630s.[130] Toward the end of the 1630s, Thomson's business connection with Massachusetts Bay was considerably strengthened when he, along with his colonial trading partner William Pennoyer, succeeded in obtaining a patent from the colony's general court to set up a fishery at Cape Ann. Pennoyer, it will be remembered, was at this time Matthew Craddock's partner in the Virginian and West Indian tobacco trade, as well as a key associate of Thomson's in a series of Caribbean privateering ventures.[131]

It is unlikely that Massachusetts was more than a marginal area of business for most of these new merchants, with the possible exception of Craddock. Their rather strong interest was based largely on a fundamental sympathy with the colony's goals and a close relationship with some sections of the colony's leadership. Matthew Craddock was in close touch with the great Puritan aristocrats who backed the Massachusetts Bay Company during the period of negotiations for its charter at the end of the 1620s, as well as afterward.[132] For the most part, however, the major connections forged by the new-merchant leaders through their participation in the trade with Massachusetts were with those gentry and trading elements of lower status who actually ruled in New England, as well as with other men like themselves from the London community of shopkeepers, ship captains, and small traders. The relevance of these relationships for English affairs would become evident, as will be seen, from the outbreak of political and religious conflict at the end of the 1630s.[133]

THE BERMUDA COMPANY

The Bermuda Company originally had been established as an offshoot of the Virginia Company by a number of the Virginia Company's most active members, and the early history of the two corporations had overlapped a great deal. The same three-way factional struggle that occurred in the

[129] See, for example, Thomson's provisioning trade in 1638 in partnership with Foote and Trerice (Trevise) (*C.S.P. Col. 1574–1660*, p. 275). Foote carried on his London ironmongering trade and large-scale New England commerce in partnership with his nephew, the Boston resident Joshua Hewes (Bailyn, *New England Merchants*, p. 35; E. Putnam, ed., *Lt. Joshua Hewes* [New York, 1913], pp. 15, 22, 55–56). For Trerice, an extremely active New England sea captain and trader, see *Aspinwall Notarial Records*, index.

[130] H. F. Waters, *Genealogical Gleanings in England*, 2 vols. (Boston, 1901), 1: 66.

[131] Shurtleff, *Records of the Governor* 1: 256; W. Kellaway, *The New England Company, 1649–1776* (London, 1961), pp. 58–59; J. Winthrop, *The History of New England*, ed. J. Savage, 2 vols. (Boston, 1825–1826), 1: 307.

[132] *Winthrop Papers* 3: 377–78, 4: 207–8; Andrews, *Colonial Period* 1: 367.

[133] For more on the colonial merchants' relations with New England, political and religious as well as commercial, see below, ch. 6.

Virginia Company took place in the Bermuda Company and, as in the Virginia Company, the Smythe-Warwick alliance ultimately prevailed over the Sandys faction. However, the Bermuda Company was not dissolved, and Sir Thomas Smythe ascended to the governorship in 1623 and was succeeded by his son-in-law, Alderman Robert Johnson.[134] Nevertheless, the victory of Smythe's merchant party could not overcome the City establishment merchants' basic aversion to colonial commerce, for it could in no way dissolve the barriers to their participation. The Bermuda Company's commercial privileges had little practical significance for the Bermudian trade, since tobacco, Bermuda's main commodity, was imported freely, without company regulation, from Virginia and the West Indies. Moreover, in Bermuda, as elsewhere, in order to market tobacco on a large scale it was often necessary to become involved in plantations—and this was something London's leading company merchants were unwilling to do. As a result, there is little sign of the participation of City company merchants in this trade after the middle 1620s.[135]

On the other hand, the Riches, led by the earl of Warwick, were quite prepared for plantation investment, and they appear to have remained major plantation owners and merchants in Bermuda throughout the pre–Civil War period. The Riches' interest in Bermuda was, of course, greatly enhanced as a result of the difficult straits in which the parliamentary oppositionists found themselves beginning in the later 1620s. The earl of Warwick took over the governorship of the company in 1628, and during the next several years numbers of his friends from the parliamentary opposition and the Providence Island project joined the company. Under the influence of Warwick and his associates, Bermuda, like Massachusetts and Providence Island, was made to function as a haven for Puritan refugees and conspirators.[136]

While assuming during the 1630s some of the aspects of a godly com-

[134] See W. F. Craven, *An Introduction to the History of Bermuda* (repr. from *William and Mary Quarterly* for 1937–1938 [Williamsburg, n.d.], ch. 7); H. G. Wilkinson, *The Adventurers of Bermuda*, 2d ed. (London, 1958), p. 398.

[135] For example, there were three Levant–East India merchants—Humphrey Browne, Robert Offley, and Humphrey Slaney—who imported Bermudian tobacco in 1626. They brought in 2,700 pounds out of a total of 70,000 pounds imported by seventy-five merchants (London Port Book for Imports, 1626, PRO, E.190/31/3). There were four Levant–East India merchants active in 1627–1628—Christopher Clitherow, Robert Johnson, Richard Middleton, and William Williams. Together, they brought in about 5,000 pounds of tobacco out of the total of some 140,000 pounds brought in by about 125 different Bermuda-trade merchants (London Port Book for Tobacco Imports, 1627–1628, PRO, E.190/32/8, which is abstracted and printed in N. J. Williams, "England's Tobacco Trade in the Reign of Charles I," *V.M.H.B.* 65 [1957]: 421–49).

[136] Wilkinson, *Bermuda*, pp. 173, 216, 398; T. K. Rabb, *Enterprise and Empire* (Cambridge, Mass., 1967), app.; G. L. Kittredge, "George Stirk, Minister," *Colonial Society of Massachusetts Transactions* 13 (1912): 47–49; J. H. Lefroy, *Memorials of the Bermudas*, 2 vols. (Bermuda, 1877–1879), 1: 590. For the Puritan experiment on Bermuda in this period, see below, ch. 6.

munity, Bermuda, in contrast with both Providence Island and Massachusetts, also successfully produced a staple export, that is, tobacco. As a result, the Bermuda Company attracted to itself, as Massachusetts and Providence Island did not, large numbers of overseas traders who took over most of the colony's commercial functions. Like the other English tobacco merchants throughout the Americas, these men were almost always originally smaller traders from outside the ranks of the City's company merchants. Not unexpectedly, they included a number of men at the core of the new-merchant leadership who were thus brought together in still another context. Prominent among them were Matthew Craddock and Maurice Thomson, as well as such leading partners of Thomson's as Elias Roberts, Thomas Stone, Richard Bateson, and Samuel Warner. In two of the three years in which Thomas Stone's name was listed in the port books as a trader in Bermudian tobacco, 1627–1628 and 1634, he was Maurice Thomson's partner in the tobacco trade with St. Kitts and Virginia. It is probable, therefore, that the port book entries under his name stand for a Stone-Thomson partnership. In both of these years Stone's shipments were the largest ones recorded (17,633 pounds in 1627–1628, 14,040 pounds in 1634); and, in fact, they are the two largest tobacco shipments recorded for Bermuda for any of the years between 1625 and 1640 for which there are port books.[137]

Unfortunately, it is not possible to follow directly the interaction between merchants and aristocratic elements within the Bermuda Company during the pre–Civil War period. But there can be little doubt that in jointly operating the company the two groups forged connections that influenced their subsequent collaboration, not only commercial but also political. It is probable that the Virginian tobacco merchant Thomas Allen was the person of that name who held the post of Bermuda Company treasurer around 1640. Moreover, in 1641, the new merchant Owen Rowe was appointed to the company's deputy governorship to serve alongside the earl of Warwick, who remained the governor.[138] Rowe, the son of a yeoman from Bickley, Chester—and also, apparently, a relative of Susanna Rowe, the earl of Warwick's second wife—originally had been apprenticed to the Haberdashers Company and set himself up as a silk mercer in the City. During the 1630s, he became active commercially both in New England (where he planned to settle) and in Virginia. At the time he became deputy governor of the Bermuda Company, Rowe was emerging as one of the leading figures in both the colonizing leadership and the City

[137] London Port Books for Tobacco Imports, 1627–1628 (see above, note 135) and London Port Book for Imports, 1634, PRO, E.190/38/5.

[138] Lefroy, *Memorials*, 1: 590; Wilkinson, *Bermuda*, p. 398.

Puritan opposition. He served as an important link between the ever more closely connected colonizing aristocracy and new-merchant leadership.[139]

THE PROVIDENCE ISLAND COMPANY

The Providence Island Company was founded in late 1629 as an offshoot of the Bermudian venture. Capt. Philip Bell, who was the Bermuda Company's governor on the island and under Warwick's patronage, informed the Riches of the discovery of Providence Island and of its great potential as a colony. Warwick then gathered his associates and formed a joint-stock company to operate the project.[140]

The company was composed almost entirely of nonmerchant nobles and gentry who hoped to establish a godly Puritan community that was also a profit-making commercial venture. During its early years, the company concentrated on establishing staple-producing plantations on the island. The earl of Warwick, Lord Saye, Lord Brook, John Pym, and their partners financed and directed this endeavor, so London merchants had little opportunity to involve themselves.[141] In 1635, however, the company radically altered its priorities. After the Spanish attacks on the island that year, the company decided to put the bulk of its investments into privateering and to make the island an armed base for a campaign to dismantle Spain's Caribbean empire.[142] In 1636, the company received permission from the Crown to engage in private war against Spain in the West Indies. At the same time, the company began to make plans for removing its planters from Providence Island and to establish new settlements on the mainland of Central America.[143]

With the Providence Island Company's reorientation, outsiders gained the opportunity for the first time to participate in its activities. During the later 1630s the company issued a series of commissions to private parties entitling them to establish their own plantations and engage in privateering ventures in the Caribbean under company auspices. In this way, Maurice Thomson, along with several of his colonial trading partners, began his collaboration with the Providence Island leadership, forging still another bond between the new-merchant leadership and the colonizing aris-

[139] Haberdashers Company, London, Apprenticeship Bindings, 1602–1611, 11 August 1609; Pearl, *London*, p. 324; M. Noble, *The Lives of the Regicides*, 2 vols. (London, 1798), 2: 150–51; J. E. Farnell, "The Usurpation of Honest London Householders: Barebones Parliament," *E.H.R.* 82 (1967): 26. Rowe imported 6,000 pounds of Virginian tobacco in 1640 (London Port Book for Imports, 1640, PRO, E.190/43/5). For the collaboration between new merchants and colonizing aristocrats on religious policy inside the Bermuda Company, see below, ch. 6, pp. 279–80.

[140] Newton, *Colonising Activities*, pp. 52–59.

[141] Ibid., pp. 60–79, 146–50.

[142] Ibid., pp. 186–235, 248–71.

[143] Ibid., p. 248.

tocrats. Indeed, during the later 1630s these two groups suddenly escalated their joint activities in the Americas, setting in motion a series of spectacular initiatives throughout the hemisphere.

Maurice Thomson obviously was already well known to the company leadership when it first approached him for aid. In 1638 at a meeting of the company directors, a Mr. Samuel Border told John Pym, Benjamin Rudyerd, Lord Mandeville, and the earl of Warwick that there was a major silver mine to be exploited in the Bay of Darien. They went promptly to consult with Maurice Thomson about what to do. Thomson proposed that a voyage be organized under his direction to investigate the mine's potential. The company concurred, and the membership subscribed a separate joint stock of £350 to finance the venture. Thomson personally led this expedition in 1639.[144]

In the next couple of years Thomson seems to have carried out most of the Providence Island Company's provisioning tasks, and in 1641 he secured a contract from the company that formally put him in charge of this function. He also ran, on occasion, special business ventures of his own within the company's privileges. In 1640, for example, the company granted him the "liberty by his ships and agents to take what camphera wood he can get within the extent of the company's patent, provided he allow the company one-nineth part of what he shall procure."[145]

It will be recalled that in the spring of 1638, the privy council issued its final ruling against William Claiborne and his friends, defeating, at least for the time being, their long struggle to retain Kent Island as a private colonial base against Lord Baltimore and his Maryland Colony. About a month later, in May 1638, the Providence Island Company granted the same William Claiborne a commission to found a new English settlement on the island of Ruatan off the coast of Honduras. It has reasonably been suggested that Maurice Thomson, a partner of Claiborne's in the Kent Island project, was one of Claiborne's chief backers in this venture, but no direct confirmatory evidence has been discovered. Claiborne's colony, called Rich Island, endured until 1642 when it was overrun by the Spanish.[146]

Meanwhile, Claiborne and his friends had shown no sign of relinquishing their interest in the region to the north of Virginia, and they appear to have enlisted the aristocratic Puritan colonizing leadership to help them further their ambitions. In 1639, William Claiborne and his fellow Virginia councilor Samuel Matthews, along with the London merchants

[144] PRO, C.O.124/2/357–59.

[145] PRO, C.O.124/2/387, 389, 390; *C.S.P. Col. 1574–1660*, pp. 296, 309, 317, 318.

[146] Newton, *Colonising Activities*, pp. 267, 315; Hale, *Virginia Venturer*, pp. 232–33.

Maurice Thomson, George Fletcher,[147] and William Bennett, applied for a new grant encompassing a very large section of land between the Potomac and the Rappahannock rivers in the unsettled area between Virginia and Maryland. What is most intriguing about this endeavor is that in making their bid these men took as their partner the Bermuda Company itself, which joined them in their petition to the privy council.[148] This request seems never to have been acted on. But it does give some indication of the growing aspirations, as well as the growing collaboration, of the new-merchant leadership and colonizing aristocrats in this period. The new men were, of course, deeply preoccupied at this time with Virginian plantations and land speculation—and increasingly involved with the colonizing aristocrats in their Caribbean projects. It is impossible to know just what the aristocratic leaders of the Bermuda Company had in mind when they helped seek this grant to the north of Virginia. But they, too, appear to have been increasingly interested in mainland plantations, as is indicated by the Providence Island Company's plans for new settlements on the coast of Central America. In fact, in 1638 William Woodcock, who was the Providence Island Company's husband (its chief executive officer), is listed in the port book of that year as importing the enormous load of 164,000 pounds of *Virginian* tobacco into London![149] This shipment must surely have been related to plans of the colonizing aristocrats for expanding their colonial interests onto the North American mainland, just how remains unclear.[150]

Finally, in this same period between 1638 and 1641, Maurice Thomson, in collaboration with the American-trade merchant and Levantine trade interloper William Pennoyer, Thomas Frere (a one-time apprentice of William Tucker's brother-in-law and Thomson's sometime partner William Felgate), and some privateering traders of Cornwall, organized and financed a string of spectacular raids on Spain's West Indian possessions.[151] These voyages were carried out under the intrepid leadership of Capt. William Jackson, an apprentice of William Tucker in the Cloth-

---

[147] Fletcher, a merchant of very diverse commercial interests, was a close associate of the Kent Island leader William Cloberry and his brother Oliver Cloberry; together they traded with the Barbary Coast and the West Indies (PRO, H.C.A.24/105/5; PRO, will of William Cloberry, 1640, PCC Coventry 4).

[148] Hale, *Virginia Venturer*, p. 236; Andrews, *Colonial Period* 2: 284 n. 1; Lefroy, *Memorials* 1: 724.

[149] London Port Book for Imports, 1638, PRO, E.190/41/5.

[150] For other, parallel developments at this same time, see ch. 6, p. 301ff.

[151] V. T. Harlow, ed., *The Voyages of Captain William Jackson*, Camden Miscellany 13 (London, 1923), pp. v–vii; Newton, *Colonising Activities*, pp. 267–71; Stock, *Proceedings and Debates* 1: 110–14, 135–38. Frere was the son of a Suffolk yeoman (Skinners Company, London, Apprentices and Freemen Book, 1601–1694, fol. 102; Woodhead, *Rulers*, p. 74).

workers Company.[152] The venture was sanctioned by letters of reprisal issued by the Providence Island Company and was remarkably profitable. The company received £3,000 as the one-fifth share of the venture's booty to which it was entitled by virtue of its commission. Even so, it was underpaid. Indeed, the extraordinary success of this venture led the earl of Warwick to attempt a similar, but larger and ultimately more famous, project of his own beginning in 1642, and to secure the collaboration of Maurice Thomson and William Pennoyer, as well as Captain Jackson, in carrying it out.[153] By that time, the new-merchant leadership and the colonizing Puritan aristocrat had expanded the range of their joint activities well beyond the sphere of commerce and colonies.

The New Merchants on the Offensive:
West Indian Sugar Capitalism, Virginian Expansion, and East Indian Interloping, 1640–1649

Something of the social character, modes of operation, and commercial career of that emerging group of traders who constituted what I have called the new-merchant leadership should now be evident. I have traced the rise of an entirely new and significant overseas commercial group, separated by differences in origin, outlook, and forms of economic action from the City's chief overseas traders, the mere merchants of the regulated companies. These new men were, in particular, poles apart from the Levant–East India Company merchants who formed the core of the City company merchant establishment. Hailing from social strata far inferior to those from which the company merchants came, the new-merchant leaders had initially entered the colonial field as a second choice, because they lacked the economic endowments and political privileges to enter the better-established and apparently more lucrative company trades. Nevertheless, by 1640, after two decades of commercial innovation and political manipulation in the Americas, the new-merchant leaders had amassed both the economic resources and the commercial experience to

---

[152] Clothworkers Company, London, Apprentice Register, 1606–1641, 7 May 1637. William Tucker was, almost certainly, a leading backer of this venture.

[153] Harlow, *Captain William Jackson*, p. xi; Newton, *Colonising Activities*, p. 271. For Warwick's venture, see below, ch. 8. The Jackson ventures were only part of a series of such privateering voyages undertaken in this period by Maurice Thomson in collaboration with his colonial merchant friends, in particular William Pennoyer and Gregory Clement, as well as Richard Bateson and Edward Wood (the latter two, as noted, were also working at this time with the major colonial trader Samuel Vassall). These voyages are difficult to sort out, but they seem to have begun in 1637, after Thomson and Clement had won from the Crown the right to seek reprisal for the loss of their ship *Merchant Bonaventure*, to the Dunkirkers in 1634, and they continued well into the 1640s (*C.S.P.D. 1636–1637*, pp. 350, 554; PRO, C.2/Ch.I/C.59/29; PRO, H.C.A.24/108/62–65, 116).

recognize and exploit avenues for gain that eluded even the company merchants. Having taken over the colonial field by default, they were better positioned than any other merchants to profit from the spectacular opportunities which that field suddenly came to offer. What is perhaps most indicative of their increasing commercial power is that they were also prepared by this point to exploit the ensuing political instability in order to invade the privileged ground of the company merchants and to confront them on their own special terrain, the trade with the East Indies.

It is crucial to reemphasize, then, that the new-merchant leaders were not simply merchants in the sense of specialized overseas traders. Unable to secure apprenticeships from wealthy company merchants and lacking major investment funds, they were often obliged at the start of their careers to enter less certain and less lucrative occupations: they were ship captains, shopkeepers, domestic traders, and, of course, American colonists. But even their success in the transatlantic commerical world could not result in their smooth promotion into the ranks of the mere merchants of the company-organized trading community. The mere-merchant qualification clause of the company charters prevented these men from entering the established regulated companies—unless they would agree to relinquish their London shops and give up their former occupations.

On the other hand, the new merchants' activities, not only in the colonial sphere but in their domestic London businesses as well, clearly sensitized them to a broad spectrum of economic opportunities requiring innovation and diversification. The takeover of the colonial field by these traders cannot, therefore, be explained merely in terms of their restricted opportunities. Men from their middling stratum were, in this period, involving themselves in a wide range of entrepreneurial initiatives, not only in overseas commerce but throughout England, and not only in trade but in industrial production. The degree and character of this involvement are far from clear and need much more investigation. But it is worth noting that one of the major Virginian tobacco traders, Richard Bateson, a partner of Maurice Thomson's and Samuel Vassall's in a broad variety of American ventures, was also very much involved in the glassware trade.[154] The cheesemongers and American tobacco traders William Harris and Thomas Deacon, who took part with Maurice Thomson and his friends in the purchase of the great Berkeley Hundred plantation, collaborated with another of Thomson's associates, the Anglo-Dutch American trader Nicholas Corsellis, in carrying on an active lead trade from the Mines Royal in Cardigan, Wales.[155] Joshua Foote, the London ironmonger who was an associate of Maurice Thomson's in the New England sup-

---

[154] House of Lords MSS, 21, 30 July 1641, 5 August 1641.
[155] *H.M.C., Sixth Report, Appendix*, pp. 109, 118; *L.J.* 8: 415–16.

ply trade, was also active in the 1630s in establishing an ironworks in Tancready, Ireland.[156] During the 1640s he followed this up, in partnership with such other leading London traders with New England as Robert Houghton, William Hiccocks, and John Pocock, by opening up the famous ironworks in Braintree, Massachusetts.[157] The fact remains that the most spectacular and revolutionary commercial-industrial development of the Interregnum was the introduction of sugar planting to the West Indies. The same new-merchant leadership group that already dominated American enterprise provided much of the energy and capital behind this development.

SUGAR PLANTATIONS AND TRIANGULAR TRADES

During the early years of their colonization, the West Indies had been dominated almost exclusively by tobacco, produced on small plots by a yeoman population. By the end of the 1630s, however, European markets for tobacco were becoming saturated, and enterprising businessmen began a search for new crops. In the early 1640s, a number of Dutch merchants introduced sugarcane into the islands' economy after having familiarized themselves with its production in Portuguese Brazil. Since sugar was immensely more profitable than tobacco, the innovation was copied wherever possible, with catastrophic social consequences.[158]

The social changes that followed the introduction of sugar were implicit in its basic unit of production. "The sugar plantation was a factory set in a field." The typical plantation, described by Richard Ligon in somewhat exaggerated terms, cost in the neighborhood of £14,000 and consisted of five hundred acres, of which two hundred acres were devoted to sugar planting. Besides a dwelling house, fixed capital included an ingenio, a still house, a boiling house, a filling room, and a carding room, as well as stables, a forge, and huts for slaves. The plantation was manned by ninety-six black slaves, three Indian women, and twenty-eight white servants. There were, in addition, forty-five draught cattle, twelve horses, sixteen asses, and eight milk cows.[159] Given such extraordinary capital, labor, and technical requirements, it is not difficult to comprehend why the spread of sugar planting throughout the West Indies brought about the transformation of the islands' social and economic organization. It opened the way for the decline of small-scale production, the replacement of free white by

---

[156] PRO, C.24/733/33.

[157] E. N. Hartley, *Ironworks on the Saugus* (Norman, Okla., 1957), pp. 65–77.

[158] Williamson, *Caribee Islands*, pp. 137–39, 157–58; R. S. Dunn, *Sugar and Slaves: The Rise of the Planter Class in the English West Indies, 1624–1673* (Chapel Hill, N.C., 1972), pp. 61–62.

[159] R. Pares, "Merchants and Planters," *Ec.H.R.*, supp. (1960): 23; Williamson, *Caribbee Islands*, p. 156; Dunn, *Sugar and Slaves*, pp. 66–73.

black slave labor, and the concentration of land and capital in the hands of a relatively small number of businessmen who could afford to invest and innovate.[160]

The growth of sugar planting in the West Indies during the 1640s and the socioeconomic changes it entailed were at once the cause and the consequence of the simultaneous reorientation of the transatlantic trade routes and the activities of the merchants who followed them. Even before 1640, English tobacco importers had begun to reexport American tobacco to the markets of Europe and the Near East. The merchants who developed the West Indian sugar economy were led further to enlarge the scope of their dealings in order to encompass the various segments of a highly complex but integrated system of production. To fill the manpower needs of the plantations, the merchants expanded the slave trade in West Africa. To secure the cattle and horses needed by the plantations, they increasingly resorted to Virginia or New England. Perhaps most important, to supply the unprecedented capital requirements for founding plantations, the merchants relied on the wealth they had already accumulated in American enterprise (although a number of substantial English gentry who emigrated to the West Indies during the Interregnum also supplied funds).[161] Overall then, during the 1640s and 1650s, there was an accelerated development of what have been loosely called the triangular trades, directly centered on and stimulated by the growth of sugar production in the West Indies.[162]

The new-merchant leadership was obviously the group of traders best prepared to take up the task of developing sugar plantations. They were used to trading with Virginia and the West Indies in provisions and tobacco; they had strong links with New England; and they were accustomed to investing in production, often through advances to planters, but sometimes by way of direct ownership. From the early 1640s, many of these men bought plantations while carrying on the subsidiary trades necessary to supply themselves and the other sugar producers. In these processes, Maurice Thomson and his various circles of friends once again took the lead.

A petition of 1647 from twenty-nine "merchants and planters adventuring to the island of Barbados" who claimed to have "either totally or at least principally planted the island" provides evidence of the identity of the colony's entrepreneurial leaders.[163] The petitioners included Maurice Thomson as well as Thomas Andrews, Elias Roberts, Jeremy Blackman,

---

[160] Williamson, *Caribee Islands*, pp. 157–58; Dunn, *Sugar and Slaves*, pp. 73–80.

[161] Pares, "Merchants and Planters," p. 4.

[162] For some aspects of the early development of the triangular trades, see Bailyn, *New England Merchants*, pp. 84–91; V. T. Harlow, *Barbados, 1625–1685* (Oxford, 1926), ch. 6.

[163] *L.J.* 9: 50.

William Pennoyer, Richard Bateson, and Thomas Frere—all experienced in the Americas and all partners in the colonial leadership group in the prewar period.[164] Also among the signers were Michael Davison, a former apprentice of William Pennoyer's, who seems to have represented Pennoyer in Barbados from around 1640,[165] and Robert Wilding, an agent of Thomson's and Thomas Stone's on St. Kitts in the late 1620s. Beginning in the later 1630s, Wilding became a major tobacco trader in his own right,[166] and by 1647 was the partner of another of the petitioners, Martin Noel, in the sugar and tobacco trade from Montserrat. Noel was at this juncture emerging as one of the entrepreneurial leaders of the field. He did not, it seems, become connected with Maurice Thomson and his associates until the 1640s, but from that time on was one of their most important partners in both the East and West Indies.[167] All of these men seem to have been landowners in Barbados, and many of them already had, or were about to, set up sugar plantations.[168]

Most of these Barbadian merchant-planters, as well as a number of Thomson's other friends, were at this time also penetrating and developing the slave trade.[169] The main source of slaves for English traders was Guinea, on the west coast of Africa. In 1631, Charles I had granted a patent for trade with this area to a syndicate headed by the courtier-merchant Sir Nicholas Crispe. Crispe's partners in his Guinea Company were

[164] For the backgrounds and previous careers of all of these men, see above, this chapter.

[165] Woodhead, *Rulers*, p. 57. Davison was the son of a Plumber of London (Clothworkers Company, London, Apprentice Register, 1606–1641, 24 January 1635–1636). See also below, note 168.

[166] Bodleian Library, Rawlinson MSS C.94, fol. 9. Wilding was apprenticed to Stone in the Haberdashers Company (Haberdashers Company, London, Freemen Book [chronological], 1638). He imported, for example, 12,000 pounds of Virginian tobacco in 1640 (London Port Book for Imports, 1640, PRO, E.190/43/5). For Wilding's early career with Stone and Thomson on St. Kitts, see above, p. 128.

[167] PRO, H.C.A.24/109/56; *C.S.P. Col. 1574–1660*, p. 348. Noel was the son of a Mansfield, Staffordshire, "gent." (Pares, "Merchants and Planters," p. 6 n. 29; Woodhead, *Rulers*, p. 122). See also below, pp. 175–76.

[168] Later in the year 1647, almost identical petitions were presented to Parliament by Maurice Thomson and William Pennoyer requesting permission to transport horses and cattle from Virginia and New England to Barbados in order to facilitate building their sugar works there. (*H.M.C., Sixth Report, Appendix*, pp. 202, 203). It is almost certain that Davison was Pennoyer's partner in this enterprise (*C.S.P. Col. 1574–1660*, p. 379). He was involved in trade with Barbados from at least 1640 (Royal Commonwealth Institute, Darnell Davis Collection, box 7, no. 5). For Martin Noel's involvement with Barbadian sugar planting, see Pares, "Merchants and Planters," p. 6 n. 29; Royal Commonwealth Institute, Darnell Davis Collection, box 7, no. 2; PRO, will of Martin Noel, 1665 PCC Hyde 120. For Richard Bateson's extensive plantation interests in Barbados, see PRO, will of Richard Bateson, 1667 PCC Carr 79. For those of Thomas Andrews and his son Jonathan, see Royal Commonwealth Institute, Darnell Davis Collection, box 15, book 1, 143. For those of Thomas Frere, see Woodhead, *Rulers*, p. 74.

[169] For the slave trade in general in this period, see E. Donnan, *Documents Illustrative of the Slave Trade in America*, 4 vols. (Washington, D.C., 1930–1935), 1: 73ff.

Humphrey Slaney, Slaney's apprentice John Wood, and Slaney's son-in-law, the ubiquitous William Cloberry, the Kent Island Company leader.[170] In 1638, Maurice Thomson attempted to break into this trade illegally, but his ship was stopped, on the request of the Guinea Company, by order of the privy council.[171] With the meeting of the Long Parliament, however, Nicholas Crispe came under attack as a monopolist. When Crispe subsequently was forced to withdraw from the trade, the Guinea Company effectively lost its privileges.[172] Although Crispe's old company continued in the trade with a somewhat fluctuating membership, the parliamentary government failed to enforce its monopoly, and this left the way open for the new-merchant leadership.

Throughout the 1630s, the Guinea Company had been mainly concerned with the direct import of redwood, elephants' teeth, hides of all sorts, and, above all, gold.[173] But as new opportunities emerged in the West Indies in the early 1640s, the company sought to reorient itself toward the slave trade. By this time, however, it had to contend with a growing horde of competitors. In the years between 1642 and 1645, the leading colonial merchant Samuel Vassall carried out at least one voyage to Guinea and Barbados[174] and, at about the same time, a syndicate led by Michael Cawton, a sea captain and merchant previously active in the Virginian and West Indian trades,[175] also traded along this route.[176] The remaining members of the Guinea Company attempted to get court action to block Cawton's venture and to confirm their monopoly, but there is no evidence that they succeeded.[177] From the mid-1640s, therefore, a succession of shifting partnerships, often involving individuals from the Thomson connection and concentrating entirely on the new triangular trades,

[170] For the early history of the English trade with Guinea, see Blake, "Guinea Trade," pp. 86–106. For a summary of the trade in the 1630s, see Oliver Cloberry's account in his suit in Chancery, PRO, C.2/Ch.I/C.52/38. Nicholas Crispe was the son of the London alderman Ellis Crispe and throughout the 1620s and 1630s was a major financier and customs farmer (R. Ashton, *The Crown and the Money Market, 1603–1640* [Oxford, 1960], index). For Humphrey Slaney, see above, pp. 101, 103, 110. John Wood and William Cloberry were both former apprentices of Slaney (Blake, "Guinea Trade," p. 95).

[171] *C.S.P. Col. 1574–1660*, p. 273; *C.S.P.D. 1637–1638*, pp. 406, 417.

[172] For Crispe's appearance in Parliament and its results as far as the Guinea Company is concerned, see W. Notestein, ed., *The Journal of Sir Simonds D'Ewes from the Beginning of the Long Parliament to the Opening of the Trial of Strafford* (New Haven, 1923), p. 540; *C.J.* 2: 33, 278, 970; Blake, "Guinea Trade," p. 97.

[173] See PRO, P.C.2/41/378, for a list of products commonly imported from Guinea in the 1630s. See also Blake, "Guinea Trade."

[174] PRO, H.C.A.24/108/356.

[175] PRO, H.C.A.24/98/212, 214 and PRO,H.C.A.24/104/285. Cawton was the son of a Surrey gentleman, (Clothworkers Company, London, Apprentice Register, 1606–1641, 9 May 1635).

[176] PRO,H.C.A.24/108/7, 8.

[177] Ibid.

was able to enter the commerce with Guinea. From 1645 to 1647, for example, William Pennoyer organized a series of voyages, first in partnership with Richard Hill,[178] and then in partnership with his brother Samuel, his apprentices Michael Davison and Joseph Terringham, Maurice Thomson's brother Robert and Thomson's brother-in-law Elias Roberts, and William Fletcher.[179] Meanwhile, Samuel Vassall continued in the trade in association with his brother-in-law Peter Andrews, Maurice Thomson's old associate Jeremy Blackman, and his own sometime partner Richard Cranley.[180] John Wood, the only surviving member of the original Guinea Company, seems to have constructed a new group, based to some extent on old company connections, to carry on the trade. This included, at one time or another in the 1640s, John Ballow, Thomas Walter, William Crispe, Rowland Wilson, Sr., Rowland Wilson, Jr., and John Brett.[181] By 1648 Maurice Thomson himself had become associated with this latter syndicate.[182]

Their deepening involvement in the total process of West Indian economic development led the new merchants to demand a total transforma-

---

[178] PRO, H.C.A.24/108/165. Hill was active during the pre–Civil War period in the American tobacco and Newfoundland fish oil trades, as well as the trade with Spain. From 1642 he was involved with Richard Cranley in Newfoundland. He was the son of a tanner of Moretonhampstead, Devon (R.H.E. Hill, "Richard Hill of Moreton, Alderman of London," *Devon Notes and Queries* 4 [1907]: pp. 49–51, 145–48; BL, Add. MSS 5489, fol. 46; London Port Books for Imports, 1633–1640). Hill was probably a pre–Civil War associate of Pennoyer's. The two of them were constant partners in parliamentary finance and politics from the early 1640s (*C.J.* 3: 333, 367, 568).

[179] PRO, H.C.A.24/108/362. For the earlier activities of Samuel Pennoyer, Robert Thomson, and Elias Roberts, see above, this chapter. For Davison, also see above. For Terringham's apprenticeship to Pennoyer, see Clothworkers Company, London, Apprentice Register, 1606–1641, 11 May 1632. Terringham was the son of a Northamptonshire gentleman (ibid.).

[180] PRO, H.C.A.24/109/255; PRO, H.C.A.24/110/35. For Blackman, Cranley, and Andrews and their earlier activities in the Americas, see above, this chapter.

[181] For the Guinea Company in the 1640s under the leadership of John Wood, see PRO, H.C.A.24/108/7, 8, 232, 247; PRO, H.C.A.24/109/151, 190, 342; and PRO, H.C.A.24/110/74, 75. John Ballow was an old associate of William Cloberry's and had been the agent of the Guinea Company in Barbados in 1641 (Royal Commonwealth Institute, Darnell Davis Papers, box 7, no. 2 [Deeds, vol. 1, fol. 202]). For the early connection with Cloberry, see PRO, Index to High Court of Admiralty Papers for 1616–1624. Thomas Walter and Rowland Wilson, Sr., both had been involved during the prewar period in the Spanish trade (London Port Book for Exports, 1640, PRO, E.190/43/4). Wilson, who was also a leading trader with France, became in 1640 a director of the East India Company (*C.C.M.E.I.C. 1640–1643*, p. 61). He was a son of an old armigerous family of Grese Garth in Kendal, Westmoreland (*Visitation of London, 1633–1635* 2: 356). His daughter Mary married a brother of Nicholas Crispe (ibid.). Thomas Walter was John Wood's brother-in-law (PRO, will of Thomas Walter, 1657/8 PCC Wootton 5). William Crispe was probably the cousin by that name of Nicholas Cripse (PRO, will of Ellis Crispe, 1625 PCC Clarke 120). Brett, from Dinsdale, Staffordshire, was apprenticed in London to his father-in-law the American-trade merchant Randall Mainwaring. On Brett's relationship to Mainwaring and Mainwaring's extensive connections among the colonial merchant leadership, see above, p. 138, and note 80.

[182] PRO, H.C.A.24/109/151.

tion of the political arrangements through which the colony was governed. This was because the existing political-institutional structures stood in the way of a full implementation of their commercial program. The earl of Carlisle, the proprietor of the West Indies, saw the islands merely as a source to be milked, and his government functioned mainly to that end. The proprietor tolerated no local representation, such as existed at that time in Virginia. All opposition was violently suppressed. The governor in the colony, appointed by the proprietor, ruled by decree and did his best to extract for his own and the proprietor's benefit a maximum return by any means that could be made to work. During most of the period before the Civil War, the colonial merchants and planters were subjected to an endless variety of poll taxes, transfer fees, levies on production, and customs on trade, while having to face, from time to time, the outright expropriation of their land.[183]

Under such conditions neither persons nor property were entirely safe, and the long-term investments required for sugar plantations were a dubious proposition at best. Understandably, the Barbadian merchant-planters wanted security from proprietary caprice before fully immersing themselves in all phases of the new West Indian economy. They sought, therefore, a new political order in which ultimate control of the land and its uses would lie in the hands of the planters themselves. The parliamentary petition organized in March 1647 by Maurice Thomson's merchant-planter leadership was directed to precisely this end. The petitioners presented two essential demands: (1) the possession of their lands in freehold tenure, and (2) the installation of their own system of government on the islands.[184] They called, in short, for the dismantling of the landholding and political arrangements of the West Indian proprietorship and the creation of a favorable politico-legal environment for the commercial development they hoped to bring about.

The implementation of the merchants' programs would have necessitated a small revolution. It would also have directly affected the complicated structure of English aristocratic interest in the Caribbean—involving no less a personage than the earl of Warwick—that had developed during the pre–Civil War era.[185] A Parliament preoccupied with its own domestic political crisis was unable to take decisive action. The disposition of the West Indian proprietorship had to wait upon a final settlement of the Civil War.[186]

---

[183] On the government and administration of the West Indies before the Civil War, see Williamson, *Caribbee Islands*, pp. 83–93, 135–49. For a full résumé of the conflicts between the proprietary interests and the merchants and planters, see Bodleian Library, Rawlinson MSS C.94.

[184] *L.J.* 9: 50. See also Williamson. *Caribbee Islands*, pp. 119–20, 125–28.

[185] Williamson, *Caribee Islands*, pp. 109–11, 118, 129, 140–43, 159–62.

[186] See below, ch. 12.

VIRGINIAN EXPANSION

Maryland was a second area in which the new merchants took direct action during the 1640s against a colonial institutional structure that had proved unfavorable to their commercial-expansionary interest. There, as noted, the proprietary regime provoked opposition not as a result of its arbitrary absentee exactions, but as a result of its too-powerful controls over the process of development and of the barriers it posed to Virignia's expansion. Led by the Kent Island organizers William Claiborne, William Cloberry, and Maurice Thomson, Virginia's merchant-councilors had made every effort to overthrow the Calvert patent. But despite their opposition, and that of the Virginian planter class as a whole, the Maryland Colony had successfully established itself and had incorporated Kent Island within its borders. This outcome did not win the acceptance of either William Claiborne or the others of the Virginian merchant-planter-councilor clique, and they remained prepared to reverse it should the occasion arise.

At the outbreak of civil war, the Calverts supported the king, and this led to a severe weakening of their proprietary authority in Maryland. Sections of the Virginian merchant-planter-councilor leadership quickly saw an opportunity to regain control. Richard Ingle, a merchant and sea captain who had been trading with Maryland in partnership with the London colonial merchants Thomas Allen and Anthony Pennyston,[187] seized St. Mary's in 1644. Almost simultaneously, William Claiborne captured Kent Island.[188] Both men claimed to represent Parliament against the royalist and papist proprietary government, and Calvert's patent was immediately brought into question before the earl of Warwick's parliamentary commission on plantations.[189]

Sections of the colonial merchant leadership almost certainly had known beforehand of these attacks on Maryland. Not long after the actions of Ingle and Claiborne had raised a challenge to proprietary control, they sought to deliver a knockout blow. On 4 March 1647, eighteen London merchants "trading to Virginia and other English plantations" petitioned Parliament to demand the abrogation of the Baltimore proprietorship. They submitted their remonstrance only two days after the Barbadian merchant-planters had brought in their very similar petition, with some of the same signatures, against the Carlisle proprietorship. It is very

[187] PRO, H.C.A.24/102/190. For Thomas Allen, see above, pp. 147, 155. Anthony Pennyston was one of the few Levant Company merchants to enter the new trades with the Americas (see above, ch. 3).

[188] Andrews, *Colonial Period* 2: 308–9. For a full narrative of these events, see B. C. Steiner, *Maryland during the English Civil Wars*, John Hopkins University Studies in Historical and Political Science, ser. 24, nos. 11, 12, and ser. 25, nos. 4, 5 (Baltimore, 1906–1911).

[189] Stock, *Proceedings and Debates* 1: 171–74.

likely, therefore, that the two were planned together. Once again, Maurice Thomson was prominent among the signers, who included such old associates of Thomson's as William Pennoyer, Oliver Cloberry (brother of William), George Fletcher, Thomas Deacon, and Richard Chandler (a onetime apprentice of Thomas Stone), as well as Ingle's partner Anthony Pennyston.[190] The future of the Calvert proprietorship was not to be finally decided for a number of years. But, once again, the American merchant-planter leadership had set in motion a political attack on a colonial institutional order that had proved incompatible with their interest in continuing commercial expansion.

EAST INDIAN INTERLOPING

During most of the pre–Civil War period, the new-merchant leadership had of course operated in different spheres from those of the City merchant establishment. Nevertheless, the expansionary and diversifying dynamics of their commercial enterprises increasingly led these men to break into territory already carved out by the City elite and protected by the state. The resulting commercial conflicts would have important political implications.

Even outside the sphere of overseas commerce proper there are some tantalizing examples. It should be noted in passing that the colonial trader Richard Bateson carried on his aforementioned trade in glass while waging a battle against the glassmaking patent that had been granted to Robert Mansell.[191] Similarly, during the mid-1630s the girdler Stephen Estwicke, who was later to work with Maurice Thomson in East Indian interloping, was active in opposing the newly formed Company of Silkmen.[192] Michael Herring and Richard Hill, leaders from approximately 1640, if not before, in the colonial tobacco and sugar trades, seem to have come into conflict during the 1630s with the Company of Soapboilers.[193]

Of course, it was in the realm of overseas commerce that the new-merchant leadership found itself most constricted by the already established structures of commercial organization and privilege. A number of the key new-merchant leaders had engaged in quarrels with the chartered com-

[190] Ibid., pp. 194–95. For Pennoyer, Fletcher, Deacon, and Cloberry, see above. For Chandler, see Haberdashers Company, London, Apprenticeship Bindings, 1611–1630, 8 May 1625. He was also a Virginian trading partner of Robert Wilding, another leading colonial merchant and former apprentice of Stone's. For Wilding, see note 166.

[191] See above, p. 160. See also H. Price, *The English Patents of Monopoly* (Cambridge, Mass., 1906), pp. 72–81.

[192] Pearl, *London*, p. 315.

[193] BL, Add. MSS 5489, fol. 46. For Hill's career and connections, see above, p. 165 and n. 178. Herring's background is obscure. For his tobacco-trade involvement, see PRO, E.122/230/9.

panies. William Pennoyer, the major partner of both Matthew Craddock and Maurice Thomson, got in trouble for persistent interloping in the Levant Company's privileged areas. But he long refused to join the company, since this would have required him to relinquish his London shop.[194] Andrew Hawes, a partner of the colonial traders Thomas Deacon and William Harris in their London cheesemongering business, also had been in difficulty with the Levant Company for interloping;[195] so had Jonathan Andrews, son and partner of the shopkeeping new merchant Thomas Andrews;[196] so had William Fletcher, a City clothdrawer who would later collaborate with William and Samuel Pennoyer, Robert Thomson, Elias Roberts, and Richard Bateson in the West Indian trade.[197] In fact, by the end of the 1630s, the new merchants had powerful economic incentives for breaking into the Levantine commerce, besides their desire as shopkeepers to get around the Levant Company's merchant middlemen and purchase lucrative eastern imports directly. During this period, the Levant emerged as a significant market for tobacco, and Matthew Craddock and William Pennoyer were among the first to link the American tobacco commerce directly with the Levant. Pennoyer ultimately gave up his London shop and joined the Levant Company to do this. But in the same period, Maurice Thomson and his brother George, along with William Tucker, refused to observe such formalities, and together simply launched a large-scale voyage into the Mediterranean in direct defiance of the Levant Company's patent.[198]

The most enticing opportunities, however, lay to the south and the east—in Africa and the East Indies. The new merchants Samuel Warner and Gregory Clement had gotten in trouble for violating the East India Company's privileges in the late 1620s. But at that early point, men such as these posed no real threat to the merchant elite who controlled the company.[199] Nevertheless, by the early 1640s, much had changed. The new merchants had gone from strength to strength and had developed considerable cohesiveness and resources of their own. While their major triumphs had thus far been registered in areas ignored by the great London

[194] PRO, S.P.105/149/253.

[195] PRO, S.P.105/148/194. Hawes was also an interloper during the 1630s in the privileged sphere granted the Greenland Company (PRO, P.C.2/42/55). For Hawes's partnership with Deacon and Harris, see *C.S.P.D. 1639–1640*, p. 563; PRO, will of Andrew Hawes, 1642 PCC Cambell 70. Hawes was from an Ipswich family (*Visitation of London, 1633–1635* 1: 368).

[196] PRO, S.P.105/149/92.

[197] PRO, S.P.105/150/267. For Fletcher's West Indian operations, see PRO, H.C.A.24/108/362, and above, p. 165.

[198] PRO, H.C.A.24/102/37. This voyage, which took place in 1638–1639, touched at the ports of Patamos, Scanderoon, Marseilles, Leghorne, Morea, and Malaga.

[199] *A.P.C. 1627–1628*, pp. 220–21; *C.S.P.D. 1627–1628*, p. 531; *C.S.P. Col. E.I. 1625–1629*, pp. 49, 488, 491; *C.S.P. Col. E.I. 1630–1634*, pp. 148, 156, 164–65; Pearl, *London*, p. 327.

merchant magnates, they were now ready to challenge the established elite on its own ground. The treatment of colonization as a total process combining production and trade had provided the basis for the new merchants' success in the Americas during the 1620s and 1630s. Starting in the late 1630s, and especially after the Civil War had created a greater opening, they resolved to extend the same approach to the East Indies.

The incursion of the new-merchant leadership with America into the commerce of the East Indies was the last and most formidable in a long series of attacks on the monopoly privileges of the East India Company during the reign of Charles I.[200] As early as 1630, Charles had shown his willingness to ignore the company's privileged status when he dispatched his own privateering vessel to prey on the native trade between the Red Sea and India. The company was always held responsible for depredations made by Englishmen in this area, and when the king's ship captured a Malabar junk, the company was compelled to pay full compensation. Still, from the king's point of view the voyage had been a success, and in 1635 one of the most powerful men of Charles's court, Endymion Porter, attempted to follow suit. In cooperation with two young London merchants, Thomas Kynnaston, the cashier to the government financier Sir Abraham Dawes, and Samuel Bonnell, an agent of the great Anglo-Dutch merchant Sir William Courteen, Porter sent out two vessels, the *Samaritan* and the *Roebuck*, under the command of William Cobb, which were licensed under the privy seal to prey on ships and goods of any state not in league and amity with His Majesty. The *Roebuck* made its way to the Red Sea, where it plundered two native junks. This proved disastrous for the East India Company because the local authorities, making no distinctions among English ships, soon imprisoned the company's factors and forced them to make full reparation to those who had been harmed. It is probable that Sir William Courteen himself was involved in Cobb's privateering venture. Courteen, a Crown lender and one of London's great merchant princes, previously had traded throughout Europe and in 1625 had attempted, without success, to colonize the West Indies. In any case, when the Convention of Goa shortly thereafter opened up the Indo-Portuguese markets to English traders, Courteen certainly did decide to organize an interloping expedition.[201]

John Weddell and Nathaniel Mountney, two ex-employees of the East India Company, apparently first put forward the plan for a major voyage

---

[200] In the following section on the East Indian trade, I have relied heavily on the excellent narrative provided by William Foster in his introductions to the calendars of the court minutes of the East India Company for the years 1635–1660. I am also indebted to the stimulating article by J. E. Farnell, "The Navigation Act of 1651, the First Dutch War, and the London Merchant Community," *Ec.H.R.*, 2d ser., 16 (1964).

[201] *C.C.M.E.I.C. 1635–1639*, pp. xiv–xvi.

of trade to Goa, Malabar, China, and Japan.[202] They made contact with Endymion Porter through Sir William Monson and Secretary Francis Windebank, and an association that included Bonnell, Kynnaston, and Porter, but that was mainly backed and financed by Sir William Courteen, was quickly organized.[203] On 12 December 1635, Courteen's syndicate obtained a license to trade with all areas in the East not previously exploited by the East India Company. In the preamble to this document, the organizers justified their voyage by reference to the new opportunities opened up by the Convention of Goa and the hope of finding a northwest passage. They rationalized their launching of an independent venture within the East India Company's chartered privileges by reference to that company's failure to settle and fortify areas in the East, with the consequent forfeit of important English commercial positions.[204]

Shortly thereafter, Sir William Courteen died and his company was reorganized under the leadership of his son William. By the new articles of agreement drafted in the late spring of 1636, Courteen was to receive something over one-half the profits from the venture; Endymion Porter, one-quarter; and Captain Weddell, Thomas Kynnaston, and Nathaniel Mountney, the remainder. The king, who had been secretly bribed with a £10,000 interest in the venture, granted the association a full royal patent in 1637.[205]

About the time that Courteen's ship set sail, another interloping venture was in preparation, this time to the island of Madagascar.[206] The East India Company had used Madagascar for many years as an important stop-off for its ships on their way to the East; there crews took on fresh water, cut billets for firewood, and bartered brass wire, beads, and calicoes with the natives for oxen and provisions. Nevertheless, the company had refused to consider a permanent settlement on Madagascar because its directorate, like the rest of London's company merchant establishment, was unalterably opposed to investment in colonization. The East India Company's officers were, in fact, hostile to any expenditures not immediately productive of profit and were constantly urging their agents to spend as little as possible on fortifications or buildings of any sort. This policy was in marked contrast with that of the Dutch, who were in this period

[202] For this paragraph, in general, see *C.C.M.E.I.C. 1635–1639*, pp. xvi–xix, xxi.

[203] Courteen did not supply all the money from his own resources. Paul Pindar, the great London financier, reportedly advanced £35,000–36,000 for the venture and John, earl of Shrewsbury, another £2,500 (W. R. Scott, *The Constitution and Finance of English, Scottish, and Irish Joint-Stock Companies to 1720*, 3 vols. [Cambridge, 1910–1912], 2: 113).

[204] *C.C.M.E.I.C. 1635–1639*, pp. 127–29.

[205] *C.C.M.E.I.C. 1635–1639*, pp. 123, 188, 191, 275–76.

[206] For the following paragraph, see W. Foster, "An English Settlement in Madagascar in 1645–1646," *E.H.R.* 27 (1912): 239–40.

[171]

constructing an Asian commercial empire on the basis of forts, armed ships, and the encouragement of settlers. As a later seventeenth-century English commentator phrased the distinction: "The Dutch as they gain ground, secure it by vast expenses, raising forts and maintaining soldiers; ours are for raising auctions and retrenching charges; bidding the next age grow rich, as they have done, but not affording them the means."[207]

Consequently, as in so many previous colonizing efforts of the late Elizabethan and early Stuart periods, the original initiative for the creation of a permanent settlement on Madagascar came from the landed classes. In 1637, Prince Rupert, the king's nephew, "having a desire to put himself upon some honourable action" and having obtained an account of Madagascar that fully satisfied him as to its possibilities for becoming "the balance of all the trade betwixt the East Indians and these parts of the world," resolved to colonize the island and to go there himself as soon as the initial settlement had been made. King Charles gave the venture his enthusiastic support, but Rupert's mother, the queen of Bohemia, compared his plan to "one of Don Quixote's conquests," and when a "blunt merchant, called to deliver his opinion, said it was a gallant design but such as wherein he would be loath to venture his younger son," Rupert decided to go off to fight on the Continent instead.[208] The idea of a half-way-house colony on the route to the East Indies was not, however, allowed to drop. In early 1639, the earl of Arundel revived Rupert's project with the king's backing, and set about organizing a voyage of his own. Simultaneously, the earl of Southampton developed an almost identical plan for a colony on Mauritius.[209]

By the end of the 1630s, under the hammer blows of one after another incursion within its chartered privileges, the East India Company was in serious crisis, in danger of collapsing. Only in December 1639 did Charles I finally respond to the company's desperate pleas and call a halt to Arundel's and Southampton's colonizing ventures and demand that William Courteen wind up his project. Nevertheless, Charles was not able to back up his own orders.[210] By 1640–1641, Parliament had returned to launch its onslaught on courtiers and special interests. Because Charles was himself secretly entangled with Courteen, he seems to have been unable to force him to cease trading or restore the East India Company's monopoly. Early in 1641, negotiations between the company and Courteen were attempted, only to break down over Courteen's insistence that he be repaid in full for his entire project in return for relinquishing his claims in the

[207] J. Fryer, *New Account of East India* (London, 1698), p. 46, quoted by Foster, "Madagascar," p. 239.

[208] *C.C.M.E.I.C. 1635–1639*, pp. 244–45, 257, 264.

[209] Ibid., pp. 315, 322–23, 337, 340, 349, 350.

[210] Ibid., pp. 274ff., 296–97, 302, 351–52.

East. The East India Company was naturally unwilling to accede to such "vast" demands, and Courteen, faced with only a minimal threat of executive or judicial reprisal, had no incentive to call his venture to a halt.[211]

Nevertheless, while Courteen's ability to carry on the trade was in little legal danger during the early 1640s, he was by this time in deep financial difficulty. His father, Sir William, had saddled him with enormous debts, and the disastrous failure of his own early East Indian voyages had made matters a great deal worse.[212] Courteen attempted to recoup his losses by continuing to invest in his East Indian association, but as a result of his financial situation was compelled, increasingly, to give over control to a group of his partners, drawn largely from the new-merchant leadership and headed by Maurice Thomson.

How and when the new-merchant leaders, and close allies of theirs, first involved themselves with the Courteens is not precisely clear. There are, however, fragmentary and indirect, though not conclusive, pieces of evidence that some of these merchants were working with the Courteens either from the time that their project was initiated or very soon thereafter. Gregory Clement, who, as noted, had been in trouble for trading illegally in the East India Company's privileged areas as early as 1631, was by the later 1630s up on charges in the High Court of Admiralty stemming apparently from his involvement in the initial voyage of plunder of Samuel Bonnell and Thomas Kynnaston and their ship *Samaritan*, which had caused much damage to the company. Already in September 1635, the East India Company board of directors had delayed honoring a cash obligation to Clement, "having heard of his private trade," and shortly thereafter began to pursue proceedings in court against the privateering syndicate. Clement was, of course, one of Maurice Thomson's leading partners and in these years was working with Thomson not only in the colonial tobacco trade but also in a series of privateering efforts in the West Indies. Similarly, John Fowke, a Levant Company trader who carried on a thirty-year legal battle with the East India Company over disputed debt obligations, became involved with Sir William Courteen when Fowke and his partner William Cloberry, the great colonial trader and Kent Island leader, fitted out their ship *Dragon* for Courteen's use in his interloping fleet of 1635–1636. It has been impossible to discover pre-

---

[211] *C.C.M.E.I.C. 1640–1643*, pp. xiv–xvi, 143, 144, 145, 146, 147, 151, 155. Similar negotiations failed in 1642 (ibid., pp. 241, 242).

[212] The story of the Courteens' business enterprises and resulting financial problems during the first half of the seventeenth century is related with full detail in a number of contemporary pamphlets. See *Lex Talonis; or the Law of Marque or Reprizals* (London, 1682); J. Darrell, *Strange News from the Indies* (London, 1652); E. Graves, *A Briefe Narrative of the Cases of Sir William Courteen and Sir Paul Pindar* (London, 1679); and other untitled, undated works collected in the British Library (515. K. 21).

cisely what Fowke's relationship was to the interloping venture in subsequent years. It seems clear, however, that he continued to be involved, or at some point became reinvolved, in the project, for he was throughout the period one of the closest collaborators of the new merchants in a wide range of endeavors. In February 1647, he presented to the House of Lords the interloping syndicate's crucial petition demanding the end of the joint-stock charter and the opening up of the East Indian trade.[213]

A series of events that took place shortly after the king had patented Courteen's syndicate is also intriguing. In May 1638, Maurice Thomson, in association with Oliver Cloberry, brother and recently estranged partner of William Cloberry, attempted, as noted, to illegally break into the Guinean trade. They were stopped by the government, but not for long. Also in May 1638, the government gave a monopoly of trade with Morocco to much the same group of merchants, led by the courtier-financier Sir Nicholas Crispe, that already held the Guinean patent.[214] This grant immediately met fierce opposition from a combination of forces whose full character and interrelationships remain unclear. Leading the opposition to the Morocco Company patent was none other than William Courteen, backed by his trading associate Samuel Bonnell. Among their colleagues was, first of all, Nathaniel Andrews, son of the shopkeeper—colonial merchant Thomas Andrews. Both Thomas and Nathaniel Andrews would soon, certainly, be partners in the East Indian interloping venture. Also an opponent of the Morocco Company on this occasion was the very same Oliver Cloberry who was at that very moment Maurice Thomson's partner in the invasion of the Guinean trade.[215] From the very start of his venture, Sir William Courteen had incorporated trade with both Morocco and Guinea within his overall East Indian interloping project, for these places were major sources of gold and ivory, as well as other products, that could be picked up en route to and exchanged in the East.[216] Cour-

---

[213] For Clement's connection with the venture of Bonnell and Kynnaston, see PRO, H.C.A.13/55/219–219v, 230ff., and *C.C.M.E.I.C. 1635–1639*, p. 85, although it must be stated that the actual nature of his involvement is far from clear. For the leasing of the *Dragon* by Fowke and Cloberry to Courteen, see PRO, H.C.A.24/92/153; PRO, H.C.A.24/93/169; PRO, H.C.A.24/102/245; PRO, H.C.A.13/55/267. For Fowke's delivery of the interloping syndicate's petition for opening the East Indian trade, see *H.M.C., Tenth Report, Appendix*, 6, p. 167.

[214] *C.S.P.D. 1637–1638*, pp. 406, 417; *C.S.P. Col. 1574–1660*, p. 273; H. Castries, *Les sources inedites d'histoire du Maroc*, 5 vols. (Paris, 1908), 3: 409.

[215] For these merchants and their struggle against the Morocco Company in this period, see *C.S.P.D. 1638–1639*, pp. 69, 130, 136, 329, 356–57, 363, 501; *C.S.P.D. 1639*, p. 120; *C.S.P.D. 1639–1640*, pp. 379, 513; PRO, P.C.2/49/107–8; PRO, P.C.2/50/29, 30, 40, 101, 124, 130–32, 335–37, 579, 641, 649, 673; PRO, H.C.A.24/100/102.

[216] For the connection that developed among Guinea, Morocco, and the East Indies in Courteen's interloping voyages, see PRO, H.C.A.24/93/79; PRO, H.C.A.24/110/317; *E.F.I. 1642–1645*, pp. xxii, 185.

teen's opposition to the Moroccan patent certainly stemmed from his concern for his East Indian project, and it is very possible (though not proved) that the simultaneous incursion by Oliver Cloberry and Maurice Thomson into the Guinean trade was also linked to the Courteen venture.

There is direct evidence that from 1641 to 1642, Thomson and his friends were working with Courteen. In those years, Maurice Thomson's long-time partner Jeremy Blackman was serving as master of the ship *William*, owned by the colonial merchants Richard Bateson, Simon Turgis, and Thomas Cox (also partners of Thomson's), and sent out by Courteen.[217] According to James Darrell, writing about a decade later:

> Mr. Courteen . . . was so weakened in his estate, that (for the better support of his trade) about *Anno* 1642, he was constrained thereby as well as by advice of his friends to associate with Mr. M. T. [Maurice Thomson] and J. B. [Jeremy Blackman] and other adventurers who were altogether strangers in that trade, but made such use of his necessity . . . by clandestine, private and prejudicial contracts.[218]

By 1642 Courteen had, in fact, gone bankrupt and shortly thereafter fled to the Continent, leaving full control of his East Indian operation in the hands of his partners.[219] These merchants can be divided into four different categories:[220] (1) traders previously involved in the American colonial trades, including Maurice Thomson, William Pennoyer, Robert Thomson, Edward Thomson, Richard Bateson, Jeremy Blackman, Martin Noel, Nathan Wright, Samuel Moyer, and Thomas Andrews and his son Nathaniel; (2) foreign merchants living in England who were Dutch associates of Courteen's, including Joas Godschalk, John La Mott, Derrick Hoast, Adam Laurence, Waldegrave Lodovicke, and John Rushout; (3) John Fowke, the early collaborator of Sir William Courteen's who later associated himself with the new merchants' syndicate; and (4) new recruits from the mercantile community. Among the new recruits were John Dethick, a domestic trader with his home county of Norfolk;[221] Stephen Estwicke, a London "haberdasher of small wares";[222] James Russell, apparently involved in both the Spanish and the Merchant Adventurers'

[217] PRO, H.C.A.24/108/50/54; PRO, H.C.A.24/110/317.

[218] Darrell, *Strange news from the Indies*, p. 24.

[219] *Fraud and Oppression Detected and Arraigned.* . . . (London, n.d.), p. 3.

[220] The following lists are derived from *C.C.M.E.I.C. 1644–1649*, pp. 116, 305 n. 1, 382; *L.J.* 10: 617, 624; *H.M.C.*, *Seventh Report, Appendix*, p. 66; PRO, H.C.A.24/108/51, 265. For Fowke, see above.

[221] *C.C.M.E.I.C. 1644–1649*, p. xxii. Dethick may also have been involved in the trades with the Americas in the 1630s. On his background and early career, see above, p. 139, and note 83.

[222] Pearl, *London*, p. 315.

trades;[223] William Ryder, a Southwark sea captain;[224] and Thomas Boone, a West Country merchant.[225] Considering the large sums required for the interloping syndicate's extensive undertakings, it would be surprising if this list exhausted its membership. In fact, there is strong indirect evidence that a substantial number of other men shared the risk, most of them recruited from Maurice Thomson's colonial merchant leadership group. One document, in particular, gives this impression—a petition of 17 August 1649 from "diverse adventurers in the Second General Voyage," in which the demand is made for better terms in settling the accounts between investors in the "Second General Voyage," organized in 1647, and the old joint-stock owners. The list of twenty signers includes William Pennoyer, Robert Thomson, Martin Noel, and Adam Laurence—all definitely involved in the interloping scheme. Among the others were Samuel Pennoyer, William Thomson, Michael Davison, John Wood, and William Harris—all of whom were relatives of Maurice Thomson's, his partners in the trade with the Americas, or both—as well as Nicholas Corsellis, a Virginian tobacco trader from a Dutch family whose son married Maurice Thomson's daughter. Also listed are a group of foreign merchants who almost certainly had been associated with William Courteen— James Houblon, John Casier, William Boene, and Ahaseurus Regemont (Jeremy Blackman later married the widow of the last named). There can be no doubt that this connection was associated with Thomson. It clearly functioned, as will be seen, as an opposition "party" inside the company, led by Thomson and based in the Second General Voyage. It seems almost certain that some if not all of its members were also involved with Thomson in the interloping project.[226]

The program of trade and colonization launched by the new merchants' East Indian interloping association found its origin in Sir William Courteen's interloping and colonial projects of the 1630s, as well as those of Arundel, Rupert, and Southampton. The new merchants naturally pur-

---

[223] *C.J.* 4: 101. London Port Book for Cloths, 1640, PRO, E.190/43/4. Russell was apparently the son of a Hertford gentleman (Drapers Company, London, Apprentice Register, 1615–1625, alphabetical index).

[224] *C.C.M.E.I.C. 1644–1649*, p. 218 and index.

[225] *C.C.M.E.I.C. 1644–1649*, p. 360; *Dictionary of Seventeenth-Century Radicals*, vol. 1, s.v. "Thomas Boone."

[226] See, for example, the syndicate's plans for investing £80,000 in a project on the Malabar coast (*C.C.M.E.I.C. 1644–1649*, p. 369). For the petition, see *C.C.M.E.I.C. 1644–1649*, pp. 342–43 n. 1. For Nicholas Corsellis, and his relationship with Maurice Thomson, see PRO, will of Nicholas Corsellis, 1665/1666 PCC Mico 5; Society of Genealogists, Boyd's Index: 14503. Corsellis brought in, for example, some 11,000 pounds of Virginian tobacco in 1640 (London Port Book for Imports, 1640, PRO, E.190/43/5). Corsellis worked with Maurice Thomson's colonial-trading partner Thomas Deacon in the domestic lead trade. For Blackman and Regemont, see PRO, will of Jeremy Blackman, 1656 PCC Berkley 380.

sued the direct trade, begun by Courteen, to the Far East. But the experience of many of these men in the American trades induced them also to devote a good deal of attention to the colonizing possibilities that, until that time, had been ignored by the East India Company. The connection between the interlopers' new plans for the East Indies and their previous practice in the colonial trades with the Americas was clearly seen by their contemporaries. As Richard Boothby reported: "A great talk and rumour hath happened this last spring . . . about divers of His Majesty's subjects adventuring to Madagascar . . . and there to plant themselves as in other parts of America."[227]

In 1645 the Thomson-led interlopers dispatched an expedition under Capt. John Smart with the object of establishing the long-projected colonial settlement off the east coast of Africa.[228] In the new merchants' grandiose vision, this colonial base would function not only as a provisioning and supply point on the route to the East, but also as a center of colonial production—especially of sugar, but also of indigo, cotton, and tobacco. In fact, they later advertised their plantation colony in the Indian Ocean by emphasizing the similarity of its productive potential—soil, geography, climate, and the like—to that of the island of Barbados in the Caribbean (where they were, of course, already active). Ultimately, they intended this settlement to form the focal point of a complex, multilateral trading network, encompassing not only the local port-to-port commerce with India, East Africa, and the Indies, but stretching as far away as the English colonies in America.[229] Smart landed first at the old stop-off in St. Augustine Bay, Madagascar. He set his 140 colonists to building houses and planting corn and dispatched two of his ships to attempt to establish further colonies on the eastern coast of Madagascar, on Mauritius, and on the island of Assada (Nossi-Be). None of these undertakings, however, succeeded. The crops failed; provisions ran short; many of the planters fell ill; and none of the other prospective sites for colonies panned out. Late in 1646, Smart was forced to abandon the settlement and evacuate his decimated population of colonists.

The new-merchant syndicate was not discouraged by this initial colonial failure, and during the later 1640s it stepped up its activities within the sphere of East Indian commerce. The interlopers were not content with the simple bilateral route rigidly followed by the old company and so began to exploit the potentially lucrative port-to-port trade on the Indian subcontinent. They took up, moreover, Courteen's idea of integrating a

[227] R. Boothby, *A Brief Discovery . . . of Madagascar* (London, 1646), p. 1.

[228] The following brief narrative account of this expedition is based on Foster, "Madagascar," pp. 242–50.

[229] R. Hunt, *The Island of Assada* (London, 1650); C.C.M.E.I.C. *1644–1649*, pp. xxii–xxiii; Foster, "Madagascar," p. 245. See also Farnell, "Navigation Act," p. 444.

regular trade with Guinea within the regular commerce to the East. These men were, of course, already active in West Africa in connection with the slave trade and West Indian plantations. They now hoped to use gold from Guinea to finance the purchase of commodities in the Indies, thereby solving the problems of bullion supply and bullion export that had long plagued English East Indian commerce.[230] Nor did the interlopers abandon their intention (in the words of one of their contemporary chroniclers) to "settle factories and plant colonies after the Dutch manner." In fact, by 1649, they had organized and sent out a new voyage to Assada. It is notable that they placed this expedition under the command of none other than Col. Robert Hunt, a protégé of Lord Brook who only recently had served as governor of the aristocratic Puritan opposition's colony on Providence Island.[231] At the same time, they began to project a second colonial base, this time on Pulo Run, an island in the East Indies seized by the Dutch but legally belonging to the English and, they hoped, recoverable by themselves.[232]

Meanwhile, the old East India Company had come to the edge of dissolution. Following the king's failure during the early 1640s to call off Courteen's venture, Parliament had granted the request of Maurice Thomson, alderman Thomas Andrews, Samuel Moyer, and James Russell to have liberty to trade with the East Indies in April 1645, had refused the plea of the company to put a stop to the interlopers' activities in the winter of 1645, and, following very extended deliberations, had decided against renewing the old company's patent in March 1647.[233] Without a privileged position in the trade, the company had little possibility of attracting continued support from the traditional company merchant sources, and was forced to contemplate the end of its permanent joint stock. Meanwhile, to keep the trade alive while renewed attempts were made to secure a charter from Parliament, the company decided to issue, under separate administration, an autonomous "terminable" joint stock covering a limited set of operations and running for a limited period of time. The company's success in raising funds for the Second General Voyage was in marked contrast with its continuing failure with its old joint stock, and the explanation is not far to seek. The new men of the interloping syndicate were at this time sending private ships to the East on their own, but they were willing to provide substantial support, in terms of

[230] *E.F.I. 1642–1645*, pp. xxii, 146; *E.F.I. 1646–1650*, pp. 27, 48. Guinea was also a source of ivory, highly valued in the east.

[231] Darrell, *Strange News from the Indies*, p. 4; *C.C.M.E.I.C. 1650–1654*, pp. ix, 10, and index. Newton, *Colonising Activities*, pp. 217, 219, 252.

[232] *C.C.M.E.I.C. 1644–1649*, pp. xvi, xxiii, xxiv, 166, 212, 370, 377.

[233] *C.J.* 4: 101; *C.C.M.E.I.C. 1644–1649*, p. 12; *L.J.* 9: 61. For details on the parliamentary deliberations on the East India Company, see below, ch. 12.

finance and leadership, to this separate and independent venture, while naturally refusing to back the old joint stock.[234] The stockholders of the Second General Voyage established a board of sixteen special directors to manage its affairs, to be chosen from among those men who had invested at least £1,000 in the venture. Six of the directors they elected were leading members of the new-merchant leadership's interloping syndicate— Thomas Andrews, Nathan Wright, Maurice Thomson, Samuel Moyer, Jeremy Blackman, and Capt. William Ryder.[235] Maurice Thomson and Jeremy Blackman were, moreover, among the eight merchants chosen to represent the Second General Voyage in negotiations with holders of old joint stock.[236]

The commercial operations of the Second General Voyage seem to have been quite successful,[237] but in 1649, when by the original agreement they had to be brought to a close, the directorate of the old company was forced again to face the problem of carrying on the trade. The old company's failure once more between January and August 1649 to raise sufficient funds for a new joint stock left it seriously weakened and unable to counter the attack that now came from both within and without its ranks.[238] On 15 August 1649 a "General Court of All Freemen and Adventurers" in the East India Company was called to decide the company's future. No decision was taken at this meeting, but it was agreed to refer the problem to a joint committee composed on the one hand of representatives from the company's generality and, on the other, of the company's directorate. The fact that at least six of the nine delegates representing the generality were members of the Thomson connection is indicative of the influence the new-merchant leadership had by now acquired even inside the company.[239] Indeed, a short time later, when the interloping syndicate petitioned Parliament for sanction of its own commercial plans for the East Indies, the old directorate found itself hopelessly outflanked.[240] Clearly, the interlopers were the most dynamic element active in East Indian enterprise at this time. It was largely through their contributions to the Second General Voyage that the old company had been able to sustain itself at all. Consequently, neither the old directorate's denial of the interlopers' claims nor

[234] On the financial support for the Second General Voyage, see *C.C.M.E.I.C. 1644–1649*, pp. xv–xvi.

[235] Ibid., p. 218.

[236] Ibid., p. 227.

[237] Ibid., p. xix.

[238] Ibid., p. 342.

[239] Ibid., pp. 341–42. William Barkeley, Samuel Moyer, Maurice Thomson, Nathan Wright, Capt. William Ryder, Capt. Jeremy Blackman.

[240] Ibid., p. xxiii.

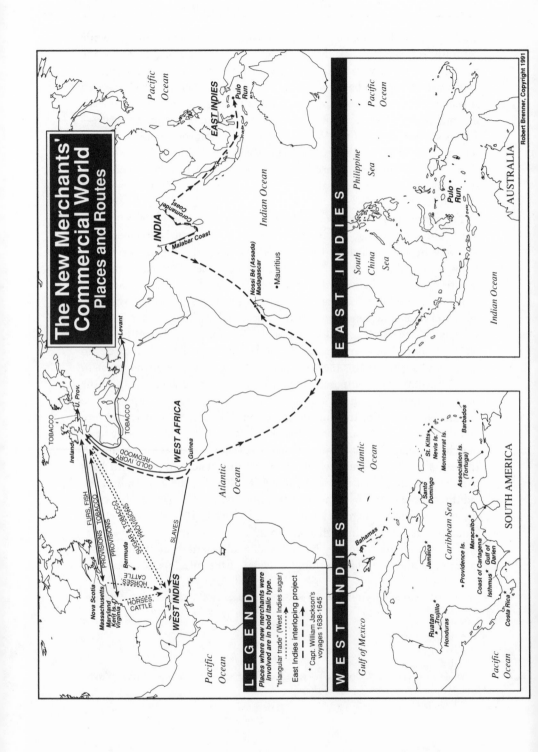

The New Merchants' Commercial World
Places and Routes

L E G E N D

Places where new merchants were *involved are in bold italic type.*

"triangular trade" (*West Indies sugar*)

East Indies interloping project

* Capt. William Jackson's voyages 1638-1645

Pacific Ocean

Atlantic Ocean

Indian Ocean

EAST INDIES

Pulo Run

INDIA

Coromandel Coast

Malabar Coast

Nossi Be (Assada)
Madagascar

•Mauritius

WEST AFRICA

Guinea

GOLD, IVORY, REDWOOD

SLAVES

Levant

U. Prov.

Ireland

TOBACCO

TOBACCO

Nova Scotia

Massachusetts
Maryland
Kent Is.
Virginia

FURS, FISH

PROVISIONS

TOBACCO

SUGAR, TOBACCO

PROVISIONS

Bermuda

HORSES, CATTLE

HORSES, CATTLE

WEST INDIES

EAST INDIES

Philippine Sea

South China Sea

Pacific Ocean

Pulo Run

Indian Ocean

AUSTRALIA

Robert Brenner, Copyright 1991

WEST INDIES

Gulf of Mexico

Atlantic Ocean

Caribbean Sea

Pacific Ocean

Bahamas

Santo Domingo

St. Kitts
Nevis Is.
Montserrat Is.

Association Is. (Tortuga)

Barbados

Jamaica *

•Providence Is.

Maracaibo *

Coast of Cartagena *

Isthmus * Gulf of Darien

Costa Rica *

Ruatan
Trujillo *

Honduras

SOUTH AMERICA

its plans for a new monopoly charter carried conviction. The old guard's only hope lay in a merger of the two groups.

The interlopers were inclined, in general, toward a "free, well-regulated trade" rather than a joint-stock monopoly.[241] They had very little to gain from a joint stock that was not totally devoted to their program. As the precondition for their acceptance of a merged joint-stock organization, therefore, they demanded that the old company directors agree to implement a series of projects that they had always rejected in the past:[242] (1) the establishment of an island colony off the east coast of Africa; (2) the pursuit of the port-to-port trade in the Far East; (3) the settlement of colonies in India and the East Indies, in particular on the island of Pulo Run; and (4) a general policy of encouraging settlers at all East Indian outposts. The interlopers required, in addition, assent to (5) the purchase and incorporation into the East India Company of the Guinean trade as a valuable source of gold and other commodities marketable in the East; (6) the right to send independent voyages to China, Japan, and other areas if the company itself refused to do so; and (7) compensation for certain losses the interlopers had sustained in their own venture.

The old company directorate naturally objected to all of these proposals. Their weakened position, however, left them little ground for effective opposition. They were obliged to accede to the settlement substantially worked out between the new merchants and the national government. This agreement retained the joint-stock organization that the new men had originally opposed, but adopted in its entirety the remainder of the interlopers' program for the operation of the trade.[243]

The New-Merchant Leadership

The new merchants' potential for such wide-ranging activities derived in part from the economic success they had already achieved. In terms of wealth, it is obvious that these men could not by 1640 begin to rival the top Levant–East India merchants. But the socioeconoimc standing, in the very rough terms in which it can be measured, of the the new-merchant leadership—which represented, by and large, the leading layer within a much larger overall group of colonial traders—did not compare unfavorably with that of the average Merchant Adventurers (here taking into account the Adventurers' whole commercial group) (see table 4.1). Moreover, a small, but still quite pivotal, group among the new merchants had

[241] Ibid., p. 369.

[242] The following program has been derived from the interlopers' propositions to the government of 10 November 1649 (PRO, C.O.77/7/6; *C.C.M.E.I.C. 1644–1649*, pp. 369–72).

[243] *C.C.M.E.I.C. 1644–1649*, pp. 377–78. See also below, ch. 12, pp. 608–13.

profited by their trading activity to such an extent that they had achieved by 1640 a position that might be described as the top of the second rank within the merchant community—that is, just below the aldermanic–East India Company elite. These men included the Levant–East India colonial traders Matthew Craddock and Samuel Vassall, as well as John and Samuel Warner, Thomas Stone, Maurice Thomson, and Thomas Andrews. Craddock and Vassall would be elected London MPs in 1640; and Craddock had actually become by this time an East India Company director. John Warner was the only new merchant elected to the aldermanic court in the prerevolutionary period, achieving his office in 1640. His brother Samuel Warner became an alderman in 1643.[244] Thomas Andrews chose to pay a fine rather than take the office of sheriff, but he did become an alderman in 1642.[245] Thomas Stone also paid a fee to avoid having to become sheriff, and when, in 1640, the most substantial citizens of his ward (Cripplegate Within) were ranked into four classes according to their wealth, Stone was included among the men of the top class.[246] A similar four-class division was made in Maurice Thomson's Billingsgate Ward, and Thomson was listed among the three men designated as "the first and best sort."[247] The high position achieved by these few individuals is evidence of their impressive commercial success over the previous period, and also helps to explain some of the political and social influence they and their group were able to exert during the following years.

It seems reasonable to argue, however, that in the last analysis the new merchants' growing strength was basically attributable to their internal cohesiveness and their wide-ranging connections. Great stress has been laid on the common origins and direct family and business ties that defined the colonial merchant leadership. Of course, there were many other colonial traders with the Americas, including a number of quite important ones, who, as far as is known, were outside this core network. But these men shared the new-merchant leadership's economic interests. Moreover, they do not seem to have differed very greatly from the new-merchant leadership in their background (see table 4.1) or their overall modes of operation. As a contemporary described the colonial trading group as a whole, "These are not merchants born, or versed in foreign ports, or any trade, but to those plantations, and that from either planters there or wholesale tobacconists and shopkeepers retailing in England."[248] For these reasons, it is not surprising that the new-merchant leaders' general course

---

[244] Pearl, *London*, pp. 185–87, 189–91, 325–27.

[245] Ibid., p. 310.

[246] Harvey, *List of Principal Inhabitants of London, 1640*, p. 13.

[247] Ibid., p.2.

[248] "The Humble Remonstrance of John Bland of London Merchant," *V.M.H.B.* 1 (1894): 144. See also below, ch. 6.

TABLE 4.1

Socioeconomic Position of London's Overseas Merchants, Pre−Civil War

	New Merchants 1 (no. = 82)	New Merchants 2 (no. = 60)	Levant Company (currants traders, 1640) (no. = 61)	Merchant Adventurers (exporters of 100 + cloths, 1640) (no. = 74)
Percentage armigerous according to *Visitation of London, 1633−1635*	42	33	59	39
Percentage included in leading inhabitants of 1640[a]	31	21	49	42
Geographical Origins				
Born in London	15 (25%)	4 (20%)	23 (58%)	21 (40%)
Born out of London	45 (75%)	20 (80%)	17 (42%)	30 (60%)
No information on birthplace	20	36	21	23

NOTES

New Merchants 1 All members in American colonial partnerships through 1640 (derived from table 4.2): Thomas Allen, William Allen, Jonathan Andrews, Nathaniel Andrews, Peter Andrews, Thomas Andrews, Jr., Thomas Andrews, Sr., William Barkeley, Richard Bateson, Edward Bennett, Richard Bennett, William Bennett, Jeremy Blackman, Anthony Briskett, Richard Buckham, William Capps, William Chamberlain, William Claiborne, Gregory Clement, Oliver Cloberry, William Cloberry, Thomas Combes, Nicholas Corsellis, Matthew Craddock, Richard Cranley, Thomas Deacon, John de la Barre, James Dobson, Edward Downing, William Felgate, Timothy Feltoñ, George Fletcher, Joshua Foote, Thomas Frere, Ralph Hamor, William Harris, Andrew Hawes, Joseph Hawes, Nathaniel Hawes, Anthony Hilton, John John, John Johnstone, Thomas King, Roger Limbrey, Cornelius Lloyd, Randall Mainwaring, Samuel Matthews, George Menefie, Edward Meredith, Ralph Marrifield, George Payne, Samuel Pennoyer, William Pennoyer, Richard Quiney, Elias Roberts, John Sadler, Humphrey Slaney, George Snelling, Robert South, Thomas Stegg, Andrew Stone, James Stone, Thomas Stone, William Stone, Edward Thomson, George Thomson, Maurice Thomson, Nicholas Trerice, William Tucker, Simon Turgis, John Utie, Samuel Vassall, William Vassall, Robert Wilding, William Wilkinson, William Willoughby, Edward Wood, Nathan Wright.

New Merchants 2 Traders of 10,000 + lbs. of tobacco in 1627−1628, 1630, 1633, 1634, or 1640 (as recorded in London Port Books for Imports): Thomas Allen, William Allen, Thomas Armstone, Margaret Barker, Edward Barton, Richard Bateson, Edward Bennett, Jeremy Blackman, John Bradley, Henry Brooke, Capt. William Button, John Constable, Thomas Cornwallis, Nicholas Corsellis, Edward Davies, John Davies, Humphrey Farley, John Flowes(r?), Thomas Gower, Robert Grimes, Alex Harewood, Edward Harris, Joseph Hawes, George Henley, Anthony Hopson, Francis Huffe, Edward Hurd, James Jenkins, Thomas Jennes(ings?), Richard Johns, Edward Maior (Meyers), Samuel Matthews, William Melling, George Menefie, John Osborne, Richard Perry, William Pierce, John Preene, John Prim, Richard Quiney, Samuel Rastell, Elias Roberts, Israel Scarlet, George Smith, John Southwood, Richard Stephens, Thomas Stone, Robert Swinnerton, George Thomson, Maurice Thomson, William Thomson, William Tristram, Robert Tucker, John Turner, William Underwood, William Watts, William Webb, John White, Robert Wilding, Richard Wilson.

[a] Harvey, *List of Principal Inhabitants of London, 1640*. See above, n. 84.

of action across a wide range of activities tended to prove congenial to the whole group of colonial traders, and that these traders by and large were willing to follow their lead.

Finally, the new-merchant leaders were able to stretch their sphere of influence far beyond that of mere colonial traders. On the one hand, they were closely related to that loosely defined middle layer of London shop-keepers, ship captains, and domestic traders, which, once organized, would be capable of challenging the City's political order. On the other hand, they were tied to that group of colonizing aristocrats who would help lead the parliamentary attack on the Caroline regime. It was thus their dual role—not only as leaders of an American colonial interest, but also as partners with and mediators between the parliamentary leadership and the City popular classes—that gave the new-merchant leaders the strength in the following years to launch powerful initiatives not only in the sphere of commerce, but also in politics and religion. In these revo-lutionary decades, successful campaigns in one sphere were often impos-sible without correspondingly effective initiatives in the others.

TABLE 4.2

The New-Merchant Leadership:
Partnerships in the Colonial-Interloping Trades, 1616–1649

	Partnership	Purpose	Year
1.	William Tucker Elias Roberts Ralph Hamor	Foundation of Virginia plantation	1616

Va. Co. Recs. 3: 58; Brown, *Genesis* 2: 1034.

2.	William Tucker William Capps	Virginia sassafras trade	1620

PRO, H.C.A.24/79/98.

3.	Sir Thomas Warner Ralph Merrifield (Maurice Thomson)	Initial colonization of the West Indies	ca. 1625

Williamson, *Caribbee Islands*, pp. 21–22, 27–29.

4.	Maurice Thomson Sir Thomas Warner Thomas Combes Thomas Stone Robert Wilding	St. Kitts plantation and tobacco and provisioning trade	1626–1628

A.P.C. Col. 1613–1680, p. 22; PRO, C.2/Ch.I/T.24/64;
Bodleian Library, Rawlinson MSS C.94, fols. 8–9.

TABLE 4.2 (*cont.*)

	Partnership	Purpose	Year
5.	Maurice Thomson Thomas Stone	Virginia and West Indies tobacco and provisioning trade; reexportation of tobacco to Middleburg, Flushing and Amsterdam	late 1620s–1630s

Pagan, "Growth of the Tobacco Trade," 3: 261 n.89.

6.	Thomas Stone William Stone	Virginia plantation	late 1620s–1640s

Ames, *Records of Accomack* 7: *xxx, 162–63.*

7.	Anthony Hilton Edward Thomson	Founding first colony on the Isle of Nevis	1628

Williamson, *Caribbee Islands*, pp. 66–68; PRO, H.C.A.24/90/101.

8.	William Cloberry Sir William Alexander	Settlement of Nova Scotia and development of Canadian fur trade	1628

Rogers, *Earl of Stirling's Register*, p. 256; Andrews, *Colonial Period* 1: 314–15, 328, 329.

9.	Samuel Vassall Peter Andrews	Virginia and West Indies tobacco and provisioning trade	1620s–1630s

PRO, will of Peter Andrews, 1650 PCC Pembroke 152; *C.S.P. Col. 1574–1660*, p. 190 and index.

10.	Samuel Vassall Peter Andrews George Menefie	Virginia plantation and tobacco and provisioning trade	1620s–1640s

PRO, H.C.A.24/92/299; PRO, will of George Menefie, 1647 PCC Fines 31.

11.	Edward Thomson Thomas King Thomas Wilkinson	St. Kitts tobacco and provisioning trade	1631–1633

PRO, H.C.A.24/89/128.

12.	William Cloberry Maurice Thomson John de la Barre Simon Turgis William Claiborne	Kent Island Project	1631

"Cloberry Transcripts," *Md. Hist. Mag.* 26 (1931), 27 (1932).

13.	Jeremy Blackman George Thomson	Shipping services for Kent Island Project	1631

Md. Hist. Mag. 27 (1932): 17.

14.	Maurice Thomson John de la Barre	Interloping in Canadian fur trade	1631

A.P.C. Col. 1613–1680, pp. 134, 169–85; *C.S.P. Col. 1574–1660*, pp. 103, 106–7, 114, 119, 120, 128, 139, 143, 145, 151.

[185]

TABLE 4.2 (*cont.*)

	Partnership	Purpose	Year
15.	William Tucker Maurice Thomson Thomas Stone	Syndicate given right to market entire Virginia tobacco crop	1632–1633

PRO, C.O.1/6/54; *C.S.P. Col. 1574–1660*, p. 151.

16.	George Thomson Jeremy Blackman	Virginia tobacco and provisioning trade	1633

PRO, H.C.A.24/89/129.

17.	Maurice Thomson Gregory Clement Robert South William Willoughby	Virginia tobacco and provisioning trade	1634

C.S.P.D. 1636–1637, pp. 350, 554; PRO, C.2/Ch.I/C.59/29.

18.	Thomas Stegg Maurice Thomson	Stegg is Thomson's factor in Virginia	1634 on

PRO, H.C.A.24/97/51; PRO, H.C.A.13/55/268, 312.

19.	George Thomson Anthony Briskett	Founding colony on island of Montser- rat and tobacco and provisioning trade there	1635

PRO, H.C.A.24/92/26; PRO, H.C.A.13/53/19, 295; Williamson, *Caribee Islands*, p. 94.

20.	Thomas Stone William Stone Andrew Stone	Virginia plantation and tobacco and provisioning trade	ca. 1635

Nugent, *Cavaliers and Pioneers*, pp. 211ff.

21.	John Warner Samuel Warner	Virginia tobacco and provisioning trade	1635

PRO, H.C.A.24/92/37.

22.	William Harris Thomas Deacon Andrew Hawes	Virginia plantation and tobacco and provisioning trade; London cheese- mongering business	1630s

New York Public Library, Smyth of Nibley Papers, no. 40; "Abstracts of Virginia Land Patents," *V.M.H.B.* 6 (1899): 91; *C.S.P. Col. 1574–1660*, p. 281; *C.S.P.D. 1639–1640*, pp.
563–64; PRO, S.P.105/148/194; PRO, will of Andrew Hawes, 1642 PCC Cambell 70.

23.	Richard Bateson Samuel Vassall Edward Wood	Virginia and West Indies tobacco and provisioning trade	1630s

PRO, C.2/Ch.I/C.90/28.

24.	Richard Cranley Edward Thomson	Virginia and West Indies tobacco and provisioning trade	1630s

PRO, S.P.105/149/255; PRO, H.C.A.24/91/22–23.

TABLE 4.2 *(cont.)*

	Partnership	Purpose	Year
25.	William Cloberry Humphrey Slaney	Newfoundland, Guinea, and American tobacco trade	1630s

Cell, "Newfoundland Company," p. 615; Cell, *English Enterprise in Newfoundland*, p. 77 n. 106; Blake, "Guinea Trade," pp. 87ff.

26.	Matthew Craddock Nathan Wright	Massachusetts Bay subcompany provisioning and trade with Massachusetts	1630s

Bailyn, *New England Merchants*, pp. 19, 26 n. 35; Andrews, *Colonial Period* 1: 398.

27.	John Winthrop Edward Downing Francis Kirby	Fur trade with Massachusetts Bay	1630s

Bailyn, *New England Merchants*, pp. 26–27 nn. 38–39; *Winthrop Papers* 3: 55–56.

28.	Edward Bennett Richard Bennett John Utie	Virginia tobacco and provisioning trade	1630s

Ross, "Bennett Family."

29.	Thomas Andrews, Sr. Thomas Andrews, Jr. Jonathan Andrews Nathaniel Andrews	Trade with Massachusetts Bay; West Indies plantation and trade; London shopkeeping	1630s–1640s

Barbados Record Office, Deeds (recopied), 2/658, 3/922; PRO, S.P. 105/149/92.

30.	Samuel Vassall William Vassall	Trade with Massachusetts Bay	1630s–1640s

Bailyn, *New England Merchants*, pp. 36, 38, 88, 107.

31.	Maurice Thomson Nicholas Trerice Joshua Foote	Trade with Massachusetts Bay	1630s–1640s

C.S.P. Col. 1574–1660, p. 275.

32.	Maurice Thomson Roger Limbrey	St. Kitts tobacco trade	1636–1640

PRO, H.C.A.24/101/190.

33.	Matthew Craddock William Pennoyer Edward Meredith Grace Hardy	Virginia and Barbados tobacco and provisioning trade; owners of ship *Abraham*	1636–1638

PRO, H.C.A.24/95/203.

34.	William Tucker Maurice Thomson George Thomson James Stone		

TABLE 4.2 (*cont.*)

Partnership	Purpose	Year
Jeremy Blackman William Harris Thomas Deacon Cornelius Lloyd James Dobson	Syndicate that received "Berkeley Hundred" plantation	1637

Nugent, *Cavaliers and Pioneers*, p. 53.

35.	Richard Quiney John Sadler	Syndicate that received "Martin's Brandon" plantation; London grocery business	1637

Nugent, *Cavaliers and Pioneers*, p. 55; Grocers Company, London, Index of Freemen, 1345–1645.

36.	Samuel Pennoyer William Pennoyer Matthew Craddock	Virginia-England-Levant tobacco reexport trade	1637

PRO, C.2/Ch.I/A.13/69; PRO, H.C.A.24/95/203; PRO, H.C.A.24/101/246.

37.	William Chamberlain Samuel Vassall Richard Bateson Edward Wood George Menefie	Virginia tobacco and provisioning trade	1637

PRO, C.2/Ch.I/C.90/28.

38.	William Harris Thomas Deacon William Tucker Maurice Thomson	Virginia tobacco and provisioning trade	1637–1638

Ames, *Records of Accomack*, p. 105; PRO, H.C.A.24/94/155.

39.	Maurice Thomson Providence Island Company	Projected silver mine project in Bay of Darien	1638

PRO, C.O.124/357–59.

40.	William Claiborne Providence Island Company Maurice Thomson (?)	Founding of colony at Ruatan, Honduras	1638–1642

Newton, *Colonising Activities*, pp. 267, 315; Hale, *Virginia Venturer*, pp. 232–33.

41.	Maurice Thomson William Pennoyer Thomas Frere William Tucker (?)	Capt. Jackson's raiding voyage to Spanish West Indies	1638–1641

Harlow, *Captain William Jackson* 13: v–vii; Newton, *Colonising Activities*, pp. 267–71.

TABLE 4.2 (*cont.*)

	Partnership	Purpose	Year
42.	Maurice Thomson Richard Buckham Thomas Deacon	Virginia tobacco and provisioning trade; owners of ship *Rebecca*	1638

Ames, *Records of Accomack*, p. 105.

43.	William Tucker William Harris	Virginia tobacco and provisioning trade	1638

PRO, H.C.A.24/94/155.

44.	Richard Bateson Edward Wood Richard Cranley	Barbados tobacco and provisioning trade (using ship *Diamond*, owned by Maurice Thomson)	1638–1640

PRO, H.C.A.24/101/122.

45.	William Barkeley Timothy Felton John John Elias Roberts	Virginia, Bermuda, Greenland, and New England trade; owners of ship *Charles*	1638–1647

PRO, H.C.A.24/108/286; PRO, H.C.A.3/43/15v, 24v, 25v, 27v.

46.	Maurice Thomson Oliver Cloberry Oliver Reed George Lewine	Attempted interloping voyage to Guinea	1638

C.S.P.D. 1637–1638, p. 406; *C.S.P. Col. 1574–1660*, p. 273.

47.	Maurice Thomson Samuel Vassall George Snelling	Virginia and St. Kitts tobacco and provisioning trade	1639

A.P.C. Col. 1613–1680, p. 305.

48.	William Allen Thomas Allen William Harris Thomas Deacon	Virginia tobacco and provisioning trade	1639

A.P.C. Col. 1613–1680, p. 259.

49.	William Claiborne Maurice Thomson Samuel Matthews George Fletcher William Bennett Bermuda Company	Application for great land grant encompassing land between Potomac and Rapahannock rivers (never acted on)	1639

Hale, *Virginia Venturer*, p. 236; Andrews, *Colonial Period* 2: 284 n. 1; Lefroy, *Memorials* 1: 724.

Table 4.2 (cont.)

	Partnership	Purpose	Year
50.	Maurice Thomson William Pennoyer	Patent for fishery at Cape Anne from Massachusetts Bay Colony	1639

Shurtleff, *Records of the Governor* 1: 256; Kellaway, *New England Company*, pp. 58–59; Winthrop, *History of New England*, 1: 307.

	Partnership	Purpose	Year
51.	Maurice Thomson Providence Island Company	Thomson provisioning Providence Island	1639–1641

PRO, C.O.124/2/387, 389, 390; *C.S.P. Col. 1574–1660*, pp. 296, 309, 317, 318.

	Partnership	Purpose	Year
52.	Oliver Cloberry George Fletcher	Barbary and West Indies trade and owners of ship *Martha*	1639

PRO, H.C.A.24/105/5.

	Partnership	Purpose	Year
53.	William Allen Thomas Allen Richard Quiney John Sadler	Virginia tobacco and provisioning trade	late 1630s

C.S.P. Col. 1574–1660, p. 321.

	Partnership	Purpose	Year
54.	Randall Mainwaring Joseph Hawes Nathaniel Hawes George Payne	Virginia and West Indies tobacco and provisioning trade	late 1630s

PRO, H.C.A.24/92/33; Shilton and Holworthy, *Admiralty Examinations, 1637–1638*, p. xxvii and index; Stock, *Proceedings and Debates* 1: 181, 197–200, and index.

	Partnership	Purpose	Year
55.	Thomas Stegg Jeremy Blackman	Supplying West Indies with horses from Virginia	late 1630s

Nugent, *Cavaliers and Pioneers*, p. 118; *C.S.P. Col. 1574–1660*, p. 308.

	Partnership	Purpose	Year
56.	George Snelling Maurice Thomson Edward Thomson	Virginia and West Indies tobacco and provisioning trade	1640

C.S.P. Col. 1574–1660, p. 195; PRO, C.O.1/8/42.

	Partnership	Purpose	Year
57.	Maurice Thomson Samuel Vassall William Felgate	Virginia and West Indies tobacco and provisioning trade	ca. 1640

C.S.P. Col. 1574–1660, p. 305.

	Partnership	Purpose	Year
58.	William Tucker John Johnstone	Barbados trade	1640

Barbados Record Office, Deeds, 1/851.

	Partnership	Purpose	Year
59.	Anthony Pennyston Richard Ingle Thomas Allen	Maryland tobacco trade; owners of ship *Richard and Anne*	1641

PRO, H.C.A.24/102/190.

TABLE 4.2 (*cont.*)

Partnership	Purpose	Year
60. Oliver Cloberry George Fletcher Henry Taverner	St. Kitts tobacco and provisioning trade	1642

H.M.C., Fifth Report, Appendix, p. 30.

61. Michael Cawton Robert Shapden	Guinea and Barbados slave trade	1642–1644

PRO, H.C.A.24/108/7, 8.

62. The earl of Warwick Maurice Thomson William Pennoyer	Capt. Jackson's second marauding voyage to Spanish West Indies	1642–1645

PRO, H.C.A.24/108/7, 8.

63. William Barkeley Henry St. John John De Bayley	Provisions trade with Canada and New England	1643–1644

Stock, *Proceedings and Debates*, 1: 160–67.

64. William Pennoyer Richard Hill	Guinea-Barbados slave trade; owners of ship *Phillip*	1645–1647

PRO, H.C.A.24/108/165.

65. William Pennoyer Michael Davison	Barbados plantation	1640s

Clothworkers Company, London, Apprentice Register, 1606–1641; *C.S.P. Col. 1574–1660*, p. 379; Royal Commonwealth Institute, Darnell Davis Collection, box 7, no. 5.

66. John Wood James Houlder, factor	Guinea slave trade	1640s

PRO, H.C.A.24/108/247.

67. John Brett John Ballow Thomas Walter William Crispe John Wood	Guinea-Barbados slave trade	1646–1648

PRO, H.C.A.24/109/190.

68. William Pennoyer Robert Thomson Elias Roberts Samuel Pennoyer William Fletcher Michael Davison Joseph Terringham Richard Bateson	Guinea-Barbados slave trade	1646–1647

PRO, H.C.A.24/108/362.

TABLE 4.2 (*cont.*)

	Partnership	Purpose	Year
69.	Maurice Thomson Rowland Wilson, Sr. Rowland Wilson, Jr. John Wood Thomas Walter	Guinea gold trade; owners of the ship *Star*	1647–1648

PRO, H.C.A.24/109/151; PRO, H.C.A.24/110/74, 75; PRO, T.70/169, fols. 34–36.

70.	Samuel Vassall Richard Cranley Benjamin Cranley Jeremy Blackman Peter Andrews	Guinea-West Indies slave trade; owners of ships *Mayflower*, *Peter*, and *Benjamin*	1647

PRO, H.C.A.24/109/255; PRO, H.C.A.24/110/35; PRO, E.163/19/25.

71.	Samuel Vassall Richard Shute Roger Vivian Gilbert Morewood Richard Cranley	Trade to Brazil with license from king of Portugal; owners of ship *Concord*	1648

PRO, S.P.46/101/?; PRO, H.C.A.24/109/154.

72.	John Dethick Richard Shute Gilbert Morewood	Owners of ship *Mayflower*; perhaps also traders to Guinea (see above, no. 70)	1649

C.S.P.D. 1649–1650, p. 349.

73.	Gregory Clement William Pennoyer	Barbados-New England trade	1649

PRO, C.24/733/51.

74.	Maurice Thomson William Pennoyer	West Indies-New England trade	1649

Aspinwall Notarial Records, pp. 255, 356–57.

75.	Robert Wilding Martin Noel	Montserrat sugar and tobacco trade	late 1640s

PRO, H.C.A.24/109/56; *C.S.P. Col. 1574–1660*, p. 368; Pares, "Merchants and Planters," p. 6 n. 29; Woodhead, *Rulers*, p. 122.

76.	Maurice Thomson William Pennoyer Robert Thomson Edward Thomson Richard Bateson Jeremy Blackman Martin Noel Nathan Wright Samuel Moyer		

TABLE 4.2 (*cont.*)

Partnership	Purpose	Year
Thomas Andrews	East Indian interloping and Assada	late 1630s?–1650
Nathaniel Andrews	plantation	
John Fowke		
Stephen Estwicke		
James Russell		
William Ryder		
Thomas Boone		
Joas Godschalk		
John La Mott		
Derrick Hoast		
Adam Laurence		
Waldegrave Lodovicke		
John Rushout		
and most probably		
Samuel Pennoyer		
William Thomson		
Michael Davison		
John Wood		
William Harris		
Nicholas Corsellis		
James Houblon		
John Casier		
William Boene		
Ahaseurus Regemont		

C.C.M.E.I.C. 1644–1649, pp. xxii, 116, 218, 305 n. 1, 342–43 n. 1, 360, 382; *C.J.* 4: 101; *L.J* 10: 617, 624; *H.M.C.*, *Seventh Report, Appendix*, p. 66; *H.M.C.*, *Tenth Report, Appendix*, pt. 6, p. 167; PRO, H.C.A.24/108/50, 51, 54, 265.

TABLE 4.3
Some Family and Apprenticeship Connections Among the New Merchants

Names	Relationship	Specification	Source (ch./fn)
Thomas Allen and William Allen	son		4/110
Jonathan, Nathaniel, and Thomas Andrews	brothers	sons of Thomas Andrews, new merchant	4/84
Thomas Andrews (Jr.) and Matthew Craddock	son-in-law	marr. Damaris, dtr. of Matthew Craddock	4/84
Randall Mainwaring and Matthew Craddock	cousins	Matthew Craddock's father's sister Jane Craddock marr. Randall Mainwaring's father Edward Mainwaring	4/77
Thomas Frere William Felgate	app. Skinners		4/151
Randall Mainwaring and Joseph and Nathaniel Hawes	brothers-in-law	marr. Elizabeth Hawes, sister of Joseph and Nathaniel Hawes	4/78
George Snelling and Joseph Hawes	app. Drapers		4/78
John Brett and Randall Mainwaring	son-in-law and app. Grocers	marr. Mary, sister of Randall Mainwaring	4/80
John Jolliffe and Randall Mainwaring	nephew	son of Elizabeth Mainwaring Jolliffe sister of Randall Mainwaring	4/81
Michael Davison William Pennoyer	app. Clothworkers		4/165
Samuel and William Pennoyer	brothers	sons of Robert Pennoyer of Bristol	4/75
Joseph Terringham and William Pennoyer	app. Haberdashers		4/179
Thomas Alderne and Owen Rowe	son-in-law	marr. Dorothy, dtr. of Owen Rowe	10/60
Thomas Alderne and James Russell	app. Drapers		10/60
Richard Quiney and John Sadler	brothers-in-law	marr. Ellen Sadler, sister of John Sadler	4/60

TABLE 4.3 *(cont.)*

Names	Relationship	Specification	Source (ch./fn)
William Cloberry and Humphrey Slaney	son-in-law app. Haberdashers	marr. Dorothy Slaney dtr. of Humphry Slaney of London, merchant	4/24
Richard Chandler and Thomas Stone	app. Haberdashers		4/190
William Stone and Thomas Stone	nephew		4/44
Robert Wilding and Thomas Stone	app. Haberdashers		4/45
Elias Roberts and George, Maurice, Paul, Robert, William Thomson	brothers-in-law	marr. Dinah Thomson, sister of George Thomson et al	4/12
Edward Thomson and George Thomson et al	kinsman		
George, Maurice, Paul, Robert, William Thomson	brothers	sons of Robert Thomson of Watton, Hertfordshire	4/7
William Tucker and George, Maurice, Paul, Robert, William Thomson	brothers-in-law	marr. Mary, sister of George Thomson et al	4/10
William Felgate and William Tucker	brothers-in-law		4/17
William Jackson and William Tucker	app. Haberdashers		4/152
Peter Andrews Samuel Vassall	brothers-in-law	marr. Rachel Vassall, sister of Samuel Vassall	4/68
Thomas Vincent and Thomas Andrews	app. Leathersellers		8/20
John Warner and Samuel Warner	brothers	sons of John Warner of Bucknell, Oxon.	4/64
William Thomson and Samuel Warner	son-in-law	marr. Elizabeth, dtr. of Samuel Warner	4/63

PART TWO

THE EMERGENCE OF POLITICAL
CONFLICT, 1620–1642

[V]

The Rise of Merchant Opposition

in the 1620s

THE KEY to the London merchants' politics in the later sixteenth and early seventeenth centuries was to be found in the nature of their relationship with the royal government. This was no chance or temporary arrangement. It had deep roots in the quite permanent needs of both the overseas traders and the monarchy. The merchants derived their income from the carrying of commodities. To maintain their profits, they had to limit the supply of goods they sold with respect to the level of demand and control the demand for goods they bought with respect to the existing supply. They needed, therefore, to control entry into commerce—how many traders and how much they could trade—so as to limit the inherent tendency to overtrading and to secure favorable prices for both their sales and their purchases. The Merchant Adventurers were, of course, the classic case. In some few commercial lines, such as the Levant Company's import trade in raw silks, the purely economic barriers to entry were, in themselves, perhaps high enough to limit competition from other English merchants. But even in cases such as this, noneconomic barriers to entry were often required in order to limit competition from wealthy retailers, as well as from increasingly threatening foreign merchants. Indeed, in the early years of the seventeenth century, Dutch traders and shippers were offering a growing challenge to the English in almost every commercial area. Most of the London merchant community therefore needed government intervention—to sanction privileged trading companies and, increasingly, to keep foreign competitors out of the domestic market.[1]

On the other hand, the monarchy suffered from what might be called a structural tendency to financial crisis, resulting from its limited capacity to tax—especially to tax the land—and its secularly increasing expenses. The Crown was under continuous pressure to hand out royal resources as patronage to ensure political support. The Crown's apparently self-destructive tendency to conspicuous consumption and to the enlargement of

---

[1] See above, ch. 2.

the court had the same rationale: to cement the king's support around him. Finally, there was the ever-present propensity to the royal game of war. War did not, of course, generally result merely from the whim of the monarch. Organizing for war was a fundamental form of organizing the aristocracy and, in particular, of solidifying the aristocracy's backing for the king. Moreover, the pressures arising from an international system of states organized for war sometimes made military conflict unavoidable. It is true, and worth emphasizing, that neither aristocratic military organization and lifestyle nor external pressures for war occupied the central position in English political life that they held throughout much of the Continent at this time. The fact remains that the Crown was unable or unwilling, for extended periods, to avoid involvement in foreign warfare, and this placed intolerable strains on the royal treasury.[2]

The material foundations of the merchant community's alliance with the Crown were therefore crystal clear: the Crown could, and did, create economic privileges for the merchants; the merchants offered loans and taxes, as well as political support, to the Crown. I have already noted the profound strengthening of the Crown-merchant alliance during the second half of the sixteenth century, under the complementary pressures of the Crown's growing financial exigencies, resulting especially from war, and of the merchants' increasing need for protection, resulting especially from the stagnation of the short-route cloth export trade to northern Europe. The Merchant Adventurers, it will be recalled, had been more than willing to provide greater loans and stepped-up customs payments in exchange for a significant tightening of their monopoly. Of course, conflicts inevitably arose over the terms of the partnership between the Crown and the merchant community. But the partnership itself was never in question.

In the early seventeenth century, pressures for cooperation between the merchant community and the Crown were, if anything, increasing. The Crown emerged from the wars of the later sixteenth century in a disastrous financial condition, at least £400,000 in debt. James I made things much worse when, under pressure to consolidate his new regime, he launched an enormous shareout of royal resources with the court. By 1618, the Crown's debt had reached £900,000. Meanwhile, the potential returns from the Crown's traditional sources of revenue had decreased. Crown lands had been sold off at a rapid pace during the sixteenth century. Returns from the subsidy, the traditional parliamentary tax, had declined dramatically as a result of corruption in assessment and collection, as well as of inflation. Income derivable from one subsidy fell from £130,000 in the early sixteenth century to about £55,000 in the later 1620s (even dis-

---

[2] Cf. C. Russell, "Parliament and the King's Finances," in *The Origins of the English Civil War*, ed. C. Russell (London, 1973).

counting inflation). The outbreak of political conflict in the Stuart Parliaments only exacerbated this problem.[3]

In this situation taxes on trade appeared to provide the Crown the best way out. Such levies could be regularly adjusted for inflation. Above all, they offered certain political advantages, unavailable with other forms of revenue raising. They did not fall on the landowners; they did not require local governments controlled by landowners to collect them; and they could, at least in the view of the Crown, be levied without Parliament's approval. At the same time, although hardly welcome to the merchant community, taxes on trade could nonetheless be made acceptable, if they were sensitively levied and if the appropriate quid pro quo was offered. The Merchant Adventurers experienced something of a boom in cloth exports in the early years of the seventeenth century, but as their trade plunged into crisis after about 1614, they were willing to pay a heavy price to see that their privileges were protected. The Levant–East India Company merchants enjoyed an enormous expansion of their trade throughout the period. But their prosperity only enhanced their ability and willingness to pay for increased protection. The overall trend throughout the pre–Civil War period—especially when the Crown and the merchant community could cooperate without interference from Parliament—was thus toward rising levies on trade and greater protection for the merchants' companies.

There was a further bond that overlapped with and tended to strengthen this fundamental link between the City's company merchants and the royal government—the intimate connection between the Crown and what I have termed the merchant political elite, as represented on the court of aldermen, the customs syndicates, and the East India Company directorate; which included the top leadership elements within the chartered companies, especially those among the traders with the East. These top merchants had access to some of the best court plums, occupied many of the highest positions in the City government, and served on most royal commissions concerning trade. They were thus drawn, unavoidably, into perpetual contact, and collaboration, with the royal government.

The royal customs farms offered the great City merchants their best opportunity for holding royal office. In order to provide patronage, the Crown was led to create all sorts of income-generating licenses and monopolies that allowed for the collection of fees in exchange for the sanction of economic activities. But most of these privileges normally went to courtiers, not to City merchants. At the same time, because of the weakness of royal administration, the Crown was obliged to give over certain public functions to private parties who performed them for private profit.

[3] Russell, "Parliament and the King's Finances," pp. 96–99.

The great City merchants had better access to offices of the latter type, and the royal customs farms are the primary case in point. Leading merchants from the main City overseas trading companies controlled these farms from their inception early in the seventeenth century.[4]

The City government traditionally provided unshakable support for the monarchy because the Crown was itself historically a mainstay of the City's corporate privileges. And the same layer of top company merchants provided the primary, though not the exclusive, pool of candidates for the aldermanic court, the City's main ruling body. It is true that by the early seventeenth century, the overseas company merchants were less numerous in aldermanic offices than they had been a half century previously, when the Merchant Adventurers were overwhelmingly predominant. The aldermanic court was still dominated by wholesalers; but the wholesaling overseas company traders now had to share their positions with domestic cloth wholesalers and wholesale distributors of goods to and from the provinces, as well as a handful of large manufacturers. Even so, on the eve of civil war overseas company traders still held well over half of all the aldermanic positions, and the Levant–East India Company merchants held the great bulk of aldermanic positions occupied by overseas company merchants.[5]

The East India Company board of directors, as emphasized, was a virtual representative institution for London's greatest company merchants, allowing the leading figures in the various trades to meet together on a regular basis and to strengthen already existing business and family connections. As responsible for London's greatest single overseas commercial undertaking, the company's directors were obliged to develop the most intimate relationship with the Crown in order to secure the company's privileges and a favorable government policy toward the trade. As very rich and influential citizens in their own right, many of them developed further ties with the Crown by virtue of their participation in the customs farms and their service on the court of aldermen, or both.

As top City magistrates and, in many cases, royal officeholders, the City merchant political elite tended to constitute a small but pivotal core of strong London supporters of the Crown. Moreover, as leaders within the

[4] See above, ch. 2, p. 82.

[5] Of the twenty-eight men who held aldermanic posts between October 1640 and December 1641, sixteen were overseas merchants, among whom thirteen were Levant Company traders or East India Company officers or both. These figures were derived by comparing the list of aldermen for this period in V. Pearl, *London and the Outbreak of the Puritan Revolution: City Government and National Politics, 1625–1643* (Oxford, 1961), pp. 285–308, with lists of overseas merchants derived from the London port books and company records. For the composition of the aldermanic court in the period 1600–1625, see R. G. Lang, "London's Aldermen in Business, 1600–1625," *Guildhall Miscellany* (1971), 3: 242–64. See also R. G. Lang, "Social Origins and Social Aspirations of Jacobean London Merchants," *Ec.H.R.*, 2d ser., 27 (1974).

chartered trading companies, they were particularly well placed to influence in favor of the Crown the broad ranks of their overseas trading colleagues. The latter were, of course, predisposed to support the Crown because of their dependence on royally sanctioned trading privileges.

If London's company merchant community and the royal government were thus natural allies, Parliament and the City's overseas traders tended to be natural opponents. This was because, from one point of view, Parliament was an amalgam of grower, manufacturing, and outport interests, and because each of these interests had an understandable desire for freer trade and thus for the weakening of the London merchants' companies and privileges. Both the growers, whose wool had to be manufactured into cloths, and the clothiers, whose cloths had to be sold in overseas markets, wished to break up what appeared to them to be the monopsonistic middleman position occupied by the London merchants, especially the Merchant Adventurers, by virtue of their royally sanctioned charters. The merchants of the outports wanted to reduce what seemed to be the disproportionate share and unwarranted control of the trade held by the London merchants by means of their domination of the chartered companies. It was hardly an accident that during the early seventeenth century, the House of Commons launched attack after attack on every aspect of the City merchants' commercial privileges. To make matters worse, the very same figures who provided the leadership and ideological justification for the struggle for free trade tended also to provide the leadership for parliamentary opposition to the Crown. The result was to drive the overseas traders even further into the arms of the monarchy.[6]

The fact remains that despite this powerful preexisting structure of politico-economic interest, by 1628–1629 the majority of overseas company traders of London had been profoundly alienated from the Crown and had gone into various sorts of political opposition. How and why did this occur? Robert Ashton has argued that the merchants' opposition should not, after all, be so surprising, since the merchants shared Parliament's concern with the monarchy's abuses and supported Parliament's attack on the monarchy's arbitrary exercise of power. As similarly conservative but reform-minded social forces, Ashton argues, the parliamentary classes and the London merchants could be expected to arrive at similar political positions. It is indeed Ashton's thesis that the parliamentary landed classes and the London company merchants followed quite parallel political trajectories from 1624 right through the parliamentary revolution of 1640–1641.[7]

---

[6] A. Friis, *Alderman Cockayne's Project and the Cloth Trade* (London, 1927), p. 151. See also R. Ashton, "The Parliamentary Agitation for Free Trade in the Opening Years of the Reign of James I," *Past & Present*, no. 38 (1967).

[7] R. Ashton, *The City and the Court, 1603–1643* (Cambridge, 1979), pp. 111, 121–22, 210–12, 214.

It is perhaps true that—all else being equal—the City company merchants would have wished to follow the oppositionists in Parliament along the road of conservative reform. But all else was emphatically not equal. The company merchants, like many others, did, in specific instances, oppose the Crown's creation of privileges and the corruption this tended to encourage. Nevertheless, they could hardly straightforwardly and consistently condemn the practice by which the Crown exchanged privileges for political and financial support, since they were themselves among the Crown's chief beneficiaries. The merchants must also have disliked the Crown's increasing resort to arbitrary methods of rule during the later 1620s. But, again, they could stand in no pure and simple way against unconstitutional government, since they were by then so profoundly dependent on an implicit arrangement whereby they exchanged *unparliamentary* taxes on trade for monopoly commercial privileges of various sorts. Had the City's company merchants had the clear option of opposing the Crown's arbitrary government *and* maintaining their privileges on the basis of support from Parliament, they might well have backed more assiduously Parliament's struggles against royal constitutional abuses, especially unparliamentary taxes on trade. But in view of Parliament's continuing failure to recognize and protect their company privileges, they found it difficult to break away from the traditional arrangement.

The City's company merchants thus remained dependent on direct political intervention for their basic economic well-being. Their very economic position was indeed in part politically constituted in a way that the economic position of the landed classes in Parliament no longer was. Unlike their counterparts in many places on the Continent, the English landed classes no longer required immediate and direct access to political power and position in order to maintain themselves economically. Unlike the lords of eastern Europe, they needed no capacity to exert extra-economic compulsion buttressed by their local and national estates, in order to collect rents from their tenants; nor had they come to depend on central and local governmental offices and gifts, financed largely through state taxation, in order to support themselves, as did the aristocrats who lived off the French state. On the contrary, they were able to subsist very well off broad commercialized landed estates, from which they collected rising economic rents deriving from what were roughly free markets in land and in labor. As a result, they were free to oppose arbitrary government in general and unparliamentary taxation in particular as straightforward threats to their absolute property in a way they could not have done had they been more economically dependent on property in state offices or other sorts of privilege granted by the Crown. Conversely, precisely because Crown-sanctioned privileges constituted such a crucial component of their own private property and because the latter were so explicitly premised on the payment of unparliamentary levies on trade, the company merchants could hardly construe arbitrary taxation as unambiguously in conflict with their interests.

In sum, the City merchant community and the parliamentary oppositionists found it difficult to forge an alliance. During the later 1620s, these two forces did come together for a brief period. But, as I will try to show, their relatively short-lived entente is understandable largely in terms of the special political conditions that prevailed in those years— above all, the royal government's extreme disregard of the merchants' commercial interests, exemplified not only in the Crown's profound neglect of their traditional chartered privileges, but also in its inexplicable involvement in disastrous and commercially destructive warfare. Over the course of the pre–Civil War period as a whole, *pace* Professor Ashton, the forces represented in Parliament and the City's company merchants ended up following divergent political paths in consequence of their differing sociopolitical interests and options.

Merchants, Crown, and Parliament, 1600–1624

The early years of the seventeenth century brought sharp political conflict between the Crown and Parliament, however one evaluates its ultimate significance. Understandably, the Crown's attempt to levy unparliamentary taxes on trade became a pivotal political issue, because revenues from customs had the potential of offering the Crown financial independence, and thus of allowing it to dispense with Parliament. Indeed, the fight over impositions was perhaps the most serious struggle between the Crown and the House of Commons during the first quarter of the seventeenth century. It brought to the surface the most fundamental questions concerning the locus of political authority within the state and the nature of the subjects' liberties, especially what were viewed by many MPs as the interrelated rights of property and of Parliament.[8] Naturally, taxes on trade were also close to the heart of City merchants. But the merchants do not appear to have given strong support to opposition in Parliament at any time before 1625, even on the issue of unparliamentary customs. In fact, despite major increases in taxes on trade during the first quarter of the seventeenth century, the Elizabethan alliance between the Crown and the City merchant community was extended and strengthened.

Taxes on trade first became an issue in 1600 when Elizabeth I took over revenues from an imposition of 5s. 6d. a hundredweight that the Levant

---

[8] See, for example, C. Russell, "Parliamentary History in Perspective," *History* 61 (1976): 9; M. Prestwich, *Cranfield: Politics and Profits under the Early Stuarts* (Oxford, 1966), p. 181; J. P. Sommerville, *Politics and Ideology in England, 1603–1640* (London, 1986), pp. 151–55 et seq.

Company had formerly levied on all currants brought into England by noncompany traders. In 1605, after several years of negotiation and conflict over the question, the Crown regranted the company its charter and the company agreed to a royal levy of 5s. 6d. a hundredweight on all imported currants, including those imported by members of the Levant Company.[9] No doubt, the Crown had used an element of coercion to win this settlement, and numbers of Levantine-trade merchants remained dissatisfied. In April 1606 the Levant Company merchant John Bate took the case to Parliament, complaining that the currants imposition was unparliamentary and thus unconstitutional. In so doing, he received the active support of a number of leading Levant Company traders, including John Eldred, Thomas Cordell, and Roger Ofield. In November 1606, the court of exchequer, in a famous decision, ruled against Bate. Henceforward, impositions were at the center of parliamentary concerns, and the issue emerged as a point of bitter constitutional conflict in the Parliaments of both 1610 and 1614.[10]

Nevertheless, it is doubtful if many of the City's company merchants regarded the payment of impositions as an issue of principle, and the Crown seems to have realized this. Upon his accession to the position of lord high treasurer in 1608, Salisbury could not resist the new potential for royal revenue raising opened up by the favorable decision in Bate's case. Salisbury devised what came to be known as the general impositions, but before he attempted to impose them, he made a point of consulting and compromising with England's leading overseas traders. In June 1608, Salisbury presented his proposal to a special assembly of top merchants called from all over the country. He emphasized that the government aimed to avoid the impositions' interfering with trade. Indeed, orders had already gone out to reduce certain impositions that were felt to be a burden. In particular, as a concession to the Levant Company merchants, Salisbury reduced the controversial currants levy by some 40 percent, from 5s. 6d. to 3s. 4d. a hundredweight. He also lowered the taxes on tobacco and sugar. If Sir Julius Caesar's account of the meeting with the merchants can be trusted, Salisbury's efforts at conciliation were successful, and the merchants "after some little contradiction consented to this general imposition new."[11]

[9] F. C. Dietz, *English Public Finance, 1558–1641* (London, 1964), pp. 88–89; M. Epstein, *The Early History of the Levant Company* (London, n.d.), pp. 40–51; Friis, *Alderman Cockayne's Project*, pp. 193–95, 201–5; S. R. Gardiner, *A History of England from the Accession of James I to the Outbreak of the Civil War*, 10 vols. (London, 1883–1884), 2: 2–5.

[10] D. H. Willson, ed., *The Parliamentary Diary of Robert Bowyer* (Minneapolis, 1931) pp. 118–19; W. Notestein, *The House of Commons, 1604–1610* (New Haven, 1971), pp. 169–72, 179; Gardiner, *History* 2: 6–10.

[11] Friis, *Alderman Cockayne's Project*, pp. 196–98. The quotation is from J. Spedding, ed., *Lord Bacon's Works*, 16 vols. (London, 1861–1872), 11: 58.

In the years immediately preceding, the major company merchants had been made to appreciate, if they had not previously, their special relationship with the Crown. In 1604, the House of Commons launched the first of a series of powerful assaults on chartered companies in general and the Merchant Adventurers in particular, when it voted for the bill for free trade. However, the Crown was able to use its influence in the House of Lords to see that the free-trade bill did not pass into law. Shortly thereafter, the Crown defied the express wishes of the Commons by renewing the charter of the Levant Company and by issuing a new charter to the Spanish Company. But the Commons replied in 1606 by declaring free trade with Spain, Portugal, and France. This act must have been particularly distressing to the City's merchants, for both the traders with Spain and with France had gone out of their way to win Parliament's favor by lowering the barriers to entry into their corporations and by providing places for the outport merchants on their companies' directing boards. Parliament, on the other hand, showed its total disdain for the company merchants' interests when, in the preamble to the act for free trade with Spain, Portugal, and France, it condemned as unjust the chartered companies' systematic exclusion of shopkeepers, shipowners, mariners, handicraftsmen, clothiers, and fishermen. The confining of trade to mere merchants was, of course, a central raison d'être of the chartered companies. In 1609, the Crown once again overrode Parliament and issued a charter to the French Company. The merchants' total dependence on the Crown for their privileges could hardly have been made more explicit.[12]

It was almost certainly the merchants' understanding of the quid pro quo by which they held their corporate privileges from the Crown that led them to stay clear of the fierce conflicts over impositions that wracked subsequent Parliaments. In the Parliaments of 1610 and 1614, impositions were a main, if not the central, issue. In 1610, the Commons presented a petition to the king "that all impositions set without assent of Parliament may be quite abolished and taken away." By 1614, the members of the House of Commons had made the parliamentary levy of impositions an issue "of right," and the king dismissed them for their defiance.[13] Nevertheless, there is no evidence that the City merchants supported the Commons' fight on impositions in these years.[14] The Com-

---

[12] The foregoing progression can be followed in Friis, *Alderman Cockayne's Project*, pp. 150–65.

[13] E. R. Foster, ed., *Proceedings in Parliament, 1610*, 2 vols. (New Haven, 1966), 1: xv–xvi; 2: 267 (for quotation); Friis, *Alderman Cockayne's Project*, pp. 204–6; T. L. Moir, *The Addled Parliament* (Oxford, 1958), pp. 97–133; Gardiner, *History* 2: 65–74, 236–49.

[14] This conclusion is derived from perusing Foster, *Proceedings in Parliament, 1610*, *C.J.*, and M. Jansson, ed., *Proceedings in Parliament, 1614 (House of Commons)*, Memoirs of The American Philosophical Society, vol. 172 (Philadelphia, 1988), as well as the standard narrative sources, such as Moir, Gardiner, and Notestein. It is notable that the Levant Company's governor, Sir Thomas Lowe, was a London MP in both 1610 and 1614, but so far as the records show, uttered not a word

mons' ongoing opposition to unparliamentary taxation on trade offered these merchants an extraordinary political opening to protest their increased customs payments, but they could hardly have failed to realize that to have done so would have been to renege on their implicit bargain with the Crown and to endanger their special relationship. In the words of Thomas Hedley, a leading parliamentary opponent of impositions and theorist of parliamentary liberties, "The merchants are so compounded with or dealt with, that they will not, or dare not, bring any action against the king or his officers." On the other hand, in 1614 the Commons reemphasized its contempt for the merchants' interests, when it called for the abolition of the recently chartered French Company.[15]

Meanwhile, the royal government was attempting to rationalize its levies on trade in order to make them more palatable to the merchants as well as to respond to Parliament's protests. In 1608, as has been noted, Salisbury lowered the especially burdensome imposition on currants, as well as those on tobacco and sugar. In 1610, he initially removed the impositions on most manufactured exports (excepting only tin, lead, pewter, and bays), and later in the year went on to lift the duties on a great mass of imports. Whereas 1610 had begun with impositions on some 1,200 items, the year ended with impositions on just 264. Lord Treasurer Sir Lionel Cranfield took up where Salisbury left off.[16]

In 1615–1616, Cranfield reaffirmed the policy of shifting impositions from exports to imports to help the balance of trade and to place the burden on those commodities (and merchant importers) best positioned to be taxed. Cranfield called, moreover, for limiting impositions to a relatively small number of high-cost luxury products, the burden of which could be passed on to the consumer. He demanded, finally, that both impositions and customs be raised rather sharply on a number of import items, like raw silks, that had been seriously undervalued in the book of rates (by as much as one-third).[17] In order to win the merchants' support for these changes, in January 1616 the privy council appointed a committee of major London traders to consider Cranfield's proposed alterations in the book of rates, "whereby an ease will follow His Majesty's subjects in taking away some part of the impositions, and yet without over-much loss to His

in Commons against impositions. See also Friis's conclusion that "[the London merchants] were not unwilling to pay customs when kept within reasonable limits, and they could obtain compensation from the government in other ways" (*Alderman Cockayne's Project*, p. 201).

[15] Foster, *Proceedings in Parliament, 1610* 2: 185 (and 170–97, for Hedley's full speech at this juncture against impositions). For Hedley, see Sommerville, *Politics and Ideology*, pp. 134, 135, 148, 164. For the Commons' action against the French Company, see Friis, *Alderman Cockayne's Project*, pp. 167–68.

[16] Friis, *Alderman Cockayne's Project*, pp. 198–204, 209; Prestwich, *Cranfield*, p. 187.

[17] R. H. Tawney, *Business and Politics under James I* (Cambridge, 1958), pp. 180–90; Prestwich, *Cranfield*, pp. 180–90; Friis, *Alderman Cockayne's Project*, pp. 170–213.

Majesty in his revenue." With Cranfield as its chairman, this committee brought together some of London's greatest merchants, including the Levant–East India Company leaders William Garway and Morris Abbot, the important Merchant Adventurers George Lowe, Richard Venn, Thomas Dalby, and Samuel Hare, the leading Eastland merchants Christopher Clitherow and William Greenwell, and the customs farming magnates John Suckling and John Wolstenholme. It does not appear that Cranfield's proposals on impositions were actually implemented, but the episode does express the royal government's ongoing wish for constructive collaboration with the company merchants on the delicate matter of taxes on trade.[18]

The Crown also remained intensely conscious of the need to compensate the merchants for further levies on them. In 1619, the government managed to reimpose the 2s. 2d. on each hundredweight that Salisbury had cut from the impost on currants in 1608, bringing the tax back to its original level of 5s. 6d. Currants were at this time valued officially at 30s. a hundredweight, so the imposition now amounted to some 16 percent of the rated value (over and above the usual 5 percent customs fee). But Cranfield reasoned that the Levant Company could afford to pay a higher levy on a very lucrative item. He pointed out that currants were in fact selling at some 70s. a hundredweight at Christmas 1617, up from a normal selling price of 50s.[19]

The government had, in any case, gone out of its way to ease the burden of the increased tax on the Levant Company merchants. In 1615, in direct response to the Levant Company merchants' request, the Crown issued a navigation act that required that all Levantine commodities be imported in English ships and be brought directly from their place of origin. This measure outlawed the indirect trade in Levantine commodities by way of northern Europe, cut off the Venetians' import of currants using Dutch ships, and effectively confined the trade to the Levant Company. In 1617, the government buttressed this act by denying the Merchant Adventurers' request that they be allowed to continue importing currants from Holland. Moreover, the government ordered that the Levant Company be allowed to post a company representative at customs to enforce the new regulations. Finally, in 1619, when the Levant Company was informed of the government's intention to raise the levy, the company appears to have made the best of this by working out an agreement with the customs farmers to help ensure that no currants be allowed into the country except those brought by the company's (temporary) joint stock. In this light, it

---

[18] *A.P.C. 1616–1617*, pp. 353–55, 366; Prestwich, *Cranfield*, pp. 186–88; Friis, *Alderman Cockayne's Project*, p. 212 n. 2.

[19] Cranfield Papers, KCA, U.269/M.692; KCA, U.269/ON.6348; Friis, *Alderman Cockayne's Project*, p. 198.

is hardly surprising that the Levant Company raised no protest against the increased currants imposition itself, but merely asked that those currants it had brought into the country before the issuance of the order for raising the levy be allowed through customs at the old rate. Clearly the company understood that its ever-increasing privileges required some recompense to the Crown.[20]

This is not to contend, of course, that Crown-merchant relations were smooth and untroubled. That was far from the case. In 1614, the king leveled a devastating attack against the Merchant Adventurers when he suddenly agreed to suspend the Adventurers' privileges and to prohibit their main trade, the export of undyed and undressed cloth, in order to charter an entirely new, competitive company that was to take over the export of cloth, but in a more finished form. This was an unspeakable betrayal of the Adventurers, and it revealed an underlying tension that would disrupt, time and again, the merchant-Crown alliance. The Crown approved the so-called Cockayne Project for a number of reasons, including the possibility that it would help English producers capture control of cloth-finishing manufacture from the Dutch. There can be no question, however, that at the center of the Crown's considerations stood the hope of substantially improving its income from the cloth trade. If successful, the Cockayne Project, through taxes, customs, and other revenues, promised to add some £47,500 per annum to the Crown's income.[21]

In the last analysis, the Crown supported the privileges of the chartered companies because the merchants, directly or indirectly, would provide financial and political support to the Crown in return. There was always the chance therefore that the Crown might simply dump one or more of its merchant company clients in favor of other groups, if by that means it could improve its income or strengthen itself politically. The Crown's backing of the Cockayne Project demonstrated that this was no mere theoretical possibility, and there were to be subsequent instances of the same phenomenon.

The fact remains that the political cost to the Crown of mistreating particular groups of merchants was normally strictly limited. This was because Parliament was never willing to step in to protect the merchants when the Crown was abusing them. The House of Commons was simply unalterably opposed, both by interest and principle, to the chartered commercial companies. Even when the Crown, for its own narrow financial and political purposes, chartered the unpopular Cockayne Project, Parlia-

[20] PRO, S.P.105/148/27, 27v (15 Mar. and 15 Apr. 1619), 43 (20 Mar. 1620); Ashton, *City and the Court*, pp. 101–2; Friis, *Alderman Cockayne's Project*, pp. 180–84. See also above, ch. 2, p. 66.

[21] B. E. Supple, *Commercial Crisis and Change in England, 1600–1642* (Cambridge, 1959), pp. 34–36; Friis, *Alderman Cockayne's Project*, pp. 224–304.

ment failed to take the opportunity to side with the Adventurers. On 20 May 1614, the Merchant Adventurer MP Robert Middleton denounced Cockayne's company before the House of Commons as a far-reaching monopoly designed mainly to line the projectors' pockets, and he called on the House to intervene against Cockayne before it was too late. But the MPs could muster little sympathy for the Adventurers; in fact, some of them used the occasion to attack the company once again. These MPs expressed their concern that (then-stagnant) sales of cloth be increased, but showed only indifference as to which merchants, Merchant Adventurers or Cockayne projectors, should make the purchases.[22] The company merchants simply had little to hope for from Parliament. But, all else being equal, they could expect to build mutually beneficial ties with the Crown, for the royal government, though unreliable, had every interest in supporting the merchants' privileges in exchange for financial and political support. This was a critical difference.

When the Cockayne Project collapsed, the Crown quickly regranted the Adventurers their charter. Naturally, there was a price. According to one well-informed source, the Crown originally extracted an annuity of £20,000 a year for granting the charter in 1617, but Cranfield persuaded Buckingham to accept in its place a lump-sum payment of £80,000. This was in addition to gifts and bribes to courtiers. Typically, as further compensation for rechartering the Adventurers, the Crown levied the so-called pretermitted custom in 1619, essentially a new imposition on cloth exports.[23]

Over the following years, the merchants' dependence on the Crown was even further strengthened. The early 1620s were one of the worst periods of cloth-trade depression in English history, and the free-trade forces in the House of Commons were driven to launch an all-out attack on merchant privileges. But the Crown did not waver in its traditional support for the merchants' companies.

In 1620–1621, the privy council's committee to deal with the cloth crisis failed to suggest any major policy departures, let alone a loosening of the companies' charters. But when the House of Commons reconvened in 1621, it subjected just about every merchant company to fierce attacks. A bill for general free trade was introduced, and there was another for

---

[22] *C.J.* 1: 491ff.; Friis, *Alderman Cockayne's Project*, pp. 253–58.

[23] PRO, S.P.16/285/46; Prestwich, *Cranfield*, pp. 176–77; Friis, *Alderman Cockayne's Project*, pp. 218–19, 382. According to testimony in the Parliament of 1624, the king ultimately agreed to accept £50,000 in exchange for the restoration of the Adventurers' charter (see Friis, pp. 367, 369). More generally, see the comment by William Towerson, the Merchant Adventurers' London deputy, before the Parliament of 1621: "We have furnished the king and late queen with great sums of money, yea many £100,000 when we had but mere credit" (W. Notestein, F. H. Relf, and H. Simpson, eds., *Commons Debates, 1621*, 7 vols. [New Haven, 1935] 2: 364–65).

free trade with France. The Muscovy Company's restrictive joint-stock organization came in for criticism. Even the East India Company, traditionally immune from the attacks of the House of Commons, was reproved for allegedly exporting bullion. In the end, it was only the king's intervention that saved the merchants, above all the Company of Merchant Adventurers. On 3 May 1621, James I stepped in to prevent the House of Commons from examining the Adventurers' patents and rule books, proclaiming that "there have been diverse things between them [the Adventurers] and me not so fit for you to see and deal in. Meddle not with those things that belong to me and the state." The Parliament of 1621 was compelled to content itself with a mild bill allowing the outports free trade in the new draperies.[24]

In the spring of 1622, with the trade crisis at its peak, the privy council did go so far as to demand that the Merchant Adventurers not only buy up cloth at Blackwell Hall, but allow interlopers to trade temporarily within the Adventurers' privileged territory. However, when the Adventurers raised objections, and a stalemate developed, the royal government was unwilling to force the issue.[25]

Only in 1624 did the House of Commons finally succeed in dealing a substantial blow to commercial monopolies in general, and to the privileges of the Merchant Adventurers in particular. Peculiar conditions appear to have made this possible. In this Parliament, as in previous Parliaments, much of the leadership in the struggle for free trade was supplied by the parliamentary chieftains Sir Edwin Sandys, Sir Edward Coke, Sir Dudley Digges, and Sir Robert Phelips. In 1621, these men had led opposition to the Crown on foreign policy and freedom of speech, and had fought vigorously against the Merchant Adventurers and for free trade; but they had been no more successful at that time in overcoming the king's steadfast defense of the Adventurers than any of their predecessors, going back to 1604. However, in the Parliament of 1624, these MPs entered into an alliance with the duke of Buckingham and Prince Charles, with the goal of bringing about a new anti-Spanish foreign policy, long cherished by important elements in Parliament and on the privy council but opposed by the king. And in this Parliament, for the first time, they were able to get their way concerning free trade.

Buckingham's support was undoubtedly the new factor that allowed the old free-trade forces to turn the tide and to succeed, where they never had before, in passing powerful legislation against the Merchant Adventurers. It is likely, moreover, that the Buckingham-inspired attack on Lord

[24] Friis, *Alderman Cockayne's Project*, pp. 402–11; Supple, *Commercial Crisis*, pp. 64–69; Ashton, *City and the Court*, pp. 106–9 (the quotation is from p. 107).

[25] Friis, *Alderman Cockayne's Project*, pp. 414–20. Supple sums up: "Once more action had to await parliamentary initiative" (*Commercial Crisis*, pp. 69–70).

Treasurer Lionel Cranfield, by this time earl of Middlesex, helped prepare the way for this reversal. This attack proceeded simultaneously with the Commons' assault on the Adventurers and, in neutralizing Cranfield, eliminated one of the most influential supporters of the Adventurers' privileges and of merchant privileges in general. The bill, which was drafted by Sir Edwin Sandys, who was working closely at this time with Buckingham against Cranfield, opened up admission to the Merchant Adventurers to any wholesaler who wished to join and who would pay a reasonable fee, as determined by the privy council; it declared full freedom of trade in kerseys, western dozens, northern dozens, and new draperies; and it allowed the outports to trade freely in dyed, dressed, and colored cloths "to all places except those limited to the Merchant Adventurers" (presumably the Adventurers' mart towns). Reversing his long-standing position, James ultimately allowed the bill to pass into law.[26]

Even so, there is reason to believe that things might have gone even worse for the Merchant Adventurers had it not been for James I. Aside from Sir John Savile and a handful of MPs who were themselves Adventurers, the only MPs who spoke in favor of the Adventurers' privileges were representatives of the royal government: Sir Humphrey May, chancellor of the Duchy of Lancaster; Sir Francis Nethersole, English agent at the court of Elizabeth, electress Palatine; Sir Heneage Finch, recorder of London (traditionally a Crown appointee); and Sir Henry Mildmay, master of the Jewel House. In early May 1624, these men carried out a spirited, if ultimately futile, defense of the Adventurers' privileges before the House of Commons' committee on trade. Although the king would not, in this case, go so far as to reverse Parliament's decision, James apparently wished to have his opinions made known, and it may have been royal influence that kept the Commons from going even further than it did.[27]

It has been argued by Robert Ashton that the middle 1620s, and specifically the Parliament of 1624, marked a dramatic turning point—a fundamental change of direction—in the evolving interrelationships among the Crown, Parliament, and the City's overseas traders. According

[26] J. P. Cooper, "The Fall of the Stuart Monarchy," in *The New Cambridge Modern History of Europe*, vol. 4, ed. J. P. Cooper (Cambridge, 1970), pp. 551–52; Friis, *Alderman Cockayne's Project*, ed. S. R. Gardiner, pp. 428–30; Supple, *Commercial Crisis*, pp. 70–71; S. R. Gardiner, ed., *Commons Debates in 1625* (London, 1873), pp. 39–40.

[27] Diary of Proceedings of the House of Commons by Sir Edward Nicholas, PRO, S.P.14/166/ 127, 169v, 192v–94, 199–200v. In this and all subsequent references to the Nicholas Diary for 1624, I have relied on transcripts very generously sent to me by Prof. Robert Ruigh. I wish to thank Professor Ruigh for putting this material at my disposal. For the official and political identification of these men, I have relied on R. Ruigh, *The Parliament of 1624* (Cambridge, Mass., 1971), pp. 51, 120, 162, 170, 318 (May); 82–83, 227, 298–99 (Nethersole); 110, 201–2, 206, 207, 222, 226–27 (Finch); 52, 206, 309 (Mildmay).

to Ashton, from this point onward the Commons showed significantly greater tolerance of the merchants' privileges than it previously had done, and the Crown weakenened in its support of the merchants' privileges. This reversal allegedly paved the way for a longer-term realignment in which the City overseas traders came to side with Parliament and oppose the Crown. Nevertheless, in view of what actually happened in the Parliament of 1624, this thesis is very difficult to credit, even on the basis of Ashton's own excellent account.[28]

Quite possibly, as Ashton asserts, "the temper of the Commons in 1624 was quieter than it had been in 1621." But this difference in tone could be explained by the fact that by 1624 the cloth trade had partially recovered from the terrible depression that had gripped it in 1621; in consequence, the MPs may have felt somewhat less urgency about the matter of free trade.[29] However this may be, the Parliament of 1624 showed no softening in its attitude toward the merchants' corporate privileges. Quite the contrary. This Parliament represented something of a high point in the long-term parliamentary offensive against the City merchants' companies. The overriding fact, as has been emphasized, is that *for the first time*, Parliament actually was able to deal a serious blow to the privileges of the hated Adventurers. The damage could hardly have been much greater: the Merchant Adventurers' company was, for all practical purposes, left open to all comers; the company's trading monopoly, for what it was now worth, was restricted to undressed white cloths; and whoever wished to do so was free to trade in most other varieties of cloth. As a result, for years to come, the Adventurers could expect much-increased competition and much-reduced profits in a commercial line that was, at this time, already suffering from a serious contraction of markets and rising overseas competition. The passage of the anti-Adventurers bill alone makes it hard to believe that the Parliament of 1624 initiated a rapprochement between the House of Commons and the Adventurers, rather than a reaffirmation of their old enmity.

Nor did Parliament confine itself to profoundly weakening the company's chartered privileges. It ordered the Adventurers to submit for examination their court book, their register book, their ledger book, and books of accounts showing all disbursements since they had first laid their own private imposition on cloth exports. The company had been obliged to levy this latter impost on its own members to recoup the huge sum it had been compelled to pay the Crown for the renewal of its charter; but the House of Commons showed its near-total lack of sympathy for the

[28] Ashton, *City and the Court*, p. 111.
[29] Ibid., p. 109; Supple, *Commercial Crisis*, pp. 86–98.

[214]

Adventurers' position by terming this duty "unlawful and unjust" and declaring it a grievance to be submitted to the king.[30]

It is probable that the House of Commons would have gone even further in its attacks on the Adventurers had it been allowed to do so. As Ashton points out, the Commons' committee on trade, as reported in Pym's parliamentary diary, was desirous "that the House would deliver a final sentence against the Merchant Adventurers' patent and that it might be presented to His Majesty as a grievance." On 8 April Sir Dudley Digges, the old oppositionist (now in league with Buckingham) who had for many years led the fight against the Adventurers, demanded before the committee of trade not only that "every one that will" for a small sum "be admitted of their company," but also that the traditional restriction of membership to mere merchants be dropped. A month later, after the House of Commons had carried through its attacks on most aspects of the Adventurers' privileges, Digges reportedly believed that "the Merchant Adventurers are by what we have done dissolved already in a manner and he would have trade opened and left at liberty for all men to transport white and other cloths though he believed it will overthrow all trade." This was hardly a stance designed to conciliate the Merchant Adventurers, and Digges was hardly alone in these sentiments; almost certainly, he was speaking for a large part of the House of Commons, which, had it possessed the power to do so, would have revoked the Merchant Adventurers' privileges in their entirety.[31]

Nor did MPs confine their offensive against the City merchants to a powerful attack on the Merchant Adventurers. They resumed their assault on the Muscovy Company's privileges. They went after the Guinea Company, declaring its patent a grievance and inducing the Crown to allow proceedings against it in the courts. They attacked the Eastland Company and succeeded in ending its monopoly of the import of shipbuilding materials and timber from eastern Europe. Finally, they fought against the New England Company's recently granted monopoly of offshore fishing and, in the end, they got the Crown to declare free trade in fishing off the whole North American coast. By the time it was dissolved, Parliament had left few of London's great merchant corporations unmolested.[32]

As telling, perhaps, as its attacks on merchant privileges, and equally formative of political attitudes toward Parliament among the London merchant establishment, was the Commons' unswerving support in 1624 for Sir Edwin Sandys and his "gentry party" in their bitter conflicts with some of the City's greatest merchant leaders inside the East India and the

---

[30] Ashton, *City and the Court*, pp. 109–10.

[31] Ashton, *City and the Court*, pp. 109–110 (the first quotation is from Pym's parliamentary diary for 1624), 113, 111; Nicholas Diary for 1624, fols. 127v–28, 206, 207v.

[32] *C.J.* 1: 793–94; Gardiner, *Commons Debates in 1625*, pp. 39–41.

Virginia companies. Sandys had been quarreling with the great merchant prince Sir Thomas Smythe and others of the East India Company leadership since 1618, and it was likely Sandys' influence, as well as that of the duke of Buckingham, that explains the Commons' motion of 1 March 1624 for the seizure of the East India Company's ships that were then preparing for their annual voyage. At the same time, the Commons backed Sandys and his gentry collaborators when they appealed to the House in late April for its support in their struggle to retain control of the Virginia Company, petitioning against Cranfield for his having backed the Sandys party's opponents inside the Virginia Company. The opponents in this case were, of course, that company's "merchant party," led again by Sir Thomas Smythe, which consisted of a representative sample of the City's very top company traders, as well as the Rich faction, led by the earl of Warwick. Quite clearly, the alliance between Buckingham and the formerly oppositionist MPs extended beyond their uniting in favor of an anti-Spanish foreign policy and in opposition to Cranfield, as well as against merchant company privileges; it encompassed the addition of their mutual agreement to support gentry interests against those of the merchant elite within the great joint-stock companies.[33]

In complete contrast, the king and Cranfield gave the great City merchants full and consistent support in their disputes with Sandys and his friends in both the East India Company and the Virginia Company, from 1618 through 1624. In the summer of 1619, when Sandys' faction inside the East India Company sought to oust governor Sir Thomas Smythe and his supporters from the company's directorate, James I informed the company that he would "not have any alteration of them," and had Smythe and his friends duly reelected. In 1620, James also stepped in to stop Sandys from being reelected Virginia Company treasurer (although this did not prevent the company from choosing Sandys' close collaborator, the earl of Southampton, for the position). Then, between 1622 and 1624, James and Cranfield destroyed Sandys' tobacco monopoly, dissolved the old Virginia Company so as to break Sandys' leadership, and appointed a commission dominated by Smythe's "merchant party," along with the Riches and their friends, with the purpose of reconstituting the Virginia Company under the joint leadership of the merchants and the Rich faction. Finally, on 28 April 1624, James personally intervened to cut short the House of Commons' proceedings in support of the Virginia Company's pro-Sandys and antimerchant petition.[34]

[33] Ruigh, *Parliament of 1624*, pp. 82, 123–24, 185–86, 318–19, 318 n. 39; Prestwich, *Cranfield*, pp. 436–38; Gardiner, *History* 5: 238–39. All of these issues—the anti-Spanish foreign policy, the attack on Cranfield, and the opposition to the City merchant elite—were, in fact, closely interrelated. See below, ch. 6, pp. 271–72.

[34] The quotation is from India Office Library, Court Minutes of the East India Company, vol. B/

The Commons' solid backing of Sandys and his "gentry party" friends against the merchant elite leadership of both the East India and Virginia companies must have been highly disconcerting to the City's company merchants. It demonstrated to them, in yet another context, that they had much to fear from Parliament, and could look for security only to the Crown.

In view of the House of Commons' harsh assault on the Adventurers' privileges, its serious attacks on the other companies, and its support for Sandys' gentry party against the great merchant leaders of the Virginia and East India companies, it is impossible to go along with Professor Ashton's conclusion that, with the completion of Parliament's proceedings in 1624, "the way was paved for a new state of affairs in which the company [of Merchant Adventurers] . . . might hope to remain unmolested" and in which, presumably, there could henceforth be amity between the City's company merchants and the Commons. Nor can one agree with Professor Ashton that, given "the crown's apparently complete withdrawal of protection from it," the Adventurers (and, presumably, also the other great City merchants) "had, in fact, little else to hope for."[35] In fact, the Adventurers could not resign themselves to the catastrophic measures of the Parliament of 1624; nor could the other company merchants rest easy concerning the possible actions of future Parliaments; nor could the merchant community as a whole give up hope for aid from the Crown. Following the assaults on their privileges by the Parliament of 1624, the Adventurers may have felt they had little more to lose, but this could hardly have been very comforting to them. In any case, the Adventurers did not, from this point, enjoy full security from further parliamentary attack, nor could the other City companies count on Parliament's protection.

The Parliaments of 1626 and 1628 came out for maintaining free trade in the fish trade with the Americas. The Parliament of 1628 attacked the privileged access to the trade in whale oil and whale fins enjoyed by the Muscovy and Greenland companies and declared the Greenland Company's patent to be a grievance. In 1629, Parliament again assaulted the Guinea Company's monopoly.[36]

6, fol. 374, in T. Kiffin, "Sir Dudley Digges: A Study in Early Stuart Politics" (New York University, Ph.D. diss., 1972), pp. 168–69; Prestwich, *Cranfield*, pp. 437–38; W. F. Craven, *The Dissolution of the Virginia Company* (New York, 1932), pp. 319–21. See also above, ch. 3, pp. 99–102.

[35] Ashton, *City and the Court*, p. 111.

[36] *C.J.* 1: 863; R. C. Johnson et al., eds., *Commons Debate, 1628*, 6 vols. (New Haven, 1977–1983), 3: 429, 430, 438, 440, 441 (American fish trade); 1: 126, 343, 433, 434, 610, 611, 612, 614, 616, 618, 619; 4: 59, 71, 467, 468, 472, 474, 476 (Muscovy and Greenland companies); W. Notestein and F. H. Relf, eds., *Commons Debates for 1629* (Minneapolis, 1921), p. 225; *C.J.* 1: 931 (Guinea Company). Professor Ashton reports these examples of parliamentary attacks on merchant companies in *City and the Court*, pp. 123–29. On the other hand, he provides only one case

Meanwhile, in May 1626, the House of Commons once more declared the Adventurers' "imprest money" to be a grievance. Imprest money was the charge the company imposed on its own members' export of cloths in order to recover the very large sum it had been obliged to pay to the Crown for the renewal of its charter. Shortly thereafter, a bill began to proceed through the House for the "better venting of white cloths." This measure was most likely aimed at what remained of the Adventurers' export monopoly of that commodity. But it never passed the House, for Parliament was dissolved shortly thereafter.[37] Even so, the Adventurers could hardly accept a situation in which their trade had ceased to grow but in which their formerly privileged domain was invaded by massive numbers of new merchants. By the late 1620s and early 1630s, there were no fewer than three times as many merchants trading with the Adventurers' privileged areas as there had been in 1622 before their monopoly had been weakened; yet the volume of trade remained the same as in 1622. The Adventurers could find no new equilibrium and build no new relationship with Parliament so long as Parliament failed to support their company. Since Parliament made no move to protect them by restoring any of their privileges, the Adventurers had no choice but to continue to look to the Crown.

James I, as noted, had successfully defended the Adventurers in 1621 and was likely sympathetic to them in 1624. But in the latter year he was unable to resist the pressure of a House of Commons that now had the powerful behind-the-scenes backing of the duke of Buckingham. However, once Parliament had been disbanded and the duke of Buckingham had been eliminated, the Adventurers had every reason to expect they could regain their privileges from the king. In 1634, the Crown did, in fact, re-grant the Adventurers their charter on something like the old terms. In any case, the reign of James I almost certainly ended much as it had begun, with the City's company traders allied with the Crown and deeply suspicious of Parliament. The profound alienation of the merchants from the Crown that took place between 1624 and 1629 would find its causes largely in the events of the reign of Charles I.[38]

---

that might evidence Parliament's backing for merchant company privileges in this period, that of the East India Company's quarrel with the courtier Sir Thomas Smethwicke. However, in my opinion, the East India Company's appeal to Parliament against Smethwicke is not evidence of a more general move by the company to forsake the monarchy's protection and to look to Parliament for support of its privileges, a point that Professor Ashton himself makes clear. (Of course, Parliament and the merchants did make common cause in the later 1620s on issues other than company control of trade; namely, royal financial depredations, especially the Forced Loan, tonnage and poundage, and impositions.)

[37] *C.J.* 1: 863 (24 May 1626), 865, 866 (1, 3 June 1626). On imprest money, see Friis, *Alderman Cockayne's Project*, p. 372 n. 5.

[38] To qualify this slightly, one could say that to the extent that the merchants were beginning to

The Rise of Merchant Opposition

Merchant opposition to the royal government emerged in the later 1620s in the wake of opposition initially mounted in Parliament. As has been emphasized, the company merchants had stood largely aloof from Crown-parliamentary conflict during the first two decades of the seventeenth century. When they did finally move against the Crown, they took their lead, at almost every point, from their parliamentary counterparts, who very much intensified their attacks on the Crown from 1625 to 1626. Even then, exceptional circumstances and special grievances were critical in pushing the merchants over the brink.

It is true that as early as 1624, one finds, for the first time since 1605–1606, City merchants bringing into Parliament a protest against impositions. Even so, the manner in which they raised the question makes it evident that the merchants were merely seeking to exploit an unusually favorable situation, in which they could oppose impositions without apparently defying the Crown, and had no very fundamental political purpose in mind. Parliament had made impositions an issue of right in 1614, and this had led to Parliament's dismissal by James I. But by 1621, apparently in an effort at conciliation, the parliamentary leaders had decided to play down impositions as a constitutional question. Similarly, in 1624 the parliamentary leaders vowed not to challenge the government on the rightfulness of impositions, so as to maintain their alliance with Buckingham and avoid provoking King James.[39] Nevertheless, in order to prepare the ground for the assault in this Parliament on Lord Treasurer Cranfield, Buckingham's allies in the House of Commons could not avoid raising the question. This not only offered MPs who had been recently in opposition an opportunity to make pointed, though strictly circumscribed, references to the underlying issues of principle raised by unparliamentary customs but also provided the company merchants of London with an extraordinary chance to protest levies on trade in a politically unoffensive manner.

On 9 April 1624, Sir Edwin Sandys, one of Buckingham's main allies in the attack on Cranfield, reported to the Commons from the committee on trade a series of grievances linked to Cranfield concerning the recent levies on commerce—the composition on groceries, the new imposition on wine, and the pretermitted custom on cloth. He pointed out, in particular, that although the royal government had initiated the wine imposition as a short-term emergency measure to supply the king's children in the

---

become alienated from the royal government by the end of the reign of James I, the causes were to be found in the increasing influence of Buckingham and Charles, and their policy initiatives.

[39] See C. Russell, *Parliaments and English Politics, 1621–1629* (Oxford, 1979), pp. 93, 99, 136, 150–51, 198–99; Gardiner, *Commons Debates in 1625*, p. 81.

Palatinate and had intended for it to expire by the time of the current Parliament, Cranfield had had this levy extended indefinitely, without legal warrant or even an act of the privy council. Richard Spencer, Sir Robert Phelips, and Sir Edward Coke immediately followed Sandys and vigorously condemned the imposition on wine as a violation of Magna Carta, and as tending to the overthrow of the liberties and property of subjects. Nevertheless, all three of these MPs were careful to draw back from asking Parliament to consider impositions as a constitutional issue. They recommended instead that Parliament move against Cranfield, who was behind the levying of the impositions and who had stifled protests against them. As Nicholas recounted Phelips's advice, which was ultimately adopted: "He would have us at this time decline the dispute of the right of the laying new impositions but would have us appoint a select committee to examine the wrong done to the king and the subject by those that have been the movers and causers of these new and late impositions . . . and also to hear those merchants that complain that they have been deterred from complaining against these new impositions."[40]

The Commons' blaming the lord treasurer for the recent unparliamentary customs offered the company merchants of London an unprecedented opportunity. They could come out against costly levies on trade without appearing either to oppose the government, or to ally with parliamentary oppositionists against the Crown, or to make taxes on trade into a constitutional issue. The merchants of the French Company seem to have been the first to act, protesting that the government's new imposition of £3 per tun of wine, amounting to a doubling of the former levy, constituted an unbearable burden on their trade. However, as John Glanville reminded the House, Cranfield had eased the weight of the increased levy on the merchants by ordering the retailers of the Vintners Company to buy up all the wine the merchants imported. This assured the importers a market, and allowed them to pass on much of the burden of the impositions to domestic purchasers in the form of higher prices. Still, the House of Commons ended up condemning the wine levy as a grievance.[41]

Nor could the Levant Company resist this opening. On the very day that Sandys made his report to the House against the imposition on wine and the pretermitted customs, the company's directors decided to recommend to the company's general court that it complain to Parliament about the increase of 2s. 2d. per hundredweight in the imposition on currants, as well as the recent additional 3d. per pound duty on silk. The increased currants imposition had been levied for some five years without hitherto

[40] Nicholas Diary for 1624, fols. 128v–31, 142v–43v; Russell, *Parliaments*, p. 199; Prestwich, *Cranfield*, pp. 437–38; Ruigh, *Parliament of 1624*, pp. 317–23.

[41] Dietz, *English Public Finance*, p. 195; Nicholas Diary for 1624, fol. 143v.

[220]

having elicited the company's protest. Within four days, the company had voted to present its grievances to the Commons, and its petition was referred to Sandys and his committee on trade.[42] A month later, on the recommendation of the committee on trade, Parliament declared the Levant Company's complaint concerning the 3*d*. increase in the duty on silk to be unjustified, since the increase merely corresponded to the increase in the value of that commodity. On the other hand, Parliament added the 2*s*. 2*d*. increase in the currants imposition to its list of particular grievances, which also included the impost on wine.[43] There was no attempt to construe these grievances as an issue of constitutional principle.

Over the following two years, with the intensification of political conflict, the House of Commons came to give much more profound political significance to the question of taxes on trade, especially impositions. In the Parliament of 1625, the House of Commons confined itself, in formal terms, to dealing with the increased impositions on wines and currants as specific grievances, just as the Parliament of 1624 had done. The king, for his part, was still hoping to minimize conflict with Parliament; so, while he refused to concede the issue, he, too, went out of his way to avoid raising any point of principle. He justified the 2*s*. 2*d*. increase in the currants impost by stating correctly that the imposition was no higher than it had been in the time of Elizabeth. He explained that the levy on wines had been raised in order to finance the defense of the Palatinate. Nevertheless, in the debate over the tonnage and poundage bill, the Commons indicated that it was no longer willing, as it had been in 1621 and 1624, to refrain from questioning the constitutionality of unparliamentary impositions in the interest of Crown-parliamentary unity. In fact, when the MPs granted tonnage and poundage for only one year, they sought to have explicitly inserted into the bill for tonnage and poundage the proviso that its passage not exclude further parliamentary consideration of the propriety of impositions.[44]

By the time the Parliament of 1626 met, Crown-parliamentary relations had sharply deteriorated and the emerging opposition in Parliament was ready to treat the issue of impositions once again as a question of principle. The failure of Parliament and the Crown to come to agreement over foreign policy, over the toleration of recusants, over Arminianism and, above all, over Buckingham led to the impeachment of Buckingham and a sharp intensification of conflict. In 1626, therefore, Parliament was no longer willing to consider the various impositions merely as specific griev-

---

[42] PRO, S.P. 105/148/113, 113v (9, 13 Apr. 1624).

[43] *C.J.* 1: 793–94; Nicholas Diary for 1624, fol. 229.

[44] Gardiner, *Commons Debates in 1625*, pp. 41, 43–44, 62; Gardiner, *History* 5: 364–65. Cf. G. A. Harrison, "Innovation and Precedent: A Procedural Reappraisal of the 1625 Parliament," *E.H.R.* 101 (1987): 44–46.

ances, as it had done in 1621, 1624 and even in 1625 to avoid confrontation with the king. On 24 May 1626, the House of Commons claimed
that all impositions not approved by Parliament were unjustified.[45]

Parliament's action in turning the merchants' simple economic grievance into a constitutional issue, in connection with the general deterioration of Crown-parliamentary relations, apparently had a significant impact
on merchants' political consciousness. Even so, what appears actually to
have pushed merchants into opposition at this time was a series of disastrous policies already imposed by Buckingham and Charles in the brief
period of their ascendancy. These policies hurt the community of company
merchants as a whole, and proved particularly destructive to some of the
most influential elements within the city's merchant elite.

Even before the end of the reign of James I, Buckingham and Charles
had been willing, as noted, to give their blessing to the assault on the
Merchant Adventurers' privileges. By dissuading King James in 1624
from playing his accustomed role in support of the chartered companies,
they enabled Parliament's free-trade forces to win a victory that would
otherwise have been beyond their power. That Charles and Buckingham
were so willing to sacrifice the Adventurers' interests to the tactical exigencies of their alliance with Parliament must have proved immensely dis-
maying to the great City merchants. And since Buckingham retained his
commanding position in the new reign, the Adventurers could hardly
have been optimistic that they would, in the short run, find renewed support from the government.

At roughly the same time, Buckingham's financial extortions were caus-
ing serious damage to the whole East India Company operation. In 1622,
ships of the East India Company had taken Hormuz from the Portuguese
for the Shah of Persia, and, in the process, had seized a rich booty for the
company itself. James I advised the company to make Buckingham, who
was lord admiral, a present of some of the goods, and the company did
offer him £2,000. But this was not nearly enough for Buckingham. He
implied that 10 percent of the company's profit on all prizes was due him
as lord admiral. To induce the East India Company to increase its payment
to him, Buckingham also claimed that the company's seizure had been
illegal, insisted that he had never issued it letters of marque, and actually
charged the company with piracy before the High Court of Admiralty.
To tighten the screws on the company even further, in early 1624 Buckingham did not hesitate to prevent the departure of a company ship bound
for the East Indies. And, in the end, he managed to extract from the
company not only a payment of £10,000 for himself, but an additional
£10,000 for the king.[46]

[45] *C.J.* 1: 863–64.
[46] M. B. Young, *Servility and Service: The Life and Work of Sir John Coke* (London, 1985), pp.

Shortly thereafter, Charles I definitively disrupted the great merchants' plans for the Americas when he refused to renew the commission for Virginia that his father had authorized. Elite City merchants led by Sir Thomas Smythe, Sir Morris Abbot, and many other major Levant–East India traders, as well as some principal Merchant Adventurers, had dominated this body. Backed by James I and Cranfield, the commission for Virginia had been moving toward the reestablishment of the Virginia Company under elite-merchant domination. But in May 1625 Charles put Virginia directly under royal control and set up a new Crown-appointed council for governing the colony instead of reviving the company. Two years later, Charles granted the proprietorship of the West Indies to the earl of Carlisle, a dependent of Buckingham. Taken together, these two actions destroyed the possibility of company organization for the trade with the Americas, and effectively excluded the greater City merchants from a potentially valuable field of commerce.[47]

Meanwhile, in April 1626, Charles I took away the Great Farm of the customs from the City merchant syndicate that had controlled it since its inception. The Levant–East India Company magnates Morris Abbot and William Garway were the key figures in the old syndicate, which originally had been led by William's father, William Garway. But these merchants lost out when the Crown, apparently at Buckingham's request, decided to grant the farm to a new group led by Sir Paul Pindar and Sir William Cockayne, merchants closely connected with the court.[48]

To add to all these assaults, the greater part of the merchant community suffered badly when Charles I and Buckingham allowed England to drift into war with France as well as Spain in 1626–1627. War with Spain was damaging not only to the traders with Spain, but also to the Levant–East India Company merchants who traded through the Mediterranean. War with France was simply incomprehensible to most of the City's traders and really disastrous to those trading with France. Through disruption of trade and destruction of goods and shipping, these wars probably caused more damage to the merchants than did any other government policy.[49]

129–30; Ruigh, *Parliament of 1624*, pp. 82, 185–86; *C.S.P. Col. E.I. 1625–1629*, p. 174; K. N. Chaudhuri, *The English East India Company* (London, 1965), p. 64; Ashton, *City and the Court*, pp. 114–15, 123; Gardiner, *History* 5: 237–41.

[47] *C.S.P. Col. 1574–1660*, pp. 73–74, 85–86. See also above, ch. 3, pp. 99–106.

[48] R. Ashton, *The Crown and the Money Market, 1603–1640* (Oxford, 1960), p. 255; Dietz, *English Public Finance*, pp. 333–34; R. Ashton, "Government Borrowing under the First Two Stuarts, 1603–1642" (University of London, Ph.D. diss., 1953), pp. 95–97.

[49] For accounts of the disruption of trade brought on by war, see Supple, *Commercial Crisis*, 101–2, 104–7; Russell, *Parliaments*, pp. 261–62; A. M. Millard, "The Imports of London, 1600–1640" (bound TS BL Reading Room, n.d.), pp. 97–101. As Russell points out, the outbreak of hostilities also led to the issuing of letters of marque to Dunkirk privateers, and thus further damage to English commerce and shipping in these years. Moreover, when the English navy was preoccupied

By 1626, the City's merchants were ready to take their first steps toward open opposition to the Crown. Several of the City's top traders got an initial opportunity to strike back at the royal government by coming to the aid of the Commons in its impeachment of Buckingham. Early in the Parliament of 1626, Robert Bateman, who was a leader in the French trade, a Levant–East India Company director, and an alderman and MP of London, brought into the Commons the complaint of the merchants trading with France that Buckingham's unwarranted seizure of the French ship *Peter* had caused the French to take terrible reprisals against English vessels. Similarly, Morris Abbot, who was the East India Company's governor, a Levant Company director, an alderman of London, and a customs farmer, as well as a London MP, was only too happy to testify in support of the Commons' charge that Buckingham had extorted large sums from the East India Company.[50]

It is difficult to uncover the inner workings of merchant-parliamentary collaboration at this juncture, but one key link between the opposition forces in London and those in Parliament appears to have been supplied by the long-standing connection between Morris Abbot and Sir Dudley Digges, who, with Sir John Eliot, managed the Commons' proceedings against Buckingham. Morris Abbot's brother, Archbishop George Abbot, had been Digges's mentor at Oxford and remained an intimate of Digges and his family throughout his life. Like Digges, George Abbot was a close ally of the earl of Pembroke's inside the privy council, and Pembroke, of course, was perhaps the pivotal figure among the anti-Buckingham forces at this time. Equally significant, Digges had worked alongside Morris Abbot in City commercial affairs for over a decade. One of the few country gentlemen who took a leading role in the day-to-day affairs of the great London companies, Digges had been an initiator of the ventures for a northwest passage between 1610 and 1616, a founder of the Bermuda Company, and a director and leading spokesman for the East India Company, in which he worked closely with Abbot, who was the East India Company's deputy governor between 1615 and 1624 and governor beginning in 1625. In 1615, Digges wrote *The Defence of Trade*, a tract defending the East India Company. In 1620–1621, Digges and Abbot served together on the English embassy to Holland, which sought to secure restitution from the Dutch for the damage caused by Dutch attacks on the East India Company's outposts in the Far East. Digges's son Thomas married Abbot's daughter.[51] In March 1626, Buckingham was actually warned of the dangers posed by the Abbot-Digges connection by

with military engagements, the vulnerability of English trade to privateering, and also piracy, was only increased.

[50] Russell, *Parliaments*, pp. 277–78, 305; R. Lockyer, *Buckingham* (London, 1984), p. 305.

[51] Kiffin, "Sir Dudley Digges," pp. 77–89, 94, 112–16.

his spy Sir James Bagg. Bagg reported that Digges was Archbishop George Abbot's man and "particularly dangerous" and called Morris Abbot a "dangerous plotter." It seems reasonable to assume that Morris Abbot provided a direct link between the anti-Buckingham leadership in the council and in Parliament and those leading elements within the City's merchant community who were at this point becoming alienated from the Crown.[52]

The Parliament of 1626 marked a turning point in the rise of the merchants' movement. In the context of the stepped-up political opposition by Parliament, Charles I and Buckingham's extreme disregard for the company merchants' privileges and interests, combined with their commercially disastrous foreign policy initiatives, appears to have driven the merchants toward full-fledged resistance. Moreover, the open participation of elite merchants like Abbot and Bateman in the attack on Buckingham in Parliament made it a good deal easier for others to resist. For the first time, large numbers of the City's overseas traders began to come out into open opposition, although even now much of the merchant political elite, represented in the customs farms, on the aldermanic court, and on the East India Company's board of directors, remained steadfastly loyal to the Crown.

In June 1626, to avoid the impeachment of Buckingham, Charles I dissolved Parliament and immediately accelerated his preparations for war. The Crown's attempts to finance its military operations by unparliamentary methods very quickly provoked widespread resistance in both London and the country at large. Shortly after the dismissal of Parliament, the royal government asked a convocation of three hundred of London's wealthiest citizens, especially called for the purpose, to contribute £100,000 to the Crown. That they refused to lend the money is a sign of the rapidly developing opposition in the City. On the other hand, the aldermanic court did come through with its own loan of £20,000, which indicates that the Crown still had a strong core of supporters among the City's business leaders. Several weeks later, the king demanded that the City supply the government with twenty ships to aid in the effort against Spain. The cost to the City of supplying these ships would have been quite small, but there was enormous resistance within the common council and beyond. Here again the aldermen went out of their way to help the king, personally lending the £5,000 that was needed for the twenty ships.[53]

[52] C.S.P.D. 1625–1649: Addenda, p. 113.

[53] Pearl, London, p. 72; M. C. Wren, "London and the Twenty Ships, 1626–1627," A.H.R. 55 (1950): 322, 325–27. In his discussion of the very widespread merchants' opposition of the later 1620s, Professor Ashton, in my view, understates the degree to which critical elements within the elite—especially on the aldermanic court and within the Levant and East India Company leaderships—continued to back the Crown. Cf. Pearl, London, pp. 71–79.

Nevertheless, the citizenry in the parishes stubbornly resisted paying even the small sums demanded of them to cover the aldermen's advance payment to the king.[54]

During the second half of 1626, the king imposed and began to collect the Forced Loan. This levy provoked widespread opposition by the gentry, which eventuated in the imprisonment of many leading parliamentary resisters and, ultimately, in the famous constitutional confrontation over the Five Knights case. In fact, it has been estimated that some 5 percent of the MPs who sat in the subsequent Parliament had been in prison for refusing the Forced Loan. Nevertheless, the court of aldermen came, once again, to the aid of the Crown. In late March 1627, refusing to support the growing resistance in the counties, they agreed personally to subscribe to the Forced Loan and consented to submit lists of men in their wards who were able to contribute.[55]

Still, the opposition by the parliamentary classes to the Forced Loan did elicit a significant response in London. There was a great deal of protest against the court of aldermen's support for the loan, with the citizens calling "the Guildhall the *Yield all*." Just how deep and broad the resistance was is hard to say. But according to one report, "Concerning the loan demanded here of the City, there are very few willing to subscribe thereunto, and it hath hitherto been generally refused by the commons [the City freemen]; who, beside their plea and objection of the great charge . . . do fear to make a precedent thereof against themselves."[56] It is known that many of the City's handicraftsmen and shopkeepers refused to pay the Forced Loan, and it is worth noting in passing that a number of retailers who were at just this time entering the new trades with the Americas were among them. These included Thomas Stone, who was already a leading partner of Maurice Thomson's in Virginia and the West Indies; Stone's partner and cousin Andrew Stone; the cheesemongers Thomas Deacon and William Harris, later partners of Thomson's in the purchase of Berkeley Hundred in Virginia, as well as in many other ventures; Thomas Andrews, a Plymouth and Massachusetts Company backer, a New England trader, and later a partner of Thomson's in the West Indies and East Indies; and Joshua Foote, William Hitchcock, and John Pocock, all of

---

[54] In his account of these events, Professor Ashton does not make clear that it was not the official City government that turned down the request for the £100,000 loan. Nor does he mention the court of aldermen's loan to supply the money needed for the twenty ships. It should also be noted that, in the case of the twenty ships, the initial refusal of the Crown's request came, as on so many subsequent occasions, from the common council, not from the court of aldermen itself.

[55] Pearl, *London*, pp. 74–75; R. F. Williams, ed., *The Court and Times of Charles I*, 2 vols. (London, 1848), 1: 209; J. H. Hexter, "Power Struggle, Parliament, and Liberty in Early Stuart England," *Journal of Modern History* 50 (1978): 45.

[56] Williams, *Court and Times of Charles I* 1: 211, 217.

whom were to become major traders with New England. Far more important at this point, however, was the opposition of a number of leading company merchants. The substantial Levant Company merchants Thomas Soames, Henry Austin, Samuel Vassall, and Giles Martin all refused to pay the Forced Loan. And they were joined by the important Merchant Adventurers William Angel, Robert Palmer, Gabriel Newman, Humphrey Berrington, and William Spurstow.[57]

The resistance of this large handful of substantial overseas traders to the Forced Loan was symptomatic of deepening discontent among all layers of the London merchant community, right up to the top level, during the first half of 1627. At the same time that many citizens were refusing to pay the Forced Loan, others were continuing their resistance to the levy for the twenty ships.[58] Meanwhile, the government had further contributed to the heightening of tensions when the privy council ruled on 28 February 1627 that it would henceforth vigorously enforce the 2s. 2d. increase in the imposition on currants. The House of Commons had of course made clear its opposition on principle to unparliamentary impositions the previous May, and certain Levant Company merchants were now refusing to pay and were summarily thrown in jail. On 15 March 1627, the Levant Company's general court met to "decide whether to submit themselves to the late order of the council on the currants imposition." It was indicative not only of the Levant Company merchants' feelings at this point, but of the general political mood in the City and the country at large, that the company decided to draw up a declaration of "dissent to this imposition for the present, so as to free them from any imputation that may be cast upon them if they should consent without complaining."[59]

Over the following months, constitutional opposition and political conflict rapidly intensified. In the summer of 1627, the royal government launched the attack on the Île de Ré, but by autumn the expedition had ended catastrophically, and the troops were withdrawn in humiliation. Shortly thereafter, in early December 1627, the court of aldermen exasperated the opposition forces in both Parliament and the City by granting the royal contract estates loan to the king. It is probable that the magistrates' action was motivated, in part, by the excellent terms offered by the king. Still, the aldermen had to be aware that, in agreeing to advance the Crown another £120,000 at this absolutely critical moment when the Crown's financial distress was about to force the recall of Parliament, they

---

[57] For the lists of London loan refusers on which these identifications are based, see A.P.C. 1626–1627, pp. 217–18; PRO, S.P.16/58/? (Apr. 1627); PRO, S.P.16/71/15, 39; PRO, S.P.16/72/60, 64, 65, 71; and PRO, S.P.16/73/13.

[58] Wren, "London and the Twenty Ships," pp. 328–29ff.

[59] A.P.C. 1627, pp. 103–4, 136, 151; Johnson et al., Commons Debates, 1628 3: 447 n. 10, 449; PRO, S.P.105/148/163.

were taking a political action and making a political statement that would undercut the opponents of the government's policies. Nor did they betray the slightest ambivalence about their decision. When one of their number, the alderman John Chamberlain, refused to pay his loan contribution and jeered his colleagues for their collaboration with the government, the court of aldermen had him thrown in prison and ultimately dismissed him from the bench. The aldermen went on, moreover, to raise the royal contract estates loan within the City in the strictest possible manner: they jailed refusers for their disobedience in a period when large numbers of the magistrates' counterparts among the governors of the counties were themselves suffering imprisonment for defiantly refusing the Crown's demand for the Forced Loan.[60] At about this same time, the East India Company—loyally responding to the same urgent requests to bail out the king as did the court of aldermen—lent the crown £30,000.[61]

In spite of these loans, the Crown failed to raise sufficient funds and had to recall Parliament. In early 1628, with Parliament about to meet, a number of Levant Company merchants again began to refuse to pay the 2s. 2d. increase in the currants impost. The Crown replied by seizing their goods in customs. On 4 February 1628, these merchants brought their case before the Levant Company. It is notable that it was one of the company's directors and a very important trader, Humphrey Browne, who asked the company, "in behalf of himself and others interested in the deposited currants," to provide political and legal assistance to the resisters. The company debated the issue, but thought it best to postpone a decision for fourteen days.[62] Before the Levant Company could meet again, however, the Crown had imprisoned nine merchants in the French trade for similarly refusing to pay impositions. The traders with France and the Levant Company merchants were now united not only on impositions, but also because two of the men arrested, Henry Lee and Martin Bradgate, were among the few London merchants who traded to a signif-

---

[60] Pearl, *London*, pp. 75ff.; Williams, *Court and Times of Charles I* 1: 314–15. Professor Ashton does not believe that the City's loan should be interpreted in political terms, since the loan represented such an excellent opportunity for the City to collect its former advances to the Crown (Ashton, *City and the Court*, pp. 180–81). This would appear more plausible had the political stakes been less high and less evident to contemporaries, and had the magistrates shown any sympathy whatsoever for the London opposition in a period when much of the national political elite was also resisting. Contemporaries certainly saw the loan as a betrayal; witness not only the resistance of Alderman Chamberlain, but also the widespread refusal to advance money by the livery companies, as well as Nicholas Clegate's famous case against the City, which was taken up by the House of Commons in 1628. On the Crown's desperate search for revenue in the period before Parliament met, see Russell, *Parliaments*, pp. 330–31, 337–38.

[61] Williams, *Court and Times of Charles I* 1: 304.

[62] PRO, S.P. 105/148/152.

icant extent with both France and the Levant.[63] On 26 March, the merchants trading with France petitioned the House of Commons for the release of their arrested colleagues and against the impositions. They had no hope of paying, they added, because their ships were being held in France, and the government was doing nothing about their recovery. By 7 April 1628, the Levant Company also had brought in a petition to Parliament, in this case against the currants imposition.[64]

During the spring of 1628, the parliamentary leadership made the question of impositions a central constitutional issue. On 11 April 1628, the House of Commons agreed to petition against the wine imposition and for the freeing of the imprisoned wine merchants. The privy councilor MPs were asked to carry this petition to the king and, at the same time, to intercede on behalf of the Levant Company merchants for the release of their seized currants. Eventually, the MPs temporarily accorded the impositions question a secondary position when they failed to include their opposition to impositions in the Petition of Right.[65] Even so, as the royal government stumbled toward a semblance of compromise in the late spring of 1628 on the Petition of Right, it appears to have moved hesitantly toward agreement on the issue of impositions as well. On 10 May, the House of Commons once again raised the question of the currants impost, asking why the lord treasurer had refused to release the Levant Company merchants' goods even after the House had petitioned to this end. A week later, on 17 May, there was a major debate on impositions in which Sir Edward Coke, Sir Robert Phelips, and Sir Nathaniel Rich all proclaimed that unparliamentary impositions were unconstitutional and demanded, once again, the release of the Levant Company merchants' currants, as well as the freeing of the imprisoned wine merchants. Then, on 19 May, the chancellor of the Duchy of Lancaster, Sir Humphrey May, speaking for the Crown, announced that the government would release the Levant Company merchants' goods if the merchants would give bond to pay whatever customs ultimately were ruled to be legal.[66] However, five days later, the House of Commons was informed that "notwithstanding His Majesty's message to the House . . . for delivering the Turkey merchants' currants . . . yet they cannot get them." It turned out that a warrant had indeed been made out by the lord treasurer providing for the release of the merchants' goods. But at the last minute there came a

[63] *A.P.C. 1627–1628*, p. 315 (25 Feb. 1628).

[64] Johnson et al., *Commons Debates, 1628* 2: 55 (22 Mar. 1628), 125–26, 132, 136, 138–39 (26 Mar. 1628); 329, 330, 331 (7 Apr. 1628).

[65] Ibid. 2: 144–45, 152–53, 177, 183, 211, 216, 329, 374, 376, 387, 411, 540, 546, 550; 3: 171–72, 175, 181.

[66] Ibid. 3: 354, 357, 358 (10 May 1628); 449, 450, 452, 453, 456 (17 May 1628); 463, 468, 471 (19 May 1628).

"verbal message from the lord treasurer to forbear . . . in respect of a special command of His Majesty."[67]

During the last, climactic days of the session, the issues of unparliamentary impositions and of tonnage and poundage were catapulted to center stage. Charles gave his assent to the Petition of Right on 7 June, but, ten days later, he rejected Parliament's remonstrance of grievances. Meanwhile, on 15 June, Charles's government once again announced that it would strictly enforce the 2s. 2d. currants impost and, on 20 June, the Levant Company petitioned the Commons for relief yet again.[68] The House had already, in fact, been focusing its attention on unparliamentary taxes on trade: on 14 June, it had revived the bill for tonnage and poundage (originally presented in April, but subsequently set aside), and it now referred the Levant Company's petition on the currants imposition to the committee in charge of the bill for tonnage and poundage. When it became clear that it could not pass the tonnage and poundage bill, the House sought to avoid a head-on collision with Charles by trying to induce him to adjourn Parliament rather than prorogue it; had he done so, their bill declaring that unparliamentary impositions and tonnage and poundage were illegal could have been discussed at the next session, and, if passed, been made retroactive to the start of the Parliament of 1628. Nevertheless, on 23 June, Charles announced that he would prorogue, not adjourn, the Parliament. After a series of dramatic speeches on 24 June by Phelips, Coke, Rich, and others, declaring the need to take a principled stand on unparliamentary customs in order to protect the basic rights of subjects, the House of Commons passed, on 25 June, a new remonstrance on tonnage and poundage and impositions. Declaring, in part, "that the receiving of tonnage and poundage and other impositions not granted by Parliament is a breach of the fundamental liberties of this kingdom, and contrary to your Majesty's royal answer to their late Petition of Right," the remonstrance went on to "most humbly beseech your Majesty to forbear any further receiving the same; and not to take it in ill part from those of your Majesty's loving subjects who shall refuse to make payment of any such charges without warrant of law demanded." This was a clear incitement of the City merchants to disobedience. The king prorogued Parliament the next day.[69]

Charles was still in deep financial difficulty, requiring funds to send his fleet to relieve La Rochelle. But now London's company merchants refused to bail him out. On 2 July 1628, the Levant Company flatly turned down the king's request for a loan. At about the same time, the East India

[67] *C.J.* 1: 904; Johnson et al., *Commons Debates, 1628* 3: 595.

[68] Johnson et al., *Commons Debates, 1628* 4: 388, 390, 393; Gardiner, *History* 6: 309, 316–17, 320.

[69] Johnson et al., *Commons Debates, 1628* 4: 388, 390, 393, 477ff.; Gardiner, *History* 6: 323–25.

Company board of directors also refused the Crown's request for a loan, pleading poverty. The East India Company directorate constituted, of course, the very heart of the merchant elite.[70]

The Commons' remonstrance on tonnage and poundage and impositions had amounted to an invitation to the merchants to take the law into their own hands and to refuse henceforth to pay customs. Soon, importers of French wine and of currants from the Levant were, once again, resisting the payment of impositions. To head off this movement, Charles, in full council, declared on 20 July that the impositions were his "by a solemn and legal judgement." On 13 August the privy council issued an order to seize all goods landed without payment, and on 31 August it commanded that assistance was to be given the customs house officers in the execution of their duty and that those who resisted customs payment were to be arrested.[71]

Shortly thereafter came perhaps the turning point in the entire struggle in London. In the first part of September 1628, fourteen Levant Company merchants took it upon themselves to break into the customs house to seize currants taken from them by the royal government in consequence of their refusal to pay the 2s. 2d. currants imposition.[72] The men involved, immediately imprisoned, were not just substantial traders, but among the wealthiest and most influential citizens in London, long associated with directing circles in the Levant–East India combine and in the City government itself. Prominent among them was Nicholas Leate, along with his son Richard Leate and his sons-in-law John Wilde and Henry Hunt. Nicholas Leate had married the daughter of Richard Staper, who was, with Edward Osborne, the founder of the Levant Company (1581) and a key figure in the development of the East India Company (1599–1600). Leate himself had played a central role in the development of the eastern trades from the late sixteenth century, holding for many years the deputy governorship of the Levant Company, as well as an East India Company directorship. The connection around him was one of those critically important business and family groups that composed the core of the Levant Company and that helped to give the company's membership the ability to act so cohesively.[73]

Even more important than the appearance of the Leate connection among those merchants who broke into the customs house in October 1628 was the presence of Morris Abbot and William Garway. Abbot had

[70] PRO, S.P. 105/148/185 (2 July 1628); *C.S.P. Col. E.I. 1625–1629*, p. 529.

[71] Gardiner, *History* 7: 3–4.

[72] PRO, S.P. 16/117/20; Pearl, *London*, pp. 77–78.

[73] Society of Genealogists, Boyd's Index of London Citizens: 1650; PRO, S.P. 105/148/137; *Visitation of London, 1633–1635*, Harleian Society Publications 15 and 17 (London, 1880–1883), 1: 403; 2: 376. See also above, ch. 2, note 58.

been apprenticed to Garway's father, William, one of the founders of the Venice Company. Both men were longtime directors of both the Levant and East India companies; in fact, Abbot was currently governor of the East India Company. Abbot was also an alderman of London and had been an MP; Garway's brother Henry was an alderman as well. Finally, both Abbot and Garway had, for many years, been leaders in a series of merchant syndicates that controlled most of the king's customs farms. Both these men were unquestionably among the City merchant community's most important and influential political leaders.[74]

That magnates such as Garway and Abbot were now willing to take violent action against the government indicates that the City opposition movement had penetrated the highest levels of the merchant community. Before the merchants' campaign was over, no fewer than ten of the twenty-seven merchants on the Levant Company board of directors in 1628–1629 would involve themselves in violent, illegal actions. Never again would so large a section of the leading men in the Levant–East India combine so openly to confront the Crown.[75]

The forcible break-in by Abbot, Garway, Leate, and their merchant colleagues galvanized merchant opposition in the City. By the time Parliament had been recalled in early 1629, the merchants' movement had entered a new, more radical phase, broadening its scope to encompass opposition not merely to specific impositions but to any customs payment whatsoever that had not previously been sanctioned by Parliament. Whereas Abbot, Garway, Leate, and their friends had confined their protest to the specific grievance of the 2s. 2d. increase in the currants imposition, a number of Levant Company merchants now began to oppose the collection of tonnage and poundage by Charles I's government for the principled reason that it lacked parliamentary approval, and they refused to pay this levy. These men thus explicitly associated the merchants' movement with the House of Commons' remonstrance against tonnage and poundage of the previous June, with its call to citizens to refuse to pay unparliamentary customs, and openly identified the merchants' movement with Parliament's constitutional claims. The leaders of this more principled merchants' opposition were Samuel Vassall, John Fowke, Richard Chambers, Bartholomew Gilman, and John Rolle. All were important traders with the Levant, although none was of the first rank among City merchants. In contrast with the majority of their colleagues in the Levant–

---

[74] For these men, see above, ch. 2, p. 73 n. 58. Basic biographical information on Abbot can be found in Pearl, *London*, pp. 285–88.

[75] Thomas Symonds, Humphrey Browne, William Garway, Richard Leate, John Wilde, Samuel Vassall, Bartholomew Gilman, Richard Chambers, Giles Martin. It might also be noted that Morris Abbot, Nicholas Leate, and Henry Hunt were three onetime directors, although not directors in these years, who took illegal action.

East India group, all of these men were to remain steadfast supporters of the parliamentary opposition. Fowke, Chambers, and Vassall, in particular, came to play key roles in organizing the City's parliamentary revolution in 1640–1642. Chambers had made himself a cause célèbre when, upon being hauled before the privy council on 28 September 1628 for refusing to pay the currants impositions, he defiantly cried out, "Merchants are in no part of the world so screwed and wrung as in England. In Turkey they have more encouragement." For this he was promptly jailed, although he was bailed out a month later. In any case, when these five merchants had their goods seized for refusing to pay customs in the autumn of 1628, they launched suits of replevin for their recovery in the sheriff's court of London, claiming the right to resist any levy not warranted by Parliament. To counteract this move, the Crown quickly took the case to the court of exchequer. In making the government's argument, the lord treasurer made sure to point out that the "five merchants had unmannerly and ungratefully . . . disturbed his majesty's gracious intentions; ungratefully . . . because that company, viz. trading for Turkey, received continual favors from his majesty, having their petitions daily granted at the council board." The court of exchequer ruled on 27 November 1628 against releasing the merchants' goods, although it explicitly left the question of principle to the king and Parliament.[76]

The action of the court of exchequer seems only to have further inflamed a merchant opposition now strongly identified with Parliament and its general struggle against unparliamentary customs. Some merchants apparently had already begun a general strike against tonnage and poundage. In the words of one observer, "Our merchants of late, grounding themselves upon the Petition of Right have taken home goods without paying tonnage and poundage, offering their bonds to the customers to pay His Majesty what was due by law." During November, ships of the Levant Company and the East India Company had arrived in port, but "the generality of the merchants" of both corporations simply refused to claim them from the king's storehouse, "say[ing] they will let their goods lie and will pay neither tonnage nor poundage till his majesty do evict it from them by law" and "pleading for their so doing the Petition of Right." By early December, in the words of the Tuscan ambassador Salvetti, "every day disputes arise between sailors and His Majesty's customs house officers. The sailors refuse to pay the usual duties, insisting that Parliament did not grant them to this king as it did to his father. There is great embarrassment at court as to the best means of amending this, seeing that Parliament is about to meet. It is a question of the greatest consequence

[76] Pearl, *London*, pp. 78–79; Gardiner, *History* 7: 1–7, 28, 30–34, 82–87, 108, 114–15, 167–68; Williams, *Court and Times of Charles I* 1: 438–39 (quotation).

and, unless a remedy is found, the royal power will suffer, as day by day there are symptoms of the growing and daring opposition of the people."[77]

A short time later, Gilman and Fowke, perhaps in part to help ensure that the Parliament planned for 20 January 1629 would actually be allowed to meet on schedule, further escalated the struggle by bringing their goods forcibly through customs without payment. According to one report, "To free themselves from the customers' hands and compulsions, [these merchants] went, with two or three hundred armed men, aboard their ships, and brought from thence great store of merchandise, namely currants to land which they had already laden upon carts to carry them to their private houses." On 5 January 1629, the privy council, "not a little troubled . . . to see these bold refractory courses used by the subjects to the open condemning of the king's authority," ordered these merchants arrested and went on to demand that the Levant Company call a special meeting for the purpose of compelling its members' obedience to the ruling of the court of exchequer. When the company met, however, it explicitly defied the privy council's order to call on its members to pay the duties. Moreover, the company's general court did not stop there. Its members went on to vote that they would not merely refuse to pay the 2s. 2d. that the Crown had added in 1619 to the original 3s. 4d. impost on currants, which had been their initial grievance; they now announced their unwillingness, as a company, to pay any duties on currants whatsoever.[78]

The situation was now getting out of hand, and certain elements within the top directing circles of the great overseas companies sought to halt the escalation. When the Levant Company next met, on 22 January 1629, Anthony Abdy, the deputy governor, and John Williams, the company husband, tried to engineer a compromise. They presented to the company's general court a draft petition that once more limited the company to demanding that the 2s. 2d. currants imposition be removed. Nevertheless, not only the Levant Company's general membership, but also its board of directors, rejected the proposal of Abdy and Williams. According to the company minutes, the proposed petition "was wholly disliked by this court, for as much as it mentioned only the impost of 2s. 2d. . . . whereas they now intend to make a general complaint as well for all duties upon other commodities as for this of currants." At this point, the company's governor, Hugh Hamersley, along with Deputy Governor Abdy, tried to assert authority, desiring "the court to be very well advised what they should do therein." But "after long dispute and divers opinions given and many questions moved, whether to petition or not, whether in general by

[77] Williams, *Court and Times of Charles I* 1: 433–34, 437; *H.M.C.*, *Eleventh Report, Appendix*, 1, Skrine MSS, p. 172.

[78] *A.P.C. 1628–1629*, p. 293 (5 Jan. 1629); Williams, *Court and Times of Charles I* 2: 5–6 (quotation); PRO, S.P. 105/148/193v–94.

the company or by private men, whether for the easing of this impost upon currants only or concerning all other commodities, it was at length concluded by most of the assistants and the generality present to petition in the name of the company and in general for the discharge of all their goods now detained from them." The company had thus, apparently, joined in fully, as a body, with the growing movement against all unparliamentary customs, led by their colleagues Vassall, Chambers, Gilman, Fowke, and Rolle, and they directed their officers to present their petition to Parliament. It was symptomatic of the general explosiveness of the situation that several days later still another Levant Company director, Thomas Symonds, broke into the customs house to seize his goods.[79]

The opposition movement in Parliament and that in the merchant community had now become fully merged. The House of Commons took up with great intensity the resistance to tonnage and poundage of Gilman, Rolle, Chambers, Vassall, and Fowke on 22 January 1629, the very day of the Levant Company's declaration. Two days later, Charles appeared open to compromise when he informed the House that he had been collecting tonnage and poundage by necessity and did not claim it by right of his prerogative. He requested that Parliament now grant him tonnage and poundage. Nevertheless, on 28 January 1629, the House of Commons received a petition from the Levant Company merchant Richard Chambers protesting that he had been unlawfully imprisoned and had had his goods taken by the officers of the customs despite his offer to pay whatever ultimately was lawfully decided to be due. The Levant Company merchant John Fowke presented a similar petition on 5 February, asking for the release of his goods seized by the customs farmers.

Shortly thereafter, it was learned that the government was proceeding in star chamber against the Levant Company merchant John Rolle, who happened to be an MP, as well as the others, for their refusal to pay. And on 12 February, Chambers, Fowke, and Gilman petitioned the House of Commons for relief. The House now demanded to know why, if His Majesty admitted that unparliamentary tonnage and poundage was not his by right, the king's officers were moving against these merchants. It refused to pass tonnage and poundage until proceedings against the merchants were dropped and their goods restored. Several weeks later, the king moved to dismiss Parliament, and the House of Commons made its historic appeal to the country, concluding with the warning that "if any merchant or other person whatsoever shall voluntarily yield or pay the said subsidies of tonnage and poundage, not being granted by Parliament, he

---

[79] PRO, S.P. 105/148/196v; *A.P.C. 1628*, p. 319. The top company officers saw these actions as a direct vote of no confidence, as is indicated by the refusal of Abdy and Williams to continue to serve in their former positions at the Levant Company elections that took place two weeks later (PRO, S.P. 105/148/197v [2 Feb. 1629]).

shall likewise be reputed a betrayer of England, and an enemy to the same."[80]

The merchants' struggle now reached its climax. The majority of traders refused to ship any goods, and the king was, for a time, deprived of all customs revenue. Even now, however, there was not unanimity: critical sections of the merchant elite refused to join the protest and to confront the Crown. On 13 March 1629, at a meeting of the East India Company's board of directors, called to decide whether to join in the general refusal to pay customs, the company's governor Morris Abbot advised strongly against it, "conceiving the case of the India Company and other merchants are not alike for many reasons, and to contest with the king, as was observed by Mr. Treasurer, on a business of this nature and at this time were no way fit, considering the many occasions they have now with the king, from whom the company cannot expect any favor if herein they show themselves refractory." The board of directors put off a decision, and sought to avoid offending either the king or Parliament by securing a "bill of sufferance" from the customs house, which would allow them to send out their goods without paying, but also without the implication that they were refusing to pay.[81] However, the customs officers turned down this request. So on 18 March, at a further meeting of the board of directors, "Mr. Governor [Abbot] desired the court now plainly and directly to declare their resolution that this voyage may proceed." At this point, "to show their obedience and conformity to His Majesty . . . the Court . . . by erection of hands agreed and ordered that the entry of their goods [at customs] shall be no longer delayed but presently performed." Moreover, they reaffirmed this resolution to submit openly to the Crown, even after the company's representatives returned with the news that the customs farmers had finally agreed to their request for a "bill of sufferance."[82]

With Parliament gone, it was difficult for the many merchants on strike to continue resisting; they could hardly refuse to ship indefinitely. Even so, the movement appears to have been surprisingly effective and long

[80] For this and preceding paragraph, Notestein and Relf, *Commons Debates for 1629*, pp. 7–9, 10–12, 18, 22, 60–62, 81, 129, 135–37; Gardiner, *History* 7: 30–34, 75 (quotation).

[81] Court Minutes of the East India Company, India Office Library, vol. B/13, pp. 363–65 (quotation from p. 363). It is very relevant in this context that, in the period immediately preceding the opening of Parliament, Morris Abbot's intimate political allies, his brother Archbishop George Abbot and the archbishop's close collaborator Sir Dudley Digges (whose son married Morris Abbot's daughter), both had made their peace, at least for the time being, with Charles I and had ceased to support the parliamentary opposition. In the Parliament itself, Digges had come out explicitly in support of the Crown's policies (P. A. Welsby, *George Abbot: The Unwanted Archbishop, 1562–1633* [London, 1962], p. 136; Kiffin, "Sir Dudley Digges," pp. 336–37, 340–41).

[82] Court Minutes of the East India Company, India Office Library, vol. B/13, pp. 366–67.

lasting.[83] By the following autumn, however, most seem to have begun to send out their goods again. It is suggestive of the new mood that, on 20 August 1629, when the Levant Company next raised the issue of customs, it confined itself to attacking the 2s. 2d. currants impost and the 3d. added customs on silk as mere grievances, as it had at the very beginning. The constitutional and political implications of these levies were simply ignored. The king had survived a major test, and was already on the offensive.[84]

There can be no doubt that by the end of the 1620s, the relationship between the Crown and the City merchant community had become profoundly strained. Nevertheless, the political significance of this estrangement—the degree to which it was the result of structural or merely short-term conjunctural causes—needs to be carefully assessed. The Crown's increased customs duties had struck the Levant Company, the French Company, and the Merchant Adventurers. But it is impossible to believe that these levies were so economically burdensome as to have provoked, by themselves, serious merchant opposition. The 2s. 2d. increase in the currants levy was at the very heart of the conflict, but when the government first imposed it in 1619 the Levant Company accepted it without a murmur. Indeed, the Crown had collected this duty for five years before the Levant Company had even protested, and when the company finally did raise the issue, it did so in a most opportunistic and nonthreatening manner. The Merchant Adventurers, for their part, had gladly accepted the pretermitted custom in 1619 as a condition for the renewal of their charter and had never protested to Parliament against this impost. The French Company merchants were perhaps most affected economically due to the burden of the wine impost; but even they received major compensation for the new imposition in the form of assured purchase of their imports.

On the other hand, it is quite clear that the Crown's arbitrary exercise of authority that so troubled Parliament in the later 1620s also seriously disturbed the City merchants. They could hardly have been pleased with forced loans, arbitrary imprisonment, martial law, the illegal impress-

---

[83] At the end of May, according to one observer, "the courtiers brag more of the merchants condescending to trade than [there] is cause." By the end of June, it was still being reported that "our greatest home business hangs still in suspense. The merchants cannot be brought on to trade so freely as they were wont. Monies come in slowly." Even in October, the Venetian ambassador noted that "although many consent to the payment [of customs duties], many others refuse it, not only to avoid exposing themselves to censure, but because they conscientiously believe they would be committing a very serious sin in contravening the privileges of liberty" (Williams, *Court and Times of Charles I* 2: 15, 20; *C.S.P. Ven. 1629–1632*, p. 205.

[84] PRO, S.P. 105/148/205v.

ment of soldiers, billeting, and the like. The fact, moreover, that the Parliaments of 1628 and 1629 made unparliamentary taxes on trade a basic question of principle and central to their opposition to Charles I obviously contributed to the stubbornness and explosiveness of the merchants' opposition.

Still, it needs to be remembered that even at the height of the conflict, the Crown retained a hard core of merchant support, well situated in some of the most influential positions within the merchant community. In January 1629, with Parliament about to meet, the top Levant Company officers did their best, as noted, to head off the company's mounting constitutional opposition. Two months later, in a similar manner, the East India Company directorate refused to back the widespread movement against the Crown from within the City merchant community. In the Merchant Adventurers, too, the Crown had important agents among the company's leaders. When the Adventurers were finally induced to ship their cloths in May 1629, breaking the strike, Secretary Coke reported that the resolution was narrowly gained "by two hands," with a leading Adventurer who happened also to be Coke's brother-in-law playing an influential role in support of the Crown.[85] The court of aldermen, as emphasized, stood solidly behind the Crown throughout the whole course of the crisis, as did, of course, the farmers of the customs.

It is difficult to believe, moreover, that the Crown could not have commanded substantially more support among the company merchants, especially within the merchant political elite, had it not been brutally disregarding their interests since the middle 1620s. The company merchants differed from their landed-class counterparts in Parliament in their overwhelming dependence on the government for their livelihood; so whatever their constitutional ideas, they were in a much worse position to act on these ideas than was the parliamentary aristocracy. It is thus only superficially paradoxical that the parliamentary classes who were hardly touched economically by unparliamentary levies on trade fundamentally opposed them, while the company merchants of London who largely paid these taxes long accepted them, fighting them only very belatedly and for a brief period. For the landed classes, arbitrary taxes on trade, though economically relatively painless, constituted a real danger to their fundamental liberties of property and of Parliament, and concomitantly their power within the state. For the merchants, in contrast, these levies were the necessary condition—the quid pro quo—precisely for the maintenance of an indispensable politically constituted element of their property, their companies' commercial privileges. As has just been noted, Governor Morris Abbot successfully appealed to his fellow East India Company

----

[85] *C.S.P.D. 1628–1629*, p. 550.

directors to break the strike against unparliamentary customs on the ground that they were too tied to the king to act on Parliament's principles. Analogously, according to a report to the privy council on "the private feelings of the Merchant Adventurers" at this time, there was "speech among them of a petition to the council," to the effect "that if they pay their duties, the king will protect them against future Parliaments."[86] Had the king more assiduously protected the Adventurers against *past* Parliaments, the Crown might, all along, have been receiving their support.

As it was, the Crown had unceremoniously dropped its traditional backing for the Merchant Adventurers' privileges in 1624, and so long as Buckingham was in the saddle, it gave no sign that it wished to renew them. In addition, in less than two years from the start of the reign, Charles I and Buckingham had totally undermined the great company merchants' control of trade with the Americas, extracted £20,000 from the East India Company, and taken the customs farm from its traditional possessors within the merchant elite. Perhaps most damaging of all, the government had opened the way to the radical disruption of trade, the reduction of commerce, and the outright loss of the merchants' goods by its incomprehensible foreign wars. All these actions struck particularly hard against that pivotal group of Levant–East India Company leaders who were in these years replacing the Merchant Adventurers' top traders at the heart of the merchant elite. Had these merchant chieftains consistently supported the government of Charles—rather than, at times, lashing out against it—their less substantial though still quite well off colleagues in the chartered companies would have found it a good deal more difficult to go into opposition. Indeed, if the government of Buckingham and Charles had been less than totally insensitive to the company merchants' fundamental needs, the Crown might have found the company merchant community as a whole far less determined in its resistance in the first place.

By the end of 1629 the king's tasks with respect to the City's company merchants were crystal clear. He had to reconsolidate the support he traditionally had enjoyed among the company elite. He had to take advantage of Parliament's antipathy to merchant privileges by using the grant of favors to woo the rank-and-file members of the chartered companies. The degree to which Charles had succeeded, by his own efforts, in realizing these goals by 1640 is a question to which I will return.

[86] Ibid., p. 525.

The Merchant Community, the Caroline Regime,

and the Aristocratic Opposition

THE GENERAL strike against nonparliamentary taxation on trade marked the high point of resistance to the Crown by the City's overseas company merchants during the pre–Civil War period. During the 1630s, different merchant groups protested various royal financial and economic policies, but never again were the company merchants' protests linked so systematically to a broader politico-constitutional opposition as they had been during the struggles of the late 1620s. Even as merchant opposition was reaching its zenith, forces were in motion tending both to alienate the City's company merchants from the parliamentary leaders with whom they hitherto had been allied, and to pull those merchants back in the direction of the Crown.

Practically from the moment of Parliament's dismissal in 1629, the Crown launched a counteroffensive, lasting throughout the 1630s, which aimed to win back the overseas traders by wooing their leaders and by granting concessions to their corporations. In these years, Charles attempted to rule without Parliament. And this policy had enormous implications for the political relationship between the monarchy and the City and its merchants.

First of all, in view of his more or less permanently straitened circumstances, Charles simply could not afford an adventurous foreign policy. If at all possible, he had to avoid getting into wars, and this meant above all avoiding military conflict with Spain. Charles's policy of peace was hugely beneficial to the company merchants as a whole, and peace with Spain was especially conducive to the good health of that ever more powerful and assertive group of merchants who traded with southern Europe and the Near East by way of the Mediterranean.

Meanwhile, Charles was forced to develop a basis for financing monarchical government independently of the landed class. Since taxing the land without parliamentary consent was so difficult, Charles found himself compelled to fall back on the money-raising tactic that had been increasingly used by his predecessors: the exploitation of and dependence on London commercial sources of income, taxes as well as loans. Under James I, of course, the monarchy had turned to increased taxes on trade to supplement declining and undependable revenues from the land, particularly to get around the stalemate with Parliament. Charles carried this approach to its logical conclusion. Whereas the impositions levied by Salisbury in the first decade of the seventeenth century were worth £70,000 a year to the Crown, Charles's impositions netted £218,000 a year in the 1630s. By 1637–1640, overall revenues from the customs amounted to some 35–40 percent of royal income, around £300,000–£400,000 annually out of a total Crown revenue of perhaps £900,000.[1] Since Charles was thus compelled to milk City resources, he had little choice but to enhance the privileges of various commercial groups. This was the necessary quid pro quo for maintaining the merchants' backing.

The merchants, for their part, were open to royal advances. This was especially true of the merchant political elite within the organizations they dominated: the customs farming syndicates, which were the direct creation of the royal government; the court of aldermen, which was bound to the court as a result of the City's historical dependence on the Crown for its privileges and its oligarchic constitution; and the East India Company board of directors, which constituted the organizational stronghold of the City's very top company traders and which depended on the Crown for the company's chartered monopoly. But it was also the case for the run of company merchants who could not help but be aware of the significance of politically protected regulation of trade for their economic well-being. During the ascendancy of Buckingham in the later 1620s, the royal government had failed to live up to its side of the long-standing arrangement whereby it guaranteed merchant privileges in exchange for the merchants' financial support and political allegiance. It had poisoned Crown-merchant relations still further by its incomprehensible involvements in Continental warfare, which disastrously disrupted trade. But Parliament had done little to fill the vacuum. So the potential remained for a renewal of the traditional Crown-merchant partnership. Whether the Crown could realize this potential through consistent support for the merchants' privileges was, of course, an open question.

While the Crown was attempting to restore its working relationship with the City's company merchants, the greater City merchants and critical sections of the parliamentary leadership were moving apart. One of the most significant developments of the early years of Charles's rule was the emergence of what might be called a responsible opposition leadership in Parliament. During the latter part of the 1620s, these men sought,

[1] C. Russell, "Parliament and the King's Finances," in *The Origins of the English Civil War*, ed. C. Russell (London, 1973), p. 100; D. Thomas, "Financial and Administrative Developments," in *Before the English Civil War*, ed. H. Tomlinson (London, 1983), pp. 106, 120, 121.

under conditions of increasingly severe political conflict, to reach a principled political agreement with the Crown so as to restore the traditionally close working relationship between the monarch and the leading representatives of the landed class on the privy council and in Parliament. The settlement they envisioned would have cut short what they believed to be the Crown's unconstitutional assaults on the proprietary, parliamentary, and personal liberties of the subject, and reversed what they felt to be a crypto-Catholic and effectively pro-absolutist Arminian trend within the church. On that basis, they hoped to restrengthen royal finances and to inaugurate militantly Protestant foreign and domestic policies, to be highlighted by a naval and colonial war against Spain, as well as by the repression of papists at home. As all of these goals came to appear less likely to be realized as the decade drew to a close, these men increasingly devoted their efforts to constructing their own extensive network of colonial outposts for political refuge, Puritan experiment, and plantation development in Bermuda, Providence Island, and Massachusetts Bay. From the end of the 1630s on, this same group would take the lead in the revived opposition to Charles's policies, assume much of the leadership of the parliamentary legislative revolution, and come to compose the core of the parliamentary middle group.

During much of the 1620s, some of the City's greatest merchants had supported the political struggles of these and other parliamentary oppositionists, while working alongside them in certain colonial company undertakings. But toward the end of the 1620s, this alliance began to break down when the overwhelming majority of the City's overseas company merchants refused to support the aristocratic oppositionists in their Puritan colonial schemes and when some of the most important merchant leaders entered into open conflict with them over control of the East India Company, the traditional stronghold of the merchant elite, while effectively withdrawing from the struggle against the Crown. These processes were fraught with political implications, and they paved the way for a critical realignment.

Thus, one of the most spectacular, yet largely unnoticed, political developments of the late 1620s and the 1630s was the creation of a close working relationship between the noble and gentry political groups that operated the Puritan colonizing companies and the new-merchant leadership of the colonial trades. This alliance had its origins during the late 1620s in the intense struggles over unparliamentary taxation and Arminianism and was sealed during the 1630s when future middle-group parliamentary oppositionists and key new-merchant leaders worked together not only on commercial, but also on political and religious, initiatives inside the colonizing companies. From the start of the parliamentary legislative revolution in 1640, the parliamentary leadership was obliged to look beyond London's traditional ruling groups for allies because the City's merchant elite stood strongly behind the Crown and succeeded in exerting a powerful pro-royalist political influence on the generality of company merchants. In these circumstances, John Pym and his friends were willing and able to ally with a tumultuous London mass movement composed largely of nonmerchant citizens, in large part because they had forged a close working relationship with new-merchant leaders who stood at the head of this movement. The alliance of parliamentary leaders with London radicals only increased Parliament's difficulty in gaining and holding the support of the City's company merchants.

The remainder of this chapter will trace the complex evolution of conflict and alliance during the reign of Charles I among the Crown, the landed-class leaders of the colonizing companies, the City's company merchants, and the new-merchant leadership. In the first section, I will briefly examine the coalescence of what has been termed alternatively a responsible, colonizing, or middle-group opposition in Parliament during the course of the 1620s. In the second section, I will discuss the emerging conflicts between the aristocratic oppositionists and key sections of the merchant elite and the ensuing alignment of aristocratic oppositionist with the new-merchant leadership. In the third section, I will follow the Crown's attempt to woo the company merchants and examine some of the contradictory aspects of this quest. In the final section, I will examine the political outcome of these processes by discussing merchant politics during the crisis of the regime at the end of the 1630s.

The Rise of the Aristocratic Colonizing Opposition

Many of the MPs who came in 1640 to form the heart of the parliamentary leadership learned to work together, developed their politico-religious ideas, and created what turned out to be a critical relationship with the new-merchant leadership by means of their joint activity in the Massachusetts Bay, Bermuda, and Providence Island companies during the 1630s.[2] Nevertheless, the organization of the colonizing ventures was itself only a stage in a complex political evolution that had begun earlier. It was in the course of the interconnected political struggles and colonial initiatives of the later 1620s that what might be called the "aristocratic colonizing opposition" came together, began to separate itself from its

[2] My discussion of this group takes as its point of departure the accounts by C. Thompson and C. Russell: Thompson's "Origins of the Parliamentary Middle Group," *T.R.H.S.*, 5th ser., 22 (1972), and Russell's "Parliament and the King's Finances," as well as Russell's *Parliaments and English Politics, 1621–1629* (Oxford, 1979). See also, of course, A. P. Newton, *The Colonising Activities of the English Puritans* (New Haven, 1914).

former allies among the City's merchant elite, and started to forge ties with the new men of the colonial trades. The solidity of this responsible opposition, and the breadth of its support—even the degree to which it was a self-conscious group at various points during the 1620s—is not entirely clear. But its representative figures—Nathaniel Rich, the earl of Warwick, Lord Saye and Sele, Dudley Digges, Benjamin Rudyerd, and John Pym—were all among the top parliamentary leaders of the 1620s. Moreover, these men did distinguish themselves by a commitment to a distinctive set of policies and principles; they did through most of the decade work together to implement these policies and principles (although Digges in 1629 ceased to do so); and they did (except for Digges) join together in the Puritan colonizing companies. Finally, Pym and Rudyerd, as well as Saye and Warwick, all ended up within the parliamentary leadership in 1640, and Rich certainly would have been there, too, had he lived that long.

First and perhaps most distinctively, then, these individuals were devoted to a militantly anti-Spanish foreign policy. Although most of their colleagues in Parliament held similarly anti-Spanish religio-political beliefs, many were uncertain about how to implement them, reluctant to pay the costs of war, or both. In contrast, throughout the 1620s what would become the aristocratic colonizing opposition led the struggle to have implemented some version of the "diversionary strategy" for war with Spain, and they were willing to pay the price. Specifically, they sought to make war on Spain in a way that would minimize the English commitment to landed conflict on the Continent itself. This could be accomplished by financing a foreign force to attack Spanish Flanders—thereby compelling Spain to divert some of its troops from the Palatinate—and especially by directing English (and perhaps Dutch) naval power against Spain's fleet for the Americas and particularly Spain's West Indian colonies. Indeed, success at sea might provide the wherewithal for undertaking the military effort on land. From 1616, the earl of Warwick and his kinsman Sir Nathaniel Rich had pursued large-scale privateering ventures against Spain's Caribbean fleet and made quasi-legal attempts at colonization within Spain's empire in the Americas, notably in Guiana; but they had had to do these things mostly unofficially and on their own private initiative because of the Crown's commitment to making an alliance with Spain. Over the following three decades, the aristocratic colonizing group was in the forefront of the battle to have the monarchy forsake the alliance with Spain and make the "Western Design" an official plank of government policy.[3]

[3] Russell, *Parliaments*, pp. 13, 98, 129–32, 168, 217, 288, 293–94, 299–300, 429; Thomson, "Origins," pp. 73–74; S. L. Adams, "Foreign Policy and the Parliaments of 1621 and 1624," in

Second, even while they opposed Charles I on a long string of political issues during the later 1620s, these men also sought to help the king solve some of his major problems of governance. Indeed, through much of this period they sought to win over the king to their perspectives and policies partly by means of helping him to overcome the financial weaknesses that threatened to paralyze the monarchy—in particular, by making large additions to his regular (nonparliamentary) income. These men were strongly committed to Parliament as an institution, and they were quite willing to employ the power of the purse, to the extent they were able, to impose their policies on the Crown. But they sharply distinguished themselves from those of their colleagues in Parliament for whom cheap government and low taxes were ends in themselves. In contrast, these leaders appear to have believed that they could not get the king to rule as they wished him to rule if they did not allow him more funds. It was clearly their hope that they could have both a monarchy with improved financial resources and a king who would use those resources for ends they favored.[4]

Finally, these men maintained an overriding commitment to the orthodox Calvinist principles that they thought formed the core of English Protestant belief, and that they saw fairly well exemplified in Archbishop Abbot's governance of the church. They were for the most vigorous enforcement of the laws against Catholic recusants. They were, moreover, among the earliest and most violent opponents of the new Arminian trend in the church; for they saw Arminianism as the leading wedge of an all-out popish assault on English Protestantism and, in the end, on English parliamentary and proprietary liberties.[5] And especially in order to reach a broader, sometimes popular, audience with their political ideas, they established close working relationships with Calvinist ministers.

The foregoing positions formed a reasonably coherent perspective. On the basis of their Calvinist doctrine, these men interpreted world affairs largely as a struggle of the united Protestant churches against the papal Antichrist. From the time of Elizabeth, the Spanish monarchy had constituted the most powerful international agency of the Catholic church, so English Protestants had tended to promote a militantly anti-Spanish policy internationally. With the outbreak of the Thirty Years War in 1618, and

---

Faction and Parliament, ed. K. Sharpe (Oxford, 1978), pp. 143–47, 151–52; Newton, *Colonising Activities*, pp. 26–27.

[4] Russell, "Parliament and the King's Finances," pp. 106–8; Russell, *Parliaments*, pp. 32, 246–47, 283; Thompson, "Origins," pp. 78–79.

[5] Russell, *Parliaments*, pp. 29–30, 231, 375, 381–82, 411, 429; Thompson "Origins," pp. 74–75, 78–79. On Archbishop Abbot's Calvinist and tolerant rule in the church, as well as the Calvinism and anti-Armininianism of these men, see also N. Tyacke, "Puritanism, Arminianism, and Counter-Revolution," in Russell, *Origins of the English Civil War*, pp. 119–40.

the ensuing intensification of trans-European warfare, these men saw the danger of Catholicism as reaching crisis proportions, and they understandably called on the state to respond accordingly. In order to pursue an effective Protestant, anti-Spanish policy internationally and domestically, these men realized that it was necessary to have strong and effective government. The heightened sensitivity of at least some of these men (notably Warwick, Rich, and Digges) to the need for a stronger state also probably derived, in part, from their longtime active involvement in colonial and commercial affairs, an involvement that was relatively unusual among the greater landed classes. More acutely than most of their parliamentary colleagues, these men saw an expanding commercial and colonial empire as a key to England's economic and political power, as well as desirable in itself. They understood that English commercial and colonial interests would have to be defended and expanded by politico-military means against the Spanish, and naturally also appreciated the fact that Parliament would have to raise the money to cover the cost. But finally, even as they aimed to construct a stronger and more effective state, these men also sought to combat what they came to believe was a clerically inspired Arminian, crypto–Catholic, and crypto–Spanish drive to destroy not merely their Calvinist church but also their parliamentary liberties. A powerful and financially sound state would only be desirable if they, and the greater landed classes more generally, could exert some control over it by way of the king's council and Parliament.

These men could command the confidence to push for a more effective government, even as they opposed Charles I on specific policies, because of their great personal influence and their powerful connections with the centers of power. They themselves held high rank, as did Warwick and Saye, and/or maintained strong ties with the privy council. Warwick's brother was the influential privy councilor Henry Rich, earl of Holland. Rudyerd's patron was the earl of Pembroke, who was the lord chamberlain and, after Buckingham, perhaps the most influential aristocrat in England. Digges had Archbishop Abbot as his friend and mentor. Indeed, one way to understand the parallel and collaborative activities of these men through much though not all of the 1620s is in terms of an at least implicit entente between the great Pembroke-Abbot faction on the privy council and the increasingly influential connection around the Riches, itself closely allied with Lord Saye and his friends.[6] By virtue of rank, wealth, and connections, these men had the assurance to press for new departures in policy. They expected to have a part in governing the nation and, while naturally reluctant to innovate in constitutional terms, would not happily

[6] Adams, "Foreign Policy," pp. 143–47; R. Ruigh, *The Parliament of 1624* (Cambridge, Mass., 1971) pp. 127ff.

tolerate a situation in which they were denied what they conceived to be their proper role. Their overriding goal appears to have been merely to induce the Crown to depend more systematically on the counsel of the leading landed classes, especially themselves. They doggedly pursued the rights of Parliament, but largely as a means to their main end, and even then not intentionally at the expense of the royal prerogative. It was only after a long series of failures to induce more systematic cooperation between the king and his natural counselors that these men turned decisively to constitutional innovation, and this did not occur until Parliament returned in 1640.

James I's dogged pursuit of a Spanish alliance and a Spanish match appears to have provided the initial context and stimulus for the coalescence of these forces. James favored an alliance with Spain as a guarantee of social order and monarchical legitimacy in a world threatened by Dutch and Presbyterian republicanism, as a means of avoiding costly Continental entanglements, and as a way possibly to reverse the disastrous condition of royal finances through a rich Spanish dowry. But James's policy provoked increasing opposition among broad elements within the landed classes, especially following the acceptance in September 1619 of the Bohemian crown by James's son-in-law, Elector Frederick of the Palatinate. Opposition intensified as it became clear that James would have to grant increasing toleration to recusants as the price of the Spanish marriage. The upshot was, indeed, a certain religio-political polarization during the years 1619–1623 that foreshadowed in significant ways the polarization of the later 1620s.

Pro-Calvinist elements on James's council, among the parliamentary classes more broadly, and within the episcopal hierarchy became more openly critical of the Spanish match. As they did, they organized allies among the Calvinist clergy and the London citizenry to aid them in a series of voluntary money-raising campaigns to defend the Palatinate that proved embarrassing to James. They also encouraged ministers to preach ever more insolently against the government and its ungodly policies. In response, James's government moved sharply to repress all dissent, issuing a series of proclamations against "lavish speech" and arresting a significant number of his clerical opponents, while sharply restricting preaching. It also ordered the suspension of the penal laws against Catholics. Most striking, James seems to have thrown his support toward anti-Calvinist members of the church hierarchy, who were much more tolerant than the Calvinists of James's pro-Spanish policy, but who hitherto had seen their influence limited by the power of Archbishop Abbot and other like-minded people within the episcopal establishment, as well as by James himself. James thus threatened to overturn a long-standing balance of power between Calvinists and anti-Calvinists within the church hierarchy, with the result that those Calvinists who sought most fervently to oppose James's pro-Spanish course in foreign policy became even more concerned about the threat to religion at home.

The recall of Parliament in 1621 provided the individuals who would come to constitute a responsible, aristocratic, colonizing opposition a major opening to put forward some of their fundamental ideas. In the years since the Bohemian Revolution, James had witnessed the collapse of his pro-Spanish strategy in foreign policy. James had not approved of the acceptance by his son-in-law of the Bohemian throne, but he had found it difficult to avoid defending Frederick when Frederick came under attack from Emperor Ferdinand II. James's tactic was thus to avoid at all costs any commitment to a war for religion, for the "Protestant Cause," but to defend the Palatinate by inducing Spain to intervene with the emperor in support of Frederick's hereditary position there. However, in August 1620, Spain's Army of Flanders had invaded the Palatinate; in November 1620 Frederick was defeated at the battle of White Mountain, virtually destroying his position in Bohemia; and in the summer of 1621, Ferdinand II had promised the Palatinate and its electoral dignity to Maximilian, duke of Bavaria. To make matters worse, during roughly the same period the Huguenots' position in France was seriously weakened, under the assault of Louis XIII. With the Truce of Antwerp between Spain and the United Provinces expiring, it seemed that the Protestant Cause throughout Europe was in profound danger, and James was thus more or less obliged to allow some expression of parliamentary opinion on foreign policy alternatives if he hoped to raise the funds needed to finance military operations of any sort in the Palatinate's defense.[7]

On 26 November 1621 Sir Dudley Digges, apparently speaking for the Pembroke-Abbot connection on the privy council, opened a large-scale parliamentary debate on foreign policy. He defined the struggle as a war for religion against Spain and suggested to Parliament that it consider "whether a diverting war may be fit." Two years previously, Digges's patron, Archbishop Abbot, had interpreted the Bohemian Revolution explicitly in terms of Protestant apocalyptic history, as the beginning of the

[7] For the preceding three paragraphs, see Adams, "Foreign Policy," pp. 139–42, 146–52, 160–62; S. L. Adams, "Spain or the Netherlands? The Dilemmas of Early Stuart Foreign Policy," in Tomlinson, *Before the English Civil War*, pp. 95–97; K. Fincham and P. Lake, "The Ecclesiastical Policy of King James I," *J.B.S.* 24 (1985): 198–207; T. Cogswell, "England and the Spanish Match," in *Conflict in Early Stuart England*, ed. R. Cust and A. Hughes (London, 1989), pp. 112–122. On these developments, I have also found very helpful S. L. Adams, "The Protestant Cause: Religious Alliance with the West European Calvinist Communities as a Political Issue in England, 1585–1630" (Oxford University, Ph.D. diss., 1973). Page references to this work are from a revised version of the foregoing dissertation, kindly lent to me by Simon Adams. I wish to express my gratitude to Dr. Adams for allowing me to consult, and to refer to, his unpublished study.

final struggle between the godly and the papal Antichrist. In Abbot's words, "I do . . . foresee the work of God, that by piece and piece, the Kings of the Earth that gave their power unto the Beast (all the work of God must be fulfilled) shall not tear the whore, and make her desolate, as St. John in his revelation hath foretold." Abbot had warmly and outspokenly welcomed Frederick's acceptance of the Bohemian throne, had led the effort to propagandize and raise funds for the elector's cause, and had rather openly opposed the Spanish match while encouraging militant clerics to do the same—all against the express wishes of James I. Digges himself had custody of the papers of the great Elizabethan secretary Sir Francis Walsingham, and he seems to have developed his views on foreign policy partly from them. In addition, Digges was one of those few landed-class leaders who was extremely active in London commerce, and his support for an anti-Spanish offensive may have derived, in part, from his experience in the Bermuda and Virginia companies. When Digges and his close friend and politico-commercial collaborator Morris Abbot, Archbishop Abbot's brother, had served in 1620–1621 as English ambassadors to the United Provinces to discuss the resolution of Anglo-Dutch commercial conflicts, they had reportedly informally scouted the possibility of establishing a joint Anglo-Dutch West India Company for trade with the Caribbean and war against Spain.[8]

Sir Benjamin Rudyerd spoke next. His patron, the earl of Pembroke, was the most powerful leader of the anti-Spanish forces on the privy council. Pembroke, Archibishop Abbot, and Lucy Harington, countess of Bedford, were perhaps the leading figures in an informal English pro-Bohemian party, whose prominent members also included the Scottish peers the marquis of Hamilton and the duke of Lennox, the East Anglian gentry associated with the earl of Warwick and his kinsman Sir Nathaniel Rich, and the earl of Southampton, who headed a powerful faction that included the earl of Essex, Edmund, Lord Sheffield, Lord Cavendish, Sir Edwin Sandys, Sir Thomas Roe, and Sir John Danvers. Rudyerd strongly seconded Digges and was supported, in turn, by Sir James Perrot, apparently also under Pembroke's patronage, and Sir Miles Fleetwood. Shortly thereafter, following interventions from Sir Edward Sackville and Sir

[8] W. Notestein, F. H. Relf, and H. Simpson, eds, *Commons Debates, 1621*, 7 vols. (New Haven, 1935), vol. 2 ("X"), p. 445; and vol. 3 (Barrington), pp. 445–47; Russell, *Parliaments*, pp. 129–30; Fincham and Lake, "Ecclesiastical Policy of James I," pp. 198, 200; Adams, "Foreign Policy," pp. 146–47 (quotation from p. 147); Adams, "Protestant Cause," pp. 281, 290, 311, 324. *C.S.P. Ven. 1619–1621*, pp. 487–88. A seven-member English delegation, including four merchants, had apparently discussed a proposal for an Anglo-Dutch West India Company during the earlier conference on Anglo-Dutch commercial disputes that was held in the winter of 1619–1620. (*C.S.P. Ven. 1619–1621*, pp. 350–51, 404). The Dutch ambassadors to England had placed an Anglo-Dutch West India Company on the agenda once again in February 1621, but had been rebuffed by James (ibid., p. 569).

Robert Phelips (who appears to have urged a slower progress toward a war with Spain), Sir Edward Giles recommended the House "to consider that there may be a combat with the King of Spain as with the King's navy from the Indies which . . . will make us rich enough." Sir George Hastings, following the same line, recommended that "30,000 troops be sent into Flanders because [Spain's] Spinola . . . hath taken the Palatinate." He went on to point out that "there is younger brothers enough to accomplish it and to stop the Spaniards upon the sea." Sir George Moore and John Glanville spoke next, and both opposed war. But Sir John Crew once again returned to the idea "that, if we had trade to the West Indies, as we have had to the East Indies, . . . we might march with the Protestant princes and not with Spain. It were excellent that we might crop the House of Austria, and stop the Indies from him. [Then] we would give more than enough." Digges chimed back in, saying, "that if the King of Spain's navy were intercepted from the West Indies, if he were kept from it two years, he would be bankrupt as he was in the Queen's time."[9]

Acting, apparently, in collaboration with the Pembroke-Abbot faction on the privy council, Digges and Rudyerd had thus stimulated the presentation of the so-called diversionary strategy as an alternative approach to that of the king for recovering the Palatinate. English ships would attack the Spanish fleet and the West Indies and allow for the establishment of direct trade with the West Indies. This would undermine Spain's ability to make war on the Continent. It would provide, in turn, a much expanded financial base to support further military actions, perhaps an Anglo-Dutch attack on Spanish Flanders or merely increased English financial aid to Continental allies. In any case, it had the enormous advantage of allowing for a much cheaper anti-Spanish war than any full-scale campaign on land on the Continent: a war by diversion would apparently have cost in the neighborhood of £200–300,000 per annum, in comparison to the £1,000,000 per annum or more that a Continental land war would have required. James I already had made clear his wish to avoid *any* military confrontation with Spain, to stay clear of alliances with the Dutch that might be interpreted in ideological terms, and to confine military action on the Continent to the immediate purpose of winning back the Palatinate.[10] In direct contrast, Digges and Rudyerd, supported by the

[9] Notestein, Relf, and Simpson, *Commons Debates, 1621*, vol. 2 ("X"), pp. 445–51; and vol. 3 (Barrington), pp. 447–58; Adams, "Foreign Policy," pp. 143–45, Ruigh, *Parliament of 1624*, p. 130. On the pro-Bohemians, see also Adams, "Protestant Cause," pp. 285–86. It is not clear to me that Sir Robert Phelips opposed the war, as Russell contends. Cf. Russell, *Parliaments*, pp. 129–30 with Notestein, Relf, and Simpson, *Commons Debates, 1621*, vol. 2 ("X"), pp. 448–49 n. 5. Cf. Adams, "Foreign Policy," pp. 162–63.

[10] See Adams, "Foreign Policy," pp. 162–63. The calculation of the likely cost of war by diversion is from L. J. Reeve, *Charles I and the Road to Personal Rule* (Cambridge, 1989), pp. 230–31.

connection around the Riches, would, through much of the rest of the decade, push hard for an attack on Spain by way of the Atlantic and the Caribbean with strong support from Parliament.

The following day, 27 November, John Wilde opened debate with another demand for a general war against Spain. Sir Thomas Edmondes countered by stating that James I wished to see how Spain would act vis-à-vis the Palatinate before deciding policy, and asked the Commons to advance funds for the defense of the realm. John Pym, backed up by others, argued that the country was too poor to afford expensive military operations in Germany unless it could finance them through naval war against Spain. He put forward a compromise proposal that the Commons withhold full financial support until a declaration of such a war, but in the meantime approve a gift to the government.[11]

Pym's approach eventually carried the day. But Nathaniel Rich wanted to go much further to give a coherent ideological and political gloss to the anti-Spanish proposals. Already in the previous session of Parliament, in February 1621, Rich had gone on record with the demand for the establishment of a West India Company. Rich now claimed that "we have showed sorrow for the affliction of the [international Protestant] church, but we have showed no public testimony thereof," and requested that James I appoint a day of fasting and prayer for the church. Rich then proposed that "there be a league between England and the other princes as there is betwixt the Catholics," precisely the sort of explicitly Protestant foreign policy that James sought most fervently to avoid. Finally, and perhaps most provocatively, Rich demanded that the proposed Protestant league in Europe be confirmed by an act of Parliament. Rich's kinsman Robert Rich, the second earl of Warwick, had been hurt badly in the preceding period by James's pro-Spanish policies, particularly the revival of negotiations for the Spanish match in May 1620. In 1620, James I, supporting Sir Edwin Sandys, had stepped in to prevent the Riches from using the Virginia and Somers Island (Bermuda) colonies as bases for their privateering ventures against the Spanish West Indies. About the same time, yielding to the pressure exerted by the Spanish ambassador, Gondomar, James compelled the Riches to abandon their fledgling colony in Guiana. The temporary breaking-off of negotiations for the Spanish match two years previously, in 1618, had induced the Riches to initiate both their American privateering and their Guianan ventures. Clearly, Nathaniel Rich now wished to leave as little as possible to chance in establishing a militantly anti-Spanish, pro-Protestant foreign policy, and saw parliamentary confirmation of a Protestant alliance as a means to that end.

---

[11] Adams, "Protestant Cause," p. 325.

But at this point Rich was probably far ahead of his colleagues in the House, and no one took up his suggestion.[12]

Two days later, on 29 November, Sir George Goring, speaking for the duke of Buckingham, made his famous intervention in the House of Commons, in which he demanded that England declare war on Spain if Philip IV continued to assist the emperor in the Palatinate, and he implied that the government would welcome a militant show of anti-Spanish sentiment from the House. The House quickly passed its petition of 3 December, in which it asked James to declare war for the defense of the Protestant religion, to employ a diversionary strategy for the restoration of the Palatinate, to forge an international Protestant alliance, and to marry Charles to a Protestant princess. James I was outraged at Parliament's presumption, and the resulting conflicts quickly led to its dissolution.[13]

Over the following period, James continued to pursue his pro-Spanish diplomacy, but this broke down once again when Buckingham and Charles returned from their mission to Spain in the autumn of 1623. The determination of Buckingham and Charles to end the Spanish match seemed, in fact, to signal a reversal in policy and to offer a temporary opening to anti-Spanish forces long alienated from the seats of power. Buckingham and Charles moved to restore to favor the earl of Southampton and the earl of Oxford, both of whom had pursued militantly anti-Spanish courses from the time of the previous Parliament, and had been imprisoned by James for their pains. They also welcomed back to the court William Fiennes, Lord Saye and Sele, who had fiercely resisted the royal benevolence of 1622. The earl of Warwick and his kinsman Sir Nathaniel Rich came back into the fold as well, bringing with them, most probably, their powerful East Anglian Puritan gentry connection. Meanwhile, the prominence at court of the great Puritan minister John Preston further symbolized the new situation. Preston, who had extraordinarily broad connections among the Calvinist ministry, maintained a relationship with the earl of Warwick, whose son he had tutored at Cambridge, and he had especially close ties to Lord Saye, to whom he made a special bequest in his will composed in 1618, as well as to the Northampton Puritan Richard Knightley, a close friend of Saye's who also entered into alliance with Buckingham at this time. Perhaps most striking of all, Buckingham arranged an alliance with those MPs who had led the opposition to James in the previous Parliament, notably Sir Dudley Digges, Sir Edwin Sandys,

---

[12] Notestein, Relf, and Simpson, *Commons Debates, 1621*, vol. 2 ("X"), pp. 445, 458, 459; and vol. 3 (Barrington), pp. 464–65, 465 n. 17, 470–71; Russell, *Parliaments*, pp. 130–32; Newton, *Colonising Activities*, pp. 26–27, 34–37.

[13] See Russell, *Parliaments*, pp. 133–37, and Adams, "Foreign Policy," pp. 163–64, which differ on the interpretation of Goring's intervention and the ensuing developments.

Sir Robert Phelips, and Sir Edward Coke. By the time Parliament met, Buckingham and Charles seem to have achieved some sort of working arrangement with the mighty earl of Pembroke, who had long sought Buckingham's ruin.[14]

The basis for this newly emergent alliance of hitherto anti-Buckingham forces around the favorite was the apparent commitment of Buckingham and Charles to wage war against Spain and to convert James I to their position. As Professor Cogswell has pointed out, in December 1623, Sir Edward Conway, a secretary of state and protégé of Buckingham, put on paper a full-scale program for an anti-Spanish military offensive aimed apparently to win over James and the council to Buckingham and Charles's position. This document amounted to Buckingham and Charles's program and included ambitious plans for a broad network of alliances on the Continent and for the pursuit by England of war by diversion to recover the Palatinate. The diversionary war envisaged by Conway and Buckingham involved a commitment of English troops to support the Dutch against Spain in Flanders and, in particular, a joint Anglo-Dutch naval offensive against the Spanish Caribbean fleet and the West Indies. James I, Conway suggested, should "be pleased . . . to waste the king of Spain's shipping upon his coast, interrupt the returns of his plate, and share as deeply with him as occasion and fortune will give leave." Meanwhile, the English should join the Dutch "to supplant him [Spain] in the West Indies." On this basis, it might be possible to conduct "a diversive war upon Flanders" or, in the best case, to march directly on the Palatinate. At any rate, if James pursued a diversionary war, largely at sea, then the recovery of the Palatinate "in less than three years will easily be effected." Such phrases would, of course, have been music to the ears of those former parliamentary oppositionists who had proposed pretty much the same diversionary strategy in 1621 and who were just now moving into alliance with Buckingham. Indeed, even before Parliament convened, elements on the council had unleashed a whole series of new, anti-Spanish foreign initiatives that, they must have hoped, would soon be ratified in full by the king and Parliament.[15]

In the Parliament of 1624, the alliance of anti-Spanish forces won a minimal commitment from the Crown to an anti-Spanish foreign policy.

[14] Adams, "Foreign Policy," pp. 164ff.; Russell, *Parliaments*, pp. 145–54; Ruigh, *Parliament of 1624*, pp. 16–42; Thompson, "Origins," pp. 73–78; I. Morgan, *Prince Charles's Puritan Chaplain* (London, 1957), pp. 27, 31, 42, 43, 67–68, 70–71.

[15] The quotations are from T. E. Cogswell, "Crown, Parliament, and the War, 1623–1625" (Washington University of St. Louis, Ph.D. diss., 1983), p. 72 (I have also appropriated a few of Professor Cogswell's connecting phrases); see also pp. 67–74ff. I wish to express my gratitude to Professor Cogswell for allowing me to consult his work before publication. See also Ruigh, *Parliament of 1624*, pp. 37–39.

Probably speaking with the approval of the earl of Pembroke, Rudyerd initiated the debate over foreign policy on 1 March 1624 with a demand that the Spanish match be broken off and a war by diversion initiated. His Four Propositions called for the militia to be readied, Ireland to be reinforced, England "really and roundly [to] assist the Low Countries," and "the navy [to] be placed on a war footing." Two days later, Buckingham himself went on record explicitly in support of war against Spain by way of the Atlantic and the Caribbean. As he explained to the House, "What remained [in their design] must be gotten with arms, arms maintained by money, money with the Indies, the profit of the Indies must come by sea, and if the King and the Low Countries joined, they shall be master of the sea and Spain's monarchy will have to stop." This must, again, have done much to encourage those militantly anti-Spanish, prowar groups that were at this time allying with Buckingham and Charles.[16]

James ultimately approved the Four Propositions, but only under the most severe pressure and as the unavoidable price for a large financial advance from Parliament. Nevertheless, despite assurances from Buckingham and Charles, the anti-Spanish, anti-Catholic "blue water" policy the Commons thought it had approved began to unravel even before Parliament had completed its deliberations. Apparently doubting James's willingness to carry through a Protestant program at home and abroad, the Commons petitioned James to agree "that upon no occasion of marriage or treaty, or other request in that from any foreign prince or states whatsoever," he would "take off, or slacken the execution" of the recusancy laws. James did ultimately approve what he termed this "stinging petition" in response to the Commons' implicit threat to withhold funds. However, when the Commons, led by John Pym, launched an investigation of Richard Montague, a chaplain of the king, as a result of his publication of the anti-Calvinist tract *A New Gagge*, and then fired off a petition of protest against Montague directly to Archbishop Abbot, bypassing the House of Lords (not to mention Convocation), James angrily intervened, arresting Francis Yates and Nathaniel Ward, two East Anglian Puritan ministers who appear initially to have called Montague to the Commons' attention. James also came to the defense, in this Parliament, of the Bishop of Norwich, Abraham Harsnett, who had been attacked in the Commons for repressing Puritan lectures in Norwich and condoning what Puritans regarded as superstitious images.[17] To make matters worse,

---

[16] Ruigh, *Parliament of 1624*, pp. 177–80; Russell, *Parliaments*, pp. 171ff.; Cogswell, "Crown, Parliament, and the War," pp. 160–61. The quotation of Buckingham is from Ruigh, pp. 191–92 n. 61. Note, also, Sir John Eliot's call at this time for war with Spain and his point that this would be self-financing: "Let us remember that the war with Spain is our Indies, and there we shall fetch wealth and happiness" (Ruigh, p. 220; Russell, *Parliaments*, p. 188).

[17] Cogswell, "Crown, Parliament, and the War," pp. 257, 267–69; K. N. Shipps, "Lay Patron-

James soon made it clear that he had never really committed himself to fight against Spain, let alone to pursue the naval and colonial strategy that Parliament thought had been approved. The upshot was that, despite the fact that Buckingham and Charles had achieved a certain unity with leading forces on the privy council, in the nobility, and in the Commons in support of an anti-Spanish approach, the king and the parliamentary leadership remained seriously at odds over foreign policy and religion, with enormous consequences in both the short and medium run.

As it turned out, during his lifetime, James I succeeded in confining England's war effort to Count Ernst von Mansfeld's weak and solitary mercenary venture of 1624–1625 toward the Palatinate. This expedition went more or less directly against Parliament's express desire to defend the Palatinate by ways other than land engagements on the Continent; it was, in any case, doomed from the start by James's insistence that Mansfeld avoid attacking Spanish troops. To further compound the situation, Buckingham and Charles were soon obliged to go back on the promise not to ease up on the repression of recusants because toleration of Catholics was the unavoidable price of the French marriage and alliance that James demanded as the condition for breaking with Spain. Ironically, when Buckingham finally readied some ships, these were sent to the French government in the summer of 1625 and used against the Huguenots.

It is not surprising that the early days of the Parliament of 1625 were marked by a Commons petition against recusants—a scarcely veiled attack on the government's concessions in the interest of a French alliance— as well as a call to examine the accounts of the previous subsidy kept by the parliamentary treasurers (as demanded by the 1624 subsidy act). Sir Nathaniel Rich proposed that silenced ministers should be allowed to preach on all points agreeable to the doctrine and discipline of the Church of England; it was most probably also Rich who put forward the subscription bill, according to which ministers would only be forced to subscribe to those among the Thirty-nine Articles that had been confirmed by act of Parliament. John Crew, a strong advocate of the anti-Spanish naval war in 1621, supported Rich, as did Sir Thomas Hoby. But both Sir Benjamin Rudyerd and Sir Dudley Digges opposed this suggestion, with Rudyerd asserting that "moderate bishops" could be trusted to do on their own what Rich desired of them. Here, it appears, was a significant division of opinion among the allied anti-Spanish forces, and the matter was not pursued.

Intense conflict then broke out over the question of Arminianism, spe-

age of East Anglian Puritan Clerics in Pre-Revolutionary England" (Yale University, Ph.D. diss., 1971), pp. 43–46; K. N. Shipps, "The 'Political Puritan,' " *Church History* 45 (1976): 197–99; H. Schwartz, "Arminianism and the English Parliament, 1624–1629," *J.B.S.* 12 (1973): 43–47.

cifically Richard Montague's second book, *Appello Caesarum*, which hewed steadfastly to the anti-Calvinist position the Commons had already found offensive in his first book, as well as his manifest contempt for the concerns expressed in the Commons in 1624. On this issue, all those elements most prominent in support of the anti-Spanish war stood united. John Pym seized the initiative, and the Pembroke, Abbot, and Rich connections—notably Abbot and Pembroke themselves, along with Sir Dudley Digges and Sir Nathaniel Rich—came to Pym's aid. On 7 July, the Commons judged Montague guilty of contempt of the House. But Charles I provoked a head-on confrontation when he came to Montague's defense, claiming him to be his personal aide. Sir Nathaniel Rich, in response, insisted that Montague's books deserved censure; that he should be released only on £2,000 bond; and that he should again come before Parliament.[18]

In the second session of the Parliament of 1625, as Buckingham was coming under attack, Sir Nathaniel Rich put forward a program that may be taken to represent the central concerns of the emergent aristocratic colonizing group, or responsible opposition. He asked that the king calm Parliament's worries about the rise of recusancy and Arminianism. As to the war, he requested that the government specify who it was intending to fight and accept the "advice of this grave counsel" [Parliament] in the war's conduct. In particular, Rich demanded that Buckingham be replaced as admiral, a suggestion that no doubt reflected the overriding desire of the entire Rich connection for a naval war against Spain and its belief that Buckingham could not be relied on to carry this out effectively. But Rich also went on to make clear his concern that the king's finances be put on a more secure footing. He proposed that the Commons be permitted "to look into the King's estate, how it may subsist of itself," and also that there be a committee appointed to consider the impositions question. It was a performance in every way characteristic of the emergent aristocratic colonizing group, manifesting the group's distinctive interest in a naval war with Spain for both commercial-colonial and Protestant ends, its willingness to strengthen the king's finances if he would support its policies, its concern to defend Calvinist orthodoxy, and its expectation that the king would work out policy in consultation with the leading representatives of the landed classes on the council and in Parliament. Rich's proposals were not explicitly rejected, but in the end they came to nothing.[19]

Even so, most of the key anti-Spanish forces that had adhered to Buckingham in 1623–1624 appear to have remained largely loyal to him

[18] For the preceding two paragraphs, see Russell, *Parliaments*, pp. 222–23, 231–33; Shipps, "Lay Patronage," pp. 49–54; Shipps, "The 'Political Puritan,' " p. 200; Schwartz, "Arminianism," pp. 49–53.

[19] Thompson "Origins," pp. 76–79; Russell, *Parliaments*, p. 247.

throughout 1625. These included not only Sir Benjamin Rudyerd and Sir Dudley Digges, associated respectively with the earl of Pembroke and Archbishop Abbot, but also Sir Nathaniel Rich and the earl of Warwick, who were connected with Warwick's brother the earl of Holland.[20] These men were perhaps pleased that Buckingham was at least going to attack Spain. They were also, no doubt, happy that the de facto state of war with Spain promised to provide an opening for launching new colonizing efforts in hitherto forbidden territories of Spanish America and new privateering assaults on Spanish shipping. Finally, these men probably felt that they still had reason to hope that Charles and Buckingham would ultimately turn their military forces seaward against the Spanish fleet and Spain's West Indian colonies.

At the end of 1623, Secretary Sir Edward Conway had, as noted, made a naval and colonial war in the Atlantic and the Caribbean a cardinal element within an overall strategic plan for attacking Spain and, at the same time, had proposed that the English and Dutch join together in a West Indian enterprise. It was widely believed at the time that Buckingham was committed to this plan. In any case, just after James's death, Sir John Coke, who was perhaps Buckingham's key agent at this point and, with Conway, charged with preparing the fleet, sought to revive Conway's strategy. In April 1625, he set forth a proposal for the creation of a privately financed and privately operated fleet to "abate the pride and terror of the Spanish pretended empire" and, specifically, "to intercept his plate fleets, to invade his countries, to fortify and plant there, and to establish government, confederacy and trade." Coke's program was nothing less than a more fully worked-out version of the project that the anti-Spanish groups around Pembroke and Abbot and around the Riches had been putting forward in Parliament since 1621. Coke's idea that the expedition be carried out under private control with private financing would, moreover, be taken up, time and again, by the anti-Spanish forces over the following decades. Coke proposed that the enterprise "be undertaken by a common charge of the kingdom by a company incorporated for the West, as there is already for the East," and he went on to suggest that the estimated £361,200 that the project would require during its first two years could be raised through private subscriptions by various individuals, classes, companies, and organizations in English society. The very existence of Coke's plan, along with a complementary proposal by Secretary Heath, also presented to the government in April 1625, that the English attack the West Indies, indicates that Charles and Buckingham may not yet have

---

[20] Russell, *Parliaments*, pp. 216–17ff. Lord Saye, by contrast, appears to have deserted Buckingham in this period (Russell, pp. 238–39).

ruled out undertaking the sort of expedition that the anti-Spanish forces so fervently desired.[21]

The aforementioned anti-Spanish forces on the privy council and in Parliament apparently retained some sort of alliance with Buckingham through the end of 1625. Nevertheless, they could hardly have been pleased when Buckingham badly botched the military offensive against Spain, refusing to adopt the diversionary "blue water" strategy and suffering a disastrous defeat at Cadiz in the autumn of 1625. Buckingham's failure to consolidate a French alliance, and his drift toward open hostilities with France, must have been similarly disconcerting. Just before the meeting of Parliament in 1626, Warwick and Saye sought at least to achieve a favorable settlement of the issue of Arminianism. They insisted on having Richard Montague defend his doctrines in debate before Bishop Morton, as well as their own favored representative, John Preston. But, despite the efforts of Preston and Morton, Buckingham and Charles ended up siding with Montague. This was, apparently, the last straw.

When Parliament met in 1626, the House of Commons quickly made clear its desire to move against Buckingham. At the same time, Sir John Eliot, backed up strongly by Rudyerd, Digges, Rich, and Pym, as well as others, took the lead in suggesting once again that Parliament should move "to settle the king's estate," if the king would deal with Buckingham. Conditional upon Buckingham's punishment, they offered to make a substantial permanent addition to the king's revenue so that he could live on his own in times of peace. A whole series of alternative proposals were put forward to this end, including plans for settling the question of impositions and increasing the king's revenue through a new book of rates, passing an act of resumption of Crown land, reforming the administration of recusancy finances, and reviving the Great Contract of 1610.[22]

These same parliamentary leaders seem to have hoped that their flexibility on the government's finances would induce the king to look more favorably on their own priorities, in particular the anti-Spanish naval war and the suppressing of Arminianism. They therefore put before the Parliament of 1626 an innovative scheme for a privately financed war against Spain's fleet and West Indian colonies to be directed by themselves, beyond the control of Buckingham, through a company to be erected for this purpose and sanctioned by Parliament. Sir Dudley Digges, who in 1621 had called for a diversionary war while declaring that "the root is the money of the West Indies," first raised this idea on 14 March 1626, and justified it as a way of financing the war against Spain without burdening

[21] PRO, S.P. 16/1/59, quoted in M. B. Young, *Servility and Service: The Life and Work of Sir John Coke* (London, 1985), p. 135. See also Newton, *Colonising Activities*, pp. 28–29.

[22] Russell, *Parliaments*, pp. 282–83.

the poor with taxes. Digges may have been attempting to meet the objections of those MPs whose concern to prevent increased taxes inclined them to oppose any war. Secretary of State Sir John Coke had, of course, floated at court a quite similar plan for a West India Company to carry on private war against Spain less than a year previously, and the parliamentary backers of this project appear to have believed that they actually could now get government support for it. It was obviously the expectation of government backing that led Sir Benjamin Rudyerd to express his hope to Sir John Nethersole, during the Easter recess of the 1626 Parliament, that the "storms of this Parliament . . . now well are overblown," and to predict that Parliament would not only grant the king "an orderly warrantable revenue . . . proportionable to his ordinary charge," but "greatest of all," that there would be a West India Company established, "so that the subjects shall make war against the King of Spain and his majesty shall have no more to do at sea, but to defend the coasts." This company, explained Rudyerd, would be established by act of Parliament, so as to prevent the interference of any "powerful hand," an obvious reference to Buckingham.[23]

Sir Dudley Digges presented the private-enterprise war as the first item of business when the House of Commons returned from recess on 13 April 1626. He argued that "a great league and union had been made by the papists generally against the Protestants," but that "the only chief support of the King of Spain's ambition [is] his returns from the Indies." Digges therefore proposed that patriotic Englishmen privately raise £200,000 a year for four years for a new corporation, modeled after the Dutch West India Company and designed specifically to make war on the Spanish West Indies. An independent council of war, elected by the stockholders, would manage it.

Sir Benjamin Rudyerd immediately spoke in support of Digges, arguing:

This is a noble and profitable enterprise. Not the great territories of the King of Spain make him potent. Spain is weak and barren; his other territories far. Like the giant that had a hundred hands but had fifty bellies to feed, so no more powerful than another. His money from the West Indies barely enables him to all his enterprises, and

[23] Quoted in Russell, *Parliaments*, p. 293, see also pp. 294, 299–300. Further evidence that, at the time of Parliament's Easter recess, the aristocratic colonizing leaders believed they would secure approval for their project for a West India Company and war against Spain is found in a letter from the Bermuda Company to Capt. Henry Woodhouse, the governor of the island, informing the latter of the "purpose and consultation by so many of his company . . . to raise a stock to furnish out some ships of war for the defense of the island and for the West Indian coast, which [ships] shall make their rendezvous to and from the Somers Island." J. H. Lefroy, *Memorials of the Bermudas*, 2 vols. (Bermuda, 1877–1879), 1: 378.

being taken from him he will soon be brought down. But this way I doubt not but the king shall be made safe at home and feared abroad.

Looking ahead, Digges replied with the added provision that any peace treaty that ended the proposed war with Spain should ensure that this company be established on a permanent footing and have from Spain the right to free trade in the West Indies. If this was accomplished, said Digges, it would be the "famousest company in Christendom." Sir Robert Mansell, a protégé of the earl of Pembroke, and Sir Walter Earle, a promoter of the Dorchester Company's colonizing effort in New England and by this time closely connected with Lord Saye, followed in support. Next, Sir Nathaniel Rich revived the old idea that Bermuda, where he and his kinsman the earl of Warwick were already deeply involved, should be used as a privateering base under the auspices of the new company. He also went so far as to demand that the company be free not only of all impositions, but of the usual requirement to pay the admiral's tenth. This was patently a swipe at Buckingham and a further sign of the determination of this alliance to have him out of the picture. John Pym moved that Sir Nathaniel Rich's proposals be read and sent to committee.[24]

A few days later, on 17 April, Pym reported the findings of the committee on Arminianism—a committee that once again included, among others, Sir Nathaniel Rich, Sir Benjamin Rudyerd, and Sir Walter Earle—and catalogued Richard Montague's offenses in a two-hour speech. On 29 April, the Commons resolved that Montague had published doctrine contrary to the Thirty-nine Articles. On a motion by Sir Nathaniel Rich, the Commons then chose Pym as its sole messenger to the House of Lords, "it being said to be the greatest business that hath come into the House since *primo* Elizabeth." Meanwhile, on 26 April, Charles had given the Commons his consent to the inquiry into Buckingham. Speakers and two assistants were assigned responsibility for each of the charges against the duke, and the proceedings were once again led by representatives of the Pembroke, Abbot, and Rich factions, notably Sir Dudley Digges.[25]

The House of Commons went on to impeach Buckingham. In response, Charles I dismissed Parliament before receiving a subsidy. He was therefore obliged to employ his prerogative to raise money to organize

[24] For the previous two paragraphs, see Cambridge University Library, Whitelocke, Dd. xii. 20–22, fols. 128–31v (Yale transcript). I wish to thank Christopher Thompson for originally calling this material to my attention. See also Thompson, "Origins," p. 80. On Mansell and Earle, see Russell, *Parliaments*, pp. 16, 404, 405, 408; M. F. Keeler, *The Long Parliament, 1640–1641* (Philadelphia, 1954), pp. 165–66; Adams, "Protestant Cause," pp. 382–83; C. M. Andrews, *The Colonial Period of American History*, 4 vols. (New Haven, 1934–1938), 1: 347–48.

[25] Shipps, "Lay Patronage," p. 57; Adams, "Protestant Cause," pp. 390–91; Schwartz, "Arminianism," pp. 55–56.

for war and ended up resorting to the Forced Loan and to collecting un-parliamentary tonnage and poundage by order of the privy council. Meanwhile, as tensions grew with France, Buckingham's enthusiasm for war with Spain seems to have lessened, and, from the summer of 1626, there were new Anglo-Spanish contacts and negotiations. The growing resort to the prerogative and the increasing likelihood of improved relations with Spain created the conditions, as they had during the early 1620s, for a dramatic tightening of the alliance between the Crown and the Arminians. Anti-Calvinist clerics were now increasingly taken onto leading policy-making bodies, and they assumed a key role in propagandizing for the new royal policy departures. This was in part because, unlike their Calvinist opponents, the Arminians rejected the conception of the pope as Antichrist that had come to justify the Protestant Cause and recognized the church of Rome as a true church, and therefore had no principled difficulties in coming to terms with Spain. It was also in part because the Arminians were almost entirely dependent politically on the Crown's support and therefore willing to argue for the claims of the prerogative to a degree that would have been difficult at this juncture for their Calvinist counterparts. In July 1626, Charles issued "A Proclamation for the Peace and Quiet of the Church," which effectively outlawed Calvinist teaching on a national basis and constituted a major victory for the Arminians. Buckingham's appointment a short time before as chancellor of Cambridge conduced to the same effect within that university. By the following summer, the Crown had promised the archbishopric of Canterbury to Laud, had elevated Laud and Richard Neile to the privy council, and had deprived Archbishop Abbot of his powers, delegating them to a commission weighted in favor of Arminian bishops. Meanwhile, the clerics Robert Sibthorpe and Roger Mainwaring had proved their value to the Crown by producing major sermons and written works in support of the Forced Loan in particular and royal absolutism in general.[26]

During the winter and spring of 1626–1627, large sections of the landed class refused to pay the Forced Loan, and many of the same allied forces that had pushed for an anti-Spanish war in the Atlantic and West Indies, had fought against Arminianism and the toleration of Catholics, and had sought Buckingham's removal also took the lead organizing resistance to the loan in the localities where they were influential. The earl of Warwick refused to lend, and the Riches' allies Sir Harbottle Grimstone and Sir Francis Barrington helped ignite opposition to the loan in Essex. Lord Saye and Sele was also a loan refuser, as were Saye's friends Sir Richard Knightley, who helped mobilize resistance in Northampton-

---

[26] Adams, "Protestant Cause," p. 400; Tyacke, "Puritanism, Arminianism, and Counter-Revolution," pp. 133–34, 137; Schwartz, "Arminianism," pp. 56–57.

shire, and Sir Walter Earle, who worked against the loan in Dorset. Saye's son-in-law, the earl of Lincoln, one of the most militant opposers of the loan, incited opposition in Lincolnshire. The House of Commons' organizers of the attack on Buckingham, Sir Dudley Digges and Sir John Eliot, also opposed the loan, Eliot and Sir William Coryton leading opposition in Cornwall. Both Eliot, who in the Parliament of 1624 had come out explicitly for a naval and colonial war against Spain, and Coryton had recently entered into alliance with the earl of Warwick, after their great patron the earl of Pembroke had apparently reconciled with Buckingham when the earl of Montgomery married Buckingham's daughter in August 1626.[27]

Meanwhile, just as the Crown turned at this point increasingly to Arminian clerics to help frame, enforce, and publicly justify royal policies, key figures in the aristocratic colonizing opposition turned to certain Calvinist divines to aid in organizing and propagandizing against the government's new religio–political policies, in much the same way they had done in the struggle against the Spanish match from 1620 to 1623. These clerics were, at this time, apparently seeking to improve coordination among themselves in order to respond better to the royal government's attacks. In this effort the earl of Warwick, helped by his kinsman Sir Nathaniel Rich, appears to have played the leading role. Through direct appointment to twenty-two livings in his gift and through many other forms of encouragement and protection, Warwick was well placed to support, to influence, and to help organize for various political and religious initiatives an unusually large number of Puritan ministers, among whom were some of the most prominent Calvinist divines in the kingdom, as well as some of the most radical.[28]

In February 1626, following Charles I and Buckingham's rejection of the Calvinists John Preston and Bishop Morton at the York House Conference and their endorsement of the Arminians, key Calvinist ministers and laymen in London, reputedly inspired by Preston, secretly reorganized and revitalized an organization known as the Feoffees for Impropriations, with the purpose of buying up livings around the country in which to install clerics sympathetic to their cause. The four-person clerical contingent among the twelve feoffees included Richard Sibbes, lecturer at Gray's Inn and master of St. Catherine's Hall, Cambridge; William

---

[27] Adams, "Protestant Cause," pp. 395–97; R. Cust, "The Forced Loan and English Politics, 1626–1628" (University of London, Ph.D. diss., 1984), pp. 70–73, 137–38. Sir Dudley Digges seems ultimately to have paid the loan.

[28] See W. Hunt, *The Puritan Moment: The Coming of Revolution in an English County* (Cambridge, Mass., 1983), pp. 196ff. On Warwick's patronage and general support for ministers, see B. Donagan, "The Clerical Patronage of Robert Rich, Second Earl of Warwick, 1619–1642," *American Philosophical Society Proceedings* 120 (15 October 1976): 390.

Gouge, rector at St. Anne's Blackfriar's; and John Davenport, who in 1624 had been elected pastor of the militantly Puritan parish of St. Stephen's Coleman Street over the protests of the pro-Arminian bishop of London George Mountain. All three of these ministers maintained a close link with Preston and, along with such other London clerical leaders as Thomas Taylor and Thomas Gataker, had been among the most prominent ministerial figures behind the pro-Palatinate and anti-Spanish cause since the time of the Bohemian Revolution. Charles Offspring, the fourth clerical feoffee, was minister at St. Antholin's parish, the home of the famous St. Antholin's lectureship, long a Puritan stronghold. The eight laymen among the feoffees included Christopher Sherland, one of the leaders of the struggles against Arminianism in the House of Commons, and George Harewood, whose brother Edward was a colonel of the English contingent in the Low Countries, strongly interested in the Bermudian colonizing adventure, and a close friend of the earl of Lincoln's and Lord Brooke's, as well as Samuel Browne and Robert Eyre, two lawyers from Lincoln's Inn, where John Preston held the lectureship. The Feoffees for Impropriations functioned not only to secure the appointment of Puritan ministers around the country, but as an organizing center for further projects of the Protestant Cause at home and abroad.[29]

At least a number of the aristocratic colonizing opposition leaders, including the Riches, Lord Saye, and Sir Richard Knightley, most probably kept closely in touch with the activities of the Feoffees for Impropriations through John Preston. The earl of Warwick and Sir Nathaniel Rich were also able, most likely, to keep on top of the feoffees' efforts through both Sibbes and Gouge, who were close friends of both of them. Lord Saye probably also maintained contact with the feoffees via his close relationships with both Sibbes and John Davenport.[30] In any case, the earl of Warwick secured a direct link with the feoffees and their activities when he brought his protégé, the militant preacher Hugh Peter, to London in the fall of 1626 for what appears to have been the express purpose of

---

[29] I. M. Calder, "A Seventeeth-Century Attempt to Purify the Anglican Church," *A.H.R.*, 53 (1948): 760–75; P. Seaver, *The Puritan Lectureships* (Stanford, 1970), pp 184, 236–38; Adams, "Protestant Cause," pp. 316–17; Shipps, "Lay Patronage," p. 56; R. P. Stearns, *The Strenuous Puritan: Hugh Peter, 1598–1660* (Urbana, Ill., 1954), p. 39; I. M. Calder, *The New Haven Colony* (New Haven, 1934), pp. 5–8; Morgan, *Prince Charles's Puritan Chaplain*, pp. 111, 152–53.

[30] Morgan, *Prince Charles's Puritan Chaplain*, pp. 31, 42, 43. The earl of Warwick and Sir Nathaniel Rich had been schoolmates of Gouge's. Sibbes was "the special friend" of Warwick, who often attended his lectures at Gray's Inn, and he appointed Sir Nathaniel Rich a supervisor of his will, leaving him a ring (Hunt, *Puritan Moment*, p. 199; Donagan, "Clerical Patronage," pp. 399, 400, 401). Sibbes and Davenport published some of John Preston's sermons at the request of Lord Saye (Seaver, *Puritan Lectureships*, pp. 236). Davenport speaks of the "sundry testimonies of [Lord Saye's] special favor toward me when I was in London" (I. M. Calder, ed., *Letters of John Davenport, Puritan Devine* [New Haven, 1937], pp. 190–91).

organizing opposition to royal political and religious policies, and perhaps most especially the Forced Loan (against which the Riches and others were agitating at just this time). Peter had attended the academy in Rotherhithe of the aforementioned outspoken anti-Spanish preacher Thomas Gataker (author of a series of powerful tracts against the Spanish match and in support of the Bohemian cause), had attended the lectures of the London ministers Sibbes and Gouge, among others, and had achieved a sense of election through the inspiration of the great Essex Puritan minister Thomas Hooker, another close friend of the Riches (and later a beneficiary of their protection), before he had become curate at Leighs, Essex, around 1623, apparently at the behest of the earl of Warwick, who owned the rectory.[31]

Shortly after Peter's arrival in the City, Warwick had Peter preach at a private St. Andrews Day fast at Christ Church, London; on this occasion, Peter is described as making the rhetorical pleas that God would commune with the king's "heart in secret and reveal unto him those things which were necessary for the government and his kingdom" and would also intervene with the queen "that she would forsake idolatry and superstition wherein she was and needs perish if she continued in the same." Other ministers closely connected with the Riches, and with one another, were preaching rather similar sermons on the same theme of the danger within at about the same time. Only a few weeks before, in a sermon at court, John Preston had warned Charles that God would destroy him if he did not further exert himself in support of the Protestant Cause at home and abroad. (This sermon was later dedicated by Preston's editors to Sir Nathaniel Rich.) In parallel manner, on Guy Fawkes Day Thomas Hooker of Chelmsford also warned that "wickedness in high places," the countenancing of idolatry, and the reviling of the godly would, if not soon corrected, lead God to bring about the fall of Protestant England at the hands of Spanish military might.[32] It is evident that the court, London, and East Anglian wings of political puritanism were functioning in the closest coordination.

Because of his sermon, Peter was soon brought up on charges before Bishop Mountain. Warwick, however, was able to intervene personally with Mountain to secure Peter's freedom, and Peter was soon offering a monthly lecture at St. Sepulchre's parish in London. In the meantime, Peter had become a chief agent for the Feoffees for Impropriations. In the

---

[31] Stearns, *Strenuous Puritan*, p. 30: Shipps, "Lay Patronage," p. 171; Hunt, *Puritan Moment*, p. 197.

[32] The quotation of Peter is from Stearns, *Strenuous Puritan*, p. 41. See also Shipps, "Lay Patronage," pp. 171–72. See Hunt, *Puritan Moment*, p. 201 and ch. 8 in general for the Puritan offensive that began on the eve of the Parliament of 1626 and continued through the following period of intensifying conflict.

spring of 1627, he helped the feoffees Gouge, Sibbes, and Davenport, along with their old London associate Thomas Taylor, in their independent project to raise funds for refugee ministers from the Palatinate, an effort that recalled the analogous initiatives of the early 1620s. This was a cause the royal government had no desire to see furthered, and it soon summoned these ministers before star chamber, ostensibly because they had preempted the official collection.[33]

By August 1627, Peter was once again in trouble with Bishop Mountain, this time for Nonconformity, and by the winter he had been suspended from preaching and had fled to Holland. In November 1627, John Preston delivered his final sermon before the court, in which he proclaimed that "God is angry and He is never angry but for sin" and went on to blame an enemy within for "striking at the root of this Church and Commonwealth." Following this outburst, Laud forbade Preston to preach in London ever again.[34]

While resistance continued at home, the earl of Warwick took advantage of the undeclared Anglo-Spanish war to launch his own large-scale privateering project in the West Indies. On 17 April 1627, Charles I awarded Warwick a commission to plunder or colonize the king of Spain's possessions in Europe, Africa, and the Americas. A short time later, however, Buckingham sought to have his agent Sir James Bagg, who had replaced Sir John Eliot as vice admiral of Devon, prevent Warwick's ships from leaving Plymouth. Bagg had reported to Buckingham that Warwick was constantly in the company of Sir John Eliot, "that pattern of ingratitude." But relying on his commission from Charles, Warwick defied Bagg and Buckingham and sailed away. Warwick's goal was to capture the Spanish treasure fleet off the coast of Brazil. But he barely escaped disaster when his ships were attacked by a superior Spanish force in the Azores. The expedition ended in total failure, but Warwick enhanced his reputation as a daring fighter against the Spaniards, arch-supporters of the papal Antichrist.[35]

In November 1627, King Charles won an important test when the judges refused to rule against imprisonment without trial in the famous Five Knights case. But in the wake of the military disaster at the Île de Ré, Charles was forced to recall Parliament. In the Parliament of 1628, the aristocratic colonizing opposition took a leading part in the struggle for the Petition of Right. As Christopher Thompson has shown, all these

---

[33] Stearns, *Strenuous Puritan*, pp. 37–41; Shipps, "Lay Patronage," p. 172.

[34] Stearns, *Strenuous Puritan*, pp. 42–43. The quotation is from Hunt, *Puritan Moment*, p. 208, and Adams, "Protestant Cause," p. 408. See also Morgan, *Prince Charles's Puritan Chaplain*, pp. 188–91.

[35] The previous paragraph closely follows Hunt, *Puritan Moment*, pp. 207–8. See also Newton, *Colonizing Activities*, pp. 37–38.

men played a pivotal role in working out the compromise between the more conservative forces located primarily in the House of Lords and the more radical elements in the Commons that allowed the Petition of Right to pass through Parliament. Warwick, Saye, Rich, Pym, Rudyerd, and Digges all distinguished themselves by their insistence on the tactical necessity of both Houses acting together and by their argument that the rights of the subject could be secured without any explicit curtailment of the king's prerogative. They refused the absolute assertion of the subject's rights proposed by the militants in the House of Commons, and they resisted the explicit defense of the prerogative demanded by the conservatives in the House of Lords, while leaving the king's discretionary power in times of emergency unimpaired. Clearly, by this time, these men had developed an impressive capacity to work together and, apparently, to influence events. They were compelled to defend the liberties of the subject and the place of Parliament, but they refused to believe that their so doing would lead, of necessity, to a complete break with the king. There was no viable alternative, in their view, to collaboration between Crown and leading subjects in governing the kingdom. It was no accident, therefore, that even during the conflict-ridden Parliament of 1628, Rich, Digges, and Pym sought to renew the grant of tonnage and poundage to the king (without sacrificing parliamentary rights), while Rich and Digges tried to get the Commons to draw up a new book of rates.[36]

Even so, Charles's hesitation in accepting the Petition of Right seems to have strengthened the resolve of all these leaders to pursue their established political priorities—to combat the growing strength of Arminianism and popery in church and state (as well as the absolutist political direction to which, they believed, these theological positions naturally gave rise), to revive the assault on Buckingham, and to pursue opposition to unparliamentary taxation. All these figures (with the exception of Rudyerd) were thus among the most prominent supporters of the remonstrance against Arminianism and (ultimately) Buckingham, which passed on 17 June 1628; the Commons' impeachment of Dr. Roger Mainwaring for his denial of parliamentary rights (in which Pym played the leading role); and the final remonstrance against tonnage and poundage.[37]

It was, finally, entirely characteristic of this same group of men that, at the very height of Crown-parliamentary confrontation, in the waning days of this Parliament when the final remonstrance over tonnage and pound-

[36] Thompson, "Origins"; J. A. Guy, "The Origins of the Petition of Right Reconsidered," *H.J.* 25 (1982): 306; Russell, *Parliaments*, pp. 385–89; Russell, "Parliament and the King's Finances," pp. 106–8.

[37] Adams, "Protestant Cause," pp. 416–18; Russell, *Parliaments*, pp. 378–87; S. R. Gardiner, *A History of England from the Accession of James I to the Outbreak of the Civil War*, 10 vols. (London, 1883–1884), 6: 301–10.

age was about to be framed, they would bring forward, once again, the plan they had enunciated in the Parliament of 1626 (and before) for a new West India Company and a naval-colonial war against Spain. On 21 June 1628, speaking immediately after Sir Dudley Digges had suggested that the king be asked not to prorogue but merely to adjourn Parliament, Sir Nathaniel Rich strongly endorsed Digges's proposal and went on to call on Parliament to use the recess to prepare "a society of trade, plantation and defense" in the West Indies, which would "much advantage the king's revenue." This company, said Rich, would "increase trade, breed up mariners, weaken the great power that oversways Christendom and turn war from Rome to Carthage again." Rich went on to state that he "had a bill already drawn up to that purpose," which he would perfect during the recess for consideration by the king and by Parliament at its next sitting. According to Grosvenor's parliamentary diary, "this was proposed with much applause."[38] Again and again, over more than two decades, Rich and his friends, with amazing persistence, would bring forward analogous proposals at similarly decisive moments. Clearly, to their way of thinking the anti-Spanish offensive was in no way a peripheral element in the overall program for reform.

In the period following the dismissal of Parliament in 1628, the king confirmed the worst fears of the aristocratic oppositionists. He brought back into leading places in his councils and into important government offices such longtime supporters of pro-Spanish courses in foreign policy and actual or suspected Catholics as the earl of Arundel, Richard Weston, and Francis Cottington. It now seemed more than likely that the royal government would move quickly to reconcile with Spain. At the same time, the king once again began to collect unparliamentary impositions and tonnage and poundage. Meanwhile, Charles did not shrink from raising to high office in church and state some of the very Arminian clerics whom Parliament had singled out for attack, notably Richard Montague, while pardoning the same Roger Mainwaring whom the Commons had just impeached.

When Parliament met again in late January 1629, Sir Nathaniel Rich and John Pym—backed up by such longtime associates of theirs in the struggle to impose a militantly anti-Spanish foreign policy and to root out Arminianism as Christopher Sherland, Richard Knightley, and Walter Earle—sought to lead the Commons not only to deny the king's right to collect tonnage and poundage without parliamentary consent, but also to make the grant of tonnage and poundage contingent on Charles's abandonment of the Arminians. But in so doing, they, along with their colleagues

[38] R. C. Johnson, et al., eds., *Commons Debates, 1628*, 6 vols. (New Haven, 1977–1983), 4: 410, 413, 416.

[267]

in what we have called the responsible, middle group, or colonizing opposition, pursued, once again, a distinctive line that divided them from
other leading opponents of royal policies in the Commons. In contrast
with Eliot and Selden, they went to great lengths to avoid direct constitutional confrontation with the king in the interest of securing, by way of
compromise and financial contributions to the Crown, a specific reform
package, which included not only the defeat of the Arminians, but the
pursuit of diversionary war against Spain. Nevertheless, conflict was
soon intensifying once again. Even so, the colonial aristocratic oppositionists must have retained hope until the last minute that they could
reach an agreement with the king. Even as they were opposing royal policies, they prepared to bring before the Commons Nathaniel Rich's proposal of the previous June for a new version of the West India Company
project, to be presented when Parliament reconvened. These men may
have believed that, with the duke of Buckingham out of the way, the
chances of governmental approval were enhanced. They must, in any case,
have felt confirmed in the rightness of their proposal by the spectacular
success of the Dutchman Piet Heyn in seizing the Spanish treasure fleet
the previous August; this was reportedly worth about £1,200,000,
enough to finance an anti-Spanish sea war for several years. As the Venetian ambassador reported on 2 February 1629:

> Parliament is now sitting and good results are hoped. . . . There is
> already talk about this West India Company previously proposed in
> Parliament but put aside by the duke who as admiral did not want
> the shareholders to have exemptions granted to them prejudicial to
> his office. It is now brought forward owing to the capture of the plate
> fleet by the Dutch. The plan is to keep fifty ships always in the Indies,
> and, as many more, now being fitted out, to replace the others when
> under repair. If this is done, actum est forever as far as peace with
> Spain is concerned, but there will be a risk of a rupture with the
> Dutch, as two dogs at one bone must necessarily bite each other.

Of course, this plan came to nothing, as king and the Commons soon came
figuratively if not literally to blows and the parliamentary supporters of
western designs were left to proceed with these privately and on their
own.[39]

---

[39] Russell, *Parliaments*, pp. 392–416; C. Thompson, "The Divided Leadership of the House of
Commons in 1629," in Sharpe, *Faction and Parliament*; *C.S.P. Ven. 1629*, pp. 518–19; Newton,
Colonising Activities; Adams, "Protestant Cause," p. 420; Reeve, *Charles I*, pp. 80, 84, 92, 94–95.
Cf. R. F. Williams, ed., *The Court and Times of Charles I*, 2 vols. (London, 1848), 1: 406, 435.
According to a Spanish agent; the earl of Warwick had readied his fleet, hoping for a favorable outcome
to the parliamentary session (Reeve, 81). It should be noted in passing that just previous to the

As the conflict between king and Parliament approached its climax at the end of the 1620s, the same groups of aristocratic oppositionists who continued to provide much of the leadership in Parliament took the crucial steps to found their network of overseas colonies as refuges for possible exile or retreat and as bases for continuing religio-political opposition. In 1628, the earl of Warwick took over the governorship of the Bermuda Company. By 1630, John Pym and Sir Benjamin Rudyerd had also joined the Bermuda Company, and Lord Saye, Lord Brook, and Sir Richard Knightley entered soon thereafter. A short time previously, toward the end of 1629, Warwick had initiated the Providence Island project as an offshoot of the Bermuda Company, and by 1630 he had gathered his celebrated associates as stockholders in this new company: these included Sir Nathaniel Rich, Lord Saye, Lord Brook, Sir Benjamin Rudyerd, Sir Richard Knightley, and John Pym, as well as Sir Christopher Sherland, Sir Gilbert Gerrard, John Robartes, and Sir Thomas Barrington, who were all leading oppositionist MPs in 1628–1629. Almost all of these men were, of course, veterans and leaders in the struggles against Arminianism in the church, in favor of a militantly anti-Spanish war in the Atlantic and West Indies, and for the defense of the rights of the subject. Meanwhile, over the years 1628–1630, the earl of Warwick, Sir Nathaniel Rich, and Lord Saye made it possible for the Massachusetts Bay Company to establish itself and to secure its royal charter.[40]

The Aristocratic Opposition, the Company Merchant Establishment, and the New-Merchant Leadership: A Critical Realignment

Through most of the later 1620s, the aristocratic oppositionists and an important section of the City merchant elite followed parallel courses. They appear to have cooperated directly, moreover, in a number of political initiatives against royal policies, although there is as yet only relatively little evidence on the inner workings of their collaboration. By the end of the decade, however, it is apparent that the aristocratic opposition and the City merchant elite were not only taking divergent political and commercial paths, but actually entering into direct conflict—opening the way for the new-merchant leadership.

---

opening of Parliament in January 1629, Sir Dudley Digges deserted his former allies and went over to the Crown, as did his old patron Archbishop George Abbot. See above, ch. 5, note 81.

[40] H. G. Wilkinson, *The Adventures of Bermuda* (London, 1958), pp. 173, 216, 398; Newton, *Colonising Activities*, pp. 52–79; *The Winthrop Papers, 1498–1649*, 5 vols. (Boston, 1929–1947), 2: 329.

The aristocratic colonizing group around the Riches and pivotal sections of the City merchant elite originally came together in the course of the bitter conflict that wracked the Virginia Company. From 1621 to 1622, following a major reordering of forces inside the company, Sir Thomas Smythe's merchant party and the Rich group united together in order to attack Sir Edwin Sandys' tobacco contract, as the first step in removing Sandys' "gentry party" from the company's leadership. They succeeded in getting the tobacco contract suspended in 1623 after a hearing before Lord Treasurer Cranfield. In 1623–1624, the two groups brought about the downfall of the old company as a prelude to taking it over, and they seemed on the verge of achieving their goal when James placed leading representatives of both groups in charge of the new commission for Virginia assigned to establish a new Virginia Company.[41]

In the Parliament of 1624, both the elite merchants grouped around Sir Morris Abbot and the landed-class faction around the Riches were conspicuously neutral or ambivalent concerning the impeachment of Sir Lionel Cranfield, probably because he was such a staunch defender of their interests in Virginia, and of merchant company interests more generally. Unfortunately for both groups, Cranfield was removed from office and Charles I never did charter a new company, but instead set up a royal council for Virginia. Both groups were further damaged when Charles granted the West Indies as a proprietary colony to Buckingham's follower the earl of Carlisle in 1627.[42]

From 1626 on, both the colonizing aristocrats in Parliament and many of the leading company merchants in the City followed roughly similar courses in opposing Buckingham and Charles. In 1626, Sir Dudley Digges led the attack in Parliament on Buckingham, and he not only received the support of Rich, Rudyerd, Pym et al., but also worked directly with his longtime City associates Morris Abbot and Robert Bateman, who testified against Buckingham in Parliament. Many of the same parliamentary forces helped push through the Petition of Right, and the remonstrance against Arminianism and Buckingham in 1628. Then, after the Commons passed the remonstrance against tonnage and poundage and Charles prorogued Parliament, Morris Abbot and his elite merchant colleagues came to the aid of Parliament when they detonated a new explosion of merchant resistance by breaking illegally into the customs house to seize their goods. As Parliament and the king entered their climactic confrontations of 1629 over Arminianism and tonnage and poundage, opposition forces in Parliament and in the City seemed to be proceeding along the same lines.[43]

[41] See above, ch. 3, pp. 99–102. For these developments in detail, see W. F. Craven, *The Dissolution of the Virginia Company* (New York, 1932).

[42] Ruigh, *Parliament of 1624*, pp. 330–31.

[43] See above, ch. 5.

Nevertheless, by the winter of 1628–1629, certain fundamental bases, both economic and political, for the continuing collaboration between the colonizing aristocrats and the elite merchant oppositionists had begun to erode. During the later 1620s, the parliamentary oppositionists, especially those around the earl of Warwick and Sir Nathaniel Rich, not only continued to demand strong action against Spain in the Atlantic and the West Indies, but also took dramatic steps to reorganize their colonizing enterprises for both economic and political purposes. But the leading City merchants were moving in the opposite direction.

In the later 1620s, the generality of company merchants definitively withdrew from colonial commerce, ceding the field to the new-merchant leadership. Once company organization for the Americas had collapsed after 1624, the company merchants lost interest in the colonial tobacco and provisioning trades, and they had never wished to invest in plantations. It is doubtful, moreover, if the Levant–East India Company merchants who collaborated with the opposition to Charles and Buckingham during this period were, at any point, desirous of the anti-Spanish war that their colonizing aristocratic allies in Parliament so fervently supported. In 1623–1624, Sir Lionel Cranfield had opposed the breaking off of negotiations for the Spanish match in part because he realized that war with Spain would drastically disrupt trade. The major City merchants, who were in this period achieving great success on the basis of their lucrative trades with the Mediterranean and the Near and Far East, almost certainly shared Cranfield's worries. It is probably because they feared the consequences for the intra-European and Mediterranean trades of war against Spain in the Atlantic and the West Indies that the company merchants of London failed, apparently, to lend much support to the plans to start a new company for the West Indies that were presented at court and in Parliament in 1625 and 1626, and again in 1628. In fact, the war with Spain that took place during the later 1620s did turn out to be very damaging to trade. It must have confirmed the City merchants in their support for a policy of peace with Spain and may have proved a point of growing friction between the London oppositionists and those in Parliament.[44]

The irony is that in the very period in which major forces in Parliament, led especially by the colonial aristocratic opposition, were struggling most militantly for a systematically Protestant anti-Spanish and pro-Dutch foreign policy, the leadership of the overseas merchant community of London, focused increasingly on the Levant–East India combine, was becoming not only more devoted to friendship with Spain, but more committed to opposing the Dutch. After all, it was the Dutch, and no longer

[44] For the company merchants' withdrawal from the American trades in the late 1620s, see above, ch. 3, pp. 102–6. On Cranfield's attitude toward the Spanish match, see Ruigh, *Parliament of 1624*, p. 33.

the Spanish, who posed the greatest obstacle to the expansion of the increasingly prosperous English long-distance trades with the south and east, above all in the Far East. From the early 1610s, the Dutch had been tightening their grip on the trade with the East Indies, and by the mid-1620s, following the Amboina Massacre, the Dutch succeeded in expelling the English from the Moluccas. It was no wonder that the Levant-East India Company merchant Thomas Munn, the great theorist and propagandist of English national power through English commercial power, devoted some of the climactic sections of his *England's Treasure by Forraign Trade*, written during the 1620s or 1630s, to a scathing attack not only on the Dutch, who in the guise of friends were eating away the very foundations of English prosperity, but also on a naive English political nation that continued to consider the United Provinces its true ally. That the aristocratic colonizing opposition placed such a premium on an anti-Spanish foreign policy founded on an alliance with the United Provinces at a time when key sections of the merchant elite were demanding more decisive government action against the Dutch must have put some strain on the de facto political alliance between these forces in the latter part of the 1620s.[45]

That the elite merchant and the colonizing aristocratic wings of the opposition to Charles and Buckingham were moving apart, not only in terms of commercial interests but also in terms of ideological orientation, became evident when the great company merchants refused to give their support to the aristocratic oppositionists' new colonizing initiatives at the end of the 1620s. Had these projects had only commercial goals, the London merchants' failure to support them would be hardly worth mentioning. But the raison d'être of these ventures was primarily religious and political.

The Massachusetts Bay Company in particular was meant to constitute an ideological and political response by London citizens, militant ministers, and lesser gentry from East Anglia and the West Country to the growing threat to Calvinism from an increasingly Arminian and intolerant establishment. It was therefore significant that among the one hundred or so investors in the Massachusetts Bay Company in 1628–1629, only four were Levant Company merchants, and none of these could really be called a leading figure in the trade with the Levant. On the other hand, three of the four Levant Company merchants who did invest in the Massachusetts Bay Company were at this point opening wide-ranging careers in colonial commerce and would soon emerge among the new-merchant

[45] T. Munn, *England's Treasure by Forraign Trade* (1664), in *Early English Tracts on Commerce*, ed. J. R. McCulloch (London, 1856), ch. 19. On Anglo-Dutch conflict in the Far East in this period, see K. N. Chaudhuri, *The English East India Company* (London, 1965), pp. 61–63, 65–70; K. R. Andrews, *Trade, Plunder, and Settlement* (Cambridge, 1984), pp. 268–69.

leadership of the trades with the Americas. Company merchants were also essentially absent from the Bermuda and Providence Island companies.[46] A fissure had apparently opened up between the aristocratic colonizing leadership and the City merchant establishment.

The turning point in the relationship between the great City merchants around Morris Abbot and the colonizing aristocratic opposition appears to have come at about the time of the dissolution of the Parliament of 1629. In the period just before the start of the Parliament of 1629, Abbot's closest political associates, his brother Archbishop George Abbot and the archbishop's intimate friend Sir Dudley Digges, made their peace with Charles I, with the result that in Parliament itself Digges supported the court. Almost certainly, Morris Abbot followed their path and, very likely, threw his considerable influence behind the attempt by top officers of the Levant Company in late January 1629 to call a halt to the intensification and radicalization of that company's protest against unparliamentary customs. In any case, by 13 March 1629, Abbot, as governor of the East India Company, was strongly advising the company's directorate against supporting the general strike against unparliamentary customs called for by the Commons. This could not but have helped to alienate the colonizing oppositionist lords. In fact, two weeks previously, the colonizing nobles and leading sections of the City elite had entered into open and direct conflict.

On 2 March 1629, the very day that the Commons were physically resisting the king's attempt to dismiss them and making their historic appeal to the country, the great opposition nobles Lord Saye, the earl of Warwick, and Lord Brook suddenly launched a full-scale assault on the elite merchant leadership of the East India Company. These aristocrats aimed not only to impose a series of new policies, but to shift fundamentally the balance of power within the company—away from the old, elite merchant leadership and in the direction of an alliance headed by themselves and supported by the company's smaller investors. Opening a battle that would go on for many years, Lord Saye in particular led the company's shopkeepers and lesser gentry in putting forward the following demands: (1) quarterly general courts to replace the annual general court; (2) a quarterly accounting of the company's finances, to be carried out by auditors appointed by the general court; (3) a one-year maximum term for

---

[46] The Levant Company merchants who invested in the Massachusetts Bay Company included Francis Flyer, Matthew Craddock, Samuel Vassall, and Nathan Wright, the last three of whom were also active in the American trades. This result was obtained by comparing the list of Massachusetts Bay Company investors in F. R. Rose-Troup, *The Massachusetts Bay Company and Its Predecessors* (New York, 1930), ch. 16, with full lists of Levant Company merchants derived from the Levant Company Court Minute Books and the London port books. For the Bermuda Company, see above, ch. 4, pp. 153–56.

the governor, or at least a revision of the old practice of reelecting the governor until there was a strong reason to get rid of him; (4) rules to limit the terms of the directors; and (5) use of the ballot box at all elections.[47]

Over quite a few years, the company's overseas merchant investors, represented by the company's board of directors, had been chronically in conflict with the company's gentry and shopkeeper investors over the company's price and dividend policies. The merchants controlled the large-scale reexport trade in East Indian pepper with Europe and the Levant, and they naturally pressed the company to set low prices for its pepper. The nonmerchant, generally smaller stockholders, whose income from the trade depended mostly on stock dividends, naturally fought for higher pepper prices. Nevertheless, struggles arising from this sort of conflict of interest tended to be short-lived, especially because the smaller investors had to confine their opposition to the infrequent meetings of the company's general court. At most times, the company's merchant interest, which totally dominated the company's board of directors, simply dictated the policy it desired.[48]

The power play by the Puritan lords that began in March 1629 transformed the sporadic resistance of the small investors and gentry into a systematic movement of opposition to the old-merchant leadership of the company. Nevertheless, it is far from clear just why the colonizing lords launched their assault at the time they did, and precisely what they ultimately hoped to gain from it. Very likely, the refusal of the East India Company's directorate, at just that moment, to support the mobilization of the majority of the company merchants behind Parliament's struggle against unparliamentary customs was a major factor in provoking the revolt of the noble oppositionists. What is certain is that the nobles' attack posed a serious threat to the great merchants' domination of one of their most important commercial undertakings. The City's merchant elite considered the East India Company its special province and must have interpreted the lords' opposition as an attack on its fundamental interests and mode of life.

By the mid-1630s, the East India Company directorate had succeeded in weathering the storm and the noble dissidents withdrew.[49] But it is

[47] *C.S.P. Col. E.I. 1625–1629*, pp. 635–38, 639.

[48] Chaudhuri, *East India Company*, pp. 147–48ff. See also R. G. Lang's comment: "At every election court from 1614–1621 (except possibly those of 1616, 1617, 1620, the minutes of which have not survived), the status quo was threatened by an opposing alliance of gentlemen and shopkeepers" ("The Greater Merchants of London, 1600–1625" [Oxford University, Ph.D. diss., 1963], p. 236).

[49] The struggle can be followed in India Office Library, Court Minutes of the East India Com-

doubtful if the lessons of this conflict were soon forgotten by the great merchants who ran the corporation. For merchant magnates like Morris Abbot, this experience may well have been decisive. Abbot had helped to spark the opposition to the Crown over the currants imposition, but had sought to prevent the East India Company's joining the movement against unparliamentary tonnage and poundage and had borne the brunt of the nobles' attacks throughout the following period. How could these lords, who presumed to lead the parliamentary opposition, be entrusted with the political order when they were so ready to overturn the merchants' traditional rule within their own established sphere of authority and so willing to appeal to the people to gain their ends?

Whatever merchants like Sir Morris Abbot actually felt about the conduct of the Puritan lords inside the East India Company, that conduct turned out to be paradigmatic. Over the following decade, the aristocratic oppositionists created the same kind of partnership between top landed-class leaders and small London traders that they had essayed within the East India Company, as they forged ever-closer ties with the new-merchant leadership of the colonial trades inside their own colonizing companies. This colonizing experience went well beyond that commercial cooperation between colonizing lords and new-merchant leaders that was sketched earlier; it involved a critical political and religious collaboration as well. As noted, during the later 1620s, the colonizing aristocrats were continuing their efforts to support and to shelter — as well as to organize behind their own religio-political opposition — Puritan religious dissidents of various stripes. Partly as an extension of these efforts, they helped to make all three major colonial companies — Massachusetts Bay, Bermuda, and Providence Island — centers of religio-political initiatives in direct defiance of Archbishop Laud. The colonizing aristocrats did not identify with all of the political and religious developments that took place in the Puritan colonies any more than they agreed with all of the opinions of the ministers they patronized and worked with. Nonetheless, they strongly defended these proceedings, just as they strongly defended those clerics. In so doing, they showed their willingness to collaborate closely in religio-political oppositional activities with people like the new merchants who were normally outside the political nation, as well as with radical ministers — notably, though hardly exclusively, from the ranks of religious Independency (or "non-separating congregationalism") — whose leading supporters seem to have come largely from outside the ranks of the landed classes. In this manner the colonizing aristocrats prepared the way for an

pany, vol. B/12, p. 297 and B/13, pp. 110, 131; *C.S.P. Col. E.I. 1630–1634*, p. 268; *C.C.M.E.I.C. 1635–1639*, pp. 13, 16–17, 18, 63–64.

alliance between relatively conservative constitutional reformers like themselves and a popular movement in London that would aim to overthrow the City constitution and to transform the church root and branch.

The first major steps in constructing the alliance between colonizing lords, new-merchant leaders and Puritan ministers, most especially those associated with religious Independency, seem to have been taken in the course of setting up the Massachusetts Bay Company in connection with the organization of the more general movement of religio-political opposition to the Crown at the end of the 1620s. Here, the Puritan lords showed their willingness to patronize a militantly Puritan project that they could influence but not effectively control. On 9 March 1628, the earl of Warwick made the grant of land in Massachusetts that established the New England Company, the unincorporated predecessor of the Massachusetts Bay Company. Warwick, it seems, had initially received this land in 1623 from the Council for New England (of which he was president by 1628), and he now regranted it to a coalition consisting of London citizens, activists from the old Dorchester Company, and East Anglian gentlemen. Warwick's protégé the minister Hugh Peter, who had major links with all three groups that came to constitute the company, played a critical role in helping to forge this alliance and in sending out its first expedition, led by John Endecott, in May–June 1628, at the time of the climactic parliamentary struggle over the Petition of Right. Peter had only just returned from temporary exile in the United Provinces to begin preaching, clandestinely, in his old parish of St. Sepulchre's London. The New England Company chose Matthew Craddock as its first governor, and Craddock led it until the decision in the summer of 1630 to transfer the charter and the government of the company to the Americas. In this capacity, he appears to have taken primary responsibility for mediating between the colonizing aristocrats, who were especially needed to defend the project against royal repression, and the company's small-trader, small-gentry leadership. Craddock, already a well-established Levant Company merchant, was at this time developing his own large-scale private plantation on the Mystic River in Massachusetts, and opening a wide-ranging career as a great trader with the Americas.[50]

By early 1629, Craddock was busy recruiting the company's first ministers, with the advice of the radical Puritan cleric John Davenport, a member of the Feoffees for Impropriations, and the Dorchester patriarch John White. As Craddock wrote John Endecott on 19 February 1629, "It is fully resolved by God's assistance to send over two ministers at least

---

[50] Andrews, *Colonial Period* 1: 352–59, 363–64, 380–84ff.; Newton, *Colonising Activities*, pp. 42, 47; Stearns, *Strenuous Puritan*, p. 39. For Craddock's career as a trader with the Americas, see above, ch. 4.

with the ships now intended to be sent thither. But for Mr. Peters, he is now in Holland, from whence his return hither I hold uncertain. Those we send you shall be by approbation of Mr. White of Dorchester and Mr. Davenport." Craddock and his advisers clearly had sought Hugh Peter as their top candidate for the job, but at this time Peter was in no position to accept an appointment. During the summer of 1628, Peter had once again gotten into trouble for preaching disrespectfully about the Catholic Queen Henrietta Maria. He had to spend six weeks in jail before the earl of Warwick succeeded in bailing him out and assisting his flight to Holland. By April 1629, then, Craddock and his advisers had chosen as the company's first ministers Francis Higginson and Samuel Skelton. Both of these men recently had been silenced by the government for Nonconformity and both, moreover, appear to have been tending toward religious Independency or "non-separating congregationalism" even before their arrival in Massachusetts to help governor John Endecott organize the colony's first church at Salem. If so, this would hardly be surprising, since Hugh Peter, the company's first choice as minister, and John Davenport, one of those in charge of selection, would openly adopt this theological position within a short time.[51]

The colonizing aristocrats could hardly have been displeased by the company's ministerial selections. After all, the earl of Warwick and his friends were at this time doing their best, overtly and covertly, to keep preaching and employed, or at least out of the hands of the authorities, a number of other ministers of the same stripe as those sent to Massachusetts. Warwick almost certainly sought to protect Peter when Peter returned briefly to his old position at Rayleigh, Essex, in early 1629. But Peter was soon obliged to flee again to Holland. There he became minister of the English church in Rotterdam and succeeded, within a few years, in transforming that church into a pioneer center of experimentation in religious Independency. By 1633, heavily influenced by the English Independent theologian William Ames, exiled for may years in Holland, Peter had remodeled the Rotterdam church as a democratically organized congregation, confined to godly members who would sign a "new" covenant, and had begun to attract to Rotterdam the first in a long line of leading lights of non-separating congregationalism who would temporarily settle there, notably John Davenport and William Ames himself. Meanwhile, the earl of Warwick had helped to hide the militant Essex minister Thomas Hooker and ultimately assisted Hooker's flight from England.

[51] Stearns, *Strenuous Puritan*, pp. 40 (quotation), 44, 45–53ff.; Shipps, "Lay Patronage," pp. 174–75; N. B. Shurtleff, ed., *Records of the Governor and the Company of Massachusetts Bay in New England*, 5 vols. (New York, 1853), 1: 356; Andrews, *Colonial Period*, pp. 377–81; P. Miller, *Orthodoxy in Massachusetts* (Cambridge, Mass., 1959), pp. 130–31, 137; Calder, *New Haven Colony*, pp. 13–23.

Hooker had come under attack when, beginning in spring 1629, Laud sought to impose conformity on the Puritan preachers of Essex. But, like Peter, Hooker refused to bend, and by 1631 he was obliged to follow Peter to Holland. Hooker was prevented from becoming copastor of the English congregation in Amsterdam because of his Independent proclivities, but, following a brief stay in Rotterdam with Hugh Peter, he did secure the post of assistant to John Forbes, minister of the Merchant Adventurers' church in Delft. At Delft, Hooker worked closely with Forbes and Peter to introduce forms of congregational organization much like those installed at Rotterdam, before ultimately migrating to New England. Meanwhile, in 1630, Warwick, as president of the Council for New England, had secured a second charter for the separatists of the Plymouth Colony.[52]

Over this same period, of course, the colonizing aristocrats had taken charge of the difficult task of seeing the Massachusetts Bay Company's charter through the royal government, which they accomplished in March 1629, and of overseeing the successful transfer of the company to America. The charter was obtained, according to Matthew Craddock, by "His Majesty's especial grace, with great cost, favour of personages of note and much labour." As John Humfrey remarked in 1630 at the end of the process, "We are all much bound to Lord Saye for his cordial advice and true affections. As also my Lord of Warwick. Sir Nathaniel Rich deserves very much acknowlegement for his wise handling of Sir Ferdinando Gorges."[53]

After the Massachusetts Bay Company moved to America, its governance offered decreasing opportunity for ongoing contact between the new merchants and colonizing aristocrats. Meanwhile, however, the Bermuda Company came to provide a very important vehicle for their growing collaboration. Unlike either Massachusetts Bay or Providence Island, Bermuda was not merely the scene of a large-scale Puritan experiment; it was also a major producer of a staple crop. Many of the leading new merchants entered the Bermuda Company in order to trade in tobacco, including, among many others, Matthew Craddock and Maurice Thomson, as well as Thomas Stone, Samuel Warner, Richard Bateson, and Elias Roberts, all of whom were, at one time or another, major partners of Thom-

[52] Shipps, "Lay Patronage," p. 175; Stearns, *Strenuous Puritan*, pp. 44–52ff.; Donagan, "Clerical Patronage," p. 407; Hunt, *Puritan Moment*, pp. 254–60; Calder, *New Haven Colony*, p. 24; Newton, *Colonising Activities*, p. 37; K. L. Sprunger, *Dutch Puritanism: A History of English and Scottish Churches of the Netherlands in the Sixteenth and Seventeenth Centuries* (Leiden, 1982), pp. 163–72, 237–39; K. L. Sprunger, "The Dutch Career of Thomas Hooker," *New England Quarterly* 46 (1973).

[53] Craddock is quoted in Andrews, *Colonial Period* 1: 367. The Humphrey quotation is from *Winthrop Papers* 2: 329.

son's. As a result, in the Bermuda Company, more than in any of the other Puritan colonizing ventures, the colonizing aristocrats and the new-merchant leadership were obliged to function together on a day-to-day basis.[54]

The earl of Warwick assumed the governorship of the Bermuda Company in 1628, and, under his direction and that of his colleagues in the aristocratic colonizing opposition, the company was made to function during the ensuing political crisis in closest coordination with the newly founded Massachusetts Bay and Providence Island companies. In 1630, the Bermuda Company appointed Roger Wood its governor on the island, and Wood pursued from the start a conscious policy of recruiting English Nonconforming clergy, hoping to divert some ministers headed for New England to his own island. Wood was clearly sympathetic to the circle of non-separating congregationalists that was so influential in Massachusetts, and in the early 1630s he made a strong attempt to attract to Bermuda its most illustrious representative, William Ames.[55] Ames had intended to emigrate to New England in 1629–1630. However, instead of going to Massachusetts, Ames, as noted, traveled to Rotterdam to join Hugh Peter in the Independent church that Peter had organized there in 1633. Wood, therefore, still had hopes of inducing Ames to come to Bermuda when in late 1633 he wrote:

> As there is a supposition that you intend to come for New England, and Mr. [Hugh] Peters, as many reverent divines are gone from England before you . . . then let me desire you to leave that resolution and come to the Bermudas where you are most entirely beloved and reverenced. . . . We are also far more secure from the hierarchical jurisdiction than New England is, for no great prelate will leave his pontifical palace to take his journey to live upon a barren rock. And all our islands are not worth a bishopric and there are many men of great wealth and estates and almost whole congregations gone with their pastors, where they build towns and call them according to those from whence they come, as Boston, Yarmouth, etc.
> . . . When they have well settled themselves they must be brought under the Archbishop of Canterbury and have a suffragan sent to reduce them into the fold of their old shepherds for the King will not *be quit* of his subjects wheresoever they live under his laws and obedience. All this discourse I relate to you to divert you away from any thoughts to *seek liberty* that way.[56]

[54] See above, ch. 4, pp. 153–56.

[55] G. L. Kittredge, "A Note on Mr. William Ames," *Colonial Society of Massachusetts Transactions* 13 (1912): 60–69. See Wood's comment: "I wish some of those that fly so fast into that climate [clerics fleeing to New England to escape persecution in England] would come more southerly to us" (Lefroy, *Memorials* 1: 535–36).

[56] Lefroy, *Memorials* 1: 535–36 (emphasis in text).

Ames died before he could go to Bermuda, but the colony had no trouble attracting individuals in sympathy with his teachings. Roger Wood, Josiah Foster, and William Sayle, the governors appointed to run the colony between 1630 and 1647, were all men of marked Puritan opinion and, under their rule, Bermuda, like the New England colonies, became an important haven for Puritan refugees from religious persecution.[57] In fact, by the early 1640s, Bermuda's ministry was entirely composed of congregationally-inclined ministers—including John Oxenbridge, Patrick Copeland, Nathaniel White, and William Golding—who spared no efforts in order to reform the colony's religious life, according to their conceptions of the best reformed ideals.[58]

Warwick, along with his kinsman Nathaniel Rich, Lord Saye and Sele, and Lord Brook, appears to have taken primary control of the Bermuda Company's religious policy. Rich, Brook, Saye, and the company's treasurer Gabriel Barber handled the company's negotiations with the Bermudian Puritan minister George Stirk when Stirk threatened to quit the colony in 1634. Nathaniel Ward, one of the company's ministerial appointees, had held the rectory of Stondon Massey, Essex, in the gift of Sir Nathaniel Rich, before he was deprived of his living for Nonconformity in 1633. Moreover, Ward and Nathaniel Bernard were "translated" from their ministerial positions in Bermuda to Essex church livings under the patronage of the earl of Warwick.[59]

It seems clear that new-merchant leaders worked with the Puritan aristocrats in making religious policy inside the Bermuda Company during the 1630s, although there is little information available on company decision making for that period. A document of 1644, in which the colonizing lords and new-merchant leaders jointly promulgate directions for the colony's religious life, provides direct evidence of such collaboration.[60] The signers of this document include the Providence Island Company nobles and gentry the earl of Warwick, Lord Saye, Sir Gilbert Gerrard, Sir Benjamin Rudyerd, Sir Richard Knightley, and Gabriel Barber and the new-merchant leaders Owen Rowe, Maurice Thomson, Thomson's brother-in-law Elias Roberts, Thomson's trading partner William Felgate (William Tucker's brother-in-law), Nathaniel Hawes, and Robert Haughton. That close collaboration had been occurring during the 1630s is indicated by the fact that by 1640–1641, the new-merchant leaders

---

[57] Andrews, *Colonial Period* 1: 228–35. A Capt. Thomas Chaddock also held the position of governor of Bermuda in this period (1637–1640), but I have not discovered anything about his religious orientation.

[58] Lefroy, *Memorials* 1: 569–70, 585; Andrews, *Colonial Period* 1: 231.

[59] G. L. Kittredge, "George Stirk, Minister," *Colonial Society of Massachusetts Transactions* 13 (1912): 42–49, 38–40 n. 2.

[60] Lefroy, *Memorials* 1: 590.

Owen Rowe and Thomas Allen had acceded to the company's deputy governorship and treasurership respectively, alongside the earl of Warwick, who was governor.[61] Little has been discovered about Thomas Allen, aside from the fact that he was an active tobacco trader with the Americas in partnership with his father, William Allen. Rowe, who traded with New England and Virginia as well as Bermuda, was a founder of the Massachusetts Bay Company and a backer of the Puritan New Haven Colony. From the late 1630s, he would play a significant role in the City opposition movement.[62] By that time, as will be described, the new-merchant leaders and colonizing aristocrats were cooperating on a broad range of common projects, including a privateering war against Spain in the West Indies conducted from Providence Island, a colonizing enterprise north of Virginia, and joint political resistance in the City and Parliament.

The Company Merchants and the Crown

While the colonizing aristocrats were loosening their connections with the City's company merchants and constructing links with the new-merchant leadership, the Crown was seeking to attract the company merchants back in the direction of the court. This fact has sometimes been neglected as a result of the quite proper recognition of the real alienation of the majority of the company merchants from the Crown in the late 1620s and of the merchant's grievances, both economic and political, against royal policies in the late 1630s. I have, of course, emphasized the natural affinity of the Crown and company merchants for one another, rooted in the traditional exchange of royal commercial privileges for merchant financial and political support, as well as in their common interest in defending the City's sociopolitical order under its royal charter and its oligarchic government. Even at the height of the Crown-merchant conflicts of the 1620s, the Crown had been able to retain the loyalty of a majority of the City's merchant elite as represented on the aldermanic court and the East India Company directorate, as well as the customs farming syndicates. Still, a pivotally important group of elite merchants had turned against the Crown, joining the great majority of company merchants in opposition. With the death of Buckingham, the dismissal of Parliament, and the ending of the

[61] Ibid. 1: 590; Wilkinson, *Bermuda*, p. 390.

[62] Haberdashers Company, London, Apprenticeship Bindings, 1602–1611, 11 Aug. 1609; V. Pearl, *London and the Outbreak of the Puritan Revolution: City Government and National Politics, 1625–1643* (Oxford, 1961), p. 324; M. Noble, *The Lives of the Regicides*, 2 vols. (London, 1798), 2: 150–51. Rowe imported 6,000 pounds of Virginian tobacco in 1640 (London Port Book for Imports, 1640, PRO, E.190/43/5).

wars, there was a significant easing of tensions, and the Crown, inevitably, sought to renew its old alliance with the merchants on the traditional basis.

THE LEVANT COMPANY MERCHANTS

The Crown was fortunate in the commercial trends of the 1630s. These were years of unprecedented growth for the trades with southern Europe, the Mediterranean, and the Near East, and years of enormous prosperity for the eastward-trading merchants, especially the Levant Company traders. While the Merchant Adventurers suffered crisis and decline, the Levant Company took over the top position within the City merchant community, as their leading members consolidated their power within all of the elite bodies—the customs farms, the court of aldermen, and the board of directors of the East India Company. The entrenchment of these merchants at the top of the City's commercial hierarchy had real political significance, for it strengthened their capacity to wield broad influence within the merchant community as a whole.

The Levant Company merchants had played a leading role in the customs farms since their inception. The Levant Company founder William Garway had headed the original syndicate that controlled the farms for most of the first quarter of the seventeenth century. In December 1625, as noted, William's son William Garway and Morris Abbot, both Levant Company magnates, lost their stranglehold on the customs, although they did manage to renew their control of the currants farm, which they maintained until 1632. Even then, Paul Pindar, who led the new syndicate that by 1632 had taken over all the farms, was also a leading Levant Company merchant (although by the 1630s, he was probably better known for his close ties with the court than for anything else).[63]

From the start, the leading Levant Company traders had been politically influential within the City government, but during Charles I's reign the group emerged as by far the leading merchant force within the municipality. Between 1600 and 1625, only eight Levant Company merchants were elected to aldermanic positions in comparison with thirty Merchant Adventurers. But between 1631 and 1640, no fewer than eight Levant Company merchants were chosen for positions on the aldermanic bench, in comparison with two Merchant Adventurers. Of the twenty-eight individuals who occupied aldermanic positions between October 1640 and December 1641, no fewer than nine were Levant Company merchants, while sixteen were either Levant Company merchants or East India Company directors or both.[64]

---

[63] R. Ashton, *The Crown and the Money Market, 1603–1640* (Oxford, 1960), pp. 87–98, 107–8.

[64] Lang, "Greater Merchants of London," pp. 149–50, 200; Pearl, *London*, pp. 285–308. See above, ch. 2, pp. 81–82.

Leading Levant Company merchants had always controlled the East India Company directorate, a central meeting place for members of the City's merchant elite. During the 1630s, they strengthened their hold. Among the forty-seven persons who held positions on the East India Company's board of directors between 1630 and 1639, no fewer than twenty-eight were Levant Company merchants. Those great merchants from other trades who also sat on this board were linked to the top Levant Company merchants through their collaboration inside the company and in a variety of other ways. They were thus brought within a coherent merchant elite given its dominant coloring by the Levant Company traders.[65]

The enormous progress of the eastward traders was a boon to the Crown. As a result of their increasing commercial success over an extended period and their growing preponderance within the key City and mercantile institutions, as well as the virtually unparalleled support they had received from the Crown throughout most of their companies' existence, the eastward traders naturally tended to assume a highly conservative sociopolitical outlook. Because they stood at the center of great and long-standing family and commercial networks, they were, moreover, in a strong position to influence the other company merchants in favor of their own political positions. This group of merchants offered Charles I an indispensable political resource—a potential power base within the City from which to organize the merchant community as a whole behind the Crown. It was up to the royal government to realize this potential.

In view of the pivotal role played by the Levant Company traders in the merchant opposition of the 1620s, it is not surprising that during the 1630s the Crown went to some lengths to cater to their needs. Certain of Charles's policies considered most objectionable by the majority of his subjects were actually favorable to the Levant Company's interests. The monarchy's controversial policy of peace with Spain, inaugurated with the Treaty of Madrid in 1630, was particularly helpful to the Levant Company merchants, for they needed, above all, a secure route to the eastern Mediterranean. Moreover, the Crown, at least ostensibly, originally levied ship money in order to raise the navy that the Levant Company merchants had long demanded to protect English shipping in the Mediterranean from the depredations of the Algiers pirates.[66] The new book of rates issued in 1635, which raised the levies on a wide range of commodities, left the Levant Company merchants relatively unscathed, as the Crown failed to raise the duty on either raw silk or currants, the Levant Company's chief imports. In fact, the government actually cut 1s. 2d. from the long-disputed currants imposition, a considerable concession in view of the lengths to which the Crown had gone during the 1620s to defend its

[65] See above, ch. 2, pp. 75–79, 89–91.
[66] Gardiner, *History* 7: 176–77, 370–71.

[283]

earlier 2s. 2d. increase. Meanwhile, in 1634, the Crown had granted the Levant Company the right to post an agent at the customs house who would inspect and approve all cargoes to and from the Levant. This was a useful weapon against interlopers. No doubt the Levant Company felt the weight of royal taxation on trade, as it had in the past. But the compensation the company received was, as usual, considerable.[67]

THE FRENCH COMPANY MERCHANTS

Along with the Levant Company merchants, the French Company merchants had led the attack on the Crown in the 1620s. And if the government had perhaps less to offer the French Company traders, it still went out of its way to help them. Indeed, the Crown's endeavors to win the allegiance of the wine traders typified its entire policy toward the merchant community in this period. Beginning in May 1638, the Crown forced the Company of Vintners—under the threat of depriving them of their traditional privileges of dressing meat and selling beer—to agree to pay to the government an annual rent of £30,000, to be raised by a tax of 40s. per tun on all wine imported. The process by which this plan was put into effect, and the intermediary groups that were able to use it to their private advantage, do not require detailed explanations here. It is sufficient to state that either as a result of pressure from the Crown or through the connivance of certain leading Vintners (or both), the Company of Vintners organized from among its members a syndicate to farm the 40s. tax for the Crown: the Crown was to receive a flat annual payment of £30,000 from the farmers, and the farmers were to collect the 40s. per tun payment on all wine imported.[68]

The wine contract might have meant another burden on the already heavily taxed wine trade. However, the Crown was able to make sure that it worked out, in practice, in the wine merchants' favor. On 15 March 1638, at the Vintners Company court, the merchants of London trading in wines with France and Spain demanded that the wine retailers of the Vintners Company be required to take a certain quantity off their hands every year at set prices. This was tantamount to demanding that the retailers ensure the merchants' markets. Not surprisingly, the wine sellers of the company refused to agree, and shot off a petition of protest to the Crown the next day. But the government, probably implicated in advance in the merchants' scheme, proved unsympathetic. The Vintners Company

---

[67] Bodleian Library, Bankes MSS (catalogue) 38/8, 65/38. See also *Book of Rates for 1635* (London, 1635); A. C. Wood, *A History of the Levant Company* (London, 1935, repr. 1964), p. 51.

[68] Vintners Company, Court Book, 1629–1638, AC/3, pp. 154–65; PRO, C.66/2813/20–25; Pearl, *London*, pp. 289–91; Gardiner, *History* 8: 286–87. I wish to thank Michael Zell for transcribing for me sections of the Vintners Company records.

officers met with the French- and Spanish-trade merchants, Secretary Sir John Bankes, and the marquis of Hamilton (a key promoter at court of the wine contract) to discuss the issue. But, as the Vintners' officers reported to the membership on 21 March 1638, the government did indeed desire that the retailers be forced to buy up a certain amount of wine at a set price, just as the merchants had proposed. The government conceded that there might be yearly discussions of the price to be set. But there could be no compromise over the amount to be purchased. On 21 May 1638, this amount was fixed at 5,000 tuns annually, but by 9 January 1639, the figure had been increased to 10,550 tuns a year.[69]

This agreement to set prices and purchases in advance was clearly beneficial to both the Crown and the wine merchants. It helped to ensure that the farmers of the wine tax could collect enough taxes to be able to afford to pay the Crown its annuity for the contract. In turn, by guaranteeing the merchants that their wines would be purchased at a known price, the Crown assured them of markets they could not otherwise have counted on.

Of course, in the end this policy was not without its contradictions. By shifting the real burden of the monopoly from the importers to the shoulders of the retailers, the government had assisted the wine merchants. But this was only at the cost of alienating the wine sellers. As a result, this policy exacerbated, in one more sphere, the inherent conflict between the City's mere merchants (the overseas trading wholesalers) and the City's shopkeepers that, as noted earlier, also manifested itself in the struggles over the proposed corporation for the Spanish trade and in the Levant Company merchants' relations with their grocer customers, as well as with those shopkeepers who tried to interlope within the Levant Company's privileged areas.

THE MERCHANT ADVENTURERS

Finally, in much the same way as the government attempted to minister to the needs of the Levant Company and the French Company, it also sought to assist the Merchant Adventurers. This may, indeed, have been the Crown's most significant initiative of the 1630s with respect to the merchant community. Because of the ease of entry into their trade, the Merchant Adventurers were, more than any other company, directly dependent on their corporate privileges. Moreover, because of the deepening crisis in the cloth export trade, their dependence became greater as the seventeenth century wore on. Nevertheless, the Merchant Adventurers sustained the most damaging political attack suffered by any major mer-

[69] Vintners Company, Court Book, 1629–1638, AC/3, pp. 156–58 (15 Mar. 1638), 158–59 (16 Mar. 1638), 159–61 (21 Mar. 1638), 165 (21 May 1638), 181 (9 Jan. 1639).

chant group when Parliament suspended many of the company's most cherished privileges in 1624, opening the way for a massive invasion of the Adventurers' markets by new traders at the very time when these markets were contracting most rapidly. From that point onward, the company had little choice but to preoccupy itself with regaining its privileges.

During the later 1620s, as noted, the Adventurers played a role in the movement against unparliamentary taxation, alongside the Levant Company and French Company merchants. But, as has been observed, the Adventurers were not, even at that point, beyond compromising their political principles if they could thereby gain the king's support for their privileges. There is no reason to doubt that, all else being equal, a majority of Adventurers would have wished to support the political thrust of the parliamentary oppositionists. Yet these very same parliamentary oppositionists were the sworn enemies of the Adventurers on the issue that most affected these merchants—the regulation of trade. The Adventurers had, therefore, to consider any royal offer to restore their privileges, even if there were strings attached.[70]

The Crown well understood the Adventurers' predicament, and in 1634 the government restored essentially all of the Adventurers' old privileges, a tremendous gain for the company. By the privy council's order of 16 November 1634, the government gave to members of the Company of Merchant Adventurers the sole right to export cloths to Germany and the United Provinces, restricted this trade to the Adventurers' mart towns, and imposed a company admission fee of £100 for London merchants (£50 for outport merchants).[71] The Crown rarely granted favors without some material compensation. But it is possible that, in this case, the government was willing to bestow its bounty free of charge in order to make up to the Adventurers for the rough treatment they had suffered over the previous two decades, and to help win them back to their traditional support for the Crown.

By the end of the 1630s, however, the Crown, under enormous financial pressure, found it increasingly difficult to resist imposing new financial exactions, and the Merchant Adventurers did not remain immune. From 1635, the company had engaged in a heated dispute with the duke and duchess of Lennox over their license to export cloths within the Merchant Adventurers' chartered area. This license was essentially another charge by the king on the company, this time indirect, to help him finance favors for his courtiers. The privilege originally had been granted to the earl of Cumberland in 1600 and had since undergone a number of changes in its terms. By the later 1630s, the contract called for the company to pay

[70] See above, ch. 5, pp. 205, 210–15.
[71] PRO, P.C. 2/44/224 (16 Nov. 1634).

the Lennoxes £2,600 a year for the license. In view of the decline in their trade, the Adventurers felt this to be unreasonable and tried to get the terms of the contract changed. They first proposed a rent of £2,000 a year, but ultimately agreed to pay £2,200. Yet the licensees would not agree to any compromise and, in 1640, the duke seized a company cloth shipment in order to extract his fee.[72]

Despite Lennox's intransigence and willingness to disrupt trade in pursuit of his own narrow interest, the king seems to have stood firmly behind him. The Crown even went so far as to affirm the duke's right to license interlopers if the Merchant Adventurers refused to come to an agreement with him.[73] It is apparent, too, that the monarchy itself hoped to squeeze the Merchant Adventurers a little further in its own behalf. In January and February 1640, with financial pressure on the Crown constantly mounting, the king seems to have agreed to entertain a proposal by Edward Misselden, former Merchant Adventurer representative in Delft, not only to settle the license "to the good contentment of the Duke," but also "to make it beneficial to the King." It was almost certainly Misselden who had written to the court in 1635 that

> if . . . your Majesty do account the royal gift of license to the late Duke of Richmond, now continued to the Duchess, which yieldeth but 3000 or 4000 per annum, to be a bar to all further question of this matter [that is, of what further monies could be extracted from the Merchant Adventurers] then your humble servant presumeth not to move your Majesty's settled patience therein. Otherwise, he humbly prayeth your Majesty to respect what herein may fairly be advanced to your profit, without the wronging the merchants, or making any stop of trade or impeaching of the Duchess her interest.

The precise nature of Misselden's proposals has not been discovered. All that is known is that when Misselden placed the proposals before the company in 1640, they caused "such a disorder in [the Merchant Adventurers'] court" that they had to be given up.[74]

Even so, the government does seem to have succeeded in wrenching additional money from the Adventurers, now in exchange for a proclamation bolstering their monopoly. This seems to be the significance of a letter of 25 January 1640 from Secretary Windebank to the Adventurers' governor, deputy governor, and five of the other chief men of the company, informing them that the king was anxious for the procurement of

[72] *C.S.P.D. 1636-1637*, p. 106; *C.S.P.D. 1639*, p. 539; *C.S.P.D. 1639-1640*, pp. 333-34. R. Ashton, "Charles I and the City," in *Essays in the Social and Economic History of Tudor and Stuart England*, ed. F. J. Fisher (Cambridge, 1961), p. 156.

[73] *C.S.P.D. 1639-1640*, pp. 333-34; Ashton, "Charles I and the City," p. 156.

[74] PRO, S.P.16/285/46 (26 Mar. 1635); *C.S.P.D. 1639-1640*, pp. 328, 333, 334, 417-18.

the "£3000 behind owing by the town of Rotterdam [the Merchant Ad-venturers' factory in the Netherlands], having graciously granted a new proclamation and diverse privy seals on the humble petition of the Mer-chant Adventurers."[75]

THE EAST INDIA COMPANY

Ironically, the Crown showed least sensitivity to the commercial corpo-ration that had shown it the greatest loyalty during the crisis of the late 1620s. The East India Company's board of directors, as a central institu-tion of the City's merchant elite, was no doubt expected by the Crown to offer unquestioning obedience, and it had done so in 1629. Perhaps for this reason, the Crown had few qualms about rather mercilessly exploiting this company during the 1630s. Indeed, the government's taxes on trade hit the East India Company especially hard, as the new book of rates, promulgated in 1635, raised duties significantly on pepper, the company's main import, even though pepper prices had fallen off significantly.[76]

But what hurt the East India Company most was the Crown's lack of concern for its chartered commercial privileges. In 1630, Charles I showed his disdain for the company when he dispatched his own priva-teering vessel to prey on the native trade between the Red Sea and India.[77] A few years later, a court favorite, Endymion Porter, probably in collab-oration with the great Anglo-Dutch merchant and Crown lender Sir Wil-liam Courteen, received the king's consent to launch his own privateering voyage to the same area. Then, near the end of 1635, Sir William Cour-teen organized a truly major company, intending to carry on commerce in areas not yet developed by the East India Company, but squarely within its privileges. Courteen's was no one-shot effort, and his competition posed a grave threat to the old company's very survival.[78] Finally, be-tween 1637 and 1639, the king approved proposals by Prince Rupert, the earl of Arundel, and the earl of Southampton to develop a halfway-house colony off the east coast of Africa, on the East India Company's route to the Far East. None of the latter efforts really got off the ground, but they were nevertheless very troublesome to the East India Company, since their very existence indicated the king's willingness to ignore company privileges.[79]

---

[75] *C.S.P.D. 1637–1638*, p. 328. The proclamation had been issued in spring 1639 (PRO, P.C.2/50/170–71).

[76] *C.C.M.E.I.C. 1635–1639*, pp. xx–xxi.

[77] For the series of incursions into the East India Company's privileged areas starting in 1630s, see the narratives provided by Sir William Foster in his introductions to the calendars of the court minutes of the East India Company for the period 1635–1650. See also above, ch. 4, pp. 168–74.

[78] *C.C.M.E.I.C. 1635–1639*, pp. xiv–xix, 123, 127–29, 188, 191, 275–76.

[79] Ibid., pp. 244, 245, 257, 264; 322–23; 315, 337, 349, 350.

The East India Company looked on these invasions into its privileged domain with increasing alarm. In 1637, the company's leadership had been able politely to refuse Prince Rupert's plea for assistance, while confidently giving his project their blessing. But when the earl of Arundel made a similar request for help in 1639, the company immediately protested to the king: it demanded that Arundel's project, as well as the earl of Southampton's planned venture to Mauritius, be brought to a halt.[80] By this time the company's position had deteriorated considerably, for its monopoly privileges, which formerly had functioned so effectively in attracting investors, had ceased to carry much weight. Largely as a result of the Crown's refusal to back the company's charter, its investors experienced a major crisis of confidence during the late 1630s.[81] Indeed, by early 1639 the leading government financier, Philip Burlamachi, who had excellent connections in City and court circles, was reporting that the East India Company was planning to wind up its current joint stock and would have difficulty getting additional capital for a new issue. At the same time, anticipating the company's imminent demise, promoters of a new joint-stock company for the East Indies, to be financed primarily in Holland and perhaps connected with the Courteen projectors, petitioned the king for his support.[82]

Perhaps the indication that the trade was in serious danger of falling into foreign hands alarmed the Crown. In December 1639, Charles I finally gave a favorable response to the East India Company's petitions and remonstrances that he had ignored for years. He called a halt to the colonizing plans of both Arundel and Southampton, and ordered William Courteen to send eastward only those ships needed to bring back the goods he had already sent out. Even so, as the political crisis deepened, Charles had real difficulty actually enforcing this order.[83]

All told, the Crown's commercial policies during Charles I's personal monarchy added up to a significant gain for the City's main overseas commercial companies, with the notable exception of the East India Company. Nevertheless, in attempting to maximize its financial and political backing, the government, as always, found it difficult to avoid sacrificing one interest to another, and this was especially so during periods of financial stringency, when the weight of Crown exactions in general tended to become less tolerable. In all probability, during much of the decade follow-

---

[80] Ibid., pp. 248–49, 249 n. 1; 328, 330, 338, 339.

[81] For signs that the East India Company was in serious trouble as early as mid-1637, see "Informations and Observations that the East India Company are resolved to divide and leave the trade," and other similar papers presented to the government at that time concerning the company's problems, (ibid, pp. 247ff.).

[82] Ibid., pp. 302, 296–97.

[83] Ibid., pp. 351–52; *C.C.M.E.I.C. 1640–1643*, pp. xiv, 143, 144, 145, 146, 147, 151, 155.

ing the assassination of Buckingham, the Crown significantly improved its political standing with London's company merchant community. Just how fully it won back their loyalty, and retained it through the financial and political crisis of 1639–1642, is considered in the remainder of this chapter and in the one that follows.

The Merchant Community and the Crisis of the Regime

Through much of the 1630s, comparative calm and political stability prevailed nationally and in London, following the fierce conflicts of the 1620s. Still, the Crown was unable to solve its long-term financial problems and therefore remained vulnerable to unexpected shocks, whether internal or external in origin. The first signs of difficulty for the government came in 1635, when the government's extension of ship-money levies to the countryside provoked significant opposition from leading sections of the landed classes, as well as from citizens in London. Whether or not the Crown could have succeeded in making ship money a permanent, unparliamentary tax remains an open question. But after the king's ill-advised attempt to impose religious uniformity on Scotland in 1637, the government faced a deepening financial and political crisis.[84]

During the 1630s, the Crown had sought to milk London sources of revenue. As emphasized, the merchants felt the pressure of increased customs levies, as well as other forms of direct and indirect taxes. Meanwhile, the City as a whole was squeezed in a variety of ways. The Crown launched a series of assaults on City privileges and properties, the most significant of which were directed at the municipality's Irish lands and the royal contract estates (conveyed to the City in 1627 to repay previous loans).[85] With the onset of the Scottish war, the situation became unbearably difficult: the Crown had to intensify its financial demands from London, while attempting to maintain the citizens' loyalty.

In Robert Ashton's view, the Crown's levies on the merchants and the municipality, compounded by its arbitrary policies in church and state, brought about a renewal of the opposition movement in London as a whole. This movement was, according to Professor Ashton, essentially a continuation of that of the 1620s, with the opposition to the Crown encompassing the highest levels of the merchant elite. The merchants, says Professor Ashton, took up a position of conservative opposition that could be likened to that of Edward Hyde and Lord Falkland in the period up to, say, June 1641.[86]

[84] See J. Morrill, *The Revolt of the Provinces* (London, 1980), pp. 23–30.

[85] For these attacks on the City, see Pearl, *London*, pp. 79–88; R. Ashton, *The City and the Court, 1603–1643* (Cambridge, 1979), pp. 157–76.

[86] Ashton, *City and the Court*, pp. 204ff.

Nevertheless, Professor Ashton seems to have derived from the undoubted facts that the Crown abused the City and the City had real grievances the unwarranted conclusion that London must have supported the parliamentary political opposition. This conclusion is especially dubious with respect to the merchant elite as represented on the court of aldermen and the directorate of the East India Company, not to mention the customs farming syndicates. Professor Ashton fails to bring out the point that even at the height of merchant opposition in the 1620s, probably a majority of the merchant elite remained loyal to the Crown. The fact is, moreover, that the court of aldermen enforced arbitrary royal policies from 1635 right through 1640, even as opposition elsewhere in the country as well as in London itself rapidly mounted. Even when Parliament's return was assured in April 1640 and again in September 1640, the court of aldermen and the East India Company directorate failed to issue any sort of statement of grievances and refused to support those protests that did come in this period from the court of common council, from independently petitioning citizens, and from the East India Company's general court. Finally, neither the court of aldermen nor the East India Company directorate protested to Parliament against any of the Crown's policies of the 1630s or gave any explicit support for the parliamentary political agenda at any point during the entire first phase of the parliamentary legislative revolution, from November 1640 to June 1641, even though this revolution was backed by Hyde, Falkland, and a strong majority of the parliamentary classes.[87]

The refusal of the municipality, or any other organized section of the merchant elite, openly to support Parliament or to oppose the Crown had a great impact on political developments in London. It meant that opposition had to proceed largely outside the official institutions. This gave an enormous opening to radical elements normally outside the political nation, locally and nationally. Even by 1640, the bulk of the company merchants had to confront a situation in London in which the parliamentary movement was headed to a great extent by members of the new-merchant leadership of the colonial trades and composed largely of nonmerchant citizens, while the majority of the merchant elite backed the Crown.

SHIP MONEY

The ship-money writs, as is well known, provoked opposition from some of the core leaders of the colonizing, or middle-group, aristocratic opposition. In 1636, Lord Saye and the earl of Warwick refused to pay, and

[87] Cf. R. Ashton, *The English Civil War: Conservatism and Revolution, 1603–1649* (London, 1978), pp. 92–93. I will try to document the assertions of this paragraph in the remainder of this chapter and the one that follows.

both attempted to rouse their tenants to further resistance. In 1637, John Hampden made his famous challenge to ship money before the king's courts, defended by Oliver St. John. All these men were active members of the Providence Island Company.[88]

Meanwhile, London citizens took their own, parallel actions against ship money. Unfortunately it is difficult to get at the composition of the City movement, but the bits of evidence that exist are tantalizing. First, two of the five merchant resisters to tonnage and poundage who ignited the final, more radical phase of merchant opposition in 1628–29 figured prominently among the leaders of the opposition to ship money—the Massachusetts Bay leader Samuel Vassall and Richard Chambers, both Levant Company merchants. Second, several key new-merchant leaders were among the small number of known ship-money resisters. These included Vassall and Thomas Stone, both leading tobacco traders and partners of Maurice Thomson, as well as Michael Herring and John Brett, two lesser figures in the American trades, along with Stephen Estwicke, later an interloper in the East Indies. Finally, a good number of the known ship-money refusers would play a leading role in the City revolution of 1641–1642, while none so far discovered would end up on the side of the Crown.[89]

If the London resistance to ship money constitutes evidence for a certain limited continuity of opposition to the Crown within the citizenry from the late 1620s to the early 1640s, the magistracy's vigorous enforcement of ship money manifests the very strong continuity of allegiance to the Crown within the London elite over these years. In the later 1620s, as emphasized, the court of aldermen carried out the collection for the twenty ships, imposed the Forced Loan, rigorously exacted the royal contract estates loan, and made several other signal contributions to the Crown's fund-raising efforts. Similarly, from 1635 through 1640, in the face of widespread opposition in the City, the municipality's top officers did what they could to bring in ship money.[90]

Even before the ship-money crisis, the merchant elite in general, and the aldermanic court in particular, had distinguished themselves during the period of Charles's nonparliamentary rule by their backing of, if not enthusiastic support for, royal policies. This was so to a surprising degree even in the realm of religious affairs. In the previous period of religious

---

[88] Gardiner, *History* 8: 92–94; Newton, *Colonising Activities*, pp. 175, 236–47; N. P. Bard, "The Ship Money Case and William Fiennes, Viscount Saye and Sele," *B.I.H.R.* 50 (1977): 177–84; V. A. Rowe, "Robert, Second Earl of Warwick and the Payment of Ship-Money in Essex," *Transactions of the Essex Archaeological Society*, 3d ser. 1 (1962): 160–63.

[89] For these men as ship-money refusers, see CLRO, C.C.A. 1/3, fols. 52–53, and 1/4, fol. 46; CLRO, Aldermanic Repertories 55, fol. 32; *H.M.C., Fourth Report, Appendix*, p. 29.

[90] See Pearl, *London*, pp. 88–91. See also above, ch. 5, pp. 225–28.

laxity under Archbishop Abbot, members of the aldermanic court had patronized the famous lectureship at St. Antholin's parish, a center of Puritan preaching. But with the advent of Archbishop Laud, they thought better of continuing this support. There was a similar evolution with respect to Sabbatarianism. Having enforced the Sabbatarian laws during the 1620s, the aldermen ceased to do so in the 1630s.[91]

The foregoing actions of the City magistrates do not, of course, prove that they were devoted to the Laudian experiment. But the willingness of the aldermen to go along without protest with the government's ecclesiastical innovations and their withdrawal of support for anti-Laudian projects like the St. Antholin's lectures may have tended to alienate them from politically disaffected elements in London. There is, in fact, some evidence that from the end of the 1620s, significant numbers of company merchants were becoming less comfortable with religious positions that, though perfectly respectable a decade earlier, were now increasingly associated with political dissidence and, following the advent of Laud, identified as Nonconformist.

First of all, only a small number of company merchants appear as supporters of the projects of the Feoffees for Impropriations. Of the four nonclerics and nonlawyers among the twelve feoffees, none appears to have been a company merchant; of the sixty or more contributors to the feoffees between 1625 and 1632, only a large handful were company merchants.[92]

The clerical patronage of the Levant Company constitutes evidence that a not insignificant section of the merchant elite, and perhaps of the company merchant community more broadly, was actually willing to give positive support to the government's religious policy. As early as 1622, the Levant Company in its general court was making what might be called anti-Puritan ministerial appointments to its overseas factories. In that year, the company chose Christopher Newstead as its preacher at Constantinople. Newstead's religious orientation is evidenced by the fact that Archbishop Laud appointed him rector of Stisted, Essex, in April 1642. That he was unacceptable to his Puritan parishioners would be a gross understatement. He was not allowed to enter the church, and, apparently, was stoned by the women of the parish. An Arminian, Newstead was soon up on charges: that he had preached that God had sparing mercies; that he

[91] Pearl, *London*, pp. 79–80; Ashton, *City and the Court*, pp. 192–98.

[92] The company merchants I have been able to identify among those contributors listed in "A Summary of the Accounts of the Feoffees for the Purchase of Impropriation" include William Ashwell, Thomas Hodges, Richard Mantell, and Caldwell Farrington of the Levant Company, and Daniel Hudson of the Merchant Adventurers (I. M. Calder, ed., *Activities of the Puritan Faction of the Church of England, 1625–1633* [London, 1957], pp. 28–33. See also D. A. Williams, "Puritanism in the City Government, 1610–1640," *Guildhall Miscellany* 1: 4 [1955]).

had promoted ceremonies; that he had buried bodies with crosses on their breasts; and that he had blotted out scriptures put up by the parishioners on the wall of their local church to counteract the idolatrous pictures of God the Father and of purgatory that Newstead had placed there.[93]

No evidence has been discovered concerning the religious leanings of either Charles Robson or a Mr. Hunt, the preachers next appointed by the Levant Company. But in 1630, the company's governor, Hugh Hamersley, nominated Edward Pocock for a post. Hamersley and "others of the company . . . [had] received very good testimony and recommendations [of Pocock] both for his ability in learning, soundness in the study of divinity, conformity to the constitutions of the Church, and integrity of life and conversation." Pocock, as was customary, preached a trial sermon before the general court and apparently passed the test, for he was approved for the position on 31 March 1630. Pocock had received his B.A. and M.A. degrees from Corpus Christi College, Oxford, and became a fellow there. His religious orientation may be surmised from the fact that, following his return from the Levant, when he resumed his career in Arabic studies at Oxford, he was patronized by Archbishop Laud and ultimately became professor of Arabic. With the outbreak of hostilities, Pocock may have come under suspicion for his connection with Laud. He retained his professorship throughout the Interregnum but was ejected from his canonry in 1651 for his refusal to take the Engagement.[94] The Levant Company's selection of Edward Pocock, as well as of Christopher Newstead, could conceivably be understood in terms simply of expediency, that is, as ministerial appointments of which the government would approve. But such an interpretation seems unlikely to be correct, for the Levant Company continued to choose ministers of the same sort as Pocock and Newstead even after the fall of Laud—in fact, right through the Civil War, in the face of considerable contrary pressure from outside.[95]

That a not insignificant element within the City merchant elite, and perhaps the company merchant community generally, had at least some sympathy with the Crown on matters of religion is further evidenced in scattered data on ministerial patronage that survives for individual traders, especially the foremost merchants. Both Hugh Hamersley and Anthony Abdy, as governor and deputy governor, respectively, of the Levant Company, had attempted, against insuperable odds, to win their company membership to the side of the Crown in the crisis of 1628–1629. And both patronized ministers closely identified with the royal government. Hamersley bequeathed a ring of remembrance to Dr. William Fuller,

[93] J. B. Pearson, *Biographical Sketches of the Chaplains to the Levant Company, 1611–1706* (London, 1883), pp. 14, 48; A. G. Matthews, *Walker Revised* (Oxford, 1948), pp. 47–48.

[94] Pearson, *Chaplains*, pp. 19–21; Matthews, *Walker Revised*, p. 24.

[95] See below, ch. 7, pp. 376–78.

vicar of St. Giles Cripplegate. As dean of Ely, Fuller was cited by the House of Commons in November 1641 for "dangerous and scandalous matters delivered by him in several sermons," and subsequently discharged from his curacy. According to a London newssheet, Fuller got into serious trouble when a supply of money and muskets to be sent to the king was found at his house. For his pains in the cause of the Caroline regime, he was appointed dean of Durham in 1646.[96] Similarly, Abdy left "remembrance of my love" to Dr. Thomas Westfield, rector of St. Bartholomew the Great and archdeacon of St. Albans. Westfield was sequestered from his positions by Parliament in 1642, but his value in the eyes of the episcopal establishment is indicated by his selection as bishop of Bristol in the very same year.[97]

Christopher Clitherow, who held the governorship of both the East India Company and the Eastland Company in this period, apparently had religious leanings similar to those of Hamersley and Abdy. This, at any rate, would be a legitimate deduction from the fact that the Arminian minister John Gore dedicated his Paul's Cross sermon of December 1635, entitled *The Oracle of God*, to Clitherow, who was lord mayor of London when it was published in 1636.[98]

The leading Levant Company merchant Thomas Bowyer represents an analogous case. Bowyer's grandfathers on both sides, Francis Bowyer and Thomas Cordell, had been London aldermen and central figures in the Elizabethan expansion; his father, Robert Bowyer, was a director of both the Levant Company and the East India Company. Bowyer bequeathed money to Thomas Lant, rector of Hornsey, and to Dr. Richard Dukeson, rector of St. Clement Dane's. The only thing about Lant that has been discovered is the fact that he was sequestered from his living sometime before 1645. Dukeson was also deprived of his position after his parishioners charged him with extorting excessive burial fees, observing ceremonies, and denying the congregation's request to allow their lecturer to preach. Dukeson was obviously a strong promoter of London royalism in the early Civil War years. He was imprisoned in 1642 for refusing to admit that he had read royalist declarations in his church, and again in 1643 for circulating a petition for peace in his parish of St. Clement Dane's and attempting to bring it to the king at Oxford. Dukeson regained his living at the Restoration.[99]

It is difficult to say precisely how far a process of identification with the

[96] PRO, will of Hugh Hamersley, 1636 PCC Pile 11; Matthews, *Walker Revised*, pp. 47–48.

[97] PRO, will of Anthony Abdy, 1640 PCC Coventry 120; Matthews, *Walker Revised*, p. 1.

[98] N. Tyacke, *Anti-Calvinists: The Rise of English Arminianism, c. 1590–1640* (Oxford, 1987), pp. 216–19, 221.

[99] PRO, will of Thomas Bowyer, 1659 PCC Pell 149: Matthews, *Walker Revised*, pp. 46, 260. For Bowyer's background, see above, ch. 2, p. 72 n. 58.

more extreme ideological tendencies in the Caroline church actually progressed within the City merchant elite, now dominated by the eastward-trading leaders. Perhaps a majority of these men were still, in religious terms, middle-of-the-road, orthodox Calvinist conformists. At least a small but important minority seems to have retained strong Puritan sympathies, giving some support to militant opponents of the Caroline religious offensive. These included such great merchant magnates as Morris Abbot, Henry Andrews (an alderman and a Levant Company and East India Company director), and James Cambell (at one time governor of the French and Stapler companies, as well as an alderman and East India Company director). Like most of their colleagues on the aldermanic bench, these merchants were already quite old in the 1630s. Much of their adulthood had been spent under the rule of King James and Archbishop Abbot, and it is perhaps to these years of comparative religious laxity and moderate Puritanism of the establishment that they owed the staunch Calvinism and apparent concern for further reformation that they retained until the end of their lives. But their Calvinism did not prevent these same men from backing the court and sometimes even Laudian church policies.

Morris Abbot was the brother of Archbishop Abbot. He was active in the Puritan proceedings that took place in the parish of St. Stephen's Coleman Street in the 1620s, and he may have lent his support to the appointment of John Davenport, later a leading émigré to New England.[100] Yet, Abbot was, as noted, from the end of the 1620s, a pivotal supporter of royal policies in the City. Henry Andrews left money for John Downham, the important Puritan lecturer at St. Bartholomew's London. But this did not stop him from supporting, in addition, Dr. Thomas Howell, rector of St. Stephen's Walbrook and of Horsley, Surrey, as well as canon of Windsor. Howell was sequestered by Parliament for delinquency and absence in 1642 and promptly appointed by the Caroline court first to the rectory of Fulham, then to the bishopric of Bristol.[101] Sir James Cambell is described in a eulogy by his clerk as one who had studied the great Calvinist divines William Perkins and Richard Greenham, and who kept his household according to their teachings. That Cambell remained in some way strongly committed to his old beliefs until his death, perhaps encouraged in this by his Dutch wife, is indicated by his bequests to one Mr. Smith, a "silenced minister," and to the Dutch and French reformed congregations of London. Cambell's Puritanism did not, however, prevent him from remaining closely in touch with the increasingly Laudian establishment. He willed £1,000 to Laud's St. Paul's rebuilding project.

[100] D. A. Kirby, "The Radicals of St. Stephen's Coleman Street, London, 1624–1642" *Guildhall Miscellany* 3 (1970): 100–101.

[101] PRO, will of Henry Andrews, 1638 PCC Lee 127; Pearl, *London*, p. 166; Matthews, *Walker Revised*, p. 1.

He also made a bequest to the cleric Dr. Richard Hall, who was sequestered from his living by Parliament.[102]

It is probable that the extremism of the Laudian establishment, its in-
tolerance of even conformist Calvinism, caused men such as Abbot, Andrews, and Cambell some qualms of conscience—and there were certainly others like them even in this topmost level of London merchant
society.[103] The point, however, is that hardly any of these moderately Puritan magistrates came close to drawing the political conclusions from
their religious beliefs that were to become so obvious to their less exalted
citizen co-religionists. Like most of the rest of their colleagues on the
aldermanic court and the East India Company board of directors, they
remained loyal to the Crown throughout the period of crisis, which began
with the imposition of ship money.

Professor Ashton doubts that the City magistrates' obedience in the case
of ship money can safely be taken as indicative of their political attitudes.
He notes that the Crown put constant pressure on the aldermen to support
and enforce its policies. He points out further that sheriffs might have
found it very costly to refuse to collect ship money (for they could be
constrained to pay uncollected dues out of their own pockets). Indeed,
there were sheriffs elsewhere in the country who also enforced ship money
but who ended up supporting Parliament. Obedience on ship money was
no certain sign of a political position favoring the court.[104]

Professor Ashton has a point. Still, it is worth noting, as he himself
points out, that the committee of aldermen originally appointed by the
aldermanic court to consider how to respond to Charles's demand for ship
money presented a report that was rejected by the common council. It
would not be the last time that the common councilors would seek to over-
ride the senior body when it failed to resist royal policies that the councilors saw as unacceptable, or the last time that the councilors would go on
to put forward a position of their own that was more oppositional than that
of the aldermen. Indeed, it was only under the prodding of the common
council that the City initially came out against ship money in 1634.[105]

Second, even in London it was not impossible for a leading officer of
the City to resist, as was shown by the example of Alderman Thomas

---

[102] PRO, will of Sir James Cambell, 1641 PCC Cambell l; Matthews, *Walker Revised*, pp. 51–
54. Pearl, *London*, pp. 294–95.

[103] See, for example, the case of the East India Company director Hugh Perry who patronized the
outstanding Puritan ministers Charles Offspring and John Downham, as well as the subsequently
sequestered ministers Jeremiah Leach of St. Mary Le Bow and John Grant of St. Bartholomew's,
(PRO, will of Hugh Perry, 1634 PCC Seager 108; Matthews, *Walker Revised*, pp. 48, 53; Pearl,
London, pp. 163, 165–66, 231).

[104] Ashton, *City and the Court*, pp. 185–88.

[105] Ibid., pp. 189–91.

Soames, who, as sheriff of London in 1638, refused to collect ship money. One would have thought, moreover, that as resistance to payment by the London citizenry became widespread toward the end of the 1630s those magistrates who really desired to make a stand against the Crown would have found it easier to do so. Whereas the City government succeeded in bringing in nearly 100 percent of its quota on the first ship money writ, by the time of the writ of 1639 the figure had fallen off disastrously. Furthermore, from the summer of 1639, when the king made new demands for men and money to fight his highly unpopular war against the Scots, many local governments throughout the country defiantly and openly ceased to collect ship money. The court of aldermen might have joined this resistance with less risk than before. Yet, even in 1640, both immediately before and even after the meeting of the Short Parliament, the City magistrates went right on with their attempts to collect.[106]

Are the actions of the aldermen to be interpreted as merely expedient, and no indication whatsoever of their real political sentiments? It is, in the end, difficult to avoid seeing a good deal of significance in the sharp contrast between the defiant, and often blatantly illegal, conduct of those elite citizens who were bent on resisting the Crown in the later 1620s and the obedient behavior of the overwhelming majority of the merchant elite at the end of the 1630s. It will be recalled that the great merchant princes Morris Abbot and William Garway led a score or so of their fellow merchant magnates in the violent customs house break-in, which was perhaps the most dramatic expression of elite merchant resistance to the Crown in 1628–1629. In 1639 and 1640, in some contrast, Abbot and William's brother Henry Garway, as successive lord mayors of London, led the crackdown against opponents of ship money in the City, as well as against other resisters of royal policy.[107] Had significant sections of the City merchant elite wished to oppose ship money (and other Crown policies) at the end of the 1630s, it is hard to believe that they could not have found a way to do so, just as they had done a decade earlier.

ABORTIVE RECONCILIATION AND A NEW OFFENSIVE

Even while they organized opposition to ship money, the aristocratic oppositionists sought one last time to come to terms with Charles I. At the death of Weston in March 1635, and with the entry of France into war with Spain not long afterward, the so-called French party at court was given a renewed chance to exert influence, after a relatively extended pe-

---

[106] M. D. Gordon, "The Collection of Ship Money in the Reign of Charles I," *T.R.H.S.*, 3d ser. 4 (1910): 159; Morrill, *Revolt of the Provinces*, pp. 28–29; P. Zagorin, *The Court and the Country* (New York, 1969), pp. 115–16.

[107] See above, ch. 5, pp. 231–32, and Pearl, *London*, pp. 187, 300.

riod in which court politics had been dominated by Weston's pacific, pro-Spanish approach. Beginning about this time, such longtime pro-French courtiers as the earl of Holland, Lord Montague, Henry Jermyn, Henry Percy, and the earl of Northumberland joined with the faction around Charles's sister Elizabeth, electress Palatine, to push for a military alliance with France so as to pursue war with Spain. Most crucially, Queen Henrietta Maria seemed to come to their support. The result was a clear opening to the colonizing aristocrats and their allies in the City.[108]

In 1635, in the wake of a powerful Spanish attack on Providence Island, as well as its sister colony Association Island, the colonizing aristocrats who led the Providence Island Company were obliged to alter their program. The company began to move in the direction of using Providence Island primarily as a base for privateering and general war against the Spanish and, in turn, for shifting their colonizing efforts to the mainland of Central America.[109] At the same time, they revived their strategy of the middle 1620s and sought to ally with anti-Spanish forces at court, in order to win Charles's support for entering into political collaboration with Parliament and for undertaking a sea war against Spain in the Caribbean. In return, the aristocratic oppositionists would have agreed not only to end resistance to ship money but to push for a substantial addition to the Crown's regular income. It looked like 1624 or 1626 all over again.

In September 1635, Salvetti, the Tuscan ambassador, was found complaining that the French ambassodor Seneterre "practices with these puritans and with the queen. . . . He always proposes new leagues . . . and . . . as a thing that would perfect all the designs of France, he tries to persuade the king, by means of the queen and puritan officials, that it would be wise to convene a Parliament, by which the king could regain the affection of his subjects and obtain a great sum of money." In October, the Venetian ambassador noted that "the greater part of the nobility" was gathering in London. "The one thing they all join in maintaining with vigor is the report that Parliament will meet soon."[110] In January 1636, the Venetian ambassador reported:

> The most ardent parliamentarians think of renewing their activities and of devoting their last efforts to induce the king, if possible, to convoke Parliament. They use many means to this end. . . . The reluctance to pay the contribution for the fleet [that is, resistance to

[108] In the paragraphs that follow, I rely heavily on R. M. Smuts, "The Puritan Followers of Henrietta Maria in the 1630s," *E.H.R.* 93 (1978). See also C. Hibbard, *Charles I and the Popish Plot* (Chapel Hill, N.C., 1983), as well as Newton, *Colonising Activities*, for similar accounts.

[109] Newton, *Colonising Activities*, pp. 186–235.

[110] BL, Add. MSS 27962 and *C.S.P. Ven. 1632–1636*, p. 466 (19 Oct. 1635), both quoted in Smuts, "Puritan Followers," p. 37.

ship money] is not placed among the least, while on the other side everything is done to show the king the necessity of being well armed at sea . . . [and] to uphold the cause of the Palatinate.[111]

During 1636, mounting pressure seemed to be having a positive effect. By October, Salvetti was reporting "a great inclination to war" within the court. At the same time, Sir Thomas Roe, the protégé of Electress Elizabeth, was politicking for a voluntary war in the West Indies to be supported through the issuance of letters of marque—a re-adaptation of the parliamentary plans for private war in 1626. By the winter of 1636–1637, the Crown had agreed to prepare a fleet to be commanded by Elizabeth's sons and used against Spanish shipping.[112]

Meanwhile, the Providence Island Company, in expectation of increasing government support, had begun to carry through its new policy. In January 1636, the king, heeding the warning of Sir John Coke that the Providence Island Company could survive only if the company took up privateering, granted the company the right to make reprisals against Spanish ships, informally sanctioning unrestricted private war. The company now made a decision to float an entirely new stock for £10,000 and by mid-1636 had collectd £4,900. Then, in pursuance of its main objective, the company provisioned three ships for a long-term privateering cruise in the West Indies, to operate from the base at Providence Island. It also removed Capt. Philip Bell as governor of Providence Island and replaced him with Capt. Robert Hunt, a godly Puritan recommended by Lord Brook from among his dependents.[113]

As the Providence Island Company was reorienting itself, the earl of Warwick and his associates were doing everything possible to come to an agreement with the Crown. In January 1637, the Venetian ambassador reported a rumor that "many of the leading men of the realm were holding secret meetings," so as to bring about "a final effort to bring the forms of government back to their former state." At just this moment Warwick led a delegation of lords before Charles to assure him that "Parliament would readily consent to supply him with all he might desire to ask of it," if Charles would declare war on Spain.[114] The colonizing oppositionists apparently were still hoping that they could win Charles's support for a settlement whereby they would relinquish their resistance to ship money if the government would seek to raise money by way of Parliament and back their own plans for an anti-Spanish war. Meanwhile, the West India Company of Holland was approaching Warwick and his partners with the

---

[111] *C.S.P. Ven. 1632–1636*, p. 500 (11 Jan. 1636), quoted in Smuts "Puritan Followers," p. 37.

[112] Smuts, "Puritan Followers," pp. 38–39; Newton, *Colonising Activities*, pp. 236–37.

[113] Newton, *Colonising Activities*, ch. 9.

[114] *C.S.P. Ven. 1636–1639*, p. 125 (16 Jan. 1637), quoted in Smuts, "Puritan Followers," p. 39.

request that the Dutch be allowed to buy their colony from them in order to use it as a base against the Spanish. Warwick was at this time discussing his plans for the Providence Island Company's private war with the French ambassador Seneterre, asking him if Cardinal Richelieu would lend financial support. By mid-March 1637, Cottington reported to the French ambassador that the king did indeed plan to lend some ships to the Providence Island Company "to make a stronger war in the Indies."[115] Finally, in the summer of 1637, the privy council appointed Sir Thomas Roe, Sir Edward Conway, and Sir Dudley Digges to a six-man committee to see about establishing a new West India Company.[116] All three of these men had been among the leading advocates of war by diversion against Spain in the Atlantic and West Indies in the mid-1620s, the first two at court, the third in Parliament. It seemed as if the old court and country anti-Spanish alliance of the mid-1620s might actually be renewed.

In the end, of course, the king did not adopt an anti-Spanish foreign policy. On the contrary, during the course of 1637 the Crown moved back firmly in the direction of a pro-Spanish perspective. The court rapidly came under the domination of militantly Catholic, pro-papal forces. Moreover, the king continued to collect ship money in the face of resistance by Warwick, Saye, Hampden, and other Providence Island oppositionists. By July 1637, riots had broken out in Edinburgh in response to Charles's ill-fated plan to impose the English prayer book on Scotland. These developments appear only to have induced the colonizing lords, in close collaboration with their friends among the new-merchant leadership, to step up radically their continuing efforts to break apart Spain's empire, once again on a solely private basis, as well as to seek ways of further resisting royal policies.[117]

In April 1638, the Providence Island Company sent out Capt. Nathaniel Butler on a mission of conquest and pillage that culminated in an attack on Truxillo in Honduras. A few months later, in June 1638, the company issued a charter of incorporation to the old Kent Island promoter William Claiborne to found a colony on Ruatan in the Bay Islands off the coast of Honduras. Claiborne's project, perhaps undertaken in collaboration with Maurice Thomson, lasted through 1642. At just about the same time, the

[115] Smuts, "Puritan Followers," p. 39; Newton, *Colonising Activities*, pp. 238–39. When the Providence Island Company contacted the earl of Holland to find out if the king would allow it to sell the colony to the Dutch, the king, apparently going along with the sentiment at court for an anti-Spanish policy, agreed to help the company.

[116] *C.S.P. Col. 1574–1660*, p. 257.

[117] Gardiner, *History* 8: 200–211, 269–80, 314–20; Newton, *Colonising Activities*, pp. 248–71. Even by May 1637, Salvetti was reporting that those who wanted an anti-Spanish war were doing all they could "to force His Majesty to take them into his service by means of a Parliament. But as this scheme is very well understood by His Majesty, there is no sign that they will succeed." Quoted in Hibbard, *Charles I and the Popish Plot*, p. 76.

Providence Island Company itself, directed at this point by Warwick, Pym, Rudyerd, and Lord Mandeville, organized a private subcompany and placed it under the leadership of Maurice Thomson, to exploit a silver mine recently discovered in the Bay of Darien. In July 1638, the company sent out another privateering mission, led by Capt. Samuel Axe. In October 1638, the earl of Warwick bought out the rights of the earl of Pembroke to Trinidad, Tobago, St. Bernard, and Barbados and, shortly thereafter, sent out several pinnaces to begin a plantation on Trinidad.[118] Meanwhile, at some point in 1638 Maurice Thomson and his partners had secured the Providence Island Company's license to send Capt. William Jackson on what turned out to be an extraordinarily successful three-year voyage of plunder throughout the Caribbean. Over this period, Thomson also took over all of the Providence Island Company's provisioning functions, and in 1640 he sent still another private voyage into the region, this time to secure camphor wood.[119] Having failed to win the government's support of their naval war against Spain, the aristocratic oppositionists, working in the closest collaboration with the top new-merchant leaders, simply began to undertake this rather major project on a private, voluntary, and piecemeal basis. It was a pattern, established in the 1620s, that would be followed, in many different spheres, throughout the next decade.

Not too surprisingly, in these years the Caroline government sought to aim its repressive policies more directly at the colonizing oppositionists and their Puritan colonial experiments. In July 1637, as part of his and Charles's general campaign for religious uniformity throughout the Crown's jurisdictions, Laud secured the abrogation of the Massachusetts Bay Company charter.[120] In April 1638, the privy council ruled that William Claiborne and his partners must hand over Kent Island to the Catholic Lord Baltimore.[121] By August 1638, moreover, the Bermuda Company had apparently come under surveillance by the government.[122] In August 1639 the company received word that the "Lord Grace of Canterbury hath been informed that a great part of [the] company in general . . . the council [in Bermuda] . . . and others here [in England] in special, are non-conformists and men opposite to the government and discipline of the Church of England." The Bermuda Company members pro-

[118] Newton, *Colonising Activities*, pp. 258–68; PRO, C.O. 124/2/357–58.

[119] PRO, C.O. 124/2/387, 389, 390; *C.S.P. Col. 1574–1660*, pp. 296, 309, 317, 318; V. T. Harlow, ed, *The Voyages of Captain William Jackson*, Camden Miscellany 13 (London, 1923), pp. v–vii; Newton, *Colonising Activities*, pp. 267–71. See also above, ch. 4, pp. 156–59.

[120] H. R. Trevor-Roper, *Archbishop Laud* (London, 1965), pp. 258–61; *C.S.P. Col. 1574–1660*, p. 256 (23 July 1637).

[121] *C.S.P. Col. 1574–1660*, pp. 167–68 (7 Apr. 1638).

[122] Ibid., p. 282 (9 Aug. 1638).

tested that they had "not been acquainted with any such complaints as are intimated in his Grace's letters," but were "altogether strangers to them."[123] As if to prove their innocence, they immediately dispatched a letter to their council in Bermuda, informing the council of Laud's charges ("notwithstanding the care which you know we have taken that the discipline of our church should be used in all churches throughout those islands"). The company ordered that conformity henceforth be enforced, and specifically ordered the use of the Book of Common Prayer, kneeling at the sacrament, using the cross at baptism, and "accustomed prayers and decent ceremony." Obviously, this message betrays a certain disingenuousness, in view of the Bermuda Company's longtime patronage of Bermuda's militantly Puritan ministers and its continuing support of their religious experiments.[124] That the company had any real intention of paying more than lip service to the privy council's strictures is hardly likely. In fact, it took no action to enforce the order. Religious reformation, indeed revolution, went on unabated in the colony.

The government's increasing threats may have provoked something of a crisis in the ranks of the colonizing opposition. It is known that, for a time at least, some of the oppositionists contemplated emigration to their Puritan colonizing bases. In January–February 1638, Lord Saye, Lord Brook, and the earl of Warwick, among other leading members of the Providence Island opposition, signified their intention to emigrate.[125] Even before this time, Owen Rowe, the trader with New England and Virginia who would soon become deputy governor of the Bermuda Company and an outstanding leader of the opposition in the City, had informed John Winthrop that he, too, was about to leave for the Americas.

> I have received yours . . . being very glad to hear of your welfare, it doth somewhat rejoice my heart when I consider and think what you enjoin: my heart is with you. I shall . . . be glad if the Lord make me a way . . . that I may come see you and behold the beauty of our God . . . I have now put off my trade, and as soon as it shall please God to send in my debts, I am for your part.[126]

Rowe never did go to New England, but he did play an important role in founding the congregationalist colony in New Haven, where he sent his son. This project was organized in Rowe's Puritan parish of St. Stephen's Coleman Street and had among its chief guiding figures the Independent

[123] *A.P.C. Col. 1613–1680*, p. 241; *C.S.P. Col. 1574–1660*, pp. 302, 303; Lefroy, *Memorials* 1: 558.

[124] Lefroy, *Memorials*, 1: 560. See also above, pp. 279–81.

[125] Newton, *Colonising Activities*, pp. 244–47.

[126] *Winthrop Papers* 2: 225–26.

divines John Davenport and Henry Whitfield.[127] One of Maurice Thomson's chief American trading partners, Thomas Stone, the ship-money resister, was Whitfield's father-in-law and remained closely in contact with him throughout the period. Stone may also have entertained the idea of going with him to New England. At any rate, for his pains in the cause of Puritan Nonconformity, Stone was in trouble by 1640 before the High Commission Court.[128]

Maurice Thomson himself and his partner William Pennoyer were also planning to emigrate, specifically to Massachusetts Bay. This was the explicit condition for a fishing patent they were granted toward the end of 1630s by the general court of the Massachusetts Bay colony. As Governor Winthrop wrote, "This [grant] was not done to encourage foreigners to set up fishing among us (for all the returns would be returned to the place where they dwelt) but to encourage our own people to set upon it, and in expectation that Mr. Thomson would ere long here settle with us."[129] A government-backed fishing industry in the colony seems to have been suggested first by the Massachusetts émigré minister Hugh Peter; it is possible that it was through the Massachusetts fishing project that Maurice Thomson first established what was to be a long-lasting and pivotal relationship in England with that radical preacher.[130]

SCOTTISH WAR

As it turned out, none of these men was compelled to emigrate. By 1638, war with the Scots had become inevitable, and the government faced its greatest crisis: it had to raise, organize, and finance an army in the face of the mounting opposition of the governing classes. Perhaps in preparation for deepening conflict, the Crown made some attempt to mend its fences with the City's leading merchants. In June 1638, the government regranted the City its charter, renewing most of those privileges it previously had challenged, at a cost to the municipality of the Irish lands plus

[127] Calder, New Haven Colony, pp. 14, 30, 55, 207, and, in general, ch. 1.

[128] E. Stone, "The Ancestry of William Stone, Governor of Maryland," New Eng. Hist. Gen. Reg. 49 (1895): 314–16. For Thomas Stone, see above, ch. 4.

[129] J. Winthrop, The History of New England, ed. J. Savage, 2 vols. (Boston, 1825–1826), 1: 307. See also Shurtleff, Records of the Governor 1: 256; W. Kellaway, The New England Company, 1649–1776 (London, 1961), pp. 58–59.

[130] J. B. Felt, Annals of Salem, 2 vols. (Boston, 1845–1849), 2: 211. Maurice's brother Robert Thomson actually did emigrate to Massachusetts during the 1630s, becoming an intimate of many of the leading figures of New England congregationalism. Robert Thomson was a beneficiary and trustee of the Connecticut founding father Edward Hopkins. He purchased the house of the aforementioned minister Henry Whitfield when Whitfield returned to England (New Eng. Hist. Gen. Reg. 38 [1884]: 315–18; J. Savage, Genealogical Dictionary of the First Settlers of New England, 4 vols. [Boston, 1860–1862], 4: 287–88; Andrews, Colonial Period 2: 141; Calder, New Haven Colony, p. 237).

£12,000. About the same time, the Crown worked out its aforementioned contract with the wine merchants by which it guaranteed them a minimum market for their imports. Shortly thereafter, in March–April 1639, the government issued a proclamation strengthening the Merchant Adventurers' charter and, apparently, granted the Adventurers' request to post their own representative at the customs to guard against interlopers. In December 1639, the Crown agreed to halt the Courteen project, and ordered the licensees to send out no further vessels except those required to bring back their property from the East.[131] Meanwhile, however, faced with rapidly intensifying financial pressures, the Crown was finding itself unable to avoid making new demands on London for loans and gifts.

Following the outbreak of the Scottish War, the Crown approached the City for money and soldiers in March 1639. The municipality initially agreed to raise the money by means of contributions from the citizens of every ward. But in the end, the City came up with the meager sum of £5,000 and failed to supply the three thousand soldiers the Crown had requested. Out of the resulting impasse, the common council took the significant step of drawing up a petition of grievances to the Crown, complaining of the multitude of patents and monopolies and the infringement of the City's right to confine the use of London's trained bands to the defense of London. Nevertheless, as Edward Rossingham reported, the City was far from united on even this relatively mild expression of opposition. "The main part of the aldermen and the moderate men of the common council were utterly against the petition, and the rather because the sum to be given [the £5,000] was contemptible." The common council majority insisted on carrying through its decision. But, "since the aldermen refused to present the money and the petition together, some of the commoners undertook it, but . . . the king . . . sent a command to that committee that they should forbear to meet upon that business for he would receive neither their £5,000 nor their petition."[132] Henceforward, when the king came to the City for help, he was careful to direct his requests exclusively to the court of aldermen and to demand that the common council be excluded from the considerations. It is, in part, the failure to distinguish (as the king did not fail to do) the political attitude of the bulk of the aldermen from that of the majority on the common council that allows Professor Ashton to conclude that nearly all of the City opposed the Crown and favored Parliament.

In April 1639, the customs farming magnate Paul Pindar raised

---

[131] R. R. Sharpe, *London and the Kingdom*, 3 vols. (London, 1894), 2: 116–17; Pearl, *London*, pp. 85–86 (City); Vintners Company, Court Book, 1629–1638, AC/3, pp. 154–67 (French merchants); P.C.2/50/170–71 (Merchant Adventurers); *C.C.M.E.I.C. 1635–1639*, pp. 351–52 (East India Company).

[132] Pearl, *London*, pp. 94–95, for quotations, and in general.

£100,000 for the Crown. Then, in June 1639, the Crown returned to the City, first with a demand for a £100,000 loan, then with a request that the aldermen raise £30,000 a month from among themselves and wealthy commoners in the City ("always provided that they did not call their common council, nor put it to the commons, which his majesty would by no means endure"). The aldermanic court replied in the negative, with fifteen aldermen refusing outright to lend. A few days earlier, when the privy council had called the aldermen and other wealthy citizens before it to discuss raising funds, only two aldermen and two sheriffs had even appeared. [133] It is somewhat difficult to interpret these acts of resistance by the aldermanic court, for among the loan refusers were such archroyalists as the Levant–East India Company magnates Sir Henry Garway, Sir Anthony Abdy, Sir Christopher Clitherow, and John Cordell, as well as Sir Richard Gurney: all of these men were leading organizers of the king's party throughout the period. In any case, this was the greatest (and only real) show of opposition by the aldermen, or any organized section of the City elite, for the entire period, through the revolution of 1640–1642. [134]

SHORT PARLIAMENT

By the end of 1639 the king was obliged to recall Parliament. Shortly thereafter, in early April 1640, in a further attempt to secure money, Charles asked the aldermen to make up lists of the richest men in their wards, "provided [as he added] that the common council not meddle in it." Even with Parliament about to sit, all but seven of the twenty-four aldermen agreed to compose their lists. However, the fact that seven refused to do so shows that opposition to the king was, at this point, hardly impossible to carry through. Indeed, in the period leading up to the meeting of Parliament, the county governing classes throughout England, especially those of the southeast, were drawing up petitions of grievances for presentation to Parliament. It would have been an ideal occasion for the City to register its dissent from royal policies from a conservative standpoint, but it is more than doubtful that it wished to do this. [135]

Neither the official City nor, for that matter, any other section of the London merchant elite made any sort of protest against Crown policies to the Short Parliament. On the contrary, the East India Company directorate indicated the political priorities of the top City merchants at this point when it quashed a proposal by some of the company's members to present a petition of economic grievances.

[133] Ibid., pp. 96–97.
[134] Ibid., pp. 97–98 and app. 1. See also below, ch. 7.
[135] Pearl, *London*, pp. 99–100; Morrill, *Revolt of the Provinces*, pp. 29–30.

During the 1630s, the East India company directors had, on several occasions, conveyed their many grievances to the king: the royally sponsored privateering venture within their privileges carried out by Cobb and Ayres in 1630, the king's backing of Courteen's interloping project, the monarchy's raising of the impositions on East India Company goods in 1635–1636, and the government's failure to win compensation from the Dutch for their attacks on the East India Company in the Far East. Nevertheless, the king had done little, concretely, to address these complaints. It was therefore natural that some of the company's members should attempt to take advantage of the convening of Parliament to seek redress.

On 17 April 1640, at a general court called by the East India Company directorate to launch the subscription for a new joint stock, several stockholders spoke up about "the wrongs and injuries committed by the Dutch, especially Amboina, for which, in spite of promises made by the King and the States, no satisfaction has been given." For these reasons, they stated, they and others would "not be persuaded to underwrite for a new stock." They proposed instead that "a petition be presented to the House of Commons, complaining of the sufferings caused by the Dutch and of the depredations of Cobb and Ayres in the Red Sea, and imploring aid and direction for reparation and satisfaction." The company's directors saw, however, that any move to take the company's case to Parliament would reflect dissatisfaction with the royal government at a time when the king's position was already weakened. The directors therefore told the general court that, on that very morning, they themselves had discussed the question of going to Parliament and had resolved to follow the advice of the City recorder Sir Thomas Gardiner, a royal appointee and one of the City's staunchest supporters of the royal government. Hardly surprisingly, Gardiner had recommended against the company's petitioning Parliament. Governor Clitherow therefore expressed "his hearty sorrow that . . . the generality will not rely on the King's gracious promises [to redress their grievances] and underwrite for a subscription sufficient to prosecute the trade," and the matter was summarily dropped. Clearly, the great City merchants who sat on the East India Company's board of directors wished to avoid taking action that might undermine the king's political position at this critical moment merely for the sake of some economic grievances.[136]

On the other hand, the king's decision to recall Parliament did open the way for an emerging London opposition, operating largely outside the official City, to make its greatest show of strength up to that time. Common hall, composed of the City's liverymen, met to choose London's four

136 For the preceding two paragraphs, see *C.C.M.E.I.C. 1640–1643*, pp. 32–33.

representatives to Parliament. The men they elected had all previously distinguished themselves in the anticourt opposition in both the 1620s and 1630s, and two of them, Matthew Craddock and Samuel Vassall, were leading representatives of the colonial merchant leadership. The careers of these two traders were not, however, typical of the new-merchant leadership as a whole. Both Craddock and Vassall had been heavily involved in the trade with the eastern Mediterranean, and both had become officers in the Levant–East India combine. Both also rose to high positions in their livery companies. However, with neither Craddock nor Vassall did commercial success in the chartered companies result in the sort of conservative approach to commercial life and politics that was so characteristic of the company merchant establishment.

Both Craddock and Vassall were leaders in American colonization from the late 1620s, deeply involved in Virginia and the West Indies, and, at one time or another, Maurice Thomson's partners. Craddock was the pre-eminent figure from the City behind the oppositionist Massachusetts Bay Company and that company's first governor, as well as one of its representatives before the privy council when the government brought quo warranto proceedings against it in 1635. He was also a leading force in the antidirectorate, anticourt faction within the East India Company. Vassall, too, was a supporter of the Massachusetts Bay Company and colony, and he also represented that company before the government. In addition, Vassall was one of the handful of outstanding leaders in the City campaigns against the Forced Loan in 1627, impositions and tonnage and poundage in 1628–1630, and ship money in the middle 1630s. Vassall's political career is neatly captured in his own account of his damages, submitted to the House of Commons on 2 December 1640, and summarized by Sir John Northcote: "Sixteen times committed, £5,000 damages. Loss of his trade, £10,000 more. His credit impaired. Total £20,000." By 1640, Craddock and Vassall had gained position and experience that were rare among the colonial-interloping merchants—a combination of longtime identification with opposition forces in the City and real prominence within the City's leading institutions. They were natural choices, therefore, for the first City-wide challenge to the court and the municipal political establishment.[137]

With the convocation of the Short Parliament, the emerging parliamentary opposition wasted little time in putting forward its program, not only for political and religious reform, but for a new approach in the sphere of colonization. In his famous speech shortly after the opening of

---

[137] Pearl, *London*, pp. 175, 185–87, 189–91. For the commercial activities of these men in partnership with Maurice Thomson and, more generally, in trades with the Americas, see above, ch. 4.

Parliament, Pym exhaustively cataloged the grievances in church and state that had piled up during the long years without Parliament, and called for their reformation.[138] At the same time, in the tradition of the anti-Spanish opposition going back to the 1620s, Pym did not, at this critical political juncture, pass up the opportunity to set forth the main points of the commercial program of the allied colonizing aristocrats and new-merchant leaders:[139] (1) he asked for lower import duties on colonial products; (2) he demanded customs-free reexports; and (3) he called for an aggressive anti-Spanish foreign policy in the West Indies that might ultimately be linked to the recovery of the Palatinate. The customs levies on the American tobacco monoculture, said Pym, were confiscatory. "The adventurers in this noble work have for the most part no other support but tobacco upon which such a heavy rate is set, that the king receives twice as much as the true value of the commodity to the owner." These excessive burdens had forced merchants to take their goods directly to the European markets, bypassing London, "but now hath been lately endeavored to set an imposition upon this trade, so that the king will have a duty even out of those commodities which never come within his dominions." Most important of all:

> The differences and discontents betwixt His Majesty and the people at home have in all likelihood diverted his royal thoughts and counsels from those great opportunities which he might have, not only to weaken the house of Austria and to restore the Palatinate, but to gain a higher pitch of power and greatness than any of his ancestors; for it is not unknown how weak, how distracted, how discontented the Spanish colonies are in the West Indies. There are now in those parts, in New England, Virginia, and the Carib Islands, and in the Bermudas, at least sixty thousand able persons of this nation, many of them well armed, and their bodies seasoned to that climate, which, with a very small charge, might be set down in some advantageous parts of these pleasant, rich, and fruitful countries, and easily make His Majesty master of all that treasure, which not only foments the war, but is the great support of popery in all parts of Christendom.

These demands had been impossible to fulfill during the 1630s because of the interlocking financial, political, and commercial requirements of Caroline absolutism. Customs could not be lowered because of the monarch's constricted financial base in a period of nonparliamentary government. A strong anti-Spanish policy was also probably impossible, simply

---

[138] Gardiner, *History* 9: 101–6.

[139] L. F. Stock, ed., *Proceedings and Debates of the British Parliaments Respecting North America*, 5 vols. (Washington, 1924), 1: 97–98.

because of its cost. From another viewpoint, peace with Spain was desirable in order to protect the lucrative, customs-bearing trades with the Mediterranean (Spain, Italy, the Levant), and, equally important, to help ensure the continuing financial and political support of that key group of mercantile magnates who were commercially involved in the Mediterranean area. But the return of Parliament transformed all these priorities.

Before any action could be taken on these colonial-commercial issues or any others, the king dissolved Parliament. But this move did little to put off the deepening national crisis or to disrupt the accelerating organization of a movement for political change on both the parliamentary and the municipal levels. Even before the meeting of the Short Parliament, the City opposition, with leadership from the new merchants, had begun to show its strength, and in some unexpected places.

In late 1639 the colonial merchant leader John Warner was elected sheriff of London and then, in March 1640, was chosen City alderman. Warner was a well-known political Puritan who worked in partnership with his brother Samuel, an interloper in the East Indian and Merchant Adventurers' trades who happened also to be the father-in-law of Maurice Thomson's brother William. The Warners ran a shop in Bucklersbury, London, from which they carried on a retail tobacco business as well as a long-distance colonial trade with the Americas. Warner's election to the aldermanic board helped the City opposition create a small but strategic fifth column within the heart of the largely royalist magistracy.[140] Warner was one of the seven aldermen who in April 1640 refused to make up lists of wealthy citizens in his ward, joining the alderman-MPs Isaac Pennington and Thomas Soames, as well as John Gayre, John Wollaston, Thomas Atkins, and Sir Nicholas Rainton.[141]

Similarly subversive forces were also at work even within the archconservative East India Company directorate. In January 1640, Matthew Craddock had raised a challenge to the directorate's program for issuing a new joint stock. Craddock reported that "many adventurers except against the government of the company." This was very likely an attempt to revive the opposition to the company leadership that had been sparked by the Puritan lords beginning in 1629. Its objective was to reform the company by limiting the power of the members of the merchant elite who dominated the directorate. Craddock's initiative was defeated by the company's directors.[142] But it was a portent, of things to come, both within the East India Company and London generally, an early crossing of swords between representatives of the merchant elite drawn largely from

[140] For the Warners, see above, ch. 4, p. 134, as well as Pearl, *London*, pp. 167, 325–27.
[141] Pearl, *London*, p. 100.
[142] *C.C.M.E.I.C. 1640–1643*, pp. 1–2.

the Levant Company and the East India Company directorate, who would form the heart of City royalism, and the new-merchant leaders, who would help lead an emergent London parliamentary movement.

Following the dissolution of the Short Parliament, City opposition forces went immediately into action. By June, citizens were circulating a petition reciting their grievances and calling for the return of Parliament. The privy council's response was to arrest for "seducing the king's people" the two men thought to be the main organizers of the petition—Samuel Vassall, the recently elected City MP, and Richard Chambers, famed for his resistance to tonnage and poundage as well as his opposition to impositions and ship money. Both had been symbols of constitutional resistance in the City since the 1620s and both were by this time closely connected with the new-merchant leadership of the colonial trades. The government's action served only to provoke heightened resistance: the Venetian ambassador referred at this juncture to "an open revolt against the government," while Salvetti reported that the court feared a popular uprising. On 11 June, common council, responding to the growing popular movement in London, refused the Crown's request to lend four thousand troops.[143]

Meanwhile, proroyal forces in the City were attempting to help the Crown shore up its finances in order to stave off the recall of Parliament. In the early summer, the customs farming syndicate—which included at least five aldermen, among them the great Levant Company merchants Anthony Abdy and John Cordell, as well as the elite Merchant Adventurer William Whitmore—lent the huge sum of £250,000. On 23 July a hybrid assembly composed of the aldermen, the sheriffs, and two leading representatives from each ward volunteered £20,000 to the king, but the government refused to accept this pittance.[144]

Then, in August, the Crown and the leading officers of the East India Company engineered the famous pepper loan, by which the Crown obtained some £50,000 in ready money through buying up the company's recently landed pepper shipment on credit and reselling it at a loss to several merchants. It has been argued that this loan/sale actually benefited both parties, since the Crown paid the price the company had stipulated and offered reasonable security.[145] Nevertheless, as Professor Ashton has explained, this argument is difficult to sustain. The Crown was allowed a significantly longer time to repay than the company had offered to its mer-

---

[143] Pearl, *London*, pp. 102, 108–9; Hibbard, *Charles I and the Popish Plot*, p. 150 (quote from Venetian ambassador).

[144] Pearl, *London*, pp. 100–101, 102.

[145] William Foster, "Charles I and the East India Company," *E.H.R.* 19 (1904); W. Foster, "Introduction" to *C.C.M.E.I.C. 1640–1643*, pp. viii–xiv; M. J. Havran, *Caroline Courtier: The Life of Lord Cottington* (London, 1973), pp. 148–49.

chant purchasers. Moreover, the Crown'a ability to repay the loan even in the time designated was quite doubtful. Third, the Crown was not required to pay interest. Finally, the security offered by the crown—tallies on the great customs and bonds by a number of private sureties—was, in view of the profound crisis of royal policy and the catastrophic condition of royal finances at this point, dubious to say the least.[146]

As it was, on 22 August 1640, two days following Charles's departure northward for his campaign against the Scots, Lord Cottingham, counting on the loyalty of the East India Company's directorate, directly approached a few of its leading officers about the loan, "representing the King's many and urgent occasions, especially against the Scotch." They, in turn, explained to their colleagues on the company's board of directors the pivotal importance of the loan to the Crown's tottering position. According to the minutes of the East India Company Court of committees for 26 August: "Mr. Governor [Christopher Clitherow] reports. . . . Their lordships [of the privy council] advised that this [pepper] business be handled very tenderly at general court, that so no affront be put to the King or the proposed securities." Appreciating the Crown's situtation, and having heard presentations favoring the loan from their governor, as well as Lord Mayor Henry Garway, the company directors quickly approved the loan and deftly pushed it through the general court in the face of some opposition from the membership.[147]

Nevertheless, by late summer 1640, the Scots once more had succeeded in pushing the Crown over the brink, and the stage was set for the kind of powerful demonstration of cooperation between the London radical citizenry and the great parliamentary magnates that was to become common over the following years. The twelve peers presented on 5 September 1640 their petition calling for the return of Parliament. This document was the work of the parliamentary opposition leadership, heavily drawn from the colonizing companies. It was written by John Pym and Oliver St. John, and its presentation to the king at York followed immediately upon a secret meeting in London of the earl of Warwick, the earl of Bedford, Bedford's son Russell, Lord Brook, Lord Saye, the earl of Essex, John Hampden, and Pym.[148]

The leaders of the London opposition obviously were in close touch with developments at the conference of magnates. As the peers delivered their petition to Charles I, citizens began circulating a parallel document in the City. The Londoners' petition was fuller than that of the peers. It expressed opposition to ship money, impositions, and monopoly patents;

---

[146] Ashton, *Crown and the Money Markets*, pp. 178–80; Ashton, *City and the Court*, pp. 140–41.
[147] *C.C.M.E.I.C. 1640–1643*, pp. 80–81, 82–83.
[148] Gardiner, *History* 9: 198–200.

protested innovations in religion; attacked the war against the Scots; and derided the "sudden calling and dissolving Parliaments without the redress of grievances."[149]

The City opposition leaders were to make the mass petition one of their favorite weapons. Their frequent resort to the London populace was no doubt one factor tending, over time, to alienate the City's company merchants who were politically conservative in the municipal context—profoundly concerned with social order and deeply attached to the City constitution—but potentially favorable to parliamentary reform at the national level. In contrast, the parliamentary leaders' supreme confidence in their ability to use the mass movement is striking. It must have been based in large part on their longtime intimate working relationships with some of the leading new merchants, as well as with some of the more radical Puritan ministers, who were leaders of the City popular forces.

Having attracted no fewer than ten thousand signatures, the citizens' petition was carried to York by Londoners with no legitimate connection to the official seats of power. Maurice Thomson and Richard Shute were the two men who presented it to the king, and both were to become major figures in the City's proparliamentary movement, especially its radical wing. They were also, of course, leading representatives of the colonial-interloping leadership. Maurice Thomson was the preeminent colonial merchant of his day, active in every developing commercial area. Interestingly enough, he never seems to have become a London citizen, but was apparently content to influence the course of political events by organizing popular pressure and popular institutions, through his direct contacts with the parliamentary aristocracy, and through holding national office in the parliamentary regime. Richard Shute's early career is obscure, but he was closely associated with Thomson throughout the period, both commercially and politically. He was probably Thomson's commercial factor, and he seems to have functioned as Thomson's representative in the political arena as well.[150]

John Venn was a third Londoner mentioned by contemporaries as instrumental in organizing the citizens' petition. The son of a yeoman family of Somerset, Venn traded in wool and silk with the west of England and Ireland. Although Venn apparently was not an active trader with the Americas, he did work with some of the members of the colonial-interloping merchant leadership in the founding of the Massachusetts Bay Com-

---

[149] Pearl, *London*, pp. 174–75.

[150] For Shute's commercial position and activities, see W. J. Harvey, ed., *List of the Principal Inhabitants of the City of London, 1640. From Returns Made by the Aldermen of the Several Wards* (London, 1886), p. 14, as well as, for example, PRO, S.P.46/101/274–77; PRO, H.C.A.24/109/154. The latter documents concern Shute's partnership in the trades with the Americas with Samuel Vassall, Richard Cranley, and others during the late 1640s.

pany and in the defense of that company against the government's quo warranto proceedings against it. Moreover, he remained in close touch with the Massachusetts Bay Colony during the 1640s, especially through correspondence with John Winthrop. A Puritan militant in his parish of All-Hallows Bread Street, Venn, like Maurice Thomson and Richard Shute, would be prominent in many similar militant mass actions by the London citizenry over the following decade.[151]

The citizens' mass petition, while hardly radical, failed to win the approval of the municipality. On 22 September 1640, the court of aldermen condemned the petition. A few days earlier, Lord Mayor Henry Garway had refused even to accept the petition or to present it to Parliament.[152] This response by the official municipality was essentially the same one it had given to the common council's petition of grievances a year and a half earlier. If, as Professor Ashton thinks, the aldermen were essentially pro-Parliament, though politically conservative, it is hard to understand why they refused either to support this effort, which did not go beyond protesting the worst abuses of Charles I's unparliamentary rule, or to frame a parallel protest of their own. Given their enormous political influence in London, they could have played a powerful role in creating a politically moderate, yet proparliamentary, party in London, had they actually desired to do so. The fact is, however, that no significant section of the City elite, at any time during the struggle, would lend its open and explicit support to the parliamentary cause. Not only did elite merchants fail, as described, to protest royal policies in the crises of the spring and the fall of 1640—i.e., in the periods immediately leading up to the Short Parliament and just before the Long Parliament when they could presumably have taken action with little fear of reprisal. They would also refuse to support parliamentary reform at any time during the period of the parliamentary legislative revolution between November 1640 and the summer of 1641. All proparliamentary initiatives in London throughout the period had to come from outside the official municipality.

The refusal of the City's merchant political elite to break from the Crown and to back Parliament was fraught with political implications. First, it meant that most of the chief leaders of London's merchant community were unavailable to Parliament. Parliament's ability during the later 1620s to attract the support of key merchant magnates, it will be remembered, had been a critical source of strength for London's parliamentary opposition. Second, it meant that to back Parliament successfully in London, it would be necessary, to some extent, to attack the City government,

[151] Pearl, *London*, pp. 175, 187–89.
[152] Ibid., pp. 113, 174.

for the aldermanic court was, of course, the legitimate seat of authority in London. Third, it meant that Parliament could not simply count on London's support: it had to search the City for allies and forge alliances. All this naturally had enormous consequences for the political actions and alignments of the community of overseas traders.

The overriding result was that those overseas company merchants who might have wished to support Parliament and national reform, but from a generally conservative political standpoint, found it difficult to do so. On the one hand, they would have had to resist the pressures emanating from the merchant elite to remain loyal to the Crown, despite the fact that the elite merchants were their relatives and longtime friends and their accustomed leaders in both commercial and political affairs. On the other hand, they would have had to find a way to ally with radical citizens of lower rank in support of Parliament, while at the same time opposing those citizens' extremist political and religious projects. This would have been no easy path to follow.

At the same time, the merchant elite's loyalty to the Crown obviously offered a large political opening to the mass of proparliamentary citizens from outside and below the ranks of the company merchants, above all the new-merchant leadership. Parliament had little choice but to work with these citizens if it wished to avail itself of London's enormous resources, both financial and political. Moreover, because the official City refused to support Parliament, the London parliamentary movement found an immediate justification for carrying out a powerful attack, not only on individual proroyal magistrates, but on the whole structure of authority in the City. From the start, the militant citizens were able to combine steadfast support for Parliament with a powerful assault on the City constitution. They would be hard to resist.

Merchants and Revolution

THE POLITICAL activities and alignments of London's merchant community both expressed and helped determine the character of City and national conflict in the period leading up to the outbreak of the Civil War. From November 1640, London politics and national politics became ever more inextricably intertwined, and overseas merchants played key roles at both levels. Nevertheless, the struggles in Parliament and the City, though forming a unified whole, were not entirely analogous; at each level different types of men fought different sorts of opponents for different goals. In Parliament, men long accustomed to rule headed an opposition to the Crown that into the summer of 1641 had the support of a strong majority of the English landed classes. They sought through parliamentary legislation and through representation on the king's council to ensure powers and privileges that they felt to be theirs by custom, but to be endangered by an innovating monarchical authority. In London, in contrast, citizens largely excluded from the centers of governmental authority provided much of the leadership of the parliamentary movement from its inception. They aimed not only to secure proparliamentary reform, but also to radically alter the City's constitution and to reform the church root and branch. They were opposed from the first by the City's governing elite and, as time went on, by increasing numbers of substantial citizens who sought to defend the City's oligarchic government.

Civil war became inevitable when City and parliamentary conflicts became fully merged through the consolidation of alliances between the City radical movement and the opposition in Parliament, on the one hand, and the City conservative movement and the Crown, on the other. These alignments did not take place spontaneously or immediately but only through complex and extended disputes in which fundamental interests were clarified, while certain strategic options were foreclosed. In these processes the City merchant elite, based heavily on the Levant–East India combine, and the new-merchant leadership stood at opposite political poles and played key organizing roles.

Representatives of the merchant elite were, of course, at the core of proroyal forces in London from the return of Parliament in 1640. But a City royalist movement was fully consolidated only from the second half of 1641. It came to include both longtime supporters of the court and former backers of antiabsolutist reform who chose to ally with the Crown in order to oppose the increasingly radical aspirations of a London popular movement led by nonmerchant citizens and tied ever more closely to the opposition in Parliament. An overwhelming majority of company merchants ultimately fell into one of these two allied political categories. But it is difficult to be sure how they were distributed between them—specifically, to determine at what point in time each ultimately royalist merchant definitively came to identify with the Crown—because surviving evidence on the political orientation of large numbers of citizens is available only for the period beginning in July 1641. By this time the separation between ex-supporters of Parliament from a conservative political position and outright backers of the court had been largely superseded by the rise of a movement in the City devoted to the maintenance of the established sociopolitical order and tied to the king. This is a problem to which I will return. In any case, through the course of the struggle for power in London that took place during the autumn and winter of 1641–1642, the overseas company merchants were overwhelmingly royalist and formed the core of the proroyal forces in the City. The defection of the company merchants from their position of the later 1620s of overwhelming support for the parliamentary opposition was one of the main factors determining the course of political conflict in London and nationally in the period leading up to the outbreak of the Civil War.

In much the same way that the merchant elite derived to a large degree from the Levant–East India trades, stood at the center of London conservatism, providing the key political links between the emerging City and national royalist movements, the traders of the colonial-interloping leadership stood at the head of the City popular movement and played a critical role in connecting that movement to the national parliamentary opposition. The new merchants' continuing intimate ties with London's domestic trading community (from which many of them had come) put them closely in touch with a City parliamentary movement that was overwhelmingly composed of nonmerchants. Meanwhile, their activities in the colonial field gave them pivotal links with those Puritan colonizing aristocrats who constituted a key component of the national parliamentary leadership. Although the parliamentary movements at the City and national levels differed significantly in their ultimate goals, they were able to work closely together during the opening phases of the revolution, and the new-merchant leadership was instrumental in making this possible.

It was thus a coordinated, City-parliamentary opposition movement that struggled against Charles I and the conservative municipal authorities in 1640–1642. In these conflicts, the leading role of the new merchants and the colonizing aristocrats was evident at every important turning point. During the period from November 1640 through the summer of 1641, these groups gave one another mutual support in moving toward the reform of the monarchy and the alteration of traditional constitutional practices in the City. Ultimately, from November 1641 onward, they worked together toward City and national revolution: parliamentary control over the king's councilors and the army; the destruction of the aldermanic oligarchy and the elevation of the common council to a dominant decision-making role within the City government; and the root and branch Puritan reformation of the church.

Over the same period, these same two groups also moved together toward the fulfillment of objectives in the colonizing field that had long been frustrated by the monarchy's pacific, cost-conscious foreign policy. It would be absurd to argue that these groups provoked revolution and civil war simply to achieve their commercial-colonial aims. Nevertheless, as has been emphasized, since the early 1620s the colonizing aristocratic leadership had viewed the assault against Spain's fleet and its West Indian colonies as integrally tied to the general struggle for the fundamentally important "Protestant Cause"—a foreign policy of alliance with Protestant states against the papal Antichrist represented by Spain, especially to recover the Palatinate, which was closely linked to a domestic policy of suppressing English Catholics. The centrality of the anti-Spanish struggle had only become more salient for the colonizing aristocrats during the late 1620s and the 1630s, as the Caroline government combined a pro-Spanish foreign policy with fiercely anti-Calvinist religious courses, the open toleration of Catholics, a disdain for the rights of subjects, and, at last, the dispensing with parliamentary institutions. When, in the latter part of the 1630s, the Caroline government showed its willingness to enter into regular diplomatic relations with the papacy, to countenance the increasingly open practice of Catholicism at court, not only by foreigners around the queen but by leading English aristocrats, and, finally, in 1639–1640, to seek aid from Spain against its domestic opponents, while threatening them with Strafford's papist army in Ireland, it confirmed the deepening conviction of the aristocratic colonizing oppositionists that the struggle against Spain and popery was fundamental to the struggle for the rights of the subject and in defense of Protestant religion.[1]

By 1640, then, the emergent parliamentary leadership, headed by Pym and notably supported by the leading figures from among the colonizing lords and gentry, considered the reform of the monarchy inseparable from the reform of a church that had both promoted Charles's personal, non-parliamentary rule and subverted Calvinist religion. They conceptualized their cause as, fundamentally, a struggle against an international popish

[1] C. Hibbard, *Charles I and the Popish Plot* (Chapel Hill, N.C., 1983).

conspiracy, associated domestically with arbitrary government in church and state and the semi-Catholicizing of religion (Arminianism) and internationally with Spanish hegemony. In the eyes of the colonizing aristocratic opposition and their new-merchant allies, the plan for an attack on Spain's Atlantic fleet and its West Indian colonies formed an indispensable element within an overall program for politico-Protestant reform. They never, even for a moment, lost sight of its importance, and they brought it to the fore at each successive stage of the developing struggle.

Parliamentary Reform, the Rise of
City Radicalism, and the Colonial Offensive

Between November 1640 and July 1641, the greater landed classes represented in Parliament carried out what amounted to a legislative revolution. The parliamentary legislation of 1640–1641 was precise in its accomplishments. It destroyed the most potent instruments of judicial, financial, and administrative absolutism and formally established Parliament as a regular, permanent, and self-sustaining institution of government. Had this legislation taken effect, it would have radically reduced the king's freedom to act without the direct cooperation of the greater landed classes; nevertheless, its authors pretended to avoid any direct attack on royal authority or the institution of monarchy itself. In the minds of its supporters, who included a strong majority of the nobles and gentry represented in Parliament, the thrust of this legislation was fundamentally conservative: to root out abusive innovations imposed by the monarchical government in order to restore the traditional forms of shared authority between Crown and Parliament. At first, relatively few in Parliament thought of formal constitutional controls over the king's council or his army. The strong majority sought to consolidate and enforce their legislation simply through having the king accept their parliamentary leaders as his primary councilors. The cry of "evil councilors" was a true reflection of their own understanding of the nature of the problem, as well as of their self-imposed boundaries of reform.

In some contrast, as early as the fall of 1640 the parliamentary movement in London was beginning to assume a more explicitly innovative and radical character. This evolution in London toward greater radicalization was, from one standpoint, simply a natural response to the extreme separation of most of the citizenry from the City's profoundly oligarchic political and ecclesiastical institutions. The result was that, even by 1640, the opposition movements located in Parliament and London were voicing divergent aspirations, in large part in consequence of the different positions occupied by their constituents in relation to the sources of political and ecclesiastical authority.

In the countryside, two centuries of sociopolitical transformation had left local political and ecclesiastical institutions strongly under the influence of the greater landed classes, while endowing national representative institutions with a pivotal, if ultimately ambiguous, place in national governance. Through Parliament, the county commissions and militias, and parish church patronage, the greater landed classes already had a firm grip on the basic institutional mechanisms they needed for the assertion of their political and religious domination. All that was necessary for the full realization of their potential power was to put an end to the limitations on these mechanisms that were set by overarching centralized hierarchies in church and state. Once the encrustation of (relatively little developed) independent monarchical and episcopal administration had been torn away, or at least brought under control, the powerful aristocratic structures of governance that had grown up beneath it could function unimpeded. The parliamentary opposition did not consciously seek sovereignty, let alone the destruction of monarchy or episcopacy in what it considered to be their purified or moderated forms; in fact it was committed to both as authoritarian symbols and safeguards of the established social order. Only a tiny handful of MPs were republicans, and an overwhelming majority were opposed to tampering with the church beyond eliminating the innovative abuses of the Caroline regime—Arminianism and Laudianism, the incursion of bishops into national politics (including the settlement of religion, which they saw as a parliamentary prerogative), and the encroachment of the ecclesiastical courts into secular affairs.

The situation in London, in contrast, seemed to lead more directly and naturally toward revolutionary alternatives. The City government's bicameral aldermanic court–common council structure, headed by the lord mayor who was assisted by two City sheriffs, was analogous in form to the national governing structure, but it was quite different in substance. Despite the constitutional tradition by which the court of common council—composed of some 237 citizens elected (theoretically) by all the City's freemen—"claimed to make by-laws independently of any other power in the kingdom," the largely self-recruited and intensely oligarchic twenty-six-man court of aldermen, along with the lord mayor, actually dominated City government. The common council could not convene unless it was called by the lord mayor, who also had the right to dissolve it. The aldermanic court had veto power over common council rulings, and the aldermen even claimed the right to set common council agendas. The aldermen sat more or less continuously, while the common council rarely met more than five or six times a year, sometimes only twice. As a result, with relatively rare exceptions, the aldermanic court ran London.[2] The common council's place within City governance simply was not comparable to that of the House of Commons on the national level.

The institutions of ecclesiastical authority were even more cut off from the control of the citizens than were the institutions of secular authority—and more directly tied to the royal and episcopal hierarchies. The Crown and the bishops between them held patronage rights over more than two-thirds of the parishes; lay impropriators, including the City government and City companies, controlled appointments for most of the rest. The parishioners themselves had the right to select their own minister in only six parishes. At least within the City's official church structure, there was no analogy to that local control exercised by the landed classes that did so much to mitigate the impact of the episcopal hierarchy in the counties.[3]

RADICAL ELECTORAL INITIATIVES

If a tendency to strive for religio-political revolution was thus, in a general sense, inherent in a City parliamentary movement composed mainly of citizens largely cut off from effective participation in secular and ecclesiastical government, that movement's radicalization actually took place primarily as a practical response to the problem of giving support to Parliament's drive for reform in the face of the hostility of the aldermanic court. The court of aldermen's strong allegiance to the Crown forced the City's supporters of Parliament to go outside the official structure of government, and ultimately to attack the municipality's very principles of organization.

While the twenty-six-man aldermanic court, acting as a nearly solid block, had taken responsibility for enforcing royal policy throughout the entire period between 1625 and 1640, the court of common council had provided a more favorable terrain for expressing popular protest and organizing the parliamentary opposition. The common council's precise political makeup in the period before 1642 is difficult to decipher because of the rarity of its meetings and problems in ascertaining its membership. But Dr. Valerie Pearl's statement that the common council "appears to have had little sympathy with Pym and the parliamentary opposition" probably implies more willingness to go along with the aldermen in support of royal policies than was present in this body. As Dr. Pearl herself points out, the common council did express strong opposition to royal policies in the crisis of 1639–1640, and this recalcitrance in the face of

[2] V. Pearl, *London and the Outbreak of the Puritan Revolution: City Government and National Politics, 1625–1643* (Oxford, 1961), pp. 57–64.

[3] D. A. Williams, "London Puritanism: The Parish of St. Stephen's Coleman Street," *Church Quarterly Review* 160 (1959): 464–65.

royal command was quite evident to the royal government, which consistently warned the City authorities to leave the common council out of any consultation concerning City efforts, financial or otherwise, designed to help the king.[4] At least eight out of the twelve common councilors who were to serve on the committee of safety that would lead the City revolution starting in January 1642 already held common council seats in 1640–1641.[5] Moreover, about 40 percent of those common councilors who sat on the City's court of requests in 1640–1641 and who can be politically identified ultimately allied themselves with Parliament; that is, roughly twenty-four were proparliamentary and about thirty-four were royalist. The eighteen-man court of requests was chosen monthly by statute from among the common councilors and may perhaps be taken as representative of the common councilors.[6]

Still, to assert that the common council contained a relatively large number of members who opposed the royal court is in no way to argue that this body could become a primary focus for opposition activity. The common council was de jure and de facto unable to act independently of the court of aldermen, which remained the seat of City authority. In consequence, the parliamentary movement in London was forced to base its operations almost entirely outside the City governing structure, to challenge City customs, and, finally, to carry out a constitutional revolution. Before that revolution took place in December–January 1641–1642, the only official City-wide governmental institution that offered the parliamentary movement the potential of an effective political base inside the City itself was common hall, the electoral body composed of all of London's freemen.[7]

On 28 September 1640, common hall met for the annual election of the lord mayor. According to City custom, the citizens were obliged to nominate the senior alderman, and in this case the candidate should have been Sir William Acton, a staunch supporter of the court who was infamous for his refusal in 1629, while City sheriff, to grant a replevin to the

---

[4] Pearl, *London*, pp. 114–15. See above, ch. 6, pp. 305–6.

[5] Randall Mainwaring, Francis Peck, Stephen Estwicke, John Fowke, Nathan Wright, James Bunce, Samuel Warner, William Gibbs. The four others were William Barkeley, Owen Rowe, Alexander Normington, and James Russell. For the London Committee of Safety of January 1642, see below, pp. 370–71.

[6] The membership of the court of requests can be reconstructed from the repertories of the aldermanic court in the Corporation of London Record Office. Every month, eighteen men were chosen to compose the court of requests for that month, and their names were recorded in the aldermanic repertories. The fifty-eight men whose political affiliation has been established (on the basis of various sources listed in the notes to this chapter) obviously compose only a "sample" of the total number of individuals who sat on the court of requests in the twenty-four months between January 1640 and December 1641, but not an insignificant sample.

[7] Pearl, *London*, pp. 51–53, 110ff.

merchants imprisoned by the Crown for refusing to pay tonnage and poundage. But common hall refused to put Acton forward. The citizens nominated instead Alderman Thomas Soames, a Levant Company merchant famed for his refusal in 1638, when sheriff, to enforce ship money, and Alderman John Gayre, who (like Soames) was a Levant Company merchant who had been imprisoned the previous May for failing to submit the names of the citizens in his ward with the resources to pay the government's forced loan. Common hall's insubordination naturally caused extreme consternation in court circles. The crisis was ultimately resolved through the selection of a third candidate approved by both sides. But the citizens had shown their power, and had begun to assume the initiative.[8]

Not long after the election of the lord mayor, the citizens in common hall elected to the upcoming Parliament the same four oppositionist MPs they had chosen the previous spring for the Short Parliament. These included not only the new-merchant leaders and longtime City oppositionists Matthew Craddock and Samuel Vassall, but also the key Puritan leader Isaac Pennington. Pennington, a minor Levant Company trader and London brewer, was not apparently active in the trades with the Americas or an outstanding militant in the parliamentary opposition in its early phases. Nevertheless, he was soon to emerge as perhaps the foremost leader of London's parliamentary movement, no doubt partly by virtue of the intimate ties he had established with both colonizing aristocrats and the new-merchant leaders. From the late 1620s, Pennington played a prominent part in the Calvinist cause and, apparently in this way, forged connections with the aristocratic colonizing opposition. Pennington was a strong supporter of the London ministers' project for raising money for clerical refugees from the Palatinate in 1627 and, at about the same time, made clear his belief in the indispensability of Protestant war against Spain. As he wrote to his cousin Capt. John Pennington, "I pray God incline the heart of the King to yield that which may further God's glory . . . and tend to the reformation of that which is amiss, that so we may live and enjoy peace and prosperity under him. I mean peace with all the world but war with Spain for I am confident that we shall never have peace with them but to our prejudice." During the 1630s, Pennington was active in the militantly Puritan London parish of St. Stephen's Coleman Street, where the Independent John Davenport and the soon-to-be Independent John Goodwin were successively ministers. It may have been through Goodwin that Pennington established ties with John Hampden and John Pym. In any case, by 1640 Pennington was, in Clarendon's words, "a man in the highest confidence of the party," working closely

___

[8] Ibid., pp. 110–12.

with the parliamentary leadership. By this time Pennington also had almost certainly built substantial links with the new-merchant leadership,
in part through his kinsman Randall Mainwaring, a relative of Matthew
Craddock and a leading trader with the Americas. Mainwaring would
serve as Pennington's right-hand man in numerous radical initiatives
throughout the following decade.[9]

The election of the four oppositionist London MPs turned out to have
enormous significance. Over the following months, the court of aldermen
refused to support parliamentary reform in any way and was obliged to
abdicate its traditional role of representing the City in national politics.
The East India Company directorate similarly refused to break with
Charles. With the City's traditional political elite thus immobilized, the
City's four oppositionist MPs were able to take over the part of mediators
between London and Parliament. In collaboration with the rising mass
movement in the City, they were able to make sure that the City's enormous financial and political resources were mobilized behind Pym and
against the royal government in the first period of legislative revolution.[10]

THE ROOT AND BRANCH PETITION

With the assembling of Parliament in early November, the London citizens, fresh from their first partial victory in revising City political institutions, wasted little time in forwarding plans for radical change in the
realm of religion. During the years of Charles's rule, the government's
close control over local ecclesiastical institutions had made it essentially
impossible to implement even moderate reform within the official parish
structures. Puritan counterstructures offered the only viable alternative.
Reformation was therefore pursued through the foundation of lectureships
and the endowment of sermons by godly citizens; less respectably it was
carried on through an underground network of illegal sectarian congregations; or, most desperately, it proceeded through the support of overseas
havens for Puritan émigrés. None of these approaches could be entirely
satisfactory—although at times the construction of something like an alternative system of City lectureships appeared to offer a way out—and
during the darkest days of the Laudian period all became more difficult to
implement.

As soon as political breakdown in 1640 offered the opportunity, the
London citizens were ready to push forward their demands for greater
control of their own religious life. From the parishes came petitions de-

---

[9] Ibid., pp. 176–84, 191–93. For Pennington's relationship with Mainwaring, see e.g., below,
p. 373.

[10] Pearl, *London*, pp. 113–19.

manding parliamentary sanction for all sorts of changes in church practice, government, and personnel. Most strikingly, on 11 December 1640, an impressive contingent of respected and well-to-do citizens, numbering perhaps seventy-five, carried into Parliament a petition calling for the abolition of episcopacy "root and branch," signed by some fifteen to twenty thousand Londoners. Alderman Pennington presented it to the House. Within the Puritan movement in London there was no unanimity on what type of religious settlement should be instituted. But most were agreed that the destruction of bishops and the hierarchy they dominated was a necessary precondition for any true reformation. In 1640–1641, such a proposal could have won the support of only a small minority of the greater landed classes who dominated the opposition to the Crown. For this reason the parliamentary leaders had tried to get their citizen supporters to hold back on the root and branch petition, so as to avoid provoking division in Parliament. They were unsuccessful, and differences on the nature of the required religious reformation became a serious source of conflict between the movement in Parliament and that in the City.[11]

ANTI-SPANISH INITIATIVES

The new merchants and colonizing aristocrats in the City and parliamentary opposition never lost sight of their commercial aims, even for a moment. Shortly after Parliament reconvened, they took the initial steps to have put into practice the long-neglected, long-desired program for aggression against Spain in the Caribbean that Pym had raised again in the Short Parliament. On 11 December 1640, "divers merchants and citizens of London" active in the trades with the Americas petitioned Parliament to send down a favorable ruling in the case of the tobacco merchant Joseph Hawes, who had suffered the loss of some £12,000 in a trading voyage to Virginia when the ship he had hired was captured by the Spanish West Indian fleet. Hawes was one of the great colonial merchants of the day, the major figure in a pivotally important partnership that included his brother Nathaniel Hawes and his brothers-in-law Capt. George Payne and Randall Mainwaring. Mainwaring, as just noted, was a relative and close collaborator of both Matthew Craddock and Isaac Pennington, and was at this time becoming a key figure in both the trade with the Americas and the City opposition. Hawes had attempted to recover his loss by extracting reprisals from a captured Spanish ship brought from Bermuda into an English port, but had been prevented from doing so by the suc-

[11] Pearl, *London*, pp. 211–13; B. Manning, *The English People and the English Revolution* (London, 1976), p. 5.

cessful intervention with the English court of Roger Kilvert, a Spanish agent. According to the petitioners, "By these and like practices the English merchants are much discouraged and disabled in their trading, whilst the Spanish boldly surpriseth them, and they are ruined one after another abroad and want redress at home." They therefore requested that Parliament rule so as to "encourage the petitioners to continue their trade to America."[12]

The threat of Spanish attack had long been a stumbling block to the development of American commerce. Maurice Thomson and his partners had lost an enormous boatload of tobacco to the Spanish not long before Hawes's loss, and many other merchants had suffered the same fate at the hands of either the Spanish or the Dunkirk privateers. Both St. Kitts and Nevis were temporarily lost to Spain in 1629. The Providence Island Company itself had sustained a great setback when Spain captured its island of Association in 1635. The military defense of commercial enterprise in the Americas was clearly a top priority for the colonial entrepreneurs, both aristocrats and merchants.

As a symbol of the Caroline government's capitulation to Spain and of its betrayal of the Elizabethan heritage, Hawes's case called forth an impressive show of concern by the merchants and gentry behind the colonial projects. The new-merchant leadership organized the petition in favor of Hawes, and the petition's signers included most of the top colonial traders of the pre–Civil War period. In addition to Hawes's partners and brothers-in-law Randall Mainwaring and Capt. George Payne (who would pursue the case in Parliament over the following decade), the petitioners included Maurice Thomson, Maurice's brother-in-law William Tucker, Maurice's brothers George, Robert, and William Thomson, William Thomson's father-in-law Samuel Warner, and Samuel's brother John Warner; the Berkeley Hundred purchaser Thomas Deacon; the Martin's Brandon purchasers and longtime partners, the brothers-in-law John Sadler and Richard Quiney; the Kent Island promoter Simon Turgis, who was also a partner of Sadler and Quiney; the trader with Canada William Barkeley and his partner Timothy Felton; Thomas Frere, who was a collaborator of Maurice Thomson's and William Pennoyer's in Capt. Wil-

---

[12] House of Lords MSS, 11 December 1640. Hawes's case can be followed in L. F. Stock, ed., *Proceedings and Debates of the British Parliaments Respecting North America*, 5 vols. (Washington, 1924), 1: 101, 105, 106, 114–16, 198–200, 208, 211, 212, 214, 268, 287. See also House of Lords MSS, 11 June 1641, for a summary of the affair up to that point. For the case's progress into the late 1640s, see the history in "The Humble Petition of Randolph (Randall) Mainwaring, Nathaniel Hawes, George Payne, and Company," PRO, S.P. 16/49/66. For Hawes's partners—his brother Nathaniel and his brothers-in-law Randall Mainwaring and Capt. George Payne—see above, ch. 4, p. 138.

liam Jackson's marauding venture in Central America; and forty other colonial traders.[13]

The broad support for Hawes's petition shows that the new-merchant leaders could organize the mass of colonial traders around their common commercial interests, at the same time that they were helping to build the London parliamentary movement. Many of the petition's signers were already active—or soon to be active—alongside one another in the London popular movement. It is particularly worth noting, in this respect, that among the traders who signed the pro-Hawes petition was the outstanding parliamentary oppositionist Richard Chambers, famed for his unyielding resistance to the Crown on tonnage and poundage, ship money, and a host of other issues. The new-merchant leaders do not appear to have worked previously with Chambers, who was active in the Levantine trade. But their ability, in ways such as this, to continually broaden their circle of collaborators was one important key to their growing influence.[14] It was another sign of the times that the new merchants' petition supporting Hawes was brought into Parliament and presented to the House of Commons by none other than John Pym.[15]

At the same time that the parliamentary leaders were moving to help themselves and their merchant collaborators by beginning to implement a more militant policy toward Spain in the Americas, they were taking action on another grievance that Pym had raised in his speech to the Short Parliament, that of the customs in general, and the tobacco imposition in particular. On 11 November 1640, in response to another petition by Joseph Hawes, Parliament granted a stay of all extents (seizures) on bonds given by merchants to the customs farmers for the custom and impost on tobacco.[16] The order resulting from Hawes's petition was almost as good as a declaration that debts by merchants to the customs farmers arising from failure to pay their customs immediately would now be void. It opened the way for a series of actions against the customs farmers by new-

[13] For all these men, see above, ch. 4. The other signers included Maximillian Bard, John Barker, Raphe Barrett, John Bewley, Lawrence Brinley, Richard Brooke, Jeremy Browne, Peter Carmon, Richard Chambers, Raphe Childe, John Cocke, Robert Collines, Christopher Emerson, Humphrey Farley, Richard Finch, John Griffeth, Thomas Grindon, Richard Handson, T. Harrison, Jonathan Hervy, Thomas Hollum, Richard Hunt, Edward Hurd, Samuel Ironside, Samuel Leigh, Samuel Moyer, Thomas Norwood, Edmund Peisley, Philippe Perry, Henry Sanders, Richard Wake, Richard Waring, Edward Watkin, Thomas Watty, Will Webster, Richard Weston, William Whiting, Robert Winch, Anthony Wither, and [?] Thomson.

[14] In this respect, note that the merchant Samuel Moyer, another key figure, who was at this time linking up with the new-merchant leadership on both London political and colonial-interloping projects, also signed the pro-Hawes petition. For Moyer, see above, ch. 4, pp. 175, 178, 179.

[15] Stock, Proceedings and Debates 1: 30.

[16] "The State of the Case Concerning Customes of Tobaccoe," House of Lords MSS, 1641; H.M.C., Fourth Report, Appendix, p. 112.

merchant leaders who had long been waging an overt and covert war on the whole system of taxation on their trades. Although there is no way of assessing the extent of smuggling, it is known that such leading colonial merchants as Maurice Thomson, Edward Thomson, William Tucker, Jeremy Blackman, Samuel Vassall, and Vassall's brother-in-law Peter Andrews were all cited before governmental bodies for customs evasion at various points in the 1630s. The return of Parliament gave men such as these the opportunity to carry their fight into the open.

Shortly thereafter, the merchants trading with the Americas and their friends in the Commons made a coordinated effort to get Parliament to take more formal action against the tobacco imposition. On 6 January 1641, Oliver St. John, the famed ship-money protester who was also a Providence Island patentee and now a leading collaborator of Pym's, "moved that he had a petition of great moment to prefer" from the "merchants, shipowners, planters and adventurers to America," which "concerned the good and welfare of all the plantations in America," and wherein "was set forth what cruel exactions the customers demanded and took of such as went into any of those plantations or came from them . . . compelling such as went to enter into great bonds so to bring their goods; with divers other great extortions and oppressions." St. John "did further explain those exactions and oppressions," but the petition was sent to committee and did not reemerge until the following summer.[17]

Meanwhile, on 25 January 1641, the tobacco merchant Samuel Warner, brother of the new-merchant alderman John Warner and father-in-law of Maurice's brother William Thomson, called on Parliament to go a bit further than it had for Hawes, and force the customs farmers to hand over goods of Warner's they already had seized for his failure to make good on his bonds. Parliament responded favorably to Warner's plea, ordering the release of his goods, but a counterpetition by the customs farmers forced a more extended debate on the matter. The customs farmers rested their case on the strict formalities of the law. They were officially in charge of collecting the customs and therefore had the right to demand that the merchants pay their bonds and, if they refused, to seize their goods directly in lieu of payment. Warner, now together with Joseph Hawes (who also had had his tobacco taken by the customs farmers), responded by attacking the very legality of the duty. The custom and impost on Virginian and West Indian tobacco, said Warner and Hawes, at 4d. a pound and 6d. a pound respectively, were at the same level that they had been in the time of James I, when the price of tobacco had been ten times higher, and now amounted to more than the retail price of the tobacco. The constitutional customs rate was 5 percent ad valorem; the book of rates

[17] Stock, *Proceedings and Debates* 1: 103–4. See also below, p. 349.

and the tobacco imposition derived from it were thus, in their view, clearly illegal.[18]

It seems as if Hawes and Warner won their argument, if not a final resolution of the whole issue. Warner's goods were ordered released on 2 February 1641. On the same day, in a very similar case, Parliament ordered the customers to show cause why they should not release the goods of the new-merchant leader and MP Samuel Vassall, who had been one of the leaders of the constitutional struggle against the currants imposition and tonnage and poundage during the late 1620s. A month later, the House of Commons passed a similar ruling on the petition of the new merchants and colonizing aristocrats of the Somers Island (Bermuda) Company, thus bringing to fruition a protest launched by John Pym as long before as the Parliament of 1628.[19]

Finance, the Scots, and Strafford

During the winter and spring of 1640–1641, Parliament began the process of reform, and the City MPs and the London citizens were crucial in making this possible. Practically from the point of the meeting of Parliament, the London MPs, led by the militant oppositionist alderman Isaac Pennington, set themselves up as the main mediators between Parliament and the City on the question of City advances to Parliament. Massive amounts of money were needed to pay the Scottish army still encamped at the border. The City MPs' control over loans from London allowed the parliamentary leadership headed by Pym to raise enough money to make Parliament indispensable to the king for paying off the army, yet not enough to allow the Scots to be sent home. In this way, the City MPs and their supporters in London allowed Pym and his friends to use the Scottish army to maintain pressure on the king while they were moving to realize their program. As Clarendon put it, "The task of borrowing money gave them [the parliamentary leaders] opportunity of pressing their own designs to facilitate their work; as, if anything they proposed in the House was crossed, presently the City would lend no more money because of this or that obstruction."[20]

The success of the City MPs in establishing themselves early on as go-betweens was aided by the reluctance of the court of aldermen to speed the lending process. On 16 November 1640 Pennington reported that the City had agreed to lend only £25,000 of the £50,000 Parliament had

[18] "Case Concerning Customes of Tobaccoe."

[19] *H.M.C., Fourth Report, Appendix*, p. 44; *C.J.* 2: 77; Stock, *Proceedings and Debates* 1: 106–7.

[20] Edward Hyde, Earl of Clarendon, *History of the Rebellion*, 6 vols. (Oxford, 1888), 1: 274, quoted in Pearl, *London*, p. 199; see also pp. 197–98.

asked for (although he said that he expected they would soon consent to the rest, if the right security was granted). The City MP and new-merchant leader Matthew Craddock immediately warned that "he feared it might hinder the business to rely upon the aldermen." After some cajoling the aldermen did come through with the remaining £25,000. But Pennington solidified the position of the City MPs by having himself and Alderman Soames chosen to be the two treasurers of the loan from the City. Shortly thereafter Pennington achieved a real coup by getting the House to go, via the MPs, directly to common hall for the next loan from the City of £60,000.[21] This was an absolutely pivotal tactical breakthrough, for common hall, with its broad-based membership, was the only official City institution in which the London parliamentary militants, still a minority on the common council (not to mention the court of aldermen), were politically dominant.[22]

While the City MPs and their citizen allies thus provided the parliamentary leadership with an indispensable weapon against the Crown, they could wield the same weapon for their own ends. At crucial moments, they did not merely diverge from the policies of Pym and his friends, but sharply opposed them. Conflict arose not only over the root and branch reformation of the church, but also over the handling of the Scottish army and the disposition of the earl of Strafford. The resolution of the latter two interrelated issues was the condition for consolidating parliamentary revolution. Yet, at critical junctures during the spring of 1641, Pym and those closest to him seem to have found themselves dangerously squeezed between an alliance of London militants and House of Commons radicals, which was bent on preventing any agreement between Charles and the parliamentary leadership that might save Strafford's life, and an emergent crypto-royalist group in the Commons, which sought to extricate the king from the vulnerable position in which he found himself.

On 23 January 1641, Alderman Pennington announced to the House of Commons that the citizens would refuse to hand over the £60,000 they had promised because the king had not only countenanced the delinquents Lord Keeper John Finch and Secretary of State Sir Francis Windebank, but also had reprieved the condemned priest John Goodman. The citizens were obsessed with the pardon of Goodman because they saw it as establishing a precedent for a much more important reprieve they believed to be contemplated by the king, that of the earl of Strafford. Both houses of Parliament were clearly impressed by the citizens' threat to withhold

---

[21] W. Notestein, ed., *The Journal of Sir Simonds D'Ewes from the Beginning of the Long Parliament to the Opening of the Trial of Strafford* (New Haven, 1923), pp. 36–37, hereafter shortened to *D'Ewes*(N); Pearl, *London*, pp. 198–200.

[22] Pearl, *London*, pp. 53, 199. The common council traditionally had authority over loans from the City, although there was not, apparently, a hard-and-fast rule.

funds, and they rushed to remonstrate with the king, urging him to have Goodman executed and the laws against papists strictly enforced. [23] Meanwhile, probably to assuage the citizens, they ordered the dispatch of a commission to deface, demolish, and take away altars on 23 January, accepted and read the London ministers' petition on religion on 23 January and 2 February, and gave a first reading to the bill brought in by Alderman Pennington for abolishing superstition and idolatry and for settling true religion on 5 February. [24]

Under pressure, the king finally agreed, in his speech of 4 February 1641, to leave Goodman to the will of Parliament, and he ordered all priests to leave London within a month; meanwhile, the queen proclaimed her desire to collaborate with Parliament. Apparently satisfied, Parliament allowed Goodman to languish in prison. But on 6 February, Pennington announced to the House of Commons that the citizens of London were unhappy with the king's speech, since it had not resulted in Goodman's execution. Parliament, however, would not be bullied, and the Commons ordered the Speaker to inform the citizens that it was perfectly content with the king's speech and to request of the lord mayor that the money underwritten by the citizens be collected and paid. This did not, however, resolve the matter. [25]

Two days later, renewed conflict broke out between the citizen oppositionists and a goodly number of moderate MPs. When Parliament turned to the consideration of the citizens' root and branch bill on 8 February, a group in the House led by Digby, Falkland, Hyde, and Culpepper sought to prevent the bill from even being considered, not only because of its contents, but because of the petitioners' brazen appeal beyond the duly constituted City authorities to the London masses. Speaking "not to have the London petition committed, because tumultuarily brought," Digby said that he looked "upon this petition not as a petition from the City of London, but from I know not what 15,000 Londoners, all that could be got to subscribe." The new-merchant MP Samuel Vassall promptly replied "that many able men's hands were to the petition." And the next day Alderman Pennington took up Digby's challenge head-on. As Simonds D'Ewes reported, Pennington

> stood up and justified the London petition to have been warranted by the hands of men of worth and known integrity. And if there were any mean men's hands to it, yet if they were honest men, there was

[23] D'Ewes(N), pp. 277–79, 283, 287, 289, 294; C.J. 2: 72–73; A. Fletcher, *The Outbreak of the English Civil War* (London, 1981), pp. 4–5; Pearl, *London*, p. 200.

[24] C.J. 2: 72, 79; D'Ewes(N), pp. 313ff., 327, 329.

[25] S. R. Gardiner, *A History of England from the Accession of James I to the Outbreak of the Civil War*, 10 vols. (London, 1883–1884), 9: 272; D'Ewes(N), p. 33; C.J. 2: 80; Pearl, *London*, p. 201.

no reason but their hands should be received. And for the delivery of it himself was one of them who received it from persons of quality and worth. It was done without tumult. . . . There was no course used to rake up hands, for he might boldly say, if that course had been taken instead of 15,000 they might have had fifteen times fifteen thousands.

Nevertheless, Digby's telling distinction between London's official governors, who did not support the root and branch petition, and the constitutionally unauthorized citizens movement, which had brought it into Parliament, undoubtedly hit a nerve, and would become a source of ever greater political embarrassment and strategic difficulty for Pym and his friends. As an emerging crypto-royalist party would pound home with ever increasing effectiveness over the following year, the parliamentary opposition depended upon popular forces in London that were not only devoted to unacceptably radical religious alternatives, but bent on overthrowing traditional authority and hierarchy in the City and who knew where else. The parliamentary leadership made sure that the moderates' attack on the root and branch petition was turned aside and that the bill went to committee. However, the committee was instructed for the time being not to consider the question of the abolition of episcopacy.[26]

Pennington did not quickly let the House forget the insult to the citizens. On 10 February, the Commons requested a further £15,000 from the Londoners to pay for the navy. Pennington replied the next day that the citizens would bring in the money, but that "they took themselves much injured that it was said that the names subscribed to their petition were tapsters and ostlers," and subsequently added that "they were much discouraged by some malevolent speeches."[27]

As it was, the citizens continued to withhold the money they had promised, and this led to sudden open conflict with their erstwhile allies among the parliamentary leadership. On 18 February 1641, Sir William Uvedale, treasurer of the money for the king's army and the Scots, complained to the House that although Alderman Pennington had claimed the previous day that the greater part of the £60,000 promised by the citizens had been brought into the chamber of London, in fact only £21,000 had been collected.[28] Speaking on this problem on 20 February, Sir Simonds D'Ewes pointed out that the citizens' money would quickly be forthcoming if the two main barriers to its provision were summarily removed— the king's failure to execute Goodman and his refusal to disband Strafford's army in Ireland. Others explicitly proclaimed that there was no

---

[26] *D'Ewes*(N), pp. 335–44; Fletcher, *Outbreak*, pp. 97–99: Pearl, *London*, pp. 213–16.
[27] *D'Ewes*(N), pp. 345, 351, 356–57.
[28] Ibid., pp. 367, 371.

hope for money from London until some final action was taken on Strafford.[29] At this point, a frustrated John Pym suddenly moved that "in respect of the great necessity of the public, we might compel the Londoners to lend money."[30]

The House would not hear of Pym's shocking proposal. But the underlying conflict immediately flared up again, now around the issue of the subsidy. By this point, the more militant MPs, apparently in collaboration with the London citizens, were refusing to approve, even in principle, the further raising of money until something was done about Goodman, the Irish army, and, by clear implication, Strafford. Led by the anti-Scottish moderates Sir John Strangeways and Sir Robert Pye, the Commons, only with relative difficulty, passed the act for two additional subsidies. The vote was 195 to 129, with the later regicide John More and the militant parliamentarian John Wray tellers for the noes.[31]

The refusal of Pennington and his citizen allies to bring in funds gave a giant opening to moderate, anti-Scottish forces in the House of Commons and, apparently, in the City. On 23 February, the House appointed a twelve-person committee dominated by known moderates and later royalists to "treat with merchants and such other persons as they shall think fit" about raising a loan.[32] On 24 February, Sir Arthur Capel, speaking for the committee, reported that members had visited the City and were hopeful of raising funds there. Sir John Strangeways, another of the committee's members, then took the opportunity to make an inflammatory call for the removal of the Scots from England by 16 March.[33] This linking of City money with the Scots' withdrawal was not fortuitous. A few days later, on 27 February, Sir Edward Hyde reported that the committee had conferred "with the most substantial and best reputed men of the City." They had promised money, he said, but only if certain demands were met. These men (according to Hyde, writing later) were "very much troubled and melancholy to see two armies kept on foot at so vast a charge within the bounds of the kingdom, where . . . all danger of war was removed; and they who were very able to make good what they promised had frankly undertaken that if a peremptory day was appointed for being rid of those armies, there should be not want of monies to discharge them." Hyde

[29] Ibid., pp. 381–82; Gardiner, *History* 9: 292. When Sir Henry Marten had protested, on 18 February, the House of Lords' dawdling over Strafford by allowing him extra time to present his case, he was speaking for militant forces in Parliament *and* the City (*D'Ewes*[N], p. 371).

[30] *D'Ewes*(N), p. 382 (20 Feb. 1641).

[31] Ibid., pp. 388–89; *C.J.* 2: 87.

[32] *C.J.* 2: 91. Among those at the core of the emergent anti-Scottish and perhaps crypto-royalist group on this eleven-person committee were Sir John Strangeways, Sir Robert Pye, Sir Arthur Capel, and Edward Herbert.

[33] *D'Ewes*(N), pp. 398, 398 n. 11.

reported to the House that the committee had mobilized twenty-five persons in the City who would lend a total of £50,000, but who held back from doing so because of their objections to the recently released "Scotch paper." This document was a statement by the Scottish commissioners that proclaimed their desire to have episcopacy abolished and Strafford executed, but that had been intended for limited circulation only within the House of Commons. Its broad public circulation is something of a puzzle. It is possible that Isaac Pennington, or one of the other radical City MPs, sensing that power was slipping from the hands of the militant citizens and their parliamentary allies, leaked this document so as to bring Scots' pressure directly to bear on Parliament in support of the militants' program. But its publication in the City played into the hands of those who opposed the Scots and sought to stem the parliamentary tide.[34] Obviously, the citizens with whom these MPs had consulted had the opposite political perspective from that of Pennington's supporters; strongly sympathetic to the Crown, they were almost certainly drawn, as Pennington's supporters were not, primarily from among the City's company merchant establishment.

The proposal to use City money to pay for the removal of the Scots represented the efforts of an emergent faction around Sir Robert Pye, Sir John Strangeways, Sir Henry Jermyn, Sir Arthur Capel, Sir Edmund Waller, and others who, from early February 1641, sought to lift the pressure from the Crown by securing the withdrawal of the Scottish army and, in that way, to moderate the parliamentary offensive. Their apparent success, in the wake of the boycott of funds by the City's radicals, in mobilizing a similarly royally-inclined group inside the City in support of their cause posed a mortal threat to those in Parliament who feared the king and wished to push further parliamentary reform. During the previous month, Alderman Pennington and his friends in the City had sought to withhold City funds in order to increase the threat of a Scottish invasion and, in that way, to pressure Parliament for Strafford's execution. Now, in a rather analogous way, the parliamentary moderates were attempting to use the same sort of financial bludgeon from London for the opposite purpose—to rid the country of the Scots, an action that would have had the effect of depriving the parliamentary leadership of its main weapon against the king. The quandary thus posed for the parliamentary leadership was well stated by Clarendon in his *History*. "If the governing party embraced the opportunity to procure a supply of money which was really wanted, it would be too great a countenance to the persons who had pro-

34 Ibid., pp. 417, 417 nn. 9–19; Clarendon, *History* 1: 284, quoted in Pearl, *London*, p. 202; D. Stevenson, *The Scottish Revolution 1637–1644* (London, 1973), pp. 218–219. As Stevenson points out, "the Scots, embarrassed by the publication of what had been intended as a private paper, agreed to issue an explanation stating that they had no wish to interfere in English affairs."

cured it, and whose reputation they were willing to depress; besides, it would imply their approbation of what had been said of the disbanding, at least would be a ground of often mentioning and pressing it . . . which . . . was the thing they most abhorred."[35]

The moderates' attempt to use City money to force the withdrawal of the Scottish army appears to have precipitated something of a crisis for Pym and those great parliamentary nobles, notably the earl of Bedford, with whom he was working. Pym and his friends were walking a narrow line in this period. On the one hand, they were trying to use the City radicals and their control of funds to force the king to make a settlement. On the other hand, since any settlement of the conflict acceptable to the king might require saving Strafford's life, Pym and his friends were also seeking to prevent the citizens and their parliamentary collaborators from using their financial leverage simply to force through Strafford's execution.[36] Nevertheless, the life-and-death threat represented by the parliamentary moderates' and crypto-royalists' attempt to raise funds in the City may have forced them, at least temporarily, back into the arms of Pennington and the radicals. On 1 March 1641, in an effort to recover his position, Pennington declared that the citizens would now forward the promised funds if certain MPs named by him would visit the lord mayor and the aldermanic court. He went on to designate the parliamentary leaders John Pym, John Hampden, Denzil Holles, Nathaniel Fiennes, Sir Walter Earle, and Sir Henry Vane the younger, along with the four City MPs, Matthew Craddock, Samuel Vassall, Thomas Soames, and himself. This was a delegation in which parliamentary militants enjoyed substantial representation. Pennington also took this opportunity to cast aspersions on the group in the City from whom the parliamentary moderates were attempting to raise money, calling it a *colloquintida*, or polluted source.[37] Pennington's comments, and especially his subsequent failure to come up with the promised funds, provoked the bitterest conflict, "so much heat . . . as had scarce happened before in the House." The radical MP Henry Marten, along with Nathaniel Fiennes, was obliged to rush to Pennington's defense. Sir Edmund Waller and Sir Thomas Jermyn violently attacked him, and Jermyn demanded that Thomas Soames, the one relative moderate among the City's four MPs, henceforth replace Pennington as

[35] Clarendon, *History* 1: 284, quoted in *D'Ewes*(N), p. 421.

[36] For Pym's collaboration with Bedford and other leading nobles at this time, see Fletcher, *Outbreak*, pp. 7, 34–35, 38–39.

[37] Pearl, *London*, p. 203; *D'Ewes*(N), pp. 420–22. On the delegation named by Pennington, Earle, Vane, Craddock, Vassall, Fiennes, and Pennington himself were certainly or most likely working for Strafford's execution in this period. D'Ewes's and Falkland's comments make it fairly clear that Pennington's "colloquintida" referred to the citizens who were to raise the money (not the Commons committee negotiating with them).

the representative of the House to the City. To stem the conservative tide, a number of more militant MPs, including D'Ewes, Sir Thomas Barrington, Sir Henry Marten, Sir Arthur Hasilrig, and others, seem to have hastily improvised a plan whereby members of the House would *themselves* bring in the needed funds.[38]

It would be very useful to know with whom in the City the conservative MPs were negotiating for funds at this point. Unfortunately, there appears to be little surviving evidence on this score.[39] In any case, as it turned out, they were unable to come up with any money in London, and the effectiveness of the radical citizens' boycott only increased.[40]

The parliamentary leadership was now caught in a tightening vise. The pressure from the north was increasing. On 17 March, the Scottish commissioners declared that unless funds were soon forthcoming, the Scottish army might have to march south. The possibility of a confrontation between it and the English army seemed to be mounting daily, increased by the desire of some in the English army to attack the Scots. To compound the problem, as Pym soon learned, some of the officers in the north were plotting with the king to march on London and Parliament.[41] Meanwhile, the radicals in both London and Parliament were increasing their resolve to hold back funds. On 20 March, after the House had been informed that it still owed the armies the staggering sum of £278,000, Sir Henry Marten made the explicit proposal that Parliament advance no more money for any purpose until justice was done to the earl of Strafford. The fiery spirits Sir Walter Earle and William Strode immediately seconded his proposition. On the same day, the House of Lords passed a motion to prevent people from massing at Westminster. The Commons' radicals and City militants were working in close coordination.[42]

A few days later, on 24 March, Parliament made one more desperate plea to London. To prepare the ground, they sent a delegation to the king requesting he disband the Irish army, disperse all Catholics from around

[38] D'Ewes(N), p. 433 and nn. 13–20. For the MPs' attempt to raise funds among themselves, see pp. 434–35, 435 n. 29 (3 Mar. 1641), 438–40 (4, 5 Mar. 1641).

[39] The only name mentioned in the parliamentary diaries' report of these proceedings is one "Captain Langham," who is perhaps the John Langham who became alderman in 1642. A citizen of relatively conservative politics, Langham was a mild parliamentarian who later became a leader of political presebyterianism in the City. (D'Ewes[N], p. 420).

[40] See D'Ewes(N), p. 461, for Sir Arthur Capel's report that the mayor and aldermen had failed to lend (9 Mar. 1641).

[41] Fletcher, *Outbreak*, p. 20; Gardiner, *History* 9: 310–18, 324, 325.

[42] D'Ewes(N), pp. 513–14; *L.J.* 4: 193; Gardiner, *History* 9: 301. "The Scots do much press for their monthly pay, and threaten daily their falling into new quarters if they be not paid, and, on the other side, the City nor any private men will furnish the House of Commons with any advance, though they never be so secured to be paid out of the coming subsidies" (W. Hawkins to the earl of Leicester, *H.M.C., De L'Isle and Dudley* 6: 390 (8/18 Mar. 1641).

the court, and disarm all recusants. But on 30 March, Digby, who headed the delegation of both houses to London, was obliged to report that "the Recorder [of London, Sir Thomas Gardiner] had made a long speech, the effect of which was, in brief, that the lord mayor etc. had called a common council. . . . But, in fine, no monies would be promised. . . . The lord mayor, and court of alderman, and himself were willing to yield their best endeavors to the furtherance of the service; but they were no constitutive body, nor able to make laws for the lending of monies; and therefore could but persuade, and not compel."[43] Apparently, the lord mayor, the recorder, and the aldermen could not persuade the court of the common council or common hall, the bodies in the City that did have constituted authority to raise money from the citizens.

Digby's account reveals much about the constellation of forces in London (and nationally) at this crucial moment. The aldermen were more than willing to help undercut the City's militants and come up with the needed funds. But they were unable to do so in the face of the resolve of the common council and—behind the common council and placing great pressure on it—the radical mass movement, based in common hall and the London streets, which was bent on destroying Strafford. Whatever the wishes of the official City government, no loan could, at this point, be collected over the opposition of the London militants.

Shortly after the opening of Strafford's trial on 22 March, the citizens further tightened the screws by starting to circulate a petition calling for the earl's execution and the reform of the church. On 10 April, Hasilrig made his fateful motion for Strafford's attainder. On the very same day, recognizing the potentially decisive role of pressure from the citizens in resolving this issue, the king called on London's lord mayor to curtail all mass petitioning in the City, and to repress in particular the citizens' petition against Strafford. Nevertheless, the Londoners' campaign could not be stopped, and on 21 April a great multitude of citizens, numbering perhaps ten thousand, brought their petition against Strafford into Parliament. This was the very day that the House of Commons approved Strafford's attainder.[44]

The citizens' petition contained between ten thousand and thirty thousand signatures, depending on the estimate. The identities of the two citizens who are named by the *Journals of the House of Commons* as presenting the petition to Parliament gives a further idea as to who was leading the City movement at this critical juncture, besides the three militant London MPs, Isaac Pennington, Matthew Craddock, and Samuel Vassall. One of the presenters was John Venn, who, along with Maurice Thomson and

[43] *C.J.* 2: 112–13, 114.
[44] Gardiner, *History* 9: 329–30; Manning, *English People*, p. 9.

Richard Shute, had gained prominence the previous autumn as a leading organizer of the citizens' petition of grievances. Venn, a militant Puritan and Massachusetts Bay backer, would replace Matthew Craddock as City MP when Craddock died in May 1641, and would play a leading part in the City radical movement throughout the revolutionary period. The other presenter named was Capt. John Bradley. A citizen of obscure origins, Bradley was a leader in the trade with the Americas, having imported sixty thousand pounds of Virginian tobacco in 1640. By June 1641, Bradley would be helping to lead a new push by common hall to revise the City constitution. Aside from Venn and Bradley, two other citizens can be identified as among those heading up the City movement in those tumultuous days—first, John Fowke, a longtime opponent of the East India company and an interloper in its trade, who, as a Levant Company trader, had been prominent in the struggle against arbitrary taxation in the late 1620s; second, Randall Mainwaring, the kinsman and close collaborator of both Matthew Craddock and Isaac Pennington who had recently petitioned Parliament against Spanish privateers, along with his brother-in-law Joseph Hawes and many other new merchants. Further direct evidence of the leadership of the London movement in those critical days would certainly be desirable. Nonetheless, even from the information available, it can hardly be doubted that its composition was largely the same as it had been from the beginning of the conflict; indeed, much the same group of people would maintain leadership in London throughout the period of deepening revolution, right through to the middle of 1643. Over this whole period, they would prove indispensable to the parliamentary leadership, but also, at certain critical moments, quite intolerable to it.[45]

It is difficult to say how far the parliamentary opposition leaders originally planned to take the legislative revolution. They must have been aware, however, that to try to go much further than they did during the summer of 1641 would invite division in what had been, until that point, a tolerably unified parliamentary force. It is, in fact, fairly clear that, from a comparatively early stage, the parliamentary leaders were looking for ways simply to protect what they already had gained. The limits of their political and ideological vision are implicit in their plans of the winter and spring of 1641 to consolidate the parliamentary revolution by replacing Charles's leading advisers with their own representatives. The chief instigators of this plan were John Pym and the earl of Bedford, who was probably the real chief of the parliamentary party. Even as the trial of Strafford

45 C.J. 2: 125, 127; Pearl, London, p. 205. For Venn, see above, ch. 6, pp. 313–14. For Bradley, see London Port Book for Imports, 1640, PRO, E.190/43/5; Manning, English People, p. 92 and n. 120. For Mainwaring, see above, pp. 334–35, and ch. 4, p. 138. For Fowke, see above, ch. 4, pp. 173–74 and n. 213; also Pearl, London, pp. 316–20.

was reaching its climax in late April and early May, Bedford and Pym were negotiating with the king to bring about a settlement and seeking to win influential men in Parliament to its support. In exchange for the appointment of Bedford as lord treasurer and Pym as chancellor of the exchequer, the king demanded, first, adequate revenue for the Crown (in place of the extraparliamentary taxes of the 1630s that had been condemned by Parliament); second, the maintenance of episcopacy; and third, the saving of Strafford's life (though not, it seems, his political life). Apparently, Bedford and Pym were willing to satisfy the king on all three points, but Bedford died in early May 1641, and the arrangement was never finalized.[46]

It is not entirely clear why this agreement was not consummated, although many possible reasons have been brought out. The king himself was, in this period, under strong pressure from his courtiers to promote all sorts of plots, with the army and others. He may never really have accepted the plan. On the other hand, some MPs believed that if the "great men" got positions, they would do little to reduce the cost of the court, and would become "desirous more to pacify the irate prince and to comply with his desire in keeping up bishops and other things" than to carry out "the thorough reformation of church and state." Then there was the oft-cited veto of the plan by the great earl of Essex, whose support Pym and Bedford appear to have felt they needed.[47]

Any or all of these factors may have caused the failure of the negotiations. Nevertheless, it is questionable whether the plan had a chance of success in any case. The king demanded, above all, the reprieve of Strafford, but, as has been described, the parliamentary movement in London was set on Strafford's execution. It is not clear how Pym and his friends could have struck a bargain with the king given, on the one hand, the mounting pressures for funds from both the king's army and the Scottish forces in the north and, on the other, the citizens' refusal to grant a loan unless Strafford's execution was assured. During the last week of April the citizens, once again, affirmed this condition: immediately after the House of Commons had voted Strafford's execution, the City suddenly agreed to advance the long-requested £120,000 on the security of the sub-

---

[46] For discussions of the parliamentary program in 1641 and the attempts to strike an agreement with the king, especially through the policy of "bridge appointments," see C. Russell, "Introduction" and "Parliament and the King's Finances," in *The Origins of the English Civil War*, ed. C. Russell (London, 1973), pp. 28–29, 110–16; B. Manning, "The Aristocracy and the Downfall of Charles I," in *Politics, Religion, and the English Civil War*, ed. B. Manning (London, 1973), pp. 37–80; Fletcher, *Outbreak*, pp. 6–7, 14, 15, 34, 41, and, in general, chs. 1 and 2. See also B.H.G. Wormald, *Clarendon* (Oxford, 1951), pp. 5–10, and P. Crawford, *Denzil Holles, 1598–1680* (London, 1979), pp. 38–43.

[47] Manning, "Aristocracy," pp. 56–57.

sidy; but as soon as the House of Lords expressed its hesitation about condemning Strafford, the City immediately reneged on its commitment. According to the Venetian ambassador, "The City presented a paper to Parliament . . . stating that they will not be able to find the loan of £120,000 promised unless this minister [Strafford] pays the penalty for his alleged crimes with his life, as the people express a determination not to contribute before they obtain this satisfaction." Nor is it obvious how Pym and his friends could have dealt with the mounting pressure from those masses of Londoners who crowded into the streets of Westminster in the early days of May and succeeded in frightening the House of Lords into changing its mind and approving Strafford's attainder. Indeed, it has been plausibly argued that the citizens' demonstrated ability to mobilize the London masses for the direct application of force made it impossible for the Commons, the Lords, or the king successfully to come to Strafford's defense. Finally, there is reason to think that, in the face of the plots against Parliament unleashed at this time, from within London and within the army—after all, it had no coercive, military capacity of its own— Parliament was quite dependent on the London parliamentary movement for its defense, and therefore had little choice but to grant the citizens' wishes.[48] In a way, the crisis of Strafford's trial represented a preview of the drama that would be more fully played out during the following winter, when the fate of the parliamentary revolution was entirely in the hands of the City mass opposition movement.

During the first crisis-filled week in May, the parliamentary leadership seems to have been functioning in close harmony with the London citizens. On 3 May, as thousands of citizens were lining the approachways to the House of Lords to ensure Strafford's conviction and execution, the City MPs Isaac Pennington and Matthew Craddock brought word to the House of Commons that the Crown was seeking to seize the Tower of London on the pretext of fortifying it and that Sir John Suckling was bringing armed men into the City. The parliamentary leadership used this news, along with the by now widely perceived threat of an army plot, to win parliamentary approval of the Protestation—a loyalty oath to Parliament aimed at mobilizing the country against the danger of a counter-

---

[48] *C.S.P. Ven. 1641*, pp. 140, 141. As Sir John Coke the Younger wrote his father, "The same day [3 May] the tumultuous assemblies of citizens began at Westminster, which continued for the most part every day, until the Lords had changed their intentions that were conceived of them and passed the bill. The citizens presented themselves at Whitehall on Saturday, when both Houses went to His Majesty to desire that he would come and give his assent to the bill" (*H.M.C., Twelfth Report, Cowper MSS*, p. 281). For the narrative, and analysis, of events surrounding Strafford's execution, see Manning, *English People*, pp. 9–20. On the conspiracies against Parliament at this time, see Gardiner, *History* 9: 342–44, 348–49, 351, 355, 356, 360, 362; C. Russell, "The First Army Plot of 1641," *TRHS* 5th series, 38 (1988).

coup—on the day after it was proposed in the Commons. The City radicals quickly saw that they could use the Protestation to provide themselves with parliamentary sanction for continuing to organize the London populace under their own leadership. So on 4 May, the colonial merchant MPs Matthew Craddock and Samuel Vassall, accompanied by several ministers and captains of the City's trained bands, brought in a new mass petition from the citizens requesting that Parliament allow the Protestation to be administered to every citizen of London. This was tantamount to direct resort by Parliament to the London masses, but the Commons immediately approved it. On 11 May, the court of aldermen took the Protestation. But they refused to sanction the idea of administering it to the citizens, despite the fact that the House of Commons itself had explicitly ordered this. The citizens circulated the Protestation despite the aldermen's disapproval. There could hardly be a clearer expression of the chasm that persisted between the City elite and the London parliamentary movement.[49]

On 5 May, the citizens further flexed their muscles when Isaac Pennington brought in a bill stating that Parliament could not be dissolved without its own consent. There is no evidence that this idea had previously been part of the agenda of the parliamentary opposition. The citizens justified it as a means to assure potential creditors of Parliament that they would be repaid before any dissolution of Parliament by the king. But it also fit in with their desire for further constitutional revolution. The House of Commons approved it unanimously. On 8 May the House of Lords approved Strafford's attainder; the king followed suit on 10 May, and Strafford was executed two days later. The London movement had gotten its way.[50]

Deepening Radicalization

The collapse of the proposed arrangement between the king and the parliamentary leadership and the subsequent execution of Strafford opened a period of profound uncertainty at the top and increasing mobilization below; in consequence, it was a time of intensifying political conflict. In mid-May, Charles announced his plan to go to Scotland, an idea viewed with profound suspicion by Parliament and its supporters. Meanwhile, he plotted with all parties. To make matters worse, during June and July the House of Lords, under the influence of its strong contingent of bishops, seemed to make it clear that it would oppose any thorough reform of

[49] Pearl, *London*, p. 218; Gardiner, *History* 9: 351–54; *C.J.* 2: 132–33; Russell, "First Army Plot of 1641," pp. 95–106.

[50] *C.J.* 2: 136, 139, 140; Fletcher, *Outbreak*, p. 40; Gardiner, *History* 9: 359–60, 361, 366–69.

the church. By early June, the Lords had rejected the proposal, originating in the Commons, to remove the bishops from their House. By the end of July, the Lords had also turned down the bill for "securing true religion," an attempt to root out Catholics from offices in church and state. In response, the Commons' leaders reintroduced the root and branch bill on 27 May. They appear to have done so initially to provide themselves with a tactical weapon to compel the Lords either to expel the bishops or to face the abolition of the episcopal hierarchy altogether. Nevertheless, the root and branch bill was framed so as to radically strengthen the control over the church's policy, administration, and wealth exerted by the leading landed classes and, largely for that reason, it appears to have attracted the rather strong support of the House of Commons. Indeed, during much of the summer, the root and branch bill appeared to be proceeding toward passage.

It is obvious that most of those MPs who supported the root and branch bill did so for purposes very different from those of the forces in London that sought root and branch reformation in order to bring in Presbyterian or Independent forms of ecclesiastical organization so as to strengthen popular, local control of the church. Nevertheless, the unintended consequence of the Commons' support for the root and branch bill and for a variety of other initiatives aiming to reform the church was to further discredit the established church authorities and thereby encourage radical religious forces to pursue reformation on their own. The rising wave of popular initiatives for unilateral reform of local church practices, or, worse, the organization of sectarian congregations, naturally called forth, in reaction, the increasing alarm of the political nation.

On 24 June, desperately seeking a settlement before conflict heightened further, Pym put forward the Ten Propositions, in which the king was promised ample funds if he would disband the army, cancel his trip to Scotland, remove evil counselors, and appoint those in whom Parliament could trust. But Charles demonstrated little interest in such a bargain. In late July he reaffirmed his intention of proceeding to Scotland, and on 10 August he departed over the protest of Parliament. Meanwhile, the promotions to high office that Charles made on 8 August gave no evidence of any desire on his part to build bridges to Parliament.[51]

Unable to force a settlement on the king or to remove the danger of a royal countercoup, Pym and his friends appear to have been decreasingly able or willing to hold off their militant supporters, especially those in London on whom they ultimately depended for protection. In the words

[51] For the preceding three paragraphs, see esp. Fletcher, *Outbreak*, pp. 42–53. See also W. M. Abbott, "The Issue of Episcopacy in the Long Parliament, 1640–1648" (Oxford University, Ph.D. diss., 1981), pp. 203–5, 211–12, 253; Pearl, *London*, pp. 120–21; *L.J.* 4: 292.

of one of Charles I's advisers, London's mobilized masses had by now become Parliament's "anchorhold and only interest,"[52] and the summer of 1641 did indeed witness a significant radicalization. Militant citizens stepped up their drive to reform the City constitution. Merchant companies came under increasing pressure. The proposal for an anti-Spanish war was renewed. Perhaps most ominous of all, militant forces in Parliament and in London pushed harder for further religious reformation. The outcome was a serious increase of political and religious polarization.

REVISING THE CITY CONSTITUTION

The City opposition movement did not hesitate to exploit the momentum it had gained in the crisis-filled days around Strafford's execution and the continuing inability of Parliament to reach an agreement with the king. In the last week of June, directly defying City custom, the London freemen meeting in common hall attempted to elect both sheriffs, even though by tradition the lord mayor had the right to choose one. Characteristically, the lord mayor and the aldermen quickly shot off a petition of protest, not to Parliament but to the privy council. But the king, well understanding the sensitiveness of the issue, refused to rule in favor of the magistrates and referred the case to the House of Lords. After a further meeting of common hall failed to produce an agreement, the Lords instructed common hall to choose six representatives to negotiate a compromise with the lord mayor and aldermen.[53]

The names of the six men chosen by common hall are further evidence of who was leading the City parliamentary movement at this time. Five of these six were active with the new-merchant leadership in the colonial and interloping trades. These included Capt. John Bradley, the tobacco trader who, on 21 April, along with John Venn, had carried into the House of Commons the citizens' petition demanding Strafford's execution; Stephen Estwicke, a partner in Maurice Thomson's project for interloping in the East Indies, who during the 1630s had fought against the Crown's silk monopoly and suffered imprisonment for resisting ship money; and Randall Mainwaring, the relative of both Matthew Craddock and Isaac Pennington, who, along with his partner and brother-in-law the great trader in American tobacco Joseph Hawes, had petitioned Parliament in December 1640 for the right to take reprisals from a Spanish ship and, more generally, for a more militant English policy in the West Indies. Also among common hall's delegates were Richard Chambers and John Fowke,

---

[52] Quoted in Russell, *Origins*, pp. 28–29.

[53] For this episode, see House of Lords MSS, 6, 16, 29 July 1641 and 14 August 1641; *H.M.C., Fourth Report, Appendix*, pp. 84, 88, 90, 92, 97.

Levant Company traders who had been among the most prominent of the London oppositionists to impositions, tonnage and poundage, and a host of similar oppressive measures since the 1620s. Like those other Levant Company oppositionists, the colonial traders Matthew Craddock and Samuel Vassall, both Chambers and Fowke had established ties with the colonial-interloping combine by the time of the Civil War. Chambers was among the traders with the Americas who signed the anti-Spanish petition in support of Joseph Hawes in December 1640. Fowke, an archrival of the East India Company, carried on a personal suit against that company from the late 1620s through the 1640s, was involved with Sir William Courteen's interloping venture, and during the Civil War years helped lead the struggle against the company's monopoly privileges.

The decision of the House of Lords to invite representatives of common hall to negotiate with the lord mayor and aldermen came as a tremendous blow to the City oligarchy and its supporters. It gave prima facie legitimacy to the citizens' claims and, equally important, recognized common hall's right to negotiate with the lord mayor and court of aldermen on what was effectively an equal basis. In response, on 21 July 1641, the City's leading citizens brought in their own petition; they demanded that the House of Lords uphold the lord mayor's traditional right to appoint one sheriff and, in the process, sought to disparage the six citizens representing common hall as persons "not well affected to the present government." The organizers of this petition would form the heart of a conservative movement in the City that would grow in strength and audacity over the succeeding months. Of the petition's 172 signers, no fewer than 90 would also support, in February 1642, a parallel mass petition containing 330 signatures of protesters against the legality of the newly established committee of public safety, the City's chief revolutionary institution.[54] Of these 90, more than 50 percent were overseas company merchants. At least 22 were Levant Company traders; at least 13 were Merchant Adventurers; at least 10 were past, present, or future East India Company directors; at least 5 were French wine traders; and at least 3 were Eastland Company merchants. Clearly, the City's company merchants strongly identified with the City's traditional constitution and saw it was in danger. Over the next six months or so, they would openly ally with the Crown to defend their oligarchic government from a radical parliamentary movement in London composed almost entirely of citizens from outside the ranks of the overseas trading companies.

The House of Lords' ultimate verdict turned out to be a major victory for the City oppositionists. The Lords ruled that, in this specific case,

[54] *H.M.C., Fourth Report, Appendix*, pp. 91–92; House of Lords MSS, 26 July 1641, 24 February 1642.

common hall did have the right to elect both sheriffs, although the Lords were quick to state that their ruling established no precedent. They recommended, moreover, that common hall elect the person the lord mayor had nominated, and common hall complied with this request. Nevertheless, the lord mayor and court of aldermen were not appeased. On 26 August 1641 they appeared as a body before the House of Lords and threatened to resign their positions unless the House revoked its order. But the House of Lords stuck to its decision, and the City counterrevolution began to gather momentum.[55]

COMPANY MERCHANTS UNDER PRESSURE

While Parliament was showing unprecedented sympathy for the claims of the largely nonmerchant citizenry who dominated common hall, it was demonstrating a correlative lack of sensitivity for the needs of the City's overseas company merchants. Parliament could not, of course, have been expected to go out of its way to protect the East India Company. That company's directorate had steadfastly backed the Crown throughout the entire period of crisis. In April 1640, the company's directorate, as noted, had cut short an attempt by members of the company's general court to forward a petition of grievances to Parliament against the Crown's policies toward the company. In August 1640, the directorate again had come to the Crown's aid when it forced the famous pepper loan through the general court.

It is true that, in December 1640, the East India Company had actually gone so far as to draw up a petition for presentation to Parliament against Endymion Porter and his associates for their marauding voyage of 1630 in the Red Sea (for which the company had been held responsible) and another against Sir William Courteen for his interloping voyages in the company's privileged trading areas. Had these petitions actually been presented, they might have proved sorely embarrassing for the king, since Charles himself had been deeply involved with Porter's privateering venture and had, of course, directly sanctioned Courteen's interloping project. Occurring during the House of Commons' vigorous campaign against courtiers and promoters, the exposure of the king's close connection with Endymion Porter would likely have proved particularly damaging. In consequence, when he heard about these petitions, the king called in the company's governor Sir Christopher Clitherow and its deputy governor William Cockayne and pleaded with them to have the peti-

[55] See above, note 53; *L.J.* 4: 373; Pearl, *London*, p. 121. It may be significant that the five-person committee that took charge of the City's petition and complaint in the House of Lords included the parliamentary militants Lord Saye and Lord Wharton.

tions withdrawn, stating that Porter had "nothing to do in the business, his name only being used, and that what was done was His Majesty's act." Although the East India Company had already placed its petitions in the hands of the City MP Sir Thomas Soames for delivery to the House, Clitherow and Cockayne succeeded in having them recalled before they could be presented, so as to save the king from harm. When the board of directors was the next day apprised of what had transpired, it heartily approved of Clitherow and Cockayne's withdrawal of the petitions and, three days later, it got the Company's general court to sanction this action.[56]

Despite its sympathy for the Crown and the knowledge that it could expect little support from Parliament, the East India Company must have found the House of Commons' decision in the spring of 1641 to give consideration to the petition against it of one Thomas Smethwicke especially galling. Smethwicke's chief claim to fame had been his persistent attacks on the East India Company directorate's management of the trade over a period of more than a decade. These attacks were not particularly representative of either popular or proparliamentary forces in the company. On the contrary, Smethwicke had won the support of the Crown for his schemes beginning in 1628 when he sought to have the company credit the king with £10,000 of company stock free of charge. When Smethwicke's petition first came before Parliament in December 1640, the East India Company's directorate sought to have it dismissed by demonstrating to the House of Commons that Smethwicke had no support among the members and by informing the House of Smethwicke's "insolences and disturbances." But this effort failed when the House of Commons' committee on trade, headed by Sir Robert Harley, "ordered all books, letters, etc. concerning the management of the East India trade be brought into Commons"—which, in the words of the company's minutes, "will cause a great deal of trouble, especially now that the ships are about to be despatched." Smethwicke did not, it seems, ultimately win his case: the House of Lords entertained a further petition from him in June 1641, but he died later that year or in early 1642, and nothing further was done. Nevertheless, Parliament's willingness to countenance Smethwicke's petition as a way to attack the company was a painful blow at a time when the company was attempting to raise money for a new joint stock and was already having difficulty maintaining the public's confidence.[57]

[56] *C.C.M.E.I.C. 1640–1643*, pp. xv, 124, 128, 130–32.

[57] *C.C.M.E.I.C. 1640–1643*, pp. 126 (18 Dec. 1640), 156 (24 Mar. 1641); *D'Ewes*(N), p. 527 (16 Mar. 1641). For Smethwicke, the Crown, and the East India Company in the late 1620s, see R. Ashton, *The City and the Court, 1603–1643* (Cambridge, 1979), pp. 127–28. For later developments in the Smethwicke case, see *C.C.M.E.I.C. 1640–1643*, p. xxvii; *L.J.* 4: 265, 271; *H.M.C., Fourth Report, Appendix*, pp. 71, 74.

Nor did Parliament show great concern for the Merchant Adventurers over this period of deepening parliamentary reform and rising City radicalism. As soon as Parliament was recalled, the House of Commons took up the offensive against the Merchant Adventurers that had reached a high point in the middle 1620s. In January 1641, the Commons' committee on trade called in all of the Adventurers' patents and books "since 1406." The issue was not immediately pursued. Indeed, at the end of May 1641, the Adventurers appear to have stemmed the tide against them by offering a huge loan to Parliament of some £150,000 or £200,000. Nevertheless, on 18 June, the House of Commons resolved that "the contract between the House and the Company of Merchant Adventurers for the loan of £200,000, upon the terms formerly agreed shall be dissolved," and ordered that "Sir Robert Harley shall bring in the petition exhibited to the grand committee of trade against the Merchant Adventurers." On 14 July 1641, there was the familiar order to the committee on trade to "take into consideration of the several patents granted the Merchant Adventurers concerning the transport of cloths and . . . to examine all complaints that are made touching the abuse by that company in particular." As late as 27 October 1641, the Commons' subcommittee to consider the Adventurers' patents was still examining petitions and complaints against the company.[58]

Parliament did not, in the end, carry through its attack on the Merchant Adventurers, but the immediate reason for its failing to do so is not far to seek. As the crisis deepened in the fall of 1641, Parliament was desperate for money and willing to confirm the charters not only of the Merchant Adventurers, but even those of its sworn enemies, the Levant and East India companies, in exchange for loans. By December 1641, the Adventurers had already forwarded Parliament £30,000, and over the following two years they advanced £110,000 more.[59]

The merchants importing French and Spanish wine did not get off so easily. It will be remembered that in 1638 Charles had entered into a contract with certain courtiers and leading wine merchants whereby he had imposed an additional tax on wine. In turn, over the bitter protests of

[58] *D'Ewes*(N), p. 526; *C.J.* 2: 160–61, 179, 210, 214, 295–96.

[59] The bargaining process by which the Adventurers advanced money to Parliament can be followed in *C.J.* 2: 357, 358, 363, 364, 380, 384, 388, 415, 480, 522, 542, 552, 557, 558, 565, 567, 569, 574, 578, 580, 583, 587, 588, 590, 591, 592, 595, 625, 629, 635, 699, 798, 893, 897, 922, 957, 982 and 3: 44, 48, 222, 235, 236, 237, 239, 255, 265; *C.S.P.D. 1641–1643*, p. 492. A summary of their advances between January 1642 and January 1644 is given in PRO, S.P.28/237, on a loose sheet called "The Merchant Adventurers Account." The Merchant Adventurers had their charter confirmed by a House of Commons ordinance in late 1643. See also H. Parker, *Of a Free Trade* (London, 1648), p. 35; M. James, *Social Problems and Policies during the Puritan Revolution, 1640–1660* (London, 1930), pp. 148–50. For more on the attitude of the Levant and East India companies toward Parliament, and vice-versa, see below, esp. pp. 374–80.

the wine sellers, Charles had compensated the wine import merchants by ordering that the City wine sellers be directed to buy up annually a certain minimum amount of wine at a price set by the government. Not surprisingly, with the recalling of Parliament in the spring of 1640 and the subsequent national resistance to paying taxes to Charles's government during the following summer, the Vintners Company retailers saw a chance to turn the tables. On 21 April 1640, a committee inside the company was formed to consider the grievances of the wine sellers. But because the major merchant leadership of the Vintners Company had packed this committee with participants in the wine contract, the generality of the membership refused to recognize it. Nor would the generality agree to a petition to the Crown that was subsequently drawn up by the Vintners Company directors. Moreover, from about this time, wine sellers (as well as merchants) began refusing to pay the tax on wine. Finally, when Parliament returned in November, the retailers defied the Vintners' leadership by bringing into the House of Commons their own petition against the wine contract without having first gotten the approval of the company.[60]

The House of Commons appears to have taken swift initial retribution against the leading wine contractors, jailing William Abell and certain of his main collaborators. But after that, the complex case wandered through Parliament for close to ten months.[61] However, in August 1641, the House of Commons finally came to a decision. It took the very substantial step of declaring some forty wine importers—French Company merchants and traders in Spanish wine—to be delinquents for taking part in the wine contract, and threw a good number in prison. This was strong medicine indeed. Parliament had sided decisively with City shopkeepers against Crown-supported company merchants. Ironically, two of the men declared delinquents were none other than Henry Lee and Martin Bradgate, two of the leading wine traders whose refusal to pay impositions had sparked the merchants' opposition in the City in the later 1620s.[62]

Of course, much had occurred in the interim. Buckingham had passed from the scene. The Crown had sought to entice the merchants from their support for Parliament through the grant of privileges. A chasm had opened up between formerly allied aristocratic parliamentary leaders and London elite merchants. But no doubt most important, London's elite merchants had refused to back Parliament, and a City radical movement

---

[60] Vintners Company, Court Book, 1639–1658, pp. 28–29 (21, 24 Apr. 1640), 29, 30–31 (4 June 1640), 43 (25 Nov. 1640).

[61] D'Ewes(N), p. 73 (27 Nov. 1640); Pearl, London, pp. 289–91. William Abell and certain of his leading collaborators were initially jailed for abusing the retailers who had dared to take their case to court without getting the sanction of the company and its directorate.

[62] C.J. 2: 254, 265.

drawn from the same *nonmerchant* social layers from which the wine sellers came was ferociously attacking the City's constitution. Parliament's action of 13 August 1641 against the wine merchants was followed within less than two weeks by its decision against the court of aldermen and in support of common hall in its dispute over the election of sheriff. It is not unlikely that the City's wine sellers, like the citizens in common hall, saw their grievance against the wine merchants as connected with a more general complaint against a structure of City authority that was dominated by company overseas merchants (and other wholesalers) and that largely excluded people like themselves. On the other hand, the company merchants probably viewed the persecution of the French Company merchants and traders in Spanish wine as part of a more general pattern of parliamentary support for the City's popular forces. In any case, from the late summer of 1641 political polarization and constitutional conflict in the City rapidly intensified.

THE WEST INDIAN OFFENSIVE

While helping to pursue further the reform of the City constitution during the summer of 1641, the new-merchant leaders did not forget their colonial interests. On 3 August, they finally succeeded in getting a very favorable resolution of the issue of tobacco customs. After having neglected the issue for many months, the House of Commons settled the question of seizures:

> This House holds it fit, that all such petitioners about tobaccos of Somers Islands, and other English plantations etc. as have had their ships and tobacco taken on the seas, or by commanders of any of His Majesty's forts and castles, and men put into them; or by any of them enforced to enter bond to bring their ships and goods to London; or otherwise enforced to land their tobaccos in any other port, and by any of the farmers' officers detained; ought to have their tobaccos delivered them, without payment of any customs, or other duties, for warehouseroom or otherwise; and such of them as have been compelled to pay any sums of money, or given bonds for the payment of monies, that the officers, which received their monies or bonds, ought to make them restitution therefor.[63]

On 13 August, the Commons voted by a narrow margin to lower the total duty on tobacco from 6*d.* a pound and 4*d.* a pound for Virginian tobacco and West Indian tobacco, respectively, to a uniform rate of 2*d.* a pound.[64]

[63] Stock, *Proceedings and Debates* 1: 120; *C.J.* 2: 234.

[64] Stock, *Proceedings and Debates* 1: 120–21; *C.J.* 2: 255. Nevertheless, it is not clear that this motion actually went into effect. See Stock, *Proceedings and Debates* 1: 121 and n. 80.

Several weeks later the new merchants and colonizing aristocrats followed up their victory on the customs issue by coming forward to present their long-delayed plan for a full-scale offensive in the West Indies. Here, once again, they used the familiar tactic of new-merchant initiative coupled with parliamentary support. On 30 August 1641, "divers merchants of quality about London" presented a petition to Parliament that called for the implementation of the anti-Spanish program in almost exactly the same terms as John Pym had employed in his opening speech to the Short Parliament. Pointing out that the "Spanish party is now grown weak," they declared that it was an appropriate time to send out a number of armed ships to the Americas and Africa under a new company to be erected for that purpose in order "to possess ourselves with the riches of those countries," gain "command of the north and south seas, and make us formidable to our enemies abroad." If Parliament did not act swiftly and decisively, they warned, the English would be quickly preempted in the Caribbean and the Atlantic by the French, Portuguese, and Dutch—an interesting commentary on the rapidly changing balance of power in the region and on the need for a changing English policy toward it.[65]

The new merchants undoubtedly had received prior sanction for their petition from their allies in Parliament. For close to two decades the colonizing aristocrats had been advancing similar plans for a state-sanctioned war in the West Indies to be undertaken by a private company of patriotic Englishmen who would subsequently take over trade with the region. They had put forward, with broad encouragement from the Commons as a whole, quite analogous initiatives in the Parliaments of 1621, 1624, 1626, and 1628, and had done so again at the time of the so-called French opening at court in 1636–1637, in the Short Parliament, and in the current Parliament when Joseph Hawes had presented his petition. In the late spring of 1641, the Providence Island Company had suffered a great blow when the Spanish had captured its island of Providence, and its members, who included, of course, much of the top parliamentary leadership, must have been anxious to try to recoup. It was therefore to be expected that when the new-merchant MP Samuel Vassall brought in the merchants' petition, it was "well approved of by the House" and "especially committed to Mr. Pym and Sir John Culpepper." As John Pym cautiously commented, "Tis very hopeful if the Spanish party at court undermine it not." Pym and Culpepper headed up a twenty-six-man committee that included such veteran supporters of the Puritan colonizing adventures and anti-Spanish offensive as Sir Benjamin Rudyerd, Sir Thomas Barrington, Sir Henry Vane, Oliver St. John, and Vassall him-

---

[65] Stock, *Proceedings and Debates* 1: 121–22. For Pym's speech and his program in the Short Parliament, see above, ch. 6, pp. 308–10.

self.[66] During the last days of the session, the revelation that the king of Spain was hindering English shipping at Calais produced a further ground swell of support for the West Indian project. "This puts the House into a great rage," said one newsletter, "everyone being desirous to consent to a war with the Spaniard in the West Indies." At the adjournment of Parliament, the members of interim committees of each house—including Warwick and Mandeville for the Lords and Pym, Barrington, St. John, and Gerrard for the Commons—were directed, among other things, to "consider of forming and constituting a West India Company."[67]

DEEPENING REFORMATION?

Meanwhile, perhaps exploiting the heightened tension and fear that resulted from the king's rejection in early August of Parliament's request that he postpone his departure to Scotland, militant forces in Parliament and in the City sought to push forward religious reformation, if necessary on a piecemeal basis. On 8 August, Alderman Isaac Pennington, reporting from the committee for abolishing idolatry and superstition, established the previous February, succeeded in getting the House of Commons to order the pulling down of altar rails and the removing of communion tables in local churches. On 1 September, the House went further, passing an order that enjoined the parishes to reverse Laud's altar policy, to eradicate superstitious ceremonies such as bowing at the name of Jesus, to eliminate candles, images, and the like, and to enforce strict Sabbatarianism. This move provoked such intense opposition and division in the Commons that it had to be reconsidered, but the House eventually issued the order on 8 September.[68]

Meanwhile, on 6 September, the House had taken the significant step of sanctioning, on its own authority, the petition of the citizens of Stepney parish in London to hire lecturers at their own expense for Sunday mornings and afternoons and for Thursdays. This petition was brought into the Commons by Sir Gilbert Gerrard, a Providence Island Company activist, veteran parliamentary oppositionist, and son-in-law of the Essex Puritan Sir Thomas Barrington. The ministers Stepney parish appointed were the militant Independents William Greenhill and Jeremiah Burroughs, two East Anglian clerics who had been expelled from their positions for their

---

[66] The Parliamentary Diary of Sir Simonds D'Ewes, BL, Harleian MSS 164, fol. 74v; Stock, *Proceedings and Debates* 1: 122. The quotation of Pym is from BL, Harleian MSS 5047, fol. 79v, in Fletcher, *Outbreak*, p. 72.

[67] The newsletter quotation is from Fletcher, *Outbreak*, p. 64; A. P. Newton, *The Colonising Activities of the English Puritans* (New Haven, 1914), pp. 317–18.

[68] Fletcher, *Outbreak*, 114–17; Abbott, "Issue of Episcopacy," pp. 238–39.

Nonconformity during the 1630s and who would soon play leading roles, in close collaboration with the new-merchant leadership, in the radicalization of the City revolution. Within two days, Oliver Cromwell was demanding that the order of 6 September be generalized. Cromwell moved that "it shall be lawful for the parishioners of any parish in the kingdom . . . to set up a lecture and to maintain an orthodox minister at their own charge, to preach every Lord's day, where there is no preaching, and to preach one day in every week, when there is no weekly lecturer." Under the prodding of Pennington and others—including Jeremiah Burroughs who preached before the House on that day—the Commons passed Cromwell's proposal on 8 September. As Dr. Pearl has pointed out, if this bill had become law, the whole vexed question of ecclesiastical structure could have been bypassed, and "the victory of Puritanism . . . achieved painlessly and even without further parliamentary action."[69]

As it was, the House of Lords rejected both of the Commons' orders of 8 September. The Lords' reversal of the general order on Laudian innovations provoked a strong protest from six leading parliamentary opposition peers—Bedford, Warwick, Mandeville, Wharton, Clare, and Newport. In turn, the House of Commons' committee for the recess used its own temporary authority to see that the orders were nonetheless circulated throughout the nation between sessions.[70]

From Reform to Revolution

When Parliament returned from adjournment on 20 October 1641, Pym and his colleagues faced the same problem that had plagued the parliamentary leaders since they had begun to pass their legislation in November 1640: how to come to some arrangement with the king that would conclude and consolidate their reform of government. It had long been obvious that legislation in itself meant little. From the time of the Petition of Right, Charles showed with what ease he could ignore parliamentary enactments that he himself had approved. In order to have their reforms actually implemented and indeed to secure the safety of the reformers themselves, Pym and his friends were obliged to obtain more concrete controls over Charles's government. Yet Charles would, on his own, agree to none of these. This posed a conundrum that Pym and his friends would

[69] Parliamentary Diary of Sir Simonds D'Ewes, fols. 91, 101; *C.J.* 2: 281; K. N. Shipps, "Lay Patronage of East Anglian Puritan Clergy in Pre-Revolutionary England" (Yale University, Ph.D. diss., 1971), pp. 337–38. The Pearl quotation is from *London*, p. 220. See also Gardiner, *History* 10: 14–16, 29-30. For Burroughs and Greenhill, see below, ch. 8.

[70] Fletcher, *Outbreak*, pp. 114–15, 117–18ff.

never solve. On the one hand, were they to trust the king, they would risk not only their legislation but Parliament's safety. Not only had Charles made it clear that he had accepted a good part of Parliament's legislation only under duress, and possessed no personal commitment to the principles that lay behind it; he had also, on a whole series of occasions, entered into or sanctioned plots that, if successful, would have overthrown Parliament. On the other hand, were they to seek to impose the controls they required on the king, they would tend to alienate their own supporters within Parliament and among the landed classes more generally. This was, in part, because direct controls on the monarch, however minimal, were almost bound to appear innovative to parliamentary reformers acutely desirous of framing their reforms in conservative terms. More significantly, it was because any attempt to impose controls on the king required coercive means that could be had only outside Parliament, specifically through reliance on the London mass movement. Yet any move toward dependence on the citizens was naturally seen as fraught with danger, for it could threaten hierarchy, endanger the oligarchic control of politics traditionally exercised by the landed classes and urban elites, and place new, unwanted programs on the political agenda—above all, radical religious reformation. Pym and his colleagues thus faced a double bind: they could not trust Charles without endangering reform and their own safety; yet they could not move to safeguard reform and themselves against Charles without weakening their own position with their parliamentary supporters.

Initially, Pym and his colleagues had sought a settlement by attempting to get the king to agree to the removal of Strafford and other leading ministers and to the appointment in their place of leading members of the parliamentary opposition. But the parliamentary leadership had secured Strafford's removal and their own safety in the face of the king's plotting only by turning to the London mass movement. This appears to have helped precipitate the formation of the first royalist party, the pro-Straffordians. Then, with the apparent failure of the policy of bridge appointments, Pym had sought to achieve further reform and to consolidate a settlement by advancing the Ten Propositions and ejecting the bishops from the House of Lords. But Charles had engaged in the second army plot and had departed for Scotland. As a result, largely for strategic reasons—to confront and get around the resistance of the House of Lords, as well as of Charles himself—Pym and the other parliamentary leaders were obliged to resort to even stronger measures, notably the reintroduction of root and branch and the implicit sanctioning of local forces, especially in London, to pursue certain religious reforms on their own. But this de facto collaboration with popular elements had brought about further polarization.

By the end of the parliamentary recess of September–October 1641, Pym and his colleagues faced further complication. Over the period since the Long Parliament had first sat, the meaning of religious reformation had, for growing sections of the parliamentary classes, been essentially transmuted. In November 1640, an overwhelming majority of the parliamentary classes had strongly supported far-reaching religious reformation. They were deeply committed to removing the bishops and church courts from influence over secular affairs, to recovering royal and parliamentary supremacy from a usurping ecclesiastical hierarchy, to rooting out Arminianism and restoring Calvinism to its rightful place at the center of the religious order, and to eliminating Laudian innovations in church practice, while placing preaching at the core of day-to-day religious observance. Initially, none of the changes they desired seemed to require major alterations in the ecclesiastical structure, let alone a root and branch upheaval. Nor did these changes seem to pose a threat to the sociopolitical order, for one of their main objectives was to endow the parliamentary classes with firmer control over the church. Nevertheless, by the time Parliament returned from its recess almost a year later, many in the landed classes were coming to view religious reformation as inseparable from social subversion. In seeking to carry out ecclesiastical reform in the face of the implacable opposition of the House of Lords and King Charles, the House of Commons had, largely unintentionally, encouraged forces normally outside the political nation to take unilateral initiatives to reform religion and, even worse, had accelerated the formation of sectarian congregations, not to mention the rise of lay preaching. The process of religious reformation seemed to be getting out of hand, opening the way to popular revolution.[71]

The fact is that, at the start of the new session, Pym and the parliamentary leadership seemed to be in danger of losing support within Parliament and among the parliamentary classes more broadly as a result of their own close association with both religious reform and the London movement that especially supported it. One widely circulated pamphlet charged that the parliamentary leadership had "protected the ignorant and licentious sectaries and schismatics to stir up sedition, to bring in atheism and discountenanced all reverend ministers, and have endeavored to take away the common prayer book." Especially singled out for condemnation was "Saye the Anabaptist," who was alleged to be the leader of a "pack of half-witted lords" that included Bedford, Warwick, Mandeville, Brook,

---

[71] For excellent accounts of the way in which further religious reformation came to appear inseparable from and provocative of sociopolitical subversion in the eyes of a growing section of the parliamentary classes, especially during the second half of 1641, see Fletcher, *Outbreak*, pp. 108–14ff, and D. Hirst, "The Defection of Sir Edward Dering, 1640–1641," *HJ* 15 (1972). See also Abbott, "Issue of Episcopacy," pp. 203–5, 207, 229ff.

Wharton, and Essex, along with the MPs John Hampden, Denzil Holles, Arthur Hasilrig, Henry Marten, Isaac Pennington, Oliver St. John, Henry Vane the younger, and John Venn.[72] This sort of attack, despite its hyperbole, was not constructed out of whole cloth, and for this reason it posed serious dangers to the parliamentary leadership. The earl of Warwick, for example, had long shown his willingness to work with radical Puritans, even separatists, to strengthen political opposition and to further religious reformation. Saye and Brook were themselves Independents of some sort. Perhaps more to the point, since Parliament's return, these leaders had proved themselves ready to risk a certain amount of religious disorder in order to pursue religious reformation, especially in order to satisfy their radical supporters within London's militant proparliamentary movement, and they were loath to discourage zealous reformers, even those who held extremist views. Above all, at the time of Strafford's trial, the parliamentary leaders had not only worked closely with London radical leaders like Pennington, Vassall, Craddock, and Venn, but had depended on the street action of the London mass movement to achieve their ends and to defend themselves against the king.

There was no reason to believe that the parliamentary leadership would refrain from resorting once again to the London citizens were that to prove necessary. Yet growing numbers among the parliamentary classes, faced with rising popular initiatives, especially in the realm of religion, appear to have been increasingly willing to place their reforms in the hands of the king, if the only alternative was to place the future of their project in the hands of the London populace. Acutely aware of the rising fear of social subversion within the parliamentary classes, Charles seems, by the end of the summer, to have taken the advice of such confidantes as Sir Edward Nicholas and to have placed the protection of order and social hierarchy at the core of his program, making the defense of a non-Laudian episcopacy and of the prayer book the central plank on which to build a royalist party. This strategy posed a grave threat to the parliamentary leadership.[73]

THE SPLIT IN PARLIAMENT

At the start of the new session on 20 October 1641, Pym and his colleagues, faced with the potential defection of their supporters, apparently sought to moderate their policies in order to consolidate their position and to concentrate their forces on pressuring the king for a settlement. In par-

---

[72] "The Protestants' Protestation" (9 Sept. 1641) in *H.M.C.*, *Salisbury MSS*, 24: 277, quoted in Fletcher, *Outbreak*, p. 129.

[73] Fletcher, *Outbreak*, pp. 120–24.

ticular, they appear to have pulled back from their more controversial proposals for the reform of the church of the previous summer—notably root and branch and the Commons' orders of 8 September—and to have focused their energies on winning control of the House of Lords by eliminating the bishops and lay Catholics from that body.

Just after Parliament's return, the City radical MP and Massachusetts Bay Colony backer John Venn sought to have the Commons continue to enforce the order of 8 September by which parishes were given the right to hire their own lecturers, with or without the House of Lords' sanction. On 21 October, Venn brought into the House of Commons a motion against one Thomas Both, minister at St. Giles Cripplegate in London, for his having attacked a parishioner who was attempting to implement the House's order for the taking away of innovations and, in particular, for his having blocked the parish's attempt to appoint a lecturer under the order of 8 September. Because the House of Lords had rejected it, the order of 8 September for parish appointment of lecturers was without legal standing. Nevertheless, radical forces within London and Parliament seem to have wished to pose a test case, either of Parliament's will to further the reformation or of the Commons' willingness to give force to its own act over and against a House of Lords controlled by bishops and papists, or both. The radical MP Henry Marten and the root and brancher Sir Simonds D'Ewes leaped to Venn's aid. Nevertheless, although they may well have agreed with the views advanced by Venn and company, Pym and his colleagues appear to have wished to avoid a confrontation over explosive questions such as these, and the moderate forces easily won the day in the House.[74]

Radical elements not only in Parliament but also in London soon fell in line with the desire of the parliamentary leadership to focus on the elimination of the bishops from the House of Lords and to avoid any appearance of extremism. Demands for further religious reform ceased, for a significant period, to emanate from London. In fact, shortly after Parliament's return, City Independents and mainstream London Puritans held a crucial meeting on strategy at the home of the leading London minister Edmund Calamy, an important protégé of the earl of Warwick. They agreed to unite in the attack on bishops in the House of Lords and

---

[74] W. H. Coates, ed., *The Journal of Sir Simonds D'Ewes from the First Recess of the Long Parliament* (New Haven, 1942), pp. 19–20, hereinafter shortened to *D'Ewes*(C). The case was originally raised via a petition of 16 October from the parishioners of St. Giles to the parliamentary committee for the recess against Dr. William Fuller, Dean of Ely, and the vicar Timothy Hutton and his curate Timothy Bogh. It was initially brought into the House of Commons on 20 October by Sir Roger Burgoyne, a militant Puritan opposer of Caroline ecclesiastical innovations *D'Ewes*(C), (pp. 7, 17; M. F. Keeler, *The Long Parliament, 1640–1641* [Philadelphia, 1954], pp. 122–23). See also Pearl, *London*, p. 220.

to avoid raising disputed questions. They also agreed to use the prayer book to the extent possible in order to placate moderate Anglicans, while the Independents took it on themselves to try to persuade lay preachers not to discredit the Puritan cause by preaching in public.[75]

Nevertheless, with the outbreak of the Irish rebellion at the end of October, Pym found his options radically reduced. Now, the king and Parliament had to raise an army for Ireland, and the question of control over coercive power could not be put off much longer. As Professor Russell has put it, "From this time onwards, disputes increasingly concentrated on three issues: the winning of a majority in the House of Lords, control of the militia, and control of the London streets. Of these it was probably the third which was most important."[76]

On 8 November, Pym issued his revised Additional Instruction. This declared that if the king did not agree to the principle of parliamentary approval of royal officers, "though we would continue in that obedience and loyalty to him which was due by the laws of God and his kingdom, yet we should take such a course for the securing of Ireland as might likewise secure ourselves." The bitterly contested vote of 151 for and 110 against on the Additional Instruction showed how deeply divided the House had become.

With the decision to revive the Grand Remonstrance, Pym and his group made it abundantly clear that they no longer believed that they could both protect themselves and the parliamentary reforms already achieved and at the same time maintain the unity of the parliamentary classes. They had, they felt, no choice but to turn to London to defend their position, and they could not, as a result, avoid profoundly splitting Parliament and the parliamentary classes more generally. The content of the Grand Remonstrance was decidedly and intentionally moderate, but in this case the medium was the message. A detailed justification of Parliament's program and actions, the remonstrance was an open appeal from the parliamentary leadership to the people—above all the citizens of London—and as such it horrified much of the political nation. As Sir John Coke ironically remarked, whereas other remonstrances had been complaints of the people to the king, "some say this is a complaint of the king to the people." Sir Edward Dering, who only the previous spring had been willing to reintroduce into Parliament the root and branch bill, expressed very well the widespread fears of impending sociopolitical breakdown when he remarked that he "did not dream that we should remonstrate downward, tell stories to the people and talk of the king as of a third

[75] M. Tolmie, *The Triumph of the Saints: The Separate Churches of London, 1616–1649* (Cambridge, 1977), pp. 88–89.

[76] Russell, "Introduction," in *Origins*, p. 30.

party." But Pym, refusing to hide the intentions of the parliamentary leadership, resolutely affirmed that the remonstrance would "bind the people's hearts to us, when they see how we have been used."[77]

It is significant that at this climactic moment, the parliamentary leaders were careful to bring out the critical place of policy toward Spain in their dispute with the Crown and to reaffirm their devotion to the anti-Spanish offensive in the West Indies as the best way to advance the Protestant Cause. The government's reneging on its commitment to fight Spain in the West Indies in the middle 1620s, they made clear, was an important initial source of the conflict. The Grand Remonstrance therefore bitterly protested "the diverting of his majesty's course of war from the West Indies, which was the most facile and hopeful way for this kingdom to prevail against the Spaniard, to an expenseful and successless attempt upon Cadiz; which was so ordered, as if it had rather been intended to make us weary of war than to prosper in it."[78]

The decision by Pym and his colleagues to revive the Grand Remonstrance had far-reaching political consequences. But the split within Parliament and the parliamentary classes generally that thereby resulted represented no division over basic principles. Pym and his colleagues did not have the goal of making further constitutional innovations, nor did many of them differ irreconcilably even on religious conceptions from most of those who opposed them. They ultimately moved toward parliamentary control of the king's councilors and the militia only very reluctantly, and only out of what they judged to be a strategic necessity. What therefore distinguished Pym and the parliamentary leadership from those opting for the Crown was less their general ideology or specific program than their willingness to embrace a *strategy* of entrusting the parliamentary cause to an alliance with London citizens, which risked further political and especially religious radicalization. In contrast, those who became royalists chose, in essence, a strategy of placing the reform program of 1640–1641, which they basically shared with Pym and his colleagues, in the hands of Charles I, rather than risk losing control of the political process to popular forces.

To explain just what brought those who became parliamentarians to act as they did, in contrast with those who chose to support the Crown, still requires further research. But what must have been a central facilitating factor for the aristocratic colonizing oppositionists who formed such a crucial element within the parliamentary leadership was their long-term working relationship with the new-merchant leadership, with leading City

[77] For the two preceding paragraphs, see Fletcher, *Outbreak*, pp. 144–50 (the quotations are from p. 150). For Dering's change of heart, see Hirst, "Defection of Sir Edward Dering."
[78] Stock, *Proceedings and Debates* 1: 128.

Puritan clerics, and, through those groups, with the London mass movement. Led in particular by the earl of Warwick, the colonizing aristocrats had worked hand in hand, from the later 1620s through the whole period of Personal Rule, with new-merchant citizens and radical clerics like Hugh Peter in opposing arbitrary royal policies such as the Forced Loan, in resisting the Arminian and Laudian movements within the church, in furthering the Protestant Cause both at home and abroad, in developing commercial and privateering projects for the West Indies, and in building exile colonies in the New World for Puritan experimentation and resistance. That whole experience was undoubtedly crucial in making it possible for the parliamentary leadership to work closely with the new-merchant leaders and the City mass movement in furthering the cause of political reform, of Protestant reformation, and of the anti-Spanish offensive in the West Indies during the first phase of parliamentary struggle. The parliamentary aristocratic leaders had become used to collaborating with radical citizens and clerics normally outside the political nation, not only in commercial and colonial projects but also in political resistance to Charles I and, above all, in the movement against Arminianism and Laudianism and for a fully Calvinist settlement of religion during the years of arbitrary government. Such collaboration had proved especially fruitful in the pursuit of reform once Parliament had returned. As a result, these men had a much firmer basis for confidence than did many of their colleagues in Parliament and among the parliamentary classes in general that they could trust their militant lower-status allies outside Parliament and keep them within bounds.

REVOLUTION IN LONDON

Such confidence must have been vitally important, for, in turning to London in November 1641, Pym and his friends unquestionably were aware that they were placing their cause in the hands of a City parliamentary movement largely controlled by radicals. This was because, by the time of the Grand Remonstrance, the London citizenry had become totally polarized. Since the previous summer, the king had sought with growing openness and success to woo the increasingly cohesive and audacious London conservative movement, which had rapidly emerged to head off the radicals' offensive and to defend the City constitution. By late November 1641, therefore, London constitutional conservatism was almost entirely royalist, just as London support for Parliament was very heavily constitutionally radical.

The City's merchant political elite, as has been emphasized, at no time during the crisis that began at the end of the 1630s had given their allegiance to Parliament. But significant numbers of company merchants outside the elite probably did desire, at least for a time, from a politically conservative standpoint, to gain some type of reform of the monarchy. Despite the Crown's support for their privileges, these merchants could hardly have welcomed Charles's arbitrary rule, and must have hoped that Parliament could moderate his policies. The Levant Company, unlike the East India Company, did not refrain from presenting its grievances to Parliament, despite the risk of embarrassing the king. Its petition, forwarded on 22 December 1640, protested among other things the raising of customs duties. The second-generation Levant–East India Company magnate Thomas Soames went much further. An opposer of ship money while serving as sheriff in 1638, Soames stood as one of the four opposition candidates for City MP in April 1640 and November 1640 and refused to submit the names of wealthy citizens in his ward as payers of the government's Forced Loan in the spring of 1640. John Gayre was another top Levant Company trader who, as alderman, refused to cooperate in the spring of 1640 with the government's Forced Loan. He also stood as a popular candidate for lord mayor in September 1640. How many other politically conservative company merchants at least covertly sympathized with Gayre and Soames is impossible to say, but there may have been a significant number.[79]

Nevertheless, pressured on one side by a merchant political elite that refused to oppose the king or support parliamentary reform, and repelled on the other by an increasingly radical City parliamentary movement, company merchants who were politically conservative in the London context but who supported reform at the national level seem to have found working openly for Parliament rather difficult at every stage. The problem was only exacerbated by their dependence on the Crown for their privileges. It is possible that many company merchants hoped to have their cake and eat it too: to have Parliament impose reforms on the Crown without their having to take such overt and militant action against the king as to endanger their commercial charters. But for whatever reason, it is striking how relatively few of London's overseas company merchants were at all prominent in the City's parliamentary movement *at any time* between April 1640 and July 1641, especially in view of their wealth and preeminent position within London's political life. The result was that the City parliamentary movement was, from its inception, largely beyond the control of the company merchants: it brought the incursion of new socioeconomic forces into City and national political life and represented a shift in the locus of power within the City, not only away from the City's traditional elite merchant rulers but away from the company merchant community as a whole.

[79] PRO, S.P. 105/149/396; *D'Ewes*(N), p. 523; Pearl, *London*, pp. 191–92, 301–2.

Certainly, once common hall opened its attack in June 1641 on the lord mayor's traditional privilege of appointing one City sheriff, most of those conservative citizens who at first had identified with the parliamentary cause rushed to embrace the king as the best means to maintain the City's oligarchic political order. Within the space of a few months, the overwhelming majority of the City's overseas company merchants, along with many other substantial citizens, had definitively entered the king's camp.

On 23 July 1641, at the very time the conservative citizens were protesting the House of Lords' countenancing of common hall's attempt to elect both sheriffs, the king was promising the East India Company that he would renew its charter and remedy its grievances. A month or so later, when Parliament made an ill-considered decision not to renew the highly prized rebate of customs on reexports, the king took the opportunity to further endear himself to the merchants. When the merchants asked Parliament to reverse itself on the reexport issue, the king told his lord keeper to "tell the City in my name that though their own burgesses forget them in Parliament, yet I mean to supply that defect out of my affection to them, so that they need no mediators to me."[80]

From the fall of 1641, the king's secretary Edward Nicholas made every effort to bring the king and the leading citizens together. Meanwhile, at the election for lord mayor held on 28 September the conservative citizens gave renewed evidence that they were on the offensive. When common hall once again sought to elect its own candidate for mayor in place of the senior alderman Richard Gurney, Sheriff George Clarke simply dismissed the freemen and carried Gurney's name to the aldermanic court for approval. Clarke was one of the City's leading overseas traders, a second-generation elite merchant. A Merchant Adventurer who had exported more than two thousand cloths to the Netherlands and Hamburg in 1640, he had also served for several years as a director of the East India Company and had just that August been elected alderman.[81]

The king's decision of early November 1641 to return to London constituted an open threat to Parliament. But the lord mayor and the aldermanic court pushed forward preparations for a City banquet in the king's honor, despite the attempt by the City MP John Venn to prevent this "as a thing displeasing to Parliament." On 22 November, the Commons passed the Grand Remonstrance. But three days later, on 25 November, the City magistrates feted the king in London amid pomp and parade designed to awe a restive populace. Shortly thereafter a deputation of top City magistrates visited the king at Hampton Court. There they received

[80] Pearl, *London*, pp. 122–23; Fletcher, *Outbreak*, pp. 159–60.

[81] Pearl, *London*, pp. 124–25, 295–96. On Clarke's trade, see London Port Book for Cloth Exports, 1640, PRO, E.190/43/4, as well as *C.C.M.E.I.C. 1640–1643*.

honors, offices, and promises of favor for the City. The counterrevolution was in motion, and the battle for London would decide its fate.[82]

As early as the beginning of November, when Parliament had approached the City for a loan of £50,000 to suppress the Irish rebellion, the City recorder Sir Thomas Gardiner had complained of Parliament's failure to back up the City magistrates against the London militants. "There is now such a slighting of the government of the City that there is an equality between the mayor and the commons, the power of the mayor being no more than that of the commoners of the City." As something of a counterpoint to Gardiner's remarks, the citizens of common hall attached to their approval of the loan to Parliament proposals "that the persons of the great lords of the popish religion and other papists of quality . . . be . . . secured" and that the bishops' votes in the House of Lords be taken away. These demands were, of course, designed to put pressure on the House of Lords to pass the Commons' bill for the removal of the bishops from the upper house. It showed the degree to which the broadly representative common hall had diverged from the aldermanic court. Shortly thereafter, in a provocative action that could only raise suspicions as to his ultimate intentions, Charles dismissed the guard Parliament had appointed as its protection at Westminster, despite pleas from the House of Commons not to do so. On 29 and 30 November, violent confrontations broke out at the House of Lords when an angry crowd assembled in order to protest the new guard that the king had appointed to replace that of Parliament and to put force behind the demand to get rid of the bishops in the House of Lords.[83]

During the first week in December, the City oppositionists continued to mobilize the populace. Their aim was plainly to break the stalemate imposed by the House of Lords and to counteract the king's increasingly menacing actions. They started circulating a petition that conjoined Parliament's main demands with their own call for the reformation of City government: it called for the removal of the bishops and popish lords from the House of Lords, demanded parlimamentary control over the militia, and protested "abuses which had crept into the ancient constitution of the City." The petitioners added that "whereas it had been divulged upon the King's late entertainment in the City that the City had deserted the Parliament, they abhorred the same and should always be ready to spend their estates and lives for [its] safety." On 11 December, John Fowke, the

[82] Pearl, *London*, pp. 126–28; Fletcher, *Outbreak*, pp. 161–62.

[83] Gardiner is quoted in Pearl, *London*, p. 125. The quotation from the common hall petition is in *D'Ewes*(C), p. 133. Fletcher, *Outbreak*, pp. 171, 175; P. Zagorin, *The Court and the Country* (New York, 1969), p. 272 n. 7. For the mass mobilizations and mass pressures at the House of Lords at the end of November, and their upshot, see Manning, *English People*, pp. 53–61.

longtime City oppositionist and opponent of the East India Company, brought the Londoners' petition into the Commons, with some fifteen thousand signatures appended. There it was presented by Alderman Pennington. After this, Fowke was called in; he reported obstructions put by the lord mayor and aldermen to the petition's circulation, and the House promptly promised to look into them. On 15 December, in an open call for mass support, clearly designed to further encourage their militant supporters in London, the Commons had the Grand Remonstrance printed and distributed.[84]

On 20 December, the Commons warned the House of Lords to cease its delay on the bill to impress troops for Ireland. And, on the same day, it pursued its investigation of the City authorities for having impeded the circulation of the citizens' petition of 11 December. On 21 December, the Commons gave the militia bill a first reading. On the same day, at the annual elections to the common council, the City oppositionists won a signal victory, decisively reversing the political composition of that body in their favor. In the words of one contemporary, "By the concurrence and number of the meaner people, all such who were moderate men and lovers of the present government" were rejected, and in their place were elected citizens who were ready to take their direction from the leading faction in the House of Commons "and as forward to encroach upon their superiors, the mayor and aldermen, as the other upon the house of peers."[85]

The very same day, 21 December, the king precipitated the final showdown with his ill-conceived dismissal of Sir William Balfour, famous in the City for his heroic defense of the Tower against the incursion of troops sent by the king and the Army plotters at the time of the crisis over Strafford the previous spring, and his appointment in Balfour's place of the notorious royalist Sir Thomas Lunsford as lieutenant of the Tower. This was an open play for power, tantamount to a declaration of war. Following a fast day on the twenty-second, the House of Commons, on 23 December, issued a sharp protest against Lunsford's appointment, but the House of Lords, still resisting the Commons' demands for a parliamentary veto of the king's appointments and for the exclusion of the bishops from secular employment, refused to go along. Simultaneously, the king announced his rejection of the Grand Remonstrance. The situation was now at a breaking point, with the key constitutional and strategic questions inextricably intertwined, and still to be resolved. It was at this point that the City opposition forces, with the new merchants in the forefront, un-

---

[84] D'Ewes(C), pp. 270–72; Pearl, London, pp. 131, 222; Manning, English People, pp. 64–67; Zagorin, Court and Country, p. 271.

[85] Clarendon, History 1: 501, quoted in Manning, English People, p. 74; Pearl, London, pp. 132–39; Fletcher, Outbreak, p. 166; Gardiner, History 10: 103–4; D'Ewes(C), pp. 319–20.

leashed a powerful series of petitions, demonstrations, and armed confrontations that ultimately proved decisive.[86]

On 23 December, the very day of the Commons' protest of Lunsford and of the Lords' defiance, "divers common councilmen and others of the City of London" sought to throw their weight against Lunsford. They brought in a petition to the Commons declaring

> their fears of some dangerous designs from that citadel [the Tower]. And whereas the petitioners are informed that Sir William Belfor [Balfour], a person of honor and trust, is displaced from the office of the lieutenant and the same place bestowed upon a man outlawed and most notorious for outrages [Colonel Lunsford] and therefore fit for any dangerous attempt. The petitioners and many more, who have intelligence thereof, are thereby put into such a fright for fear and jealousy as makes them restless till they have discharged their duty in representing the same to this honorable house.[87]

An examination of the eighty-three signatures on the petition against Lunsford gives an excellent indication of the composition of the City's revolutionary leadership at this high point in the struggle. Not one Levant–East India Company merchant is among the signers. Nor does there seem to be a single Merchant Adventurer or French Company merchant. The only overseas traders who signed were from the colonial-interloping trades. The petition is indeed testimony to the numerical preponderance within the opposition movement of men not at all involved in overseas trade—and, in particular, to the special political position occupied by the new merchants, by virtue of their long-standing ties with the City's domestic tradesmen. The trader in American tobacco and interloper in the East Indies Samuel Warner, Maurice's brother George Thomson, Randall Mainwaring, and Stephen Estwicke were the core members of the new-merchant leadership who signed the petition. Additional colonial merchant signers included: William Underwood, a trader in Virginian tobacco who imported some 18,500 pounds in 1640 and who kept a shop on the same street as John and Samuel Warner's;[88] George Henley, another major colonial trader, who brought in 32,430 pounds of Virginian tobacco in 1640 and was also very active in the Moroccan and Spanish trades, as well as in privateering;[89] John Pocock, a prominent dealer with

[86] Manning, *English People*, pp. 74–76; Zagorin, *Court and Country*, p. 271; Gardiner, *History* 10: 108ff.

[87] House of Lords MSS, 23 December 1641.

[88] H. A. Dillon, ed., "MS. List of Officers of the London Trained Bands in 1643," *Archaeologia* 52, pt. 1 (1890); London Port Book for Imports, 1640, E.190/43/5.

[89] See, for example, *A.P.C. Col. 1613–1680*, pp. 242–44; PRO, C.2/Ch.I/H.75/61. Henley was

New England;[90] the tobacco seller Maximillian Bard;[91] Michael Herring, a substantial tobacco trader involved during the 1630s in the Newfoundland fish oil trade with the American-trade merchant Richard Hill;[92] Richard Hutchinson, another leading trader with New England where he owned land;[93] Lawrence Brinley; John Cocke; Richard Hunt; Richard Warner; and Robert Winch. It is notable that among the traders with the Americas who signed the anti-Lunsford petition, Samuel Warner, Richard Warner, George Thomson, Randall Mainwaring, Richard Hunt, Lawrence Brinley, Maximillian Bard, John Cocke, and Robert Winch all had signed the new-merchant leadership's petition of the previous December in support of Joseph Hawes and in favor of an anti-Spanish offensive in the West Indies.[94] Clearly, these men were working together along a broad front, going well beyond their economic interests in the Americas to City and parliamentary revolution. Tellingly, it was none other than John Pym who brought their petition against Lunsford into the House of Commons, where it was naturally very well received.[95] The alliance between the aristocratic colonizing parliamentarians and the new-merchant leadership was operating in high gear.

Seeing that all hopes for parliamentary unity had been shattered, the City oppositionists felt no further need to hold back on their plans for religious reformation. Even as they came to the aid of the parliamentary leadership, they began, once more, to push for the root and branch reconstruction of the national church and, in the meantime, carrying out local reformation on a piecemeal basis. In late October 1641, the citizens ap-

---

the second son of a Taunton, Somerset, armigerous family (*Visitation of Somerset, 1623*, Harleian Society Publications 11 [London, 1876], pp. 48–49).

[90] F. Rose-Troup, *The Massachusetts Bay Company and Its Predecessors* (New York, 1930), p. 152; *Notebook Kept by Thomas Lechford, Esq., Lawyer in Boston, Massachusetts Bay, from June 27, 1638 to July 29, 1641*, American Antiquarian Society Transactions and Collections, 7 (Worcester, Mass., 1885), p. 355. Pocock was a leading investor in the Braintree, Mass., ironworks in the 1640s (*New Eng. Hist. Gen. Reg.* 40 (1886): 170; E. N. Hartley, *Ironworks on the Saugus* (Norman, Okla., 1957), pp. 70, 286.

[91] PRO, E.122/218/25 (retail tobacco-seller licensees). Bard was the son of a minister of Staines, Middlesex (J. R. Woodhead, *The Rulers of London, 1660–1689* [London, 1965], p. 223).

[92] For Herring's tobacco imports, see PRO, E.122/230/9. For his trade with Hill, see BL, Add. MSS 5489, fol. 46.

[93] PRO, H.C.A.24/100/57; Will of Richard Hutchinson, 1670, printed in *New Eng. Hist. Gen. Reg.* 20 (1866): 359. Hutchinson was later an active interloper in the East Indies (M. P. Ashley, *Financial and Commercial Policy under the Cromwellian Protectorate* [Oxford, 1934] p. 113; *C.C.M.E.I.C. 1650–1654*, p. 340). Hutchinson was a brother of William Hutchinson, the husband of Ann Hutchinson. He had a number of sons who emigrated to New England, in partnership with whom he may have traded. His will lists houses, lands, a sawmill, and the like among his possessions in New England.

[94] See above, p. 327 n. 13.

[95] *D'Ewes*(C), p. 339.

pear, as noted, to have shelved their divisive demands on religion in deference to Pym. But on 20 December 1641, the radical London MP John Venn, a longtime supporter of the Massachusetts Bay Puritan experiment, along with the minister Cornelius Burges, brought into Parliament a petition from London's Puritan ministers, asking that they no longer be required to use prayers against their conscience and calling for a free, national synod to decide on religion.[96] Then, on 23 December, the very day that the citizens' petition against Lunsford was submitted, Alderman Isaac Pennington presented to the Commons still another petition, organized and brought in by London apprentices, this time for reforming the church root and branch; it was said to have been signed by thirty thousand Londoners. The apprentices had already announced their intention "if need be to overmatch a royal coup," and they appended to their petition a complaint that the City authorities had hindered them in their collection of signatures. They asked for the House's sanction of their proceedings. It is a sign of the parliamentary leadership's collaboration with the London movement and of its dependence on the unauthorized mass activities of the citizenry at this point that Sir Simonds D'Ewes was able to push through a motion, reported by the speaker of the house to the apprentices, that approved their "orderly manner" and promised redress against the City authorities while saving consideration of the petition's content to a later date.[97] Also on 23 December the aforementioned John Venn, along with the colonial merchants John Warner and John Brett and several other citizens of St. Benet Gracechurch parish, took the opportunity to deliver yet one more petition, to get rid of their "scandalous" minister William Quelch. John Warner was the only new-merchant leader to have gained the position of alderman in the period before the revolution. He and his brother Samuel (father-in-law of Maurice's brother William Thomson) were partners in a grocer's shop from which they sold the tobacco they imported from Virginia and the West Indies. John Brett, a brother-in-law and apprentice of Randall Mainwaring (partner and son-in-law of Joseph Hawes and relative and close political collaborator of Matthew Craddock and Isaac Pennington), was also a London grocer and had been involved in the triangular trades with Africa, the West Indies, and New England from about 1640.[98]

On 24 December, the House of Commons gave the militia bill a second reading and went on to resolve that "this House hold Colonel Lunsford unfit to be lieutenant of the Tower of London; as a person in whom the Commons of England cannot confide." They also addressed a sharp re-

[96] Ibid., p. 325; Pearl, *London*, p. 223.

[97] *D'Ewes*(C), pp. 337–38.

[98] Ibid., p. 338; House of Lords MSS, 23 December 1641. For Warner and Brett, and their colonial trades, see above, ch. 4.

buke to the House of Lords, condemning the "delays and interruptions . . . we have received in the House of Peers . . . by the great number of bishops and papists, notoriously disaffected to the common good." If Lunsford continued in his office, they warned, "we hold ourselves bound in conscience to declare and protest, that we are innocent of the blood which is likely to be spilt, and of the confusion which may overwhelm the state."[99]

The Lords defiantly put off considering the Commons' demands. But, in response, the London citizens brought in yet another petition on the same day, 24 December, that demanded that the Lords cease to procrastinate and, specifically, that they pass the impressment bill and stop holding up the effort to raise an army for Ireland. The petitioners protested the Lords' "long . . . and unseasonable delay whilst the life, liberties, and estates of the Protestants of that kingdom" were destroyed and their own Irish "estates to the value of above a million of monies" lay threatened with ruin. They called on the Lords to "lay aside all things that may trouble the way" and to "give instant dispatch for the relief of that miserable realm and people." It is likely that some of the signers of this petition actually did have Irish holdings. But the timing of this petition, as well as the identity of its signers, leaves no doubt that its function was primarily political. The City oppositionists, with new-merchant leaders prominently among them, were once more coming to the aid of their allies in Parliament. Among the signers are found, once again, Maurice Thomson and his brother William, William Thomson's father-in-law Samuel Warner, Maurice Thomson's longtime trading partner Thomas Stone, Randall Mainwaring, and Maximillian Bard, as well as one William Melling, an active trader in Virginian tobacco about whom little is known. Company merchants were once again conspicuous by their absence. The petition's signers were overwhelmingly domestic traders, a good many of them already established leaders in the City opposition who would be heard from on many occasions in the subsequent period.[100]

On 26 December, Lord Mayor Richard Gurney informed the king that Lunsford would have to be replaced or order would be entirely lost. This was a definitive sign that the aldermanic elite could no longer control the situation, and the king was compelled to dismiss Lunsford. The next day a crowd of citizens gathered at Whitehall to find out the response to their petition against Lunsford, but even on learning of the king's capitulation, they remained to press for action on their petitions against the bishops and popish lords brought in earlier in the month by John Fowke and Isaac

[99] Gardiner, *History* 10: 110–11; Zagorin, *Court and Country*, p. 274; *C.J.* 2: 356; *D'Ewes*(C), pp. 341–48.

[100] House of Lords MSS, 24 December 1641; *H.M.C., Fourth Report, Appendix*, p. 109; Zagorin, *Court and Country*, p. 275; *D'Ewes*(C), p. 342.

Pennington. Later the same day, 27 December, the subsequent Leveller John Lilburne violently confronted Lunsford with a band of armed men, the first of several clashes in this climactic period in which Lilburne would be involved. Crowds repeatedly gathered in Westminster during the next two days. Meanwhile the king and the archbishop of York busily gathered troops of their own. The House of Commons, now entirely dependent on the citizens for its security, stood behind the citizens, refusing to support declarations from the House of Lords that would have banned the citizens' assemblies. As John Pym is reported to have said, "God forbid that the House of Commons should proceed in any way to dishearten people to obtain their just desires in such a way." In this atmosphere of impending conflict, the archbishop of York, with the backing of the king, led twelve bishops to declare that the citizens' intimidation had prevented a "free Parliament" over the previous several days. The Commons responded by impeaching the bishops, and the House of Lords, now feeling itself provoked, had the bishops thrown in jail. Perhaps expecting a showdown, the Commons decided on 31 December to adjourn to Guildhall in London.[101]

It now came down to a question of force, and Parliament had placed itself firmly in the hands of its supporters in London. On 3 January, the king accused John Pym and four other leading MPs of treason. But on 4 and 5 January the Londoners closed their shops, stood armed at their doors, sheltered Pym and his colleagues, and rebuffed the king's efforts to seize the Five Members. On 4 January, the day of the king's coming into Parliament to demand the surrender of the Five Members, the common council, on the order of the House of Commons sitting at Guildhall, elected a committee of public safety for the City. This body assumed broad powers of initiating legislation in London, took the authority to call and dissolve the common council, and put itself in command of the City's militia. During the critical days of the winter and early spring of 1642, this committee guided the consolidation of the City revolution. London's militant mass movement, having provided both the indispensable instrument for defending Parliament's program and the underlying cause of Parliament's dividing against itself, had thus saved Parliament from the King's coup d'état, and it is important to look a bit more closely at the citizens who made this possible, and how they operated.[102]

I have already brought out the prominent place of the colonial-interloping merchants among the leaders of the City petition campaign and the mass mobilization in defense of London. What especially needs emphasizing is the fact of broader political organization—the existence of some

[101] Manning, *English People*, pp. 76–87; *D'Ewes*(C), pp. 352–53; Zagorin, *Court and Country*, pp. 277–78.

[102] Pearl, *London*, pp. 139–46ff., 224; Manning, *English People*, pp. 96–98.

sort of "party"—which is manifest in this series of actions, and particularly in the ability of the London oppositionists to respond, sometimes within hours of an event, with significant numbers of signatures on a petition or with a mass demonstration. This can be seen clearly with respect to the petition (with 83 signatures) against Lunsford, which came just one day after his appointment as lieutenant of the Tower, as well as the petition (with 108 signatures) in favor of the impressment bill that was delivered on the very day of the Lords' deliberations on postponing action on that bill. Obviously, there was at least a hard core of organizers with a well-developed network of followers who could be counted on at short notice. These men can be glimpsed in action in a royalist report of 9 December 1641 "concerning undue practices by citizens to get signatures to a petition to be presented in the name of the City to the House of Commons."[103] According to this source:

> William Hobson, mercer at the Maidenhead in Ave Maria Lane summoned the parishioners into his own house with a constable betwixt 9 and 10 at night and told those that refused to sign the petition that they were neither good Christians nor honest men, nor well affected to the Commonwealth; telling them he would despatch his part, and then send it to the next common councilman. This Hobson is a dangerous and factious man, and used many false persuasions to draw men to write their names. In the next ward Deputy Taylor, dwelling at the Hen and Chickens in Paternoster Row, warned most of the parish to his house, and there exhorted them to set their hands to the petition.

It so happens that both this "dangerous" Mr. William Hobson and Deputy (Daniel) Taylor were connected with the new-merchant leadership, and both may already have been active in colonial undertakings. Hobson was the father-in-law of Maurice Thomson's collaborator in the Americas and the East Indies Samuel Pennoyer.[104] Taylor's uncle Robert Taylor migrated to Bermuda and his stepbrother Edward Rawson would become secretary of the Massachusetts Bay Colony.[105] Both Hobson and Taylor would function as political intimates of the colonial-interloping merchants throughout the following decade.

There can be little doubt that much the same group responsible for the petition campaign—of which the new-merchant leadership was one, but by no means the only, important component—guided the London crowds

---

[103] *C.S.P.D. 1641–1643*, p. 193.

[104] Society of Genealogists, Boyd's Index of London Citizens: 34837. Pennoyer chose Hobson as an overseer of his will (PRO, will of Samuel Pennoyer, 1654 PCC Alchin 388).

[105] *New Eng. Hist. Gen. Reg.* 42 (1898): 178; H. F. Waters, *Genealogical Gleanings in England*, 2 vols. (Boston, 1901), 1: 170–71; PRO, will of Daniel Taylor, 1655 PCC Aylett 384.

in the decisive days of later December 1641 and early January 1642. This is not at all to say that the masses of London citizens were, at every moment, acting at the behest of the radical leadership; unquestionably, there was much spontaneity and independent initiative, and the massed citizens, at times, had their own demands. The fact remains that the demonstrations of the London citizenry, at almost every critical juncture, complemented the programs and the tactics of the parliamentary leadership and of the City oppositionists, and this was not accidental. William Lilly later stated that the demonstrators were "set on by some of better quality," and the Venetian ambassador thought that the apprentices took part "with the connivance of their masters, puritans for the most part." In the words of one commentator, "There was a kind of discipline in disorder, tumults being ready at command, upon a watch-word given." And as another drily remarked, "But how it came to pass that these multitudes should come down in such disorder, and yet be sent back and dissolved so easily at a word or beck of some men, let the world judge."[106]

Who, then, was in charge? The king accused the two City MPs, Isaac Pennington and John Venn, of bringing down "their myrmidons to assault and terrify the members of both houses, whose faces or whose opinions they like not, and by that army to awe the Parliament." Another observer thought the leadership of the crowds was the same as it had been in the crisis-filled days before Strafford's execution the previous May, and he said that the organizers of the tumults were John Fowke and Randall Mainwaring, "who went from house to house and brought this Hydra's Head to Westminster, and put in their mouths to cry 'No Bishops, No Popish Lords', as they had formerly in the same tumultuous manner caused them to cry for justice against the Earl of Strafford." No doubt both the king and the other commentator were right.[107] Indeed, it seems fairly obvious that when the House of Commons, in cooperation with the common council, constituted the City committee of public safety to take charge of London during the emergency, it merely elevated to formal political authority those in the City who had long been exercising it informally through their petition drives and their mass mobilizations.

The committee of safety, or militia committee as it came to be called, originally consisted of eighteen members, but three of these—Alderman John Gayre and Alderman John Garrard, both directors in the Levant–East India combine, and Alderman Nicholas Rainton (replaced by John Warner)—were clearly opposed to the principle and practice of the committee and did not serve.[108] The remaining group of sixteen was domi-

---

[106] The quotations are from Manning, *English People*, pp. 91–92.

[107] Ibid., p. 92 (emphasis added).

[108] CLRO, J.Co.Co.40, fols, 11, 16, 17, 17v; Pearl, *London*, pp. 140–41.

nated by the new-merchant leadership. Included were the new-merchant leaders and City oppositionist organizers John Warner, Samuel Warner, Randall Mainwaring, and Stephen Estwicke, along with Owen Rowe (the trader with Massachusetts Bay and in Virginian tobacco who had recently been elected deputy governor of the Bermuda Company), William Barkeley (the Canadian-trade merchant and partner of Maurice Thomson's brother-in-law Elias Roberts in the trades with the West Indies and New England), James Russell (a Spanish-trade merchant and apparently also a Merchant Adventurer, who was, in addition, a partner of Maurice Thomson's in the interloping project in the East Indies), and Nathan Wright (the trader with New England and Newfoundland interloper who was also a member of Thomson's East India interloping company). John Fowke, the Levant Company trader, collaborator of Sir William Courteen's, opponent of joint-stock monopoly organization in the East Indies trade, and City oppositionist who recently had established connections with the new-merchant leadership, was also among the members of the committee. None of the remaining members was an overseas company merchant. But most of the militia commissioners had been leaders in the City movement from early on, as is indicated, for example, by the fact that four of the six persons who had represented common hall in the dispute over the right to choose sheriffs the previous June were also on the militia committee.[109] Finally, perhaps to ensure the closest coordination between Parliament's own committee of safety and the committee of safety in the City, Maurice Thomson's commercial and political partner Richard Shute was appointed treasurer of the parliamentary committee of safety.[110] Shute, with Thomson, had delivered the citizens' petition of grievances to the king in September 1640. He would play a major leadership role in the City radical movement over the following two years, as would most of the members of the City committee of safety.

CONSOLIDATING THE REVOLUTION

On 11 January 1642, the king fled London, but London's leading citizens were not yet quite prepared to admit defeat. In a last-ditch effort, they circulated a petition against what they saw as the committee of safety's unlawful usurpation of the rightful powers of the City's magistracy. Presented to Parliament on 17 February 1642, this document confirms again

[109] For all these merchants, see preceding chapters. The other members of the committee of safety were Thomas Atkins, John Wollaston, John Towse, William Gibbs, Alexander Normington, James Bunce, and Francis Peck. The representatives from common hall had been Francis Peck, John Fowke, Randall Mainwaring, and Stephen Estwicke.

[110] M.A.E. Green, ed., *Calendar of the Proceedings of the Committee for Advance of Money, 1642–1656*, 3 vols. (London, 1888), 1: 3.

the social character of the forces behind a City conservative movement now firmly aligned with the Crown. Among the petition's 330 signers, there were at least 46 Levant Company merchants. No fewer than 25 of the 26 Levant Company merchants who had signed the petition of the previous summer against common hall's attempt to elect both City sheriffs also signed this petition against the militia committee. Also among the signers there were at least 15 past, present, or future East India Company directors, at least 22 Merchant Adventurers, at least 14 French Company wine traders, and at least 6 Eastland Company traders. The City's merchant community had once again shown itself firmly conservative, and, by now, fully royalist.[111]

But without the king's person or the king's army, the conservative citizens had few real sources of power. On 9 March 1642, twenty-one radical Londoners presented a petition to the common council to urge that body to disclaim the citizens' petition against the militia committee, to express to Parliament its support of the militia ordinance, and to endeavor to have the petitioners against the militia ordinance properly punished. Notable among these radical petitioners were a handful of lesser traders with the Americas, as well as the later Leveller William Walwyn. As it turned out, however, the militants had little to be concerned about. During the spring and summer of 1642, the City oppositionists had no difficulty consolidating their position by carrying through a full-scale constitutional revolution to break the old form of oligarchic rule. They abrogated the veto power of the court of aldermen over the common council, leaving the individual aldermen to cast their 26 votes together with 237 votes of the common councilors. They broke the lord mayor's power to convene and dissolve common council meetings. They took an important series of steps to destroy the stranglehold over elections to the common council hitherto exercised by small oligarchic cliques in the precincts and the wards. This helped ensure that all City freemen could exercise their right to vote. From the summer of 1642, the common council, for the moment led by its militia committee, assumed unquestioned leadership in the government of the City.[112]

During July and August 1642, the City parliamentary movement removed the last obstacle to its complete hegemony within the City when it got Parliament to bring to trial and to remove the archroyalist lord mayor Sir Richard Gurney. Gurney had continued to deny the common council's right to call and dissolve itself without the lord mayor's approval and had led a rearguard struggle by the aldermanic bench to maintain the old City

[111] Pearl, *London*, pp. 149–51; House of Lords MSS, 24 February 1642. For details concerning this petition and, more generally, the political affiliation of the different groups of overseas company merchants, see below, pp. 374–89.

[112] Pearl, *London*, pp. 143–48, 152–54. CLRO, J.Co.Co.40, fols. 25–26v.

constitution, obstruct Parliament's military preparations in the City, and support the Crown. On 9 July 1642, sixty-four common councilors petitioned the House of Lords to have Gurney stopped from hampering their proceedings. Symptomatically, among this petition's signers there were nine colonial-interloping merchants, including William Barkeley, Owen Rowe, Samuel Warner, Randall Mainwaring, Stephen Estwicke, and James Russell (all militia commissioners), as well as Samuel Vassall, Michael Herring, and Richard Waring. There were, however, only three company merchants. All of the rest of the signatories were nonmerchants. When Gurney was brought up for trial before Parliament, five of the seven magistrates who gave evidence against him were new-merchant militia commissioners, including John Warner, Randall Mainwaring, Stephen Estwicke, Owen Rowe, and James Russell. It was only fitting that on 12 August 1642 common hall elected Alderman Isaac Pennington the new lord mayor and that Pennington had his kinsman, the colonial trader and radical organizer Randall Mainwaring, chosen deputy mayor.[113] Over the following year these two officials, now in the highest seats of authority in the City, would lead London behind Parliament and toward further radicalization.

What transpired in the course of political conflict in London from the winter of 1641 through the summer of 1642 can be briefly summarized. The City oppositionists, through their petition campaigns and mass rising, had made it possible for Parliament to secure its legislation, indeed its continuing existence, against the king. In the process, they had carried out a revolution in London itself. The municipal revolt of 1641–1642 involved no mere replacement of "ins" by "outs." The citizen militants shattered the old oligarchic constitution; in the process, they achieved at least a partial transformation in the social foundations of political power in the City.

In attacking and destroying the traditional structure of governance dominated by the lord mayor and the court of aldermen, the London militants had essentially destroyed the hegemony in the City of the overseas company merchants, who traditionally had controlled the municipality precisely through controlling the court of aldermen. Over the previous period, overseas merchants had held a majority of the aldermanic positions, while wholesalers had held most of the rest. Not surprisingly, therefore, company merchants were at the heart of the two main mass petitions organized in London to stem the revolutionary tide, the first with 172 signatures against common hall's attempt to elect both sheriffs, the second with 330 signatures in February 1642 against the newly appointed militia

[113] House of Lords MSS, 9 July 1642; Pearl, *London*, pp. 155–58.

committee. All told, 412 people signed these petitions, and between one-quarter and one-third were company merchants.[114] Similarly, around 245 people signed the four main proparliamentary petitions put forward during this period and mentioned above. But among these signers, there were no more than about 15 company merchants.[115]

At the same time, in elevating to power the common council, initially led by their own special committee of public safety, the City revolutionaries carried near to the center of authority in London, and to a very influential position nationally, the new-merchant leaders who headed a powerful movement of citizens drawn from the ranks of London's domestic traders, shopkeepers, and artisans. As noted, there were nine colonial-interloping merchants (if John Fowke is included within the group) among the active militia commissioners, while the two company merchants appointed to this committee refused to serve. Similarly, of the twenty-eight common councilors who served on common council committees over the revolutionary period between the beginning of January and the end of July 1642, only two were company merchants.[116] Finally, new-merchant leaders were at the heart of all four of the aforementioned proparliamentary petitions, and these four petitions were signed, almost exclusively, by nonmerchants.

It is true that greater numbers of company merchants ultimately would change sides or come out for Parliament, once the issues of the City's constitution and its political allegiance had been firmly settled. Moreover, as described below, the radical and (except for the new merchants) largely nonmerchant citizens who dominated City politics until the middle of 1643 would see their power recede significantly after that time. Nevertheless, the London militants who overthrew the old oligarchy and secured the City for Parliament had, by the summer of 1642, achieved a truly fundamental change, and they had done so on the basis of a movement composed almost entirely of nonmerchants, over the opposition of the great mass of company merchants. Nor were they yet, at that point, ready to bring the revolutionary process to a halt.

The Politics of London's Overseas Traders at the Outbreak of Civil War

THE LEVANT–EAST INDIA COMBINE

The Crown's greatest success in London during the 1630s was in strengthening and consolidating the support—over and against Parliament—of

---

[114] See above, pp. 344, 371–72.

[115] The petition of 9 March 1642, with signatures, is in CLRO, J.Co.Co.40, fol. 25. For the other petitions, see above, pp. 364–67, 372–73.

[116] The list of the twenty-eight councilors is from CLRO, J.Co.Co.40, for the period indicated.

the majority of the City merchant elite, as represented on the customs farms, the aldermanic court, and the East India Company directorate. By 1640, the merchant elite was dominated largely by Levant Company merchants. This meant that, from the very start, a critical group of Levant–East India Company elite merchants was at the heart of the City conservative movement. From the summer of 1641 at the latest, the great bulk of the Levant–East India Company merchants threw in their lot with royalism. On the basis of the two main conservative petitions of this movement, forty-seven different Levant Company members associated themselves with the forces for order. Using additional scattered scources, it is possible to identify at least six more Levant Company members (whose names do not appear on the petitions) as allying themselves with London conservatism. This total of fifty-three does not, of course, exhaust the entire Levant Company membership, but it does include about half of those men who are known to have been active in the currants trade between 1634 and 1640, and about the same proportion of major men in that trade. Of some eighty-five Levant Company members who traded in currants between 1634 and 1640, and who were alive in 1641–1642, a total of forty-nine left evidence of their political orientation: of these, thirty-five were royalists,[117] eleven were parliamentarians,[118] and in three cases the indications are contradictory.[119] Of the twenty-two Levant Company members still alive in 1641–1642 who traded 1,000 hundredweight or more of currants in any single year during the decade 1631–1640, eleven can be identified politically: eight with royalism,[120] and one with Parliament,[121] while two left contradictory evidence.[122] (See table 7.1.)

The case of the East India Company directorate, at the core of the merchant elite, is naturally even more clear-cut. On the basis of the petitions, as well as additional evidence, no fewer than twenty-four of the thirty-three men who held positions on the East India Company governing board in 1640–1641 (including the governor, deputy governor, and treasurer)

[117] Royalists: Morris Abbot, William Ashwell, Nicholas Backhouse, Richard Bateman, Edward Bostock, Thomas Bowyer, Humphrey Browne, John Browne, William Cockayne, John Cordell, Henry Garway, John Garway, William Garway, John Gayre, Thomas Hamersley, Job Harby, Daniel Harvey, Henry Hunt, Joseph Keble, William Leader, James Mann, Thomas Marsham, Samuel Mico, Richard Middleton, Hugh Norris, Nicholas Penning, Marmaduke Rawden, Andrew Riccard, Robert Sainthill, Roger Vivian, John Wardall, John Watkins, Richard Whitbred, John Williams, William Williams.

[118] Parliamentarians: Thomas Barnardiston, Richard Chambers, Gregory Clement, Caleb Cockcroft, Matthew Craddock, Richard Cranley, Simond Edmonds, Samuel Elliot, Caldwell Farrington, Samuel Moyer, Benjamin Whetcomb.

[119] Henry Hunter, John Langham, Thomas Soames.

[120] Thomas Bowyer, John Cordell, Henry Garway, William Garway, John Gayre, Samuel Mico, Hugh Norris, Richard Middleton.

[121] Matthew Craddock.

[122] John Langham, Thomas Soames.

can be identified with the antiparliamentary cause.[123] Only two were parliamentarians.[124]

It is significant that on 26 November 1641, at the very height of the City and national political crisis, the East India Company membership elected as governor of the company Sir Henry Garway, one of London's most notorious royalists, and they reelected him the following summer, just before the outbreak of the Civil War. Despite a parliamentary order of 10 April 1643 demanding Garway's immediate dismissal from all his commercial company positions, the East India Company directorate retained Garway as governor until the regular company elections of July 1643. Even more recalcitrant, the Levant Company membership kept Garway as governor until 1644.[125] During the spring of 1643, when London was preparing its defenses against the king's armies, the East India Company's general court voted to deny Parliament's request for the use of its ordnance on the bulwarks then being erected around the City. In July of the same year, the company refused to lend six guns for the equipment of parliamentary ships.[126] In light of this defiant royalist posture, it is understandable that Parliament kept a close surveillance on the company's correspondence.[127] The loans granted by the Levant and East India companies to Parliament in 1643 can be understood only in terms of the company merchants' anxiety to be sure that their charters would be renewed. Although this quid pro quo was explicitly spelled out by Parliament, the Levant Company still had some difficulty raising the money from its members, and the House of Commons had to threaten reluctant subscribers with the immediate suspension of their privileges before the funds were forthcoming.[128]

The ideological commitments of the Levant–East India Company merchants were further expressed in their religious policies, particularly in the Levant Company's appointments of ministers. As already noted, the company chose clerics in sympathy with the anti-Puritan wing of the hierarchy even before the rise of Laud, and continued to do so in the period of Laud's ascendancy. It is not surprising that a company so strongly de-

[123] Governor Christopher Clitherow, Deputy Governor William Cockayne, Treasurer Robert Bateman, Anthony Abdy, Morris Abbot, William Ashwell, Richard Bateman, John Bludworth, George Clarke, John Cordell, George Franklin, Henry Garway, William Garway, John Gayre, John Holloway, Richard Middleton, Gilbert Morewood, Abraham Reynardson, Thomas Stiles, John Trott, Rowland Wilson, John Wolstenholme.

[124] Matthew Craddock, William Spurstow. Again, John Langham and Thomas Soames were ambivalent about their political orientation.

[125] *C.C.M.E.I.C. 1640–1643*, pp. xxi, xxv, 331; PRO, S.P.105/150/103; Pearl, *London*, pp. 300–301.

[126] *C.C.M.E.I.C. 1640–1643*, pp. 309–10, 317, 333.

[127] W. Foster, *East India House* (London, 1924), p. 16.

[128] A. C. Wood, *A History of the Levant Company* (London, 1935, repr. 1964), p. 52 n. 2.

pendent on royal support as was the Levant Company failed to risk controversial clerical appointments during the eleven years of nonparliamentary rule and Laudian religious repression. Nevertheless, in view of the company's appointment of ministers so closely connected with Laud in the period before 1640 and its continuing identification with royalist and Anglican ministers in the years following the fall of Laud, it is hard to believe that it would have pursued anything but an anti-Puritan religious policy, even had it been given the opportunity.

The first preacher to be nominated by the Levant Company in the Civil War period was one William Bull. No direct evidence of Bull's religious orientation has been found, but the company's deliberations on his appointment bring out something of the motivation behind his hiring. Bull presented himself for the post of preacher at the Levant Company's factory at Smyrna on 7 April 1645 and was requested to give the customary sermon to the general court. On 17 April, his election was deferred, exception being taken to "some passages in his prayer." A week later, at a meeting of the company's general court, the City radical MP Isaac Pennington and one John Langley expressed their strong opposition to Bull. But the court overrode their objections and by a show of hands appointed Bull to a five-year term. Still not satisfied, Pennington returned to the company several weeks later with the claim that some of the members of the House of Commons had attested to Bull's unfitness, and another company member, Thomas Barnardiston, produced a letter to the same effect. They suggested that Bull's appointment be referred to the Assembly of Divines for approval. However, this motion failed to get the court's support and Bull's election was confirmed.[129]

The objections to Bull were undoubtedly based on his failure to conform to Puritan standards. Isaac Pennington, John Langley, and Thomas Barnardiston, the three Levant Company members who pressed the attack, were all committed Puritans, and both Barnardiston and Pennington were in these years playing leading roles in the Puritan parish of St. Stephen's Coleman Street.[130] Langley, a recent entry into the Levant Company, was also a Puritan militant and in later years was apparently involved with the Anabaptists.[131] Clearly, these men were offended by the content of Bull's sermon and, more broadly, by his religious orientation. Their appeal to the judgment of the Assembly of Divines was an attempt to place the case before a body that, unlike the Levant Company, was puritanically inclined and might support their case. At the general court,

[129] J. B. Pearson, *Biographical Sketches of the Chaplains to the Levant Company, 1611–1706* (London, 1883), pp. 61–62. The following section leans heavily on the compilations from the Levant Company court books, as well as the biographical material, presented by Pearson.

[130] Guildhall Library MSS 4458.1, pp. 147, 332.

[131] W. C. Abbott, *The Writings and Speeches of Oliver Cromwell*, 4 vols. (1937–1947), 3: 49.

Bull was defended by a "Mr. Brown," almost certainly Humphrey Browne, a leading trader and a director at one time or another of both the Levant and East India companies. Browne had been a leader in the anti-impositions agitation within the Levant Company in the late 1620s. But by this time, like most of his colleagues, he had become a strong defender of the established political order and of an emerging Anglican orthodoxy.[132] He seems to have had little difficulty in getting the company members to maintain their support for Bull.[133]

The remaining Levant Company appointments before the Restoration, in a period when it was probably somewhat risky to support proroyal, Anglican ministers, provide further strong evidence of the company's establishment-oriented religious views. A "Mr. Dillingham," elected in 1648, cannot be identified. But Nathaniel Hill, appointed minister at Aleppo in 1650, was probably the vicar of Renhold who had been ejected from his post in 1643 because of his "long absence in the Royal army."[134]

Of the last four ministers appointed in this period, three—Samuel Rogers, John Dalton, and Robert Frampton—can be identified,[135] and were clearly royalist Anglicans. At the Restoration, Rogers and Dalton each received an honorary B.A. degree by the king's mandate in recognition of the inconveniences each had suffered in giving support to the royal cause. Frampton, who took a B.A. degree at Christ Church in 1641, had to defer his M.A. degree as a result of his refusal to take the Covenant. During the Protectorate, he was warned by the government that he was preaching too freely for his own personal safety. He was made bishop of Gloucester after the Restoration.[136]

The foregoing picture of the Levant Company merchants' anti-Puritanism accords well with what has been shown to be their conservative political orientation. Substantial involvement in the Levant—East India trades tended to be accompanied by a whole constellation of socioeconomic characteristics, as well as a wide variety of family and business associations with other merchants in the group, and these all led in a conservative direction. It was, indeed, by the totality of his socioeconomic position— his politically privileged commercial position, his high place in London's economic and social hierarchies, his solidarity with other company traders like himself, his self-definition in contradistinction to the City's shopkeepers, mariners, and small producers—that the typical Levant Company merchant's conservative worldview was determined.

Seen from this perspective, most of the apparent exceptions to the gen-

---

[132] See PRO, will of Humphrey Browne, 1670 PCC Penn 165.

[133] Pearson, *Chaplains*, pp. 61–62.

[134] Ibid., pp. 50, 56; A. G. Matthews, *Walker Revised* (Oxford, 1948), p. 65.

[135] Pearson, *Chaplains*, pp. 12, 18, 28; the fourth was one "Mr. Winchester," appointed in 1654.

[136] Ibid., pp. 15, 22.

eralization that the Levant–East India Company merchants held antiparliamentary, anti-Puritan positions actually tend to prove the rule. By and large, the Levant–East India Company parliamentarians and Puritans were at best marginal members of the group and exhibited social characteristics atypical of the group as a whole. They tended to be smaller traders, from non-London, low-status backgrounds, who entered the company by paying a fee rather than as apprentices to other company merchants. Most significant, however, is the fact that a majority of the parliamentary and Puritan Levant traders was actively connected with the new colonial-interloping merchant leadership. Thus, Samuel Vassall, Matthew Craddock, and Nathan Wright, three out of only a handful of really prominent Levant–East India Company merchants who opted for Parliament, were all leaders in the trades with New England, Virginia, the West Indies, and Africa, in conjunction with the other new merchants (Wright was also involved in interloping in Greenland and the East Indies). Similarly, Richard Chambers and John Fowke, substantial Levant Company traders and leaders in the constitutional opposition to unparliamentary taxation in the late 1620s, also seem to have forged ties with merchants trading with the Americas before the outbreak of the Civil War. Other Levant Company parliamentarians included Gregory Clement, William Pennoyer, Samuel Moyer, and Richard Cranley—all of whom were involved with the colonial-interloping group beginning in the 1630s, had joined the Levant Company in the 1630s by paying a fee, and were unconnected with other Levant Company families.[137] Finally, the Levant Company parliamentarians Thomas Barnardiston and Benjamin Whetcomb were, respectively, a member during the 1630s of the Providence Island Company and later an interloper in the East Indian trade, and a Massachusetts Bay trader by the 1640s at the latest.[138] That men such as these opposed the court and London's political establishment despite their Levant Company membership is congruent with the basic analysis presented here of the social and political structure of the merchant community.

The only other Levant–East India Company merchants (here I am including all Levant Company members, not just those who participated in the currants trade, as well as all East India Company directors) for whom evidence has been found of parliamentary sympathy were Henry Hunter, John Langham, Samuel Elliot, Caleb Cockcroft, Caldwell Farrington, Simond Edmonds, Isaac Pennington, Thomas Soames, and William Spurstow. Hunter had signed the antiparliamentary petition of the summer of 1641, although by late 1642 he was serving as a tax assessor in the

[137] For all these individuals, see above, ch. 4.

[138] For Barnardiston, see Newton, *Colonising Activities*, p. 127; *C.C.M.E.I.C. 1650–1654*, p. 340. For Whetcomb, see *Aspinwall Notarial Records, 1644–1651*, Boston Record Commissioners Report, 33 (Boston, 1903), pp. 24, 28, 223, 390.

London parliamentary bureaucracy. He was a son-in-law of the leading trader with Virginia, William Allen.[139] Little is known about Elliot, a small trader. What is interesting about all the other parliamentarian Levant Company merchants is that every one of them was a Puritan activist. Spurstow, Cockcroft, Farrington, and Pennington all participated together in the Puritan experiments at St. Stephen's Coleman Street throughout the period.[140] Edmonds was involved at the same time with the minister Edmund Calamy's Puritan reformation in the parish of St. Mary Aldermanbury.[141] John Langham's religious inclinations were apparent in the support he received for the mayoralty of London in 1646 from the Scottish Presbyterian minister Robert Baillie. Moreover, he maintained as his personal chaplain, Thomas Burroughs, a leading Puritan minister who was ejected from his position at the Restoration.[142] Finally, Thomas Soames's Puritanism was manifest in his association with the leading Puritan militants John Warner and John Venn (and others of their parish of St. Benet Gracechurch, London) in a petition of 23 December 1641 against their "scandalous" minister, William Quelch.[143]

It is more than likely that the religious solidarities formed by these Levant Company traders had much to do with inclining them toward Parliament, even in the face of the antiparliamentary politics of most of their Levant–East India Company colleagues. By the early 1640s, at least in London, political and religious dissent had effectively merged. Just as political opponents of the court were led to enter into religious opposition to combat the uses of the ecclesiastical hierarchy against political nonconformity, those who fervently wished for godly reformation must have seen that this could not be achieved unless Parliament prevailed. This said, it needs to be emphasized that most of the aforementioned Puritan parliamentarians among the Levant–East India Company establishment (who were not colonial-interloping traders) were in no way radicals. Both Thomas Soames and John Langham, the most substantial of these figures, were at best lukewarm and temporary backers of Parliament.[144] Among

[139] PRO, S.P.19/A.1/42; *Visitation of London, 1633–1635*, Harleian Society Publications 15 and 17 (London, 1880–1883), 1: 405.

[140] St. Stephen's Coleman Street Vestry Minute Book, Guildhall Library MSS 4458.1, p. 147; PRO, will of Caleb Cockcroft, 1645 PCC Rivers 55; PRO, will of William Spurstow, 1646 PCC Twisse 26.

[141] St. Mary Aldermanbury Vestry Minute Book, Guildhall Library MSS 3570/2, fol. 58; PRO, will of Simond Edmonds, 1656 PCC Berkley 374.

[142] Pearl, *London*, pp. 321–23; PRO, will of John Langham, 1671 PCC Duke 79. However, Langham was apparently also patronizing Anglican ministers before the end of the Interregnum. See J. E. Farnell, "The Politics of the City of London, 1649–1657" (University of Chicago, Ph.D. diss., 1963), p. 42.

[143] *D'Ewes*(C) pp. 338, 339 n. 18; *H.M.C., Fourth Report, Appendix*, p. 109; *C.J.* 2: 54.

[144] See Pearl, *London*, pp. 192, 322.

the others, only Isaac Pennington can be described as either a leader of the London revolution of 1641–1642, or a radical at any later date.[145] Like most of their colleagues within the Levant–East India combine, they were probably socially and politically rather conservative. But unlike most of their colleagues, including a few with strong Puritan sentiments, they seem to have been willing to back Parliament in the hope of achieving constitutional reform and, perhaps more especially, godly religious reformation—probably with the expectation that the truly revolutionary forces within London could be held within bounds. It seems clear that most of the Levant–East India merchants were simply unwilling to believe that the achievement of reform of the state and church hierarchies and the maintenance of stability and the established order in London were really compatible goals.[146]

THE MERCHANT ADVENTURERS

In the broadest terms, the Merchant Adventurers must be categorized with the Levant–East India Company merchants in their alienation from the radical and largely nonmerchant forces that dominated the City parliamentary movement in 1641–1642. It is true that by 1640 the Adventurers had lost their once predominant position within the merchant community, but they were still, by any measure, the most important group of company merchants aside from the Levant–East India combine. Indeed, the Adventurers' decline should not be exaggerated. In 1640, their trade may still have exceeded that of any other commercial line in total value, even if it no longer yielded the greatest profits. The Adventurers still included among their ranks a significant, if sharply reduced, number of major traders, while on average their membership undoubtedly ranked very high economically in relation to the whole of the merchant community. Finally, the Adventurers constituted a highly protected company, with politically santioned restrictions on entry that were vital to their operations. While no longer at the very top, the Adventurers were still a substantial group of privileged merchants with much to lose from serious political or social

---

[145] Ibid., pp. 176–84, 198–206, 210–21, 260–65.

[146] As I have noted, Puritan sentiments survived, at least to some extent, even among the elite royalists of the group. See above, ch. 6, pp. 296–97. For other examples of Levant Company merchant Puritans who sided against Parliament, supporting London royalism, see the cases of William Ashwell and Hugh Norris. Ashwell was a backer of the Feoffees for Impropriations, an elder in the Presbyterian system in the 1640s and 1650s, and a patron at his death of the Presbyterian minister Edmund Calamy (I. M. Calder, ed., *Activities of the Puritan Faction of the Church of England, 1625–1633* [London, 1957], p. 28; Sion College, Records of the Provincial Assembly of London, 1647–1660, MSS Acc. L40.2/E17, fol. 123; PRO, will of William Ashwell, 1656 PCC Berkley 319). Norris, whose will reads like a Puritan moral tract, left money to the Puritan preacher William Spurstow (PRO, will of Hugh Norris, 1661 PCC May 188).

disruptions. Like the bulk of the company merchants, they could not have looked with equanimity on the popular, militant upheavals of the London revolution of 1641–1642. They must have been strongly attracted to the conservative pole, which was to a large extent organized by the City merchant elite, now led by the Levant–East India Company merchants but certainly still including an important number of their own members.

Both the Levant–East India Company merchants and the Merchant Adventurers thus fell within the same broad social category of politically privileged company merchants, and this tended to lead the two groups in roughly similar politically conservative directions. On the other hand, it is essential to recognize the important socioeconomic distinctions between these groups. In the first place, by 1640 the Company of Merchant Adventurers contained significantly fewer members of the merchant elite—as represented on the customs farms, the court of aldermen, and the East India Company directorate—than did the Levant Company, and included, on average, merchants of somewhat lower economic standing. At the same time, the Merchant Adventurers do not seem to have included—at least to anything like the same degree—those extensive networks of interlocking family-cum-business connections that constituted the Levant–East India group, nor as many multigenerational ties with their company or with the City. As a result, by 1640 the few elite—and royalist—Adventurers appear to have been less well placed than were their counterparts in the Levant Company to win over a membership that was, in any case, less firmly predisposed to a fully consistent royalist standpoint than were the Levant Company merchants. Still, while a majority of the Adventurers, like most of the other company merchants, supported Parliament in the constitutional struggles of the late 1620s, but by 1641–1642 they had moved into opposition to the mass-based London revolution.

Nevertheless, the Adventurers were significantly less willing than were the Levant Company merchants to align themselves permanently and definitively against Parliament. It was not only that the handful of elite royalists in the company found it more difficult to organize a large and unwieldy membership. Perhaps feeling themselves in some sense to be "out," numbers of Adventurers appear to have been prepared in the end to accept the attack on the aldermanic elite—particularly when it became clear (after 1643) that it would be held within bounds—in order to improve their own opportunities to gain office or personal privilege. While practically no Merchant Adventurers took part in the City revolution of 1641–1642, many more Adventurers than Levant Company merchants were ultimately willing to come to terms with the parliamentary side as the City revolution came to seem less threatening than it had originally appeared.

Finally, the Adventurers' political position was immensely complicated by the problem of their chartered privileges. With their markets sharply contracted, the company's formal barriers to entry into their trade—already far more crucial for the Adventurers than for the Levant Company merchants because of the comparatively easier access to the north European cloth trade than to the Middle Eastern import commerce—became an overriding political issue. As a result, a significantly greater element of pure economic interest may have entered into the determination of the Adventurers' political position than in the case of the Levant Company traders. All else being equal, the Levant–East India Company traders' economic objections to the government's unparliamentary taxes on trade naturally tended to predispose them in favor of the reform of the monarchy. But when it came to the crunch, their fundamental concern was to hold their own Crown-protected privileged position and to defend the established sociopolitical order in the City. They were thus more than willing to sacrifice the ephemeral advantages of a more favorable policy on customs perhaps attainable via Parliament for the long-term security of their overall sociopolitical position in their company and in the City, supported by the king. In some contrast, perhaps because the very economic viability of their trade was so much more directly dependent on government-backed privileges, the Adventurers' response was more equivocal, and they tended to be more opportunistic. Paradoxically, their opportunism was extremely difficult to put into practice. The fact was that Parliament remained by and large hostile to the Adventurers' privileges. It was only in 1642–1643, as Parliament became ever more desperate for funds, that it reconciled itself to sanctioning the Adventurers' charter. Parliament changed its mind when it was able to secure a series of major loans from the company as the quid pro quo for renewing the Adventurers' privileges. When this happened, some Adventurers did undoubtedly come to look more favorably on the parliamentary cause.

In view of the Merchant Adventurers' complicated situation, it is not surprising that they turned out to be less steadfast supporters of London royalism than were the Levant Company merchants—although there was no tendency whatsoever among the Adventurers to support the City revolution. Of the seventy-four men who were active Merchant Adventurers in 1640 (that is, who exported one hundred or more cloths that year) evidence has been discovered on the political orientation of thirty-eight. Of these, eighteen can be identified only with the city conservative and royalist movement;[147] five were one-time royalists who had moved to sup-

---

[147] Anthony Bateman, Richard Bateman, William Bateman, William Christmas, George Clarke, Richard Clutterbuck, James Fenn, Robert Fenn, George Franklin, Lawrence Goffe, Robert Gore, Edward Knightley, Gabriel Newman, Thomas Northey, Francis Tichborne, George Warner, William Williams, James Yard.

port Parliament by the end of the Civil War;[148] and fifteen eventually joined the parliamentary forces, apparently never having been connected with royalism.[149] However, these figures need to be explained further if they are to be properly interpreted. (See table 7.1, p. 388.)

What is most striking in the first place is the Adventurers' overwhelming refusal to support the City's antiroyal forces during the period of constitutional revolution that secured London firmly for Parliament. Only three Adventurers can be identified as having taken part in the City's parliamentary revolution between July 1641 and July 1642;[150] meanwhile, some twenty-three Adventurers supported the conservative movement organized to oppose it.[151] Only one Adventurer, the noted Leveller radical William Walwyn, was among some 175 or so different signers of the popular petitions—first, against Lunsford's control of the Tower of London and, second, against the Lords' delay of the impressment bill—that highlighted the immediate preinsurrectionary period of late December 1641. A second trader, James Russell, was the only Merchant Adventurer who secured a place in January 1642 on the revolutionary committee of safety (militia committee) or who was among the twenty-one citizens who petitioned in early March 1642 against the royalists in support of the militia committee. Russell was also active not only in the Spanish trade but in Maurice Thomson's East Indian interloping project. The third and last Merchant Adventurer of 1640 for whom there is evidence of participation in the City revolution is Caleb Cockcroft. Cockcroft and James Russell were the only Merchant Adventurers among sixty-four common councilmen who petitioned Parliament in July 1642 against the lord mayor's refusal to put to the vote Parliament's order for war preparations in the City and, by implication, his right to control the common council's proceedings.

As would be expected, the twenty-three Adventurers who originally supported royalism included a strategic core with close family and commercial connections with the City aldermanic–East India elite. No fewer than eleven of the twenty-three Adventurers who opted at first for royalism maintained such connections. Anthony, Richard, and William Bateman were sons of Robert Bateman, who had been chamberlain of London and

[148] Anthony Biddulph, Lawrence Halstead, Andrew Kendrick, Robert Lowther, Walter Pell.

[149] Samuel Avery, Andrew Cade, Caleb Cockcroft, William Clough, James Cook, Robert Gale, William Hawkins, Daniel Hudson, Christopher Packe, Joseph Parker, Bartholomew Reymes, James Russell, Thomas Stubbing, William Tristram, William Walwyn.

[150] William Walwyn, James Russell, Caleb Cockcroft. A fourth Adventurer, Joseph Parker, may have been the citizen of that name who appears among the twenty-one signers of the promilitia committee petition of early March 1642. Bartholomew Reymes, who backed a militant anti-Laudian petition to Parliament in December 1641, at the height of the crisis, should probably also be included among the prorevolutionary Adventurers.

[151] See above, notes 147 and 148.

on the directing boards of both the Levant Company and the East India Company.[152] Sir George Clarke was one of the few Merchant Adventurers of the immediate pre–Civil War period who held an aldermanic position, and he was also an East India Company director.[153] Anthony Biddulph was Sir George Clarke's brother-in-law, and the son-in-law of a great Merchant Adventurer, Alderman Robert Palmer.[154] Robert and James Fenn were sons of the alderman and East India director Richard Fenn (Venn), another of the topmost Merchant Adventurers of the previous generation; moreover, both married into other aldermanic families. James Fenn married the daughter of Henry Andrews, an alderman, Merchant Adventurer, Levant Company magnate, and East India Company director; Robert Fenn married the daughter of alderman Edmund Wright.[155] George Franklin was an East India Company director, and the son of the leading Merchant Adventurer and alderman Thomas Franklin.[156] William Williams, himself a Levant Company trader, was the son of the East India Company director and one-time treasurer of the Levant Company, John Williams.[157] Finally, Robert Gore was most probably the son of alderman William Gore, who was a chief Merchant Adventurer and himself the son of one of the great Elizabethan merchant aldermen, Gerard Gore.[158]

These eleven elite royalist Adventurers were undoubtedly among London's most influential merchant citizens. It is therefore especially notable that they were distinctly unable—in sharp contrast with their elite counterparts within the Levant Company—to prevent a significant section of the Adventurers from ultimately moving to support Parliament. While twelve Adventurers without elite connections (along with these eleven) did at first support the royalist movement, four of these (along with one elite Adventurer, Anthony Biddulph) changed sides.[159] They joined fifteen other Merchant Adventurers who had not previously been associated with royalism (and who, significantly, included not a single merchant with al-

[152] *Visitation of London, 1633–1635* 1: 55.

[153] A. B. Beaven, *The Aldermen of the City of London*, 2 vols. (London, 1908), 2: 65.

[154] Society of Genealogists, Boyd's Index of London Citizens: 10657; PRO, will of Sir George Clarke, 1649 PCC Fairfax 47.

[155] PRO, will of Richard Venn, 1639 PCC Harvey 190; Society of Genealogists, Boyd's Index: 7862, 15622; A. Friis, *Alderman Cockayne's Project and the Cloth Trade* (London, 1927), pp. 96–98; PRO, will of Henry Andrews, 1638 PCC Lee 127.

[156] *Visitation of London, 1633–1635* 1: 290; Friis, *Alderman Cockayne's Project*, pp. 96–98.

[157] *Visitation of London, 1633–1635* 2: 353; PRO, S.P.105/149/267.

[158] Because they are so numerous, the Gores are difficult to sort out. See G. E. Cockayne, *Some Account of the Lord Mayors and Sheriffs of the City of London . . . 1601–1625* (London, 1897), pp. 73–74, 99–101; Friis, *Alderman Cockayne's Project*, pp. 96–98; T. S. Willan, *Studies in Elizabethan Foreign Trade* (Manchester, 1959), pp. 127–30, 202–5, and index.

[159] See above, notes 147 and 148.

dermanic or East India Company directorate connections) behind the parliamentary cause.[160] This made a total of twenty Adventurers who ended up as parliamentarians—that is, about half the number who can be identified politically.

What thus distinguished the Adventurers' politics from those of the majority of the Levant–East India Company merchants in this period was not any obvious difference in fundamental political attitude or ideology; both groups, like the bulk of London's company merchants, tended to be conservative in their overall outlook. The difference between the two groups is rather to be found in the Levant Company merchants' deeper involvement with the leadership of royalism and the correlatively greater tactical flexibility and adaptability displayed by the Adventurers. Especially from the autumn of 1642, the Adventurers were significantly more attracted to the parliamentary side than were the Levant Company merchants. Their relatively weak connections with the City elite, and with company and City institutions in general, partly account for their relative openness to Parliament. But there seem also to have been positive forces at work. There was first of all the need to win their privileges. There were also the political demands of the Puritan movement.

It should not be overlooked, therefore, that nine of the fifteen Merchant Adventurers who supported Parliament (and had not been associated with constitutional royalism) were active Puritans, while only one of the twenty-three Merchant Adventurers who were at some time royalists was involved in the Puritan movement. Samuel Avery, Caleb Cockcroft, and James Russell were all members of St. Stephen's Coleman Street parish and participated in its Puritan activities of the 1640s.[161] Thomas Stubbing took part in a series of Puritan initiatives at St. Dunstan's-in-the-East, serving on the "Committee of Thirty" that replaced the closed vestry.[162] Daniel Hudson was a contributor to the Feoffees for Impropriations and an original investor in the Massachusetts Bay Company.[163] Christopher Packe was elder of the Seventh London Classis and left money for Nonconforming ministers.[164] Joseph Parker left bequests to "poor godly ministers that . . . have been silenced" and had family connections in New England.[165] William Walwyn was the well-known sectarian Leveller rad-

[160] See above, note 149.

[161] St. Stephen's Coleman Street Vestry Minute Book, Guildhall Library MSS 4458.1, fol. 147; PRO, will of Caleb Cockcroft, 1645 PCC Rivers 55; Society of Genealogists, Boyd's Index: 47695.

[162] St. Dunstan's-in-the-East Vestry Minute Book, Guildhall Library MSS 4887, fol. 257. See also below, ch. 8, pp. 448–50.

[163] Calder, *Activities of the Puritan Faction*, pp. 28, 147; Rose-Troup, *Massachusetts Bay Company*, pp. 145–46.

[164] Sion College, Records, MSS L40.2/E17, fol. 21v; PRO, will of Christopher Packe, 1682 PCC Cottle 74.

[165] PRO, will of Joseph Parker, 1644 PCC Rivers 21.

ical. And, finally, Bartholomew (Barney) Reymes petitioned Parliament in December 1641 with five fellow Puritan citizens against the "scandalous" minister William Quelch.[166] In contrast, the only royalist Merchant Adventurer who has been identified with the Puritan movement was Andrew Kendrick, another of the St. Stephen's Coleman Street Puritans. By 1644, Kendrick had aligned himself with Parliament.[167]

This is not to argue that Puritan religious sentiments resulted automatically in proparliamentary politics. As in the case of numbers of the Levant–East India Company merchants, the increasingly intimate tie between Puritanism and popular revolution in London in the pre–Civil War period caused many citizens to relinquish any desire they might have had for religious as well as political reform in the interest of political privilege and social order. The point, therefore, is not so much that proportionally greater numbers of Merchant Adventurers than Levant Company merchants were affected by Puritan ideas (although one does indeed get that impression). It is rather that the Adventurers, far more than the Levant Company merchants, were ultimately free to come to terms with Parliament; naturally they would have to align with Parliament if they wished to see Puritanism put into practice. The close involvement of the Levant–East India Company merchants not only with the pre–Civil War City ruling groups but with the leadership of City royalism left relatively few of them by autumn 1642 either willing or able to follow a political course that had now to be carried out entirely within a parliamentary framework. In contrast, an important group of Adventurers—who had been tied neither to the radical parliamentary thrust nor to City royalism in the first stage of the conflict in 1641–1642—were able to play a leading role in organizing a "middle course." When the revolutionary movement began to subside, after reaching its crest in the summer of 1643, these men were free to help consolidate a proparliamentary regime in the City, while at the same time pursuing their goals of moderate political and especially religious reformation. These merchants would, however, reaffirm their fundamental conservatism in the middle 1640s when they stood, once again, against rising popular movements for revolution, but this time in positions of authority within a politically presbyterian City magistracy.[168]

THE COLONIAL-INTERLOPING MERCHANTS

It is, unfortunately, not possible to provide the same sort of quantitative analysis of the whole mass of merchants participating in the colonial trades

---

[166] House of Lords MSS, 23 December 1641.
[167] Guildhall Library MSS 4458.1, p. 147; A.O. 1: 388.
[168] See below, ch. 9.

as can be provided for the Levant–East India Company traders and the Merchant Adventurers. This is because the colonial traders were, in general, much more obscure men than were the company merchants and because the sort of numerously signed conservative petitions that give the best evidence of the company merchants' political identification have no real counterpart in the London opposition movement. On the other hand, there can be no doubt that major figures from the new-merchant leadership played key roles in the City opposition at every pivotal moment in the struggle. Nor is there any question but that the new-merchant leadership overwhelmingly supported the City opposition and Parliament. Of the leadership group of eighty-two identified earlier in this work, twenty-five can be identified with the City opposition and Parliament and none firmly with royalism. The one new-merchant leader who seems to have leaned toward royalism was Richard Cranley. He, in fact, joined the parliamentary side, but certainly from a politically conservative position. (See table 7.1.)

Although little can be said in a positive way about the hundreds of other traders who were active in commerce with the Americas during the pre–Civil War period, the evidence on City constitutional royalism does allow a political characterization of this group of merchants, at least in negative terms. It is worth pointing out that of some four hundred or more different citizens who associated themselves with the constitutional royalists' petitions of July 1641 and February 1642, only about ten can be found to have been active in the colonial trades.

TABLE 7.1
The Civil War Politics of London's Overseas Merchants

	Total	Royalist	Royalists Who Became Parliamentarian	Parliamentarian	No Information
New-Merchant Leadership[a]	82	1	1	25	55
East India Company Directors, 1640–1641	33	24	0	2	7
Levant Company Currants Traders, 1634–1640	85	35	3	11	36
Merchant Adventurer Cloth Traders, 1640 (100 + cloths)	74	18	5	15	40

NOTE
[a] "New Merchants 1," see above, chapter 4, table 4.1.

The new merchants certainly had little interest in the cause of royalism. Their powerful attachment to the movement of opposition would be abundantly confirmed, moreover, in their heavy participation in the new institutions of parliamentary government that were constructed beginning in 1642, especially those of state finance. The nature of their contributions to the parliamentary cause will be traced in detail later in this work. At this point, it will be sufficient to note that, in sharp contrast with the bulk of the company merchant establishment, the new merchants and their friends played especially pivotal roles in the vast new parliamentary structure of direct taxation (assessments), in the machinery developed to milk the royalist estates for the parliamentary cause, in the provisioning of the parliamentary army, and in the new commission of customs. In January 1643, an eight-man syndicate, composed entirely of new merchants and led by Maurice Thomson, captured the new parliamentary customs commission. Their success well exemplifies the radical transformation that had been brought about by the City revolution in the structure of power and privilege of London's merchant community. Before the Civil War, of course, the customs had been, to a large extent, the private preserve of the Levant—East India Company elite. But the royalism of most of this group disqualified them from parliamentary service. It was entirely in keeping with the new balance of political forces that their places should be taken by the new-merchant revolutionaries.[169]

[169] See below, ch. 8.

[PART THREE]

RADICALIZATION, REACTION, AND REVOLUTION, 1642–1653

The Radicals' Offensive, 1642–1643

THE CONSTITUTIONAL revolution that shook the City and Parliament during the winter and spring of 1641–1642 represented the convergence of two different political tendencies, an alliance between parliamentary-reformers-turned-reluctant-revolutionaries and City radical oppositionists. Pym and his colleagues pushed for constitutional innovation, specifically for parliamentary control over the king's councilors and the army, only as a strategic necessity in order to protect the parliamentary reforms already carried out. Indeed, consistent adherence to roughly the program sketched out in the Grand Remonstrance—and little more—was to remain the defining characteristic of Pym's party and its various middle-group successors right through to 1648, distinguishing them from their parliamentary opponents, both more radical and more moderate. Unlike the parliamentary radicals, these men refused to admit that further substantive constitutional change in the direction of the reduction—let alone the destruction—of the monarchy was necessary to secure permanent peace and the protection of parliamentary liberties. Unlike the peace party, Pym's group would not sacrifice the gains of the legislative revolution of 1641 merely to restore order and social tranquillity.[1]

The attitude of Pym and his colleagues to the London revolutionaries was dictated by their general political objectives. They sought to make use of the City's political, financial, and military resources to achieve their own program with a minimum of sociopolitical disruption. They were willing to countenance revolution in the City, but only when this became indispensable to ensure that London's resources would be put at Parliament's disposal. They accepted autonomous action by the popular masses, but only as a necessary evil, for it posed a real threat, not only to their own fundamental conceptions of order and hierarchy, but to the short-term requirements of maintaining the support of as many as possible of the country's easily frightened gentry. As it was, the turn to London symbolized by the printing of the Grand Remonstrance probably lost Pym and

[1] On the middle group and its politics, see J. H. Hexter, *The Reign of King Pym* (Cambridge, Mass., 1941); V. Pearl, "Oliver St. John and the 'Middle Group' in the Long Parliament: August 1643–May 1644," *E.H.R.* 81 (1966); V. Pearl, "The 'Royal Independents' in the English Civil War," *T.R.H.S.*, 5th ser., 18 (1968).

his friends something like half of their former allies in Parliament and among the parliamentary classes in the country.

Of course, the alliance between the City radicals and the parliamentary oppositionists was not simply a tactical makeshift, emerging haphazardly under the pressures of the moment. To an important extent it had been prepared in advance, through the forging of ties between the colonizing aristocrats and the new-merchant leadership from the late 1620s onward. Pym and his friends were willing to resort to the London mass movement because they believed they could control it. Their confidence was founded, at least in part, on their close relationship with the colonial-interloping merchants. It was based, more generally, on their successful collaboration with militant clerics and laymen outside the governing class in the Puritan opposition to Arminianism and Laudianism in London, Essex, and elsewhere, dating from the middle 1620s. Certainly, the experience of 1640–1642 confirmed the hopes and expectations of the parliamentary leadership. It was able for the most part—although not at all points—to hold the City movement within bounds. Meanwhile, the movement's militancy served it time and again in securing its goals. This was true at the time of Strafford's trial and the army plots in spring 1641, and again during the political crisis of the winter of 1641–1642; it would be true once more during the construction of a new parliamentary financial bureaucracy beginning in mid-1642.

Nevertheless, while it was the agreement and cooperation between the party of Pym and the new-merchant leadership that was perhaps most in evidence during the first phase of revolution, between 1640 and 1642, the major differences in outlook and sociopolitical position that divided these two forces and that led them at crucial moments in divergent political directions should not be overlooked. Due to lack of evidence, it is difficult to be precise about the new merchants' ideological positions at the outset of the Civil War. Nevertheless their entire situation, in all its aspects— especially their subordinate relationships to the deeply entrenched aldermanic court, to the ecclesiastical hierarchy, and to the privileged London trading companies—led them to contemplate the thorough transformation of the old order. Each of these existing institutional structures restricted their freedom, channeled their activities in directions unacceptable to them, and ultimately provoked their opposition.

Moreover, in struggling to weaken or overthrow the old institutional order, the new merchants found themselves obliged to make organizational innovations and to create new forms of solidarity that had in themselves radical political implications. These new organizational forms at first served as bases of activity within, and means of attack on, the ruling institutions; but often they ended up as substitutes for them. Thus, in commerce, religion, and politics—from the new merchants' East Indian interloping company, to their Puritan congregations and colonizing organizations, to their City committee of public safety—these men consistently employed autonomous and voluntary modes to break the monopolies of the dominant official institutions and to begin to replace them. It cannot be denied, of course, that there were important ideological forces at work—above all, the Independent ministers, with their knowledge of the governmental and ecclesiastical systems of Holland and New England, and especially their experience with the religio-political experiments carried on by the exile English communities in these places. These would shape in important ways the new merchants' consciousness. But the new forms of political, religious, and commercial *practice* that these men initially developed as pragmatic and momentary weapons of struggle had, in themselves, significant ideological effects. It would therefore be a mistake to separate too sharply the new merchants' ultimate ends from the means they developed for achieving them.

Finally, it must be emphasized that the colonial-interloping leadership, considered simply as an interest group of overseas traders with a specific experience and specific goals, was relatively small and narrowly based, and this limited its power. To some extent its members overcame this weakness through their own internal solidarity: their ability to act cohesively allowed them to exert an influence far beyond their numbers. In the long run, however, these men depended for their power not only on the alliances they could forge with political groups deriving from other social strata but also on their own direct social involvement with a much broader social layer. The parliamentary leaders were one group of indispensable allies. But the new merchants could exert their own powerful influence on the parliamentary nobles and gentry because they also maintained an intimate relationship with, and of course helped to lead, the City popular movement. The new merchants' social origins and their continuing participation in domestic commercial activities gave them strong and extensive ties to that broad layer of City shopkeepers, mariners, and artisans who largely made up the City radical movement. The majority of new merchants could, in fact, in 1640, be properly regarded as belonging to that layer. It was the new merchants' sociopolitical base in a City radical movement composed for the most part of nonmerchant citizens that provided the new merchants much of their political strength, especially insofar as they wished to achieve goals to which the leaders in Parliament were either indifferent or opposed. At the same time, the new merchants were hardly unaffected by the movement that they helped to lead. Their own actions and ideas had been to a large extent shaped within the social milieu of the City's middling elements. Moreover, their political dependence on these elements could lead them to take positions that they might otherwise have avoided.

The new merchants' powerful interest in overthrowing the core institutions of the City's old political and ecclesiastical order, their involvement in the largely ad hoc structures through which the opposition movement usually was obliged to express itself, and finally their social connections with broad strata of London's radical citizenry put them, from the start, both ideologically and strategically, at least a step ahead of their middle-group allies in Parliament. Moreover, the new merchants did not prove reluctant to embrace new political and religious conceptions when the logic of the struggle seemed to make this imperative. In sharp contrast, the defining characteristic of the parliamentary middle-group leadership was to adapt radical means to relatively conservative political and ideological ends. The new-merchant leaders could not, in the end, trust their friends within the parliamentary middle group, for they viewed the constitutional innovations that accompanied the City-national revolt of 1641–1642 as signaling the opening phase of a new period of revolution, rather than as the last unavoidable additions to an essentially completed program of reform. From that time onward, therefore, the new-merchant leaders, with their allies in London, would find it necessary time and again to act on their own initiative, apart from and to some extent in opposition to their old parliamentary associates, not only in colonial and imperial affairs, but in the fields of religion and politics as well. Beginning with the City revolution of 1641–1642, they pursued with energy and independence their anti-Spanish offensive in the Caribbean and launched a policy of imperial conquest in Ireland, while developing their East Indian interloping venture. At the same time, they radically transformed the City constitution in the direction of popular control; moved to implement a thorough Puritan reformation in their localities so as to fashion a loosely defined "Independency"; allied with the war-party elements in Parliament for a more vigorous fight against the king; and pushed ultimately for parliamentary supremacy, something like a republican settlement in the state.

The City Revolution and the Origins of City Radicalism

The revolutionary upsurge of the winter and spring of 1641–1642 marked a pivotal moment in the development of the opposition movement in the City, particularly for the colonial-interloping group within it. It was at this point that the nature of the position that the new-merchant leadership would come to occupy throughout the ensuing struggle began to be more sharply defined. Already the previous spring, in the struggle to protect Parliament while it passed its reform legislation and sought to rid the king of his evil counselors, the radical citizens had proved their worth to the parliamentary leaders, both through their well-timed advances of money and through their mass mobilizations. At the same time, however, in the complex struggles over parliamentary finance, the Scottish army, and Strafford's execution, they had shown themselves to be a powerful independent force, unwilling to tarry for their more cautious parliamentary allies. It appears to have been the City oppositionists, in alliance with radical forces in the Commons, who, in the last analysis, made it impossible for Bedford and Pym to conclude that agreement with the king through which they hoped to settle the conflict in the late spring of 1641. In the winter of 1641–1642, the radical citizens had proved themselves, once again, absolutely indispensable for defending the parliamentary leadership. The Londoners' mass petition campaign, their revolutionary rising, and their overthrow of the aldermanic oligarchy had headed off a royal coup backed by a City-based counterrevolution. But as the price of their support, the radicals had demanded and received Parliament's tacit approval of both their antioligarchic constitutional revolution in London and their renewed campaign for the root and branch reformation of the church—two efforts that must have profoundly disturbed, if they did not totally horrify, the majority of the political nation.

This study has already dwelled at length on the leading role of the colonial-interloping leadership in organizing the City petition campaign, the London mass rising, and ultimately the London committee of safety (militia committee), which was the chief instrument of the City revolution in the winter of 1641–1642. Such traders with the Americas and interlopers in the East Indies as, in particular, Randall Mainwaring, John and Samuel Warner, John Fowke, Maurice, William, and George Thomson, William Barkeley, Owen Rowe, James Russell, Stephen Estwicke, Nathan Wright, Thomas Stone, William Underwood, Richard Hutchinson, and Lawrence Brinley all were prominent in the crucial weeks of conflict. It needs to be emphasized once again, however, that these new-merchant leaders were associated with a broader political organizing network—an admittedly amorphous "party"—which, *as a whole*, carried through the London revolution. What still needs to be asked, therefore, is which citizens—aside from the tightly connected group of new merchants that must have formed one pivotal component—made up the organization of London militants, and what were their general characteristics?

Because so many of the activists are not identifiable—and because in any case their viewpoints or interconnections cannot be fully confirmed simply on the basis of their signatures on one petition or involvement in a single action—it is impossible to answer this question as completely as one would like. Still, a number of features of this group that have not hitherto been adequately noticed do stand out, and indicate a pattern. Most important, the group of activists visible in this climactic period of struggle during the winter of 1641–1642 appears to have contained a disproportionate representation of citizens who associated themselves throughout the entire Civil War period with the radical sections of the London parliamentary movement. Perhaps most striking in this respect is the prominence in these events of three of the most famous representatives of what was later to become the Leveller movement—John Lilburne, William Walwyn, and Richard Overton. Overton signed both the petition of 23 December 1641 to remove Lunsford from his command of the Tower and the petition of 24 December 1641 urging immediate passage of the impressment bill. As a common councilor, he also backed the petition of July 1642, signed by sixty-four common councilors, asking Parliament to confirm the council's newly won right to convene itself and take action without the consent of the lord mayor. Lilburne carried out an armed provocation against Lunsford a few days after the anti-Lunsford petition. Walwyn turned up several weeks afterward, along with twenty other citizen militants, petitioning the common council to take repressive action against those conservative royalist citizens who had dared petition Parliament against the City's revolutionary committee of safety. It should be noted in passing that among Walwyn's colleagues on this occasion were the colonial traders Richard Hutchinson, John Jurin, and Lawrence Brinley.[2] In addition to these three later Levellers, some of the chief leaders of what was later to emerge as the extremist Salters Hall committee for volunteers were also prominent among the revolutionary militants of 1641–1642, including Richard Turner, Jr., Heriot Washburn, Tempest Milner, Martin Pindar, and John Kendricke. In 1643 and 1644, the Salters Hall committee would try to create a City army outside the control of the official parliamentary and municipal machinery and place it in the hands of the militant citizens themselves.[3] Finally, there was among the leading activists of the City revolution of 1641–1642 a disproportionately large number of citizens who were later to become political independents, relative to the number who would later emerge as political presbyterians. Signers of the three key petitions of the winter of 1641–1642 advanced by the citizen militants—(1) against Lunsford, (2) in favor of the impressment bill, and (3) opposing the conservative petitioners against the London committee of safety—include twenty-one future political independents,[4]

---

[2] For the four petitions mentioned here, see above, ch. 7, pp. 364–67, 372–73. For Lilburne's action, see V. Pearl, *London and the Outbreak of the Puritan Revolution: City Government and National Politics, 1625–1643* (Oxford, 1961), p. 224.

[3] For the Salters Hall committee, see below, pp. 448, 452–58. For these names, see CLRO, J.Co.Co.40, fols. 67, 89v.

[4] The future political independents included Maximillian Bard, Stephen Estwicke, Richard Hutchinson, Randall Mainwaring, John Norwood, Richard Overton, Edward Parkes, John Pocock, Richard Price, Henry Robinson, Francis Rowe, George Thomson, Maurice Thomson, William

but only ten future political presbyterians.[5] Perhaps most significant of all, on the committee of safety (militia committee) itself, which was certainly the City's central revolutionary institution, there were no fewer than fourteen future political independents[6] and only a single future political presbyterian,[7] as well as two citizens who fell somewhere in between, either trying to play both sides or to form a sort of bridge or conciliatory group between the two.[8]

Not only did the committee of safety take charge of London at the height of the rising of December–January 1641–1642; equally important, it played the leading role in carrying through the subsequent constitutional revolution that broke the power of the oligarchy, introducing some of its most radical provisions. In particular, the militia committee took the initiative in attacking abuses that had crept into the City's electoral procedures, specifically the oligarchic control that small cliques in the precincts and wards had come to exercise over the common council elections. In their report on elections to the common council on 2 March 1642, the committee declared that common councilmen "ought to be freely chosen every year in the wardmote by *all . . . freemen* of the City who do pay scot and lot." It went on to affirm that "although precincts do meet . . . to consider who they think are fit to be common council men . . . yet we conceive their power extends only to present the names of such persons to the wardmote and then the said inhabitants of the ward may in part or in whole approve or reject that nomination or name others to be in election with them as they find cause."[9] As Dr. Pearl has commented, this ruling, approved by the common council, "struck directly at the power of the vestries with whom the rulers of the precincts were practically synonymous."[10] It was only a first step toward the greater popular political participation that many of these militia commissioners would continue to ad-

---

Thomson, John Towse, Richard Turner, William Underwood, William Walwyn, Samuel Warner. The sources for the political identifications in this and the following notes are the numerous lists and petitions of the late 1640s, which manifested either political independent or political presbyterian orientation.

[5] The future political presbyterians included William Barton, Edward Bellamy, Lawrence Brinley, Thomas Evershed, Richard Floyde, Nathaniel Hall, Michael Herring, Edward Hooker, John Jones, Nicholas Widmerpole.

[6] The future political independents included Thomas Atkins, William Barkeley, Stephen Estwicke, John Fowke, Randall Mainwaring, Alexander Normington, Francis Peck, Owen Rowe, James Russell, Philip Skippon, John Towse, John Warner, Samuel Warner, Nathan Wright. Compare *A.O.* 1: 5 with *A.O.* 1: 1007 (political independent militia committee of 2 Sept. 1647) and CLRO, J.Co.Co.40, fol. 215v (political presbyterian militia committee of 26 Apr. 1647).

[7] The future political presbyterian was James Bunce.

[8] The trimmers were William Gibbs and Sir John Wollaston (both of whom ended up, ultimately, with the political independents, but had wavered significantly).

[9] CLRO, J.Co.Co.40, fol. 20 (emphasis added).

[10] Pearl, *London*, p. 139.

vocate. Men from the militia committee and their allies would soon be launching direct attacks on the local vestries themselves. Indeed, during 1642–1643 this body would provide the pivotal institutional base for a radical political offensive that would threaten to further revolutionize not only the politics of the City, but those of the entire nation.

Especially in light of the overwhelming dominance of London politics by moderates, that is, political presbyterians, during the middle and later 1640s, the predominance of future radicals and political independents during the determining stages of the City revolution of 1641–1642 is a fact to be reckoned with. This is not of course to say that no citizens of relatively moderate political persuasion took an active part in the City revolution or that all of the City militants who were radical in outlook in these revolutionary days remained radical throughout the 1640s, rather than drifting over to political presbyterianism. But the overturn of the old City oligarchy by means of mass mobilization in December–January 1641–1642 was indeed an extreme step—perceived as such by contemporaries and in fact largely, though not exclusively, led by citizens who would remain at the radical end of the political spectrum. Here in the process of formation was something like a loose "party" of radical opposition that would retain a roughly consistent identity—a set of continuing, if often mutually antagonistic, core components—throughout the whole period. Including types like the majority of new-merchant leaders, most of whom would end up in the less-radical wing of political independency, as well as more-radical future political independents, along with outright future Levellers—and melding together political militants from diverse social strata (colonial-interloping merchants, domestic traders, shopkeepers, artisans)—this radical alliance of forces would work together, even while its constituents fought more or less continuously among themselves, to push toward revolution right through to 1649. To explore the character and early development of this alliance, and especially the new merchants' place within it, will be the object of the remainder of this chapter.

Puritan Imperialism: Ireland and the West Indies

THE ADDITIONAL SEA ADVENTURE TO IRELAND

Perhaps the most striking evidence that the new merchants and their London collaborators had formed by 1642 something like a party of radical opposition—a party that would in many ways achieve substantial victory with the political independents' triumph in 1648—is to be found in their leadership of one of the period's most spectacular undertakings, the "Additional Sea Adventure" to Ireland. This venture, which manifested at once the group's commercial, political, and religious aspirations, demonstrates not merely the refusal of these men to wait for their colleagues in Parliament in order to achieve their goals, but also the impressive resources in men, money, and organizational ability already at their command.

The Irish rebellion, and the constitutional questions it raised, had been at the center of the developing political conflict in late 1641. Pym and his friends had had relative success in using this issue to discredit the king, strengthen their parliamentary allies, and push forward their program for reform.[11] But the Irish revolt was not merely a problem to be manipulated politically; it had to be dealt with practically. As early as the Grand Remonstrance, Parliament had recognized that it might be necessary to provide material incentives in order to raise the financial means necessary to send a military expedition to Ireland. Perhaps the proposition inserted into this document that the king set aside lands of Irish rebels "that out of them . . . some satisfaction [may be] made to [his] subjects . . . for the great expense they are like to undergo in the war" was originally suggested by radical London citizens.[12] What is certain is that when, in early 1642, Parliament ran into difficulty raising loans through the official City government to finance an army for Ireland, "divers well-affected persons from London" were prepared to petition the Commons on 11 February 1642 for the right to "raise forces upon their own charge and to maintain them for the reducing of the rebels of Ireland into obedience, and after to receive such recompense out of the rebels' estates as Parliament should think fit."[13] It was to become a familiar pattern: the most politically forward sections of the London trading community would step in to substitute their own private initiative and daring for the chronic passivity and caution of the official municipal authorities. Their plan envisioned the setting aside of two and a half million acres in Ireland, which would eventually be turned over at specified ratios of loans to land, for those who would help finance the military expedition to Ireland. The citizens proposed that the expedition itself should be privately organized and carried out by promoters who would have the right to handpick the officers.[14]

No list has been discovered of the original London backers of the Irish

[11] See J. R. MacCormack, "The Irish Adventurers and the English Civil War," *Irish Historical Studies* 10 (1956): 21–58.

[12] MacCormack, "Irish Adventurers," p. 25; S. R. Gardiner, *Constitutional Documents of the Puritan Revolution, 1625–1660* (Oxford, 1900), pp. 204–5.

[13] Quoted in R. P. Stearns, *The Strenuous Puritan: Hugh Peter, 1598–1660* (Urbana, Ill., 1954), p. 189.

[14] *The Propositions Made by the Citie of London for Raising a Million of Money . . . for Ireland. . . .* (London, 11 Feb. 1642); MacCormack, "Irish Adventurers," p. 30; Stearns, *Strenuous Puritan,* p. 189.

adventure. There can be little doubt, however, that they were drawn to a large extent from those colonial mercantile circles that played the leading role in directing this operation throughout its existence. According to R. P. Stearns, the key parliamentary supporters were those "lords and gentlemen already familiar to Puritan enterprises at home and abroad," especially Lord Brook, Lord Saye, and the earl of Warwick.[15] This adventure was, quite clearly, another project of the chief country and City backers of expansion in the Americas, the same men who took so great a part in the leadership of the City and national opposition movements. Two of the four treasurers for the adventure appointed by Parliament were leading colonial-interloping traders, as well as important City militants who were soon to become leading parliamentary financiers, John Warner and Thomas Andrews.[16] Parliament insisted on asserting its own ultimate control over the project, but it recognized the venture's citizen promoters as the "Committee of Adventurers in London" and gave this body a good deal of the responsibility for actually organizing the expedition. The total membership of this committee has not been discovered (it was apparently quite large) but it did contain much of the heart of the colonial-interloping leadership, including Maurice Thomson, William Thomson, Samuel Warner, Thomas Andrews, Samuel Moyer, William Pennoyer, Gregory Clement, and Robert Wilding.[17]

From the spring of 1642, investments in Irish rebels' lands began to trickle in from all over the country. By July, the Irish adventurers were ready to dispatch to Munster a major force of five thousand foot and five hundred horse led by an officers' corps that they themselves had chosen (with the approval of Parliament), under the supreme command of Philip, Lord Wharton. However, the committee's troops never reached Ireland. With the outbreak of civil war in England, Parliament could not spare such a significant force outside the kingdom, and it ordered the adventurers' troops to join the parliamentary army under Lord Essex. At the same time, Parliament extracted the very large sum of £100,000 from the London committee of adventurers to support its domestic efforts against the king. The colonial-interloping leaders remained at the center of the official parliamentary effort in Ireland. But from mid-1642, their role, and that of the London committee of adventurers as a whole, was reduced to advising Parliament on Ireland, to provisioning what parliamentary forces were already there, and to collecting and advancing money, only part of which was used in Ireland (the remainder being al-

[15] Stearns, *Strenuous Puritan*, p. 189.

[16] *C.J.* 2: 463–65.

[17] See the list of members of the London Adventurers Committee, House of Lords MSS, 24 October 1645; see also "Orders Passed by Parliamentary Committee of Adventurers for Ireland," BL, Egerton MSS 2519, fol. 81v.

located to support the main parliamentary army).[18] This would not be the last time that the parliamentary leadership would absorb an independent initiative by its militant City followers and turn their energies and resources to its own ends.

Nevertheless, Maurice Thomson and his friends were not about to allow the exigencies of parliamentary politico-military strategy to prevent them from carrying out their plans for Ireland. During the spring of 1642 the main Irish adventure had difficulty getting organized, and for a time it looked as if it might never get off the ground. As a result, Parliament was disposed to regard favorably a proposal put forward on 19 April 1642 by "some persons desirous to further the conquest of Ireland and relief of their brethren there" to "fit out five, six or seven ships with five hundred soldiers" for what came to be known as the Additional Sea Adventure to Ireland. The promoters of this subsidiary plan for a privately run military expedition to Ireland asked for, and this time were granted, the same conditions initially requested for the original, main adventure: repayment of their expenses by "an allotment of land according to their several subscriptions," as well as "a commission securing them entire independence in their proceeding" and, further, the right to "hold and enjoy to their own use, without any account whatsoever . . . all ships, goods, wares, plate, pillage and spoil" that they might seize in the voyage.[19]

The Additional Sea Adventure to Ireland was the private project of the new colonial-interloping leadership and its nonmerchant political and religious allies, an early and spectacular project of London's radical party or

---

[18] MacCormack, "Irish Adventurers," pp. 34, 37–39; *H.M.C., Fifth Report, Appendix*, p. 40; *The State of Irish Affairs . . . from the Committee in London for Lands in Ireland* (London, 1646), pp. 1–3. There is massive documentation for the pivotal role of the colonial-interloping leadership in support of official parliamentary activities in Ireland in these years—especially in providing advice, in war contracting and provisioning, and in money-raising efforts. Here, as elsewhere, the lead was taken by Maurice Thomson and William Pennoyer, but a good number of their friends such as Gregory Clement, Nicholas Corsellis, Richard Cranley, Stephen Estwicke, William Harris, Richard Hill, Owen Rowe, William Tucker, Samuel Vassall, and Nathan Wright were also prominently involved. For the activities of these men in Irish provisioning, see, for example, *C.S.P.D. 1641–1643*, pp. 299, 327; *C.S.P.D. 1644*, pp. 164, 169, 170, 234; *C.S.P.D. 1644–1645*, pp. 360, 590–91; *C.S.P.D. 1645–1647*, pp. 210, 410, 416; *C.S.P.D. Addenda 1625–1649*, pp. 643, 657, 670; *H.M.C., Fifth Report, Appendix*, pp. 6, 69, 72; *C.J.* 2: 799, 906, 939; *C.J.* 3: 333, 548, 568, 620–21, 622; *C.J.* 4: 78, 106, 115, 186, 231, 278, 316, 330, 404, 522; *C.J.* 5: 11, 74, 92, 164; *L.J.* 5: 392, 573, 600, 706; *L.J.* 6: 154, 155, 157; *L.J.* 7: 632, 676–77; *L.J.* 8: 484, 487; *L.J.* 9: 30, 35, 37, 70, 98, 180. Also, in general, BL, Add. MSS 4771 and Egerton MSS 2519. For their role as investigators and advisers on Irish affairs, see, for example, *L.J.* 5: 395; *H.M.C., Fifth Report, Appendix*, pp. 51–53. For their fund-raising on behalf of the parliamentary effort in Ireland, see *A.O.* 1: 70–71, 220–21. The amounts of money involved could be staggeringly large, as with Thomson's loan to Parliament of £10,000 for the raising of Jephson's new regiment in the winter of 1645–1646. PRO, S.P. 63/216/9, p. 92.

[19] *H.M.C., Fifth Report, Appendix*, p. 18; *A.O.* 1: 9–12.

alliance. Appointed by act of Parliament on 17 June 1642, the venture's sixteen commissioners, besides Maurice Thomson, included George Thomson, William Thomson, Gregory Clement, William Pennoyer, William Willoughby, Samuel Moyer, and Richard Hill, all of whom were relatives or business partners of Thomson's in the colonial-interloping trades; Richard Shute, probably Thomson's closest political companion and a colonial trader himself; Richard Waring, a signer of the colonial merchants' petition supporting the trader with the Americas Joseph Hawes; and Thomas Vincent, formerly an apprentice in the Leathersellers Company to the major new-merchant leader Thomas Andrews and at this time a shipowning partner of Maurice Thomson's and Gregory Clement's who was just becoming involved in the famous ironworks project in Braintree, Massachusetts.[20] Three other men on the commission—Sir Nicholas Crispe, John Wood, and Thomas Chamberlain—had been leaders in developing the Guinean trade during the late 1620s and 1630s.[21] Also among the commissioners was Thomas Rainsborough, a seaman who as colonel in the New Model Army was later to play a leading role among the more radical political independents and Levellers.[22] The last of the sixteen commissioners was the great Providence Island and Saybrook projector Robert Greville, Lord Brook, a well-known Puritan radical.

By 29 June, within two weeks of Parliament's approval of their project, these undertakers had gathered together and dispatched an expedition of a thousand foot soldiers, about five hundred seamen, and fifteen vessels. Six months of private war and plunder in Ireland followed. Although it actually took part in a number of military and naval engagements, the Additional Sea Adventure had only a small impact on Irish affairs because it soon ran out of funds, especially as money promised from the main adventure to Ireland was never forthcoming.[23] Nevertheless, the Additional Sea Adventure is an extremely important expression of the new merchants' capacity, at this point, to organize themselves and their allies for their special political and religious, as well as their commercial, goals. Aside from the Guinea Company members John Wood, Thomas Chamberlain, and Nicholas Crispe (a royalist monopolist whose participation was probably motivated by a desire to save his own skin and to gain political sup-

---

[20] A.O. 1: 11. For all these men, except Thomas Vincent, see above, ch. 4. Vincent was the son of a Begwith, Leicester family (Society of Genealogists, Boyd's Index of London Citizens: 14223). For his relationship to Thomas Andrews, see Leathersellers Company, London, Freemen Book, 13 October 1629. For Vincent's activities in the ironworks project, see E. N. Hartley, *Ironworks on the Saugus* (Norman, Okla., 1957), p. 77. For his shipping partnership with Thomson and Clement, see PRO, H.C.A.24/105/62–65.

[21] J. W. Blake, "The Farm of the Guinea Trade in 1631," in *Essays in British and Irish History*, ed. H. A. Cronne, T. W. Moody, and D. B. Quinn (London, 1949).

[22] Stearns, *Strenuous Puritan*, pp. 190–91, 288, 293, 313, 315.

[23] Ibid., pp. 191–200.

port for his Guinea Company monopoly, then under attack), all of the aforementioned commissioners of the Additional Sea Adventure were important participants in London's parliamentary cause, and all were to emerge as leaders of its more radical and ultimately political independent wing.

The individuals charged by the commissioners with actually carrying out the Irish expedition further evidenced the radical Puritan orientation of the project as a whole.[24] The Independent minister Hugh Peter accompanied the voyage as its chaplain and was one of the project's guiding figures. A former dependent of the earl of Warwick, Peter had, of course, worked closely with Warwick and the Puritan Feoffees for Impropriations and the Massachusetts Bay Company in religio-political oppositional activities in London in the later 1620s. At the end of the decade, he had been removed from his Essex living for Nonconformity. During the 1630s, Peter had exiled himself from England and had carried out pioneering experiments in Independent church organization in both Holland and New England. In September 1641, Peter had returned from Massachusetts to England in order to represent the Massachusetts Bay Colony as its English agent and to support the parliamentary cause. Peter probably first had made contact with Maurice Thomson in the course of their various activities in Massachusetts, and he was to remain a very intimate political associate of Thomson's and of the new-merchant leadership throughout the 1640s. From the start one of the leaders of London's radical party, or alliance, Peter would emerge by the end of the period as one of the most important ministerial spokesmen for *both* the New Model Army (especially its less radical, though strongly Independent, officer-led wing) and the London political independents, and would provide a crucial link between them.[25]

The Additional Sea Adventure's overall commander was Lord Brook, but he did not actually accompany the voyage. The land commander and practical leader of the expedition was Alexander Lord Forbes, an old friend of Lord Brook's and a kinsman of John Forbes's, a Puritan minister who had collaborated with Hugh Peter in establishing the congregationalist organization of the church of the English Merchant Adventurers' overseas community in the Netherlands (Delft) during the early 1630s.[26] Second in command of the land forces was John Humfrey, one of the leading lights of the Massachusetts Bay Colony and its first deputy gov-

---

[24] The list of the leadership of the Additional Sea Adventure is given in H. Peter, *A True Relation of the Passages of God's Providence in a Voyage for Ireland with the Additional Forces. . . .* (London, 18 Nov. 1642), pp. 1–4.

[25] Stearns, *Strenuous Puritan.* See above, ch. 6, pp. 263–65, 276, 277.

[26] Ibid., pp. 190–91; A. P. Newton, *The Colonising Activities of the English Puritans* (New Haven, 1914), p. 246.

ernor. Humfrey had married the daughter of the earl of Lincoln and during the 1630s was in close contact with the colonizing activities of the Puritan nobles Lord Saye, Lord Brook, and the earl of Warwick. In 1641 Humfrey was appointed governor of Providence Island, but his plans to emigrate were disrupted when the colony fell to the Spanish.[27] The admiral of the fleet was Hugh Peter's brother Benjamin. The vice admiral was the commissioner Thomas Rainsborough, the later Leveller; Rainsborough's brother William, also involved in the voyage, had lived in Charlestown, Massachusetts, before the Civil War.[28] The rear admiral was Maurice Thomson's brother Robert, a resident of Boston, Massachusetts, during the 1630s.[29]

The investors in the Additional Sea Adventure were of pretty much the same political stripe as were the active promoters and military leaders. The promoters organized the project in a remarkably short space of time, so they undoubtedly were obliged to rely to a large extent on previous acquaintances. That they were able so quickly to raise a total of £43,400 from some 180 subscribers gives an indication of the extent and quality of their network; this was a larger amount of money than the Virginia Company could attract for investment in its joint stock in some twelve years of operation.[30] Although it is not possible to give an exhaustive account of the subscribers here, some striking characteristics are clearly evident. In the first place, colonial-interloping merchants made a very large contribution. In addition to the twelve previously listed colonial-interloping traders who were commissioners of the project and naturally also investors in it, the project's financial backers included at least twenty-one other merchants active in the Americas, in interloping in the East Indies, or both. All told, these thirty-three colonial-interloping trading investors committed some £12,460, close to 30 percent of the project's total fund. Of their number, no fewer than twenty-three were later political independents, as compared with five who were later political presbyterians (five cannot be identified as to political orientation in the later 1640s).[31]

[27] Newton, *Colonising Activities*, pp. 41, 45, 46, 80, 81, 83, 211, 286, 292.

[28] Stearns, *Strenuous Puritan*, p. 191.

[29] H. F. Waters, *Genealogical Gleanings in England*, 2 vols. (Boston, 1901), 1: 66.

[30] For a list of subscribers in the Additional Sea Adventure, with their investments, see J. P. Prendergast, *The Cromwellian Settlement of Ireland* (Dublin, 1871), pp. 443–48. For the Virginia Company joint stock, see above, ch. 3.

[31] The following are the colonial-interloping merchant investors in the Additional Sea Adventure to Ireland, with the amounts of their investments. The political independents are marked (I), the political presbyterians are marked (P), and those who cannot be identified in political terms are marked (U). William Allen (I): £200; Thomas Andrews (I): £500; Thomas Barnardiston (I): £50; John Brett (I): £300; Lawrence Brinley (P): £200; Thomas Chamberlain (P) and Abraham Chamberlain (U): £1,000; Gregory Clement (I): £1,300; Richard Cranley (P): £300; Dennis Gawden (I): £600; Michael Herring (P): £200; Richard Hill (I): £700; Robert Houghton (I): £400; Richard

Aside from the colonial-interloping merchants, there was only a tiny handful of overseas company traders among the investors, a further indication of the sharp divide that separated the politically and commercially radical new-merchant group from the City's correspondingly conservative company merchants.[32] Among the remaining citizen subscribers, there were a substantial number of those leading nonmerchant London oppositionists who, alongside the colonial-interloping merchants, would identify themselves with the City radical movement of 1642–1643 and especially the victorious political independent army on its invasion of London at the end of the 1640s. In addition to the aforementioned later Leveller Thomas Rainsborough, these included Edmund Harvey, Richard Turner, Sr., Richard Turner, Jr., Thomas Hussey, Joshua Woolnough, John Strange, Abraham Babington, Hogan Hovell, Francis Webb, Samuel Harsnett, Nathaniel Lacy, and Fulke Wormelayton, as well as Thomas Prince, the later Leveller. These men would help lead the citizens' radical offensive of 1642–1643 and take leading posts in the new political administration set up nationally and in London by the political independents at the close of the 1640s—the militia and assessment committees, the high courts of justice, and the Commonwealth finance commissions.

Significantly, there were four identifiable ministers associated with the Additional Sea Adventure, and at least three of them were religious Independents who had worked closely with one another, as well as other leading Independent clerics, during the 1630s—Hugh Peter, William Greenhill, and Jeremiah Burroughs. Peter's career has already been discussed; the careers of both Greenhill and Burroughs ran along similar lines. Like Peter, Burroughs had been a protégé of the earl of Warwick. Burroughs also had enjoyed the support of the great Puritan patroness Lady Jane Bacon, and so had Greenhill. Both Greenhill and Burroughs, like Peter before them, had been deprived of their livings for Nonconformity; both were suspended in 1636 by Bishop Wren of Norwich, as were William Bridge and John Ward, two other Independent clerics from East Anglia. Following the loss of their ministries, Burroughs and Greenhill, as had Bridge and Ward, fled to Rotterdam, where all four associated themselves with the centrally important English Independent congrega-

---

Hutchinson (I): £100; John Jurin (P): £200; Samuel Moyer (I): £300; Samuel Pennoyer (I): £450; William Pennoyer (I): £350; Richard Shute (I): £300; George Snelling (I): £100; Thomas Stone (U): £200; Maurice Thomson (I) and George Thomson (I): £1,000; Robert Thomson (I): £100; William Thomson (I) and his father-in-law Samuel Warner (I): £600; Thomas Turgis (U): £200; William Underwood (I): £100; Thomas Vincent (I): £1,000; Richard Waring (I): £660; Benjamin Whetcomb (U): £500; William Willoughby (I): £50; and Edward Wood (U): £500.

[32] The only overseas traders I have been able to identify among the 180 investors who were *not* new merchants are William Methwold, an East India Company director; Nicholas Crispe, the Guinea Company trader; and Richard Clutterbuck, a Merchant Adventurer.

tion founded and developed there by Hugh Peter, in collaboration with William Ames, Thomas Hooker, and John Davenport. After Peter and Davenport had left the Rotterdam church for New England in 1635–1636, Bridge and Ward were chosen ministers in their place. By early 1639, Bridge and Burroughs had assumed leadership of the Rotterdam church. Just previously, Sydrach Simpson and Joseph Symonds, two London Independents who had been deprived of their livings and had initially joined the Rotterdam church, had broken from the main body to found their own "purer" congregation. Meanwhile, Philip Nye and Thomas Goodwin, along with John Archer, were heading a closely allied Independent congregation at Arnhem. Most of those clerics who would emerge as the central leaders of London Independency in the early 1640s had worked closely together in the congregational experiments in Rotterdam and Arnhem. Hugh Peter, William Greenhill, and Jeremiah Burroughs were all part of that leadership and would soon be collaborating with the "Five Dissenting Divines" of the Westminster Assembly; in fact, Burroughs—along with Sydrach Simpson, Philip Nye, Thomas Goodwin, and William Bridge—was himself one of the "five."

Burroughs and Greenhill were especially close friends and, with the backing of Lady Jane Bacon, had been leaders of the Puritan community in Norfolk. In the fall of 1637 they participated in a dangerous mission, smuggling back into Norfolk several barrels full of seditious books and pamphlets. After they had landed clandestinely at Great Yarmouth, disguised as soldiers returning from the Battle of Breda, the militant Puritan and future regicide MP Miles Corbet gave them protection and hospitality at his house. During the late 1620s and early 1630s, Corbet, as corporation recorder of Great Yarmouth, had led a long fight by the town against the ecclesiastical hierarchy to retain as its minister the militant Puritan John Brinsley, and throughout the 1640s Corbet would remain close to these Independent clerical radicals.[33]

By 1641, Burroughs and Greenhill had returned from Holland, and, as noted earlier, they were the two ministers appointed by the radical London parish of Stepney when that parish secured from the Commons the right to appoint its own lecturers in September 1641. By 1644, Greenhill had gathered his own congregation. Burroughs never actually gathered a congregation, and this appears to have left him the freedom for a more

[33] For the foregoing two paragraphs on Greenhill, Burroughs, and the other Independent ministers, see K. N. Shipps, "Lay Patronage of East Anglian Puritan Clerics in Pre-Revolutionary England" (Yale University, Ph.D. diss., 1971), pp. 152–66, 175–83, and K. L. Sprunger, *Dutch Puritanism: A History of the English and Scottish Churches of the Netherlands in the Sixteenth and Seventeenth Centuries* (Leiden, 1982), pp. 163–70, 227–31. On Corbett, see Shipps, pp. 219–33. See also, below, pp. 422–23.

active and direct role in radical politics.[34] Even by the end of the 1630s, Burroughs was enunciating some of those extreme political opinions for which he and a number of the other Independent ministers would later become well known. In fact, by the winter of 1642–1643 Burroughs and Peter, along with a third leading Independent cleric, John Goodwin, would be providing some of the key political and ideological leadership for the radical wing of the London parliamentary movement, with a critical core of new-merchant leaders right beside them.

Finally, there appear to have been only three MP backers of the Additional Sea Adventure to Ireland, but two of these were significant figures indeed, Oliver Cromwell and Arthur Hasilrig. These two men may originally have become associated with the new-merchant leadership as a result of their involvement with Puritan undertakings in New England. Hasilrig was Lord Brook's brother-in-law and had been an important backer of the Saybrook Colony; both Hasilrig and Cromwell seem to have planned to emigrate to Massachusetts.[35] The collaboration of both these leading figures with the new merchants and their London friends in the Additional Sea Adventure to Ireland signaled an emerging alliance among the war-party radicals in Parliament, those in the City, and ultimately, those in the army that would span the entire period, reaching its height in the Commonwealth.

The Additional Sea Adventure to Ireland was, in the words of R. P. Stearns, a "distinctly parliamentary force" that "proceeded on the premise that the Irish and the Royalists were united" even though civil war had yet to be declared in England. As Hugh Peter put it in the day-by-day journal he kept of the Additional Sea Adventure's progress in Ireland, "an Irish rebel and an English cavalier in words and action we found as unlike as an egg is to an egg." The commander of the venture, Lord Forbes, co-operated only with parliamentary garrisons in Ireland, or with those who, when challenged, claimed their allegiance to Parliament and indicated their willingness to accept officers appointed by that body.[36] The Additional Sea Adventurers thereby showed themselves in practice to be politically a step ahead of their compatriots in England. The group was to occupy a similarly advanced position throughout the Civil War. Linking new-merchant and nonmerchant radicals, future political independents, and a few future Levellers, the Additional Sea Adventure may be considered in some respects the first autonomous project of that City militant

---

[34] M. Tolmie, *The Triumph of the Saints: The Separate Churches of London, 1616–1649* (Cambridge, 1977), pp. 95, 98, 107, 122.

[35] Newton, *Colonising Activities*, pp. 172ff.; M. F. Keeler, *The Long Parliament, 1640–1641* (Philadelphia, 1954), p. 213; *Dictionary of Seventeenth-Century Radicals*, vol. 2, s.v. "Arthur Haselrige."

[36] Stearns, *Strenuous Puritan*, p. 192.

Puritan party, or alliance of forces, buoyed up by new recruits from New England and very much religiously Independent in character, that was to form the hard core of City radicalism, political independency, and republicanism throughout the 1640s.

CAPTAIN JACKSON'S VOYAGE TO THE CARIBBEAN

The Additional Sea Adventure to Ireland, like many similar ventures of the new merchants and their radical friends, expressed not only a refusal to wait for Parliament in order to act, but also a reliance on autonomous and voluntary forms of organization. It should not be forgotten that in this very same period the new merchants were also stepping up their large-scale interloping project in the East Indies that had, typically, the dual purpose of allowing for innovative activity that was not possible within the officially established institutional and policy framework, and of providing a base for attacking and ultimately altering that framework.[37] In much the same way, in precisely the same months that these men were launching the Additional Sea Adventure to Ireland, a number of them were carrying out an equally impressive, imperial venture in the West Indies.

The Grand Remonstrance had made an anti-Spanish campaign of conquest in the West Indies a high priority for Parliament, but the parliamentary leadership's preoccupation with preparations for war against the king obliged it to postpone such a mission indefinitely. Parliament's failure to act did not, however, prevent Maurice Thomson and his friends from dramatically stepping up their activity in the West Indies. At the start of the 1640s, these men had begun to involve themselves in the rapidly developing sugar plantations on the islands, and in the associated growth of the triangular trades in sugar, slaves, and provisions. Meanwhile, between 1638 and 1641, Thomson, William Pennoyer, and some West Country merchants had dispatched Capt. William Jackson, an apprentice of Thomson's brother-in-law William Tucker, on a highly successful series of raids on Spain's possessions in the Caribbean.[38] Then, beginning in 1642, much the same group of men, this time in collaboration with the earl of Warwick and other Providence Island backers, sent out Captain Jackson once again on an expanded version of his earlier marauding voyage. Jackson's campaign of pillage lasted for three years, during which time he took and ransomed Maracaibo, temporarily captured the island of Jamaica, captured Truxillo, raided the smaller towns of Costa Rica and the Isthmus, and carried out various expeditions on the coast of

[37] See above, ch. 4, pp. 169–81.
[38] See above, ch. 4, pp. 158–59 and notes 151–53.

Cartagena and attacks against Guatemala and the small towns off the Gulf of Mexico. In March 1645, Jackson returned home via Massachusetts to divide the booty with his sponsors.[39]

While both the Additional Sea Adventure to Ireland and Captain Jackson's voyage to the Caribbean should be seen, from one vantage point, as at least partially successful attempts by the new merchants and their associates to implement policies and strategies on which the parliamentary leadership was as yet unwilling or unable to act, these projects should also be viewed, from a different angle, as privately-run forerunners of more thoroughgoing government-sponsored ventures that were to take place following the political independents' victory in 1649. Both the Additional Sea Adventure to Ireland and Captain Jackson's voyage took on the aspect of colonial voyages of conquest; but they were of necessity limited to temporary occupations and short-term campaigns of pillage. With the political independents' triumph, however, the new merchants and their friends would no longer have to satisfy themselves with such halfway measures as these, for the state was then prepared to take up where private initiative had left off. Indeed, the Cromwellian conquests of both Ireland and Jamaica can be seen, in important respects, to have grown out of the earlier campaigns initiated by the new merchants—and these traders would be closely involved with and profit from each.

Of course, during the early 1640s, the new-merchant leaders were hardly confining their thoughts and concrete initiatives to the sphere of imperial affairs, while passively awaiting more favorable political developments at home. The necessity of acting to secure a government that in structure and policy would be accessible to and sympathetic with their commercial interests had been brought home to them time and again through the 1630s and into the 1640s. On this ground alone they were probably more than normally fearful of a parliamentary compromise with the Crown for the sake of order, and a consequent return to the old type of foreign policy making in which commercial concerns were subordinated to the desires of court factions, the needs of government finance, dynastic considerations, and the monarch's ideological preferences. Equally salient, however, these men and their associates saw the City revolt of the winter of 1641–1642 as the opening step toward religio-political reformation. From that time onward, with or without Parliament, they showed no hesitation in pushing forward their plans for furthering the revolution. During 1642–1643, they would work to implement their own ideas about religion, intervene in the disputes over the preparations

---

[39] V. T. Harlow, ed., *The Voyages of Captain William Jackson*, Camden Miscellany 13 (London, 1923), p. xi n. 2; Newton, *Colonising Activities*, pp. 268, 315–17. See also PRO, H.C.A.24/106/149, for a reference to the employment in this venture of Thomson's ship *Ruth* under the command of Capt. Edward Thomson, Maurice's longtime collaborator.

for and the conduct of the Civil War, and, ultimately, try to determine the specific form of political settlement.

Toward Religious Independency

The new-merchant leadership was strongly in favor of root and branch Puritanism and the end of episcopacy, as were almost all of the City oppositionists, whatever their precise political and religious positions. This preference was a natural response to the grip maintained by the Crown and the hierarchy over London parish patronage, and it expressed the citizens' desire for ecclesiastical forms that would allow them to shape their own religious lives. On this issue, the militant citizens were inherently more radical in terms of religion than their colleagues in Parliament whose local patronage and control over ecclesiastical legislation already gave them a high degree of power over church affairs and who were, for the most part, repelled by both the Presbyterian and Independent alternatives favored by most of the leaders of the City's mass movement. From November 1640, with their root and branch bill, and again in August and September 1641, with their bill for parish appointments of weekly lecturers, the City oppositionists had tried to push their parliamentary allies toward more rapid and far-reaching reformation. But in both these instances, a parliamentary leadership still striving for unity had induced the citizens to hold back. By the end of the autumn of 1641, however, with the Grand Remonstrance issued, the City revolution in full swing, and Parliament firmly dependent on the citizens for its survival, London oppositionists, led once again by the radical London MPs John Venn and Isaac Pennington and their new-merchant colleagues, saw no reason to continue to wait. They took advantage of the profound political crisis of late December 1641 to renew their call for root and branch reformation and began to implement once more their strategy for reformation on a parish-by-parish basis.[40]

As noted, on 20 December 1641, John Venn, along with the minister Cornelius Burges, brought into the House of Commons a petition from the City's Puritan ministers that requested that they no longer be required to use prayers against their conscience and that called for a free, national synod to decide the religious settlement. Then, on 23 December, Alderman Pennington presented a petition from the City's apprentices, demanding root and branch reformation. On the same day, 23 December, Venn, the colonial merchant leader Alderman John Warner, and John Brett, the New England trader and son-in-law of Pennington's close as-

---

[40] For the foregoing, see above, ch. 7.

sociate Randall Mainwaring, along with several other citizens of St. Benet Gracechurch parish, took the opportunity to carry into the Commons a petition to eject their "scandalous" minister William Quelch.[41] These petitions seem to have set the agenda for the citizens' movement for reformation in London. Especially after the City revolution had been consolidated in the spring of 1642, the citizens sought to achieve reform directly by means of local, autonomous initiatives in the parishes, even while continuing to press for a national settlement via Parliament and the Assembly of Divines. Here, as elsewhere, the colonial-interloping traders were in the forefront of revolution, as is evident in their roles in their own local parishes, most especially in St. Dunstan's-in-the-East.

In late March 1642—at just about the time they were launching their Additional Sea Adventure to Ireland and their marauding voyage to the West Indies under Captain Jackson—key new-merchant leaders were working with other "inhabitants" of St. Dunstan's-in-the-East to present to Parliament the following petition, reciting their frustrations at the hands of their own parish minister in the pursuit of the godly cause during the previous years:

> Humbly showeth that Dr. John Childerly parson of [St. Dunstan's-in-the-East] for divers years last past hath not preached unto them himself, and his place (for the most part) was supplied with negligent and scandalous ministers who were paid for all those sermons that were preached on the Lord's day by the parishioners of the same parish. And whereas he that preached in the afternoon on the Lord's day is lately dead, the inhabitants desired leave of the Doctor to choose another to supply his room at their own charges to which the Doctor consented, and thereupon they chose one Mr. [John] Simpson whom they presented to the Doctor who refused to receive him. Whereupon they procured the order of this Honourable House made the 8 September 1641 . . . and presented it to the Doctor together with the names of the inhabitants that desired Mr. [John] Simpson to be their lecturer (who were the major part) desiring the Doctor to accept him, if not for his promise yet upon that order, notwithstanding he doth still refuse to permit him to preach unto us.[42]

The offending recalcitrant minister, Dr. John Childerly, had been chaplain to two archbishops before his appointment to the St. Dunstan's living by order of James I. In his will he professed himself "to have lived in the

---

[41] W. H. Coates, ed., *The Journal of Sir Simonds D'Ewes from the First Recess of the Long Parliament* (New Haven, 1942), p. 338; House of Lords MSS, 23 December 1641. See also above, ch. 7, pp. 365–66.

[42] House of Lords MSS, 22 March 1642. See also *Manuscripts of the House of Lords*, n.s., 11, *Addenda, 1514–1714* (London, 1962), no. 3579.

faith and unity of the holy Catholic Church." Childerly was declared by Parliament to be a royalist and dismissed from at least one of his livings, although he apparently stayed on at St. Dunstan's until his death in 1645.[43] John Simpson, the minister the parishioners had chosen to be their lecturer, was characterized by Calamy as "a great antinomian."[44] During the Interregnum he was one of the most prominent and more radical of London's congregationalist ministers. He served in the New Model Army, and then became a strong radical opponent of the Protectorate. During the 1650s he was involved in one of the City's fiercest local sectarian conflicts, a popular struggle between Independent and Presbyterian factions for control of the parish of St. Botolph without Aldgate.[45]

The St. Dunstan's petition that called for Simpson's appointment was signed by more than 150 parishioners on separate sheets circulated within the several parish precincts. Notable among the signers were the colonial merchants Maurice Thomson, his brother George Thomson, their brother-in-law William Tucker, William Allen, Richard Bateson, and George Payne.[46]

As had many others in the City, the Puritan parishioners of St. Dunstan's-in-the-East had sought to initiate reformation in their parish under the sanction of the Commons' bill of 8 September 1641, which authorized parish appointments of weekly lecturers. Having apparently been thwarted temporarily by their minister John Childerly, they now sought to exploit the favorable political situation to have Parliament approve their selection of John Simpson as their lecturer. In this they succeeded, and Simpson's appointment was indeed confirmed by the Commons on 22 March 1642.[47]

The struggle to appoint the congregationalist minister John Simpson at St. Dunstan's-in-the-East offers striking evidence concerning the religious aspirations of an important group of new-merchant leaders and the way it went about achieving them. In the realm of religious affairs, the new merchants of St. Dunstan's showed the same willingness to rely on ad hoc organization reflecting newly created solidarities and on the mobilization of the citizenry that was so characteristic of the initiatives of the group as a whole in every other field. It was through carrying out such organizing that these men could first put their conceptions into practice,

[43] A. G. Matthews, *Calamy Revised* (Oxford, 1934), p. 49; R. Newcourt, *Reportorium Ecclesiasticum Parochiale Londinense*, 2 vols. (London, 1708–1710), 1: 334.

[44] Matthews, *Calamy Revised*, p. 443.

[45] G. Nuttall, *Visible Saints: The Congregational Way, 1640–1660* (Oxford, 1957), pp. 36, 105, 146; J. A. Dodd, "Trouble in a City Parish under the Protectorate," *E.H.R.* 10 (1895): 41–54.

[46] House of Lords MSS, 22 March 1642.

[47] W. A. Shaw, *A History of the English Church during the Civil Wars and under the Commonwealth, 1640–1660*, 2 vols. (London, 1900), 2: 301.

and, ultimately, impose them over fields of activity from which they had formerly been excluded by relatively closed institutions. It is, in part, in such practical terms that one should interpret the strong tendency, not only of the group at St. Dunstan's-in-the-East, but of the majority of the new-merchant leadership to prefer Independent religious forms—that is, forms of church organization and practice that called for local initiative and local control with neither bishops nor Presbyterian assemblies supervising from above; that emphasized the role of the "godly" or most forward elements; that elevated the role of the laity vis-à-vis the clergy; and that tended to disperse authority in religious affairs relatively widely among the laity of the church (however this was defined).

What might be termed "de facto," or informally independent, Puritanism was, it seems, the more or less natural form by which popular—meaning nongentry—forces could carry out Puritan reformation in England throughout a whole epoch. The state's failure to impose a more purely Protestant religion—and its sometimes intense opposition to moves in this direction—meant that Puritan reform had, of necessity, to be carried out piecemeal. In some instances, Puritan nobles and gentry, using their rights to appoint ministers and their other direct controls over local political and ecclesiastical life, could, on their own initiative, directly carry through aspects of the reform program on an official basis. But in the absence of such support from ruling-class elements, and sometimes even in its presence, popular forces were obliged to pursue reformation by means of voluntarily constructed groups, which normally were local in scope, usually were distinct from the official parish, and often were composed of only a minority within it. It was only through unofficial autonomous organizations, involving highly participatory forms of church practice, that "the godly"—the self-appointed initiators of reformation and the self-styled exemplars of the Protestant ideal—could achieve a Protestant religious practice free from popish remnants and, most particularly, carry on those multifarious preachings, Bible expositions, and religious meetings so integral to their conception of a fully reformed church, but so difficult to come by within the state religious structure.

Of course, in line with fundamental Calvinist principles, it was always the mission of the godly to reconstitute and discipline the whole society in accord with God's Word. It was therefore always their intention, in the long run, to enforce universal acceptance of their purified religious practice on a national basis, backed up by the state's full political sanction. But in the face of the monarchy's apparently unshakable opposition to additional official steps to further purify the church as a whole at the national level, there was always an immanent tendency on the part of the godly to attempt to articulate and reinterpret to themselves, in religious terms, their anomalous situation as a minority of saintly practitioners exemplify-

ing true Protestantism amid an unregenerate mass of "neuters" and outright "papists."

Such pressures for self-identification through theoretical self-clarifica-
tion and more-formal church organization became particularly strong in
periods of religious reaction and persecution by the official state church.
At such moments, not only did the sustaining hope and expectation for a
slow but steady reformation through bit-by-bit penetration of the established church structure appear illusory, but the felt need to harden and
consolidate organizationally, as well as to explain and justify theoretically,
the existing associations of the godly seemed absolutely essential. Explicit
articulations of Independent, or congregational, religious conceptions,
with their distinctive and clearly non-Calvinist ideas of "gathered"
churches confined to "visible saints" and of the autonomy of individual
churches, thus appear to have had a basis in the actual religious practice
of already functioning Puritan collectivities, congregations of self-selected
minorities that almost always functioned somewhat apart from the rest of
the parish. But it is no accident that the drive to theorize and formalize de
facto godly religious practice became most intense in those periods of
sharpest religious repression—toward the end of the reign of Elizabeth,
during the early years of James I's rule, and, in particular, from the onset
of Laudianism in the later 1620s.[48]

At least a pivotal core among the new-merchant leaders originally became attracted to Independent religion in the course of their support for,
and involvement with, the Puritan experiments in New England and
Holland. The need to protect not only particular Puritan ministers but
also already formed Puritan associations—indeed whole godly communities—from intense attack by the church and state authorities at the end
of the 1620s was behind the movement to Massachusetts Bay, as well as
emigration to the United Provinces. And it is notable that, particularly
with the government's assault on their well-developed network of semiofficial reformed institutions in London and East Anglia, many Puritans
from these areas moved rapidly to develop, accept, and put into practice
Independent conceptions of church order—most extensively, of course,
in the Americas and Holland where they were adapted to new contexts.
During the late 1620s and 1630s, such key new-merchant leaders as Matthew Craddock, Samuel Vassall, Owen Rowe, Thomas Andrews, Mau-

---

[48] For the foregoing see especially the works of P. Collinson, notably *The Elizabethan Puritan
Movement* (London, 1967) and "The Godly: Aspects of Popular Protestantism in Elizabethan England," originally in papers presented to the *Past & Present* Conference on Popular Religion (7 July
1966), reprinted in *The Godly People: Essays on English Protestantism and Puritanism* (London, 1983).
See also Tolmie, *Triumph of the Saints*, pp. 31–33. I have also benefited greatly from a manuscript
by O. Kalu on Puritanism in Essex in the early seventeenth century. I wish to thank Dr. Kalu for
allowing me to read this work before publication.

rice and Robert Thomson, William Pennoyer, and Thomas Stone forged very intimate connections with the Independent militants who formed the lay and clerical leadership of the colonizing movement to New England; this is prima facie evidence of their general sympathy with, though not their exclusive attachment to, Independent ideas in this period, especially since many of these merchants, along with many of their colleagues, continued to express similar religious preferences throughout the subsequent era of revolutionary turmoil.[49]

[49] Cf. P. Collinson, "The Early Dissenting Tradition," in *Godly People*; Shipps, "Lay Patronage"; Sprunger, *Dutch Puritanism*; S. Foster, *Notes from the Caroline Underground* (Springfield, Oh., 1978); R. P. Stearns and D. H. Brawner, "New England Church 'Relations' and Continuity in Early Congregational History," *American Antiquarian Society Proceedings* 75 (21 Apr. 1965–20 Oct. 1965). Craddock had been, of course, one of the leaders of the Massachusetts Bay Company and key supporters of the colony; he had been directly responsible for choosing the Massachusetts Bay Colony's first ministers, Francis Higginson and Samuel Skelton, both Independents; and he left a bequest of £50 for Harvard College. See above, ch. 6, pp. 276–77, and *The Winthrop Papers, 1498–1649*, 5 vols. (Boston, 1929–1947), 3: 225–26. Samuel Vassall not only played a leading role in the founding and governance of the Massachusetts Bay Company but also remained active commercially in Massachusetts through his partnership with his brother William, who migrated to the colony at the transfer of the charter. William Vassall, a sometime Massachusetts magistrate, helped lead the struggle for greater toleration in the colony. The two brothers accumulated a huge estate in Massachusetts, and Samuel eventually migrated there (B. Bailyn, *The New England Merchants in the Seventeenth Century* [Cambridge, Mass., 1955], p. 107; Pearl, *London*, pp. 190, 191 n. 128). Owen Rowe remained in close touch with John Winthrop throughout the 1630s, purchased goods in Massachusetts, and, by the mid-1630s, appears to have decided to emigrate. Although he never went to Massachusetts, he did play an important role in the founding, during the late 1630s, of the explicitly congregational project for New Haven, which was chiefly organized in Rowe's parish of St. Stephen's Coleman Street and had among its chief guiding figures the leading Independent divines John Davenport and Henry Whitfield. Whitfield was minister in Guilford, Surrey, before he helped found Guilford, Connecticut, in order that he and his company "might settle and uphold all the ordinances of God in an explicit congregational Church way." Rowe's son did emigrate to New Haven (I. M. Calder, *The New Haven Colony* [1934], pp. 1–31, 55, 87, 207). Thomas Andrews's continuing sympathy with the objectives of the Massachusetts Bay venture is evident in his direct financial contributions to the general support of the colony as well as to Harvard College. His support of the separatist colony at Plymouth during the 1620s is another indication, in the colonial context, of his partiality to congregational forms of Puritanism (*New Eng. Hist. Gen. Reg.* 36 [1882]: 68; 39 [1885]: 179–81; W. Bradford, *A History of Plymouth Plantation, 1620–1647*, ed. W. C. Ford, 2 vols. [Boston, 1912], 2: 6). Maurice Thomson was, as noted, planning to migrate to Massachusetts by the late 1630s. He maintained close ties with his brother Robert, who did go to New England and who became an intimate associate of many of the leading figures of New England congregationalism. Robert Thomson was a beneficiary and trustee of the Connecticut founding father Edward Hopkins, and purchased the house of Henry Whitfield when that congregational minister returned to England. Both Maurice Thomson and William Pennoyer must have enjoyed the warmest relations with Massachusetts Bay, for they were awarded a special patent to establish a fishery off Cape Ann by the Colony's suspicious magistrates. Pennoyer exhibited his sympathies for the colony's aims through an important contribution to Harvard College (*New Eng. Hist. Gen. Reg.* 38 [1884]: 315–18; J. Savage, *Genealogical Dictionary of the First Settlers of New England*, 4 vols. [Boston, 1860–1862], 4: 287–88; C. M. Andrews, *The Colonial Period of American History*, 4 vols. [New Haven, 1934–1938], 2: 141; Calder, *New Haven Colony*, p. 237; PRO, will of William Pennoyer, 1671 PCC Duke 25). Throughout the period of

It is hardly surprising that the tendency to embrace Independent religious views on the part of the new merchants, as well as significant numbers of their collaborators in the leadership of the City radical opposition, only intensified following the collapse of Laudian repression and the successful consolidation of City revolution. The failure of Parliament to establish a new form of religious settlement to replace the old, disintegrating ecclesiastical order left the new merchants and their friends little choice but to carry forward reformation on their own. For this they needed little encouragement. And the mere practical fact that they were thus obliged to pursue reformation by means of the initiatives of the most forward (godly and active) elements and on a parish-by-parish basis naturally intensified the predilection of a critical core among them to interpret reformation in Independent terms. It must be emphasized, of course, that London's citizens could view their moves toward reform in other ways. And in this period especially, a great many saw local reformation as merely a first step in what they assumed would be an overall development toward a national Presbyterian framework.[50]

Whatever the mixture of practical and ideological elements that went into shaping their religious conceptions—and I would assert the fruitlessness of attempting to separate these elements too sharply—the strong preference on the part of a majority of new-merchant leaders for Independent religion, which was manifested in their close association with Independent ministers, had enormous political significance. The Independent ministers and their congregations composed only a small section of the City's reforming religious community, but they could exert an influence far out of proportion to their numbers. First, the Independent churches that arose in London during the 1640s were enormously cohesive bodies, with memberships capable of taking coordinated action at a moment's notice. As strictly voluntary organizations, they "gathered" their members out of the parishes to form ongoing and tightly knit religious groups; moreover, they selected new recruits only from among those who were already in close fellowship with their congregations and who had undergone close scrutiny during an extended period of testing. Second, although officially autonomous and self-sufficient, the City's Independent churches maintained close, and apparently somewhat formalized, associa-

Laudian repression Thomas Stone maintained close connections with the Reverend Henry Whitfield, the congregationalist leader of the New Haven Colony. Stone also was very likely the merchant of that name who was responsible for the concealment and escape to Holland of John Davenport in 1633. For his involvement with Puritan Nonconformity, Stone was in trouble before the Court of High Commission by the end of the pre–Civil War decade (E. Stone, "The Ancestry of William Stone, Governor of Maryland," *New Eng. Hist. Gen. Reg.* 49 [1895]: 314–16; Calder, *New Haven Colony*, p. 23).

[50] See above, ch. 6, pp. 275–80.

tions with one another. The Independent churches, as a group, therefore could easily take action together on issues of common concern. Finally, although they made every effort to distinguish themselves from the more radical and openly separatist sectarian congregations, the Independents were in fact, in significant respects, close to the sects in terms of their fundamental religious views. Indeed, to many contemporaries they were indistinguishable from the separatists. In particular, both the Independents and the separatists differed sharply from the rest of the reforming religious community in that they endowed each local church with the capacity for self-government and restricted church membership to those who were godly "visible saints." Both the Independents and the sects, therefore, broke in practice from the Calvinist conception of the church as a comprehensive body that included, and could therefore govern, the whole population and that, by virtue of its catholicity, possessed the capacity to carry out, in a unified way, its primary function as an agency to enforce uniformity, discipline, and social control.

Because so much of the Puritan community was fiercely and irrevocably Calvinist, the Independents tried to play down their congregationalism, and they emphasized that, unlike the separatists, they favored a state church and strongly supported the national reformation of the existing parish churches. But in the end the Independents could deny neither the autonomy of their individual churches, nor the factual separation of their congregations from the parish churches, nor a certain kinship with the separatists, with whom they actually retained close ties. As a consequence, the Independents tended to be grouped with the separatists—especially by hostile contemporaries—and came under attack for many of the same reasons that the separatists were assailed. The Independents and the sects were therefore often compelled to collaborate, if only to defend themselves, and the consequences were far-reaching. The relatively better-off commercial elements, typified by the new-merchant leadership, which apparently tended to constitute the core of the Independent congregations, ended up working in tandem with the small tradesmen and artisans who seem to have populated the separatist churches. This was an explosive sociopolitical combination, able, when internally unified, to exert a powerful influence on public affairs.[51]

As close associates of the Independent ministers and churches, many of the new-merchant leaders became involved with their highly developed organizations. Here they found still another source of solidarity to bind their own group together. Equally important, they found in the Indepen-

---

[51] For the foregoing discussion of London Independency, I have relied on Tolmie's excellent account in *Triumph of the Saints*, especially pp. 85–102. See also pp. 39–46, on the social composition of the Independent in contrast with the separatist churches.

dent congregations a further basis for reaching out and consolidating those ties with other nonmerchant City radicals—of disparate political, religious, and social backgrounds—with whom they had to work if they wished to exert significant political influence. Indeed, the emerging radical political alliance in the City would find one essential source of its organizational and ideological cohesiveness in the participation of a significant proportion of its members in the London Independents' religious initiatives.[52]

As noted, a key group of new-merchant political militants was instrumental in the choice of the Independent minister John Simpson as lecturer at St. Dunstan's-in-the-East in the spring of 1642, including Maurice Thomson, his brother George Thomson, their brother-in-law William Tucker, Richard Bateson, George Payne, and William Allen. Allen, a citizen of Tower Street, London, provided a direct link between the St. Dunstan's petitioners and perhaps the most politically pivotal Independent church in London, that of John Goodwin.[53] Goodwin had succeeded John Davenport as vicar of St. Stephen's Coleman Street parish when Davenport left England in 1633. St. Stephen's was one of the few parishes in London in which the parishioners maintained the right to appoint their own minister. Not coincidentally perhaps, St. Stephen's turned out to be a key organizing center for both political radicalism and Independent Puritanism throughout the period.

During the 1630s and early 1640s, many of its parishioners seem to have regarded the St. Stephen's Coleman Street parish church, in Tolmie's words, "as an implicit congregational church with an implicit congregational ministry." Even so, when John Goodwin moved in 1643 not merely to "gather" a congregation out of the parish but also to include within it certain outsiders and to exclude as unqualified a number of St. Stephen's parishioners, he aroused the opposition of some of the parish's leading members, notably the London MP and City radical political leader Alderman Isaac Pennington. By the middle 1640s, the parish was split into two conflicting factions. On one side was John Goodwin, supported by those who had joined his gathered church. On the other side were those of the parish exemplified by and led by Pennington. The latter parishioners appear to have gone along with the experiment of giving the St. Stephen's parish church an explicitly congregational form, of gathering it so to speak, and they were content, in the process, to admit godly persons from outside the parish into their congregation. However, because they wished to retain the parochial character of their congregation,

---

[52] See above, p. 395.

[53] For Allen's membership in Goodwin's gathered church, see Tolmie, *Triumph of the Saints*, p. 115.

they balked when Goodwin and his followers sought to assume authority over admission to the newly constituted church, with the right to reject those members of St. Stephen's parish church whom they judged to be insufficiently godly. "Parochial Independents," typified by Pennington, thus agreed with the Presbyterians, in contrast with the congregational Independents, in supporting a *parish-based* church, and here they drew the line against John Goodwin and his followers. On the other hand, they were parochial *Independents* because they agreed with the congregational Independents, in opposition to many mainstream Presbyterians, in supporting the voluntariness and the autonomy of the local churches (specifically in relation to any classical or synodal hierarchies), in backing lay (as opposed to clerical) control of the church and especially of admission to the sacrament, and, perhaps above all, in supporting toleration for the gathered churches. They thus maintained a large area of agreement with the congregational Independents, and this provided the basis for continuing collaboration.[54]

This is not the place for a detailed account of the conflict at St. Stephen's Coleman Street. What is important for present purposes is that, although Goodwin was ousted from his position in 1645, there was never the sort of break between the two sides that would prevent their political collaboration. Both sides continued to supply numbers of leading figures in the radical, and later political independent, movements in the City. From Goodwin's gathered church came such major radical leaders as Mark Hildesley, Nathaniel Lacy, Daniel Taylor, Thomas Lambe, John Price, Richard Price (the mercer), and his nephew Richard Price (the scrivener). Lacy, Taylor, and Hildesley all worked with the new-merchant leadership in the Additional Sea Adventure to Ireland and, by the middle 1640s, one of the Richard Prices appears to have entered the trade with the West Indies. Among those who remained with the official parish were the colonial-interloping merchants James Russell and Owen Rowe, both City militia commissioners, as well as Thomas Alderne, who was Rowe's son-in-law and Russell's apprentice and, by the end of the 1640s, a trader with the West Indies in his own right. The Providence Island Company member Thomas Barnardiston was also a parochial Independent in St. Stephen's Coleman Street parish. It is indicative of the nature of the conflict at St. Stephen's that all of these men, on both sides of the conflict, ended up as political independents and that Rowe, Alderne, and Barnardiston, as well as Alderman Pennington, were among those who backed Goodwin's return to St. Stephen's parish in 1649.[55]

---

[54] See Tolmie, *Triumph of the Saints*, pp. 111–16, for the foregoing discussion of developments at St. Stephen's Coleman Street.

[55] Tolmie, *Triumph of the Saints*, pp. 114–15; St. Stephen's Coleman Street Vestry Minute Book, Guildhall Library MSS 4458.1, pp. 147, 161; Matthews, *Calamy Revised*, pp. 227, 479. On Al-

Aside from those connected with John Simpson at St. Dunstan's-in-the-East and with John Goodwin at St. Stephen's Coleman Street, other groups of religiously Independent new-merchant leaders associated themselves directly with the national leadership of the Independents' movement by gathering around the ministers Sydrach Simpson, Thomas Goodwin, and William Bridge, all of whom had been leaders in the Rotterdam and Arnhem Independent congregations during the later 1630s and ended up among the Five Dissenting Divines of the Westminster Assembly and as authors of the *Apologeticall Narration*. Simpson was curate and lecturer at St. Margaret New Fish Street parish during the 1630s, and prominent among his followers was the new merchant Thomas Andrews, who supported the separatist-backed Plymouth Colony during the 1620s, traded with and patronized the New England colonies in the 1630s, and got involved in both interloping in the East Indies and trading with the West Indies in sugar during the 1640s. In 1642 Andrews became one of the few new merchants to gain the position of alderman, and, also in that year, his son Thomas married Damaris, a daughter of the great colonial merchant MP and London oppositionist Matthew Craddock. When Sydrach Simpson had left St. Margaret's for Rotterdam in the late 1630s, Thomas Andrews followed him there to join his congregation. When Simpson returned to London and assumed his lectureship at St. Margaret's, his congregation met at Andrews's house. Two of Andrews's sons and business partners, Thomas Andrews, Jr. and Nathaniel Andrews, were also close to Simpson and both left him bequests. The colonial leader Samuel Warner (brother of the new-merchant alderman John Warner and father-in-law of Maurice's brother the new merchant William Thomson) was also an intimate of Simpson's, an overseer of his will, and most probably also a member of his congregation.[56] The great Independent leader Thomas Goodwin had left Yorkshire for exile in Arnhem, where he was co-pastor of the English congregation along with Philip Nye. Like Sydrach Simpson, Thomas Goodwin returned to London in 1641, and he brought his congregation from Arnhem with him. It seems to have met, in fact, at St. Dunstan's-in-the-East. Among the influential members of Goodwin's congregation was the leading new merchant Samuel Moyer. A

---

derne, see PRO, will of Thomas Alderne, 1657 PCC Ruthen 218; Society of Genealogists, Boyd's Index: 13156. Alderne left bequests to John Goodwin and "the poor of Mr. Goodwin's congregation." On Barnardiston, who was not typical of the colonial-interloping merchant group in that he was a son of a rich old Essex gentry family and married the daughter of a London merchant, see Newton, *Colonising Activities*, pp. 127–28.

[56] Tolmie, *Triumph of the Saints*, pp. 104–5; J. E. Farnell, "The Politics of the City of London, 1649–1657" (University of Chicago, Ph.D. diss., 1963), p. 59; J. C. Whitebrook, "Sir Thomas Andrews, Lord Mayor and Regicide, and His Relatives," *Congregational Historical Society Transactions*, 2d ser. (1938–1939), 13: 155, 160, 161; *D.N.B.*, s.v. "Sydrach Simpson"; will of Sydrach Simpson, printed in Waters, *Genealogical Gleanings* 2: 1186.

signer of the new merchants' petition supporting the trader with the Americas Joseph Hawes and a key partner in Maurice Thomson's East Indian interloping project, Moyer was also a patron of the Independent ministers John Owen and John Collins.[57] William Bridge had been pastor of the Rotterdam congregation—at which Jeremiah Burroughs (also one of the Five Dissenting Divines and an *Apologeticall Narrator*) had served as teacher—before he returned to England and gathered a church in Yarmouth. Maurice Thomson's partner William Pennoyer, who may have had family connections with Yarmouth, left money to Bridge, as well as to William Greenhill, and also made a bequest of £30 a year for two scholars and two fellows at Harvard College in Massachusetts.[58] Greenhill, a major participant in the congregationalist experiments in Holland during the 1630s, was a most intimate associate of the Independent clerical leadership, as well as the new-merchant leadership. His appointment, along with his close collaborator Jeremiah Burroughs, in September 1641 as co-lecturer for Stepney parish, one of London's main centers of religio-political radicalism throughout the Interregnum, had initiated the effort to carry through a Puritan reformation of the church on a voluntary, parish-by-parish basis. Since that time, Greenhill had participated in the new merchants' Additional Adventure to Ireland and would soon form his own gathered congregation in Stepney, eventually becoming Stepney's official parish minister. Like his partner William Pennoyer, Maurice Thomson was closely connected with Greenhill, although, like some others among his new-merchant colleagues, he appears to have leaned toward "parochial Independency," seeking to avoid rending the parish by using it as the basis for forming a congregation. Thomson became a churchwarden in Greenhill's Stepney church, but seems never to have joined his gathered congregation. Nevertheless, Thomson's daughter Maria was baptized in Greenhill's gathered church in 1648. Maurice's relative and trading partner Edward Thomson, and Edward's wife, were also members of Greenhill's gathered church, as was William Pennoyer's wife.[59]

---

[57] *D.N.B.*, s.v. "Thomas Goodwin"; Matthews, *Calamy Revised*, pp. 228–29; Tolmie, *Triumph of the Saints*, p. 105; PRO, will of Samuel Moyer, 1683 PCC Drax 96; *Dictionary of Seventeenth-Century Radicals*, vol. 2, s.v. "Samuel Moyer."

[58] Tolmie, *Triumph of the Saints*, pp. 89, 95, 107; PRO, will of William Pennoyer, 1671 PCC Duke 25; *Dictionary of Seventeenth-Century Radicals*, vol. 1, s.v. "William Bridge," and vol. 3, s.v. "William Pennoyer"; R. W. Lovett, "The Pennoyer Scholarship at Harvard," *Harvard Library Bulletin* 4 (Spring 1950).

[59] For the basic religious identification of Maurice Thomson, see Tolmie, *Triumph of the Saints*, pp. 140–141. For Thomson as churchwarden in Stepney, see G. W. Hill and W. H. Frere, *Memorials of Stepney Parish* (Guildford, 1890–1891), p. 148. It might be noted in passing that Col. John Okey and his wife also belonged to William Greenhill's congregation. The data concerning the members of Greenhill's gathered church is from Stepney Meeting House, "A Book of Church Affaires at Stepney," and Register of William Greenhill's church at Stepney, PRO, RG4/4414. I am

From the late 1640s the Independent minister George Cockayn operated a gathered church at Soper Lane, London, and among its members
were the important tobacco merchant William Underwood and Maurice
Thomson's Guinean-trade partner Rowland Wilson. In 1648 the Independent minister Thomas Brookes transformed the parish church of St.
Margaret New Fish Street, where Sydrach Simpson had been lecturer,
into a gathered congregation, and it is probable that William Pennoyer's
brother and colonial-interloping partner Samuel Pennoyer, who left
money to Brookes and maintained a host of New England Puritan connections, was one of its members.[60] Stephen Estwicke, the London militia
commissioner and the interloping partner of Maurice Thomson in the
East Indies, who was one of the City's leading Independent militants, also
was a patron of Brookes. Estwicke attended the gathered congregation of
Matthew Barker in his parish of St. Leonard's Eastcheap. At his death,
he left money for the Independent ministers Joseph Carryl, George Griffith, Ralph Venning, and William Tuttie. Another key activist in the colonial trades, the City goldsmith and Bermuda Company officer Francis
Allein, also patronized Carryl, Griffith, and Venning, as well as two other
Independent ministers, Thomas Elford and Thomas Gilbert.[61] Venning,
along with William Cooper, presided over the parish of St. Olave's
Southwark, one of the centers of religio-political radicalism throughout
the Interregnum. Venning, as did Cooper, received a bequest from still
another of the colonial-interloping leaders, Jeremy Blackman, who was a
resident of St. Olave's (and brother-in-law of Thomas Prince, later to
become a Leveller).[62] Finally, it seems that several important new merchants had, by the end of the 1640s, ended up in the Baptist wing of the
Puritan movement. These included Samuel Moyer, Maurice Thomson's
brother George, and Richard Shute.

This evidence about the new merchants' proclivities for Independent
religion is of a relatively general type. It does not reveal precisely how
well formed or inflexible were their attitudes on some of the key theological questions that so agitated the City's ministry in this period: the nature

---

grateful to Dr. Bernard Capp for this material. In 1649, Maurice Thomson contributed a commending epistle to a pamphlet authored by the Particular Baptist Samuel Richardson. Thomson's collaborator Richard Shute was also a religious Independent (Tolmie, loc. cit.).

[60] J. B. Marsh, *The Story of Hare Court* (London, 1871), pp. 38, 77; C. B. Cockett, "George
Cockayn," *Congregational Historical Society Transactions* 12 (1933–1936); 225–35. Matthews, *Calamy Revised*, p. 79; PRO, will of Samuel Pennoyer, 1654 PCC Alchian 388.

[61] J. E. Farnell, "The Usurpation of Honest London Householders: Barebone's Parliament,"
E.H.R. 82 (1967): 27–28; PRO, will of Stephen Estwicke, 1658 PCC Wootton 520; PRO, will of
Francis Allein, 1659 PCC Pell 472; *Dictionary of Seventeenth-Century Radicals*, vol. 1, s.v. "Francis
Allein." Allein named Carryl and Venning executors of his will.

[62] Matthews, *Calamy Revised*, pp. 135, 501; PRO, will of Jeremy Blackman, 1656 PCC Berkley
380.

of the church's membership—whether it should include all of the parish-ioners or just the "visible saints"; the role of the laity vis-à-vis the clergy; the distribution of authority within each church; the connection of one church to another; and the relation of church and state. It is not improb-able that a good number of these traders would have embraced any sort of church framework that enjoined a fully reformed Puritan practice, al-lowed the congregations a modicum of local autonomy, gave the laity a leading role within the church, and allowed toleration for the gathered churches. Thus, while only relatively few of the new-merchant leaders were outright Presbyterians,[63] at least a number of those who were appar-ently Independents nonetheless retained close ties with Presbyterian min-isters. Moreover, others with Independent attachments were willing to take part in the watered-down and rather loose Erastian Presbyterian set-tlement established by Parliament in late 1645.[64] Nor is this surprising; Independents, both congregational and parochial, had important things in common with Presbyterians. Like Presbyterians, Independents were committed to maintaining a state church to ensure order, and parochial Independents were even in favor of keeping the parish as the basis for establishing autonomous congregations. Also like Presbyterians, Inde-pendents were concerned with completing the reformation of religion on

[63] The new merchant religious Presbyterians so far identified are Thomas Gower, Lawrence Brin-ley, Michael Herring, Richard Quiney, John Sadler, and Robert Wilding, as well as John Warner and John Fowke (the only really major figures among them). Gower, Brinley, Herring, and Warner were elders in the London Presbyterian system and representatives to the London Provincial Assem-bly (Sion College, Records of the Provincial Assembly of London, 1647–1660, MSS Acc. L40.2/E17, fols. 3, 17, 21, 123, 245). All appear to have patronized Presbyterian ministers: PRO, will of Thomas Gower, 1676 PCC Bence 101; PRO, will of Lawrence Brinley, 1662 PCC Laud 151 (be-quest to Edmund Calamy); PRO, will of Michael Herring, 1657 PCC Bence 101 (bequests to Laz-arus Seaman, James Cranford, Thomas Manton, Simon Peck); PRO, will of Richard Quiney, 1657 PCC Ruthen 6 (bequests to Thomas Watson and Alexander Beane); PRO, will of John Sadler, 1659 PCC Bell 7 (bequests to Thomas Watson and Alexander Beane); PRO, will of Robert Wilding, 1673 PCC Pye 107 (bequests to Peter Ince, Arthur Barham, Samuel Rolles). John Warner maintained as his chaplain the noted Presbyterian minister Christopher Love (Pearl, *London*, p. 167). For Fowke's Presbyterianism, see V. Pearl, "London's Counter-Revolution," in *The Interregnum*, ed. G. E. Ayl-mer (London, 1972), p. 31.

[64] See, for example, the aforementioned cases of William Underwood, who became a member of the congregation of the Independent minister George Cockayn (who preached Underwood's funeral sermon), and of Francis Allein, who supported a stable of Independent ministers. During the 1640s, both had participated in the national Presbyterian structure, Underwood as an elder of St. Stephen's Walbrook and as the representative of St. Stephen's to the London Provincial Assembly, and Allein as an elder of St. Dunstan's-in-the-West (Sion College, Records, MSS fols. 17, 106v; Marsh, *Hare Court*, p. 77; PRO, will of William Underwood, 1657 PCC Wootton 147; *Dictionary of Seventeenth-Century Radicals*, vol. 1, s.v. "Francis Allein"). The aforementioned James Russell, Thomas Barnar-diston, and possibly even Owen Rowe, appear to have pursued an analogous path at St. Stephen's Coleman Street, participating in the national Erastian Presbyterian structure in the mid-1640s, even if perhaps preferring religious Independency.

a national and official basis. They therefore shared with Presbyterians an aversion to the complete separation of church and state, and this point of agreement could have broad political, as well as religious, implications. Indeed, had the new parliamentary church allowed a certain degree of toleration and established the basis for a modicum of religious pluralism, the Independents among the colonial-interloping traders could almost certainly have lived with the basic structure it defined and might very well have sought to achieve some sort of unity with the City's Presbyterians (as they actually did under the Commonwealth). As it was, however, by the middle of the 1640s, London's governing authorities were employing the new parliamentary church and Presbyterian religion as central *political* weapons against both the City and army radicals and attempting to repress them as "dangerous sectaries," hoping to outlaw both religious Independency and separatism alike precisely in order to consolidate a political presbyterian settlement of the conflict.

This is not to say that the political presbyterians' charge of religious sectarianism, with its implication of political radicalism, was entirely wide of the mark. Many of the new merchants and their London political allies certainly did favor religious Independency and, from early on, they worked hand in hand with some of the period's key Independent ministers in the leadership of a City radical political movement that would gather strength in 1642–1643. Further, a common religious involvement with congregational religious activities did help some of the economically more substantial City radicals, typified by the new merchants, to forge political ties with those less substantial citizen religious separatists who, throughout the entire period, provided a critical element within every radical political mass upsurge. It is certainly false that all of the City's leading political radicals were also Independents or separatists, or that citizen Presbyterians were unrepresented in the radical leadership.[65] Nonetheless, religious Independents did dominate the leadership of London's political radical movement to a striking degree, especially given their very minor position in the City in comparison to that of the religious Presbyterians; moreover, separatists do appear to have constituted a disproportionately large element within that movement's rank and file. Depending as they did through much of the 1640s on the mobilization of masses of militant Londoners, the new merchants and their friends in the emerging radical movement could dispense with the separatists only at great cost. By the same token, precisely because those moderate forces in London that would emerge during the middle 1640s as political presbyterians saw religious Indepen-

---

[65] Leading radicals who were also religious Presbyterians so far identified (aside from the new-merchant radicals who were Presbyterians, or sympathetic to Presbyterianism, mentioned in notes 63 and 64) included Sir David Watkins and Tempest Milner.

dency as leading inexorably to political subversion, they could not but make demands concerning the religious settlement part of their political program. In their view, Independency would, first of all, corrode the national church and the local parish structures through which they hoped to enforce order and repress opposition; it would, in addition, give rise to a religious pluralism that would inexorably lead to political insubordination, most particularly among the citizens of the lower orders that populated the separatist congregations. Many of the City's political moderates saw no alternative therefore but to demand that a strict Presbyterian discipline and absolute religious uniformity (antitoleration) be essential parts of any Civil War settlement. It was not that religion could be reduced to politics. It was just that, from very early on in the struggle in London, the two were rightly seen as inextricably intertwined.

The Radical Offensive, 1642–1643

By the winter of 1642, what I have called the radical wing of the London parliamentary movement had begun to put forward the essential elements of what would ultimately constitute a full-scale alternative program for carrying on the war. Radicals were demanding, in the first place, that the weight of war finance be shifted from those godly elements that had so far borne a disproportionate share of the cost by virtue of their voluntary contributions, that more equitable money-raising arrangements be devised, and, in particular, that Parliament put the squeeze on royalists to raise funds. They were asking, second, that delinquents be removed from all official positions, both secular and ecclesiastical, and that godly persons be put in their places. Finally, they were requesting that Parliament transform the whole conduct of the war by replacing the present wavering aristocratic military leadership with more resolute commanders and by allowing the radicals to finance and organize their own independent army of godly citizens.

Insofar as this program tended to ensure the financial strength and military preparedness of the parliamentary forces, it fitted in perfectly with, and in fact buttressed, the policies Pym and his friends were already pursuing. Indeed, the close working relationship between the parliamentary leaders and the radical London citizens, facilitated by the long-standing ties between the colonizing aristocrats and the new-merchant leadership, continued to constitute one vital feature of political development in this period. But the dilemma posed for Pym's middle group was how to make use of these very helpful citizens while preventing them from gaining the power to impose policies that the middle groupers opposed. This task was to prove especially difficult in the face of King Charles's absolute refusal to agree to a compromise settlement and the recurrent military emergencies. During the winter, spring, and early summer of 1642–1643, as in so many other revolutionary situations throughout history, the threat of disastrous military defeat gave increased credence to radical demands for a drastic reorganization of Parliament's military effort that had clearly revolutionary political implications. In these months, London militants sought to exploit what was perhaps Parliament's greatest politico-military crisis to gain their own independent citizens' army and to secure the removal of the earl of Essex as commander in chief of the parliamentary forces. Lacking the support of either Pym or the official City government, they could not achieve these goals without conflict, but were obliged to seek to impose them by means of the mass mobilization of the London citizenry, the forging of an alliance with Parliament's war-party wing, and the enunciation of the ideal of parliamentary supremacy based on popular sovereignty.

SUPPORTING THE WAR EFFORT:
THE ARMY AND THE ASSESSMENT

The City radicals secured from the start a pivotal position within the parliamentary military effort by virtue of their control of London's militia committee and, in addition, the dominant place of Londoners within Parliament's army. In July 1642, London provided ten thousand volunteers to constitute Parliament's army, under the command of the earl of Essex. The following September, London contributed, as well, two more regiments of foot and four of horse for the parliamentary force. Not only was the regular parliamentary army for the most part composed of Londoners; in addition, during the initial phase of the conflict, the London militia played an absolutely indispensable military role, alongside the main force under Essex. Following Parliament's early defeats at the hands of the royalists, the City's trained bands marched out of the City to save the day at Turnham Green in mid-November. Meanwhile, in the days just before the first major confrontation between the king's and Parliament's armies at Edgehill, it had been agreed that a new army of sixteen thousand men should be raised to act in conjunction with the City's trained bands, with the whole force to be placed under the command of the earl of Warwick. It would be wrong to say that the City's radicals entirely controlled London's contributions to these military and troop-levying efforts, for the officers of the City's trained bands included a number of citizens who had played no leading role in the London revolution during the winter of 1641–1642 and who would end up as political presbyterians. The fact remains that the radicals were able to use their domination of the militia committee to gain a disproportionate share of the very top officer positions in the City's armed forces. No fewer than five of the six colonels who headed the six London-trained bands were themselves members of the militia committee, and four would end up as political independents. Their control of this commanding position within the City's military establishment provided a critically important initial base on which the radicals would build their power over the course of 1642–1643, both in London and within the newly emerging parliamentary administration.[66]

In order for Parliament to succeed militarily it had to go about constructing an effective money-raising machine. Through assuming a central role in this process, the City radicals consolidated for themselves, at least for a time, an absolutely indispensable place in the parliamentary cause. During the year following the outbreak of armed conflict, working closely with the middle-group parliamentary leadership, the City radicals succeeded in winning acceptance of almost the entirety of their program for financing the parliamentary military effort, and they themselves assumed a major part in putting that program into effect. They gained in this way an extraordinarily powerful foothold within the new parliamentary administrative apparatus, an achievement to be noted time and again by (often envious and resentful) contemporaries. As Clement Walker would remark, these men, later political independents, became "the publicans and sinners that handled most public treasure, the layers on, exactors, treasurers, etc., of taxes, the far more numerous and busy party in all money committees and gainful employments, engrossers of all great offices, and the great sharers of public monies amongst themselves for compensations for losses and rewards for services pretended."[67] From this position, they were able to gain a leverage on the course of affairs far out of proportion to their influence within the official City government.

The process of constructing a parliamentary financial machine began in June 1642, when Parliament passed its ordinance for "bringing in plate, money, and horses." Although the act was not specific in this regard, it seems that all "well affected" Englishmen were expected to contribute voluntarily in proportion to their wealth, with the promise that their advances would eventually be refunded, with interest paid at 8 percent. Clearly, the same City oppositionists who had already taken outstanding parts in the City revolution, the committee of safety (militia committee), and the Lon-

---

[66] Pearl, *London*, pp. 250–51; S. R. Gardiner, *History of the Great Civil War*, 4 vols. (London, 1893), pp. 38, 40, 52–60; H. A. Dillon, ed., "MS. List of Officers of the London Trained Bands in 1643," *Archaeologia* 52, pt. 1 (1890): 134–41. The colonels who were militia committee members included Isaac Pennington, Thomas Atkins, Sir John Wollaston, John Towse, and John Warner, all of whom were future political independents, except for Wollaston, who was something of a trimmer. The sixth colonel was Thomas Adams, a future political presbyterian.

[67] C. Walker, *Anarchia Anglicana; or, The History of Independency, The Second Part* (London, 1661), p. 5.

don committee of adventurers for Ireland, were expected to play a major role under this act. Two of the four treasurers appointed to administer the act on a national basis, John Warner and Thomas Andrews, were leading new merchants and members of the militia committee (while the other two, John Towse and John Wollaston, were also City militia committeemen although not new merchants).[68] Parliament already had chosen Andrews, Warner, and Towse to be treasurers for the Irish money, and all four men would occupy a long succession of such treasurerships throughout the Civil War years. To collect the contributions coming in under the act for plate, money, and horses, Parliament set up receiving commissions in the various counties, and in London established a large-scale administration consisting of committees of eight to twelve persons in every ward. The composition of these committees gives an excellent idea of the City's leading supporters of Parliament at the outbreak of the Civil War in the summer of 1642. That no fewer than thirty individuals from the colonial-interloping trades held positions shows the pivotal place these men already occupied.[69]

Since it called for no machinery for assessment or forced collection, the act for bringing in plate, money, and horses, not very surprisingly, elicited insufficient funds for Parliament, and the burden of financing the war fell most heavily on those citizens most strongly committed to the cause. On 21 November 1642, the leading City militant, Richard Shute, brought in a petition to Parliament, demanding that the costs of war cease to be paid only by the "good and godly" party. Shute was, as noted, one of the key political representatives of the new-merchant leadership and its radical citizen allies. He had, with Maurice Thomson, delivered the mass City petition for the recall of Parliament in the autumn of 1640, and from that time on the two had been constant companions. Shute, Maurice Thomson, and their friends were, of course, deeply involved in the original Irish project and had been entirely responsible for the Additional Sea Adventure to Ireland. They had undoubtedly also contributed more than their share under the act to collect plate, money, and horses. Perhaps most important, as will be seen, Shute and his friends had, in early November 1642, just succeeded in gaining parliamentary consent to raise by voluntary means their own small independent cavalry force in the City. Obvi-

[68] A.O. 1: 7–9.

[69] PRO, S.P. 16/491/47. William Thomson, William Tucker, Thomas Frere, Maurice Thomson, George Payne, John Dethick, Edward Hurd, John Pocock, William Kendall, Maximillian Bard, Randall Mainwaring, William Underwood, Samuel Warner, Lawrence Brinley, Thomas Barnardiston, James Russell, Richard Shute, Thomas Gower, Michael Herring, Stephen Estwicke, George Henley, William Pennoyer, Richard Waring, Nathan Wright, William Barkeley, Nicholas Corsellis, Richard Hill, George Snelling, and William Hitchcock are the colonial-interloping merchants who served on the "plate, money, and horses" ward committees.

ously, they wished now to devote their scarce resources to their own project. They wanted, moreover, to shift the burden of war finance onto the royalists, by means of forced levies on "malignants" (royalists), a proposal to which I will return shortly.[70]

Richard Shute and the radical citizens were at this point almost certainly working in close coordination with Pym and his friends in Parliament on the problem of financing the parliamentary cause. The parliamentary leaders were only too glad to take up the militants' grievances and to use them as the occasion to install the permanent system of taxation that they long had desired. On 26 November 1642, recognizing that the parliamentary army "hath been hitherto for the most part maintained by the voluntary contributions of divers well-affected persons, who have freely contributed according to their abilities," Parliament enacted the ordinance for a weekly assessment on the City of London, a law that was soon extended to the country as a whole.[71]

Naturally, the City militants who applied the original pressure in favor of the assessment act were very well represented among the Londoners chosen to administer it. The twelve commissioners appointed to oversee the act in the City included the new-merchant leaders Maurice Thomson, Thomas Andrews, Samuel Vassall, and John Warner, along with John Fowke and Richard Chambers, the Levant–East India Company oppositionists who had become associated with the colonial-interloping group by 1640, as well as Richard Waring, an associate of Thomson's who had signed the American-trade merchants' petition favoring the colonial trader Joseph Hawes and served as a commissioner heading the Thomson-led Additional Sea Adventure to Ireland. The other commissioners were the City radical MPs John Venn and Isaac Pennington, the London treasurers and militia committeemen John Wollaston and John Towse, and the Levant Company trader Thomas Soames. The new merchants Andrews and Warner, along with Towse and Wollaston, were chosen to be treasurers to receive the money coming in under this act, the same post these four men previously had held for the Irish adventure and under the ordinance for bringing in plate, money, and horses. Of the twelve City commissioners for the assessment act, eight also sat on the City's militant committee of safety (militia committee). Except for Chambers, Soames, and Vassall, all of the commissioners would end up as political independents (although, again, Wollaston should be viewed as something of a trimmer).[72]

To carry out the assessment act in the localities, assessors were ap-

---

[70] *C.J.* 2: pp. 857, 847.

[71] *A.O.* 1: 38–42; Hexter, *Reign of King Pym*, pp. 16–18. Shute and his friends may actually have been the first explicitly to propose the weekly assessment system. See *C.J.* 2: 858–59. The meaning of their proposals of 22 November 1642 is not clear from the *Commons Journal*.

[72] *A.O.* 2: 38–42.

pointed in each ward, and once more the significant role of the colonial-interloping merchants should be noted. The assessors included such immediate members of Maurice Thomson's circle as William Pennoyer, Samuel Moyer, Nicholas Corsellis, John Dethick, George Snelling, Richard Hill, Thomas Vincent, and John Brett. Richard Hutchinson, John Sadler, Edward Hurd, Lawrence Brinley, Michael Herring, John Pocock, and George Henley were other traders with the Americas also appointed assessors.[73]

SUPPORTING THE WAR EFFORT:
THE NAVY AND THE CUSTOMS

During the subsequent months, Parliament put its assessment system into place, but collection was inefficient and took time. Parliament was therefore obliged to devise ad hoc arrangements to assure a steady flow of money in order to cope with what became a permanent financial crisis. Charles I had used the customs system as a source of advances on government income. But the Caroline customs farmers were at the core of City royalism and could hardly be expected to lend their support to the parliamentary cause. When in late December 1642 the old customers refused Parliament's request for a loan, Parliament promptly dismissed them and, in January 1643, appointed its own commission for customs. This new body was established with the explicit purpose of advancing money to the parliamentary government, especially the navy, and it was entirely in the hands of the new-merchant leadership. The customs commission of eight included Maurice Thomson and his partners in interloping in the East Indies Stephen Estwicke, James Russell, and Thomas Andrews, along with John Fowke and Richard Chambers, as well as William Barkeley, the trader with the Americas who had worked from the 1630s in partnership with Thomson's brother-in-law Elias Roberts. The last member of the commission was the London goldsmith Francis Allein, an active participant in the Bermuda Company. Six of the eight customs commissioners were also City militia commissioners. All but Chambers were in the more radical wing of the City parliamentary opposition, all but Chambers ended up as political independents, and Thomson, Estwicke, Andrews, Russell, and Allein can be identified as religious Independents of one sort or another.[74]

The special function of the customs commission was to support the parliamentary navy. In fact, in providing advances for the navy, the new-

[73] PRO, S.P.19/A.1/37.

[74] Lawrence Whitacre's Parliamentary Diary, BL, Add MSS 31116, fol. 16v.; *C.J.* 2: 937–38; *A.O.* 1: 104–5. On Francis Allein in the Bermuda Company, see J. H. Lefroy, *Memorials of the Bermudas*, 2 vols. (Bermuda, 1877–1879), 1: 590.

merchant customs commissioners appear, to a significant extent, to have been providing the financing for their own critical role, and that of other colonial-interloping traders, in organizing and actually carrying out Parliament's naval effort. At the start of the conflict, in the late spring of 1642, Parliament had succeeded in constituting the core of its navy by winning over to its support almost all of the officers of the existing permanent royal navy, who brought their ships with them. At the same time, it had seized control of national naval administration from the king. It secured the position of admiral of the fleet for the earl of Warwick, and officially appointed him in early July. Then, on 15 September 1642, Parliament appointed a twelve-person commission, composed half of MPs and half of civilians and led by Sir Henry Vane, to take charge of actually organizing and administering the new navy.[75] This commission included the leading new merchants Samuel Vassall and Richard Cranley, who were partners in shipowning and in the American trades, as well as Vassall's relatives and sometime shipping partners Squire and Alexander Bence, both MPs. Simultaneously, Parliament appointed Thomas Smythe as secretary to its newly established admiralty, led by the earl of Warwick. Smythe had been secretary to the old admiral the earl of Northumberland, and was a close collaborator of Maurice Thomson's. He had been one of the commissioners of Thomson's Additional Sea Adventure to Ireland in June 1642, was a partner of Thomson's in anti-Spanish privateering, and was a part owner, with Thomson and the earl of Warwick himself, of the ship *Discovery*.[76]

In order to secure the wherewithal to carry out simultaneously the imposing tasks of waging war at sea against the king, of protecting its supporters' trade, and of preventing navigation to enemy ports, Parliament had to supplement its small permanent navy by hiring armed merchant vessels from private individuals. As was to be expected, the City's company merchants, overwhelmingly opposed to Parliament, were less than willing to offer their ships for Parliament's naval effort. In consequence, Parliament was obliged to turn for assistance once again to traders outside the City's merchant establishment, and in particular to the new-merchant leaders. These men provided, by way of private contracts with the government, a large part of the parliamentary navy, and they also supplied, in Groenveld's words, "naval officers of a new type, who had been trained in merchant ships and replaced the old aristocratic commanders in Parliament's navy," under the command of the earl of Warwick.[77] Within a

---

[75] H. C. Junge, *Flottenpolitik und Revolution: Die Enstehung der englishen Seemacht wahrend der Herrschaft Cromwells* (Stuttgart, 1980), pp. 40–41, 45–47.

[76] *A.O.* 1: 28; Junge, *Flottenpolitik*, pp. 54–56; PRO, H.C.A.24/108/62–65.

[77] S. Groenveld, "The English Civil Wars as a Cause of the First Anglo-Dutch War, 1640–1652" *H.J.* 30 (1987): 548; Junge, *Flottenpolitik*, pp. 48–53.

month of its appointment, in October 1642, the parliamentary navy commission is found signing an agreement with Maurice Thomson to hire his ship *Hopewell* for the parliamentary navy. Over the course of the Civil War years, Parliament would hire for its navy no fewer than eight vessels belonging in whole or in part to Maurice Thomson, including the aforementioned *Discovery*, owned by a partnership that included Thomson, Thomas Smythe, and the earl of Warwick. Parliament also hired at least six other ships owned wholly or in part by Thomas Smythe and four more ships owned wholly or in part by Samuel Vassall. Overall, no fewer than sixty ships belonging to new merchants have been identified as serving in this manner in Parliament's navy during the Civil War.[78]

The ordinance that had installed the new-merchant led syndicate as commission for the customs, at a salary of £10,000 a year, made it clear that the commissioners would be expected to perform important lending functions, and they were in fact called on incessantly to keep the parliamentary navy from collapsing. The commissioners were obliged to advance £20,000 in the first place just to obtain the customs commission for a period of three years. In March 1643, Parliament required them to advance an additional £20,000 to hold onto their offices.[79] In May 1643, they were told that another £45,000 was needed: would they advance this sum "upon their own credit or otherwise?" They turned down this request, but in September, the customers lent £30,000 to the navy treasurer, Sir Henry Vane.[80] During 1644—in March, September, October, and November—they lent an additional total of £61,000. Finally, in February 1645, after a year in which Parliament had begun to requisition the customs receipts directly, thereby preventing the customers from repaying themselves for their loans, Parliament demanded another advance of £70,000. Apparently this was too much for the syndicate, and it decided to withdraw in favor of a new group.[81]

---

[78] *C.S.P.D. 1641–1643*, p. 402; Junge, *Flottenpolitik*, pp. 54–56; Groenveld, "First Anglo-Dutch War," pp. 548 n. 26 and 551 n. 37.

[79] *Mercurius Aulicus*, 18 January 1643; Whitacre's Diary, BL, Add. MSS 31116, fol. 33v.; PRO, Declared Accounts, Customs, E.351/643 (1643).

[80] *C.J.* 3: 72, 243, 246, 253, 254; *L.J.* 6: 221; PRO, E.351/643.

[81] *C.J.* 3: 505; *H.M.C., Sixth Report, Appendix*, p. 16; *L.J.* 6: 609; PRO, E.351/644 (1644); L. A. Harper, "Public Borrowing 1640–1660, with Special Reference to the City of London between 1640 and 1650" (University of London, M.S. thesis, 1927), pp. 133–34. For the previous paragraph, I have been much aided by Harper's work. The figures given should be fairly complete, as they have been checked against the customs commissioners' declared accounts for these years, in PRO, E.351/643–44. The loss of the customs commission by the syndicate of colonial-interloping radicals appears also to have had political significance. The five-man group that now took over the customs was composed entirely of leading political moderates, men who would soon emerge as leaders of political presbyterianism in the City. It also included four Merchant Adventurers. Its members were Samuel Avery, Christopher Packe, Walter Boothby, Richard Bateman, and Charles Lloyd, among

SUPPORTING THE WAR EFFORT:
DELINQUENTS' ESTATES

Finally, between March and September 1643, Parliament began to put into effect the proposal, originally advanced by Richard Shute and the City radicals the previous autumn, that the property of royalists ("malignants") be sequestered to help finance the war and, in particular, to pay back sums lent by godly citizens. Parliament did not fully implement this program until mid-1644, but most of the commissioners who ultimately took over the task of compounding with delinquents were once again recruited from the same group of radical citizens that had first proposed the measure. It is not surprising that when Parliament faced such tasks as rooting out and registering all royalists within the lines of communication, this was the commission of militants it assigned to the job. Its members included the London new-merchant radicals Maurice Thomson, Maurice's brother Robert Thomson, Randall Mainwaring, Richard Shute, Richard Hill, John Bradley, and Samuel Moyer, as well as such militant City allies of theirs as Sir David Watkins, Daniel Taylor, Mark Coe, Richard Salway, and William Hitchcock. Of the commission's twenty-three citizen members, eight had taken part in the Additional Sea Adventure to Ireland and twelve were later political independents (while three were later political presbyterians).[82]

THWARTED REVOLUTION

Pym and his friends in Parliament had no objection to adopting the proposals for finance and administration put forward by the City radicals and recruiting these same men to implement them. They probably had little choice in any event, for during the early years of the Civil War, the official City government, now dominated by the common council, although basically sympathetic to Parliament, took a very cautious political stance for both political and economic reasons. Many common councilors did not wish to be too prominently identified with the parliamentary leadership for fear of reprisals by a possibly victorious monarch. At the same time, they did not wish to sink too much of their own or the City's money in a

---

whom the first four were Merchant Adventurers (Bateman was also a trader with the Levant) (*A.O.* 1: 667).

[82] M.A.E. Green, ed., *Calendar of the Proceedings of the Committee for Compounding, 1643–1660,* 5 vols. (London, 1889–1892), preface; *A.O.* 1: 802–3. The Additional Sea Adventurers among the commissioners included Sir David Watkins, Maurice Thomson, Robert Thomson, Thomas Prince, James Storey, William Hitchcock, Richard Hill, and Samuel Moyer. The last seven of these were to become political independents, as were the commissioners Randall Mainwaring, Richard Salway, Daniel Taylor, Mark Coe, and John Bradley. The political presbyterians on the commission were Sir David Watkins, Alexander Jones, and Gabriel Beck.

potentially fruitless cause. Then, too, they naturally worried about the disruptive and possibly destructive effects of war on the economy. Finally, the City magistrates continued to face strong opposition from well-organized conservative and crypto-royalist forces in London itself, which were powerfully rooted in the City's overseas company trading community. During the fall and winter of 1642–1643, London opponents of Parliament were able to organize very effectively in favor of the king by helping lead struggles in the City for a speedy peace (with conditions unspecified) and to resist the new financial pressures on the citizenry emanating from Parliament's rigorous new tax machine. On both of these issues, they were able to mobilize significant support not only from among the broader populace, but also from what appears to have been a not insignificant minority within the City magistracy itself, thereby seriously threatening the pro-parliamentary common council majority and, more broadly, the parliamentary leadership.

Even through much of the winter of 1642–1643, then, long after the overturn of the old aldermanic oligarchy, numerous London magistrates, even among those strongly favoring Parliament, remained predisposed to search for an accommodation with the king on the basis of fewer assurances than the parliamentary leaders were prepared to settle for.[83] These men were inherently cautious, for they knew that their own position within the City was still shaky, subject as it was to the powerful conflicting pressures of London's well-organized crypto-royalists and of its rising radical movement. It was, indeed, the sluggishness of the official City government in responding to parliamentary financial and military needs that gave the radicals their opening. The radicals were only too happy to make up for the lack of militancy on the part of the magistrates. But their personal and financial sacrifices on behalf of Parliament were not made without strings attached.

The opening of negotiations for peace with the king in November 1642 was the occasion for the initial salvo in the radicals' political campaign. On 11 and 13 November, "the godly and active part of the City," led by the leading radical and new-merchant representative Richard Shute, deplored before Parliament the current moves toward accommodation with Charles I. The petitioners "speak in the language of many thousand," said Shute, "but they fear they are bought and sold." The godly citizens offered to raise at once a thousand light horse and three thousand dragoons, proposed to finance this force through voluntary contributions by establishing their own special independent committee in the City, and nominated as their commander Sir Philip Skippon, head of the City militia. Skippon had established a reputation not only for military competence,

---

[83] See Pearl, *London*, pp. 254–57.

acquired in service with the Dutch under Sir Horace Vere in the Palatinate, but also for his militantly Puritan and parliamentary sentiments, demonstrated throughout the crisis of December–January 1641–1642. Skippon was able, by virtue of his honesty and courage, to retain the confidence of parliamentarians of all shades of opinion in the factional conflicts of the subsequent period. Nevertheless, he was especially close politically to the City's radicals, and largely for this reason they selected him for their commander. At the height of the City revolt of late December and early January 1641–1642, on the initiative of the London radical MP John Venn, the committee of safety (militia committee) had turned to Skippon for his advice on how to proceed with the rising, and had associated him, on an ad hoc basis, to their body. During the late 1640s, Skippon would make vitally important contributions to the radicals' efforts, especially by organizing official and unofficial forces to save the City from the political presbyterians in the summer of 1648 and (as a political independent recruiter MP) by pushing forward in the House of Commons the radicals' program for electoral reform in London the following winter.

The radicals accompanied their proposals with a sharp criticism of Parliament's war effort. Not only was the army badly paid and equipped, they said, but its leadership was weak, its officers being "not so careful and diligent as they ought, nor all of them so trusty." Here was the first intimation of what would eventually emerge as an explicit demand for the replacement of the earl of Essex and the vacillating military policy he represented with godly officers and a reorganized army that could be counted on to prosecute the war with vigor.

Pym and his parliamentary allies, who would try to stick by Essex to the end, could hardly have welcomed such a caustic attack by lowly and disrespectful citizens, but at this point they were in no position to stand on ceremony. The king's army appeared to be carrying the day and his soldiers were already raiding the outskirts of London, while the official City government had failed to come through with needed financial aid. So the MPs swallowed their pride. Recognizing in their ordinance of 14 November 1642 that the petitioners already had "advanced large sums of money and other supplies . . . and have set forth many soldiers under the earls of Essex and Warwick," they accepted the citizens' proposals, and designated the radical lord mayor Isaac Pennington, along with his two sheriffs, to set up a committee to help put these into effect. The identity of the men appointed to this volunteer committee for raising a new City cavalry gives a further indication of the character of the forces behind the radical thrust at this point. Included were such radicals and future political independents as Christopher Nicholson, John Dethick (an interloper in the East Indies), Hogan Hovell, Mark Hildesley, and John Kendricke, as well as the future Leveller William Walwyn. The radicals had taken a small first step toward gaining an independent military potential.[84]

By the end of November 1642, with the negotiations with the king already collapsing, the radicals were determined to press their advantage and at the same time to head off mounting sentiment for peace in the City. On 1 December they brought in a new petition[85] that called on Parliament to give up all moves for accommodation, to send forth immediately into battle the earl of Essex with an additional force of six thousand men, to recall to the field the local forces from Kent and Essex, and to begin to finance these actions out of the estates of papists and malignants. Finally, they repeated a demand they had already presented on 13 November—that the ministers in the City and country that had been declared delinquents, "especially such as have been judged unworthy of their places, may be seized on, and so kept from opening their mouths against God, the Parliament and all goodness . . . and other godly ministers appointed to supply their places." The approach of the petitioners was indeed peremptory. "Ever since the sitting of this present Parliament," they stated, "they had been ready . . . to contribute, subscribe, and lay out themselves in all those ways which they did either discern or were directed did tend to the maintenance of the cause." They had just recently advanced £30,000 and would be willing to raise £10,000 more immediately, but only "so as it may be employed in the more speedy and effectual prosecution of the war which . . . would not have been drawn out to this length, had it not been for giving ear to those counsels of accommodation." In closing, their threat to withhold funds and to take action on their own could hardly have been more clear and insulting: "The contemplation of their eminent danger . . . enforceth them humbly to remonstrate that if the destructive counsels of accommodation be reassumed they shall think it necessary to look to their own safety and forbear to contribute to their own ruin."

According to one hostile pamphleteer, this remonstrance was framed by the "now principal designers and managers of public affairs of the City." But he correctly pointed out that the official City government explicitly had rejected it. The gap that separated the radical movement from the bulk of common councilors is evident. If one could discover the names of

---

[84] For the previous three paragraphs, see *C.J.* 2: 844–45, 847–51; Pearl, *London*, pp. 251–53; M.A.E. Green, ed., *Calendar of the Proceedings of the Committee for Advance of Money, 1642–1656*, 3 vols. (London, 1888), 1: 1–2. On Skippon, see *Dictionary of Seventeenth-Century Radicals*, vol. 3, s.v. "Philip Skippon"; "A Letter of Mercurius Civicus to Mercurius Rusticus: or London's Confession," in *Somers Tracts*, 16 vols. (London, 1748–1752) 1: 411, 413.

[85] For this and the following paragraph, see Whitacre's Diary, BL, Add. MSS 31116, fol. 12v; *The True and Original Copy of the First Petition Which was Delivered by Sir David Watkins. . . .* (London, Dec. 1642). For this document, see BL, E.130 (7 and 26).

the "four score and fifteen citizens" who reportedly delivered the radical petition to Parliament, it would be possible to construct an in-depth profile of the composition of the City radical movement's leading members at this point. Still, in view of even the mere handful of individuals definitely linked with the petition, there can be little doubt about the constellation of forces behind it. Maurice Thomson's collaborator Richard Shute once again was the man who presented the petition before Parliament. Accompanying Shute was Sir David Watkins, who also had backed Maurice Thomson's Additional Sea Adventure to Ireland and was to remain an outstanding leader of the radical offensive throughout 1642–1643. Lord Mayor Isaac Pennington, probably the most influential figure among the City radicals, was also a strong supporter of the petition, as was his deputy lord mayor and close political associate, Randall Mainwaring, a leading representative of the new-merchant group. But the most striking set of names singled out by contemporaries as leading supporters of the petition were the Independent divines Hugh Peter, John Goodwin, and Jeremiah Burroughs: all three were closely connected with the new merchants and major architects of the radicals' offensive.[86] The prominence of these men at the head of the delegation that delivered the petition to Parliament points to the central role of at least certain key Independent clerics in the development of the City radical movement and to the significance of Dutch and New England examples in shaping not merely the religious, but also the political, ideas on which this movement was based.

Hugh Peter, who, as noted, had been associated with religio-political experiments in both Holland and New England during the 1630s, had at this point only recently returned from playing a major role in the new merchants' Additional Sea Adventure to Ireland. He was to remain a key spokesman for the new-merchant group and, more broadly, for City radicalism and political independency throughout the period. By the later 1640s Peter would be putting forward ideas for social and commercial, as well as political, reform, derived explicitly from Dutch examples, which corresponded closely to the new merchants' interests and aspirations. John Goodwin was, of course, the minister of St. Stephen's Coleman Street London, "the Faubourg St. Antoine" of the English Revolution. In his tenure as vicar of that parish and his subsequent leadership of the gathered church there, Goodwin became associated with such new-merchant militants as Owen Rowe, James Russell, Thomas Barnardiston, and William Allen, as well as such other major City radical figures as Lord Mayor Isaac Pennington, Mark Hildesley, Nathaniel Lacy, Daniel Taylor, John Price, the two Richard Prices, and Thomas Lambe. Just a short time before the delivery of the radicals' December petition, in October 1642,

---

[86] See *The True and Original Copy.*

Goodwin appears to have been among the first to put forward publicly a justification of the war that went beyond the strictly legalistic and constitutional ideology of the parliamentary leadership. He had declared that, in its essence, it was a war for religion, and appealed specifically to "Christians of ordinary rank and quality" to support it for this reason.[87]

By 1648–1649, both Goodwin and Peter would emerge as pivotal figures in the triumph of the political independents and the establishment of the Commonwealth. Still, at this earlier juncture, in the winter of 1642–1643, Jeremiah Burroughs probably was playing an even more crucial part than either of them in shaping City radicalism. This former dependent of the earl of Warwick and Lady Jane Bacon had by this time, as noted, become lecturer in the radical suburban parish of Stepney and had recently backed the new merchants' Additional Sea Adventure to Ireland. Most tellingly, Burroughs appears to have been one of the very few English theorists to come out explicitly for popular sovereignty and parliamentary supremacy even before the onset of the English Revolution. The reported occasion for Burroughs's striking pronouncement was a conversation he had had with John Michaelson, parson at Chelmsford, Essex, concerning the revolt of the Scots and the possible grounds for justifying it.[88] This took place in August 1638, following a sermon Burroughs had delivered at the house of the earl of Warwick. Michaelson, whose testimony is the basis of our knowledge of this discussion, apparently had claimed that those who formed and supported the Scottish covenant in 1638 had no legitimate authority to do so, since they were not magistrates and had no deputation from the supreme magistrate, the king. In response, Burroughs put to him the time-honored question, "What if the supreme magistrate refuse or neglect that which he ought to do and is necessary to be done, may not the people give power to some other to supply his neglect and defect?" Michaelson replied strongly in the negative. "Supreme power is in the supreme magistrate," he said, citing Romans 13 as had a long line of political theorists before him, and went on to claim that the supreme magistrate had this supreme power "immediately from God." As Michaelson recalled it, this argument hardly satisfied Burroughs, who once again fell back "upon the point of the people's power; that they did originally choose their kings and prescribe them conditions and limited their power by laws," and buttressed his position by propounding the "cases of elective princes as of the King of Poland, the

---

[87] P. Zagorin, *The Court and the Country* (New York, 1969), p. 346. For Peter and Goodwin, in relation to the new merchants and their friends, see above, pp. 405, 407, 420–21.

[88] Essex Record Office, T/B, 211/1, no. 39. I owe this reference to Christopher Thompson, who generously furnished me with a full transcript. The document has been printed in Shipps, "Lay Patronage," pp. 406–8 (see also pp. 178ff.). For Burroughs's earlier career and relationship with the new merchants, see above, pp. 407–8.

Duke of Venice, and especially of a *people going to the West Indies*" (emphasis added). Burroughs could not see how Michaelson could fail to answer affirmatively the question "If a king at his coronation should swear to observe ancient laws and liberties of the kingdom, yet afterward should exercise tyranny upon his people and make no conscience of his oath, whether it were not lawful to refuse obedience unto him to resist him by force and to defend ourselves and liberties by arms?"

Burroughs was subsequently brought up on charges of sedition for expressing these views and naturally claimed in his own defense that he had been misunderstood. Still, by the early 1640s, he was again putting forward very similar arguments in favor of popular sovereignty, views that not only justified parliamentary supremacy but that opened the way for a democratic interpretation. It is hard to avoid the conclusion that Burroughs, and perhaps others too, were in fact developing this viewpoint well before it became at all safe to express it with the flight of the king from London. In any case, the radical citizens were soon to express closely analogous opinions in almost identical language, and there is no doubt that Burroughs and certain others among his fellow Independent ministers, who worked closely with the radical citizens and who were familiar with the Continental and American religio-political experiments, had a powerful impact on the citizens' formulations.

On 1 December 1642, the very day the City radicals, with Burroughs in their lead, had petitioned against any accommodation with the king and in favor of a more effective prosecution of the war, Burroughs brought forward to Parliament his tract *The Glorious Name of God* explicitly in order to provide the citizens' action with a theoretical rationale. In this work, Burroughs marshalled many of the arguments that the City militants would later advance to justify their mobilization of the citizenry for the purposes of defeating the king and establishing some form of parliamentary supremacy. Burroughs left no doubt whatsoever about the immediate, practical motivation for his work: "The City being in great fear of a great army coming against it in the name of the King," it was necessary to set about "vindicating the commission from this Lord of Hosts to the subjects . . . to take up arms."[89] Burroughs not only provided a theoretical basis for parliamentary authority and parliamentary resistance to the king, but, equally significant for present purposes, called on Parliament to recognize that the "burden of the great work in this state [hath] lain upon . . . the religious party" and to see that their greatest strength in the coming battles lay in "those that are called *Round heads*."[90] Who,

---

[89] *The Glorious Name of God, The Lord of Hosts* (London, 1643). See the title page, preface, and last page of the preface, which contains the parliamentary order of 1 December 1642 to print the book.

[90] Ibid., pp. 23–24.

according to Burroughs, were these "Roundheads," and what was the "religious party"? Burroughs left no doubt that at least its City component was concentrated in that radical group which has been identified here with the new-merchant leaders and their nonmerchant radical citizen allies. As he stated,

> They pray more for the King, than any people do; yea, they do more for him and his, in a right way, than any people do. Who have ventured so much of their estates to reduce Ireland to the obedience of the King, as those that are called *Roundheads?* Will it not be found that some few of these in the City of *London* have disbursed more for the King's service in this thing to keep this his lawful inheritance in his possession . . . than all those thousands that are now with the King in his army?[91]

It is likely that Burroughs's ideas about resistance and parliamentary rights had already gained a certain currency within the City radical movement he was helping to lead. But despite their threats, the citizen radicals were not at this point yet ready to break with the parliamentary middle-group leadership. In their petition to Parliament of 1 December, they refused to specify their political principles and long-term goals, and continued to voice the middle group's tenaciously held fiction that the royal government's crimes were the fault solely of "evil counsellors" and not the king. Still, it was indicative of things to come that when Richard Shute yet again came before Parliament on 9 December to deplore all moves toward compromise with the king, he drew his most vocal support from the republican extremist Sir Henry Marten. On this occasion, Marten provoked the revulsion of most of his fellow MPs when, on welcoming Shute, he proclaimed to the House of Commons that "we ought to receive our instructions . . . from the people."[92]

At this early stage, in December 1642, neither Parliament nor the London magistrates were prepared to countenance the radicals' program. The Commons refused to consider it until it had received the official backing of the City, so the radicals took their petition before the common council. But, despite its endorsement by Lord Mayor Pennington, the petition was rejected by the City government. Indeed, during December and January, Pennington and his friends had their hands full warding off a powerful counteroffensive for peace, emanating especially from influential forces in London itself. Charles I made a pivotal contribution to the radicals' efforts when, in early January 1643, he not only rudely rejected a very moderate petition for peace that had come from the City, while failing to give the

---

[91] Ibid., pp. 63–64 (emphasis in original).
[92] *The True and Original Copy*; Whitacre's Diary, BL, Add. MSS 31116, fol. 14.

slightest evidence of a willingness to compromise, but also made the provocative demand that, as a condition for a settlement, Parliament hand over to be tried as traitors the City radical leaders Lord Mayor Isaac Pennington, the London MP John Venn, the opponent of the East India Company and Courteen collaborator John Fowke, and the new-merchant leader and deputy lord mayor, Randall Mainwaring, as well as citizen militants Robert Tichborne, Edmund Harvey, and Richard Browne. According to the royalist newssheet *Mercurius Aulicus*, Tichborne, Harvey, and Browne were "three seditious subjects who had committed several outrages" on citizens of London. Over the following months, they, too, would emerge as prominent figures within the City radical leadership and, along with Randall Mainwaring, would constitute a whole series of commissions, organized by Parliament, that had as their purpose either the collection by force of money or supplies required for the military effort or the repression or surveillance of groups of citizens thought to be hostile to Parliament.[93]

Following Charles's dismissal of the Londoners' moderate proposals for peace, the City radicals once more brought before the Commons their petition of 1 December 1642, with its demands for a volunteer army and, more generally, for a more militant prosecution of the parliamentary cause. And this time they made somewhat more headway. On 26 January 1643, the Commons constituted an eighteen-person committee to treat with the citizens and directed this body to present to the House a revised ordinance for an army of volunteers, "so we be not troubled for money and always be borrowing." But after that, the plan for a volunteer army appears to have died in committee.[94]

Although a majority of the House was at this point still unready to entertain the radicals' program, the Commons' reception of the citizens' petition does evidence the growing collaboration between the London radical movement and Parliament's war-party wing. John Blackiston appears to have brought the citizens' proposal into the Commons, and Alexander Rigby moved the appointment of the committee; both were war-party men

[93] Pearl, *London*, pp. 253–57; Gardiner, *Civil War* 1: 74–75, 78, 79–81, 84, 85ff.; *Mercurius Aulicus*, 22 January 1643. For the tasks carried out by Mainwaring, Tichborne, Harvey, and Browne for Parliament, see *C.J.* 2: 933 (seizure of Sir Nicholas Crispe's horses, 21 Jan. 1643); *A.O.* 1: 77 (distraining nonpayers of assessments, 8 Feb. 1643); *Mercurius Aulicus*, 21 March 1643 (repressing apprentices' demonstration against paying assessments); *C.J.* 3: 55 (searching for dangerous people within the parishes, 21 Apr. 1643); *C.J.* 3: 94–95 (collecting unpaid customs, 20 May 1643); *C.J.* 3: 166, 175 (searching for dangerous persons within the City, 15, 19 July 1643).

[94] Pearl, *London*, p. 257; *The Humble Petition of divers of the best affected Ministers of the Citie . . . Also the Humble Petition of many grave citizens of London; being both delivered the 21st day of this instant January 1642* (London, 1643); Hexter, *Reign of King Pym*, p. 110; *C.J.* 2: 943; Diary of Walter Yonge, BL, Add. MSS 18777, fol. 133v (26 Jan. 1643). I want to express my gratitude to Christopher Thompson for his generosity in lending me his transcript of this diary.

and fiery spirits, both were later appointed to the High Court of Justice to try the king, both were religious Independents, and Blackiston was later a regicide. The eighteen-man committee that was established was dominated by radicals; of its seventeen members still alive in 1648, twelve took their seats in the Rump, ten were appointed to the High Court of Justice, seven are among those characterized by David Underdown as "revolutionaries," and three were regicides.[95]

It was only in the middle of March 1643 that the radicals were able to take a substantial step toward the realization of their program. In the previous weeks, the king had once again destroyed all hope of a settlement by declaring Parliament's county associations traitorous and rejecting the House of Lords' proposal for a cessation of hostilities. Then, on 11 March 1643, when Pym went to the official City government for additional supplies of men and money for the parliamentary army, the magistrates told him that they had had great difficulty even in collecting the funds already promised and that they could make no further levies. This was the opening the radicals needed, and the same group of City militants that was behind the moves of the previous autumn and winter for an independent volunteer army came forward to make up for the official municipality's lack of fervor for the cause. On 15 March, it was reported in Common Council that "divers well affected citizens did lately . . . make offer to the committee of the militia . . . to raise at their own charge three regiments of foot consisting of 10,000 men or thereabouts for the better safety of the City." In view of the City's own failure to come up with funds, it was not an offer the magistrates could refuse.[96]

The City radicals were now moving toward the crest of their power. No longer willing to keep their struggle within the narrow bounds set by the middle groupers in Parliament, they were ready to try to dictate terms. As *Mercurius Aulicus* reported, on 29 March Hugh Peter preached a fast day sermon in which he "came to tax the Parliament . . . whom he accused . . . for abusing the people in that they had fooled them all this while with hopes and promises of a *reformation*, and now would leave the work and make peace without them." "Therefore," concluded Peter threateningly, "it did concern all of them that had taken the *Protestation*

---

[95] Hexter, *Reign of King Pym*, p. 110 n. 25. The committee members were William Purefoy, Henry Marten, John Blackiston, Cornelius Holland, Godfrey Bosvile, Sir Henry Mildmay, Alexander Rigby, William Strode, John Gurdon, William Heveningham, John Wilde, Sir Thomas Barrington, Sir William Strickland, Edmund Prideaux, John Rolle, Peter Wentworth, Sir Henry Heyman, and William Cage (d. 1645), of whom the first three were regicides and the first seven are on Underdown's list of "revolutionaries," that is, among those who openly committed themselves to the revolution while it was in progress during December and January 1648–1649 (D. Underdown, *Pride's Purge* [Oxford, 1971], p. 210 and app. A. For Blackiston and Rigby, see also Keeler, *Long Parliament*, pp. 109, 323).

[96] CLRO, J.Co.Co.40, fol. 55v; Pearl, *London*, p. 260; Hexter, *Reign of King Pym*, pp. 23–24.

to hold up their hands and stick unto the cause themselves"—a statement that, according to *Aulicus*, "hath so wrought upon the factious and unruly rabble . . . that it is thought they will ere long as furiously affront the two Houses of Parliament, as by the instigation of some of the two Houses, they have done His Majesty." *Aulicus* correctly observed that the City radicals were now entirely fed up with the middle group's dogged insistence that "all the wrongs they had suffered proceeded from evil counsellors" (but not the king himself), and were moving into firm alliance with the war party MPs, backed up by masses of London militants. It was not by chance that *Aulicus* singled out the fiery spirit Miles Corbet, MP, as one of the sympathetic listeners at Peter's sermon. The close link between Corbet and the Independent ministerial radicals was of long standing. It was one of those key connections around which the emerging network linking war-party parliamentarians and City radicals was now being constructed.[97]

The very next day, 30 March 1643, the City radicals brought in a new *Petition and Remonstrance to Common Council and to Parliament* in which they sought to spell out for the City and for Parliament their political platform. This document shows the significant distance they had traveled, in constitutional theory, beyond the narrow conceptions of the parliamentary middle group and toward support of a more or less full-fledged Parliamentary supremacy and, in political and strategic practice, in the direction of a link-up with the war-party militants in the House of Commons and the mass mobilization of the citizenry of London. To begin with, very much like Jeremiah Burroughs in his discussion with Michaelson, the citizens found that much of the confusion over the question of the locus of sovereignty and the rights of the subjects arose from "the usual misconstruing and perverting the supposition of law, *that kings can do no wrong*, which being never intended (as we conceive) of his personal commands and actions is notwithstanding made of to maintain them, and thereby in a mysterious manner to deceive the people."[98] According to Burroughs, the sovereign had supreme authority from God by virtue of his office, but only so long as he acted lawfully. As Burroughs had written in *The Glorious Name of God*, the sovereign's higher powers, that is, "that authority

[97] *Mercurius Aulicus*, 2 April 1643. For Corbett's ties to Jeremiah Burroughs and William Greenhill, see above, p. 408. In the sarcastic words of one contemporary observer the radicals "will no longer wrong our King secretly, through the sides of his evil *counsellors*, or *Cavaliers*, but charge him *directly*, and *point blank*, as in that most seditious declaration, or whatever you will call it, presented by Sir *David Watkins*, and that broken citizen, out at elbows, called *Satten* [Richard] *Shute*, to the common council, and by them to the remainder of the *Lower House*, if it be not a breach of privilege to call it so" (*A Letter from Mercurius Civicus to Mercurius Aulicus*, p. 417; emphasis in original).

[98] *Remonstrans Redivivus: An Account of the Remonstrance and Petition. . . .* (London, 25 July 1643) (emphasis in original); Pearl, *London*, p. 260.

that God and man have put upon such a man . . . must be subjected to, and not resisted . . . but if one that is in authority command out of his own will, and not by law, I resist no authority at all, if I neither actively nor passively obey." Even so, as long as it was admitted (by Burroughs and others) that supreme power did lie with the king, and that the king's power derived immediately from God, many found it difficult to conceive of the king's making an actually illegal command and equally hard to admit of the subject's right of resistance. This was the weakness of Burroughs's biblically founded arguments, as his opponents were quick to point out. As the Essex minister Edward Symmons put the question: Does God really grant supreme power to the office of kingship, but not the king's person, as Burroughs seemed to be contending? *"That authority which God and man hath put upon a man* [the ruler]: I demand again, is it only naked authority so put, without any relation to the man on whom put, that must be subjected unto, and not resisted?"[99]

The City radicals now cut through this entire complex of problems with a sharply antitraditional and rationalist rephrasing of the question of legitimate rule. Their politico-theoretical "apprehensions," they asserted, were "grounded as well upon *right reason* as your own [that is, Parliament's] declarations." And they continued,

> That originally the supreme power being in the whole people, Parliaments were by them constituted to manage the same for the preservation and well-being of the commonwealth: So as properly in the Parliaments of England, acting for the same doth the supreme power reside; from whose judgments there is no appeal being presumed ever to intend the proper interest of the commonwealth, that is the safety and freedom thereof, it being the highest of treasons through fear or favor to neglect the same.

From these fundamental assumptions, it clearly followed that the king's calling and dissolving of Parliament and, in particular, "the usage" of passing bills of right and justice in Parliament by the king "is but a matter of form annexed to his office and not a matter of will." Here was nothing less than a declaration of parliamentary supremacy founded on popular sovereignty as the goal of the revolution.[100]

The radicals' phraseology was intimately linked with their strategic aim of harnessing the people's power to the parliamentary cause. As they reminded the MPs in the preface to their remonstrance, much of Parliament's strength resided in "the affections of the people still manifested by

[99] The two previous quotations are given in R. Tuck, *"Power* and *Authority* in Seventeenth-Century England," *H.J.* 17 (1974): 50, 52 (emphasis in original). In this section, I have been much aided by Tuck's stimulating article.

[100] *Remonstrans Redivivus*, pp. 4–5 (emphasis added).

their readiness from *all quarters to rise and appear in considerable bodies* for the carrying of this just and undoubted cause."[101] Clearly, these men were banking a great deal on the mobilization of the City masses. That they were aware of, or prepared for, the more explicitly democratic conclusions that might be drawn in thought and action from their own populist constitutional and organizational principles may however be doubted.

From the leading names involved, from the nature of the proposals, and from the ideological statement that accompanied them, there can be no doubt that the political forces behind the drive in the City and in Parliament for an independent citizens' volunteer army were essentially the same ones that had dominated the revolutionary City committee of safety (militia committee), had organized the Additional Sea Adventure to Ireland, had taken the dominant role in constructing the parliamentary financial machine, and had striven since the previous autumn for a reorganization of the parliamentary military effort—that is, what I have called the City radical alliance, with a central core consisting of many of the new-merchant leaders and their nonmerchant collaborators, and including, quite prominently, certain leading Independent ministers. Once more at the center of the project were the leading radicals of the offensive of the previous autumn, Richard Shute, Isaac Pennington, Sir David Watkins, and Randall Mainwaring. John Fowke, the militant opponent of the East India Company and former associate of Sir William Courteen, presented the radicals' petition of 15 March to the common council. According to the royalist newssheet *Mercurius Aulicus*, the key new merchants, John Warner and Thomas Andrews, as well as John Towse and Fowke, "were like to have had the greatest hand in promoting" the associated *Petition and Remonstrance* within the City government. They were, in *Aulicus*'s estimation, "four of the most seditious in the whole pack." All four of these men were members of the City militia committee, and the first three of them had consistently taken over the key treasurerships in the parliamentary financial apparatus. The twelve-person committee that was charged by the common council with considering the petition for a volunteer army, and that ultimately approved it, was obviously packed with known supporters of the radicals' project. In addition to Warner, Fowke, and Towse, it included the new merchants and City militia commissioners James Russell, Stephen Estwicke, and Owen Rowe, along with the colonial tobacco merchant Michael Herring, as well as John Kendricke and Richard Turner, both of whom were soon to assume directing roles in the volunteer army project. *Mercurius Aulicus* reported that when William Steele, the deputy City recorder and a leading promoter of the petition, was asked who had composed the petition, he replied, "It was drawn up by the advice

[101] Ibid., p. 2 (emphasis added).

of the best lawyers and divines in the City." *Aulicus* added that "[Hugh] Peter, one of the Amsterdamians that now rules the roost, and passeth in the number of their best divines, stood at the hall door and earnestly pressed every man as he went in to have a care of that petition." According to the later Leveller William Walwyn, leading political activists who would soon join the gathered congregation of the radical Independent minister John Goodwin were also prominent among the key supporters of the petition for the volunteer army project and the accompanying remonstrance. These prominently included Richard Price (the scrivener) and Price's uncle Richard Price (the mercer). William Walwyn himself also backed the project.[102]

In view of the pressing need to prepare for war, especially in the wake of the now-imminent collapse of the Oxford negotiations (which were formally called off on 14 April), not only the City government but Parliament as well had little choice but to accept the radicals' proposal for a volunteer army. On 12 April 1643, Parliament passed an ordinance establishing a subcommittee to sit at Salters Hall to carry out this project under the jurisdiction of the militia committee, which was the radicals' main official stronghold within the City. As Dr. Pearl has pointed out, this was a great victory for the radicals, for they now had what was practically their own financial and military organization within the City, with official status.[103]

The rising radical tide was evidently by now engulfing much of the City. In the very same period that the militant citizens were presenting their volunteer army project to the City and to Parliament, the same group of City radicals that has already been observed in action securing the appointment of the Independent minister John Simpson as lecturer of St. Dunstan's-in-the-East was carrying out a local revolution in that parish. Before the Civil War a small, self-selected committee of substantial parishioners ruled St. Dunstan's-in-the-East; this body carried on most of the parish's business and appointed its leading officers. Local government by such "closed vestries" appears to have been the London norm during this period. In the spring of 1643, however, the generality of inhabitants of St. Dunstan's decided that they could no longer tolerate this oligarchic rule. Their own account of their parish revolution is worth reciting in full.

Whereas at a vestry held the 9th of April last Mr. William Browne and Mr. Bernard Hide were then chosen church wardens of the same parish for the year ensuing and the same day the major part of the

[102] *Mercurius Aulicus*, 2 April 1643, CLRO, J.Co.Co.40, fol. 57; Tolmie, *Triumph of the Saints*, pp. 115, 224 n. 147.
[103] Pearl, *London*, p. 260; *L.J.* 5: 715–16.

rest of the inhabitants meeting in the same church and conceiving the choice of the vestry men concerning choosing of church wardens *without the consent of the rest of the inhabitants* of the same parish to be *illegal although customary* made their choice and elected Mr. Robert Foote and Sargeant-Major William Tucker to be church wardens and a difference arising by reason of a double choice and being presented to the Honorable House of Commons was by them referred to the Committee for Examinations who upon due hearing of both sides reported that [in] their opinion . . . the selection of the said Mr. Robert Foote and Sargeant-Major William Tucker to be church wardens of the same parish church was a due election . . . which report the major part of the parishioners now present do well like of and submit unto accordingly. At which meeting the 9th of April last a committee consisting of 30 persons inhabiting of the parish were elected and chosen instead of vestry men to govern the affairs of the same parish church for the year ensuing which are hereafter particularly named. (emphasis added)

Two phrases stand out in this account: "without the consent of the rest of the inhabitants" and "illegal though customary." These echo the rationalist and antitraditionalist formulations just then being employed by the London radical leadership in its *Petition and Remonstrance* to justify its plan for a volunteer army; they indicate that the parishioners of St. Dunstan's-in-the-East held similarly advanced conceptions of popular rule. That the St. Dunstan's parishioners actually succeeded in their struggle to break the closed vestry demonstrates, moreover, that they had further strengthened a well-organized radical movement that already, a year previously, had been able to impose the selection of the Independent John Simpson as parish lecturer over the objections of the parish minister John Childerly. Many of the same people led the fight to destroy the rule of the closed vestry as had initiated the struggle to hire Simpson, including once again a number of important new-merchant leaders. Maurice Thomson's brother-in-law and partner William Tucker was one of the two new church wardens chosen by the parishioners to replace the old representatives of the closed vestry. The new Committee of Thirty, the annually elected body set up by the inhabitants to replace the closed vestry as the basic parish governing body, included the colonial-interloping traders William Tucker, Maurice Thomson, William Allen, Richard Bateson, and George Payne (all active in the move to hire Simpson), as well as Edward Wood. It was expressive of the rising political temperature in the City that the St. Dunstan's parishioners appear to have petitioned the House of Commons to approve their small revolution in parish governance on 12 April 1643, the very same day that Parliament gave its assent to the citizens' project for a volunteer army.[104] No doubt many of same people were behind both of these initiatives.

It was probably no coincidence that at precisely this moment several key groups of City Independents broke from their previous policy and constituted public practicing congregations. At the start of the 1640s, those in London committed to religious Independency seem to have consciously decided to refrain for the time being from gathering new congregations out of the parishes while undertaking to avoid controversy over the form of church government. They apparently chose this course not only in order to maintain their common front with the broader Puritan community in opposition to Laudianism and episcopacy and in support of Parliament and the City revolution, but also to prevent their adversaries from tarring the parliamentary political cause in general and the London radical party in particular with the Independent-sectarian brush. As recently as their previous major petitioning initiative, in November–December 1642, the radicals had gone out of their way to complain to Parliament of "the imputation cast upon the godly part of the City by the malignant party that they desire an Independent government may be set up in the church." This was a charge given prima facie credence by the disproportionate role within the radical political leadership, especially in relation to their small numbers in the City, of Independent ministers such as Jeremiah Burroughs, Hugh Peter, and John Goodwin, as well as of Independent laymen. Nevertheless, in the first two weeks of April, perhaps feeling that with the radical movement in full swing there was both less to be risked and more to be gained for both the religious Independent and radical political causes by their coming out into the open, the Independents changed course. Dr. Nathaniel Homes and Henry Burton became the first London Independents publically to gather congregations out of the parishes, and this could only have enhanced the radicals' momentum.[105]

In the months following the collapse of the Oxford treaty, supporters of Parliament were obliged to confront not merely the end of all hope of peace but the greatest military emergency of the war: royalist troops appeared, increasingly, to be carrying the day throughout the country. As the politico-military situation became more threatening, the radical movement appears to have gathered force, and much of London appears to have been overtaken by a new wave of Puritan religious fervor, manifested

---

[104] St. Dunstan's-in-the-East Vestry Minute Book, Guildhall Library MSS 4887, fol. 257; *C.J.* 3: 41.

[105] Tolmie, *Triumph of the Saints*, pp. 90–95; *C.J.* 2: 857 (12 Nov. 1642). Previously existing Independent congregations in London, notably those of Thomas Goodwin and Sydrach Simpson, had had an earlier existence in exile in the United Provinces. In consequence, they had been able to return to London fully formed and thus able to avoid gathering members and disrupting the parish churches.

especially in a rising tide of iconoclasm. On 27 April, the common council moved to have Cheapside Cross pulled down and demolished, "in regard of the idolatrous and superstitious figures there set about." About a month later, the House of Commons called on its committee for "pulling down and abolishing all monuments of superstition and idolatry" to take into its custody the copes in the cathedrals of Westminster, St. Paul's, and Lambeth. Meanwhile, the common council extended somewhat further the City constitutional revolution that it had carried out during the spring of 1642. On 28 April 1643, it ruled that all aldermen's deputies, hitherto appointed at the will of the aldermen, should be chosen from among the (elected) common councilors. On 21 June, it ordered that, although common hall had previously been obliged to choose the City chamberlain from among two nominees of the court of aldermen and the two City bridgemasters from among four nominees of the court of aldermen, common hall should now have the authority both to nominate and to elect these officials.[106]

The growing royalist threat from without had its counterpart within London itself, for the City contained, as emphasized, a large group of wealthy and influential crypto-royalists. In early May, a number of leading Londoners were implicated in the plot against Parliament of Sir Edmund Waller. These prominently included Sir George Benion, Robert Alden, and Marmaduke Rawden, all of whom had been among the chief organizers of the conservative citizens' petition of February 1642 protesting the new revolutionary City committee of safety and, more generally, the City constitutional revolution. It will be recalled that company merchants made up a large proportion of the signatories of Benion's antimilitia committee petition; similarly, a major group of top company merchants revealed themselves to be among London's bitterest opponents of Parliament at this point, either as direct backers of Waller or as refusers to pay the parliamentary assessment. The latter included the customs farmers Sir Paul Pindar and Sir Nicholas Crispe, the great Levant–East India Company merchants Sir Henry Garway, John Gayre, William Ashwell, Robert Abdy, Daniel Abdy, and Elias Abdy, and the important Merchant Adventurer Lawrence Halstead. The East India Company went so far, at this perilous time, as to resist Parliament materially, refusing Parliament's direct order to lend ordnance to the City militia committee and ignoring Parliament's call to dismiss Sir Henry Garway from his company offices. The Levant Company also expressed its political sympathies by similarly retaining Garway as company governor until early 1644.[107]

[106] Gardiner, *Civil War* 1: 135ff.; CLRO, J.Co.Co.40, fol. 58v, 59, 65v; *C.J.* 3: 110 (quotations).

[107] Pearl, *London*, pp. 265–67.

As they had since the start of the conflict, polar political groups—one essentially royalist and dominated by company merchants as well as other wealthy citizens, the other politically radical and conspicuously including colonial-interloping traders as well as nonmerchant shopkeepers, ship captains, and artisans—continued largely to set the terms of political conflict in the City. The great mass of citizen parliamentary moderates who would take control of London during the middle 1640s remained in the background, seeking to prevent either royalists or radicals from getting their way.

Meanwhile, the Salters Hall committee for volunteers was attempting to raise troops and money under the ordinance of 12 April 1643. Before long, however, there developed an intense jurisdictional dispute among the radicals themselves over the precise limits of the authority of this body. The Salters Hall committeemen were proposing to establish in the City and suburbs a voluntary collection to the value of one weekly meal from every inhabitant. They were aiming to use the proceeds to raise their own regiments of "honest and well-affected persons . . . under command of known and trusted officers," to be appointed by themselves. However, this plan provoked the immediate opposition of the City militia committee, whose leading members had originally been among the chief organizers of the project and indeed the whole radical offensive. As these men quickly pointed out, Parliament had delegated the right to raise troops in the City to the militia committee alone, and had extended the militia committee's authority so as to cover the new volunteer army under the very ordinance that had established the committee at Salters Hall in the first place. In fact, the Salters Hall committee was technically a subcommittee of the militia committee.[108]

It has so far been impossible to discover the full character of this dispute and precisely who supported each side. However, given an understanding of the groups involved in the conflict, one may hazard an interpretation as to what was actually occurring, especially in light of what appears to have been the somewhat analogous conflicts that took place in the later 1640s between London's mainstream political independents and their more politically extreme allies. The situation and complaint of the Salters Hall committeemen should have been easily appreciated by those City radical leaders, prominently including a big group of militia commissioners, who had first been responsible for setting up that committee, for those men had found themselves in a similar position with respect to the moderate leadership in Parliament (not to mention the City) over the past year or more.

[108] *A Declaration and Motive of the Persons trusted usually meeting at Salters Hall in Bread Street . . . for Contributing the Value of a Meale Weekly, towards the forming of some Regiments of Volunteers, to be payd during these times of Danger* (London, 6 May 1643); Pearl, *London*, p. 268.

The Salters Hall committee, having taken over direct administrative responsibility for raising both men and money for the volunteer army, did
not see why it should be deprived of the political authority to direct the
army. But the City radical leadership—exemplified by such militia committee leaders as Randall Mainwaring, John Fowke, John Warner, John
Towse, and Thomas Andrews, and including such militant colleagues of
theirs as Richard Shute, Sir David Watkins, and Isaac Pennington—had
no intention of ceding control over the new volunteer army to a different
set of individuals of almost certainly lower social position and perhaps
more extreme political convictions than their own, who might use this
force for ends different from those they themselves desired. Ironically,
however, there was substantial, if inexplicit, warrant for the Salters Hall
committee's initiative in the very remonstrance by which the radical leadership had originally justified and explained that body. In their *Petition
and Remonstrance*, the radicals had argued "that the safety of the people is
the supreme law and is the foundation and end of all just government,
even parliaments themselves." They had admitted further that all just
magistracy "is a matter of trust only for the good of the people." They had
been careful, however, to conclude from these premises that it was "most
agreeable to reason that those who by the consent of all are entrusted with
the making of laws should direct those that are to put the same in execution."[109] But a different conclusion was also possible: since the safety of
the people is the supreme law and since governments are established only
for the good of the people, then the people themselves, should they feel
their interests and safety endangered, might act directly to protect themselves. This is what the Salters Hall committee appeared to be about in
the period of developing military crisis of the spring of 1643 (whether or
not it worded the matter in this way) and what the militia committee was
unprepared to grant. Just as the middle-group parliamentarians had created the potential basis for their own displacement by establishing the City
radicals at the center of Parliament's financial-military apparatus, so, in
the same way, the radical leadership itself had created the potential condition for its own supercession by similarly installing representatives of
the extreme radical wing within its own movement at the center of a new
and vigorous City financial-military machine.

Here, then, was the defining dilemma of what might be called—rather
imprecisely and for lack of a better name—the moderate republicans and,
indeed, the abiding problem of republican theory throughout the whole
period. Here also was the characteristic dilemma of the new-merchant
leaders, who were perhaps the representative sociopolitical group within
this moderate republican trend, although not by any means its only com-

---

[109] *Remonstrans Redivivus*, pp. 4–5.

ponent.[110] Those who wished to push the revolution beyond the limits set by the constitutionally conservative parliamentary leadership toward the supremacy of Parliament based on popular sovereignty and a decisive demotion (not necessarily demolition) of the monarchy could do so only by way of the mobilization of the populace. But once the people were mobilized they might become a force of their own that could turn the revolution from the goal of rule by Parliament to that of rule by the people. Similarly, in the realm of theory, those who dared to put forward a rationalist theory of legitimacy by popular consent (popular sovereignty) to replace divine right and custom-based conceptions opened the way not merely for parliamentary supremacy and republicanism, but for democracy. It was in part for this reason that most of those essentially conservative reformers-turned-revolutionaries in Parliament, typified by Pym and his colleagues, had stuck tenaciously to their less elegant, but less dangerous, method of justifying their reforms—that is, by way of detailed reference to historical and legal precedent, however fictitious, and by attributing all the deficiencies of the Caroline regime and its policies to Charles's "evil counsellors." Correspondingly, these parliamentarians did actually attempt in practice to keep the revolution within certain strict political bounds, and thus within constitutional limits that could conceivably be justified by precedent, by tradition. Their aim to retain monarchy on something like the terms of the Grand Remonstrance did not therefore correspond only to their desire to maintain kingship as a source of social and political stability. It was also a way of keeping their actual political practice from too sharply discrediting a theory that was of great practical use to them precisely because it could be employed to put restraints on monarchy without opening the way to popular radicalization.

In contrast, the new-merchant leadership and its radical friends among the citizenry had less reason to be satisfied with the goals envisioned by Parliament. They thought they had much to gain from further revolution and saw the possibilities as well as the dangers inherent in their reliance on the City masses. They were therefore willing to take greater risks in theory and practice to win advances in politics and religion, as well as in commerce. They were the natural advocates of a clear-cut parliamentary supremacy and in this limited sense the natural republicans of the period; but, like the republicans of many periods, they occupied an inherently unstable political position. This was due to their restricted social base— they and their immediate allies were themselves substantial men—and their correspondingly narrow theoretical position. Between the moderate

[110] I shall henceforth use the term *moderate republican*, as explained in this paragraph, to refer to supporters of full parliamentary supremacy based on popular sovereignty, not necessarily the total elimination of the monarchy.

middle-group forces working for an ill-defined parliamentary monarchy and the democratic dynamism of sections of the London populace, they had constantly to maneuver within narrow limits, for to win a favorable settlement, they required the neutralization of the forces on both extremes simultaneously.

In order to head off the drive for autonomy of the Salters Hall committeemen, the City's militia commission and its friends at the center of the radical leadership had an obvious route to follow. They brought their dispute before the common council, a body that they knew was far more conservative than they were themselves. There was little doubt which way the common council would rule, once it had appointed a fourteen-person committee to consider the question. This committee was loaded with well-known conservative figures, of whom at least eight would end up as leading political presbyterians, even neo-royalists. Indeed, the essential elements of that moderate political combine that would come to dominate City governance throughout the middle and late 1640s were, even now, beginning to be assembled. On the recommendation of this committee, the common council ruled that the militia committee was to have full authority over all troops levied in the City, including the new volunteer army. The Salters Hall committee might help the militia committee levy troops, but it was to be clearly subordinate to it.[111] Perhaps in an attempt to co-opt the extremist political forces concentrated at Salters Hall, the common council further ruled that the Salters Hall committee should nominate twenty-one of its members, seven of whom would be chosen to be added to the militia committee itself.[112]

If the City's radical leadership—specifically, its less extreme wing centered in the City's militia committee—was thus moved to thwart the drive for autonomy by the Salters Hall committeemen, it did not draw back from the struggle for a City army of volunteers that it had set in motion and wished to continue. Indeed, from this time onward, the militia committee appears to have become even more radical in its political composition. The addition to the militia committee of seven Salters Hall radicals, if somewhat discouraging to the subcommittee, served to sharpen further the militancy of the senior body. Moreover, at the very same time that the

[111] CLRO, J.Co.Co.40, fols. 62v–63. The future political presbyterians on the fourteen-man common council committee that ruled that the Salters Hall committee had to remain subordinate to the militia committee included Thomas Adams, Richard Chambers, Christopher Packe, Richard Bateman, Alexander Jones, Richard Glyd, Thomas Cullum, and Theophilus Riley (a royalist even in 1643).

[112] CLRO, J.Co.Co.40, fol. 67. The seven men added to the militia committee, out of the twenty-one nominated by the Salters Hall committee, included Edward Cole, Richard Turner, Jr., Robert Tichborne, Tempest Milner, William Antrobus, Thomas Player, Sr., and Samuel Harsnett—all future political independents.

militia committee was adding the seven men from Salters Hall, it was receiving a further six-man infusion to its membership, which was also heavily weighted with radicals and future political independents. Among these six further additions to the militia committee were the lord mayor, Isaac Pennington, probably the key leader of the City radical movement; John Kendricke, soon to serve as a treasurer for the war party's committee for a general rising; Richard Turner, Sr., father and constant political and economic collaborator of Richard Turner, Jr., the Salters Hall committeeman simultaneously being added to the militia committee; and William Hobson (father-in-law of the leading new-merchant and radical Samuel Pennoyer), who has already been described as a key organizer in the revolutionary petition campaign of December 1641. All of these men, except perhaps for Kendricke, would end up as leading political independents.[113]

Still, it is unlikely that the militia committee's move against the committee at Salters Hall was achieved without some cost to the radical offensive as a whole. To achieve victory, the radical leadership had been forced to fall back on the conservative common councilors (presumably its opponents) in order to defeat its own (godly) followers. It had thus revealed the limits of its independent power, as well as the boundaries of its radicalism. It had no doubt alienated in the process some of those very militant citizens whom it would still need in order to build a truly effective army and to provide a basis for its own power.

Over the following period, the struggle to create an independent volunteer army in the City continued. Moreover, in the early weeks of July, the radicals added a new element to their program. Following a series of disastrous defeats of the parliamentary army under the earl of Essex and some spectacular revelations concerning Essex's own equivocal attitude toward the Civil War struggle, war-party elements in both Parliament and the City began openly to advocate Essex's dismissal from the supreme command and his replacement by the godly general Sir William Waller.[114]

On 13 July 1643, the new-merchant leader and City MP Samuel Vassall, who appears to have been working very closely at this point with the parliamentary radicals, spoke before the House of Commons and presaged what was about to occur. As reported by *Mercurius Aulicus*,

> Master Vassall moved exceedingly earnestly that their general [Essex] should be pressed to speak more plainly: and that if after the expense of two millions of treasure without any effect he had a mind to lay down arms . . . there wanted not as good soldiers which would take them up. Which motion, though it took not in the House for

[113] CLRO, J.Co.Co.40, fol. 67.
[114] Hexter, *Reign of King Pym*, chs. 5–6.

the present, yet generally (all about the City), they have designed Waller for the place, whose conquest are their daily discourse.[115]

The dual thrust to replace Essex and to reconstruct the army reached its climax in mid-July with the project for a committee for a general rising. On 20 July, a petition with some twenty thousand signatures was brought into the House of Commons, calling for the establishment of a new ten thousand-man citizens' volunteer army to be organized by a committee of MPs to be set up for this purpose. The petitioners did not hesitate to designate the names of those who would lead the committee for a general rising or to demand its full independence. That was clearly an affront to the authority of Parliament. But this was also a time of the most extreme military emergency, probably the very lowest point in the war for the parliamentary forces, as the House of Commons obviously well knew. As the *Commons Journal* reports, the House deemed the petition "irregular, and contrary to the proceedings and privileges of Parliament, yet, notwithstanding, considering the great and invincible necessity the kingdom was in at this time wherein safety was to be preferred before privilege of Parliament, they took no further notice of it." The Commons went on to accept the petitioners' proposals, agreeing to a committee composed almost entirely of war-party militants who would organize the new army and choose the new commander. Prominently included were such "fiery spirits" as Sir Henry Marten, Alexander Rigby, Dennis Bond, John Blackiston, William Strode, John Gurdon, Thomas Hoyle, and the MP lord mayor Isaac Pennington. No fewer than ten members of the thirteen-man committee would end up as political independents. Eight would be nominated to the High Court of Justice, which tried the king.[116]

The general rising initiative represented the culminating effort of that same City radical group that had been aiming to create an autonomous army since the previous autumn, and whose goal had already been partially realized through the establishment of the City's volunteer force the previous April. The new structure of authority that emerged at the height of the military emergency in July 1643 could hardly have been more to its liking. The parliamentary war-party chiefs, prominent among them London's radical lord mayor and MP Isaac Pennington, had seized the initiative in the Commons from the vacillating middle group, which still clung to the earl of Essex. As *Mercurius Aulicus* put it, were their project

---

[115] *Mercurius Aulicus*, 13 July 1643. For Vassall, see *C.J.* 3: 159.

[116] *C.J.* 3: 175–76. The future political independents were Isaac Pennington, Herbert Morley, John Blackiston, Dennis Bond, John Gourdon, Henry Marten, Alexander Rigby, William Massam, Thomas Hoyle, and Henry Heyman, among whom the first eight were nominated to sit as judges at the king's trial. The application of the term political independent to these MPs follows David Underdown's categorization in *Pride's Purge*, app.

to succeed, it "would quickly ease [Pym's] *close committee* of all further trouble and draw the strength and riches of the kingdom to . . . that one City under the command of this new authority." The meeting that organized the petition and mass demonstration that brought about the establishment of the general rising committee and volunteer army was held at Grocers Hall, the City militia committee headquarters; and it is probable that the militia committee, the stronghold of the City radicals and the new merchants, was one of the main forces behind the new enterprise. Moreover, at the same time that the City radicals were establishing the general rising committee, Parliament was calling on the City militia committee to exercise martial law in the City, thus elevating this body's authority above that of the City government itself, at least for the time being. The new merchant Randall Mainwaring, the Salters Hall committee leader Robert Tichborne, and Edmund Harvey—three of the more radical among the militia commissioners and officers of the City-trained bands—were asked to take charge of this effort. That the war-party radicals in Parliament, and their compatriots in the City who were organized around Richard Shute, Isaac Pennington, and the City militia committee, were now closely coordinating their actions is further indicated by the appointment of the key new-merchant radical and militia committeeman Samuel Warner to be one of the new treasurers for the committee for a general rising. Warner was the brother and business partner of the colonial tobacco trader and City radical alderman and militia commissioner John Warner and father-in-law and business partner of William Thomson, Maurice's brother.[117]

For a short time, it looked as if the entire radical movement had unified itself at last and had finally consolidated an institutional base within the City. No doubt in order to provide the ideological rationale for the whole undertaking, the City radicals, now on the verge of realizing their long-sought objectives, chose this moment—25 July—to republish their remonstrance of the previous spring, their basic programmatic document.[118] On 27 July, the committee for a general rising, now called the committee at Merchant Taylors' Hall, appointed Sir William Waller to be general of the volunteer army. Shortly thereafter, the London militia committee followed suit, picking Waller to head all of the forces already under its jurisdiction. If all went according to plan, the radicals would soon have under their joint command an army far larger than that led by the earl of Essex. But, once again, for reasons that remain unclear, the radicals fell to quarreling among themselves. There seems to have been a competition between the militia committee and the committee for volunteers over re-

---

[117] *Mercurius Aulicus*, 25 July 1643; *C.J.* 3: 175; *C.S.P.D. Addenda, 1625–1649*, p. 652.
[118] *Remonstrans Redivivus*; Pearl, *London*, p. 260 n. 98.

cruits. The two bodies may also have differed about military tactics—whether to march out boldly as Sir Henry Marten seems to have wished, or to remain in place to protect London. In the end, the committee for a general rising simply disintegrated through its inability to construct an army of volunteers, and by the following autumn, it had ceased to exist.[119]

With the collapse of the committee for a general rising the radicals lost their best opportunity to establish a real base of independent power in London. Given the moderation of the proparliamentary majority within the common council, they needed to focus the potential strength and revolutionary élan of the City populace by means of the creation of new institutions on a broad scale. It appears that at least part of the reason for their inability to do this successfully, except in such local instances as the small revolt at St. Dunstan's-in-the-East, can be found in divisions among themselves, perhaps in particular over the question of how far it was safe to go in allowing popular participation without jeopardizing their own position of leadership. On the other hand, it is probable that, in this situation of unsurpassed military emergency, the London citizenry as a whole was more prepared than at any other time during the Civil War years to follow the radicals' political leadership. As the politico-military crisis was transcended over the subsequent period, the radicals' political influence waned correspondingly.

At any rate, from late 1643, the City radicals, in particular those moderate republican types who, I have argued, found their chief representatives among the committee of public safety (militia committee), the commissioners for the Additional Sea Adventure to Ireland, the chief architects of Parliament's financial administration, and the leadership of the City campaign for an independent citizen army, were in sharp eclipse as a political force. So were the colonial-interloping merchants, who were at the center of all of these efforts of the radicals. It was only from 1646–1647, with the onset of a new period of popular mobilization, this time heavily concentrated in the army rank and file, that these men would get another chance. By 1648–1649, they would come to power in London and nationally, riding the coattails of an analogously radical military officers' group that made good use of the power of the genuinely democratic forces in the army, before finally destroying them as a threat to the new order.

[119] Hexter, *Reign of King Pym*, pp. 124–28ff.

Political Presbyterianism

DURING the middle and later 1640s there was a significant reordering of political forces in London, or, more exactly, a full working out and clarification of the broad political divisions between royalists and parliamentarians that had emerged by the autumn of 1642. At each end of the political spectrum there continued to exist political groups that refused fully to reconcile themselves to the newly emergent City regime. One was basically royalist and covertly or openly devoted to the restoration of the prewar status quo; the other was radical, tending to desire parliamentary supremacy ("moderate republicanism"), if not further democratization. But the most striking development of the middle and later 1640s was the eclipse of both of these political tendencies within the official municipal government and London politics more generally and the emergence of a massive, if heterogeneous, representation of essentially moderate elements. The new balance of forces had significant implications for the political positions and roles of the different sections of the merchant community.

The constitutional royalists made their major bid to retain City power in the winter and spring of 1641–1642. But this was thwarted by the City's revolutionaries, and London was secured as a stronghold of Parliament. Henceforth, the royalists gradually receded from the picture as an open political group, although they were able to make their influence felt covertly and indirectly when openings presented themselves. In turn, that alliance of City radicals, which had played the leading part in organizing the antiroyalist struggle and City revolution in 1641–1642, had attempted during the military crisis of 1642–1643 to push through a drastic reorganization of parliamentary military and financial institutions that would have further revolutionized political institutions both nationally and within the City. However, the radicals' plan to crystallize a new center of political power by means of the creation of a citizens' army under their own control collapsed, and they were henceforth obliged to organize themselves largely outside official City institutions. Although it is difficult to be certain of this, the radicals' capacity to win political support and more generally to exert power in the City appears to have been heavily based on their ability to link their politico-ideological program to building the parliamentary war effort and staving off defeat by the king. They accrued their greatest strength at the time of Parliament's greatest military emergency, when their dedication to the cause and their ability to organize in its support seemed most indispensable. As the military threat from the king declined after 1643, as the parliamentary war machine was perfected and put on a more solid political and financial footing during 1644 and 1645, and especially as the fundamental political problem ceased, after Naseby, to be victory over the king in order to avoid losing the Civil War and became settlement with the king in order to secure peace and stability, the radicals saw their influence steadily decline.

The moderates who came forward to dominate official City politics during the middle 1640s wished neither to restore the pre–Civil War political structure nor to push the revolution further, except in one critical respect: they wanted to complete the Puritan reformation of religious institutions. They were the primary beneficiaries of London's constitutional revolution of 1641–1642, although they were not, by and large, its chief creators. The primary makers of the revolution had been those allied radical forces that had established a base in the temporarily all-powerful committee of safety (militia committee), among which the new-merchant leadership was one important element. The new merchants and their allies failed to extend their power into the official municipality. Nevertheless, the radicals' revolution had curbed the veto of the aldermanic court, had cleared that body of most (though not all) of its outright royalists, and in this way had broken the strength of the old City elite, centered especially on the merchants of the great overseas companies. It had therefore paved the way for the elevation of the common council to a dominant position in City decision making, and with it those moderate political forces that had made the common council their political base.

The moderates certainly opposed royalism in London. In their view, the official City government of the pre–Civil War era—dominated as it had been by direct recipients of Court favors (customs farmers and monopolists), as well as merchant magnates from the privileged overseas companies—had been far too willing to sacrifice the citizens' interests to the needs of royal policy. The rebirth of absolutist rule in both church and state had to be prevented. This would require not only the preservation of parliamentary liberties and the newly won prerogatives of the common council. It would necessitate in particular the destruction of episcopacy and the creation of religious institutions, especially at the local level, under the control of citizens like themselves. From one viewpoint, then, the City moderates saw themselves as protagonists in that struggle for limited reform which had set off the revolutionary process in 1640–1641, and they were committed to defeating the king militarily in order to bring it to a successful conclusion. Their devotion to the cause, and effectiveness in supporting it, undoubtedly helped them draw support in London away from the radicals. Once the war had been won, they appeared well placed to consolidate their rule fully by helping underwrite a stable peace.

At the same time, however, feeling themselves increasingly threatened by the rising movements of political and religious radicalism that had been unleashed by the Civil War, the City moderates saw the need for monarchy as the bulwark of the political order. Ideally, a restored monarchy would stand behind their own magistracy. Equally crucial, it would guarantee the imposition of that full-fledged Presbyterian religious system which they projected not only as the key instrument of godly reformation on a national basis, but also as the basic organizational form for transferring control of local church government into their own hands and as the central mechanism for the enforcement of discipline and order within the City. As newcomers to positions of authority in a situation of profound instability and continuing rebellion, London's political moderates could hardly feel confident of their hegemony. The apparatus of control offered by the Presbyterian church courts and supervisory assemblies was perfectly designed to supplement their authority. The fundamentally localist perspective from which these men viewed the world can therefore hardly be overemphasized. They were the archetypical burgher Calvinists, and only their obsessive preoccupation with City problems can account for their sometimes bewildering—and, in retrospect, perhaps naive—political maneuvers. The inseparability of godly magistracy and Presbyterian church polity was the basic ideologico-institutional premise from which they derived their rather variable political strategies for securing a national Civil War settlement.

From the near-collapse of the parliamentary forces in the summer of 1643 through the parliamentary military victory in 1645, the London moderates did not hesitate to mobilize the City's financial and military resources in support of Parliament's war effort, but they rejected the radicals' plans for further institutional innovation in the City. Once the war was over, however, London's moderates confronted a difficult strategic dilemma. In certain respects, their predicament was analogous to that of the so-called parliamentary middle group: how to use, but control, the popular energies unleashed by the Civil War in order to defeat, but then come to terms with, a monarch who disagreed fundamentally with their goals. But the City moderates found their position considerably complicated by the lack of enthusiasm in Parliament for the pure Presbyterian church settlement that they, unlike the middle group, regarded as indispensable for any political settlement. Relatively few among the parliamentary classes wished to tamper with the distribution of power within the ecclesiastical structure, except in order to limit the authority of the bishops and church courts, and to ensure Parliament's ultimate control over the settlement of religion. Unlike the newly empowered political moderates

in the City, the parliamentary nobles and gentry had traditionally dominated their parishes and their counties and, for the most part, had long
controlled their local churches; moreover, few of them faced, during the
Civil War and its sequels, significant threats to their authority from religio-political movements drawn from lower social strata in the countryside
normally outside the political nation. As a result, they had little need
for—and a good deal of suspicion of—the congregational consistory
courts and the decentralized hierarchy of classical assemblies that were the
defining features of the Presbyterian church order, for these institutions
seemed to pose a not insubstantial threat to parliamentary and landed-class
control over religion, not only over the theological settlement but also
over the government of the church at the national and, especially, the
county and parish levels. Perhaps most directly problematic for the City's
political presbyterians, the powerful leadership of Parliament's middle
group not only was overwhelmingly Erastian, as were the parliamentary
classes more generally, but also contained pivotally important figures who
were sympathetic to religious Independency or separatism. Men of the
middle group, like Lord Saye and Sele, Nathaniel Fiennes, and Oliver
Cromwell, were strongly opposed to the Presbyterians' new disciplinary
order from a mildly tolerationist perspective, and they were willing to ally
with religious radicals from the war party, notably Sir Henry Vane, to
ensure a settlement that was both sufficiently Erastian and sufficiently careful of tender consciences. As a result, the long-term basis for any working
arrangement between the middle group and the City's moderates proved
increasingly tenuous. With Parliament's decisive military victories over
the king in the middle of 1645, the magistrates moved to consolidate a
new alliance with both the political descendants of Parliament's peace
party, now led by the earl of Essex, and the Scots, in what emerged as the
tripartite coalition constituting political presbyterianism.

In the same way that the religious term "Independency" is a misnomer
for the parliamentary wing of political independency—and for analogous
reasons—the religious term "Presbyterian" is a misleading name for the
parliamentary wing of the political presbyterian movement. The political
presbyterians in Parliament, like their predecessors of the peace party,
contained relatively few religious Presbyterians within their ranks. They
defined themselves vis-à-vis their parliamentary adversaries, notably
those of the middle group, by their willingness, in the last analysis, to
entrust the constitutional settlement to a monarch whom they knew could
not be counted on to defend that settlement, rather than seek to *impose* a
settlement on the Crown and endure the risks of political disorder and of
the breakdown of social hierarchy that would be entailed. In contrast, it
was the distinguishing feature of the middle group that its members were
willing to accept the risks entailed by the military and popular mobiliza-

[463]

tions required to impose a peace on Charles I in order to secure a satisfactory politico-constitutional settlement. The peace-party and moderate factions that would ultimately form the core of political presbyterianism had thus initially—in late 1643 and the first part of 1644—opposed Parliament's alliance with the Scots precisely because it meant intensifying the military conflict, and thus increasing the risks of political instability. However, in one of the more striking political reversals of the Civil War, they had themselves moved into alliance with the Scots during the autumn and winter of 1644–1645. The Scots had deserted their former middle-group allies especially in response to the attempts by the middle-group leadership, beginning in mid-1644, to ensure toleration for tender consciences, as well as in reaction to the rise of religious conflict within the parliamentary armies and to what appeared to them to be the growing likelihood that a parliamentary victory over the king would open the gates to political and religious radicalization. The Scots' overriding strategic objective was to impose a Presbyterian settlement in England, in order both to ensure that their own Presbyterian settlement would be safe from the sort of attack undertaken by Charles during the late 1630s and to secure social order against the sects. The old peace-party and moderate factions that came to constitute political presbyterianism in Parliament had little or no sympathy for religious Presbyterianism; but, as the Scots alienated themselves from the middle-group/war party alliance and made clear their lack of concern about imposing constitutional guarantees on Charles, these factions agreed to accept the Scots' insistence on a Presbyterian religious settlement in order to secure the Scots' alliance and what they hoped would be the resulting ability to negotiate a settlement with the king.[1]

It was the Scots insistence on Presbyterianism that, in the first instance, makes it at all sensible to term the Scots–Essex peace-party alliance political presbyterian. In turn, it was precisely the centrality of the Presbyterian religious goal for the partnership between the Scots and peace-party and moderate factions in Parliament that attracted London's moderates. The Londoners' adherence to what became the three-sided political presbyterian alliance—constituted by the Scots, Parliament's peace-party and moderate elements, and themselves—only made the Presbyterian church settlement that much more central a goal for that alliance. If political presbyterianism is thus a misnomer for the parliamentary party that provided such a visible section of the political presbyterian leadership, it is more appropriate for the political presbyterian alliance as a whole; this is be-

[1] For the previous paragraph, and for the development of political presbyterianism more generally, see M. P. Mahony, "The Presbyterian Party in the Long Parliament, 2 July 1644–3 June 1647" (University of Oxford, Ph.D. diss., 1973). See also D. Underdown, *Pride's Purge* (Oxford, 1971), pp. 59–75, and V. Pearl, "The 'Royal Independents' in the English Civil War," *T.R.H.S.*, 5th ser. 18 (1968).

cause the parliamentary wing of this coalition turned out, in the last analysis, to be dependent on the Scots and the City to win its program and because these forces were indeed centrally committed to religious Presbyterianism.

London's magistrates, as had the Scots before them, began to forsake their former parliamentary allies during the summer of 1645 in order to secure the Presbyterian settlement that was their top priority. Ironically, however, the old peace-party and moderate factions in Parliament with whom the citizens ultimately cast their lot were perhaps even less likely than their old middle-group partners to succeed in securing their preferred ecclesiastical program. This was because the king, with whom they hoped to negotiate a settlement, could be expected to be even less willing to accept a Presbyterian religious order than was the middle group. Even so, by the spring and summer of 1646, much of the core leadership of the City's moderate forces, exasperated by Parliament's continuing rejection of its demands for an undiluted Presbyterian discipline, would actually move toward entrusting its program to the king and the old royalist party of the City, rather than risking further revolution and endangering its own newly consolidated position. The citizens' turn in the direction of Charles I and the City's royalists is understandable only as the outcome of some very wishful thinking and their increasingly desperate search for order. In the long run, the City moderates could count only on their own strength and, by the spring of 1647, they would take decisive steps to construct an army of their own to enforce the kind of settlement they preferred. To understand the evolution of the City moderates' politics, especially in relation to the various sections of the merchant community with which this work has been concerned, it will be necessary to narrate somewhat more extensively their rise to power within the City and to analyze the group of magistrates that assumed the leading roles.

The Moderates' Offensive: From Military Victory to Civil War Settlement

Although the City moderates' program was not fully articulated until after the decisive victory at Naseby, the general thrust of their politics was evident long before then. It was, intrinsically, neither reactionary nor revolutionary, but designed to consolidate their newly established political power. Between 1642 and 1645, the moderates were concerned with confirming the constitutional arrangements that had emerged from the City revolution of 1641–1642; with prosecuting the war; and with beginning the process of articulating the additional institutional bases they felt were needed for the successful maintenance of their authority.

The majority of the common council had sought to contain the radicals' offensive in 1642–1643, for this would have threatened both City and parliamentary political authority.[2] Similarly, in January 1644, the common council voiced strong objections when the still-active Salters Hall committee radicals brought before Parliament their old plan for an independent volunteer army under their own control, to be financed by an assessment worth one meal a week on every London citizen. In response to the magistrates' appeal, Parliament promptly quashed the Salters Hall propositions. Meanwhile, the City government had taken it on itself to order that no citizens' petitions should be presented to Parliament without the consent of the common council.[3]

On the other hand, the City majority's opposition to the radicals' proposals throughout the period cannot be taken to indicate any unwillingness on their part to prosecute the war, or any underlying tendency to give in to the king. In the very days of late July and early August 1643 when the City magistrates were doing their best to undermine the radicals' committee for a general rising, they did not hesitate to raise some £50,000 for Parliament to cope with the military emergency. Less than a month later, they played a pivotal role in turning aside a major royalist threat when they sent out four regiments of the City's militia under the earl of Essex to relieve the besieged town of Gloucester. Meanwhile, on 6 August 1643, the common council denounced in the strongest terms the House of Lords' attempt to negotiate a peace treaty with the king, which, in the eyes of the magistrates, "if yielded unto would be utterly destructive to our religion, laws, and liberties." The councilors expressed the hope to the House of Commons "that you would be pleased to persist in your former resolutions whereupon the people have so much depended, and wherein you have so deeply engaged yourself." The City mobs that two days later disrupted the parliamentary motions toward peace may have had at least the tacit blessing of the City officials.[4]

Over the following year, the City leaders actively supported the parliamentary efforts to improve the war effort. During the early months of 1644, they gave their blessing to the Scottish alliance and to the committee of both kingdoms.[5] Meanwhile, they pressured Parliament to reform Essex's army by replacing "scandalous," "profane," and "unfaithful" officers

<hr />

[2] See above, ch. 8. See also V. Pearl, *London and the Outbreak of the Puritan Revolution: City Government and National Politics, 1625–1643* (Oxford, 1961), pp. 250–73.

[3] CLRO, J.Co.Co.40, fols. 82v–83v (10 Jan. 1644), 86v–87 (22 Jan. 1644).

[4] CLRO, J.Co.Co.40, fols. 69v (6 Aug. 1643), 70 (11 Aug. 1643), 73 (9 Sept. 1643); *Mercurius Aulicus*, 12 August 1643; R. R. Sharpe, *London and the Kingdom*, 3 vols. (London, 1894), 2: 192–95.

[5] CLRO, J.Co.Co.40, fols, 84v–85v; Mahony, "Presbyterian Party," pp. 55–56, 77–78; Sharpe, *London and the Kingdom* 2: 198, 203.

with "well-affected" ones.[6] They did not even hesitate, between January and April 1644, to adopt the radicals' plan to raise new City troops by way of a weekly meal assessment, once they had made certain that the additional forces would be firmly under the control of the properly constituted authorities.[7] In mid-May 1644, through official City petitions backed up by a mass demonstration outside Parliament, the magistrates brought the full power of the City into play to induce the House of Lords to agree with the Commons and renew the committee of both kingdoms.[8] From late 1644 through the first half of 1645, they continued to support parliamentary efforts to reorganize the army and to appoint a new and more vigorous leadership. Indeed, during the politico-military crisis that followed the fall of Leicester in early June 1645, they intervened sharply to demand that Fairfax's army immediately be completed, as well as that Oliver Cromwell be appointed head of new forces to be raised in the Eastern Association, a request that fed directly into the army's call to make Cromwell lieutenant general.[9]

Throughout this whole period, in fact, the City's magistrates could be seen from one point of view as fairly consistent supporters of what has been described as middle-group politics: the adoption of innovative and sometimes radical military and political strategic alternatives to prevent the king's victory in order to impose a settlement that realized the principles originally set out in 1641–1642, but did not go beyond them. The whole trend was symbolized by the election of Sir John Wollaston to replace the radical Isaac Pennington in the fall of 1643. Indeed, Wollaston's political orientation was probably a good deal closer to that of his middle-group counterparts in the parliamentary leadership than it was to that of the majority of his more fanatical religiously Presbyterian and politically repressive colleagues in the City's magistracy. A wealthy goldsmith by occupation, Wollaston had been sufficiently committed to the cause of Parliament and City revolution to take up a post on the committee of safety (militia committee) in January 1642. On this heavily radical body, Wollaston represented a moderate wing; yet, especially because he sympathized with Independency in religion, as indicated by his patronage of a host of Independent ministers, he could not give his unqualified support to the political presbyterian offensive that gathered force following his retirement from the mayoralty. Like his fellow goldsmith and militia committee moderate William Gibbs, as well as such common councilors

<hr />

[6] CLRO, J.Co.Co.40, fols. 88–88v.

[7] CLRO, J.Co.Co.40, fols. 86v, 88v, 90, 90v, 93a, 94; *Mercurius Aulicus*, 25 January 1644; Sharpe, *London and the Kingdom* 2: 199.

[8] CLRO, J.Co.Co.40, fols. 96v, 97, 97v, 98; *Mercurius Aulicus*, 16 May 1644.

[9] CLRO, J.Co.Co.40, fols. 125, 131–131v; Sharpe, *London and the Kingdom* 2: 199, 214, 217–18; S. R. Gardiner, *History of the Great Civil War*, 4 vols. (London, 1893), 2: 233–37.

as Thomas Noel and Thomas Viner (both, incidentally, also goldsmiths), Wollaston occupied a swing position in City politics, between the political presbyterians and more radical forces on the militia committee and elsewhere. Wollaston approved of the political presbyterians' moderate political goals, yet at critical moments, he was obliged to ally with the radicals in order to prevent the political presbyterians from seeking to achieve their preferred settlement by means of either relying on Charles I or entering into a disastrous military confrontation with the army.[10]

The City did not wait until the war was over to begin to advance its own positive program for a settlement. As early as 22 January 1644, the common council appointed a committee to consider a petition to Parliament,

> that they would be pleased to speed the settlement of church government for the quieting of the minds of the people, and that private persons may be prohibited to anticipate the wisdom of both Houses of Parliament by assembling themselves together and exercising of church discipline without the warrant of the civil power, which tends much to the dishonour of Parliament and the disturbance of the peace of the church, City, and kingdom.

During the previous months, a number of London's Independent ministers had, more or less suddenly, begun to take the audacious step of gathering congregations out of the parishes, sending a wave of panic and revulsion through the heavily Calvinist and Presbyterian ranks of the City's clergy. In late November 1643, London's Presbyterian ministers had organized a protest against the Independents for their implicit attack on the parish churches, and the City's petition was designed to back them up. It was a harbinger of things to come; the magistrates would ally with the Presbyterian ministers of London to repress the Independents and the sects for undermining the church's control over the parish and for thereby threatening the enforcement of social discipline and political order.[11]

In May 1644, in preparation for the forthcoming negotiations with the king, Parliament asked the magistrates to consider what they wished to have included in any peace settlement. The City initially presented a twenty-eight-point program, but the magistrates pared this down at Parliament's request to six central planks, and then ultimately sent it back to Parliament in October 1644 for consideration in the upcoming Uxbridge negotiations. The City's demands reflect very clearly the City magistrates'

---

[10] Pearl, *London*, pp. 328–31. For Wollaston's support for Independent ministers, notably Thomas Brookes, George Griffith, and Joseph Carryl, see PRO, will of Sir John Wollaston, 1658 PCC Wootton 248. On Gibbs, see Pearl, *London*, pp. 320–21.

[11] CLRO, J.Co.Co.40, fol. 86; M. Tolmie, *The Triumph of the Saints: The Separate Churches of London, 1616–1649* (Cambridge, 1977), p. 95.

fundamentally corporate and localist consciousness and their concern to protect the municipality from threatening forces, both above and below, that might infringe on their powers and privileges. The magistrates asked not only that Parliament confirm the City's charter, customs, and liberties, but also that Parliament cede authority over London's defensive forces to the City itself. The City was to control its own militia and the Tower of London; moreover, City forces were not to be sent outside London without the consent of the municipality. Finally, echoing a continuing fear of the religio-political radicalism of the City's suburbs, the magistrates requested that the militias of the parishes beyond the City but within the bills of mortality should be regulated by the common council. This demand would emerge as a central point of contention in the struggle between political presbyterians and radicals in the City over the Civil War settlement.[12]

At the same time, despite their intense fear of the radicals, the moderates understood the gap that separated them from the prewar City ruling groups, in terms of both their social origins and their political methods. In early 1645, the court of aldermen, which still included a significant knot of covert royalists, attempted to reclaim its old veto over the common council's proceedings, but the common council majority firmly rebuffed it.[13] The problem that continued to haunt the moderates, however, was how to consolidate their newly won position of hegemony in London in a period of rising radicalism and social disorder without throwing themselves back into the arms of the old City elite.

It was only following the final military defeat of the Crown, in the autumn of 1645, that the City moderates began to put forward the most distinctive point of their program, namely their support for a full-fledged Presbyterian religious settlement that would preclude any sort of toleration. The City first enunciated its views on the reformation of the church in November 1645 in response to Parliament's decision to institute its newly-arrived-at religious settlement despite objections from the Scots and the London Presbyterian ministry. To the City magistrates, the new parliamentary program was nothing less than a betrayal of the Covenant. Parliament had accepted, in principle, the Presbyterians' demand for the establishment of parish elderships, whose holders would have the power to excommunicate. However, it had gone on to rule that, under the new dispensation, these elders would have the right to judge and punish only with respect to a small number of specified offenses; a standing committee of Parliament, especially appointed for the task, would exert authority in

[12] CLRO, J.Co.Co.40, fols. 95v, 104, 104v, 105v, 108–10, 115–115v; Sharpe, *London and the Kingdom* 2: 209–10. See below, ch. 10, esp. pp. 502, 514, 550–51.

[13] CLRO, J.Co.Co.40, fols. 120v, 123, 126 (24 Jan., 24 Feb., 24 Apr. 1645).

all other cases. In response to the parliamentary order of 23 September 1645 that called for the selection of elders, the City clergy had noted five objections to the mode of election of these officers and the extent of their powers. But the City magistrates needed little prompting from the ministers to see that the effect of the parliamentary settlement would be to deprive the consistorial courts of their full disciplinary powers and thus to deprive the whole Presbyterian structure of its raison d'être as an instrument of political repression and social control. They were therefore only too happy to frame their own petition protesting Parliament's new ecclesiastical structure and to forward it to the Commons, along with two other major petitions, one from eighty-seven London Presbyterian clergymen and the other from fifty-nine fervently Presbyterian citizens, which similarly questioned the legitimacy of the new religious settlement.[14]

In these London petitions of November 1645 one can see the connection between abstract theology and practical religious problems in the minds of the citizens and clerics. Parliament's failure to recognize Presbyterianism as biblically directed was, at this juncture, the root of the problem. Given the assumption of Presbyterianism by divine right, the citizens and clerics felt fully justified in challenging Parliament across the board. They questioned, in particular, the following aspects of the proposed settlement: the elders' lack of power to test the communicants' biblical knowledge before administering the sacrament; the limited number of "scandalous" actions that would warrant suspension from the sacrament; the establishment of a standing committee of Parliament to take care of all cases of unenumerated scandals brought by any of the classes; and the lack of provision for rooting out schism.

As the City magistrates realized, if the proposed parliamentary ecclesiastical structure was allowed to stand, the two-sided thrust of their own program for reform would be severely blunted. If the number of enumerated scandals was limited, the real power of the consistory court would be restricted. If control of unenumerated scandals was placed in the hands of a parliamentary committee, ecclesiastical power would be removed, once again, from the local level, as it had been before the Civil War. The citizens had not fought to destroy episcopal domination in London in order to deliver full control of their churches into the hands of Parliament.

---

[14] W. A. Shaw, *A History of the English Church during the Civil Wars and under the Commonwealth, 1640–1660*, 2 vols. (London, 1900), 1: 269–70, 293; CLRO, J.Co.Co.40, fols. 148–148v and 151–53 (where petitions are recorded with names of signers). See these references for the following two paragraphs. For the London political presbyterians' political offensive overall, the standard work is V. Pearl, "London's Counter-Revolution," in *The Interregnum*, ed. G. E. Aylmer (London, 1972). See also M. Kishlansky, *The Rise of the New Model Army* (Cambridge, 1979), ch. 4. Kishlansky's work is especially valuable for its bringing new evidence to bear on City politics in the middle 1640s, derived from the newly discovered Diary of Thomas Juxon, Dr. Williams's Library, MS 24.50.

Nor did they intend to cede the task of imposing religious discipline and conformity, so critical for urban social control and political order, to a parliamentary committee. Such a body might be unsympathetic and, in any case, could hardly be expected to manage the enormous judicial task that would be thrust upon it. Only a fully empowered eldership could ensure that the Londoners exercised sufficient local control over religion and that the new church commanded sufficient disciplinary force at the level of the parishes.

The House of Commons responded to these London petitions of November 1645 with extreme irritation and outrage, labeling the City's petitioning a breach of parliamentary privilege. The parliamentary leadership was, at just this moment, moving in precisely the opposite direction from that desired by its erstwhile London allies. Having revived Cromwell's committee of accommodation, it was seeking, once again, to forge Presbyterian-Independent unity through securing toleration for at least the Independents within its new Erastian Presbyterian ecclesiastical system. The Commons betrayed its growing distrust of London by refusing to honor the City's request that it maintain control not only of its own militia, but also of those in the suburbs.

Not surprisingly, these rebuffs by the Commons further inflamed the Londoners' opposition. The magistrates' response was, openly and provocatively, to strengthen their relationship with the Scots, as well as to more tightly coordinate their activities with the political presbyterians in Parliament, led by the earl of Essex and his lieutenant Denzil Holles. The political presbyterian alliance was beginning to operate in high gear. On 14 January, the magistrates made a great public show of taking the Covenant with the Scottish commissioners in London. A few days earlier, they had begun to weed out dissidents in their own ranks by moving to require all common councilors to retake the Covenant. Rumors were already flying that the king would come to London, catalyzing a political takeover led by the Scots and the City, and based in an organized political presbyterian citizenry. The parliamentary leadership, for its part, was doing its best to fan the flames of anti-Scottish sentiment by exposing, through the revelation of captured documents, the Scots' secret and independent negotiations with the royalists, while decrying the Scottish army's misconduct in the north.[15]

On 16 January, the magistrates presented a new petition to Parliament, demanding not only strict Presbyterian discipline, but the repression of

[15] For the previous two paragraphs, see Shaw, *English Church* 1: 284; CLRO, J.Co.Co.40, fols. 170–170a; Mahony, "Presbyterian Party," pp. 196–99, 208–12, 237–38; Gardiner, *Civil War* 3: 5–10.

Independent as well as separatist congregations. The common council thus complained that

> private meetings, especially on the Lord's day, of which they are at least eleven in one parish, are multiplied whereby the public congregations' ordinary and godly orthodox ministers are very much neglected and condemned, as if they were like the primitive persecutions or as if we were still under the tyranny of the prelatical government; and by reason of such meetings and the preaching of women and other ignorant persons, superstition, heresy, schism are much increased, families divided, and such blasphemies as the petitioners tremble to think on uttered to the dishonour of Almighty God.

Worse still, the City had been informed that "diverse persons have an intention to petition the honourable House for a toleration of such doctrines as are against our covenant under the notion of liberty of conscience." In response, reported the magistrates, many of the City's local wards had used the occasion of the recent City elections in December 1645 to petition their aldermen "for a speedy settling of church government within this City and against toleration." As the City itself had "no power . . . to suppress or overcome this growing evil" of Nonconformity, the magistrates were asking Parliament to institute speedily its new religious order "according to our most solemn covenant with the most high god," to prevent toleration, and to restrain private meetings contrary to the Covenant. As the arch-Presbyterian Scotsman Robert Baillie assessed the situation:

> We have gotten it thanks to God, to this point that the mayor, aldermen and common council and most of the considerable men are grieved for the increase of sects and heresies and want of government. They have yesterday had a public fast for it, and renewed solemnly their Covenant by oath and subscription; and this day have given in a strong petition for settling of church government and suppressing of all sects without any toleration. No doubt if they be constant they will obtain all their desires, for all know the Parliament here cannot subsist without London; so whatsoever they desire in earnest and constantly it must be granted. Wherefore albeit they gave them a baffling answer to their former petition a month ago, yet considering the address of this in all its progress, they have thanked them for it and promised a good answer speedily. The Independents and all sects are wakened much upon it, and all will stir, which way we do not know yet.[16]

[16] CLRO, J.Co.Co.40, fols. 160v–161. Baillie is quoted in Shaw, *English Church* 1: 284. See also Kishlansky, *New Model Army*, pp. 81–82.

Apparently acting in response to the City's request, the House went back to reconsider the powers they had placed in the Presbyterian eldership and the question of unenumerated scandals. Nevertheless, relations between the magistrates and the House of Commons were soon inflamed once again, when the City accepted from the Scots, without informing Parliament, a letter discussing the Scots' program for a settlement and thanking the City for its steadfast struggle for Presbyterian church order. When, in early February, the parliamentary leaders learned of this transaction from a common councilor MP opposed to the political presbyterians, they expressed extreme anger at the citizens' pretension in functioning as an independent political authority and at their having hidden their actions from Parliament. Shortly thereafter, the House of Commons expressed its growing distrust of the City by again refusing the common council's recently renewed request to control the militia of the suburbs.[17] Meanwhile, the City's political presbyterian leadership continued its drive to consolidate its control of the common council by starting to investigate those councilors who had refused to retake the Covenant.[18]

Parliament's ultimate resolution of the problem of how to enforce ecclesiastical discipline—that parliamentary commissioners be appointed in every province to judge unenumerated scandals—was even less acceptable to the Presbyterians than the original proposal for a single standing parliamentary judicial committee. On 11 March 1646, on receiving a petition from a number of Presbyterian citizens protesting the new parliamentary religious amendments, the common council sent to Parliament a strong complaint against the proposed civil commissions.

[The City] . . . being informed that commissioners are to be chosen in every province to have some superintendant power in church government . . . the same tends much to the discouragement of such as are willing to submit to the Presbyterial government established by both Houses of Parliament and that this and the want of further directions concerning the choice, employment, and indemnity of special elders is like to obstruct the prosecution of the votes passed the 20th of February last, the petitioners have thought it their duty to make the same known.

In this instance, the common council initially directed its petition to the House of Lords, expecting from that body, where support for the political presbyterians was growing, a more favorable response than from the Commons. But the Lords rejected the magistrates' actions as a breach of

---

[17] Mahony, "Presbyterian Party," p. 213; Diary of Thomas Juxon, Dr. Williams's Library, MS 24.50, fols. 59, 59v, 60v, 61.

[18] CLRO, J.Co.Co.40, fol. 166v; Diary of Thomas Juxon, Dr. Williams's Library, MS 24.50, fol. 60v.

parliamentary privilege. The citizens did not even attempt to deliver their document to the Commons, but Parliament did not let the matter rest and, on 17 March, sent a delegation to the City to explain to the magistrates just why it found their petition so offensive. Parliament reaffirmed its commitment to its recently passed church settlement and, by the end of the month, to Baillie's dismay, the common council had decided to back down and call off its campaign to alter that settlement.[19]

By April 1646, then, the City's magistrates had been obliged to adjust their strategy to take into account Parliament's unrelenting Erastianism. Henceforth, they focused ever more single-mindedly on the problems of order and the post–Civil War political settlement. To the despair of Robert Baillie, the magistrates largely gave up their demand that Parliament make the church settlement more perfectly Presbyterian in structure and practice. At the same time, however, they sought more systematically to use the newly established Erastian Presbyterian ecclesiastical order as a vehicle to suppress all dissenting opinion in politics and religion and to achieve the sort of political settlement they desired. Correlatively, they assumed an ever more open and provocative role in national politics, seeking, in close coordination with the political presbyterian leadership in Parliament and their Scottish allies, to pressure the Commons to agree to peace terms that were favorable to the king by threatening covertly, or even openly, to negotiate directly with Charles or even to welcome him back to London. As a result of this shift in political approach, the City political presbyterian leadership alienated a number of its former supporters who had been ready to press for a Presbyterian reformation of the church, but who were unwilling to accept the politically reactionary, if not openly royalist, drift of the leading magistrates. On the other hand, it came to attract a number of former constitutional royalists, who saw a growing convergence, in terms of strategy if not ultimate goals, between their own political desires and those of the increasingly repressive political presbyterians.[20]

The total merger, by spring 1646, of politics and religion, and of political presbyterianism in Parliament and in London, was manifest in the City's declaration of 14 April, which delivered a new message to Parliament, laying out the City's newly revised program, and which sharply accelerated party-political polarization nationally. The common council noted:

[19] CLRO, J.Co.Co.40, fols. 173v–174; Shaw, *English Church* 1: 285–86, 293; Mahony, "Presbyterian Party," pp. 214–15, 225; Kishlansky, *New Model Army*, pp. 83–85; Diary of Thomas Juxon, Dr. Williams's Library, MS 24.50, fols. 66, 66v, 68.

[20] On the drift of political presbyterianism toward the royalists in 1646–1647, see Pearl, "London's Counter-Revolution," pp. 35–37. See also below, pp. 478, 485–86.

the many scandalous and vicious pamphlets printed and published within the City, the frequent unlawful meetings of assemblies in private, the increase of heresies, sects and schisms, matters of a very high nature and of ill and dangerous consequences conferring much division and contention amongst the people endeavoring (if possible) a division between Parliament and this City and of both kingdoms of England and Scotland, and this chiefly for want of settlement of church government.[21]

Then, "having their instructions," according to City militia captain Thomas Juxon, "from Sir Philip Stapleton to petition no more but to put forth a remonstrance, the [political presbyterian] party in the City" took the audacious step of deciding to present its own program for the Civil War settlement to Parliament, and appointed a committee to draw up the document. The City was already, at this point, arousing suspicion that its lord mayor, Thomas Adams, was secretly intriguing to bring the king to London, and Adams was soon called for interrogation before Lord Saye, Oliver St. John, and others. The political presbyterians' strength was meanwhile increased, as the House of Lords came, more or less systematically, to support the political presbyterians' side.

On the other hand, the anti–political presbyterian leadership in the Commons seems to have been able to solidify its control of that House in this period by politically exploiting the political presbyterians' association with, and apparent dependence on, the Scots. The Scots' clear willingness to seek a settlement with the king independently of Parliament, already exposed on a whole series of occasions by the parliamentary leadership, appears to have exacerbated already widespread anti-Scottish feeling in the Commons and to have alienated a decisive section of uncommitted opinion from the political presbyterians. Anti-Scottish sentiment was significantly strengthened following the publication in mid-April of the Scots' objections to Parliament's propositions for a settlement, before Parliament had had the opportunity to reply to them and following the king's flight to the Scots at the start of May 1646. In this situation, in order to secure the sort of settlement they desired, the logical strategy for the political presbyterians—and especially the City—was to increase their pressure on the House of Commons from the outside, or even to seek to get around it. As Baillie had put it earlier, "All know that the Parliament here cannot subsist without London."[22]

On 22 May, the common council approved the draft presented by its

---

[21] CLRO, J.Co.Co.40, fol. 176.

[22] For the previous two paragraphs, Diary of Thomas Juxon, Dr. Williams's Library, MS 24.50, fol.71 (quotation); CLRO, J.Co.Co.40, fols. 176, 181–82v; Mahony, "Presbyterian Party," pp. 216, 260, 262, 273.

committee and, four days later, this document was presented to Parliament as the City remonstrance. A day earlier, on 25 May, Charles bypassed Parliament and directly approached the common council with a compromise plan for a peace settlement. Meanwhile, the City's opponents of political presbyterianism had begun to circulate their own petition to counter the City remonstrance, and the magistrates immediately responded. On 1 June 1646, "after long and serious debate," the common council therefore resolved "that the manner of getting of hands unto a petition by divers citizens and others in and about the City of London and especially by some few members of this court in a clandestine manner intended to be presented to the Parliament is prejudicial to the City, tending to sedition and to the disturbance of the peace thereof."[23]

London had come full circle from the revolutionary days of 1641–1642. At that time supporters of Parliament had seized the municipal institutions after a radical campaign conducted outside the official City, very often by popular petitions that the City authorities (at that time royalist) had refused to sanction. In mid-1646, the heirs (if not the creators) of City revolution and civil war sought to impose order and to short-circuit a process of political radicalization in order to maintain the status quo that they had come to control. The City had relinquished its demands for a more perfectly Presbyterian church structure in favor of making the parliamentary church a more perfect instrument of its political goals.

To the minds of these magistrates a durable settlement was thus predicated on two basic conditions: first, the establishment of a repressive Presbyterian church order to enforce religious uniformity, impose political order, and exclude from government as many as possible of the political presbyterians' potential opponents; second, the restoration of monarchy to secure political obedience. The central points of their program, presented in their remonstrance to Parliament of 26 May, clearly reflect their position as newcomers to power anxious to consolidate their recently won hegemony. Their principal demands included (1) the suppression of all separatist and private congregations; (2) proceedings against all Brownists, heretics, schismatics, blasphemers, and the like; (3) the enforcement of obedience to the Covenant on a universal basis; (4) the exclusion of all those disaffected from the Presbyterian government from any place of public trust; (5) the hastening of peace with the king; (6) a pledge by Parliament to study all means to preserve the Scottish union and Scottish friendship; and (7) the application of the estates of delinquents to the discharge of the great public debts owed to the City and the citizens.

The City's remonstrance provoked great consternation in the House of

[23] CLRO, J.Co.Co.40, fols. 181–82v (City remonstrance), 183 (quotation); Mahony, "Presbyterian Party," pp. 279, 281.

Commons, which ultimately came out against it, although the House of Lords approved it. In response, the City stepped up its pressure by organizing a petition among the citizens in support of its remonstrance and another against the parallel London petition to Parliament that was opposing the remonstrance. To squeeze Parliament even further, the City also showed itself perfectly willing to negotiate as an independent power. In late June 1646, the magistrates took the extraordinary step of drafting their own letter to the king expressing their desire for his return. This was an extreme provocation, for, as was well understood, the king's presence in London could serve as a rallying point for all strands of proroyal opinion. Not surprisingly, a House of Commons aware of the danger and jealous of its prerogatives intervened to prevent the City from sending this letter.[24]

Meanwhile, in driving to eliminate all dissent and disorder, the City government may have had an effect precisely the opposite to what it intended. The newly emerging Leveller movement appears to have succeeded, during the spring and summer of 1646, in exploiting growing fears of repression and of a constitutional sellout to the royalists in order to attract increasing numbers of Londoners to its campaigns and its program. The magistrates, for their part, sought to impose order by themselves, as well as they could. In particular, the common council did its best to come to the aid of the City's Presbyterian clergy who, led by Mr. Thomas Edwards, continued to spearhead the counterrevolution. On 23 June, the common council appointed a City committee to root out persons involved in producing "scandalous, base, and horrid pamphlets and books." And in August, the magistrates set up another committee to try to do something about ministers going away and leaving their parishes unoccupied due to the refusal of many people to pay tithes.[25]

Over the summer of 1646, the political presbyterians in Parliament and in the City appear to have reached the conclusion not only that they could not hope to implement their program until they disbanded the army, but also that they could not disband the army until the Scots had left the scene. This was because a decisive number of MPs continued to look to the army as a counterweight to Scottish influence in England. The political presbyterians therefore adopted a plan to remove the Scots precisely as a means to win parliamentary support to dissolve the New Model Army. In this scenario, the City was to provide the political, and if necessary the military, muscle to back up the political presbyterians' initiatives in Parliament. During the autumn of 1646, with the help of the City, Parlia-

---

[24] CLRO, J.Co.Co.40, fols. 187–98(?); Sharpe, *London and the Kingdom* 2: 234–37; Mahony, "Presbyterian Party," pp. 216–19.

[25] CLRO, J.Co.Co.40, fols. 184, 190v.

ment did vote to send the Scots back home with a very large ransom, made possible by a loan from the Londoners of £200,000, and by late December 1646, the Scottish army had crossed back into Scotland. Many MPs now felt free for the first time to join the hard-core political presbyterians in a move against the New Model Army.[26]

Meanwhile, the City was pursuing its drive for order with ever-increasing single-mindedness. In October 1646, the City passed up the senior alderman traditionally in line for the position, and selected as lord mayor the noted royalist and anti-Presbyterian Sir John Gayre. Gayre would patronize Anglican ministers throughout the Interregnum. His election shocked Baillie, who had hoped for the victory of John Langham, a man who could have been expected to work more closely with the Scots and give greater consideration to the Presbyterians' special religious interests. The election showed how far things had gone toward a reconciliation of the political presbyterians and the outright royalists, and indeed toward the reassertion of royalist power within the City.[27]

The real crisis was not, however, reached until the following winter.[28] On 10 December 1646, "diverse well-affected freemen and convenant engaged citizens" brought in two new petitions that asked the common council to present certain grievances to Parliament. This action set off the chain of events that resulted in the final split with the army and, ultimately, the army's invasion of London in the summer of 1647. The petitions, delivered to the magistrates "by a great number of considerable citizens of known worth and of approved integrity to the Parliament," substantially repeated the City demands of the previous twelve months, except for one major addition: "the enemies now being subdued, the armies may be disbanded that the so much complained of oppression by their means may be redressed." Eight days later the common councilors approved the citizens' demands and agreed to forward them to Parliament as their own. As they explained their central request that the army be dismissed,

> There are some officers and many common soldiers . . . who either have never taken the Covenant or are disaffected to the church government held forth by the Parliament . . . the pulpits of divers godly ministers are often usurped by preaching soldiers and others who

[26] Mahony, "Presbyterian Party," pp. 287–89, 290–325; Bodleian Library, Clarendon MSS, no. 2475; Gardiner, *Civil War* 3: 183, 186, 216; Pearl, "London's Counter-Revolution," pp. 43–44.

[27] Pearl, "London's Counter-Revolution," p. 38; Diary of Thomas Juxon, Dr. Williams's Library, MS 24.50, fols. 91, 91v; Pearl, *London*, pp. 302, 321–23; PRO, will of John Gayre, 1649 PCC Fairfax 133; J. E. Farnell, "The Politics of the City of London, 1649–1657" (University of Chicago, Ph.D. diss., 1963), p. 38.

[28] For the following paragraph, see CLRO, J.Co.Co.40, fols. 199v–203.

infect their flock, and all places where they come, with strange and dangerous errors. And then we humbly submit it to your lordships to consider what security or settlement can be expected, while they are masters of such a power, and what example, if not encouragement, the people may take from them, to refuse the Covenant or if they have taken it to condemn the same, to the great derogation of that church, which the Parliament has declared.

A few days later London's political presbyterians appear to have tightened their grip on the municipal government by winning a smashing victory over their political independent opponents at the common council election of December 1646. The political presbyterian alliance, strongly abetted by a revived royalism in London, was now ready to attempt to take power.

In early March 1647, the City forwarded to Parliament a copy of a recently circulated Leveller petition and called for the repression of its initiators. At the same time, the magistrates expressed once again their opinion that social rebellion within the City or elsewhere could not finally be eradicated until the army, which gave it sanction, was irrevocably dispersed. Within the month, a joint City-parliamentary committee was negotiating the details of the army's dissolution. As it turned out, however, disbanding the army was easier to demand than to accomplish, and a test of strength became inevitable. On 16 April 1647, Parliament gave the City permission to take full control of its own armed forces and to reorganize them from the top down as it saw fit. The common council then appointed a new militia committee to replace the now unreliable commission that originally had been chosen in the revolutionary days of January 1642 and then supplemented with extremist militants at the height of the radicals' campaign for an independent volunteer army in the spring of 1643. This new body, fully in sympathy with the political presbyterians' intentions, took charge of the climactic phase of the City's political offensive.[29]

The new militia committee actually attempted to construct a citizens' force that could stand up to the New Model Army. But for both practical and political reasons, it was never able to create a really potent and steadfast City defense.[30] Certainly, the enormous risks to both persons and property that could have been entailed by an armed confrontation must

---

[29] CLRO, J.Co.Co.40, fols. 207–10, 212, 214, 215. For the radicals' domination of this committee to 1647, see below, ch. 10, pp. 512–14.

[30] The City's political and military preparations to confront the army can be cursorily followed in Bodleian Library, Clarendon MSS., nos. 2528, 2534, 2547, 2565. The Clarendon correspondent was at all points doubtful of the City's ability to develop a serious military capability. See nos. 2528 and 2565 (7 June, 2 Aug. 1647).

have proved a major discouraging factor. It was, moreover, one thing to support a strategy of disbanding the army on the assumption that the army would act constitutionally and obey Parliament's order to dissolve. It was quite another to seek to impose the dissolution on the army by force. Once the army had made clear that it would resist, many supporters of the political presbyterians' general political perspectives must have seen little choice but to desert the political presbyterian cause simply because they believed that the City forces could not possibly prevail in combat against the New Model Army.[31] It is apparent, in addition, that even within the moderates' leadership there were wavering individuals who, in the end, like many of the parliamentary middle groupers, felt that the destruction of the army before the conclusion of a definitive settlement with the king would do more harm than good, and might open the way for the return of an unrestrained monarchy.[32] The upshot was that in August 1647, the army was able to march into London unopposed and to place the municipal government firmly under its thumb. It selected its own lord mayor, appointed its own militia committee, and ultimately imprisoned five key City leaders of the political presbyterians' anti-army offensive.

The following spring and summer, the same conflict was more or less reenacted. The army was forced to leave London to deal with new royalist risings. The municipality, once more free to pursue its own political aims, reinstituted the old, imprisoned political presbyterian leadership, once again took control of the militia committee, brought cryptoroyalists from the old elite into key directing roles as it had in 1647, and pressed Parliament to agree to a personal treaty with the king. When the army had dealt with its enemies in the counties, it returned once again to enforce its will on the City; this time, however, it more thoroughly and more permanently remodeled its government.[33]

---

[31] As one observer remarked at this time, "The City is still subject to be ridden by every party and will be so rather than endanger trade and stock" (Bodleian Library, Claredon MSS, no. 2460). On the impact of the army's decision to resist disbandment on the political presbyterians and their prospects, see Mahony, "Presbyterian Party," pp. 363–64, 385.

[32] It should be noted, for example, how many members even of the political presbyterians' own militia committee, appointed by the City in April 1647 with the express purpose of preparing the City's forces against the political independents, went over to the political independents at their victory. These included, at the least, Sir John Wollaston, William Gibbs, Philip Skippon, John Bellamy, Nathaniel Camfield, Tempest Milner, Maurice Gethin, and Richard Turner out of a twenty-eight-man committee. It may be doubted if any of these men were convinced political presbyterians to the extent of supporting a military confrontation with the political independents. Indeed, it may be doubted if the City's militia itself, especially its officer corps, was ever very well cleansed of opponents of the political presbyterians (See Bodleian Library, Clarendon MSS, no. 2565).

[33] CLRO, J.Co.Co.40, fols. 273–74, 280v–81; Sharpe, *London and the Kingdom* 2: 259–67, 270–98; and, especially, I. Gentles, "The Struggles for London in the Second Civil War," *H.J.* 26 (1983). See also below, ch. 10, pp. 528–33.

The Composition of the Political
Presbyterian Leadership

A full analysis of political presbyterianism in the City would have to extend its purview beyond the confines of City government. The political presbyterian party often displayed the aspect of a mass movement, notably in its attempt to raise an army to counter the political independents and in its efforts through mass demonstrations to overawe Parliament. Ideally, one would investigate not only those who led the movement, but also those who composed its rank and file, and would try to find out just how the movement was organized. For practical reasons, in what follows I confine my analysis to the movement's leadership—the City magistrates who, alongside the City's Presbyterian clergy, constituted the movement's main directors and organizers.[34] In so doing, I will pay special attention to the place of the different merchant groups within the movement. In this way, I hope to lay the basis for comparing London's political presbyterians with the City's political independents, whom I will discuss in the chapter that follows.

The common council leadership of the political presbyterian offensive can easily be identified by examining the handful of key committees that were in charge of all the most important City actions during the period. The first of these committees was appointed in October 1645 to consult with those ministers and citizens who objected to the new parliamentary religious settlement. This committee drew up the City petition on church government of 14 January 1646. It was also given responsibility for carrying out the investigations of the Independent ministers Hugh Peter and William Hawkins for their attacks on the City government, as well as of those common councilors who had refused to take the Covenant.[35] This committee was succeeded on 9 March 1646 by a new body including many of the previous committee's members, which was appointed to write the City's petition of protest against the proposed county church commissions for unenumerated scandals. This latter group of men also produced the City remonstrance to Parliament of 22 May. In addition, it was charged with composing the letter to the king of 30 June 1646, which called for his return and the settling of a well-grounded peace.[36] In December 1646, a third committee was set up to organize the City's political offensive against the army. This committee was responsible for drawing up the

[34] For an interesting analysis of how the political presbyterian movement was organized in the parishes, see M. Mahony, "Presbyterianism in the City of London, 1645–1647," *H.J.* 22 (1979). The conclusions of Dr. Mahony's in-depth study of the parish-level leadership of political presbyterianism coincide very closely with those concerning the City-wide leadership presented here.

[35] CLRO, J.Co.Co.40, fols. 148, 151–53, 160v–61, 166v.

[36] Ibid., fols. 173v, 174–80, 181–82v, 186.

City's petition of 18 December 1646, which called for the army's dissolution. In March 1647, it composed the remonstrance that requested once again that the army be disbanded, and that those responsible for a recent Leveller petition be punished. The same men were also in charge of the City's negotiations with Parliament to work out the details of the army's dismissal.[37] Finally, on 26 April 1647, the common council appointed a fourth committee to direct the City militia and to see to the defense of the City and Parliament against the army.[38]

Apart from these four committees, there were only three others that carried out any task that was politically relevant to the presbyterian offensive of 1645–1647. These included a twelve-man committee of 23 June 1646 to suppress subversive pamphlets; a twenty-three-man committee of 10 August 1646 to try to protect tithes; and a twenty-three-man committee of 26 March 1647 to see what was necessary to secure the City's defenses.[39]

A total of fifty-three men served on the foregoing seven committees, which directed City politics between October 1645 and April 1647.[40] Certainly, not all of these committeemen were in sympathy with their committee's purposes. But in view of the overwhelming dominance of political presbyterianism within the City government, it is reasonable to assume that most of them, especially those who were regularly appointed throughout the period, were in general accord with the political line that the committees consistently espoused. Undoubtedly, the whole group of committeemen included most of the core leaders of the City's political presbyterian offensive. Discovering its political, commercial, and religious characteristics can deepen an understanding of political presbyterianism in the City and determine the place of the major merchant groups in relation to it.

[37] Ibid., fols. 199–203v, 207–10, 212.

[38] Ibid., fol. 215v.

[39] Ibid., fols. 184v, 190v, 211v.

[40] The following is a list of the members of these seven committees of 1645–1647. The number of committees on which each man served is given in parentheses: Thomas Adams (3), [?] Allen (1), Thomas Andrews (1), Thomas Arnold (5), Thomas Atkins (1), Samuel Avery (7), Edward Bellamy (5), John Bellamy (2), John Bide (3), Walter Boothby (3), Lawrence Bromfield (4), Edwin Browne (1), James Bunce (7), Nathaniel Camfield (2), Thomas Chamberlain (1), Stafford Clare (2), Sir George Clarke (2), [?] Coates (1), George Dunn (1), Thomas Foote (1), John Fowke (3), John Gase (5), Maurice Gethin (2), William Gibbs (3), Richard Glyd (3), John Glyn (1), Thomas Gower (1), Nathaniel Hall (1), Michael Herring (1), William Hobson (2), Edward Hooker (6), Alexander Jones (3), John Jones (5), Peter Jones (1), William Kendall (4), John Kendricke (2), John Langham (6), Christopher Meredith (1), Tempest Milner (2), Thomas Noel (2), Christopher Packe (7), James Russell (2), Philip Skippon (1), Thomas Steane (2), Edward Story (2), Richard Turner (1), Richard Venner (7), Thomas Viner (2), John Warner (1), Francis West (2), George Witham (3), Sir John Wollaston (5), Richard Young (1).

POLITICS

In political terms, the group of committeemen was overwhelmingly parliamentarian in sympathy, composed of individuals who had played active roles on the parliamentary side from the outbreak of the Civil War in the autumn of 1642. As Dr. Pearl had justly commented, "It is false to imagine that they were deeply conservative or neoroyalist in the early days of the conflict."[41] Only two of the fifty-three committeemen can be identified with the royalist movement of 1641–1642.[42]

On the other hand, however, it needs to be emphasized that few of the leaders of political presbyterianism in the City had been prominent in the London revolutionary movement that, in late 1641 and early 1642, not only saved the City from royalism but also carried out the constitutional revolution that elevated the common council to the central position in City decision making. Of the fifty-three committeemen, twelve served on four or more of the committees and were *not* selected for the political independent militia committee appointed by the army in September 1647; they may thus be taken to constitute a representative sample of the very top leadership of political presbyterianism in the City.[43] Among them, four had been either members of the sixteen-person City militia committee that led the revolution of the winter of 1641–1642 or among the 175 or so different signers of the three key revolutionary petitions of that period— against royalist control of the Tower of London, against the House of Lords' delay over the impressment bill, and against those who had dared to oppose the establishment of the committee of safety.[44] Similarly, twenty-six committeemen served on at least one of the three committees that took charge of the political presbyterian offensive against the army between December 1646 and the spring of 1647 and were *not* selected for the political independent militia committee chosen by the army in September 1647, and may therefore be taken as a further sample of leading City political presbyterians.[45] Among them, only four were on the revolutionary militia committee of the winter of 1641–1642 or signers of any of the

---

[41] Pearl, "London's Counter-Revolution," p. 30.

[42] Sir George Clarke, Edwin Browne. For this result and those that follow, consult table 9.1.

[43] Thomas Arnold, Samuel Avery, Edward Bellamy, Lawrence Bromfield, James Bunce, John Gase, Edward Hooker, John Jones, William Kendall, John Langham, Christopher Packe, Richard Venner.

[44] Edward Bellamy, James Bunce, Edward Hooker, John Jones.

[45] Thomas Adams, Thomas Andrews, Samuel Avery, Edward Bellamy, John Bellamy, John Bide, Walter Boothby, Lawrence Bromfield, Edwin Browne, James Bunce, Thomas Chamberlain, Sir George Clarke, John Gase, Richard Glyd, Thomas Gower, Edward Hooker, John Jones, Peter Jones, William Kendall, John Langham, Robert Mainwaring, Christopher Packe, Richard Venner, Thomas Viner, Francis West, George Witham.

three aforementioned revolutionary petitions.[46] Finally, the political presbyterians' militia committee of April 1647, the main directing body of
their counterrevolution, included twenty members who were not also
members of the political independents' army-appointed militia committee
of the following September;[47] among them, only four were either members of the revolutionary militia committee of the winter of 1641–1642
or signers of any of the three revolutionary petitions of that period.[48] The
leadership of London political presbyterianism thus contrasted sharply
with that of the leadership of political independency in the City: as I will
try to demonstrate fully in the next chapter, the latter did find its roots, to
a very large extent, within the leadership of the City revolution of 1641–
1642, as well as in the radical offensive of 1642–1643. For example,
among the twenty-seven members of the army-appointed political independent militia committee of September 1647 who had *not* also served on
the political presbyterian militia committee of April 1647,[49] ten had been
members of the revolutionary militia committee of the winter and spring
of 1641–1642 or signers of the revolutionary petitions,[50] and at least another two had assumed other top directing roles in the London uprising
of that period.[51]

In this light, Dr. Pearl's assertion that the "political presbyterians were
men who challenged and displaced the aldermanic elite in 1641–2 and
now wished to preserve their established position"[52] needs modification.
In fact, future political presbyterians played only a limited role in the
direct challenge to the aldermanic elite that took place during London's
revolution of the winter and spring of 1641–1642, although they ultimately took a major part in the displacement of the aldermanic elite that
resulted from the success of that revolution and that came with the elevation of the common council to a position of hegemony within the City
government. The political presbyterians, as emphasized, had thus been

[46] Edward Bellamy, James Bunce, Edward Hooker, John Jones.

[47] Thomas Adams, Samuel Avery, Edward Bellamy, John Bellamy, John Bide, Walter Boothby,
Lawrence Bromfield, Edwin Browne, James Bunce, John Gase, Maurice Gethin, Richard Glyd,
Thomas Gower, Edward Hooker, John Jones, William Kendall, John Langham, Robert Mainwar-
ing, Richard Venner, Francis West.

[48] Edward Bellamy, James Bunce, Edward Hooker, John Jones.

[49] Isaac Pennington, Thomas Atkins, John Warner, John Fowke, Thomas Andrews, Thomas
Foote, Simond Edmonds, John Venn, Francis Allein, Rowland Wilson, Edmund Harvey, Richard
Salway, Richard Turner, Samuel Warner, William Barkeley, William Hobson, James Russell,
Owen Rowe, Thomas Player, Stephen Estwicke, Robert Tichborne, William Antrobus, Thomas
Noel, Samuel Moyer, Alexander Normington, Alexander Jones, Mark Hildesley.

[50] Thomas Atkins, John Warner, John Fowke, William Hobson, Samuel Warner, William Barkeley, James Russell, Owen Rowe, Stephen Estwicke, Alexander Normington.

[51] Isaac Pennington, John Venn.

[52] Pearl, "London's Counter-Revolution," p. 34.

less the makers of the revolution of 1641–1642—a role largely occupied by what I have termed London's radical alliance—than its inheritors and consolidators. During the earlier 1640s, they had certainly been parliamentarians in opposition to the royalists, but they had not, by and large, been revolutionaries. From the middle 1640s, they were increasingly obsessed with the rising tide of radicalization and with the restoration of political order—and were ever more willing to go to any lengths to achieve this, often against the original instigators of the London revolution.

The increasingly reactionary political trend that marked the political presbyterian offensive between the fall of 1645 and the summer of 1647 was to some extent a reflection of the changing composition of the City's political leadership over this period—that is, of the common council committees that made policy. As the political presbyterians stepped up their campaign, they secured an ever tighter stranglehold on City governance and became decreasingly tolerant of the participation in government of potentially hostile political forces. Nineteen of the fifty-three aforementioned committeemen were unable to secure committee posts after the summer of 1646;[53] they were apparently excluded from an active role in City government in the climactic phase of the political presbyterian assault on the army that began in December 1646. Among these nineteen committeemen, seven had taken part in the revolution of 1641–1642, either as members of the militia committee of January 1642 or as signers of the three major revolutionary petitions.[54] As their offensive approached its most critical stages, the political presbyterians thus relied more and more on conservative citizens and sought to cleanse their ranks of possibly unreliable individuals, especially the militants of the earlier, more radical, phases of the struggle.

Finally, it appears that this reactionary trend was significantly accentuated with the renewed political presbyterian offensive of the summer of 1648. The City leadership in this period can be identified once again by references to the key committees in charge of the short-lived City campaign: (1) a thirteen-man committee of early May 1648 that drew up the petition to Parliament asking for City control of its own militia; (2) the new thirty-one-man political presbyterian militia committee itself; and (3) an eighteen-man committee of 22 June 1648 that instigated the petition to Parliament calling for a personal treaty with the king.[55] A total of forty-

[53] [?] Allen, [?] Arthur, Thomas Atkins, Stafford Clare, George Dunn, Thomas Foote, John Fowke, John Glyn, Nathaniel Hall, Richard Herring, William Hobson, Alexander Jones, [?] Meredith, Thomas Noel, James Russell, Thomas Steane, Edward Story, John Warner, Richard Young.

[54] Thomas Atkins, John Fowke, Nathaniel Hall, Richard Herring, William Hobson, James Russell, John Warner.

[55] CLRO, J.Co.Co.40, fols. 273–74, 274v, 281.

one common councilors served on these committees. Twenty-four of them had been among the committeemen of 1645–1647, so it is clear that there was no very great political discontinuity.[56] But it is notable that among the seventeen who had not served on the committees during the City's original offensive of 1645–1647, but joined the political presbyterians only in 1648, there were at least five royalists.[57] The core political presbyterian leadership of London thus entered into ever closer alliance with the old forces of royalism in the City. Apparently, it was willing to risk not only the restoration of untrammeled royal power at the national level, but even the return of the old City ruling groups in order to ensure order in the City.

RELIGION

In view of the fact that their activities were, in large part, aimed at achieving a more perfect form of Presbyterian church, it is legitimate to assume that most of these committeemen, for one reason or another, supported a Presbyterian religious settlement. On the basis of supplementary information, moreover, it is demonstrable that the core leadership of London political presbyterianism was closely tied to leading Presbyterian ministers and deeply involved in the construction of the official Presbyterian ecclesiastical structure in London, from the time of the promulgation of the parliamentary religious settlement in 1645–1646. Of the aforementioned twelve committeemen who served on at least four of the seven committees, and who have been taken as representative of the top leadership of the political presbyterian movement,[58] at least ten were religious Presbyterian activists outside the municipal governmental framework, as well as within it:[59] six were ruling elders in the London Presbyterian Provincial Assem-

[56] The following is a list of the members of these three committees of 1648. The number of committees on which each man served is given in parentheses. For the continuity and discontinuity with the committeemen of 1645–1647, compare this list with that in note 40: Thomas Adams (1), Thomas Andrews (1), Thomas Arnold (1), [?] Arthur (1), Samuel Avery (3), Anthony Bateman (2), William Bateman (1), Edward Bellamy (3), John Bellamy (1), John Bide (1), Edwin Browne (3), James Bunce (1), Thomas Chamberlain (1), [?] Chamberlain (2), Robert Chambers (1), Philip Chetwin (2), Sir George Clarke (1), Thomas Foote (2), John Fowke (1), John Gase (1), John Gayre (1), William Gibbs (3), Richard Glyd (2), Nathaniel Hall (1), Edward Hooker (1), [?] Jackson (1), William Jesson (3), Peter Jones (2), John Jurin (1), William Kendall (1), John Langham (1), Peter Mills (2), Thomas Player (2), Abraham Reynardson (1), Philip Skippon (1), Richard Venner (1), Thomas Viner (1), John Warner (1), Francis Waterhouse (1), Francis West (1), Sir John Wollaston (1).

[57] Anthony Bateman, William Bateman, John Gayre, Philip Chetwin, Abraham Reynardson.

[58] See above, note 43.

[59] Thomas Arnold, Samuel Avery, James Bunce, John Gase, Edward Hooker, John Jones, William Kendall, John Langham, Christopher Packe, Richard Venner.

bly,[60] and four others can be identified as patrons of, and close collaborators with, Presbyterian ministers.[61] The City moderates' moves to consolidate their power in London are incomprehensible without reference to their overriding concern for specifically Presbyterian church forms. The leading magistrates' close connections with the Presbyterian ministers explain the relatively smooth coordination between the lay and clerical wings of the Presbyterian movement throughout the period, and help to account for the movement's power and effectiveness.

On the other hand, although the leaders of the political presbyterian movement were at all times closely wedded to Presbyterian church forms, the opposite cannot be assumed. There was, it is clear, a substantial minority of magistrates, including a number of committeemen, who were religious Presbyterians, but who were not willing to go along with the increasingly reactionary political goals to which the movement for Presbyterian religious reformation became connected during the middle of 1646. At least half a dozen committeemen of the period 1645–1647—including such central figures as John Warner and John Fowke, and also including Stafford Clare, Michael Herring, Alexander Jones, and Thomas Steane—were proponents of Presbyterian religious forms, but refused to support the political presbyterians' increasingly overt collaboration with the royalists. These men are not found among the committeemen who took charge of the offensive against the army beginning in December 1646; Warner, Fowke, Jones, and Steane sided with the political independents.[62]

SOCIOECONOMIC CHARACTERISTICS

Perhaps the most striking feature of the political presbyterian leadership is the sharp decline in influence of both those polar overseas merchant

[60] John Gase, Edward Hooker, John Jones, William Kendall, Christopher Packe, Richard Venner (Sion College, Records of the Provincial Assembly of London, 1647–1660, MSS Acc. L40.2/E17, fols. 3v, 21v, 101v, 105v, 109).

[61] That is, Samuel Avery, John Langham, Thomas Arnold, James Bunce. For Avery, see his activities in St. Stephen's Coleman Street during the Presbyterian restructuring of the mid-1640s (Guildhall MS 4458, fol. 134). For Langham, see the support he received from the arch-Presbyterian Robert Baillie (Pearl, *London*, pp. 321–23). For Arnold, see his bequest to Presbyterian ministers (PRO, will of Thomas Arnold, 1660 PCC Coke 118). For Bunce's Presbyterianism, see Pearl, "London's Counter-Revolution," p. 32.

[62] Warner, Steane, and Herring were ruling elders of the London Presbyterian classes (Sion College, Records, MSS fols. 3, 101, 109, 123). For the patronage of Presbyterian ministers by Warner and Herring, see above, ch. 8, note 63. Steane left money in his will to the Presbyterian minister Lazarus Seaman (PRO, will of Thomas Steane, 1674 PCC Dycer 103). Alexander Jones left bequests to the Presbyterian ministers Edmund Calamy, Matthew Haviland, Thomas Watson, William Jenkins, and James Nalton (PRO, will of Alexander Jones, 1660 PCC May 1571). For Fowke's Presbyterianism, see Pearl, "London's Counter-Revolution," p. 31.

[487]

groups that played such essential roles in setting the terms of political conflict in 1640–1643. Political presbyterianism evidently did not strongly attract either one. The overseas company merchants were far less prominent among the new moderate City leadership that emerged in the mid-1640s than they had been under the old order. Only three Levant Company traders and East India Company directors (not also part of the colonial-interloping leadership) were among the fifty-three committeemen of 1645–1647, and two of these men had in fact been royalists in 1641–1642.[63] Although few of the Levant–East India Company merchants actually gave up their businesses and left London to join the royalist camp following the defeat of City royalism, most withdrew from political activity and lapsed into a hostile "neutrality," a crypto-royalism, waiting for better days. Better days did in fact come in the spring and summer of 1647, and again in the spring and summer of 1648, when the City government attempted, albeit hesitantly and inconsistently, to confront the army and impose a national settlement according to its own lights. During both of these periods there was a dramatic reemergence of City royalists, and these were to a significant extent recruited from among the Levant–East India combine. It is indicative of that trend that the neo-royalist Levant–East India Company magnate John Gayre was chosen lord mayor in the autumn of 1646, and played a key political role in the political presbyterian onslaught of 1647. In 1648, among the five neo-royalist committeemen, there were no fewer than four major Levant–East India Company merchants.[64]

The colonial-interloping merchants were also almost entirely absent from the political presbyterian offensive. There were just four new merchants among the fifty-three committeemen. Two of them, John Warner and James Russell, were clearly political independents: they served on no common council committees after the middle of 1646; they were expelled from the militia committee in the political presbyterian purge of April 1647; and they were appointed to the new army-sponsored militia committee of September 1647.[65] The other two—Michael Herring and Thomas Gower—each served on only one committee. Only Gower took part in the climactic political presbyterian thrust starting in December 1646. It is notable that at least three of these men—Warner, Herring, and Gower—were religious Presbyterians, and it is quite possible that the committee involvement of at least the first two of these was largely an expression of their religious concerns. The colonial-interloping leadership, as a group, was to a great degree religiously Independent and, ulti-

---

[63] John Langham, Sir George Clarke, Edwin Browne—of whom the last two were royalists.

[64] Anthony Bateman, William Bateman, John Gayre, Abraham Reynardson. See above, note 57.

[65] For the militia committees, see A.O. 1: 5, 1007; CLRO, J.Co.Co.40, fol. 215v.

mately, politically independent, too. Connected with the radicals from the start, they consistently lost political influence with the growing predominance of the moderates, to regain their strength only with the army's rise to power.

There were, on the other hand, five identifiable Merchant Adventurer committeemen—Christopher Packe, Samuel Avery, Walter Boothby, George Witham, and John Kendricke. All five had become leading London parliamentarians during the Civil War, although none of them had played a noticeable part in the City revolution of 1641–1642. Two of these men, Avery and Packe, were among only four citizens to serve on all seven of the key political presbyterian committees, and were certainly among the most important, if not the most steadfast, leaders of the political presbyterian offensive. At least four of the five (Packe, Avery, Boothby, and Witham) were strongly religious Presbyterians, playing leading roles in the restructuring of the church in London.[66] In their moderate politics and strongly disciplinary Puritan religion, these men were representative of those Merchant Adventurers who had sided against the king.

To sum up: the City political presbyterian leadership included a far smaller proportion of overseas traders than had previous City ruling groups. Only about a quarter of the committeemen were merchants, and if those known to have been either royalists or political independents are removed, the proportion is even smaller. Overseas traders composed perhaps half of the aldermanic court that ruled London in the pre–Civil War period. In contrast, the new governors of London appear to have been recruited to a far greater extent from the City's domestic trading community. The distribution of occupations among those twelve common councilors who served on at least four of the seven key committees and formed most of the central core of the political presbyterian leadership is probably typical of the top level of the movement. Apart from three merchants (the Merchant Adventurers Packe and Avery, as well as the Levant Company trader John Langham), there was a woolen draper (James Bunce, who was Langham's brother-in-law), a goldsmith (John Wollaston), a distiller (Edward Hooker), a fishmonger (Edward Bellamy), a cutler (Lawrence Bromfield), and a hosier (Richard Venner, who appears to have been a member of the Barber Surgeons Company and bequeathed £300 to his daughter Magdalene for her work on "distilling of waters and making of surgical salves"), as well as members of the Haberdashers (Thomas Arnold), Turners (John Gase), and Grocers (John Jones) companies who

---

[66] For Packe and Avery, see above, notes 53 and 54. Boothby was a ruling elder in the London Provincial Assembly (Sion College, Records, MSS fol. 3v). Witham was a leading supporter of the Presbyterian minister Edmund Calamy in his proceedings in the parish of St. Mary Aldermanbury (Guildhall Library MS 3570.2, fol. 58).

were not overseas traders, but whose occupations cannot be more precisely identified.[67]

The reduced political role of the overseas merchant community during this period was probably inevitable, given the reduced role of the aldermanic court in relation to the common council, which undoubtedly at all times had a higher percentage of nonmerchants within it. But the decreased prominence of the overseas merchants in the City's leadership unquestionably also reflected the new political realities of this period and indeed helped to determine them. This aldermanic court was demoted in the course of the same process of revolutionary conflict that brought about the decreased influence of the City merchant establishment, based in the great overseas companies. The leading overseas traders, dismayed by the alterations in the City constitution that reduced their influence, assumed for their part a very cautious political stance starting in 1642. They adopted a low profile and refused to commit themselves politically until the time was right. It cannot be said that the men who took their place in governing the City were drawn from very far down on the socioeconomic scale. Indeed, some 60 percent of the committeemen are found among the list of London's leading inhabitants drawn up in 1640 for the king's tax purposes, a figure quite comparable to that for the overall group of Levant Company active traders in this period.[68] But these men were of a different type from the old City ruling elite, and undoubtedly distinguished themselves from it. Primarily local in the scope of their businesses and unconnected with the great overseas trading corporations, they differed from the City's establishment merchants in having no reason to support the monarchy and its court as a source of protection for foreign trade monopolies or a favorable foreign policy. At the same time, unaccustomed as they were by family tradition to rule, they need not have mourned the passing of the old domination of the aldermanic court. There may have been little in their situation to push them toward revolution, but there was no reason for them to refuse to identify with Parliament or to disdain to take over City leadership by means of the common council, once that body had been elevated to the central position in City decision making. On the other hand, the relatively narrow sphere of their daily activities and

[67] For Bunce and Wollaston, see Pearl, *London*, pp. 313, 315, 328–31. For Hooker and Bellamy, see W. J. Harvey, ed., *List of the Principal Inhabitants of the City of London, 1640. From Returns Made by the Aldermen of the Several Wards* (London, 1886), pp. 2, 4. For Jones, see V. Pearl, "London Puritans and Scotch Fifth Columnists: A Mid-Seventeenth-Century Phenomenon," in *Essays in London History Presented to P. E. Jones*, ed. A. E. Hollander and W. Kellaway (London, 1969), p. 323. For Gase, see PRO, will of John Gase, 1668 PCC Herne 105. For Venner, see PRO, will of Richard Venner, 1656 PCC Berkley 17; see also Pearl, "Scotch Fifth Columnists," p. 323. For Bromfield, see PRO, will of Lawrence Bromfield, 1668 PCC Hene 113. For Arnold, see Society of Genealogists, Boyd's Index of London Citizens: 6520.

[68] Harvey, *List of Principal Inhabitants of London, 1640*.

their relative unfamiliarity with the commanding heights of governance may have left these men relatively unprepared to assume power. In their own insecurity as rulers, as well as the actual precariousness of their position in a period of political upheaval, we may discern perhaps the roots of their restrictive, repressive, and ultimately reactionary politics.

TABLE 9.1
Political Presbyterian Committeemen

	Nov. 1645–Aug. 1646				Dec. 1646–April 1647			June–Aug. 1648		
	(1)	(2)	(3)	(4)	(5)	(6)	(7)	(8)	(9)	(10)
Thomas Adams					X	X	X		X	
(?) Allen	X									
Thomas Andrews					X					X
Thomas Arnold (IM)	X	X			X	X	X			X
(?) Arthur									X	
Thomas Atkins (IM)	X									
Samuel Avery	X	X	X	X	X	X	X	X	X	X
Anthony Bateman								X		X
William Bateman									X	
Edward Bellamy			X	X	X	X	X	X	X	X
John Bellamy	X						X			X
John Bide		X				X	X			X
Walter Boothby	X				X		X			
Lawrence Bromfield	X				X	X	X			
Edwin Browne							X	X	X	X
James Bunce	X	X	X	X	X	X	X		X	
Nathaniel Camfield (IM)						X	X		X	
Thomas Chamberlain					X					X
(?) Chamberlain								X	X	
Richard Chambers										X
Philip Chetwin								X	X	
Stafford Clare		X		X						
Sir George Clarke					X	X				X
(?) Coates			X							
George Dunn				X						
Thomas Foote	X							X		X
John Fowke (IM)	X	X		X				X		
John Gase	X	X		X	X		X			X
John Gayre									X	
Maurice Gethin (IM)						X	X			

TABLE 9.1 *(cont.)*

	Nov. 1645–Aug. 1646				Dec. 1646–April 1647			June–Aug. 1648		
	(1)	(2)	(3)	(4)	(5)	(6)	(7)	(8)	(9)	(10)
William Gibbs (IM)	X	X					X	X	X	X
Richard Glyd	X	X					X		X	X
John Glyn				X						
Thomas Gower							X			
Nathaniel Hall				X						
Michael Herring		X								
William Hobson	X	X								
Edward Hooker	X	X	X	X		X	X		X	
(?) Jackson										X
William Jesson								X	X	X
Alexander Jones (IM)	X	X		X						
John Jones		X		X	X	X	X			
Peter Jones						X		X		X
John Jurin										X
William Kendall	X	X			X		X			
John Kendricke		X		X						
John Langham	X	X	X	X	X		X		X	
Robert Mainwaring							X			
(?) Meredith			X							
Peter Mills									X	X
Tempest Milner (IM)						X	X			
Thomas Noel		X	X							
Christopher Packe	X	X	X	X	X	X	X			
Thomas Player									X	X
Abraham Reynardson										X
James Russell (IM)	X	X								
Philip Skippon (IM)							X			X
Thomas Steane		X		X						
Edward Story				X		X				
Richard Turner (IM)							X			
Richard Venner	X	X	X	X	X	X	X			X
Thomas Viner					X	X				X
John Warner (IM)	X									
Francis Waterhouse										X
Francis West						X	X			X
George Witham			X	X	X					
Sir John Wollaston (IM)	X	X		X		X	X			X
Richard Young	X									

Table 9.1 (*cont.*)

The Committees

(1) 20 October 1645 to 14 January 1646, originally appointed to consult with ministers and citizens who objected to a parliamentary settlement of religion. See above, this chapter, note 35.

(2) 9 March 1646 to 30 June 1646, originally appointed to write the City protest petition against a proposed county church commission for unenumerated scandals. See above, this chapter, note 36.

(3) 23 June 1646, appointed to suppress subversive pamphlets. See above, this chapter, note 39.

(4) 10 August 1646, appointed to protect tithes. See above, this chapter, note 39.

(5) 10 December 1646 to April 1647, originally appointed to draw up the City petition of 18 December 1646 calling for the army's dissolution. See above, this chapter, note 37.

(6) 20 March 1647, appointed to see what was necessary to secure the City's defenses. See above, this chapter, note 39.

(7) 26 April 1647, appointed to take charge of the City militia (the new political presbyterian militia committee). See above, this chapter, note 38.

(8) Early May 1648, appointed to draw up a petition to Parliament requesting City control over its militia. See above, this chapter, note 55.

(9) May 1648, appointed to take charge of the City militia (the new political presbyterian militia committee). See above, this chapter, note 55.

(10) 22 June 1648, appointed to petition Parliament for a personal treaty with the king. See above, this chapter, note 55.

Note

IM = Member of the political independent militia committee of September 1647.

The New Merchants Come to Power

URING the later 1640s the City's political presbyterians dominated London with comparatively little difficulty. Within the City government, opposition to political presbyterianism was never significant. In fact, the City's political independents owed little of their ultimate triumph to their own political base in London, but depended almost entirely on the intervention of the army. It was the army that installed its City allies in power in 1647 and again in 1648; it was the army that ultimately allowed them to consolidate their position beginning in the winter of 1648–1649. Precisely because political independency was so weak within the official City before the army triumph and so dominant thereafter—because its moments of political defeat and victory were so clear-cut—it is not difficult to identify the composition of its leadership. At the same time, because the continuities, in terms of personnel and program, between sections of the City radical movement of the early 1640s and London political independency were so pronounced, one can fairly well specify the political significance of the political independents' movement.

Political independency as it emerged in London during the middle 1640s must be sharply distinguished, in terms of political ideology, religious orientation, and social composition, from the alliance in Parliament that was also termed political independent, although misleadingly so. Political independency in Parliament was led, through most of the later 1640s, by "royal independents," largely descended from the parliamentary middle group, who were neither politically radical, nor, for the most part, religiously Independent (nor for that matter even religiously Presbyterian). The royal or middle-group independents had entered into an alliance, in 1644–1645, with descendants of the parliamentary war party, who were significantly more radical than they, both politically and religiously. The political independent alliance in Parliament had as its goal defeating the royalists militarily. But the terms it sought in a settlement of peace went only a bit beyond the constitutional limitations that the middle group had been seeking to impose on the Crown since the winter of 1641–1642, although it was, by this time, prepared to grant some degree of religious toleration. The parliamentary wing of political independency, least of all its critically important middle-group component, should therefore no more be understood as "Independent"—given that term's religious meaning and its connotation of political radicalism—than the parliamentary wing of political presbyterianism should be thought of as "Presbyterian."

On the other hand, just as one *can* appropriately apply the term "Presbyterian" to the extraparliamentary Scottish and City components of the political presbyterian political alliance, one can also, if one is careful, usefully apply the term "Independent" to the crucial extraparliamentary components of the political independent alliance, not only in the army but also in London. Political independency in London is thus best understood as composed of the politically less extreme and economically more substantial elements within that contradictory coalition of forces that composed what I have called London radicalism, or the London radical alliance, from 1642–1643 onward. One wing of this broader radical alliance was constituted by the economically substantial, war-party, quasi-republican, and, to a great extent (though not exclusively), religiously Independent elements that composed the mainstream of City political independency, among whose most important representatives were to be found the colonial-interloping merchant leaders. The other wing of this alliance was constituted by the socially and economically less substantial, religiously separatist, and more democratic elements, prominently including the Levellers and their (sometime) political allies among the sects. The struggle against political presbyterianism in London during the later 1640s thus ultimately involved a coalition of London's radical forces that was rather analogous to the alliance behind the City's radical offensive of 1643. However, during the later 1640s, London's political independents succeeded in taking power in the City as a direct consequence of the army's capture of the national state. They were, as a result, able to achieve a dual goal that previously had been beyond their capacity: to defeat the political presbyterians and, with the bloody destruction of the Levellers shortly thereafter, to dispatch the democratic wing of the radical alliance. The Commonwealth thus carried to a position of unprecedented strength both nationally and locally an enlarged version of much the same set of militant forces that had led the successful City revolution in the winter of 1641–1642 and the unsuccessful City radical offensive to carry that revolution further in 1642–1643. The political independents' accession to power in London brought the colonial-interloping merchants to the pinnacle of their influence. It will be the objective of this chapter to analyze the political independents' path to power, and of the two that follow to examine the consequences of their victory.

Political Independents on
the Defensive, 1645–1647

Throughout the period of the political presbyterians' ascendancy in London, the City's political independents maintained a relatively uncombative stance. This was especially true of the economically more substantial and politically more moderate elements among them, typified by the new-merchant leadership. Despite their pivotal position at the heart of the parliamentary financial-administrative machine, the City radical leadership, especially its top new merchants, never enjoyed great influence within the central City governing institutions. It had based its once substantial influence in London largely on its powerful grip on the City militia committee. That body played a dominant role in the City revolution in 1641–1642 and helped spearhead the radicals' offensive of 1642–1643. But the radicals' initiative had failed when the mass movement on which they had sought to build their power disintegrated, and henceforth their impact on City governing circles was in decline.

As that broad grouping of political moderates that would form the core of political presbyterianism in the City gained ever greater strength during the middle 1640s, those radicals who retained positions within the City government became progressively more alienated from the vast majority of magistrates, and ultimately were buried beneath the political presbyterian avalanche. Especially from 1645 City radicals in general and colonial-interloping merchants in particular played hardly any role in governing the City. The political presbyterian leadership that rose to power from this point included, as noted, relatively few of those who actually made the City revolution, or, it may be added, those who led the City radical offensive of 1642–1643. Since political presbyterians essentially monopolized the common council committees that took charge of the political presbyterians' initiatives and excluded most individuals who were hostile, City radicals in general and new merchants in particular were essentially absent from the common council committees after the summer of 1646.[1] Even that handful of new merchants who continued to hold the influential post of alderman in these years were rendered essentially impotent. Both Alderman William Barkeley and Alderman Samuel Warner, leading colonial traders, actually gave up their offices in 1645, almost certainly because their political positions clashed so strongly with those of the overwhelmingly political presbyterian majority. Two other new-merchant leaders, Thomas Andrews and John Warner, did retain their alder-

[1] For the common council committeemen of 1645–1647, see above, ch. 9, pp. 481–93. Among those common council committeemen designated as constituting the political presbyterian leadership, not a single one appears to have been active in the radicals' offensive of 1642–1643. See notes 43–48.

manic posts, but were almost entirely inactive. Even Alderman John Fowke, the City militant leader and new-merchant ally most willing to compromise with the political presbyterian trend, was excluded from the key political presbyterian committees after the summer of 1646.[2]

Given their weakness within the City, London's political independents had little choice but to look to the middle-group war-party alliance that maintained a majority in the Commons until the end of 1646 and, in the last resort, to rely on the army officers to provide a shield against political presbyterianism and a capitulation to royalism. Meanwhile, they sought to help secure an acceptable resolution of the conflict by means of winning away from political presbyterianism those London citizens who were moderate in politics and Presbyterian in religion, but who were nonetheless uncomfortable with the political presbyterians' accelerating drive toward a peace settlement that lacked constitutional guarantees and toward religio-political repression.

To pursue this strategy, the London political independents had to avoid all taint of revolutionism: to stress conciliation, to place responsibility for the current divisions on the political presbyterians, and to highlight the dangers both to Parliament and to the City inherent in the political presbyterians' intolerant and crypto-royalist political approach. These erstwhile radicals no longer could aspire, as they had in 1643, to help dictate terms of a national political settlement. They had built their power and popular support for their program on their vanguard role in securing London for Parliament in the revolution of 1641–1642 and in seeing to the military and financial security of the cause in the perilous times of 1642–1643. But their popularity with the citizenry, as well as with the MPs, appears to have waned precipitately as the overriding problem ceased to be winning a military victory over the king and came instead to be negotiating a stable peace with him. Doubtless, these men still held out hopes for a political settlement that would bring about parliamentary supremacy and the serious demotion (or perhaps even the demolition) of the monarchy. But, in practice, they had to resign themselves to the relatively conservative constitutional compromise envisioned by the middle-group or royal independents who held the balance of power within the parliamentary political independent alliance through most of the period. They made clear, moreover, that, despite the preference of a majority among them for religious Independency, they could live with Parliament's formally Presbyterian church settlement. In fact, some of the leading religious Independents among the political independents actually took part in the new Parliamentary ecclesiastical system. But the one demand the City's

[2] V. Pearl, *London and the Outbreak of the Puritan Revolution: City Government and National Politics, 1625–1643* (Oxford, 1961), pp. 313–17; see also above, ch. 9, p. 485.

political independents could not afford to relinquish was for toleration in religion, since this was the critical condition for their own political survival and especially the survival of their allies among the sects.

To as great an extent as possible, the political independents now eschewed the old tactic of mobilizing their citizen supporters en masse, for this would have tended to alienate their allies within the parliamentary leadership and to repel those citizen moderates with whom they hoped to ally. Sitting uncomfortably between the increasingly dangerous political presbyterians, on the one hand, and, on the other, an emerging movement of religiously separatist and democratic radicals that arose in response to the political presbyterians' offensive, the bulk of London's political independents clung to the hope that the Erastian, mildly tolerationist, antipolitical presbyterian leadership in Parliament would secure for them a favorable settlement. The result was that, as the political presbyterian offensive gathered steam, especially from the summer of 1646, the political independents found themselves under increasingly strong political pressures.

From that time, if not before, what appears to have been a long-standing division within that wing of the City radical alliance that had come to constitute political independency in London began more openly to manifest itself. One group comprised men who may, for descriptive purposes, be roughly termed the more conservative political independents. They appear to have remained more fully dependent on the parliamentary independent leadership, to have sought more diligently to pursue an alliance with religiously more tolerant and politically less royalist and repressive political presbyterians, and to have had greater reluctance to resort to mass mobilization and alliance with the City's most militant forces. The other group contained those who may be termed the more radical political independents. These men appear to have been more willing to risk reliance on the populace and alliance with the separatist congregations and Levellers; they also seem to have remained somewhat more open to relatively democratic ideas. Which individuals fell into each of these categories—which were, in any case, hardly airtight—is difficult to say. Nevertheless, there is reason to believe that the new-merchant leaders, with their multifarious ties of office and interest to the parliamentary regime—forged through service in state finance, army provisioning, and the navy, as well as through participation in Irish and American colonial policy-making—were, before the revolt of the army, especially chary about charting a course independent from that of the parliamentary leadership and were thus, for the most part, to be found among the more conservative political independents. The Independents of John Goodwin's gathered church may be taken, in contrast, as representatives of the more radical political independents, drawn, as they tended to be, from further down the social scale than the "uppermost Independents" and more willing to involve themselves in the mass organizing of the citizenry, to reduce the disciplinary role of the state in religious affairs, and, eventually, to work with the Levellers. These two groups within London's political independency did pursue somewhat divergent tactics, especially in 1647. Nevertheless, all things considered, no section of London's political independency could amass the power to hold off the political presbyterians. All of the City's political independents possessed one last potential trump card, on which all remained in the last analysis entirely dependent—namely, their tightening alliance with an army officer corps, including significant numbers rather close to them ideologically, that became increasingly troubled by the political presbyterians' growing strength.[3]

From December 1645, London's political independents found themselves increasingly endangered by and compelled to respond to the City political presbyterians' ever more daring attempts to impose on Parliament their now explicitly anticongregational, antitolerationist program. Over the previous two months, they had very likely placed their hopes in the revived parliamentary committee for accommodation—established precisely to achieve Presbyterian-Independent unity—to defend them against the political presbyterians and to secure toleration for them. To this purpose, some of the leading Independents held meetings in London with less repressive Presbyterians to discuss what sort of toleration might be mutually acceptable. In this connection, the politically influential, moderate Presbyterian minister Stephen Marshall—father-in-law of the Independent minister Philip Nye—sought, as he had previously, to achieve an agreement with the Independents by granting them toleration, although denying this to the other, explicitly separatist, congregationalists. But in the end, these efforts came to nothing.[4]

Before the end of January 1646, the Independent minister Hugh Peter was thus obliged to return from the army to London to assume a central role in organizing a political independent counterattack. Peter, it will be recalled, had served since the early 1640s as a leading representative of the London radical alliance in general and of the new-merchant leadership in particular. During the middle 1640s he had, in addition, become perhaps the chief public spokesman for the New Model Army, especially its top officers. Peter may have forged his initial connections with Maurice Thomson and William Pennoyer as early as their Massachusetts Bay fishing venture at the end of the 1630s. During the summer of 1642, he had

---

[3] See M. Tolmie, *The Triumph of the Saints: The Separate Churches of London, 1616–1649* (Cambridge, 1977), pp. 142–44ff.

[4] Tolmie, *Triumph of the Saints*, pp. 128–30.

served as chaplain for the new-merchant leadership's Additional Sea Adventure to Ireland, and on his return from Ireland he had published a major propaganda document celebrating its achievements. From the autumn of 1642, along with those other Independent clerical militants John Goodwin and Jeremiah Burroughs, Peter helped give political and ideological leadership to a London radical movement in which new merchants played a central role. He was, in particular, a leading promoter of the radicals' important petition and remonstrance, their statement of political principles of March–April 1643. After the radicals' offensive had largely collapsed in the summer of 1643, Peter joined Maurice Thomson once more, this time in collaboration with three of Thomson's Anglo-Dutch East India interloping partners, on a commission sent out by Parliament to Holland to raise money there for "distressed Protestants in Ireland." This commission returned to England in March 1644, having raised perhaps £30,000 for the cause. Over the following years, Peter was a leading promoter of Parliament's military and political effort, assuming a wide range of organizing and propaganda tasks. During the spring of 1644, he worked with parliamentary committees seeking ways to shut off the king's supplies from the Continent and, partly to this end, served for a time with the parliamentary navy under the command of his longtime patron and political collaborator, the earl of Warwick. On this latter task Peter very likely collaborated, still another time, with the new merchants. Between December 1643 and February 1644, Parliament had passed a series of acts to encourage private individuals to provide ships for the parliamentary navy and to set themselves up as privateers, especially to attack ships trading with ports held by the royalists. The twelve-person committee it established to supervise the sale of prizes taken included the new-merchant leaders Maurice Thomson and Thomas Andrews. From December 1643, Thomson was personally active as a privateer, seeking to intercept ships coming from Amsterdam and Rotterdam to royalist ports and making use of the business agents he maintained in these places to supply intelligence on movements of vessels. From the spring of 1645, Peter served as radical chaplain and propagandist for the New Model Army, attempting to inspire its troops for battle, defending the adherence of many of the soldiers to sectarian religious ideas, and, from time to time, reporting for General Fairfax and the army to Parliament. He thereby won plaudits, and some material compensation, from the parliamentary majority, while earning from the political presbyterians the sneering title of "metropolitan of the Independents." By early 1646, then, Peter had not only reassumed the role he had played in 1642–1643 as a leading organizer and propagandist for London's radical alliance, in particular its emergent political independent wing; he was also providing perhaps the key political link between the army officers and London's political independent leadership.[5]

On 14 January 1646, the magistrates of the City and the Scottish representatives in London, it will be recalled, had taken the Covenant together, and two days later the City government had presented to Parliament a petition that demanded, among other things, the suppression of all private and separate congregations, explicitly including those of the Independents. This ended, for the time being, all hopes for Presbyterian-Independent accommodation, and over the period that followed, in a series of politically charged sermons, Hugh Peter threw down the gauntlet to political presbyterianism in the City. On 23 January, Peter reported to Parliament on Fairfax's success at Dartmouth, and made a point of emphasizing how unified and active were the troops in support of Parliament, even "though their judgments might differ." On 1 February, at Magnum Church in London, Peter argued that "the word uniformity is not in all the scripture, but the word unity [is]." Going on to invoke the Dutch example, as he would again on countless occasions over the next several years, Peter pointed out that "in Holland, an Anabaptist, a Brownist, an Independent, a papist could all live quietly together, and why should they not here? [In] the Army, there are twenty several opinions and they could live quietly together." Peter then took up the City's recent petition for the outlawing of the Independent and separatist churches and preventing toleration. He asserted that the magistrates "were not fit for government," demanded "why an Independent may not be a common councilman," and asked rhetorically, as he would again and again of the common councilors, "Will ye bring yourselves into bondage?"[6] About the same time, in his Thanksgiving Day sermon celebrating the army's capture of Bristol, Peter preached that

> we have overcome Strafford, he was one mountain; we have taken Bristol, that was another mountain; and now the mountains to be overcome [are] slavery and tyranny. [I am] persuaded that if ever this Kingdom [be] brought into slavery, this City [will be] the cause of it. The Parliament [has] voted ease or liberty for tender consciences, and what [has] the common council to do with matters of church government [that] they must petition forsooth [so that] they

[5] L.J. 6: 155, 158; C.J. 3: 198; R. P. Stearns, *The Strenuous Puritan: Hugh Peter, 1598–1660* (Urbana, Ill., 1954), pp. 218–19, 224–33, 235ff.; A.O. 1: 347–52, 392–93; PRO, H.C.A.24/106/100/349, and H.C.A.24/102/119. The ship *Discovery*, jointly owned by Maurice Thomson, Thomas Smythe, Gregory Clement, and Robert South, as well as the earl of Warwick and several others, was granted no fewer than twenty-seven prizes between May 1645 and June 1646 (S. Groenveld, "The English Civil Wars as a Cause of the First Anglo-Dutch War, 1640–1652," *H.J.* 30 [1987]: 551 n. 27; PRO, H.C.A.24/108/62–65). See also above, ch. 8, p. 434.

[6] T. Edwards, *The First and Second Part of Gangraena*, 3d ed. (London, 1646), pt. 1, p. 107.

will have this and they will have that; and if ever this kingdom be brought into bondage, we may thank them.[7]

The City was quick to respond. On 9 February, taking notice of some "strange passages delivered of late in some sermons and otherwise by Mr. [Hugh] Peter, Mr. [William] Hawkins [another leading Independent minister of London] and others within the City tending to the scandal and reproach of the court," the common council appointed a committee to launch an investigation of Peter, Hawkins, and any other like offenders and, at the same time, to examine those members of the common council who had failed to take the Covenant with the rest of the magistrates on 14 January. In late February, to head off the growing wave of repression in the City, representatives of London's gathered churches apparently held a series of meetings for the purpose of organizing a mass petition to Parliament containing between forty thousand and fifty thousand signatures of those opposing political presbyterianism. Nevertheless, this campaign never got off the ground, perhaps because the City's more conservative "uppermost" independents, who appear to have maintained control of the radical cause throughout 1646, still hoped to carry out their battles through more conventional channels.[8]

At least through the end of the winter of 1646, via their own maneuvers and with the help of Parliament, the City's political independents did in fact largely succeed in thwarting the political presbyterians' initiatives. Already wary of the City's political pretensions, the parliamentary majority as noted, had refused, in November 1645, to include the City's demand to control London's suburban militias among the proposals it was to present to the king in the upcoming treaty negotiations. The City would not, however, accept that result, and in mid-December it called on Parliament to reconsider. About a month later, to counter the City, George Snelling, recently elected radical MP from Southwark, presented to Parliament a petition from his district that asked the MPs to allow Southwark to control its militia on its own. Snelling, significantly enough, was an important figure among the new merchants. A former apprentice of the major colonial merchant Joseph Hawes, he had worked in partnership with Maurice Thomson and Samuel Vassall in the trade with Virginia as early as 1639 and with Thomson and Edward Thomson in sending supplies to the Caribbean in 1640, and he had supported the Thomson-led Additional Sea Adventure to Ireland in 1642. In February 1646, Parliament refused again to place the suburban militias under City control.[9]

[7] Ibid.
[8] CLRO, J.Co.Co.40, fols. 166a–166b; Tolmie, *Triumph of the Saints*, p. 146.
[9] M. P. Mahony, "The Presbyterian Party in the Long Parliament, 2 July 1644–3 June 1647"

In mid-March 1646, Parliament also turned down the City's protest against the provision allowing lay commissioners to try unenumerated scandals that had been included in Parliament's proposal for the new church order, and went on to approve its own settlement of the church.[10] Shortly thereafter, to Baillie's dismay, the new merchants' longtime collaborator, the militant opponent of the East India Company John Fowke—who had, in fact, broken politically from the great majority of new merchants in order to support, until this point, the City's petitioning campaign—succeeded in convincing a cautious common council majority to cease its protests over Parliament's new ecclesiastical structure. Apparently hopeful that the City could now be induced to compromise, on 2 April Hugh Peter delivered before Parliament and the City government a thanksgiving sermon for the army's recent successes in Cornwall in which he proposed a political marriage between Parliament and the City and called on the magistrates to be wary of the king's intention to come to London. "Remember what we fought for, prayed for, adventured for," he pleaded, "[and] let not all be lost in the kiss of a royal hand, nor suffer your eyes to be put out with court-glitter and glory."[11]

The fact remains that, by mid-April, the common council, in close concert with the political presbyterian leadership in Parliament and aided and abetted by the Scots, had decided to present its own program for a political settlement to Parliament in the form of the City remonstrance. The City's political independents were thus suddenly obliged to step up their organizing both inside and outside official institutions, and to coordinate their activities to as great an extent as possible with the political independent alliance that still retained leadership in the Commons. On 19 May, having been several times revised in committee, the remonstrance was brought before the common council for a vote. At this point conflict erupted when some of the magistrates sought to interrupt the speech by the common councilor Stephen Estwicke, who was inveighing not only against the remonstrance but more generally against the court itself for having (in Estwicke's opinion) dealt unfairly with Parliament. Estwicke at first refused to back down, asking by what right he was prevented from speaking, but he was obliged eventually to agree to "say nothing to the prejudice of the court" and "the thing was passed over." Estwicke had been an organizer of the City revolution of the winter of 1641–1642 and

---

(University of Oxford, Ph.D. diss., 1973), pp. 196, 251; *C.J.* 4: 429, 441. See also above, ch. 9, pp. 471–72. For Snelling's background, see above, ch. 4, pp. 138, 189, 190 and note 79.

[10] R. Baillie, *Letters and Journals*, ed. D. Laing, 2 vols. (Edinburgh, 1841), 2: 361; Mahony, "Presbyterian Party," pp. 196, 214–16; See also above, ch. 9, pp. 472–74.

[11] V. Pearl, "London's Counter-Revolution," in *The Interregnum*, ed. G. E. Aylmer (London, 1972), p. 35; Baillie, *Letters and Journals* 2: 358; H. Peter, *God's Doing and Man's Duty* (London, 1646), quoted in Stearns, *Strenuous Puritan*, p. 279.

a member of the revolutionary committee of safety appointed at that time, and had emerged in the subsequent period as a leading City radical, a well-known religious Independent, and a major organizer of the new-merchant leadership's projects for interloping in the East Indian trade and for organizing a colony on the island of Assada in the Indian Ocean. Before the vote was taken, the small phalanx of political independents within the common council did its best to support Estwicke and to stem the tide. Alderman Thomas Andrews, like Estwicke a radical militia commissioner, a religious Independent, and a new-merchant leader, active in both the East and West Indies, came out strongly and openly against the remonstrance, as did John Fowke and Robert Tichborne, a leading radical organizer since 1643 (along with eleven others who cannot be identified by name).[12]

The interventions of these councilors did not, of course, prevent the magistrates from approving the remonstrance and presenting it on 26 May to a rather hostile House of Commons. On the day the remonstrance was delivered to the Commons, the radical London MP Isaac Pennington sought to convince Lord Mayor Adams to deliver unopened to the House the letter (proposing terms of a settlement) the City had received the previous day directly from the king. When Pennington reported to the Commons that Adams had refused his request, Col. George Thomson bitterly remarked that had such a thing been done by a lord mayor a year earlier he would have been subject to censure before the House and imprisoned. Thomson, brother and business partner of Maurice Thomson, had recently been chosen recruiter MP for Southwark and would, over the subsequent period, play a leading political role among the more radical forces within the House of Commons.[13]

Meanwhile, led by Hugh Peter and others, the City's political independents had held a series of protest meetings and had launched their own petition campaign to counter the political presbyterians' remonstrance. They initially presented their petition to the common council on 22 May, but the magistrates, led by Lord Mayor Adams, refused to give it serious consideration and advised the petitioners simply to present their document to Parliament themselves. On 31 May 1646, in a sermon at the Three Cranes, Peter attacked the common council's meddling in affairs beyond its jurisdiction, mocked supporters of the Covenant as wishing to make of it an "idol," and denounced those who would compromise everything merely to achieve a settlement with the king. Characterizing the political presbyterians as "refined malignants," he declared that he saw "no more

---

[12] Diary of Thomas Juxon, Dr. Williams's Library, MS 24.50, fols. 78–78v. On Tichborne, see below, note 15.

[13] Diary of Thomas Juxon, Dr. Williams's Library, MS 24.50, fol. 79v.

difference between these times and the first times of troubles than a half crown piece and two shillings and sixpence," and made clear that the political independents' hopes now rested heavily with the godly army. He concluded by voicing his concern that, although the New Model Army, like Jesus, "went about doing good and working miracles," just as "at length the people crucified him, so will men do with this army."[14]

On 2 June 1646, the City's political independents delivered their petition, apparently drawn up by Hugh Peter and reportedly containing twenty thousand signatures, to Parliament. The two men noted by contemporaries as heading this delegation are indicative of the radicals' leadership at this stage. One was Robert Tichborne, a religious Independent, a Salters Hall committeeman, and a City militia commissioner, who had played a leading role in the City's radical offensive in 1643. Although apparently not yet active in the new colonial-interloping trades, Tichborne, a linen draper, would within a few years organize his own interloping syndicate for commerce with the East Indies. In the meantime, he would head one after another of the political independents' initiatives in London. The other presenter appears to have been Samuel Warner, a religious Independent and representative figure from the new-merchant leadership who traded American tobacco in partnership with his brother John Warner and was the father-in-law of Maurice Thomson's brother William. Warner, one of the small number of new merchants and political independents who secured the post of London alderman, had been a militant in the City revolution of 1641–1642 and a member of the original City committee of public safety (militia committee), as well as a leader in the City radical offensive of 1643, having been a treasurer for the committee for a general rising. Both Tichborne and Warner typified the economically more substantial and politically more moderate wing of the London radical alliance that came, in this period, to constitute the leadership of political independency in the City. A deeply divided House of Commons agreed, by the narrow margin of 112 to 108, to thank the petitioners. Sir John Evelyn and Arthur Hasilrig, leaders of the middle-group/war-party alliance, served as tellers for the yeas, evidencing the ongoing cooperation in this period between the independent alliance in the Commons and a London radical movement under the control of the City's political independents.[15]

Perhaps to avoid provoking a confrontation, or in deference to the

[14] T. Edwards, *The Third Part of Gangraena* (London, 1646), pp. 121–22; Diary of Thomas Juxon, Dr. Williams's Library, MS 24.50, fols. 78v–79.

[15] The political presbyterian leaders Denzil Holles and Philip Stapleton were tellers for the noes. (*C.J.* 4: 561; Tolmie, *Triumph of the Saints*, p. 135). On Tichborne, see *D.N.B.*, s.v. "Robert Tichborne," and *Dictionary of Seventeenth-Century Radicals*, vol. 3, s.v. "Robert Tichborne"; see also above, ch. 8, p. 443 and n. 93 and below, note 79.

wishes of the political independent alliance in Parliament, London's political independents at this point cut short their campaign of mass mobilization. Indeed, even as the City was seeking to negotiate directly with the king as an independent authority and welcoming Charles's provocative proposal to come to London, Hugh Peter went to great lengths to propose a compromise. Peter's *Last Report of the English Wars*, published in the summer of 1646, may be taken to represent the political perspective, at that juncture, of at least an important section of London political independency. Its content was clearly designed to appeal to moderate London citizens who feared that a political presbyterian settlement with the Crown would lack constitutional guarantees and who were willing to compromise somewhat on the issue of religious uniformity in the interest of avoiding political confrontation.

Above all, Peter stressed his willingness—and by implication the willingness of his political independent allies—to accept the parliamentary ordering of the church, despite its outwardly Presbyterian structure. Parliament had, of course, diluted the Presbyterian character of the new religious settlement by significant concessions to Erastianism and the promise of mild tolerationism. Even so, for the new-merchant leaders and their nonmerchant allies, many of whom preferred religious Independency, the agreement to go along with a parliamentary settlement that was Presbyterian in structure represented a real concession. Peter could thus appear in a conciliatory light when he called for an end to all criticism of either Presbyterianism or Independency until both of these concepts were better defined.

What was unacceptable, Peter argued, was the political presbyterians' use of Presbyterian religious structures and ideas in the service of political repression and crypto-royalism. This was most evident, he asserted, in the City's demand to exclude all who were not religious Presbyterians from political office. Peter called on the political presbyterians to cease to "make religion a stalking horse to politick ends" and pleaded that the "hispaniolized statesmen" (with the king) then being courted by the City were a far greater threat to the kingdom than the "anabaptists" (in the army, as well as in London).[16]

In the heat of battle the previous spring against the City remonstrance, Peter had already let slip his barely concealed preference for parliamentary supremacy and a moderate republicanism, when he had denounced those Londoners who made a fetish of the need to come to terms at any cost with the king, "as if we could not live without one." Yet in the summer of 1646 Peter was anxious to play down the dilemma of the precise

---

[16] For the previous two paragraphs, see *Mr. Peters Last Report of the English Wars* (London, 1646), pp. 5–8; Stearns, *Strenuous Puritan*, pp. 288–89.

form of constitutional settlement and to stress instead the devastating consequences for London itself of a political presbyterian accommodation with the king. As he warned those still undecided moderates in both London and Parliament, such a settlement would leave their fundamental liberties undefended. In Peter's words, "The influence of the City is such that we could not have wanted it, and therefore their highest design now is to make it royal. . . . I pray improve your interests and let London know that if they think a Parliament sits the quieter by being so near them so I think when the Parliament doors are shut up at Westminster, their shops will hardly stand open in London."[17]

In his *Last Report* Peter did not hesitate to lay out, in some detail, far-reaching plans for the postrevolutionary period, offering invaluable evidence of the programmatic thinking at this point of those political independent, quasi-republican elements in the City and the army that Peter represented. Perhaps the most remarkable aspect of Peter's *Last Report*—especially in view of the fact that the politico-constitutional character of the Civil War settlement was still so uncertain—is the extraordinary prominence given to long-term strategic issues of English foreign affairs. Peter demanded in the first place an immediate invasion of Ireland "to teach the peasants liberty." This proposal may have had as one of its aims unifying leading City political independents and political presbyterians around their common interest in the original Irish adventure and the conquest of Ireland. Both political presbyterians and political independents in London had watched with increasing frustration as Parliament had seemingly lost interest in the takeover of Ireland and the promised shareout to Londoners of massive quantities of Irish lands that would accompany that conquest. Meanwhile, Peter proposed, the nation should send delegations to Sweden, the United Provinces, the Swiss cantons, and other religiously sympathetic powers to begin forging an international Protestant alliance. Such an alliance, he added, would be far more attractive to any of these potential allies if England could offer a strong navy; indeed, as Peter would have occasion to reemphasize at numerous points in the following period, building English naval power had to be a top priority. Finally, Peter did not hesitate to put forward, in explicit terms, a vision of the sort of large-scale imperialist campaign about which the new-merchant leadership had fantasized for years—a two-pronged attack in the West and East Indies. As he stated, "If our back door were well-shut at home, how might Euphrates be dried up; I mean the West Indies and the East too offer themselves to our devotion. . . . Let us still remember the support of trade is the strength of the island; discountenance the merchant and take beggary by the hand." For Peter, Protestant imperial warfare would long

---

[17] Edwards, *Third Part of Gangraena*, p. 121; *Mr. Peters Last Report*, p. 11.

since have occupied England's energies "were we not more effeminate than our predecessors in Queen Elizabeth's time." As he continued, "I must confess I am divided between Ireland and the Palatinate, only I quiet myself in this that we may do both." Such sentiments are explicable only by reference to Peter's longtime intimate connections with both the new-merchant and landed-class wings of England's Puritan commercial imperial leadership. Both the colonizing aristocrats and the new merchants had, of course, been voicing similar demands using similar rhetoric for at least a quarter of a century, and Peter was now undoubtedly functioning, at least partly, as their mouthpiece. Peter's emphasis on these ideas at this time is indicative of the prominence they continued to occupy in the plans for a settlement of at least some of the important sections of City political independency—sections that would in fact gain the power to begin to implement them under the Commonwealth.[18]

Of course, despite Peter's pleas, the overwhelming majority within the City government persisted in its royalist-tinged quest for a repressive Presbyterian settlement—a course that, to Peter and his friends, was supremely self-destructive. As Peter had complained on another occasion, the political presbyterians who ruled London were men "that never lived beyond the view of the smoke of their chimneys, that measure States and Kingdoms with their interests, by their private shopwards"—an evaluation that accords very well with the interpretation of political presbyterianism presented in the previous chapter. The political presbyterians failed to share the vision held by Peter and his friends of a world to conquer under a new regime in which parliamentary liberties were secure. Equally to the point, they continued to be blinded, in their single-minded obsession with order, to the dangers even to their own continued rule that might result from the restoration of an untrammeled monarchy. As Peter's longtime collaborator Jeremiah Burroughs, the Independent minister and political radical, put it in a sermon presented at his St. Michael's Cornhill lectureship just after the publication of Peter's *Last Report*, the City was "unthankful to the army, the instruments of their deliverance, by whose means they enjoyed the clothes they wore, the bread they eat, the trading they had. . . . [If] the [army] would stand upon terms or capitulate . . . what might they [the Londoners] have then?" In this situation, the fate of the political independents of the City came increasingly to depend, explicitly or implicitly, on the fate of the army. Peter therefore made sure to emphasize in his *Last Report* that the dissolution of the army "ought not to be a work of haste"; it "was hardly gotten, and I wish it may be as hardly disbanded."[19]

[18] *Mr. Peters Last Report*, pp. 6–10.
[19] Peter is quoted in Pearl, "London's Counter-Revolution," p. 34; for Burroughs, see Edwards, *Third Part of Gangraena*, p. 107; *Mr. Peters Last Report*, p. 5 (for final quotation).

During the remainder of 1646, as the political presbyterians pursued their plans for the removal of the Scottish military forces from England in preparation for an all-out attack on the army, the political independent leaders persisted, by and large, in projecting an image of responsible moderation. In June and July, certain elements within the more radical wing of London political independency, notably those from the gathered congregation of the Independent minister John Goodwin, apparently attempted for a time to work more closely with the Levellers. In roughly the same period, John Price, another John Goodwin Independent, put forward arguments going far in the direction of a full-fledged parliamentary supremacy. But, ultimately, the political independent leadership in the City went out of its way to head off a series of petition drives, emanating from the separatist congregations, to protest the imprisonment of the Leveller leaders William Larner, John Lilburne, and Richard Overton.[20]

In the meantime, the City's political independents seem to have sought to forge closer ties with the New Model Army. In fact, throughout the summer of 1646, while projecting a compromise settlement in London, Hugh Peter and other Independent ministers simultaneously sought to prepare the army for a London-led onslaught. Peter is reported in June, at Hedington Fort, as "incensing the army against the City, telling them that after you have done all this, they would not have you live nor enjoy any places." In July, he warned the soldiers again that "though you have conquered the kingdom, done all this service" and now might "expect your arrears, look to enjoy your liberties, yea and expect preferments, . . . it may be you shall be cast into a stinking prison." Finally, in August, preaching at the Stepney pulpit of the Independent radicals Jeremiah Burroughs and William Greenhill, Peter actually expressed the belief that a new war was in the offing. "Though now [you] had a month or two, a time of cessation . . . yet [you] must look shortly for war." The king had rejected the Newcastle propositions, said Peter, and "for refusing the offer of peace, he might never have it more, but he and his children . . . ere long might beg their bread."[21]

Nevertheless, whatever their attempts to ready the army for conflict with the political presbyterians, the City's political independents themselves offered little overt leadership against the growing wave of repression in London. Their temporizing stance in the face of the increasingly unrestrained campaign launched by the municipality against religious and political dissidents of all kinds became the object of bitter recrimination from rising, militant forces in the City. Indeed, the Levellers and their allies won increasing credibility and support for their political ideas in this

---

[20] Tolmie, *Triumph of the Saints*, pp. 146–49; J. Price, *The City Remonstrance Remonstrated* (London, 1646), pp. 7ff.

[21] Edwards, *Third Part of Gangraena*, pp. 24, 27, 122–24.

period precisely because of their willingness to stand up against the political presbyterians' onslaught—as the political independents would not. [22]

In the end, however, the political independents were forced back into the arms of the sectarian and democratic radicals by the political presbyterians' unremitting attack. As late as February 1647, London's political independents decided to quash a proposed radical petition campaign to counter the City's very threatening petitions of the previous December. These petitions had called for the disbanding of the army, the repression of separate congregations and of lay preachers, and the removal from all government positions of those who refused to take the Covenant. During the winter of 1646–1647, moreover, following the Scots' withdrawal from England, the middle-group/war-party alliance definitively lost its majority in the Commons, and the City's political independents, who had so much relied on the power of that alliance, found themselves in a highly exposed position. Meanwhile, the Leveller leaders, strengthened by the adherence to their cause of a significant section of the separatist community, had launched their own courageous campaign and appear to have attracted the support of a growing number of lower-class, congregationally inclined citizens. The upshot was that at least some important elements within the more radical wing of City political independency reached the conclusion that they had little choice but to throw their support behind the Levellers' important March petition. [23]

The fact remains that London's radical alliance lacked the requisite power to turn back a political presbyterian attack, which disposed of the authority of the City government, and appears to have commanded wide support throughout London's politically active population. As the political presbyterians reached the peak of their influence, the City's political independents in general and the new merchants in particular were obliged to watch helplessly as the last bastion of their power within the official City was demolished. As late as the early spring of 1647, the old City militia committee, established in early 1642 and enlarged during the radical offensive of the spring of 1643, continued to control the City's armed forces. But in view of the radical political makeup of this body, the political presbyterian magistrates could not possibly leave it in place. On 26 April 1647, with Parliament's approval, the magistrates selected a new thirty-one-man militia committee, which included only eight of the men who had been serving on the committee until that point. Only four of the commissioners appointed by the political presbyterians had served on the original, revolutionary committee of public safety (militia committee) of

[22] Pearl, "London's Counter-Revolution," p. 37.
[23] Tolmie, *Triumph of the Saints*, pp. 150–53; Mahony, "Presbyterian Party," p. 334.

January 1642.[24] Among the commissioners removed was the entire contingent of colonial-interloping merchants from the old committee, including John Warner, Samuel Warner, Randall Mainwaring, James Russell, Nathan Wright, William Barkeley, Owen Rowe, and Stephen Estwicke, as well as John Fowke, the Levant–East India Company oppositionist and Courteen collaborator who had become allied with them.

At the same meeting of the common council at which they remodeled the militia committee, the political presbyterians sought to have all of the councilors retake the Covenant as a requirement for retaining their positions. When the councilors Stephen Estwicke and John Brett attempted to resist this test, the common council expelled them from the court and had them forcibly thrown out of the meeting, citing "their misdemeanors in the court and willful disobedience to same, to the great disturbance and disquiet of the whole court and retardation to the right proceedings thereof in great contempt of this court." Estwicke, a central figure among the City's political independents and a new-merchant leader, had come under fierce attack by the magistrates a year previously for having sought to oppose the City remonstrance. John Brett, who was the son-in-law of the longtime City radical and new-merchant leader Randall Mainwaring, had, during the 1640s, entered into the new trades with New England, Guinea, and Barbados (and would end up a major landowner in Massachusetts, as well as a patron of Dissenters, after the Restoration).[25]

During the spring of 1647, the Levellers and their sectarian allies brought one after another petition to Parliament, but, according to William Walwyn, "the uppermost Independents stood aloof and looked on, whilst Mr. Stasmore, Mr. Highland, Mr. Davis, Mr. Cooper, Mr. Thomas Lambe of the Spital and very many more for many weeks plied the House." It was only when the ranks of the army began to move decisively against the political presbyterians that the City's leading political independents decided to come out openly and definitively in opposition. On 22 May 1647, the royalist lord mayor John Gayre received information that a number of the City's key political independents, who previously had opposed doing so, had made a decision to take advantage of the army's discontent to join the London mass movement against political presbyte-

[24] Compare A.O. 1: 990–91 (the full committee which was serving until Apr. 1647), with CLRO, J.Co.Co.40, fol. 215v (the political presbyterian militia committee of Apr. 1647) and A.O. 1: 5 (the original militia committee of Jan. 1642). The eight holdovers on the political presbyterians' committee were John Langham, John Bellamy, Tempest Milner, Richard Turner, Sir John Wollaston, James Bunce, William Gibbs, and Philip Skippon, of whom the last four had served on the original militia committee of January 1642.

[25] Diary of Thomas Juxon, Dr. Williams's Library, MS 24.50, fols. 107v–108; CLRO, J.Co.Co.40, fol. 215v. On Brett, see PRO, S.P. 16/496/59; PRO, will of John Brett, 1685/6 PCC Lloyd 1. See also above, ch. 4, pp. 138, 165.

rianism. About the same time, the army grandees, notably Oliver Cromwell, under pressure from the rank-and-file, decided to assume leadership of the army revolt, and their decision undoubtedly had a decisive impact on London's political independents. A series of meetings was held at Cromwell's house in London at the end of May between Cromwell and other army officers, and other meetings brought together City political independents, Levellers, and apparently Cromwell himself. The upshot was that the army leadership decided to secure the artillery at Oxford and to seize the king. Shortly thereafter, a newly united City radical movement launched its "sharp" petition against the political presbyterians in the City government and in Parliament, presenting their document to the Commons on 2 June 1647. A day later Cornet Joyce captured the king at Holmby and Oliver Cromwell left London to return to the army. Hugh Peter seems to have played a decisive role at this critical juncture in convincing Cromwell to respond positively to the demands of the soldiers and to take the lead of the army. Peter fled London for the army with Cromwell on 4 June, and, during the course of their journey, according to some sources, sought to convince Cromwell to bring the king to justice, try him, and cut off his head. Over the following period he sought to give inspiration to the soldiers' revolt and, very likely, helped ensure coordination between the army and London political independency.[26]

London's Political Independents Come to Power

THE ARMY'S INVASION OF LONDON

In late July 1647, the army began its march on London to unseat the political presbyterians. Predictably, one of its first demands was the reestablishment of the old City militia committee, which had been dominated by political independents. An overawed Parliament passed an ordinance to that effect on 23 July 1647. By this time, however, Parliament's actions merely reflected the real contest for power being waged between the army and the City. When a crowd of political presbyterian citizens besieged the Houses for their capitulation to the army, the MPs meekly reinstalled the political presbyterian militia committee. Consequently, at the time the army finally entered London on 6 August 1647 it had still to confront a hostile City government that retained control of its own armed forces.

The army's political initiatives after capturing London in 1647 may be

[26] W. Walwyn, *Walwyn's Just Defence* (1649) in *The Leveller Tracts, 1647–1653*, ed. W. Haller and G. Davies (New York, 1944), p. 356; Mahony, "Presbyterian Party," p. 398; Tolmie, *Triumph of the Saints*, p. 155. On Peter and Cromwell, see R. W. Pacy, "Spiritual Combat: The Life and Personality of Hugh Peter, a Puritan Minister" (State University of New York at Buffalo, Ph.D. diss., 1978), pp. 198–200.

viewed as constituting the preliminary steps toward the completion of the City revolution that the radicals had failed to achieve on their own in 1642–1643. The army's first move was to establish its own City militia, and the militia commission appointed by Parliament at the army's behest in September 1647 provides striking evidence for the continuity between the City radical leadership of the early 1640s and that of City political independency, for the close ties between the army officer leadership and the more moderate, political independent wing of the City's radical alliance, and for the central position within the leadership of London political independency of the new-merchant leadership. Of the thirty-six persons appointed to the new army committee, no fewer than twenty-one had served on the City militia committee during 1642–1643, the period in which that body provided the key institutional base for the City radical movement.[27] Considering that the army-appointed committee included, in addition, such established revolutionaries of the 1641–1643 period who had not previously served on the London militia committee as Edmund Harvey, John Venn, and Mark Hildesley, it can be seen how far the invading army leadership looked to the long-eclipsed alliance of City radical forces to represent its political needs.[28]

Among the longtime radicals on the army-appointed militia committee, new-merchant leaders occupied a very prominent place. The army-appointed militia committee included all the colonial-interloping merchants who had served on the militia committee during the period of City revolution and rising radicalism of 1642–1643, except for Randall Mainwaring and Nathan Wright—that is, John Warner, Samuel Warner, James Russell, Owen Rowe, Stephen Estwicke, Thomas Andrews, and William Barkeley, as well as their friend John Fowke. Joining these traders on the militia committee were two additional new-merchant leaders who were partners of Maurice Thomson's: the colonial trader and interloper in the East Indies Samuel Moyer, and Rowland Wilson, a wealthy City trader from a company merchant family, but also a religious Independent who was at this time becoming associated with Maurice Thomson in the Guinea trade. Also among the militia commissioners were Francis Allein, the

---

[27] A.O. 1: 1007 for the militia committee of 2 September 1647. For militia committee appointments of the 1642–1643 period, see A.O. 1: 5; CLRO, J.Co.Co.40, fols. 37v–39v, 47, 67. The holdovers from the militia committee of 1642–1643 were Isaac Pennington, Sir John Wollaston, Thomas Atkins, John Warner, Thomas Andrews, John Fowke, William Gibbs, Philip Skippon, Richard Turner, Sr., Samuel Warner, William Barkeley, William Hobson, James Russell, Owen Rowe, Thomas Player, Stephen Estwicke, Robert Tichborne, Richard Turner, Jr., Tempest Milner, William Antrobus, and Alexander Normington.

[28] For Venn, see above, ch. 7, pp. 313–14, 337–38; Pearl, London, pp. 187–89. For Harvey, see above, ch. 8, p. 443 and n. 93; M. Noble, The Lives of the Regicides, 2 vols. (London, 1798), 1: 337–38. For Hildesley, a follower of John Goodwin, see J. E. Farnell, "The Usurpation of Honest London Householders: Barebone's Parliament," E.H.R. 82 (1967): 29.

Bermuda Company activist who had been a partner in Maurice Thomson's original customs farming syndicate of 1643; William Hobson, the father-in-law of Maurice Thomson's partner Samuel Pennoyer; and Richard Salway, not himself a colonial trader but an interloper in the Merchant Adventurers' trade and the son-in-law of the new merchant Richard Waring. If the latter three are included within the new-merchant group, the new-merchant leadership controlled more than one-third of the positions on the political independents' militia committee.[29]

Shortly after taking power, the army also deprived the political presbyterians of their control over the militias of the City's suburbs. In early 1647, the newly emergent political presbyterian majority in Parliament had granted the City's long-standing demand to control the suburban militia committees. But when it entered London, the army reversed this decision, restored the suburban militias to suburban control, and had new suburban militia commissions appointed. Among the members of these new army-appointed suburban militia commissions, there were small knots of important new-merchant leaders. On the Tower Hamlets body were Maurice Thomson and his radical colonial-interloping associates William Pennoyer, Samuel Moyer, William Willoughby, and Martin Noel. The large Southwark commission included Maurice's trading partner, George Snelling, a recruiter MP, as well as such other colonial merchants as George Pasfield, Maurice's brother George Thomson (also a recruiter MP), and Robert Haughton, a backer of Thomson's Additional Sea Adventure to Ireland who was active in the Bermuda Company, as well as in the trade with New England, where he had relatives and business partners and where he had recently invested in the Saugus Ironworks project. The inclusion of these men on these bodies points once again to the new merchants' pivotal position in the nucleus of the City radical movement and their importance in welding together the diverse elements of which that movement was composed.[30]

Aside from refashioning the City's armed forces to its own liking, the army carried out a small but well-aimed purge of top municipal office-holders. On 24 October 1647 Parliament impeached, at the army's instigation, five men who had played a leading role in the political presbyterian thrust of the previous summer, charging them with threatening the Com-

[29] For all of the aforementioned, except for Salway, see above, ch. 7 and ch. 8. For Salway's family connections, see Society of Genealogists, Boyd's Index of London Citizens: 28675. For his trade with Amsterdam, see PRO, S.P.46/80/136, 143. Cf. *Dictionary of Seventeenth-Century Radicals*, vol. 3, s.v. "Richard Salway."

[30] *A.O.* 1: 1010, 1057–58. For Haughton, see J. H. Lefroy, *Memorials of the Bermudas*, 2 vols. (Bermuda, 1877–1879), 1: 590; E. N. Hartley, *Ironworks on the Saugus* (Norman, Okla., 1957), pp. 71–73; B. Bailyn, *The New England Merchants in the Seventeenth Century* (Cambridge, Mass., 1955), pp. 79–80.

mons and fomenting a new war. These included the leading Levant–East India Company merchants and crypto-royalists John Gayre, who had been lord mayor during the antiarmy offensive of 1647, and Alderman John Langham. Four days later a body of soldiers was sent to common hall to make sure that the choice of a new lord mayor would conform to the army's wishes. The man elected was none other than the leading colonial tobacco trader and longtime leading radical politician (though religious Presbyterian) John Warner.[31]

While attempting to weaken the grip of the political presbyterians and royalists in the City, the army leadership and London's political independents also sought to distance themselves as much as possible from their sometimes indispensable, but politically problematic, allies among the separatists and Levellers. Immediately following the army's march into London, several Leveller leaders demanded that the army council establish popular citizens' militias for the City, the Tower, and Southwark. This proposal revived, in a different form, the old Salters Hall project for an autonomous citizens' army. But neither the army leadership nor the City's mainstream political independents could approve this plan, for they were painfully aware of the fragility of their own position within a City still strongly influenced by the political presbyterians. The army instead established a new Tower regiment under the command of Robert Tichborne, the former Salters Hall militant and religious Independent who, as noted, had emerged during the middle 1640s as one of the top leaders of London's political independents. The underlying conflict between the more moderate and more extreme wings of the long-standing but always tenuous London radical alliance had thus resurfaced.[32]

By the autumn of 1647, the Levellers were approaching the height of their influence, marked by the circulation of the *Agreement of the People* and the Putney debates. On 9 November 1647, Parliament rejected the *Agreement of the People* and immediately thereafter the Levellers countered with a mass petition. At just this juncture, a pamphlet entitled *A Declaration by Congregational societies in and about the City of London, as well of those commonly called Anabaptist as others* was published. In the name of "the generality of people fearing god," this work repudiated such outrageous doctrines as polygamy, the community of property, and parity, while interpreting liberty narrowly as religious liberty. It was a scarcely concealed attempt by leading congregationalists to discredit the Levellers by implying that the Levellers adhered to these awful notions, and, in the process, to distance the congregationalists from their former radical allies. Although the *Declaration* was published anonymously, its authors later

[31] R. R. Sharpe, *London and the Kingdom*, 3 vols. (London, 1894), 2: 266–67.
[32] Tolmie, *Triumph of the Saints*, pp. 162–63.

identified themselves, and among them were several of London's leading political independents. They included Richard Shute, a religious Independent and colonial commercial and political partner of Maurice Thomson's, who had helped lead the City's radical offensive of 1642–1643; William Greenhill, the Independent pastor and lecturer of Stepney who had long collaborated closely with the recently deceased Independent minister Jeremiah Burroughs, and was himself a leading London radical and new merchant ally (with Maurice Thomson himself among his flock); John Simpson, the Independent ministerial radical, whom the militant inhabitants of St. Dunstan's-in-the-East, prominently including Maurice Thomson and his friends, had nominated to be their lecturer; and Thomas Brookes, the Independent lecturer who became minister in 1648 of St. Margaret New Fish Street and who was patronized by such new-merchant leaders as William Pennoyer, Samuel Pennoyer, and Stephen Estwicke.[33]

While attempting at one and the same time to displace the political presbyterian–royalist alliance and to hold off the Levellers, sections among the City's political independents now sought to exploit the growth of the mass radical movement in the army and the City to begin to advance their own preferred political alternatives. Their first efforts in this direction took place inside the East India Company at the beginning of September 1647, less than a month following the army's entry into London. It will be remembered that at this very moment the new merchants were nearing the high point of their attack on the old guard of the East India Company. From the mid-1640s, they had been attempting to plant a new colony off the coast of East Africa on the island of Assada, while sending out a series of interloping trading voyages to India in violation of the East India Company's old monopoly privileges. Simultaneously, they were infiltrating the company itself in preparation for taking it over from the inside.

Lacking secure monopoly privileges, the company's old leadership had been unable to attract money to its joint stock, and when Parliament refused in early 1647 to renew the company charter, it looked as if the corporation might collapse entirely. The East India Company temporarily saved itself in the summer of 1647 by launching the so-called Second General Voyage independently of the main joint stock. But for members of the company's old guard this was a Pyrrhic victory, for they succeeded in raising this "temporary" joint stock only by turning for assistance to the colonial-interloping leadership. The new merchants seized on the old leadership's desperate situation, supplied massive investment funds to the new undertaking, and thereby secured for themselves powerful positions within the company's directorate. No fewer than six of sixteen special di-

---

[33] Ibid., pp. 170–71. See above, ch. 8, p. 424.

rectors chosen to manage the Second General Voyage were drawn from among the new-merchant leadership, including Maurice Thomson, Thomas Andrews, Nathan Wright, Samuel Moyer, Jeremy Blackman, and William Ryder. The first four of these merchants would serve on one or another of the army-appointed political independent militia committees in the London area in 1647. Their struggle inside the East India Company was heavily commercial in character, but it also had an important and explicit political thrust.[34]

According, then, to the East India Company court minutes of 1 September 1647, some of those merchants who had just been "chosen to be managers of the affairs of this general voyage do refuse to take the oath which every man that is admitted into the freedom of this society takes. Whereupon some of these gentlemen declared that there were some things mentioned in the said oath which they conceived were not requisite." A "great debate" reportedly followed, which ended with the appointment of a committee, consisting of representatives of each side, to mediate the conflict. What was at stake was quite clear: as the interloper in the East Indies Alderman Thomas Andrews would explain, some of the new directors whom he represented refused to take the oath to become company freemen so long as this oath contained the "expression of allegiance to the King's majesty." Those who would not take the oath were none other than the colonial-interloping leaders who had just joined the company. This is evidenced by the fact that the new merchants Maurice Thomson, William Pennoyer, William Harris, and Jeremy Blackman, as well as Alderman Thomas Andrews, were the ones chosen to sit on the mediating committee as representatives of the oath refusers. These men were all very active in the trades with the Americas, as well as interloping in the East Indies. They can be taken to represent the whole group of interlopers who had recently entered the company, and they obstinately refused to compromise on this issue. It is a sign of the new merchants' intransigence at this point in their stand against the monarchy, as well as of their indispensability to the company, that the old, heavily royalist leadership was forced to give in to them. Despite the threat of such diehard representatives of the company's old guard as Thomas Rich and John Holloway to withdraw their investments in the joint stock if the oath requirement was dropped, the old directorate agreed to allow the new men to enter the Second General Voyage and to take up leadership positions without having to declare their allegiance to the king.[35]

A good idea of the new merchants' thinking at this point concerning a

[34] *C.C.M.E.I.C. 1644–1649*, pp. xv, 218, 227.

[35] India House Library, East India Company Court Minutes, vol. B/24, pp. 7–10 (1–8 Sept. 1647). For Alderman Andrews's formal refusal to take the oath, 22 September 1647, see *H.M.C., Tenth Report, Appendix*, pt. 4, p. 167.

political settlement comes from the pronouncements of their longtime intimate, political collaborator, and effective spokesman, the Independent minister Hugh Peter. In his *A Word for the Armie*, published in London in the early autumn of 1647, Peter sought first to defend the army's unconstitutional actions—its defiance of Parliament, its entry into London, and its remodeling of the City government. "The first force ever put upon the Parliament was long before this, and that nearer hand: did not the City *Remonstrance* hang like a petard upon the Parliament door week after week . . . till [Parliament] were forced to speak pure *London?*"[36]

Peter went on to sketch the outlines of a Civil War settlement. He began by repeating his long-standing demand for a tolerationist religious order, although one backed up by the state. To ensure that religious practice stayed within decent Christian limits, Peter proposed establishing "a committee for union betwixt all men truly godly, that we may swim in one channel . . . with free and loving debates allowed in every county that we may convince not confound one another." The idea was that "no magistrate in matters of religion meddle further than as a nursing father, and then all children shall be fed, though they have several faces and shapes." To support preachers, he suggested "tithes or something of analogy to them brought into a common stock in every county." Finally, to bring the reformation to completion, especially by bringing the Word of God to "the dark corners of the land," Peter outlined a proposal he had first presented in the spring of 1646. "Two or three itinerant preachers [should] be sent by the state into every county," he asserted, "and a committee of godly men, ministers, gentlemen, and others [should] send out men of honesty, holiness, and parts into all counties recommended." Overall, Peter's program constituted precisely the sort of Independent religious settlement generally desired by the more substantial and less radical elements among London's political independents, for it combined a significant degree of religious pluralism with enough state intervention to ensure religious order, official support for ministers, and the vigorous propagation of the gospel.[37]

Although Peter stopped short of an outright call for a republic, asserting that not "good laws but good men must save kingdoms," his references to republican Venice and the United Provinces were indicative of the models he was working from. That Peter intended at least a severe demotion—if not outright elimination—of the monarchy was evidenced in his proposal for a council of state of ten or thirteen persons to serve as a permanent executive advisory committee, not to the king but to Parlia-

---

[36] H. Peter, *A Word for the Armie and Two Words to the Kingdome* (London, 1647), pp. 5–6.

[37] For this and the following three paragraphs, see *A Word for the Armie*, pp. 10–14. For Peter's advancing of proposals for propagating the gospel, see C. Hill, "Propagating the Gospel," in *Historical Essays, 1600–1750*, ed. H. E. Bell and R. L. Ollard (London, 1963), pp. 39–43.

ment. A version of this plan would, of course, actually be implemented with the establishment of the council of state for the Rump Parliament. Peter also called for frequent parliamentary elections and the redrawing of parliamentary electoral districts, demands that would draw strong support from among the more radical political independents during the following period. Significantly absent from Peter's program was any provision for the extension of the franchise so central to the concerns of the Levellers.

Aside from state-guided tolerationism and a nondemocratic version of parliamentary supremacy, Peter put forward a series of broad-ranging proposals for the reform of governmental administration and the law. To combat corruption, he asked that sufficient "salaries be appointed to all places of trust that temptations to deceit not take hold of officers." He demanded the reform of the laws concerning imprisonment for debt. Above all, he stressed the importance of "quick justice," the reform of legal procedures to make them swifter, cheaper, and less exploitable by lawyers.

Finally, Peter returned to his old theme of Puritan commercial imperialism. He repeated his desire that "merchants may have all manner of encouragement." He suggested that English commerce would be the stronger "if strangers even Jews be admitted to trade" through the relaxation of civil and commercial restrictions on resident aliens. No doubt in part with his new-merchant allies in mind, he demanded, once more, "that the work of Ireland may not thus still be made a mock work, but that the business be carried on strenuously and vigorously by men to be confided [in]." He called again, moreover, for renewed imperial action in the Americas, asserting that the time and energy being spent in legal quarrels "were better bestowed upon the West Indies to which we have been so often called, and would soon make an end of Europe's troubles by drying up that Euphrates."

Peter's program was aimed to appeal to, and enunciate a program for, that broad alliance of radical, but non-Leveller, forces—especially in London, notably the new-merchant leadership—that had supported the army's march into London and that now looked to the army as the catalyst for reform, if not revolution. None of Peter's proposals was a utopian dream. All would, in fact, be implemented, or at least put forward with some chance of success, under the Commonwealth, with the active involvement and support of the City radicals, new-merchant leaders prominently in the forefront.[38]

One final proposal advanced by Peter in *A Word for the Armie* seems at first to be somewhat out of context, namely, that the "customs [from ex-

[38] See below, chs. 11 and 12.

ternal trade] . . . may be in very choice hands." But this suggestion appears less anomalous when it is noticed that Peter's pamphlet was published on 11 October 1647. On that very day, the fiery war-party radical Miles Corbet, a longtime friend of Peter's and of the City radical movement, brought into Parliament a proposal from the radical new-merchant leaders Maurice Thomson, Thomas Andrews, Richard Shute, Stephen Estwicke, and Thomas Smythe that they be given the customs commission in place of the syndicate of political presbyterians and neo-royalists that had taken it over in 1645. Peter's reference to the customs was surely inserted into his pamphlet to coincide with and to support the petition by these men. It shows just how closely Peter and the new-merchant leadership were working at this critical juncture.[39]

The army's invasion of London in 1647 and the uncompleted revolution it initiated there marked a crucial phase in the maturation of political independency in the City. The easy collaboration between the City's political independents and the army at the time of the army's invasion revealed the close working relationship that already existed between the politically less extreme and economically more substantial leaders of the old City radical movement and sections of the army's officer leadership. It also foreshadowed the alliance of radical forces, nationally and in London, that ultimately would carry through the revolution of 1648–1649, forsaking its middle-group allies on the one hand, while holding off and ultimately destroying the democratic and separatist movement within its own ranks on the other.

To explain fully how the political independents in London had forged ties with the political independents in the army and Parliament during the course of the 1640s would require further research. However, part of the answer is certainly to be found in the collaboration that took place between the City trained bands (militia), which were to a significant degree under radical leadership, and the regular army. Important City radicals such as Owen Rowe, Robert Tichborne, William Underwood, John Venn, John Warner, John Towse, and Rowland Wilson, who held top officer positions in the City militia, built up close associations with some of the politically influential officers of the New Model Army (and its predecessors) through joint military operations and related activities. Some of them, such as Venn and Wilson, as well as other leading radical citizens such as Richard Salway, actually became officers in the parliamentary army itself. Contact between leading City and army political independents may also have been

---

[39] *A Word for the Armie*, p. 11; *C.J.* 5: 331. Thomas Smythe was, as noted, a shipowning partner of Maurice Thomson and the new-merchant leaders Thomas Vincent and Gregory Clement, along with the earl of Warwick, and was active with them in anti-Spanish and antiroyalist privateering. (See above, note 5.) For further evidence on the collaboration between Smythe and the new-merchant leadership, see below, pp. 525, 526, 529, 554.

established through the work of such key City new-merchant radicals as Owen Rowe, Stephen Estwicke, William Pennoyer, Richard Hill, Maurice Thomson, Richard Shute, Thomas Andrews, Samuel Vassall, and a number of others in army provisioning. Rowe actually became the central arms administrator for Parliament's army under the earl of Essex and supervised the officers of the ordnance. Common ties to the gathered churches of London and to their ministers offered still another basis for building connections between army and City political independents.[40]

Finally, there can be little doubt that the multifarious organizations, committees, and associations that grew up in this period to oversee religious and political, as well as commercial, activities in the English colonies in America were essential to consolidating that alliance of political independents which connected army, parliamentary, and City radicals in 1647–1649. The Additional Sea Adventure to Ireland of 1642 marked a crucial stage in the construction of a network of activists interested in Puritan imperial designs; that network would serve as a basis for radical political organizing throughout the whole course of the 1640s. This project involved not only all the new-merchant leaders and many of their militant London friends, but also key Parliament- or army-based leaders such as Sir Arthur Hasilrig and Oliver Cromwell. In addition, Parliament's committee on plantations proved disproportionately attractive to radical elements; twenty-two of its members during the Civil War period were from the House of Commons, and these included such war-party radicals as Sir Arthur Hasilrig, Sir Henry Vane, Dennis Bond, Miles Corbet,

[40] For the militia officers, see *Names, Dignities, and Places of All the Colonels . . . of the City of London* (London, 1642). For Venn's, Wilson's, and Salway's military careers, see *Dictionary of Seventeenth-Century Radicals*, vol. 3, s.v. "John Venn," "Rowland Wilson," and "Richard Salway." On the provisioners, see, for example, *C.J.* 3: 200, 204, 490, 492; *L.J.* 6: 174, 175, 179, 180 (Estwicke); *C.J.* 3: 316, 330–31 (Pennoyer and Hill); PRO, S.P. 16/539, pt. 4/503; *C.J.* 5: 513 (Thomson, Andrews, Shute, Estwicke); *H.M.C., Fifth Report, Appendix*, p. 104; *L.J.* 6: 104 (Rowe); *L.J.* 9: 180 (Vassall); *C.J.* 2: 753 (John Bradley). For Rowe in the central arms administration, see *Dictionary of Seventeenth-Century Radicals*, vol. 3, s.v. "Owen Rowe." Citizens and officers came together in such London gathered congregations as, for example, Thomas Goodwin's church, of which the militant army leader Col. Edward Whalley, and perhaps also the officers Sir William Constable and Sir Matthew Boynton, as well as the colonial-interloping trader Samuel Moyer, were members (Tolmie, *Triumph of the Saints*, pp. 105, 188). Col. John Okey was a member of the gathered church of the leading Independent William Greenhill, who was himself closely connected with such new merchant radicals as Maurice Thomson, Edward Thomson, and William Pennoyer. See above, ch. 8, p. 423. The important London congregation of George Cockayn included the citizen radical leaders Robert Tichborne and Rowland Wilson, along with Henry Ireton's brother John Ireton. Cockayn became chaplain to the army leader Gen. Charles Fleetwood (although it is not clear whether the Fleetwood-Cockayn relationship dated back to the 1640s, the relevant period in this context). See J. B. Marsh, *The Story of Hare Court* (London, 1871), pp. 38, 77; C. B. Cockett, "George Cockayn," *Congregational Historical Society Transactions* 12 (1933–1936): 225–35; *Dictionary of Seventeenth-Century Radicals*, vol. 1, s.v. "George Cockayn" and "Charles Fleetwood."

Cornelius Holland, Richard Salway, William Purefoy, Francis Allein, George Snelling, and Alexander Rigby, as well as, again, Oliver Cromwell. The committee on plantations had extensive dealings with the new-merchant leadership, especially concerning Parliament's proposals for settling the governance of the Caribbean islands and for Virginia, and in this process important political and personal connections were undoubtedly solidified.[41]

In fact, indirect but tantalizing evidence strongly suggests that Cromwell's connection with the new-merchant leadership may have been even closer than it appears. Cromwell's personal secretary from 1646–1647 was Robert Spavin, a militant Puritan republican of humble rural origins. Spavin turns out to have been a rather substantial colonial trader, closely associated with the new-merchant leadership in a whole series of ventures in both the Eastern and Western Hemispheres. A significant investor in the Second General Voyage of the East India Company, Spavin also was a backer of the new merchants' colonizing project on Assada in the Indian Ocean and was, in addition, a partner with Maurice Thomson and others in what was apparently a private plantation, independent of the main venture, on that island. Spavin was, furthermore, a partner of Thomson's close friend William Pennoyer in the related trade with Guinea. Finally, Spavin was a partner of Martin Noel's and one of Noel's relatives in the West Indies, in plantation businesses in Barbados and Montserrat. In his will, apparently written in 1650, Spavin named Thomson, Pennoyer, and Noel trustees of his estate. Of course, the relationship secured by the new merchants with Oliver Cromwell was not necessarily as close as that with his secretary. Still, according to one government report submitted after the Restoration, Maurice Thomson "had always been violent against the kingly government [and] was intimate with Cromwell." Maurice's brother, Maj. Robert Thomson, according to this source, "was so great with Cromwell that he nearly married his daughter." The capacity of these traders to build connections—by means of their colonial-interloping ventures and in other ways—with the very top army leadership was impressive indeed. Heading the interlopers' petition two years later to the Commonwealth government for their own patent to trade in the East Indies was no less a figure than Lord General Sir Thomas Fairfax himself![42]

Certainly, contemporaries were well aware of the central place of colonial affairs in the evolution of political independency, not only in the City,

---

[41] *A.O.* 1: 331; L. F. Stock, ed., *Proceedings and Debates of the British Parliaments Respecting North America*, 5 vols. (Washington, 1924), 1: 175. Cf. above, ch. 4, pp. 165–68.

[42] G. E. Aylmer, *The State's Servants* (London, 1973), pp. 263–64 and n. 80; *C.C.M.E.I.C. 1650–1654*, pp. 14, 93; PRO, will of Robert Spavin, 1651 PCC Grey 165; PRO S.P. 29/159/108 (quotations); *C.C.M.E.I.C. 1644–1649*, p. 361.

but in Parliament and the army as well. As Clement Walker bitterly commented, the political independents

> have provided themselves of places of retreat in case they cannot make good their standing in England: Ireland is kept unprovided for, that they may find room in it when necessity drives them thither. If their hopes fail in Ireland, they have New England, Bermuda, Barbados, the Caribbee Isles, the Isle of Providence, Eleutheria, Lygonia, and other places to retreat to and lay up the spoils of England in.[43]

Beyond the close personal and political relationships that already linked certain of the City's political independents with their counterparts in the army and Parliament, there appears to have been emerging, even at the time of the army invasion of London, some sort of ideological consensus uniting them. This was in evidence, as has been seen, in the writings of the army spokesman and new merchant representative Hugh Peter. It was also manifested in a remarkable political initiative that took place in the summer of 1647, the launching of the *Articles and Orders* of the Bahamas. The longer-term origins of this document are to be found in the series of sharp religious conflicts that wracked the colony of Bermuda during the 1640s, provoked largely by the group of militant Puritan ministers that was attempting to impose on the colony a pure, congregational-type church structure. Apparently, these clerics and their followers had, by the middle 1640s, encountered insurmountable opposition from other factions on the island, and some of them, led by Capt. William Sayle (a former governor of Bermuda), began to plan an alternative colony of their own to be situated in the Bahamas. The *Articles and Orders* of the "Company of Adventurers for the Plantation of the Islands of Eleutheria" was thus, in the first instance, simply a founding document for the colonial project of this group of dissatisfied Bermudans.[44] One cannot ignore, however, that the *Articles and Orders* was published in London as a political broadside on 9 July 1647 and presented to Parliament a week later. This was at the very height of the confrontation between political presbyterians and political independents, between the City magistrates and the army. In view of the document's sharply radical religio-political contents, and particularly of its very special group of English backers, it could easily have been viewed in some quarters as a political provocation. Certainly, one can hardly avoid the conclusion that its publication was in-

---

[43] C. Walker, *The History of Independency*, pt. 1 (London, 1660), pp. 143–44.

[44] H. W. Miller, "The Colonization of the Bahamas, 1647–1660," *William and Mary Quarterly*, 3d ser., 2 (1945); J. T. Hassam, "The Bahamas: Notes on an Early Attempt at Colonization," *Massachusetts Historical Society Proceedings*, 2d ser., 13 (Mar., 1899): 4–58.

spired at least as much by the pressing ideological requirements of political conflict in England as by the projected needs of the new colony.

The *Articles and Orders* of the Bahamas was, in fact, no mere colonial charter but a tract for the times—a political intervention in the struggle between political independents and political presbyterians, consciously aimed to win English support for the Bahamas project more on the basis of its ideological thrust than of its commercial and colonial promise. This is indicated in both the document's relative neglect of actual conditions in the islands and its elaborate articulation of the venture's religio-political premises. To begin with, at a time when the political presbyterians were fighting most uncompromisingly for the recognition of religious uniformity as the founding principle of the state, demanding the withdrawal of all political rights from those who refused to conform to the established religion, the *Articles and Orders* gave explicit support to the principle of religious toleration and the separation of church and state:

> Whereas experience hath shewed us the great inconveniences that have happened, both in this kingdom of England, and other places, by a rigid imposing upon all an uniformity and conformity in matters of judgment and, that practices have been made, factions fomented, persecutions induced and the public peace endangered. And for that we well know that in this state of darkness and imperfection, we know but in part. That there are both babes and strongmen in Christ: And that every member who holds the head and is of the body of *Jesus Christ*, hath not the same place and office nor the measure of light, who yet desire and endeavor to increase in knowledge. And in the meantime walk according to what they have received, in all godliness, justice and sobriety. . . . It is therefore ordered . . . that there shall be no names of distinction or reproach, as Independent, Antinomian, Anabaptist, or any other cast upon any such for their difference in judgment, neither yet shall any person or persons, assume or acknowledge any such distinguishing names, under the penalty of being accounted (in both cases, either imposing or accepting or assuming any such name or names) as enemies of public peace. . . . That no magistracy or officers of the republic, nor any power derived from them, shall take notice of any man for his difference in judgment in matter of religion or have cognizance of any cause whatsoever of that nature.[45]

That the proposed colony is here referred to as a "republic" may or may not be significant. But the specific constitutional structure prescribed, and

---

[45] "Articles and Orders, made and agreed upon the 9th day of July 1647," *Colonial Society of Massachusetts Transactions* 32 (1933–1937): 81–82.

the language in which it is proposed, is so republican in form that it is hard to read the tract as anything else but an endorsement of this type of political order.

> The government . . . shall be continued in a senate of the number of one hundred persons. . . . And whensoever any of them shall die or sell away his interest in the said plantations; then there shall be another elected in his room . . . by the major part of the said senate out of the other adventurers and planters resident in the said islands. And the same elections shall be made in this manner (viz.) First, 20 fit persons shall be nominated. Then those 20 reduced to the number of 4, by scrutiny, and out of those 4 one to be chosen by ballotines. . . . And that the same senate shall . . . make election of all officers for doing of justice, and distributing and setting out of lands, and for the care and oversight of all public monies . . . there shall be yearly a governor and 12 counsellors chosen out of the said number of 100 senators, who shall take the daily care of things necessary for the prosperity of the *plantation*.[46]

This, then, is an explicit plan for establishing in the Bahamas a self-perpetuating oligarchic republic clearly derived from Continental models, Dutch and Venetian, with religious toleration as a first principle. It is impossible to prove beyond doubt that its author and its supporters intended at this very moment to push for such a settlement in England itself. That these men did, however, actually desire such a government is a reasonable presumption, especially in view of what is known about their political orientations and their subsequent political careers. Among them there were some of those figures from Parliament and the army, as well as the City, who would be instrumental in furthering the revolutionary overthrow of 1648 and essential to carrying on the work of the Commonwealth itself. Of the twenty-six citizens, parliamentarians, bureaucrats, and army men who were the chief backers of the *Articles and Orders*[47] of the Bahamas project (or the "Eleutheria" project, as it was called), there are only three men who can be termed central figures within the new-merchant leadership—namely, Owen Rowe, Gregory Clement, and Thomas Smythe—but they are major figures indeed. Rowe had been a backer of the New Haven project, which was largely organized in his London parish of St. Stephen's Coleman Street, and served through much of the 1640s and 1650s as deputy governor of the Bermuda Company. A leading London

---

[46] "Articles and Orders," p. 85 (emphasis in text). It is also worth noting the close analogy between the place of the council vis-à-vis the senate of the Bahamas and the place of the council of state vis-à-vis the House of Commons under the Commonwealth.

[47] For the backers of the Bahamas project, with brief biographies of each one, see Hassam, "Bahamas."

radical and apparently a parochial Independent, Rowe became a member of the original City committee of public safety (militia committee) in January 1642, assumed the position of sergeant major in the City's trained bands, became the chief of arms administration for the parliamentary army, was appointed to the army-backed City militia committee of 1647, and eventually became a regicide. Gregory Clement was a very close collaborator of Maurice Thomson's; he was a partner of Thomson's in privateering and colonial activities, and a commissioner for the Thomson-led Additional Sea Adventure to Ireland. Elected recruiter MP for Fowey in 1648, Clement soon became a regicide. Thomas Smythe was also a commissioner for the Additional Sea Adventure to Ireland and a partner of Thomson's in shipowning and privateering. Originally secretary to the old admiral of the navy, the earl of Northumberland, Smythe became secretary to the parliamentary admiralty committee in September 1642 and then in December 1643 to the admiral of the parliamentary navy, the earl of Warwick. Later, Smythe was appointed to the parliamentary navy commission, joined Maurice Thomson and his friends in an attempt to take over the customs commission in October 1647, and, under the Commonwealth, again became a commissioner of the navy, as well as a commissioner for the sale of prize goods.[48] Two other Bahamas investors were also involved in enterprises in the Americas and/or connected with the new-merchant group. One was Robert Haughton, the Southwark militia commissioner, Additional Sea Adventurer to Ireland, and trader and investor in Bermuda and New England; the other was John Humfrey, the onetime Massachusetts Bay deputy governor and Providence Island appointee for governor who had also been a leading figure in the Additional Sea Adventure to Ireland.[49]

The Eleutheria project is significant because it shows the aforementioned London-based colonizing radicals working together with a group of similarly radical City, army, parliamentary, and bureaucratic personages in an explicitly oligarchic republican and tolerationist project a year and a half before the advent of the Commonwealth. Most of these figures would continue to cooperate with one another in establishing the Commonwealth regime on similarly oligarchic republican and tolerationist lines. Among the leading nonmerchants involved in the Eleutheria project were Cornelius Holland, a backer of the New England ironworks project in the 1640s and a Bermuda Company stockholder who, as "link boy" between Parliament and the army, was one of the MPs most active in the

---

[48] For these men, see above. On Smythe's activities in parliamentary naval administration, see W. G. Cogar, "The Politics of Naval Administration, 1649–1660" (Oxford University, Ph.D. diss., 1983), p. 44.

[49] On Haughton, see above, note 30. On Humfrey, see A. P. Newton, *The Colonising Activities of the English Puritans* (New Haven, 1914), pp. 41, 45, 46, 80, 81, 83, 286, 292.

army's ultimate drive for power in 1648 and one of the handful of the Commonwealth's most influential politicians in the early period of the Rump; Gualter Frost, another major backer of the New England ironworks project in the 1640s, who first became politically active in 1639–1640 as a secret courier between the English opposition leaders and the Scottish Covenanters, who subsequently served as co-secretary of the committee of both kingdoms, as swordbearer and chronologer of London, and as commissary of provisions for Ireland, who assumed the sensitive positions of secretary of the Derby House committee in the later 1640s and secretary for the Commonwealth council of state in 1649, and who authored propaganda works for the new republic against the Levellers; Owen Rowe's brother William Rowe, secretary to the commissioners with the army in the north in 1644 and later scoutmaster general of the New Model Army, who married the daughter of the Commonwealth leader Thomas Chaloner and ultimately became another of the republic's influential politicians; John Rushworth, secretary to the army generals; John Blackwell, son of a London grocer and a Puritan sectarian who became a captain in Cromwell's regiment, a deputy treasurer of war for Parliament in the mid-1640s, then a Commonwealth treasurer of war; Arthur Squibb, a Puritan sectarian who became an influential commissioner for the advance of money under the Commonwealth, a Fifth Monarchist and a nominee for the Barebone's Parliament; John Hutchinson, an MP for Nottingham, who became a regicide and a member of the Commonwealth council of state; and Thomas Westrow, a close friend of Cromwell's who became a Commonwealth MP.[50]

Certainly, much more needs to be discovered about the aforementioned individuals and their interconnections, as well as about the other backers of the Eleutheria project. But it seems reasonable to view them as a representative group within an emergent alliance of City, army, and parliamentary radicals, which, while stopping far short of the demands of the Levellers, was aiming at a significant reconstruction of the English polity. This goal was unacceptable to the great majority of the gentry, and in particular to that special set of middle-group or royal independent leaders who had hung on so tenaciously to leadership in Parliament and held out so unyieldingly for a settlement roughly along the lines of what they had proposed in 1642. It was the achievement of these radicals in 1648–1649 to wrest power, albeit partially and temporarily, from the middle-group leaders, long accustomed to rule, and to move toward, if never quite to

---

[50] For the biographical information presented here, see the biographies in Hassam, "Bahamas," and especially, Aylmer, *State's Servants*, pp. 261–68 (on Squibb), 242–46 (on Blackwell), 254–56 (on Frost), and 260 (on Rushworth). Hartley, *Ironworks on the Saugus*, includes brief biographies (pp. 71–73) of those Bahamas projectors who were also backers of the ironworks project, namely, Robert Haughton, Cornelius Holland, and Gualter Frost.

consolidate, a new form of rule in church, state, and the economy for England.

DEFEATING COUNTERREVOLUTION, 1648

Neither London's political independents, nor their allies in the army and Parliament, were as yet in 1647 at the point of seizing power. By the spring of 1648, John Warner, the army-sponsored colonial-merchant lord mayor, was encountering difficulties maintaining order in the City in the face of riots inspired by political presbyterians. Around the country preparations were in progress for a new round of royalist and political presbyterian risings. During the spring and summer of 1648, much the same sort of political drama as had been played out in 1647 had to be reenacted. Royalist revolts broke out in various parts of the country, forcing the army to vacate London. The City political presbyterians took advantage of the resulting power vacuum to reassert its authority in the City government. It released its former leaders who had been imprisoned by the army the previous fall, appointed again its own militia committee, and took the initiative once more to force Parliament to reopen negotiations with the king. The Scots made the decision to invade, and the struggle between the political presbyterians and their enemies had, once again, to be fought out on the field of battle.[51]

Parliament's Derby House committee, now largely shorn of political presbyterians and Scots, took charge of coordinating the military and political struggle against the royalist rebels in the spring and summer of 1648. By this time, there was no possibility of trusting a virtually royalist City government to help put down the various neo-royalist risings that were threatening Parliament and the army. At the very time of the Kentish rebellion in May and June 1648, the City government was petitioning Parliament for the creation of an association of Kent, Essex, Middlesex, Hertfordshire, and Sussex—the very counties most unsettled by royalist discontent—and thereby signaling its sympathy with the rebels, if not its willingness to support them directly. In these circumstances, the political independent alliance in Parliament and the army leadership had little choice but to turn for support to the old radical leadership in the City, prominently including the new merchants.

Only a month and a half previously, in March 1648, the Derby House committee had negotiated what must have been one of the largest loan and provisioning contracts of the entire Civil War era with a syndicate headed by new-merchant leaders and a handful of their City radical friends. This

---

[51] For this and the following paragraph, see D. Underdown, *Pride's Purge* (Oxford, 1971), pp. 88–89, 94–100; Gentles, "Struggle for London"; Sharpe, *London and the Kingdom* 2: 270–88.

contract called for the delivery of some £83,000 in "money, corn, ammunition and other provisions, to make the soldiers in the Kingdom of Ireland [under the command of Lord Inchiquin in Munster] take the field with cheerfulness" that summer. The ten-person syndicate[52] constituted a representative sample of the forces making up political independency in London. It included, in the first place, Maurice Thomson, Stephen Estwicke, Richard Shute, Thomas Andrews, Thomas Smythe, and Thomas Vincent. All six of these men were at this time partners of one another in various colonial-interloping projects, and the first five had joined together in October 1647 in an attempt to take over the parliamentary customs commission. All six of these contractors were also veterans of the City radical movement, as were at least three of the remaining four men who made up the syndicate, namely, Thomas Player, Tempest Milner, and Maurice Gethin. Player and Milner had been leaders of the extremist Salters Hall committee in 1643, and Gethin had been a leading activist in the City revolution of the winter of 1641–1642, a signatory of both the petition of December 1641, which demanded that the House of Lords take immediate action on the impressment bill, and the petition of March 1642, which called for sharp reprisals against those citizens who had dared to come out against the revolutionary committee of safety. All three of these men had been appointed to London's political independent militia committee of the previous September.[53]

As the royalist revolt gathered steam during the late spring, contemporaries became aware of the "the continual endeavor of the grandees of Derby House and the army to put all the arms, garrisons, ships and strengths of the kingdom into the hands of antimonarchical, schismatical independents."[54] In these processes, the new merchants took a leading part, carrying out a series of crucial military operations in support of Fairfax's army. On 29 May 1648, just a few days before Fairfax dispersed the main force of the proroyal Kentish rebellion, Maurice Thomson and his old business partner William Willoughby were called in to help in the pacification of the county. The Derby House committee asked them to "produce 30 faithful men, such as you can be confident of" to take over the defense of the fort at Tilbury, and to make sure that these fighters were well paid and provisioned during the emergency. Then, on 3 June, Thomson and Willoughby were requested to take into their possession all the ferryboats on the Thames, as well as all those in Kent and Essex, in order to prevent those who had been in arms against Parliament in Kent from passing into Essex to cause new disturbances there. On the same

[52] PRO, S.P.16/539, pt. 4/503; C.J. 5: 513.

[53] CLRO, J.Co.Co.40, fol. 67 (Player and Milner); House of Lords MSS, 24 December 1641; CLRO, J.Co.Co.40, fol. 25 (Gethin).

[54] Walker, *History of Independency*, pt. I, p. 106.

day, Maurice Thomson's brother George and his old partner George Snelling, the two MPs from Southwark, were called on by the House of Commons to take charge of securing the safety of that borough during the emergency.[55]

Three weeks later, the Derby House committee once again approached Thomson for help on a similar mission of pacification, this time in the wake of the revolt of the parliamentary navy. Thomson was now asked to call together two of his Anglo-Dutch East India interloping partners, Nicholas Corsellis and Adam Laurence, as well as the colonial trader Capt. John Limbrey, and to travel with them into Holland in order to try to secure "the recovery and reducement" of the ships that had been taken over by the royalists in the naval mutiny in late May. In 1643, Parliament also had sent Thomson, Corsellis, and Laurence on a mission to Holland, accompanied on that occasion by the minister Hugh Peter, to raise money for "distressed Protestants in Ireland." Thomson had wide-ranging connections in Holland, which probably originated with his reexport business in tobacco (for which he maintained a factor in Amsterdam) and which no doubt multiplied as a result of his involvement with the Anglo-Dutch merchants of the Courteen project and its sequels. And this fact was clearly well known to the political independent leadership in Parliament.[56]

During the next two months of crisis, other City radicals took a prominent part in securing London itself for the army. Here, Philip Skippon, a longtime political collaborator of the London radicals in general and of the new merchants in particular, played the decisive role. Skippon had made a central military contribution to securing London for Parliament at the time of the City revolution of the winter of 1641–1642, had worked with new-merchant leaders (among others) on the revolutionary militia committee established at that juncture, and had assumed the office of commander in chief of the City's militia, or trained bands. In the spring of 1642 Skippon had invested in the new merchants' Additional Sea Adventure to Ireland. During the following autumn, the City radicals, led by Richard Shute, nominated him to serve as head of their independent citizens' volunteer army. Shortly thereafter, Skippon was appointed sergeant major general in Essex's army and served with great distinction. He retained his rank and regiment in the New Model Army and became military governor first of Bristol and then, in January 1647, of Newcastle. In the spring of 1648, Skippon was again appointed commander of the City

[55] C.S.P.D. 1648–1649, pp. 86, 92–93.

[56] PRO, S.P.21/9/181–82; C.S.P.D. 1648–1649, p. 139. Limbrey was a leading figure in the Bermudian and West Indian trades, as well as the colonizing of Jamaica. See C. M. Andrews, British Committees, Commissions, and Councils of Trade and Plantations, 1622–1675 (Baltimore, 1908), p. 45; Lefroy, Memorials 2: 67, 81, 88, 91, 103; D. C. Coleman, Sir John Banks (Oxford, 1963), p. 10.

militia with the implicit task of keeping London secure from the attacks of the political presbyterians and outright royalists. Over the following summer, working closely with the Derby House committee and also, apparently, the London sectarian congregations, Skippon managed to maintain control of most of London's official armed forces in the face of determined efforts by the City government to remove him. He was also able to raise, at the behest of the Derby House committee, a less official supplementary cavalry force under the control of the City's political independents for the explicit purpose of countering the offensive of royalists and political presbyterians. Skippon's efforts, perhaps more than those of anyone else, prevented the City's political presbyterians from translating their political hegemony in London into military control.[57]

Other radical citizens were also playing a part. On 4 July 1648, Rowland Wilson, the Guinean-trade partner of Maurice Thomson, was informed by the Derby House committee that the enemy had plans to surprise several fortified houses in Surrey. He was therefore asked to take charge of raising a force of men and engaging in the defense of Marton Abbey.[58] At the end of August, with the threat of rebellion still a reality, Thomas Alderne and Richard Price were sent a warrant by the Derby House committee to "apprehend all . . . persons engaged in the late rebellion in Kent" and "also to seize all arms, ammunition, and other provisions of war . . . sent from this City or parts adjacent . . . not having the authority of Parliament for their passage."[59] A parishioner of radical St. Stephen's Coleman Street, Thomas Alderne was active in the trades with New England and the West Indies and was closely connected with the new-merchant leadership through the Bermuda Company deputy governor Owen Rowe, a fellow parishioner who was his father-in-law, and the East India interloper James Russell, also a parishioner at St. Stephen's Coleman Street, to whom he had been apprenticed (both Rowe and Russell had been members of the original City committee of public safety of January 1642, and had taken part in countless subsequent activities in the radical cause).[60] It cannot be determined which of two related Richard Prices was working with Alderne on this occasion—whether the uncle Richard (the mercer) or the nephew Richard (the scrivener). Both were members of John Goodwin's gathered church and one of them had recently entered the trade with the West Indies. Like many others in Good-

---

[57] Gentles, "Struggle for London," pp. 292–99; Tolmie, *Triumph of the Saints*, pp. 174–76; *Dictionary of Seventeenth-Century Radicals*, vol. 3, s.v. "Philip Skippon."

[58] *C.S.P.D. 1648–1649*, p. 161.

[59] Ibid., pp. 190, 248.

[60] PRO, will of Thomas Alderne, 1657 PCC Ruthen 218; Coleman, *Sir John Banks*, pp. 6, 10–12; *Aspinwall Notarial Records, 1644–1651*, Boston Record Commissioners Report, 32 (Boston, 1903), pp. 396–97; Society of Genealogists, Boyd's Index of London Citizens: 13156.

win's congregation, both Richard Prices were to play important roles in the establishment of the Commonwealth, as was Alderne.[61]

Meanwhile, at the end of June 1648, under heavy pressure from the City, the House of Commons reversed its vote of no addresses and began to move toward renewal of the personal treaty. Shortly thereafter, the House of Lords endorsed a petition from sixty officers in the London trained bands urging that the king be brought to London for the opening of talks and, at the same time, took steps to undermine Skippon's control of the City's armed forces. Skippon was, however, able to retain a hold on London's militia, allowing the radicals of the City to attempt to mount a counterattack. In early July several of the most substantial of the "uppermost independents" went into action. In collaboration with the Independent minister Philip Nye, son-in-law of the moderate Presbyterian cleric Stephen Marshall, the East India interloping traders Thomas Andrews and Stephen Estwicke, both of whom were leading City radicals and religious Independents, as well as their old collaborator John Fowke and the usually cautious middle-group trimmers Sir John Wollaston and William Gibbs, began circulating a petition that explicitly opposed the "personal treaty" with the king, which the official municipality so fervently desired.[62]

According to Clement Walker, the aforementioned effort by these men and "others who hold rich offices by favor of the Grandees" proved that the political independents had "no intent to make peace with the King."[63] However, Walker at least partially contradicts himself when he points out that even following the army's victories, leading political independents still had hopes that the Treaty of Newport (which would start in October 1648) would bring about a satisfactory settlement with the king.[64] Walker's inconsistency lay in his insistence on treating political independency, especially including its parliamentary wing, as a unified political party. What had, of course, been operative since 1644–1645 was a strategic alliance in Parliament between some of the more resolute middle-group politicians, led by such aristocratic "royal independents" as Lord Saye and Sele, who were in the last analysis constitutional moderates, and politically more thoroughgoing war-party radicals. This alliance initially had been constituted to prevent a royalist military victory or a political sellout to the king by the political presbyterians, and had until this point retained the

---

[61] For the American trade of one of the Richard Prices, see PRO, C.O. 1/12/5, 96. For the Prices' careers and connections, see Tolmie, *Triumph of the Saints*, pp. 115, 139–40, 179, 184; Walwyn, *Walwyn's Just Defence*, pp. 361–65, 368, 388, 395.

[62] Walker, *History of Independency*, p. 116.

[63] Ibid.

[64] C. Walker, *Anarchia Anglicana; or, the History of Independency, The Second Part* (London, 1661), pp. 11–13.

support of both the army officer corps and London's political independents. But its constituent elements differed among themselves on the preferred character of the Civil War settlement.

TOWARD REVOLUTION

In fact, by the end of the summer of 1648, following the New Model Army's crushing victories at Preston and Colchester, the political independent alliance was finally beginning to break apart. The middle-group or royal independents saw some sort of deal with the king as unavoidable, despite Charles I's many misdeeds. In contrast, radicals in Parliament, backed up by compatriots in the army and London, were at this time beginning to view the king's defeat, following a series of useless bloodlettings for which Charles I could be held directly responsible, as opening the way toward a resolution of the conflict in which the king would be made to pay for his crimes, and the monarchy would perhaps be jettisoned altogether. As Walker comments, "The victory [over the Scots] did work like bottled ale with [Thomas] Scot, [George] Thomson, [Cornelius] Holland, [Sir Henry] Mildmay, and many others of the light-hearted saints who were so puffed with the windiness of it, that they began to swell with disdain and malice against the personal treaty."[65]

Walker's juxtaposition of these four men is significant, for at just this point, in late August–early September 1648, radical forces in the army, Parliament, and the City were beginning to make preparations to forsake definitively their middle-group friends and to move toward a revolutionary takeover. Holland, Scot, and Mildmay were clearly among the pivotal figures in Parliament behind this thrust, and they would continue to provide some of the top leadership for the new republic in its early days. Maurice's brother George Thomson, an army colonel, an MP from Southwark, and a core member of the new-merchant leadership, may be assumed to have represented an analogous group in London, as well as to have provided an important link among the radical forces in the army, Parliament, and the City. In mid-September, negotiations took place among key army and parliamentary radicals, notably Henry Ireton and Edmund Ludlow, concerning the strategy for revolution and the most desirable form of political settlement, and it is possible that these negotiations ultimately included representatives of the London radical leadership.[66] Certainly, when the army moved to invade London in November–December 1648, its radical City allies were well prepared.

[65] The quotation is from Walker, *Anarchia Anglicana*, p. 10. For the general political alignments at this time, see Underdown, *Pride's Purge*, introduction and chs. 4 and 5. See also V. Pearl, "The 'Royal Independents' in the English Civil War," *T.R.H.S.*, 5th ser., 18 (1968).
[66] Walker, *Anarchia Anglicana*, p. 10; Underdown, *Pride's Purge*, pp. 107–8.

What made it possible in the late summer of 1648 for the radical wing of the political independent alliance in Parliament and the political independents in London to contemplate breaking from the middle-group parliamentary leadership once and for all is perfectly clear: it was the emerging likelihood of an army revolt against Parliament. During the summer and fall of 1647, when the army also had effectively taken political control, the top army leadership, most notably Cromwell supported by Ireton, had managed to hold the political independent alliance together and to keep the army ranks in tow, so as to allow the royal independents to seek, still another time, to come to terms with the king. At that juncture, led by Lord Saye and Sele and the earl of Northumberland, royal independents had advanced the *Heads of Proposals* as the basis for a settlement, proposing, among other things, that Parliament choose the king's executive officers for ten years, after which time the king would be allowed to choose one of the three parliamentary nominees for each position; that Parliament control the militia for twenty years, and, even after that, have the right to veto any directives to the militia the king might give; that all peers created by the king after 1642 be prohibited from sitting in the House of Lords unless Parliament explicitly approved them; and, perhaps most important from the standpoint of the City's political independents, that the parliamentary Presbyterian church be continued, but that Independents and moderate Anglicans who wished to form churches outside the Presbyterian structure be allowed to do so.[67] In view of the fact that not only Parliament, but also, and above all, the army officers, approved propositions to the king roughly in keeping with the *Heads of Proposals*, the less extreme sections of the radical alliance that constituted City political independency had little choice but to go along, for they had no desire to throw in their lot with the Levellers and had no other significant force of their own. By the autumn of 1648, however, radical elements in the army's leadership led by Henry Ireton had decided that they were no longer willing to pursue negotiations with the king along the lines pursued in 1647. It was the army's break from the long-standing political independent alliance in Parliament that provided the indispensable politico-military basis for a parallel and associated break on the part of the City's political independents, the new merchants prominently among them. For the first time since the summer of 1643, the less-extreme wing of the City radical alliance could reasonably make a fight for a political settlement directly in accord with its own interests and conceptions.

The army's ultimate decision to move against both the king and Parliament was conditioned by a powerful upsurge of the democratic and sectar-

[67] For a recent interpretation of these developments, see the important article by J.S.A. Adamson, "The English Nobility and the Projected Settlement of 1647," *H.J.* 30 (1987).

ian movement in the army rank and file and in London, as well as in the counties. First there was a Leveller petition of 11 September demanding the abolition of the veto power of the king and the House of Lords; then there were three mass petitions from the counties presented to the Commons on 10 October that called for an end to the personal treaty; and finally, in mid-November, came a series of petitions, sent by several regiments to the army council, demanding justice against the king. In the absence of this popular movement—the pressure it placed on the top officers for action and the power it generated for the army as a whole—the army council might never have taken its decisions of mid-November 1648 to defy Parliament and to accept Ireton's army remonstrance to justify its actions.[68] At this point, the position of the radical leaderships among the army officers (headed by Ireton) and in London in relation to their Leveller and extremist sectarian supporters appears to have been rather analogous to that of the leadership of the City radical offensive of the spring of 1643 in relation to some of the more militant representatives of its popular following. What distinguished the two cases, however, was the outcome of each. In 1643, the City radical leadership, centered especially in the militia committee, refused to grant the demands for autonomy of the very militant Salters Hall committee. As a result, it seems to have caused a certain degree of demoralization and disunity among the City's most active and enthusiastic political forces, thus contributing to the dispersal of its own key sources of power before it had been able to achieve its goals.

In 1648, by contrast, the radical leadership did not make the same mistake. During the first part of November, apparently at the suggestion of Cromwell—urged on, very likely, by Ireton—a group of City political independents invited Leveller leaders to hold a series of meetings at the Nags Head tavern in London with the goal of achieving political unity before the army took action. On 15 November, this group—which included, at various points, the City political independents Robert Tichborne, Col. John White, Daniel Taylor, John Price, and Dr. William Parker—agreed to recommend that the date of Parliament's dissolution should be part of an agreement "above law" that would be drawn up by representatives of the army and the counties. This proposal was then sent to army headquarters where Leveller agents secured certain additions to Ireton's army remonstrance; specifically, future parliaments, "as near as may be, an equal representative of the whole people electing," with the representative body forbidden to interfere with the fundamental liberties set forth in a "settlement and agreement." Even then, the Levellers were not satisfied. They wanted a firmer grant of toleration and more tangible

---

[68] Underdown, *Pride's Purge*, pp. 109–10, 113, 116–19, 121–22.

assurances that a new tyranny by the army and Parliament would not replace that of the king. It was necessary, said the Levellers, before the army marched on Parliament, for the army leadership, along with its friends in Parliament and the City, to take concrete steps toward accepting a revised *Agreement of the People*. The Levellers presented their demands to the London political independents Hugh Peter, Robert Tichborne, Samuel Moyer, and Col. John White and pressed them to communicate these to Ireton and the army leadership. To satisfy the Levellers and to ensure unity, the army officers, even as they were making their final preparations to march on London, agreed on 26 November to establish a committee of sixteen, composed of four representatives each from the council of officers, the City political independents, the House of Commons radicals, and the Levellers, to draw up a new *Agreement of the People*. The four men chosen to represent London's political independents were Robert Tichborne, Col. John White, Daniel Taylor, and Richard Price.[69]

The eight persons identified as representing the London political independents in the foregoing series of meetings were all representative figures within a City radical alliance that went as far back as the City revolution of 1641–1642 and the radical offensive of 1642–1643 and that now, at least for this brief moment, included the Levellers. Hugh Peter was, of course, a representative of the army, as well as the London political independents. Robert Tichborne, as noted, was by this time among the top leaders of City political independency. Samuel Moyer, a representative of the new-merchant leadership who was at this point active in interloping in the East Indies, was a member of Thomas Goodwin's congregation and had served on both the London and the Tower Hamlets militia committees appointed by the political independents in the fall of 1647. Dr. William Parker was one of the most prominent lay leaders of London's gathered churches and, like Samuel Moyer, apparently a follower of the Independent divine Thomas Goodwin. Col. John White was a stalwart of the political independents in the City militia and was perhaps a member of Sydrach Simpson's gathered church. Daniel Taylor, a member of John Goodwin's congregation, had been a militant organizer for the City radicals as early as their petition campaign of December 1641 and a backer in 1642 of the new merchants' Additional Sea Adventure to Ireland, while maintaining a host of connections in the colonies, including an uncle, Thomas Taylor in Bermuda, and a stepbrother, Edward Rawson, who was secretary for the Massachusetts Bay Colony. Richard Price (the scrivener) was also a member of John Goodwin's congregation and one of London's

---

[69] J. Lilburne, *The Legall Fundamentall Liberties of the People of England*, in Haller and Davies, *Leveller Tracts*, pp. 415–24; B. Taft, "The Council of Officers' *Agreement of the People*, 1648/9," *H.J.* 28 (1985): 171–72; Underdown, *Pride's Purge*, 123, 128–29; Tolmie, *Triumph of the Saints*, pp. 178–80.

most prominent political independent leaders, as was his kinsman John Price, the radical pamphleteer.[70] Selected for their capacity to negotiate and reach a settlement with the Levellers, these men, with the exception of Peter (and perhaps Tichborne), were drawn from the more radical wing of London political independency, within which John Goodwin's gathered church seems to have played a central leadership role.

The outcome of these high-level last-minute meetings between the formally allied political independent, or moderate republican, and democratic-sectarian wings of the emerging revolution was ostensibly to grant the Levellers much of what they had asked. Indeed, political friendship between the political independents and Levellers reached something of a high point in this period. The Levellers turned the mid-November funeral of the assassinated Leveller hero Thomas Rainsborough into a political demonstration, and, significantly, the Independent cleric Thomas Brookes, patronized by such new-merchant political independents as Samuel Pennoyer and Stephen Estwicke, gave the funeral oration.[71] Nevertheless, despite their mutual sympathy and solidarity at this point, it is doubtful whether the Levellers and the political independent leaders actually interpreted their hastily reached political agreement in precisely the same way. By this point, the political independents and Levellers had reached divergent understandings of the crucial notion of popular sovereignty and, in turn, of what was the most desirable form of political settlement.

In 1643, the concept of popular sovereignty was still at the stage of initial formulation, and in the wave of mass mobilization that swept the City at that time, it remained open to a possibly democratic interpretation. By late 1648, however, the political independent leaderships in both the army and London were defining the idea in highly restricted terms and articulating, from a variety of standpoints, notions of an oligarchic or guided republicanism—or perhaps more strictly speaking, since it was not necessarily proposed to abolish the monarchy, of parliamentary supremacy without much democracy, based on a limited franchise. As early as their important *Petition and Remonstrance* of spring 1643, the radicals of London had tended to emphasize the leading role and final responsibility not of the people but of their representatives. Still, they had left undefined the ultimate political implications of their central premise "that the safety of the people is the supreme law." By 1648, however, this ambiguity was well on its way to resolution, at least in the minds of the revolution's leadership.

[70] Tolmie, *Triumph of the Saints*, pp. 56, 105, 122, 179–80 (Parker); 104–5, 179, 184 (White); 115, 179, 184, 187 (Taylor). On Taylor's American connections, see *New Eng. Hist. Gen. Reg.* 42 (1888): 178–79; PRO, will of Daniel Taylor, 1655 PCC Aylett 348.

[71] Tolmie, *Triumph of the Saints*, p. 178.

In a pamphlet plausibly attributed to Hugh Peter and published in those critical moments of October 1648 when the parliamentary, City, and army leaderships were formulating their plans for their own particular kind of revolution, the dilemma was resolved in no uncertain terms: "It is not *vox*, but *salus populi* that is the supreme law. . . . If the common vote of the giddy multitude must rule the whole, how quickly would their own interest, peace and safety be dashed."[72] The people's representatives, working from "common plain, general and universal reason and moral principles," should retain authority, not the people themselves. Shortly thereafter, Henry Ireton, apparently working in close collaboration with Hugh Peter, made *salus populi* and popular sovereignty the central premises of the army remonstrance, probably the central ideological statement of the revolution of 1648. On the basis of these principles, he justified the army revolt and went on to argue for parliamentary supremacy, biennial parliaments, redrawn electoral districts to undermine the electoral influence of king and lords, and a written constitution. In combination with the somewhat expanded but still rather restricted franchise that was known to be preferred by Ireton and most of the army leadership, these provisions, if implemented, would have made for a radically transformed political order in England, but one in which popular sovereignty would have assumed an effectively oligarchic form.[73]

It was the ambiguity of the army remonstrance—and their knowledge of their differences with Ireton and his colleagues within the army, parliamentary, and London radical leaderships—that accounted for the Levellers' great anxiety to impose constitutional limitations on any new government before the army could take control. But the Levellers were, in the end, unable to resist demands for unity, and with the enthusiastic support of its rank-and-file militants, the army marched in powerful and united fashion into London. The army commanders, and their political independent supporters in Parliament and in London, were thus able to solve the crucial question of power in the manner they desired, via the installation of a purged Parliament, based ultimately on the army's force. In early January 1649, expressing the consensus of the revolutionary leadership in the army, Parliament, and London, the Rump promulgated the theoretical foundations of the new regime: sovereignty lay with the people, but popular sovereignty was to be subsumed under the sovereignty of the Commons.[74]

---

[72] *Salus Populi Solus Rex* (London, 19 Oct. 1648), quoted in H. N. Brailsford, *The Levellers and the English Revolution* (London, 1961), pp. 345–46. Brailsford attributes the document to Hugh Peter.

[73] Underdown, *Pride's Purge*, pp. 125–26. For evidence that Peter assisted Ireton in writing the army remonstrance, see Stearns, *Strenuous Puritan*, p. 323 n. 15.

[74] Underdown, *Pride's Purge*, pp. 172–74, 262–64. See also below, ch. 11, pp. 563–65.

With the establishment of the Commonwealth, the alliance of radical forces that had carried through the revolution thus decisively rejected the Levellers' alternative. But its rejection of a democratic constitution should not be understood as expressing merely the cynical self-interest of a newly empowered ruling clique, although that was probably part of the story. In December 1648 the army council did debate and ultimately ratify a revised version of the *Second Agreement of the People*, forwarding it to Parliament in January 1649. Moreover, a significant group within political independency in London, drawn apparently from its more radical wing, did throw its support behind the revised *Second Agreement*. This is evidenced by the apparent willingness of the longtime City militants and religious Independents Samuel Moyer, William Hawkins, Daniel Taylor, Mark Hildesley, Richard Price, Col. John White, John Langley, and Abraham Babington to serve on the twelve-man commission, named in the document, to carry out the task of electoral redistricting and to collect signatures for the *Second Agreement*. The revised *Second Agreement* did not, of course, fully meet the Levellers' demand for the democratization of the franchise, but it did go some way toward satisfying the Levellers by including quite radical provisions on toleration, the reapportionment of electoral districts, and the protection of individual liberties. Still, the telling fact is that, in the end, the revised *Second Agreement* attracted little enthusiasm from any quarter, either within the army or in London, and the reason does not seem hard to find.[75]

As almost all sections of the alliance of forces that made the revolution of 1648 were aware, any fully democratic settlement would have restored the conservative gentry to power. This was simply because, with the important exception of London (and of course the army), relatively few areas in the nation had experienced significant radicalization during the Civil War years. In fact, in view of the ideological hegemony exercised by local landlords over most of the countryside and the relative immunity of agricultural laborers to radical politics in this epoch, relatively little mass radicalization could have been expected at this time from rural England, except perhaps for the rural industrial districts, under any conditions. In this situation, the militant minorities in Parliament, the army, London, and the counties who made the revolution tended to feel obliged to explain their actions, in various ways, precisely as the justifiable deeds of militant minorities. As "a plain man" had analyzed the practical implications of the Levellers' democratic politics at a Leveller meeting in Wapping in

[75] D. M. Wolfe, ed., *Leveller Manifestoes of the Puritan Revolution* (New York, 1944), p. 344. Taylor, Price, White, and Moyer had represented the City's political independents in the negotiations with the Levellers over the *Second Agreement of the People* in November and December 1648. Taylor, Price, and Hildesley were members of John Goodwin's congregation, probably the core of radical political independency in London. Moyer and Langley would end up as Baptists.

January 1648: "We know that the generality of people are wicked . . . and if (by the sending abroad of your [Leveller] agents into all the parishes of the kingdom) they come to have power and strength in their hand, we may suppose, and fear, that they will cut the throats of all those that are called Roundheads, that is, the honest, godly, faithful men in the land." Correlatively, in defending the revolution against its political presbyterian critics in late January 1649, the Baptist minister Samuel Richardson had no qualms about admitting that the army and its friends were no more than a "small part" of the nation, "but the better part"; as a result, he asserted, even if the people "declared against what they [the army] have done, yet it is to be justified, to be necessary, good, and lawful." Hugh Peter had said pretty much the same thing in his *Salus Populi Solus Rex* of the previous autumn. Symptomatically, even the very radical separatists who flocked to the Levellers' banner and were attracted to their democratic program tended to end up viewing their revolution as a revolution of saints, the creation of a godly few. If some of the Levellers' firmest supporters thus saw the necessity of downplaying democracy precisely to secure the revolution and open the way to further reform, it is hardly surprising that the political independents failed to raise a protest when the revised *Second Agreement* was ignored. Even when out of power and threatened by repression, the political independents had been dubious about the very radical ideological conceptions advanced by the Levellers and their sectarian friends. Now that they had themselves moved close to the seats of authority by virtue of the establishment of the Rump, they had little motivation to fight for them.[76]

[76] Tolmie, *Triumph of the Saints*, pp. 169–72, 181–91 (the quotation is from p. 172). I have been much aided here by Tolmie's stimulating analysis. It should be noted that at least certain of those elements on the more radical wing of political independency did continue to agitate strongly for further democratization during the Commonwealth period. But, symptomatically, they appear to have confined themselves largely to the municipality of London where the expansion of the electorate was much more likely to increase the base of support for further political radicalization than it was in the country as a whole (especially given that royalists and political presbyterians were excluded by law from political participation in London). Led especially by John Price and other members of John Goodwin's church, as well as certain representatives of the separatist congregations, there were, at the time of successive mayoralty elections in 1649, 1650, and 1651, quite powerful agitations to reform City electoral procedures so as to allow the rate-paying inhabitants of the wards to elect the mayor and sheriffs, instead of common hall, which was composed of the liverymen of the companies and which thus excluded from participation not only the yeomen of the companies that possessed a livery but all the members of those companies that had no livery. There was also, especially during the summer of 1651, a related attempt to curtail certain of the lord mayor's powers over procedure in the common council. Ultimately, in late 1651, the Rump had to intervene to prevent this movement from achieving victory on the election question. In so doing, it defended the position in power of those less-radical political independents (moderate republicans)—apparently including most, though not all, of the new merchants (Samuel Moyer was a notable exception, as were a few others from Goodwin's gathered church) who had come to power in the City with the revolution of 1648–1649 and who had sought

In the revolutionary process that reached its climax with the execution of Charles I and the establishment of the Commonwealth, it was, not accidentally, the minister Hugh Peter who at every crucial moment set forth in pamphlet and sermon what was to be the next step. In these climactic moments Peter's pivotal role as link between, and mouthpiece for, the allied army, City, and parliamentary radical leaderships was fully revealed. Peter helped inspire the army's march on London. In the period following the march, he helped effect and preached in favor of Pride's Purge, justified the republican settlement, called on the army "to root up monarchy not only here but in France and other kingdoms about," and came out strongly behind Ireton in calling for the trial and execution of King Charles. In view of Hugh Peter's central role in shaping and propagandizing for it, it is hardly surprising that the new republic Peter helped to usher in turned out to be the very best government his collaborators in London, especially within the new-merchant leadership, could have hoped for.[77]

The City Radicals Consolidate Their Power

The army's victory brought the colonial-interloping leadership and its political independent allies in London to a position of unprecedented influence both locally and nationally. This is understandable from several vantage points. First, during the latter part of the 1640s, London had emerged as perhaps the greatest stronghold of political presbyterianism and neo-royalism in the country. Almost the entirety of the overseas company merchant community had, sooner or later, associated itself with the Crown; in turn, a very strong majority of the most substantial citizens doing business domestically had come out strongly for political presbyterianism, if not open royalism. More generally, the new regime had only limited support among socioeconomically substantial and politically influential layers anywhere in the country; above all, the landed class of the nation was largely aliented from the revolution of 1648. In consequence, the invading army and its allies in Parliament had little choice but to look

---

to defend existing electoral and governing procedures in London and the new political and religious status quo established during the early Commonwealth period (CLRO, J.Co.Co.41, fols. 7v [Oct. 1649], 35, 35v, 36v, 37, 38, 38v, 39v, 40 [Sept.–Dec. 1650], 55, 57, 60 [July 1651], 65v [Nov. 1651]; Farnell, "Usurpation," pp. 36–37, 40). For analogous, and related, religious conflict under the Commonwealth, see below, ch. 11, note 15.

[77] For Peter's preeminence in this period, see Walker, *Anarchia Anglicana*, pp. 31, 49–50, 67; Stearns, *Strenuous Puritan*, pp. 315–36; Underdown, *Pride's Purge*, 147–48, 156, 158, 164, 170, 188, 198; H. R. Trevor-Roper, "The Fast Sermons of the Long Parliament," in *Religion, the Reformation, and Social Change* (London, 1972), pp. 331–38. Trevor-Roper also brings out the important role played by other Independent ministers in this period.

for support to the City's political independents, its moderate republicans, with the new merchants prominently among them. London's political independents were the most influential political force still available to the new regime in what was undoubtedly the most strategically important locale in the country. In fact, the new merchant leaders and their London friends offered the revolution one of its few discernible sources of political support among the relatively wealthy and educated classes, that is, outside those artisan and craft layers from which much of the revolution's most militant support had been drawn, both in London and the army, among the separatist churches and the Levellers. Of course, the emergent alliance between the national rulers of the Rump and the less extreme wing of the London radical alliance was no mere marriage of convenience. Long in preparation, it manifested a well-established network of political, religious, and business connections among political and religious radicals in Parliament, the army, and London, as well as an emerging ideological consensus.

In 1647, when they had first neared the seats of power, the City's political independents had tried for, but failed to secure, a dominant position in London—and a pivotal supporting role nationally—by destroying their major competitors on both sides, the political presbyterians and the Levellers. By 1649, however, they were perfectly placed to complete their unfinished task; the requirements for securing the new regime, at least as these were conceived by the Commonwealth's national leadership, corresponded very closely to the requirements for consolidating their own position. With the help of the army's intervention in the electoral process, the City's political independents seized power in London through carrying out a mild revolution in the structure and functioning of City government. Simultaneously, they provided one of the pivotal sociopolitical bases for the Rump regime. They played a key role in helping to establish the republic and in the rooting out of its enemies in the immediate postrevolutionary period. They supplied much of the personnel for the financial and administrative apparatus of the new regime, especially in state taxation, the navy, and the City militias. On the basis of their newly acquired power, they carried out important political reforms and religious changes in the City, while pushing for analogous measures on a national scale, where their influence was more restricted. Finally, and most significantly for England's politics, they were a central force in enacting and implementing that dynamic military-commercial offensive that was perhaps the most characteristic feature of the Commonwealth's rule.

THE CITY REVOLUTION

When the army invaded London in December 1648 for the second time in a little over a year, it carried out a reorganization of City politics designed to ensure the permanent hegemony of its own supporters. This meant not merely the replacement of its army's enemies by its allies in important individual positions (as in 1647), but enabling its London supporters to retain their political power over the long run. Throughout the middle and later 1640s, the influence of radical political forces within the official institutions of City government had steadily diminished, and at least part of the explanation for this trend clearly must lie with the radicals' inability to attract widespread support among the City's electorate. Those who held the (limited) franchise, assuming the elections were relatively free, must have favored, overwhelmingly, the political presbyterians; otherwise, the political presbyterians' extraordinary dominance of the common council is hardly comprehensible. Those who took power at the national level in 1648–1649 were clearly well aware of the political weakness of their London supporters within the official City, and especially of their inability to win substantial backing at the polls. One of their first actions on seizing power, therefore, was to manipulate qualifications for voting and officeholding so as to guarantee electoral victory by their City backers. A parliamentary ordinance of December 1648 deprived of the franchise all malignants, supporters of the king, and signers of the Engagement for a personal treaty with the king, and prohibited them from holding positions on the common council. Its implementation drastically transformed the balance of power inside the official municipality. No fewer than two-thirds of the common council's incumbents lost their seats in the first elections under the Commonwealth held in late December 1648. The way was thus opened for a big influx of new common councilors—in particular, for the rise to dominance of the City's moderate republicans, with representatives of the colonial-interloping leadership prominently among them.[78]

James Farnell has identified the figures who took control of City politics in 1649. Of the seventeen persons he lists as composing the common council's new leadership, no fewer than seven were colonial and/or East Indian interloping merchants—namely, Owen Rowe, William Pennoyer, Stephen Estwicke, Richard Hutchinson, Samuel Moyer, Richard Shute, and James Russell. All seven had long associations with the new-merchant leadership in a wide variety of commercial and radical political projects, and all (with the possible exception of Russell) were identifiable as religious Independents, congregational or parochial. Among the remaining ten common council leaders listed by Farnell, there were at least five others who, while not necessarily participants in the colonial and interloping trades before 1649, had nevertheless worked alongside the new-merchant leaders in a long series of political and religious activities within the political independent movement—that is, Robert Tichborne, Daniel

[78] Farnell, "Usurpation," p. 24.

Taylor, Mark Hildesley, Edward Parks, and Nathaniel Lacy. Tichborne is familiar as a leading City "uppermost independent," active in radical campaigns from at least 1643. In the 1650s Tichborne would join with the aforementioned Richard Hutchinson, along with John Dethick, a partner of Maurice Thomson's in East Indies interloping, in a new private company for trade with the East Indies. Taylor and Parks, though not overseas merchants, maintained close connections with Bermuda and New England. Both Parks and Taylor had been outstanding activists in the mass petition campaigns that highlighted the City revolution of 1641–1642. Both Taylor and Lacy had been backers of the new merchants' Additional Sea Adventure to Ireland. All of these men (with the possible exception of Parks) were connected with Independent ministers: Hildesley, Taylor, and Lacy were members of John Goodwin's gathered church, and Tichborne belonged to the congregation of George Cockayn.[79] Along with the new-merchant leaders and a relatively small number of other relatively substantial citizens not too different from themselves, they would not only dominate the City government in the first years of the republic, but share the Commonwealth's key administrative positions, especially in finance, the navy, and local military administration.

The new common councilors made clear their radical politics and their intimate ties with the new regime at the national level in their very first actions as magistrates in early January 1649. When the newly elected citizens presented themselves for swearing in as common councilors before the royalist lord mayor Abraham Reynardson, Reynardson attempted to extract from them the traditional oath of allegiance to the king. The common councilors immediately protested to Parliament, and the House of Commons promptly forbade Reynardson to persist with this requirement. Then, at the next common council meeting, held 13 January 1649, the new councilors brought in a major petition for approval by the City and presentation to Parliament. The central demands of this remonstrance represented the top priorities of the new rulers of the City and were at that very moment being echoed throughout the kingdom: (1) execution of justice against the king ("upon all the good and capital authors, contrivers of and actors in the late wars against the Parliament and kingdom from the highest to the lowest"); and (2) the placing "of the militia, navy and all places of high office" into the hands of none but "constant and uniform" supporters of the present government. Lord Mayor Reynardson did everything in his power to obstruct this petition. According to the common council's own narrative of the day's proceedings:

[79] On Tichborne's participation in the East Indian trading syndicate, see Coleman, *Sir John Banks*, pp. 7, 16, 22; KCA, U.234/B1 (records of East Indies trading syndicate led by John Dethick). On Hildesley, see Farnell, "Usurpation," p. 29; Tolmie, *Triumph of the Saints*, pp. 114–15, 184, 187. Hildesley was executor of Daniel Taylor's will (PRO, will of Daniel Taylor, 1655 PCC Aylett 348).

Though [the petition] was often and earnestly pressed for a long time by the major part of the court that it might be read to receive the sense of the court, yet the lord mayor wholly refused to suffer the same or that the question should be put whether it should be read yea or no. After the fruitless expense of many hours another question being drawn up the major part of the court required it to be put . . . to be decided according to the right and custom of the court and being denied therein declared how unjust and of what a destructive nature to the being of the court such a denial would be yet notwithstanding the lord mayor with the two aldermen departed and left the court sitting to the great grief and dissatisfaction of the same.[80]

According to City custom, the attendance of the lord mayor and a certain number of aldermen was required for a common council quorum. By their withdrawal the magistrates thus hoped to terminate the meeting. But the common council continued to meet without the aldermen and the lord mayor. They elected their own chairman and went on to approve the petition for presentation to Parliament. Parliament not only accepted the petition, but voted to sanction the procedural innovation implicit in the council's action. Henceforth, only common councilors (forty in number) were necessary to constitute a quorum, and ten commoners could by themselves call a common council meeting. The lord mayor's consent was no longer to be necessary for either action.[81]

Thus was finally settled a long-standing dispute concerning the distribution of authority among the major bodies that composed the City government. At the time of the City's constitutional revolution of 1641–1642 the common council had taken over, de facto, ultimate decision-making power in the City. Hitherto, meetings of the common council had had to be called by the lord mayor, and the aldermen had held veto rights over all decisions taken. But at a common council meeting held in early 1642, the votes of the twenty-six aldermen were for the first time counted together with those of the 237 common councilmen, and the court of aldermen was thereby deprived of its veto. From that time onward, the magistrates adhered to this precedent, but without any explicit constitutional decision on the matter. In early 1645 when the tide was running strongly in favor of political moderation, the majority of the court of aldermen tried to reassert its old veto power. Only five aldermen opposed this initiative, and it is significant that these included all four of the colonial-interloping merchants who were members of the aldermanic court, Thomas Andrews, Samuel Warner, William Barkeley, and John

---

[80] CLRO, J.Co.Co.40, fols. 313v–314; Farnell, "Usurpation," p. 25.
[81] Sharpe, *London and the Kingdom* 2: 298–99, 303–5; *A.O.* 3: cxi–cxii.

Warner.[82] In 1645, the common council was hardly ready to admit the aldermanic claims, and the matter was left in abeyance until the triumph of the army and the series of events just recounted.

The leading participants in the common council's actions of 13 January 1649, which put the City government strongly on record against the king while at the same time accomplishing a small constitutional revolution in the municipality, can be deduced from the list of twenty men who were chosen to carry the petition to Parliament. They included the colonial-interloping traders Owen Rowe, Richard Shute, William Pennoyer, Thomas Barnardiston, Richard Hutchinson, Samuel Moyer, and Nathan Wright, as well as their aforementioned political independent friends within the common council leadership, Robert Tichborne, Edward Parks, Mark Hildesley, and Daniel Taylor.[83]

Having refashioned the common council to its own taste, the new national government went on to cleanse the aldermanic court of potential opponents. During the spring of 1649, all those who refused to proclaim the establishment of the Commonwealth or the abolition of monarchy were excluded from its ranks. The lord mayor was replaced first, and it is striking that in April 1649 as in September 1647 the choice of his successor was made from the circle of new-merchant leaders. Whereas when the army first invaded London the tobacco trader John Warner replaced the Levant–East India magnate John Gayre, on this occasion the colonial trader and interloper in the East Indies Thomas Andrews took over from the Levant–East India magnate Abraham Reynardson. Both of these purges manifested the dramatic shift in the locus of power in London that had been brought about by civil war and revolution, especially within the ranks of the overseas trading community.[84]

Subsequently, seven other aldermen were forced out, including the Levant–East India establishment merchants John Gayre, John Langham, and Thomas Soames, as well as the famous Levant Company parliamentary oppositionist Richard Chambers, a former friend of the new merchants. Chambers had served on the political presbyterian militia committee of 1648, apparently having become alarmed by the radical turn of politics at the end of the 1640s.[85] This purge left only the radical Isaac Pennington, the old parliamentarian Simond Edmonds, and the royalist trimmer Richard Bateman as Levant–East India Company representatives on the aldermanic court. The political presbyterians Samuel Avery

---

[82] CLRO, Adlermanic Repertories 57, fol. 45v. Alderman John Fowke, the Courteen collaborator and East India Company opponent who had become connected with the new merchant leadership, was not apparently an opponent of restoring the veto.

[83] CLRO, J.Co.Co.40, fol. 313.

[84] Sharpe, *London and the Kingdom* 2: 308, 312; *C.J.* 6: 177.

[85] Sharpe, *London and the Kingdom* 2: 308–11.

and Christopher Packe also trimmed their sails and remained the only aldermen identifiable as Merchant Adventurers. These last four men—Edmonds, Bateman, Avery, and Packe—were all, in 1649, still members of the syndicate in possession of the customs commission. It is not improbable that their desire to hold onto the customs helps to account for the willingness of such prominent political presbyterian leaders to come to terms with the new regime.

SECURING THE NEW REGIME AGAINST ITS ENEMIES

London's revolution of the winter and spring of 1649 had a dual purpose: to establish the political independents in power, and then to bring the weight of what was by far the most important constituency in the country behind the revolution in progress and in support of the republican regime. London's newly installed rulers, as their first act, had placed the City government on record in support of bringing the king to justice. Meanwhile, many of the same persons, as well as others drawn from similar City political groups, were also taking part, as individuals, in the king's trial. Indeed, in the proceedings against Charles I, as well as the subsequent series of state trials by means of which the Commonwealth disposed of its leading enemies, radicals of the City, with new merchants prominently among them, assumed the sort of leadership role at the level of national politics that hitherto had been inconceivable for citizens of London outside the top elite.

Two of the three lawyers selected by Parliament to serve as its prosecutors in Charles's trial, John Bradshaw and William Steele, had long been prominent representatives of London's radical alliance. Bradshaw had established his political credentials very early in the Civil War. In 1643–1644, he was a leading militant of the very radical Salters Hall committee and represented its demands before the common council. In 1645, he served as counsel for John Lilburne in Lilburne's successful appeal to the House of Lords to overturn the star chamber sentence against him for publishing seditious books. Shortly after his nomination to the government's commission for prosecuting the king, Bradshaw was promoted to the presidency of the high court. Not long thereafter, he became the first president of the Commonwealth's new council of state. Steele had been a leading participant in the radicals' offensive of the spring of 1643 and was a promoter of their quasi-republican petition and remonstrance. He was unable to serve as prosecutor in Charles's trial due to illness, not for lack of desire. In the summer of 1649, Steele was chosen London's first recorder under the republic. It might be noted in passing that at the same time Steele was appointed, John Sadler, another radical lawyer from the same political circles, was chosen London's town clerk. Sadler was a member of Samuel Hartlib's group of reformers and, under the new regime, became an important advocate of the Rump's new departures in commercial policy and a leading propagandist for the republican form of government, authoring *Rights of the Kingdom* (London, 1649), a defense of the Commonwealth. Archetypical representatives of what I have termed moderate republicanism in the City, both Steele and Sadler would play important roles in the movement for the progressive reform of the law under the Commonwealth.[86]

The high court chosen to try Charles I was very large, consisting of about 130 persons. Among them, there were about twenty well-established London radicals, including Philip Skippon, Isaac Pennington, Thomas Atkins, Thomas Pride, Richard Salway, Robert Tichborne, Robert Lilburne, Robert Overton, Josias Berners, John Bradshaw, Edmund Harvey, John Venn, John Fowke, Owen Rowe, Randall Mainwaring, Thomas Andrews, Thomas Boone, Francis Allein, Gregory Clement, and Rowland Wilson, of whom the last eight were involved in the colonial-interloping trades.[87]

Radical Londoners were significantly better represented on the thirty-four-person court, also headed by John Bradshaw, that tried the duke of Hamilton, the earl of Holland, and several others for treason two months later. In these trials, the aforementioned William Steele played a leading role in the prosecution, and later published his argument in Hamilton's case. Among the judges in these proceedings were the new merchants Samuel Moyer, William Underwood, Richard Shute, Owen Rowe, William Barkeley, and Stephen Estwicke, as well as their collaborators in the common council leadership Daniel Taylor, Mark Hildesley, and Robert Tichborne, along with two other prominent London radical citizens, William Wyberd and George Langham. It was expressive of the new constellation of power under the Commonwealth that joining these citizens on the high court were a large handful of individuals who as early as 1647 had backed the tolerationist and republican *Articles and Orders* for Eleutheria (Bahamas), including William Rowe, Robert Norwood, John Sparrow, and John Blackwell (who was the son of a London grocer and himself a citizen).[88]

Over the following period, while the army roamed the kingdom putting down its enemies, the City's moderate republican rulers continued to help the new regime maintain internal security. In March 1650, a new

---

[86] *D.N.B.*, s.v. "John Bradshaw," "William Steele," and "John Sadler"; *Dictionary of Seventeenth-Century Radicals*, vol. 1, s.v. "John Bradshaw"; vol. 3, s.v. "William Steele," and "John Sadler." For the movement for law reform under the Commonwealth, see below, ch. 11, pp. 571–76. Steele and Sadler are also notable for their advocacy of toleration for and acceptance of the Jews in England.

[87] *A.O.* 1: 1254–55.

[88] *H.M.C., Seventh Report, Appendix*, p. 71.

High Court of Justice was established to investigate and bring to justice plotters against the government, mutineers, and adherents of the king; no fewer than half of its members were Londoners. The justices included the new merchants William Underwood, Samuel Moyer, Maurice Thomson, Richard Shute, William Pennoyer, Maximillian Bard, Owen Rowe, Thomas Andrews, Stephen Estwicke, and William Barkeley; their common-council collaborators Daniel Taylor, Nathaniel Lacy, and Robert Tichborne; such established London radicals as William Steele (recorder of London), John Sadler (London town clerk), John Langley, William Wyberd, Silvanus Taylor, Josias Berners, Nathaniel Whetham, and Abraham Babington; and the Bahamas project backers John Blackwell, John Sparrow, Robert Norwood, and William Rowe.[89]

While helping the new regime prosecute seditious representatives of the old order, the republican rulers of London were also aiding it in the repression of extremist radicals. The Levellers had hoped to revive their movement in the spring of 1649 by organizing a new campaign around their pamphlet, *The Second Part of Englands New-Chaines Discovered.* But their hopes were irrevocably dashed when their onetime supporters within the Particular Baptist churches refused to come to their aid. In seeking to win over the Levellers to the new republic, the Particular Baptist minister Samuel Richardson assumed the leading role, much as he had done a few months earlier in the efforts to justify the establishment of the Commonwealth by a radical minority and to reconcile the political presbyterians to the revolutionary takeover. For his services in the cause of the new regime, Richardson must have won the appreciation of the newly dominant moderate republicans of London. It was probably no coincidence that, when Richardson published his *Divine Consolation* in 1649, Maurice Thomson wrote a commending epistle.[90]

The social gulf that separated the group of "silken independents," typified by the cosmopolitan nouveaux riches of the new-merchant leadership, from the artisan-based Leveller militants now fully manifested itself in the political arena. Many of the new-merchant leaders and their friends had begun life among the City's humble shopkeeping and mariner elements. It was in fact their close and continuing connection with the City's "middling" and "industrious sorts of people" that had in part inspired their ideals, and that had enabled them to work so intimately and relatively successfully with the City's mass movements and sectarian churches, as well as with the extremely radical politicians who had emerged from them, during the greater part of the 1640s. But those days were now long past. As the Leveller William Walwyn sarcastically described the political in-

[89] *A.O.* 2: 364–67.
[90] Tolmie, *Triumph of the Saints*, pp. 181–84, 141.

dependents' rapid rise to riches and office and their tendency to trumpet their success as a sign of God's favor, "It seems your congregation is of near relation to those that hold prosperity a mark of the true church."[91] Walwyn oversimplified, but he was not entirely off the mark when he bitterly charged the political independents with betraying their former friends and supporters. They "had but run with the stream, and turned with the times . . . changed principle with their condition."[92]

Quite appropriately, it was the colonial-interloping leader Thomas Andrews, a longtime member of Sydrach Simpson's gathered congregation, who, as first Commonwealth lord mayor of London, met with Oliver Cromwell to arrange a City feast for Parliament, the council of state, and the army officers, after they had bloodily destroyed the Leveller dissidents at Burford in May 1649. Nor was it surprising that the preacher at that feast was the longtime comrade in arms of both the new-merchant leadership and their political independent friends within the army, the Independent minister Hugh Peter.[93] When the House of Commons arranged its own occasion to thank God for "reducing the Levellers," it chose, in similar manner, the great Independent clerics Thomas Goodwin and John Owen. Peter, Goodwin, and Owen, with their Independent clerical colleagues Joseph Carryl and Philip Nye, became the leading political propagandists for the Commonwealth.[94] These were the ministers supported by the new merchants and many of their political independent friends in the City. On the issue of Leveller subversion, as on the general question of who was to rule under the Commonwealth, they and their patrons were as one.

STAFFING THE NEW REGIME: THE MILITIA

While carrying through their small constitutional revolution, cleansing their own house of opponents of the regime, and helping the new government destroy its more radical and more conservative opponents, the moderate republicans of London played an important role in the purges carried out by the Commonwealth at all levels of government and took a truly pivotal position in the new national administration. One of the London radicals' first demands on coming to power within the City was that places of public trust, especially in the militia and the navy, be cleansed of unreliable elements and replaced by trustworthy men like themselves. For this, the new regime needed no urging, and in the restaffing of strategic

---

[91] Walwyn, *Walwyn's Just Defence*, p. 372.
[92] Ibid., p. 371.
[93] *Mercurius Elencticus*, no. 6 (28 May–4 June 1649).
[94] B. Worden, *The Rump Parliament, 1648–1653* (Cambridge, 1974), pp. 122, 195.

governmental positions that followed, the colonial-interloping merchants and their radical City friends were assigned the central role.

Given the pivotal importance of London's armed forces to the Commonwealth's security, especially in view of the festering hostility to the regime within London, the City and suburban militia committees had, of necessity, to be revamped. In May 1648, London's political presbyterians had, once again, installed their own City militia commission, so the new regime was obliged to turn once more to its allies in the City to create a new one. On 17 January 1649, Parliament appointed its own militia commission and, as in September 1647, this body was dominated by that radical leadership which had launched the City offensives of 1641–1643, which had formed political independency in London from the middle 1640s, and which had come to constitute the core of the City's newly empowered ruling group. Of its thirty-seven members, fifteen had been members of the City militia committee in 1642–1643, and three others had been leaders of London's radical upsurge of that period; similarly, twenty-four had been members of the army-appointed militia committee of 1647. Looked at from a slightly different angle, the committee included twelve activists in the colonial-interloping trades—Thomas Andrews, Rowland Wilson, Gregory Clement, Owen Rowe, William Underwood, John Dethick, Samuel Moyer, Stephen Estwicke, Richard Shute, Francis Allein, John Pocock, and the Courteen collaborator and East India Company opponent John Fowke; one additional overseas trader with whom they often worked on both commercial and political affairs— Richard Salway; and three other citizens with whom they were closely allied politically on the new Commonwealth common council—Robert Tichborne, Mark Hildesley, and Daniel Taylor.[95] As on the occasion of the army's previous invasion of London in 1647, the City's suburbs were given control of their own militias; and once again, small groups of new-merchant radicals were strategically placed on the new commissions. In Tower Hamlets, Maurice Thomson, Samuel Moyer, William Pennoyer, and William Willoughby were again appointed, as were George Thomson, George Snelling, George Pasfield and Robert Haughton in Southwark.[96]

STAFFING THE NEW REGIME: THE NAVY

As had the City militia, the parliamentary navy had been filled with subversive elements. To confront the problem, the new regime turned immediately to its friends among the new merchants. This was to be ex-

[95] *A.O.* 1: 1261.
[96] *A.O.* 2: 123, 195.

pected, in view of their service to the parliamentary navy throughout the Civil War period, as well as their close connections with the new leaders of the navy under the Commonwealth.

At the outbreak of the Civil War, much of the English navy had taken Parliament's side. Nevertheless, Parliament had nowhere near enough ships to confront the royalists and interrupt shipping to royalist strongholds, and was obliged to turn to private shipowners for help. Colonial-interloping traders, as noted, appear to have provided a disproportionate number of the ships for the parliamentary navy and, in addition, to have carried out themselves, on a private basis, a great number of privateering ventures under parliamentary commissions to capture ships bound for royalist ports. In this way, they achieved positions of influence and trust within the earl of Warwick's naval administration.[97]

It was only natural, then, that in late May 1648, in the wake of the royalist naval uprising, the Derby House committee called on Maurice Thomson and some of his friends to go to Holland to seek to recover the ships in revolt. Nor was it surprising that, half a year later, the new republican government turned to the new merchants for the task of politically cleansing its navy and helping to organize a new naval administration—and even less so in view of the fact that the leadership of Commonwealth naval policy making and administration was in the hands of intimate friends of theirs. In the earliest days of the republic, Miles Corbet, who had collaborated closely with the new merchants and the City's Independent ministers on a long series of radical political and religious projects during the 1640s, headed up Parliament's committee of the navy, which was in charge of financing the navy and overseeing naval administration. During the course of the following year, George Thomson, Maurice's brother, succeeded Corbet, and in 1650 formally became the navy committee's chairman.[98] Meanwhile, shortly after Pride's Purge, on 15 December 1648, the House of Commons ordered its committee of the navy to "confer with Mr. William Pennoyer, Col. William Willoughby, Mr. Samuel Moyer, alderman John Fowke, William Barkeley, and Maurice Thomson and such other persons as they think fit for the present supply of the navy with money or any other navy business."[99] All these men were, of course, at the heart of the new-merchant leadership, and this parliamentary order gave the signal to hand over to the new merchants a dominant role in all aspects of Commonwealth naval policy and administration.

[97] Groenveld, "First Anglo-Dutch War," pp. 548–51. See also above, ch. 8, p. 432–34.

[98] Worden, *Rump Parliament*, pp. 59, 166–67; Cogar, "Politics of Naval Administration," p. 36. The Commonwealth's navy is referred to in February 1649 as "Miles Corbett's fleet" by *Mercurius Pragmaticus*, quoted in V. Rowe, *Sir Henry Vane the Younger* (London, 1970), p. 159.

[99] *C.J.* 6: 97.

In order to assure the navy's loyalty to the new regime by removing its former political presbyterians and royalists at all levels, the Commons appointed, on 16 January 1649, a sixteen-person commission for the "regulation of the navy and the customs." It was entirely in the hands of Maurice Thomson and his new-merchant friends and included, besides Maurice Thomson, Robert Thomson, William Willoughby, Thomas Andrews, Thomas Andrews's son Jonathan Andrews, William Barkeley, Stephen Estwicke, Richard Hill, Samuel Moyer, the brothers Samuel and William Pennoyer, James Russell, Richard Shute, and Richard Hutchinson. John Langley and John Holland were the only commissioners who were not colonial-interloping merchants. No fewer than ten of these commissioners had been among the backers of the new merchants' Additional Sea Adventure to Ireland in 1642; ten were also contemporaneously participants in Maurice Thomson's challenge to the East India Company, both inside and outside that corporation.[100]

In the first uncertain months of the new regime, the committee for regulating the navy and the customs, or the "committee of merchants" as it was sometimes called, not only sought to ensure the political reliability of the parliamentary navy but also took initial responsibility for creating a new, more efficient naval administration for the Commonwealth. The committee members prepared a model of all positions and personnel in the navy and shipyard, and saw to it that salaries were raised and that workers were paid more promptly. In an effort to reduce corruption, they banned the old custom whereby workers accepted perquisites for their work. Simultaneously, they sought to carry through a political purge designed to root out elements sympathetic to the recent royalist rising within the fleet.[101]

Meanwhile, on 15 February 1649, the parliamentary navy committee had called on the commission for regulating the navy and the customs to nominate what was to be a permanent committee in charge of day-to-day administration of the navy and the shipyards. All five of the persons ultimately chosen to constitute this navy commission were also members of the regulating committee, and they included Maurice's brother Robert, the New England merchant, and Maurice's longtime business partners

---

[100] *A.O.* 1: 1257. The Additional Sea Adventurers on the regulating commission included Thomas Andrews, Richard Hill, Richard Hutchinson, William Pennoyer, Samuel Moyer, Richard Shute, Samuel Pennoyer, Maurice Thomson, Robert Thomson, and William Willoughby (among whom Maurice Thomson, Shute, William Pennoyer, Willoughby, and Hill were among the commissioners who directed the Adventurers' project). The East Indian interlopers on the regulating commission included Thomas Andrews, William Barkeley, Stephen Estwicke, Richard Hill, William Pennoyer, Samuel Moyer, James Russell, Richard Shute, Samuel Pennoyer, Maurice Thomson, and Robert Thomson.

[101] Cogar, "Politics of Naval Administration," pp. 74–88.

William Willoughby and Thomas Smythe. Willoughby, a ship captain and shipowner with many ties to New England, had worked closely for many years with Thomson and Gregory Clement in privateering in the Americas, as well as in the tobacco trade with Virginia. Smythe had been a promoter of the republican Bahamas project of the summer of 1647; had petitioned with Maurice Thomson, Stephen Estwicke, Richard Shute, and Thomas Andrews in their (unsuccessful) bid to take over the customs in September 1647; and was a member of Maurice Thomson's ten-person syndicate that undertook the £83,000 Irish army provisioning contract in March 1648. For a time, the navy commission and the regulating committee worked together on naval administration, but eventually the navy commission alone assumed this task, directly implementing the policies decided on by Parliament—contracting for vessels for the state's service; constructing, repairing, and supplying ships; providing ordnance; and so on.[102]

During the summer of 1648, Trinity House, the corporation of shippers, had taken part in the movement to bring back the king and supported the navy's revolt against Parliament. On 29 June 1648, Trinity House had petitioned Parliament "that since His Majesty's evil council were removed from him, and no face of an enemy appearing to obstruct, that, by the settling of His Majesty in his just rights, this miserable distressed Kingdom might [enjoy] a happy and lasting peace." A few weeks later, the earl of Warwick referred to rumors circulating in Holland that Trinity House was encouraging seamen to join the service of the ships in revolt.[103] When the political independents came to power, therefore, they had to put the government of Trinity House into commission in order to destroy its royalist influence. On 23 February 1649, a committee of nine, expanded to twelve later in the year, was appointed to govern Trinity House.[104] In view of his service to Parliament against the rebellious ships, it is understandable that Maurice Thomson was appointed to this committee. Joining him were his partners in East Indian interloping, Samuel Moyer and Jeremy Blackman. George Pasfield, a trader with the West Indies, was another member of the committee.

The importance of the parliamentary commission for Trinity House during the early years of the Commonwealth has sometimes been missed; in fact, this body played a part in formulating Commonwealth commercial policy. This becomes less surprising when it is noted that alongside the new-merchant leaders on the Trinity House commission sat a number of truly pivotal figures in the Commonwealth with whom the new merchants

[102] *C.J.* 6: 144; Cogar, "Politics of Naval Administration," pp. 44–48.

[103] *L.J.* 1: 352; G. G. Harris, "The History of Trinity House at Deptford, 1514–1660" (University of London, M.A. thesis, 1962), p. 27.

[104] *C.J.* 6: 150, 290.

would collaborate on many occasions—in particular, the republican king-pin Thomas Scot, as well as Col. Richard Deane, appointed in February 1649 (with Robert Blake and Edward Popham) one of the three commanders of the fleet.

To fill out the foregoing picture of new-merchant domination of Commonwealth naval administration, it should be added that the commission for the sale of prize goods, as well as the new syndicate organized in 1650 that won the navy supply contract, were both under the influence of colonial-interloping traders and their moderate republican political allies. The sixteen-person prize goods commission included the new merchants Robert Thomson, Maurice Thomson, Robert Dennis, William Barkeley, Nathaniel Andrews, George Pasfield, and Owen Rowe, as well as their political allies on the common council Mark Hildesley and Daniel Taylor.[105] The eight-man syndicate that took control of the lucrative business of supplying the navy included the colonial-interloping traders Thomas Alderne, Nathaniel Andrews, John Limbrey, and Dennis Gawden (as well as Col. Thomas Pride).[106] Finally, it should be pointed out that the man appointed to be treasurer of the Commonwealth navy, perhaps the key figure in naval administration under the Commonwealth, was the New England merchant, interloper in the East Indies, and Commonwealth common council leader, Richard Hutchinson.[107]

STAFFING THE NEW REGIME: FINANCE

To finance the Commonwealth, the new government felt obliged to re-model the entire financial administration and to place its friends in the most crucial positions. This meant appointing, once again, essentially the same group of individuals that had taken leadership in the common council, that had staffed the City militia, and that had assumed charge of the navy. Basically, there were three categories of financial administration: taxation on internal and external trade (customs and excise); sale of property formerly in the hands of persons or institutions opposed to or dissolved by Parliament (delinquents, bishops, deans and chapters, the Crown); and direct taxation (the assessment). Leaving aside the Crown lands (which were allocated to paying off the army's arrears) and the bishops' lands (which by 1649 had been mostly sold off), administration in all of these areas was placed in the hands of much the same interlocking groups, with the new merchants again in a central position.

In January 1643, at the time of the radicals' offensive, the parliamen-

---

[105] A.O. 2: 75.

[106] Coleman, *Sir John Banks*, p. 10.

[107] C.J. 6: 438–40; Rowe, *Sir Henry Vane*, pp. 170–71. Hutchinson was appointed in October 1650. For biographical information on him, see Aylmer, *State's Servants*, pp. 247–50.

tary customs commission had been captured by representatives of the new-merchant leadership and their friends, specifically Maurice Thomson, Stephen Estwicke, Thomas Andrews, William Barkeley, Francis Allein, James Russell, John Fowke, and Richard Chambers. In 1645, these men had lost the commission to a group of wealthy political presbyterians. Even following the army's invasion of London in 1647, Thomson, Andrews, and Estwicke, along with Richard Shute and Thomas Smythe, had failed in their effort to get back the commission. However, with the triumph of the political independents, the new government felt obliged to reward its friends. Maurice Thomson's committee for regulating the navy and the customs was given charge of nominating the new five-person customs commission. Chosen were the interloper in the East Indies Stephen Estwicke, along with Robert Tichborne, Mark Hildesley, Daniel Taylor, and Edward Parks, the common council leaders who worked with the new-merchant leadership on so many other political and administrative bodies in these years. When Parks died in 1652, he was replaced on the customs commission by Maurice Thomson's brother George.[108]

The excise commission was the only one of the financial plums that had eluded the new-merchant leadership entirely in the early years of the Civil War. It had gone to a heterogeneous syndicate of London citizens, including several of the few establishment company merchants who chose to support Parliament rather than the king. But in September 1650, the Commonwealth bestowed the excise commission on a six-man syndicate led by Maurice Thomson and his former colonial merchant partner George Snelling, the MP and militia commissioner from Southwark.[109]

The former committees in charge of overseeing national taxation (the assessment) and of compounding with delinquents were consolidated during the Commonwealth into a single seven-person body—the commission for the advance of money of 1650. The leading colonial-interloping radicals, Samuel Moyer and James Russell, served on this body, alongside the New England trader and colonist Edward Winslow (who was the agent in England for the Plymouth Colony) and the Bahamas project promoter Arthur Squibb.[110] The fifteen trustees for deans and chapter lands included the new merchants Owen Rowe, Stephen Estwicke, and Rowland Wilson, their radical friends from the common council leadership Robert Tichborne, Daniel Taylor, and Mark Hildesley, and Samuel Pennoyer's father-in-law William Hobson.[111]

---

[108] B. Capp, *Cromwell's Navy* (Oxford, 1989), p. 50; *C.J.* 6: 193 (24 Apr. 1649); *C.J.* 7: 118 (8 Apr. 1652).

[109] *A.O.* 2: 422.

[110] *C.J.* 6: 395.

[111] *A.O.* 2: 82–83.

The remarkable eminence achieved under the Commonwealth by the new merchants and their London radical colleagues, both nationally and in London, reflected the pivotal position they had come to occupy as backers of the revolutionary government. That England's new rulers not only understood and appreciated their supporting role but sympathized with many of their aims and ideals was to be amply demonstrated in the policies considered and adopted by the new republic.

[XI]

Political Independents, New Merchants,
and the Commonwealth

T HE ESTABLISHMENT of the Commonwealth, I have tried
to argue, represented the triumph of an emergent alliance of radical forces in the army, Parliament, and the City. In part, of
course, this alliance consolidated itself in power simply in response to
short-term tactical exigencies. The hardening belief, following the Second
Civil War, that Charles I would never abide by any peace agreement,
along with the intensifying pressures exerted by the army's rank and file,
induced these forces to break definitively from their former middle-group
allies and to seize state power. Subsequently, the threat posed by democratic militants to the new regime's stability, in the face of its already
narrowed sociopolitical base, led them effectively to destroy the Levellers.
These steps were motivated, in the first instance, by immediate, practical
considerations; nevertheless, they had far reaching consequences for im-
parting political definition to the new Commonwealth government. Taken
together, they meant the defeat and loss of influence of an extraordinary
range of political tendencies across the entire spectrum of political forces
that had fought against the king since 1642. Almost the whole of the old
parliamentary party that had defeated the royalists lost control over the
political process—from crypto-royalists through political presbyterians to
the most radical of the middle-group independents, and excepting only
.the radical wing of the political independent alliance. Simultaneously,
what might be generally termed the democratic wing of the revolution
suffered definitive defeat. The victorious revolutionary alliance thus defined itself, in negative terms, as constituted by those elements that had
refused both to bargain further with the king and to accede to the demands
of Leveller radicalism. The fact remains, as I have tried to argue, that the
coalition of forces that came to power in the Commonwealth was hardly a
tactical makeshift constructed on the spur of the moment. Nor were the
steps it took to consolidate its rule merely pragmatically motivated. Nor
was the political outcome it achieved—by which its more moderate parliamentary and political presbyterian opponents and its more radical sectarian and democratic opponents were simultaneously dispatched—acci-

dentally arrived at. The radical alliance that made the revolution and then crushed the democratic movement within its ranks had been long in preparation and, by 1648, possessed certain rough and ready political and organizational foundations—a functioning network of political connections and an emergent agreement on certain ideological conceptions, reform ideas, and policy departures. As a result, the Commonwealth took on a rather distinctive political character—and projected a definite if limited radicalism—that distinguished it from all English governments that preceded and followed it.

Of course, from the standpoint of the Levellers and their allies among the sects, the radicalism of the Commonwealth was pale indeed. Once they had seized power, the leaders of the new government showed little interest in allowing the people greater political participation or in instituting social reforms that might restrict property rights. Nevertheless, the conservatism of the Rump can be and has been exaggerated, especially when its political character has been compared only with that of the democratic and separatist militants and not with that of what had been, and what was again to become, the established political mainstream. In comparison with any of the other English governments of the seventeenth century, before or after the Interregnum, always dominated by the greater landed classes, the Commonwealth represented a truly radical departure. This was so with respect to the political attitudes of a significant section of its leadership, the social and political character of its main supporters, the institutions through which it governed, the constitutional ideas by which it justified those institutions, the religious conceptions and policies that it expressed and implemented, the range of reforms it seriously considered, and its positive political achievements, above all in the realm of commercial and foreign affairs.

In the first place, then, compared with any regime that preceded or followed it in the seventeenth century, the Rump possessed a very radical leadership. The men who seized power with the army's march on London in December 1648 and who determined the character of the revolution in the period through the king's execution were, in their overwhelming majority, war-party radicals, radical political independents, and regicides. According to Blair Worden, the triumvirate of Thomas Scot, Thomas Chaloner, and Henry Marten, all self-conscious republicans, composed the revolution's top political leadership during this period. Among their most important collaborators at this juncture were the long-established parliamentary radicals, reformers, and architects of the revolution of 1648 Cornelius Holland and Sir Henry Mildmay. Their allies at this point also included John Blackiston, John Carew, Sir John Danvers, Gilbert Millington, Humphrey Edwards, Sir Gregory Norton, John Venn, Miles Corbet, William Purefoy, Augustine Garland, Lord Grey of

Groby, Sir James Harrington, John Lisle, Nicholas Love, Sir Thomas Wroth, Luke Robinson, and Alexander Rigby, along with the army leaders Oliver Cromwell, Henry Ireton, and Thomas Harrison. This list reads like a roll call of Parliament's most radical activists during the whole of the Civil War period. It is quite true, and needs to be emphasized, that the republicans Chaloner, Marten, and Scot and their radical friends did not, for long, rule by themselves, but were soon obliged to integrate into the top Commonwealth leadership a number of very major figures who were politically more moderate than themselves. The fact remains that, throughout the Commonwealth period, these radical figures exerted a powerful and often dominant influence on the formation of government policy. That persons with their political outlook could, through so much of this epoch, maintain the political initiative—even if they were often frustrated in the achievement of their goals—had an enormous impact on the political complexion of the Commonwealth and would have been unheard of in any other English government of the seventeenth century, before or after the Interregnum.[1]

The same point can be demonstrated from a slightly different angle. Worden has singled out from among the Rump's 220 to 230 members the Commonwealth's leading parliamentary activists. Of the 33 MPs he lists, 14 were regicides and 22 were among those categorized by David Underdown as revolutionaries. Correlatively, almost half were either religious separatists or parochial or congregational Independents. The Rump leadership was thus constituted in large part by what was, in ideological terms, a tiny radical minority within England's political class. Representatives of that radical minority had carried through the revolution of 1648, with the help of militants in the army and London drawn largely from social layers well beneath their own.[2]

Second, the organized political groups on which the Commonwealth rested were significantly more radical politically and religiously and were drawn from layers far lower on the socioeconomic scale than were any of the primarily noble and gentry groups on which all seventeenth-century governments before 1647–1648 and after 1660 were essentially founded. Above all, of course, the Commonwealth depended on the army. The army's officer corps, recruited mostly from the lower ranks of the landed class or from entirely outside it, was notoriously heterogeneous ideologically and far from uniformly radical in either political or religious

---

[1] B. Worden, *The Rump Parliament, 1648–1653* (Cambridge, 1974), pp. 35–38. This chapter is much indebted to Worden's work, as well as to D. Underdown, *Pride's Purge* (Oxford, 1971), ch. 9.

[2] Worden, *Rump Parliament*, pp. 387–91. I have added to Worden's most-active list Rowland Wilson, who died in 1650. For the political and religious characterizations of the individuals on Worden's most-active list, I have relied on Underdown's categorizations in *Pride's Purge*, app. A. Only 5 percent of the MPs in 1648 fell in Underdown's category of "revolutionaries."

terms—witness its leader, Oliver Cromwell. The fact remains that the army leadership had distinguished itself precisely by its willingness to break from even the most politically adventurous of the middle-group or royal independents in order to make the revolution and found the new regime. In so doing, it embraced, at least formally—though not, in the case of a number of its top leaders, really substantively—the very radical ideological outlook expressed in Henry Ireton's army remonstrance, adopted by the army council in November 1648, and in the revised *Second Agreement of the People*, approved by the army council in January 1649. In the years that followed, moreover, both at the behest of its own membership and sometimes in response to pressure from its rank and file, the army officer corps gave serious consideration to a range of opinion and actual backing to concrete proposals for political, legal, and religious reforms that would have been dismissed as extremist by the majority of the political nation either before 1648 or after 1660.

Besides the army, the Commonwealth relied politically, to a far greater extent than did any other English government before or after the Interregnum, on citizens of London from outside the City's established governing circles, that is, outside that aldermanic elite, heavily composed of great merchant leaders of the overseas chartered companies, which had traditionally ruled. In fact, as has been emphasized, the new ruling group in London on which the Commonwealth depended excluded not only the heavily royalist old City elite, but also those magistrates, drawn largely from what might roughly be called the second rank of London citizens, who had constituted the political presbyterian leadership. The Rump was thus obliged to look to the long-standing City radical alliance, now largely shorn of its democratic and separatist wing, not only to staff important administrative posts and to offer financial support, but also to provide crucial assistance on internal security and general political collaboration. Prominently included among these newly ascendant political independent groups were, of course, representatives of the new-merchant leadership, as well as a number of other important City sociopolitical forces.

It is true that, precisely because its main sources of support were so narrow, and its roots within those broad landed-class layers that composed the traditional political nation so restricted, the coalition of forces that made the revolution and led the Commonwealth government found that there was a large gulf between what it wanted in the abstract and what it could hope to achieve yet still retain power. In order to consolidate the regime, on the one hand against royalist and political presbyterian resistance and on the other against the Levellers' subversion, the Rump had to find allies. In particular, to have a hope of stabilizing the new government, the Commonwealth government had to find some way to neutralize, and to win at least the passive support of, the staunchly conservative and largely alienated mass of the nation's gentry, which held the key to the success of any English government. To consolidate their rule, the new Commonwealth governors thus had little choice but to welcome back to the House of Commons well over one hundred MPs who had more or less explicitly rejected all aspects of the revolution of 1648–1649. This large antiradical block put major direct constraints on what the Rump leadership could hope to do. At the same time, the Commonwealth leadership had little alternative but strictly to *self-limit* its own radical program so as not too much to offend and provoke moderate opinion in the country at large. As a result, partly in consequence of the opposition from returning conservative MPs and partly in consequence of their own concern to achieve stability for the regime, the radical leaders of the Rump either failed to have passed or found themselves actually opposing not only the series of reform demands that had initially emanated from the Levellers, but also less extreme if still highly controversial reform proposals that were forwarded from the army and from the often still militant separatist churches of London.[3] These latter propositions were largely designed to help the poor at the expense of the rich, especially through changes in the law and in judicial procedure, to eliminate government interference in religion and moral conduct through granting unrestricted toleration and abolishing tithes, and to increase popular participation in government, especially in London. But they made relatively little headway within the Commonwealth government, and the result was that those militant elements from inside the army, as well as from the sectarian churches of the City, that continued to agitate for such reforms became progressively more alienated from the regime.

The ultimate result of the aforementioned constraints on Rump policy-making, in the context of the Commonwealth's initial defeats of its democratic-sectarian, its political presbyterian, and its parliamentary middle-group opponents, was, however, less to eradicate the Rump's radicalism than to give it a highly distinctive form. What the Rump leadership wanted that it could also achieve—the new regime's actual ideological coloring and the policies it was able to implement—turned out to correspond, to an extraordinary degree, to the ideals and aspirations of that rather narrow alliance of political independent forces that had assumed power in London in consequence of the revolution of 1648. The perspec-

---

[3] This follows Worden, *Rump Parliament*, and Underdown, *Pride's Purge*, both of whom attribute the Rump's failure to realize the radicals' hopes in large part to the resistance of the generally conservative returning MPs. Worden also emphasizes that the radicalism of the Rump's ostensibly radical leaders turned out in practice to be rather limited (pp. 41–42). However, he does not make adequately clear to what extent he attributes this to the genuine beliefs and desires of these men, and to what degree he attributes it to their understanding of the need to compromise in order to retain power, given the sociopolitical realities.

tives and policies that were acted on by the Commonwealth leadership—especially by those self-styled republican and radical groups in Parliament that continued to play a central role in governing the nation, strongly supported by the political independent coalition that ruled London—had this in common: they were largely unacceptable to, or inadequate for, *both* the overwhelming majority of the conservative gentry *and* the plebeian Levellers, as well as the less radical though still politically extreme saintly radicals, heavily recruited from the ranks of artisans and small tradesmen, who remained politically active in the army and London. The moderate republicans who ruled the Rump and the City wanted parliamentary supremacy, rejecting both the balanced constitution of the gentry and the Levellers' democracy. They wanted sanction for voluntary gathered autonomous churches and a significant degree of toleration, but also a state-regulated and state-supported religious settlement and government control of moral conduct; this was in some contrast with both the religious uniformity required by the gentry and the untrammeled liberty for religious experimentation and the abolition of tithes demanded by the Levellers and the separatists. They wanted the moderate reform of the law and of government in the interests of progress, economy, and efficiency, in opposition both to the gentry, which steadfastly supported the maintenance of privilege and the common law, as well as the lawyers' vested interests, and to the groups of Levellers and some of the sectarian churches, which wanted legal reforms in the interests of the poor, however these might threaten property and the common law, and which were overtly antilawyer. Finally, and perhaps most characteristically, the moderate republican alliance that made the revolution and, to a large extent, ruled the Commonwealth wanted commercial expansionism and imperial aggression on the world scale.

It has been rightly argued that, under the Commonwealth, the Rump leadership found itself very limited in what it could achieve. It has, however, been less clearly seen how relatively radical the Commonwealth still turned out to be and very closely what it did attempt and actually accomplish conformed to the hopes and dreams of London's newly ascendant political independent ruling group, in particular of the new-merchant leadership. The aim of this chapter and the one that follows is to make that demonstration.

Oligarchic Republicanism

It would be wrong to argue that, in constructing the revolutionary institutional foundations of the new regime, the revolutionaries of 1648–1649 were self-consciously applying well worked out and clearly understood political theories. But it would also be misleading to understand their actions as purely pragmatic responses to situational pressures. By the end of the 1640s, most of those who actually made the revolution of 1648 knew that they wanted parliamentary supremacy. They understood that this meant the severest restriction on, if not the total abolition of, the constitutional powers that had formerly accrued to the king and his nobles; they had gone at least some way toward articulating the constitutional ideas that might justify and satisfactorily explain their actions; and they knew they had the support of influential social forces for both their political conceptions and the revolutionary constitutional innovations that followed from them—not only in the officer corps of the army but also in the new leadership of London. Indeed, London's political independents, or moderate republicans, had played a not insignificant role in advancing the ideas through which the revolution was justified.

As early as 1643, war-party militants, especially in the City, had begun to advance conceptions of parliamentary supremacy based on popular sovereignty. In fact, the quasi-republican *Petition* and *Remonstrance*, which highlighted the Londoner's campaign for an independent citizens' army in the spring and summer of 1643, was specifically designed to oppose and go beyond, both tactically and ideologically, the strategic perspectives of the middle-group leaders in Parliament and the vague conceptions of a traditional balanced constitution that they used to justify those perspectives. By the end of the 1640s, in such documents as the *Articles and Orders* of the Bahamas, which was jointly supported by new-merchant, army, and parliamentary radicals, as well as in the writings of the new merchants' and army officers' intimate associate Hugh Peter and in the declarations of Peter's close collaborator Henry Ireton, these ideas had been further articulated and given a somewhat oligarchic definition, especially in opposition to the democratic conceptions of the Levellers. Specifically, Parliament's own understanding of *salus populi*—rather than any direct expression of *vox populi* through more democratized institutions—was to be the practical principle of legitimacy. In this revised form, which I have termed in a rough and ready way moderate republican, these conceptions provided the basis for the series of epoch-making political and institutional transformations through which the Commonwealth was established—the execution of the king, the abolition of the House of Lords, the abolition of the monarchy, and the declaring of England a "free state."

It is crucial, then, to emphasize that the radical alliance that came to power in 1648–1649 distinguished itself politically, and not just tactically, from its former allies of the middle group and that it went about justifying its actions in terms of its own ideological perspectives. During the first year or so of the new regime, the Commonwealth debated and decisively rejected schemes for the preservation of kingship and the

House of Lords that had been advanced by various more moderate political forces. The revolutionary ruling group also ensured the continued influence of its own political perspectives by defeating moves to readmit all members ousted in Pride's purge and for an act of oblivion for the Rump's enemies.[4] Moreover, the Commonwealth's new rulers did not hesitate to frame these actions in terms of their own particular version of popular sovereignty. On 4 January 1649, in overriding the Lords' refusal to cooperate in trying the king, the Commons proclaimed that "the people are, under God, the original of all just power," a foundational political principle that could have been accepted by only the tiniest minority of the traditional political nation. But, in the very same resolution, the Commons also declared that "the Commons of England, in Parliament assembled, being chosen by, and representing the people, have the supreme power in the nation," a proposition that, in the eyes of the Leveller democrats and their separatist allies, rendered the acceptance of popular sovereignty without much practical significance. Underdown writes that "the Commons had proclaimed the sovereignty of the people in the 4 January resolution, but by declaring themselves the repositories of that sovereignty, they had at once sought to escape from the dangerous logic of their own principles." His sentence captures precisely the position and outlook of the new Commonwealth ruling group, and most particularly its supporters in London.[5] The Commonwealth's new leaders had achieved, by way of revolution based heavily on popular mobilization, an extraordinary, if still quite restricted, freedom of action over and against the country's traditional rulers. They now sought to make use of what they emphasized was a popularly derived parliamentary supremacy in order to govern without popular interference, according to their own lights. In so doing, they received the dynamic, and unreserved, support of the City's new rulers who, as noted, took the lead both in demanding the king's execution in January 1649 and in celebrating the Levellers' destruction the following June.

Religious Reformation

The Rump's religious perspectives were, in crucial respects, analogous to its political principles. They amounted on the one hand to a disavowal of the religious programs of almost all sections of the old parliamentary party, and, more specifically, to a rejection of episcopacy, of a national Presbyterian structure in any form, and of religious uniformity. On the

---

[4] Worden, *Rump Parliament*, pp. 170–71.

[5] *C.J.* 6: 109–11; Underdown, *Pride's Purge*, pp. 173, 263 (quotation). Underdown provides quotations from Commonwealth officials of the same period to similar effect.

other hand, they meant a dismissal of the demands of the Levellers and the separatists for the full separation of church and state. Grossly speaking, the Commonwealth's religious settlement represented the victory of congregational and parochial Independent perspectives: it brought mild toleration, complemented by the continuation of a national church, and state intervention to enforce and regulate social behavior. As such, it conformed, almost perfectly, to the specifications of London's new rulers, who used their newly won hegemony to establish an analogous regime in the City, with the goal of installing a new religious pluralism within a context of state-assured social discipline. In fact, London's magistrates played a not insignificant role in constructing a new religious order in the City, while they also helped establish national religious policy.

During its first two years, the Commonwealth established the main lines of its state-backed tolerationist perspective. On 7 August 1649, the Commons defeated an ordinance calling for the endorsement of Presbyterian government and use of the Directory, recommitting this legislation as showing "insufficient respect for tender consciences." This negative action was confirmed a year later when the Commons passed the so-called Toleration Act repealing compulsory churchgoing. Nevertheless, the Commons proved unwilling to go any further than this in reducing state intervention in religious affairs, passing a bill in June 1649 for maintaining ministers partly out of state funds and refusing on a series of occasions to abolish tithes.[6]

London's new political independent rulers clearly approved this direction, but wanted the state to take further steps to regulate public behavior. It also wanted the Commonwealth to assume greater responsibility for propagating the gospel. On 23 January 1650, the City drew up for presentation to the Commons a petition to the following effect: "As this Parliament hath expressed their tender care of men conscientiously dissenting, so you would be pleased to improve your authority to the uttermost for the interest of true religion and suppressing of all such principles and practices as would raze the foundations of piety and civil government. And that more clear and numerous laws be made or supplied against unlawful swearing, cursing . . . and profaning of the Lord's day." The City went on, in its petition, to express its joy at the recent act for propagation of the gospel to the Indians in America. However, it demanded that similar efforts also be made within England itself, calling for the "spreading of the gospel to dark corners of this land." Here London's new political independent rulers were taking up the proposals of the new merchants' old friend Hugh Peter, who had become during the later 1640s perhaps the

[6] Underdown, *Pride's Purge*, pp. 271–72, 275; Worden, *Rump Parliament*, pp. 121, 206–7, 238.

country's most prominent supporter of systematic internal missionary work and had made it a cornerstone of his program for the postrevolutionary settlement. Peter proposed that the government take responsibility for funding and organizing the perambulations through every county of full-time intinerant ministers, and his idea appears to have won the enthusiastic support of various wings of religious Independency, in London and elsewhere.[7]

Within a week of the City's petition, the Commons had called for the framing of a series of bills to implement the City's requests and, during the following spring, these bills were put forward, considered, and passed into law. In April, the House approved a new law better to enforce the Sabbath; in May, it passed a harsh act, carrying the death penalty, against incest, adultery, and fornication; and in June, it legislated against swearing and cursing. In addition, it sought to repress Ranter publications and activities.[8]

During the same period, the House also moved to have the gospel propagated throughout the British Isles. It had already established a commission for such missionary work in New England, among whose sixteen members were the colonial merchants Robert Thomson (Maurice's brother), Robert Haughton, Edward Winslow, and Richard Hutchinson, along with the new merchants' ally from the London common council Edward Parks, also well connected in New England, and the republican City recorder William Steele.[9] In the early months of 1650, the Commons established committees to propagate the gospel not only in the country's religiously backward and outlying regions, the so-called dark corners, but also in such heartland areas as Wiltshire and even Southwark (the committee for which was taken charge of by new merchant MP George Snelling). But, in the end, commissions were established only for Wales, the four northern counties, and Yorkshire.[10] Apparently, more conservative MPs opposed their extension into England for fear that the itinerant preachers might disrupt the sociopolitical stability of the counties.

The transformation in the official religious outlook that was the consequence of the revolution of 1648 and the installation in power of new ruling groups at the levels of both the central state and the City govern-

---

[7] CLRO, J.Co.Co.41, fols. 118v–19. For Peter's proposals, and their acknowledged influence on Commonwealth legislation concerning the propagation of the gospel, see C. Hill, "Propagating the Gospel," in *Historical Essays, 1600–1750*, ed. H. E. Bell and R. L. Ollard (London, 1963), pp. 39–44. Cf. C. Hill, "Puritans and the Dark Corners of the Land," *T.R.H.S.*, 5th ser., 13 (1963). For their initial presentation in 1646–47, see above, ch. 10, p. 518.

[8] *C.J.* 6: 354, 359, 385, 396–97, 410–11, 424, 427, 433, 453–54; Worden, *Rump Parliament*, p. 233; Underdown, *Pride's Purge*, p. 275.

[9] *A.O.* 2: 197–200.

[10] *C.J.* 6: 335–37, 352, 365 (Southwark, Wiltshire), 370, 396, 416, 420, 421; Underdown, *Pride's Purge*, p. 273; Worden, *Rump Parliament*, pp. 120–21, 234–36, 271–73.

ment was manifested in governmental clerical appointments, both nationally and in London. During 1649–1650, the first two years that the London moderate republicans held power, the common council hired twenty-three different ministers to preach before it on various occasions; among them, at least sixteen were either parochial Independents, congregational Independents, or separatists. Then, in March 1651, the common council chose as its more or less permanent preacher the Independent minister George Griffith.[11] In contrast, of the fourteen different ministers hired by the common council to preach before it at various feasts, fasts, and special occasions during 1646–1647, the high tide of political presbyterianism in the City, ten can be identified as religious Presbyterians.[12] Presbyterian ministers were, of course, overwhelmingly dominant in number during the whole Interregnum period in London, while Independents constituted a small minority. That the common council, now dominated by political independents, made the appointments it did was hardly surprising; its leaders were themselves, for the most part, parochial or congregational religious Independents and were already, as individuals, patronizing the very same ministers or others of much the same stripe.[13]

The national government's clerical appointments show how closely the Commonwealth and the City's new rulers were in tune with one another on religious matters. During the course of its existence, between December 1648 and April 1653, the Rump made sixty-nine preaching assignments for fasts, thanksgivings, and humiliations. Of these, at least fifty-five appointments went to parochial Independents, congregational Independents, or separatists, and about the same number went to ministers who were also hired by the London common council in 1649–1650.[14] The

---

[11] Compiled from CLRO, C.C.A.1/6, fols. 258–59, and C.C.A.1/7, fols. 58–59, 135, 145. The congregational and parochial Independent ministers included Joseph Carryl, Philip Nye, George Cockayn, Sydrach Simpson, Thomas Goodwin, John Owen, William Greenhill, John Warren, Peter Sterry, Matthew Barker, Nathaniel Homes, Samuel Lee, Thomas Harrison, John Bond, John Cardell, and William Strong. There were three Presbyterians appointed, Stephen Marshall, Obadiah Sedgewick, and Lazarus Seaman. I am not able to pinpoint the religious orientation of John Arthur, William Cater, and "Mr. Eaton" so as to categorize them as Presbyterian, Independent, or separatist. For the appointment of Griffith, CLRO, J.Co.Co.41, fol. 46.

[12] CLRO, C.C.A.1/5, fols. 255–56, and C.C.A.1/6, fol. 46. The Presbyterian ministers appointed included Anthony Burgess, Cornelius Burges, Francis Roberts, Richard Dyer, William Jenkins, Walter Bridges, Richard Vines, Simon Ashe, Samuel Bolton, and Edmund Calamy. There was one Independent, Joseph Carryl. The religious orientations of "Mr. Hicks," "Mr. Hill," and "Mr. Ward" have not been discovered.

[13] For the support of these men by the political independents, and notably the new-merchant leaders, see above, ch. 8, pp. 413–27.

[14] A list of the Rump's ministerial appointees is found in J. F. Wilson, *Pulpit in Parliament* (Princeton, 1969), pp. 251–54. They are as follows, with the number of times appointed in parentheses; (I) indicates Independent, (P) indicates Presbyterian, and (L) indicates that person was also a ministerial

council of state's ministers came from the same Independent group. They included the congregational Independents John Owen and Thomas Goodwin and the parochial Independents Joseph Carryl and Peter Sterry, as well as the new merchants' intimate friend Hugh Peter. Peter was eventually chosen as official preacher of the council of state.

The Commonwealth religious establishment, its outlook and personnel, was not of course extremely radical. Nevertheless, it represented quite a sharp departure from everything that had come before, for it reflected a standpoint that had been held by only a tiny part of the old political nation, or for that matter of the old parliamentary party. This standpoint happened, of course, to be the one preferred by London's political independent rulers, the new merchants prominently among them.[15]

Progressive Reform of the Law and Governmental Administration

Radical elements within the Commonwealth leadership sought significant changes in the law and in governmental administration, just as they had in the Constitution and in official religious outlook and practice. These changes were not, once again, extremely radical if the standard for radicalism is taken to be what was desired by or acceptable to the Levellers

---

appointee of the City of London: Joseph Carryl (I)(9)(L), Stephen Marshall (P)(4)(L), Hugh Peter (I)(3)(L), George Cockayn (I)(1)(L), John Rawlinson (P)(1), Thomas Brookes (I)(2), Thomas Watson (P)(1), Lazarus Seaman (P)(1)(L), T. Temple (?)(1), J. Cardell (I)(1)(L), John Ley (P)(2), [?] Carter (?)(1), John Owen (I)(9)(L), J. Warren (?)(1)(L), Thomas Goodwin or John Goodwin (I)(4)(L), [?] Knight (?)(2), Ralph Venning (I)(1), John Bond (I)(4)(L), William Strong (I)(6)(L), W. Cooper (I)(1), William Greenhill (I)(1)(L), Peter Sterry (I)(2)(L), V. Powell (I)(1), William Bridge (I)(1), Philip Nye (I)(3)(L), Sydrach or John Simpson (I)(1)(L), Nicholas Lockyer (I)(2), Christopher Feake (I)(1), Matthew Barker (I)(1)(L), William Ames (I)(1). Feake, Powell, and John Simpson ended up as Fifth Monarchists.

[15] It should be noted that once they had won political influence, had prevented the implementation of a state-backed Presbyterian settlement, and had achieved a policy of toleration for the Commonwealth, most of the Independent ministers and their supporters among the laity were quite ready to seek an alliance with Presbyterians. During the 1640s, when the Presbyterians had aimed to repress them, the Independents had been obliged to ally with the separatist congregations for interrelated political and religious ends. But now that they constituted the heart of the new religious establishment and had made religious pluralism the order of the day, they were anxious to emphasize those ideas they held in common with the Presbyterians, both to win the Presbyterians' support for the new regime and to secure the Presbyterians' help in controlling religious experimentation on the part of the sects that might threaten order and decency. For this development, as well as the drive on the part of the majority of Independents to maintain the religious status quo established by the Commonwealth against certain more radical Independents, notably John Goodwin and his followers, and some of the separatist churches, see Worden, *Rump Parliament*, pp. 123–24, 191–92, 292–96; J. E. Farnell, "The Usurpation of Honest London Householders: Barebone's Parliament," *E.H.R.* 82 (1967): 43–45.

and some of their separatist allies. The Levellers and their friends wanted changes in the law that would have infringed on property rights and that would have undermined legal professionalism, and very few who were influential within Commonwealth governance wanted such things. Nevertheless, as in the cases of both political ideology and religious outlook, what was distinctive, as well as genuinely radical, about Commonwealth legal and governmental reform efforts easily can be missed if the reference point is the Levellers and the sects, rather than the traditional political nation before and after the Interregnum. Here again, the Commonwealth's specific reform thrust was significantly shaped by what I have termed moderate republican forces and was especially congenial to, and influenced in important ways by, the new political independent ruling group in London and its close allies.

CHEAP AND EFFICIENT GOVERNMENT

Something of the general direction of reform desired by the City's political independents can be gathered from their efforts to clean up and streamline City government. During their first year or so in office, London's new rulers revamped the effective salary and expenditure structure for City offices. With the goal of making offices accessible to more citizens, as well as reducing corruption, they raised the salaries attached to some offices and, in particular, reduced the enormous entertainment requirements that had hitherto attached to the offices of sheriff and lord mayor. The magistrates went on, moreover, sharply to curtail the sale of offices so as to prevent extortion and help ensure that persons who were appointed were chosen on the basis of their ability. Finally, the common council, through the establishment of a standing committee, took direct control of the City chamber away from the court of aldermen, while banning the former practice whereby the aldermen received from the chamber interest-free loans. By thus reducing privilege, cutting down corruption, and opening careers to the talented, the new common council leadership hoped to pave the way for a cheaper and more effective administration of the City. This was precisely the sort of serious reform in the interest of progress and efficiency—next to impossible to carry out under the pre–Civil War aldermanic elite, but by no means socially revolutionary—that conformed most closely to the ideals of the new-merchant moderate republicans now so firmly ensconced near the sources of power.[16] It seems also to have been

[16] CLRO, J.Co.Co.41, fols. 8v–9, 12v–14, 32v–33, 41, 53; Farnell, "Usurpation," pp. 31–33. As commissioners for regulating the customs and the navy, members of the new-merchant leadership were introducing very similar measures, at just this time, in the administration of the Commonwealth navy. See above, ch. 10, p. 553 and below, ch. 12, p. 583.

just the sort of reform most seriously considered by the Commonwealth government in the content and administration of the law.

LAW REFORM

During its first year of existence, the Rump, concerned basically to consolidate its rule, achieved little in the way of changes in the law. However, from the fall of 1649, led by the republican politicians Thomas Chaloner and Henry Marten, radicals in the Commons did mount a serious drive for reform. In the period from September 1649 to April 1650, these forces managed to pass a series of reforms in the laws for the relief of poor men imprisoned for debt, but overall their efforts met with defeat and their campaign soon petered out. The next flurry of activity in support of the reform of the law seems to have been given its impetus, at least to a significant degree, by the City.[17]

On 23 January 1650, at the very same meeting at which it drew up its aforementioned plans for religious reformation, the City framed a program for the reform of law, to be presented to the Commons. It proposed "that all the statutes may be so clearly collected . . . that every man may know his duty and danger and the laws be so devised . . . that no mere form or subtlety of words may undermine or destroy the people's just rights." To these ends, it demanded "that no writ of error may issue out of any court till the same court hath heard and allowed all the errors to be assigned and that writs and proceedings of law may be plainly written in English and . . . so expressed that people may know both how and when they may receive their right." In addition, the City asked that local commissions in every county and City be established to register all land transfers.[18]

During the following year, the Rump responded positively to at least part of the City program. Under the leadership of Sir Arthur Hasilrig, the Commons effectively gave its approval on 4 February 1650 to a new law "for redress and prevention of mischiefs and delays arising to people" out of the cumbersome procedure of appeals by writs of error, and officially passed it on 11 March.[19] A push from the army in the aftermath of Dunbar appears to have been required for the Commons to act on the City's demand that proceedings of law, both oral and written, be in English; but this too was incorporated in law in November 1650.[20] The Commons failed to act on the question of county registries.

The City's proposals had not, obviously, come from nowhere. Every

---

[17] Worden, *Rump Parliament*, pp. 204–6; Underdown, *Pride's Purge*, p. 277.

[18] CLRO, J.Co.Co.40, fols 18v–19.

[19] *C.J.* 6: 357, 380.

[20] Underdown, *Pride's Purge*, pp. 277–78; Worden, *Rump Parliament*, p. 238.

one of them, and others like them, already had been, or were in the process of being, placed on the agenda by a loose alliance of legal innovators who composed a distinct stream of legal reform opinion. This trend has been termed "moderate," but again, that appellation is appropriate only if the reference point for "radical" is Levellers and separatists.[21] A better label might be "progressive." The movement's leading figures were drawn, to an important extent, from that distinctive minority at the radical end of the political spectrum that had given outright support to the revolution of 1648 but had opposed the Levellers. In fact, it included some of the revolution's leading ideologists, theorists of precisely the position—that parliamentary supremacy was based on popular sovereignty but that Parliament was itself the self-sufficient repository of sovereignty—to which much of the Rump's radical leadership and its political independent supporters in the City were committed. Prominent among them was the City and army radical Hugh Peter. So was John Bradshaw, president of the High Court of Justice that tried the king, who had justified the proceedings and parliamentary sovereignty in terms of popular consent. Also included in this group was the attorney John Cook, a leading publicist for religious Independency and in favor of the army, who had defended John Lilburne before the House of Lords and who had gained national prominence in January 1649 when he assumed the positions both of the government's solicitor, directed to prepare the charge against the king, and its prosecutor before the High Court of Justice. A theorist of republican rule, Cook defended the Commonwealth in his pamphlet *Monarchy No Creature of God's Making* (1652). Henry Parker, another of the same group of legal reformers, had served from 1645 with John Sadler, London's republican town clerk under the Commonwealth, as secretary to the House of Commons and, from 1649, as secretary to Cromwell's army in Ireland. One of the era's leading radical political theorists, Parker was perhaps the first in the Civil War period, clearly and publically, to offer a theory of parliamentary supremacy based on popular sovereignty. In common with much of the Commonwealth leadership, however, he saw Parliament as the ultimate authority, with no appeal permitted beyond it to the people. Finally, Henry Robinson, also part of this group, was another of the period's most prominent theorists of religious toleration and oligarchic republicanism, and a leading reform writer in the fields of commerce, medicine, education, and the law.[22]

[21] The group is identified, and termed "moderate," by D. Veall, *The Popular Movement for Law Reform, 1640–1660* (Oxford, 1970), pp. 111–22, but his point of reference is explicitly the Levellers.

[22] *Dictionary of Seventeenth Century Radicals*, vol. 1, s.v. "John Bradshaw" and "John Cook"; vol. 3, s.v. "Henry Parker" and "Henry Robinson." Cf. W. K. Jordan, *Men of Substance* (Chicago, 1942).

Besides their commitment to religious toleration and oligarchic republicanism, all of the aforementioned writers had in common the goal of reforming the law so as to make it more accessible and effective by streamlining, shortening, and reorganizing its cumbersome and obscurantist procedures and institutions. That goal was certainly in keeping with the aim of the Levellers and separatists to make the law more accessible to the poor and to prevent it from being used to exploit the poor and line the pockets of the lawyers. Yet these reformers did not, for the most part, share the anti–common law and antiprofessional bias of the Leveller and separatist wing of the legal reform movement and were explicitly hostile to demands for democratizing legal institutions or decentralizing state power. They sought above all the rationalization and professionalization of the law in the interests of efficiency. [23]

It was only with the establishment of the Hale Commission in December 1651 that the drive for legal reform under the Commonwealth was renewed, having apparently run out of steam temporarily with the enactment of the law for legal proceedings in English. In view of the twenty-six-person House of Commons committee that chose it, the Hale Commission appears to have been the product of a joint effort by radical forces in the Commons, the army, and the City. The nominating committee included, on the army side, the radical officer MPs Thomas Harrison, Nathaniel Rich, and Philip Jones, along with the proreform grandees Charles Fleetwood and Oliver Cromwell. Among its civilian members were the long-established radicals John Carew, Augustine Garland, John Dove, Miles Corbet, Dennis Bond, Henry Mildmay, Henry Heyman, Francis Allein, Thomas Westrow, Arthur Hasilrig, and Gregory Norton. Carew, Garland, Dove, Corbet, Bond, Mildmay, Allein, Harrison, Norton, and Cromwell were all among those MPs designated by Underdown as revolutionaries at the time of Pride's Purge. Corbett, Bond, and Heyman had been prominent collaborators with the London radicals in their struggle for an autonomous citizen army in 1643, as well as on many subsequent occasions. Hasilrig and Cromwell were both longtime promoters of colonial enterprise and both had been supporters of the new merchants' Additional Sea Adventure to Ireland in 1642. Francis Allein was the London goldsmith active with the new merchants in the Bermuda Company, as well as on countless political and financial committees over the entire period. Thomas Westrow was a promoter of the republican-oriented Bahamas project, which had significant support among the radical citizens. Finally, John Danvers, a regicide MP who was acquainted with the new-merchant leadership through his numerous activities relating to the Bermuda Colony, played an especially important role in desig-

---

[23] Veall, *Popular Movement for Law Reform.*

nating the Hale Commission's membership, and he helped to give it its radical composition.[24]

The Hale Commission's membership reflected the radical opinions of its nominators, and the oligarchic republicanism associated to an important degree with London's new ruling group was well represented. The commission's twenty-one members included the new merchants' clerical collaborator Hugh Peter; the colonial-interloping leader Samuel Moyer; Josias Berners, a Baptist republican attorney of London who was a friend of Moyer's and served with Moyer on the Commonwealth committee for compounding, sequestration, and advance of money; the East India Company oppositionist and longtime associate of the new-merchant leadership John Fowke; the Commonwealth town clerk of London John Sadler, a leading republican propagandist for the Commonwealth; the Commonwealth City recorder William Steele, who had backed the radicals' petition and remonstrance in spring and summer of 1643 and had been appointed in 1649 a solicitor for the government in the trial of Charles I; and John Sparrow and John Rushworth, who were both promoters of the quasi-republican Eleutheria project starting in 1647.[25]

The Hale Commission's proposals have been interpreted as an expression of the aforementioned movement for progressive legal reform. In view of the fact that the commission's chief, Matthew Hale, was a major figure in that movement, as were two of its three other leading members, the moderate republicans John Sadler and William Steele, that seems hardly controversial.[26] This characterization also fits, of course, with the fact that much of the commission's membership was derived from London political independency. The program proposed was quite radical in its attack on the slowness and inaccessibility of legal procedure, as well as its assault on the privileges of the lawyers. But it was far from what the Lev-

[24] *C.J.* 7: 58; Worden, *Rump Parliament*, pp. 271–73.

[25] For the Hale Commission's membership, see Veall, *Popular Movement for Law Reform*, pp. 80–83; M. Cotterell, "Interregnum Law Reform: The Hale Commission of 1652," *E.H.R.* 82 (1968): 689–704. For Josias Berners, see G. E. Aylmer, *The State's Servants* (London, 1973), pp. 210–13. The commission's radical contingent also included the army officers William Packer and Thomas Blount.

[26] "The Hale Commission proposals were a fair consensus of the opinions of the moderate reformers" (Veall, *Popular Movement for Law Reform*, pp. 120, 115–17). Cotterell indentifies Hale, Sadler, Steele, and John Fountain as "the leading members of the Hale Commission" (see "Interregnum Law Reform," 691). Cotterell argues that the Hale Commission was not "radical," but clearly her standard for radicalism is, again, basically Leveller. She does not deny that the Hale Commission proposals marked a sharp break with dominant legal opinion, but, because she believes that "the essence of radical law reform programs was anti-professionalism" (p. 696), she is unable to recognize the distinctive, radical, but proprofessional and non-Leveller movement for legal reform that was behind these proposals. She thus fails to grasp the radical contribution of those often City-based moderate republicans who wanted to make radical legal reforms in the direction of increased professionalism and efficiency, while eliminating privilege and corruption.

ellers and the sects desired, in that it was not decentralizing, democratic, or antiprofessional, nor did it reduce the role of lawyers.

Echoing the Levellers, the Hale Commission proposed new county courts possessing wide jurisdiction so as to make justice more accessible to people who lived outside London. But whereas the Levellers had wanted these courts to be self-sufficient, decentralized, and staffed by elected laymen, the Hale Commission proposed courts in which the judges were appointed by and firmly under the control of the central government and from which appeal could be made to the central courts. The commission also suggested the formation of a new court of appeals. This, too, had been a proposal of the Levellers and Fifth Monarchists, who saw it as a way to control and discipline judges. But a court of appeals could also be conducive to more efficient and effective justice, especially since the only method of appeal in common law had been on technical grounds, by writ of error. This writ was not only unsuitable for the purpose of a substantive appeal, but could be manipulated by lawyers to delay proceedings. As noted, both the City leadership and the law reformers in Parliament had sought the reform of the writ of error; it appears to have been their concerns and desires that were motivating the Hale Commission when it called for the abolition of the writ of error and the establishment of a court of appeals. The Hale Commission also proposed county commissions to register land transactions similar to those already suggested to the Commons by the London common council, the complete abolition of fines on original writs, and the liability of copyhold land for debt. Finally, the Hale Commission recommended that limitations be placed on lawyers' incomes; it also presented a program for improving legal education and raising the standards of legal practice. As the Hale Commission's most recent historian concluded, the commission's work clearly disappointed the Levellers and Fifth Monarchists, but also "appalled conservatives." This was no doubt just what was intended by the commission's antidemocratic but moderate republican supporters.[27]

It is true that the Rump ultimately approved nothing of the Hale Commission's program for the reform of the law. The commission's proposals were apparently thwarted by conservative forces in the House, supportive of the common lawyers, drawn heavily from among the many late-returning MPs.[28] Nevertheless, the fact that the Commonwealth government could even place this set of proposals seriously on the agenda shows how significantly the political universe had been transformed. Neither the Stuart Parliaments before the Civil War, nor the middle-group MPs who

[27] Cotterell, "Interregnum Law Reform," pp. 696–702.

[28] Veall, *Popular Movement for Law Reform*, pp. 84–85; Worden, *Rump Parliament*, pp. 107–17, 271–73, 279–83.

often led Parliament in the 1640s—influenced as both were by the common lawyers and conservative opinion more generally—would seriously have considered these legal departures any more than they would the Rump's parliamentary supremacy (oligarchic republicanism) or its pluralist, tolerationist religious settlement.

The New Merchants and Commercial Policy

under the Commonwealth

IF THE RUMP'S policy accomplishments were to a significant extent restricted by its narrow sociopolitical base, there remained one field in which it was able to achieve really striking successes, and that is the realm of commerce and diplomacy. England's dramatic rise as a military-commercial power in this era was perhaps the achievement most characteristic of the Rump's overall political orientation. Contemporaries saw a clear connection between republican politics and overseas commercial and military power, and the Rump was a prime piece of substantiating evidence. Nor was this a coincidence, for the radical political groups that came to power in 1648–1649, both nationally and in London, placed commercial and colonial expansion near the top of an agenda that also included, as has been described, oligarchic republican governing institutions in politics; Independent, tolerationist, and a settlement of religion; government discipline of social conduct; and the progressive reform of judicial procedures and institutions of the law.

The ideological republicans Thomas Scot, Thomas Chaloner, and Henry Marten, in association with their radical allies in the House, provided the Commonwealth's leadership in the initial period of its consolidation; nevertheless, as has been emphasized, these forces were soon obliged to share power, as well as to compromise their goals in one sphere after another. Still, in the field of overseas policy, the republicans and their friends do seem to have retained the initiative and, to a very great extent, to have succeeded in implementing their plans. By the fall of 1649, these men had succeeded in constituting what was an effectively coordinated radical party. This party's core was composed of Marten, Chaloner, and Sir Henry Neville, all friends, "the most closely knit grouping in the house;" it prominently included such intimates of theirs as Edmund Ludlow, Cornelius Holland, Henry Smyth, Lord Grey of Groby, Augustine Garland, Luke Robinson, and James Chaloner; and it achieved its cohesion and identity through the common commitment of its members to a republican political outlook. Over the following year, the Marten-Chaloner-Neville group expanded its influence by forging close ties with a

House of Commons faction around Herbert Morley and by strengthening its working relationship with its old republican ally Thomas Scot, as well as with Arthur Hasilrig. Still, as explained, despite their organization, the Rump's republicans showed themselves ever more clearly limited in their ability to win significant domestic reforms. In Worden's view, the result was that, as these factions found themselves increasingly frustrated on the home front, they devoted themselves ever more single-mindedly to the promotion of ambitious diplomatic and commercial initiatives. In so doing, they were able to draw especially broad support in the Commons from MPs who were not perhaps self-conscious ideological republicans but who had long been attached to the successive wings of parliamentary radicalism—the old parliamentary war party and its successor, the radical wing of the parliamentary political independent alliance. As "the architects of the Rump's diplomacy," these men, working together, appear to have exerted a powerful influence over foreign and commercial policy-making throughout the entire Commonwealth period.[1]

The "imperialist republicans" of the House did not act alone. Their confidence and competence in the field of commercial and foreign affairs appears to have derived, at least in part, from their ability to forge close connections with that powerful mercantile nexus that had come near to the centers of both national and municipal power with the revolution of 1648–1649, namely, the new-merchant leadership. Throughout the Commonwealth, new merchants played a very direct and immediate role in the processes of commercial and foreign policy-making at all levels. This influence was made possible, in part, by the predominant position they, and powerful nonmerchant political independent allies of theirs, had achieved when they captured the City's government. It was also partly conditioned by their extraordinary penetration, already discussed, of all levels of militia, naval, and financial administration within the Commonwealth. It was actually realized not only by way of the direct advisory role played by new-merchant leaders for Parliament and for the council of state on all aspects of commercial policy-making, but also by the ability of key new-merchant MPs and close London allies of theirs to participate directly in policy-making within the Commons itself, in close collaboration with Rump republican factions.

Of course, even under the Commonwealth, relatively few merchants or Londoners were members of Parliament, which remained overwhelmingly a landed-class institution. It has not been widely noticed, however, that beginning in 1645 a small but significant contingent of London citizens were elected as recruiters to the House of Commons and that, almost

[1] B. Worden, *The Rump Parliament, 1648–1653* (Cambridge, 1974), pp. 174, 218–19, 256–57, 259–60.

to a man, they strongly supported the political independents and became leading backers of the Rump. These included Francis Allein, Thomas Atkins, Thomas Boone, Gregory Clement, Nicholas Gould, Edmund Harvey, Thomas Rainsborough, Richard Salway, Philip Skippon, George Snelling, George Thomson, and Rowland Wilson. All of these men, except Boone, are on Underdown's list of parliamentary revolutionaries. Along with a few other earlier-elected MPs recruited from the ranks of the overseas and domestic trading community, they were able to exert an influence on the Commons' policy-making in general and overseas affairs in particular far beyond what their numbers would seem to warrant.[2]

The disproportionate influence exerted by businessman MPs within the Rump appears to have derived primarily from two sources. In the first place, these men had the ability to work very cohesively with one another, a capacity undoubtedly related in part to the membership of many of them in the same new-merchants' commercial and political networks. George Thomson (Maurice's brother) and George Snelling, the two MPs from Southwark, as well as Gregory Clement, were longtime major partners of Maurice Thomson's going back to the pre–Civil War era. Rowland Wilson, the trader with Guinea, and Thomas Boone, a member of the Assada interloping syndicate, became associates of Thomson's in the later 1640s. Francis Allein was a City goldsmith who had played an active role alongside the new merchants in the Bermuda Company and had been in close touch with Maurice Thomson from the early 1640s when he took part in Thomson's customs syndicate. Richard Salway was another citizen who was often politically active with the new-merchant leadership, although he does not seem to have participated in their trade.

In the second place, these businessman MPs were either themselves among the leading politicians of the Rump, or had established close ties with a Rump leadership that was itself unusually well-connected with commercial and colonial affairs, most notably the imperialist republicans. As Dr. Worden has shown, the groups of merchant MPs were able to build their influence especially as they forged ever-closer connections with the powerful Marten-Chaloner-Scot and Morley factions in the House. It might be noted in passing that Thomas Chaloner himself, perhaps the key figure in shaping Commonwealth commercial policy, was particularly closely connected with both the new-merchant MP Thomas Boone and the new merchants' close friend Richard Salway. At the same time, perhaps a third of the thirty-three persons designated by Dr. Worden as constituting the Rump's activist core—including Francis Allein, George Thomson, and Rowland Wilson, as well as Thomas Chaloner, Miles Corbet, Sir John Danvers, Sir Arthur Hasilirig, William Lenthall, Richard Salway,

[2] D. Underdown, *Pride's Purge* (Oxford, 1971), app. A.

Henry Vane, and John Venn—were either themselves active in commercial or colonial affairs or both, or very closely tied politically to others who were so active.[3]

Commonwealth commercial policy was thus, to a great extent, an expression of the aims of the imperialist republicans and the new-merchant leadership. The new merchants sought to influence the government so as to further their own immediate interests. But since the new merchants represented the most dynamic areas of English commerce, their success in shaping policy in their own interests tended, to a striking degree, to further the interests of English commerce more generally. The Rump's republican factions sought to make commercial policy serve the goal of enhancing English world power, especially in order to validate their own leadership, to give legitimacy to the Commonwealth, to prove the superiority of the republican form of rule, and, not least, to protect the republic from its many enemies abroad. But since the growth of English power tended, at this historical juncture, to depend directly on the construction of a powerful navy and indirectly on the growth of English commerce, the effect of their interventions tended to be very favorable to the development of all facets of English trade. The upshot was that government support for commercial development tended, under the Commonwealth, to be raised almost to the level of a principle.

Military Security and Naval Buildup

Initially, beginning in the winter and spring of 1649, the Commonwealth was obliged to focus its military efforts on Ireland, which, among other things, provided the main base for royalist privateers. The government immediately established the revolutionary goal of constructing a permanent fleet, breaking with Parliament's previous reliance on hired merchant ships to constitute its navy. To this end Parliament did not hesitate to authorize the expenditure of vast sums, raising the money largely through increases in customs revenues. S. R. Gardiner estimated that the Commonwealth government devoted 20 percent of its budget to the navy. Between 1649 and 1654, the navy added 147 ships to its arsenal. Meanwhile, the Rump was able to recruit well-trained and politically committed officers, most notably the republican-oriented generals-at-sea, Robert Blake and Richard Deane, but also including ideologically driven radicals at less-exalted ranks. In addition, by offering higher pay, providing for a fairer distribution of the yield from captured prizes, and cam-

---

[3] Worden, *Rump Parliament*, pp. 30–32, 256, 389–91.

paigning to root out corruption in naval administration, it was able to attract more competent and devoted ship commanders, sailors, and ship-yard workers.[4]

As Cromwell brought the Irish under control in the period between the spring of 1649 and the spring of 1650, the Commonwealth was increasingly able to frame objectives for its naval campaigns against the royalists that furthered not only the immediate military defense of the new state, but also the improvement of conditions for the pursuit of commerce. Indeed, naval operations initially designed for military defense became, over time, more oriented toward commercial expansion and maritime hegemony. From the time of the royalist naval revolt in 1648, royalist privateers and their European allies had succeeded in partially paralyzing English trade. Yet a healthy commerce was seen by Commonwealth policymakers as indispensable, not only to the nation's wealth and to government finance, but also to the maintenance of those marine capacities on which the navy itself depended. To the primary end of making the European shipping lanes once again safe for English trade, over the course of the summer and autumn of 1650 Blake carried out a devastating naval campaign in Iberian waters. He succeeded in blockading, then destroying, Rupert's royalist fleet, which had taken refuge in Lisbon under the protection of King John IV. Meanwhile, in retaliation against the Portuguese for protecting Rupert, Blake seized the Portuguese sugar fleet in September 1650. He then imposed a humiliating peace on the Portuguese government in order to demonstrate to other European nations how the Commonwealth intended to treat countries that harbored disrupters of English commerce. The upshot, within a few years, was the opening of the Portuguese colonies to English trade and religious toleration for English merchants in Portugal. Blake's intimidating actions also succeeded in inducing the king of Spain to allow the English the crucial right to use Spanish ports not only in Spain itself but also in Italy and Sicily for supplying their military and commercial operations in the Mediterranean and, ultimately, by the end of 1650, to grant diplomatic recognition to the Commonwealth. They set the stage, in addition, for William Penn's marauding voyage to mop up French privateers in the Mediterranean in early 1651. Taken together, the naval campaigns of Blake and Penn largely succeeded in reopening English trade along its traditional routes,

[4] S. R. Gardiner, *The History of the Commonwealth and the Protectorate*, 3 vols. (London, 1894–1901), 1: 25–26, 331, 340–42; W. G. Cogar, "The Politics of Naval Administration, 1649–1660" (University of Oxford, Ph.D. diss., 1983), pp. 1–2, 23–24, 28–29, 37–41, 47–49, 57–58, 74–88; M. P. Ashley, *Financial and Commercial Policy under the Cromwellian Protectorate* (Oxford, 1934), p. 155; S. Groenveld, "The English Civil Wars as a Cause of the First Anglo-Dutch War, 1640–1652," *H.J.* 30 (1987): 558–60.

above all with the lucrative regions of southern Europe and the Mediterranean.[5]

It was the new revolutionary leaders of the Commonwealth, with their reformed naval administration, who were most responsible for the rapid naval buildup and the spectacular destruction of royalist opponents at sea, a fact well understood by contemporaries, even hostile ones. By the autumn of 1650, Crouille, the unofficial agent in England of the French government, was warning Cardinal Mazarin to establish relations with the Commonwealth, describing the republic's new governors as follows:

> Not only are they powerful by sea and land, but they live without ostentation, without pomp, without emulation of one another. They are economical in their private expenses, and prodigal in their devotion to public affairs, for which each one toils as if for his private interests. They handle large sums of money, which they administer honestly, observing a severe discipline. They reward well, and punish severely.[6]

The Commonwealth alliance of ideological republican leaders, longtime (if not necessarily ideologically republican) radicals in Parliament, and colonial-interloping merchants in London, provided the initiative at all levels for building up and deploying the navy. The admiralty committee of the council of state took charge of naval policy-making. On this body, Sir Henry Vane was, at least for a time, the dominant force, but he was joined in leading the committee by Col. Valentine Walton, Col. William Purefoy, Dennis Bond, Anthony Stapley, Thomas Scot, and Thomas Chaloner.[7] Chaloner and Scot were at the core of the emerging imperialist republican leadership. Stapley was a mainstay of the republican faction around Herbert Morely that worked closely with Chaloner, Scot, and their friends, especially on overseas policy. Stapley was also actively involved in the movement for law reform.[8] Bond had, from early on, established a reputation for himself as a fiery spirit and was among the very close parliamentary collaborators of the new-merchant leadership. All of these men except Vane and Bond were regicides, and all but Walton were in the forefront in framing Rump overseas policy.

---

[5] Gardiner, *Commonwealth and Protectorate* 1: 331–46, 349; 2: 188, 386–87; Cogar, "Politics of Naval Administration," pp. 23–24, 39.

[6] Quoted in Gardiner, *Commonwealth and Protectorate* 1: 346. See, in this regard, the Venetian ambassador's earlier comment (1644) that "France is exceedingly concerned to support a moderate monarchy in this kingdom as against a republic, which . . . would be more formidable, especially for its naval strength" (*C.S.P. Ven. 1643–1647*, p. 129, quoted in C. Hill, *God's Englishman* [New York, 1970], p. 131).

[7] Cogar, "Politics of Naval Administration," pp. 25–27.

[8] Worden, *Rump Parliament*, pp. 29, 281, 313–14; *Dictionary of Seventeenth-Century Radicals*, vol. 3, s.v. "Anthony Stapley."

The Commons' committee of the navy, alongside the admiralty committee of the council of state, also had a leading part in naval policy-making, and assumed special responsibility for naval finance, as well as for overseeing naval administration. The initial chairman of this committee, during the Commonwealth's early search for security, was the new merchants' close collaborator, the parliamentary radical Miles Corbet. Maurice's brother George Thomson succeeded Corbet as chairman in 1649–1650, and brought before the Commons most of the main measures for raising money for the navy and for administering the buildup of the fleet. As to the committee itself, in the words of a recent authority, it "was dominated by those MPs who were connected with the City and the mercantile world." In fact, twelve of the twenty MPs most regularly in attendance at the navy committee during the Commonwealth were merchants. Led by George Thomson, this body explained to the Commons the very large increases in financing that would be needed to construct the navy, recommended how this money should be obtained, and took charge of its expenditure in overseeing naval construction and naval operations.[9]

The committee for regulating the navy and customs, appointed at the recommendation of the Commons' committee of the navy, was, as noted, totally in the hands of the new-merchant leadership, headed by Maurice Thomson. This body initiated the reorganization of the navy's administration and, in 1649, handpicked a new five-person standing commission of the navy entirely from its own membership to finish the job. It was these two committees, in concert with the Commons' committee for the navy, that took charge of actually constructing the Commonwealth navy.

These bodies assumed, in the first place, the job of overseeing the dockyards, fitting out, hiring, and manning the ships, and paying the seamen. In so doing, they implemented the reform of salaries, the rationalization of shipyard personnel, and the attack on corruption in the name of efficiency and careers (roughly) open to talents that had been authorized by the Commonwealth's political leadership. At the same time, these bodies succeeded in fundamentally reconstituting the navy's leadership, bringing in a largely new corps of officers that was remarkably favorable to the new republican order, a stronghold of political and religious radicalism. This they appear to have accomplished, to a striking degree, by appointing shipmasters from their own immediate politico-commercial circles. Two of their most typical appointees were also among the small group of senior commanders, just below Blake and Deane—viz., Robert Moulton and Edward Hall. Moulton had temporarily emigrated to New England in 1629 and would later collaborate with the earl of Warwick, Maurice Thomson, and others in anti-Spanish and anti-royalist privateering. Tell-

[9] Cogar, "Politics of Naval Administration," pp. 35–42.

ingly, in 1636, Moulton had been appointed second in command of Sir William Courteen's interloping venture into the privileged territory of the East India Company. Hall, too, had commanded a ship in Courteen's interloping fleet, and, by the mid-1640s, had become notorious as an outspoken republican. More generally, it is the conclusion of the most recent historian of the Commonwealth navy that "very few former masters in the Levant and East Indies trades served [as naval officers] under the Commonwealth"—which is not too surprising, in view of who appointed the officers. On the other hand, the socio-political complexion of the new Commonwealth leadership of the navy was directly expressed in the "striking predominance of American traders among the more senior [officers]," with "at least 30 captains belong[ing] to this group."[10]

From Military Defense to
Commercial Aggression: The American Colonies

Taken together, the Commonwealth's naval buildup and its early campaigns against royalists at sea and those who would shelter them constituted a powerful lever for commercial expansion. It was, however, only from the late summer and early autumn of 1650, with the destruction of its royalist enemies at sea and the defeat of the political presbyterians at Dunbar, that the Commonwealth could begin to consider the explicit reallocation of its growing naval power from military-defensive to commercial-offensive purposes. Even then, much of its commercial foreign policy remained, of necessity, bound up with its drive for security, for royalist forces continued to pose a threat both from within the British Isles and from abroad. This was even true in America. Here, almost from its inception, the Rump was obliged to take cognizance of a series of full-fledged colonial revolts. Throughout the colonies, a self-styled royalist politics prevailed, and Virginia, Barbados, Antigua, and Bermuda refused to submit to the illegitimate governors of the Commonwealth. Nevertheless, the widespread willingness within the colonies to defy Parliament should be understood less in terms of planters' royalist proclivities than in terms of their commercial aspirations. The colonists' real objective was to take advantage of political disarray in the home country in order to gain freedom for their trade from English domination. This set them directly against those London colonial merchants who commanded such influence within the Commonwealth, and Commonwealth policy toward

[10] B. Capp, *Cromwell's Navy* (Oxford, 1989), pp. 50–55, 165–166 (quotations), 396; Cogar, "Politics of Naval Administration," pp. 43–49, 74–88. See also above, ch. 10, p. 553 and ch. 11, p. 570.

Barbados and Virginia assumed the avowed goal of reconsolidating London merchant hegemony over colonial commerce.

During the pre–Civil War period, the royal government had imposed ever more stringent commercial controls on the American plantations. These restraints were aimed at increasing customs revenue, and also at promoting English trade (insofar as this was conducive to increased customs). That well-entrenched group of merchant-planter-councilors, led by Maurice Thomson, William Tucker, Thomas Stone, and their Virginia-based friends, which dominated the pre–Civil War government of colonial Virginia, had pushed strongly and persistently—against the express interests of the majority of the planters represented in the Virginia Assembly—for a policy of excluding all foreigners from the trade with Virginia. Largely because of the financial advantages that would accrue to the customs farmers in particular, but also of course to the English government, these merchant-planters were able to get their way. By the mid-1630s, foreigners had been excluded from all trade to any of the colonies on the American mainland and in the Caribbean. On the other hand, to the chagrin of both merchants and planters, the Crown ruled that colonial products had to be exported to England only. The purpose of this ruling was to cut off the direct trade between America and Europe in order to integrate the colonial reexport commerce within the English customs systems. Its effect was greatly to increase the sale price of colonial tobacco reexported to European markets. Both of these restrictive policies seriously exacerbated an already difficult situation for the planters. They tended to limit further an already overstocked market and to bring down even more the selling price of tobacco in the colonies, thus reducing many of the planters, especially the smaller ones, to the brink of economic ruin. It was inevitable that, given the chance, the colonists would seek to assert their independence in order to gain free and open trade.[11]

From the outbreak of the Civil War, the English government was able to exert decreasingly effective control over the American colonies. On 2 November 1643, Parliament appointed a commission for plantations, which was headed by the earl of Warwick and included such other Providence Island colonizing nobles and gentry as the earl of Manchester, Lord Saye and Sele, John Pym, Sir Gilbert Gerrard, and Cornelius Holland, as well as the colonial merchant MP Samuel Vassall.[12] This body assumed broad authority over colonial affairs, but the actual power it could apply was highly circumscribed as a result of the distractions at home. The planters thus gained substantial control of their own govern-

[11] G. L. Beer, *The Origins of the British Colonial System, 1578–1660* (New York, 1908), pp. 197–211, 233–40; J. A. Williamson, *The Caribbee Islands under the Proprietary Patents* (Oxford, 1926), pp. 96–98, 100–102. See also above, ch. 4, pp. 129–33.

[12] *A.O.* 1: 331.

ments and, in the leading colonies, Virgina and Barbados, they pursued similar policies, especially in the sphere of commerce.

In 1643, Virginia's colonial government passed an act making it "free and lawful for any merchants, factors or others of the Dutch nation to import wares and merchandises and to trade or traffic for the commodities of the colony in any ship or ships of their own or belonging to the Netherlands."[13] Barbados adopted the same approach, though less explicitly. As early as February 1645, English merchants there were complaining that "diverse worldly-minded persons, willfully neglect to ship their merchandise in English vessels." Two years later, the earl of Warwick protested the damage inflicted on English trade by "the trade and habitation of the Dutch" in Barbados.[14] These complaints were, of course, ignored by the planters.

The free-trade policies instigated by the colonial authorities during the 1640s opened the way to a drastic revision of the international distribution of commerce within the colonies. In a period in which the commercial requirements of the colonies continued to expand, while the ability of the English merchants to meet them was somewhat hampered by the effects of the Civil War, Dutch mercantile power came in to fill the vacuum. In the West Indies, especially Barbados, there was a rapid transformation of the economy from tobacco to sugar during the period. The Dutch played a major role in this process, and by 1649 they were, by all accounts, the dominant merchants in the islands. In Virginia the change was less dramatic, but there, too, Dutch penetration was significant. During the late 1630s, the Dutch had been largely absent from the trade. By 1643, the Dutch trader DeVries found in Virginia, alongside thirty vessels from England, "four Holland ships which make a great trade here." At Christmas 1648, he reported that there were thirty-one ships in the colony: twelve were English; twelve were Dutch; and seven came from New England. In the same year, it was reported that a fleet of twenty-five Dutch ships was being readied for voyages to the colony. Similar policies, in similar situations, led to similar Dutch advance throughout the West Indies, in Bermuda, and in Maryland.[15]

Both Virginia and Barbados, as well as their neighboring English colonies, enjoyed unprecedented prosperity during the 1640s, and the planters did not fail to grasp the connection between political independence, free and open trade, and more profitable sales. The execution of the king provided the final pretext, if any was needed, for the colonies to declare

[13] Quoted in Beer, *British Colonial System*, p. 356.
[14] Quoted in V. T. Harlow, *Barbados, 1625–1685* (Oxford, 1926), pp. 37–38.
[15] Harlow, *Barbados*, pp. 38–44; Beer, *British Colonial System*, pp. 356–57. Cf. J. R. Pagan, "Dutch Maritime and Commercial Activity in Mid–Seventeenth Century Virginia," *V.M.H.B.* 90 (1982): 491–93.

their open defiance of the English government. "Royalism thus became the stalking-horse for the accomplishment of a policy which was essentially economic." By 1650 Barbados, Antigua, Virginia, and Bermuda had risen in revolt, making clear that they would not submit to the revolutionary usurpers at Whitehall.[16]

The Commonwealth government devised and implemented its policies for the rebellious colonies in the closest collaboration with the colonial merchants. What the new merchants needed in the Americas was entirely straightforward: the reassertion of political and commercial control over the colonial economies. This required, in the first place, the creation of colonial governments favorable to the new merchants, the installation in leading colonial governmental positions of men who could be trusted to protect new merchants' interests, and the destruction of proprietary authorities where they still existed. It meant, in the second place, direct action by the English government itself to exclude Dutch merchant competitors. As it turned out, the Commonwealth did tailor its policies to achieve precisely these goals. Examining the policy-making processes by which the new regime responded to the new merchants' demands, offers some idea of how this came about.

The first reference of the republican government to the problem of colonial unrest came on 15 March 1649, when the council of state asked the "committee of merchants" in charge of regulating the navy and the customs to take into consideration the condition of Barbados and to decide whether it was safe to continue to license the exportation of horses there in case of the colony's disaffection.[17] Although Barbados had yet to declare its defiance explicitly, the government was well aware of the obstinacy with which the Barbadians had resisted the commands of the parliamentary committee on plantations during the previous years and therefore sought to deprive them of any strategic matériel for military resistance. The council of state's referral of the problem to the committee for regulating customs and the navy gave an immediate and decisive indication that the new government intended to work hand in hand with the leading merchants of the colonial field. This sixteen-person committee, it will be recalled, was entirely controlled by the new-merchant leadership: its membership included the traders with the Americas and interlopers in the East Indies Maurice Thomson, Robert Thomson, Thomas Andrews, Jonathan Andrews, William Barkeley, Stephen Estwicke, Richard Hill, Richard Hutchinson, Samuel Moyer, William Pennoyer, Samuel Pennoyer, James Russell, Richard Shute, and William Willoughby.

On 26 July 1649, the Commonwealth dispatched a letter to all of the

[16] Williamson, *Caribbee Islands*, p. 162.
[17] *C.S.P. Col. 1574–1660*, p. 328; Williamson, *Caribbee Islands*, p. 165.

colonies that announced the change in English government and required the inhabitants to continue their obedience. Barbados was still a year away from revolt, but, inspired by its strongly royalist governor Sir William Berkeley, Virginia had assumed an openly royalist stance starting in the middle 1640s. As early as 1644, the House of Commons had instructed its committee of the navy to report on the best course for reducing Virginia to the obedience of Parliament, but nothing could be accomplished while domestic politics remained unsettled.[18] Now, however, in the midsummer of 1649, with the new regime firmly installed, the government was at least ready to begin consideration of the matter, if not yet prepared to take action, and several important interested groups were at this time feverishly evolving plans for what they hoped would be the Commonwealth's settlement in Virginia.

That famous group of intellectual reformers, led originally by Comenius and at this juncture by John Dury and Samuel Hartlib, was especially concerned with what would happen in Virginia. These so-called utopian writers had long promoted economic, technical, and educational reform, as well as the propagation of the gospel, while spreading the idea of religious toleration. Through the agency of Benjamin Worsley, probably their chief representative on commercial and colonial matters, they now put forward to the new government a far-reaching program for reformation in Virginia, involving on the one hand the introduction of new commodities and manufactures and on the other the preaching of the Word and the conversion of the Indians. As Worsley wrote John Dury on 27 July 1649, "If the government [in Virginia] be altered, the Parliament's authority instituted . . . free preaching of the gospel, civility and industry countenanced, many a good preacher might there find a call . . . trading very much advanced . . . and the knowledge of God among the Indians as well there as in New England promoted."[19]

Apparently Worsley, Dury, and their friends hoped that the position they had taken against political presbyterianism in the later 1640s would stand them in good stead with the new government. In particular, they seem to have expected the influential MP John Trenchard and his son-in-law John Sadler, as well as John Bradshaw, president of the council of state, to help them get the government to listen to them. To implement their plans in Virginia, they wanted the government to set up a new parliamentary commission to take charge of the colony, and it is significant indeed that the men they proposed for this body came to a very large extent from the ranks of the new-merchant leadership. Worsley made Maurice

[18] Williamson, *Caribbee Islands*, pp. 165–66; Beer, *British Colonial System*, p. 359.

[19] Sheffield University Library, Hartlib MSS, 30 (2). I owe this and the following references to the Hartlib MSS to Dr. Toby Barnard, who generously sent me transcripts from this collection. I want to express my gratitude for his assistance. See also J. P. Cooper, "Social and Economic Policies under the Commonwealth," in *The Interregnum*, ed. G. E. Aylmer (London, 1972), pp. 133–34.

Thomson, William Pennoyer, and Martin Noel his prime nominees for the commission, and he also prominently mentioned William Willoughby and Thomas Andrews.[20] All of these traders, except perhaps for Noel, were at the heart of the new-merchant leadership. It is not really surprising that Worsley should have sought out these men, for the new merchants were already connected with Worsley's influential friends John Sadler and John Bradshaw, both of whom, as noted, were oligarchic republicans, longtime activists in the City radical movement, and associated with such men as William Steele, Henry Parker, Henry Robinson, and John Cook in the promulgation of republican and tolerationist ideas and in the Commonwealth movement for the progressive reform of the law. Moreover, although Worsley himself was apparently not yet personally acquainted with the new-merchant leaders, he knew of their reputation as "great plantation and Parliament men," who, he no doubt realized, shared many of his own ideas about commercial and colonial development, as well as religious reformation in the colonies.[21] Worsley would, in fact, soon be intimately allied with a number of the top new-merchant leaders and working closely with them in the creation of Commonwealth colonial policy.

Worsley did not hesitate to get directly in touch with a number of the new merchants. On 17 August 1649, in a letter to Dury, he refers to "some merchants . . . willing to subscribe a stock for to send to Virginia," apparently in support of the parliamentary mission of conquest.[22] By the following autumn, alongside Maurice Thomson, William Pennoyer, and a number of their colonial merchant friends, Worsley was taking the leading role in helping the council of state's admiralty committee construct the Commonwealth's policy for Virginia.

On 29 November 1649, the following decision was noted in the council of state's admiralty committee minutes:

> In pursuance of an order of the council of state of the 13 October last to consider the case of Virginia plantation this committee upon consideration thereof and for the better settling of the said plantation in such way as may be for the best advantage of this Commonwealth and the good of merchants trading to those parts ordered that Mr. Maurice Thomson and such other merchants as he shall think fit to advise with be desired to attend this committee upon Monday next . . . to be conferred with concerning the same and to bring with them such proposals in writing as they shall conceive most conducing to the well settling of so public a work.[23]

[20] Hartlib MSS, 30 (2); 50 (2); 61 (h).

[21] Hartlib MSS, 30 (2).

[22] Ibid.

[23] PRO, S.P.25/123/78v. See J. E. Farnell, "The Navigation Act of 1651, the First Dutch War,

A week later, the scheduled meeting on Virginia was postponed when the admiralty committee was informed that "Mr. Maurice Thomson could not be here by reason of sickness preventing him." It was rescheduled instead for the following week, at which time Thomson was desired to appear with "such merchants trading to Virginia as he should think fit," and to "bring with him such writings as he hath in his hands concerning the Virginia business."[24] Thomson nominated as additional merchant advisers his old trading associates William Pennoyer and William Allen. After a number of postponements, the admiralty committee ordered Thomson, Allen, Pennoyer, and Benjamin Worsley to attend its meeting on 9 January 1650 "to offer what they shall conceive requisite for reducing [Virginia] to the interest of the Commonwealth, and to be placed in such hands as this state may confide in, that the trade to that plantation may not be destroyed by the disloyalty of that plantation to this commonwealth."[25] On the appointed day, the admiralty committee approved a policy for Virginia that, in its essentials, called for the establishment of a special commission, apparently along the lines originally suggested by Worsley, to be chosen by Parliament to take over the government of Virginia and to oversee the appointment of a new governor and council in the colony more favorable to the Commonwealth's interests.[26] This recommendation was apparently forwarded to the council of state. With additions, it served as the basis for the policy that was ultimately adopted.

The Commonwealth's preoccupation with its enemies nearer home, both within the British Isles and at sea, prevented it from taking action concerning the rebellious colonies before the summer of 1650. The particular occurrence that set off the chain of events that led to actual legislation and military operations against the colonies was the return to England at that point of certain Barbadian supporters of the Commonwealth who had been banished from the island by the overtly royalist party that had taken power there in the spring of 1650. These men reported that Barbados was now firmly in the hands of an extreme anti-Commonwealth faction led by the brothers Walrond, and that Lord Willoughby, who had purchased a lease on the West Indian proprietorship from the earl of Carlisle in 1647, had arrived in the islands to organize resistance.[27] On 16 August 1650, the council of state once again referred the problem of colonial recalcitrance to its admiralty committee, which was instructed to "take into consideration the petitions, papers, and propositions concerning

---

and the London Merchant Community," *Ec.H.R.*, 2d ser., 16 (1964): 441.

[24] PRO, S.P.25/123/84v.

[25] PRO, S.P.25/123/97v. See also PRO, S.P.25/123/92v, 105v.

[26] PRO, S.P.25/123/107.

[27] Harlow, *Barbados*, p. 61 and, in general, ch. 2, pt. 2. Cf. Ga Puckrein, *Little England. Plantation Society and Anglo-Barbadian Politics, 1627–1700* (New York, 1984), pp. 104ff.

the business of Barbados and to advise with such as are from thence and any other merchants trading thither."[28] These propositions were read at the committee meeting of 27 August 1650 "in the presence of divers merchants trading to the Barbados as also . . . of divers persons who came from thence." The committee then ordered the merchants to "draw up reasons they have to offer against these propositions," and present them in writing at the next meeting, at which time the committee would reconsider the matter "upon a full hearing . . . on both sides."[29]

The merchants' objections to the original propositions for Barbados, advanced, apparently, by the planters who had fled from the island are not known precisely. There can be no question, however, that the policy ultimately arrived at and forwarded to the council of state was largely in accord with the merchants' interests and contrived with their full participation. Three days later, after having heard the merchants' proposals, the admiralty committee ordered that an act be drawn up for presentation to Parliament specifying the prohibition of all trade to Barbados, either by foreigners or Englishmen. At the same time it resolved that a parliamentary commission to govern Barbados should be appointed and that a squadron of six ships, "four to be merchant ships set forth at the charge of the merchants who are interested in the island," should be sent to subdue the colony. By 10 September, the scope of the policy had been broadened to include the other royalist colonies of Bermuda and Virginia, and the committee's proposals along with additional "propositions brought in by Mr. Maurice Thomson concerning the reducing of Barbados" were forwarded to the council of state for presentation to Parliament, to be turned into legislation.[30]

When Parliament took up the council of state's proposals on the colonies shortly thereafter, the new-merchant leadership continued to exert a powerful influence on the formation of policy. On 27 September 1650, the "act for prohibiting trade and commerce to Barbados, Antigo, Virginia, and Bermudas" was read in the Commons for the first and second times and sent to its committee of the navy, referred to the "special care" of Col. George Thomson. Thomson was, of course, Maurice's brother and the navy committee chairman. The committee of the navy was also authorized to contract for ships and provisioning for the expedition to the colonies. Colonel Thomson reported the act back to Parliament on 3 October 1650 and it was passed on that day. At the same time, and quite significantly, Parliament moved to call in the proprietary patents for Barbados, Ber-

[28] *C.S.P.D. 1650*, p. 290.
[29] PRO, S.P.25/123/223.
[30] PRO, S.P.25/123/223v–224, 228v.

muda, and the West Indies. These had long been opposed by the new-merchant leadership.[31]

Parliament's decisions of late September–early October 1650 gave the colonial merchants just about everything they had requested. The decision to take the colonies by force and to put control of the colonial governments in the hands of commissions appointed by Parliament assured them, in the first place, the destruction of the West Indian proprietorship that they had so long pursued. With their increasing involvement as sugar planters in the domestic economy of Barbados during the 1640s, the new merchants had sought to protect themselves from the proprietors' arbitrary exactions and expropriations. In 1645–1647, they had taken their case to court, as well as to Parliament, but had not quite succeeded in having the Carlisle patent nullified. Under the Commonwealth, however, with Lord Willoughby, Carlisle's successor, at the head of a colonial rebellion, the English governing authorities had little choice but to grant the new merchants their wish and abolish the proprietorship. Still, from the point of view of the colonial merchants, the removal of proprietary parasitism from the West Indian economy would have been relatively insignificant had it not been accompanied by the permanent exclusion of the Dutch from the trade with the colonies in the Americas that was provided by the Act of 3 October 1650.[32]

The Act of 3 October 1650 prohibiting trade with the colonies has sometimes been treated as merely a temporary wartime measure, designed to apply only until the colonies were subdued. It was, in fact, intended from the start to be permanent and was clearly aimed at the restoration of English merchant hegemony throughout the British empire. That this should be so is hardly surprising in view of the colonial merchants' heavy participation in the forming of the act. It can be verified from the act itself, as well as from the testimony of contemporaries and the actions of the Commonwealth government. The first section of the act describes the British empire in the Americas ("Virginia . . . the Islands of Barbados, Antigua, St. Christopher's, Nevis, Monteserrat, Bermudas, and divers other islands and places in America"); asserts its rightful subordination to English law; names Barbados, Antigua, Bermuda, and Virginia as the specific plantations that have "most traitorously, by force and subtlety usurped a power of government"; and goes on to "forbid to all manner of persons, foreigners and others, all manner of commerce, traffic and correspondency whatsover" with these four colonies. This is the antiroyalist, anti-insurrectionary part of the act. There is, however, a later section that explicitly goes beyond the purely punitive intent of the first part and ex-

[31] *C.J.* 6: 474, 478.
[32] *C.J.* 3: 607. See also above, ch. 4, pp. 165–66.

tends the application of the act beyond the rebellious colonies to include the entire empire in the Americas. Here the government "forbid[s] and prohibit[s] all ships of any foreign nation whatsoever, to come to, or trade in, or traffic with *any of the English plantations in America, or any islands or places thereof, which are planted by, and in possession* of this Commonwealth, without license first had from the Parliament and Council of State" (emphasis added). There is nothing in the act to indicate that its application was merely to be temporary.[33]

The colonies themselves were well aware that the Act of 3 October 1650 was to be applied on a permanent basis. The remarkably similar declarations of defiance framed by Barbados and Virginia attest to the planters' common understanding of the ordinance. They provide, in addition, a clear indication of the real significance of the colonial rebellions, as well as of the English actions to subdue them. In March 1651, Virginia's governor Sir William Berkeley responded to the news of the English government's legislation and plans for the suppression of the colony with a defiant address to the Virginia Assembly in which he clearly linked the colonial demands for a royalist settlement in England, political autonomy, and free trade. As he concluded, "We can only fear the Londoners, who would fain bring us to the same poverty, wherein the Dutch found and relieved us; would take away the liberty of our consciences, and tongues, and our right of giving and selling our goods to whom we please. But gentlemen by the grace of God we will not so tamely part with our king, and all these blessings we enjoy under him."[34] The colonial government in Virginia followed its governor's inspiration to frame a full justification for rebellion. It answered the Act of 3 October 1650, point by point, denying that Virginians were either traitors or lawbreakers and affirming that this was well known to the English government. As it concluded the declaration,

> We think we can easily find out the cause of this excluding us the society of nations, which bring us necessaries for what our country produces. And that is the avarice of a few interested persons, who endeavor to rob us of all we sweat and labor for. Therefore on the whole matter we conclude: We are resolved to continue our allegiance to our most gracious king, yet as long as his gracious favor permits us, we will peaceably (as formerly) trade with the Londoners, and all other nations in amity with our sovereign; protect all foreign merchants with our utmost force from injury in the rivers; give letters of reprisal to any injured within our capes; always pray for the happy

[33] *A.O.* 2: 424–29. For a different view, see Ashley, *Financial and Commercial Policy*, pp. 132–33.

[34] "Speech of Sir William Berkeley, and Declaration of the Assembly, March, 1651," *V.M.H.B.* 1 (1894): 77.

restoration of our king and repentance in them, who to the hazard of their souls have opposed him.[35]

The arrival of the Act of 3 October 1650 in Barbados several weeks earlier had occasioned a very similar response. The council there asserted the legality of its own government in traditional terms, but went on, in more original fashion, to question the right of the English Parliament, in which Barbados had no representative, to legislate for it. As to the concrete provisions of the act, the council proclaimed:

> Whereas all the old planters well know how much they have been beholding to the Dutch for their subsistence, and how difficult it would have been (without their assistance) ever to have settled this place and even to this day are sensible what necessary comforts they bring us and how much cheaper they sell their commodities to us than our own nation; but this comfort must be taken from us by them whose will must be our law. But we do declare that we will never be so ungrateful to the Dutch for former helps as to deny them or any other nation the freedom of our ports and protection of our laws whereby they may still (if they please) embrace a free trade and commerce with us.[36]

The new merchants played a major role in seeing to the execution of the antiroyalist, antiproprietor, and anti-Dutch colonial policies enacted by Parliament in September–October 1650 and in molding the political settlements in the colonies that followed the Commonwealth's conquest. Less than a week after the passage of the act forbidding trade with the colonies, acting on the advice of Maurice Thomson, the admiralty committee of the council of state ordered the stay of ten or twelve English ships that Thomson had learned were about to embark for Barbados from Middleburgh and Flushing in defiance of the new law. Of course, no full enforcement was possible until the colonies had been subdued. The parliamentary navy committee was, therefore, immediately charged with organizing the military expedition and in this process Maurice's brother, the committee's chairman Col. George Thomson, played a leading part.[37]

On 27 November 1650, thirty-seven merchants and planters, including such business associates of Maurice Thomson's as William Pennoyer, Richard Bateson, John Wood, Edward Wood, Michael Davison, Jonathan Andrews, and Thomas Frere petitioned the council of state "to give way to the said merchants at their own charge to provide 5 or 6 . . . able

[35] Ibid., p. 81.

[36] *A Declaration set forth by the Lord Lieutenant the Gentlemen of the Councell and assembly occasioned from the view of a printed paper Entitled an Act prohibiting trade. . . .* (London, 1651), p. 4.

[37] *C.S.P. Col. 1574–1660*, p. 344; *C.J.* 6: 474, 526.

ships with competent cargos in them . . . to exercise all acts of hostilities against the islanders," in case the islanders refused to submit to the Commonwealth regime. The merchants proposed four conditions for a political settlement on Barbados designed to bring the colony into obedience to the Commonwealth and asked to be allowed to enforce them against the colony. They further asked permission to trade with the colony immediately after it had been subdued.[38] This plan would have placed the whole process of suppressing the colonial revolts in the hands of the new merchants; in its merger of the political and military with the strictly economic aspects of the project it typified their preferred approach to commercial development. In their privateering ventures of plunder under the Providence Island Company, in their Additional Sea Adventure to Ireland (1642), and in Capt. William Jackson's marauding voyage to the West Indies (1642–1645), these men already had carried out, on a smaller scale, much the same kind of private wars for economic aggrandizement that they were now suggesting. They well understood the significance of direct political control for any subsequent commercial settlement worked out for the colonies. The council of state, however, saw the threat to its sovereignty implicit in the merchants' propositions and declared that "both in respect of matter and manner they are dishonorable" to the government. Still, the government accepted at least the commercial part of the merchants' proposal, and the merchants supplied five of the seven ships that ultimately composed the expeditionary fleet for the West Indies.[39]

The three parliamentary commissioners who were chosen to carry out the reduction of Barbados at the end of 1651 do not seem to have been closely connected with the colonial-interloping merchants. However, all four men who were placed in charge of the expedition against Virginia— Robert Dennis, Thomas Stegg, William Claiborne, and Richard Bennett—were themselves longtime colonial merchants; moreover, three of them (Dennis, Stegg, and Claiborne) had long been close associates of the new-merchant leadership, and three (Stegg, Claiborne, and Bennett) had been leading Virginia colonial officials. Robert Dennis, the commander of the fleet to Virginia, had been employed throughout the 1640s by Maurice Thomson's brother-in-law Elias Roberts, William Berkeley, and Timothy Felton (all three major colonial merchants) as master of their ship *Charles* on its voyages to Bermuda, the West Indies, and the North American continent.[40] Thomas Stegg had been the Virginia factor of both Maurice Thomson and the important American trader and London mili-

---

[38] PRO, C.O.1/11/23.
[39] *C.S.P.D. 1650*, p. 444; *C.J.* 6: 526.
[40] PRO, H.C.A.3/43/15v, 24v, 25, 27v; PRO, H.C.A.24/108/286.

tant MP Matthew Craddock. In partnership with one of Thomson's leading trading partners, Jeremy Blackman, he imported horses into Virginia in the late 1630s, by which time he had entered the narrow circle of colonial councilors. William Claiborne had been one of the leading merchants, planters, and politicians in Virginia beginning in the 1620s, and was at the center of its political and commercial development. In partnership with William Cloberry, Maurice Thomson, and others, he had organized the private syndicate for colonization and trade based on Kent Island in the Chesapeake, and from this position, as well as his place on the Virginia Council, he had led the fight against the Calvert proprietorship in Maryland. By the end of the 1630s, like Maurice Thomson, Claiborne had become involved in new colonizing ventures in the Caribbean under the aegis of the Providence Island Company, but he maintained his contacts with Virginia and kept a sharp eye on Maryland, ready to strike. Finally, Richard Bennett, although not, apparently, so directly connected with the new-merchant leadership as the others, appears to have represented similar interests in Virginia. A major colonial planter and official, he was also a longtime leading merchant and thus tended to side with the merchant-planter-councilor clique against the planters, and against the Calvert proprietorship.[41]

The composition of the four-man parliamentary commission for Virginia evidences the success of the new merchants and their friends in convincing the Commonwealth government to restore to power in the Chesapeake colonies the old pre–Civil War merchant-planter-councilor clique, with its anti–free trade and anti-Calvert program. There can be little doubt, in fact, that one of the major purposes of this commission was to reimpose that expansionist, anti-Calvert policy for Virginia which had been temporarily suspended in the 1630s under Charles I, but which had been revived by aggressive new-merchant action during the troubled era of the Civil War. A coalition of English traders and Virginia planters, led by the merchant-planter-councilor clique, had of course bitterly contested Lord Baltimore's proprietorship from its inception in 1632, basing its opposition in part on its desire to protect the trading colony on Kent Island led by Capt. William Claiborne, William Cloberry, and Maurice Thomson, but more generally on its concern to keep open the expansionary potential of the Virginia colony toward the north. From the early 1640s, first the London merchant Richard Ingle, then William Claiborne himself, had launched military assaults on the Maryland colony. The London traders with Virginia, led by the new merchant leadership, had followed up these military attacks by petitioning Parliament against Lord Baltimore in

---

[41] For Stegg, Claiborne, and Bennett, see above, ch. 4. Bennett was for many years closely associated with the leading Virginia councilor and opponent of Maryland, John Utie.

March 1647. The pressure exerted by these men, including Maurice Thomson, William Deacon, William Pennoyer, Richard Chandler, Thomas Gower, and Oliver Cloberry, seems to have induced the parliamentary committee for plantations, already no doubt perturbed about the royalist activities of Baltimore's brother Leonard Calvert in the colony, to call in Baltimore's patent, although not yet formally to revoke it.[42]

In 1649, Baltimore's old nemesis Richard Ingle revived his attack on the proprietorship and the matter was referred to the admiralty committee of the council of state, which once again called on Maurice Thomson and his friends for advice. At the meeting of 9 January 1650 in which the committee approved, on the merchants' counsel, its policy for the reduction of Virginia to the obedience of the Commonwealth, one of the specific proposals adopted called for the attorney general to redraft a grant for Virginia "in which . . . the confines of the said plantation [Virginia] were to be particularly expressed according to the ancient limits."[43] This provision was almost certainly put in at the suggestion of merchants dealing with Virginia in order to restore the old claims of Virginia to Maryland and of the merchant-planter clique to Kent Island. Its approval was, by implication, a demand by the committee for the abolition of Lord Baltimore's proprietorship, on the grounds that the Maryland colony was clearly within the bounds of the original Virginia patent.

When, in late 1651, the fleet to pacify Virginia was dispatched from England, the Rump's commission in charge of the expedition carried instructions to "reduce all of the plantations within the Bay of Chesapeake to their due obedience to the Parliament of the Commonwealth of England." This was clearly meant to include Maryland, and contained an implied threat to Baltimore's control of the colony. That threat was, of course, greatly magnified by the fact that the commission was directly in the hands of London merchants trading with Virginia, the old merchant-planter-councilor combine.[44]

By the end of 1652, the new-merchant leadership could hardly have been more satisfied with the evolution of colonial policy under the Commonwealth. The royalist revolts had been put down and a policy of total exclusion of the Dutch from the colonial trade had been adopted. Throughout the colonies,[45] moreover, parliamentary commissions had

---

[42] For these developments, see above, ch. 4, pp. 167–68.

[43] PRO, S.P.25/123/107.

[44] "Instructions to the Commissioners, 26 September 1651," *V.M.H.B.* 11 (1904): 38.

[45] It might be noted that, in broad outline, developments in Bermuda appear to have followed the pattern of those in the other colonies in this period. The outcome was to place the government of the island in the hands of a seventeen-man commission appointed 25 June 1653. This body included a strong representation of new-merchant leaders who had previously played an important role under the Bermuda Company, including Owen Rowe (formerly deputy governor and treasurer of the com-

been installed whose main purpose was to ensure the necessary conditions for merchant-led colonial development: the reduction of proprietary parasitism on the plantation economies and the enforcement of an anti-Dutch, anti-free trade regime against the interests of the great majority of the colonial planters.

Commercial Policy and World Power

Narrowly viewed, the policies implemented by the Commonwealth in the Americas reflected the new-merchant leaders' powerful influence over policy-making in these spheres, the result, in turn, of their close connections with Commonwealth decision makers, as well as their indispensable role in Commonwealth governance. Nevertheless, these same policies are incomprehensible unless they are interpreted as well in terms of that drive for English commercial supremacy in the name of imperialism and world power that was undertaken by those key groups of Rump moderate republicans and radicals that were so central in establishing the regime and in providing much of its leadership. It follows that *both* of those traditional interpretations of the Commonwealth's commercial dynamism—as the special creation of a relatively small group of newly ascendant imperialist republicans in Parliament and as the product of the unusually powerful influence exerted by merchant groups—are not only correct but entirely complementary.[46] It was the durable alliance between the newly installed radical leaderships in Parliament and in the City that was most responsible for the unusually attentive, experimental, and aggressive approach to commercial policy that was pursued under the Commonwealth. This was in evidence not only in the formation of policy for the Americas, but also in that for the Mediterranean and East Indies as well. It was manifest, moreover, in those more general programmatic departures which gave the Commonwealth's overall approach to commercial policy its distinctiveness—the council of trade, free ports, the navigation act, and the Dutch war.

Two closely interrelated problems, both results of a century of English commercial transformation, posed themselves for solution to Common-

pany), Maurice Thomson, Elias Roberts, Nathaniel Hawes, and Matthew Bateson, as well as their friend, the City goldsmith and Bermuda Company investor, Francis Allein (J. H. Lefroy, *Memorials of the Bermudas*, 2 vols. [Bermuda, 1877–1879], 2: 42).

[46] See H. R. Trevor-Roper, "Oliver Cromwell and His Parliaments," in *Religion, the Reformation, and Social Change* (London, 1972), pp. 357–61; G. N. Clark, "The Navigation Act of 1651," *History* 7 (1922–1923); Farnell, "Navigation Act"; Gardiner, *Commonwealth and Protectorate* 1: 120 n. 1; Groenveld, "First Anglo-Dutch War," pp. 559–60. Cf. C. Wilson, *Profit and Power* (London, 1957), pp. 149–57.

wealth policymakers: first, the increasing complexity of English trade; second, the overpowering competition of the Dutch. For centuries English trade had been, for the most part, bilateral commerce dominated first by the wool-exporting Staplers, then by the cloth-exporting Merchant Adventurers. Both the English customs system, which continued to involve direct levies on all imports and exports whatever their source, and the characteristic institution for the organization of trade, the regulated corporation of merchants covering single two-way trading lines, remained premised on that ideal type. Yet almost all of the newer trades originating in the second half of the sixteenth century—especially the long-distance commerce with the Levant, the East Indies, Africa, and the Americas—were essentially import trades that integrally involved not only reexports but also internal multilaterality, that is, triangular trades. Both the operation of the traditional customs system and that of the typical commercial corporation came, therefore, in some respects, to fetter the newly developing commerce. The government's practice of levying customs on goods imported into England for the purpose of reexport seemed irrational and unnecessarily discouraging to merchants, and gave rise to the call for free ports (in other words, duty-free reexports). Similarly, the chartered companies' various restrictions on entry, as well as the narrow and traditional forms of trade the companies sometime dictated, seemed to some merchants to limit unnecessarily the play of capital and entrepreneurship, and thus gave rise to the demand for a freer trade. Both of these policy alternatives—free ports and free trade—were to preoccupy Commonwealth policymakers.

Correlatively, the long-dominant Merchant Adventurers' commerce had traditionally involved trade in partnership with the Dutch as a defining characteristic. But almost all the newer trades had as their raison d'être either the bypassing of Dutch middlemen or the opening up of entirely new sources of import commodities, and therefore increasingly had to be built up in commercial struggle against the Dutch. Until the 1640s the English had, for long periods, enjoyed an artificial insulation from their commercially superior Dutch competitors, due to the Hollanders' almost perpetual involvement in war with their key trading partner Spain. With the Peace of Munster in 1648, however, the Dutch were finally freed to capitalize fully on their enormous commercial and maritime resources. To make matters worse, English trade was, at this very moment, seriously disrupted by the Civil War, especially by royalist privateering. As a result, a commercial situation very favorable to the English, in which as late as the outbreak of the Civil War, English merchants appeared to be the dominant force in European commerce, deteriorated disastrously in the space of just a few years. Even in 1641, Sir Thomas Roe had been able to see that the recent successes of English commerce were very largely attributable to the involvement of the European states in war. "Our great trade depends upon the trouble of our neighbors," said Roe, "but if a peace happen between France, Spain, and the United Provinces, all these will now share what we possess alone." Roe had, if anything, underestimated the commercial carnage that would follow peace between Spain and the United Provinces. By the early years of the Commonwealth, the Dutch had recovered their near-monolopy of the Baltic trade, essentially eliminating the English as serious competitors. They had regained their hegemony in the lucrative commerce with Iberia, especially in American reexports, reversing the position attained by the English during the years in which the Dutch had been distracted by war with Spain. Most shockingly, perhaps, the Dutch had demolished the English merchants' position of predominance in the Mediterranean and were now threatening to exploit the disruption of English commerce by the royalists and their confederates to gain a position at least of parity in the rich trades to Italy and the Levant. Simultaneously, while maintaining their long-dominant position in the East Indies, the Dutch had, as noted, taken advantage of the Civil War to invade the trades with the English colonies in Virginia and the West Indies. Finally, and least surprisingly, once war with Spain had ended, the Dutch had little difficulty reasserting their fundamental preeminence in the international carrying trades within Europe and beyond. Indeed, by the middle of 1651, they were making serious inroads as middlemen in the English market itself, bringing in commodities from distant ports that only recently had been monopolized by London company merchants. By this time, one knowledgeable commentator had reason to warn that the Dutch, "(after they had settled their liberty) . . . have . . . for some years aimed to lay a foundation to themselves for engrossing the universal trade not only of Christendom, but, indeed, of the greater part of the known world." Coping, in one way or another, with potentially devastating Dutch competition had to be a top priority for the policymakers of the new regime.[47]

The problems of increasing commercial complexity and of Dutch competition were thus in reality inseparable from one another. The Hollanders' overwhelmingly powerful position was based, in large part, on their capture of multilateral, reexport trades, both inside and outside Europe,

---

[47] See "Sir Thomas Roe's Speech in Parliament (1641)," *Harleian Miscellany*, 12 vols. (London, 1809), 4: 456; *The Advocate* (London, 1652), reprinted in R.W.K. Hinton, *The Eastland Trade and the Commonweal* (Cambridge, 1959), pp. 205–13 (quotation on p. 205); Hinton, *Eastland Trade*, pp. 84–85; Wilson, *Profit and Power*, pp. 40–47; H. Taylor, "Trade, Neutrality, and the 'English Road,' 1630–1648," *Ec.H.R.*, 2d ser., 25 (1972); J. I. Israel, "The Phases of Dutch *straatvaart* (1590–1713)," *Tijdschrift Voor Geschiedenis* 99 (1986): 11–23. Israel's article is especially important in that it reverses earlier impressions that, even following the Dutch peace with Spain, English hegemony in the Mediterranean remained secure and the Dutch posed no serious competitive threat.

largely by means of their superior shipping and, as a by-product of that, the predominance in Europe of the Amsterdam customs-free entrepôt. To deal with this situation, England had no choice but, in one way or another, to follow the Dutch example. Yet, in theory at least, there were two alternative modes by which this might be accomplished: either in conflict or in collaboration with the Dutch. The first course was perhaps the most obvious one, and was, in both the short and the long run, the one put into practice. It meant powerful state intervention to rationalize English economic and financial organization, to protect English commerce and shipping from Dutch competition, and, ultimately, to destroy the Dutch competitors through war. But the path of alliance and cooperation, despite its prima facie implausibility, appears also to have been seriously mooted by Commonwealth policymakers. The facts of roughly common republican political systems and of generally similar Protestant religious systems seemed to make the Dutch and the English natural allies against the threat posed by the monarchical Counter-Reformation powers, Spain and France. Moreover, at least to the English, the prospect of improved commercial collaboration with the Dutch was a real attraction; the Dutch had at hand both manpower and capital resources that were much in demand by a very vital, yet still comparatively underdeveloped, English merchant community.

With hindsight, the possibility of really close political and commercial collaboration between England and the United Provinces appears remote, since the Dutch had an enormous commercial competitive advantage and appear to have had little to gain from cooperation. Yet, starting in the latter part of 1650, the Commonwealth government, at the crest of its strength following a powerful buildup of both its army and navy and the crushing defeat of royalist foes throughout the British Isles and around Europe, appears to have considered the closest alliance and even some form of unification with the United Provinces to be at least a possibility, at least for a time. This is not to deny that the Commonwealth government continued, throughout the period, to promote English commercial interests aggressively over and against those of the Dutch, as it did, for example, in its colonies in the Americas. But it was apparently hoped that the threat posed by English naval power to Dutch trading operations would help to make the Dutch see the long-run economic advantages of politico-commercial cooperation.

As Dr. Worden has pointed out, Thomas Chaloner and Thomas Scot, especially from the period following the great victory at Dunbar, were working together on intimate terms, seeking to accelerate further the Commonwealth's new commercial overseas offensive in the Americas and elsewhere, and collaborating closely with London's merchant community in seeking to find cheaper ways to finance and supply the navy. As Chaloner wrote Scot in December 1650, "I pray present my humble service to my Lord General [Cromwell], who I wish had settled his [military] business there, that he might look a little toward the sea, which being our main business now, will never be carried by men of such narrow hearts, as for the most part been formerly employed." In the early months of 1651, a cult of enthusiasm for the Venetian republic seems to have developed, and the Commonwealth leadership sought to establish a link from the government's impressive string of military and diplomatic successes to its republican form of rule. Meanwhile, in this same period, it attempted to enhance further the Commonwealth's international political and commercial position by embarking on a series of striking new diplomatic and trade policy departures.[48]

As I will try to show, then, the Commonwealth gave serious consideration during the first half of 1651 to establishing customs-free ports in the fullest sense of the term, as open to foreign as well as English shipping, and to freer trade. This initiative toward trade liberalization appears to have been premised to a large degree on the parallel negotiations for the closest sort of political alliance, indeed political union, with the Dutch. Union was intended to bring about the most intimate political, as well as commercial, unity between the two countries. The rise and fall of the Commonwealth council of trade marked this period of perhaps utopian attempts at liberalization. The collapse of the negotiations with the Dutch in mid-1651 rendered useless the main policy alternatives this council was created to develop and brought swiftly in its train the navigation act and the Dutch war. Combat replaced cooperation toward the unchanging goal of empire and commercial supremacy.

THE CREATION OF THE COUNCIL OF TRADE

The origins of the Commonwealth council of trade are apparently to be found in two orders of the winter of 1649–1650. On 21 December 1649, the House of Commons ruled that the issue of establishing free ports in England be referred to the parliamentary committee of the navy, chaired by Maurice Thomson's brother George Thomson. This body was ordered to "send for and advise with such merchants or others as they shall think fit therein; and to consider the conveniences and inconveniences thereof: wherein they are to have special care that the Commonwealth be not prejudiced in their customs and excise." Several weeks later, on 11 January 1650, Col. Richard Hutchinson, the trader with New England, interloper in the East Indies, and soon-to-be treasurer of the navy, informed

---

[48] Worden, *Rump Parliament*, pp. 252, 256, 260; J. Nickolls, *Original Letters and Papers of State . . . of Mr. John Milton* (London, 1743), p. 43.

the House of Commons that the council of state had received petitions from the East India, Levant, and Eastland traders for the renewal of their corporate privileges, "which carry with them some restraint of general liberty of trade." Hutchinson reported that, in the view of the council of state, "such grants of restraint, if they shall be judged necessary" was the sort of question of general policy that the Commons should itself decide. The Commons' response was to order that an act be prepared for establishing a standing council for ordering and regulating commerce to the best advantage of the Commonwealth. It was recognized from the start that the question of free trade, as well as that of free ports, would centrally preoccupy this council.[49]

Specially charged by the Commons with planning the council of trade and with framing its instructions were two MPs who were to stand at the very center of commercial policy formulation throughout the life of the Commonwealth, Thomas Chaloner and Richard Salway. Both had been at the core of the revolutionary movement that installed the new regime; both were to remain until the end among the Commonwealth's very top leaders and most stalwart supporters; both had already shown a strong interest in commercial affairs. They are typical of the republican radicals who helped to impart to Rump commercial policy its particularly aggressive character.

Thomas Chaloner had, according to Anthony à Wood, returned from foreign travel a "well-bred gentleman, but tinged, as it seems, with anti-monarchical principles." Ultimately "one of Henry Marten's gang," he became "a great stickler for their new Utopian Commonwealth."[50] As early as 1646, Chaloner had argued that Parliament should "first settle the honour and safety and freedom of the Commonwealth, and then . . . of the King, so far as the latter may stand with the former and not otherwise." In 1647, he was accused of claiming that "the Houses are accountable to none but God Almighty."[51] Along with his republicanism, Chaloner developed a serious concern for commercial matters, as he demonstrated in the crudely imperialist introduction he wrote in 1648 to Thomas Gage's A New Survey of the West Indies.[52] In this work, Chaloner assured his readers that although the Civil War was still continuing to bring misery, peace was not far off, and that with peace would come a new era of English overseas conquest, especially in the West Indies. In this regard, a few lines of Chaloner's doggerel may be worth quoting:

[49] C.J. 7: 336, 346–47.

[50] A. à Wood, Atheniae Oxoniensis, ed. P. Bliss, 4 vols. (London, 1813–1820), vol. 3, fols. 531–32; D.N.B., s.v. "Thomas Chaloner."

[51] Worden, Rump Parliament, p. 37.

[52] T. Chaloner, Upon the Worthy Work, of his Most Worthy Friend the Author (London, 1648). I owe this reference to the kindness of Dr. Blair Worden.

You the worthy Patriots of this land
Let not your hearts be drowned in despair . . .
You shall again advance with reputation
And on the bounds of utmost Western shore
Where English colours ne'r did fly before.
Shall them transplant, and firmly fix their station.

Richard Salway, a close political collaborator of Chaloner's especially in the support of an aggressive approach to commercial affairs, was the son-in-law of the colonial trader Richard Waring, who was a collaborator of Maurice Thomson's and an important representative of the new-merchant leadership. Like his father-in-law, Salway became a London grocer and, in the early 1640s (as did another key new-merchant grocer, Samuel Warner), he illegally interloped within the privileged areas of the Merchant Adventurers. Apparently a leader in the antiroyalist City apprentice riots of the early revolutionary period, Salway had, by the late 1640s, won an important place among London's political independents, and he was appointed to the City militia committees of September 1647 and January 1649.[53] In the meantime, Salway had joined the army and become a major. It was no doubt politically significant that in his political independent manifesto, *Last Report of the English Wars*, written in the summer of 1646, Hugh Peter singled out Richard Salway for special praise, along with such other prominent radical officers as Edward Whalley, Thomas Pride, and Thomas Rainsborough. With ties in London and the army, as well as Parliament, which he entered as a recruiter MP in 1645, Salway was, like Hugh Peter, undoubtedly one of the key figures who forged the radical alliance that seized power in 1648 and provided the revolution with its political rationale. A religious Independent and apparently an oligarchic republican, Salway worked with Thomas Chaloner and Henry Marten in drafting the Commons' resolution of 4 January 1649 that proclaimed the legitimacy of the Commonwealth in terms of popular sovereignty, while reserving to the Commons full authority with no appeal beyond it.[54]

On 16 March 1650, the act for establishing the council of trade was read for a second time. The Commons resolved that this body should consist of fifteen men, that two of its members should be Richard Salway and Thomas Chaloner, and that a third should be Sir Henry Vane, long an important figure in the colonizing movement. Parliament also took this

[53] Society of Genealogists, Boyd's Index of London Citizens: 26875; PRO, S.P.46/80/136, 143 (interloping); M. Noble, *The Lives of the Regicides*, 2 vols. (London, 1798), 2: 158–63; A.O. 1: 1007, 1261.

[54] *Mr. Peters Last Report of the English Wars* (London, 1646), p. 4; *Dictionary of Seventeenth-Century Radicals*, vol. 3, s.v. "Richard Salway."

opportunity to select as secretary for the new council that leading member of the "Hartlib Circle" Benjamin Worsley.[55] Worsley, it will be recalled, had established direct ties with the new-merchant leadership at least by the summer of 1649 and was, at this point, in the winter and spring of 1650, working closely with Maurice Thomson, William Pennoyer, William Allen, and the council of state's admiralty committee in formulating Commonwealth policy for the rebellious colonies in the Americas, especially Virginia. In addition, the Commons ruled that a broadened, twenty-three-person committee of the House should take charge of completing the establishment of the council of trade, its personnel, and its instructions.

The composition of the Commons' committee for completing the establishment of the council of trade provides further evidence as to who was behind Commonwealth commercial policy. Including twelve of Underdown's revolutionaries and twelve of Worden's thirty-three most active Rump MPs, this committee was once again heavily recruited from among those I have termed radicals and moderate republicans—strong political backers and leaders of the Rump, often intimates of the new-merchant leadership, and committed promoters of a vigorous overseas policy for the new regime.[56] In the first place, alongside Thomas Chaloner and Richard Salway on this committee sat their brothers James Chaloner and Humphrey Salway, both of whom could be counted on to support their siblings' initiatives. In addition, there were two immediate members of the new merchant leadership, Gregory Clement and Thomas Boone, as well as Francis Allein, the London goldsmith who had long worked closely with them.[57] Gregory Clement had been in trouble as early as 1631 for illegal trading in the East Indies. Over the next two decades, Clement was one of Maurice Thomson's most important political and commercial collaborators in the trades with the Americas, in privateering, and in the Additional Sea Adventure to Ireland, and he worked with the new-merchant leaders on a long string of City and national political committees, most recently the London militia committees of September 1647 and January 1649 and the High Court of Justice that tried the king (December 1648). Thomas Boone was, like Clement, with whom he was often allied, a West Country merchant with London connections, who only recently had joined the new-merchant leadership in its Assada–East Indies interloping proj-

[55] *C.J.* 6: 383.

[56] Ibid. The members of the committee to establish the council of trade were Sir Henry Vane, Thomas Boone, Mr. Ashe, Mr. Stephens, Mr. Goodwin, Gilbert Pickering, Mr. Hodges, Sir John Hippesley, Philip Jones, Richard Salway, Charles Fleetwood, Dennis Bond, Richard Darley, Francis Allein, James Chaloner, John Lisle, Miles Corbet, John Danvers, John Venn, Humphrey Edwards, Thomas Chaloner, John Jones, and Gregory Clement. The twelve last named were the "revolutionaries" designated in Underdown, *Pride's Purge*, app. A—among whom the last seven were regicides.

[57] For most of the following information on Clement, Boone, and Allein, see above.

ect. He appears to have been another of those pivotal figures who provided indispensable personal connections between the City and the parliamentary wings of the radical movement, for he was also one of the closest political friends of Thomas Chaloner.[58] Francis Allein was a religious Independent and parliamentary radical who, as a judge of King Charles, took a hard line on the fourteen occasions he attended the king's trial (although he did not sign the death warrant). Allein had worked with the new merchants Maurice Thomson, Thomas Andrews, Stephen Estwicke, James Russell, and William Barkeley as early as 1643 on their commission for the customs, and on numerous occasions since then. Not surprisingly, he was also a very close political collaborator of Richard Salway,[59] with whom he worked constantly in the Rump, and probably also of another member of the committee for establishing the council of trade, the radical Sir John Danvers. Both Allein and Danvers were active members of the Bermuda Company and served on various governmental bodies established to deal with Bermuda affairs.[60] Finally, on this committee were John Venn, Miles Corbet, and Dennis Bond, all well-known fiery spirits and radical supporters of the Commonwealth who, though not themselves apparently directly active in overseas trade, had long worked in collaboration with the new merchants, not only on common political projects but on matters concerning the new merchants' special commercial and financial interests. Venn, Corbet, and Bond had been leading figures in the City radical movement of 1643 and Bond had been chosen by the City militants to be a member of the committee for a general rising that climaxed that offensive. Bond's intimate connections with the new merchants were evidenced in 1646, when he led a small battle in the House of Commons to stay proceedings at law against the major trader with the Americas and new-merchant radical politician John Warner, and to allow him to reclaim some tobacco of his which had been seized by the customs farmers.[61] Miles Corbet, a longtime friend of Hugh Peter and Jeremiah Burroughs, had brought into the House of Commons in autumn 1647 the proposal of Maurice Thomson, Thomas Andrews, Stephen Estwicke, Richard Shute, and Thomas Smythe to have the customs commission restored to them. Corbet had been the dominant parliamentary figure in the initial reorganization of the Commonwealth navy, serving as chair of the Commons' committee for naval affairs. He appears to have taken a leading role in establishing the Commonwealth's council of trade, for on 1 August

---

[58] Worden, *Rump Parliament*, p. 31.

[59] According to Worden, the alliance of Allein and Salway "was as intimate and consistent as that of any two Rumpers" (*Rump Parliament*, p. 31).

[60] Lefroy, *Memorials* 1: 590, 2: 42; *C.S.P.D. 1651*, pp. 454–55.

[61] *C.J.* 4: 431, 508.

1650 he brought back into Parliament the final redrawn act for this body, with the names of the commissioners and their instructions.[62]

The membership of the council of trade, which by 11 April 1651 had come to include seventeen members,[63] was made up of three distinct, but closely interrelated, groups. In the first place, there was the new-merchant leadership, represented on the council by Maurice Thomson, the MP Thomas Boone, the India Company opponent John Fowke, and John Limbrey, the colonial merchant who had gone to Holland in 1648 as a parliamentary commissioner to recover the rebellious ships along with Maurice Thomson and Thomson's Anglo-Dutch East India interloping partners Adam Laurence and Nicholas Corsellis. Second, there were the imperialist republican MPs, represented by Thomas Chaloner and Richard Salway (as well as by Thomas Boone). Finally, there was the so-called Hartlib Circle, represented on the council by Benjamin Worsley, who was the council's secretary and one of its key moving spirits, by Robert Honeywood, who was Sir Henry Vane's brother-in-law and later the translator of a tract on the virtues of the Venetian republic, and by Sir Cheney Culpepper.[64] All three of these groups were closely tied to one another, and were supportive of roughly the same policy directions.

It did not take long for the council of trade to make an impact. By the autumn of 1650, it had forwarded to the council of state for presentation to Parliament what is in certain respects the most characteristic piece of Commonwealth commercial legislation, the act ordering English government convoys for Levant Company shipping in the Mediterranean. Previous governments had seriously contemplated this policy, but had never put it into effect, largely because of its cost. To make this program practicable, the republic had to raise customs rates by 15 percent. That it unhesitatingly did so shows how far the alliance of imperialist republicans and their radical friends in the House and the new-merchant leadership had been able to take the Commonwealth beyond the traditional premises of English foreign policy—making. Perhaps for the first time, English government fiscal policies were being consciously and systematically shaped to fit the needs of commercial development, rather than vice versa, as for example during the reign of Charles I. Appropriately enough, the ordinance was led through Parliament by that imperialist republican par excellence Thomas Chaloner and passed on 31 October 1650.[65]

---

[62] *C.J.* 6: 451–52.

[63] *A.O.* 2: 403 (original fifteen members); *C.J.* 6: 560 (additions of John Limbrey and Dr. Aaron Gourdain).

[64] On Honeywood, see *D.N.B.*, s.v. "Robert Honeywood." On Culpepper, see Cooper, "Social and Economic Policies," p. 133.

[65] *C.J.* 6: 488–89; Gardiner, *Commonwealth and Protectorate* 1: 339–43; T. Violet, *Mysteries and Secrets of Trade* (London, 1653), p. 177. See in this context Cardinal Mazarin's earlier observation

The council of trade's original twelve-point set of instructions designated two major areas of potential innovation in policy that the parliamentary committee felt should be given special attention: first, the possibility of loosening the corporate organization of commerce, that is, free trade; second, the idea of encouraging the English entrepôt trade through setting up free ports.[66] Most probably, the parliamentary committee responsible for establishing the council and writing its instructions supported both a freer trade and free ports. Clearly, too, the new-merchant leadership, undoubtedly quite influential within that committee, also supported these commercial policy directions. But the question that historians have rightly asked is the degree to which such groups as these were able actually to have their way, in relationship to possibly opposed commercial interests and, more generally, the Commonwealth government as a whole.[67]

FREE TRADE

It has often been pointed out that despite the possible intent of the council of trade's instructions, the Commonwealth government did not in fact move to abolish corporate companies. The government explicitly sanctioned company organization for both the East Indies and Guinea, each a major area of activity of the pro–free trade new-merchant leadership, and these actions have been taken as strong evidence against the idea that the new regime was especially favorable to a freer trade.[68] Nevertheless, to interpret the government's chartering of the East India and Guinea companies as indicating the continued force of traditional principles of company organization under the Commonwealth is, in my view, to mistake the form for the substance of these decisions.

Consider, in particular, the trade with the East Indies, by far the most crucial case. Here government pressure was indeed responsible for the establishment of a unitary joint-stock organization—against the express wishes of the new-merchant leadership for a freer commercial regime, a regulated company in which members would trade individually under rules and regulations set by the corporation. Yet what has not perhaps been well enough understood is how closely the government-imposed settle-

(1646) to the effect that "in a republic, taxation being voluntary and coming by consent and by agreement of everyone for a policy unanimously agreed, they will pay without murmurings or regrets whatever is necessary to make that policy succeed" (quoted in Hill, *God's Englishman*, p. 131).

[66] The council of trade's instructions are printed in C. M. Andrews, *British Committees, Commissions, and Councils of Trade and Plantations, 1622–1675* (Baltimore, 1908), app. 1.

[67] See the thorough critical survey of the historiography by Cooper, "Social and Economic Policies."

[68] Ibid., p. 132. Cf. D. Massarella, " 'A World Elsewhere': Aspects of the Overseas Expansionist Mood of the 1650s," in *Politics and People in Revolutionary England*, ed. C. Jones et al. (Oxford, 1986).

ment of the trade with the East Indies nonetheless conformed to the new merchants' desires by requiring a complete break from the traditional modes of carrying on the trade precisely so as to achieve the effects generally intended by the demand for free trade.

It will be recalled that by the later 1640s, the old East India Company was in deep crisis. The interloping syndicate under the leadership of Maurice Thomson was invading all aspects of the company's trade, and using its influence in Parliament to prevent the company from stopping the practice. In 1645, the company had sought to have Parliament intervene to stay a new voyage being prepared by the interlopers, but it had failed to do so, and Thomson and his friends had expanded the scope of their activities, notably to include a projected colony on the island of Assada, off the east coast of Africa.[69]

Even so, it had looked for a time as though the company might ultimately recover its privileges. In the period beginning in late 1643, despite the company's open royalism, a Parliament desperate for funds had seemed willing to restore its patent, more or less explicitly in exchange for financial contributions to the parliamentary cause.[70] After a long, drawn-out process, the Commons did ultimately approve the renewal of the East India Company charter on 5 December 1646.[71] But that was as close as the East India Company came to regaining its privileges. On 13 February 1647, Alderman John Fowke, representing Thomson's interloping syndicate, brought before the House of Lords' committee charged with considering the renewal of the company's patent reasons why the trade with the East Indies should cease to be governed by a joint-stock company. Fowke, a bitter enemy of the old company who had been involved in interloping in the East Indies from the time of Courteen's initial venture, was of course a longtime collaborator of the new-merchant leadership in a wide range of activities. On 27 February, the Lords' committee actually recommended that the House of Lords approve the Commons' bill for the renewal of the patent. At this point, however, the House gave the new merchants' interloping syndicate a final chance to state its case, and the new merchants' intervention seems to have tipped the balance against the old company. On 16 March 1647 the House of Lords, with only eleven persons in attendance, voted down the company's privileges. In view of the fact that seven of the Lords who had served on the committee that initially had recommended that the House approve the patent were in at-

[69] See above, ch. 4.

[70] *C.C.M.E.I.C. 1640–1643*, pp. xv–xvii, 365; *C.J.* 3: 313, 376. For the general pattern of parliamentary grants of company privileges in exchange for company loans to Parliament, see W. R. Scott, *The Constitution and Finance of English, Scottish, and Irish Joint-Stock Companies to 1720*, 3 vols. (Cambridge, 1910–1912), 1: 237–38.

[71] *C.J.* 3: 395, 4: 38, 330, 5: 1.

tendance that day, it seems evident that outside influence, specifically, that of the new merchants, had turned the tide.[72]

By the autumn of 1647, especially following the army's invasion of London, the old company had no choice but to recognize the new commercial and political balance of forces. It agreed to collaborate with the new merchants in the establishment of a new, temporary joint stock that would be independent of the old company and be governed by a separate board of directors on which the new-merchant leadership would be heavily represented. Then with the victory of the political independents in 1648–1649, the new merchants felt strong enough to ask the government for a charter for their own separate company. It is a sign of the new merchants' extraordinary influence in the highest circles of power that heading up their petition of the autumn of 1649 for government sanction of their own new company was no less a personage than Thomas, Lord Fairfax, the parliamentary commander in chief. The old company directorate had meanwhile forfeited all trace of political influence as a result of its staunchly royalist stand in the two civil wars. Even so, the old directorate responded to the interlopers' petition by calling on the government to renew the old company's charter and to "hinder the proceedings of the pretended planters to Assada."[73] At this point, the government intervened in order to secure an agreement that would include both warring factions. Nevertheless, the settlement imposed by the council of state represented an overwhelming victory for the new merchants, for it embodied the near-totality of their program for opening up and transforming the trade.[74]

What the new merchants really wanted, in place of the East India Company's old operation, was what they called a truly "national settlement," organized by means of a regulated company in which members would be free to allocate their commercial resources as they saw fit, under the general supervision of the corporation. In their words, the old company's 1649 proposal for

> a subscription for 5 years . . . is not for a *national* settlement. . . . There shall not be a considerable stock underwritten to carry on that trade, yet all other Englishmen will be prohibited to the prejudice of navigation and trade . . . this being absolutely against our national liberties and destructive to the public good to hold more places than you can well plant, fortify, and manage.[75]

The new merchants argued that the unitary joint-stock monopoly proposed by the East India Company's old guard would both limit the capital

[72] *L.J.* 8: 643, 9: 41, 81; *C.C.M.E.I.C. 1644–1649*, pp. xiii, xiv; *H.M.C. Tenth Report, Appendix*, 6, p. 167. For Fowke's involvement with Courteen, see above, ch. 4, pp. 173–74.

[73] *C.C.M.E.I.C. 1644–1649*, pp. xxiii, 361, 365–67; PRO, C.O.77/7/5.

[74] PRO, C.O.77/7/6, 7, 8; *C.C.M.E.I.C. 1644–1649*, p. 370.

[75] PRO, C.O.77/7/6 (emphasis added).

input that might otherwise flow into the trade, and restrict the manner and direction in which capital might be used within the trade. These were obviously closely related points: if there was a freer organization of trade, more capital would be able to come in; if there was more capital, it would be possible to take better advantage of the full range of opportunities offered by the trade with the East.

In developing their argument, the new merchants could and did refer to their own experience. The old company's monopoly privileges had long hindered their ability to bring vast new capital resources to the trade, capital investment that was premised on major innovations—in the manner of operating the trade, in the areas to be exploited, and in the mode of exploitation. The company's monopoly had been used not merely to cut out potential competitors within its own specific sphere of operations, which was bad enough; it had also been used systematically to stymie those who wished to promote other, undeveloped aspects and regions of the Eastern trade. In particular, the East India Company leadership had refused to plant colonies in the East and tried to prevent others, notably the new merchants, from doing so; it had confined its trade to India, whereas the new merchants and others had long been intent on once again penetrating the East Indies, and particularly on establishing trade with the island of Pulo Run; it had ignored the Guinean trade, which the new merchants had already used for its gold and ivory to complement the East Indian commerce; and it had refused to establish well-fortified settlements in India itself. Most generally, the company had hampered entrepreneurship and innovation, and this is what the new merchants most wished to encourage in their drive for a freer trade.[76]

The agreement imposed by the government on the old directorate recognized as valid every one of the new merchants' objections to the manner in which the trade had been operated by the old company. The new merchants' proposal for a settlement of the trade had consisted of twelve points, and the old company was obliged to agree to all twelve: (1) that a joint stock of £300,000 immediately be raised; (2) that the government be asked to recover Pulo Run from the Dutch and that the island be planted; (3) that former agreements as to the value of company assets in India be recognized; (4) that Assada be planted under the auspices of the joint stock and that settlers there be given liberty to trade freely in the commodities of that island; (5) that the Guinea trade in gold and teeth be united with the East Indian trade, under the government of the company, as soon as this was possible; (6) that fortifications be built in India; (7) that all company decisions be made by majority vote of the adventurers and possession of £500 of company stock be required for voting eligibility; (8) that the new merchants' proposals for company employees and their

[76] See above, ch. 4, pp. 178–81.

salaries be adopted; (9) that planters be encouraged to settle in India and have the right to engage in the port-to-port trade there; (10) that the company monopolize the reexport trade from India to Europe in the chief commodities of India; (11) that the interlopers be compensated by the company for their previous loss of the ship *Ruth* in India; and (12) that Maurice Thomson's agreements for trade in saltpeter with the government be recognized and agreed to.[77]

The government did establish a new united joint stock in 1650, but since at least six of the thirteen members of the new company's board of directors were representatives of the new-merchant leadership,[78] the interlopers could be assured that their program would be implemented. Moreover, the new united joint stock was set up on an explicitly experimental basis: no new shipping was to be sent out by the company after the summer of 1653, unless there was a new decision to continue the joint-stock form. In fact, when the united company's original stock did run out, the trade was allowed to lay open for some four years, during which time the new merchants reverted to their old policy of independent shipping.[79] Meanwhile, Maurice Thomson and some of his friends had taken advantage of the liberty granted under the agreement imposed by the government for individuals freely to create their own plantations and commerce on the island of Assada. In February 1650, Thomson, along with his brother William Thomson and his old interloping partners Nathan Wright, Thomas Andrews, Nathaniel Andrews, Jeremy Blackman, and Samuel Moyer, as well as Oliver Cromwell's secretary Robert Spavin and several others, organized a joint stock syndicate in which each invested £1000, and, on that basis, pursued the development of a private 600 acre plantation on Assada, exporting its produce. Finally, and equally relevant to the issue of the Commonwealth's outlook on a freer trade, the settlement imposed by the government on the East India Company, as part of the agreement for the new united stock, included a final crucial operating limitation on the company's monopoly, forced through by the new-merchant leadership: "If any of [the Adventurers] shall propose a new voyage to the generality [and] if they should dislike it, it [is] not unlikely but that upon

---

[77] PRO, C.O.77/7/6, 7, 8, 9; *C.C.M.E.I.C. 1644–1649*, pp. 369–72, 374–76, 377–78.

[78] *C.C.M.E.I.C. 1650–1654*, p. 49; Maurice Thomson, Samuel Moyer, Thomas Andrews, Nathaniel Andrews, Capt. William Ryder, and Jeremy Blackman.

[79] *C.C.M.E.I.C. 1650–1654*, p. xvii; *Brittania Languens* (1680), in *Early English Tracts on Commerce*, ed. J. R. McCulloch (London, 1856), p. 335. In this period, the new merchants took up where they left off. In December 1655 they were ready to dispatch no fewer than fourteen ships to the East (*C.C.M.E.I.C. 1650–1654*, p. xxiv). For details of their operation in this period, which included the incorporation of the Guinean trade within the trade with the East, see PRO, C.9/24/167.

good caution liberty would be given to such persons to prosecute the same on their own account."[80]

In sum, while the form of government of the East Indian trade remained technically the same, its content was changed beyond recognition, in the direction of greater freedom of movement for capital and entrepreneurship. This was the basic intention of those who wanted free trade. It was because the new merchants' program, enforced by the government, entailed so sharp a break from past practice that the old company struggled so long and so bitterly against it. It was a sign of the times—of the predominance of new policymakers with new ideas and new friends—that the East India Company's old guard was so soundly defeated.

FREE PORTS AND THE NAVIGATION ACT

The place of the free-ports proposal within English commercial policymaking during the Commonwealth has long been the subject of debate and confusion. Controversy has centered, in particular, on two problems: (1) who backed this proposal; and (2) what was the relationship between the free-ports plan and other aspects of English policy, especially the navigation act and Anglo-Dutch relations more generally. Was the free-ports proposal the project of the traditional company merchants, the new-merchant "free trading" types, or neither (or both)? Was it complementary to, or in conflict with, the navigation act, a pro- or anti-Dutch policy? These are important questions. But answering them can compound confusion unless one is very explicit about the radically different ways in which the free-ports proposal was actually framed by different groups of supporters. Depending on how it was stated, the demand for free ports could complement policies either relatively favorable or violently hostile to the Dutch, and thus, in different versions, elicit the support or hostility of different and sometimes opposed commercial groupings.

The divergent implications of different versions of the free-ports proposal can be seen in the debates on this issue that were carried on before the council of trade. Parliament had ordered the council to "advise how free ports or landing places for foreign commodities imported (without paying of custom if again exported) may be appointed in several parts of this land, and in what manner the same is to be effected."[81] The idea was to reduce the financial burden of customs on reexports to the end of encouraging the development of an English entrepôt. Insofar as a record exists, it appears that most of the council of trade's proceedings on this question were held in the spring of 1651. It is unlikely that this was acci-

[80] *C.C.M.E.I.C. 1650–1654*, pp. 14, 93; PRO, C.O.77/7/7, 9 (quotation).

[81] Andrews, *British Committees*, app. 1.

dental, for this was the precise period of the Anglo-Dutch negotiations concerning a possible alliance, indeed union. The considerations on free ports were almost certainly meant to tie in with these negotiations, for the specific form in which the free-ports idea was implemented would imply much concerning England's approach to her potential ally and competitor, whether it was to be hostile or cooperative.

The very first free-ports proposal presented to the council of trade, "Considerations Concerning Free Ports or Scales in England,"[82] possibly the council's own conspectus on the basic issues at stake, set down, in its first two articles, the contradictory conditions that were to determine the competing definitions of free ports. According to article 1:

> Experience hath showed that free scale is and will be beneficial to any commonwealth where it is admitted. It is conceived that little objection be made or any valid reason showed why all foreign commodities whatsoever may not be admitted to that free scale set up and allowed of in this commonwealth for exportation as well as importation . . . *if imported or exported in English bottoms.* (emphasis added)

In essence, this narrow version of the free-ports idea involved no more than freeing the English reexport trade from the fiscal impediments of the customs. In its specification that free ports should be open to English shipping only, it implicitly recognized the fact that the English could not compete on equal terms with the Dutch under present conditions of superior Dutch shipping. It followed that the objective of free ports should be to encourage English trade, and with it the improvement of English shipping, through making this more competitive by way of lower customs, while in the meantime giving it government protection through a navigation policy.

In contrast, however, article 2 of "Considerations" went as follows:

> It is conceived necessary that all nations in amity be admitted the benefit of the free scale *in their own vessels*, and coming in laden, may land part, or all, and relade their own or any other foreign goods using the said free scale. (emphasis added)

In this form, the Dutch were clearly invited in; the navigation policy was ruled out. By itself, such a program of really open free ports would appear to have been highly unrealistic from the English standpoint, for there would have been nothing to prevent the Dutch from simply taking advantage of the English free-port facilities to erode even further the position of English commerce and shipping. Since few at this point could have had illusions about the ability of the English to compete with the Dutch on

[82] BL, Add. MSS 5138, fol. 145.

even terms, it would seem reasonable to suspect that this broader free-ports plan was meant to go along with additional complementary policy departures that could make it more feasible. Apparently, this was the case.

On 14 April 1651 the council of trade referred the issue of free ports to a variety of different, interested groups, especially merchants, for their viewpoint. The first report came back within two weeks.[83] It clearly represented the position of the great London company merchants. Its signatories included the leading Levant Company merchants William Cockayne, Robert Burdett, Samuel Mico, William Vincent, and Richard Bateman; the governor of the Eastland Company Richard Chiverton; the leading French-trading merchant Rowland Wilson; and one of the top merchants involved with Spain, Robert Lant. Since most of these merchants represented commercial fields in which reexports were significant, they could hardly have been expected to disapprove of the free-ports idea of eliminating or reducing customs on reexports.[84] Nonetheless, it seems quite clear that these merchants would approve the free-ports proposal only so long as a clearly anti-Dutch reading was implied, so long, that is, as foreign shipping would be excluded from its benefits. As they wrote in their report, "Freedom of landing goods imported without payment of any customs for such part as shall again be exported . . . will increase the shipping, navigation, and trade of this nation *especially if all goods so to be exported may be exported in English ships*" (emphasis added). For all practical purposes, this proviso would have excluded foreigners from the use of the entrepôt. Moreover, it is a fact that both the Levant Company and the Eastland Company had already explicitly called on the Commonwealth government to implement full-fledged navigation policies in their own trades. Indeed, as earlier noted, both companies had, for many years previously, enjoyed the benefits of just such a policy. The Levant Company's position on this question was presented in its petition to the government of 28 December 1649 and is worth quoting at length, for it pretty well summarized the generally held viewpoint among the English company merchants:

> Whereas amongst many necessary provisions heretofore made against the employment of strangers shipping, all persons (as well subjects of this land as strangers) have for above 30 years past been prohibited to import into this land commodities of the Levant but such as were free of the Levant Company and *in English ships only*. Since which prohibition this trade unto those parts hath been abundantly ad-

[83] Ibid., fols. 146–47.

[84] PRO, S.P.105/144/30–30v; Hinton, *Eastland Trade*, pp. 84–94; A. Friis, *Alderman Cockayne's Project and the Cloth Trade* (London, 1927), pp. 181–92; L. A. Harper, *The English Navigation Laws* (New York, 1939), pp. 40, 44.

vanced, and many great ships built and employed by your petitioners in so much that the serviceable shipping of this land were within a few years after increased three fourths parts . . . [o]f late diverse persons, subjects and strangers, do invade your petitioners' privileges and *indirectly import* hither currants and other commodities of the Levant *from the Netherlands* and other places, which being a ready means to set strangers' bottoms on work, or at best to employ small barks and vessels of no force, will assuredly (if not prevented) not only tend to the destruction of our great shipping which have been constantly maintained by freight of currants, cottons, etc. (being goods of small value but of great bulk), but will also occasion the overthrow of this trade, and expose the same into the hands of the Hollanders who frequenting the Levant seas with store of great ships and cheap freights and easier charge, buying also their commodities with ready money which we have in exchange for our English manufacturers, and being not so subject to those difficulties and surprisals which we are liable to as well from the French fleet and the revolted ships, when they have by these advantages worn out our shipping, will raise these commodities to very high rates.[85] (emphasis added)

Here in a nutshell was the case for the navigation policy. In order to improve their competitive position vis-à-vis the Dutch, the English company merchants of London primarily involved in the import (and reexport) trades called for what became, in essence, the two major provisions of the navigation act of 1651: that goods of an area be imported in English vessels (or in ships of the country of origin) and that they be brought directly from their place of origin, so as to cut out the Dutch middlemen. If company merchants could obtain for themselves in addition free ports—that is, customs-free reexports—so much the better, for this would further enhance their ability to compete.[86]

Further evaluations of the free-ports proposal were subsequently submitted to the council of trade by other groups of merchants. One such

[85] PRO, S.P. 105/144/30–30v. The Levant Company presented these same demands to the government once more in December 1650. The Eastland Company made analogous requests in 1649 and 1651 and, apparently, so did the Greenland and Russia companies at about the same time. Hinton, *Eastland Trade*, pp. 86–91, 187–94; Harper, *English Navigation Laws*, pp. 43–44; Wilson, *Profit and Power*, pp. 54–56.

[86] In light of the foregoing evidence, it is difficult to accept Dr. Farnell's argument that the major company import merchants failed to support the free-ports idea, at least in the restricted sense (see "Navigation Act," pp. 447–48). Indeed, the adoption of a policy of customs-free reexports would seem to have represented an unqualified gain for the major company import (and reexport) merchants, especially the Levant and East India company merchants. It is, on the other hand, certain that these same major merchants would have opposed free ports that were open to foreigners, especially the Dutch.

position paper came in from certain alien merchants living in England, another from a group of "other merchants."[87] However, the styles and contents of the position papers of these two sets of merchants are so similar that it is hard to avoid the conclusion that the two sets of advocates drew them up in close consultation with one another. The wording of large sections of each proposal is identical; moreover, the second proposal, that of the aliens, explicitly refers to the first for a fuller expression of its own position on certain points. The general intent of both proposals is clearly the same, and they are mutually reinforcing—but quite at odds with the position paper submitted by the company merchants. The specific common content of the two proposals, as well as what is known of the signers of the alien merchants' report, provides a clue as to the probable identity of the "other merchants."

The alien merchants were, naturally enough, enthusiastic about the free-ports idea. They claimed, in encouragement, that "it will draw trade over hither from all parts in regard of the natural situation and commodiousness of these harbors for an universal magazine." They were careful to request, of course, that the free-ports proposal should not, as the company merchants had proposed, be tied to a ban on foreign shipping. One of the advantages of the free-ports idea, they said, would be to "increase and encourage [native] merchants to be as ready to adventure the transportation of [commodities] as is now done by other nations." But they insisted that it should "be at the liberty and choice of the merchant to export the goods either in English or foreign ships."

There were six signers of the report from the alien merchants.[88] Significantly, at least two of these signers, Nicholas Corsellis and Derrick Hoast, maintained the closest personal relationship with Maurice Thomson and the new-merchant leadership. Corsellis had worked with Thomson in the trade with the Americas, the interloping project in the East Indies, and the Additional Sea Adventure to Ireland. His son had married Thomson's daughter.[89] Hoast, like Corsellis, and indeed a whole group of alien merchants living in England, also had worked with Thomson in the interloping project in the East Indies and related ventures. Moreover, Hoast and Corsellis, along with a third Anglo-Dutch interloper in the East Indies, Adam Laurence, had served with Thomson on two parliamentary missions to Holland. In 1643–1644, the four of them had gone there, along with the radical minister Hugh Peter, to raise money for distressed Protestants in Ireland; in 1648, they had traveled to Holland along with the colonial merchant John Limbrey (by 1651 a member of

---

[87] BL, Add. MSS 5138, fols. 147–49 ("other merchants") and 149–150v (aliens).

[88] Ibid., fol. 150v.

[89] For Corsellis, and his family and commercial connections with Thomson and the new-merchant leadership, see above, ch. 4, pp. 160, 176, 183, 193.

the council of trade) to help get aid in recovering the rebellious ships.[90] In view of the intimate connections of these foreign merchants with Thomson, the close correspondence of their proposal to that of the "other merchants," and the specific content of the proposal of the "other merchants," it is difficult to avoid the conclusion that the proposal of the "other merchants" was representative of the new-merchant leadership, and perhaps presented by Thomson himself.

The propositions of the "other merchants," presented 26 May 1651, do not suggest excluding foreign shipping from the free ports. On the contrary, the main thrust of their proposal is that foreigners must in all respects be given equal treatment, and indeed special encouragement. One of the best reasons for free ports, they said, was to "invite over ingenious merchants and handicraftsmen." To achieve this, they argued, foreigners should pay the same customs as Englishmen paid; they should have equal access to the English legal system (except officeholding and voting), with all laws presently in force against aliens repealed; and they should, at least at first, be given special privileges and grants to attract them. The concluding statement of the "other merchants" constituted such a vigorous defense of a free-trade position as to make it difficult to connect it with any other merchants besides the colonial-interloping leadership.

> Something more may be said for the encouragement of strangers which may be held a fundamental means to increase trade, but for that it will be looked upon as being too much for a stranger it is here concluded with this position. That trade being the basis and well-being of a commonwealth the way to obtain it is to make it free trade and not to bind up ingenious spirits by exemptory privileges which are granted to some particular company and men that will not adventure and take pains as ingenious as other laborious spirits will do.[91]

It remains to be asked, however, on what basis the new-merchant leadership could possibly have supported truly open free ports. For certainly they, as much as the company merchants, appreciated the threat posed by the Dutch merchants' superior competitiveness. Had not these men themselves pushed vigorously and continuously to exclude all Dutch merchants from their main area of commercial involvement, the English colonies in the Americas? Two closely interrelated possibilities suggest themselves as the underlying premises for the new merchants' daring free-ports proposal, one rather narrow and connected with the particular character of the new merchants' commercial interests, the other quite broad and related to the most general problems of English commercial policy-making.

[90] For missions to Holland, see A.O. 1: 220–21; PRO, S.P.21/9/181–82. See also above, n. 89.

[91] BL, Add. MSS 5138, fols. 147–49.

The new merchants' very success in having already entirely excluded the Dutch from trade and shipping to the American colonies by means of the Act of 3 October 1650 may have been one major factor in allowing them the luxury of proposing free ports without special anti-Dutch provisions. At the same time, in their trade with the East Indies, the new-merchant leadership had already shown itself most anxious to collaborate with Dutch merchants. It had been quite willing, first of all, to ally with the Anglo-Dutch merchant Sir William Courteen and Courteen's Dutch partners against the English company. And it will be recalled that, in the late 1630s, proposals almost certainly emanating from the Courteen interloping syndicate were advanced to place the East Indian trade in the hands of a new Anglo-Dutch company to be organized in Holland.[92] Subsequently, in developing their own multifaceted East Indian interloping venture throughout the 1640s, the new merchants worked in the closest partnership with alien, especially Dutch, merchants living in London. The new-merchant leaders were obviously not only very impressed with the Dutch example and anxious to imitate it, but also desirous of making use of Dutch skills and resources in order to do so. They had developed a most grandiose plan for building up the East Indian commerce, which included establishing colonies on Assada and Pulo Run, incorporating the Guinean trade in gold and ivory, and expanding commerce beyond India into the South Seas and perhaps to China and Japan. Especially in view of the lack of interest in their program on the part of the great company merchants, the new merchants may well have hoped to get help from Dutch merchants to implement it. Their proposal for free ports, bound up as it was with their call for the removal of all legal restrictions on the operation of alien merchants in England, should most likely be viewed, as least in part, in this light.

Even so, the new merchants must certainly have realized that implementing their free-ports proposal, implying as it did the increased exposure of English commerce to Dutch competition, would involve enormous risks. No English government could agree to so dangerous a proposal, and it is unlikely, in fact, that the new merchants meant it to be put forward in isolation from additional policy departures. They must have known quite well that safeguards were essential. Especially in view of the timing, as well as the content of their propositions, it seems likely that they hoped that adequate security could in fact be achieved through the Anglo-Dutch negotiations for an alliance, which were occurring at precisely the moment they put forward their free-ports plan. Certainly, the new merchants' free-ports proposal appears more realistic and comprehensible if it is seen as connected with the English proposition at these nego-

[92] *C.C.M.E.I.C. 1635–1639*, pp. 296–97.

tiations for an "intrinsical union" between England and the United Provinces, an actual political unification. At the same time, the Commonwealth's consuming preoccupation in this period with England's commercial problems, manifested in particular in the intensive discussions of free ports and related proposals, helps to make more understandable the sometimes puzzling character of the Anglo-Dutch negotiations themselves.

The negotiations carried out during the spring of 1651 by Oliver St. John and Sir William Strickland with the Dutch representatives at the Hague have been rightly understood, broadly speaking, in terms of the common political and religious outlook of the two nations, which seemed to dictate an alliance against the Catholic and monarchical powers of Europe. More specifically, they have been quite properly interpreted in relation to the immediate security problems of the new English republic. In fact, successive leaderships of the parliamentary side had sought, since the early 1640s, to forge an alliance with the United Provinces and to secure their support against the royalists; and the Commonwealth, from its inception, continued those efforts. Nevertheless, the methods adopted by the English in the course of the negotiations with the Dutch in the spring of 1651 often have been treated as mysterious and irrational. S. R. Gardiner thought the conduct of these discussions showed how little the new regime understood about diplomacy; the negotiations seemed to him to manifest the worst excesses of English patriotic zeal.[93] But if one appreciates the difficulties of the English position arising from English commercial inferiority to the Dutch, it may perhaps appear that the negotiators pursued the most reasonable course open to them.

It has sometimes been overlooked that unless the English representatives at the Hague could achieve a cooperative solution to the mass of outstanding commercial questions that divided the English from the Dutch, stemming from their head-on trading competition throughout the world, they would have difficulty negotiating even a truly stable peace, let alone a satisfactory political alliance. For even if the English negotiators settled the most pressing politico-strategic issues—specifically the questions of mutual military aid and the disposal of proroyalist forces in Holland—English commerce would still face the necessity of coping with overpowering Dutch economic competition. The English government would then have virtually no choice but to adopt a strongly protective and aggressive stance toward Dutch trade, and this would, in the end, undermine hopes for political alliance. It is in that light, it seems, that the apparently extreme and utopian English insistence on some sort of actual

---

[93] Gardiner, *Commonwealth and Protectorate* 1: 352–67 (esp. pp. 358–59); Groenveld, "First Anglo-Dutch War."

political union between the nations should be viewed. Union appears, in retrospect, as an alternative to hostility and the probability of war. Only through union could English and Dutch commercial capital overcome the barriers that separated them. Only if the political division between England and Holland was erased could English and Dutch merchants resolve the zero-sum competitive commercial game in which they were matched. The English, at a distinct disadvantage in that game, needed to unite with the Dutch, or else they very likely would have to fight them.

Whatever its logic in purely strategic terms, the English proposal for the unification of two essentially separate national cultures and historically evolved societies was very radical. And all the individuals actually responsible for conceptualizing the plan and the sort of considerations that went into their thinking still need to be discovered. In this regard, it would be important to know a great deal more than is known at present about the actual contacts that existed between Dutch and English citizens that may have formed the practical background to this program—and, in particular, about the connections between the merchant communities of these two trade-conscious republics. Here, the new merchants' continuing involvement in joint Anglo-Dutch operations in the East Indian trade may very well have been relevant. And the personal experience of Maurice Thomson, who had widespread connections in Holland and whose daughter married the son of his Dutch partner Nicholas Corsellis, may have been especially significant. (Thomson was not, by the way, the only important new merchant with Dutch relatives; one of his leading partners, Jeremy Blackman, who was nominated but not approved for the council of trade, married a Dutch woman, the widow of another of his and Thomson's Anglo-Dutch partners in East Indian interloping, Ahaseurus Regemont).[94]

During the 1640s Thomson had made great use of the contacts he had built up in Holland to carry out important missions for the parliamentary government. In 1644 Thomson launched a large-scale venture to take royalist ships off the coast of Holland as prizes, and on this occasion he ordered his commander to consult with Zegar Corsellis and Laurence Coighen in Amsterdam to get information on the movement of royalist vessels. Corsellis was probably a relative of the aforementioned Nicholas Corsellis. From the later 1630s, Coighen had been serving as Thomson's agent in Amsterdam to handle that end of Thomson's reexport trade in American tobacco. It was undoubtedly Thomson's knowledge of Dutch affairs and his extensive network of connections in Holland that made him the logical person to carry out the aforementioned parliamentary missions

[94] PRO, will of Jeremy Blackman, 1656 PCC Berkley 380; *C.J.* 6: 451–52. For Blackman's commercial activities, see above, ch. 4.

of 1643 to raise money for distressed Protestants in Ireland and of 1648 to try to recover the rebellious ships.[95] Most fascinating in this respect is a spy report, submitted to the Restoration government in June 1666 at the time of the second Dutch war, in which Maurice Thomson and his brother Major Robert Thomson were accused of passing military intelligence to the Dutch. As this spy reported,

> It was my chance to be where I saw and overheard three men who seemed to be persons of quality, and one of them in a travellers habit, and spake his English with a Dutch pronunciation, mighty careful and serious in their discourse, wherein they much rejoiced that the Dutch had done so well, and attributed much of their good success to the care and diligence of Maurice Thomson and his brother Major for that they gave them such timely intelligence of the dividing of our English fleet, with all the motions thereof, and an account how they were fitted out, etc. And that Maurice Thomson and his brother were the men that held the intelligence and supplied them throughout, from time to time, and highly recommended their great care and circumspection in performance of the same. And that it was of great advantage to their state, to have two such sure friends that never failed in their intelligence, and that [the "Rumper-republican" Thomas] Scot for his 1000 guilders a year did not service in comparison with them.[96]

Whether or not the foregoing charges concerning the Thomsons' conduct after the Restoration are true is essentially beside the point. What is significant is that they possessed a certain prima facie plausibility, in view of the actual experiences of the Thomsons during the Civil War and the Commonwealth, recalled in great detail in the remainder of this report— their advocacy of republicanism, their central role as organizers of the navy, and, most especially, their close connections with the Dutch community. As the spy recalled, "Thomson and Hugh Peters and one Nicholas Corsellis a Dutchman were at the beginning of the war sent over to the states of Holland to collect their charitable benevolence for the distressed Protestants in Ireland, and obtained a great sum, *and was ever in great favor with the Dutch, and it seems he hath a greater kindness for them still than for England*" (emphasis added).

It should not, of course, be concluded that under the Commonwealth Thomson and his friends wished to sell out English interests to the Dutch. Rather, because of their admiration for Dutch institutions, both political

---

[95] PRO, H.C.A.24/106/100, 349 (prize venture); PRO, H.C.A.24/102/119 (reexport trade to Amsterdam).

[96] PRO, S.P.29/159/108.

and commercial, and their goal of increased collaboration with Dutch merchants, especially perhaps on their projects in the East Indies, these traders appear to have hoped that the deep competitive commercial divide that separated the two merchant communities could be transcended by a political friendship, indeed merger, between the two nations, rather than resolved through conflict. In fact, it is not entirely implausible, as their enemies charged, that during the Commonwealth period, the new merchants and their political independent friends had lent what influence and resources they possessed to the pro-Holland, anti-Orange factions in the Netherlands, centered especially in Amsterdam; for, in some contrast with the proroyalist stadtholder, these factions aimed to build friendly relations with the new English republic. According to Clement Walker:

> Observe [the political independents'] practices in the Low Countries, where having by their spies and emissaries, found burghers of the same humor with themselves: They propagated their doctrines so far as to endeavour to strike the aristocratical members out of the commonwealth, by abetting some of the states provincial to lessen (and so to abolish by degrees) the lord states general (the optimates of that state) to ruin the Prince of Orange, to whose family they owe their liberty, to dissolve the general union of the said United Provinces, and so to take in pieces the whole frame of that republic.[97]

Until his death in 1650, William II supported a policy favorable to the Stuarts, and had given aid and comfort to royalist exiles in the Netherlands. With his demise came the ascendancy of Holland and the revolution in foreign policy, which opened the way to much closer relations between the Netherlands and the new English republic.[98]

The English government's proposal in 1651 for a closer union with Holland almost certainly was the indispensable premise of, and complement to, the new merchants' proposals that legal restrictions on Dutch merchants living in England be lifted and that free ports be established. This impression is given further weight when one takes notice of a pamphlet, *A Good Word for a Good Magistrate*, published by Hugh Peter, the new merchants' close collaborator, on 7 June 1651[99] at the height of the Anglo-Dutch negotiations for union—and less than two weeks following the submission to the council of trade of the new merchants' own pro-alien free-ports program on 26 May 1651. (On 3 May 1651, the English government already had decided at least to offer the Dutch a waiver of the

[97] C. Walker, *The High Court of Justice: Being the Third Part of the History of Independency* (London, 1661), pp. 21ff.

[98] Gardiner, *Commonwealth and Protectorate* 1: 352–57; Groenveld, "First Anglo-Dutch War," pp. 542–43, 551–55.

[99] H. Peter, *Good Work for a Good Magistrate* (London, 7 June 1651).

[623]

prohibition against aliens holding real property in England.)[100] Peter's document is, from one point of view, little more than a paean to the Dutch example and a plea for the English to follow it. Peter repeats the new merchants' demands for free trade, free ports, and the removal of all legal restrictions on alien merchants, and goes on to call for a policy of wholesale imitation of the Hollanders across a wide range of institutional spheres—political, legal, cultural, and commercial. He proposes not only a Dutch-type national bank and a Dutch-type single tax system, but in addition (for example) the establishment of fire-fighting brigades and road gutters inspired by Dutch models. As Peter grandly remarked, "This nation is not barren altogether of self-denying spirits, and ingenious patriots: and though Holland seems to get the start of us, yet we may follow, as to stand at length upon their shoulders, and so see further."[101]

It seems reasonable to conclude, therefore, that in Commonwealth England there existed an influential section of public opinion (the limits of which still need to be defined) that was actually quite serious about union with Holland, despite the difficulties it would obviously entail. The proponents of unification—among them, the new merchants and their political allies—saw in Holland the most promising model for the general reform of English institutions in the interests of economic and social development, under the aegis of a stable, commercially oriented oligarchic republic. The apparent willingness of these men to make substantial changes in order to bring English institutions into line with those of the Dutch helps one understand how they could so readily conceive of an actual union between the two national cultures.

The English, of course, could have had no illusions that the Dutch would easily accept their proposal for union. They realized, certainly, that in the short run the Dutch would be sacrificing a great deal should it actually come to pass. It is perhaps for just this reason that they carried on their diplomacy in an aggressive manner, threatening to break off talks at the slightest sign that the Dutch were holding back. Gardiner thought St. John's ignorance of commercial and diplomatic matters accounted for his haughty attitude toward the negotiations. It may be more reasonable to explain St. John's approach in terms of the English feeling that only a scarcely veiled threat of outright attack on the Dutch could induce the Hollanders even to consider a political union.

In the end, the Dutch refused to yield. Instead of the political alliance the English wanted, the Dutch proposed a "commercial union"—a series of propositions designed to ensure and increase the equal opportunity of English and Dutch merchants in common spheres of activity, including

[100] Gardiner, *Commonwealth and Protectorate* 1: 357–58 n. 6.
[101] Peter, *Good Work*, preface.

even the English colonies in the Americas.[102] The Dutch proposal was, of course, intolerable to the English; it was equivalent to a proposal that both nations move politically to ensure that the Dutch commercial competitive advantage over the English should have its fullest effect. The only way the English could agree to equal competition between English and Dutch merchants was to erase the distinction between the two, to make them part of the same national community by way of union. When the Dutch showed they would not agree to this, the English knew they had little choice but to take a protectionist and combative stance.

THE NAVIGATION ACT

By August 1651, within weeks of the breakdown of negotiations, the English were moving quickly toward passage of the navigation act, evidence perhaps that the failure to achieve unity was what directly triggered the stepped-up aggressiveness.[103] As Oliver St. John put it when the negotiations collapsed, in expressing his regrets that the Dutch had rejected the English demands for "a nearer union": "In a short time, you will see our dispute with Scotland at an end, and you will then send envoys to ask what we have now offered you cordially; but believe me you will then repent of having rejected our offers."[104] If they could not have collaboration through unification, the English well knew they must have competition through aggression.

Writing in 1654, the Dutch ambassador who came over to London for the negotiations which climaxed the Anglo-Dutch War asserted "that some few persons interested in the highest degree in the East Indies and in the new plantations of this nation . . . gave the principal impulse to the making of the [navigation act of 1651]." A royalist commentator had slightly earlier remarked, "As for sea affairs the war at first was set on by those men that were the procurers of the act prohibiting trade [navigation act] which act was procured by some few men for their interest."[105]

Technically speaking, these assessments are almost certainly correct. In view of their central participation in almost all other aspects of Commonwealth commercial policy-making, it would have been surprising indeed had the new-merchant leaders failed to play a major role in the framing of the navigation act, expecially given their economic interests. The council

[102] Gardiner, *Commonwealth and Protectorate* 1: 364–65; *H.M.C., Thirteenth Report, Appendix* 1, p. 605.

[103] *C.J.* 6: 617 (5 Aug. 1651). Even as early as March–April 1651, the English were preparing the anti-Dutch navigation act, in case the negotiations for a closer union with the Dutch failed (Violet, *Mysteries and Secrets of Trade*, p. 178; see also *C.S.P.D. 1651*, p. 119).

[104] Gardiner, *Commonwealth and Protectorate*, 1: 365.

[105] Both statements are quotations from Clark, "Navigation Act," p. 285.

of trade produced two drafts of the navigation act for presentation to the council of state, and this body was, as noted, composed largely of new-merchant leaders and colleagues of theirs. The author of the navigation act—as well as of the pamphlet *The Advocate*, which was initially presented in August 1651 and which ultimately constituted the council of state's main public justification of the act—was Benjamin Worsley, secretary to the council of trade.[106] Worsley was, of course, one of the new merchants' chief collaborators in the making of Commonwealth commercial policy. Worsley had worked in concert with the new-merchant leadership in framing the Act of 3 October 1650 for excluding the Dutch from the trade with the colonies in the Americas, in planning the military expeditions to put down the royalist revolts in Virginia and the West Indies, and in establishing and operating the council of trade. There is every reason to think that he continued to work with them on the council of trade in the case of the navigation act.

Nevertheless, it would be extremely misleading to deduce from the important facts of the new-merchants' influence on Commonwealth policy-making in general, and the new-merchants' participation in the framing of the navigation act in particular, that the navigation act and the Dutch war are comprehensible mainly as an expression of the narrow desires of the new-merchant leadership. First of all, it should be clear that, by this time, even taking into account only the trading lines in which they were directly active, the new merchants could hardly be said to represent a mere special interest. Their private commercial needs were in an important sense national commercial needs. If the navigation act is understandable, to an important degree, as a response to the new merchants' difficulties with Dutch competition in the long-distance trades with the Americas, Africa, and the East Indies, it must be admitted that their special problems were now the general problems of the nation. Moreover, the colonial-interloping traders were hardly the only group of merchants strongly supporting the navigation act. Both the Levant and the Eastland companies had, as noted, already been calling for the act's two main provisions: that goods be brought in directly from their country of origin and that they be imported in English ships (or those of the country of origin). In the wake of the peace between the United Provinces and Spain, devastating Dutch competition had, with shocking suddenness, imposed itself in every one of the dynamic import trades that had grown up since the reign of Elizabeth and assumed such a central place in English overseas commerce. The English merchants who operated these trades were obliged to do so almost entirely on the basis of English ships; at a serious competitive cost disad-

---

[106] Hinton, *Eastland Trade*, pp. 89–90.

[626]

vantage and legitimately fearful, they had to see the navigation act as an indispensable first step to protect at least their English market against a Dutch commercial invasion that was already underway.[107]

Even so, to interpret particular commercial policy departures of the Commonwealth, the navigation act included, simply as responses to pressure exerted by specific merchant groups on the government from the outside, would still miss the point. In consequence of the central role of imperialist republicans and other longtime radicals in its leadership and of its close collaboration with London's political independent rulers and the colonial-interloping merchants, the Commonwealth government had adopted the view that the expansion of commerce was a fundamental means of enhancing England's international strength and its own legitimacy. At the same time, it had come to envision the secret of commercial success— as revealed by the Dutch example—as the state's systematic support of trade. This was made abundantly clear in *The Adovocate*, by Benjamin Worsley, which was not merely a public justification of the navigation act, but a semiofficial declaration, published by the council of state, of the government's general approach to commerce in relation to international politics.

It is by trade, and the due ordering and governing of it [by the state] and by no other means that wealth and shipping can . . . be increased and upheld, and consequently by no other [means] that the power of any nation can be sustained by land or sea, it being not possible . . . for any nation . . . to make itself powerful in either of these without trade or a thorough inspection into trade and the course of it.[108]

The Dutch had thus achieved commercial preeminence not only through "the great number of shipping that they constantly built," but also by "the manner of [the government's] managing their trade and shipping in a conformity and direction to their grand end" of "engrossing the universal trade." Consequently, the Dutch government had seen to it that "their fleets were and have been always carefully and constantly attended with a

[107] See above, pp. 615–16. See also Taylor, "Trade, Neutrality, and the 'English Road,' " pp. 259–60. Here I differ with both Dr. Farnell and Dr. Hinton, who argue that the major company merchants were not strong supporters of the navigation act (Farnell, "Navigation Act," p. 446; Hinton, *Eastland Trade*, pp. 90–92). On the other hand, it should be noted that the Merchant Adventurers, as cloth export specialists trading with the United Provinces, opposed the navigation act. Cf. Wilson, *Profit and Power*, pp. 54–56.

[108] Quotations in this and the following paragraph are from *The Advocate*, reprinted in Hinton, *Eastland Trade*, pp. 205–13. This pamphlet bore the subtitle "A Narrative of the state and condition of things between the *English* and the *Dutch* Nation, in relation to Trade and the consequences depending thereupon, to either commonwealth, as it was presented in August 1651," and was "printed by William Du-Gard, printer to the Council of State."

convoy at the public charge." It had also made sure of the "smallness of their custom or port duties" so as to encourage the growth of shipping and offer Dutch merchants a competitive advantage. Furthermore, it had provided for the "prudent laying on and taking off impositions for the furtherance of their own manufacturers and for the encouragement of bringing in some and discouragement of bringing in other commodities," notably dressed and dyed English cloths, thus providing a systematic policy of protection. Finally, the Dutch government had sought the improvement of trade "by their treaties or articles of confederation with other princes" and, in general, "by making . . . care and protection of trade abroad in all places their interest of state."

In *The Advocate*, the English council of state made explicit its program of using Dutch methods to beat the Dutch at their own game. The English government had already been attempting to do just this with the passage of the Convoy Act of 1650, its consideration of free ports, and its angry demand that the Dutch relinquish their special privilege of passing through the Sound toll-free, secured through their recent treaty with Denmark. "If the nature of those courses which [the Dutch] have taken . . . for the encouragement of trade be looked into," said *The Advocate*, "it cannot be imagined but that they shall make any people great, rich and flourishing in trade that useth them." "Nor will our neighbors therefore . . . take it . . . ill," it went on, "if we see the necessity of providing for the defense of the commonwealth by shipping . . . or . . . if we take up some of the like courses as they for the encouragement of trade." As *The Advocate* ominously concluded, "It is by a knowledge of trade and commerce . . . that one nation or state knows perfectly how to straighten and pinch another and to compel a compliance from them." The latter might be achieved "either by . . . depriving the course of some necessary commodities from them, as [by] war for shipping or food, etc.; or by obstructing the sale or vent of the native commodities belonging to them; or by weakening them in their shipping and draining them . . . of their treasure and coin." The passage of the navigation act followed directly from this line of thinking; in a matter of months, so would the Anglo-Dutch war.

NAVAL WAR AGAINST THE DUTCH

The Commonwealth possessed the resolve and the capacity to move so quickly and decisively against the Dutch because it had, from its inception, prepared for and implemented an increasingly aggressive and expansionist commercial and naval policy. It had maintained this approach even in the face of, and to some extent in aid of, the negotiations for Anglo-

Dutch unity. As the Venetian ambassador pointed out in June 1651, "Owing to the care of Parliament [the English] have 80 men of war, which are certainly the finest fleet now afloat whether for construction, armament or crews. They can increase their numbers with incredible facility to 150, 200, or more sail."[109] On the basis of its growing naval power, the Commonwealth's defensive naval strikes to gain security for the new republic against royalists and their allies had assumed ever broader commercial purposes—to reestablish traditional English trading lanes and, beyond that, to assert British maritime hegemony.

The series of missions of Blake, Penn, and (later) Ayscue to the Iberian peninsula and the Mediterranean were basically aimed at destroying Rupert and punishing those who had protected royalists or who had launched privateering attacks on British shipping. But they ended up, as noted, as attempts to extract major commercial concessions from Portugal and Spain and to reestablish English power beyond the Straits. In parallel manner, English maritime aggressiveness was, before long, leading to serious assaults on Dutch shipping, and these had the effect, intended or not, of eroding by forceful political means the Dutch commercial competitive advantage and of pressuring them to take more seriously the English demands for a closer unity. The Commonwealth's attempts from early 1651 to implement the Convoy Act of 1650 led to a series of warlike encounters with Dutch vessels in the Mediterranean. Its naval voyages of 1651–1652 to break the self-styled royalist governments in the West Indies and Virginia had the larger goal of enforcing the Act of 1650 for monopolizing trade with the American colonies, and they were highlighted by Ayscue's seizure of fourteen Dutch ships in Barbados in October 1651. Meanwhile, under the cover of British embargoes of 1649–1650 against Scotland, Portugal, and France in retaliation for these nations' varying levels of support for the royalist cause, English privateers had been carrying out increasingly numerous assaults against Dutch shippers in the face of the continued insistence on the part of the United Provinces that they retained the right, as neutrals, to trade with all parties. Between 1649 and 1651, the number of Dutch ships taken by English privateers more than tripled. (It is of more than passing interest that new-merchant leaders were in the forefront of the privateering campaign to enforce the embargoes; the Commonwealth commission for the sale of prize goods was, moreover, composed largely of new merchants and close collaborators of theirs from among London's political independent rulers.) Even while negotiating for closer union, the English government had, as noted, during the spring of 1651 drawn up preliminary drafts of the navigation act in case those ne-

---

[109] *C.S.P. Ven. 1647–1652*, pp. 187–88.

gotiations failed. As it was, the passage of the navigation act in August 1651 constituted merely one further provocation in an ongoing pattern of escalation by the English designed to bring the Dutch, in one way or another, to terms. The Dutch, for their part, had no intention of relinquishing the fruits of their commercial superiority, built up over many decades. By the middle of 1652, following a six-month period in which English privateers had captured a further 106 Dutch vessels, the English government had once again made clear its continued dissatisfaction with the Dutch lack of interest in a closer union and with their continued failure to deal with English royalists in Holland. The outbreak of war could no longer be avoided.[110]

The Commonwealth's imperialist republican leaders, most prominently Marten, Chaloner, Neville, and Morley, bent on aggression, controlled overseas policy in the period of growing tension between mid-1651 and mid-1652, during which the Anglo-Dutch negotiations disintegrated and ultimately collapsed.[111] And they were to a great extent directly responsible for the moves toward war. As it turned out, the English navy did not find warfare with the Dutch an easy option. A series of defeats in the opening phases of the conflict appears to have thrown English overseas policy-making into something of a crisis. One outcome was a sweeping reform in the leadership of the navy—the radical demotion of Chaloner, Marten, and their friends in the interest of the professionalization of the war effort. In the wake of the defeat of General Robert Blake at Dungeness at the end of November 1652, the government moved to concentrate responsibility for naval policy and administration in a new six-person admiralty and navy commission, endowed with wide powers and recruited mostly from outside Parliament. This commission included the colonial-interloping leaders George Thomson and James Russell, as well as their intimate City friends and collaborators the MP Richard Salway and John Langley (a member of the new merchants' committee for regulating the customs and the navy), along with the MPs Sir Henry Vane and the militant John Carew.[112] The first four of these men were representative City radicals or moderate republicans. Characteristically, they carried out their assignment with extraordinary energy and efficiency, and, in the space of a few short months, they succeeded in transforming the operations of the

---

[110] For this and the preceding paragraph, see especially Groenveld, "First Anglo-Dutch War," pp. 555–64, as well as Gardiner, *Commonwealth and Protectorate* 2: 75–87, 108–18ff., and Wilson, *Profit and Power*, ch. 4. I have been much aided throughout this chapter by Groenveld's important article. For the preparation of the navigation act as early as March–April 1651, see Violet, *Mysteries and Secrets of Trade*, p. 178.

[111] Worden, *Rump Parliament*, pp. 301–2; Cogar, "Politics of Naval Administration," pp. 100–103.

[112] Cogar, "Politics of Naval Administration," pp. 109–20; *C.J.* 7: 225, 228.

navy. They ironed out and stepped up the provision of the fleet; solved the crisis of naval manpower that had been brought on by the pile-up in arrears of sailors' pay; and, finally, established the closest working relationship with the admirals of the fleet, notably Robert Blake and Richard Deane, moderate republicans like themselves. There is reason to doubt that the English victories in the first Dutch war, which followed the initial period of setback, could have been achieved had it not been for the work of the men on this committee.[113]

The ability of the Commonwealth leadership to integrate so systematically and successfully the quest for world power with the drive for commercial hegemony was not missed by contemporaries. And at least some of them attributed this capability to the close interpenetration and cooperation of politicians and merchants in the governance of the republic. In assessing the sources of strength of the Commonwealth, the Venetian ambassador made sure to point out

> the facility with which the English increased their fortunes by trade, which has made great strides for some time past, and is now improved by the protection it receives from Parliament, *the government of the Commonwealth and that of its trade being exercised by the same individuals*. . . . The advantage of this was formerly recognized by other nations who are now impoverishing themselves because in our time the source of our greatness is considered dishonorable.[114] (emphasis added)

The distinctive traits of the Commonwealth government were most obvious to those who participated most intimately and who benefited most directly from the new regime. As the parliamentary diarist Goddard commented, the Rump was "an iron parliament, a trading parliament" in contrast with the Protector's Parliament, whose members sided against the "citizens and late Parliament men." The republican leaders Henry Neville and Thomas Scot were even more specific. According to Neville, the Protectorate was created to make peace with the Dutch and war with Spain, and the *Humble Petition and Advice* made another Dutch war impossible. "It is not for a hierarchy," he said, "to maintain that War."[115] Correlatively, Scot argued that it had been the special mission of the Commonwealth to defeat the Dutch and force them to unite with England. Only Cromwell's intervention had prevented this. According to Scot,

[113] V. Rowe, *Sir Henry Vane the Younger* (London, 1970), pp. 178, 190. The assessment of the committee's work is that of Dr. Rowe.

[114] *C.S.P. Ven. 1647–1652*, pp. 187–88. For this and contemporary quotations linking republicanism with commercial and imperial potency, see Hill, *God's Englishman*, p. 131.

[115] The foregoing quotations are in Cooper, "Social and Economic Policies," pp. 121–22.

The Dutch War came on. If it had pleased God and his Highness to have let that little power of a Parliament sit a little longer . . . we intended to have gone off with good savour, and provided for a succession of parliaments; but we stayed to end the war. *We might have brought them to oneness with us.* Their ambassadors did desire a coalition. This we might have done in four or five months. We never bid fairer for being masters of the whole world (emphasis added).[116]

[116] J. T. Rutt, ed., *The Diary of Thomas Burton*, 4 vols. (London, 1828), 3: 111–12.

 [XIII]

The New Merchants and the Fall
of the Commonwealth

T HE COMMONWEALTH period represented the high point
of power for London's political independents, or those I have
loosely termed moderate republicans—that is, the long-standing
City radical alliance, shorn of its politically most extreme elements, the
Levellers and their separatist allies. It was also, of course, the moment of
greatest influence for the new-merchant leadership, which formed one important element in that alliance. In contrast, the merchants of the City's
overseas companies saw their political power reach its lowest ebb under
the Commonwealth. Most of the traditional company merchant establishment, centered on the Levant–East India combine and, to a lesser extent,
on the Merchant Adventurers, had stood in the vanguard of City constitutional royalism and had, as a result, seen its hegemony in London destroyed by the City revolution of 1641–1642 and the City's alliance with
Parliament. What remained of company merchant political influence was
largely demolished during the later 1640s when the City's political presbyterians, ultimately allied with resurgent London royalists, were removed from power by the invading New Model Army. The near-total
absence of both Levant–East India merchants and Merchant Adventurers
from influential political positions within the Commonwealth government
is, in fact, powerful proof of the near-total implication of both of these
groups with the forces arrayed against political independency in the City.

The alienation of the company merchant community from the Commonwealth was so striking that the author of the royalist newssheet *Mercurius Elencticus* could discover in it what he believed to be the basis for
an (optimistic) prognosis of ill health for the new regime. "They [the
political independents in power] want the heart of the *merchants* (I think
I may safely say) of all *interests* and they are the Vena-porta: If they flourish
not a kingdom may have good limbs, but empty veins and nourish little"
(emphasis in original).[1] Of course, in making that assertion, *Mercurius
Elencticus* overlooked one merchant interest, and a very important one

[1] *Mercurius Elencticus*, no. 7 (4–11 June 1649).

indeed: the new-merchant leadership. It was, of course, no accident that the new-merchant leaders and their friends could command such a central position among the supporters of the Commonwealth. This was their pay-off for years of political collaboration with the republic's new rulers, and for most of the new merchants it was well-earned compensation for a long period in the political wilderness. The new men were, moreover, uniquely equipped for the job: alongside the other London political independent leaders, they could offer a crucial political base for the republic, as well as an outstanding source of administrative personnel and significant funds to finance the government. In view of the fact that almost the entire community of overseas company merchants was disqualified from holding office, that made them almost indispensable. Finally, the new merchants' success under the Commonwealth must be attributed, to a large degree, to the common outlook and interest that they seem to have shared with some of the most powerful elements among those who governed the Rump. In its nondemocratic republicanism, its relative religious toleration, its partiality toward Independency, the desire of at least some of its key leaders to make the law more efficient and progressive, and its militant commercial imperialism, the Commonwealth was a near-perfect embodiment of the new merchants' interests and ideals. From their standpoint it represented the most favorable conceivable outcome of the revolutionary struggles.

But those very aspects of the Commonwealth regime that made it so perfect a realization of the new merchants' aspirations were, from a wider perspective, grave weaknesses. Any government that reflected so closely the new merchants' interests and ideals was bound to represent only a very narrow constituency of the nation—and this narrowness was the Commonwealth's Achilles' heel. The Rump had been established by a radical, mass upsurge in the army; it was the irresistible force of the army rank and file that made possible the defeat of the old parliamentary parties, the purging of Parliament, the execution of the king, the destruction of the House of Lords, and the consolidation of the new republic. Nevertheless, during the first half of 1649, the Commonwealth deprived itself of a significant section of its mass support when it dispersed the democratic and sectarian wing of the army. What popular radical backing it still retained, located largely in London and among the army rank and file, was further dissipated when the Rump was unable to take positive action even on certain relatively moderate proposals for religious and social reform. On the other hand, the Commonwealth earned itself the permanent distrust of most of the traditional landed class when it destroyed the monarchy, the House of Lords, and the episcopal hierarchy, and granted limited toleration. This distrust hardened into hatred as the maintenance of the army and the government's involvement in overseas military adventures brought continued high levels of taxation.

The Commonwealth had to construct a social base for itself. But in the long run it could secure this base only by making concessions either to popular participation and social reform, thus acceding to the radicalism of artisans and small tradesmen, or to institutional and constitutional conservatism, which would appeal to the traditionalism of the old landed-class rulers. Taking either course would tend not only to further alienate either radicals or conservatives, but also would likely lead to the regime's own dissolution. The Commonwealth's vulnerabilities and incapacities were all too evident to the army officer corps, which in the last analysis pulled the strings. Yet, while the Commonwealth was entirely dependent on the army, the army could not easily dispense with the Commonwealth. The Rump offered the army at least the fig leaf of legitimacy, whereas direct army rule would appear to be the rule of naked force. A frustrated officer corps did ultimately dissolve the Commonwealth in 1653 in a halfhearted attempt to respond to popular forces within the army and London. The officers then abruptly destroyed the Barebone's Parliament, which had replaced the Rump, when that body showed signs of passing into law some of the somewhat radical social reform ideas that had originally inspired its establishment. By the end of 1653, the army, and especially its top leadership, was having to face in even starker form essentially the same problem of the disjunction between political and social power as had the Rump.

Taken together, the dissolutions of the Rump and of Barebone's Parliament in 1653 amounted to a blanket rejection of the various segments of London's radical Commonwealth ruling group. It has become an historical commonplace that few in the nation mourned the Rump's demise. This assessment, it is true, has not gone entirely unchallenged, and as early as 1659 the Commonwealth leader Thomas Scot felt called upon to rebut it. Scot was, of course, one of those "Rumper-republicans" who best represented the antidemocratic, yet relatively radical, republicanism that seems to have inspired the original core leadership of the Commonwealth regime. As Scot asserted,

> That gentleman says the Parliament went out, and no complaining in the streets, nor enquiry after them. That is according to the company men keep. . . . A petition, the day after Parliament was dissolved, from 40 of the chief officers, the aldermen of the City of London, and many godly divines besought to have that Parliament restored. But the Protector, being resolved to carry on his work, threatened, terrified, and displaced them; and who would for such a shattered thing venture their all?[2]

[2] J. T Rutt, ed., *The Diary of Thomas Burton*, 4 vols. (London, 1828), 3: 112.

Nevertheless, the very substance of Scot's defense contradicts his own argument. The inconsequentiality of the protest against the Rump's dissolution to which Scot refers attests far more to the weakness than to the strength of the Rump's support. Still, Scot helps make it possible to pinpoint the specific character of the narrow backing that body did enjoy: the new merchants and their London political independent friends, the City's Independent ministers, and the Rump leadership itself.

On 21 May 1653, a petition demanding the recall of the Rump and signed by forty London citizens was presented to Oliver Cromwell by Alderman Thomas Andrews, abetted by Alderman Stephen Estwicke, who delivered a speech in its behalf.[3] Both of these men were leaders of City radicalism and political independency going back to the early 1640s, prominent religious Independents, longtime commercial and political associates of Maurice Thomson's, and currently participants in Thomson's interloping project in the East Indies. According to one contemporary observer, the Londoners' petition was "put on foot by the routed members and some Independent ministers."[4] This is quite plausible, since the rule of the Commonwealth was marked by the closest collaboration between key sections of the Rump's leadership, the City's political independents and new merchants, and the Independent divines. Certainly, the citizens' petition reflects the fundamental concern of London moderate republicanism to maintain the very favorable Commonwealth regime, and it is not surprising that the signers included many of that political group's most prominent leaders. Among the petition's forty signers, in addition to Estwicke and Andrews, were the colonial-interloping traders and longtime City radicals and political independents Maurice Thomson, his brothers Robert and William, William's father-in-law Samuel Warner, Thomas Allen, Edward Winslow, Richard Waring, William Pennoyer, Pennoyer's old apprentice Michael Davison, James Russell, and James Wainwright, as well as their close associates William Hobson (Samuel Pennoyer's father-in-law) and the goldsmith and Bermuda Company leader Francis Allein. Further evidence for the long-term continuity of the City's radical "party" may be found in the fact that the forty petitioners included four persons who had been original members of the revolutionary City committee of safety of January 1642 (Estwicke, Warner, Russell, and John Wollaston); four who had been leaders on the Salters Hall committee and/or the committee for a general rising, which spearheaded the City radical offensive for an independent volunteer army in 1643 (Warner, John Kendricke, Edward Story, and Tempest Milner); and ten who had

---

[3] C. H. Firth, ed., *The Clarke Papers*, Camden Society Publications, 4 vols. (London, 1891), 3: 6.

[4] *H.M.C., Fourteenth Report, Appendix 2*, p. 201.

been on the army-appointed militia committee of September 1647 (Andrews, Estwicke, Warner, Russell, Wollaston, Milner, Alexander Jones, Thomas Foote, Thomas Arnold, and William Hobson).[5]

The failure of these men to affect even slightly the government's decision revealed their ultimate political impotence and their fundamental dependence on the army. Cromwell emphasized the point by abruptly dismissing all the petitioners from their governmental offices. Most of them were ultimately taken back into the fold and allowed to hold onto individual positions of influence through the remainder of the Interregnum. Henceforward, however, their ability as a group to affect the course of political development was strictly limited.

[5] *A Catalog of Eminent Names* (London, 26 May 1653) (BL, 698 [16]); *C.S.P.D. 1652–1653*, pp. 351, 345, 363; Firth, *Clarke Papers* 3: 6. James Wainwright was an apprentice of Maurice Thomson's old colonial trading partner Thomas Stone (Haberdashers Company, London, Apprenticeship Bindings, 1630–1652, 20 May 1631). Also among the petitioners was Samuel Lee, ship captain, who was master of the ship *Discovery*, sent out by Maurice Thomson, Gregory Clement, and others from 1637 on (*C.S.P.D. 1636–1637*, p. 554).

Postscript

THIS STUDY has proceeded from commercial change, considered as a sociopolitical and not simply an economic process, to the formation of merchant groups, to the character of merchant ideology and politics, to the nature of merchant commercial and political ties with nonmerchant political forces, and finally to merchant political interventions in successive phases of political conflict during the first half of the seventeenth century, and the broader impact of those interventions. Perhaps it is now appropriate to take the final, necessarily much more speculative, step of asking explicitly how the results of this inquiry might bear on the broader interpretation of the political conflicts of the Stuart period. The intent here is less to summarize achieved results than to suggest tentative hypotheses for further research and analysis.

The Traditional Social Interpretation
of the English Revolution

During the middle decades of the twentieth century, what might be termed the traditional social interpretation dominated the historiography of the political conflicts of the Stuart era. In this view,[1] a rising bourgeoi-

[1] What I am here calling the traditional social interpretation is an amalgamation of the conceptually interrelated arguments put forward by C. Hill, R. H. Tawney, and L. Stone in the following works: C. Hill, *The Revolution of 1640* (London, 1940); R. H. Tawney, "The Rise of the Gentry," *Ec.H.R.* 11 (1941); R. H. Tawney, "Harrington's Interpretation of His Age," *Proceedings of the British Academy* 27 (Oxford, 1941); R. H. Tawney, "The Rise of the Gentry: A Postscript," *Ec.H.R.*, 2d ser., 7 (1954); L. Stone, "The Anatomy of the Elizabethan Aristocracy," *Ec.H.R.* 18 (1948); and L. Stone, "The Elizabethan Aristocracy: A Restatement," *Ec.H.R.*, 2d ser., 4 (1952). Neither Stone nor Hill would today adhere to this synthesis. More recent statements of position by Hill can be found in "Recent Interpretations of the Civil War," in *Puritanism and Revolution* (London, 1958); *Reformation to Industrial Revolution* (London, 1967); "A Bourgeois Revolution?" in *Three British Revolutions*, ed. J.G.A. Pocock (Princeton, 1980); and "Parliament and People in Seventeenth-Century England," *Past & Present*, no. 92 (1981). Hill's current version of the social interpretation focuses on the revolution's *unintended outcome*, which, he argues, "was the establishment of conditions far more favorable to the development of capitalism than those which prevailed before 1640. The hypothesis is that this outcome, and the Revolution itself, was made possible by the fact that there had already been a considerable development of capitalist relations in England." "A Bourgeois Revolution?" p. 111ff. Stone's *Crisis of the Aristocracy* (Oxford, 1965) constitutes, in important respects, a critique of the traditional social interpretation that he helped develop. For Stone's revised position, see "The Social Origins of the English Revolution," in *The Causes of the English Revolution, 1529–1641* (New York, 1972), and "The Results of the English Revolutions of the Seventeenth Century,"

sie, composed of traders and industrialists in the towns and gentry and yeomen in the country, grew up in the interstices of the old order, came into conflict with an old aristocracy that had been unable to adapt to the new pressures and opportunities of the emerging market economy, and ultimately overthrew that aristocracy in the English Revolution. By this account, the rise of trade plus the price revolution provided the original motor of capitalist development in Tudor England. But commercialization and rising prices had an impact on the nascent bourgeois class quite different from their impact on the old feudal class (or at least a significant part of that class) because each of these classes occupied a distinct social position, maintaining itself in its own distinctive way and possessing its own characteristic interests. A new urban and particularly a new rural entrepreneurial bourgeoisie composed of gentry and yeomen took advantage of new markets and sticky rents to grow increasingly rich and powerful. In contrast, much of the old feudal landed class was unable to respond. The traditional aristocracy, it was argued, maintained itself by its military feudal following; this necessitated retaining paternalistic relations with tenants, who were often also political clients. But paternalism was, of course, the opposite of what was required to take the maximum commercial benefit from the land. To make matters worse, the price revolution especially penalized those landlords unable or unwilling to raise rents, while it benefited tenants and aggressive rack-renters. Finally, leading sections of the aristocracy were hurt by their high consumption requirements. Bastard feudal magnates had to live like lords to maintain standing with their followers. Court nobles had to assume heavy diplomatic costs, while also keeping up conspicuous consumption for prestige purposes. In sum, bastard feudal, passive, and court aristocrats suffered in the new economic environment engendered by the growth of commerce and the rise of prices, while nonfeudal, active, and country gentry, as well as yeoman tenants and owner-operator farmers, profited.

By the late sixteenth century, the aristocrats' immobility had left them in financial crisis, while the gentry and yeomen grew from strength to strength. To compensate for its economic difficulties the aristocracy sought political remedies and was obliged to turn to the monarchy for support. The monarchy provided succor to the crisis-bound aristocracy through the creation of court offices and other perquisites, and it financed these sinecures by granting commercial and industrial monopolies and by levying unparliamentary taxes on the newly developing bourgeois economy, fettering the growth of production. In response, the bourgeoisie,

in Pocock, *Three British Revolutions*. As should be obvious, I depend in many important ways on the works of both Hill and Stone and share many of their conclusions, although the character of the general interpretation I put forward may differ from each of theirs.

notably the gentry, was obliged, in its own material interest, to fight for commercial freedom and parliamentary liberties, and it ultimately precipitated revolution against the absolutist state and the feudal aristocracy supported by it.

The traditional social interpretation has suffered from certain disabling weaknesses. Above all, it has been unable to specify for the relevant period—roughly from the reign of Elizabeth to the English Revolution—economically distinct feudal and capitalist classes that were, respectively, structurally prevented from and structurally capable of gaining from the new economic conditions and, as a result, ultimately driven into political conflict with one another.[2] It is true that bastard feudal lords who applied their lands to the maintenance of politico-military followers or who made large consumption expenditures so as to live nobly and reward their supporters would, all else being equal, have been disadvantaged with respect to other landed elements who did not have these burdens. But the traditional social interpreters have been unable to explain why those lords could not, under the economic pressures and opportunities of the period, shed their followers and transform their households so as to make use of their lands and other resources in more profitable ways, or why those who failed to adjust would not, over more than a century of rising prices and stagnant incomes, have gone under. The fact is that, by the end of the sixteenth century, there were very few such old-style magnates left in England.[3]

It is also true that "active" tenants who secured long leases early in the sixteenth century were able, for a time, to profit at the expense of their "passive" landlords from rising food prices and land prices. But again, this temporary difference in structural position could not determine a long-term difference in capacity to make a successful economic response; it is clear that by the end of the century most long leases had fallen in, and landlords could now easily profit (probably at the expense of tenants) from rapidly rising rents.[4]

[2] For the critique of the traditional social interpretation, the locus classicus is J. H. Hexter, "Storm over the Gentry," in *Reappraisals in History* (New York, 1961). Hexter builds on H. R. Trevor-Roper, "The Elizabethan Aristocracy: An Anatomy Anatomised," *Ec.H.R.*, 2d ser., 4 (1952); H. R. Trevor-Roper, "The Gentry, 1540–1640," *Ec.H.R.*, supp. 1 (1953); and J. P. Cooper, "The Counting of Manors," *Ec.H.R.*, 2d ser., 8 (1956). Cf. J. H. Hexter, "The English Aristocracy, Its Crises, and the English Revolution, 1558–1660," *J.B.S.* 8 (1968): 22–78, for an illuminating discussion of Stone's *Crisis of the Aristocracy*. I have offered an analysis of the debate in "Bourgeois Revolution and Transition to Capitalism" in *The First Modern Society*, ed. A. L. Beier et al. (Cambridge, 1989).

[3] For the elimination of the magnates by the end of the sixteenth century through processes of transformation and attrition, see L. Stone, "Power," in *Crisis of the Aristocracy*, ch. 5, and P. Williams, *The Tudor Regime* (Oxford, 1979), pp. 428–52. Cf. J. Goring, "Social Change and Military Decline in Mid-Tudor England," *History* 60 (1975).

[4] On the landlords' adjustment to the new conditions and their profit from rising rents, see Stone,

As for the supposedly greater consumption requirements of courtier aristocrats in comparison to country gentry, it is not easy to see why these would not have been met, or more than met, by the courtier aristocrats' access to lucrative offices and gifts. In fact, the argument that court life was especially burdensome for the nobility refers mainly to the reign of Elizabeth, when the monarch's expenditures on her officers and courtiers were unusually low. This situation was reversed during the reign of James I and the first part of Charles I's reign, when spending at court skyrocketed.[5]

The upshot is that, by the era of the Civil War, it is very difficult to specify anything amounting to a class distinction of any sort within the category of large holders of land, since most were of the same class. In England the distinction between "nobles" and "gentry" was inadequate to specify distinct social classes, given that nobles were generally recruited from the greater gentry, while nobles' younger sons were non-nobles and mostly gentry. More to the point, by the middle decades of the seventeenth century, after a long evolution, a strong majority of English landlords, titled and untitled, great and small, were maintaining themselves in the same way, deriving the bulk of their income from taking competitive rents from commercial farmers for the lease of their absolute landed property.

The failure, so far, to discover convincing evidence that feudal and capitalist classes took divergent economic paths and entered into conflict during the half century or so before 1640—indeed the inability even to identify such classes in those years—has led to the emergence of a very different picture of socioeconomic and political evolution in that epoch than the one originally envisioned by the traditional interpreters.

First, it is now rather clear that, far from suffering economic crisis in the period before the Civil War, the peers, who included most though by no means all of the greatest landlords of England, enjoyed very striking economic success, a long-term substantial improvement in their economic position. Indeed, if anything, this was an era of rise, not decline, for the aristocracy and for the landlord class as a whole. But this should not be surprising in view of the fact that the years between 1580 and 1640 were ones of rising rents and food prices, as well as of agricultural improvement. Both nobles and gentry should have done very well, so long as they had ceased to maintain themselves as military magnates and could assume the position of absolute owners and commercial landlords taking market-

---

Crisis of the Aristocracy, pp. 307–10, 314–22, 327–28, 334; E. Kerridge, "The Movement of Rent," *Ec.H.R.*, 2d ser., 6 (1953); G. R. Batho, "Landlords in England," in *The Agrarian History of England and Wales*, vol. 4, *1500–1640*, ed. J. Thirsk (Cambridge, 1967).

[5] Stone, "Anatomy of the Elizabethan Aristocracy," pp. 38–41; *Crisis of the Aristocracy*, pp. 473–75; Hexter, "English Aristocracy."

determined rents from their tenants.[6] Over the early modern period, rather than bringing about the rise of a dynamic new bourgeois class alongside and in conflict with a declining feudal class, a profound process of socioeconomic change brought about the broad transformation of the landed class as a whole. This process may, at the start of the period, have had differential effects, positive and negative, on those rooted, respectively, in emergently capitalist social property relations and those still dependent on (partially) feudal social property relations—reliant on magnate-centered affinities and/or faced with tenants with rents fixed by custom or by long leases. But by 1640, there had emerged in England a landed class that was by and large—though not of course uniformly—capitalist, in the sense of depending on commercial farmers paying competitive rents, rather than one that was sharply divided into advanced and backward sectors.

Second, as a direct consequence of their socioeconomic transformation, the greater landed classes were able, in relative terms, to constitute themselves as an extraordinarily homogeneous aristocracy. There were few sharp social or political distinctions between occupants of the top layer of the landed class, composed largely but by no means entirely of peers, and those of the layers below it. As a result, peers and other great nontitled landlords, who tended to occupy most of the top political leadership and government positions—on the king's council "at court," as well as in both Houses of Parliament and in the leading government positions at the county level—differed mainly in degree and not in kind from the other members of the English political nation.[7] This distinguished England's dominant class from the dominant classes in many other parts of Europe, where court or office-based aristocracies, who depended on central state taxation and fees, tended to come in conflict with local aristocracies that derived their income from seigneurial dues and commercial rents and offices in semiautonomous provincial or local political bodies. Moreover,

---

[6] See Stone's conclusion that "the disadvantages in estate management under which the aristocracy laboured in the late sixteenth century were therefore only temporary and were caused by features peculiar to the age. When times changed in the seventeenth century and when they set their minds to the problem of more efficient management, the many who still owned thousands of acres of underexploited land were able to make a striking recovery. The evidence of their success is writ large in the family archives of the early seventeenth century" (*Crisis of the Aristocracy*, pp. 333–34). For aristocratic recovery, see also Hexter, "English Aristocracy."

[7] Stone, "The Peerage in Society," in *Crisis of the Aristocracy*, ch. 2. "There were 121 peerage families in 1641 and there were probably another 30 to 40 upper gentry families who were as rich as the middling barons and richer than the poor ones" (p. 57). "[The] 500 upper gentry families are in many ways similar in attitudes and way of life to the lower reaches of the peerage, and it was with them, or with the leading elements among them, that social and matrimonial ties were maintained" (p. 52). "The titular peerage . . . comprised the most important element in . . . a class of very rich landlords, an association of the well-born" (p. 64).

there was no unbridgeable gap between the English landed class and its farmer-capitalist tenants such as that which divided the aristocracies of much of Europe (whether they depended on office and taxation or lordship and seigneurial dues) from their peasant tenants. The outcome was that, in England, there was relatively easy coordination among the upper layers of the landed classes, often led by peers, and the lower layers; a relatively broad understanding within the landed class as a whole of the wide range of interests shared by its members; and even a significant potential for political cooperation between landlords and farmers (both tenants and owner-operators), since farmers had many interests in common with land-lords despite the built-in conflict between landlords and tenants over the level of rent.

Third, leading nobles and other great landowners led the parliamentary legislative revolution of the period from the autumn of 1640 through the summer of 1641, and a very strong majority of the parliamentary classes fully supported the rather far-reaching religio-political program of this revolution. The king was largely politically isolated from the landed class as a whole until the autumn of 1641. The English revolution thus initially pitted a socioeconomically and politically unified landed class against the monarch and his limited number of supporters, who were drawn largely from among dependent courtiers and crown "projectors," the upper ranks of the ecclesiastical hierarchy, and the privileged merchants and magis-trates of London. This development is difficult to square with the idea of a revolution against the aristocracy, let alone against an absolutist or a feudal aristocracy tied to the monarchy.

Fourth, with respect to the landlord class of England broadly con-strued, it has yet to be shown that those who supported Parliament and those who supported the Crown during the Civil War beginning in 1642 differed systematically in social class terms or, equally to the point, that a social-class split within the landed class per se was a significant factor be-hind the political conflict.[8] But in so homogeneous a landed class as that of England in the 1640s, whence would such social differences have arisen?

Finally, the overseas company merchants, the leading burgher stratum, failed, as has been seen, to support Parliament against the Crown in 1641–1642. This does not necessarily tell against the traditional social interpretation, which can surely incorporate overseas trading groups that were economically dependent on and thus politically favorable toward the Crown. The fact remains that existing versions of the traditional social interpretation have been unable to specify just what the revolutionary bourgeoisie was (and what it was not). They have therefore been unable

[8] For a recent discussion of this question, see L. Stone, "The Bourgeois Revolution of Seventeenth-Century England Revisited," *Past & Present*, no. 109 (1985).

to go beyond the proposition that it was constituted, at least in part, by "commercial classes" broadly speaking, failing adequately to define or to distinguish among these. Most important, the traditional social interpretation has wrongly implied that these classes were inherently opposed to a somehow feudal landed aristocracy by virtue of their place in the sociopolitical structure.

The Revisionist Challenge

Nevertheless, I think it would be a mistake to draw the conclusion, as has too often been done in recent years, from the failure of the traditional social interpretation to explain the political conflicts of the seventeenth century, that these conflicts are without social foundations, let alone that they have no basis in systematic political and ideological differences. It needs to be remembered that the aim of the traditional social interpretation was initially to provide a social basis, a social logic, for what was already a broadly accepted account of seventeenth-century conflicts in terms of differences over constitutional and religious principles. Its goal was to show just why people should actually have held, consistently and systematically, the conflicting constitutional and religious ideals that, in the view of most historians, had led them into political struggle. Its argument was, of course, that these ideological conflicts could be attributed to the systematically different ways people from opposing classes with different interests had experienced and been affected by the long-term socioeconomic transformations of the epoch, especially the rise of capitalism. In view of the way in which the traditional constitutional and religious interpretation of the seventeenth century had come to be seen as dependent on the traditional social interpretation, it is no coincidence that the apparent collapse of the traditional social interpretation has led, more or less directly, to the concomitant erosion of the accepted constitutional and religious interpretation.[9]

The current Revisionist school has thus founded its challenge to historiographical orthodoxies precisely by taking as its point of departure the discrediting of the argument of the traditional social interpretation that

[9] It is interesting that J. H. Hexter, a leading proponent of the traditional political and religious interpretation, and J.C.D. Clark, a Revisionist critic of it, agree that the recent erosion of allegiance to that interpretation has been, to an important degree, the result of its association with the traditional social interpretation and the widespread criticism of the traditional social interpretation. Compare J. H. Hexter, "The Early Stuarts and Parliament: Old Hat and *Nouvelle Vague*," *Parliamentary History Yearbook* 1 (1982): 186–89, with J.C.D. Clark, *Revolution and Rebellion* (Cambridge, 1986), pp. 22, 24–29. These authors of course disagree about the conclusions to be drawn from their common observation.

the opposed constitutional and religious ideas advanced in the course of the seventeenth-century conflicts represented the ideological weapons, respectively, of a rising rural and urban bourgeoisie and a declining feudal aristocracy. If the political conflicts of the period did not, in fact, express the social conflicts of these opposing classes, how could the constitutional and religious ideas advanced in the course of those political conflicts be properly interpreted as expressing their opposed class interests? The Revisionists take it for granted that the failure of the traditional social interpretation means the impossibility of *any* social interpretation. They thus feel free to point out that, if it is indeed agreed that those who struggled against one another on the issues of Parliament's right to approve all legitimate taxes, of arbitrary imprisonment, impressment, and martial law, and of Arminianism did not actually differ from one another in terms of their position in society, their social interests, or their social experience, it becomes much more difficult to see how the differences over policy could be more than superficial and of a principled nature. For in that case, whence should differences over principle have arisen and persisted and why should conflicting principles have elicited more than temporary support from their adherents?

On the basis of their dismissal of any systematic social basis for seventeenth-century political conflicts, the Revisionists have put forward an alternative vision: that during the early decades of the seventeenth century the effective units of politics were a myriad of atomized court factions, parochial county communities, narrowly defined economic interest groups, and careerist politicians, as well of course as monarchs and their favorites. Within this framework, they have understood the ebb and flow of political events largely as the result of the disorganized and often misinformed struggles of the disparate competing units to secure their usually ephemeral private interests and achieve their ambitions, with disproportionate weight naturally allowed the greatest figures of the realm—the monarchs, the leading ministers, Buckingham, the major courtiers and churchmen, and the greatest aristocrats. In this political universe, conflict was for the most part to be explained in terms of short-run factors, the emergence of very specific conjunctures. Overt principles and ideologies were, in the Revisionists' analysis, little more than post facto explanations and justifications by the participants for their roles in momentary struggles arising from conflicting special interests and competing ambitions pursued through the construction of alliances that were generally little more than temporary marriages of convenience. The idea of relatively long-term, fairly systematic principled conflict is thus, for the Revisionists, a groundless one. Leaving aside Arminianism in the later 1620s and Puritanism in the early 1640s there was, in the Revisionists' view, a rather generalized consensus among all parties on basic constitutional and religious ideas during the first four decades of the seventeenth century.[10]

As the leading proponent of this general perspective, Conrad Russell begins by reinterpreting the conflicts of the early 1620s as mild and unsystematic and goes on to argue that the politics of these years exemplify the politics of the pre–Civil War period as a whole. In this context, Russell contends that the descent into the very sharp struggles of the later 1620s was the result of accidental or exogenous causes, specifically the nation's involvement in war. War gave rise to conflict because it exposed what Russell does believe to have been a major structural problem: the monarchy was unable to fulfill its responsibility for national security due to the systematic incapacity of the existing state apparatus to support large-scale military projects. The English state was unprepared for war in consequence of the landed class's blinkered parochialism—the lack of interest of the county communities in foreign affairs, the refusal of these communities to finance military operations, and their resentment of any interference by the central administration in their self-government—and the Crown's corresponding lack of independent financial and administrative resources. In Russell's view, then, the MPs' undeniable turn to arguments based on constitutional and religious principle during the Parliaments of the late 1620s was simply the result of their own need, and that of their constituents, to rationalize their recalcitrance vis-à-vis the financial and administrative requirements of the state and their anger at the government's sudden and largely unexplained championing of Arminianism. Correlatively, Russell agrees with John Morrill in viewing the politics of the 1630s as a return to normalcy, which Russell understands as the natural result of the nation's return to peace. Like Morrill, moreover, Russell interprets the new descent into conflict at the end of the decade as again only the consequence of outside pressures, in this case the rebellion of the Scots. Revising somewhat his earlier position, Russell does now agree that broad sections of the landed class and their parliamentary representatives resisted the Caroline regime from the later 1630s in order to defend sincerely held constitutional and religious principles. Nevertheless, he continues to insist that the failure of many parliamentary leaders to understand the financial and administrative needs of the state remained a central un-

[10] For the foregoing, see above all the series of penetrating studies by Conrad Russell: "Parliamentary History in Perspective," *History* 61 (1976); *Parliaments and English Politics, 1621–1629* (Oxford, 1979); "Monarchies, Wars, and Estates in England, France, and Spain, c. 1580–c. 1640," *Legislative Studies Quarterly* 7 (1982); and "The Nature of a Parliament in Early Stuart England," in *Before the English Civil War*, ed. H. Tomlinson (London, 1983). For the Revisionists' idea of a consensus on principles, see especially J. Morrill, "The Religious Context of the English Civil War," *T.R.H.S.*, 5th ser., 34 (1984): 160. Cf. M. Kishlansky, "The Emergence of Adversary Politics in the Long Parliament," *Journal of Modern History* 49 (1977). See also below, n. 12.

derlying cause of the inability of the crown and Parliament to find a mutually satisfactory solution. For in the last analysis, Russell contends, King Charles and Parliament could (and in a way did) come to an agreement on at least the central constitutional issues. Indeed, it is Russell's fundamental conclusion—shared with Morrill—that given the extent of the consensus on basic principles, Civil War was placed on the agenda only because of still another exogenous event—the outbreak of the Irish rebellion. It was actually fought because first the Scots (by using their leverage over the parliamentary leadership) and then King Charles (by accepting the essentials of Parliament's constitutional program) forced to the surface an already-existing major division within the landed class over religion and because militant Puritans would not agree to relinquish their goal of further reformation.[11]

Ironically, then—but not really surprisingly—the systematic disassociation within the historiography, following the discrediting of the traditional social interpretation, of political and religious ideas from their social context has led, in the hands of the Revisionists, to the denial that seventeenth-century political conflicts are explicable as a consequence of clashes of constitutional and religious principles. Instead, we have the assertion that these conflicts are largely understandable as the product of accidents and misunderstandings, occurring for the most part in situations where the outbreak of war has placed unbearable pressures on the polity, opening the way to the disruptive interventions of fanatical religious minorities.

Toward a New Social Interpretation

It seems to me that the fundamental prima facie objection to the Revisionists' conception of seventeenth-century politics as constituted by clashes among essentially particularized individual and group interests within a general political context of ideological consensus is that it is demonstrable

[11] Russell, *Parliaments*, esp. pp. 417–33; J. Morrill, *The Revolt of the Provinces* (London, 1980), pp. 24–28; Morrill, "Religious Context of the Civil War"; C. Russell, *The Fall of the British Monarchies 1637–1642* (Oxford, 1991), pp. 8–11 (on principled constitutional motivation for the political resistance of the parliamentary classes in the later 1630s); pp. 72, 113, 155, 254 (on parliamentary opposition's failure to appreciate and act upon monarchy's legitimate financial and administrative needs as an underlying cause of failure to reach agreement); pp. 400–401, 527 (on king's acceptance of parliamentary constitutional program); pp. 115, 121–22, 203–4, 400–404, 527 (on Scots then king forcing split of Parliament over religion); pp. 98–99, 268–73, 275, 527 (on the refusal of Pym and his party to compromise over religion and this as cause of split of Parliament). Cf. C. Russell, *The Causes of the English Civil War* (Oxford, 1990). Professor Russell's major studies appeared when this book was in press. I have made an initial attempt to take their results into account in this Postscript.

that analogous political conflicts over essentially similar constitutional and religious issues broke out on a whole series of occasions during the pre–Civil War period and in fact throughout the seventeenth century, and that those who opposed one another in these struggles consistently articulated their positions in terms of quite similar sets of principles, principles that are incomprehensible merely as ad hoc rationalizations for the forwarding of narrowly personal, factional, or local short-term interests. From this standpoint, wars certainly did, in many instances, provide the occasion for conflict. But this was not so much because they posed insoluble problems for an underfinanced and understaffed monarchy faced with a political nation that was oblivious to the needs of the contemporary state. It was, first of all, because, throughout the seventeenth century, monarchs tended to undertake specific wars—and pursue particular foreign policies—of which the parliamentary classes could not approve. This was true of Charles I's wars of the mid-late 1620s and could hardly have been more the case for his conflict with the Scots at the end of the 1630s. It was, more generally, because the monarchy's pursuit of war tended to bring to the surface precisely those questions of constitutional and religious principle—concerning parliamentary powers, subjects' liberties, and the character and security of the Protestant settlement—that were most in dispute. The resolution of these questions would bear very heavily on what would be the nature of the English state. Once the crown had begun to undertake wars more to the liking of the parliamentary classes, and the central issues of principle had been satisfactorily settled—as effectively happened by the end of the seventeenth century—financing and administering wars ceased to be the insurmountable problems that they previously had appeared to be.

Still, I would also contend that one of the best ways to restore principled conflict over the constitution and religion to its proper place at the center of the interpretation of seventeenth-century politics is to reassociate constitutional and religious ideas with the sociopolitical and economic contexts from which they arose—the experiences they were designed to comprehend, the interests they were shaped to further, and the structures they in effect defended or tended to transform. Without doing so, it is difficult to understand why these particular constitutional and religious conceptions came to be subject to conflict in this particular epoch, why they were supported or opposed in the manner they were and by which persons, why they were defended in a principled and systematic way throughout the seventeenth century, and why certain of the most fundamental among them were salient and successful in England but in very few other places in Europe at the time.

I would therefore argue that historians have moved too facilely from the failure of the traditional social interpretation to specify distinct and conflicting feudal and capitalist classes at the root of seventeenth-century conflicts to the general conclusion that the English Revolution has little or nothing to do with the transition from feudalism to capitalism. This negative conclusion might be warranted at this point if the only plausible model that could link transition to revolution was one in which a feudal landed class representing a feudal mode of production directly confronted a capitalist class representing a capitalist mode of production. Yet even severe critics of the traditional Hill-Tawney-Stone model have acknowledged not only that the long epoch between the Wars of the Roses and the Civil War was indeed one in which the English dominant class ceased to partake of a mode of life centrally organized around and economically dependent on the direct, local exertion of force and jurisdictional rights, and came to subsist largely on contractually founded commercial rents derived from the lease to capitalist farmers of their absolute landed property; these critics have gone on also to conclude that it would be rather surprising if this epochal transformation had failed to have significant implications for the nature of the state and the character of politics.[12]

It would therefore be my view that the exponents of the traditional social interpretation were not, in fact, misguided in one fundamental respect: they quite properly searched for the roots of the seventeenth-century political conflicts in structural problems emerging as a consequence of the long-term transformation of English society in a capitalist direction from the later medieval period. The fundamental flaws of their approach derive instead from their guiding vision of the transition to capitalism as taking place in England by way of the emergence of a bourgeois society within the womb of a largely inert, constraining feudal structure encompassing a significant part of the landed class. A secondary, though important, problem is their (implicit or explicit) conception of capitalism as virtually equivalent to commercial society (in town and country) and of the commercial classes as undifferentiatedly capitalist. In contrast, it would be my own point of departure that capitalism developed in England from the end of the medieval period by means of the self-transformation of the old structure, specifically the self-transformation of the landed classes. As a result, the rise of capitalism took place within the shell of landlord property and thus, in the long run, not in contradiction with and to the detriment of, but rather to the benefit of the landed aristocracy. At the same time, the "commercial classes," far from uniformly capitalist or ideologically unified, were divided from, and indeed in crucial ways set against, one another in consequence of their diverse relationships to production, property, and the state.[13] From this starting point it becomes possible, I

---

[12] For this explicit recognition, see Hexter, "Rise of the Gentry," pp. 142–48.

[13] I have attempted to distinguish between these two differing conceptions of transition and to

believe, to begin to understand the differing political and religious out-looks of the major sociopolitical actors treated in this work as, in crucial respects, responsive to their differing interests and experiences rooted in their differing relationships to capitalist development and its effects—or, more precisely, to the new forms of social-property relations and the new form of state that were the product of the transition to capitalism. On that basis it becomes possible, in turn, to make sense of those fundamental political alliances that have formed the foundation for the social analysis of politics advanced in this study—between patrimonial monarchy and the overseas company traders, between leading sections of the parliamen-tary aristocracy and the colonial-interloping leadership, and between the colonial-interloping leadership and London retailers, ship captains, arti-sans, and small tradesmen—as well as the conflicts among these forces thus allied. In so doing, it may be feasible to take at least the initial steps toward reconstructing a more general social interpretation of the seven-teenth-century political struggles.

What the transition from feudalism to capitalism on the land thus es-sentially amounted to was the transformation of the dominant class from one whose members depended economically, in the last analysis, on their juridical powers and their direct exercise of force over and against a peas-antry that possessed its means of subsistence, into a dominant class whose members, having ceded direct access to the means of coercion, depended economically merely on their absolute ownership of landed property and contractual relations with free, market-dependent commercial tenants (who increasingly hired wageworkers), defended by a state that had come to monopolize force. The medieval lords' ultimate economic dependence on their feudal extraeconomic powers was demonstrated in the period of population collapse from the middle of the fourteenth century on. In this epoch, the lords were obliged to revert to seigneurial reaction and parlia-mentary legislation to have a hope of maintaining their seigneurial levies, but were not able to prevent the collapse of their lordships under the pres-sure of peasant resistance and flight, losing the capacity to take coerced rents and failing to prevent the peasants from achieving free status. They were thus left to depend economically merely on their land, which they now found very difficult to valorize by way of market-determined rents in the face of the very low labor/land ratio and, to make matters worse, the peasants' claims to the right to inherit and to fixed dues. As a conse-quence, they suffered a disastrous decrease in income. The lords did suc-ceed during the subsequent era in securing absolute property in their landed estates, in part against the claims of the customary tenantry, in part

explore the differing implications of each for the interpretation of social change and political conflict in early modern England in "Bourgeois Revolution."

by maintaining broad demesnes as an inheritance from the medieval period. They thereby gained the ability to take commercial and competitive, not merely customary and fixed, rents from their tenants, and were able to take advantage not only of the rising food and land prices that marked most of the early modern period, but also of the growing competition in the land and product markets among their commercial farmer-tenants. The result of the latter change was increasing social differentiation—as more-efficient, often larger producers won out over less-efficient, often smaller producers—and significant agricultural improvement, leading to the growth of agricultural productivity. Because of their self-transformation—partly imposed on them, partly implemented by them—the greater landed classes thus succeeded in accumulating their great wealth and social power directly on the foundations of capitalist property and capitalist development.[14]

The transition from feudalism to capitalism had a formative impact not only on the nature of the aristocracy, but also on the evolution of the state during the Tudor–Stuart period. But whereas capitalism and landlordism developed more or less symbiotically, capitalist development helped precipitate the emergence of a new form of state, to which the relationships of capitalist landlords and of the patrimonial monarchy were essentially ambiguous and ambivalent and ultimately the source of immanent fundamental conflict.

The obverse side of those processes by which neo-feudal lords became commercially responsive capitalist landlords during this epoch were processes by which landed-class elements contributed to and benefited from the creation of a new form of unified state with an unprecedented level of jurisdictional and legal unity and a novel monopoly of the legitimate use of force. Lords had good reason to relinquish their coercive capacity, thus their capacity for de facto independent jurisdiction and disruption, because they could no longer effectively apply it to what had been its primary function throughout the medieval period—ensuring forced levies from unfree peasants. Furthermore, to the extent that they wished effectively to exploit their lands commercially, lords found themselves obliged to cease to use them to patronize political followers and thus to hold onto correspondingly less coercive capacity. Finally, as they succeeded in securing regular rental incomes from their estates directly on the basis of their absolute property and the workings of roughly free markets in land and labor (which facilitated roughly free contractual exchanges between themselves and their tenant farmers), they were able to give up their connec-

---

[14] R. Brenner, "The Agrarian Roots of European Capitalism," in *The Brenner Debate: Agrarian Class Structure and Economic Development in Pre-Industrial Europe*, ed. T. H. Aston and C.H.E. Philpin (Cambridge, 1985), pp. 270–72, 291–99.

tions with those bastard feudal affinities that had functioned in part to give economic support to their members (via magnate patronage and the fruits of marauding and of corrupting local government), and could refrain from depending on the monarchy to provide alternative opportunities for income through offices and other perquisites. The upshot was that, as they emerged as successful commercial landholders overseeing an emergent capitalist agrarian economy, English landlords ceased to require forms of state, of political community, either local or national, that had as one of their central functions the economic support of the members of the dominant class by means of the maintenance of *politically constituted forms of private property*—either by making possible direct lordly levies from the peasants, based on lordship, or by constituting property in central or local offices, based largely on peasant taxation. They thereby distinguished themselves from most of their counterparts on the Continent, who continued to depend on politically constituted forms of private property precisely because they were obliged to continue to maintain themselves through the coercive exploitation of possessing peasants. Typifying the latter were both the seigneurs of northeastern Europe (Poland and eastern Germany), whose income continued to depend on lordship (and rents secured by force) made possible by membership in privileged nobilities organized through local and national estates, and the dominant class of much of France, whose members were obliged to subsist, to a great extent, on income from the possession of national and local offices and jurisdictional rights, constituted by national, provincial, and local political communities. In direct contrast, by the seventeenth century, the English landed classes not only could take substantial incomes from their lands without recourse to lordship and the intra-lordly political communities on which lordship ultimately rested, but also, for the same reason, could dispense with property in office and the national or local tax/office states on which it tended to be based.[15]

No longer needing to possess what was in effect a piece of the state, be it a lordship or an office, to maintain themselves economically, what the greater landed classes of England now merely required was a state able to protect for them their absolute private property—initially, both from marauding bands of neo-feudal magnates and from peasants seeking to conquer what they believed to be their customary rights to the land; ultimately, from landless squatters. They therefore associated themselves ever more closely during the early modern period with the monarchy in the construction of an increasingly powerful and precociously unified state that

[15] For an attempt to explain why diverging forms of social-property relations established themselves in each of these regions from the end of the Middle Ages and why each of these social-property forms was systematically associated with the emergence of particular forms of state, see ibid., pp. 275–99.

succeeded, by the early seventeenth century, in securing (at least in formal terms) a monopoly over the legitimate use of force. This monopoly of force was, from one point of view, extraordinarily effective in guaranteeing landed-class property.[16]

On the other hand, the unification of the state by the early seventeenth century left the monarchy in an unprecedented position vis-à-vis the landed class. The previous epoch had witnessed the effective elimination of those semiprivate political bodies, above all the magnate affinities, that by virtue of their direct control of the means of force and consequent territorial authority had, throughout the medieval period, retained the potential to exert a signficant direct limitation on national government, especially in their localities, but also at the center. Correlatively, the state had vastly increased its effectiveness by improving its administration, extending its activity into many new spheres, and accruing massive new, especially landed, wealth in the hands of the monarch. Yet the monarchy continued effectively to control this much more powerful and much more unified state, for it maintained, as a legacy from the medieval period, considerable financial and administrative resources of its own and the right to appoint most major governmental officers, while suffering relatively few de jure limitations on what it could do. Monarchs were no mere executives, but great patrimonial lords, viewed by contemporaries as virtually inseparable from the state. As great patrimonial lords, English monarchs inherited political (prerogative) rights to economic resources sufficient to maintain themselves and to constitute their own political following—what might be called the patrimonial group—the membership of which was composed of individuals who depended on various forms of politically constituted property, created and maintained by the monarchy and the patrimonial group itself. Just as the monarchs' followers depended on the patrimonial group and their place within it to maintain themselves economically, the monarchs found in the patrimonial group the core of their own political base. On that foundation, as well as the substantial power they derived from their formal control of the state as a whole—its operation and the appointment of its officers—English monarchs derived the power to pursue their own interests and those of their followers. These

[16] On the strengthening of government under the Tudors in general, see Williams, *Tudor Regime*, in which the emergence of the state's monopoly of force is treated in chapter 4, "Force and Arms" and chapter 13, "Who Ruled?" On the latter, see also Stone, "Power." A series of studies by M. E. James on the north of England during the Tudor period provides perhaps the best account of the mechanisms entailed in the dual process by which monarchal government was strengthened and magnate-centered forms of political organization and political power were dissolved during the Tudor period. See *Change and Continuity in the Tudor North*, Borthwick Papers, no. 27 (York, 1965); "The First Earl of Cumberland and the Decline of Northern Feudalism," *Northern History* 1 (1966); *A Tudor Magnate and the Tudor State*, Borthwick Papers no. 30 (York, 1966); "The Concept of Order and the Northern Rising, 1569," *Past & Present*, no. 60 (1973).

interests—which prominently included the maintenance of the monarchs' self-defined place among the monarchs of Europe, regulating their diplomatic, military, and familial relations with those monarchs—could not be assumed always to coincide with those of the landed class, even despite the fundamental concerns monarchs and the landed class shared, notably for the maintenance of order and hierarchy and for unity *tout court*.

The sort of danger potentially constituted by a state-building patrimonial monarchy pursuing its own interests—including those of its family and dynasty, as well of its followers—was well exemplified by developments in late medieval and early modern France. Here the monarchy was obliged to construct the central state to a significant degree in conflict with and at the expense of the powers, property, and privileges of local rulers and proprietors. It therefore carried through the expansion of unified government on traditional patrimonial lines, as an extension of the household, by constructing its own dependent following of politico-military servants through granting them various forms of politically constituted private property—initially, fiefs with seigneurial dues, but, more characteristically, income-yielding offices, dependent on the monarchy's power to tax (largely peasant) land. But the growth of the monarchy's jurisdiction and taxation struck directly at the politico-legal authority and the landed resources of local powerholders and proprietors, and provoked often strong resistance. The emergent patrimonial tax/office state could consolidate itself essentially for two interrelated reasons. First, it was able to secure a vast new material base by levying ever-increasing taxes on a peasantry that had secured essentially full property in the land; this allowed it to finance a massive structure of offices held as private property and other forms of privileges and grants. Second, on that foundation, the monarchy was able to attract, as well as to construct, an aristocracy heavily dependent on offices. These processes were made possible at least partly because French seigneurs had managed to retain only relatively restricted access to demesne lands and/or feudal levies over and against the pretensions of the peasantry (in comparison to their counterparts in England and Eastern Europe) and were therefore less able and less willing to resist the expanding monarchical state and more open to becoming part of it. The absolutist tax/office state thus succeeded in establishing itself in France, as the outcome of much conflict over an extended period, not only by attacking sections of the aristocracy, but also by effectively reorganizing much of the aristocratic class within the state itself, precisely by means of constructing a vastly expanded monarchical patrimonial group, composed of proprietors of offices and other beneficiaries of royal largesse.[17]

---

[17] It therefore needs to be noted not only that numbers of the same local rulers and proprietors who were hurt by the extension of royal jurisdiction and taxation secured (compensatorily) offices and other

In England, the patrimonial monarchy posed, in the final analysis, the same underlying threat. But there, in some contrast with France, the greater landed classes could willingly assume an active role in the creation of a unified polity and an effective state precisely because the monarchy was obliged to carry through the process of state building by means of the closest collaboration with them. This was largely because the transformation of the aristocrats into successful capitalist landlords had not only relieved them of the need for a state consisting of locally based associated lordships or estates to dominate the peasants directly; it had also very much restricted the potential for the construction of an absolutist tax/office state — by limiting the landlords' need for office as a source of income and by restricting the amount of landed property that could be taxed without directly confronting the landlord class. As a result, within the unified state, the English monarchy had, in comparative terms, only limited independent sources of income and a restricted patrimonial following of dependants. It therefore had few officers it could call its own (who relied for their economic maintenance on their state offices and thus on the monarchy), and was thus dependent on unpaid officials drawn from the landed class to staff local government, administer justice, and organize the military. At the same time, the landlord class retained significant leverage over state finance: taxes were levied on its land and it retained the traditional right to approve them in Parliament. Indeed, in any trans-European perspective, what is most striking about the English localities, and especially the propertied interests based in those localities, is emphatically not their parochialism or hostility to the central government, but rather the extent to which they saw their most fundamental interests as dependent on the strengthening of the unified national state.

The greater landed classes could thus hardly view the state merely negatively as a threat to their local proprietary and political hegemony, as is implied by the one-sided notion that the gentry's politics and worldview were focused narrowly on the county and the parishes and that their main concern with national government was to prevent the intrusion of the state (and occasionally to seek its aid with local projects or problems). Despite superficial similarities, the English landed class's political interests must therefore be sharply distinguished from those of the truly locally focused

income by the same process, but also that the process of unification was, for this reason, itself decisively limited, since many of the old proprietary rights and jurisdictional powers were now effectively recreated within the "absolutist" state. The growth of royal absolutist government was thus, in part, simultaneously a process of aristocratic class (re)formation. For the contrasting evolutions in France and England, see Brenner, "Agrarian Roots," pp. 260–64, 288–90; G. Bois, *Crise du féodalisme* (Paris, 1976), pp. 203–4, 254–56, 364; P. Anderson, *Lineages of the Absolutist State* (London, 1974), pp. 85–112. Cf. E. Wood, "The State and Popular Sovereignty in French Political Thought: A Genealogy of Rousseau's 'General Will,' " *History of Political Thought* 4 (1983).

dominant classes of northeastern Europe, to which they have sometimes been misleadingly compared.[18] Local landed proprietors initially looked to a more effective national monarchical state, of which county government was an integral part, to defend their property from peasants and neo-feudal magnates. But they also closely identified their own interests with the growth of the power of the monarchy and the state in a whole series of other crucial areas. They backed the extension of the monarch's authority against the pretensions of the international papacy and the national church hierarchy. They desired the strengthening of the state's geopolitical position against threatening Catholic powers, notably Spain. They sought the increase in the monarchy's material base (and indirectly their own) by means of the spoliation of the church's lands. Finally, by virtue of their own growing involvement in the developing national capitalism, the greater landed classes had to favor a stronger government that could more effectively regulate the social economy. In particular, significant sections of the landlord class were indirectly dependent for their rents on the demand for wool and other raw materials, as well as food, emanating from a dynamic domestic cloth industry producing directly for an international market. Since the prices to be paid for agricultural products, as well as the security of the social order in the face of commercio-industrial fluctuations thus depended, to an important degree, on the health of the cloth industry, landlords had little choice but to interest themselves in government policy to regulate cloth production and cloth commerce, and especially in the state's actual capacity to make and enforce such policy. Indeed, by the seventeenth century, the political leaders of the parliamentary classes had to be, with the monarchy, more or less continuously involved with the making of commercial policy generally and, beyond that, with government regulation of dynamic nascent manufactures produced for a growing domestic market. In all of these contexts, Parliament should not be viewed merely as a guarantor of the local landlords' property and their position in the state; it served as a central means for the effective collaboration of those local proprietors with the patrimonial monarchy in operating the state and in governing the country.[19]

[18] For a powerful critique of the view that the landed classes' political outlook was locally focused, see C. Holmes, "The County Community in Stuart Historiography," *J.B.S.* 19 (1980). Cf. G. R. Elton, "Tudor Government: The Points of Contact. I. Parliament," *T.R.H.S.*, 5th ser., 24 (1974).

[19] For the landed class's grasp of the relationships between the health of the cloth trade, the level of its rents, and prosperous agriculture, see J. P. Cooper, "Differences between English and Continental Governments in the Early Seventeenth Century," in *Britain and the Netherlands*, ed. J. Bromley and E. H. Kossman (London, 1960), 1: 88. For the parliamentary classes and the regulation of the economy more generally, see Williams, *Tudor Regime*, pp. 143–45ff. For their involvement with the regulation of the cloth trade and commercial policy, see, e.g., the studies by Friis, Supple, Stone, and Ashton cited earlier in this work. For the state's support of nascent industries, see J. Thirsk, *Economic Policy and Projects: The Development of a Consumer Society in Early Modern England* (Ox-

The fact remains that the form of state that emerged in England during the early modern period was immanently problematic. Part and parcel of the same process by which capitalism emerged within the shell of commercial landlordism, coercive powers and jurisdictional rights were, for the first time, clearly separated from the private property and private proprietors, to which and for whom they had historically been integral, and concentrated in a unified state structure, formally possessed by the patrimonial monarchy. At the same time, patrimonial monarchs in England could actually exert only restricted control over the state in consequence of their restricted material resources and their quite limited patrimonial following of political dependents, as well their difficulty in taxing the land, given the ownership of most of it by a powerful landlord class, rather than by peasants. In this situation, private property was potentially threatened because what the patrimonial monarchy required to secure its viability, autonomy, and dynamism was independent access to income from the land. At the same time, institutional measures taken to guarantee the security of private property against the state could jeopardize the politico-economic strength, the very maintenance, of the patrimonial monarchy. The underlying question was not, moreover, merely that of what were to be the limits on what the state could do. Because state action had become so crucial to meet the needs of both the monarchy and the landed classes, the question was also one of who was to control the state and for what ends.

The same point can be expressed in a somewhat different manner. Sociopolitical evolution in early modern England appears to be marked by two fundamental long-term continuities extending far back into the medieval period. First, socioeconomic power in the country generally remained in the hands of the landed class. Second, government continued to be led by the monarch, as a great private lord, who continued ultimately to rely on the members of the league of landed lords to operate a governmental administration that, crucially, belonged to him. But by the seventeenth century, these two major continuities tended to mask two equally fundamental, interrelated discontinuities. First, the country's landlords no longer maintained themselves economically by their capacity directly to coerce a possessing peasantry, a capacity that had depended on membership in various kinds of local, regional, and national patrimonial political communities or groups. Instead, they had come to rely simply on their unconditional landed property and thus on the protection of their private property by the indirect coercion exerted by the state. Second, the monarch, while remaining a great lord with the capacity to maintain himself, in the first instance, by virtue of his private wealth and patrimonial

ford, 1978). Cf. G. R. Elton, "Tudor Government: The Points of Contact. I. Parliament," *T.R.H.S.*, 5th ser., 24 (1974).

following, had ceased to depend for his government on lords who, by virtue of their own political organizations, often centered on the households of great bastard feudal magnates, had private access to the means of coercion, their own authority within a limited territory, and thus an effective right and capacity to govern within a given locale. Instead, the Crown had come to monopolize the legitimate use of force and the royal government had come to constitute the only legitimate, authoritative source of governance. As a result, even the greatest members of the landed class could, as individuals, generally exercise the power to govern and the right to coerce only by securing from the Crown appointments to positions in central or local government institutions. They could ordinarily have an effect on policy formation or on the process of governing only through official and semiofficial bodies—directly through their own holding of formal or informal positions in the government, or indirectly through influencing the king's confidantes, the royal council, Parliament, and the county commissions.

The new situation contained an implicit threat to the stability of mixed monarchy, because the type of balance on which mixed monarchy had depended had been transcended. Under the medieval regime, both the Crown as leading patrimonial lord and the lords of the country could have been said (with a degree of oversimplification) to have controlled their own distinct spheres, lived off their own resources, and governed the country collaboratively. Despite a level of political unity unparalleled elsewhere in Europe, the English medieval state was held together only by the cooperation of its greatest territorial magnates and their followers, secured, to a great extent, through the leadership of the monarch. The monarch, as greatest lord, could operate the state only on the basis of the ongoing collaboration of these magnates. By the same token, because, by virtue of their coercive capacity, these great aristocrats essentially possessed a (local or territorial) piece of the state, the question of the limits and uses of state power did not pose itself as it would later. In contrast, by the time of the accession of the Stuarts, the English state had become a unitary one, and was thus no longer ultimately limited by the private powers of its relatively independent constituents, as it clearly had been as late as the third quarter of the fifteenth century, when national and local government had been paralyzed through fracture and when breakdown had, in part, assumed the form of numerous decentralized conflicts among neofeudal affinities. The result was the emergence of what was, in key respects, a very new problem, both structural and constitutional. To limit, to defend against, or to make use of the state, which had ceased to be subject to fissure into its constituent parts, could no longer be achieved through the restrengthening of local or particularist powers and privileges; it had to be accomplished by taking control of it as a whole.[20]

The question of limits to and control over the state could not, finally, easily be prevented from surfacing; for it tended to be raised, at least in an implicit manner, whenever the monarch differed with the great majority of the parliamentary classes over a policy issue regarded as fundamental. And from the start of the Stuart era, if not before, there was reason to expect such divisions to arise, especially over the interrelated questions of religion and foreign policy. Differences over foreign policy tended to bring out differences over religion, and vice versa, and both tended to bring to the fore broader, unsettled issues concerning the relationships of the monarchy and of the parliamentary classes to the state and to private property, specifically over the crown's independent money-raising capacities (taxation, as well as monopolies) and administrative resources, notably those attached to the church hierarchy.

From the time of Mary's reign and the accession of Elizabeth, the great majority of the parliamentary classes had come to see the defense of a theologically orthodox Protestant religious settlement as absolutely indispensable to the security of many of their most vital interests. These comprised not only the independence of the English monarchy from foreign control, the autonomy of the English church vis-à-vis the papacy, and the security of the crown's and the greater landed classes' formerly monastic lands. They also included the central position of the greater landed classes within the state—specifically the role of Parliament in legislation—and the hegemony of secular over ecclesiastical authority in the realm of religion—specifically the subordination of the church not only to the crown, but also to Parliament. A state defined as Calvinist Protestant had thus become a sine qua non for the parliamentary classes in large part because the construction of a state that would defend their vital interests over the course of the Tudor period had had to take place over and against opposing forces that had, systematically or episodically, defined themselves as Catholic and anti-Protestant—not only the papacy, elements within the old church hierarchy, and Spain, as well (on occasion) as magnate rebels and peasant resisters, but even (as under Mary) the patrimonial monarchy

---

[20] Again, contrast the situation in England with that of early modern France. There, members of the dominant class sought to defend their properties and privileges (which were themselves often politically constituted) from the centralizing monarchal state not so much by strengthening national representative institutions as by asserting localist and particularist privileges, such as the liberties of local estates, nobles' exemption from taxation, and the like. At the same time, they had to be at least ambivalent about the growth of the centralizing state as an absolutist state, for they saw it as constituting, through its offices and other forms of privilege (supported ultimately by arbitrary taxation), a further, critical source of income for their own maintenance.

itself. While it would be rather speculative, then, to argue that there was a straightforward elective affinity between Calvinist religion and an aristocracy that was increasingly capitalist and oriented toward local and national state service, it seems much less controversial to conclude that, because of the specific historical trajectory of the Reformation in England, the greater landed classes had come to see Calvinist Protestantism as inextricably bound up with their position in the polity and society, and with their whole mode of life.

The Protestant settlement was an irrepressible issue because the condition of Protestantism both abroad and at home appeared, throughout the period, to be highly precarious. Above all, in the international arena, Protestants seemed increasingly threatened by the growing strength of the Catholic powers. Domestically, there was less immediate danger, but Reformation religion was, even by the accession of the Stuarts, only relatively weakly rooted in some areas of the country and seemed to meet resistance in specific regions and among important sections of the population. In this situation, led by lineal and ideological descendants of the original Elizabethan exponents of what has been called the Protestant Cause, many of the most important landed-class leaders had come, by the reign of James I, to see the struggle to defend Protestant religion as indissolubly tied to the struggle against the papal Antichrist, whose most significant support came from Catholic Spain. As had the earl of Leicester, Secretary Walsingham, and their friends under Elizabeth, they therefore made the support of Protestant powers on the Continent against Spain and the systematic repression of Catholics at home their highest priorities.[21]

Some of the most important leaders of the anti-Spanish forces at court and in Parliament were willing to go to very great lengths to achieve this

---

[21] On the significance of the Protestant Cause, I am very much indebted to S. L. Adams, "The Protestant Cause: Religious Alliance with the West European Calvinist Communities as a Political Issue in England, 1585–1630" (Oxford University, Ph.D. diss., 1973), esp. pp. 1–12, 24–34, 35–73 (page references are from a revised version, kindly lent to me by Simon Adams), as well as S. L. Adams, "Foreign Policy and the Parliaments of 1621 and 1624," in *Faction and Parliament*, ed. K. Sharpe (Oxford, 1978), and "Spain or the Netherlands? The Dilemmas of Early Stuart Foreign Policy," in Tomlinson, *Before the English Civil War*. Cf. P. Lake, "The Significance of the Elizabethan Identification of the Pope as Antichrist," *Journal of Ecclesiastical History* 31 (1980). Note Lake's observation that "anti-popery provided the perfect basis for a paean of praise for the achievements of the Protestant ruling class and the godly magistrate at their head. But . . . there was no room for respectability to lead to complacency. . . . Rather . . . at home the forces of irreligion, ignorance and residual popery provided an ideal opportunity for the adversary to spread his poisonous doctrines; abroad, the power of Spain and the more general obligation of all true Protestants to come to the aid of their persecuted brethren, were ever present in the minds of the godly. Here, in short, was an activist ideology for the Protestant ruling class, both in its domestic administrative duties and in the direction of national policy in the theatre of European war and diplomacy" (p. 177). On the significance of the Protestant Settlement for the parliamentary classes, see also D. M. Loades, *Politics and the Nation* (London, 1979), pp. 239–40, 243, 246–48ff.

goal: they were disposed to support the idea that substantial additions should be made to the king's regular revenue, were he to adopt their favored policies and consult regularly with the leadership of the parliamentary classes, especially themselves. These leaders did not cease to advocate this approach of *strengthening* the state so as to achieve key foreign and domestic policy goals—in particular the more diligent defense of the Protestant Cause abroad and repression of Catholics at home—throughout the 1620s and during the 1630s, even while simultaneously seeking to induce the Crown to recognize what they believed to be their traditionally established parliamentary liberties and property rights.[22] Indeed, it was in their goals (in practice, not easily combined) *both* of building a strong state, mainly for the achievement of international military, commercio-colonial, and religious objectives, *and* of defending parliamentary liberties, that leading sections of the English parliamentary classes most distinguished themselves from their counterparts throughout most of Europe.

At the same time, because the aim of a strong parliamentary state implied increased parliamentary taxation and growing interference in the localities by the central state administration, it also constituted an important source of political division in the landed class throughout the seventeenth century and beyond. The parliamentary classes were thus united on the defense of proprietary and personal liberties, the defense of parliamentary rights to protect those liberties, and the defense of Protestantism to secure the entire sociopolitical order. They were, however, far from unanimous as to whether these goals should be combined with the pursuit of a strong military and commercial position internationally, requiring a more powerful state, or with a less ambitious, more defensive international stance, requiring a smaller, cheaper state. This difference could be merely episodic and one of degree. The fact remains that, especially as the seventeenth century wore on, those within the parliamentary classes who were committed to a more ambitious overseas program tended increasingly to find allies and supporters among urban commercial elements often associated with Puritanism and Dissent, and perhaps subversion. As a result, division within the parliamentary classes over the government's international commitments, finance, and taxation, took on a more permanent political and ideological character.

In contrast with the strong majority of the landed class, English monarchs had good reasons systematically to refuse to make the defense of the Protestant Cause a point of departure for their foreign and domestic pol-

---

[22] For these forces, see C. Thompson, "The Origins of the Parliamentary Middle Group," *T.R.H.S.*, 5th ser., 22 (1972), and Russell, "Parliament and the King's Finances," in *The Origins of the English Civil War*, ed. C. Russell (London, 1973), pp. 106–8, as well as Russell, *Parliaments*. Cf. Morrill, *Revolt of the Provinces*, pp. 16–17. See also above, ch. 6, pp. 243–47ff.

icy. First of all, to adhere in advance to a Protestant foreign policy would dangerously reduce diplomatic flexibility: specifically, it would eliminate the (in many ways) attractive option of pursuing national security through allying with either France or Spain so as to defend against the other, while opening up the ghastly possibility of having to confront both great Catholic Continential powers simultaneously. At the same time, a Protestant alliance would very likely (though not inevitably) mean an alliance with the republican power of the United Provinces, a relatively distasteful option for an English monarch. In addition, for any English monarch, there were dynastic interests and considerations of power and position within the community of European monarchs that had to be taken into account; to do so was likely to be incompatible with the defense of the Protestant interest, because the French and Spanish monarchical families—but apparently none of the ruling families of the Protestant states—could offer a daughter of a status sufficient to be the wife of an English king. Finally, an inflexible commitment to the defense of Protestantism internationally would make it difficult to stay out of war, to avoid the enormous costs of war, and to maintain financial solvency and keep from depending on Parliament. On the other hand, an alliance with Spain or France could bring with it the potential—through dowries, secret subsidies, and the like from these monarchies—of financial gains of such magnitude as to go far to repair the crown's fiscal weakness.[23]

Were the monarchy in fact, to reject a foreign policy oriented to the Protestant Cause, further points of conflict would tend to emerge. Friendship with either Catholic Spain or Catholic France might logically be pursued by means of a marriage alliance. Yet for an English monarch to secure a marriage alliance with a Catholic monarchical family was not only bound to badly frighten parliamentary classes already attuned to the rising strength of popery abroad; it could not but require significant toleration for Catholics at home, and the parliamentary classes were allergic to Catholic toleration in any shape or form. In contrast, English monarchs tended to approach the question of Catholic toleration far more flexibly and pragmatically: indeed, they often found it practical to recruit Catholics from among the elite to serve as leading councilors or servants; such men, dependent as they were upon the monarch for political protection and promotion, could usually be especially relied upon to hew closely to the monarch's political line.

Disagreements over an ideologically Protestant foreign policy tended, moreover, to reflect or exacerbate differences concerning the formally Cal-

[23] Adams, "Protestant Cause"; Adams, "Foreign Policy"; Adams, "Spain or the Netherlands?"; T. Cogswell, "England and the Spanish Match," in *Conflict in Early Stuart England*, ed. R. Cust and A. Hughes (London, 1989); Russell, *Causes*, p. 61.

vinist Protestant settlement itself, how it should be interpreted and what were its implications for policy. Of course, Calvinism could be perfectly compatible with, and intensely supportive of, monarchy, episcopal hierarchy, and social order. The fact remains that Calvinist religion required intense intellectual and practical self-conscious activity on the part of both its clerical and its lay practitioners in reading and interpreting the Bible so as to understand one's duty to God. It could, in consequence, provide a path to conclusions about the requirements in action of God's Word that were more than unwelcome to those in authority. This was especially so in late Tudor and early Stuart England: the established church itself was but "halfly reformed," its practice still containing significant popish remnants; a large part of the population was unlearned in or resistant to Protestant ideas; and the Reformation itself seemed to be endangered by the growing power of Catholicism internationally. In this context, taken seriously by godly minorities in a sea of unregenerates, disciplinary Calvinism could, paradoxically, lead to the self-organization of the godly, independent of the official church, for purposes of securing a more perfectly Protestant religion—either to (desperate) attempts actually to subvert or overthrow the episcopal order and install a fully-fledged Presbyterian order or to separation by "visible saints" to form Independent or separatist congregations.[24]

In this situation, zealously Protestant ecclesiastical authorities and secular aristocratic leaders, obliged to defend or at least go along with the established church and its imperfections, yet desirous of furthering evangelical activity at home and the defense of Protestantism abroad, might prove excessively tolerant of Nonconforming elements among the godly (on whom they depended to spread the Word). They might also prove all too self-indulgent in fulfilling their own professed obligation vigorously to advise the monarch about the requirements of God's Word with respect to international policy. They might even willingly organize not only to bring pressure from within the political nation on the monarch in an effort to induce him to change his policy, but also, with the cooperation of their friends among the Calvinist clergy, to inform people outside the governing class of the monarch's errors and even to incite them to action.

[24] For the social and psychological dynamics leading to the development and adoption of the ideas of religious Independency and congregationalism that were built into the actual experiences of minorities of "godly" Protestants seeking purer forms of religious practice than those available in the parish churches, see P. Collinson, "The Godly: Aspects of Popular Protestantism in Elizabethan England," in *Godly People: Essays on English Protestantism and Puritanism* (London, 1983). For a parallel account of the tendencies to semiseparatism among those Protestants who made predestinarianism central to their practical divinity ("experimental" as opposed to "credal" predestinarians), see P. Lake, "Calvinism and the English Church, 1570–1635," *Past & Present*, no. 114 (1987), esp. pp. 38–40, 74–75.

Not surprisingly, Tudor and Stuart monarchs tended to move in a rather different direction on religion. Elizabeth I had experienced much uncomfortable pressure from some of the country's greatest aristocratic leaders to adopt a more purely Protestant stance both domestically and in foreign policy; more than this, she had witnessed the emergence of a truly subversive Presbyterian movement among the clergy, some of the key leaders of which received significant protection (though hardly ever programmatic support) from top representatives of the church hierarchy and the parliamentary classes. Elizabeth's response had been to press for a religious settlement more or less self-consciously directed toward the maintenance of monarchical authority and social order—one that was therefore focused on ceremonies and mechanical prayers, that emphasized hierarchy in the church as well as in the state, that discouraged preaching (especially outside official venues), and that vigorously repressed Nonconforming Protestants. Her appointment of John Whitgift as archbishop had furthered all these policy directions. Meanwhile, she had resisted any systematically anti-Catholic stance in foreign policy and had sought ways to tolerate and include within the government Catholics who were loyal to the English state. She had, moreover, turned to Catholics and crypto-Catholics among the elite in order to balance overzealous Calvinist aristocrats at court and on her council and thus retain her own freedom of action.[25] The policies of James I and Charles I ultimately represented variations on the same basic themes. Indeed, both monarchs ended up pursuing interrelated initiatives of which the majority of the parliamentary classes could not approve: to ally with Catholic powers internationally, to increase toleration for Catholics at home, to place Catholics or crypto-Catholics in high positions at court and on the king's council, to follow anti-Calvinist courses in religion, to downplay or repress preaching in favor of set routines, and (at least in Charles's case) to crack down on nonconformity and to strengthen the episcopal hierarchy so as to lean to a greater extent politically and administratively on the church.

[25] On the foregoing, especially the differences in attitude and conflicts in policy toward religion between Queen Elizabeth and many of the top representatives of the greater landed classes in her council and in Parliament, the fundamental point of departure is provided by P. Collinson, *The Elizabethan Puritan Movement* (London, 1967), esp. pp. 29–30, 35–37, 60, 62–63, 69–70, 150–51, 164, 191–204, 244ff. and P. Collinson, *The Religion of Protestants* (Oxford, 1985), ch. 1, esp. pp. 5–6, 11, 31–35. Cf. C. Cross, *The Royal Supremacy in the Elizabethan Church* (London, 1969), pp. 68–94. For further discussion of the differences between Queen Elizabeth and leading landed-class leaders over foreign policy (particularly the Protestant Cause), over the protection of Puritan radicals, and over what should be the nature of officially prescribed religious practice, see also Adams, "Protestant Cause," esp. pp. 13, 25–28, 29–31, 36–42, 55–56, as well as P. Lake, "Puritan Identities," *Journal of Ecclesiastical History* 35 (1984): 119–23, where material on these issues presented by W. T. MacCaffrey in his *Queen Elizabeth and the Making of Policy* (Princeton, 1981) is reported and helpfully discussed.

It cannot, of course, be concluded that it was inherently impossible for the patrimonial monarchy and the parliamentary classes to reach agreement, or that conflict was inevitable. The fact remains that their differing sociopolitical positions within the state and with respect to private property did tend to endow them with conflicting interests and conceptions concerning the proper nature of the state, its constitution, and to lead them to differing general perspectives on foreign policy and religion, as well as state finance and administration. As a result, on what might be termed the menus of policies acceptable to the monarchy and to the parliamentary classes respectively on each of these questions, there were included major policy options quite unacceptable to one or the other. Moreover, while the Crown considered the making of foreign policy perhaps the sphere most appropriate to the exercise of the royal prerogative, differences over foreign policy had the greatest potential for erupting and for creating broad polarization. This was because, in view of what appeared to be a highly perilous international situation over a long period, the parliamentary classes found it difficult to refrain from making their opinions known. But when differences over foreign policy occurred, they tended not only to go along with disputes over religion, but also to set off serious conflicts over royal finance and administration that brought to the surface unresolved differences over the constitution, the nature of the state.

Thus, while the monarchy initially had no long-term aim for an absolutist state and the parliamentary classes no conscious goal of parliamentary sovereignty—and while both certainly saw unity as a fundamental ideal and disunity a major danger—each was almost obliged to pursue its policy goals and defend its own conception of mixed monarchy (the prerogatives and rights there defined) in ways that could easily lead in one or another of those directions. That is, merely to defend its own conception of the status quo, the monarchy was almost bound to seek to increase the financial and administrative resources it could secure by exercise of the prerogative—to build up, as it were, an independent material base for itself especially for increasing and strengthening its patrimonial following. The latter was composed of persons dependent on the Crown by virtue of their dependence upon some form of politically-constituted private property. The parliamentary classes, for their part, would tend to seek strictly to limit the monarch's capacity to raise taxes without parliamentary consent and to restrict his use of the church, notably, the upper clergy, for his political ends, implicitly restricting his policy-making freedom and limiting his own patrimonial administration. Moreover, when significant disagreements over foreign and religious policy did arise, the monarchy and the parliamentary classes could not help being tempted to turn to controversial methods to secure their aims—the Crown to use unparliamentary forms of taxation, thereby threatening the security of private property and of parliamentary liberties, while relying for councilors and administrators on leading clerics, and the parliamentary classes to exploit the power of the purse, thereby challenging the royal prerogative, as well as to seek greater parliamentary control over churchmen and religion more generally. In such instances, there did not exist agreed-on constitutional guidelines for how to resolve conflicts over policy or for what the Crown and the parliamentary classes could and could not do in pursuit of their ends. It is therefore not surprising that both the monarchy and the parliamentary classes tended to formulate divergent principles to explain and justify their actions, with the monarchy turning to divine-right justifications for its obligation to defend the public good as it saw fit, and the parliamentary classes turning to traditional ideas of proprietary and parliamentary rights. Nor is it astonishing that each sought to pursue its goals by forging alliances with other social elements with whom it shared similar or complementary social interests and ideological perspectives. The Crown would tend to build its patrimonial group or alliance by constructing bonds with other social forces dependent on politically constituted forms of property—notably representatives of the upper levels of the church hierarchy, dependent courtiers and royal "projectors" created by Crown grants of various sorts, and London's overseas privileged company merchants. The parliamentary classes would tend to seek allies among other social forces concerned with defending absolute private property, opposing arbitrary taxation, and defending the Protestant Cause, some of them well outside the political nation—especially tenant and owner-operator farmers in the countryside, Calvinist ministers, and, ultimately, the new merchants, artisans, and small tradesmen of London. The result was that, during the pre–Civil War period, and indeed throughout the seventeenth century as a whole, one witnesses a pattern of recurrent conflicts, over unparliamentary taxation (especially of trade) and over religion and foreign policy, that became inextricably intertwined, bringing to the fore major underlying differences about the nature of the state and of constitutional perspective, making for the consolidation of alliances, and leading to serious political explosions.

Unparliamentary Taxation:
The Crown and Company Merchants Allied

By the notion of mixed monarchy that continued to constitute the generally accepted conceptual framework for politics in the early part of the seventeenth century, the monarchy was, in its ordinary affairs, supposed to "live of its own," that is, on the basis of the politically sanctioned financial resources that accrued to the prerogative—lands, feudal incidents of various sorts, and (more controversially) taxes on trade called impositions. Parliament was, in theory, obliged to provide for the Crown's extraordinary needs, above all for military expenses. Nevertheless, because of Elizabeth I's very costly combat with Spain, by the time of James I's accession to the throne in 1603, the Crown found itself in dire financial straits that threatened its freedom of action and with it the political structure of dual authority and responsibility embodied in the mixed-monarchy ideal.[26] Even so, James I felt obliged to make massive expenditures on patronage to consolidate his rule, and, to make matters worse, was unable to control his generosity to his friends and his own self-indulgence. The result was that the Crown soon found itself facing an ever-increasing debt, resulting from a large annual deficit growing out of control.[27]

To cope with its financial crisis, the monarchy had essentially three alternatives. It could ask Parliament to vote it subsidies; it could come to an agreement with Parliament to make possible an increase in the Crown's regular sources of nonparliamentary income; or it could turn to unparliamentary prerogative money-raising measures. Reliance on parliamentary subsidies was problematic because it meant increased dependence on Parliament. The Crown and Parliament did make a series of attempts to arrange to raise the Crown's ordinary income, the most prominent of which was the proposal for the Great Contract of 1610, but they could never come to a mutually satisfactory agreement. The upshot was that the Crown felt obliged to turn to prerogative methods of government financing, and in this field unparliamentary taxes on trade appeared especially promising.[28]

Unparliamentary taxes on trade avoided many of the central political problems associated with taxing the landowners: they did not hurt the landowners materially; they did not depend on local government, controlled by the landowners, to collect them; and, by definition, they avoided further dependence on Parliament. They could also easily be adjusted to inflation. On the other hand, unparliamentary customs seemed to fly in the face of the constitutional tradition that taxes be approved by Parliament. The Crown sought to get around this problem by presenting unparliamentary impositions as if they were tariffs, coming under the

[26] On the mixed-monarchy ideal and parliamentary finance, see G. L. Harriss, "Medieval Doctrines in the Debates on Supply, 1610–1629," in *Faction and Parliament*; see also M. A. Judson, *The Crisis of the Constitution* (New Brunswick, 1949), pp. 122–23ff.

[27] Russell, "Parliament and the King's Finances," pp. 94–99; A.G.R. Smith, "Crown, Parliament, and Finance: The Great Contract of 1610," in *The English Commonwealth*, ed. P. Clark et al. (London, 1979), pp. 112–14, 126; D. Thomas, "Financial and Administrative Developments," in *Before the English Civil War*, pp. 103–9.

[28] Smith, "Crown, Parliament, and Finance," pp. 114–27; Thomas, "Financial and Administrative Developments," pp. 120–21; Russell, "Parliament and the King's Finances," pp. 94–99.

Crown's jurisdiction of the regulation overseas trade. The fact remains that, when challenged by merchants and MPs, James I was ready to justify unparliamentary taxes on trade on principle, for the king needed the income they would yield in order to maintain his freedom, his capacity to act as a monarch. The Crown's judges in Bate's case argued that the king had absolute power to do what was necessary for the common good, a view held by both James I and his son. And to the extent that the Crown sought to maintain this position in practice—as it would do on a series of occasions over the next three decades—it had recourse to a constitutional ideal that was unacceptable to the parliamentary classes. Sharp, principled conflict over the question of unparliamentary taxation of trade was thus a continuing major theme of English politics throughout the early Stuart period.[29]

It was therefore no accident that the Crown sought to have the weight of its unparliamentary taxes fall, for the most part, on the overseas company merchants. It believed, with justice, that it could count on these traders to accept them, because the monarchical government had historically proved such a powerful supporter of the company merchants' interests. Especially because they faced such great barriers to taxing the land, English monarchs as a rule took special care to promote overseas trade as a base for government finance, as well as for other reasons. This distinguished them from a number of their Continental counterparts, notably the French monarchs, who possessed the alternative of collecting unparliamentary land (and other) taxes and were, moreover, under severe pressure to grant commercial and industrial privileges to parasitic aristocratic courtiers, often at the direct expense of merchants and their companies (and indeed the development of French commerce). English monarchs had been ready, for centuries, to grant lucrative privileges to London's overseas companies in exchange for loans and taxes, and because the Tudors and Stuarts were particularly protective of both the Merchant Adventurers and the Levant–East India combine, the government felt it could expect the City's merchants to grant it even unparliamentary taxes as a quid pro quo.

The company merchants were more than willing to honor their side of this deal. To begin with, the company merchants' very ability to maintain themselves, to make a commercial profit, depended on their ability to buy cheap and sell dear, and thus on their ability to prevent overtrading in their markets, and thus, to a great extent, on their ability to exert privileged political control over their markets. Their profits were therefore not

[29] On the Crown's justification of unparliamentary taxation of trade in terms of the principle that it could do whatever was necessary, including levying arbitrary taxes, to defend the people's security, see J. P. Sommerville, *Politics and Ideology in England, 1603–1640* (London, 1986), pp. 151–52; Judson, *Crisis of the Constitution*, pp. 112–15, 118, 127–28, 134.

only independent of any direct participation in capitalist production, but were doubly dependent on the political organization of their economic activity. The company merchants did not trade merely on the basis of individual decisions about the allocation of their resources; they traded in close coordination with other members of their regulated companies, which collectively decided times for trading, the kind of shipping to be used, and individual and total amounts to be traded in order to keep supply and demand in balance. The companies were able to regulate commerce because they could, by political means, limit entry into their trade, and this was made possible only by chartered privileges granted by the state.

The Merchant Adventurers had risen to a position of unprecedented dominance during the century before 1550 because they were able to sell their broadcloths cheaper than could any of their competitors in the European markets, and the Adventurers remained, until the early seventeenth century, by far the most important group of merchants in London. Nevertheless, they were able to succeed in stabilizing their profits and retaining their position during the second half of the sixteenth century, in the face of a serious threat to their survival from stagnating and increasingly competitive international markets for cloth, only by greatly tightening their control over and regulation of their trade. This they accomplished by inducing the government to abrogate or severely reduce the trading privileges of their main foreign competitors (especially the Hanse merchants), by sharply raising the fee for entry into their company, and by excluding from the trade all those who were not mere merchants (retailers, mariners, and so forth). In turn, the Levant–East India combine was able to succeed the Merchant Adventurers as London's leading group of overseas traders in the decades immediately prior to the Civil War because it was able to exploit the dynamically growing English (and European) demand for imports (and reexports) from southern Europe, the Near East, and the Far East by establishing powerful positions in the ultimate markets for these goods. But these traders were able to carry through the substantial entrepreneurial activities that made possible the founding and development of their trades with Russia, Morocco, Venice, the Levant, and the East Indies as successfully as they did only because of the government's willingness to offer them sole access to new areas of commercial development, to provide the chartered privileges that formed the basis for their companies, and to give them significant commercial and political protection from foreign competitors.

Ironically, then, there remained in the very constitution of the company merchants' property and, indeed, in their whole approach to commercial development on the basis of that property, a critical, irreducibly politico-jurisdictional element of the sort that had long been transcended in the property of the landlord class. This was a crucial determinant of their perspective on politics and led, inexorably, to the closest alliance with the monarchy. The merchants were dependent on politically-constituted private property and the monarchy was prepared to create and maintain this for them in exchange for political and financial support. The company merchants, next to the ecclesiastical hierarchy, provided perhaps the best and most consistent sociopolitical base for the Crown during the pre–Civil War decades. Aside from the exceptional period of Buckingham's rule, the privileged company merchants generally went along with the Crown's unparliamentary taxation, failed to join Parliament in protesting it, and worked in close collaboration with the monarchical government. By the climatic years of crisis from 1637 to 1640, taxes on trade constituted perhaps 40 percent of the monarchy's annual income, and the merchants in that critical period showed far less desire to protest unparliamentary levies than did the parliamentary classes.[30]

The Parliamentary Classes
against Unparliamentary Taxation of Trade

In clear contrast to the overseas company merchants, the parliamentary landed classes offered consistent, militant, and principled opposition to unparliamentary taxes on trade, even though these taxes had a very limited impact on their economic well-being. Their opposition is only superficially paradoxical, for unparliamentary taxes on trade appeared to threaten the position of the greater landed classes in the state and thus their property. The parliamentary classes were free to oppose these taxes without ambivalence because their private property no longer depended directly on political powers and privileges, with the result that they did not depend for their very economic survival directly on support by the state. This set them apart from their counterparts in Europe—as well as from the company merchants of London—who secured (at least a significant part of) their material base through politically constituted private property—valuable posts, immunities, or special privileges granted by the monarchy—and who therefore had to be at least ambivalent about, if not entirely sympathetic to, increasing the monarchy's capacity to strengthen itself materially by whatever means, including arbitrary taxation. Some French aristocrats, for example, were hurt by royal levies on their lands (although much of the nobility was exempt), but many of these same aristocrats, like many others, were economically dependent on the fruits of property in

---

[30] For the preceding three paragraphs, see above, chs. 2, 5. "By 1641, customs and impositions were yielding £407,225 per annum, as against £334,480 for all other clearly legal sources of revenue" (Russell, *Causes*, p. 174 n. 49).

office, which were based, in turn, on the expansion of the monarchical state and, directly or indirectly, on the growth of taxation. In contrast, the general success of the English parliamentary classes as commercial landlords left few of them dependent on offices or court perquisites (which is not to say they did not desire them), but it left them vulnerable to arbitrary taxation. They had to view arbitrary taxes on trade as an unmitigated threat to the parliamentary liberties that were the central defense of the property rights on which they relied for their very existence.[31]

Understandably, then, between 1610 and 1629 the parliamentary classes opposed unparliamentary levies on trade consistently, implacably, and on principle. That the opposition of the parliamentary classes to unparliamentary taxes on trade was indeed a principled one can be deduced simply from the fact that taxes on trade were of little material cost to the landed class. Equally to the point, Parliament based its opposition to unparliamentary impositions on much the same principled arguments throughout the period, arguments that spoke to their actual position vis-à-vis the state and their commercial landed property.

Following the Court of Exchequer's ruling in Bate's case that taxes on trade, which always had been taken in a parliamentary way from 1340 through the middle of the sixteenth century, could indeed be levied without parliamentary consent, Parliament made impositions a central issue and an issue of right in the Parliaments of 1610 and 1614. In 1610, the Commons as a body proclaimed that impositions were a direct violation of the fundamental law or right of property, that the consent of Parliament was required for the king to tax, and that impositions were therefore void and of no legal effect. Individual MPs offered the further explanation that, were their property not secure from arbitrary taxation, people could not actually be free, but would have to be villeins. If unparliamentary impositions were permitted, it was concluded, Parliament's authority and perhaps its very existence would be threatened, and for that reason parliamentary consent was required for taxation on trade even in emergencies. In 1614, as the Commons moved again toward declaring impositions illegal, its members made almost precisely the same arguments. James dissolved both the 1610 and 1614 Parliaments in large part because of these conflicts over impositions.[32]

---

[31] See Sommerville, *Politics and Ideology*, ch. 5.

[32] The parliamentary opposition to impositions in 1610 and 1614 can be followed in *Proceedings in Parliament, 1610*, ed. E. R. Foster, 2 vols. (New Haven, 1966), and *Proceedings in Parliament, 1614 (House of Commons)*, ed. M. Jansson, Memoirs of the American Philosophical Society, vol. 172 (Philadelphia, 1988). I also depend here on the very helpful discussion of the ideas presented in Parliament to justify opposition to the king's impositions in Sommerville, *Politics and Ideology*, pp. 4, 135–36, 151–56, 160–63. Cf. D. Hirst, "Revisionism Revised: The Place of Principle," *Past & Present*, no. 92 (1981), pp. 83–84, 86–89. One should note, in passing, a further recurrent

It is true that in 1621 the House of Commons implicitly decided, in the interest of Crown-parliamentary collaboration, not to raise the issue of impositions. But in 1624, even while working closely with Buckingham and taking care to avoid confrontation on the issue, House leaders did not fail to point out that the levying of unparliamentary impositions was a violation of Magna Carta and tended to the overthrow of the liberties and property of subjects. In 1625, as political conflict began to heat up, the Commons took the extreme step of granting the Crown tonnage and poundage for only one year, and issued an implied warning that the Crown's levying of unparliamentary impositions would, once again, be subject to protest and resistance.[33]

At the end of the Parliament of 1626, the Commons did, once more, make impositions, as well as unparliamentary tonnage and poundage, an issue of right, but the crown went ahead to collect both these levies anyway. Taxes on trade became, of course, a central focus of the climactic conflicts of the parliamentary sessions of 1628 and 1629. Meanwhile, in 1626–1627, the government had levied the Forced Loan, and representatives of the Crown had presented a full-fledged case for royal absolutism, arguing in particular that the king did have the right, and the duty, to levy unparliamentary taxes to defend the people's safety, especially in case of emergency.[34] As a result, in 1628, the MPs' protests over unparliamentary taxes on trade paralleled their opposition to the Forced Loan and, not surprisingly, their arguments were much the same in both cases. In fact, the arguments they defended in that session were, as they again and again pointed out, much the same ones they had advanced in the parliamentary battles against arbitrary taxation on trade in 1610 and 1614, as well as in other struggles against the king's levies of so-called benevolences fought largely outside Parliament over the previous fifteen years. As the

---

argument of the MPs against impositions that was particularly appropriate to the emergent capitalist agrarian society: the king had an interest in refraining from arbitrary levies because the security of the subjects' property was a precondition for economic development, since without such security subjects would have no incentive to invest and there would be no increase in wealth to support either the state or society. This position was stated by Thomas Hedley and Nicholas Fuller in 1610 and by Sir Edward Coke in 1621 (Sommerville, *Politics and Ideology*, p. 135). As Sir Nathaniel Rich presented it in 1628, "If there be no propriety of the subject . . . and if there be no meum and tuum, there must be no justice; if so, no industry and then there will be a kingdom of beggars" (R. C. Johnson et al., eds., *Commons Debates, 1628*, 6 vols. [New Haven, 1977–1983], 2: 135). For a narrative of the conflicts around impositions from 1600 to 1614, see S. R. Gardiner, *A History of England from the Accession of James I to the Outbreak of the Civil War*, 10 vols. (London, 1883–1884), 3: 1–14, 70–72, 74–83, 237–41.

[33] For Parliament's treatment of the issue of impositions from 1621 to 1625, see above, ch. 5, pp. 219–21, and sources cited there.

[34] For Charles and his government explicitly identifying themselves with absolutist ideas to justify their policies in the period following the adoption of the Forced Loan and in the Parliament of 1628, see Sommerville, *Politics and Ideology*, pp. 127–31; Russell, *Parliaments*, pp. 366–68.

Commons resolved in a committee of the whole house on 3 April 1628, "it is an ancient and undoubted right of every free man to have a full and absolute propriety in his goods and estate, that no tax, tallage, loan, benevolence, or any other like ought to be commanded or levied by the king, or any of his ministers, without common assent by act of Parliament."[35]

Shortly thereafter, Parliament approved and Charles I ultimately accepted the Petition of Right, which reaffirmed this same principle. Nevertheless, only a couple of weeks later, having discovered that Charles had not in fact relinquished the right to take unparliamentary impositions, the MPs found themselves obliged to frame a new remonstrance against unparliamentary taxation on trade before the king's imminent prorogation of Parliament. With little time for detailed argument, the Commons leaders simply referred back to precedents and their previous protestations against impositions, as did Coke and Phelips, and noted that if they did not act immediately, they would, in the words of Sir Nathaniel Rich, "lose our liberties." The House of Commons' remonstrance against unparliamentary tonnage and poundage and impositions of 24 June 1628 termed these taxes "a breach of the fundamental liberties of this kingdom" and called on all subjects to resist paying them. Less than a year later, the session of 1629 concluded in tumult, with the Commons once again demanding that the country oppose arbitrary government by refusing to pay taxes on trade.[36] The parliamentary classes, composed largely of commercial landlords, could secure their absolute landed property, in the presence of a patrimonial monarchy in effective control of a state with a legitimate monopoly of the means of force and of the authority to govern, only if they could limit the monarch's independent power to tax; it was not surprising that they viewed Parliament's right to approve or disapprove of state levies as a matter of principle.

Conflict over Religion and Foreign Policy

The intensification of conflict over unparliamentary taxation during the third decade of the seventeenth century was accompanied, of course, by deepening struggles over the interrelated issues of foreign policy and religion. Indeed, by the end of the 1620s, significant differences over reli-

[35] *Commons Debates, 1628*, 2: 66, 124, 125, 130, 138, 141, 142, 289 (quotation), 380; 3: 269, 280, 340, 450, 595; Sommerville, *Politics and Ideology*, pp. 157–58; Russell, *Parliaments*, pp. 356–57. On earlier arguments against benevolences, see R. Cust, *The Forced Loan and English Politics, 1626–1628* (Oxford, 1987), pp. 152–58. Cf. M. L. Schwarz, "Lord Saye and Sele's Objections to the Palatinate Benevolence of 1622," *Albion* 4 (1972).

[36] *Commons Debates, 1628*, 4: 447–49, 470–71; Gardiner, *History* 7: 75. See also above, ch. 5, pp. 230–36.

gion and foreign policy threatened to produce an explosion precisely because these differences manifested themselves within a context of already
existing disagreements over the monarch's authority and the subjects'
rights; they were therefore irresolvable by recourse to commonly agreed-
on procedures or constitutional ideas, and led both Crown and parliamentary classes to pursue novel powers, to make innovative constitutional
claims, and to secure provocative alliances with other social forces.

The Bohemian revolution of 1618 and the subsequent attack by Catholic Habsburg troops on Protestant Bohemia and the Palatinate, ruled by
James I's son-in-law, Elector Frederick, placed the defense of the Protestant Cause urgently on the agenda and brought to the fore the implicit
differences in approach to religion and foreign policy of the monarchy and
of much of the leadership of the parliamentary classes. James I, for his
part, aimed mainly to defend family-dynastic interests in the Palatinate,
and indeed only those of his son-in-law's proprietary claims that he viewed
as legitimate. To do so, James sought to secure the intervention of the
king of Spain on Frederick's behalf in connection with his broader effort
to construct an Anglo-Spanish alliance, to be consecrated in an Anglo-
Spanish marriage. He aimed thereby to avoid the possibly disastrous costs
of war at a point at which his government was already in profound financial crisis, to keep the Crown from the increased dependence on Parliament that would surely result from a warlike policy, and to stay clear of
entanglements with the republican Dutch. Moreover, the Spanish Match
offered the possibility of a dowry of such magnitude as could go far toward
solving his financial problems and providing him independence.

On the other hand, Archbishop Abbot and a series of interlocking court
factions led by the earl of Pembroke sought to induce the Crown to come
to Frederick's defense by making foreign alliances with European Protestant powers in order to attack Spain, and they drew powerful support
from a broad range of landed-class leaders, some of them directly tied to
Abbot and Pembroke, others heading important noble and gentry connections long associated with the Protestant Cause—Lucy Harington, countess of Bedford, the earl of Southampton, the earl of Warwick, and Lord
Saye and Sele. These forces thus sought to pressure James to give up the
illusion that Spain would aid Frederick in recovering the Palatinate, and
to break off the Spanish Match. From the start of the 1620s, they began
to coordinate their activities with militant Puritan clerics, based heavily
in London, as well as certain City magistrates. They organized a series of
voluntary money-raising efforts for the Palatinate that proved highly embarrassing to the king. And, as the likelihood that the Spanish marriage
would actually be contracted appeared to increase, they unleashed a fero-
cious preaching propaganda campaign against the government's policy. In
the Parliament of 1624, leaders in the Commons used their power of the

purse, the threat to hold back approval of the subsidy bill, to induce James to approve the substance of their "stinging petition" on religion, as well as to compel the king to follow through on the commitments he had just made on foreign policy.[37]

James was thus brought to see the dangers, if he had not seen them before, of "political puritanism." His general response was a marked shift in what had formerly been his rather evenhanded and relatively inclusive policy toward religion. In order to back up his diplomacy and proceed unhampered toward the Spanish marriage, James implemented a series of increasingly repressive measures designed especially to eliminate the ministers' politically oppositional and religiously controversial "lavish speech," as well as to restrict preaching in general. Meanwhile, he suspended the laws against recusants as part of his attempt to win the alliance with Spain. In addition, reversing his long-held strategy of maintaining a rough balance of power among polar religious tendencies within the church, James began to promote leading Arminians (this despite the fact that he opposed their antipredestinary theology and previously had done his best to squelch it), and came to the defense of the Arminian cleric Richard Montague, under attack in the Parliament of 1624. These moves were politically understandable: the Arminian clerics were uncommitted to the Protestant Cause internationally, rejected the conception of the pope as Antichrist that had come to justify the Protestant Cause, and recognized the church of Rome as a true church; they were therefore quite willing to support the Catholic toleration and pro-Spanish foreign policies that were anathema to their Calvinist colleagues. But the result was that the early 1620s was a period of not insignificant political polarization, foreshadowing in important ways—though not of course inevitably issuing in— the polarization of the later 1620s and indeed that of 1639–1641.[38]

A militantly anti-Spanish position, it must be said, was not without its problems even for the landed classes. Above all, war was almost certain to be expensive, and the increased taxation and stepped-up interference from the central state that would likely accompany war undoubtedly gave im-

---

[37] For the previous two paragraphs, see Adams, "Foreign Policy," pp. 143–47; Adams, "Protestant Cause," pp. 285, 290, 296–98, 308, 315, 328–29, 331; Cogswell, "England and the Spanish Match," pp. 116–18; K. Fincham and P. Lake, "The Ecclesiastical Policy of King James I," *J.B.S.* 24 (1985): 198–202. Cf. P. Lake, "Constitutional Consensus and Puritan Opposition in the 1620s: Thomas Scott and the Spanish Match," *H.J.* 25 (1982). For the House of Commons's use of the power of the purse, see T. Cogswell, "Crown, Parliament, and the War, 1623–1625" (Washington University of St. Louis, Ph.D. diss., 1983), pp. 267–69. See also above, ch. 6, pp. 247–55.

[38] Fincham and Lake, "Ecclesiastical Policy of James I," pp. 202–7; Cogswell, "England and the Spanish Match," pp. 117–22; Lake, "Calvinism and the English Church," pp. 71–72; N. Tyacke, *Anti-Calvinists: The Rise of English Arminianism, c. 1590–1640* (Oxford, 1987), pp. 125ff. For "political puritanism," see Adams, "Protestant Cause," p. 1; K. Shipps, "The 'Political Puritan,' " *Church History* 45 (1976). See also above, ch. 6, pp. 247–48.

portant sections of the parliamentary classes misgivings about pursuing by military means even so good a cause as the recovery of the Palatinate.[39] For this reason, those on the king's council and in Parliament who supported recovering the Palatinate via the pursuit of the Protestant Cause argued that this should be accomplished by recourse to the strategy of "war by diversion." By this tactic, England would directly or indirectly support Dutch military efforts so as to force Spain to divert its troops from central Europe, thereby reducing pressure on the Palatinate; meanwhile, it would also pursue a "blue water" policy of assaulting the Spanish treasure fleet in the Atlantic and attacking the Spanish colonies in the Americas. The diversionary strategy was ideologically attractive because of the implied entente with the Dutch (and Dutch representatives had, in fact, proposed just this joint strategy to the English in 1621 at the expiration of the truce between Spain and the United Provinces). But it also had a practical appeal in that, ostensibly, it could be relatively cheap because it involved only a limited commitment to land war on the Continent and offered the possibility of paying for itself if the Spanish silver fleet could be taken (as it was by the Dutch in 1628). It goes without saying that the diversionary strategy found particular favor with that very small, but politically pivotal, section of the greater landed classes that was directly active in colonial-commercial initiatives in the Americas, notably the circle around the earl of Warwick and his kinsman Nathaniel Rich.[40]

Despite the possible costliness and inconvenience to the localities of military intervention abroad, the House of Commons did, in both 1621 and 1624, express its enthusiasm for a war with Spain that it understood to be more or less explicitly premised on one or another version of the "diversionary strategy." In the Parliament of 1621, the Commons came out for the militant pursuit of the Protestant Cause in its declaration of 4 June and, following a discussion on foreign policy in which many MPs proposed war by diversion, in its petition and remonstrance of 1 December. In the Parliament of 1624, it looked for a brief moment as if the Crown and the parliamentary classes had come together on their perspectives on foreign policy in general and how to recover the Palatinate in particular. Buckingham and Charles had entered into an alliance with anti-Spanish factions on the king's council and in the nobility generally, as well as with

---

[39] This theme is centrally developed in Russell, *Parliaments*. For further discussion of opposition among the MPs to war, see Cogswell, "Crown, Parliament, and the War," where an interpretation very different from that of Russell of the general attitudes toward foreign policy of the House of Commons in the pivotal Parliament of 1624 is presented. Cf. R. Zaller, "Edward Alford and the Making of Country Radicalism," *J.B.S.* 22 (1983).

[40] Adams, "Protestant Cause," pp. 288, 304, 309, 313, 324, 325, 327, 337–38, 340–41; Adams, "Foreign Policy," pp. 151, 161–65; Cogswell, "Crown, Parliament, and the War," pp. 71–74, 95–96, 160, 170–71. See also above, ch. 6, pp. 244, 248–54.

former opponents of royal policy in the Commons, around an anti-Spanish offensive. They appear, moreover, to have become convinced of the need for some variation of the diversionary strategy and, following the adoption of the Four Propositions, which the anti-Spanish elements in Parliament and on the privy council understood to embody that strategy, Parliament agreed to raise by taxation the not insubstantial sum of three subsidies and three-fifteenths for the Crown to begin to finance it. This unity turned out to be illusory because James I never really approved of its premises, and as that became more evident, conflict ensued. Nevertheless, landed-class leaders continued to consider, and to evince considerable support for, "blue water" initiatives even as Crown-parliamentary conflict intensified beginning in 1625. Plans were thus enthusiastically supported by the Parliaments of 1626 and 1628 for war against Spain in the Atlantic and the West Indies, to be carried out by a voluntary private national company, led and financed primarily by the parliamentary classes, which would, upon victory, continue as a company for trade and colonization in the Americas.[41]

From 1625–1626, growing sections of Parliament thus ceased to support the Crown's warlike foreign policy not because they opposed war in general due to its cost, but because that policy came to involve military adventures very different from the one they thought they had approved and financed in 1624. Even as Parliament was completing its business, Charles and Buckingham were negotiating the alliance with France that provided for the toleration of Catholics that James had ostensibly promised not to give. Count Ernst von Mansfeld's ill-fated mission to central Europe signified the government's willingness to attempt the land war that Parliament had hoped it would avoid. Ships lent by the government to the French Crown were ultimately used against the Huguenots.

The nation's involvement in war did lead to increased pressure on the polity, and intensified conflict. But this happened not so much because a monarchical government committed to securing the national interest and the safety of its citizens, but lacking the financial administration to collect the necessary funds, came in conflict with an (extraordinarily undertaxed)

[41] This follows Adams on the Parliament of 1621 (see "Foreign Policy," pp. 160–64) and Cogswell on the Parliament of 1624 (see "Crown, Parliament, and the War," chs. 4, 5). It seems to me that both Adams and Cogswell advance convincing arguments in favor of the traditional view that, in these Parliaments, the House of Commons was strongly prowar, although the issue has not yet, perhaps, been definitively settled. Cf. Russell, *Parliaments*, where the argument is made that only a very restricted number of MPs had a genuine desire for war, that most MPs (and their constituents) generally wished to avoid war because of its costs, and that the support for war that was manifested in these Parliaments expressed for the most part the readiness of the MPs to follow the lead of the king and leading courtiers. Russell does not perhaps sufficiently consider the degree to which the adoption of the much less costly diversionary strategy—at an estimated annual price one-third to one-fifth that of a land war—could have met the objection to an anti-Spanish war that it was too expensive. See above ch. 6, p. 250.

landed class as a consequence of the latter's general unwillingness to shoulder its responsibility for paying for defense. It occurred, in the first instance, because the patrimonial monarch, bent on assuming what he and his immediate collaborators held to be his proper place and power among the monarchs of Europe, adopted specific overseas policies that lacked the support of Parliament. It took place, more broadly, because the Crown sought to implement these policies by means of unparliamentary taxation, as well as other forms of arbitrary governance, while putting forward absolutist constitutional ideas, leaning politically on members of the upper clergy, promoting Arminianism, tolerating Catholics, and repressing religio-political oppositionists.

Parliament's growing opposition from 1625 to 1626 to Charles's foreign policy, and more particularly its insistence on impeaching Buckingham, Charles's leading minister, were taken by the king and some of those close to him as affronts to the king's dignity and, at least implicitly, as challenges to his right to choose his own councilors. Charles responded by dismissing Parliament. Yet in order to continue to govern and to pursue his goals without financial support from Parliament, the king was obliged from 1626 to 1628 to rely on arbitrary taxation: he promulgated the Forced Loan and began systematically and forcefully to collect unparliamentary impositions and tonnage and poundage. In so doing, Charles looked to "new counsels," sought to justify his actions in absolutist terms ("no ordinary rules can prescribe a law to necessity"), and appears to have contemplated governing over the long term on a nonparliamentary basis. Meanwhile, to further strengthen the government, Buckingham moved decisively to use his control over patronage to limit access to what hitherto had been, in relative terms, a politically pluralist king's council; for the time being, entry was largely restricted to known supporters of the government's policy or those who could be counted on to follow Buckingham's lead.[42]

Meanwhile, the government's growing alienation from France had led it to consider steps toward reducing the level of conflict with Spain. Buckingham explored these initiatives from the late summer through the early winter of 1626–1627, and they were furthered by the return to court of some of the main leaders of the old pro-Spanish faction. By the latter part of 1628, the pro-Spanish faction was, once again, predominant.[43]

In this context, differences over religion came increasingly to be seen as the heart of the conflict because they were viewed as inseparable from

[42] Cust, *Forced Loan*, pp. 17–23 (on the view of the impeachment of Buckingham by Charles and his councilors), 27–29, 62–67, 79–80, 88 (quotation), 89–90 (on the turn of the king and his advisers to ideas of arbitrary rule), and 24–26, 188–208, 317–19 (on Buckingham's tightening control over patronage at the center, as well as in the localities).

[43] Adams, "Protestant Cause," pp. 400, 418–19.

fundamental differences over the nature of the state and the place of the leading subjects in it. On the one hand, in the face of the alienation of much of the parliamentary landed classes from its policies, Charles's government carried to its logical conclusion the perspectives on religion and the church that James had begun to implement in the period of brief but intense polarization around the Spanish Match in the early 1620s. It moved to consolidate its support for and dependence on members of the ecclesiastical hierarchy, especially Arminian clerics, appointing them to leading church and governmental positions, bringing them onto the privy council, and employing them to promote royal policies within the nation at large. Over the previous decades, representatives of the upper clergy had, in general, proved much more willing than had those of other social layers to justify absolute monarchy. This is explicable, it would seem, in terms of the direct dependence of the members of the upper levels of the ecclesiastical hierarchy on the monarchy for appointment to what were effectively state offices, which they held almost as private property, and for protection against the militant Erastianism of the parliamentary classes. Monarchs, for their part, often looked to the churchmen to support and implement policies that were unpopular in the country; for the upper clergy were the closest thing they possessed to their own administration of politically-dependent, patrimonial office holders. The Crown thus had an interest in strengthening the church and it was even open to defending the clergy's jurisdictional pretensions in order to form a counterweight to the parliamentary classes. Of course, as Protestant churchmen who were willing to tolerate Catholics and even the pope (were he to drop his jurisdictional claims), and who therefore harbored no principled enmity to the Catholic powers, Arminian clerics found it easier than did their Calvinist counterparts to argue for the king's increasingly pro-Spanish line. They were similarly more willing at this juncture to invoke the divine-right principles that Charles wanted to hear in order to justify the absolutist, unparliamentary measures he was required to take to implement his policies, in particular the king's right to tax without Parliament's consent. Meanwhile, the religious practices favored by the Arminians, with their focus on the sacraments and set prayers and ceremonies and their emphasis on hierarchy and order, appeared to fit very well with the requirements of Charles's authoritarian political courses.[44]

---

[44] On the relatively broad support among the clergy in general, and among the Arminian clergy in particular, for absolutist ideas, see Sommerville, *Politics and Ideology*, pp. 118–20, 127–31; and Judson, *Crisis of the Constitution*, pp. 171–217. For monarchs and prelates, and the willingness of the former to support the jurisdictional claims of the latter, see P. Collinson, *Religion of Protestants*, pp. 3–7, 11. Collinson's description, in this regard, of Elizabeth I brings home the general point: "She had repeated occasion to thwart Parliamentary initiatives in matters of religion and to insist that spiritual matters belonged to spiritual persons. Nothing made the Queen less Erastian than the Eras-

On the other hand, as the government's foreign and domestic political initiatives, led by the duke of Buckingham, deviated ever more sharply from what the MPs thought they had approved, and especially as the Crown turned to nonparliamentary government based on unparliamentary taxation to pursue its initiatives, leadership elements among the parliamentary classes were obliged to activate extra-parliamentary resistance in the counties. In so doing, they entered into alliance with an emerging London opposition movement led by overseas merchants and came, once again, increasingly to support the propaganda activities and the religio-political organizing of militant Calvinist clerics, especially in London and East Anglia. The latter, as in the early 1620s, now preached insolently to the government about the consequences of forsaking the godly Protestant Cause—recalling, as they had earlier, the curse of Meroz; initiated, once again, provocative voluntary fund-raising efforts for the Palatinate; and helped organize the new Puritan political colonizing efforts, notably in Massachusetts Bay. By 1628 and 1629, parliamentary leaders were concluding successive, conflict-torn sessions with all-out assaults on the Arminian clergy and Arminian ideas as crypto-Catholic and as the primary threat to Parliament and private property, with demands to determine the religious settlement that came perilously close to implicit (and innovatory) claims of parliamentary control in this sphere, and with inflammatory calls on the people, especially the citizens of London, and above all the overseas merchants, to forcibly resist the Crown's illegal unparliamentary taxation. At the end of the decade, then, there was more than a grain of truth in the malicious characterizations of each side by the other—of the royal government as "popish" and arbitrary and of its opponents as "popular," Puritan, and careless of the royal prerogative.[45]

---

tianism of the House of Commons" (p. 5). For Charles I's analogous approach, see Russell, *Fall of the British Monarchies*, pp. 39–41ff. Cf. J. P. Sommerville, "The Royal Supremacy and Episcopacy 'Jure Divino,' *Journal of Ecclesiastical History* 34 (1983). For the openness of Arminians to non-Protestant foreign-policy options because of their positions on the pope and the Catholic church, see Adams, "Protestant Cause," p. 22; Fincham and Lake, "Ecclesiastical Policy of James I," pp. 202–6. For the fit between the English Arminians' theology and the religious practice that flowed from this, and the requirements of Charles I's generally authoritarian politics, see N. Tyacke, "Puritanism, Arminianism, and Counter-Revolution," in *The Origins of the English Civil War* (London, 1973), p. 140.

[45] Cust, *Forced Loan*, pp. 102ff., 170–84, 229–52; W. Hunt, *The Puritan Moment: The Coming of Revolution in an English County* (Cambridge, Mass., 1983), pp. 193–202, 208, 212, 214–18; Adams, "Protestant Cause," pp. 398, 421–22; C. Thomson, "The Divided Leadership of the House of Commons in 1629," in *Faction and Parliament*; Russell, *Parliaments*, pp. 380–82, 404–14. Note Russell's comment that "just as the 1628 House had been driven towards giving legal force to Parliamentary interpretation of the law, the 1629 House was driven towards wishing to give legal authority to Parliamentary interpretation of religion" (p. 409). See also above, ch. 6, pp. 261–69.

The Parliamentary Classes
and the Overseas Company Merchants

If the overseas company merchants and the parliamentary classes had had more in common on crucial issues of policy, they might have succeeded in fashioning a more organic, intimate, and long-term political alliance, especially on the heated questions of constitutional principle that were raised during the explosive conflicts of the later 1620s. Had they done so, the course of political struggle during the second quarter of the seventeenth century might well have been significantly altered. As it was, crucial conflicts of interest stood in the way. Most obviously, Parliament was never willing to support, and almost always militantly opposed, the overseas merchants' company privileges. To compound matters, the very parliamentary leaders who stood most strongly against the Crown's arbitrary policies—men like Digges, Sandys, Coke, and Phelips—turned out to be the most steadfast opponents of the companies' chartered rights. In almost every Parliament of the early Stuart period, the Commons fought militantly and consistently to destroy the privileges of the Merchant Adventurers, while simultaneously challenging one extant or proposed trading company charter after another. Meanwhile, through most of the pre—Civil War period, with the important exception of the years 1624 to 1629, the Crown was in theory and in practice a powerful if inconsistent supporter of company privileges and a strong backer in particular of the interests of the merchant elite. It is true and important that the Crown was often a fickle and unreliable friend of the merchants. But since Parliament was never willing to come out in favor of those privileges that were such an essential element of the company merchants' property, it left the door open, over the long run, for the Crown to retain, or to recover, the merchants' political loyalty.[46] The result was that throughout most of the first quarter of the seventeenth century the company merchants went along with the Crown's unparliamentary taxation on trade, failed to offer even minimal support for Parliament's struggles over principle in this matter, and provided a crucial political and material base for the regime, no doubt for those very reasons further alienating the MPs.

Moreover, in precisely the period beginning around 1618, during which political leaders of the greater landed classes were committing themselves ever more fervently to the pro-Dutch, anti-Spanish Protestant Cause, the Levant–East India combine, which was at this time emerging as the most powerful and influential section of the overseas merchant community, was moving in a determinedly anti-Dutch direction and finding more reasons to desire peace with Spain. As a result of the Dutch drift

[46] See above, ch. 5.

toward renewed war with Spain following the expiration of their truce in
1621, English merchants secured a major commercial opening to expand
their activities in intra-European trades, especially with Spain itself, in
which they had hitherto been severely disadvantaged by their inability
successfully to compete with Dutch traders. But to exploit these opportunities, English traders obviously needed English peace with Spain. At the
same time, the Levant–East India combine was, in this period, consolidating a position of hegemony in the Mediterranean that had already
yielded, and promised to continue to yield, enormous profits. This trade,
too, could be disrupted by war with Spain, which might threaten English
access to the Mediterranean. Finally, the Levant–East India combine
found the Dutch to be the main obstacle to its efforts to consolidate its
position in the Far East. And at just the time during the first half of the
1620s when elements at court and in the country at large were agitating
most strongly for an alliance with the United Provinces, Dutch merchants
were dealing the most devastating military and commercial blows to the
East India Company's Far Eastern outposts.[47]

It remains true, and critically important, that as opposition in Parliament intensified starting in 1625, it was able to gain significant support
among London's overseas traders. I have argued, however, that special
conditions were crucial in making this possible. Above all, from 1624 to
1625, Buckingham and Charles implemented policies that were guaranteed to alienate the City's company merchants and especially its elite political leadership—allowing Parliament to deprive the Merchant Adventurers of their privileges; breaking the control of some of London's greatest
merchants over the trades with Virginia and the West Indies; taking away
the customs farms from top Levant–East India leaders used to enjoying
their fruits; and shamelessly plundering the East India Company's treasury, while failing to respond to that company's pleas for political and
diplomatic support against the Dutch. The government delivered the coup
de grace to the merchants when it involved itself simultaneously in the
commercially disastrous wars with Spain and France. The result was that
a vitally important section of the merchant elite first gave public support
to Parliament's attack on Buckingham, then backed up Parliament's fight
against unparliamentary customs by refusing to pay them and by taking
direct, forceful action against the customs administration. Encouraged by
the defection from the Crown of some of their major leaders, company
merchants, especially those trading with the Levant and France, but also
the Merchant Adventurers, played a crucial role in support of the parliamentary opposition from 1627 through 1629.[48]

[47] See above, ch. 6, pp. 271–72.
[48] For this and the following paragraph, see above, ch. 5.

The fact remains that the alliance between company merchants and parliamentary opponents of royal policy during the later 1620s was, in significant respects, both partial and short-lived. First, leading elements in the merchant political elite continued at all points to provide Charles strong and vitally important backing. The court of aldermen gave Charles continuous financial support and vigorously enforced his policies on the citizens. The East India Company came through with a major loan to the king at an especially critical juncture in late 1628. Similarly, at the height of the crisis in 1628–1629, the top officers of the Levant Company sought to prevent it from giving full support to the movement against unparliamentary taxes. Perhaps most significant, Sir Morris Abbot, the Levant–East India magnate whose opposition to Charles and Buckingham initially had most helped to catalyze the merchants' struggle in support of Parliament, moved back to support of the Crown during the winter of 1628–1629. As governor of the East India Company, he prevailed on that corporation to refuse to back the merchants' general strike against unparliamentary customs in March 1629. This action of Abbot's was undoubtedly one important factor, though not the only one, in inducing the leading colonial aristocratic oppositionists Lord Saye, Lord Brook, and the earl of Warwick to launch their challenge to the old elite merchant directorate for control of the East India Company at the height of the merchants' movement against the Crown.

The struggle between colonial aristocrats and elite merchants for control of the East India Company seems to have reflected, directly or indirectly, broad and growing conflicts of interest and ideology between company merchants and landed-class oppositionists during the latter part of the 1620s. Not only were the company merchants entirely relinquishing what had been their rather lukewarm interest in commerce and colonization in the Americas, while moving toward an anti-Dutch and pro-Spanish stance on foreign commercial policy; they were also refusing to support the aristocratic colonizing oppositionists in those new colonial projects of theirs that had explicitly political and religious oppositional aims, notably the Massachusetts Bay Company. This refusal seems of a piece with the relative lack of support found among the company merchants for the Puritan and politically oppositionist Feoffees for Impropriations, which was backed, of course, both by citizen opponents of royal religio-political policies and by colonizing aristocrats. Indeed, at least an important section of the merchant elite was willing to go some distance in identifying with the new anti-Calvinist, anti-Puritan religious direction of the Caroline regime. By the same token, the top leadership of the final and most militant phase of London resistance during the winter and spring of 1628–1629 appears to have come disproportionately from among the very few overseas company merchants who were already involved with the Puritan colonizing companies (and who would continue to participate in commerce and colonization in the Americas).[49]

Merchant militancy was vitally important in fueling the parliamentary struggle of 1628–1629 against the Crown. The fact remains that there did not emerge in London during the later 1620s a movement with enough independent political will, enough autonomous power, and sufficiently extensive and durable ties to the parliamentary leadership to make it possible for the parliamentary opposition, and Parliament itself, to continue in defiance of the Crown. That such a movement did arise in 1640 was surely one central condition for the very different outcome of the parliamentary legislative revolution of 1640–1641.

The Aristocratic Opposition and the New-Merchant Leadership

The decade after 1629 witnessed a crucial restructuring of political alliances. The colonial aristocratic oppositionists, alienated from leading company merchants, sought new allies in order to further their colonial-commercial and religio-political goals, and they found them in the new-merchant leadership of the colonial-interloping trades. Meanwhile, especially following the elimination of Buckingham from the scene and the ending of the wars with France and Spain, the company merchants were willing to resume their old alliance with the Crown on the basis of the traditional arrangement, the exchange of company privileges for financial and political support.

The alliance between the colonial aristocratic oppositionists and the new merchants appears to have found its origins in the religio-political opposition of the later 1620s. During this period, colonizing oppositionist peers carried out joint activities with militant Puritan ministers in organizing and publicizing the proparliamentary, anti-Spanish, and anti-Arminian causes. In particular, the earl of Warwick and Lord Saye and Sele worked very closely with the ministers John Preston at court, Hugh Peter in London, and Thomas Hooker in Essex, and this collaboration was almost certainly crucial in facilitating broader cooperation between oppositionists from the greater landed class on the one hand and those from the lesser gentry and from the middle- and lower-class citizenry on the other. It was in the colonizing ventures that emerged (in part) from the religio-political opposition of this period—initially the Massachusetts Bay Company and the Bermuda Company, and later the Providence Island Com-

---

[49] See above, ch. 6.

pany—that colonizing aristocrats and new-merchant leaders learned how to work together.[50]

About the new-merchant leadership it is necessary to say little here except to reemphasize the extreme degree to which the colonial-interloping traders and the overseas company merchants contrasted in their socioeconomic origins and their subsequent occupations and careers, and the corresponding extent to which their contrasting origins, experiences, and interests led them in sharply divergent, often opposing, commercial, religious, and political directions. Coming largely from outside London, the colonial-interloping merchants generally began their careers as London domestic shopkeepers (retailers) or ship captains, or as emigrants to the colonies. Most of them lacked the wealth and connections needed to secure an apprenticeship to a company merchant. In addition, many were explicitly barred from joining the overseas trading companies, even if they had the requisite wealth, because they were retailers or mariners. The shopkeeping retailers thus found themselves directly opposed to the wholesaling company merchants as an immediate result of the latter's politically buttressed property position, not only because of the inflated sale price of the merchants' goods made possible by their government-sanctioned company privileges, but also because of the retailers' exclusion by the merchants' charters from almost the entire field of overseas trade.

The colonial-interloping traders were especially attuned to the profit potential of commerce and colonization in the Americas precisely because of their lack of trading opportunities elsewhere. In fact, the main reason the Americas remained open to them was that the company merchants of London, who could probably have dominated the field had they wished to, had ceased to interest themselves in it because its commerce was unregulated by a privileged chartered company and because its commercial exploitation required long-term, risky, and difficult-to-supervise capital investments in production. In contrast, the key to the extraordinary economic success of the new-merchant leadership can be found in the willingness and the ability of its members to take responsibility for so many aspects of the spectacular processes of commercial and productive innovation entailed by the colonization process as a whole. Whereas the company merchants thus continued to maintain themselves on the basis of property that remained to a significant degree politically constituted, and systematically to avoid involvement in production, the new merchants not only initially traded without state-backed commercial privileges but were obliged to become profoundly involved as capitalist entrepreneurs in colonial production, first in tobacco and then in sugar planting, while pio-

[50] See above, ch. 6, pp. 262–64, 276–80.

neering the Africa–West Indies–Virginia–New England trades in slaves, provisions, and staple crops.[51]

The basis for the alliance between the new merchants and the colonial aristocratic oppositionists was found, of course, in their common desire to exploit commercial, colonial, and privateering opportunities in the Americas, but it extended, more or less from the start, to their common support for what they believed to be a totally integrated program. This entailed: opposition to Spain and the papal Antichrist abroad by means of war against Spain's Atlantic fleet and its colonies in the West Indies; repression of Catholics at home; opposition to Laudianism and Arminianism in the church; and support for parliamentary rights and for the destruction of unparliamentary levies in the state. Even before the 1620s were over, the colonizing aristocrats and new merchants were collaborating in working out the complex arrangements by which the Massachusetts Bay Company was organized and chartered, as well as in the quotidian commerce with Bermuda. By the end of the 1630s, these allies were working closely together across an extraordinarily vast and complex field of activities: a long series of business initiatives in the Caribbean and North America to attack Spanish shipping and Spanish colonial possessions militarily, to colonize Providence Island and perhaps other places in the region, and to develop land around the Chesapeake Bay; the support of the Puritan colonies as places of refuge for Nonconforming or otherwise oppositional clerics and laymen, and possibly even themselves; a last-minute campaign (following the apparent discrediting of Habsburg promises that the Palatinate would be restored) to win Charles I to an anti-Spanish foreign policy in exchange for a large increase in parliamentarily granted taxation; opposition to ship money in London and the counties; and, ultimately, the movement to secure the recall of Parliament.[52]

Meanwhile, the company merchants were moving in the opposite direction from both the colonizing aristocrats and the new-merchant leadership, demonstrating their willingness to reforge their old ties with the Crown. In this epoch, the Levant–East India combine was going from strength to strength, many of its members accruing vast fortunes by virtue of their stranglehold over trade with the Levant. For them, the Crown's peaceful and pro-Spanish foreign policy was particularly welcome, and they could easily afford to pay unparliamentary duties in exchange for support of their privileges. They were even potential beneficiaries of the ship-money levy. Moreover, the 1630s was the decade in which leading representatives from the Levant–East India combine replaced those of the Merchant Adventurers Company as the dominant company-merchant in-

---

[51] For the previous two paragraphs, see above, chs. 3, 4.

[52] See above, ch. 6, pp. 299–304, 307–9, 312–15.

fluence on the aldermanic board. As leaders in their companies and top members of the City corporation, at all times in close contact with the Court, the Levant–East India aldermen were particularly well placed to induce their colleagues in their companies to see the Crown's point of view. The Merchant Adventurers, for their part, were open to a renewed alliance with the Crown because they were in a situation almost precisely opposite to that of the traders with the Levant; with their trade in profound crisis, their privileges, now renewed and strengthened by the royal government, had become indispensable. The French Company merchants, who had, with the Levant Company traders, led the merchant opposition to the Crown in the 1620s, also found themselves drawn back toward the Crown when they also received strengthened privileges, although at an increased cost.[53]

It cannot be denied that during the 1630s, the Crown–company merchant alliance was fraught with contradictions, which became unquestionably more intense as the decade wore on. As the Crown faced increasing financial and political pressures, especially with the descent into military conflict with the Scots, it showed itself unable to avoid dishonoring its commitments or making new, unreasonable demands on its political partners. Paradoxically, the elite sections of the merchant community were the worst victims of the government's search for increased income and ways to reward other clients. The City corporation was especially hard-hit, as the Crown launched a powerful series of attacks on its privileges and property. Similarly, the East India Company, whose board of directors was virtually an executive committee for London's greatest overseas traders, not only was obliged to pay increased duties on its imports, but saw its privileges radically devalued by the Crown's backing of the Courteen project, not to mention the government's failure to help it against the depredations of the Dutch in the Far East. No doubt the Crown made its greatest demands on these elite forces because it believed it could best count on them to understand its needs. The fact is that, with the exception of its refusal to come through with a loan to the king at a critical point in 1639, the aldermanic court stood solidly behind the Crown throughout the political crisis that resulted in the recall of Parliament: it raised its own loans for the Crown; it enforced ship money right through 1640 at a time when the ruling classes throughout the country were engaging in a tax strike to hinder the war effort against the Scots and to force the return of Parliament; and it refused to make any open protest against royal policies or to call for the recall of Parliament, even in the periods just before Parliament convened in April and November 1640. Meanwhile, during the spring of 1640 the East India Company directorate choked off the

53 See above, ch. 6, pp. 281–98.

attempt by its members to bring the company's rather severe commercial grievances before the Short Parliament, and during the following summer made sure that the company approved the notorious pepper loan to the Crown. Together, the aldermanic court and the East India Company directorate, along with the customs farmers, would form a solid pole of attraction for royalism in the City right through to the outbreak of the Civil War in August 1642.[54]

From the Consolidation of Alliances to the Outbreak of Civil War

The story of the descent from parliamentary legislative revolution to the coming of the Civil War is, as has often been pointed out, the story of how and why a landed class that appeared tolerably unified behind the parliamentary political and religious legislative agenda at least until the middle of 1641 came, over the course of the following year, to split apart. This story, it has been argued in this work, is also the story of the consolidation of critical alliances—for the purposes of pursuing what turned out to be life-and-death struggles—on the one hand among the Crown, the merchant political elite, and through the elite, the great majority of overseas company merchants, and on the other hand among key elements in the parliamentary leadership, the new-merchant leadership, and, through the new-merchant leadership, a London mass movement composed of nonmerchant citizens drawn from the ranks of retail shopkeepers, mariners, and artisans. Indeed, I argue that the causes of the Civil War are to be found to a very great degree precisely in the exigencies that lay behind the forging of these alliances and in the largely unintended results of their construction. By this reasoning, it is a mistake to see the split within Parliament as resulting from fundamental differences within the parliamentary classes over political or religious principles or goals. The landed class was, from a trans-European perspective, rather homogeneous in socioeconomic terms, its members possessing roughly the same interests and sharing many of the same life experiences. As a result, they held, to a very great extent, a common ideological outlook, both religiously and politically. The social and ideological unity of the parliamentary classes was expressed in the striking level of agreement among the MPs on the very extensive political and religious program passed by Parliament through the summer of 1641. The split is thus inexplicable merely in terms of dynamics internal to Parliament or the parliamentary classes alone; it must

[54] See above, ch. 6, pp. 305–12; also V. Pearl, *London and the Outbreak of the Puritan Revolution: City Government and National Politics, 1625–1643* (Oxford, 1961), pp. 79–106.

be explained in terms of forces external to and acting on Parliament and the landed classes. It needs to be understood, specifically, in terms of two facts: that Parliament could not hope to defend (let alone impose on the king) its program of 1640–1641 without the power that could be supplied by the London mass movement; and that an alliance with the London mass movement had certain unavoidable results that could not but precipitate division.

The Civil War occurred because the majority in Parliament felt obliged to make the strategic choice to secure its program of 1640–1641 by turning to the London mass movement. Parliament had little alternative but to depend on London, for, as a result of that same long-term evolution by which the members of the greater landed class had become for the most part commercial landlords, its leading representatives had ceased to command their own private military followings and the state had assumed a monopoly of the legitimate use of force. The members of Parliament and those they represented individually and as a body, were therefore without an existing military force of their own. They were, as a result, faced with an agonizing choice, one that would plague England's antiabsolutist parliamentary classes throughout the remainder of the seventeenth century. By virtue of its enormous population and its extraordinary wealth, London not only could provide the men and matériel needed to create a formidable army, but constituted what was by far the single most strategic politico-military base in England.[55] Nevertheless, to ally with citizens outside the City's traditional governing elite was to take the differences between the Crown and the parliamentary classes for a decision outside the political nation. In 1641–1642, this meant, in particular, giving parliamentary sanction to a radical mass movement to overturn the established sociopolitical oligarchy in London so as to significantly democratize London's municipal government. It also meant placing definitively on the agenda further religious reformation and very likely religious revolution—in the sense of the overthrow of episcopacy and its replacement by a more locally- and popularly-controlled church, Presbyterian or Independent. As a result, the parliamentary leadership's turning to London had to cause a split: it alienated a near-majority of MPs and of the parliamentary classes in the country, who preferred, in the interests of order and hierarchy, to trust their antiabsolutist reform program to a king who

---

[55] As Russell puts it, "Unlike the medieval barons, the peers of 1641 had no armies of their own. . . . [I]n accepting the protection of the radical Puritans of the City, they accepted the protection of a military force that was not under their control" ("Introduction," in *Origins of the English Civil War*, p. 30). On London's extraordinary place within the social economy of the seventeenth century, see A. Wrigley, "A Simple Model of London's Importance in Changing English Society and Economy, 1650–1750," *Past & Present*, no. 37 (1967): 44–70.

had proved himself entirely hostile to it, rather than to place it in the hands of the radical citizenry.

During 1640–1641, Parliament passed a legislative program that, had it been implemented, would have substantially altered the nature of government and the constitution, the state itself. Not only would the parliamentary program have cut short the Caroline experiment; it would also have largely destroyed the potential for absolutist rule, precluding its emergence. In particular, it would have removed, and prevented the further development of, absolutism's necessary material base in unparliamentary taxation. That would, in turn, have prevented the construction of any extensive royal administration independent of the parliamentary classes and, more generally, the expansion of the monarchy's patrimonial following, the members of which depended on one form or another of politically constituted private property. Correlatively, it would have insured a regular place for Parliament in the governance of the nation. In order to rule without Parliament during the 1630s, Charles had extended and deepened most of the policy departures with which he had begun to experiment in the later 1620s. He had strengthened his access to unparliamentary sources of revenue, significantly increasing the government's arbitrary levies on trade and ultimately imposing ship money. This he had accomplished by restrengthening his alliance with the company merchants of London, dependent on crown-sanctioned privileges. He had also increased his reliance on bishops as leading state servants, and at the same time sought to strengthen the church as an independent source of political and administrative power for the regime by fully backing the Laudian program. The latter included attempts to extend the wealth, administrative competence, and jurisdiction of the church, as well as correlated efforts to install a sacramentally based, ritual-centered religious practice that could buttress episcopal hierarchy and clerical pretension as bulwarks of absolutist politics. Charles had, in addition, revived his predecessors' practice of granting monopolies—thereby creating "projectors" of all sorts—so as to further expand his group of political dependants. Meanwhile, he had adopted a necessarily inexpensive, and thus cautious, foreign policy, which leaned in the direction of, but stopped short of any full commitment to, Spain. With the Scottish revolt, and the decision to subdue that revolt without recourse to Parliament, Charles was obliged to go further in all these policy directions, and he ended up seeking political, financial, and military support from various groups of Catholics at court and around the British Isles, while moving toward a real alliance with Spain.[56]

[56] On the final phases of Charles's Personal Rule and the increasing collaboration with Catholics of all sorts, see C. Hibbard, *Charles I and the Popish Plot* (Chapel Hill, N.C., 1983).

In reaction, Parliament took up where it had left off in the late 1620s, but now embarked upon a radical course that it could not previously have contemplated. It banned taxation without its consent, specifically ship money and forced loans, as well as unparliamentary taxes on trade, both impositions and tonnage and poundage. It attacked monopolists and "projectors," further undermining the crown's ability to construct a dependent following on the basis of politically constituted forms of private property. It eliminated the prerogative courts (star chamber and high commission). It established Parliament as a regular institution meeting at least once every three years and passed an act stating that the current Parliament could not be dissolved without its own consent. At the same time, it launched a devastating assault on all aspects of the Laudian religious regime, attacking its leaders, reversing its administrative and religious policies, and destroying certain of its main institutional bases. Finally, led by the aristocratic oppositionists and the new-merchant leadership, the MPs moved toward the adoption of a militant campaign against Spain in the Atlantic and the West Indies that had long been blocked by the monarchy's peaceful and cost-conscious foreign policy.[57] The upshot was in fact (an ultimately abortive) parliamentary revolution around constitutional and religious principles that had the strong support of most of the landed class but which were opposed by the Crown and a relatively restricted body of supporters, recruited, at its core, from those reliant upon politically constituted private property—the upper clergy, courtiers and clients actually dependent upon Crown offices, monopolies, and other such gifts, and great company merchants. This legislative revolution, which basically unified the landed classes in its support over and against the Crown for a couple of months short of a year, needs to be clearly distinguished from the Civil War, which manifested the subsequent division of the landed classes, not over ends but over the best means to adopt in order to secure broadly held principles.

The leaders of Parliament thus maintained a strong majority of MPs behind their program through much of the summer of 1641. Even so, there is reason to believe that the parliamentary majority would have had substantial difficulty keeping Parliament in session and getting its program through had it not been for its supporters in London and the ability of the London parliamentary movement effectively to control the City and

[57] For a balanced and sophisticated account of the parliamentary legislative revolution and its politics, see R. Ashton, *The English Civil War: Conservatism and Revolution, 1603–1649* (London, 1978). For Parliament's action in the sphere of religion during 1640–1642, see Morrill's "Religious Context," as well as his "Attack on the Church of England in the Long Parliament, 1640–1642," in *History, Society and the Churches*, ed. D. Beales and G. Best (Cambridge, 1985). Now, see also Russell, *Fall of the British Monarchies*, passim. For Parliament's anti-Spanish foreign-policy initiatives, see above, ch. 7.

Parliament-London relations. By virtue of their connection with proparliamentary forces in London, the parliamentary leaders were able, during the winter and spring of 1640–1641, to manipulate the supply of indispensable money from London so as to use the threat of invasion by the Scottish army to pressure Charles I to agree to their program. Most critically, in early May 1641, large-scale demonstrations of Londoners outside Parliament and the citizens' readiness to rise en masse to counter the army's plot appear to have succeeded in compelling the House of Lords to agree to convict Strafford and in heading off a royal coup.

Parliament was able to rely on London's financial and military resources because it had succeeded in finding allies external to the official City who had themselves worked out ways to act outside normal municipal channels. The processes by which Parliament was able to construct an alliance with proparliamentary forces in London were, of course, immensely facilitated by the close working relationship already established between the colonial aristocratic oppositionists, who provided Parliament with some of its central leaders, and the new-merchant leadership, some of whose chief figures were also political leaders of London's parliamentary movement. But that alliance was made necessary only because the court of aldermen, which dominated the City government, refused at any point between 1640 and 1642 clearly to back Parliament. Not only did the court of aldermen refuse to support and attempt to prevent protests against royal policies and demands for the recall of Parliament coming from the common council and citizen petitioners in 1639 and 1640; it failed, on its own, in any way to come out against royal policies, or to demand Parliament's reconvening, or to support Parliament's program at any point during the subsequent period. Parliament was able to get around aldermanic opposition, in part by referring to common hall, composed of the freemen of the City, in part by making use of the City's four MPs who had been elected by common hall and who were willing and able to serve as intermediaries between Parliament and London, and in part by forging ties directly with the City mass movement. Nevertheless, Parliament's inability to work through London's traditional political elite, or more generally through economically substantial and politically moderate but proparliamentary forces in the City—as it could throughout most of the counties—had enormous political implications, for it obliged the parliamentary leadership to forge an alliance with London citizens to defend the parliamentary cause against the king, the character of which turned out to be incompatible with the continuing unity of the parliamentary classes.

To get around the court of aldermen, Parliament was compelled to seek allies outside the ranks of those leading citizens who traditionally dominated London politics and was obliged to go along with radical political initiatives that clearly violated London's established constitution. The fact that Parliament could find support within common hall and among the City MPs reflected the rising power of a militant mass movement, controlled largely by radical citizens outside the ranks of the company merchants, which was provided an extraordinary opening by Parliament's need for its support. It seems evident that a significant number of company merchants would have wished to give their support to parliamentary reform, if all else were equal. Nevertheless, to do so they had, as members of the overseas merchant companies, to defy the majority of the aldermanic court, which was largely constituted by top leaders of precisely those companies; that made their task difficult from the start. As political conservatives within the context of municipal politics, they had, moreover, to find a way to support parliamentary reform while at the same time avoiding alterations in the City constitution that were not only desired in their own right by radical citizens but seemed to be tactically necessary to strengthen Parliament's base in the City; this made their task increasingly problematic over time. The result was that the City movement in support of Parliament was dominated by rank-and-file citizens drawn heavily from among shopkeepers, mariners, artisans, and craftsmen, with new merchants making up one (though only one) crucial element of its leadership. Unlike the greater landed-class leaders who guided Parliament and who dominated both government and the church at the local level, these men were largely cut off from the sources of commercial, political, and ecclesiastical power by the privileged merchant companies that controlled much of foreign trade, by the aldermanic oligarchy that dominated City government, and by the Crown and the ecclesiastical hierarchy, which exerted a stranglehold over the official parish churches of London. They were, in consequence, open to radical religio-political courses of action that the parliamentary classes would in general have found antipathetic, but which the parliamentary leadership had to consider in order to confront the alliance of the aldermanic oligarchy with the royal government. Indeed, over the course of 1641, the struggle to defend the parliamentary cause in London increasingly became in addition a struggle to revolutionize the City's constitution and to abolish episcopacy root and branch as the prelude to the introduction of a Presbyterian or Independent order in the church. This was a political conflict that had a clear social character, as the forces of order drew the core of their strength from the privileged overseas company merchants of London and the forces of revolt drew theirs primarily from nonmerchant citizens outside the ranks of London's wholesalers.[58]

Parliament's dependence on a radical mass movement of London citizens, itself in large part due to the opposition of the official City to Parlia-

---

[58] For the previous three paragraphs, see above, ch. 7.

ment, had momentous consequences for the way its leaders were obliged to go about securing the parliamentary program. Parliament's first and best chance to reach an agreement with the king appears to have come during the spring of 1641, with the efforts led by the earl of Bedford and John Pym to gain a settlement on the basis of the king's elevation of top parliamentary leaders to key positions in his government in exchange for saving Strafford's life. This plan apparently fell through because of the opposition of the earl of Essex and other elements in Parliament, and also because of the death of the earl of Bedford before the arrangement could be made final. Still, it is important to emphasize that the London parliamentary movement had probably doomed Bedford and Pym's plan from the start. The citizen oppositionists had made the execution of Strafford a non-negotiable demand and let it be known that they would withhold indispensable funds from Parliament indefinitely and bring ever-greater numbers to demonstrate outside the Houses of Parliament in order to get their way. The open coercion of Parliament by the citizens and the willingness of some elements in the House to make use of London pressure to secure their ends appears to have been responsible for the first large-scale defection from Parliament toward the king and the creation of the first royalist party, during the spring of 1641 (although it is important to note that, even before this time, unwonted pressure from the citizens, especially in favor of religious reform—unsubtly applied through mass petitions, demonstrations, and the manipulation and withholding of financial aid to Parliament—had propelled a small but important knot of leading MPs toward royalism).

The failure of the Bedford plan, Strafford's execution, the army plots, the continuing mobilization of the London masses, and finally the king's announcement that he planned to go to Scotland resulted in a period of deepening polarization during the summer of 1641 in which the search for a settlement appears to have become much more difficult. With the king apparently even less disposed than previously to reach agreement, the Parliamentary leaders were rendered, implicitly or explicitly, that much more dependent on London for the defense of Parliament and for pressuring the king to compromise. As a result, they were even less prepared than before to resist demands for further religio-political radicalization emanating from the City populace. In late June, the freemen of London in common hall, in direct defiance of City custom, attempted to elect both sheriffs, even though the lord mayor had by tradition the right to choose one, and this naturally provoked a protest from the City authorities. Although common hall had clearly violated the City constitution, Parliament felt obliged to consider its case and ultimately to rule in its favor. Shortly thereafter, Parliament began to contemplate action against the Merchant Adventurers' charter once again. A more direct symptom

of the new political situation was Parliament's positive response to the City
wine retailers' request to condemn those French Company wine merchants
and importers of wine from Spain who had agreed to participate in the
royal wine contract of 1638; it had some forty merchants imprisoned.
Meanwhile, the Commons had once again taken up the bill to abolish
episcopacy root and branch with the purpose of pressuring the House of
Lords to agree to remove the bishops from its membership, but with the
unintentional effect of encouraging local Puritan religious initiatives,
even the rise of separatist congregations, especially in London. Perhaps
most provocative of all, responding once again to citizens' demands, in
particular to the prodding of City radical leader and MP Isaac Pennington, chair of the committee for abolishing idolatry and superstition, the
Commons took a series of steps in August and early September toward
religious reformation that went beyond the mere reversal of Laudianism.
The most significant of these moves may have been the Commons' orders
of 8 September, which included an injunction to allow parishes to appoint
their own weekly lecturers. The initial call for this action had come from
the radical parish of Stepney, and the orders were forced through the
House by religious radicals like Oliver Cromwell.

It was Parliament's apparent willingness to go along with initiatives of
citizens largely outside the ranks of the City political elite and outside the
community of company overseas traders—to revise the London constitution, to attack company merchant privileges, and to pursue Puritan reformation from below—that appears to have created the conditions for the
decisive strengthening of royalist forces that took place during the second
half of 1641. It convinced conservative reformers in Parliament that the
further pursuit of reform would inevitably encourage increased popular
and radical interventions in the political arena and in religious affairs,
thereby threatening social hierarchy and political order. It induced Londoners who were conservative in the municipal context but open to parliamentary reform to come out forcefully behind the Crown in order to ensure the traditional City sociopolitical order. The rise of a powerful
royalist contingent in the City, centered on the community of company
overseas traders, was especially significant for the consolidation of the
emergent royalist party because it opened up a realistic prospect that the
king could move directly to deprive Parliament of its London base and
put an end to political resistance.

During the second half of 1641, the king thus sought to build the
power required to confront Parliament. He attempted to win the support
of the parliamentary classes by arguing, with good reason, that the parliamentary leadership was opening the way for popular religiopolitical radicalism and by calling, in response, for the reassertion of the authority of
the traditional episcopal church—and in this he was to a large degree

successful. Especially from the fall of 1641, for significant sections of the parliamentary classes, the meaning of episcopacy—and of religious symbols and practices more generally—was dramatically transformed. From an innovating instrument of absolutism and clerical pretension (requiring radical reform to make its continuing existence tolerable), the episcopal hierarchy came to appear to many as the indispensable guardian of tradition, privilege, order, and property. In this increasingly favorable context, Charles sought to consolidate his alliance with the London political establishment in preparation for a royal coup d'état against Parliament.[59]

It is difficult to believe that Parliament would have split merely because of differences over political or religious ideas within its own ranks. Political and religious radicals formed only a small minority among the MPs and they could not, on their own, have broken the consensus represented by the legislation of 1640–1641. Indeed, at every crucial juncture before November 1641, the parliamentary leadership was able to succeed in removing from the agenda radical ideological proposals that threatened unity. This was so in early 1641, when the Londoners' root and branch petition had set off impassioned debate in the Commons. This was also true in late October 1641, when Pym and his friends, so as to retain unity in order to settle with the king, appear to have called a halt to the discussions of root and branch begun the previous summer and easily quashed the House radicals' attempts unilaterally to pursue further religious reformation on the basis of the Commons' orders of 8 September. Other factors held constant, it is hard to see why Parliament should have become divided against itself on the question of religion or on political principle.[60]

[59] The transformation of religious meanings—including those of episcopacy and the prayer book—that took place in the context of the political polarization and radicalization which occurred during the second half of 1641 constitutes, it seems to me, an indispensable part of the context for the conservative resistance to parliamentary religious initiatives in the countryside, 1642–1649, discussed by J. Morrill, "The Church in England, 1642–49," in *Reactions to the English Civil War*, ed. J. Morrill (London, 1982). For the previous paragraph, see above, ch. 7, pp. 359–62.

[60] See above, ch. 7, pp. 355–57. In his recent book, Professor Russell argues, in part, that other factors were not held constant: it was pressure imposed by the Scots on Parliament to approve a Scots-type religious settlement (so as to secure religion in Scotland) that forced Parliament to split, thereby actualizing an already-existing division that might not otherwise have realized itself. As Russell puts it: "It was the Scots' special contribution to this situation that they constantly forced the divisive questions to the top of the political agenda and therefore forced the English to choose sides about them. Since their English friends owed their power to the Scots' army, they were in no position to resist such pressure" (*Fall*, p. 204 and passim). Nevertheless, as a factor explaining the actual division within Parliament and the landed classes that led to Civil War, pressure from the Scots is puzzling because of its timing. There is no doubt that the Scots placed great pressure on their British allies to reform religion according to the Scottish model; how to respond to this pressure was indeed a source of division within Parliament in the winter and spring of 1641. But, since the Scots concluded their treaty with England in August 1641 and withdrew their army shortly thereafter, it is difficult to see how Scottish pressure could have been responsible for the definitive split within Parliament and the

The Irish revolt brought to the surface the underlying difficulty in the position of Pym and his parliamentary allies. If the parliamentary leadership wished to win its program, it could no longer avoid a direct confrontation with the Crown over what now became the practical question of who was to control the army. In order to defend its position against the king, it therefore had little choice but to take, if only as practical measures, the constitutionally innovative steps of asserting parliamentary control of the king's councilors and of the militia, and to give these force by consolidating its alliance with the London proparliamentary movement. However, it could ensure the alliance with the citizens only by giving implicit parliamentary sanction to revolution in London and all that that entailed: the independent mass organization and mass rising of London citizens to head off the royal coup that culminated in the king's attempt to seize the Five Members; the overturning of the old aldermanic elite and a significant democratization of London governance; and the consideration of the further religious reformation that London mass petitioners placed on the agenda once again at the very height of the crisis of December and January 1641–1642.[61] A near-majority of the landed class found this much too high a price. It was not that they were not strongly committed to Parliament's legislation to remove the threat of absolutism, nor even so much that they found Pym's pragmatically motivated constitutional innovations impossible to accept. It was simply that they found it preferable to entrust their political reform even to the king than to open the way for what many saw as a serious challenge to social hierarchy and social order. The ultimate consequence was civil war.

Those who wished for further religious reformation were, of course, far better represented in the ranks of Parliament than in the ranks of the

---

parliamentary classes which occurred only from autumn 1641 when the Scots were out of the picture. As Professor Russell makes clear, "From [the beginning of May 1641] onwards, the Scots in English politics were, for the time being, a spent force" (p. 202). They would not again assume the capacity to so affect parliamentary politics until the latter part of 1643.

It should be added that there appears to be a certain ambiguity in Professor Russell's argument. This concerns the religious settlement that those who supported the Scots alliance did, or could have been made to, accept in order to maintain it. Professor Russell speaks of Pym and company "committing themselves to the Scots' programme for a Presbyterian settlement" (*Causes*, p. 122). But it is very unclear on what basis he makes this assertion. As he himself notes, it is highly unlikely that what became the leadership of the parliamentary side could, under any circumstances, have been compelled by the exigencies of the alliance with the Scots to support a truly Scottish settlement—viz. a Presbyterian order in which the church was (in theory) autonomous, with full control over the spiritual sphere (*Fall*, pp. 185, 183). Nor is it clear that, even at the height of the Scots' influence, that Pym and his friends ever committed themselves even to Root and Branch. The question is, then, what religious settlement would the parliamentary leaders have been prepared to agree to, and just how divisive would this have been (before religion had been politicized in the manner it was during the second half of 1641)? See below notes 62 and (especially) 63.

[61] See above, ch. 7.

king. Obviously, Parliament offered the best possibility for further purifying the church. Equally to the point, those landed-class elements who had been most active in the anti-Arminian, anti-Laudian struggles of the later 1620s and 1630s had had experience working with popular forces outside the political nation; they therefore probably felt less threatened by them than did others, more confident that they could keep these forces under control, and thus more willing to work with them in the parliamentary cause. Nevertheless, it is in my view a mistake to draw from the fact that parliamentarians and royalists were divided to a significant degree along religious lines, the inference that disagreements within the parliamentary classes over the issue of the religious settlement were what precipitated the split among the parliamentary classes, or that the parliamentary leadership provoked division within the previously united parliamentary class to secure controversial religious goals. Religion appeared to be a central dividing issue, but not because royalists and parliamentarians, in Parliament and within the landlord class generally, were unable to come to agreement among themselves on the question of religion. Most MPs, both future royalists and future parliamentarians, were agreed on what was, in fact, a very thorough and farreaching program to roll back all aspects of the Laudian experiment in the church—to wipe out the innovations in religious ceremony and practice and to drastically reduce the role of churchmen in politics and the church hierarchy in secular affairs. On the other hand, few MPs felt the need for changes in church structure, except perhaps to secure a "lowered episcopacy," plans for which were widely considered during the first part of 1641, winning very broad support.[62] Indeed, a number of leading figures among those who organized the royalist party in Parliament in the autumn and winter of 1641–1642 had been in the forefront of the push for church reform of the winter and spring of 1641, even to the extent of supporting (a highly erastianized version of) root and branch. The issue of religion appeared to be divisive because it had become politicized in a quite specific way, especially during the second half of 1641. On the one side, the newly created royalist party had made the defense of episcopacy the sine qua non for the defense of monarchical authority and social hierarchy, while identifying—not without reason—demands for further religious reform with

---

[62] For the near-unanimous support in Parliament for the thorough destruction of all aspects of the Laudian church, as well as the wide attraction of schemes for a lowered episcopacy, see Russell, *Fall*, pp. 114–116, 203, 220–221, as well as pp. 249–251. As Russell notes, "The attack on the Laudian church did not divide these people [future royalists and future parliamentarians] . . . For many of [the future royalists] further reformation meant first and foremost the purging of idolatry and Arminianism, and they wanted Root and Branch, if at all, more as a means to the end than as an end in its own right" (p. 203).

sociopolitical radicalism. On the other side, London militants had indeed made root and branch reformation of the church a central plank of their broader radical religio-political program. Civil war occurred because the parliamentary classes were obliged to seek to secure their own program by choosing between, and making the best of, these alternatives.[63]

[63] Professor Russell appears to argue that, in the last analysis, it was the refusal of those who wanted further religious reformation to relinquish their goal that forced the division that led to civil war. The crown induced Parliament to divide in this way by agreeing to accept the Parliamentary constitutional program and constituting his own party on that basis, while deciding to hold the line on religion (*Fall*, pp. 401, 527). This position appears to dovetail with, though it may not be precisely the same as, John Morrill's. Morrill contends that "an increasing number of ecclesiastical reformers argued for the fundamental reform of the Church. The Elizabethan settlement was to be dismantled and reconstituted." Thus, "it was the force of religion that drove minorities to fight and forced majorities to make reluctant choices." ("Religious Context," pp. 161, 157.) Nevertheless, this argument appears difficult to accept, even on the basis of Professor Russell's own studies. First, it is hard to see on the basis of what evidence Professor Russell concludes that the king truly committed himself to the parliamentary constitutional program at any point. As Russell's works confirm, Charles I was profoundly hostile to Parliament's constitutional program of 1640–1641 and formally accepted it only under the extreme political and financial pressures that had been created as a result of the Scots' invasion. Indeed, as Russell shows in detail, throughout 1641–1642, precisely to avoid having to implement that program, Charles pursued a strategy designed to eliminate the foundations of Parliamentary power—above all the Scots, but also the pro-parliamentary movement in London—and meanwhile launched plot after plot to overthrow Parliament. The future royalists who joined Charles from the autumn of 1641 did not do so, as Russell implies, because Charles had definitively accepted their own and Parliament's constitutional program—they had no reason to trust him, nor any lever to keep him honest; they allied with the king only because they felt that their program, and their interests more generally, were more secure in his hands than in the hands of the alliance of forces behind Parliament, most especially the Londoners. Second, there is little reason to believe that any significant section of the parliamentary leadership had a principled commitment to a religious program that went beyond what future parliamentarians and most future royalists could have agreed to through the spring of 1641. Indeed, as Russell demonstrates, future royalists and future parliamentarians were equally strongly committed to the across-the-board attack on Laudianism—Arminianism and idolatry—and, through the spring of 1641 were, according to Russell, in full agreement on religious program more generally, even if "similar views were held for . . . highly different reasons" (see fn. 62; quotation from *Fall*, p. 220). Thus, with regard to further reformation beyond what had been achieved in spring 1641, Russell makes perfectly clear that "for most of the junto . . . Root and Branch was not a fundamental issue of principle" (Russell, *Causes*, 60). Pym and the parliamentary leadership would have been more than willing to accept many of the schemes for lowered, elected bishops put forward in the first part of 1641, for, as Russell himself states, these would have achieved most of the goals with which they were primarily concerned, especially depriving the king of the use of bishops as political instruments (and for which they had considered abolishing episcopacy in the first place). (Russell, *Fall*, pp. 250–251.) Of course, "[f]or Charles such a scheme was entirely beside the point." The parliamentary leadership turned to root and branch in late May-June 1641, with the support of a number of figures who were in no way religious militants, only after the house of lords had refused to eliminate bishops from their body, setting up in this way a fundamental obstacle to further politico-constitutional reform. As Russell puts it, "It is only after the Army Plot that, for the first time, the junto showed a vigorous and united commitment to Root and Branch. In these circumstances, it was not only a religious programme: it was a constitutional one, whose major

Roots of Radicalization

As things turned out, those who had feared that, if Parliament broke with the king and allied, as it would have to, with London's popular forces, the political dispute between king and Parliament would get beyond the control of the governing class, proved correct. From 1642, in order to fight the king, Parliament had to depend on various London factions, the Scots, and ultimately the New Model Army, with the result that at many turning points during the decade its decisions expressed the influence of forces outside it as much as its own independent deliberations. The impact of the evolution of politics in London on national developments is only part of a larger story that has yet to be fully explored, but that impact is still worth reviewing.

Schematically speaking, during the middle and late 1640s, London merchant politics, and City politics generally, were heavily shaped by the struggle among three major political forces: radicals, moderate parliamentarians, and crypto-royalists. Much of the time, these political forces were obliged to secure their ends by choosing the least unfavorable political means from among an array of options presented to them by broader national forces—royalists, Parliament, the competing parliamentary factions, the Scots, and the New Model Army. Yet it is also true that each of these political forces was, at crucial turning points, able to shape political choices made at the level of national politics and thus to determine the course of intraparliamentary and royalist-parliamentary conflict.

Recruited and led by citizens from outside the company merchant community, colonial-interloping traders prominently among them, the City radicals dominated the City revolution of 1641–1642, organizing the mass petitions, mobilizing the mass demonstrations, and taking charge of the citizens' rising that secured the City against Charles I's attempted

---

object was to deprive the King of the power to control the church." (Russell, *Causes*, pp. 60, 121; Cf. Russell, *Fall*, p. 203.) Finally, as Russell himself points out, whatever their religious preferences, "the debates, and even more the reluctance privately expressed to the Scots by their friends, suggest that *most of the English did not want a further reformation badly enough to risk a civil war for it*" (*Fall*, pp. 203–4, emphasis added). In this light, it is difficult to see how a militant religious minority within the parliamentary classes could, on its own, have forced a split over, and war for, further reformation. This is especially so, in view of the fact that few if any of those noble chieftains who constituted much of the heart of the parliamentary leadership—men like Bedford, Essex, Saye, and Warwick—would have agreed to fight a war for further reformation, or could have been compelled by others in Parliament to have done so. As Professor Russell concludes at another point, "to say the parties were divided by religion is not the same thing as to say religion caused the Civil War" (Russell, *Causes*, p. 59; also pp. 21, 58). The political nation did not split and fight the Civil War in order to achieve, or prevent, further reformation (although those who wanted further reformation ended up disproportionally on the side of Parliament, while those who did not ended up disproportionally on the side of the king).

coup. It was on the basis of their militant activity, pursued for the most part outside official London institutions, that they succeeded in elevating the common council to a central position in government decision making (in place of the court of aldermen) and in constructing an initial power base for themselves within the City—in the London militia and above all on the temporarily omnipotent militia committee. During the following months, they vastly enhanced their influence, both in London and nationally, by making signal contributions, far out of proportion to their numbers, to the construction of the new parliamentary regime—its army, its navy, its military provisioning, and its finance. Meanwhile, they flexed their muscles by organizing their own Additional Sea Adventure to Ireland, an early and spectacular manifestation of the radicals' cohesiveness, of their impressive material resources, and of their vanguard political role.[64]

During 1642–1643, the London radical movement continued, as it had during the revolutionary days of the winter and spring of 1641–1642, to work in an intimate alliance with the parliamentary middle group in support of joint efforts to build the parliamentary military and financial machine, an arrangement no doubt facilitated by the long history of collaboration between a number of the leaders of the middle group and the new-merchant leadership. Nevertheless, this alliance, conjoining as it did forces drawn from extremely different social layers and holding contrasting religio-political views, was always fraught with tension, and the City radicals did not, in fact, prove reluctant to break with the middle group's politics, both strategically and ideologically, when this became necessary for the achievement of their goals. Using their newly found and rapidly growing influence within the parliamentary cause, both nationally and locally, the radicals launched an independent offensive, beginning in the late autumn of 1642 and extending through much of the summer of 1643, that aimed to transform Parliament's effort both politically and militarily. They sought to make up for Parliament's indecisive military campaigns and the halfheartedness of its aristocratic leadership by creating a new, citizen-based, revolutionary military force controlled by themselves through new revolutionary institutions. The radicals' efforts to achieve this goal were marked, most strikingly, by their willingness to turn to the mass mobilization of the citizens and to justify this turn in the most radical, indeed quasi-democratic terms—as they did in their justification of radical City electoral reform in the spring of 1642, their small revolution in St. Dunstan's-in-the-East in the spring of 1643, and in their *Petition and Remonstrance* of the same period. The outcome of the citizen radicals' efforts was to make possible the greatest challenge by war-party radical

[64] See above, ch. 7, pp. 362–74; ch. 8, pp. 397–410, 427–35.

forces in Parliament for national political leadership at any time before 1647–1648.[65]

The openness of the City radicals to relatively extreme ideological conceptions should be understood, in part, in terms of the tactical exigencies of the moment: given the war party's minimal strength within Parliament, the MPs could be induced to accept the radicals' program for reforming Parliament's military effort only under pressure from the urban masses. But the City radical leadership's openness to rather extreme religio-political conceptions and its willingness to depend on the London populace is also at least partially understandable in terms of its own derivation from socioeconomic layers below the ranks of the company merchant community, and its origins among the shopkeepers, ship captains, and smaller domestic traders that constituted, along with artisans and craftspeople, the radical movement's rank and file. Indeed, the opposition between new-merchant leaders (who for the most part came from this layer, and who made up one, though only one, crucial element of the City radical leadership) and the Levant–East India merchant leaders (who constituted much of the core of City conservatism and royalism) expressed the enormous shift, not only politically but also socioeconomically, in the locus of political initiative and influence that occurred in the City between 1640 and 1643. Finally, the ideological predilections of the radical citizens were to a significant degree influenced by—and of a piece with—their religious tendencies toward a militant Puritanism aiming for local, as well as a high degree of popular, control of the church. Independent ministers made an enormous contribution to the ideological as well as the organizational leadership of the City radical movement, and a disproportionate number of the movement's lay leaders were religious Independents, parochial or congregational.

During the winter and spring of 1643, the City radical movement was obliged to distance itself to an ever-greater degree from the parliamentary middle-group leadership in order to carry out at the level of national politics its campaign for creating its own volunteer army and especially for removing from the command of the parliamentary army the earl of Essex, to whom Pym and his friends were strongly devoted. In so doing, the radicals repudiated the middle group's insistence on justifying resistance to the king in the fictitious terms of opposition to the king's evil councilors and the defense of traditional constitutional arrangements, and put forward instead a call for parliamentary supremacy justified in terms of the principle of popular sovereignty. At the same time, they moved into ever-closer alliance with "fiery spirits" in the House of Commons with whom they worked to secure parliamentary sanction for their project. The alli-

---

[65] For this and the following three paragraphs, see ch. 8.

ance between the City radical movement and war-party militants in Parliament reached the apex of its power during the early summer of 1643. As the military fortunes of the parliamentary army reached their lowest ebb, the radicals' call for new military and political leadership as well as reorganization based on innovative forms of mass mobilization, appears to have carried increasing conviction both inside and outside Parliament. The radicals were thus able to impose on Parliament—contravening all constitutional propriety and parliamentary privilege—their plan for a volunteer army. Simultaneously with Parliament's assent to the establishment of the committee for a general rising and with the appointment of Sir William Waller to head both the volunteer army and the City militia, the Commons' war-party radicals seem to have wrested, if only for a moment, control of the parliamentary cause from the parliamentary middle group.

Nevertheless, the allied City and parliamentary radicals never realized their plans. The war-party radical MPs were dependent on the radical citizens, but the latter never consolidated a base within the official City government. As the military crisis was gradually transcended, the radicals appear steadily to have lost influence among the mass of the citizens and with it all hope of retaining their position of power. From then on, in both London and Parliament, they were forced onto the defensive.

Political Presbyterians and Political Independents

The radicals' failure opened the way for the rise to power within the City of a massive and powerful, if rather heterogeneous, alliance of forces that can be called moderate parliamentarian, which dominated the City government throughout the middle years of the 1640s. Basing their power in their control of the common council, the moderates were the chief beneficiaries of the revolution that had elevated the common council to the dominant position in City decision making; most of them had not been, however, among the revolution's makers, having identified themselves with Parliament and the new City regime for the most part only after the City revolution had been completed and London secured for Parliament. As newcomers to power, the moderates were, above all, set on creating the conditions for consolidating their rule. They were thus naturally quite committed to securing Parliament's victory and to securing the new City regime against the return of the old aldermanic oligarchy. Characteristically, however, they were determined to establish full-fledged Presbyterian rule in the City—as the instrument for furthering Puritan reformation; as the means of gaining for the citizenry municipal and parish control over their own churches; and, increasingly, as perhaps the main mechanism for repressing rising movements of religio-political radicalism that threatened further revolution.

The London moderates attracted only relatively limited support from the overseas company merchants, who remained strongly royalist and constitutionally conservative in City politics, although a handful of Merchant Adventurers did emerge among the moderates' key leaders. The moderates' leadership was for the most part recruited, instead, from citizens of what might be called the second rank, although it distinguished itself from the pre–Civil War leadership less by its smaller wealth than by its overwhelmingly local business interests. Although no doubt for the most part economically well-off, the new London leaders of the Civil War period did see that a substantial political gap—if not always an unambiguous or unbridgeable one—separated them from the old City elite.[66]

So long as the war had to be fought, the City moderates were strong backers of Parliament's military effort. Until Parliament was victorious, they were thus more or less steadfast backers of the middle-group and war-party leadership, which pushed for measures to prosecute the war more effectively, from the middle of 1643 through the middle of 1645. Indeed, interventions backed by the London moderates appear to have been crucial to the defense of the City and Parliament from royalist attack in the summer of 1643, in helping to get through Parliament the Scottish alliance and the establishment of the committee of both kingdoms in the first half of 1644, and in securing the constitution of the New Model Army in the spring of 1645. Nevertheless, as soon as the war did end, the City moderates became progressively more alienated from the parliamentary leadership. This was because the middle-group and war-party descendants who came to constitute the political independent alliance in Parliament were progressively less willing to tolerate the City's single-minded efforts to achieve a Presbyterian ecclesiastical order, for these ran counter to the MPs' goal of an Erastian settlement that would ensure and strengthen parliamentary and landed-class control over the church. The City moderates, for their part, became increasingly uncompromisingly Presbyterian in response to what they saw as a growing threat of religio-political radicalization and social disruption from below.[67]

To achieve what were in essence local goals, the City moderate or political presbyterian leaders joined the parliamentary political presbyterians and the Scots in the tripartite political presbyterian alliance for a national political settlement. The political presbyterians in Parliament had little sympathy for religious Presbyterianism per se, but hoped to use the

[66] For the previous two paragraphs, see ch. 9.

[67] See ch. 9, pp. 465–68.

strength of the political presbyterian alliance to impose on Parliament (and the king) a speedy settlement to the conflict in the interests of social hierarchy, social order, and the end of political and religious radicalism from below. The Scots, with little concern for the niceties of a constitutional settlement in England, hoped to use the political presbyterian alliance to impose a Presbyterian church settlement so as to protect the Presbyterian system in Scotland from English intervention. The Londoners would seem to have needed some sort of guarantee from the king of the rights and powers of Parliament simply to secure the survival of their own local regime; they nonetheless showed decreasing concern for parliamentary constitutional goals and greater openness to outright royalist designs in their single-minded drive for a Presbyterian religious settlement. This, despite the fact that Charles was probably even less likely to agree to a Presbyterian religious outcome than was Parliament.

The political presbyterian leaders in Parliament had little choice but to place their fate in the hands of outside forces: the Scots and London. Indeed, between 1646 and 1648, proceedings in Parliament were subject to determination as much by external forces as by the MPs themselves. When the Scottish army proved more of a political liability than a real source of power to the political presbyterians, the political presbyterian cause came to depend increasingly on London municipal backing, pressure from the City masses, and the threat of City military intervention. In fact, once the Scots had left the scene at the end of 1646, the political presbyterians, now enjoying a parliamentary majority, appeared well on their way to the successful use of their London base to secure the settlement they desired. Nevertheless, although in full control of the municipality, and able to remodel the militia and recruit their own military forces, London's political presbyterians never had enough support in the City to underwrite a highly risky, potentially catastrophic confrontation with the New Model Army.[68]

In the course of the City's political presbyterian offensive of 1646–1647—and again in 1648—crypto-royalist forces played an ever more prominent role. A powerful royalist party had, of course, made a nearly successful bid to defend the City's oligarchic constitution and keep London firmly in the king's camp in 1641–1642. The influence of the royalists did not, moreover, end when their offensive failed: possessing the self-confidence and internal cohesiveness of longtime rulers of the City, and retaining the support of much of the extraordinarily powerful overseas company merchant community, they continued, informally, unofficially, and largely sub rosa, to exert a significant influence over the course of events. During the winter of 1642–1643, when moderate, if proparlia-

---

[68] For the previous two paragraphs, see ch. 9, pp. 462–65, 468–80.

mentary, forces in London were having doubts about continuing the war, the crypto-royalists helped mount a powerful bid for an unconditional peace. Then, when the City's moderates sealed their alliance with Denzil Holles and his political presbyterian friends and began seriously to court the king during the spring of 1646, the crypto-royalists were able not only to come out into the open, but ultimately to help lead the political presbyterian assault on the parliamentary political independent alliance and the army during the first half of 1647. The latent power of London's traditional rulers—rooted especially in the community of overseas company merchants—was once again reasserting itself.[69]

The response of London radicalism to the accelerating political presbyterian steamroller of 1645–1647 was indecisive and often disunited. During the middle 1640s, leading elements in the old radical alliance, including a number of key new-merchant leaders, had established lucrative and influential positions in the new parliamentary state. They had also vastly expanded their wealth, especially by the recent development of sugar planting in the West Indies and perhaps also by their large-scale interloping venture in the East Indies. The radicals still held out hope for a revolutionary settlement that would bring parliamentary supremacy, a mild tolerationism, and a militant commercial and colonially oriented foreign policy. Yet they were reluctant to launch a struggle for these goals by means of the mass mobilization of the London populace—especially in view of the declining support for the radicals in London after the military emergency of the summer of 1643 was transcended—and were well on their way to separating their goal of some form of republican rule from any democratic trappings. As a result, they tended to rely in practice on the middle-group/war-party political independent alliance in Parliament and were correspondingly far more reluctant to chart an independent political course than they had been in the period through 1643. More militant elements of the old radical alliance—some of them apparently veterans of the Salters Hall committee of 1643–1644 and drawn from among the more radical of the Independent, as well as from certain separatist, congregations—do appear to have been willing to contemplate popular resistance to the threat from the political presbyterians. But even they were at best ambivalent about the Leveller movement that actually took this task into its own hands. As a result, the fate of London, and of England as a whole, in 1647 and 1648 was determined by decisions made inside the New Model Army.

The drive to power by the army's hesitant and ambivalent officer corps turned out to be a godsend for the less extreme among the London radicals who, by the end of the 1640s, composed the core of City political inde-

---

[69] See ch. 8, pp. 435–36; ch. 9, pp. 478–79, 485–86.

pendency—and above all for the new-merchant leadership. The inability, on the one hand, of the middle-group leaders either to impose a constitutional settlement on the king or to break decisively with him, and the pressure from a rising radical movement in the army rank and file, on the other hand, forced the army leaders to make the revolution of 1648. In order to take power, the army officers corps had little choice but vastly to reduce the influence of all of its more conservative opponents—including the political presbyterians and outright royalists in the City, as well as the entire spectrum of political factions in Parliament up to and including most of even the more adventurous among the old middle groupers. Then, in order to consolidate the new regime, it was obliged to destroy most of its more radical former allies, especially the Levellers. The result was that the City political independents, the new-merchant leaders prominently among them, found the way cleared for an extraordinary assertion of their influence. Their path to influence was made that much smoother by the many ties they had constructed with leaders both among the radical MPs and within the army officer corps, with whom they had much in common ideologically. They could firmly consolidate their new position of power in the City and nationally by virtue of the pivotally important political base they could offer a new Commonwealth government that was profoundly isolated from almost all elements within the old governing class and desperately in need of allies.[70]

The Meaning of the Commonwealth

The upshot was a new political regime that has sometimes been improperly categorized as essentially conservative. Understandably, the Commonwealth did appear conservative to its critics among the Levellers and within the separatist churches of London, for it drew the line sharply against further political democratization and against additional reforms that might threaten private property. But its leaders, its goals, and its achievements were far too radical to allow it to win the acceptance of the overwhelming majority of the parliamentary landed classes that dominated every English government before 1648 and after 1660, and that succeeded to a significant degree in moderating even the Commonwealth's politics. The Commonwealth's top leadership was drawn to a very significant extent from ideological republicans and other radicals who could not have come close to power in any government before or after the Interregnum. It represented distinctive strains of reform opinion on politics, religion, the law, and commerce that were ideologically extremist from the

[70] For the previous three paragraphs, see ch. 10.

standpoint of the overwhelming majority of the parliamentary classes, if inadequately radical from the standpoint of the artisan- and crafts-based Levellers and separatists. And it rested on—and was given its distinct political ideological coloring by—social layers nationally, in the army, and in London, significantly below or outside the traditional governing classes, most notably the newly ascendant political independent rulers of London, prominently including the new-merchant leadership.

In constitutional terms, the Commonwealth established parliamentary supremacy based on popular sovereignty, but reduced popular sovereignty to little more than parliamentary supremacy itself. It sought to use its rather limited powers to reform governmental administration and the law in the interests of efficiency and progress by opening careers to talents and reducing the role of privilege, while warding off any and all threats to legal professionalism and the prerogatives of private property. In religious affairs, the new regime eliminated all hopes of episcopal or Presbyterian hierarchical rule, and established instead a mildly tolerationist order in which mainstream Independent ministers enjoyed a hegemonic position, but where religious dissidence that might lead to public disorder or political subversion was harshly repressed. Perhaps most striking of all, the Commonwealth installed a militant approach to foreign policy that was unprecedentedly favorable to the expansion of English trade and empire. Commonwealth overseas policy thus had the following effects: it encouraged the greatest possible commercial investment, expansion, and innovation, notably by organizing the newly reconstituted East India Company according to the free-trade program of the colonial-interloping leadership; it secured English merchants' hegemony, over and against the Dutch, in the colonies of North America and the West Indies, especially via the Act of Trade of 1650 and the subsequent voyages of conquest to Virginia and the West Indies; it provided English merchants and shippers maximal protection in their traditional European and Mediterranean routes, especially by means of the Convoy Act and the naval voyages of Robert Blake and of Sir George Ayscue of 1650–1651; finally, having failed in its perhaps utopian goal of political unity (and commercial collaboration) with the United Provinces, it initiated the use of political and military force to secure commercial and colonial parity with the Dutch, especially via the navigation act and the first Dutch war.[71]

Precisely because Commonwealth policy across the board expressed so very well the distinctive perspectives, aspirations, and interests of the City political independents in general and the new merchants in particular, it could appeal only to a very narrow range of social and political interests within the nation. The alliance of what I have termed moderate republican

---

[71] For the previous two paragraphs, see chs. 10, 11, 12.

forces that governed nationally and in London under the Commonwealth exerted an influence that could not possibly be justified by its real social and political weight within English society. It was not therefore surprising that the republican regime had few resources with which to defend itself, and that when its opponents in the army moved to dismantle it, it went with a whimper, not a bang.[72]

Conclusion

The Restoration and its sequels amounted to a significant repudiation of the parliamentary legislative revolution of 1641 and of the array of forces that had stood behind it—an alliance led by a largely capitalist parliamentary landlord class, headed by great aristocrats concerned with enhancing the power of the English state for religious and commercial objectives, and notably supported by colonial merchants in the Americas and interlopers in the East Indies who helped lead a London mass movement, composed mostly of shopkeepers, artisans, ship captains, and some small wholesale traders. Between 1660 and 1688, then, as between 1618 and 1640, the Crown was able on a series of occasions to initiate political experiments with the interrelated aims of securing financial and administrative independence for the monarchy—especially by increasing revenue from customs and strengthening the episcopal hierarchy as well as London's oligarchic court of aldermen, bulwarks of royal power—and ruling without Parliament, while pursuing an alliance with—and major financial subsidies from—the leading Catholic and absolutist power of Europe, now France rather than Spain. The corresponding inability of the politics of anti-absolutism to consolidate itself—focused as it was on the assertion of parliamentary rights, the assault on Catholicism domestically and internationally (especially as a stalking-horse for absolutism), the attack on Charles's pro-French foreign policy and support for a pro-Dutch alternative, and the opposition to the political pretensions of the ecclesiastical hierarchy—was evident from the time of the Exclusion Crisis. In the years 1678–1681, a great aristocratic capitalist, the earl of Shaftesbury, with socioeconomic interests and ideological perspectives analogous to those of the great landed-class leaders who had stood at the head of Parliament in 1641, was thus obliged to organize an alliance of forces very much like that of 1641 for a Protestant and politico-constitutional program analogous to that of 1641, which had itself been adumbrated in 1628–1629 and, to a certain limited extent, even in the early 1620s. This program included, besides the Exclusion of the Catholic James Stuart and

---

[72] See ch. 13.

a turn to a Protestant anti-French foreign policy, greater parliamentary control of financial resources available to the government, church reform aimed at reducing the bishops' political influence, the disbanding and prevention of a standing army, and the safeguarding of parliamentary liberties, including regular meetings of Parliament (not simply at the king's discretion) and protection of the independence of the MPs and of the electorate from corruption by the Crown.[73] As in 1641, moreover, this program not only won the backing of a strong majority of the parliamentary classes, carrying the day ever more easily in three consecutive Parliaments, but also brought behind itself, within a broad alliance, a significant part of the London populace outside the municipal sociopolitical elite, as well as other political forces from outside the political nation throughout England. Indeed, as had Pym and his friends in 1641, the Exclusionist forces in Parliament depended on London's four staunchly Whig MPs to represent the Exclusionist cause in Parliament and to help organize a powerful citizens' mass movement to support Exclusion and overcome the opposition of the oligarchic and strongly proroyal court of aldermen. As in 1641, moreover, this movement based itself in the relatively democratic common hall, and to a lesser extent in the common council, and relied heavily on electoral struggles and citizens' mass petition campaigns, especially to secure the reversal of the king's prorogations and dissolutions of Parliament.[74]

Nevertheless, the alliance of forces behind the Exclusionist program of 1678–1681 came less close than did its predecessor of 1641 to getting the king to accepts its goals. The parliamentary classes, without military force of their own, still had no means to oblige the king, who was largely in control of a state with a monopoly of force, to agree to their program, except by imposing it through coercive means, which were accruable in turn only through the activation of social forces outside the political nation, notably in London. But having been profoundly traumatized by the highly unwelcome outcome of Parliament's alliance with political and religious radicals from London and elsewhere during the Civil War, the great majority of the parliamentary classes was even less willing than in 1641 to seek to impose its program on the king by mobilizing a mass

[73] J. R. Jones, *The First Whigs* (London, 1970), pp. 52–55. Jones comments: "It was a mark of the domination of the Commons by the Opposition that these important proposals should have received a second reading on 5 April without the Court being able to challenge them seriously either in debate or in a division. The obvious effect of these provisions . . . would have been to give Parliament a greatly increased and possibly predominant share in the government of the country. At the same time it would have been difficult for the Crown to rally opinion against them and to appeal directly to the nation" (p. 54).

[74] D. F. Allen, "The Crown and the Corporation of London in the Exclusion Crisis, 1678–1681 (Cambridge University, Ph.D. diss., 1976), pp. 93–160.

movement, even more fearful of the link between Nonconformist religion and revolutionary politics, and probably even more disposed to depend on the king and his church. The outcome of the Exclusion Crisis was indeed more like 1628–1629 than 1641: when the MPs were unable to follow up their parliamentary successes with active resistance, Parliament found itself dissolved and, after an interval, the way was opened for a new experiment in absolutist rule. By the time James II had acceded to the throne, the fundamental problem or paradox of 1641 had, if anything, become more intense: the parliamentary classes were perhaps by now even more committed programatically to antiabsolutist parliamentary rule, but they were perhaps even less willing to do what was strategically necessary in order actively to oppose an absolutist monarch to secure such rule.

On the other hand, over the second half of the seventeenth century socioeconomic developments only increased the already substantial weight within society of the forces that had stood most unbendingly and militantly behind the antiabsolutist, parliamentary legislative revolution of 1641. During the Restoration period, agrarian capitalism further consolidated itself and agricultural improvement accelerated. Larger landlords won out over smaller landlords and owner-operators, who were caught in a squeeze between falling prices and rising taxes. More efficient, often larger farmer-tenants meanwhile prevailed over less efficient, often smaller ones, as competition in all markets intensified. Consequently, agricultural improvement continued to provide the basis for an increase of population off the land, especially in industry. The upshot was that England's landlord class became during the Restoration period even more firmly rooted in agricultural capitalism and more inextricably tied to a dynamic manufacturing sector.[75]

At the same time, the commercial revolution in overseas trade, already in full flower by 1650, had matured much further, profoundly strengthening, in both absolute and relative terms, those social groups of merchants based in the newer areas of commercial penetration. Between 1660 and 1700, the cloth export trade to northern Europe continued to stagnate, as it had since 1614, even further weakening the Merchant Adventurers. To make matters worse, the trade in new draperies, which constituted the most dynamic element of the north European cloth commerce, was controlled to a significant degree by foreign merchants.[76] The Levant Company merchants, meanwhile, continued to enjoy extraordinary prosperity, milking their royal monopoly of a now quite routine trade. In 1688, as

[75] D. C. Coleman, *The Economy of England, 1450–1750* (Oxford, 1977), pp. 91–172.

[76] R. Davis, "English Foreign Trade, 1660–1700," *Ec.H.R.*, 2d ser., 7 (1954): 163, 165; D. W. Jones, "London Merchants and the Crisis of the 1690s," in *Crisis and Order in English Towns, 1500–1700*, ed. P. Clark and P. Slack (London, 1972), p. 326; G. DeKrey, *A Fractured Society: The Politics of London in the First Age of Party, 1688–1715* (Oxford, 1985), pp. 144–45.

was already the case in 1640, proportionally more merchants in the trade with the Levant than in any other line of commerce were acquiring elite status, and the term Turkey merchant had come to connote both immense wealth and political conservatism.[77]

But the most spectacular gains continued to be made by the newer long-distance trades—with the East Indies, with the West Indies and North America, and with Africa. Between the 1660s and 1700, East Indian imports, now prominently including calicoes, as well as spices and silks, grew by some 80 percent, while East Indian reexports grew much faster. In fact, opportunities in this line grew so rapidly that by the late 1670s, interlopers in the East Indies and traders from other lines were agitating to overthrow the old, royally chartered joint stock, which restricted total investment, in order to open up the trade so as to enlarge investment and increase entrepreneurship. In so doing, their approach was indeed rather similar to that adopted by the colonial-interloping leaders in the 1640s and 1650s, with the later seventeenth-century East Indian oppositionists, like the earlier ones, proposing "to make the trade more national." But the elite-merchant and predominantly Tory leadership of the old company maintained its stranglehold over the trade by securing the strong backing of the monarchy, impelling the East Indian trading opposition to confirm and extend its commitment to Whiggism.[78]

Meanwhile, over the same period—from the 1660s to 1700—the value of imports from the West Indies and North America, primarily sugar and tobacco, actually doubled, while that of reexports grew much more rapidly. Simultaneously, the wealth and political power of the traders with these regions increased correspondingly. Traders with the West Indies and North America had from the start operated under free-trade conditions, and, like their predecessors of the 1640s and 1650s, the traders with these regions of the 1680s and 1690s were intent on pulling down all barriers to the expansion of their commerce. These barriers were seen to include not only the Crown-backed Royal Africa Company, which dominated the slave trade, the Russia Company, which sought to control the tobacco reexport trade to Muscovy, and the small Hudson's Bay Company, but also the East India Company itself. Indeed, as during the Interregnum, those who led the agitation to transform the norms and institu-

[77] R. Davis, *Aleppo and Devonshire Square: English Traders in the Levant in the Eighteenth Century* (London, 1967); DeKrey, *Fractured Society*, pp. 141–44. The merchants trading with the Levant seem to have been strongly Tory at the time of the Exclusion Crisis, but had become strongly Whig by the 1690s. Jones, *First Whigs*, p. 162; DeKrey, *Fractured Society*, pp. 130–33.

[78] Davis, "English Foreign Trade," pp. 153, 163–64; Jones, "London Merchants," p. 318; DeKrey, *Fractured Society*, pp. 23–25, 123–26; H. Horwitz, "The East India Trade, the Politicians, and the Constitution: 1689–1702," *J.B.S.* 17 (1978): 2 (quote). Cf. K. G. Davies, "Joint-Stock Investment in the Later Seventeenth Century," *Ec.H.R.*, 2d ser., 4 (1952).

tions that governed the trade with the East Indies—including, as earlier, great figures in the trade with the Americas and, most especially, traders from the newly dynamic Iberian commerce—were, for the most part, not only used to operating in spheres outside company regulation, but also, as in the earlier period, closely allied with the political opposition to the court, which was by this time Whig.[79]

Taking place in the foregoing socioeconomic and political context, the Revolution of 1688 did prove both revolutionary and glorious for its backers. Thanks largely to the intervention of William III, the Revolution of 1688 and its immediate sequels were able to accomplish for the parliamentary classes the veritable miracle of securing for them their program without requiring their having to resort to much overtly subversive action or the mobilization of the masses. The events of 1688 and the period immediately following can be seen therefore to represent the victory of a program quite similar to that of 1641 and the establishment in power of an alliance of forces behind that program quite analogous to that of 1641—on the one hand, an antiabsolutist, Protestant, and agrarian capitalist aristocracy favoring a strong state for international military and commercial power and for defense against the Catholic powers, and on the other hand, a dynamic maturing entrepreneurial merchant class, oriented toward making the most of the growing opportunities that could be derived from the long-distance trades and an expanding colonial empire, as well as from war finance. One witnesses a revolution in foreign policy leading directly to war with France and, in turn, a resolution of many of the central conflicts that had agitated the polity for more than a century.

The parliamentary victory of 1688 and its immediate sequels thus marked the consolidation of certain long-term patterns of development that had already marked off sociopolitical evolution in England from that of most of the Continent during the early modern period and the establishment of certain other such trends that would, in the course of the eighteenth century, further distinguish it. The stage had been set, of course, by the precocious and exceedingly thorough development of a unified national state capable of protecting absolute landed private property, largely via the elimination of bastard feudal regionally based magnates and the monopolization of the legitimate use of force by the government. That process, largely the achievement of the Tudor period, was the joint product of an increasingly capitalist landlord ruling class and the patrimonial monarchy, and stood in marked contrast especially to French centralization, which tended to attack, but then to absorb within the monarchical state, propertied interests, as well as local and particularist jurisdictions

---

[79] Davis, "English Foreign Trade," pp. 152–53, 163, 165; DeKrey, *Fractured Society*, pp. 130, 136–41, 149–51.

and freedoms—from provincial estates to local *parlements* to municipalities and guilds.

The Revolution of 1688 and the legislation of the 1690s were what finally placed the precociously unified English state under parliamentary rule and cut short the tendency to absolutism—to the erection of a state operated by the patrimonial monarch and its following, without reference to representative institutions, on the basis of its independent revenue and autonomous financial, judicial, and military administration. This outcome was again in sharp distinction to developments in France, where the patrimonial monarchy, with political support from a massive following dependent on property in office, achieved a significant degree of authority to tax arbitrarily, established a standing army, and governed for more than a century without reference to national representative institutions. Though in a sense prepared for during a whole epoch and though no doubt abstractly desired by the great majority of the landlord class, the settlement secured in England in 1688 had been very difficult to achieve in practice because of the parliamentary classes' profound dependence on and involvement with the monarchy, and their equally deep mistrust of the urban commercial and industrial classes outside the governing elite, fatally tainted by Dissent. Henceforth Parliament gained regular, in fact annual, meetings by virtue of the Triennial Act and especially its refusal to vote more than yearly supplies to the king for his army and navy. Moreover, the House of Commons took control, through the formulation of precise appropriation clauses, of much of the money it voted the king. The upshot was the destruction, for all practical purposes, of the monarchy's independent money raising capacity and the corresponding abandonment of the ancient ideal that "the king should live of his own"—the effective end, in short, of patrimonial monarchy in England. Finally, through its financial control and its regular meetings, Parliament was able to bring about an enormous increase in what the government did by way of legislation, thereby vastly extending its own sphere of influence.[80]

The defeat of the monarchy's absolutist tendencies, the destruction of its patrimonial base, and the consolidation of parliamentary rule allowed the landed classes to take control of taxation and state finance and administration; the way was thereby prepared for the erection, during the century following 1688, of an extraordinarily powerful centralized state, organized for the more or less explicit and limited purpose of enhancing England's international power. This state, which secured perhaps higher levels of taxation and more advanced forms of bureaucratic administration

[80] See esp. H. Horwitz, *Parliament, Policy, and Politics in the Reign of William III* (Manchester, 1977), pp. 311–15, and C. D. Chandaman, *The English Public Revenue* (Oxford, 1975), pp. 279–80.

than could be found anywhere in Europe, appears to have been the special contribution of sections of England's unique capitalist aristocracy.[81] The rise of bureaucratic as opposed to patrimonial administration was made possible by the ability of the economically independent capitalist landlord class as a whole to allow for the creation of an office structure that was not primarily designed to secure the economic maintenance of the ruling class and that could thus provide for careers (very roughly) open to talent. The massive growth of taxation expressed the desire of the aristocracy to build and use the state as an instrument for the achievement of certain goals— notably military, commercial, and colonial power, as well as the defense of Protestantism.[82] Here was one more aspect of English sociopolitical development that diverged fundamentally from that of France, where the state continued, through its offices and privileges, to provide incomes so as directly to maintain, or help maintain, the dominant class on the basis of politically constituted private property.

It was the consolidation of parliamentary rule—of parliamentary control of taxation and of the disposal of much of the government's revenue— as well as the drive to international power of the English state made possible thereby, that provided the fundamental conditions for the erection of the institutional framework for the commercial revolution, as well as for the financial revolution that allowed for a permanent national debt. Parliament now assumed a central position in regulating trade and chartering commercial companies and immediately took measures to allow for freer and greater mobilization of capital in overseas enterprise. It chartered the New East India Company in 1694, thus undermining the old company; deprived the Hudson's Bay Company of its exclusive privileges in 1697; destroyed the Royal Africa Company's monopoly in 1698; and broke the Russia Company's control over the Muscovy tobacco reexport trade in 1699. Not coincidentally, in each instance it thereby honored the demands

[81] P. Mathias and P. O'Brien, "Taxation in England and France, 1715–1810," *Journal of European Economic History* 5 (1976); J. Brewer, *The Sinews of Power* (New York, 1989). I want to thank John Brewer for allowing me to read the manuscript of this work before publication.

[82] The massive international commitments assumed by the English parliamentary classes, beginning shortly after 1688 and continuing over the next century, constitute massive prima facie evidence against a central tenet of the Revisionists' case: for these commitments would appear to tell against the view that the parliamentary classes were opposed, generally and on principle, to financing major overseas adventures and to the growth of state administration thereby entailed, rather than merely to many of the specific overseas adventures undertaken by English monarchs over the course of the seventeenth century and, more generally, to their having been undertaken without parliamentary consent. (Prof. Russell seems to give much of the Revisionists' case away—and, paradoxically, to concede alot to the old Whig case—when he agrees that whereas, during the seventeenth century, "financial pressures put strain on the principle of consent to taxation everywhere in Europe. . . . England, because the principle of consent to taxation was so particularly well entrenched, was perhaps put under more constitutional strain by this process than some other powers" [*Causes*, p. 215].)

of those very significant groups of London merchants, based heavily in the long-distance and unregulated trades and closely identified with the Whigs, who had been most anxious to enter, enlarge, and transform commercial enterprise, but who until then had been prevented from doing so by the old Tory-dominated restrictive companies that now lost out. It was precisely these same traders who were also the primary mercantile protagonists of the financial revolution, constituting the core of the new Bank of England. Many of the same Whig merchants had taken control of the government of the City of London with the overturning of 1688–1689.[83] In this context, it does not seem farfetched to understand the new government's willingness to grant limited political rights to Dissenters in terms of the powerful base of political and financial support provided the new regime by London Whigs, especially City overseas merchants associated with Nonconformist Protestantism.

In sum, the Revolution of 1688 and its sequels not only realized the project of 1640–1641 of the parliamentary capitalist aristocracy; in so doing, it also realized, in a politically subordinated form, the project of 1649–1653 of its leading allies outside the landed classes, the American colonial and East Indian–interloping leadership.

[83] DeKrey, *Fractured Society*, pp. 25–27, 121–27. I want to express my great indebtedness to DeKrey's important study.

Index

Stone, Thomas (*cont.*)
133, 155, 182, 183n, 184t, 186t, 278; po-
litical position and activities of, 226, 292,
367, 397
Stone, William, 128, 145, 183n, 185t, 195t
Story, Edward, 482n, 485n, 492t, 636
Story, James, 435n
Strafford, earl of. *See* Wentworth
Strange, John, 407
Strangeways, John, 333, 334
Strickland, William, 444n, 620
Strode, William, 457
Strong, William, 569n
Stubbing, Thomas, 384n, 386
Styles, Thomas, 101
subsidy assessments, 80–81
Suckling, John, 209
sugar plantations, 161–66
Supple, Barry, 24n
Susan, 21
Sussex, earl of, 108
Swinnerton, Robert, 183n
Symonds, Thomas, 232n, 235

Taverner, Henry, 191t
taxation. *See* customs and impositions; tonnage
and poundage
Taylor, Daniel, 369, 421, 435, 536, 539, 544,
546, 548, 549, 551, 555, 556
Taylor, Harland, 30n
Taylor, Silvanus, 549
Taylor, Thomas, 263
Temple, T., 569n
Ten Propositions, 342
Terringham, Joseph, 165, 191t, 194t
Thomas, William, 176, 193t
Thomson, Edward, 128, 129, 136, 175, 183n,
185t, 190t, 192t, 195t, 328
Thomson, George, 195t, 514; and Additional
Irish Adventure, 404, 407n; company and
trade activities of, 118, 128–29, 146, 183n,
185t, 186t, 187t; and naval affairs, 583,
594, 630; political position and activities of,
326, 364, 365, 397, 398n, 504, 530, 533,
552, 579; religious position of, 414, 424
Thomson, Maurice, 115, 182, 328, 549; and
Additional Irish Adventure, 402, 403n,
407n, 435n; on customs commission of Parliament, 432, 520, 553, 556; East Indies
and Guinea trade of, 164, 165, 173, 174,
175, 178, 179, 192t, 517; family connec-

tions of, 176, 195t, 522; military affairs of,
434, 514, 529, 554, 555; other colonial activities of, 123–24, 152, 153, 156–67,
183n, 187t, 190t, 302, 304, 587, 612; political activities of, 313, 367, 397, 398n,
430n, 431, 435, 521, 636; privateering ventures of, 158–59, 191t, 500, 501n; relations
with the Dutch, 500, 621–23; religious position of, 414, 417, 423, 449; tobacco trade
of, 131, 132, 134–35, 139, 140, 155, 184t,
185t, 186t, 188t, 189t, 326; Virginia dealings of, 118, 120, 137, 146, 147, 158–59,
167, 168, 589; West Indies trade of, 125–
29, 162, 278
Thomson, Paul, 118, 128, 195t
Thomson, Richard, 186t
Thomson, Robert, 407n; company and trade activities of, 153, 165, 175, 187, 191t, 192t,
587; family connections of, 176, 195t, 522;
political position and activities of, 326, 435,
553, 555, 636; religious position of, 304n,
417, 567
Thomson, William, 195t; and Additional Irish
Adventure, 402, 404, 407n; company and
trade activities of, 118, 128, 134, 612; political position and activities of, 326, 367, 397,
399n, 430n, 636
Thorpe, George, 146
Throckmorton, William, 146
Tichborne, Francis, 383n
Tichborne, Robert, 521n, 548, 549; company
and trade activities of, 543–44; and military
affairs, 455n, 484n, 513, 515, 520, 551;
political activities of, 443, 504, 505, 536,
546, 551, 556
tobacco, 43; prices of, 129, 130; production of,
98, 129–30; taxation of, 327–29, 349; trade
in, 95, 105, 113, 125–29, 130–31, 132,
154, 155, 162
tonnage and poundage, 231–36, 266, 267, 672
Towerson, William, 21, 32n, 211n
Towse, John, 371n, 399n, 430, 431, 447, 520
Traves, James, 77n, 87n
Trerice, Nicholas, 152, 183n, 187t
triangular trades, 161–66
Trinidad plantation, 302
Trinity House, 554–55
Tristram, William, 103, 183n, 384n
Trott, John, 376n
Tucker, George, 169
Tucker, William, 195t, 326, 403n, 430n;